International Directory of

COMPANY
HISTORIES

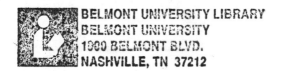

International Directory of

COMPANY HISTORIES

VOLUME 64

Editor

Tina Grant

ST. JAMES PRESS

An imprint of Thomson Gale, a part of The Thomson Corporation

THOMSON

GALE

Detroit • New York • San Francisco • San Diego • New Haven, Conn. • Waterville, Maine • London • Munich

THOMSON

GALE

™

International Directory of Company Histories, Volume 64

Tina Grant, Editor

Project Editor
Miranda H. Ferrara

Editorial
Virgil Burton, Donna Craft, Louise Gagné,
Peggy Geeseman, Julie Gough, Linda Hall,
Keith Jones, Lynn Pearce, Maureen Puhl,
Holly Selden, Justine Ventimiglia

Imaging and Multimedia
Randy Bassett, Lezlie Light

Manufacturing
Rhonda Williams

LIBRARY OF CONGRESS CATALOG NUMBER 89-190943

ISBN: 1-55862-509-7

BRITISH LIBRARY CATALOGUING IN PUBLICATION DATA

International directory of company histories. Vol. 64
I. Tina Grant
33.87409

Printed in the United States of America
10 9 8 7 6 5 4 3 2 1

CONTENTS

Company Histories

PREFACE

The St. James Press series *The International Directory of Company Histories (IDCH)* is intended for reference use by students, business people, librarians, historians, economists, investors, job candidates, and others who seek to learn more about the historical development of the world's most important companies. To date, *IDCH* has covered over 6,750 companies in 64 volumes.

Inclusion Criteria

Most companies chosen for inclusion in *IDCH* have achieved a minimum of US$25 million in annual sales and are leading influences in their industries or geographical locations. Companies may be publicly held, private, or nonprofit. State-owned companies that are important in their industries and that may operate much like public or private companies also are included. Wholly owned subsidiaries and divisions are profiled if they meet the requirements for inclusion. Entries on companies that have had major changes since they were last profiled may be selected for updating.

The *IDCH* series highlights 10% private and nonprofit companies, and features updated entries on approximately 50 companies per volume.

Entry Format

Each entry begins with the company's legal name, the address of its headquarters, its telephone, toll-free, and fax numbers, and its web site. A statement of public, private, state, or parent ownership follows. A company with a legal name in both English and the language of its headquarters country is listed by the English name, with the native-language name in parentheses.

The company's founding or earliest incorporation date, the number of employees, and the most recent available sales figures follow. Sales figures are given in local currencies with equivalents in U.S. dollars. For some private companies, sales figures are estimates and indicated by the abbreviation *est.* The entry lists the exchanges on which a company's stock is traded and its ticker symbol, as well as the company's NAIC codes.

Entries generally contain a *Company Perspectives* box which provides a short summary of the company's mission, goals, and ideals, a *Key Dates* box highlighting milestones in the company's history, lists of *Principal Subsidiaries, Principal Divisions, Principal Operating Units, Principal Competitors,* and articles for *Further Reading.*

American spelling is used throughout *IDCH,* and the word ''billion'' is used in its U.S. sense of one thousand million.

Sources

Entries have been compiled from publicly accessible sources both in print and on the Internet such as general and academic periodicals, books, annual reports, and material supplied by the companies themselves.

Cumulative Indexes

IDCH contains three indexes: the **Index to Companies**, which provides an alphabetical index to companies discussed in the text as well as to companies profiled, the **Index to Industries**, which allows researchers to locate companies by their principal industry, and the **Geographic Index**, which lists companies alphabetically by the country of their headquarters. The indexes are cumulative and specific instructions for using them are found immediately preceding each index.

Suggestions Welcome

Comments and suggestions from users of *IDCH* on any aspect of the product as well as suggestions for companies to be included or updated are cordially invited. Please write:

The Editor
International Directory of Company Histories
St. James Press
27500 Drake Rd.
Farmington Hills, Michigan 48331-3535

AB	Aktiebolag (Finland, Sweden)
AB Oy	Aktiebolag Osakeyhtiot (Finland)
A.E.	Anonimos Eteria (Greece)
AG	Aktiengesellschaft (Austria, Germany, Switzerland, Liechtenstein)
A.O.	Anonim Ortaklari/Ortakligi (Turkey)
ApS	Amparteselskab (Denmark)
A.Š.	Anonim Širketi (Turkey)
A/S	Aksjeselskap (Norway); Aktieselskab (Denmark, Sweden)
Ay	Avoinyhtio (Finland)
B.A.	Buttengewone Aansprakeiijkheid (The Netherlands)
Bhd.	Berhad (Malaysia, Brunei)
B.V.	Besloten Vennootschap (Belgium, The Netherlands)
C.A.	Compania Anonima (Ecuador, Venezuela)
C. de R.L.	Compania de Responsabilidad Limitada (Spain)
Co.	Company
Corp.	Corporation
CRL	Companhia a Responsabilidao Limitida (Portugal, Spain)
C.V.	Commanditaire Vennootschap (The Netherlands, Belgium)
G.I.E.	Groupement d'Interet Economique (France)
GmbH	Gesellschaft mit beschraenkter Haftung (Austria, Germany, Switzerland)
Inc.	Incorporated (United States, Canada)
I/S	Interessentselskab (Denmark); Interesentselskap (Norway)
KG/KGaA	Kommanditgesellschaft/Kommanditgesellschaft auf Aktien (Austria, Germany, Switzerland)
KK	Kabushiki Kaisha (Japan)
K/S	Kommanditselskab (Denmark); Kommandittselskap (Norway)
Lda.	Limitada (Spain)
L.L.C.	Limited Liability Company (United States)
Ltd.	Limited (Various)
Ltda.	Limitada (Brazil, Portugal)
Ltee.	Limitee (Canada, France)
mbH	mit beschraenkter Haftung (Austria, Germany)
N.V.	Naamloze Vennootschap (Belgium, The Netherlands)
OAO	Otkrytoe Aktsionernoe Obshchestve (Russia)
OOO	Obschestvo s Ogranichennoi Otvetstvennostiu (Russia)
Oy	Osakeyhtiö (Finland)
PLC	Public Limited Co. (United Kingdom, Ireland)
Pty.	Proprietary (Australia, South Africa, United Kingdom)
S.A.	Société Anonyme (Belgium, France, Greece, Luxembourg, Switzerland, Arab speaking countries); Sociedad Anónima (Latin America [except Brazil], Spain, Mexico); Sociedades Anônimas (Brazil, Portugal)
SAA	Societe Anonyme Arabienne
S.A.R.L.	Sociedade Anonima de Responsabilidade Limitada (Brazil, Portugal); Société à Responsabilité Limitée (France, Belgium, Luxembourg)
S.A.S.	Societá in Accomandita Semplice (Italy); Societe Anonyme Syrienne (Arab speaking countries)
Sdn. Bhd.	Sendirian Berhad (Malaysia)
S.p.A.	Società per Azioni (Italy)
Sp. z.o.o.	Spólka z ograniczona odpowiedzialnoscia (Poland)
S.R.L.	Società a Responsabilità Limitata (Italy); Sociedad de Responsabilidad Limitada (Spain, Mexico, Latin America [except Brazil])
S.R.O.	Spolecnost s Rucenim Omezenym (Czechoslovakia
Ste.	Societe (France, Belgium, Luxembourg, Switzerland)
VAG	Verein der Arbeitgeber (Austria, Germany)
YK	Yugen Kaisha (Japan)
ZAO	Zakrytoe Aktsionernoe Obshchestve (Russia)

$	United States dollar		ITL	Italian lira
£	United Kingdom pound		JMD	Jamaican dollar
¥	Japanese yen		KPW	North Korean won
AED	Emirati dirham		KRW	South Korean won
ARS	Argentine peso		KWD	Kuwaiti dinar
ATS	Austrian shilling		LUF	Luxembourg franc
AUD	Australian dollar		MUR	Mauritian rupee
BEF	Belgian franc		MXN	Mexican peso
BHD	Bahraini dinar		MYR	Malaysian ringgit
BRL	Brazilian real		NGN	Nigerian naira
CAD	Canadian dollar		NLG	Netherlands guilder
CHF	Swiss franc		NOK	Norwegian krone
CNY	Chinese yuan		NZD	New Zealand dollar
COP	Colombian peso		OMR	Omani rial
CZK	Czech koruna		PHP	Philippine peso
DEM	German deutsche mark		PKR	Pakistani rupee
DKK	Danish krone		PLN	Polish zloty
DZD	Algerian dinar		PTE	Portuguese escudo
EGP	Egyptian pound		RUB	Russian ruble
ESP	Spanish peseta		SAR	Saudi riyal
EUR	euro		SEK	Swedish krona
FIM	Finnish markka		SGD	Singapore dollar
FRF	French franc		THB	Thai baht
GRD	Greek drachma		TND	Tunisian dinar
HKD	Hong Kong dollar		TRL	Turkish lira
HUF	Hungarian forint		TWD	new Taiwan dollar
IDR	Indonesian rupiah		VEB	Venezuelan bolivar
IEP	Irish pound		VND	Vietnamese dong
ILS	new Israeli shekel		ZAR	South African rand
INR	Indian rupee		ZMK	Zambian kwacha
ISK	Icelandic krona			

International Directory of
COMPANY
HISTORIES

Acushnet Company

333 Bridge Street
Fairhaven, Massachusetts 02719-0965
U.S.A.
Telephone: (508) 979-2000
Toll Free: (800) 225-8500
Fax: (508) 979-3927
Web site: http://www.acushnet.com

Wholly Owned Subsidiary of Fortune Brands Inc.
Founded: 1910 as Peabody, Young & Weeks
Employees: 4,615
Sales: $1 billion (2002)
NAIC: 339920 Sporting and Athletic Good Manufacturer

A subsidiary of Fortune Brands Inc., Achusnet Company is devoted to producing golfing equipment and accessories. The Fairhaven, Massachusetts-based company boasts three of the most important brands in the industry: Titleist, Foot-Joy, and Cobra. Titleist produces the top selling golf ball, a favorite of touring professionals for several decades, but the logo also adorns other golf products, including clubs, gloves, bags, and accessories. Foot-Joy is best known for golf shoes and also markets dress and athletic shoes as well as golf gloves and accessories. Cobra's focus is golf clubs, but it too makes accessories. In addition to eight manufacturing, sales, and distribution centers located in the United States, Acushnet also operates facilities in countries across the world, including England, France, Germany, South Africa, Japan, and the Peoples Republic of China.

1910 Origins

Acushnet was founded in 1910 by a graduate of the Massachusetts Institute of Technology, Phillip W. "Skipper" Young, along with two college friends. Their partnership was called Peabody, Young & Weeks but subsequently became known as Acushnet Processing Company, named after the town in which they set up shop, Acushnet, Massachusetts. Although the company soon moved to New Bedford, Massachusetts, it retained the Acushnet name. Its original focus was on rubber, taking advantage of a process Young developed to reconstitute rubber waste and scraps into a workable material. Acushnet developed a

steady business with the major Akron, Ohio, rubber companies, which sent them their rubber scraps to be processed. By the end of World War I, in 1918, Acushnet was the world's largest supplier of reclaimed uncured rubber. However, with the dramatic drop in rubber prices in the early 1920s, falling from more than $3 per pound to just three cents per pound, Acushnet was forced to shift its focus. The company began to produce a number of molded rubber products, including bathing shoes and caps, toy boats, and hot water bottles. Acushnet became involved in the golfing business because of Young's fondness for, and frustration with, the game. According to company lore, he was so dismayed by the inaccuracy of his golf shots one day that he decided to x-ray some golf balls to see if the cores were properly centered. He found that most were well off the mark and prone to erratic shots. As a result, he decided to develop a better golf ball.

The first golf balls, dating as far back as the 15th century, were made of wood, either from elm or beech. Although durable, they were far from aerodynamic and could travel only around 100 yards. Next came leather spheres filled with cow's hair. The first major breakthrough in the evolution of the golf ball was the "feathery," introduced in 1618. Inside its leather sphere, painted white for better visibility, were goose feathers. The ball was packed while wet, so that upon drying it would become tight and firm and capable of being driven twice as far as a wooden ball. This process was labor intensive and thus resulted in a product that was expensive beyond the reach of average people. Next came the Gutta Percha ball, developed by Reverend Adam Paterson of St. Andrews, Scotland. It was made from rubber, the name referring to the gutta percha gum used as a raw material. The gutta percha ball could be mass produced, making golf more affordable, but it also had a tendency to break into pieces while in flight. Then, in 1898, Coburn Haskell introduced a more durable golf ball, one that had a solid rubber core around which was wrapped rubber thread that was then enclosed in a gutta percha covering. By the early 1900s, the Haskell ball became the standard in golf. As Skipper Young discovered, however, the balls were not precisely manufactured.

Introducing the Titleist in the 1930s

After introducing the x-ray machine to golfing technology, in 1930 Young patented a machine that could wind rubber string

Company Perspectives:

Titleist is committed to satisfy golfers with golf products of superior performance and quality. The Titleist culture will be one of challenging up and supporting down. Recognizing that the ultimate competitive advantage is an environment that utilizes and develops the creative energies of all associates, our objective will be to develop goal directed work teams empowered to anticipate and respond to changing consumer/market conditions. Destiny is not a matter of chance. Destiny is a matter of choice.

around a rubber core in a uniform manner, which led to the development of a "dead center" golf ball that he named Titleist. To demonstrate the effectiveness of his new ball, Young also developed the first mechanical golf swing machine, a two-headed affair that with its consistent stroke was able to show that there was only a minor variance among individual Titleist balls. As a result of this foray into the golf ball business, Acushnet split into two divisions, one devoted entirely to golf and the other to the company's remaining rubber products. An important decision made early on was to limit the sale of Titleist golf balls to golf course pro shops, thus attaining a higher margin.

With the advent of World War II, Acushnet shelved its golf business for several years, instead devoting its resources to the production of molded gas masks, for which the company became the Allies' sole supplier, as well as an oxygen mask developed in conjunction with Harvard Medical School and important war materials such as torpedo gaskets and o-rings. With the end of the war in 1945, Acushnet returned to making golf balls and other consumer products. In 1948, the company introduced what it called "dynamite thread," which along with other refinements resulted in increased yardage. A major milestone was reached the following year when Titleist became the most played ball at the prestigious U.S. Open tournament.

In the 20 years following World War II, Acushnet's golf division grew alongside the popularity of the sport. During this span, the number of golf courses more than doubled, from 4,000 to 8,700, and the number of people who played 15 or more rounds of golf each year expanded from 2.5 million to 8.5 million. The amount of money spent on golf equipment increased from around $60 million to $150 million, one-third of which was spent on golf balls. Acushnet took steps to maintain its leadership in golf ball technology by launching a research and development team that studied golf ball aerodynamics. The company also moved beyond golf balls when in 1962 it acquired John Reuter Jr., Inc., maker of the popular Bulls Eye putter. In 1969, Acushnet added other golf clubs as well as golf bags to its product line by acquiring Golfcraft Inc. It was also during this period, in 1968, that the company changed its name from Acushnet Process Company to Acushnet Company, Inc. While the rubber and golf divisions accounted for an equal share of the company's revenues of $45 million, the golf business proved to be more profitable.

Acushnet became involved in golf carts in 1975 by acquiring Shelford Group of England. A year later, Acushnet was itself

acquired, bought by American Brands, Inc., a company that was initially involved in the tobacco industry but in time added other consumer products, such as Sunshine Biscuits and James B. Beam Distilling Co. (American Brands took the name Fortune Brands Inc. in 1997.) As a subsidiary of American Brands, Acushnet continued to operate both golf and rubber products divisions for another 18 years. Finally, in 1994, management from the rubber division bought their operation from the parent company, naming it Acushnet Rubber Company, Inc. In 2002, the company dropped the Acushnet name, choosing instead to call itself Precix (pronounced "precise").

Acushnet, the golf subsidiary, continued to grow under new ownership, and in 1985 added another major brand, Foot-Joy. The company was just one of dozens of shoemakers operating in Brockton, Massachusetts, when it was founded in 1857 as the Burt and Packard Company. It was known as the Field and Flint Company in 1910 when it first became involved in the golf shoe business. The Foot-Joy line of golf shoes was introduced in the 1920s and received a major boost when the American Ryder Cup team, which played the best Europeans in a team tournament, selected Foot-Joy as its official shoes. By 1945, a majority of professionals on the U.S. PGA Tour wore Foot-Joys, a distinction the company retains until the present day. Field and Flint was acquired by the Stone and Tarlow families in 1957. As Titleist had done earlier, new management opted to limit the sale of Foot-Joy golf shoes to pro shops. The company took on the name of its signature brand in 1970, dropping Field and Flint Company for Foot-Joy, Inc. In 1975, a controlling interest in the business passed to General Mills, Inc., which two years later bought the rest of the company. As part of General Mills Fashion Group of companies, Foot-Joy became involved in golf gloves in the early 1980s, its Sta-Sof golf glove becoming the top seller. It also added golf socks, which also became number one in the category. When the corporate parent decided to reorganize to focus on its core businesses, a number of suitors made a bid for Foot-Joy, including a management group led by Richard and William Tarlow, who had sold the business to General Mills ten years earlier, as well as Converse, Inc. and Spalding. Acushnet emerged the winner, paying nearly $57 million for Foot-Joy.

Not only did Acushnet and Spalding spar over Foot-Joy, the two leading companies in golf equipment spent considerable time in court from 1981 to 1990 hashing out patent issues. The initial dispute involved Spalding's 1974 patent for a sodium and zinc golf ball cover called Surlyn. It was a major advance because it prevented excessive cracking. Titleist and a number of other ball manufacturers adopted the formula and Spalding went to court to protect its patent. After eight years of litigation, a federal judge in 1989 ruled against Acushnet. While Acushnet filed an appeal, it sued Spalding over patent violations regarding golf ball dimple patterns, fluorescent ball covering, and golf ball molding. Finally, in November 1990, the two companies settled their differences, agreeing to a cross-licensing of patents.

The 1990s and Beyond

In 1990, Acushnet reorganized its golf business, forging a single operating unit, Titleist and Foot-Joy Worldwide. A third major brand joined the fold in January 1996 with the acquisition of Cobra Golf Inc., maker of high-tech golf clubs. Cobra was a

```
┌─────────────────────────────────────────────┐
│              Key Dates:                      │
│                                              │
│ 1910:  The company is formed as a rubber     │
│        processing business.                  │
│ 1932:  A Golf Ball Division is created.      │
│ 1968:  Acushnet Company name is adopted.     │
│ 1976:  The company is acquired by American   │
│        Brands, Inc.                          │
│ 1985:  Foot-Joy, Inc. is acquired.           │
│ 1994:  The company's Rubber division is sold │
│        off.                                  │
│ 1996:  Cobra Golf Incorporated is acquired.  │
│ 2000:  Tiger Woods drops his endorsement of  │
│        Titleist balls.                       │
│ 2002:  Acushnet reaches the $1 billion mark  │
│        in annual revenues.                   │
└─────────────────────────────────────────────┘
```

much younger entity than its sister companies. It was launched in 1973 by Thomas Crow, a former Australian Amateur Champion who also had 20 years of experience in golf club design working at Melbourne-based Precision Golf. Crow emigrated to San Diego, California, and launched his own golf club company, producing a unique club called the Baffler, the first utility wood that golfers could rely on to help them escape from especially tricky lies. The company then built on a reputation for innovation. In the mid-1980s, it embraced lightweight graphite shafts. Later, it developed the first full sets of oversized irons.

At first, Cobra Golf Inc. operated as a separate unit from Titleist and Foot-Joy Worldwide, but in August 1999 Acushnet's management decided to consolidate the golf club business. Although the brands continued to maintain separation, their operations were combined and streamlined to cut costs and gain efficiencies. A year later, the Titleist and Cobra sales forces were also consolidated, a move designed to help Cobra, which lacked a large enough stand-alone sales force to achieve the level of sales Acushnet expected from the brand. In 2000, Acushnet did away with the two division format, opting instead to do business as a single entity, Acushnet Company, featuring its three premiere brands.

In the last two decades of the 20th century, Acushnet expanded its golf business internationally. In 1983, the company formed a joint venture with Tokyo Tire and Rubber Company to distribute Titleist products in Japan. Acushnet Foot-Joy Thailand Ltd. was launched in 1990 to manufacture Foot-Joy golf gloves. Acushnet GmbH became operational in Germany in 1992. A year later, operations were established in Canada, Sweden, France, Denmark, and Austria. In 1994, Acushnet Nederland BV was launched, followed in 1995 by a joint venture in Taiwan to manufacture Foot-Joy golf shoes. The Acushnet South Africa office opened in 1996. Finally, Acushnet Singapore Pte. Ltd. launched operations in Singapore and Malaysia in 2002.

Leading Acushnet into the new century was president and CEO Walter R. Uihlein, a long-time executive with the company. An avid golfer from childhood, Uihlein went to work at a local pro shop as a teenager. He was, by his own admission, entranced by the image portrayed by the Titleist sales rep, who was always better dressed than the competition and had the air of the consummate professional. One Titleist rep, Jim Kernohan, took Uihlein under his wing and helped him land a job with Dunlop after college. As soon as a sales job opened up at Titleist, however, Uihlein was quick to lobby for the position. An enthusiastic and hard worker, he quickly made his way up through the ranks. Hired as a sales rep in 1977, he was promoted to national sales manager little more than a year later. By age 33, he made vice-president, and three years later, in 1985, became the youngest general manager in the company's history. In 1989, he became president and CEO of Titleist and added the chairmanship in 1995. In that same year, he became president and CEO of Acushnet.

The emergence of Tiger Woods in the late 1990s increased golf's popularity and also added to the complexities Uihlein faced in leading Acushnet into the new century. In 2000, Woods dropped his endorsement of Titleist balls, opting instead for the new line of Nike golf balls. Although Acushnet lost some sales, Titleist continued to own a third of the market. In fact, Titleist faced greater challenges elsewhere, as a number of other companies began introducing a wide variety of high-tech balls. Titleist kept pace by offering its own advances. Acushnet as a whole had to contend with increased competition as well as the fallout of poor economic conditions that adversely impacted golf. The number of rounds of golf worldwide fell off, resulting in a glut of golf balls in inventory. In the summer of 2002, Acushnet cut nearly 300 jobs. In May 2003, the company announced further cutbacks, with another 200 jobs to be shed over the course of the next year, including the elimination of Ball Plant 1, the original ball-making facility in Acushnet, Massachusetts, which opened in 1932. Despite making fewer golf balls, Acushnet was still able in 2002 to crack the $1 billion mark in annual revenues for the first time.

Principal Competitors

Callaway Golf Company; Nike, Inc.; The Top-Flite Golf Company.

Further Reading

Brink, Bill, and Richard Sandomir, "Quest for Perfect Ball Consumes Pros and Duffers," *New York Times*, June 16, 2002, p. 8.

Seal, Mark, "Family Affair," *Golf World Business*, October 2001, p. 28.

"Steady Gains in Sales, Profits Are Par for Course at Acushnet," *Barron's National Business and Financial Weekly*, April 22, 1968, p. 30.

Sterba, James P., "Rolling Clones," *Wall Street Journal*, June 15, 2000, p. A1.

—Ed Dinger

GENERAL CONSTRUCTION COMPANY

Aegek S.A.

304 Messogion Avenue
Cholargos
Athens GR-155 62
Greece
Telephone: (+30) 210 650 9800
Fax: (+30) 210 653 5761
Web site: http://www.aegek.gr

Public Company
Incorporated: 1949
Employees: 1,400
Operating Revenues: EUR 138.65 million ($150 million)
 (2003)
Stock Exchanges: Athens
Ticker Symbol: AEGEK
NAIC: 237310 Highway, Street, and Bridge Construction;
 237110 Water and Sewer Line and Related Structures
 Construction; 541330 Engineering Services

Aegek S.A.—the company's full name is Aegek Anonymous Company of General Construction and Maritime, Tourist, Agricultural and Forestal Enterprises—is one of Greece's leading construction and engineering companies. Aegek specializes in large-scale private and public works projects, including the construction of roads and bridges, hydroelectric dams, subways—including the Athens Metro—and other projects, such as part of the infrastructure for the huge Athens-hosted 2004 Olympic Games. Founded in 1949, Aegek has participated in a wide array of joint ventures that have significantly contributed to its growth. Among the group's partners have been ABB, Campenon Bernard, Dumez, and Hochtief. Joint ventures continue to form nearly 90 percent of Aegek's total EUR 139 million in annual revenues. Another important part of the company's operations is its Aegek Energy subsidiary, which builds and operates power plants. Long focused on the Greek market, Aegek began exporting its expertise at the turn of the 21st century, winning contracts in foreign countries such as Jordan, Rumania, the Former Yugoslav Republic of Macedonia, and Cyprus. Aegek has been listed on the Athens Stock Exchange since 1993.

Rebuilding Greece in the 1950s

Aegek was founded in order to participate in the reconstruction of Greece following the Nazi occupation during World War II. By the 1950s, the company was engaged in various projects in Greece, particularly those relating to the country's development of a modern public infrastructure. Aegek quickly became one of the leading Greek engineering and construction companies, with a focus on public works projects. As such, Aegek participated in a number of important construction projects during its early decades.

One of Aegek's first major projects involved the building of the Irrigation Works of Thessaly, completed in 1955, and the related Lake Karla Tunnel project, completed in 1962, which involved the construction of a drainage tunnel diverting the waters from Thessaly's Lake Karla for irrigation purposes. That project, however, was later recognized as an ecological disaster that resulted in the death of the famed lake.

In the 1970s, Aegek branched out into the private sector. The company joined the important Steyr Hellas project, which brought automotive construction to Greece through Austrian Steyr's attempt to market its trucks and other light vehicles there, including the military-oriented G-Wagon. An automotive plant, built in Salonika, was completed in 1973.

Beginning in the late 1970s, Aegek began developing expertise in a new area when the company began building hydroelectric dams and power plants. Throughout the decade, Aegek had built a number of smaller hydro-electric dams as well as several large-scale projects, such as the hydro-electric power (HEP) unit at Assomati in 1985, the hydro-electric dam at Messohora in 1989, and the Aoos HEP complex, begun in 1990. Aegek emerged as a niche specialist in that area, ultimately forming a dedicated subsidiary, Aegek Energy, to encompass its HEP construction and operations activities.

Public Powerhouse for the New Century

In 1991, Aegek began constructing the underground power plant for the HEP dam at Thissavros. Also in that year, the company joined in the launch of another prestigious project, that of the construction of the new underground Metro in

Company Perspectives:

Throughout its long history, AEGEK has been developed from a technical company of medium size, into a contractor of large infrastructure projects and into a group numbering more than 10 large or smaller specialized corporations. The last period of the Company's development course begins in the year 2000 and coincides with the rapid development of all financial indicators, the acquisition of profound specialization in power and infrastructure projects, the growing of the group through large buy-outs and acquisition of participations in companies such as ETEP, METON and EFKLIDIS, the systematic expansion of its activities abroad.

Key Dates:

1949: Aegek Anonymous Company of General Construction and Maritime, Tourist, Agricultural and Forestal Enterprises (Aegek S.A. for short) is founded.

1955: The company completes the construction of the Irrigation Works of Thessaly.

1962: Aegek constructs Lake Karla Drainage Tunnel.

1973: Steyr Hellas automotive plant is completed.

1979: Aegek begins developing an expertise in the construction of Hydro-electric Plants (HEP) and dams.

1985: The company builds an HEP unit at Assomati.

1991: The company starts work on the construction of the Athens Metro.

1993: Aegek goes public on the Athens Stock Exchange and launches international operations.

1996: Construction operations along the Pathe Highway begins.

1999: Aegek enters the Jordanian market with the construction of two irrigation dams; the company acquires Ekter SA and Omas SA.

2000: Aegek enters Romania with the construction of Millennium Business Center in Bucharest.

2002: Diameter, Odosimansi, Axon, and Oikodomiki are acquired.

2003: Aegek acquires control of Efklidis SA, which is renamed Aegek Group SRL.

Athens, the largest construction project in Greece. Aegek later joined in on two additional phases of that project, extending its participation into the 2000s. In 1992, Aegek became part of the consortium building the Evinos Aquaduct, a project for the diversion of waters from the Evinos River to the Mornos Reservoir. This involved the building of an earthfill dam and the digging of a tunnel linking the river to the reservoir.

The Greek government stepped up its infrastructure spending in the 1990s, when the country joined the European Community. The increase in spending led Aegek to go public in 1993, listing on the Athens Stock Exchange. The public offering helped fuel the group's expansion objectives into the 2000s. Over the next decade, Aegek increased its scale more than tenfold, raising its annual revenues from the equivalent of about EUR 10 million to more than EUR 138 million ($150 million) at the end of 2003. Acquisitions formed a strong part of the Aegek's growth strategy. The company also began competing for its first contracts outside of Greece, notably in the Balkan states and Cyprus.

At the same time, Aegek continued to expand its range of competencies, in part through acquisitions, enabling it to diversify its range of projects. In 1995, the company joined in on the construction of the Tempi Railway Tunnel, which involved building a 12 kilometer stretch of high-speed railway linking Evangelismos and Rapsani along the new Athens-Thessalonika line. The following year, Aegek began work on the first of three phases of the Pathe Highway connecting Athens to Patras. This project included the construction of a railway tunnel and portions of the high-speed railroad connecting the two cities. In 1997, the company began work on another high-profile project, that of the construction of a Biological Research Center for the Academy of Athens. That project was completed in 2002. Aegek launched another major roadworks project in 1997 when it began constructing a 13-kilometer stretch of the Egnatia Highway from Grevena to Siatista.

The turn of the 21st century marked two major developments for Aegek. On the one hand, the company began a new series of acquisitions, such as its 1999 purchases of Ekter SA, another publicly listed construction group, and the engineering firm Omas SA. In 2000, the company acquired a stake in another engineering group, Efklides S.A., then, in 2001, acquired holdings in Etep SA and Meton SA, both construction companies. In 2002, Aegek continued its buying spree, picking up Odosimansi Technical Company, Axon Technical Company, and Oikodomiki SA. These three were then merged, with Diameter, into Aegek itself. By the end of 2003, the company had gained majority control of Meton and Efklidis, the latter of which was renamed Aegek Group SRL.

While pursuing its acquisition program, Aegek also launched a drive into the international construction market. In 1999, the company won contracts for two construction projects in Jordan—the Wala Dam, at the Al-Wala Wadi, and the Mujib Dam, at the Al-Mujib Wadi. In 2000, Aegek entered Rumania with the contract to build the Millennium Business Center in Bucharest, a project completed at the end of 2003. This contract led the company to step up its contracts in Rumania, which included a road improvement project on the highway between Timisoara and Lug, starting in 2002, and the repair of the DN2 roadway in southeastern Rumania, also starting in 2002.

Even as it pursued its international expansion, Aegek remained a leader in the Greek construction industry. Major projects included the construction of a new General Military Hospital in Thessalonika. Construction on that complex began in 2001, with completion expected in early 2005. Also in 2001, Aegek added the building of the Olympic Airways Hangar at the new Athens International Airport. In addition, the company picked up a number of projects related to the 2004 Olympic Games to be hosted in Athens.

In 2003, Aegek expanded its road-building operation with the launch of work on the Arta-Trikala Highway. Aegek's part of that project involved the construction of the entire roadway from the Pachtouri Tunnel up to Agia Kiriaki. By then, Aegek itself appeared on the highway to future success as a leading Greek construction and engineering company.

Principal Subsidiaries

Aegek Group SRL; Ekter S.A. (37.6%); Ergonis S.A. (40%); Dirki S.A.; Aegek Rom Construct Srl; Enet S.A.; Edafostatiki S.A. (43%); Aegek Energy S.A.; Astakos Terminal S.A. (50%); Meton S.A. (37.46%); Piraeus Prodefin Holding (26.65%); Athinaikoi Stathmoi S.A. (20%); Akaport S.A. (25%); Foxford Trading Ltd (66.67%); Aegef Group Srl (50%); Energy Electromechanical Projects S.A.; Aegek Anonymous Company Of Energy And Technology; Astakos Terminal S.A.

Principal Competitors

Consolidated Contractors Company; Aktor S.A.; Avax S.A.; Volos Technical Company S.A.; Altec Group S.A.; Pantechniki S.A.; Empedos S.A.; Alte S.A.; Atti-Kat S.A.; Athena Hellenic Engineering Industrial and Touristic Company.

Further Reading

Aggistalis, George, "Highway Across Greece," *World Tunnelling,* March 1999, p. 61.
Hope, Kevin, "Jordan Awards Dams Contract," *Financial Times,* January 20, 1999, p. 7.
"Jordan: Greek/Bosnian Team Wins Dam Contract," *MEED: Middle East Economic Digest,* January 29, 1999, p. 18.

—M.L. Cohen

SOFT DRINKS

AG Barr plc

<table>
<tr><td>

1306 Gallowgate
Glasgow
G31 4DS
United Kingdom
Telephone: (+44) 1415 541899
Fax: (+44) 1415 545768
Web site: http://www.agbarr.co.uk

Public Company
Incorporated: 1904
Employees: 915
Sales: £128 million ($217.30 million) (2003)
Stock Exchanges: London
Ticker Symbol: BAG
NAIC: 312111 Soft Drink Manufacturing

</td></tr>
</table>

AG Barr plc is the United Kingdom's leading focused soft drinks manufacturer and maker of the world-famous Irn Bru. Popularly known as "Scotland's other national drink," Irn Bru is the only soft drink in the world that has managed to maintain its leading home market position against the Coca Cola Company, although that company's rise in Scotland has put Barr under pressure in the early 2000s. Barr's response has been to make its own move on the export market, pushing south into England and continental Europe. Irn Bru has also become one of the most popular soft drinks in Russia, in part because of its suitability as a vodka mixer. AG Barr also produces another well-known "vintage" British soft drink brand, Tizer, which originated in Manchester in the 1920s. The company has been extending that brand with the launch of a new range of fruit-flavored drinks in 2004. The company also produces D&B, Findlays Natural Mineral Water, and Simply Citrus, as well as Orangina, under license from France's Pernod Ricard. AG Barr produces its syrups and bottles its drinks in four Edinburgh-area manufacturing plants, as well as operating distribution centers throughout much of the United Kingdom. The company has been listed on the London Stock Exchange since 1962, and the founding Barr family retains more than 25 percent of its shares. AG Barr is led by CEO Roger White, who, in 2004, became the

first non-Barr family member to head the company. In 2003, the company posted sales of £128 million ($217 million).

A Scottish Soft Drinks Company in the 19th Century

Although the Barr family had long been involved in manufacturing, its original business was as a cork cutter providing stoppers for local bottlers in Falkirk, Scotland. Founded in 1830 by Robert Barr, the family business thrived into the second half of the 19th century. The invention of new bottle closure systems largely replaced cork stoppers, and the Barrs were forced to look for a new area of business. In 1875, Barr's son, Robert, launched a new company producing so-called "aerated water," a precursor to modern soft drinks.

The practice of injecting carbon dioxide into water had been developed in the late 18th century; among the first to market the new carbonated water was London's Schweppes in 1792. Drink makers soon began mixing fruit juices, such as the popular lemonade, with the carbonated water, and by the mid-19th century "effervescent" drinks had become popular. The Barr family's own shift toward producing soft drinks coincided with their rising popularity, spurred in part because of the growing temperance movement in the United Kingdom at the time.

Robert Barr's son, Robert Fulton Barr, established his own soft drinks plant in Glasgow in 1887. The larger population of the Glasgow region enabled the second Barr company to flourish, and later to become the dominant of the two family-owned soft drinks businesses. Nonetheless, the Falkirk Barr company grew strongly into the mid-20th century as well.

Robert Fulton Barr turned over his company to his younger brother, Andrew Greig Barr, who left his career as a banker to join the Glasgow company at the turn of the 20th century. The two Barr companies established something of a working partnership, inventing common drink flavors. Yet Andrew Barr proved a driving force and is credited with providing the recipe for the Barrs' most lasting success, "Iron-Brew," launched in 1901.

The Barrs' Iron Brew was one of many similar—and similarly named—soft drinks available in the first half of the 20th century. Although not brewed, the drinks did indeed contain a small percentage of iron and were touted for their healthful properties. Later legislation provided for an iron content of at least 0.125 milligrams per fluid ounce. Barr's variation on the Iron Brew theme—each manufacturer had its own recipe—was backed up by a knack for advertising. The original bottle labels featured a strongman raising a bottle of Iron-Brew. Andrew Barr did not live to see the full success of the Iron-Brew brand; he died in 1903 at the age of 31. The following year, the company adopted its permanent name, AG Barr & Co.

Under the next member of the Barr family to lead the company, William Barr, who took over in 1909, AG Barr turned to celebrity endorsers, hiring popular local athletes to endorse the "brew." These included John Blair, Benny Lynch and Willie Lyon. William Barr, himself a weightlifter, was known for being able to tear a telephone directory in half. The company's talent for advertising provided such lasting slogans as "Your Other National Drink" and "Made from Girders." Early deliveries were made by cart drawn by the world's tallest working horse, Camera. In the 1930s, the company launched a highly popular comic-strip advertisement, Ba-Bru and Sandy, featuring the adventures of the Indian Ba-Bru and the Scottish Sandy in their search for a bottle of Iron-Brew. That campaign ran for more than 40 years.

World War II nearly spelled the end of AG Barr. The government led a rationalization of the country's soft drink sector, which was then nationalized and subjected to a streamlining to just six authorized "standard" soft drinks. Unfortunately for Barr and many other Scottish drinks makers, Iron Brew was not included among the standard drinks formulas, and the company was forced to cease production for the duration of the war.

By the end of the war, most of Scotland's soft drinks makers had disappeared. Both Barr companies held on, however, and prepared to return to independent production at the end of the 1940s. Yet even as the Barrs prepared to restore their own branded products and recipes, including Iron-Brew, they came under a new threat. With the war over and with the privatization of the soft drink industry in view, the British Parliament now proposed to introduce new truth-in-labeling laws. A major feature of the proposed legislation demanded that soft drink names reflect the products' true nature. This meant that such popular soft drinks as Ginger Ale, which, if it contained ginger, was not an "ale," would be discontinued.

Branding Success after World War II

In the Barr companies' case, the truth-labeling laws threatened the branding of their most popular product, Iron-Brew, which was not brewed. However, the new head of AG Barr, Robert Barr, hit on an ingenious means of skirting the impending legislation. In 1946, the company adopted the phonetic

spelling for its soft drink, renaming it Irn Bru, and therefore shielding it from the new labeling legislation. Although the labeling guidelines were not made into law until the 1960s—and existing soft drinks were allowed to keep their names under that legislation—Irn Bru quickly captured the hearts of Scottish consumers and became the region's most popular soft drink.

The success of Irn Bru encouraged the company to begin expanding. At first the company remained in Scotland, where it opened a number of new plants to support its growing sales throughout the country. In the early 1950s, however, Barr made its first move south into England, acquiring Hollows, based in Bradford, in 1954. The steadily building success of AG Barr's Irn Bru in the meantime made it the focus of the Barr family's strategic efforts, and in 1959 AG Barr finally acquired the Barr business based in Falkirk. The two companies then merged under the single AG Barr name.

With operations now spanning seven plants in Scotland, as well as the Hollows operations in England, AG Barr went public in 1965, listing its shares on the London Stock Exchange. Nonetheless, the company remained tightly controlled by the Barr family.

The public offering enabled Barr to begin expanding its operations. In 1967, the company, which previously had marketed its soft drinks only in bottles, added canning capacity with the purchase of Stotherts Ltd, based in Atherton. The company later became the first in the United Kingdom to adopt the new stay-on-can flip-top type can pull rings. Barr also released a low-calorie version of Irn Bru at the end of the decade.

Expanding Brands for
the Late 20th Century and Beyond

Barr began adding to its brand portfolio in the 1970s, including launching a short-lived fruit juice soda, Jusoda. A more lasting addition to the company came with its acquisition of another long-lived British soft drink brand, Tizer, acquired with the £2.5 million purchase of Tizer Limited, based in Manchester, in 1972.

Tizer originated from a soft drinks business set up by brothers Fred and Thomas Pickup in Portsmouth starting in 1906. The brothers moved onto Bristol the following year, then split up, with Fred Pickup settling in Yorkshire. He began producing carbonated beverages in 1919 and eventually established plants at Bradford and Leeds as well. Thomas moved back to his hometown of Manchester in 1922, and two years later he launched a new soft drink, taking its name from the word "appetizer."

Tizer grew into one of the most popular brands in the region, and Thomas Pickup opened a number of new facilities to support the rising demand. By the 1930s, he operated factories throughout northern England and into Scotland as well. In the years following the World War II, Pickup revived the Tizer brand, which became the company's sole product, and then the company's name itself. After Thomas Pickup died in the early 1970s, the company was acquired by Armour Trust, which then sold it on to AG Barr.

Tizer added a new brand pillar to Barr's portfolio. The company became determined to restore Tizer to its original

Key Dates:

1830: Robert Barr founds a cork cutting business in Falkirk, Scotland.

1875: Barr's son, Robert, founds a company selling bottled ''aerated'' water in Falkirk.

1887: Robert Fulton Barr, son of the second Robert Barr, founds his own soft drink company in Glasgow and later turns over the business to his younger brother Andrew Greig Barr.

1901: The Barr companies introduce their own Iron-Brew formula.

1904: Glasgow Barr company becomes AG Barr & Co. after Andrew Barr's death.

1940: Production of Iron-Brew is suspended after the nationalization of the British soft drinks industry during World War II.

1946: Barr adopts a new trade name for its Iron-Brew brand, using the phonetic spelling Irn Bru.

1954: Barr acquires Hollows, based in Bradford, England.

1959: AG Barr acquires Robert Barr of Falkirk.

1965: AG Barr goes public on London Stock Exchange.

1967: The company acquires Stotherts Ltd.

1972: AG Barr acquires Manchester-based Tizer Ltd, and its Tizer soft drink brand.

1983: Globe Soft Drinks in Edinburgh is acquired.

1988: Mandora St. Clements in Mansfield is acquired.

1995: AG Barr is awarded the Orangina licensing franchise for Great Britain.

1996: The company opens a new plant in Cumbernauld.

1998: The company reaches a bottling and distribution agreement with PepsiCo to sell Irn Bru in Russia.

2004: Roger White becomes the first non-Barr family member to head the company.

prewar recipe, a process hampered by the fact that the manufacturer of a primary ingredient had gone out of business. The success of the revitalized Tizer brand helped boost Barr's sales, which topped £12 million at the beginning of the 1980s. During the 1970s, also, the company began moving into the export market, selling the Irn Bru brand to popular British tourist destinations, such as the coast of Spain.

Barr made two more acquisitions in the 1980s, buying Edinburgh's Globe Soft Drinks in 1983 and Masnfield-based Mandora St. Clements in 1988. For the most part, however, the company stayed out of the massive global drinks consolidation which was gaining momentum at that time and which resulted in the creation of a small number of truly giant drinks conglomerates. Barr itself remained protected from takeover by the Barr family's controlling stake in the company.

Under new family leader Robin Barr, the company contented itself with protecting its position as Scotland's best-selling soft drink, a status that made Scotland an anomaly in a world where the Coca Cola Company had succeeded in dominating every other market. Into the late 1990s, however, Coca Cola's gaining popularity, particularly among Scottish youth, brought Barr under pressure. At one point, Coca Cola even claimed to have taken away the number one spot in Scotland, a falsehood that the U.S. company was later forced to retract.

Barr in the meantime had begun its own, if limited, export program, shipping Irn Bru to quench the thirst of the Scottish expatriate communities in Australia, Hong Kong, and Canada, among other places. The company also began promoting Irn Bru in Spain beyond its coastal tourist base. Coca Cola's difficulties in entering the Russian market also inspired Barr to enter that country as well, striking a bottling franchise agreement in the mid-1990s. That agreement, while promoting the Irn Bru brand name in Russia, fizzled out soon after, however. Instead, Irn Bru reached a new licensing agreement with the Pepsi Cola Bottling Company, which took over the bottling and distribution of the Irn Bru brand in Russia. By the 2000s, Irn Bru had grown into one of the top three Russian soft drink brands, boosted in part by its role as a popular vodka mixer.

Back at home, Barr itself had joined the licensing sector after being awarded the license to produce and distribute the Orangina brand family in Great Britain. Supporting that license, as well as increasing sales of the group's own brands, was the construction of a new state-of-the-art bottling facility in Cumbernauld in 1996. The new facility provided 122,000 square feet of production space. The additional bottling capacity encouraged Barr to add a new brand family, and in 1996 the company acquired a 40 percent stake in Findlays Spring Natural Mineral Water. AG Barr gained full control of Findlays in 2001.

Barr celebrated the end of an era when Robin Barr stepped down from the company's chief executive spot, naming in his stead Roger White, the first time someone from outside of the Barr family had been appointed to lead the company. White promised to expand the group's range of products—in particular by adding juice-based products and other bottled water products—while retaining and expanding its traditional carbonated beverage core. The first step in that expansion came in 2004 with the launch of a new range of fruit-flavored Tizer-branded soft drinks. After more than 100 years, AG Barr remained a mainstay in the U.K. soft drinks market.

Principal Subsidiaries

Findlays Spring Natural Mineral Water.

Principal Competitors

Procter and Gamble Company; PepsiCo Inc.; Coca-Cola Company; Sara Lee Corporation; Groupe Danone; Cadbury Schweppes plc; Interbrew SA-NV; SABMiller plc; Mitchell and Butlers plc.

Further Reading

''AG Barr Buys up Findlays,'' *Evening News*, December 27, 2001.

Bowker, John, ''Family Ties Weakened at AG Barr,'' *Scotsman*, January 21, 2004.

''Caps off to Irn-Bru for Russian Revelation,'' *Evening News*, June 17, 2002.

Clark, Andrew, ''Irn-Bru Invasion,'' *Guardian*, March 30, 2000, p. 21.

Dow, James, ''Barr Fails to Fizz as Sales Fall Flat,'' *Scotsman*, September 26, 2002.

Ferguson, Christine, "Continuing Thirst for Success," *Herald*, April 10, 2004, p. 18.

Harvey, Amanda, "Barr Backs Its Bru," *Scotsman*, September 27, 2000.

The History Of Barr Soft Drinks, London: AG Barr, 2003.

"Irn Man Barr Steps down for Successor," *Evening News*, January 20, 2004

"Irn Man Shows His Mettle," *Scotsman*, January 25, 2004

Lyons, William, "End of the Soft Sell as Tizer Cools Its Image," *Scotsman*, November 15, 2003.

"Row Brus as US Pulls down the Irn Curtain," *Evening News*, April 29, 2004.

Tate, Michael, "Scots Irn Man Sorts the Bru from the Blue," *Observer*, April 7, 1996, p. 3.

Yates, Andrew, "AG Barr Success Story Continues," *Independent*, January 8, 1998, p. 24.

—M.L. Cohen

Alfa Laval AB

Rudeboksvägen 1
SE-226 55 Lund
Sweden
Telephone: (+46) 36 65 00
Fax: (+46) 32 35 79
Web site: http://www.alfalaval.com

Public Company
Incorporated: 1883 as AB Separator
Employees: 9,358
Sales: SEK 13.9 billion (2003)
Stock Exchanges: Stockholm
Ticker Symbol: ALFA
NAIC: 333999 All Other General Purpose Machinery
    Manufacturing; 334513 Instruments and Related
    Product Manufacturing for Measuring Displaying, and
    Controlling Industrial Process Variables; 332410
    Power Boiler and Heat Exchanger Manufacturing

Alfa Laval AB operates as a leader in the heat transfer, centrifugal separation, and fluid handling industries. The company's heat exchangers are used for heating, cooling, freezing, ventilation, evaporation, and condensation of fluids. Alfa Laval's separation business dates back to its roots as a cream separator in 1883. Its separators are now used in the food processing and chemical industries, on ships and oil rigs, in wastewater treatment plants, and in businesses that purify industrial fluids. Its fluid handling pumps and valves are used in the production of beverages, dairy products and other foods, pharmaceutical products, and health and personal care products. Alfa Laval's products are sold in over 100 countries to customers in the process technology and equipment markets.

Early History

In 1877, the Swedish engineer Gustaf de Laval began to develop the first Swedish milk separator. A year later, he secured a patent for his design. After graduating from Uppsala University, de Laval entered the Technological Institute and passed the final examination in 1866. Times were hard, and de Laval was forced to take a position as clerk in the general store at the Falun mines; an engineer with a first-class diploma, he weighed out nails, herring, and salt to miners. In 1867, however, de Laval received a grant from the Swedish House of Lords and pursued advanced studies at Uppsala University in 1872, receiving the degree of doctor of philosophy.

The process of mechanically separating cream and milk through the physical application of centrifugal force was first exploited in 1876 by Wilhelm Lefeldt in Germany and two years later in Denmark by L.C. Nielsen. The latter technology was acquired by Burmeister & Wain of Copenhagen in 1882. Lefeldt and Nielsen's separators could not work continuously, unlike Gustaf de Laval's superior system. On February 26, 1878, de Laval entered into partnership with Swedish engineer Oscar Lamm. Together they founded the trading company Oscar Lamm, Jr., of Stockholm. The partnership was successful, with de Laval in charge of the technical side and Lamm the financial and commercial aspects of the business. Lamm tried to interest influential agents in Europe, among these H.C. Petersen & Company, Copenhagen; Bergedorfer Eisenwerk near Hamburg; Th. Pilter, Paris; the trading firm D. Hald & Company, London; and Boeke & Huidekooper of Groningen in the Netherlands. In the company's first year of business, 1879, overseas sales accounted for 50 percent of the company's turnover. Foreign demand for cream separators rose sharply, and in 1883 around 80 percent of sales were from overseas. Almost 97 percent of exports were sold through foreign distributors in the more industrially advanced countries. The product in question was the energy-intensive, power-driven cream separator. Manual cream separators were not introduced until 1887.

The company did not set up a domestic marketing division until four years after it had established its foreign distribution network. Its agents were already specialized in marketing dairy equipment, and cream separators complemented their existing product mix.

Four other European companies also manufactured power-driven cream separators in the late 1870s. They were Nielsen & Petersen—from 1882 owned by Burmeister & Wain—in Denmark, and Lefeldt, Fesca, and Petersen in Germany. The indus-

Company Perspectives:

Alfa Laval's daily work is inspired by constant effort to increase added value for customers. Satisfied customers create a company with competitive, continuous value growth for shareholders. Alfa Laval's four business principles include: optimizing the use of natural resources is our business; respect for human rights is fundamental; high ethical standards guide our conduct; and our commitment to open dialogue builds trust.

trial exploitation of this process was protected by patent. The holder of the patent for the separation method secured temporary legal protection against imitation and had the opportunity of gaining an international monopoly. The patent on the application of centrifugal force for separating milk and cream, which had been granted in 1884, expired in the countries in which it had first been granted in 1892—namely, in Sweden, Denmark, France, Germany, and the United States—and in countries where these patents had subsequently been registered. The reason no domestic cream separator industry had evolved in more industrially advanced countries like the United Kingdom and France is probably that foreign patent registrations from the late 1870s blocked the establishment of an indigenous industry until the beginning of the 1890s.

ABS Is Formed in 1883

The work that Oscar Lamm put in during his travels produced positive results, and overseas sales increased during 1880. The growth of the business demanded another form of collaboration between the two partners, and a limited company was the natural solution. On April 5, 1883, the company's statutory meeting was held, with de Laval and Lamm as the major shareholders. Oscar Lamm controlled 48 percent of the company shares and Gustaf de Laval 47 percent. The remaining 5 percent of the company was controlled by four individual members of the new board. Lamm was chairman of the board and managing director. In the same year, the company, named AB Separator (ABS), established a subsidiary in the United States. The managing director for this new company, the De Laval Cream Separator Company, was J.H. Reall of New York. He was not an engineer, nor did he own a workshop, but edited and published the *Agriculture Review* and the *Journal of the American Agricultural Association*. The Swedish separators were manufactured by P. Sharples of Westchester, New York. In 1886, Oscar Lamm left the corporation as managing director and was replaced by John Bernström in 1887. Gustaf de Laval was elected to the Royal Swedish Academy of Science and to the Royal Swedish Academy of Agriculture and Forestry. In the United Kingdom, the Dairy Supply Company, ABS's main customer, became sole agent.

At the same time, Gustaf de Laval constructed a turbine engine that could be used as a power source for the separator. A very important acquisition was the Alfa patent, bought in 1889 from a German, Clemens von Bechtolsheim.

In the years prior to 1890, the Danish company Burmeister & Wain won an ever-increasing share of the market. Burmeister & Wain was a major competitor both in Denmark, where it almost ousted ABS, and after 1883 in the international market. ABS marketed a product inferior to that of Burmeister & Wain, since its cream separator had a lower skimming capability. In the short term, however, ABS managed to increase its sales because of the high demand from small dairies overseas, which Burmeister & Wain could not yet cater to effectively. Burmeister & Wain's dominant market position in Denmark, ABS's decline in that market, and Lefeldt's inferior position in relation to foreign competitors in its home market, Germany, can be taken as evidence of the key importance of product quality to company growth.

When ABS began to find it hard to sell power-driven separators, it fitted them out with a new energy source—the turbine. At the same time, ABS launched its manual cream separators in the hope of reaching new groups of customers. Fourteen years were to pass before another Swedish company established itself in the Swedish and overseas markets. Before this competition had begun to seriously threaten ABS's future, the market was broadened to include more countries.

Overcoming Competition: 1890s–Early 1900s

More Swedish companies began to establish themselves in the home market when de Laval's patent ran out shortly after 1890. A new wave of patent registrations took place in the international market in the following decade, but these new entrants to the market produced manual cream separators.

In the mid-1890s, ABS diversified further by constructing industrial separators. The principle of centrifugal force was thus applied to a higher level of technology. At the same time, ABS diversified into technically simpler manual cream separators. Lower prices for these products ensured them a far wider market than that for power-driven separators.

By 1898, there were 35 plants worldwide manufacturing separators. Newcomers gained entry to the market by producing manual cream separators, which were not only less resource-intensive but also had a far larger market than the power-driven variety. Of the companies established after Burmeister & Wain, Lefeldt, and Fesca, the most prominent were Sharples in the United States, Mélotte in Belgium, Josef Meys in Germany, Edmond Garin in France, and Svenska Centrifug in Sweden.

The most threatening rival to the Alfa system was the Belgian Mélotte patent. ABS acquired U.S. exploitation rights for this patent but never made use of those rights; this greatly benefited the sales of its own system in the United States. In Europe, however, the Mélotte system was a major competitor.

After 1903, there came a wave of new companies worldwide that exploited the expired Alfa patent. With only a few exceptions, entry to the market for the new companies was secured via manual cream separators. By 1906, ABS was competing with 50 companies in the German market. By 1912, there were 135 firms operating in the international market, 70 of them in Germany and 16 in Sweden. The most important of these were AB Pumpseparator and AB Baltic in Sweden, ABS's former agents Bergedorfer Eisenwerk—which became a major competitor in 1904—Miele & Cie. and Westfalia in Germany, and A/S Titan in Denmark. These were mostly companies that had moved into separators after establishing themselves in other branches of engineering production.

In Stockholm, news had been received of impending bankruptcy at ABS's competitor Svenska Centrifug AB. ABS's management persuaded several major Centrifug stockholders to exchange their shares at above-par rate for Alfa shares. In 1905, a majority stake was taken in Centrifug, including its subsidiary, Gloria Separator GmbH Berlin. The next competitor to be bought by ABS was one of the most important dairy machine plants in Germany and one of the largest in Europe in the early 1900s, the Bergedorfer Eisenwerk. As in the case of Svenska Centrifug, the financial position of the enterprise was too weak for the owner Carl Bergner to demand better sales terms let alone fight a takeover bid.

The last big competitor to be bought before World War I was Burmeister & Wain, in 1910. This firm, at the time equal in reputation to ABS, and financed with capital from its U.S. subsidiary, had been bought for SEK 1.8 million so that it could be closed down; it would not have contributed anything new to ABS's existing business.

During the period 1905 to 1910, when ABS began to take over competitors, it had at its disposal sufficient capital to act without endangering its own liquidity. During the 25 years between the foundation of its first overseas subsidiary in the United States in 1883 and the takeover of Bergedorfer Eisenwerk in 1907, more than SEK 100 million had flowed into the coffers of the parent company in Stockholm.

The profits of the U.S. subsidiary company, transferred between 1895 and 1914, amounted to about SEK 46 million. This sum provided the stockholders' dividend, so that ABS could use the net consolidated profit of the whole company for reinvestment.

Production and organization techniques were also transferred from the U.S. subsidiary to the parent company and its European subsidiaries. In this way, ABS secured advantages of scale in the international separator market. Already in 1892, the U.S. subsidiary, the De Laval Cream Separator Company (Lavalco), was buying out all the U.S. shareholders and had built a new factory at Poughkeepsie, New York. This factory was highly profitable. In 1895, Francis Arend became managing director of Lavalco. The company had branches in Philadelphia and Chicago, as well as a subsidiary in San Francisco. A branch office opened in Canada in 1899 and became a subsidiary in 1912 under the name of the De Laval Dairy Supply Company. In 1899, the Swedish ABS participated in the formation of the De Laval Steam Turbine Company in the United States by contributing $240,000. In 1908, Gustaf de Laval left the ABS board of directors. He died five years later at the age of 67. In 1911, new subsidiaries were formed in Milan and Riga.

Surviving the War Years

By the time World War I began in 1914, ABS had acquired shares in Goldkuhl & Broström, Buenos Aires. This was raised to a majority interest in 1927, when the name was changed to Sociedad Alfa-Laval. In 1960, it became a wholly owned ABS company.

In 1915, ABS's John Bernström resigned as managing director and was replaced by his nephew, Captain Erik Bernström. J. Bernström left his post as chairman of the board in 1916, to be succeeded by Ernst Trygger, and his son Richard Bernström was vice-chairman until his death in 1919. The U.S. company Lavalco produced a milking machine in 1918, and four years later the first milking machine based on the Lavalco design was manufactured by ABS in Sweden. In 1922, Axel Wästfelt succeeded Erik Bernström as managing director, and the company Zander & Ingeström became ABS's sales representative for industrial separators in Sweden and Norway. In the United Kingdom, the De Laval Chadburn Company was formed in 1923 for sales of milk and industrial separators. In 1925, an ABS subsidiary was formed in Helsinki, and in 1926 British De Laval Chadburn Company changed its name to Alfa-Laval Company, a wholly owned ABS company. In the same year, subsidiaries were formed in Sydney, Australia, and Palmerston North, New Zealand. Between 1927 and 1929, subsidiaries were formed in Oslo, Warsaw, Danzig, and Zagreb, Yugoslavia.

In 1928, in cooperation with its Swedish competitor AB Pump-Separator, ABS bought the rival company AB Baltic. Only a few months later, ABS acquired its last major Swedish competitor, AB Pump-Separator itself. Both acquisitions, AB Baltic and AB Pump-Separator, had been more energetic than ABS in seeking ways to take advantage of the upswing in trade at the beginning of World War I and had expanded their capacity and grown faster than ABS. These two acquisitions were the most important mergers within the Swedish separator industry.

In 1930, Jacob Wallenberg of the Swedish banking house Stockholms Enskilda Bank was elected to the board of directors. The U.S. company Lavalco had a bad year and ceased paying dividends until 1935. The German subsidiary Bergedorfer Eisenwerk also operated at a loss until the end of 1933. In 1934, the Alfa-Laval Company (U.K.) moved to facilities in Brentford, near London. A new subsidiary was formed in Melbourne in 1936, and the last important Swedish competitor, Eskilstuna Separator, was acquired in 1939. The outbreak of World War II brought with it an upswing for the U.S. companies. During the war, Lavalco increased the number of personnel from 700 to 2,300, and the U.S.-based Turbinbolaget increased personnel from 1,100 to 2,400. The companies' sales increased by more than five times the prewar figure. More than 50 percent of the Poughkeepsie factory's capacity was taken up by precision work for defense purposes, but at the German factory in Bergedorf manufacture of munitions was extremely limited. In 1942, Francis Arend, managing director of Lavalco, died and was succeeded by Ralph Stoddard, who three years later was succeeded by his son, George. ABS acquired Arend's 10 percent share in Lavalco.

In 1939, Alfa-Laval Company at Brentford began producing industrial separators and milking machines, and increased its sales by 70 percent. During World War II's so-called Skagerack blockade, Sweden and ABS were cut off from many business partners. This period was to be a watershed between the old and the new eras in the company's history.

In the United States, Lavalco was given the task of constructing an oil separator for the U.S. Navy. Orders started pouring in from marine authorities, shipowners, and shipyards. U.K. Alfa-Laval Company became the European development center for these industrial separators. The research-and-development activities were transferred to Stockholm and several engineers were sent away on study visits—to rubber plantations in Southeast Asia, to olive groves in Italy, and aboard whalers in the South Atlantic. Thousands of owners of olive groves and vineyards in Italy and France exchanged their ancient equipment for separators. By 1945, there were hundreds of applications for separators within industry and scientific research.

Growth and Expansion: 1950s–80s

During the 1950s, the cellulose industry became the major customer group for plate heat exchangers, or PHEs, which were used in the pasteurizing process and for yeast manufacture. ABS's interest in these developments was taken care of in Germany by Bergedorfer Eisenwerk. PHEs could be used to comparable advantage in breweries and yeast manufacturing; later, distilleries, wineries, and other foodstuff industries came to appreciate their uses. One successful Swedish competitor, Rosenblads Patenter, was taken over by ABS in 1962. ABS dominated the market for PHEs in the chemical and marine sectors while the strength of its U.K. competitor, the Aluminium Plant and Vessel Company (APV), lay in the food and beverage sectors. APV was the same size as Alfa-Laval in this sector. ABS's major competitor in Europe was the family-owned company Westfalia AG in Oelde, Germany, and in the United States the Sharples Separator Company of Philadelphia. Westfalia and APV combined forces against ABS.

Production of separators began in Nevers, France, in 1947, and the U.K. manufacture of milking machines was moved to Cwmbron in Wales in 1949. A year later, the Italian subsidiary acquired plant and storage facilities in Muggio/Monza near Milan, and a subsidiary was established in Brussels in 1952. ABS formed new subsidiaries in Switzerland in 1960, in Bombay in 1961, and in Sao Paulo and Lima in 1962. In the same year, Turbinbolaget in the United States was sold to Lehrman Brothers.

In 1963, ABS (AB Separator) changed its name to Alfa-Laval AB. Further subsidiaries were formed in Santiago de Chile and Mexico City, and in the United States Lavalco

acquired G & H Products, Jay-Ro Services, and Hercules Filter. In 1966, the Spanish company Touron y Cia (Tycosa), Madrid, became a wholly owned subsidiary. A new Alfa-Laval subsidiary was formed in Amsterdam and took over industrial sales from the agent, Koopman & Company, in 1967. At the same time, a new subsidiary was formed in Zürich after Alfa-Laval's takeover of its agent, Wenger. In 1968, Bergedorfer Eisenwerk merged with STAL Refrigeration AB of Norrköping, Sweden. The new company was known as Stal-Astra GmbH. In Melbourne, H. Hamilton Pty, Ltd. was acquired and the name changed to Alfa-Laval Separation A/S. Lavalco acquired two new subsidiaries in the United States, American Tool & Machinery and Contherm Corporation. Also in 1968, a subsidiary was formed in Kuala Lumpur, and a minority interest was acquired in the Japanese firm Kurose.

In 1970, a subsidiary was formed in Algeria, and new office and storage facilities were built in Dublin and Melbourne. The Spanish subsidiary purchased property near Madrid and constructed workshops, warehousing, and office facilities there. In 1974, property and buildings were purchased in Lidcombe, near Sydney. Alfa-Laval Engineering was formed in Tokyo and another subsidiary established in Caracas. In Leewarden, the Netherlands, Tebel Maschinefabrieken was acquired for the manufacturing of machines for cheesemaking. In 1975, a subsidiary was formed in Iran in connection with the delivery of two large dairy facilities. In 1976, an office was opened in Moscow, and Lavalco established production facilities in Branchbury, New Jersey, also building workshops and offices for its spray-dryer department. In the same year, Sullivan Systems of the United States, a producer of refining systems for vegetable oil, was acquired. In 1977, a subsidiary was formed in Athens; the West German subsidiary acquired Atmos Lebensmitteltechnik, a manufacturer of machines for the meat industry; STAL Refrigeration formed a subsidiary in the United States; De Laval Company (U.K.) purchased the Ibex Engineering Company, Hastings; and the OTEC project for the utilization of temperature differences in tropical oceans was initiated. In 1979, the U.S. company changed its name to Alfa-Laval Inc. and the Canadian company became Alfa-Laval Lté.

In 1980, Alfa-Laval Company (U.K.) bought Dairy Supplies Hereford. A subsidiary was formed in Harare, Zimbabwe. In 1981, the West German company Bran & Lübbe, Norderstedt, a producer of dosing pumps and system and measurement instruments for the food industry, was acquired. This company had subsidiaries in a number of countries. The French Alfa-Laval company bought the firm Jean Pagées et Fils of Lyon, office and service center facilities were built in Singapore, a subsidiary was formed in Nairobi, and the Peruvian subsidiary constructed offices and warehouses. In the same period, Alfa-Laval increased its interest in the Japanese firm of Nagase-Alfa to 70 percent and Alfa-Laval Service was established in Japan as a wholly owned company for the sale of spare parts to the industrial sector. Alfa-Laval Contracting was formed in the United Kingdom, and in West Germany Alfa-Laval acquired 26 percent of the shares in G. Riedel Kälte- und Klimatechnik. In 1983, offices were opened in Cairo and Damascus to service the Middle Eastern market.

In early 1985, Alfa-Laval established a subsidiary in Portugal and an office was opened in Peking. In the same year, 100 percent of the free-floating shares of the Swiss company Chemap and its subsidiaries were acquired. Chemap was one of the world's largest manufacturers of fermenters. Haven Automation International, Hong Kong, along with its subsidiaries, was purchased. The company served the marine and offshore markets in Southeast Asia. In Australia, Heat Transfer Pty. Ltd., a manufacturer of a specific type of tube heat exchanger, was acquired and a majority holding was taken in Bioter S.A., one of the market leaders in fish feed in Spain. In New Zealand, Alfa-Laval purchased the company Manus Nu-Pulse.

Two companies in Sweden and one in the Netherlands, the Tebel Pneumatiek, were sold during 1985. The total number of Alfa-Laval's employees decreased by 636 to 15,394; 5,239 new employees were appointed in Sweden and 10,155 abroad. In 1986, Alfa-Laval established a finance company, Alfinal, in Belgium. Finance companies were also formed in Denmark and West Germany, and a leasing company was started in Spain.

After a long period at the helm of Alfa-Laval, since 1922, Axel Wästfelt had retired as managing director in 1946 and was replaced by the English-born Harry G. Faulkner. Faulkner had been an auditor in the U.K. subsidiary of accounting company Price Waterhouse & Company and went on in the 1930s to become managing director of Electrolux. During Faulkner's leadership, Alfa-Laval grew at a rapid pace in all traditional areas, particularly overseas. He led the company aggressively in industrial marketing, in sharp contrast with the preceding decades. In 1960, the 36-year-old Hans Stahle took over as managing director.

A principal feature of the change lay in the transfers of companies, which were carried out during the merger-happy 1960s, in consultation with Jacob Wallenberg, chairman of the board from 1960 to 1970. The factory manufacturing industrial separators was moved from the Stockholm center to Tumba, 25 kilometers southwest of the city, and in 1964 the head office followed. In 1980, Hans Stahle became chairman and was succeeded as managing director by Harry Faulkner, son of Harry G. Faulkner. During the 1980s, a large number of divisions within manufacturing and administration were formed into affiliates responsible for their own accounting. In 1989, Harry Faulkner was replaced by Lars V. Kylberg, who joined Alfa-Laval in May 1989. In October of the same year, Hans Stahle died while still executive chairman and was succeeded by Peder Bonde.

It was during the directorship of Harry Faulkner that Alfa-Laval bought the Sharples Separator Company, at the end of 1988. Sharples was until 1988 the world's largest manufacturer of decanter centrifuges, with a very strong position in the U.S. domestic market. It was the same company that had already in 1883–84 cooperated with Alfa-Laval in the U.S. market, and since 1887 had turned out to be one of the Swedish company's most aggressive competitors, particularly in the United States. Harry Faulkner pointed out that of the 20 acquisitions made between 1986 and 1988 by Alfa-Laval, Sharples was the largest. The acquisition of Sharples was of strategic importance since it greatly strengthened the separator business which forms the core of Alfa-Laval's operations. The Sharples group has subsidiaries in some ten countries and production facilities in both the United States and Europe. The group's annual sales were approximately $100 million.

Koppens Machinenfabriek in the Netherlands and Krämer & Grebe in West Germany were also integrated into the Alfa-Laval group in 1989. During the first half of 1990, Alfa-Laval acquired TW Kutter in the United States, an engineering company and food processing equipment distributor. In the heat exchanger sector, Alfa-Laval purchased the Italian company Artec. Furthermore, joint-owned sales companies were formed in Hungary and Poland and negotiations were in progress in 1990 for the establishment of subsidiaries in other former Eastern bloc countries. Between 1985 and 1989, the number of employees in the original Alfa-Laval group was reduced by 4,000 as a result of rationalization, restructuring of production, and the sale of peripheral operations, and a total of 7,500 new employees joined the group as a result of acquisitions. The total number of employees during 1989 increased by 2,561, from 17,156 in 1988 to 19,717 in 1989. In 1989, new managing director Lars V. Kylberg pointed out that "in recent years our sales have doubled in North America. In the booming Pacific Basin, we are firmly rooted in Singapore and the Asian countries. Our overall strategy for the coming years is to grow within our core business."

Changes in the 1990s and Beyond

While Alfa Laval (the hyphen in the company's named was dropped in 1993) pursued growth in the 1990s, the company dealt with several major changes. The first came in 1991, when Switzerland-based Tetra Pak Group made a $2.68 billion offer for the company. The Tetra Pak offer was attractive to Alfa Laval, largely due to the recent fall in its profits. Indeed, according to a 1991 *Wall Street Journal* article, "The union would spawn one of the world's biggest producers of food packaging and processing equipment."

After the takeover was announced, anti-competition concerns led to an investigation by the European Commission. The two companies agreed to various concessions and were eventually allowed to complete the transaction. In 1993, Alfa Laval was reorganized as an independent industrial group within the Tetra Laval group. Tetra Pak took over the company's liquid food processing business while farm equipment and related units were organized into a new division, Alfa Laval Agri.

Under its new parent, Alfa Laval spent the latter half of the decade working to develop new products. Among those was a new oil treatment system used on board ships. The ThinkTop Separation Unit and Control & Indication units were launched in 1999 and were considered some of the industry's most advanced automated valve control systems.

Another major change was on the horizon for Alfa Laval as it planned to enter the 21st century. Charterhouse Development Capital made a SEK 14.5 billion offer for the company after Tetra Laval put the firm up for sale in 1999. The sale failed to come to fruition, leaving Alfa Laval's future hanging in the balance. UBS Capital made an offer for the firm, but again buyout talks were terminated after UBS determined that Tetra Laval's asking price was too high. Finally, Industri Kapital 2000 Ltd. agreed to acquire a controlling interest Alfa Laval in 2000 in one of the largest Scandinavian management buyout campaigns in history. Under Industri Kapital, Alfa Laval focused on strengthening its Separation, Heat Transfer, and Fluid Handling business units.

After operating as a private company for over ten years, Alfa Laval re-listed on the Stockholm Stock Exchange on May 17, 2002. Industri Kapital CEO Bjvrn Savnen commented on the move in an April 2002 *efinancialnews.com* article, stating, "We have been very pleased with Alfa Laval's performance during our ownership. Already at the time of our investment we saw a listing of the company as a logical continuation of the company's future development." Alfa Laval CEO Sigge Haraldsson agreed, adding, "For us the IPO means that our financial position will be strengthened, allowing for additional growth and expansion."

Fueled by the offering, Alfa Laval made two key purchases in 2003. The firm of bioKinetics, a division of Kinetics Groups Inc., was added to the company's holdings and gave it a foothold in the high-tech integrated process solutions industry that served the biotech and pharmaceutical markets. Alfa Laval also acquired the Toftejorg Group, a leading Denmark-based tank cleaning equipment manufacturer. In addition, the company developed AlfaNova that year, a compact heat exchanger that was able to withstand high temperatures and pressures. At the same time, Industri Kapital reduced its stake in the firm from 26.9 percent to 17.9 percent.

The company expected to continue its growth in the years to come. Its business strategy was focused on six areas: the growth of its current products and services, market-driven research and development, the creation of a new marketing organization with ten customer segments, consideration of the aftermarket for growth potential, the development of new marketing concepts, and the addition of new products. Haraldsson planned to retire in late 2004, leaving Alfa Laval on the hunt for a new leader.

Principal Subsidiaries

Alfa Laval Holding AB; Alfa Laval NV; Alfa Laval Holding BV; Alfa Laval Holding GmbH; Alfa Laval USA Inc.; Alfa Laval Inc. (U.S.); Alfa Laval India Ltd.; Alfa Laval KK (Japan); Alfa Laval Philippines Inc.; Alfa Laval Copenhagen A/S; Alfa Laval France SAS.

Principal Operating Units

Separation; Heat Transfer; Fluid Handling.

Principal Competitors

Tyco International Ltd.; Emerson Electric Company; Honeywell International Inc.; Parker Hannifin Corporation.

Further Reading

"Alfa Laval Acquires Toftejorg Group," *Food Trade Review*, May 2003, p. 254.

"Alfa Laval Sold, Scandies Shut out London Lenders," *Euroweek*, June 23, 2000, p. 43.

Ascarelli, Silvia, "Alfa Laval Cuts Scope of Its IPO," *Wall Street Journal*, May 15, 2002, p. C11.

Burton, John, "Swedes Agree Alfa Laval Merger Deal," *Financial Times*, April 20, 1001, p. 10.

Bushrod, Lisa, "Industri Kapital Manages Alfa Laval IPO," *European Venture Capital Journal*, June 1, 2002, p. 1.

Dawnay, Kit, "Alfa Laval's IPO Is Biggest in Sweden for Nearly Two Years," *efinancialnews.com*, April 25, 2002.

The Growth of a Global Enterprise: Alfa-Laval 100 Years, Stockholm: Alfa-Laval AB and Esselte Wezäta, 1983.

Fritz, Martin, *Ett världsföretag växer fram. Alfa-Laval 100 år, Del II: Konsolidering och expansion*, Stockholm: Alfa-Laval, 1983.

"Haraldsson to Step down From Alfa Laval Helm," *Lloyd's List*, January 28, 2004, p. 3.

Moore, Stephen D., "Tetra Pak Proposes Friendly Takeover of Alfa-Laval Valued at $2.91 Billion," *Wall Street Journal*, January 29, 2001, p. A15.

"Packaging Crusader Wraps up Merger Deal," *Financial Times*, May 24, 1991, p.23.

"Putting Tetra Laval Together," *Business Europe*, October 18, 1993.

"Third Time Lucky for Sale of Tetra Laval Division," *Financial Times*, June 14, 2000, p. 30.

Wohlert, Claus, "Concentration Tendencies in Swedish Industry before World War I," *The Concentration Process in the Entrepreneurial Economy Since the Late 19th Century*, edited by Hans Pol and Wilhelm True, Munich: Zeitschrift für Unternehmensgeschichte, 1988.

——, *Framväxten av svenska multinationella föreag*, Stockholm: Almpvist & Wiksell International, 1981.

—Claus Wohlert
—update: Christina M. Stansell

America's Car-Mart, Inc.

1501 Southeast Walton Boulevard, Suite 213
Bentonville, Arkansas 72712
U.S.A.
Telephone: (479) 464-9944
Fax: (479) 273-7556
Web site: http://www.car-mart.com

Public Company
Incorporated: 1981
Employees: 550
Sales: $154.80 million (2003)
Stock Exchanges: NASDAQ
Ticker Symbol: CRMT
NAIC: 523999 Miscellaneous Financial Investment
Activities; 441120 Used Car Dealers; 551112 Offices
of Other Holding Companies

America's Car-Mart, Inc., operates a chain of more than 70 used-car dealerships. Car-Mart targets customers with limited or poor credit histories and offers these customers financing. Typically, a Car-Mart customer pays a down payment of between zero percent and 17 percent of the automobile's cost. The average price of an automobile on a Car-Mart lot is $6,200. Payments are made by the customer as frequently as once per week. If a payment is one day late, the customer receives a letter from Car-Mart. After three days without payment, the customer receives a telephone call from Car-Mart. Vehicles are repossessed after 40 days without payment. Approximately 18 percent of Car-Mart's customers have their vehicles repossessed. Car-Mart operates dealerships in Arkansas, Oklahoma, Kentucky, Missouri, Texas, Kansas, and Indiana. The company prefers to open its dealerships in rural communities, favoring communities with populations ranging between 20,000 and 50,000.

Origins

Car-Mart was started in 1981, when the company's first used-car dealership opened in Rogers, Arkansas. The basis of the company's business strategy from the start was to sell automobiles to customers with limited or poor credit. The first dealership focused on extending credit to individuals who could not obtain loans from conventional sources or other used-car dealers, offering itself as the only way some residents in Rogers could purchase transportation. The offer was not altruistic: The company charged high interest rates and it pursued delinquent accounts doggedly, but the offer did answer a need. The Rogers dealership recorded immediate success, prompting management to open three more dealerships in 1982, each offering the company's "Buy Here/Pay Here" financing.

Car-Mart discovered a lucrative market niche in the early 1980s and built on its sound business premise throughout the 1980s and into the 1990s. The company's business model required assiduous, daily attention to its sales, placing a premium on the financing side of the business. The cars were merely commodities, commodities that consumers wanted, and commodities that some consumers could only obtain by entering into financing agreements such as those offered by Car-Mart. The profits to be made were enticing, but much depended on the careful execution of the financing model. In this area, Car-Mart excelled, enabling the company to expand throughout Arkansas.

Car-Mart targeted rural markets, those communities with populations ranging between 20,000 and 50,000. According to the company's thinking, in these small communities the need for a car was greater than in a large metropolitan market supported by mass-transit systems such as buses or subways. In addition, individuals who failed to make payments were easier to track down in smaller communities. For Car-Mart, everything depended on recouping the money credited to its customers, an endeavor the company found far easier in rural communities.

During the first 18 years of its existence, the company opened an average of nearly two new dealerships each year, fanning outward from its starting point in Rogers. By the end of 1998, the company operated 35 dealerships, presiding over a $65 million-in-sales operation whose geographic reach extended from Arkansas into Oklahoma, Texas, and Missouri. It was at this point that the company was introduced to another company named Crown Group, Inc., forever changing the structure and strategy of Crown Group.

1999 Acquisition by Crown Group

Crown Group, which played a decisive role in Car-Mart's future from the end of 1998 forward, began its eclectic corporate life in 1983. During its first decade of existence, as Car-Mart expanded throughout Arkansas, Crown Group operated in various facets of the cable television business, owning a range of cable and cable-related programming businesses. In 1992, the Irving, Texas-based company decided to reinvent itself. It sold most of its programming businesses and began to search for new business opportunities, embarking on a path toward diversity. After exploring various businesses, the company decided to enter the casino market. In June 1993, the company acquired St. Charles Gaming Company, Inc., a company that owned, operated, and developed casino gaming properties. St. Charles's signature property, a riverboat casino located in Calcasieu Parish, Louisiana, was completed in mid-1995, by which time Crown Group already had begun to reduce its ownership stake in the casino company. Crown Group sold 50 percent of St. Charles in June 1995, making a profit on its original investment, and sold the remaining percentage in May 1996.

After the divestiture of St. Charles, Crown Group had to find a new identity for itself. The company either formed companies or acquired companies that in less than a year added numerous faces to the organization. The program to expand into variegated business interests began in June 1997, when the company added two companies to its fold. Crown Group acquired a 49 percent stake in Casino Magic Neuguen S.A., an enterprise that operated two casinos in Argentina. The company also formed Concorde Acceptance Corporation, a mortgage lender targeting customers with less than exemplary credit history. Crown Group added two more companies in February 1998. The company purchased 53 percent of Paaco Automotive Group, a used-car dealership that also owned a finance company, and 80 percent of Precision IBC, Inc., a company that rented sold, tested, and serviced stainless steel bulk containers. In May 1998, Crown increased its interest in Paaco to 65 percent and its interest in Precision to 100 percent. The company also added a fifth company in May 1998, forming Home Stay Lodges I, Ltd., a partnership focused on the development and operation of extended-stay lodging facilities.

By the end of 1998, Crown Group had completed the quick transformation from casino operator into a diversified holding company with interests in gambling, used cars, mortgage lending, bulk containers, and lodging. Its management was ready to make further additions to the company's portfolio of concerns,

and in the beginning of 1999 its sights set on Car-Mart. In Paaco, Crown Group already had an interest in used-car sales. Like Car-Mart, Paaco catered to customers with weak credit histories and offered financing to such customers, but unlike Car-Mart, Paaco focused on larger metropolitan markets, operating in Dallas/Ft. Worth and Houston, and it reconditioned nearly all of its vehicles, a practice Car-Mart did not observe. In January 1999, Crown Group added to its used-car holdings by acquiring 100 percent of Car-Mart for $41 million, purchasing the company when its annual sales totaled $65 million. Once included within Crown Group's fold, Car-Mart exuded admirable strength, quickly becoming the holding company's brightest shining asset. Within two years, the success of Car-Mart convinced Crown Group's management to change its business strategy entirely.

Crown Group's management continued to add to its holdings in the months following the acquisition of Car-Mart. In February 1999, the company took a 50.1 percent interest in CG Incorporated, S.A. de C.V., which was formed to develop and operate casinos in El Salvador. The following month, the company acquired 45 percent of Atlantic Castings, Inc., an investment-casting manufacturer of turbine engine components. In December 1999, management showed its growing appreciation for the used-car business by adding to its investment in Paaco and Car-Mart. The company acquired a 70 percent interest in Smart Choice Automotive Group, a company that sold and financed used cars and trucks in Florida. Once the acquisition was completed, Paaco became a wholly owned subsidiary of Smart Choice.

The acquisitions completed once Crown Group decided to diversify its interests led to exponential revenue growth. Having shed nearly all of its assets by 1997, the company's sales volume totaled $2 million at the beginning of its acquisition campaign. By 1999, revenues had reached $111 million. In 2000, sales totaled $237 million, a total derived primarily from the company's involvement in used-car sales and financing. Of the $237 million generated in sales in 2000, nearly $220 million came from the company's three used-car entities. The 35 dealerships operated by Car-Mart combined with the ten dealerships operated by Paaco and the 15 dealerships operated by Smart Choice represented the heart of the company.

As Crown Group entered the 21st century, it looked at its diverse holdings and began to increase its already overwhelming dependence on used-car sales and financing. The company began to retreat from its other businesses, divesting its casino holdings and lodging interests and, by April 2001, reducing its equity position in Precision to 50 percent. The divestitures left the company with its used-car operations, a 50 percent stake in Precision, an 80 percent interest in Concorde, and a 45 percent stake in Atlantic Castings. Revenues for the 12-month period ending in April 2001 totaled $342 million, $327 million of which came from the company's used-car businesses.

An Independent Entity in 2001

During the summer of 2001, Crown Group's management was involved in serious discussions about the future of the company. The discussions led to the announcement in October 2001 that the company intended to sell all of its subsidiaries

Key Dates:

1981: The first Car-Mart dealership opens in Rogers, Arkansas.
1999: Car-Mart is acquired by Crown Group, Inc.
2001: Crown Group announces it will sell all its businesses except for Car-Mart.
2002: Crown Group changes its name to America's Car-Mart, Inc.

except for Car-Mart. Further, the company intended to abandon its headquarters in Irving, Texas, and move to Car-Mart's home base in Bentonville, Arkansas. Finally, in the ultimate expression of the company's commitment to Car-Mart, it revealed that it would change its name to America's Car-Mart, Inc. The decision to stake its future entirely on Car-Mart was based on two conclusions. First, Car-Mart had proven to be the strongest asset within the company. In 2001, Car-Mart generated more profits than all of Crown Group's other subsidiaries combined. Second, Crown Group's management believed the diversity of its holdings presented a confusing picture to investors. "It was hard for investors to know what they were investing in," the company's chief executive officer explained in a September 17, 2002 interview with *Investor's Business Daily*. "So we've become one company they do understand: auto retailing."

The momentous announcement made in October 2001 set in motion the unraveling of Crown Group and its emergence as Car-Mart. Smart Choice was sold in October 2001. In the beginning of the year 2002, the company officially changed its name to America's Car-Mart, Inc. In May 2002, the company sold its 50 percent interest in Precision for $3.8 million. In July 2002, the company divested its last non-Car-Mart asset, selling its 80 percent interest in Concorde for $3 million. Meanwhile, a new management team was installed, taking the helm in May 2002. Nan R. Smith, who had served as Car-Mart's chief operating officer from 1981 to 1998 and as its president from 1999 to May 2002, was appointed vice-chairman of the board in May 2002 before being named chairman of the board in September 2002. Tilman J. Falgout, III, who had served as Car-Mart's general counsel since 1995, was appointed chief executive officer.

The new management team took control of a vibrant enterprise with an impressive record of financial growth. During a seven-year period beginning in the mid-1990s, Car-Mart's sales increased at a compounded annual growth rate of 20 percent. Its profits during the same period increased at a 21.4 percent compounded annual growth rate. During its ownership by Crown Group, Car-Mart increased the number of its dealerships from 35 to the 62 properties Smith and Falgout presided over in late 2002. Geographically, the company had expanded into Kentucky, Indiana, and Kansas since 1999, giving it a presence in seven states.

As Car-Mart prepared for its future, it planned to continue to expand the proven concept that had realized growth for more than 20 years. Much of the company's success depended on its ability to effectively prosecute its "Buy Here/Pay Here" financing model. "It requires daily execution to keep contact with customers," an analyst said in a September 17, 2002 interview with *Investor's Business Daily*. Falgout realized as much, saying in the same article, "Collections is the focus of our business—selling cars is not." By April 2003, after opening nine new dealerships during the preceding 12 months, the company owned 64 dealerships. In the years ahead, it planned to follow what Falgout referred to as a "grass fire" approach to expansion. The company intended to spread outward from its base in Arkansas, hoping to eventually make Car-Mart a genuine, nationally operating chain of dealerships.

Principal Subsidiaries

Crown Group of Nevada, Inc.; Crown Delaware Investments Corporation; Colonial Auto Financing, Inc.; Colonial Underwriting, Inc.; Texas Car-Mart, Inc.; Auto Finance Investors, Inc.

Principal Competitors

AutoNation, Inc.; CarMax, Inc.; DriveTime Automotive Group, Inc.

Further Reading

"Car-Mart Plans to Expand Presence in Oklahoma with Two New Dealerships," *Knight Ridder/Tribune Business News,* May 31, 2002.
"Crown Group Inc. of Irving, Texas, Is Changing Its Name to America's Car-Mart, Inc. and Moving to Rogers," *Arkansas Business,* November 19, 2001, p. 14.
Reeves, Amy, "America's Car-Mart Inc.," *Investor's Business Daily,* September 17, 2002, p. A12.
Sawyers, Arlena, "Dallas Firm Buys Smart Choice," *Automotive News,* September 6, 1999, p. 38.
Turner, Nick, " 'Buy Here, Pay Here' Leader in Used Cars," *Investor's Business Daily,* October 13, 2003, p. A09.

—Jeffrey L. Covell

AmerisourceBergen Corporation

P.O. Box 959
Valley Forge, Pennsylvania 19482
U.S.A.
Telephone: (610) 727-7000
Toll Free: (800) 829-3132
Fax: (610) 727-3600
Web site: http://www.amerisourcebergen.net

Public Company
Incorporated: 1985 as Alco Health Services Corp.; 1969
    as Bergen Brunswig Corp.
Employees: 14,800
Sales: $49.6 billion (2003)
Stock Exchanges: New York
Ticker Symbol: ABC
NAIC: 422210 Drugs and Druggists' and Sundries
    Wholesalers

AmerisourceBergen Corporation is one of the largest pharmaceutical services companies in the United States. The firm distributes pharmaceutical products and services to health care providers, including hospital systems, physicians' offices, alternate care and mail order facilities, independent community pharmacies, and regional chain pharmacies. It also provides logistical expertise, contract packaging services, and product marketing services to its manufacturing customers. AmerisourceBergen was created out of the 2001 union of AmeriSource Health Corp. and Bergen Brunswig Corp.

History of AmeriSource

In August 1985, the company that would become AmeriSource was incorporated as Alco Health Services and held an initial public stock offering of 4.7 million shares. The history of the predecessor Alco Health Services can be traced to 1977, when a diversified conglomerate, the Alco Standard Corporation, entered the pharmaceutical distribution business by purchasing The Drug House, a major wholesaler operating in Pennsylvania and Delaware.

Alco Standard was the brainchild of entrepreneur Tinkham Veale II, who had built a multimillion-dollar conglomerate on the principle of corporate partnership. Veale sought to acquire healthy, owner-managed companies in the $5 million to $10 million range. He allowed each company practically full autonomy, while providing support in legal and tax matters. When Alco Standard was incorporated in 1960, it was a modest $5 million chemical company. By 1968, sales were $140 million, coming from 52 subsidiaries with products ranging from stamped metal parts to wax paper.

Shortly after Alco Standard's acquisition of The Drug House, the company began to build a network of drug wholesalers. In early 1978, Duff Brothers of Chattanooga, Tennessee, was acquired, and later that year Marsin Medical Supply Company of Philadelphia, Pennsylvania, was purchased. Geer Drug, with annual sales of about $45 million, was acquired in 1979. Headquartered in Charleston, South Carolina, Geer foreshadowed an expansive drive southward. By the early 1980s, Alco Standard's pharmaceutical distribution network was the third largest in the nation.

Alco Standard soon made other acquisitions of pharmaceutical wholesalers, including Kauffman-Lattimer of Columbus, Ohio; Smith-Higgins of Johnson City, Tennessee; Strother Drug of Virginia; and Brown Drug, which operated in South Dakota, Iowa, and Minnesota. At the same time, the drug industry itself was undergoing intense change. Healthcare expenditures in the United States were on the uptrend, amounting to about 10 percent of the gross national product by 1985. As the population grew older, the health care industry promised continued growth.

Alco Health Services Grows as an Independent Operation

In 1985, Alco Standard's drug distribution operations were spun off into a separate company, Alco Health Services Corporation. Alco Standard retained approximately 60 percent of the new company's stock. The new company continued to use Alco Standard's administrative functions on a fee basis. Alco Health was led by John H. Kennedy as chairman and Joseph B. Churchman as president.

Shortly after Alco Health began to operate independently, it acquired the Valdosta Drug Company of Valdosta, Georgia, with $22 million in annual sales, and the $100-million-a-year Meyers and Company of Tiffin, Ohio. These two acquisitions helped push Alco's sales over the $1 billion mark.

In the early 1980s, drug wholesalers found new ways to support the independent drug retailers that comprised nearly 60 percent of their business. Wholesalers offered more non-drug products, including hospital supplies and health and beauty aids. Alco Health sought to strengthen its independent customers by sharing its own primary strength-marketing. By offering services such as in-store merchandising and group advertising, wholesalers could help their customers compete with the growing drugstore chains. Alco Health introduced its retail support program in 1982. Such support tactics as customized price stickers gave a boost to those independent druggists who participated. A year later, Alco introduced a complete line of medical equipment for home use, from wheelchairs to disposable syringes under the Total Home Health Care program, which provided independent retailers the marketing support they needed for such products through direct-to-customer delivery and accounting assistance.

Computer services provided by the wholesaler included management information reports, automated retail accounts-receivable systems, and shelf labels for automated inventory control. By 1985, Alco Health was marketing an in-pharmacy computer system based on an IBM personal computer that was capable of being used for total store automation.

At the same time, wholesalers, including Alco Health, began to develop the business of large drugstore chains and mass merchandisers. In 1981, 25 percent of all wholesalers' business was to drugstore chains, up from 15 percent in 1971. The opportunity arose because of the reluctance of manufacturers to maintain the costly sales force needed for direct selling to chains. The trend continued throughout the 1980s. By 1985, chain drugstores and mass merchandisers made up 18 percent of Alco Health's annual revenues.

Sales to hospitals also increased in the early 1980s, as health care facilities attempted to lower their costs by reducing their pharmaceutical inventories. Alco was able to provide rapid, often same-day, service to many facilities. By 1985, 24 percent of Alco Health's sales were to hospitals.

During the latter half of the 1980s, Alco Health continued to grow at a tremendous rate. In 1986, further acquisitions included L.S. DuBois Son and Company of Paducah, Kentucky; Pennington Drug of Joplin, Missouri; Mississippi Drug of Jackson, Mississippi; and MD Pharmaceuticals of Dothan, Alabama, adding $300 million in annual revenues. Archer Drug of Little Rock, Arkansas, and Michiana Merchandising of Mishawaka, Indiana, were also purchased.

In 1987, Alco Health reorganized several of its operating units. Smith-Higgins, Valdosta Drug, MD Pharmaceuticals, Mississippi Drug, and Duff Brothers were combined to make up the southeastern region of Alco Health. Geer Drug and Strother Drug were combined to eliminate overlap. Management of the new units remained in the hands of regional managers, and their territories were enlarged considerably.

Alco Health's marketing strategy, which focused on three areas—independent druggists, hospitals, and chain drugstores and mass merchandisers—remained constant throughout the 1980s. A major boost to the third segment came in 1987, when Alco Health was selected as the primary wholesale supplier to 1,000 of the Revco chain's 2,000 drugstores. In 1988 revenues passed $2 billion.

John F. McNamara, formerly chief operating officer, became president of Alco Health in 1987. McNamara came to the company in 1981 when Kauffman-Lattimer was acquired. Kennedy remained chairman until August 1988, when previously retired Ray Mundt returned temporarily to oversee changes in Alco Health's ownership. Mundt previously had served as president of Alco Standard and on the Alco Health board of directors.

Management-Led Buyout in 1998

In early 1988, a management group attempted a leveraged buyout of Alco Health, offering $26 per share to take the company private. Shortly thereafter, in June, McKesson Corporation, formerly Foremost-McKesson, the largest drug wholesaler in the country with 28 percent of the national market, offered $30 per share, or $508 million, for Alco Health. The deal, however, fell through three months later when the Federal Trade Commission (FTC) ruled against the acquisition on antitrust grounds. Alco Health was still 49-percent owned by its former parent, Alco Standard Corporation. Alco Health explored options with its investment banker, Drexel Burnham Lambert.

In November 1988, a group of investors, which included Citicorp Venture Capital Ltd. and a group of Alco management-level employees, proposed a cash tender offer for Alco Health's shares at $31 per share. A holding company, AHSC Holdings Corporation, was set up to handle the acquisition. The proposal was accepted and when the tender offer expired at the end of December 1988, AHSC Holdings owned 92 percent of Alco Health's stock. The merger allowed for the conversion of the remaining equity into debentures due in the year 2004. Alco Health continued its normal daily operations during the transition of ownership. John F. McNamara led the company as chairman, CEO, and president from 1989.

New Challenges and Opportunities in the 1990s

The early 1990s provided new challenges and opportunities to Alco Health Services and pharmaceutical wholesalers in general. The drug market continued its expansion, fueled by an

Key Dates:

1907: Lucien Brunswig buys out his partner and renames his business Brunswig Drug Company.

1947: Emil P. Martini creates the Bergen Drug Company.

1969: Martini successfully negotiates the purchase of Brunswig Drug Corporation; the merged company is named the Bergen Brunswig Corporation.

1977: Alco Standard Corporation purchases The Drug House.

1985: Alco Health Services Corporation is incorporated.

1988: AHSC Holdings Corporation acquires Alco in a management-led buyout.

1994: Alco Health changes its name to AmeriSource Health Corporation.

1999: The company purchases C.D. Smith Healthcare and a substantial share of ADDS Telepharmacy Solutions, Inc.

2001: AmeriSource acquires Bergen Brunswig and renames itself AmerisourceBergen.

aging population and its need for health care. The trend in pharmaceutical distribution was toward fewer competitors handling a greater market share. From 1979 to 1990, the number of U.S. drug wholesalers decreased from 150 to 90, while the role of middlemen increased. The top five companies, including Alco Health, handled about half of the business nationwide. As the field of suitable acquisitions thinned out, and as the pharmaceutical-distribution field became a battle of the giants, Alco Health placed greater emphasis on internal expansion.

In July 1994, Alco Health, one of America's top five pharmaceutical wholesalers, changed its name to AmeriSource Health Corporation. The company aimed to increase its business by driving unnecessary costs out of its distribution system and repositioning itself as a unified source of products and programs nationally. Many of the company's divisions, which until then had maintained their original identity, became part of the AmeriSource family. The company, now located in Malvern, Pennsylvania, continued to acquire other companies throughout the latter half of the 1990s: in 1995, Liberty Drug Systems, the North Carolina-based provider of pharmacy software and hardware and Newbro Drug Co. of Idaho Falls; in 1996, Gulf Distribution Inc.; and in 1997, the equity interests of Walker Drug Company LLC. AmeriSource also aimed to tighten its relationship with its retail customers via a nationwide telemarketing program instituted in 1995. However, in 1996, several of those customers were less than satisfied. In a case later dismissed in District Court, several retail pharmacies claimed that AmeriSource had conspired to deprive them of discounts offered by HMOs, hospitals, and mail order pharmacies.

In 1997, AmeriSource made national news as it joined again with McKesson, this time as part of a proposed merger. The U.S. District Court blocked the move, as it did a similar move that year to merge Bergen Brunswig and Cardinal Health. Both mergers would have reshaped the distribution picture across the United States. All four companies argued that they sought

consolidation in a move to make themselves more efficient and cut prices. However, the FTC claimed that the mergers were the companies' "chosen means to remove their incentives to cut prices." The drug wholesalers, according to the FTC, had so many distribution centers that they were forced to cut prices to keep products off their shelves.

AmeriSource responded to the court's decision by turning its attention to local objectives, signing on new customers, attempting to control costs, and investing in new marketing initiatives cumulatively known as "disease state management." "At the end of the day," according to R. David Yost, president and chief executive officer of the company, in a 1998 *Drug Store News* article, "we maintain that wholesaling is a local business. . . . In our vision for the future, we see the community pharmacy playing a key role. . . . We see the pharmacist of the future being totally involved in customers' healthcare management and being paid for it."

To this end, AmeriSource, introduced value-added programs in the late 1990s, such as MedAssess, a disease state management program to help pharmacists monitor clients' regimens, and the Diabetes Shoppe, a program designed to train the pharmacist to train the diabetic. Other programs included Family Pharmacy, American Health Packaging, Health Services Plus, and ECHO, the company's proprietary software system. In 1999, the company purchased a substantial share of ADDS Telepharmacy Solutions, Inc., a leading provider of e-commerce medications management.

The company continued to grow in size and reputation in 1999 and 2000. In 1999, AmeriSource purchased C.D. Smith Healthcare, a leading regional wholesale pharmaceutical distributor, and gained a contract with the Department of Veterans Affairs to provide services to its more than 500 pharmacies. In 2000, it purchased Pharmacy Healthcare Solution, a pharmacy consulting company. The company became a "preferred provider" in 1999 of both the Pharmacy Providers Service Corporation, representing 1,200 independent pharmacies, and Premier, Inc., the nation's largest alliance of hospitals and healthcare systems in the United States.

History of Bergen Brunswig

Lucien Napoleon Brunswig, the founder of Bergen Brunswig, was born in 1854 in France, the son of a country doctor. While Lucien felt little inclination to pursue the healing art of his father, he did develop an interest in some day providing the drugs that were vital to patients' treatment. When political turmoil in France in the 1870s prompted Lucien, and many other young French people, to emigrate, he arrived in the United States unemployed and nearly penniless. In 1871, the 17-year-old Lucien was accepted as an apprentice to a U.S. druggist.

Apprenticeship meant more than learning the drug trade; it also entailed sweeping floors, cleaning out the cages of the pets sold at the drugstore, and attending to other menial tasks. Despite his meager income, Lucien Brunswig's hard work and thrift helped him save enough to open a retail drug store in Atchison, Kansas, when he was 21 years old. His drugstore was such a success that he sold it profitably and took the train as far southwest as it would go, to a few miles outside of Fort Worth, Texas, then a small, dusty town of a few hundred people.

Brunswig's Fort Worth drugstore, serving both retail and wholesale, flourished. By 1883, less than five years after he had opened the store, his business reported $350,000 in annual sales. In 1882, George R. Finlay, the owner of a well-established wholesale drug firm in New Orleans, invited Brunswig to join him as a partner. Lucien Brunswig readily agreed to sell his own drug business and become Finlay's business partner in New Orleans. Finlay's firm, Wheelock-Finlay, became Finlay and Brunswig. Upon Finlay's death in 1885, Lucien Brunswig took over the entire wholesale drug operation and settled into New Orleans, where he served as a police commissioner of the city for four years. In 1887, Brunswig took on a partner, F.W. Braun.

The following year, Brunswig became interested in expanding west, setting his sights on faraway Los Angeles, California, a growing town of 30,000. Brunswig dispatched Braun to Los Angeles to open one of the few wholesale drug companies in the area, the F.W. Braun Company. Business opened in Los Angeles on the first floor of a two-story adobe house. Pharmaceuticals were not only sold over the counter, but a few salesmen also ventured out to visit druggists and procure their orders, which could be filled within two to three weeks. After a year, F.W. Braun Company was flourishing and moved into the Old Post Office Building next-door, the first of a series of expansions.

In 1890, while Lucien Brunswig remained in New Orleans, he ordered the opening of what would become a prosperous branch of F.W. Braun in San Diego, California, a city even smaller and dustier than Los Angeles, and one with fewer drugstores. The coming of the Spanish-American War was a boost for the drug business nationwide, and Lucien Brunswig's profits continued to soar. In 1903, deciding that the future of his company lay in the West, Brunswig sold his profitable New Orleans establishment and moved with his family to Los Angeles to preside over the continued expansion of his business. In 1907, he bought out Braun, and his business was renamed Brunswig Drug Company.

With headquarters in Los Angeles, the wholesale drug enterprise was soon expanded to include branches in Phoenix and Tucson, Arizona, as well as a short-lived store in Guaymas, Mexico. As a result of World War I, Pacific Coast business boomed, far beyond Brunswig's wildest dreams. In 1922, when other U.S. businesses were experiencing a slump, Brunswig's sale of drugs as well as cosmetics, a recent and lucrative addition to the drug line, reached a record level. In that same year, Brunswig decided the company needed a manufacturing plant that would house a laboratory and produce cosmetics. Goods that were manufactured in the Brunswig labs eventually made their way to the Philippines, Japan, and the Hawaiian Islands.

A wealthy businessman, Lucien Brunswig had also become an ardent bibliophile, art collector, and philanthropist. In 1927, he presented to the University of California at Los Angeles more than 1,000 books for its library of French language and literature. Moreover, with the onset of the Great Depression, Brunswig's company opened soup kitchens to feed the desperately poor; his own business did not suffer significantly during

this time. Brunswig died in 1943, two years after his retirement; he did not live to see his kingdom expand tremendously, as it did in the years following World War II.

Postwar Growth as a Wholesale Distributor

Roy V. Schwab succeeded Lucien Brunswig as president of the Brunswig Drug Corporation, moving the company's headquarters in 1947 to Vernon, California. By then, the Brunswig Drug Corporation had divested itself of its manufacturing plant and laboratories, concentrating solely on the wholesale distribution of pharmaceuticals. In fact, Brunswig was considered the most advanced wholesale drug operation in the United States, although by no means the largest. It was, for example, the first wholesale drug company in the United States to introduce computerized punchcards for keeping track of inventories.

In 1949, the 61-year-old Brunswig Drug Corporation merged with the Coffin Redington Company of San Francisco, the first of numerous significant mergers. The company expanded rapidly in California. In 1950, it opened its San Jose division; in 1951, its Sacramento division; and in 1954, its San Bernardino division. In 1952, it acquired the Smith-Faus Drug Company, and by 1960 it had 14 divisions in the southwestern United States.

In the eastern United States, another drug company benefited from the postwar economic boom. In 1947, Emil P. Martini founded and became the first president of the Bergen Drug Company based in Hackensack, New Jersey. A graduate of the New Jersey College of Pharmacy in 1923, Martini opened his first retail pharmacy in Hackensack five years later. A second pharmacy was acquired at the height of the Depression, and a third was acquired in 1937. A well-established member of the community and president of the New Jersey State Board of Pharmacy, Martini helped establish a wholesale drug distribution company in 1947 named after the county of Bergen in which they lived. The success of the Bergen Drug Company was phenomenal, in part because of the insatiable demand for the wonder drugs of World War II, including such antibiotics as penicillin. Despite the growing sales volume, the company continued to offer same-day service.

With the 1955 death of Emil P. Martini, Sr., leadership of the company was turned over to Martini's son, Emil P. Martini, Jr. The Bergen Drug Company then began rapidly expanding and acquiring other wholesale drug companies. In 1956, Bergen acquired Drug Service Inc. of Bridgeport, Connecticut. Between 1957 and 1958, Bergen operations were started in three California cities, Fresno, San Francisco, and Covina. In 1959, it became the first company in the nation to use computers for inventory control and accounting purposes. By the 1960s, Bergen Drug Company was among the largest wholesale drug distributors in the United States, supplying 5,000 pharmacists and hospitals.

Bergen and Brunswig Merge in 1969

In May 1969, Martini successfully negotiated the purchase of Brunswig Drug Corporation. The latter had sought to buy the former until Brunswig Drug managers realized that financially it made more sense to have Bergen buy their company, as the price-earnings figures of Bergen's stocks were more advantageous. The name of the new company would be the Bergen Brunswig Corporation.

Several acquisitions followed. In 1970 alone, the Bergen Brunswig Corporation added 12 drug companies and laboratories to its fold, transforming itself into a truly national drug distribution business. Head of the Bergen Drug Company since 1956, Martini, who had graduated with a degree in pharmacy from Purdue University, was given his original job in his father's firm with the understanding that he was to learn the drug distribution business from the bottom up, which he did. Under his direction and that of his younger brother, Robert E. Martini, also a pharmacist and vice-president of the company, the Bergen Brunswig Corporation became in the 1970s one of the most modern drug distribution companies in the United States.

Bergen Brunswig revolutionized the trade in 1971 when it pioneered the electronic transmission of purchase orders to Eli Lilly & Co. In the early 1970s, Bergen Brunswig introduced the handheld computer scanner, with which pharmacists could scan the barcodes on merchandise. Stock was then reordered on the basis of the information collected by the scanner. The inauguration in the late 1970s of an advanced computer system automated the prescription department still further, connecting hospitals and chain pharmacies electronically to Bergen Brunswig's distribution centers. Soon the majority of orders could be transmitted to Bergen Brunswig via telephone lines, and in the 1980s satellite communication replaced conventional telephone lines. One hundred years after the opening of the F.W. Braun Company wholesale drug store in Los Angeles, the distribution time of drug orders was down from two to three weeks to less than 24 hours.

The 1980s saw the explosion of pharmaceutical and health care product demand, contributing significantly to Bergen Brunswig's phenomenal growth. In 1981, the president of the National Wholesale Drug Association noted a 17 percent increase in the sales of pharmaceuticals in the first half of that year. The stock value of Bergen Brunswig Corporation increased between 1977 and 1981 by 50 percent, while its net earnings in the three-year period of 1987 to 1990 increased 316 percent, with an average annual growth rate of 25 percent. The aging of the U.S. population had something to do with this success, as did the popularity of its two biggest selling drugs, Zantac, for the treatment of ulcers, and Epogen, used in kidney dialysis treatment.

Despite the considerable increase in the number of its customers—10,000 by 1990—Bergen Brunswig could still guarantee next-day service by means of its computer system. Bergen Brunswig supplied software to some 300 hospitals, thereby linking them to the company's computer-driven distribution and pricing system. This equipment helped Bergen Brunswig become the largest supplier in the United States of pharmaceuticals to hospitals. In addition, the company attracted customers through its Good Neighbor Pharmacy plan, which catered to the particular needs of independent pharmacies.

The development in the 1980s of a new generation of automated distribution centers speeded up service and delivery to the point where Bergen Brunswig had become the model for drug distribution companies nationwide, although it was second largest in the drug distribution industry. The corporation's new distribution facility in Corona, California, could process an order every three seconds—with 100 percent accuracy—of any of the 2,500 most popular pharmaceuticals or health care products. The company then focused on getting closer to the customer—the pharmacist or store manager—in order to anticipate needs to such a degree that the customer might never have to place an order. Toward that end, Bergen Brunswig monitored the customer's stocks and automatically replenished supplies. The automated distribution system enabled Bergen Brunswig and all other wholesale drug companies to process three times as many orders as previously.

The 1980s also saw the development of another line of products, which resulted from Bergen Brunswig's acquisition in 1982 of Commtron, Inc., a national distributor of home videos as well as 4,000 consumer electronic products. By 1990, Commtron, a 79 percent owned subsidiary of the Bergen Brunswig Corporation, became the nation's number-one distributor of videos, with distribution centers and headquarters in Des Moines, Salt Lake City, and Chicago. With 1,000 employees, Commtron's sales in 1990 increased 17 percent over the previous year. However, in June 1992, Bergen Brunswig sold Commtron in an effort to return its focus to its core pharmaceutical operations. Number two video distributor Ingram Entertainment acquired Commtron for $78.3 million.

Leading the company into the 1990s was Robert Martini, company president and CEO, and Emil Martini, Jr., the chairman of the board. Later, Robert Martini took over the position of chairman, and Dwight A. Steffensen became president and chief operating officer. In addition, pharmacists occupied many of the company's top management positions.

Restructuring in the Early to Mid-1990s

In the early 1990s, Bergen Brunswig, like many pharmaceutical and health care wholesalers, was caught in a margin squeeze, as the public outcry over soaring health care costs kept drug prices from increasing. In fact, according to industry statistics, gross profit margins declined every year since 1989 because the drug wholesaling industry continued to be very competitive on pricing, and there had been reductions in the rate of drug price inflation over recent years. During this time, Bergen Brunswig went through some restructuring, including staff reductions, a move to more efficient warehouse facilities, and the elimination of duplicate operating systems resulting from mergers. The company indicated that it saved in excess of $20 million annually from its restructuring. In spite of industry trends, Bergen Brunswig was the only company in the drug wholesaling industry to post an increase in gross profit margins in the December 1994 quarter.

Analysts attributed Bergen Brunswig's success during this critical time to careful management decisions and smart acquisition moves. In 1992, Bergen acquired pharmaceutical distributor Durr-Fillauer Medical Inc. for $484 million. Durr-Fillauer was a national supplier of medical surgical products to hospitals, clinics, and alternate site health care facilities. In addition, the company acquired Southeastern Hospital Supply Company and Professional Medical Supply Company. In July 1995, Bergen signed an agreement to acquire Colonial Healthcare Supply Co., one of the ten largest full-line distributors of medical and surgical products in the country. Each of these acquisitions complemented the Durr Medical operations and expanded their presence nationally in this area. Durr Medical became the fourth largest medical-surgical distributor in the United States.

Joint ventures and agreements during the early and mid-1990s made Bergen Brunswig a more visible force in the worldwide pharmaceutical industry. In December 1994, Bergen Brunswig signed a five-year, sole source pharmaceutical distribution agreement with Columbia/HCA Healthcare Corporation, the nation's largest healthcare services provider, operating 195 hospitals and 125 outpatient centers in 34 states, England, and Switzerland. The total contract was expected to generate $2 billion in revenues for Bergen Brunswig over the life of the agreement. In addition, the company signed a five-year agreement with Safeway Stores Inc. to be its primary supplier of pharmaceuticals, pharmacy-related items, and selected over-the-counter products. The contract was expected to generate over $1 billion in revenue for Bergen over five years. Safeway operated 1,068 stores in the United States and Canada at the time and was the third largest retail grocery chain in North America.

Also known as a technology leader in the distribution industry, Bergen Brunswig focused on offering value-added services to its customers. In July 1994, the company introduced Accu-Source, a multimedia communication, product information, and electronic ordering system for retail pharmacy customers. Developed in conjunction with Apple Computer, the program allowed pharmacies to look up items by category, list substitutions available for products, see special pricing, or communicate with a local Bergen Brunswig division through email. The service also provided personalized information so pharmacies could view statistics such as their own net sales, prescription volume, or product mix. In just four months, Bergen received over 2,000 signed contracts for AccuSource, and it represented Apple's largest multimedia project for a single company. Other state-of-the-art services included OnCall*EDI, a fully-integrated on-line ordering system for the institutional pharmacy, and QuikNet, a fully functional electronic system for ordering, managing, and tracking compliance of medical and surgical products for clinics and hospitals. Moreover, the Bergen Brunswig Drug Company, a wholly owned subsidiary of the Bergen Brunswig Corporation, had converted to paperless billing several years before and was constantly refining its funds transfer and information management systems.

The latter half of the 1990s proved to be more challenging for Bergen Brunswig. A planned merger with generic drug manufacturer IVAX fell through in 1997. Cardinal Health then made a $2.6 billion play for the company. Its plans were thwarted however when the FTC ruled against the merger. Throughout 1998 and 1999, Bergen Brunswig made several expensive purchases, including Stadlander Operating Co. and PharMerica Inc. The acquisitions led to a host of lawsuits. Shareholders filed suit against Bergen Brunswig, claiming the company used false information in order to inflate its stock price. The company then filed its own claim against Stadlander's former parent company, alleging the firm overstated profits to close the deal. In 2000, Bergen Brunswig sold off its medical supplies distribution firm and the Stadlander

Pharmacy subsidiary. It also set plans in motion to settle the class action suit brought against the company.

The AmerisourceBergen Merger

Both AmeriSource and Bergen Brunswig entered the new century as two of the largest drug wholesalers in the nation. With competition biting at their heels, the two companies agreed to pair up in a multi-billion dollar union in 2001. The deal cleared regulatory hurdles and was completed in August. The newly merged company adopted the name AmerisourceBergen Corp. and took the leading position in its industry with nearly $36 billion in annual revenues. By 2003, revenues had climbed to $49.6 billion. As the largest purchaser of generic drugs in the United States, AmerisourceBergen operated as a supplier to over 25,000 chain and independent pharmacies and thousands of hospital, nursing homes, and mail-order pharmacies.

In a December 2001 *Drug Store News* article, CEO R. David Yost stated, ''When [Bergen chairman] Bob Martini and I sat down to put this thing together, it was never about being the biggest; it was always about being the best. And sometimes bigger can help you be the best.'' He went on to claim, ''We're excited about our position because, first, it gives us much larger scale than we ever had before, and we think this scale will translate into our ability to develop new programs and services for our customers.'' In addition, he added, ''We're bringing together two companies that have a large array of value-added services for the retail trade.''

Indeed, by 2003 revenues and profits had climbed substantially, and the company was well on its way to achieving the $150 million in cost savings as a result of the merger. During that year, the company acquired Anderson Packaging Inc., Bridge Medical Inc., and U.S. Bioservices Corp. It faced a minor setback when it lost the Department of Veterans Affairs contract worth $3 billion in operating revenue. Undeterred, AmerisourceBergen forged ahead, anticipating nothing but success in the years to come. A new Medicare drug benefit, expected to lead to an increase in drug use, promised to be quite lucrative for the company in the future. AmerisourceBergen appeared to be well positioned for growth in the years to come as it operated in a $200 billion industry that was expected to grow at a steady clip over the next decade.

Principal Subsidiaries

AmerisourceBergen Drug Corporation; Amerisource Health Services Corporation; Amerisource Receivables Financial Corporation; AmerisourceBergen Services Corporation; Amerisource Heritage Corporation; Anderson Packaging, Inc.; ASD Specialty Healthcare, Inc.; AutoMed Technologies, Inc.; 0Bergen Capital Trust I; Bridge Medical, Inc.; Brownstone Pharmacy, Inc.; Capstone Pharmacy of Delaware, Inc.; Compuscript, Inc.; Computran Systems, Inc.; Dunnington Rx Services of Rhode Island, Inc.; Family Center Pharmacy, Inc.; Goot Nursing Home Pharmacy, Inc.; Health Services Capital Corporation; Insta-Care Pharmacy Services Corporation; ION, L.L.C.; J.M. Blanco, Inc.; Pharmacy Corporation of America; PharMerica, Inc.; PharMerica Drug Systems, Inc.; US Bioservices Corporation.

Principal Competitors

Cardinal Health Inc.; McKesson Corp.; Owens & Minor Inc.

Further Reading

"Amerisource, A Drug Seller, to Buy Packaging Company," *New York Times*, May 23, 2003, p. C4.

"AmeriSource Shifts Management to Focus on Three Key Channels," *Drug Store News*, April 5, 1999, p. 3.

Barrett, Amy, "Bergen Brunswig: Time to Climb on Board?," *FW*, April 14, 1992, p. 14.

"Bergen Brunswig Begins to Heal," *Forbes*, November 22, 1993, p. 212.

Binzen, Peter, "One Leveraged Buyout Has Paid Off, and It Keeps On Growing," *Philadelphia Inquirer*, December 12, 1994, p. D3.

Fay, John T., *NWDA 1876–1986: Centennial Plus Ten*, Alexandria, Vir.: National Wholesale Druggists' Association, 1987.

Frederick, James, "Revolutionizing an Industry," *Drug Store News*, December 17, 2001.

Gilpin, Kenneth N., "Two Drug Wholesalers to Merge in a $2.4 Billion Stock Deal," *New York Times*, March 20, 2001, p. C8.

Heller, Al, "Formidable Four Move Ahead Separately, Optimistically," *Drug Store News*, September 21, 1998, p. 11.

"Major Drug Wholesaler Upbeat Despite Losing Big Contract," *Associated Press*, May 24, 2004.

Meilach, Dona Z., "At Home & On the Road, Pharmaceutical Distributor Uses Variety of Large-Screen Devices," *Computer Pictures*, May-June 1993, p. 14.

Moukheiber, Zina, "Easy Pill to Swallow," *Forbes*, October 29, 2001.

Reeves, Amy, "Merger Is a Year Old, but Work's Not Done," *Investor's Business Daily*, November 22, 2002, p. A6.

Roller, Kim, "AmeriSource Trade Show Leaves All 'Energized' for the Real World," *Drug Store News*, August 28, 2000, p. 16.

Werner, Thomas, " 'Without Negatives': That's How Alco Health Services' Chief Describes Its Business," *Barron's*, April 13, 1987.

Wiley, Karen, ed., *Centennial Sampler: 1888–1988*, Orange, Calif.: Bergen Brunswig Corporation, 1988.

—Thomas M. Tucker
—updates: Carrie Rothburd and Christina M. Stansell

APi Group, Inc.

2366 Rose Place
St. Paul, Minnesota 55113
U.S.A.
Telephone: (651) 636-4320
Fax: (651) 636-0312
Web site: http://www.apigroupinc.com

Private Company
Incorporated: 1948
Employees: 5,000
Sales: $800 million (2003 est.)
NAIC: 551112 Offices of Other Holding Companies;
235110 Plumbing, Heating and Air-Conditioning
Contractors; 235310 Electrical Contractors; 562910
Remediation Services; 235990 All Other Special
Trade Contractors; 332322 Sheet Metal Work
Manufacturing; 332312 Fabricated Structural Metal
Manufacturing; 33241 Power Boiler and Heat
Exchanger Manufacturing; 532412 Construction,
Mining and Forestry Machinery Leasing; 561621
Security Systems Services (Except Locksmiths);
421330 Roofing, Siding and Insulation Material
Wholesalers

APi Group, Inc., is a private holding company for about 27 subsidiaries that provide various construction, specialty contracting, and maintenance services mainly for industrial and commercial clients. The subsidiaries are grouped into five main areas of operation: Fire Protection Systems, Specialty Construction Services, Special Systems, Distribution, and Fabrication and Manufacturing. Fire protection, including installation of sprinkler systems and wildfire suppression, accounts for more than half the company's business. Other subsidiaries are active in insulation and electrical contracting, plumbing, boiler maintenance, heating and ventilation, garage door installation, asbestos abatement, building security systems, steel fabrication, distribution of construction materials, the manufacture of air ducts, and the rental of aerial work platforms. Most of the APi Group's construction and contracting-related subsidiaries are located in Minnesota and sur-

rounding states, but the company's fire protection holdings extend as far as Texas, California, Canada, and the United Kingdom. The APi Group has its roots in a small insulation contracting firm founded in the 1920s in St. Paul, Minnesota. The company attained its current scope as the result of an acquisition strategy directed by CEO Lee Anderson, son of the company's founder.

A Small Contractor Beginning to Grow: 1948–84

Although the APi Group was incorporated in 1948, it grew out of a plumbing and heating company started by Reuben L. Anderson around 1924. This contracting company was located in St. Paul, Minnesota and did business as Reuben L. Anderson-Cherne Plumbing. By the late 1920s the company also had branched out into asbestos and pipe insulation and the distribution of insulation materials. In 1948 the insulation-related activities were spun off into a separate firm known as Asbestos Products. This firm included divisions that eventually would develop into the subsidiaries APi Distribution, a wholesaler of insulation products for industry, and APi Construction Company, an insulation contractor for the utility, energy generation, petroleum, and paper industries. Anderson operated Asbestos Products as an independent sister company to his plumbing firm for about three decades. Asbestos Products changed its name to APi Inc. in the 1970s. Anderson eventually sold his interest in the plumbing firm in 1979.

Reuben's son Lee Anderson joined the firm in 1964 at the age of 25 when his father granted him a 50 percent interest in the company. At the time, APi had about 30 employees and annual revenues of $120,000 from its insulation distribution and contracting activities. Lee Anderson became president of the company and began a series of acquisitions in the 1970s that greatly expanded APi's scope of operations.

Anderson's first acquisition was the 1969 purchase of the Industrial Sprinkler Corporation, a fire protection company located in St. Paul that had been founded 15 years earlier. This was followed by the purchase of Anco Products, Inc. in 1972. Anco was a young firm in Elkhart, Indiana, engaged in the production of flexible heating and cooling air ducts. The company also made the Textrafine brand of insulation, a resilient long-fiber insulation used in cryogenic tanks for the storage of liquefied natural gas. Another subsidiary, APi Supply, Inc., was established in St. Paul in 1977 as a sales and rental firm for aerial work platforms—machines used to lift loads high into the air—including scissorlifts and boom lifts from manufacturers such as Snorkel, JLG, SkyJack, Workforce, and Upright. In 1981 APi bought Industrial Contractors, Inc. (ICI) of Bismarck, North Dakota. ICI was a construction service and maintenance firm with a particular focus on boiler maintenance and process piping in power plants. The company could be contracted to perform scheduled plant shutdowns for maintenance purposes, and also worked in steel erection, siding, metal roofing, electrical, and plumbing contracting. The Andersons also entered the banking sector during this time. Reuben Anderson bought a northern Minnesota bank in 1975 and expanded it to neighboring towns. Lee Anderson sold the chain to Norwest Corp. for a considerable profit in 1997 and retained two banks under the name Anderson Financial Corp. The banks were not part of APi, but Lee Anderson kept his main office in Golden Valley at the financial company while serving as president of APi.

Increasing the Pace of Acquisitions: 1985–95

As APi's list of acquisitions grew, Anderson's associates noted that he demonstrated a knack for good timing in his deals and for developing employee loyalty. He continued to keep his eye out for promising firms that were available for acquisition and would complement APi's existing operations. The pace of acquisitions increased in 1985 when APi gained three more subsidiaries. The first was Viking Automatic Sprinkler Company, with offices in Duluth, Rochester, and St. Paul, Minnesota. Viking had been established in 1924 and had the capability to fabricate sprinkler systems in-house for installation at new construction projects. A second acquisition was The Jamar Company, a Duluth-based contractor working in metal roofing, siding, sheet metal fabrication, piping, and ductwork for the paper, food processing, and mining industries. Jamar also constructed and repaired power boilers. The company had been established in 1913 by Walker Jamar, Sr., and had sales of $4–5 million at the time of the acquisition. APi's third acquisition that year was a building materials wholesaler located in the Minneapolis suburb of Fridley. The company was known as Reserve Supply but changed its name to APi Supply Company after the acquisition.

Of the three 1985 acquisitions, The Jamar Company experienced the most rapid growth. Jamar management wanted the company, which at the time was a straightforward union contractor, to diversify into construction businesses unrelated to union contracting. Jamar bought the Arrowhead Mechanical Contracting Company, a 45-year-old plumbing, heating, and process piping business, in 1986. The next year it acquired ASDCO, a northern Minnesota building products wholesaler that developed into Jamar's distribution division. ASDCO formerly made sales via telephone, but Jamar opened an outlet to showcase ASDCO's products. In 1988 Jamar's headquarters moved from Canal Park Drive to a 65,000-square-foot West Duluth facility that was four times as large as its former site. Jamar's construction services division started up in 1989 to sell and rent aerial lift equipment, forklifts, scaffolding, and temporary heating equipment.

Another three acquisitions joined the APi Group in 1989. Two of them worked in structural steel fabrication: L.L. LeJeune Steel Company of Minneapolis, which had been in business since 1944, and Wisconsin Structural Steel Company of Barronnet, Wisconsin. Wisconsin Structural Steel shared its management and inventory with LeJeune after the acquisition but remained a separate subsidiary. The third acquisition that year was Western States Fire Protection Company. Western had been established in Denver in 1985 and had offices in Dallas and Houston. Over the next few years, Western's scope expanded as APi acquired and merged several other fire protection companies in western states. Western gained offices in California, Kansas, Colorado, Oregon, Texas, and Nevada.

In 1990 APi became part of an alliance seeking to build a 175-mile toll road around the Twin Cities metro area. The company formed the Minnesota Tollway Authority Inc. with several partners to pursue this goal. The proposed toll road met with criticism from people who did not like the idea of paying a toll or who were concerned the project would encourage urban sprawl. APi was losing money on the venture and dropped out of the alliance as it became clear the project would not gain government approval.

APi bought Industrial Fabricators, Inc. and National Fire in 1994. National Fire was merged into Western States Fire Protection. Industrial Fabricators, in business since 1975, made large industrial silencers used for safety and environmental purposes. The firm fabricated metal silencers at a plant in Thorp, Wisconsin and sold them to power plants and other facilities worldwide. The Twin City Garage Door Company was acquired by APi in 1995. The firm had been established in 1966 and grew to be one of the largest full-service garage door companies in the Twin Cities area.

Meanwhile, The Jamar Company was continuing its decade-long path of rapid expansion. In 1990 Jamar established Sonneman Construction in Cloquet, Minnesota as a boiler maintenance and repair division. In 1992 Jamar bought Arrowhead Refrigeration, a northern Minnesota refrigerator service and repair business. Jamar opened an office in Upper Michigan in 1993 because it had won several contracts from that area in the past. In 1995 Jamar's Construction Service Division partnered with Acme Tool Crib of the North to distribute woodworking and construction tools; they were displayed in the same show-

Key Dates:

1948: Asbestos Products is incorporated to work in installation and distribution of insulation.

1964: Lee Anderson joins his father's business.

1969: APi makes its first acquisition, that of Industrial Sprinkler Corporation.

1972: Anco Products, Inc., a flexible duct and insulation manufacturer, is acquired.

1977: APi Supply, Inc. is established to sell aerial work platforms.

1981: North Dakota contractor Industrial Contractors, Inc. is acquired.

1985: The Jamar Company, Viking Automatic Sprinkler, and APi Supply Company are acquired.

1989: Western States Fire Protection and two steel fabrication companies are acquired.

1996: VFP Fire Systems and Vipond Fire Protection of Canada are acquired.

1998: About a dozen fire protection acquisitions expand the company's reach in Canada, the United Kingdom, and the western United States.

2003: Recently acquired electrical contractors Lakehead Electric and Thompson Electric are merged to form APi Electric.

2004: ABATECO, Inc. is formed to focus on asbestos and lead abatement.

room as the construction products available from ASDCO. Overall, Jamar was developing a versatile range of services to attract customers who wanted to work with a single contractor rather than dealing with separate businesses for each stage of a construction project. The company hired mechanical engineers and installed computer-aided design systems so that it could offer complete design-build services.

Late 1990s Expansion in the Fire Protection Sector

In the second half of the 1990s APi acquired more than a dozen domestic and international fire protection companies, making this the company's dominant line of business. Statewide Fire Protection of Las Vegas, which specialized in installing sprinkler systems in casinos, was bought in 1996 and rolled into Western States Fire Protection. APi also purchased VFP Fire Systems, Inc. and Vipond Fire Protection that year. VFP had been established in 1927 and did work in Ohio, Indiana, Michigan, Pennsylvania, Kentucky, Alabama, Texas, and West Virginia. Vipond, in business in Canada since 1945, had offices in the province of Ontario. Both Vipond and Western States Fire Protection expanded in 1998 when several smaller companies were acquired and merged with them. Western got RLT Fire Protection, Inc. of San Diego, which worked in residential sprinkler systems, and Universal Fire Equipment Co. of Dallas, a fire alarm and detection contractor. Vipond was enlarged with an array of Canadian fire protection firms: Sask Fire Protection and Advantage Fire Protection of Calgary, Alberta; Integrated Protection of North Bay; JP Theoret Electric, Ltd. of Montreal; Nichols-Radtke Sprinkler of Hamilton, Ontario; Ultra Alarm Services Ltd. of Moncton, New Brunswick;

and Island Electric, Regional Alarms & Security of Sudbury, Ontario.

These all became part of the parent company Vipond, Inc. In addition, Vipond bridged the Atlantic to buy A&A Fire of Glasgow, Scotland. The Canadian offices all became part of Vipond Fire Protection, Inc. while the United Kingdom site changed its name to Vipond Fire Protection, Ltd. Both divisions became part of the parent company Vipond, Inc. Ironically, amid the accumulation of fire protection subsidiaries, APi experienced a fire in 1998 at Anco, the air duct and insulation producer in Indiana. Some ductwork on the fiberglass line caught fire one afternoon and, although all employees were safely evacuated, equipment damages amounted to $2 million.

Vipond was further enhanced in 1999 with the acquisition of Cronin Fire Equipment of Ottawa, Alsask Fire Equipment of Regina, Saskatchewan, and Firestop of Belfast, Ireland. That year APi also bought Security Fire Protection Company, Inc. of Memphis, Tennessee. Security Fire Protection was founded in 1966. Because Memphis was a national distribution center, it developed particular expertise in sprinkler systems for refrigerated and frozen storage facilities, developing technologies that became industry standards. In 1999 APi also established Western States Fire Protection Company of Alaska.

By the late 1990s APi had grown to be one of the top 500 private firms in the nation. Revenues in 1998 were $423 million with a profit of $22 million. By 1999 fire protection had grown to account for 60 percent of APi's revenues, up from 30 percent five years earlier. Yet the company showed no sign of slowing down. APi bought US Fire Protection and Alliance Fire Protection, both based near Chicago, in 2000. Alliance had been founded in 1995 and did general design and installation of sprinkler systems. US Fire Protection had been in business since 1986. It worked mainly with residential systems, with a particular focus on retrofitting existing structures to comply with changing fire codes. Later in 2000 APi bought Communication Systems, Inc., with offices in Casper, Wyoming and Rapid City, South Dakota. This company had been founded in 1986 and provided design, installation, and support services related to closed circuit television, patient wandering systems, gas detection, nurse call systems, infant protection, and security. A similar company, Northern Fire & Communications of Montana, was acquired the following year. Northern Fire & Communications had been providing integration of low-voltage call, alarm, and intercom systems since 1984. The company's main office was in Kalispell, Montana, with branches in Billings and Missoula. Both Northern Fire and Communication Systems became divisions of APi Systems Group, Inc., the parent company for APi's hazard, alarm, and security system operations. Vipond also had developed a division, Vipond Systems Group, active in this sector.

Continued Growth into the New Millennium

Aside from the acquisitions related to fire suppression and alarms, APi experienced some developments in the construction and contracting fields in the late 1990s. In 1997 the company bought New Reach Co., Inc. of Wisconsin. This firm was a wholesaler that leased aerial lift equipment. New Reach was sold to Rental Services Corporation a year later. A longer-lasting acquisition in 1997 was Lakehead Electric, a contractor based in Duluth, Minnesota. Lakehead had been in business since 1963 and provided electrical design services, installation, and emergency outage support for local giants in the paper, pulp, and mining industries, including Potlatch Corporation, Northshore Mining, Blandin Paper, and U.S. Steel. With APi's backing, in 1999 Lakehead launched the Lakehead DataCom division devoted to security systems, fire alarms, fiber optics, and data communications.

In 1998 APi sold its building materials wholesaler APi Supply Company (but retained APi Supply, Inc., the aerial work platform rental company). The subsidiary was sold in part because Home Depot, which had its own distribution system, was moving into rural areas and threatening APi's territory. The sale led to a loss of about $135 million in annual revenues, but ongoing acquisitions in the area of fire protection made up for it.

APi established a new subsidiary, Halon Banking Systems, in 1999. This company's area of business was the environmentally responsible management, redeployment, and destruction of halon, a compound used in fire extinguishers. The firm was located in St. Paul and sent extinguishers to affiliates in Denver and Dallas to be refilled.

In 2001 APi bought Doody Mechanical, Inc., a St. Paul-based contractor providing services to larger institutions such as schools, housing projects, industrial sites, retail locations, and places of worship. Doody's services included heating, ventilation, air conditioning, plumbing, process piping, and sheet metal fabrication. The company had been founded in 1959 and formed a sheet metal division in 1985 so that it could fabricate HVAC duct systems in-house. Also in 2001, APi acquired Thompson Electric of Cloquet, Minnesota. Thompson had been established in 1919 to install fire alarms and police call boxes and branched out to electrical contracting in 1928. The company changed hands several times over the years; by the time it landed at APi, annual revenues were around $7 million. Two years later Thompson merged with Lakehead Electric to form APi Electric, the largest commercial electrical contracting firm in the region. Thompson's strength was in commercial electrical services, while Lakehead focused on industrial and highway lighting. Both were also active in computer cabling, security systems, closed circuit television, and other low-voltage services.

Late in 2003 APi bought Windy City Fire Protection of Chicago and merged it into Alliance Fire Protection. In 2004 the APi Construction Company, the insulation contractor in the group, spun off a new subsidiary to emphasize asbestos and lead abatement services. The company was known as ABATECO, Inc. It won a contract to register the asbestos present in Xcel

Energy's Bayport power plant. Meanwhile, APi's other subsidiaries were carrying out contracts in their respective areas of business: Viking Automatic Sprinkler company had recently installed a sprinkler system at Best Buy's new headquarters in Richfield, Minnesota; Doody Mechanical and Western States Fire Protection had teamed up to install the piping and sprinkler system, respectively, for a new Cabela's outdoor gear store in Kansas; and Jamar had recently fabricated and installed an air flow system for Willamette Paper in Kingsport, Tennessee. Each subsidiary was contributing its piece to APi's loosely related array of specialized mechanical, construction, distribution, and life protection operations.

Principal Subsidiaries

ABATECO, Inc.; APi Construction Company; APi Electric; APi Supply, Inc.; Doody Mechanical, Inc.; Industrial Contractors, Inc.; The Jamar Company; Twin City Garage Door Company; Anco Products, Inc.; Industrial Fabricators, Inc.; Lejeune Steel Company; Wisconsin Structural Steel Company; Alliance Fire Protection, Inc.; Security Fire Protection Company, Inc.; US Fire Protection, Inc.; Viking Automatic Sprinkler Company; VFP Fire Systems, Inc.; Vipond, Inc.; Western States Fire Protection Company; ASDCO; APi Distribution; APi Systems Group; Communications Systems, Inc.; Halon Banking Systems; Northern Fire & Communication.

Principal Divisions

Specialty Construction Services; Fire Protection Systems; Fabrication and Manufacturing; Distribution; Special Systems.

Principal Competitors

Grinnell Corporation; Express Garage Doors Inc.; Herc-U-Lift; United Rentals; EnviroTech Remediation Services, Inc.

Further Reading

Beal, Dave, "API's Low-Profile Empire," *St. Paul Pioneer Press,* August 4, 1999, p. 1B.

King, Marshall V., "$2 Million Fire Ravages Anco," *Elkhart Truth* (Ind.), February 10, 1998.

Laine, Burton, "Building Blocks," *Duluthian,* March 1, 1997, p. 12.

Mark, Terry T., "Anco Gets Loan," *Elkhart Truth,* February 2, 2001.

"Two Duluth, Minn.-Area Electrical Contracting Firms to Merge," *Duluth News-Tribune,* March 4, 2003, p. 1.

Whereatt, Robert, "Toll Highway Would Link I-35W with I-94 Through Northern Metro Suburbs," *Star Tribune,* November 21, 1990, p. 1A.

—Sarah Ruth Lorenz

Asahi Denka Kogyo KK

2-3-14 Nihonbashi-Muromachi, Chu
Tokyo
103-8311
Japan
Telephone: (+81) 3 5255 9002
Fax: (+81) 3 3246 2090
Web site: http://www.adk.co.jp

Public Company
Incorporated: 1917 as Asahi Denka Kogyo
Employees: 2,135
Sales: ¥104.53 billion ($1.15 billion)(2003)
Stock Exchanges: Tokyo
Ticker Symbol: 4401
NAIC: 325192 Cyclic Crude and Intermediate
   Manufacturing; 311225 Fats and Oils Refining and
   Blending; 325211 Plastics Material and Resin
   Manufacturing; 325998 All Other Miscellaneous
   Chemical Product Manufacturing

Asahi Denka Kogyo KK (the company uses Asahi Denka Co. Ltd. as an English equivalent) is one of Japan's leading chemicals producers. The company's range in this field is segmented into two categories: basic chemicals and functional chemicals. The basic chemicals Asahi Denka produces are caustic soda, liquid chlorine, hydrochloric acid, propylene glycol, hydrogen peroxide, sodium percarbonate, fatty acid, glycerine, and other related products. The company's functional chemicals consist of surfactants, lubricants, industrial and institutional detergents, polyurethane, sealants, stabilizers, flame retardants, plastic additives and plasticizers. Other functional chemicals include optical storage materials and optical hardening resins, imaging and photographic chemicals, high purity gases for the semiconductor industry, among others. Chemicals account for more than two-thirds of the Asahi Denka's revenues, which topped ¥104.5 billion ($1.15 billion) in 2003. The remainder of the company's sales come from its Foods division, which has developed as an offshoot of its chemical operations. The company produces a variety of foods, including margarine, shortening, lard and related spreads, oil and fat for the production of chocolate, mayonnaise, dressings, fillings, milk products, food additives, frozen pie crusts, and cakes and confectioneries. Listed on the Tokyo Stock Exchange, Asahi Denka has manufacturing facilities in Japan, the United States, France, Germany, Korea, Malaysia, Thailand, Taiwan, and in mainland China. The company is part of the vast Furukawa mining group, which also includes such companies as Furukawa Electric Co., Yokohama Rubber Co., Fuji Electric Co., Fujitsu Limited, Nippon Light Metal Company, and the Dai-Ichi Kangyo Bank. Asahi Denka is led by chairman and CEO Masahiro Iwashita and president and COO Hiroyuki Nakajima.

Chemicals Offshoot in the 1920s

Ichibei Furukawa founded a copper mining company in Kusukura in 1875. Two years later, he added a second mine in Ashio. By the end of the century, Furukawa had expanded into coal mining as well, a move that signaled the start of a long period of diversification for the company, which became known as Furukawa & Co. in 1905.

Furukawa initially expanded into machinery at the turn of the 20th century, setting up its own plant to support its Ashio Copper Mine operations. By the outbreak of World War I, Furukawa had extended its range into power generation. Following the war, Furukawa sought new areas for diversification.

Japans reliance on imports for its chemicals needs made that sector an attractive target for Furukawa, which joined in a national effort to boost the country's industrial self-reliance. In 1915, Furukawa outlined plans to begin production of caustic soda (sodium hydroxide) using the recently developed salt electrolysis process. One of the world's most important base industrial chemicals, the caustic soda production process provided a variety of related chemicals, including chlorine and hydrochloric acid.

Furukawa established Tokyo Denka Kogyo-sho in 1915 and began construction on a new chemicals plant. In 1917, the chemicals subsidiary was restructured and renamed as Asahi Denka Kogyo KK. Production began the following year at the new company's completed Ogu Plant in Tokyo.

Asahi Denka quickly began its own diversification as it developed a wide range of chemical products and specialties, many of which began as offshoots to the company's core production. Such was the case with Asahi Denka's launch of production of hydrogenated oils in 1919, which used the hydrogen generated through the salt electrolysis production process.

Asahi Denka entered the agrochemicals market in the early 1920s, taking over Furukawa's lead arsenate production, itself a byproduct of Furukawa's copper refinery operations. Over the next decade, Asahi Denka expanded its range of agricultural chemicals as well; by 1928, that activity had developed strongly enough to be spun off into a separate company, Nihon Noyaku Co, in a joint venture with Fujii Seiyaku Co. Nihon Noyaku then became Japan's first dedicated agricultural chemicals company.

In the meantime, Asahi Denka had continued expanding its range of products, developing chemicals and products for a variety of industries ranging from paper and textiles to the automotive, shipbuilding, and construction industries. Asahi Denka itself entered a new industry in 1929 when it launched its own Risu brand of margarine. That marked the first of a steadily growing line of food products for the company. Foods grew into a major division of Asahi Denka, accounting for some one-third of its sales by the end of the 21st century.

Postwar Expansion

Emerging from World War II, Asahi Denka prepared to take advantage of the boom in operations during the country's economic and industrial reconstruction. In 1947, Asahi Denka formed a dedicated sales subsidiary, Yoko Sangyo Co. That company also began manufacturing industrial chemicals as well as other chemical products, such as liquids for metalworking. Two years later, Asahi Denka was listed on the Tokyo Stock Exchange's main board. The company remained an important component of the Furukawa group, which had itself gone public earlier in the decade.

At the end of the 1950s, Asahi Denka began a new phase of expansion and diversification, adding new product lines and expanding its production capacity both inside Japan and abroad. In 1959, the group set up a dedicated subsidiary for its hydrogen peroxide production, Tokai Denka Kogyo Co., which emerged as the country's leading producer of this product.

Asahi Denka's expansion took off in the 1960s. The company established its own transportation and leasing subsidiary, Kyokuyu Sangyo, in 1961, then added a real estate division, Kyokuyu Real Estate KK, in the same year. The company also launched its own architectural services operation in 1964.

Meanwhile, Asahi Denka continued adding new chemical operations, such as the launch of plasticizers and plastic stabilizers through a new subsidiary, Adeka Argus, created in 1962. The company also entered fine chemicals production, launching Adeka Swift Chemical Co in 1965.

In 1966, Asahi Denka began expanding its industrial capacity with the building of its new Akashi Plant, in Hyogo. The company also took part in the construction of the Kashami Complex in Ibaraki, backing the formation of a number of companies there, such as Kashima Chlorine & Alkali Co., completing its Kashami Plant in 1970. Asahi Denka then added the Sodegaura Factory in Chiba as part of subsidiary AS Kasei in 1975, as well as a plant in Kuki in 1979.

The company's expanded capacity backed up its entry into a number of new product categories, such as the launch of industrial and domestic-strength detergents and disinfectants in 1973, fatty acids and glycerine in 1979, and plasticizers in 1980.

Continued Growth: Late 1980s and Beyond

Toward the end of the 1980s, Asahi Denka began expanding its geographic focus as well. Food products played a prominent role in the company's international development, starting with the creation of a subsidiary in Singapore in 1988, which began producing edible oils. At the end of the decade, the company, which had diversified its food products offerings to include a wide range of products, including mayonnaise and other dressings, as well as frozen bread dough, pie crusts, and cakes, stepped up expansion of its food products division both abroad and in Japan. In 1994, the company launched a new subsidiary, Asahi Fine Foods, which began producing its own line of mayonnaise and dressings.

The company's primary operations, however, remained in the chemicals industry. Asahi Denka also began developing global chemicals operations in the late 1980s and 1990s. In 1989, the company launched subsidiary Chang Chiang Chemical Co, in Taiwan, where it began manufacturing plastics. Then, in 1991, Asahi Denka formed a new company in Korea, Han-Nong Adeka Corp (renamed as Dongbu Adeka in 1997), which began producing plastic additives. Also in 1991, Asahi Denka joined Mitsui and Company Ltd. and Miyoshi Oil and Fat Company Ltd. to form the Palmoleo Inc. joint venture, which produced fatty acids.

Asahi Denka turned to the United States in the mid-1990s, forming Amfine Chemicals Co. Ltd., which began producing plastic additives in 1994. The company expanded its plastic additives operations again the following year with the launch of a new subsidiary in Thailand. Meanwhile, the company completed its domestic industrial production, opening its Soma factory in Fukushima in 1996.

Toward the end of the 1990s, Asahi Denka launched its entry into Europe as well, setting up its first European office in Germany in 1998. The company quickly added its first full-fledged European subsidiary, setting up Asahi Denka Europe in 1999. In that year, the company also began restructuring parts

Key Dates:

1875: Ichibei Furukawa establishes a copper mining company in Kusukura, Japan.

1915: As part of its diversification, Furukawa begins development of production of caustic soda (sodium hydroxide) using electrolysis process, forming Tokyo Denka Kogyo-sho.

1917: Chemicals division is reformed as Asahi Denka Kogyo.

1918: Production begins with the completion of Ogu Plant in Tokyo.

1919: The company starts producing hydrogenated oil using hydrogen byproduct of electrolysis process.

1929: Production and marketing of Risu brand margarine begins.

1947: A sales subsidiary, Yoko Sangyo, is set up.

1949: Asahi Denka goes public on the Tokyo Stock Exchange.

1959: Tokai Denka Kogyo, which produces hydrogen peroxide, is formed.

1962: Plasticizers and plastic stablilizers production is launched under Adeka Argus subsidiary.

1965: Fine Chemicals division, Adeka Swift Chemical, is formed.

1970: Kashima Factory opens in Ibaraki as part of the company's industrial capacity expansion.

1988: First international subsidiary is created in Singapore for production of edible oils.

1991: Han-Nong Adeka Corporation (later Dongbu Adeka) is formed in Korea.

1994: The company enters the United States with the creation of Amfine Chemicals Co.

1999: The company's first European subsidiary is established in Germany.

2001: The company enters China with it subsidiary Asahi Denka Shanghai.

2004: Asahi Food Sales Co. distribution subsidiary is established as part of a restructuring plan.

tions with the formation of a French joint venture, Adeka Palmarole, in partnership with Switzerland's Palmarole, in 2000. Asahi Denka then targeted an entry into the Chinese market, establishing Asahi Denka Shanghai Co. in 2001. The following year, the company set up the joint venture Kukdo Chemical Kunshan with Korea's Kukdo Chemical Co., then expanded its own Chinese operations with the creation of Adeka Fine Chemical (Shanghai) Co. that same year. In 2003, Asahi Denka acquired full control of its Korean Dongbu joint venture. Then, in 2004, the company established a new subsidiary for its Korean operations, Asahi Denka Korea, based in Seoul.

The difficult economic climate in the early 2000s led Asahi Denka to restructure parts of its operations to conform with an overall medium-range strategy adopted in 2004. As part of the restructuring, the company created a new subsidiary, Asahi Food Sales Co., which took over Yoko Sangyo's food distribution operations. Yoko Sangyo itself was merged into the group's Adeka Fine Chemicals Co. subsidiary. As it moved into the new century, Asahi Denka had grown into one of Japan's most diversified chemicals and foods manufacturers.

Principal Subsidiaries

Nihon Noyaku Co., Ltd.; Yoko Sangyo Co., Ltd.; Kyokuyu Sangyo KK; Kyokuyu Real Estate KK; Asahi Architects Office Co., Ltd.; Oxirane Chemical Corporation; Kashima Chlorine & Alkali Co., Ltd.; Kashima Chemical Co., Ltd.; Kanto Sodium Silicate Glass Co., Ltd.; Adeka Clean Aid Co., Ltd.; Tokyo Environmental Measurement Center Co.,Ltd.; CO-OP Clean Co., Ltd.; Chiba Fatty Acids Co., Ltd.; Mizushima Plasticizer Co., Ltd.; Nihon Epoxy Resin Co.,Ltd.; Allergen-Free Technology Laboratories Inc.; Asahi Fine Foods Co., Ltd.; Adeka Engineering & Construction Co., Ltd; Adeka Logistics Co., Ltd; Asahi Foods Sales Co., Ltd; Yongo Co., Ltd.

Principal Competitors

BASF AG; Bayer AG; JFE Holdings Inc.; Mitsubishi Chemical Corp.; BP Chemicals Inc.; Occidental Chemical Corp.; Merck KgaA; Clariant International AG; Rhodia Inc., Asahi Kasei Corporation.

Further Reading

"Asahi Denka Boosting Sales of Food Divisions," *Comline: Biotechnology and Medical Industry of Japan*, December 19, 1991.

"Boosting Resins," *Asia Pacific Coatings Journal*, August 2003, p. 6.

"Japan's Asahi Denka Develops Bromide-free Flame Retardant," *Asia Pulse*, February 4, 2004.

—M.L. Cohen

of its operation, merging with Tokai Denka Kogyo. In another restructuring move, the company combined its Yoko Sangyo operation into Asahi Fine Foods in 2000.

Asahi Denka continued its expansion into the 2000s. In 2001, the company acquired Yongo Co, a division of Japan Tobacco that produced edible oil and fat, as well as confectionery ingredients and other foods. The company extended its European opera-

ASDA Group Ltd.

ASDA House, Southbank
Great Wilson Street
Leeds LS11 5AD
United Kingdom
Telephone: (113) 243-5435
Fax: (113) 241-7150
Web site: http://www.asda.co.uk

Wholly Owned Subsidiary of Wal-Mart Stores Inc.
Incorporated: 1949 as Associated Dairies and Farm
    Stores Ltd.
Employees: 122,000
Sales: $21.7 billion (2004)
NAIC: 445110 Supermarkets and Other Grocery (Except
    Convenience) Stores; 452910 Warehouse Clubs and
    Superstores

ASDA Group Ltd. operates as one of the largest food retailers in the United Kingdom. The company's stores sell a wide variety of merchandise including food and apparel, along with housewares, music, videos, and books. ASDA has approximately 259 stores in its arsenal—each averaging nearly 42,000 square feet with some as large as 100,000 square feet. The company, once known as a dairy conglomerate, was acquired by Wal-Mart Stores Inc. in 1999. Under its new parent's guidance, ASDA has been adding pharmacies, opticians, jewelry, and photo departments to its stores.

Early History

The origins of the ASDA Group are to be found in the efforts of English dairy farmers to protect themselves from falling milk prices after World War I. When wartime price controls were lifted and England began once again to import large quantities of European dairy products, local milk prices fell sharply and showed every sign of continuing to do so. Various legislative remedies were devised, but in the meantime a Yorkshire dairy farmer named J.W. Hindell led a number of his fellows in the creation of Hindell's Dairy Farmers Limited, a 1920 partnership whose purpose was to acquire or build both wholesale and retail outlets for their milk, in that way securing for themselves a steady market and a floor price.

During the next 25 years, Hindell's assembled a wide variety of dairy businesses, founding or purchasing a total of nine operating companies involved in everything from the raising of dairy cattle to the processing and distribution of milk and milk products, as well as the promotion of numerous cafes, retail milk shops, and bakeries.

By the time of World War II, Hindell's, headquartered in Leeds, had extended its interests across the Midlands and diversified as far as meatpacking and even the quarrying of lime. The partnership became a public company in March 1949, as Associated Dairies and Farm Stores Limited, which included some 26 farms, three dairies, two bakeries, 42 retail shops, and pork-butchering facilities. With 1,200 employees, Associated was already an important part of the relatively quiet economy of northern England.

Success in the 1960s–70s

The next 20 years saw a veritable blizzard of further acquisitions by Associated. Dairies and creameries too numerous to mention became part of the rapidly growing northern conglomerate, but beyond expanding profits, little changed at the company until 1965, when Associated created a subsidiary called ASDA Stores Limited. In that year, the parent company, by then known as Associated Dairies Limited, with sales of £13.5 million, was highly profitable and probably did not much concern itself with the tiny food-stores division, which at best could be expected to fill one more niche in the company's overall business plan.

As it turned out, however, the stores were an immediate and immense success. Associated had come up with a merchandising concept entirely new to England, and well tailored to the working-class cities in which it chiefly operated: the company opened extremely large, rather spartan stores in abandoned warehouses or mills, offering to the public a limited selection of goods at the lowest possible prices. These "edge-of-town" stores depended for their success on the rapid proliferation of the automobile in Great Britain and the accompanying decline in local consumer loyalties. As in America, the British public soon decided that it cared less about neighborhood vendors than low prices, and the automobile allowed them to act on their preference. Associated's warehouse stores were an enormous success, and the company quickly set about the program of expansion that would make it one of the leading retailers in the country.

The company thus found itself milking two kinds of cows, dairy and cash, and the latter, naturally, proved the more attractive as time passed. Associated continued to add to its dairy holdings, but it was apparent by the early 1970s that the ASDA Stores division would soon dwarf its parent. At that time, the stores were still operated in a rudimentary fashion, with little centralized administration, primitive marketing, and no attempt at attractive floor displays. But ASDA had pioneered not one but two new ideas in British food retailing, the edge-of-town location and the superstore size, and for a long time had the market to itself.

The company opened stores in Scotland and Wales, and began casting about for opportunities to invest its growing cash reserves. In 1972, ASDA entered the travel agency business, in 1977 it had a go at furniture with its purchase of the Wade's stores, and at various times in the decade it tried its hand at a number of other diversions, none of them successful and all of them eventually eliminated. But longtime Chairman Noel Stockdale could hardly be concerned about these minor setbacks; quite reasonably, he did not try to fix what was not broken, but continued building more superstores across the northern half of the country. By 1978, ASDA had 60 of these, and two years later they passed the £1 billion sales mark.

As is usually the case, however, the rest of the marketplace had not stood still in the meantime. With ASDA's runaway success as a model, the established grocery chains began building similar superstores at out-of-town locations, while London-area stores discovered that low prices were not enough to please more sophisticated shoppers. These shoppers wanted pleasant surroundings as well as low prices, and they soon got both in the more luxurious superstores opened by ASDA's rivals. As a result, by the early 1980s the ASDA format of high volume, low price, and no frills had come to seem dated and unappealing. Customer loyalty, never strong in the economy-store sector, shifted away from ASDA toward the chains more in tune with the new wave of unabashed materialism in Thatcher's England, leaving the Yorkshire firm in danger of an early death. In a period when everyone had a superstore, ASDA's were decidedly less ''super'' than the rest.

Changes in the 1980s

Such, at any rate, was the diagnosis of John Hardman when he became managing director of stores in June 1984. Although the company was in the midst of a profitable, £1.76 billion sales year, Hardman understood that the market had moved ahead of ASDA and would soon leave ASDA floundering in its wake. Hardman, therefore, proposed a radical repositioning of the ASDA chain, to include the following improvements. First, a completely new look was to be unveiled for all of the stores, replacing their stacked-carton, industrial brown decor with a new, appetizing green palette, dramatic lighting, dropped ceilings, and imaginative display racks. Second, the chain would introduce its own ''ASDA Brand'' line of foods, since private-label merchandising generally yielded substantially higher gross margins. Third, the stores were to adopt an EPOS system—electronic point-of-sale registers—to provide more efficient records and inventory control. Fourth, the company would build a centralized network of distribution warehouses, eliminating the scores of trucks that arrived each day at store loading docks. Fifth and last, ASDA would push toward the more affluent population in southern England and the London area, where relatively few superstores had as yet been built.

Around the same time Hardman was revamping its stores, ASDA made its largest acquisition to date. In 1985 the company purchased the leading retailer of furniture in the United Kingdom, a company known as MFI, which had sales of about £300 million a year. Company spokesmen at the time pointed to the two concerns' similar positions in the marketplace, since MFI also operated large, edge-of-town stores that sold low-priced goods; but financial analysts from the beginning doubted the wisdom of the merger, and in this case they were correct. After only two years of an up-and-down marriage, ASDA sold its partner in the largest management buyout in British history, receiving £453 million in cash plus 25 percent of the newly formed ''Maxirace.''

As a matter of fact, ASDA decided at that time to sell everything: under Hardman, now chairman, the company realized that its future lay in superstores and nothing but superstores and, therefore, sold off not only MFI but also Associated Fresh Foods, the modest dairy company that at one time had been Hindell's Dairy Farmers Limited—that is, ASDA's own parent. ASDA would henceforth focus solely on its newly revamped and expanded line of food stores, with the single exception of Allied, a chain of carpet and drapery stores that the Group was unable to sell and, therefore, retained.

At first, the superstore facelift and expansion program appeared to succeed in nearly every respect. ASDA Stores became known for their innovative design, large selection of fresh foods, and equally extensive nonfood offerings, the latter accounting for some 25 percent of total store sales. A system of nine central warehouses was completed, as was the installation of EPOS and a more advanced data processing network. Profits in the new and redecorated stores were significantly higher than in the older ones, due in part to the ever-increasing number of ASDA brand items on the shelves and the more efficient distribution system. The company continued its southern assault, opening an average of 12 to 15 new superstores each year, many of them in the crowded urban areas of the South. And, in the most dramatic proof yet of its commitment to the grocery business, ASDA acquired 62 of rival Gateway's superstores for £705 million. This mammoth purchase, in a single stroke, increased ASDA's selling area by 50 percent, from 5 million to

7.5 million square feet, and further solidified its position as one of the largest operators of superstores in the United Kingdom—the new stores were on average even larger than ASDA's.

Restructuring and the Wal-Mart Purchase: 1990s and Beyond

It became apparent in the early 1990s that ASDA had perhaps bit off more than it could chew as debt related to the Gateway acquisition continued to grow. During 1991, Hardman resigned amid a host of problems and Archie Norman was named his replacement. A 1991 *Investors Chronicle* article summed up ASDA's financial position, claiming the new CEO had "inherited a dangerously listing ship whose longer term future and prosperity are far from assured."

Under new leadership, ASDA spent the next several years restructuring company operations, revamping its brand image, broadening its product mix, and lowering its prices. Norman's efforts paid off—by 1995 pretax profits had increased by nearly three times over 1992's results. Success continued over the next several years, which prompted ASDA to once again seek out merger activity. The company turned to competitor Safeway plc in 1997, suggesting a union that would create the largest food retailer in the United Kingdom. The $14.5 billion deal fell through later that year.

Undeterred, ASDA continued to look for a deal that would give it an edge in the industry. Its opportunity came when U.S. retail giant Wal-Mart Stores Inc. made a $10.8 billion takeover bid for the company in June 1999. Wal-Mart's bid thwarted efforts made by Kingfisher plc, who had entered merger talks with ASDA earlier in the year. ASDA, however, was eager to join forces with Wal-Mart, the enormously successful U.S. company on which it had based so many of its business strategies. At the same time, Wal-Mart stood to gain handsomely from the deal. The ASDA acquisition was its largest international foray to date, instantly doubling its international sales. "Indeed, the company has set its sights on becoming a leading cross-border retailer in Europe," reported a 1999 *Business Week* article. "Wal-Mart wants a third of its growth over the next five years to come from international operations." This initiative placed ASDA in an enviable position among its competitors.

Bolstered by the recent takeover, ASDA experienced success in the early years of the new millennium. Almost immediately after the purchase ASDA adopted Wal-Mart's "price roll-back" program, thus igniting price wars among U.K. supermarket companies. ASDA opened its first store under the Wal-Mart banner in 2000 and launched Smart Price, a new brand based on Wal-Mart's Great Value and Sam's Choice well known brands.

By 2003, it had usurped competitor J Sainsbury plc from its number two position in the U.K. food retailing market. It hoped to grow even larger by adding 70 Safeway stores to its arsenal. The bidding process for Safeway was subject to a variety of regulatory issues, however, and ASDA eventually lost out to Wm Morrison Supermarkets plc. As a whole, the European retail sector was expected to experience a wave of consolidation in the coming years. With Wal-Mart—whose fiscal 2004 sales were $256.3 billion—as a parent, ASDA appeared to have a bright future.

Principal Competitors

J Sainsbury plc; Safeway plc; Tesco plc.

Further Reading

"ASDA Gets in First Blow on Morrison," *Independent*, March 5, 2004.

Avery, Nerys, "Late Welcome to ASDA Cash-Call," *Investors Chronicle*, November 15, 1991, p. 34.

Ball, Deborah, "Wal-Mart Bid on Supermarkets in U.K. Is Move to Thwart Rival," *Wall Street Journal*, December 11, 2003, p. B2.

"Corporate Profile: ASDA," *Times*, October 13, 1997.

Dawley, Heidi, "Watch Out: Here Comes Wal-Mart," *Business Week*, June 28, 1999, p. 48.

Hollinger, Peggy, "Not to Be Taken for Granted: Transposing a Culture," *Financial Times*, October 1, 1999, p. 5.

Mesure, Susie, "Food Sales Bolster ASDA Success Story," *Independent*, August 14, 2003.

"New ASDA Management Plans Major Restructuring," *AFX News*, January 15, 1992.

Tooher, Patrick, "Is There Still Shelf Life in ASDA?," *Independent*, September 3, 1995, p. 7.

Wachman, Richard, "Tesco and ASDA Grow Fat at Rivals' Expense," *Observer*, November 30, 2003, p. 3.

Whysall, Paul, "Wal-Mart's Takeover of ASDA: What the Papers Said," *British Food Journal*, 2001, Volume 103, Issue 10.

—Jonathan Martin
—update: Christina M. Stansell

ATC Healthcare Inc.

1983 Marcus Avenue, Suite E122
Lake Success, New York 11042
U.S.A.
Telephone: (516) 750-1600
Fax: (516) 750-1750
Web site: http://www.atchealthcare.com

Public Company
Incorporated: 1971 as Staff Builders Inc.
Employees: 194
Sales: $148.7 million (2003)
Stock Exchanges: American
Ticker Symbol: AHN
NAIC: 621610 Home Health Care Services; 561329
   Temporary Help Services

ATC Healthcare Inc. provides temporary staff to health care facilities and private patients throughout the United States. Its 67 offices are located in 26 states and supply a wide variety of medical personnel not only to hospitals, clinics, mental health facilities, and nursing homes but also to physician practice management groups, managed health care facilities, insurance companies, schools, community health centers, and in-home patients. Among ATC's pool of health care professionals are registered nurses, licensed practical nurses, and certified nursing assistants, as well as nurses in various specialty areas such as critical care, neonatal care, and mental health care. Clients also have access to allied health professionals such as speech therapists, occupational therapists, physical therapists, and radiology technicians. ATC also provides a broad range of administrative staff such as administrative assistants, medical records clerks, collection, and personnel claims processors. ATC Travelers, the company's travel nurse program, provides long-term care givers across the nation.

A Medical Temp Service in the 1970s–80s

ATC Healthcare Inc. descended from Staff Builders, a New York City firm that specialized in providing temporary help in the medical field. Staff Builders began franchising its agencies in 1971. By the time it finally incorporated in 1978, it had 72 offices located through the United States. Staff Builders offices in New York and other large cities provided mainly in-home care for the sick and elderly. In rural areas, the company's temps were frequently used to staff hospitals, particularly where unions had not made inroads. By the mid-1980s, Staff Builders workers were also caring for growing numbers of AIDS patients.

In August 1986, it agreed to be acquired by a competitor, Tender Loving Care Health Care Services Inc. (TLC) of the New York City suburb Lake Success. The deal called for TLC to take over Staff Builders in exchange for approximately $44 million in TLC common stock.

Tender Loving Care had been founded in 1977 and went public in 1983. Staff Builders had lost $2.2 million the previous year, but its value at the time, strategically at least, was evident from the bidding war that erupted when the TLC takeover was announced. A month later, Hospital Capital Corporation, a U.K. developer of hospitals and health care facilities, made an offer estimated at $42.4 million, including over $10 million in cash. Staff Builders rejected the offer, concluding that ownership by Tender Loving Care would be better for shareholders. No sooner had the firm declined the British offer than another temporary help firm, the Norrell Corporation, attempted to purchase the company for about $33.6 million. When Staff Builders rejected the offer, Norrell launched a hostile takeover attempt, purchasing 610,000 Staff Builder shares, almost 20 percent of the company's outstanding stock. It announced that when stockholders met to vote on the TLC merger, Norrell would vote against it. Despite Norrell's opposition, however, the acquisition by Tender Loving Care was approved in January 1987.

The combined company, then known as Tender Loving Care Services, Inc., acquired another temp business, Professional Care Inc. in September 1987. The price for the 11-branch firm was approximately $3 million in cash and notes, some $9 million less than CarePlus, Inc. had been willing to spend for it—until CarePlus learned that Professional Care was under indictment for Medicare fraud in New York state. Tender Loving Care's president, Ephraim Koschitzki, was not concerned about the legal problems. His eye was on the $14 million he

Company Perspectives:

ATC's organizational philosophy combines the expertise of a major corporation with locally managed offices that promote creative responses to individual market demands. Supporting this mission are goals to constantly develop new services tailored to meet the needs of clients, employees and specific patient populations.

believed the new offices—located in Florida, New Hampshire, Texas, Michigan, Ohio, and Wisconsin—would add to TLC's annual revenues. Meanwhile, Tender Loving Care had been expanding its temp offerings into non-medical areas. To reflect the new focus, the company changed its name from Tender Loving Care Health Care Services to Staff Builders Inc. in November 1987. By that time, the company employed some 20,000 nurses in nearly 150 offices in 28 states. It had annual sales of $95 million, more than three times what it had reported in 1986.

However, rather than doubling its revenues by 1988, as the firm's leadership predicted, sales dropped nearly 20 percent. Staff Builders experienced new setbacks the following year as it attempted to expand its medical services division, an arm that accounted for less than 40 percent of the firm's annual sales. The downturn was exacerbated by the costs incurred by the closing of a number of offices and the settlement of a lawsuit with a former franchisee. In December 1989, the company reported a fourth quarter loss of $30.4 million. Until then, profits had been running on a shoestring. The year-end figures showed a total loss of $29.6 million.

By the end of 1989, shareholders were decidedly unhappy with the direction the company was taking. Management began entertaining offers to purchase Staff Builders. Instead, in early 1990, Staff Builders laid off about 10 percent of its 1000 employees and sold 125 of its personnel services offices to OTI Services for $4 million. The sale marked a change in Staff Builders' business model—that of narrowing its focus to home health care—a move that some of its biggest competitors, such as Olsten Corporation, had already made. Staff Builders also introduced a program under which the bulk of its branch offices would be franchised rather than company owned. By spring 1990, it had opened 25 franchise branches. With changes underway and its stock price still depressed, rumors circulated that Staff Builders would be targeted for a takeover.

Ups and Downs in the Early 1990s

By the summer of 1991, Staff Builders was providing staff for home health care almost exclusively. Despite the blossoming of the home care market, the company's 1990 revenues had fallen nearly 9 percent from $186 million to $170 million, and the firm was one of two home nursing companies in the country whose revenues dropped that year. The company's new CEO, Stephen Savitsky, tried to explain the decline as the result of the sale of one of the company's units. A larger problem was Staff Builder's accounting systems. When the change to home care was implemented, the system was not sophisticated enough

to process the additional paperwork and as a result scores of bills went uncollected.

On the positive side, by February 1992 Staff Builders had won Medicare certification—required by most large insurance companies of health care providers—for 37 of its facilities and hoped all of its branches would be certified by the end of the year. Staff Builders continued to develop its franchise operations. About 70 percent of its branches participated in the new program under which local operators were offered a percentage of gross profits on non-Medicare business in exchange for an equity investment. Staff Builders sought new franchisees on an ongoing basis. To finance the expansion, the firm floated a stock issue of two million shares, which raised about $11.6 million in capital for the firm. However, the new stock and warrants eventually contributed to a dilution of its stock value a few years later.

As fiscal 1992 ended, it looked as if Staff Builders had turned a corner. It reported a profit of $352,000 for the year after a loss of $5.6 million the year previous. CEO Savitsky attributed the turnaround to the new focus on home care, an area in which profit margins were higher. This segment accounted for nearly 80 percent of Staff Builders' business in 1992, double the year before. The company had also installed new computer billing systems and became involved in the area of mental health care with the establishment of the At Home Mental Health Program. Most importantly, for all its administrative problems, Staff Builders' reputation as a provider of quality care had never been questioned.

By June 1993, Staff Builders was the nation's fourth largest provider of home health care, an industry with estimated yearly revenues of $15 billion. The company had grown to 107 offices in 30 states, with 62 of its agencies franchises and 45 company owned. The company was licensing new franchises at a rate of about two each month, and it had between 30 and 50 applicants for new franchises in cities into which it planned to expand. Nurses comprised more than half of the company's franchisees.

Once Staff Builders got back on its feet financially, it began acquiring other home health care operators. In July 1993, it bought Albert Gallatin Visiting Nurse Association Inc., a company with eight offices in West Virginia and western Pennsylvania. Staff Builders paid approximately $1.9 million, most of which went toward the assumption of Albert Gallatin's debt. The additional agencies would eventually increase Staff Builders' annual revenues by $30 million. As its revenues climbed and its share price remained depressed, Staff Builders abruptly became a Wall Street favorite. Adding to its attractiveness, home health care was expected to explode as the number of senior citizens and AIDS patients increased. Moreover, it looked like the Clinton administration might enact sweeping health care reforms that could only help companies like Staff Builders, which were seen as keeping overall health costs down. All told, analysts predicted 15 to 20 percent growth rates at the company for at least five years.

In July 1994, when Staff Builders agreed to purchase ATC Services Inc. for $8.7 million, it had grown to the third-largest company in its industry. ATC became a wholly owned subsidiary of Staff Builders and continued to be based in Atlanta,

Key Dates:

1971: Staff Builders begins franchising temporary medical services.
1978: The company incorporates.
1986: Staff Builders merges with Tender Loving Care Health Care Services Inc. (TLC).
1987: TLC changes its name to Staff Builders Inc.
1989: The company begins focusing on home health care services.
1999: The company spins off Tender Loving Care home care as a subsidiary.
2001: The company changes its name to ATC Healthcare Inc.
2002: ATC begins recruiting nurses from India and South Africa.

Georgia. ATC's 13 new offices in seven states brought Staff Builders annual revenues estimated at approximately $25 million. Four months later, ATC acquired an additional seven offices spread across five states.

By December 1994, when Staff Builders moved its headquarters to a larger building, its home health care services accounted for 91 percent of its annual revenues. The company was growing at a rate of about 20 percent a year. It was making a return to hospital staffing, a sector it had largely abandoned for two years. A year later, as 1995 ended, Staff Builders had a network of some 170 branches, including 126 franchises, located in 37 states. It employed about 2,200 full-time administrative staff and boasted a pool of approximately 30,000 care givers, about 34 percent of whom were nurses and other licensed medical personnel. About 12,000 of its temporary pool was on assignment at any given time. Staff Builders made a number of acquisitions in 1995, including McdVisit Inc., Accredicare Inc., CareStar Inc., All Care Inc., and Professional Skills Inc.

Legal Difficulties in the Mid-1990s

A string of legal difficulties beset Staff Builders beginning in the mid-1990s. In May 1995, an African-American resident of New Haven, Connecticut, complained to the Department of Health and Human Services (HHS) that the company had ended service after she moved into a housing project that was barred by the company's guidelines from being visited by its personnel. Such redlining was in violation of the Civil Rights Act. As a result of the complaint, the State of Connecticut and HHS signed an agreement to deny Medicaid payments to firms that practiced redlining. Although Staff Builders maintained it had revised its guidelines, HHS gave the company 60 days to change its practices or face the loss of Medicare and Medicaid reimbursement.

In the fall of 1995, the U.S. Attorney for the Eastern District of Pennsylvania brought charges against Staff Builders' subsidiary Albert Gallatin, alleging that the company had engaged in Medicare fraud between 1987 and 1989. Staff Builders denied the extent of the over-billings Gallatin was supposed to have

made and entered into arbitration with the government over the matter, a process that dragged out over the next five years. Following an audit of Staff Builders' Medicare submissions, the HHS Inspector General brought new charges of irregularities in September 1998. The firm was charged with over-billing Medicare by approximately $3.5 million in 1994. In addition to receiving from the government $2.5 million for treatments not covered by Medicare, the company was alleged to have charged more than $750,000 for, among other things, the lease of Jaguar and Cadillac automobiles for the personal use of Staff Builders' executives. Staff Builders announced its intent to appeal the decision, maintaining the charges were the result of misunderstandings caused by a differing interpretation of Medicare laws by HHS officials. Settlements related to the mis-billings resulted in net losses of $45.4 million taken in the third quarter of Staff Builders' 1998 fiscal year.

In June 1997, Staff Builders' subsidiary ATC Healthcare Services acquired medical temp firm Nursing Management Services (USA) from the Premier Health Group plc of the United Kingdom. NMS was Premier's American arm. The purchase marked Staff Builders' entrance into the so-called travel nurse field, in which long-term nursing care is provided anywhere in the country, primarily to at-home patients. ATC purchased NMS for $1.5 million in cash and future considerations based on performance. As part of the agreement, a new company was formed, Premier Health Group (USA), to manage the unit resulting from the merger of NMS and ATC's nursing division. The new management company was to be jointly owned, with Premier plc controlling 51 percent.

In early 1999, Staff Builders launched a major reorganization, spinning off its home health care subsidiary Tender Loving Care. Under the new arrangement, TLC became an independent, separately traded company that specialized in providing staff for home health care. Under the plan, Staff Builders' shareholders received one share of TLC stock for every two Staff Builders shares held. The TLC subsidiary itself had just been formed weeks before Staff Builders' board of directors approved the spin-off plan. After the TLC spin-off was completed in October 1999, Stephen Savitsky, Staff Builders' chairman and CEO, assumed the same positions at TLC.

The costs of the spin-off coincided with a number of other major costs that contributed to another year of losses in fiscal 2000. Among additional factors for the shortfall was a major drop in revenue from Staff Builders' information technology temp services division, which was sold in late 1999, and expenses incurred from the relocation of its subsidiary ATC Healthcare Services to New York from Georgia. The company had run into new legal problems in July 1999 when the State of Massachusetts determined that Staff Builders had billed the state $4.7 million in expenses in the early 1990s that should have been paid by the federal government's Medicare program. In the wake of the Massachusetts case, the State of Connecticut launched its own audit of a decade's worth of Staff Builders charges. As a result, the firm had to set aside $11 million in capital for state liability payments. On top of its state problems, the federal government claimed that the company still owed it as much as $17 million. All this came at a time when the company was in default of its bank agreement and had had its credit facility reduced from $50 million to $40 million. In consideration of these realities, auditor Deloitte & Touche, LLP, in Staff Builders' 1999 annual report to the Securities and Exchange Commission, expressed "substantial doubt about the ability of the Company to continue as a going concern."

A New Name for the 2000s

Staff Builders did survive, however. In August 2001, the company once again adopted the name of a subsidiary when the firm became ATC Healthcare, Inc., a modification designed to show the change wrought by the TLC spin-off. The firm had begun once again to concentrate on institutional clients rather than home patients. After the name change, all the company's locations operated under a single corporate banner—ATC Healthcare Services, Inc. By the end of 2001, ATC had 63 locations spread across 25 states. Every week ATC, placed some 3,500 nurses drawn from a pool of more than 10,000 health care professionals in 50 areas of specialization. Revenues increased by 20 percent in 2002, a real turnaround for the once-troubled company. The change was reflected in ATC's share price, which climbed to $2 from lows around $0.20 in January 2001.

In January 2002, ATC completed the purchase of Direct Staffing Inc., its largest franchise, with operations on ATC's home ground of New York City and Long Island. ATC paid approximately $30.2 million to its owners, a son and two sons-in-law of ATC's CEO Stephen Savitsky. ATC said it made the purchase in order to reduce royalty payments. The company made other purchases in 2002 as well. In June, it acquired Staff One Healthcare of Tucson, Arizona, for $2 million. The following October, it bought All Nursing of Houston Texas for $200,000.

In August 2002, ATC announced partnerships with the Nurse Alliance Group and Medinnel Inc. that would assist in the recruitment of foreign nurses to ease the acute shortage of nurses in the United States. Fifty nurses from India and some 200 from South Africa were hired for the company's travel nurse arm. They were expected to add between $20 and $25 million to ATC's annual revenues. Two months later, the company assumed full control of Nursing Management Services, its travel nurse division, which was later renamed ATC Travelers. In June 2003, ATC signed an agreement with Travel Choice Staffing of Tampa, Florida, to establish what it called a traveling radiology division that would supply radiology workers where needed throughout the United States.

Principal Subsidiaries

ATC Healthcare Services, Inc.; ATC Staffing Services, Inc.; ATC Funding, LLC.

Principal Competitors

AMN Healthcare; Cross Country Healthcare; Gentiva Health Services, Inc.; Medical Staffing Network; Nursefinders.

Further Reading

Burns, John, "Regional Home-Care Firms Grow with Deals," *Modern Healthcare*, July 11, 1994, p. 22.
"CEO Interview: Stephen Savitsky–Tender Loving Care Health Care Services Inc. (TLCS)," *Wall Street Transcript Digest*, August 6, 2001.
Dallas, Sandy Lutz, "Home-Care Franchises Soar in Popularity," *Modern Healthcare*, June 7, 1993, p. 34.
"Firm Revives by Caring for Homebound," *Crain's New York Business*, January 18, 1993, p. 15.
Furman, Phyllis, "Health Care Temp Firm Aims for Recovery," *Crain's New York Business*, June 18, 1990, p. 18.
"Home-Care Firm Cited for Civil Rights Violations," *Modern Healthcare*, May 29, 1995, p. 4.
Hopkins, Susanne, "IHS Files for Chapter 11," *HomeCare Magazine*, March 2000.
——, "Staff Builders Sells Chelsea Computer, Focuses on Spinoff," *HomeCare Magazine*, November 1999.
Marcial, Gene G., "Hospital Services for Stay-At-Homes," *Business Week*, August 9, 1993, p. 69.
"Norrell Corp. Lifts Stake in Staff Builders to 19.2%," *Wall Street Journal*, January 5, 1987.
Schworm, Kimberly, "Staff Builders to Spin Off Home Care Unit," *Broadcast Engineering*, May 1999.
"Staff Builders Completes Pact," *Wall Street Journal*, August 31, 1993, p. A7.
"Staffing Firm Rules the Bedside Manor," *Crain's New York Business*, January 21, 2002, p. 4.
Strugatch, Warren, "Staff Builders Posts a $3.2 Million Loss," *New York Times*, July 2, 2000.
Tannenbaum, Jeffrey A., "Health Plan Could Boost Sales of Nursing Franchises," *Wall Street Journal*, September 30, 1993, p. B2.
"Tender Loving Care to Buy Staff Builders for About $41 Million," *Wall Street Journal*, September 23, 1986.
Wagner, Mary, "Acquisitions Add Up to Home-Care Revenue Growth," *Modern Healthcare*, May 20, 1991, p. 108.
Weissenstein, Eric, "HHS Audit Shows Staff Builders Overbilled," *Modern Healthcare*, September 14, 1998, p. 14.

—Gerald E. Brennan

Attica Enterprises S.A.

157 Kon Laramanli Avenue
Voula
GR-166 73
Greece
Telephone: (+30) 210 891 9500
Fax: (+30) 210 891 9509
Web site: http://www.attica-enterprises.com

Public Company
Incorporated: 1918 as General Company of Commerce
   and Industry of Greece
Employees: 1,000
Sales: EUR 385.5 million ($462 million)(2003)
Stock Exchanges: Athens
Ticker Symbol: ATTE GA
NAIC: 483111 Deep Sea Freight Transportation; 551112
   Offices of Other Holding Companies; 483113 Coastal
   and Great Lakes Freight Transportation; 483212
   Inland Water Passenger Transportation; 488510
   Freight Transportation Arrangement; 561510 Travel
   Agencies; 561520 Tour Operators

Greece's Attica Enterprises S.A. is the leading specialist operator of international ferry services in Europe. The company acts as a holding company for its two main shipping operations, Superfast Ferries and Blue Star Ferries. Superfast Ferries is the company's international component, with a fleet of ten high-speed ferries offering passenger and freight service across most of Europe's major seaways. Superfast is the leading provider of ferry services between Greece and Italy, serving Ancona, Brindisi and Bari in Italy across the Adriatic Sea from the Greek ports of Patras and Igoumenitsa. Since the 2000s, the company has also become the leading ferry services company on the Hanko, Finland, to Rostock, Germany, route. Superfast has also established a major on the Zeebrugge, Belgium, to Rosyth, Scotland, route. The opening up of Greece's inter-island market has enabled the company to establish a strong presence at home as well through its controlling stake in Strintzis Lines Shipping S.A., which operates under the Blue Star Ferries name. Blue Star serves most of Greece's major island groups, including the Ionian, Dodecanese, and Cyclades islands, as well as Crete. Attica Group was formed in the early 1990s by chairman and CEO Pericles S. Panagopoulos and later joined by his son, Alexandros Panagopoulos. Listed on the Athens Stock Exchange, Attica achieved revenues of EUR 385.5 million ($462 million) and net profits of EUR 28.3 million ($34 million) in 2003.

From Cruise Vessels to Ferries: 1970s–90s

Born into an Athens hotel family, Pericles Panagopoulos's own career interests turned to shipping. By the age of 15, Pangopulos had joined his uncle Eugene Eugenides' steamship company, Home Lines, working weekends and on school holidays. Panagopoulos went on to study business and economics, pursuing his education in Greece, as well as in England and Switzerland. After completing his studies, Panagopoulos worked in various positions in the shipping industry, including passenger lines, but also in cargo and reefer shipping. By the late 1960s, Panagopoulos's career had taken him to Greek cruise ship operator, Sun Lines.

Tourist travel to Greece and its islands had begun to take off in the 1960s, and by the middle of the decade the country was hosting more than three million visitors per year. Greek ship owners, largely from the country's islands, built up fleets of cruise and other ships, buying largely second-hand craft that could be converted to the tourism trade. For the most part, however, Greek cruise lines stayed close to their domestic home base, rarely venturing into international waters. This was in part because shippers preferred the high level of government protectionism that more or less blocked foreign shippers from entering the Greek market. Yet the Greek tourist trade remained highly seasonal, with a great deal of activity during the summer months and tourist traffic practically at a standstill during the off-season.

Panagopoulos decided to break this mold by launching his own cruise line company at the beginning of the 1970s. Under Panagopoulos's model, his ships would work Greece's ports during the summer, then move on to North America, serving the

Company Perspectives:

Attica Enterprises endeavors to control and operate leading modern brands in the sectors of sea transportation and leisure. Europe is our home market. We strive for the highest professional standards providing our customers with services of better value for money than any of our competitors. The services we offer must manifest our commitment to providing customers a service with safety, reliability, punctuality, technical competence, quality, flexibility and innovation.

so-called ''fly-cruise'' U.S. market along the Mexican Riviera. In order to launch his business, named Royal Cruise Lines, Panagopoulos took out a mortgage on his property in Athens. For his first vessel, Panagopoulos broke from the Greek market standards and placed an order for a vessel to be built-to-order for Royal Cruise Lines in Denmark.

Panagopoulos took delivery on the vessel, the Gold Odyssey, in 1974. The success of Royal Cruise Lines' business model, later extended to include cruises in Alaska, Scandinavia, the South Pacific, and the Far East, enabled the company to survive the difficult economic climate of the late 1970s. Panagopoulos also maintained a small fleet of cargo ships as an added source of revenues. Nonetheless, as the company prepared to expand its fleet, it was forced to opt for a second-hand vessel for its second ship. Bought from Home Lines in 1982, the new ship was re-commissioned as the Royal Odyssey.

Strong growth through the early 1980s enabled Royal Cruise Lines to commission a new ship in 1985. The Crown Odyssey, as it was called, became the company's flagship when it was delivered in 1988. Yet, less than two years later, Panagopoulos, then fifty-five years old, decided to retire. In November 1989, Panagopoulos agreed to sell Royal Cruise Lines to Denmark's Kloster Cruises, later known as Norwegian Cruise Lines. Kloster's purchase price for Royal Cruise Lines was reported as high as $300 million.

A New Career in Retirement: 1990s

Panagopoulos's plans to retire did not last long, however. By 1992, he had decided to return to passenger shipping with a new idea. In 1992, Panagopoulos bought a dormant company, known as Attica Enterprises. That company had started out in 1918 as General Company of Commerce and Industry of Greece but later focused on producing and trading flour under the name of Attica Flour Mills.

Panagopoulos renamed the company Attica Enterprises and began preparations to launch into a new shipping area—that of international ferry services, joined now by his son Alexandros. Panagopoulos's new concept involved the use of new high-speed vessels capable of transporting both freight and passengers. In 1975, Attica Enterprises set up a new subsidiary, Attica Maritime, and took delivery of its first two vessels, named Superfast I and Superfast II. The ships were put into service serving the route across the Adriatic Sea between Patras in Greece and Ancona in Italy. With speeds of up to 26 knots, the

Superfast ships trimmed some eight hours off the usual travel times. The voyage of just 20 hours allowed Superfast to begin offering daily ferry service.

Attica Maritime changed its name to Superfast Ferries as the company quickly became a major force in a revitalized Adriatic shipping market. The success of the Superfast formula permitted the company to place an order for two new ferries in 1996. Built at the Kvearner Shipyard in Finland, the new vessels, Superfast III and Superfast IV were delivered in 1998 and placed on the Patras-Ancona route. The company then shifted its original pair of ferries to serve two new routes, between Patras and Bari, Italy, and between Igoumenitsa and Bari. The company later added Brindisi, in Italy, as well.

European Ferry Leader in the 2000s

Soon after receiving its third and fourth ferries, Attica decided to branch out beyond the Adriatic Sea, eyeing routes in the Baltic Sea. In 1998, the company commissioned four new Superfast ferries at the Howaldtswerke ship yard in Germany, with an option for two additional ferries. By 1999, the company's growing business encouraged it to exercise that option in 1999. The company took delivery of the first two of the new Superfast series that year; these were put into service supporting the company's Adriatic Sea operations. By then, Superfast had firmly established itself as the leader in that market, with a more than 30 percent share.

Attica also sought to establish a position in the Aegean Sea. In 1999, the company agreed to buy a 38 percent stake in publicly listed Strintzis Lines SA, later taking control of that company with more than 48.6 percent. Strintzis, which was renamed Blue Star Ferries under Attica, had gone public in 1993 in order to support its own launch onto the Greek-Italian sea route. Yet, Blue Star's largest business remained in the Greek inter-island sector, in which Strintzis, founded by Gerasimos Strintzis, had become the market leader. Blue Star brought Attica 11 more ferries as well as a number of new vessels on order. These included a new state-of-the-art ferry, the Blue Star Ithaki, built by Daewoo Heavy Industries in Korea. That vessel was put into service in the Cyclades island chain in 2000. Two more Blue Star ferries, built by Van der Giessen de Noord, in the Netherlands, were delivered in 2000 as well.

By now, Attica had already put in an order for two new Superfast ferries to be built by Germany's Flender Werft, with delivery slated for 2002. These were needed to back up the company's winning bid for the operation of a new ferry service between Scotland's Rosyth and the European continent. In 2001, Attica decided on Belgium's Zeebrugge as the continental port of the new line. That service, which marked Scotland's first-ever direct link to the European continent, was launched in 2002.

The delivery of Superfast VII, followed soon after by Superfast VIII, enabled the company to open up a new service between Hanko in Finland and Rostock in Germany. That service was an immediate success, and Superfast became the leading ferry operator in the Baltic Sea as well.

With the delivery of the latest Superfast ferries (IX and X), Attic began seeking buyers for it original vessels. In 2002, the

Key Dates:

1918: General Company of Commerce and Industry of Greece, which later becomes the publicly listed company Attica Flour Mills, is founded.

1971: Pericles Panagopoulos sets up his own cruise line company, Royal Cruise Lines (RCL).

1974: RCL takes delivery of its first vessel, the Golden Odyssey, and enters the United States "fly-cruise" market.

1989: Panagopoulos sells RCL to Kloster Cruise Lines for $250 million.

1992: Panagapolus buys Attica Flour Mills, renames it Attica Enterprises, then places an order for two "Superfast" ferries.

1995: Attica takes delivery of Superfast I and Superfast II, launching service between Greece and Italy.

1998: The company orders four more ferries to increase its fleet to eight vessels by 2000.

1999: Attica acquires 38 percent (later 48.6 percent) of Sprintzis Lines to enter the domestic inter-islands market.

2001: Ferry service between Hanko, Finland, and Rostock, Germany, begins.

2002: Rosyth-Zeebrugge service is launched.

2004: Superfast is named the United Kingdom's best ferry operator by *Holiday Which?* magazine.

company sold Superfast III and IV to Australia's TT-Line Pty, backed by the Government of Tasmania, for $152 million. That same partnership purchased a third vessel from Attica, the Superfast II, in 2003. At this point, Attica had taken delivery on the last pieces of its Superfast fleet, with the delivery of XI in July 2002 and XII in October of that same year.

As it gained majority control of Blue Star, Attica began reorienting that company to focus on the Greek market, with new services opening in the Dodecanese islands in 2002, and a new route linking Piraeus and Crete in 2003. As part of its refocusing, Blue Star ended its ferry service between Greece and Venice that year.

Early in 2004, Attica sold off the vessel that had started it all, when the Atlantic Navigazione, part of Italy's Grimaldi Group, agreed to purchase the Superfast I. By then, Attica was celebrating steadily rising revenues, which topped EUR 385 million ($462 million) in 2003, and strong reputation for the quality of its service. In 2004, the company received recognition as the best ferry operator in the United Kingdom according to the *Holiday Which?* magazine.

Principal Subsidiaries

Strintzis Lines Shipping SA (48.6%); Superfast Ferries SA.

Principal Competitors

J Lauritzen A/S ; Navigation Maritime Bulgare; Caspian Shipping Company; Compania de Navigatie Fluviala Romana S.A.; Stena Line Scandinavia AB; A.S. Eesti Merelaevandus; Tirrenia di Navigazione S.p.A.; Stena Line UK Ltd.; Irish Continental Group plc; Scandlines Danmark A/S.

Further Reading

"Attica Deal, Exchanges Show Greece Is Open for Business," *Euroweek*, October 12, 2001, p. 20.

Clough, Juliet, "Over the Sea to Europe," *Mail on Sunday*, December 16, 2001, p. 94.

Hope, Kerrin, "Superfast Success," *Europe*, March 1998, p. 42.

"A Trendsetter That Has Put Its Rivals through Their Paces," *Lloyds List*, May 22, 2003.

—M.L. Cohen

Barclays plc

54 Lombard Street
London EC3P 3AH
United Kingdom
Telephone: (207) 699-5000
Fax: (207) 283-5055
Web site: http://www.barclays.com

Public Company
Incorporated: 1896 as Barclay & Company, Ltd.
Employees: 74,420
Total Assets: £443.36 billion ($788.51 billion) (2003)
Stock Exchanges: London New York Tokyo
Ticker Symbol: BCS
NAIC: 522110 Commercial Banking; 551111 Offices of
Bank Holding Companies

With a rich history dating back almost 300 years, Barclays plc has grown into one of the largest financial services groups in the United Kingdom. The company is involved in banking, investment banking, and investment management and operates 2,000 domestic branches and nearly 850 international branches in over 60 countries across the globe. Barclays is organized into seven business units: Barclays Africa; Barclaycard; Barclays Capital; Barclays Global Investors; Barclays Private Clients; and UK Banking. The company has over 4.5 million registered online bankers and over 10.6 million Barclaycard customers in the United Kingdom. In 2003, Barclays was the world's ninth-largest bank based on market capitalization.

Early History

Barclays takes it symbol, the spread eagle, from the Quaker goldsmithing and banking firm founded by John Freame in 1728. In 1736, James Barclay, Freame's brother-in-law, became a partner in the Black Spread Eagle. When two more of Barclay's relatives joined the firm—Silvanus Bevan in 1767 and John Henton Tritton in 1782—the banking firm took the name by which it would be known for more than a century: Barclays, Bevan & Tritton. While fledgling joint-stock banks outside London struggled to establish themselves in the late 18th and early 19th centuries, Barclays, Bevan & Tritton was still occupied with the well-established and highly lucrative commercial life of London.

A series of legislative changes enacted in the late 19th century created a new banking climate that threatened the existence of private banks such as Barclays. First, the Bank Charter Act of 1826 allowed banks with more than six partners to be formed only outside London. In 1833, the geographical restriction was removed. Stockholders of new joint-stock companies were granted limited liability for the first time in 1854. Finally, in 1879, existing joint-stock associations were allowed to convert to a limited-liability structure.

Mergers in Late 19th and Early 20th Centuries

As a result of these legislative changes, provincial limited-liability joint-stock companies started picking off private banks. After lengthy negotiations, three of the largest Quaker-run banking firms—Barclays (which had become Barclays, Tritton, Ransom, Bouverie & Company after a merger in 1888), Jonathan Backhouse & Company, and Gurneys, Birkbeck, Barclay & Buxton, along with 17 smaller Quaker-run banks, agreed to merge and form a bank large enough to resist takeover attempts. Barclays took its modern form in 1896 when the 20 private banks merged to form Barclay and Company, Ltd., a joint-stock association with deposits totaling an impressive £26 million. This marked the beginning of Barclays' tradition of service to farmers and fishermen.

Francis Augustus Bevan, grandson of Silvanus Bevan, served as the new bank's first chairman for 20 years. The company's structure and course, however, were directed for its initial 40 years by Frederick Crauford Goodenough, as first secretary, until 1917, and then as chairman after Bevan's retirement until his own death in 1934. Goodenough was the only chairman recruited from outside the original founding families until 1987. Recruited from the Union Bank of London, Goodenough remained aloof from family controversies and quickly proved his merit.

Goodenough's first task was to meld the constituent banks into a single enterprise. He took a decentralized approach that was to be Barclays' hallmark for most of the 20th century. Each

Company Perspectives:

We aspire to be one of the most admired financial services organisations in the world, recognised as an innovative, customer-focused company that delivers superb products and services, ensures excellent careers for our people and contributes positively to the communities in which we live and work.

member bank was independently operated under the control of its own board of directors. Senior partners of the constituent banks were given a seat on the Barclays board. In this way, longstanding relationships between each member bank and its customers were maintained, and the new company took advantage of the knowledge and experience of its leaders.

At the same time, Goodenough initiated a series of mergers which eventually made Barclays one of the largest banks in Great Britain. In its first 20 years, Barclays acquired 17 private banks throughout England, including Woods and Company of Newcastle upon Tyne in 1897, Bolitho Bank in Cornwall, and United County Banks, its first joint-stock bank acquisition, in 1916. The bank's merger with the London, Provincial and South Western Bank in 1918 made it one of the Big Five British banks. During this period, Barclays merged with 45 British banks and its deposit base grew to £328 million.

This era of banking amalgamations came to an end in 1919, when the Colwyn Committee recommended, and banking authorities unofficially adopted, limitations on previously unregulated bank mergers. The committee suggested that thenceforth the Bank of England and the treasury approve only those mergers that provided important new facilities to customers or secured significant territorial gains for larger banks. Mergers were no longer approved if they resulted in a significant overlap in the areas served by constituent banks without countervailing benefits to customers or if they would result in ''undue prominence'' for a larger bank. After the Colwyn Committee report, mergers were increasingly difficult to justify, and the consensus was that mergers among the Big Five would not be approved.

International Expansion in the 1910s and 1920s

After Barclays' expansionist phase ended, Goodenough turned his attention to international banking operations. Barclays' first international venture took place in 1914 when it established its French subsidiary, Cox & Company. Goodenough had a vision of a network of Barclays banks spanning the globe to the greater glory of the British Empire. As early as 1916, he started preparations for worldwide banking by acquiring the shares of the Colonial Bank, established in 1836 to provide banking services in the West Indies and British Guiana. The Colonial Bank's charter was extended by special legislation to British West Africa in 1916 and then worldwide in 1917.

Immediately after World War I, Goodenough began negotiations with the National Bank of South Africa Ltd. and the Anglo-Egyptian D.C.O., operating in the Mediterranean. Despite the opposition from the Bank of England, which feared Barclays would become overextended, Goodenough engineered the 1925 merger of the two banks with the Colonial to form Barclays Bank

(Dominion, Colonial & Overseas), later renamed Barclays Bank (D.C.O.). Although Goodenough never realized his dream of establishing banks throughout the British Empire, for decades Barclays was the only British bank to combine domestic business with a widely dispersed international branch network.

A contemporary of Goodenough speculated that the chairman became interested in expanding Barclays' international operations because domestic growth was very limited. Despite this stagnation and later the Great Depression, Goodenough's plan did not result in a disastrous overextension of the bank's assets.

Barclays survived the Great Depression relatively intact to take its place as a leading wartime financier. Goodenough died in 1934 and was replaced by William Favill Tuke, who was in turn replaced in 1936 by Edwin Fisher. Fisher saw Barclays through the boom years of World War II. When Fisher died in 1947, he was replaced by William Macnamara Goodenough.

In 1951, Anthony William Tuke, the son of William Favill Tuke, became chairman following William Goodenough's retirement that year. A.W. Tuke was essentially conservative but encouraged innovations, even those he personally disliked, that were potentially beneficial to the bank. Under Tuke's leadership, Barclays became Britain's largest bank, surpassing the Midland Bank in the late 1950s. Barclays was also a leader in introducing new banking technology. In 1959, Barclays was the first British bank to use a computer in its branch accounting; it also introduced the world's first automatic cash-dispensing machine and started a plastic revolution in Britain by introducing the Barclaycard in 1966.

Barclays Enters U.S. Market in 1965

In the late 1960s and early 1970s, when most competitors were struggling to establish international operations, Barclays enjoyed an enormous head start, since its operations in former British colonies in Africa and the Caribbean were well-established. The economies of many of these countries, however, were precarious. To offset its high exposure in developing countries, Barclays decided to enter the U.S. market. It first established Barclays Bank of California in 1965, and then, in 1971, formed Barclays Bank of New York. Together these two banks gave Barclays the unique advantage of having retail banking operations on both U.S. coasts. Another advantage Barclays enjoyed was an exemption from 1978 legislation barring foreign banks from operating branches in more than one state.

In 1967, British banking authorities clarified their position on domestic mergers. The National Board for Prices and Incomes stated that mergers would be allowed to rationalize existing networks and that further reduction in the number of independent banks would not be viewed as inherently anti-competitive. Barclays quickly took advantage of the change in policy by merging with the venerable Martins Bank in November 1968. Established by Sir Thomas Gresham, chief financial adviser to Elizabeth I and founder of the Royal Exchange, Martins Bank, the sixth-largest in the country, brought Barclays more than 700 branches, mostly in northern England.

In 1973, A.W. Tuke was succeeded as chairman by Anthony Favill Tuke, William F. Tuke's grandson. A.F. Tuke served until 1981, when he left Barclays to operate a British mining

Key Dates:

1728: John Freame forms a Quaker goldsmithing and banking firm.
1736: James Barclay becomes a partner.
1896: Twenty private banks merge to form Barclay and Company Ltd.
1918: The company merges with the London, Provincial and South Western Bank.
1968: Barclays merges with Martins Bank.
1984: The company changes its name to Barclays plc.
1985: Barclays becomes a holding company.
1995: Wells Fargo Nikko Investment Advisors is acquired.
1997: Parts of BZW are sold.
2000: The company purchases Woolwich plc.

company. His tenure was most notable for Barclays' expansion in North America. In May 1974, Barclays Bank International acquired the First Westchester National Bank of New Rochelle, New York. In the late 1970s, Barclays opened a series of branches and agencies in major U.S. cities. By 1986, North American operations had extended to 37 states. In the early 1980s, Barclays Bank International diversified into commercial credit, acquiring the American Credit Corporation, renamed Barclays American Corporation (BAC) in May 1980. Later that year, BAC acquired 138 offices from subsidiaries of Beneficial Finance and the operations of Aetna Business Credit Inc.

Restructuring in the Early 1980s

In June 1981, Timothy Bevan became chairman of Barclays and immediately, with the assistance of United Kingdom Chairman Deryk Weyer, set about restructuring domestic operations. The system of local control initiated by F.C. Goodenough had become outdated as the bank expanded and diversified. Senior managers' responsibilities were not clearly defined, and, although technically higher in authority than regional bank directors, in practice the senior managers were subject to the regional officials' control as board members. Moreover, the original structure of the company tended to produce dynasties. Weyer's strategy was to establish three basic divisions to represent Barclays' most important markets—the large corporate market, the middle market of small- to medium-sized businesses, and the traditional individual-customer and mass-consumer market. Bevan and Weyer moved cautiously, however, avoiding wholesale reorganization of the company so that the relationships of local managers with large customers were not disrupted.

Further changes in the structure of the company followed. Barclays had converted from a joint-stock bank to a public limited company in 1981, and it assumed its present name in 1984. In 1985, Barclays became a holding company and all of its assets were transferred, in exchange for stock, to its operating subsidiary, Barclays Bank International Ltd., which was simultaneously converted to a public limited company and renamed Barclays Bank plc.

In 1986, Barclays acquired Visa's traveler's check operation, becoming the third-largest issuer in the world with 14

percent of the market. That same year, in preparation for the deregulation of the British securities market, Barclays Merchant Bank Ltd. de Zoete and Bevan and Wedd Durlacher Morduant & Company merged to form Barclays de Zoete Wedd (BZW), a new investment-banking enterprise.

Challenging Environment in the Late 1980s

Chairman John Quinton, appointed in May 1987, faced a number of challenges in the late 1980s. Domestic banking had always been Barclays' strength, but the bank faced increasing competition. National Westminster Bank edged out Barclays in assets. The building societies, by offering high interest on savings, threatened the bank's traditional deposit base. Finally, American and Japanese banks entered the commercial-lending market and began to pose a threat to British banks. Barclays fought back with two formidable money-generating enterprises, Mercantile Credit and the Barclaycard, which generated about 20 percent of Barclays' domestic profits. The bank also continued to rationalize its branches to better serve the three major banking-service markets. In addition, Barclays planned to spend more than £500 million on technological advances, including the introduction of the first electronic debit card in the United Kingdom.

Barclays' future in international banking was less certain. It was dealt a number of setbacks in the late 1980s. In 1986, Barclays divested its 148-year-old, wholly owned South African subsidiary, Barclays National Bank (Barat), in response to a disastrous drop in the subsidiary's earnings from 1984 to 1986 and to losses in the lucrative student market in Britain as Barclays' presence in South Africa became more unpopular at home. Also, the steady deterioration of African economies posed a hazard because the bank's African involvement was so heavy. Barclays decreased its African investments where possible but had difficulties in removing profits and proceeds from Africa. In addition, Barclays' Hong Kong and Italian operations both suffered large losses in the 1980s, and the performance of Barclays' American operations was consistently disappointing. In the early 1980s, Barclays expanded very rapidly and tried to build earnings quickly through an aggressive lending policy. As a result, branches picked up a large volume of low-quality loans. Bad-debt ratios were very high, costs were difficult to control, and American operations only started to show a profit in the late 1980s (only 4 percent of Barclays' profits were from U.S. operations, while 15 percent of the bank's assets were invested there). As a result, Barclays began offering specialized services in the United States in an attempt to improve its position there. Nevertheless, after years of trying to make it profitable, Barclays sold its California banking subsidiary in 1988 to Wells Fargo. The following year, Barclays sold its U.S. consumer finance unit to Primerica (later known as Travelers).

On the positive side, Barclays' investment-banking operations showed promise. BZW expanded its operations by purchasing 50 percent of Mears and Phillips, an Australian brokerage firm. Barclays also formed a new bank in Geneva, Barclays Bank S.A., to develop capital markets with BZW.

A Change in Strategy in the Early to Mid-1990s

Although Barclays began the 1990s in an expansion mode, the bank was soon forced into retreat. In 1990, Barclays acquired Merck, Finck & Co., a German investment bank, and L'Europeenne de Banque, based in Paris. However, extended recessions on both sides of the Atlantic led to numerous bankruptcies in the early 1990s, and many banks—including Barclays—suffered huge losses from bad loans. Barclays was forced to set aside £1.55 billion in 1991 and £2.5 billion in 1992 against these bad loans. Profits, already hurt by continuing high operating costs, plunged as a result. Barclays, in fact, posted a pretax loss of £244 million in 1992.

The bank's difficulties led to the early—and forced—departure of Quinton, who had been expected to stay on for a couple more years. Andrew Buxton, who had worked his way up through the ranks since joining Barclays as a trainee in 1963 and was a descendant of one of the company founders, became CEO in April 1992 and then added the chairmanship at the beginning of 1993. Although a Barclays' tradition, the dual appointment provoked controversy as institutional shareholders voiced concerns that the bank had grown too large for such an arrangement. Subsequently, in the fall of 1993 Barclays made the rare move—for Barclays—of tapping an outsider when it appointed Martin Taylor as CEO, with Buxton remaining chairman. Taylor had most recently led a turnaround at U.K. textile firm Courtauld Textiles that involved closing factories and restructuring the business.

In the midst of these management changeovers, Barclays began a retrenchment—which continued into the mid-1990s—whereby it reduced its far-flung operations, at least in selected countries and regions; undertook a massive cost-cutting program; and once again restructured its domestic retail banking operations. Barclays dramatically reduced its troubled U.S. operations, starting with its exit from U.S. retail banking in May 1992, through the sale of its remaining branches and assets to Bank of New York Co. In late 1994, Barclays Business Credit, a firm that offered asset-based lending to U.S. companies, was sold to Shawmut National Corporation for $290 million. In 1996, Barclays' U.S. mortgage unit, Barclays American Mortgage Corporation, was sold to Norwest Mortgage Inc. In addition to these American divestitures, banking operations in Israel were sold off, and Barclays' Australian retail banking subsidiary was sold in 1994 to St. George's Bank of Australia.

The most visible aspect of the cost-cutting program was the elimination of 18,000 jobs between 1990 and 1995. The majority of these cuts were made in the United Kingdom, most notably as a result of the restructuring of the bank's domestic retail branches. By late 1994, Barclays' domestic branch network had been cut to 2,080, a reduction of 21.5 percent since 1989.

Like most U.K. banks, Barclays benefited from the improved economic conditions of the mid-1990s, and as a result the bank was able to enhance its loan portfolio. Barclays had to set aside only £396 million in 1995 and £215 million in 1996 for bad loans. The bank's reduced foreign and domestic operations and cost-cutting moves, in concert with the improving economic environment, led to healthy before-tax profits of £2.08 billion in 1995 and £2.36 billion in 1996. Nevertheless, during these two years, Barclays continued to restructure, this time concentrating on its Asset Management Group. In 1995, the bank bolstered its presence in the Asia-Pacific region by purchasing Wells Fargo Nikko Investment Advisers, which was integrated into the Asset Management Group. Two years later, Barclays sold its global custody business to Morgan Stanley Group Inc.

Barclays neared the turn of the 21st century (and its 275th anniversary in 2003) in its strongest position in years. Although it would continue to face serious competition at home, the bank's restructuring of its domestic retail banking network seemed to be a success. As Europe slowly moved toward integration, Barclays smartly divested many of its non-European operations while seeking opportunities for continental expansion. At the same time, Barclays had retained some geographic flexibility by maintaining an international presence in investment banking through its successful BZW unit. Merger activity in 1997 however, placed this unit in a precarious position.

Late 1990s and Beyond

Intense competition forced Barclays' reorganization to continue in 1997. Large mergers, including the tie up of Morgan Stanley and Dean Witter and the merger of Salomon Brothers and Smith Barney, had left Barclays unable to compete in the global investment banking industry. As such, the company opted to sell off parts of its BZW unit in 1997. Credit Suisse First Boston purchased the European and Asian investment banking portion of the business while ABN Amro snatched up its Australian and New Zealand operations. Barclays opted to keep BZW's debt business, renaming it Barclays Capital.

As Barclays struggled to retain its market share over the next several years it dealt with several changes in management. The sell off of BZW was considered highly controversial among Barclays' shareholders, a fact that may have played a role in Taylor's resignation in November 1998. He was replaced by Michael O'Neill, an American executive who orchestrated the merger of Bank of America and Nations Bank. His appointment was applauded by many who felt Barclays' would benefit from his merger experience. Due to health problems, however, O'Neill quit on his first day, leaving Sir Peter Middleton at the helm of what many analysts were now considering a sinking ship. Matthew W. Barrett was named CEO in 1999 while Middleton remained chairman.

With a stable management team now in place, Barclays continued to revamp its organization. In 1999, it announced that 6,000 jobs would be eliminated from its U.K. workforce. It also set plans in motion to shutter up to 200 rural branches by 2000 as part of its strategy to focus on online banking. The company continued to eye growth and moved to acquire Woolwich plc in a $7.96 billion deal. The *Wall Street Journal* summed up the advantages of the union in August 2000, reporting that it would "double Barclay's presence in the U.K. mortgage sector to 8% and boost the bank's total client base to 16 million from 13 million, making it the third-largest financial institution in the U.K. based on number of customers." The article went on to state, "The takeover also gives Barclays one of the U.K.'s most successful online-banking ventures. Though Barclays has more online customers than any other bank in the U.K., Woolwich's Internet service is considered far more advanced." Barclays completed the transaction in 2000. It made another acquisition in 2003 when it added Spain's Banco Zaragozano to its arsenal. The $1.8 billion acquisition fit nicely into Barclays' strategy to grow its business in Europe.

Chairman Middleton announced that he would retire at the end of 2004, leaving Barrett to take over as chairman. John Varley was slated to assume the CEO position. At this time, the company focused on increasing revenues, controlling costs, and maintaining a cautious approach to risk management. While it looked to organic growth to bolster sales and profits, Barclays did not rule out the possibility of future merger activity. Pre-tax profits rose by 20 percent in 2003, a sign that Barclays' actions were paying off.

Principal Subsidiaries

Barclays Bank plc; Barclays Capital Inc.; Barclays Capital Investors N.A.; Woolwich plc.

Principal Operating Units

Barclays Africa; Barclaycard; Barclays Capital; Barclays Global Investors; Barclays Private Clients; UK Banking.

Principal Competitors

HBOS plc; HSBC Holdings plc; Lloyds TSB Group plc.

Further Reading

Bailey, Martin, *Barclays and South Africa*, Birmingham: Haslemere Group, 1975.

"Barclays Set for Expansion," *Herald*, August 6, 1999, p. 24.

Bray, Nicholas, "Barclays Pursues Shrinkage to Achieve Solid Returns: Round-the-World Presence Is Played Down in Favor of U.K. Retail Banking," *Wall Street Journal*, October 31, 1994, p. B4.

Caplan, Brian, "Is Martin Taylor's Halo Slipping?," *Euromoney*, March 1996, pp. 54–58.

Crossley, Julian Stanley, *The DCO Story: A History of Banking in Many Countries, 1925–71*, London: Barclays Bank, 1975.

"The Davidson Interview: Martin Taylor," *Management Today*, April 1996, pp. 40–44.

"The Eagle Preens Itself," *Economist*, June 25, 1988, pp. 84–85.

Great Britain Commission on Industrial Relations, Barclays Bank International, Ltd., London: HMSO, 1974.

Green, Edwin, *Debtors to Their Profession: A History of the Institute of Bankers, 1879–1979*, New York: Methuen, 1979.

"Half Way up to the Top of the Hill: Barclays Bank," *Economist*, August 13, 1994, p. 71.

Hoffman, Abigail, "The Middleton Way," *Sunday Telegraph*, June 27, 2004, p. 8.

"Is Might Right?," *Economist*, April 16, 1988, pp. 97–98.

Lambert, Wade, "Woolwich Purchase Allows Barclays to Focus Elsewhere," *Wall Street Journal*, August 14, 2000, p. A14.

"The New New Look: Barclays Bank," *Economist*, December 12, 1992, p. 86.

"O'Neill to Be Chief at Barclays," *Scotsman*, February 12, 1999, p. 27.

Paterson, Lea, "Barclays Chief Predicts More Bank Deals," *Independent*, December 23, 1997, p. 19.

"Predators Eyeing up Rudderless Ship," *South China Morning Post*, April 15, 1999.

"The Shake-Up in the Barclays Boardroom," *Economist*, April 25, 1992, p. 83.

Tuke, Anthony, and P.W. Matthew, *History of Barclays Bank Limited*, London: Blades, East & Blades Ltd., 1926.

Tuke, Anthony, and R.J.H. Gillman, *Barclays Bank Limited, 1926–1969: Some Recollections*, London: Barclays Bank, 1972.

Valdmanis, Thor, "No Sacred Cows: Former Industrialist Martin Taylor Whips Barclays Back into Shape," *Financial World*, May 9, 1995, p. 34.

Watkins, Leslie, *Barclays: A Story of Money and Banking*, London: Barclays Bank, 1982.

West, Karl, "Banking on a Safe Pair of Hands," *Herald*, October 10, 2003, p. 23.

—updates: David E. Salamie and Christina M. Stansell

Bertucci's Corporation

155 Otis Street
Northborough, Massachusetts 01532
U.S.A.
Telephone: (508) 351-2500
Fax: (508) 393-8046
Web site: http://www.bertuccis.com

Private Company
Incorporated: 1984 as Bertucci's Inc.
Employees: 6,060
Sales: $162.3 million (2002)
NAIC: 722110 Full-Service Restaurants

Bertucci's Corporation, a casual-dining chain, owns a collection of full-service Italian restaurants that operate under the name "Bertucci's Brick Oven Pizzeria." During the early years of the 21st century there were roughly 80 Bertucci's restaurants scattered throughout the northeastern United States, each of which featured wood-fired brick ovens, which cook hotter than conventional pizza ovens, and served Tuscan-styled food, including gourmet pizzas, salads, soups, seafood, and pasta dishes. Founded in suburban Boston by Joseph Crugnale, Bertucci's expanded quickly during the 1980s and 1990s, growing from a single restaurant in 1981 to a sprawling restaurant chain by the mid-1990s. N.E. Restaurant Co. Inc., Bertucci's owner since 1998, adopted the Bertucci's name in 2001.

Origins

By the time Joseph Crugnale decided to invest his time and energy into building a chain of Bertucci's Brick Oven Pizzeria restaurants, he had already amassed a substantial fortune, enough to warrant an early retirement for the Italian-born restaurateur. Remarkably, Crugnale had placed himself in this enviable position, sitting atop a $4.5 million fortune after less than a decade of work, by the time he was 31 years old. His greatest success, however, was still to come. Bertucci's would be Crugnale's crowning achievement, overshadowing by far what he had accomplished during his twenties and increasing his already sizable fortune considerably. From a single restau-

rant in 1981, Bertucci's developed into a chain that, during one five-year period, grew by 3,157 percent, quickly inundating the mid-scale restaurant market surrounding the Boston area with a collection of full-service restaurants. As the chain grew, extending its presence outside of Massachusetts and then outside of New England, Crugnale's reputation grew, making both the founder and the company models of success in the U.S. restaurant industry.

Born in Sulmona, Italy, Crugnale landed his first job in the restaurant business after his family emigrated from their home country and settled in New England, where during his high school years Crugnale worked as a porter at the Sonesta Hotel in Cambridge, Massachusetts. Crugnale accumulated additional experience by working in restaurants in Massachusetts and Florida, gaining expertise in cooking from the chefs there, before making his entrepreneurial debut in 1974 when he opened his own ice cream stand. The following year, Crugnale refinanced his father's home and purchased Steve's Ice Cream from founder Steve Herrell, paying $80,000 for the enterprise that eight years later would make him a multimillionaire.

Crugnale built Steve's Ice Cream into a lucrative national chain, establishing 26 stores through franchising agreements by the time he sold the concept to Integrated Resources in 1983 for $4.5 million. Under Crugnale's stewardship, Steve's Ice Cream had become wildly popular, and it also indirectly spawned the creation of his signal success, Bertucci's. Two years before Crugnale divested himself of Steve's Ice Cream, he opened the first Bertucci's Brick Oven Pizzeria in his home town of Somerville, Massachusetts, establishing the Italian restaurant, with its wood-fired brick oven, two doors away from one of his Steve's Ice Cream stores. At the time, the reason for opening the Italian pizzeria was to eliminate the possibility of an ice cream competitor moving in; eventually, however, its existence would transcend any connection to forestalling the establishment of a competing ice cream shop.

The drive to secure prime real estate dictated Crugnale's actions after he sold Steve's Ice Cream, leading the Bertucci's founder into the real estate business. With the $4.5 million gleaned from the sale of his ice cream chain, Crugnale embarked on his new career in real estate. After less than two years, though, he became bored with malls and office buildings and reconsidered the potential of his pizzeria concept. Crugnale was convinced that Bertucci's, a name he had picked out of a magazine on a flight to New York, would work on a larger scale, with the restaurant's wood-fired brick oven and exotically topped pizzas providing the distinguishing characteristics for a chain of pizzerias. Crugnale made bold plans, resolving to open 20 Bertucci's Brick Oven Pizzerias during the ensuing five years, investing his future efforts wholly in achieving with pizza what he had previously accomplished with ice cream.

Expansion Begins in the Mid-1980s

Crugnale's ambitious expansion plans began with the opening of two restaurants in January and April 1985, each outfitted with an open-hearth brick oven fueled by hardwood logs and each serving specialty pizzas topped with an eclectic array of ingredients such as artichoke hearts and roasted eggplant. The wood-fired brick ovens, inspired by a visit to his grandmother's home in Italy, became the hallmark of Crugnale's restaurants as he expanded the chain during the mid- and late 1980s. He began by establishing units throughout the Boston metropolitan area, then moved outward in concentric circles, saturating white-collar markets in the region surrounding Bertucci's corporate headquarters in Woburn, Massachusetts. Crugnale endeavored to fulfill his objective of establishing 20 restaurant units by 1990, and he designed each restaurant differently, avoiding the presentation of Bertucci's as a chain. Crugnale also eschewed financing the expansion through franchising agreements, something he had been pressured into doing when he operated Steve's Ice Cream and for which he evidently had developed a distaste. ''Franchising is a different business,'' Crugnale explained to *Restaurant Hospitality.* ''You have to operate under a different set of rules, a set of rules I don't like.''

No two Bertucci's were alike, yet each contributed profits to one company and that company was recording explosive growth as customers flocked to Crugnale's restaurants. Although Bertucci's was expanding at a rapid rate, little was spent on advertising to promote the chain's growth. Instead, the company relied nearly exclusively on word-of-mouth recommendations to compensate for spending less than 1 percent of revenues on advertising. As the chain grew to 14 restaurants by the end of 1989, recommendations came not only from satisfied customers but also from dining publications in the Boston area and from USA Today, which listed Bertucci's as one of America's top ten pizza restaurants in 1989. As the company entered the 1990s coming off its astounding 3,157 percent five-year growth rate, expectations for the future were justifiably bright, leading Crugnale to project that in the decade ahead Bertucci's would become a publicly traded company and would expand into a 100-unit chain with restaurants scattered throughout major metropolitan markets stretching between New England and Florida.

Ambitious Plans for the 1990s

While Crugnale's expectations were high, the company was already moving resolutely toward becoming a pervasive fixture along the Atlantic seaboard by the beginning of the 1990s, having expanded its menu to include soups, salads, and an assortment of pasta dishes before moving into markets in Rhode Island and New Hampshire. To finance the realization of Crugnale's proclamation, Bertucci's became a publicly owned company in July 1991, offering the 21 units composing the Bertucci's chain on the market for $13 per share. By the end of the year, after sales had increased 30 percent from the previous year to reach $37.4 million and net income had increased a gratifying 90 percent to surpass $3 million, Bertucci's stock price had nearly doubled, selling for $24.75 per share as the company continued to thrive despite the debilitative effects of a nationwide recession.

In 1992, when the number of Bertucci's restaurants increased from 26 to 36, Crugnale inaugurated delivery and take-out services, fueling sales growth further. The company's low food costs, which amounted to roughly 25 percent of sales, kept profitability high and rounded out what was proving to be a consistently successful enterprise on all fronts. The criteria for site selection during 1992 and in the years ahead were the same as the demographic factors that governed Bertucci's expansion during the 1980s: an area populated by white-collar professionals, 100,000 people within five miles of a Bertucci's unit, and average annual household incomes of $40,000.

Bertucci's Falters in the 1990s

Adhering to these stipulations, Crugnale pushed the Bertucci's concept forward, rapidly pursuing his stated goal of establishing 100 restaurants by the end of the decade. The bigger the chain became, however, the more Crugnale and the rest of Bertucci's management had to navigate in unchartered waters, leaving the company exposed to the uncertain vagaries of operating in unfamiliar markets. For years, Bertucci's had expanded in concentric circles that rippled outward from the Boston area, but during the first half of the 1990s that strategy was abandoned to develop a more comprehensive geographic presence in the eastern United States. In 1994, when 18 new Bertucci's units opened their doors, the company moved into a host of new markets, including Atlanta, Chicago, Orlando, and Ocean Township, New Jersey, widening the chain's geographic scope substantially. The lack of familiarity with these and other new markets began to affect the company adversely. Sparking interest in some of the new units was proving to be more difficult than anticipated. By the end of 1994, when the company scaled back its expansion plans for 1995, announcing it planned to open between 10 and 12 units over the next two years instead of between 12 and 15 units in 1995 alone, the signs of wear and tear on the rapidly expanding chain were beginning to show.

Bertucci's difficulties were not made easier by a wrongful death lawsuit levied against the company in 1995. A year before the suit was filed, a New Hampshire woman, Janet Walker, had dined at a Bertucci's restaurant in Salem, New Hampshire, and ordered a chicken pesto sandwich after reportedly asking the waitress whether or not the pesto sauce contained nuts, to which Walker was allergic. The waitress, according to the lawsuit,

Key Dates:

1981: Joseph Crugnale establishes the first Bertucci's Brick Oven Pizzeria in Somerville, Massachusetts.
1985: Two additional restaurants are opened.
1991: Bertucci's goes public.
1994: As part of a major expansion phase, the company moves into the Atlanta, Chicago, Orlando, and Ocean Township, New Jersey, markets.
1998: N.E. Restaurant Co. Inc. acquires Bertucci's.
2001: N.E. Restaurant Co. adopts the Bertucci's Corporation name.

failed to mention that the pesto sauce did contain nuts, and as Janet Walker ate the sandwich she went into anaphylactic shock and then slipped into a coma. A week later, Walker died, prompting her family to file a $10.4 million lawsuit against Bertucci's in July 1995.

The charges against Bertucci's came midway through the bleakest year in the company's history. Although sales increased 17 percent in 1995, eclipsing $120 million, and nine new restaurants were opened, the company's profits plunged 43 percent during the first fiscal quarter, followed by a $2.92 million loss in the fourth quarter. By the end of the year, Bertucci's was in the red, registering an $886,000 loss for all of 1995. The company that had spent all of its corporate life growing by leaps and bounds was now stumbling after its first decade of existence, reeling from the growing pains associated with what one industry observer characterized as a promising concept that tried to become a national power too fast. Crugnale conceded that there were problems hobbling the company as it entered 1996, but his comments characterized Bertucci's difficulties as nothing extraordinary. "What happened to us is typical of what happens to anybody," he related to *Restaurant Business* in January 1996. "You get beat up, you make mistakes, you stub your toe."

In 1996, Crugnale and the rest of his management team were intent on proving that Bertucci's difficulties merely represented a minor, temporary injury. Although the company expected to open eight new units during the year, the strategy for the future included a slower pace of expansion than recorded in the past, that is, opening smaller restaurants, renovating units more frequently, marketing more aggressively, and developing a greater presence in existing markets before entering new markets.

Changes in the Late 1990s and Beyond

Despite the signs of growing too fast, Bertucci's represented a powerful force as it entered the late 1990s, buoyed by sales that had grown exponentially during the course of its existence. Over the next several years, the company worked to correct the mistakes it made in the previous years in order to shore up profits. Discouraged by Bertucci's sluggish stock price, Crugnale and his management team began to consider several options for Bertucci's. Crugnale decided that reverting back to private ownership would benefit Bertucci's in the long run. Consequently, he led a buyout group that offered $8 per share

for the company in 1998. His plans were thwarted however, when one month later N.E. Restaurant Co. Inc. came in with a higher offer at $10.50 a share. Bertucci's board of directors accepted the N.E. Restaurant Co. offer later that year.

As a Brinker International franchisee, N.E. Restaurant Co. operated 34 Chili's and several On the Border restaurants. The company was looking to expand and believed the Bertucci's concept would be a strong growth vehicle. With Crugnale no longer at the helm of the chain he founded, N.E. Restaurant Co. spent the first several years after the merger retooling its management structure, creating a new corporate culture, and promoting the Bertucci's name through advertising campaigns. Chairman and CEO Ben Jacobson commented on the company's strategy in a September 2001 *Nation's Restaurant News* article. "We've spent a full year getting our arms around [Bertucci's]," he remarked. "We had to put a solid management team together and get the operations, design and menu squared away. Now we're ready to ramp up significantly."

Indeed, N.E. Restaurant Co. proved its commitment to Bertucci's when it decided to sell its Chili's and On the Border restaurants to focus solely on the Italian concept. In 2001, the company adopted the Bertucci's Corp. name and immediately launched expansion plans that included adding new menu items and refurbishing existing stores. The firm also planned to begin franchising in the near future. To freshen up its image, the company's new restaurants were smaller and outfitted to look like Tuscan farmhouses. A $4 million advertising campaign with the tagline "Everybody Eats" was developed in April 2002. While many restaurant companies suffered in the early years of the 21st century due to a sluggish economy, Bertucci's appeared to be on solid ground. Having overcome the hardships of the mid-1990s, management was optimistic that the restaurant chain would experience success in the years to come.

Principal Competitors

Back Bay Restaurant Group Inc.; Darden Restaurants Inc.; Uno Restaurant Holdings Corporation.

Further Reading

Allen, Robin Lee, "Ad Campaign Humor Generates Bottom-Line Smiles at Bertucci's," *Nation's Restaurant News*, November 24, 1997.
——, "Bertucci's Inc. Served with $10.4M Wrongful-Death Suit," *Nation's Restaurant News*, August 21, 1995, p. 3.
——, "Bertucci's Reaches for a Bigger Slice of the Action," *Nation's Restaurant News*, October 23, 1995, p. 14.
——, "Bertucci's to Return to Private Sector," *Nation's Restaurant News*, March 2, 1998.
——, "NERC to Acquire Bertucci's Pizza Chain in $96M Deal," *Nation's Restaurant News*, May 25, 1998.
——, "N.E. Restaurant Eyes Bertucci's Growth Track," *Nation's Restaurant News*, December 4, 2000.
——, "Post-Buyout Places Focus on Chain's Trattoria Roots," *Nation's Restaurant News*, August 23, 1999.
"Bertucci's Loses $886K after $3.2M 4th-Q Charge," *Nation's Restaurant News*, March 11, 1996, p. 12.
Casper, Carol, "Bertucci's: Making a Name for Itself," *Restaurant Business*, May 1, 1989, p. 242.
Coeyman, Marjorie, "Too Much, Too Soon," *Restaurant Business*, January 1, 1996, p. 30.

Frumkin, Paul, "Bertucci's Brick Oven Pizzeria: As Pizza Concept Expands, Menu Operators Set Plans in Motion to Develop into a National Chain," *Nation's Restaurant News*, January 28, 2002.

——, "Bertucci's Expansion Plans Include Franchising Debut," *Nation's Restaurant News*, September 3, 2001.

——, "Bertucci's Turns the Corner As Repositioning Drives Sales," *Nation's Restaurant News*, June 2, 2003.

Keegan, Peter O., "Operations, Store Growth Fuel Boom at Bertucci's," *Nation's Restaurant News*, August 24, 1992, p. 14.

Mamis, Robert A., "Upper Crust: Bertucci's Inc.," *Inc.*, December 1989, p. 134.

"NE Restaurant Corp.: Bertucci's Pizza Evaluates Cash Offer of $90 Million," *Wall Street Journal*, April 6, 1998, p. A20.

Neumeier, Shelley, "Bertucci's," *Fortune*, December 30, 1991, p. 121.

Prewitt, Milford, "Bertucci's Brick Oven Pizza: A Slice above the Rest," *Nation's Restaurant News*, August 13, 1990, p. 12.

——, "Newest "Kids' on the Block Spark Analysts Interests," *Nation's Restaurant News*, March 30, 1992, p. 16.

Soeder, John, "Local Boy Makes Good Pizza," *Restaurant Hospitality*, August 1992, p. 94.

"Three Italian Stallions," *Restaurant Hospitality*, August 1992, p. 85.

—Jeffrey L. Covell
—update: Christina M. Stansell

BRISA Auto-estradas de Portugal S.A.

Edifício BRISA
Quinta da Torre da Aguilha
2785-599 Sao Domingos de Rana
Portugal
Telephone: (+351) 21 444 85 00
Fax: (+351) 21 444 91 93
Web site: http://www.brisa.pt

Public Company
Incorporated: 1972
Employees: 3,000
Sales: EUR 502 million (2003)
Stock Exchanges: Euronext Lisbon
Ticker Symbol: BRI
NAIC: 234110 Highway and Street Construction; 234120
    Bridge and Tunnel Construction; 513330
    Telecommunications Resellers; 541330 Engineering
    Services

BRISA Auto-estradas de Portugal S.A. has played a key role in bringing Portugal's once-neglected transportation infrastructure up to date. The company, which holds the largest road concession granted by the Portuguese government, constructs, maintains, and operates the country's main network of tolled expressways. Brisa's 1,100-kilometer highway network encompasses a major north-south expressway along the Atlantic coast, a circle of roads around Lisbon, and a highway that reaches east from Lisbon to the Spanish border. The company pioneered an innovative tolling system known as Via Verde that automatically deducts tolls from registered drivers without requiring autos to stop. Brisa first began constructing its network under a concession granted in the early 1970s and, three decades later, has nearly completed the planned 1,100 kilometers of expressways. The company's fortunes have been closely tied to the Portuguese economy, which both created the pressure for a better transportation system and resulted in increased traffic and higher toll revenues to pay for it. Brisa's current concession for toll road maintenance and operation extends through 2032. The company also has small holdings in Brazilian and Spanish tollway operators. Brisa's other business activities aim to provide a full array of services for drivers, including roadside assistance, periodic car inspections, and automatic payment at gas stations. Other subsidiaries are active in engineering consulting and telecommunications services.

1970s Origins: Portugal's First Expressways

Brisa was first formed under Portugal's Salazar dictatorship in the early 1970s. At the time, the country's transportation system was inadequate to support a modern economy; some towns were linked by ancient dirt roads and there was no means for fast, efficient transport of goods. On September 28, 1972 a public deed established Brisa and granted the company a 30-year concession to design, build, manage, and maintain express motorways. In the initial stage of the plan, Brisa was to construct 390 kilometers of roadways by the end of 1981. The first priority was a highway designated as A1, a 300-kilometer stretch reaching from the capital of Lisbon north to Porto, Portugal's second-largest city. This highway would become a crucial link to the industrial activity in the north of the country and experience the highest traffic volumes in Brisa's network. Construction also began on the A2, which was projected to reach from Lisbon to resort areas on the southern coast.

Two years after the establishment of Brisa, the Salazar dictatorship was overthrown by a Marxist revolution. The new regime included Brisa in a program of nationalization, first taking control of 40 percent of the company and eventually gaining a 90 percent share. Road construction continued stretch by stretch under socialist control. As the first highway sections were completed on the A1 and A2, the government concession was expanded to include adjoining stretches. In addition, concessions were granted for expansions to the network: the A3 would extend the north-south highway from Porto up to the Spanish border, the A4 would reach east from Porto to the city of Amarante, and the A5 was to reach from Lisbon about 25 miles west to the coast. However, the combined length of the network never exceeded 300 kilometers through the 1980s.

International investment in Portugal increased in the mid-1980s as part of a program to prepare Portugal to join the Euro-

Company Perspectives:

Brisa is a Portuguese company ranking by own merit among the largest private motorway operators in Europe. Brisa established high technical and managing standards regarding the construction, maintenance, and operation of the 11 motorways under its operation. Project management, the innovating Via Verde, and a growing network are three critical factors in Brisa's success joined by a fourth: corporate stability. The capacity to build motorways meeting both deadlines and budgets is a demonstration of the company's efficiency and a guarantee of return on investments. Via Verde is another instrument of Brisa's efficiency and an unquestionable demonstration of the high quality standards and innovating capacity achieved as far as road services are concerned.

pean Economic Community in 1986. Financial aid was directed at the transportation system in an effort to speed up the completion of some much-needed highway links. In 1985, Portugal received a loan of PTE 20 million from the European Investment Bank in order to complete the stretch of the A1 between Porto and Coimbra, a university town midway to Lisbon. The completion of this stretch was expected to give a boost to private industry, which was located mostly in northern Portugal, and would also link Porto to a highway reaching from the coastal town of Aveiro east to the Spanish frontier. That road was opened in 1986, which allowed business to transport goods to Spain without navigating winding, poorly surfaced mountain roads.

Investing to Jump-Start Highway Construction: 1980s–90s

In 1987, a new government led by the center-right Social Democrats came to power in Portugal and began loosening the state's control over economic activity. After years of slow progress, the government began an extensive investment program to bring the transportation infrastructure up to date. While some funds were earmarked for railroad and subway companies, the largest share went to highways. Brisa received a direct capital injection of PTE 17.7 billion in 1990. The investment was urgently needed, since traffic volume in Portugal was growing at a faster rate than any other country in the European Union. Average daily traffic volume increased at a rate about 4.5 percent more than the gross domestic product each year between 1990 and 1996. The government kept up its intensive program of annual investments, allowing Brisa's network to grow from 300 kilometers in 1990 to 600 kilometers in 1995.

The Via Verde ("green lane") automatic tolling system was first implemented during this period as well. The first Via Verde machines were installed in 1991 in four toll plazas in the Lisbon area. They worked by detecting a box in the windshield of drivers who had subscribed to the program. Fees were then automatically deducted from the subscriber's account. The Via Verde system operated on a pilot basis for the next few years.

Portugal experienced an economic crisis in 1993 that hurt Brisa's performance. Nevertheless, the company began reporting steadily rising revenues in the subsequent years. Net profit

in 1994 was PTE 6.7 billion on sales of PTE 34.7 billion, and revenues were climbing about 10 percent annually as the highway network was expanded. In 1995, Brisa's network was double what it had been five years earlier. That year, the Via Verde system, having proven its efficiency, was extended to all toll plazas in Portugal. Via Verde subscriptions were voluntary, but they accounted for about one third of revenues by the first half of 1997. A new concession agreement in the fall of 1997 provided for future highway development. Under the agreement, Brisa was to nearly double the length of its network to 1,114 kilometers by 2004. The company also received state subsidies for construction costs and was granted an income tax holiday through 2005. However, Brisa's network was reduced that year when the A7 and A8 highways were removed from the company's jurisdiction due to discontent over their progress. The state compensated Brisa for the two highways and put their maintenance contracts out to tender; they eventually went to a private operator, Auto-Estradas do Atlantico.

Privatization in the Late 1990s

Many of Portugal's state-owned firms were being privatized in the late 1990s. The electric utility and the telephone company had been partially privatized, and in 1997 Brisa was next in line. The company used the song "Somewhere Over the Rainbow" in numerous television and radio spots to advertise its upcoming stock sale. The initial public offering (IPO) occurred on November 24, 1997 on the Lisbon Stock Exchange. Brisa sold 21 million shares, or 35 percent of the company, to local and foreign investors and raised PTE 102 billion. The IPO was heavily oversubscribed; more than 5 percent of Portugal's adult population placed orders for shares. The company's shares were seen as a reliable investment promising steady revenue, since tolls and traffic were projected to increase. Brisa's net profit in 1997 was PTE 21.1 billion on sales of PTE 49.2 billion.

The second phase of privatization occurred in November 1998. The government sold another 16.6 million shares, raising PTE 136 billion and leaving it with a 36.8 percent stake in Brisa. The government went ahead with the second phase despite global economic turmoil. This second offering was also oversubscribed, even though shares were selling at almost double the price of the IPO, since Brisa was still perceived as a sound defensive investment. The company's road concession had just been extended to 2030 with a provision for toll rates to be increased in line with inflation. By the end of 1998, Brisa had completed 829 kilometers of its network. The company added 147 kilometers in 1998 alone, finishing stretches on the southern A2 and the A3 in the far north, as well as the A6 stretch, which led straight east from Portugal to the Spanish border. Sales in 1998 were up 28 percent to EUR 314 million.

The government sold a third stake in Brisa in May 1999. Another 12 million shares, a 20 percent stake, were sold to retail and institutional investors, raising about EUR 550 million. The state also extended Brisa's concession two more years until 2032. Meanwhile, competitors were starting to challenge Brisa's dominance of Portuguese highways. Besides the A7 and A8, which had been transferred to private operators, the government had launched about a dozen new road concessions. Many of the new highways would be shadow-tolled, which meant that drivers paid no direct fee; instead, the road operator received govern-

Key Dates:

1972: Brisa is established under the Salazar dictatorship.
1974: Brisa is nationalized after a Marxist revolution.
1985: International investment is targeted at Portugal's lagging transportation sector.
1990: A new center-right government begins investing heavily in transportation.
1995: The Via Verde automatic toll booth system is installed at all toll plazas.
1997: Brisa is privatized in share offerings over the next three years.
2002: The length of Brisa's highway network exceeds 1,000 kilometers.
2004: Brisa begins competing for new road concessions in the northern Portugal.

ment compensation based on traffic volume. However, since traffic across Portugal continued to increase, Brisa predicted that the new highways would bring more traffic to its own network.

Restructuring and Diversification: 1999 and Beyond

Now that it was almost fully privatized, Brisa began looking for profitable ways to diversify and restructure its operations. In late 1999, the company made its first international investment when it joined a consortium led by Edizione Holding that was bidding for a 30 percent stake in the Italian road company Autostrade. Brisa ended up with a 0.15 percent stake in the Italian firm. The company was also looking into the telecommunications sector. Brisa already operated a communications network along its highway system, and the coming liberalization of the telecom market offered possibilities for turning the network into a profitable enterprise. Initially, Brisa made an agreement with the former state company Portugal Telecom to jointly operate a network along Brisa's highways. After Portugal Telecom's monopoly was abolished at the start of 2000, Brisa made plans to build a competing high-capacity telecom network together with the mobile phone operator Telecel and fixed-line operator Oni. Ultimately, however, the deal fell apart, so Brisa set up its own subsidiary as a holding company for future telecommunications activities.

In 2001, the Portuguese government sold its remaining holdings in Brisa. Early that year, the company expanded its international connections when it bought a 20 percent stake in Companhia de Concessoes Rodoviárias (CCR), a Brazilian company with 1,300 kilometers in road concessions. In addition, Brisa was in talks with the Spanish highway operator Acesa concerning possible future cooperation. In what was viewed as a prelude to a merger between the two companies, Brisa and Acesa acquired 5 to 10 percent stakes in each other during 2002 and also planned to bid jointly for a stake in Empresa Nacional de Autopistas, Spain's state-owned highway operator. In the end, however, Acesa merged with a Spanish competitor to form Abertis, and the two companies withdrew their bid for Ena.

Brisa was also implementing an internal restructuring during the first years of the new century, spinning off many depart-

ments into separate subsidiaries. The first such reorganization occurred in 2001, when Via Verde was set up as an independent company owned 75 percent by Brisa and 25 percent by a Portuguese interbank clearing company. Over the next few years, other subsidiaries were created, including Brisa Internacional, which handled international investments; Brisa Electrónica Rodoviária, responsible for installation and maintenance of electronic tolling systems; Brisa Engenharia e Gestao, created from the former engineering and construction management department; and Controlauto, which provided periodic car inspections for maintenance purposes. Brisa also began making the Via Verde payment system available for transactions at other businesses. In May 2002, Brisa Access was set up for this purpose; its first initiatives made it possible for consumers to pay electronically at gas stations and parking lots.

Road construction continued as the 2004 deadline for completion of the entire 1,110-kilometer network neared. In July 2002, the final stretches of the A2 southern highway were completed, allowing Portuguese vacationers to reach the holiday destination of Algarve. The A4, a short spur east from the northern town of Coimbra, was completed that year as well. By the end of 2002, Brisa had just over 1,000 kilometers of expressway open to traffic. Revenues had been rising as more highways entered the network. Toll revenues were EUR 452 million in 2002, with 56 percent of this amount paid through the Via Verde system. Brisa's net profit that year was EUR 213 million.

The only parts of the planned network not yet open to traffic in 2003 were parts of the A13 and most of the A10 motorway. Both were part of a knot of highways in the Lisbon area. Brisa's investment plan called for the entire network to be completed by the end of 2005. The company was also adding lanes to some existing motorways to handle larger traffic volumes. In early 2004, Brisa entered into an agreement that set the tone for the activities in which it could engage after completion of the originally planned network. The company announced it would partner with Teixeira Duarte SA, a construction firm, to compete for new concessions in the north of Portugal. The Portuguese government was planning a number of new toll road concessions there, but Brisa would have to compete or partner with other private operators to win them. However, even without carrying out major new construction, Brisa had a dependable source of income in the toll revenues from its existing network.

Principal Subsidiaries

Brisa Internacional; Brisa Servicos; Via Verde (75%); Brisa Access (70%); Controlauto (60%); MCall; Brisa Assistencia; Brisa Electronica; Brisa Engenharia; Brisa Conservacao; ONI SGPS (17%); Abertis (Spain, 4%); CCR (Brazil, 17%).

Principal Competitors

Lusoponte; Auto-estradas do Atlantico; AENOR—Auto-estradas do Norte.

Further Reading

Baker, Mark, "Portugal Drives on with BRISA's IPO," *Privatisation International*, November 1997, p. 9.

——, ''BRISA Driving Ahead,'' *Privatisation International*, December 1999, p. 21.

Blum, Patrick, ''Portugal Announces Large Capital Investment Plan for Infrastructure,'' *Financial Times*, September 18, 1990, p. 4.

''Brisa A-E Privatization Rolls Along,'' *Wall Street Journal*, November 10, 1998, p. 9.

Burns, Erik T., ''Portugal Sells 20% Brisa Stake for $582 Million,'' *Wall Street Journal*, May 25, 1999, p. 18.

Hawkins, Paula, ''Full Speed Ahead for Brisa Sale,'' *European*, October 26, 1998, p. 43.

Rhydderch, Sarah J., ''Brisa May Offer Investors a Solid Road to Income,'' *Wall Street Journal*, December 4, 1997, p. 14.

Smith, Diana, ''Portugal's Antiquated Road System,'' *Financial Times*, September 18, 1985, p. 3.

Wise, Peter, ''Brisa in Phones Alliance,'' *Financial Times*, February 11, 2000, p. 16.

——, ''Brisa Offer Raises Euros 137m,'' *Financial Times*, July 17, 2001, p. 29.

——, ''Brisa Road Deal Points to Merger,'' *Financial Times*, September 17, 2002, p. 16.

—Sarah Ruth Lorenz

Bumble Bee Seafoods L.L.C.

9655 Granite Ridge Drive, Suite 100
San Diego, California 92123
U.S.A.
Telephone: (858) 715-4000
Fax: (858) 560-6045
Web site: http://www.bumblebee.com

Private Company
Incorporated: 1960 as Bumble Bee Seafoods, Inc.
Employees: 1,000
Sales: $500 million (2003 est.)
NAIC: 311711 Seafood Canning; 311712 Fresh and
    Frozen Packaged Fish and Seafoods

Bumble Bee Seafoods L.L.C. is a top producer and marketer of canned albacore tuna, canned salmon, and other seafood products. Its Bumble Bee brand ranks second in the U.S. tuna market, while its Clover Leaf brand is the market leader in Canada. Bumble Bee is majority owned by Canadian seafood company Connor Bros., through that company's Income Fund trust. Bumble Bee's products include solid white and chunk light albacore tuna, as well as other specialty seafood products, including canned red and pink salmon; shrimp in all sizes; crab in a variety of cuts; whole and smoked oysters; whole, chopped, minced, and smoked clams; sardines in a variety of flavors; mackerel; and scallops. The company also makes ready-to-eat products, including packaged tuna and seafood salads with crackers. In addition to activities in North America, Bumble Bee's sales and operations extend to Australia, the Caribbean, Europe, Latin America, and New Zealand. Its canning facilities are based in California and Puerto Rico.

Origins and Development of a Seafood Business

The history of Bumble Bee Seafoods can be traced to 1899, when seven canning companies along the Columbia River in Astoria, Oregon, decided to unite their operations under the auspices of the newly incorporated Columbia River Packers Association (CRPA). Salmon fishers and canners had come to Astoria in the 1860s, when the Columbia River produced abun-

dant salmon supplies. After the salmon supply peaked in the 1890s, the more than 50 businesses that had sprung up in the area began looking to Alaska for their catch of the ocean sockeye variety of salmon. When the CRPA was founded, canneries in Astoria were seeking a cooperative organization, with centralized operations, that would be better prepared to handle strikes among the local fisherman's union. Among the group's leaders was Samuel Elmore, whose Astoria plant became the main cannery for the CRPA. The group was able to purchase several new sailing vessels and establish a cannery on Bristol Bay in Alaska. It also built bunkhouses near the Astoria cannery to house the Chinese immigrant laborers it employed.

The CRPA continued to focus on salmon canning until the mid-1930s, when it was discovered that albacore tuna were plentiful off the coast of Oregon. CRPA then began catching, canning, and marketing the new product in limited quantities until tuna proved itself a popular and saleable food, at which time the group's focus begin to shift increasingly to tuna. In 1938, the CRPA added on to its main cannery in order to handle the volume of tuna being canned. During this time, both salmon and tuna were processed under the Bumble Bee label, a name inspired by a fishing vessel owned by the company. By 1940, tuna had surpassed salmon to become the CRPA's primary product.

The company continued to expand its operations as the Bumble Bee brand built a solid reputation. By the 1950s, the company was recognized as a major competitor in the seafood industry, and by the end of that decade, the Bumble Bee brand had become one of the most respected labels in canned seafood. During this time, major consolidations in the industry took place, with large consumer goods companies buying up most of the canneries in California, Oregon, and Washington. Before long, a prominent Hawaii-based seafood company, Castle & Cooke, took notice of the CRPA and struck a deal to acquire a 61-percent ownership stake in it. In 1960, the CRPA was rechristened Bumble Bee Seafoods, Inc., becoming a wholly owned subsidiary of Castle & Cooke. Eventually Bumble Bee was more fully integrated into the parent company, becoming an operating division. Under Castle & Cooke, a new Bumble Bee cannery was established in Cambridge, Maryland, adding to its existing canneries in Astoria and Honolulu.

Company Perspectives:

Families all across America have grown up on the delicious taste of Bumble Bee Seafoods. They've enjoyed our family of products in sandwiches, salads, casseroles . . . even right out of the can!

By the 1970s, Bumble Bee had experienced considerable growth. In 1975, it made a major purchase of a fleet of tuna seiners, and two years later it acquired another cannery, this one in Puerto Rico. A fishing base was also established in Ecuador. By the close of the decade, Bumble Bee had purchased an additional cannery from Sun Harbor Industry in San Diego.

1980s: Expansion and Ownership Changes

Bumble Bee underwent a series of significant changes in the 1980s. First, it shuttered its operations at its original cannery in Astoria, which was no longer a central location for operation. Interestingly, the Astoria cannery had been deemed a National Historic Landmark in 1966 and was recognized as the longest continuously-operated cannery in the country. The next change for Bumble Bee occurred in 1984, when Bumble Bee's division president, Patrick Rose, learned that the company was about to be put on the auction block. Rose decided to buy Bumble Bee from Castle & Cooke and take the division private. Rose and three managers negotiated the 1985 leveraged buyout, and then Rose took steps to help the company's bottom line. Toward that end, he declined to purchase two of the company's unprofitable plants, in San Diego and Hawaii, and decided against acquiring Bumble Bee's tuna fishing fleet. Rose also rejected Castle & Cooke's long-term contracts with domestic fishermen, and began buying tuna from less expensive Asian sources. In addition, he cut the company's advertising budget in half, increased the offshore cannery staff by 300 workers, cut 30 staff from the corporate payroll, automated office operations, and issued stock options to managers as well as performance-based incentive plans to others in the company. Finally, Rose added capital to Bumble Bee's cannery operations in Puerto Rico and moved the company's headquarters from its old San Diego waterfront structure to a new, modern hilltop office building in the city.

Rose and the others on the management team anticipated that the company would become more successful in five years. However, in only the first 29 weeks under the new operations, Bumble Bee was already able to pay down its bank debt substantially. By 1987, the company had moved up from number three to become the second most popular brand of tuna. By the end of the decade, Rose and the other three managers were ready sell the company or go public, a full two years ahead of their planned schedule. At a board meeting in Puerto Rico in 1988, the four principals reached a decision to sell, and Pillsbury agreed to buy the company as long as Rose agreed to stay on as head of the company for five years.

In 1988, Grand Metropolitan plc, a British conglomerate, took over Pillsbury following a bitter corporate battle. The next year, Grand Metropolitan ordered Pillsbury to get out of the seafood business. The decision left Bumble Bee floundering, along with Van De Kamp's, another Pillsbury purchase that had taken place less than five years before. Although Bumble Bee had pulled in sales of $285 million in 1988, Grand Metropolitan considered it a poor prospect for future growth, and Pillsbury reached a tentative agreement to sell both Bumble Bee and Van de Kamp's seafood subsidiaries in August 1989. Uni Group, a new U.S. affiliate of Unicord Company of Bangkok, Thailand, purchased Bumble Bee for $269 million in cash. The transaction marked the first time a Thai company had purchased an American concern of so great a magnitude. Uni Group kept the existing management team at Bumble Bee, and plans were set to open a new canning facility in Santa Fe Springs, California, within six months that would be responsible for accepting tuna loins cleaned in Thailand and shipped there for canning.

The 1990s Dolphin Controversy

In 1990, a national controversy arose over the method most fishermen used for catching tuna. Known as purse-seine netting, the method allowed fishermen to cast a large net around a school of tuna and pull it together to trap the fish. However, dolphin in some areas tended to school with yellow fin tuna, and the purse-seine method of netting inadvertently trapped the dolphins as well. After the controversy began, the three largest sellers of tuna in the United States moved quickly to quell a potential boycott of their products by announcing that they would no longer buy or sell tuna caught by the purse-seine method, thus protecting the dolphins. All three seafood companies, including Star Kist, Van Camp, and Bumble Bee, put "dolphin safe" logos on their cans. However, in December 1990, an ad war was begun by environmental activists from Earth Island Institute, who charged Bumble Bee with failing to comply with its agreement to not accept fish from boats that killed dolphins, even though it was still labeling its products "dolphin safe." The Earth Island group took out full-page ads accusing Bumble Bee of lying to the public. Unicord, the owner of Bumble Bee, quickly countered by threatening a libel suit, maintaining that it was complying with the dolphin-safe agreement. The battle resulted in the two sides presenting their positions on the nationally-televised morning show "ABC's Good Morning America," allowing the public to decide for themselves.

In the early 1990s, Bumble Bee also underwent changes in its warehousing and shipping methods. The company, which had been using public warehouses since 1906, and had 13 facilities to store its products, began using new machines for production, which allowed increased production, from 1,200 cans per minute to 1,400 cans per minute. The biggest change, however, was in packaging. The company eliminated corrugated cases and began using tray pack/shrink wrap, the format preferred by supermarket retailers. In 1996, Questor Management Company and the parent company of Star-Kist Foods, H.J. Heinz, announced a deal to acquire Bumble Bee from Unicord for $200 million. Under the terms of agreement, Questor would lead the marketing and own the Bumble Bee brand name, while the Star-Kist affiliate would buy Bumble Bee's tuna production facilities in Mayaguez, Puerto Rico, Santa Fe Springs, California, and Manta, Ecuador. In addition, Questor signed a letter of intent that Unicord would continue to supply Bumble Bee with tuna and salmon for packing. However, the deal fell through that December.

Key Dates:

1899: Seven fishermen in Astoria, Oregon, establish Columbia River Packers Association (CRPA) to fish and process sockeye salmon at Alaska's Bristol Bay.
1910: CRPA switches from salmon to tuna fishing.
1920: CRPA expands its Astoria cannery.
1960: CRPA becomes a wholly-owned subsidiary of Castle & Cooke and is renamed Bumble Bee Seafoods Inc.
1977: Bumble Bee acquires a fishing base in Ecuador and tuna cannery in Puerto Rico.
1980: Bumble Bee suspends its canning operations in Astoria.
1997: Bumble Bee is sold to International Home Foods, Inc. (IHF).
2000: ConAgra Foods, Inc., acquires Bumble Bee.
2003: Company is renamed Bumble Bee Seafoods L.L.C. and is spun off from ConAgra.
2004: The Canadian firm Connors Bros. acquires a majority share of Bumble Bee.

In May 1997, an announcement was made that Bumble Bee would be sold to International Home Foods, Inc. (IHF), a New Jersey-based company. The deal would allow IHF to purchase Bumble Bee's ongoing canned seafood business and acquire substantially all of its assets and subsidiaries for $163 million cash and the assumption of certain liabilities of Bumble Bee. The acquisition would give the New Jersey-based manufacturer and marketer of branded food products ownership of Bumble Bee's processing plants in Puerto Rico, Equador, and Santa Fe Springs, California, along with its procurement offices in Japan and Washington, and its corporate offices in San Diego. The same year, IHF also purchased Orleans Seafoods, Inc. This acquisition put Bumble Bee in the position of expanding its seafood products to include such specialty items as anchovies, clams, oysters, shrimp, and smoked scallops. Bumble Bee launched a major marketing campaign to advertise the new products, which included recipe contests in daily newspapers, and television and radio advertising. IHF also acquired Canadian company, BC Packers, which allowed Bumble Bee to provide the leading brand of salmon and tuna in Canada under the Clover Leaf label. Also, the company began distributing the leading brand of high-quality packed sardines, called King Oscar.

2000 and Beyond

In 2000, IHF announced that it would be acquired by ConAgra Foods, Inc., one of the largest branded food companies in North America, for $1.6 billion plus assumption of $1.3 billion in debt. Under the deal, IHF shareholders would receive $22 per share, half in cash and half in ConAgra stock. After the deal was completed, IHF would add additional brands to ConAgra's large portfolio, including the Bumble Bee Seafoods brand, and create a company with some $28 billion in annual sales. Bumble Bee, which had now acquired Tyson Seafood's surimi business, including the Louis Kemp brand, had estimated sales of $750 million at the time of the sale.

After three years, in May 2003, ConAgra announced that it would spin off its Bumble Bee canned seafood business and other seafood assets to Bumble Bee's operating senior management, along with the private investment firm of Centre Partners Management LLC and affiliates. The purchase included the Bumble Bee, Clover Leaf, Orleans, and Paramount brands, along with Bumble Bee operations in California, Canada, Ecuador, Louisiana, and Puerto Rico. Bumble Bee's management team, including President and CEO Christopher Lischewski, continued to run the company, which became known as Bumble Bee Holdings L.P. Despite numerous ownership shake-ups over the years, Bumble Bee was the number one producer of canned albacore tuna, canned salmon, and specialty seafood products sold under the Bumble Bee brand, as well as the number two brand, behind StarKist, in overall tuna products. Lischewski expressed the company's interest in continuing to expand its position in the global seafood market by capitalizing on its low-cost operations, brand name recognition, and procurement strength.

As Bumble Bee moved forward, it contracted with San Diego-based Fleishman-Hillard to serve as its public relations agency. Because both companies had their home offices in San Diego, both maintained a strong local presence as well as a strong national reach, all helping Bumble Bee to achieve a broader presence. Bumble Bee made plans to expand into new seafood categories and aimed advertising campaigns toward consumers, food retailers, and potential business partners.

In early 2004, Bumble Bee announced that it had entered into negotiations with Canadian-based Connors Bros. Income Fund, the management arm of Connors Bros., the largest producer of canned sardines in the world. The deal was signed in March of that year, being unanimously approved by all involved, and gave Connors Bros. a controlling stake in Bumble Bee, with the remaining shares retained by the company's then current owners. Bumble Bee's CEO Lischewski retained his position, while Connors CEO, Edward McLean, was named executive vice-president. When the deal was completed, Bumble Bee Seafoods L.L.C. became the largest branded seafood company in North America, a company poised for continued success and prosperity.

Principal Competitors

Ocean Beauty Seafoods Inc.; StarKist Seafood; Tri-Union Seafoods LLC.

Further Reading

Kelly, Robert, "Connors Bros. Shareholders OK Deal to Merge with U.S. Tuna Firm Bumble Bee," *America's Intelligence Wire*, March 19, 2004.
"ConAgra Sells Bumble Bee Canned Seafood Unit," *New York Times*, May 20, 2003.
"ConAgra Sells Bumble Bee Seafoods," *Seafood Business*, June 2003, p. 4.
"International Home Foods, Inc. to Acquire Bumble Bee Seafoods, Inc.," *PR Newswire*, May 2, 1997.
Nathans, Leah, "Hot for Glory," *Business Month*, January 1989, p. 52.
Our History, San Diego, Calif.: Bumble Bee Seafoods, 2004.

—Nancy K. Capace

Candle Corporation

100 North Sepulveda
El Segundo, California 90245
U.S.A.
Telephone: (301) 535-3600
Toll Free: (800) 328-1811
Fax: (301) 727-4287
Web site: http://www.candle.com

Private Company
Incorporated: 1976
Employees: 1,787
Sales: $382 million
NAIC: 334611 Software Reproducing; 511210 Software
   Publishers

As one of the world's largest independent software and services companies, El Segundo, California-based Candle Corporation specializes in helping end-users cost-effectively maximize the performance of complex computer systems and software applications. It accomplishes this via more than 250 software products for everything from mainframe systems to Web environments, as well as specialized consulting services. During the early 2000s Candle had more than 3,000 customers in 60 countries worldwide, with regional headquarters in Singapore and the United Kingdom. Encompassing 83 percent of the *Fortune* 100 and 73 percent of the Global 100, these clients included the likes of 3M, Bank of America, Coca-Cola, Ford Motor, Johnson & Johnson, McDonald's, Nestlé USA, Procter & Gamble, Prudential Financial, Sara Lee, and Sprint.

Two Lines of Good Code: 1975–78

Candle was founded in 1976 by Aubrey G. Chernick. Born in Los Angeles in 1949, Chernick was raised in the small Canadian farm town of Deloraine, Manitoba, where his parents operated a grocery store. He earned an undergraduate degree in chemistry from the University of Manitoba and found employment in an environmental analysis lab. Although the lab contained computers, Chernick did not know much about them.

Along with a fellow employee, he learned the BASIC programming language.

Although Chernick considered a career in medicine, he continued to work with computers and began developing software in the Canadian province of Ontario. After spending three months in the Canadian division of Computer Science Corporation, Chernick was laid off. Despite his growing knowledge base, Chernick was still a relative computer neophyte, and he failed to land a job with Canada's Datacrown when they determined he had little experience. Ultimately, Chernick found work at Laurentian University, a rural Canadian college that was hard pressed to attract system programmers. There, he learned the ropes by installing operating systems on IBM Model 40 mainframes and reading everything he could about them.

After another failed attempt to find employment with Datacrown, Chernick went to work for the Government of Manitoba. There, his involvement with computers continued to grow, and he learned how to program the IBM MFT operating system and eventually the IBM MVS system. While attending meetings of the Central Ontario Users Organizations, Chernick saw that many IBM mainframe users had common needs that were not being met.

This observation was Chernick's inspiration for creating a new software application. In 1975, he convinced Canada Life of Ontario to let him use the company's computer for development purposes. In return, he offered them a copy of his finished product at a reduced price. It took Chernick about four or five months to complete his work, which he named OMEGAMON for MVS. Dubbed as the first-ever real-time application for monitoring IBM mainframe operating system performance, OMEGAMON's name was inspired by the last letter of the Greek alphabet and the first letters of the word "monitoring." The application literally was supposed to represent the "last word in monitoring." In later years, Chernick would often tell reporters how he started Candle with "two lines of good code."

Armed with a new product, the 26-year-old Chernick established Candle Services Corporation in October 1976 and began making the rounds at data centers to peddle OMEGAMON. Chernick called his new enterprise Candle because of his intent to shed light on how mainframe operating systems worked. Candle operated in Toronto, Ontario, for about six months. Ironically, Chernick sold the third copy of OMEGAMON to Datacrown, where he had unsuccessfully sought employment. In 1977, Candle relocated to Los Angeles and shortened its name to Candle Corporation. Clients at this time included the likes of Warner Brothers, Southern California Edison, and U.S. defense contractors such as Hughes, Northrop, and TRW Aerospace. That year, Chernick focused on improving OMEGAMON and increased the application's functionality by 400 percent.

Candle's earliest days were humble ones, and Chernick ran the company from his apartment for about 18 months. In a somewhat pioneering move, Chernick sold his software over the telephone before that practice was widely used by software firms.

In the May 22, 2000, issue of the *Los Angeles Business Journal*, Chernick stated: "You want a war story? I had just come down here and was working out of an apartment in Marina del Rey, and I got a call from someone at Hughes. It was kind of a strange call. They asked, 'How do you sell your product?' I said, 'You get a 30-day trial.' They asked, 'What's involved in the trial?' and I said, 'You get the software and a tape with instructions.'" Chernick went on to describe how Hughes offered to send someone to his apartment to pick up the application, which he then sold for $100.

In 1978, Chernick began publishing a newsletter called the *Candle Computer Report*. According to some industry observers, this technical newsletter did much to give the company credibility among computer users and elevate its image. Candle also developed a strong reputation for providing quality technical support. As the years unfolded, Chernick remained committed to keeping Candle a private company, refusing to be pressured by a focus on quarterly profits. In addition, he did not accept money from venture capitalists and built Candle from the ground up by investing a sizable share of the profits back into the firm.

Rise to Prominence: 1979–94

Candle embarked on national tours in 1979 with the goal of providing user education regarding availability and performance issues. The following year, the company recorded its first million-dollar sales month in December and ended the year with $4.5 million in revenues. With the release of OMEGAMON for CICS, Candle's application evolved to meet the growing needs of transaction processing within the financial sector and other industries. The company also released EPILOG for MVS, which enabled system administrators to perform long-term analysis.

In 1981, sales spiked more than 200 percent from 1981 levels, reaching $10.4 million. During the same time frame, the company's employee base grew from 52 to 108. As he found success, Chernick formalized a way to share it with the world by establishing the Candle Foundation in 1982 to support humanitarian, cultural, and social projects. According to the company, these include "community investment and redevelopment initiatives, education and information dissemination programs, medical research, and drives to combat hunger and homelessness."

Heading toward the mid-1980s, Candle strengthened its reputation as a leader by providing more education to the industry than ever before. *CCR*'s readership reached 50,000 subscribers in 1984, and the company held its first user conference the following year. It also was in 1985 that Candle released its CL family of software.

Revenues reached $100 million in 1988, at which time Candle held about 32 percent of the performance measurement software market, according to a report issued by Computer Intelligence and reported in the October 1988 issue of *Software Magazine*. IBM held 33 percent of the market, followed by Boole & Babbage (13 percent), Landmark Systems (6 percent), Goal Systems (5 percent), Applied Data Research (4 percent), and Morino Associates (3 percent).

A spate of new product offerings was released in the late 1980s. In 1988, Candle released one of the industry's first console automation programs when it rolled out AF/OPERATOR, along with a related automation management tool called AF/REMOTE. These were followed by a new version of OMEGAMON designed for monitoring the performance of IBM's DB2 relational databases. OMEGAMON for DB2 was adopted quickly by leading companies worldwide.

In 1989, Candle's employee ranks grew to approximately 700. That year, the company unveiled OMEGACENTER, which it dubbed "one of the first applications designed to integrate performance management, data center automation, remote control, and communications technologies within one solution." OMEGACENTER pioneered the use of graphics to display system performance via Candle's Status Monitor tool.

Candle kicked off the 1990s with the next evolution of its flagship product. OMEGAMON II offered users a truly comprehensive performance management package, as it incorporated many of the company's existing solutions. In addition, it allowed users to view system facts via a graphic interface. A suite of DB2 tools followed in 1991, along with the OMEGAVIEW status management tool.

It was not until the early 1990s that Candle employed the services of a public relations agency. At that time, Marina del Ray, California-based Miller Shandwick was chosen to handle media relations and promotional efforts. In late 1992, Candle moved it headquarters and 900 workers from West Los Angeles to Santa Monica, California. Most employees moved into cubicles, and executives also had open offices to facilitate communication. In addition, Candle's data center relocated to a site outside Los Angeles in an effort to save money on real estate

---

Key Dates:

1975: Aubrey G. Chernick develops OMEGAMON for MVS, the first real-time application for monitoring IBM mainframe operating system performance.

1976: Chernick founds Candle Services Corporation in Toronto, Ontario.

1977: Candle relocates to Los Angeles and shortens its name to Candle Corporation

1978: Chernick begins publishing the *Candle Computer Report* newsletter.

1982: The Candle Foundation is formed to support humanitarian, cultural, and social projects.

1992: Candle moves it headquarters and 900 workers from West Los Angeles to Santa Monica, California.

1996: Candle celebrates its 20th anniversary; Robert J. LaBant is named president and chief operating officer.

1999: Candle relocates from Santa Monica to El Segundo, California.

2001: Andy Mullins is named president and chief operating officer, while LaBant becomes vice-chairman.

2004: IBM announces that it will acquire Candle and that Chernick will leave the organization.

---

costs. Sales grew rapidly during this time period, climbing from $151 million in 1990 to $210 million in 1993.

Candle unveiled other new performance management product introductions during the first half of the 1990s. These included the OMEGACENTER Gateway for MVS in 1993 and OMEGAMON II for SMS in 1994. At this time, Candle's annual revenues totaled $213 million.

Moving Beyond the Mainframe: 1995–98

In 1995, Candle introduced its CCC product family to address the industry's use of PCs and UNIX workstations. That year, the company was in the process of carrying out a $500 million research and development initiative to change its focus from mainframes to PC and desktop systems. Candle relied upon its very first trade advertising campaign to promote this transition.

It also was in 1995 that Chernick was given the Albert Abraham Michelson Award. According to a December 7, 1995 release from *Business Wire*, he received the award at the Computer Measurement Group annual conference for "technical excellence and professional contributions to the field of computer management."

In the September 25, 1995, issue of the *Los Angeles Business Journal*, Software Council of Southern California Executive Director Bill Manassero credited Candle for its longevity in the industry, remarking: "It has survived very well in a high-tech world that is changing all the time. As it has turned away from mainframe technologies to PCs, Candle has been able to handle the change and continued to thrive. It is really a testament to Chernick's management skills."

As of 1995, Candle employed 1,100 workers, approximately 550 of who worked at its Santa Monica, California headquar-

ters. Many of the remaining employees worked at one of the company's 29 regional offices, most of which were located in North American cities.

Candle celebrated its 20th anniversary in 1996, when years of steady growth culminated in annual revenues of $230 million. The company employed 1,200 workers in 42 offices throughout the world and devoted about 30 percent of its revenues to research-and-development initiatives. Much of this work was carried out at Candle's Westlake Village, California, research and operations center. It also was in 1996 that Robert J. LaBant was named president and chief operating officer of Candle.

During that same year, a major shift took place at the company that emphasized the growing importance of networked systems. This included the development of middleware, or software that allows different software applications to communicate with one another, and an emphasis on professional services. Candle dubbed its product and service offerings in this area as Solutions for Networked Applications.

In a September 24, 1996, news release, Chernick said: "We are entering a new era in business and technology. To remain competitive, businesses must break through traditional boundaries and forge new relationships internally and externally with other companies and new processes. We call it the era of Networked Businesses, which we think best reflects the new realities of commerce, competitiveness, and information technologies. . . . This is a new business dimension for Candle," he continued. "For 20 years we have focused on the back-end, managing large, deployed applications and systems. With our new initiatives, we are addressing new problems at the very beginning of the new business process and application life cycle."

Candle's push into the networked solutions arena involved alliances with other companies, as well as the acquisition of other technologies and firms. In addition to acquiring Lotus Notes management solutions developer CleverSoft Inc. in July 1996, Candle agreed to acquire MQSeries services provider AMSYS North America. The latter acquisition bolstered Candle's capabilities in the middleware arena. To connect its customers with leading middleware experts, Candle also formed the Worldwide Design Network at this time.

By 1996, Candle's software was used in 5,000 data centers, and its clients included 75 percent of *Fortune* 500 companies. According to the April 1996 issue of *Technical Support*, Candle was "the only software company to deliver systems, network, and console management solutions that span desktops, UNIX systems, and MVS-based mainframes."

Heading toward the late 1990s, Candle capitalized on a business market that was characterized by a growing number of mergers and acquisitions. It accomplished this by developing Roma BSPTM to help organizations integrate applications quickly. This was followed by the release of other award-winning products, including an application response time monitor called ETEWatch in 1998, as well as the Candle Command Center (CCC) for UNIX System Services.

The Age of E–Business: 1999 and Beyond

By 1999, Candle's revenues were $382 million. That year the company relocated its headquarters from Santa Monica to El Segundo, California. It employed 1,800 people in 55 offices throughout the world, including about 700 at its headquarters. At this time, e-business became a major focus for Candle. The company released the eBA*ServiceMonitor in 1999, which it called "the first solution introduced to monitor the effectiveness of IT strategies, initiatives, and investments for Web sites from the visitor's perspective."

Candle's sales reached approximately $400 million in 2000, at which time the company employed about 2,000 people. This led to the development of OMEGAMON XE and DE in 2001, which were designed to meet the needs of companies engaging in e-business. In addition, Candle introduced its CandleNet eBusiness Platform Powered by Roma Technology, which was designed for e-business deployment.

Andy Mullins was named Candle's president and chief operating officer in January 2001, succeeding Bob LaBant, who became vice-chairman. At this time, Chernick was focusing more on the big picture and allowing Candle managers to handle day-to-day company operations. Candle now devoted some 60 percent of its resources to non-mainframe computing. Through its consulting arm, Candle began to help companies build bridges between the their mainframe applications and the Web. Known as application integration, this pursuit accounted for about 15 percent of the firm's revenues.

In the March 19, 2001, issue of *Interactive Week*, Chernick summed up Candle's development to date and his optimism regarding the company's future, remarking: "There's a whole ecosystem of infrastructure and transactions that needs to be managed. For the last 25 years, we have worked on scalable solutions. For the last five to seven years, we added a focus on ease of use. And in the last three to five years, we've focused on the business process. The Internet is where it all comes together."

In 2002, Candle introduced the PathWAI line of software and consulting packages aimed at simplifying and streamlining the design, development, and operation of middleware and Web server infrastructures. It also was in 2002 that Candle received a bronze award in the 2001 California Awards for Performance Excellence (CAPE) competition, based on the Malcolm Baldrige national standards for excellence and quality. According to Candle, the company was recognized for exhibiting "visionary leadership and a focus on customers."

In 2003, Chernick established the National Center for Crisis and Continuity Coordination (NC4), which the company described as "an organization focused on advancing crisis management and business-continuity readiness through public-private sector collaboration." That year, the Software Council of Southern California named Chernick Software CEO of the Year. By the end of 2003, Candle's sales stood at $382 million and the company's suite of PathWAI solutions had grown from seven to 17 packages.

After passing up on hundreds of offers to buy Candle over the years, in early 2004 Chernick agreed to sell his company to IBM. Although the terms of the deal were not disclosed, one industry analyst indicated that IBM would likely pay $350 million for Candle.

In the April 1, 2004 issue of *Computerworld*, IBM Software Group Senior Vice-President and Group Executive Steve Mills said that the two companies working together would be able to "provide customers with powerful capabilities for managing end-to-end infrastructure, processes, and applications, which are key requirements for the on-demand operating environment."

As part of the arrangement, Chernick would not remain with the company he founded with two lines of good code and a vision for making computer operators' lives easier. As Candle prepared for a new era in its history, President Andy Mullins said IBM would make decisions about the structure of the combined enterprises in the first year following the acquisition.

Principal Competitors

BMC Software Inc.; Computer Associates International Inc.; Compuware Corporation.

Further Reading

"Background and Buzz on L.A.'s Richest People," *Los Angeles Business Journal*, May 21, 2001.

Brueggmann, Steve, "Aubrey Chernick: The Man Behind Candle Corporation's Success," *NaSPA News*, April 1996.

"Candle Corp. Announces Favorable Federal Jury Ruling," *Business Wire*, April 18, 1986.

"Candle Corp. Chairman Aubrey Chernick Wins Award; Named Recipient of A.A. Michelson Award at CMG," *Business Wire*, December 7, 1995.

"Candle Corporation Launches New Focus on Solutions for Networked Businesses," *PR Newswire*, September 24, 1996.

"Candle Moves to New Headquarters," *Software Magazine*, October 1992.

"Candle to Launch New Developer Tools," *eWeek*, December 3, 2003.

Cone, Edward, "Web Lights Candle's Way," *Interactive Week*, March 19, 2001.

Deady, Tin, "Mainframe Software Firm Broadens Focus. Candle Corp. Expanding into PC-Based Systems," *Los Angeles Business Journal*, September 25, 1995.

Dempsey, Michael, " 'Two Lines of Good Code' Made Him a Billionaire," *Financial Times*, September 1, 1999.

Desmond, John, "Candle Gets Mileage from MVS Mysteries," *Software Magazine*, October 1988.

Dunphy, Laura, "Soft-Spoken Software Mogul," *Los Angeles Business Journal*, May 22, 2000.

Hamblen, Matt, "Update: IBM to Buy Candle Corp. for Mainframe Management," *Computerworld*, April 1, 2004.

Lais, Sami, "Candle Sets Sights on Web," *Computerworld*, December 20, 1999.

O'Donnell, Debra, "Candle Invests in Intellectual Assets," *Software Magazine*, October 1996.

Ricadela, Aaron, "IBM to Acquire Candle," *InformationWeek*, April 1, 2004.

Umbaugh, Robert E., "Aubrey G. Chernick: On Managing the Complexities of the IS Department," *Information Systems Management*, Winter 1992.

—Paul R. Greenland

Carrefour SA

6, avenue Raymond Poincare
75016 Paris
France
Telephone: (+33) 1 53 70 19 00
Fax: (+33) 1 53 70 86 16
Web site: http://www.carrefour.com

Public Company
Incorporated: 1959
Employees: 420,000
Sales: $72 billion (2002)
Stock Exchanges: Euronext Paris
Ticker Symbol: CA
NAIC: 445110 Supermarkets and Other Grocery (Except Convenience) Stores; 452910 Warehouse Clubs and Superstores; 445120 Convenience Stores; 452990 All Other General Merchandise Stores

As the world's second largest retailer, Carrefour SA operates more than 10,300 stores in France and abroad under more than two dozen names including Carrefour, Champion, Shopi, Marché Plus, Dia, Ed, and Promocash. The company merged with Promodès SA in 2000 to become Europe's leading operator of supermarkets, convenience stores, discount stores, cash-and-carry outlets, and hypermarkets. The company's founders created the concept of the hypermarket, an expanded supermarket offering a wide variety of merchandise—including groceries, electronics, clothing, and automotive supplies—that allowed consumers to accomplish most of their shopping at one store. Hypermarkets became a rapid success, revolutionizing the retail industry in France and worldwide.

Company Origins

Carrefour emerged in 1959 as a collaboration between two entrepreneurs, Marcel Fournier and Louis Defforey, in Annecy, a city in eastern France that had become increasingly industrialized since World War II. Both men came from successful, enterprising families, and each was anxious to expand his own business by building large supermarkets. Fournier already had established the department store Grand Magasin de Nouveautés Fournier d'Annecy and had connections in the Casino supermarket company, and Defforey was president of Badin-Defforey in Lagnieu.

In the 1950s the French grocery industry consisted primarily of family operations. Traditional grocery stores, committed to providing a variety of high-quality products, accounted for 83 percent of food sales. As fewer young people entered into family businesses, however, and grocers' unions, independent wholesalers, and food cooperatives increased in number, a need for alternatives to the smaller markets developed. At the same time, big department stores, generally located in the center of cities, often proved inconvenient, and the high prices they charged for luxury items and value-added services were prompting consumers to look elsewhere for nonfood items.

Moreover, the concept of free service was becoming increasingly popular. Free service, prevalent in retail by the 1990s, was invented in 1916. Prior to its institution, consumers relied heavily on assistance from sales clerks in selecting and obtaining merchandise. Under the free service system, however, customers used bags, carts, or baskets to collect their needs—placed within easy reach and individually priced—while sales clerks served primarily as cashiers.

The supermarket, which first appeared in France in 1954, used the concept of free service. With larger facilities located outside the center of cities, supermarkets could provide fresher produce, a greater variety of products, and lower prices than the traditional grocery store. By the end of the decade, however, only 33 free service supermarkets were in operation in France, and none of them was modeled after the large discount supermarkets in the United States.

Thus, in May 1959, Fournier and Defforey decided to incorporate these virtually unexploited concepts for their store in Annecy. An offering of 7,000 shares of stock was made to ten stockholders, and a facility already under construction in Annecy was purchased. The ground floor of the building was to be used as the supermarket, while the upper floors, containing apartments, were to be sold to help finance the business. Marcel Fournier was elected president, and Denis Defforey, Louis's son, was chosen as general director. Fournier named the business Carrefour, the French transliteration of the Greek word agora, or marketplace.

During this time, a businessman named Edouard Leclerc, who was establishing supermarkets in the Rhine-Alps region, announced plans to open a store in Annecy. Fournier and Defforey knew that, to be able to compete, they had to open their store before Leclerc opened his. Thus Fournier offered the basement of his department store, Grand Magasin de Nouveautés Fournier, for Carrefour's use. This annex was opened on January 7, 1960, six months before the opening of the larger store, and was an immediate success. In fact, four days after it opened, the annex was already out of goods and had to close for one day to restock. The threat of competition from Leclerc prompted Fournier and Defforey to offer the lowest prices they could, and, as it turned out, Leclerc never built the competitive supermarket in Annecy.

To familiarize the public with supermarkets, Carrefour embarked on an advertising campaign before opening its main store. The publicity was effective. The store opened on June 3, 1960, achieving sales that far surpassed expectations and drawing 15,000 customers in the first two days. In a little more than three weeks, Carrefour had sales of FFr 290,000, a figure most independent grocers reported for an entire year. To prevent traffic jams, the store expanded its parking lot, but the company's management soon was convinced that supermarkets in urban areas were impractical.

Expansion in the 1960s

Between 1961 and 1962, business at Carrefour increased 45 percent and salaries increased as well. The following year, another supermarket was opened in Cran-Gevrier, in the Annecy region, this time with a vast parking lot. Moreover, Carrefour installed its own discount service station in the parking lot of its first store, selling gasoline without a name brand for five centimes less per liter than the average price; making neither a profit nor a loss, the company's gas station was intended as a protest against the French government's high gasoline taxes. Carrefour's discounts angered smaller business owners, a reaction that would prove typical throughout much of Carrefour's history.

During this time, the company decided to expand into the Paris region, purchasing a tract of land 30 kilometers south of the capital in Sainte-Geneviève-des-Bois, where costs were lower and more space was available. Before construction began at the new site, Louis Defforey and his brother Jacques went to the United States to observe the American commercial structure. Seminars given by Bernardo Trujillo on such modern sales practices as free service, discount prices, and large facilities convinced the Defforeys to completely modify Carrefour's initial plans for the store outside Paris. Although Carrefour did not adopt the huge dimensions of American stores with many cashiers and large aisles, they did construct a relatively large facility and integrated the idea of low prices on every product by purchasing merchandise from wholesalers and producers. They also followed Trujillo's advice about investing less in luxury construction. The store opened in June 1963 and was referred to by the press as a hypermarket, reflecting its 2,500 square meters of space, 400 parking places, and abundance of both food and nonfood merchandise. The store was an immediate success, with each customer purchasing, on average, three times more than in a regular supermarket.

Carrefour's success was based on its discount prices, decentralization of power, reduced emphasis on aesthetics and equipment costs, and accelerated rotation of stocks. The hypermarket appealed to younger people and new suburban dwellers, as well as the budget-conscious consumer affected by the high inflation rates in the 1960s. Carrefour's innovations in weighing, pricing, wrapping, cashing, and refrigerating made its hypermarket integral to the ensuing revolution in French retail. Not everyone, however, was pleased with these developments. The company had an adverse effect on small businesses, and an independent butchers' union blocked Carrefour's trucks at an abattoir in 1964 to protest the store's discounts. Moreover, some complained that shopping at the hypermarket was an impersonal experience, lacking in the traditional rapport between shopowner and loyal customer.

In January 1965, to avoid government restrictions on expansion, Carrefour formed two divisions: Carrefour Supermarché was led by Marcel Fournier and Denis Defforey, and Grands Magasins Carrefour, a subsidiary, was led by Jacques Defforcy and Bernard Fournier. A hypermarket of 10,000 square meters was opened near Lyon in 1966 as well as another of 20,000 square meters in Vitrolles. The following year, an office was opened in Paris to collect, compare, and distribute results from all the stores, and in 1968 Marcel Fournier moved his office from Annecy to Paris.

International Growth in the 1970s–80s

Carrefour also actively sought involvement with other companies in Europe, including Delhaize Fréres-Le-Lion in Belgium, Mercure in Switzerland, Wheatsheaf Investment in Great Britain, and Italware in Italy, and made major efforts to expand into Mediterranean regions in Europe. During its international expansion, Carrefour was careful to appeal to new clientele by marketing local products, rather than exporting French products. Initially developing new stores through joint subsidiary companies in partnership with local retailers, Carrefour eventually acquired full interest in these stores. Competitors such as Auchan, Casino, and Euromarchè followed Carrefour's lead over the next ten years, greatly increasing the number of hypermarkets in France.

In June 1970 Carrefour stocks went on sale at the Bourse in Paris. With high inflation in the mid-1970s, competition for food prices was fierce, and when the 1973 Royer law put restrictions on the development of large stores in France, Carrefour began to focus increasingly on expansion abroad. Between 1978 and 1982, the greatest number of new Carrefour stores was established outside of France, particularly in Latin countries. Profits proved high at its stores in Brazil, Argentina, and Spain.

By 1982 the hypermarket industry had matured, resulting in active competition for prices, standardization of product lines, and the closing of some parts of the market. The food market stagnated, and Carrefour reduced the size of some of its stores. During this time, the company entered into more partnerships with other companies, including one with Castorama, through which it sought to satisfy increased demand for leisure and hardware products. Although Carrefour reported sales nearly double those of its immediate competitors—Casino, Viniprix, and Nouvelles Galeries—the company's primary goal was to preserve existing markets and its commercial, financial, and developmental advantages.

Marcel Fournier, who had been awarded the Legion of Honor, died in 1985, and the institute of management founded by Carrefour was named after him. By that year, Carrefour had expanded to ten countries across three continents and had a net profit of FFr 520 million. As emphasis on brand image intensified on a national scale, Carrefour introduced its own private brands as a low-cost alternative, while still emphasizing quality. In 1988 Carrefour was France's leading hypermarket merchant and the top retail company in Europe, with 65 hypermarkets in France and approximately 115 in Europe and South America. In February of that year, the company opened a 330,000-square-foot hypermarket outside Philadelphia, Pennsylvania. Initial financial problems due to low customer volume were overcome, and Carrefour opened a second hypermarket in the Philadelphia area in 1991. Carrefour continued to provide autonomy to each department head through its successful policy of decentralization and continued to focus on long-term results rather than immediate successes.

Continued Growth in the 1990s

In the early 1990s all members of the founding families of Carrefour left the company's active direction and formed an advisory council. Carrefour sold its stores in Annecy and Cran-

Gevrier to Casino, and, in return, Casino sold its hypermarket in Nantes to Carrefour, so that Carrefour only managed stores of more than 2,500 square meters. In 1991 Carrefour acquired competitor Euromarché for $850 million and Montlaur, a bankrupt grocery chain, for $175 million. Although France had reached the saturation point with 798 hypermarkets and governmental regulations restricted the opening of new hypermarkets, Carrefour continued to expand in foreign markets, with its own stores or partnerships in Austria, Great Britain, The Netherlands, Switzerland, Germany, Belgium, Italy, Spain, Africa, Argentina, Brazil, and the United States.

In 1992 Carrefour planned to open two new stores in Great Britain in a joint venture with Costco, a warehouse club company. In addition, the company's discount food chain, known as Ed, was established in Great Britain and Italy, providing a limited range of products at extremely low prices. Carrefour also opened new stores in Spain, Brazil, and Argentina and began plans for stores in Taiwan, Turkey, and Malaysia.

In 1993 Carrefour faced further challenges to its expansion in France in the form of a government-enforced freeze on new hypermarkets in rural parts of the country. Nevertheless, accustomed to such legislative, noncompetitive restrictions, the company continued its pattern of growth, particularly in foreign markets. In an exception to that international expansion, the company closed its two stores in the United States in 1993 and had no plans for opening others there. It continued to pull out of the U.S. market by selling its 11 percent interest in Costco, a warehouse retailer in the United States. It retained its 20 percent stake in Costco UK, however, and as of 1998 it owned 6 percent of Office Depot, a U.S. office supply discounter, and 8 percent of PETsMART, a U.S. discount pet supply retailer.

Expansion in Central and South America was especially strong in the 1990s. Carrefour moved into Mexico in 1993, opening the first of a chain of hypermarkets. Of the 30 stores the company opened in 1996, 15 were in Mexico, Brazil, and Argentina. By 1997 Carrefour operated approximately 60 stores in South America and was generating $7 billion in sales in Brazil and Argentina alone. Hoping to build on its successful growth in the area, Carrefour planned to open ten hypermarkets in Chile over the next decade.

By 1995 Carrefour operated more stores internationally than it did in France. Asia provided another fertile ground for Carrefour's international expansion. The company opened its first store in Seoul, South Korea, in 1996, after the South Korean government lifted some of its restrictions on foreign retailers. When the financial crisis in Asia hit in the late 1990s, Carrefour was already operating 26 hypermarkets in the region. Because of its discount strategy and the steady demand for food and other basics sold by the company, Carrefour was weathering the recession. In fact, Carrefour opened 20 more stores in Asia in 1997 and 1998.

Restrictions on the company's growth in France increased in 1996. In an effort to protect small shopkeepers, the French government placed a six-month ban on the opening of any store measuring more than 300 square meters (3,230 square feet). Unable to open new stores, Carrefour continued to expand in France by acquiring its competitors. In 1996 it bought a 41 percent interest in the owner of the Cora supermarket chain, GMB.

Carrefour's performance in France was hurt by an economic slowdown in 1996 and 1997. Carrefour store sales rose in the first half of 1998, however, by 4.1 percent. The company was in the process of refurbishing its stores in 1998; it hoped to complete 19 that year and then extend the program in the following year.

Internationally, Carrefour bought eight Eldorado stores in Brazil in 1997 and converted them in 1998 to the Carrefour name. The company planned to open 34 new stores by the end of 1998, including its first stores in Colombia, Chile, and Indonesia. Carrefour thus remained committed to growth in France through increases in same-store sales and the acquisition of rival stores and to expansion internationally through both acquisitions and the opening of new stores.

Strategic Acquisitions in the Late 1990s and Beyond

Indeed, the company made two key purchases in 1998 and 2000 that would catapult it into the top spot in Europe as well as secure its position as the world's second largest retailer. Carrefour acquired the remaining shares of Comptoirs Modernes SA that it did not already own for approximately $3 billion in 1998. The acquisition added more than 790 supermarkets—operating under the Stoc, Comod, and Marché Plus names—into Carrefour's expanding arsenal.

The company began planning its next big move in 1999 when it made a $16.5 billion play for competitor Promodès SA. Founded in 1961 by Paul-Auguste Halley and Leonor Duval Lemonnier, Promodès originally started as a wholesale food distributor but over time grew into one of the world's largest operators of hypermarkets, supermarkets, convenience stores, and discount stores. Management from both firms hammered out the terms of the deal over a three week period and agreed that a union would provide the growth needed to remain competitive in the industry. Not only would the merger make it the largest retailer in Europe and the second largest in the world, it would give it a competitive edge over Wal-Mart Stores Inc., the U.S. giant that was looking to move into Carrefour's territory.

The deal cleared regulatory hurdles and was completed in early 2000. With more than 8,800 stores in 26 countries and revenues of nearly $65 billion, Carrefour entered the new millennium on solid ground. While management worked on the merger integration process, the company remained focused on growth. It formed GlobalNetXchange, an online supply house, with Sears and Oracle in 2000. It also opened its first hypermarket in Japan that year and purchased Belgium-based GB and Gruppo GS of Italy.

In 2001 the company sold its interest in Picard Surgelés. The following year it spun off its 10 percent interest in PETsMART. The firm continued to strengthen its hold over the Italian and Polish markets and also moved into the Scandinavian market in

2003. It established its first Champion supermarket in Beijing in April 2004.

Since the Promodès acquisition, Carrefour had faced increased competition and weakening sales in its homeland and its market share began to fall in France, Spain, and Brazil. Rumors began to surface that Carrefour would either become a takeover target by the likes of Wal-Mart or make another large acquisition to fend off unwanted advances. In December 2003, Paul-Louis Halley and his wife died in a plane crash—the two represented the Halley family, Carrefour's largest shareholder. Their deaths gave rise to further speculation that changes could be on the horizon for Carrefour.

Principal Operating Units

Champion; Dia; Ed; Carrefour; 8 a Huit; Promocash; Shopi; Proxi; Prodirest; Norte; GB; GS; Puntocash; Marché Plus; ooshop; DiperDi; Dock's Market.

Principal Competitors

Auchan S.A.; Casino Guichard-Perrachon S.A.; Association des Centres Distributeurs E. Leclerc.

Further Reading

''Asian Retailing: Going Cheap,'' *Economist,* August 15, 1998.

Bidlake, Suzanne, ''Ed's Cut Price Bonanza,'' *Marketing,* February 11, 1993, p. 19.

Ellison, Sarah, ''Carrefour's Net Rises, But Market Share Slips,'' *Wall Street Journal,* March 9, 2001, p. A11.

''En Garde, Wal-Mart: Retail Rival Carrefour Bulks Up,'' *Business Week,* September 13, 1999, p. 54.

''EU Gives Carrefour-Promodes Green Light,'' *Eurofood,* February 3, 2000.

''French Fusion,'' *Economist,* September 4, 1999, p. 61.

''French Retailers Create New Wal-Mart Rival,'' *Wall Street Journal,* August 31, 1999, p. A14.

Johnson, Jay L., ''Carrefour Revisited,'' *Discount Merchandiser,* August 1990, pp. 24–30.

Kamm, Thomas, ''Retailers in France to Merge,'' *Wall Street Journal,* August 31, 1998.

Mao, Philippe, ''France: Defforey Family, Halley Family,'' *Forbes,* July 18, 1994, p. 202.

''Not at Any Price,'' *Economist,* April 6, 1996.

''Retailing in South America,'' *Economist,* July 12, 1997.

Sasseen, Jane, ''France: Balladur Halts March of the Hypermarché,'' *International Management,* June 1993, p. 24.

Toussaint, Jean-Claude, *La politique générale de l'enterprise, un cas concret: Carrefour,* Paris: Chotard & Associés, 1984.

Villermet, Jean-Marc, *Naissance de l'hypermarché,* Paris: Armand Colin, 1991.

White, Erin, ''Carrefour Finds Itself in the Cross Hairs,'' *Wall Street Journal,* February 26, 2004, p. B2.

—Jennifer Kerns
—updates: Susan Windisch Brown and
Christina M. Stansell

Cesky Telecom, a.s.

Ol353 anská 55/5
130 34 Prague 3
Czech Republic
Telephone: (420) 271 411 111
Fax: (420) 271 469 868
Web site: http://www.telecom.cz

Public Company
Incorporated: 1993
Employees: 13,337
Sales: CZK 51.48 billion (2003)
Stock Exchanges: Prague
Ticker Symbol: BAATELEC
NAIC: 517212 Cellular and Other Wireless Telecommunications; 517110 Wired Telecommunications Carriers

The company Cesky Telecom, a.s. is a former state monopoly that still dominates the telecommunications market in the Czech Republic. The firm offers fixed-line voice services, broadband Internet and data services as well as mobile service through its subsidiary Eurotel. Cesky Telecom was established in the early 1990s to oversee the national telecommunications network after the fall of communist power and the breakup of Czechoslovakia. The company inherited an underdeveloped network and proceeded to modernize it at a rapid pace with the help of Dutch and Swiss partners. The firm has struggled for nearly a decade to achieve full privatization; more than one planned sale has fallen apart before it could be completed. The state still retains a 51 percent stake in Cesky Telecom while the remainder is publicly held. The company is one of the most heavily traded stocks on the Prague Stock Exchange. Since the Czech telecommunications market was opened to competition in 2001, Cesky Telecom has been striving to retain its leading position by offering professional Internet, data, and mobile services to offset the drop in usage of fixed line service.

Establishment and Privatization of SPT Telecom in the Early 1990s

Czechoslovakia's telecommunications network was neglected during the communist period. Most central planners did not consider services to be a genuine form of production, so they failed to invest in the communication infrastructure. Instead, investment was targeted at primary forms of production such as industrial enterprises. Telephone services served as a stable source of revenue that was channeled to more valued entities in the central planning system. In particular, the telephone service was used to subsidize postal services, which operated at a loss. Telephone tariffs were not related to the cost of providing service. Charges for domestic calls were low and charges for international calls were extremely high.

As a result of this neglect, there were only 1.6 million telephone lines in Czechoslovakia in 1980—10.6 lines per 100 people in the country. About 700,000 new lines were added over the next decade, bringing the average up to 14.9 lines per 100 people, but over the same period the waiting list for a telephone line nearly doubled. Only 33 percent of households had their own telephone in 1990. Residents of some remote villages hardly ever held a telephone in their hands.

In late 1989, the Velvet Revolution brought about the collapse of communist power in Czechoslovakia. That year SPT Praha (short for Sprava post a telekomunikaci Praha, the Ministry of Posts and Telecommunications) was created as a state-owned monopoly for postal and telecommunications services. In 1990, SPT entered into a joint venture with Bell Atlantic and US West to establish Eurotel Praha as a mobile telephone service provider. The American partners held a 49 percent share in the enterprise. Eurotel acquired the exclusive right to operate a network on the 450 MHz system, an analog standard.

Separatist impulses led to the dissolution of Czechoslovakia on December 31, 1992 and the formation of independent Czech and Slovak Republics. The Czech Ministry of the Economy assumed responsibility for telecommunications. In 1993, SPT Praha was split into two separate entities: the Czech Post and SPT Telecom. This finally put a stop to the subsidy of postal services with telephone revenues. SPT Telecom was now in charge of an aging analog telephone network composed of deteriorating copper wires. The waiting list for telephone installation had grown to 800,000 people. Despite these problems, the telecom entity produced a reliable profit. SPT Telecom had a profit of CZK 6 billion on revenues of CZK 18 billion in 1993.

Company Perspectives:

To implement its vision, the Group has formulated a mission statement: to be a leader on the electronic communications market in the Czech Republic and to offer its customers the best solutions to their telecommunications needs; to be a preferred employer for top professionals, whom it wants to motivate to build up value of the company further; to be a premium builder of shareholder value in the area of electronic communications; to be an active stakeholder in the development of the Czech community of which it is a part, and to promote outwardly the ethical and professional principles which it espouses and applies to its own development.

By this point, the privatization process in the former Czechoslovakia was in full swing. The government wanted a speedy transition from state to private enterprise, and starting in 1991 it sold citizens vouchers that could be used to bid at large auctions of hundreds of companies. The telecommunications enterprise was scheduled to be part of the second wave of privatization in 1994. In preparation, SPT Telecom was converted into a joint stock company, SPT Telecom, a.s., at the start of 1994. Later that year, a 26 percent share in the company was auctioned to Czech citizens, and SPT Telecom became the largest company listed on the newly established Prague Stock Exchange. Also in 1994, the Eurotel mobile phone enterprise acquired a license to operate a network on the digital GSM standard.

International Partnership and Rapid Modernization: 1995–99

The next stage in the privatization of SPT Telecom involved controversy over whether to allow foreign companies to gain control over telecommunications in the Czech Republic. Minister of Economics Karel Dyba contended that SPT Telecom needed the financial resources and technical know-how of a foreign company in order to modernize its network as quickly as possible. He managed to push his stance through over those who feared a loss of state control. In September 1994, the state set guidelines for the sale of a further 27 percent stake in SPT Telecom. The offer attracted potential investors such as France Telecom, Deutsche Telecom, Bell Atlantic, AT&T, and Stet International, many of whom joined into consortia to submit final bids. J.P. Morgan & Co. acted as investment advisor for the Czech side. SPT Telecom was an attractive investment since it had the potential to grow several times over and give its partner a strong foothold in Eastern Europe.

Amid the conflict over the proposed sale, SPT Telecom's general director Jiri Makovec was ousted at a board meeting in December 1994, ostensibly because he had awarded a lucrative telephone card contract to a firm to which he had personal ties. His departure, however, was likely related to the fact that he opposed selling to a foreign investor. Makovec was replaced by Svatoslav Novak, the former deputy minister for telecommunications at the Ministry of the Economy. Novak worked hard to reassure employees who were suspicious of the prospect of foreign involvement.

In the spring of 1995, J.P. Morgan received five final bids for the 27 percent stake in SPT Telecom. In June, the stake was awarded to TelSource, a consortium comprised of KPN NV of the Netherlands and Swisscom Ltd. of Switzerland. New shares were issued and the state's holding was diluted to 51 percent. Bessel Kok, the Dutch head of TelSource, became deputy general manager of SPT Telecom, which gave TelSource operating control despite its minority stake. A shareholders' association was subsequently formed to contest the sale on legal technicalities, but it did not succeed in invalidating the deal.

SPT Telecom's most urgent task now was to modernize its network. The company had already gotten about CZK 7 billion in loans from the World Bank and other institutions to fund a program that would wipe out the waiting list for a telephone line and replace the analog network with digital exchanges. Modernization proceeded at a rapid pace after the partnership with TelSource. The size of the waiting list went down for the first time in 1996, but it still stood at 623,000 and was about two years behind. Telephone density was up to 27 lines per 100 people. SPT Telecom was trying to shake off its bad image with an advertising campaign using the slogan, "Forget the past, look to the future." Progress continued so that by the end of 1998 the waiting list was down to 141,000 people, 70 percent of households were connected to the network, and two-thirds of lines were connected to digital rather than analog exchanges.

These rapid advances led to steady increases in revenue throughout the late 1990s. Annual revenue rose from CZK 32.5 billion in 1996 to CZK 51.9 billion in 1999. Net profit was steady at around CZK 6 billion a year. Besides the expansion of its network, SPT Telecom made large cuts in its workforce during this period and installed modern billing and service equipment. A new tariff system was introduced that eliminated the disparity between expensive international and cheap local calls. Rates were raised slightly to reflect the true costs of telephone service, which was a requirement for the Czech Republic to join the European Union. In 1998, SPT Telecom introduced ISDN Internet services, which became a small but growing part of overall revenue. The mobile phone subsidiary Eurotel also grew during the late 1990s. It began offering service on the GSM standard in 1996, which led to increasing revenues over the next few years despite the entrance of some competitors in the mobile market. The decade ended with a small skirmish between SPT Telecom managers and a newly elected Czech government whose telecommunications minister, Antonin Peltram, was trying to force changes to the supervisory board. TelSource became frustrated with what seemed like purely political maneuvers and threatened to pull out of the company. In mid-1999, Peltram's choice for a new head of the supervisory board was installed and TelSource stayed with the company for the time being.

Unsuccessful Privatization Efforts: 2000–02

At the start of 2000, SPT Telecom changed its name to Cesky Telecom, or Czech Telecom, to more clearly express the nature of its operations. The second stage in the privatization of Cesky Telecom began in December 1999, when the Czech cabinet approved a plan to sell the 51 percent state-held share in the company. At first, it was expected that TelSource would be interested in this stake, but in August 2000, KPN, the Dutch member of the consortium, announced that it would be investing in mobile licenses in Europe instead. This generated uncertainty about the future of Cesky Telecom. The government

Key Dates:

1990: Mobile phone operator Eurotel is established as a joint venture between the Czechoslovakian telecom ministry, Bell Atlantic, and US West.

1993: The Czech Ministry of Posts and Telecommunications is split into the Czech Post and SPT Telecom.

1994: SPT Telecom becomes a joint stock company and is partially sold to Czech investors.

1995: The TelSource consortium buys a 27 percent stake in SPT Telecom; a rapid modernization program is launched.

1996: Eurotel launches mobile service on the GSM digital standard.

1998: SPT Telecom introduces ISDN Internet service.

2000: SPT Telecom changes its name to Cesky Telecom.

2001: The Czech telecommunications market is opened to competition.

2002: A planned sale of the state's remaining share to a Deutsche Bank consortium falls through.

2003: Cesky Telecom acquires full control of Eurotel; TelSource sells its stake in Cesky Telecom.

2004: The full privatization of Cesky Telecom is relaunched.

needed money from the sale to make up for a huge budget deficit; meanwhile, shares in telecommunications companies were losing value in a worldwide trend. In the summer of 2001, TelSource signed a contract with the Czech government to work jointly in selling both the state's and TelSource's shares in Cesky Telecom. A call for bids was launched late that year.

By the spring of 2002, Cesky Telecom was in talks with two consortia led by Deutsche Bank and Swisscom. Then the government postponed the sale because the bids were too low. After receiving new bids that summer, the government agreed to sell its 51 percent stake to a group comprised of Deutsche Bank, TDC of Denmark, and other investors for EUR 1.82 billion. However, the TelSource stake was not part of this agreement. The deal was called off in November before a contract could be signed because the Deutsche Bank consortium failed to reach agreements with TelSource and with Atlantic West, the 49 percent partner in the Eurotel unit. Deutsche Bank had hoped to buy more than just the 51 percent stake in Cesky Telecom, but it turned out that KPN was not as eager as expected to sell its TelSource share, and neither was Atlantic West able to offer terms acceptable to Deutsche Bank and its partners. While the sale was falling apart, the Cesky Telecom supervisory board dismissed CEO Premysl Klima and replaced him with Ondrej Felix, the board chairman.

The Czech government had been planning to liberalize the telecommunications market since the early 1990s, and the need to stand up to competition was a primary motivating factor in the development of Cesky Telecom over the decade. In early 2000, the government approved a Telecommunications Act that gave Cesky Telecom a little extra time before it would have to face full competition. The market for the local and international fixed-line voice market was opened at the start of 2001, but call-by-call selection of operators would not be implemented until 2002, and pre-selection of operator would not be allowed until 2003. The act also set up the Czech Telecom Office as a regulatory entity for the telecommunications sector. The main competitive challenge for Cesky Telecom was in the area of mobile services. Start-up fixed-line operators complained that they could not make a dent in Cesky Telecom's market dominance because it was not offering reasonable interconnection agreements.

Responding to a Changing Market: 2003–04

The use of fixed-line voice services began declining after the start of the new century, putting pressure on Cesky Telecom to diversify its operations. A new ADSL broadband Internet access portfolio was introduced in early 2003. Cesky Telecom also started up wholesale operations, leasing its network to other local and international operators. The company incorporated branches in Slovakia, Austria, and Germany in 2003 to promote this service. The company also made personnel changes, reducing management levels to bring the number of employees to about half of the 1997 level. In June 2003, Gabriel Berdar took over as CEO from Ondrej Felix, who remained chairman of the supervisory board. Berdar had a successful background as the head of Dell Computer's Czech subsidiary.

The Czech government had been working on a new privatization strategy since the break-up of the Deutsche Bank deal in 2002. A sale was more likely to go through if the difficulties posed by the TelSource and Eurotel holdings were cleared up. Cesky Telecom had tried unsuccessfully to buy Eurotel from the Atlantic West consortium in 2001. Finally, in the fall of 2003, Cesky Telecom acquired Atlantic West's 49 percent share and took full control of Eurotel. In December of that year, TelSource sold its 27 percent stake to various financial investors, thus negating the joint sale agreement it had with the Czech government. These developments laid the ground for the relaunching of the privatization process at the start of 2004. Potential bidders were TDC of Denmark, Swisscom, and the Czech financial group PPF. The sale was expected to be completed in 2005. The government did not cancel out the possibility of selling Eurotel separately from Cesky Telecom.

Meanwhile, Cesky Telecom was engaged in disputes with the government. The company was fined by the Anti-Monopoly Office for alleged anti-competitive practices related to discounts and bonuses offered to clients who signed long-term contracts. Cesky Telecom, on the other hand, accused the government of failing to properly reimburse it for its statutory obligation to provide universal services such as public pay phones and emergency calls. Conflict also erupted with Eurotel, leading to the resignation of Eurotel's CEO Terrence Valeski. He was replaced by managers from Cesky Telecom. One of Cesky Telecom's complaints was that Eurotel had been planning to launch an Internet service that would compete with its own ADSL service.

Despite these disputes, Cesky Telecom remained relatively strong in its core services. Annual revenues had dropped slightly over the past few years to CZK 51.5 billion from a high of CZK 57.2 billion in 2000, but the company still controlled nearly three-quarters of fixed-line services and half of the mobile market. The challenges in the coming years would be to carry out a full privatization, stave off competitors, and emphasize newer technology to replace the drop in fixed-line usage.

Principal Subsidiaries

Eurotel Praha, spol. s.r.o.; OMNICOM Praha, spol. s.r.o.; CenTrade, a.s. (86.5%); SPT TELECOM (Czech Republic) Finance B.V.; CZECH TELECOM Austria GmbH; CZECH TELECOM Germany GmbH; CZECH TELECOM Slovakia s.r.o.; AUGUSTUS, spol. s.r.o.

Principal Competitors

Aliatel, a.s.; Contactel s.r.o.; T-Mobile Czech Republic a.s.; Cesky Mobil, a.s.

Further Reading

Anderson, Robert, "Cesky Restarts Its Search for a Partner," *Financial Times*, January 8, 2004, p. 26.

——, "Cesky Telecom Readies Itself for Revolution," *Financial Times*, January 4, 2002, p. 20.

——, "Investors Wary of Czech Upheaval," *Financial Times*, February 3, 1999, p. 34.

——, "Pace of Czech Phones Reform Irks Operators," *Financial Times*, March 13, 2001, p. 3.

——, "Speed Is of the Essence for Cesky Privatisation Plans," *Financial Times*, October 10, 2003, p. 27.

Boland, Vincent, "Contenders Fight It out for Czech Prize," *Financial Times*, October 18, 1994, p. 30.

——, "Czech Phone Group Ousts Chairman," *Financial Times*, December 31, 1994, p. 18.

——, "SPT Opens Line to Czech Phone Profits," *Financial Times*, February 6, 1997, p. 22.

——, "SPT Seeks Humility to Cope with Deregulation," *Financial Times*, September 3, 1996, p. 21.

Bouc, Frantisek, "Dial M for Monopoly," *Europe Intelligence Wire*, February 12, 2004.

"Eurotel CEO Valeski steps down," *Europe Intelligence Wire*, May 7, 2004.

Green, Peter S., "Deal Fizzles for Czech Telephone Company," *New York Times*, November 28, 2002, p. W1.

Lytle, Douglas, "SPT Telecom's Prospects Boost Image of Shares," *Wall Street Journal*, June 30, 1999, p. 14.

Taylor, Malcolm, "Czech Mate," *Communications International*, August 1995, p. 12.

"Telecom to Take over Eurotel before Privatisation," *Europe Intelligence Wire*, June 5, 2003.

Zdenek, Hruby, "Czech & Slovak Republics after Czechoslovakia," *Telecommunications*, October 1995, p. 46.

—Sarah Ruth Lorenz

The Charles Machine Works, Inc.

1959 West Fir Avenue
Perry, Oklahoma 73077
U.S.A.
Telephone: (580) 336-4402
Toll Free: (800) 654-6481
Fax: (580) 572-3527
Web site: http://www.ditchwitch.com

Private Company
Incorporated: 1958
Employees: 1,000
Sales: $180 million (2002)
NAIC: 333120 Construction Machinery Manufacturing

The Charles Machine Works, Inc. is headquartered in the small town of Perry, Oklahoma (located 60 miles north of Oklahoma City), where the company is commonly known as Ditch Witch, the name of its signature trench-digging machine. Charles Machine offers six categories of equipment. The company's trenchers and plows include pedestrian, walk-behind models for use in laying utility and communications lines; compact, maneuverable trenchers and plows designed to be used in confined areas; and heavy duty models for larger trenching projects, as well as vibratory plowing and pavement cutting. To meet a variety of underground construction needs, Charles Machine's offers a line of trenchless products, including directional drills, fluid management products, piercing tools for boring projects and pipe pushing and pulling, and rod pushers. The company's electronic products are used to located and identify buried services, as well as to track directional drilling tools and locate power and communication faults. To haul Ditch Witch equipment, Charles Machine also sells a line of custom-designed trailers. In addition, the company manufactures vacuum excavation equipment and compact utility machines such as a mini skid steer, a mini excavator, and a combination excavator and tool carrier. Almost all of the products offered by Charles Machine are researched, designed, and manufactured by the company. A key to distribution is a worldwide network of independently owned Ditch Witch dealerships, which are devoted exclusively to the sale of Ditch Witch products and also offer service and maintenance training. Charles Machine is a closely held corporation, majority-owned by its chairman, Edwin Malzahn. The employees own 30 percent of the company.

Early 20th Century Origins

Charles Machine traces its heritage to Carl Frederick Malzahn, who emigrated to America from Germany, according to his grandson Edwin Malzahn, to avoid service in the army. He then moved his family to Perry, Oklahoma, in 1902 to avoid the brutal winters of Minnesota. He set up a blacksmith shop in Perry some five years before Oklahoma became a state. He was assisted by his sons Gus and Charles, instilling in them a pride of craftsmanship and establishing a focus on quality and value that would be passed on to later generations. The shop was successful, but when Oklahoma underwent an oil boom, the Malzahns were able to transition away from smithing, which had no future, to specializing in performing repairs to the equipment used in the nearby oil fields. Charles Malzahn, father of Edwin, eventually took over the business, which became known as Charlie's Machine Shop.

Growing up, Edwin Malzahn gained practical experience working in his father's machine shop, then rounded off his knowledge by earning a degree in mechanical engineering at Oklahoma State University. After graduating in 1943, he returned to Perry eagerly "in search of things to make." Inspiration would visit the young man one day while watching several plumber's helpers using picks and shovels to dig a 50-foot trench in order to install a water line. Malzahn was convinced he could invent a machine that could do the job easier, shared the idea with his father, and the two went to work developing a compact machine that could dig a shallow, narrow trench, ideally four inches wide and 24 inches deep. There were already large trenchers designed for the installation of distribution lines for plumbing and other utilities, but these machines were ill-suited for digging the trenches between individual homes and trunk lines. At first, the Malzahns tried to make a miniature version of the larger wheel trenching machines, but the concept failed to work. Instead, they pursued a self-propelled ladder-type ditcher that relied on a vertical line of buckets with teeth that could gouge out dirt at one end of a conveyor chain and deposit it in neat piles along the trench. An innovative gear box allowed the machine to simultaneously power the digging operation and provide self propulsion.

By 1949, the Malzahns had a production model of their first service-line trencher, the DWP, which stood for Ditch Witch Power. At the time, Charlie's Machine Shop employed just ten men. It was now renamed The Charles Machine Works. To drum up business for his new product, which was priced around $750, Edwin Malzahn used his car to tow the first Ditch Witch around the state of Oklahoma, demonstrating it to plumbers. By 1951, the Ditch Witch accounted for 10 percent of Charles Machine's annual sales.

Incorporation and Expansion: 1950s–80s

Malzahn grew the Ditch Witch business through the 1950s, as the machine was instrumental in making the installation of indoor plumbing affordable to many households. It also launched a niche industry. In 1955, Malzahn received a patent for the endless conveyor ditch digging machine. During his lifetime, Malzahn would receive several other patents and develop a number of product ideas that had nothing to do with trenching machines. He sold these product ideas to other companies, opting to focus the family business on the Ditch Witch. The company was incorporated in 1958. The Ditch Witch was proving so successful that a year later the company moved out of the downtown Perry building that had housed the original blacksmith shop and opened a new 24,000-square-foot manufacturing plant, as well as an 8,000-square-foot office complex, on land a few miles west of Perry. At this stage, annual sales were in the $1.5 million range, and Ditch Witch sales accounted for 98 percent of Charles Machine's business. For a time, the company continued to repair oil field equipment, but they did this mostly as a convenience to long-time customers. The future of the business lay squarely with the growth of the Ditch Witch business. Charles Malzahn would not live to see the full extent of the success achieved by Ditch Witch, however. Several months after the ribbon-cutting ceremony for the new facilities, held on July 6, 1959, he succumbed to the long-term effects of leukemia and diabetes.

Over the next 25 years, the company grew at a steady pace, although there was a difficult stretch during the recession of the early 1970s that necessitated the laying off of 70 employees in 1974. The business recovered and by 1984 reached the $75 million mark in reported sales. It topped $100 million in 1987, when Charles Machine shipped some 5,400 Ditch Witch trenchers, which now came in 18 models, ranging in power from five horsepower to 100 horsepower. In addition, the company had expanded its product offerings to include vibratory plows,

backhoes, earth saw, road wideners, trailers, rammer, plate compactors, boring units, and earth augers. It even sold a chemical, Perma-Soil, that could be mixed with soil in order to stabilize it. In the late 1980s, it became involved in directional drills by buying the navigational boring system of Pierce Arrow. The Ditch Witch machine was honored in 1988 when it was named by *Fortune* magazine as one of the "100 products America makes best." Charles Machine now employed approximately 700 people, a significant increase over the 56 employees who worked for the company when it was incorporated in 1958. Moreover, the company had built up a network of 105 dealers spread across the United states and Canada, and another 25 overseas dealers located in 22 countries.

Charles Machine grew even faster in the 1990s after the economy picked up following a recession. According to press estimates, the company reached $170 million in sales in 1994 and a year later approached $200 million, about half of which came from the sale of trenchers. Nevertheless, management did not necessarily see the firm as a trencher manufacturer, viewing it more as a business that installed underground utilities. In this way, Charles Machine was not threatened by new trenchless technologies and became involved in products that could be considered a threat to its traditional product line. The company was also forward looking in its approach to design and manufacturing. Long gone were the days when the design staff would develop a product, then simply hand it over to the manufacturing side to produce. Instead, the company adopted a cross-functional team approach that brought in as many people as possible—from manufacturing, marketing, product support, and service—as soon as possible in the design process. As this approach evolved, input from major vendors would be sought. Manufacturing also employed important new tools, such as computer-aided capabilities and statistical process control. In addition, Charles Machine made a commitment to service. In the early 1990s, the company opened a new Ditch Witch Training Center in Perry to train factory and dealer personnel as well as owners of Ditch Witch equipment, especially the new trenchless technology products.

From Hiring Spree to Lay Offs: Late 1990s and Beyond

Business for Charles Machine thrived in the late 1990s, spurred in large part by the efforts of telecommunications companies to lay dramatically increasing numbers of fiber optic lines. Charles Machine went on a hiring spree, adding some 500 new people in a short period of time. Employment peaked at 1,700. In early 2000, the company announced that it planned to hire another 1,000 workers to its headquarters in Perry, a town of little more than 5,000 people. About 70 percent of the employees already had to commute to Perry. The company conducted a survey on the town and concluded that Perry could support 900 new single-family houses, 250 single-family rental houses, 190 mobile homes, and more than 350 apartments, as well as two more motels and five more restaurants. In April 2000, Charles Machines and the city of Perry hosted a conference for builders, architects, developers, and contractors to promote new building in Perry to meet the needs of the community when hundreds of more people came to work at Charles Machine.

Key Dates:

1902: Carl Frederick Malzahn opens a blacksmith shop in Perry, Oklahoma, with sons Gus and Charles.
1949: Charlie's Machine Shop becomes Charles Machine Works with the introduction of the Ditch Witch.
1955: A patent is received on the Ditch Witch.
1958: The company is incorporated.
2002: A fifth-generation member of the Malzahn family is named CEO.

Plans for expanding Charles Machine and its hometown would soon be put on hold, however, as the company experienced a severe drop in business, the result of a downturn in the economy that had a particularly adverse impact on telecommunications firms, some of Charles Machine's most important customers. In addition, the telecommunications industry was now laying fewer land lines because of earlier overbuilding, a situation exacerbated by the rising popularity of wireless products that cut into land line sales and produced the trickle down effect of eliminating the need to buy new Ditch Witch equipment. In May 2001, Charles Machine cut 75 temporary and part-time jobs, and 75 full-time positions were eliminated after employees were offered an early retirement package. Subcontract work was also brought back to the Perry Plant. Later in the same month, the company laid off 225 full-time workers. Five months later, in October 2001, another 250 employees were laid off, including plant and office personnel, dropping total employment to just over 1,000.

Charles Machine also faced the issue of succession, as Malzahn reached 80 years. Although he remained highly active with the company, in June 2001 he turned over the chief executive officer role to David O. Woods, who had been serving as the chief operating officer since 1995. Woods joined Charles Machine after graduating from Oklahoma State University in 1980 with a degree in business management. Malzahn held onto the presidency and chairmanship, thus continuing to be very much in charge. In the meantime, members of his family were also moving up in the ranks of the organization. His son served as vice-chairman; a granddaughter, Tiffany Sewell-Howard, who held an MBA from Oklahoma State University, was the head of information technology; and a grandson was involved in product development.

In February 2003, only two years after becoming CEO, Woods resigned to pursue other business opportunities, according to a company spokesperson. Despite his advanced years, Malzahn added the duties of the chief executive officer to those of president and chairman. He maintained that coming to work was, in fact, his favorite hobby, better than fishing or golf. His granddaughter, Sewell-Howard, took over the chief operating officer position. A year later, in February 2004, she was named Charles Machine's new chief executive officer, after joining the company just four years earlier. She faced some challenges ahead, as the company attempted to recover from the lingering effects of a recession. Charles Machine was already looking to further diversify its business, bringing out the mini skid steer and five mini excavators, but there was also considerable untapped potential for the traditional Ditch Witch products. Most of the world lacked the kind of underground infrastructure enjoyed by the United States. It was very likely that the greatest opportunities for Charles Machine in the future lay overseas.

Principal Competitors

Astec Industries, Inc.; CNH Global N.V.; Vermeer Manufacturing Company.

Further Reading

Brezonick, Mike, "Trencher Firm Still Breaking New Ground," *Diesel Progress Engines & Drives*, September 1993, p. 64.
Johnson, Bill, "Maker of Ditch Witch Keeps Roots Planted in Hometown of Perry," *Journal Record*, June 10, 1989.
Landberg, Lynn, "Ditch Witch Trencher Changes Utility Installation," *Construction Equipment*, August 2002, p. 149.
Wiley, Elizabeth Camacho, "Machine Works Business Marks 100 Years in Perry, Okla.," *Daily Oklahoman*, September 22, 2002, p. 1.

—Ed Dinger

clarion®

Clarion Company Ltd.

50 Kami-Toda
Saitama
335-8511
Japan
Telephone: (+81) 48 443 1111
Fax: (+81) 48 445 3810
Web site: http://www.clarion.co.jp

Public Company
Incorporated: 1940 as Hakuson Wireless Electric
   Company
Employees: 9,594
Sales: $1.54 billion (2003)
Stock Exchanges: Tokyo
Ticker Symbol: 6796
NAIC: 334310 Audio and Video Equipment Manufactur-
   ing; 423620 Electrical and Electronic Appliance,
   Television, and Radio Set Merchant Wholesalers

Clarion Company Ltd. is one of the world's leading producers of in-car entertainment systems. The Saitama, Japan-based company has long played the role of leading edge in developing automotive sound and information systems—the company claims credit for being the first in the world to place a radio in a car in the 1940s. Clarion continues to develop and adapt new technologies for in-car use, including the company's latest line of DVD, television, GPS, and wireless Internet and telephony products. Clarion's automotive systems are manufactured and distributed throughout the world, with 20 manufacturing facilities in Japan, Taiwan, China, Malaysia, the Philippines, France, Great Britain, Mexico, and the United States, and distribution operations in more than 50 countries. While Clarion's automotive systems are sold worldwide, the company also produces a range of home audio and karaoke systems for the domestic market, as well as audio and video systems, including rear-view cameras, for busses and boats. The company's production is separated into two primary divisions: OEM Business Division, which develops and distributes in-car systems directly to the world's major automobile makers; and the Aftermarket Sales Division, which focuses on developing, manufacturing, and distributing products for retail channels. Clarion Company is listed on the Tokyo Stock Exchange and is led by President Tatsuhiko Izumi.

Auto Radio Pioneer in the 1940s

Clarion was founded in 1940 as the Hakuson Wireless Electric Company, one of many Japanese companies formed during the period to produce battery-powered radios for household use. In 1943, the Hakuson company merged with another radio builder, Takizawa Wireless Electric Industries Co., and the newly enlarged company took on a new name as Teikoku Dempa Company.

Following the end of World War II, Teikoku began formulating future plans to enter the export market as well, and adopted a new brand name, Clarion, for use on its radios. At the same time, the company's engineers began working on a bold new project—that of adapting the household radio for installation into an automobile. Work began in 1948, and by 1951 Teikoku Dempa succeeded in becoming the first in the world to produce a car radio, the model A-214. That radio—which featured a single button—launched a revolution in the auto market, creating a new equipment category, In-car Entertainment (ICE).

Although targeting its traditional consumer market, Teikoku Dempa also sought agreements to place its radio in automobiles as OEM equipment. In 1953, Renault Japan became the first in the world to feature a Clarion-branded auto radio, known as "Le Parisian," featuring factory installation in its 4CV model. The following year, the company reached an agreement with the United States' RCA devising industry standards for AM/FM radio reception, which marked another milestone in the global auto radio market. By 1958, the company had begun exporting its first car radios to the United States.

Teikoku Dempa adapted the fast-developing transistor technology of the 1950s to its car radios, and by 1959 had produced the world's first fully transistor-based radio. Among the company's first clients for the new generation of car radio was Nissan Motor, which accorded Teikoku Dempa's radio with the company's genuine parts specification.

<table>
<tr><td>

Company Perspectives:

Clarion strives to improve society by seeking to develop the relationship between sound, information, and human interaction, and by creating products to meet those needs.

</td><td>

Key Dates:

1940: Hakuson Wireless Electric Company begins with production of battery-powered home radios.
1943: The company merges with Takizawa Wireless Electric Industries Co. and becomes Teikoku Dempa.
1947: The Clarion brand name is registered.
1951: The company introduces the world's first car radio.
1953: Renault Japan introduces the first car featuring a factory-installed Clarion radio.
1958: The company begins exporting its car radio to the United States.
1959: The first fully transistorized car radio is introduced.
1962: The company goes public on the Tokyo exchange's secondary market.
1963: The first stereo car radio system is introduced.
1967: The company opens new headquarters in Saitama.
1968: The company introduces its first car cassette player.
1969: The company's stock is listed on the Osaka secondary index.
1970: The company changes its name to Clarion Company Ltd. and changes its listing to the Tokyo and Osaka main boards; the first foreign manufacturing plant opens in Malaysia.
1980: Clarion opens a semi-conductor development facility.
1983: The company builds factories in France and Mexico.
1987: Production begins at a factory in the United States.
1995: Manufacturing subsidiaries open in Hong Kong and mainland China.
1998: The company debuts its AutoPC in partnership with Microsoft.
2001: Company headquarters are moved to Hakusan.

</td></tr>
</table>

Teikoku Dempa went public in 1962, listing on the secondary section of the Tokyo Stock Exchange. The listing helped fuel continued product development for the company. The invention of stereo sound recording and broadcasting technology led the company to adapt its products to meet the new transmission capability. The company's model CA-802, which debuted in 1963, was the first stereo car radio in Japan. That product began shipping in 1964.

Teikoku Dempa moved to new headquarters in Saitama in 1967, as work began on developing a new generation of car radios featuring the latest in consumer audio technology, tape cassettes. The first Clarion radio featuring a built-in cassette player debuted in 1968. The following year, Teikoku Dempa listed its stock on the Osaka Stock Exchange's secondary board. Then, in 1970, the company switched its listings to the main index of both exchanges. The company opened new headquarters in Tokyo soon after, and, at the end of that year, changed its name, to Clarion Company Ltd.

International Growth in the 1980s

Clarion by then had established itself as one of the top names in car audio equipment. To meet the rising international demand, the company opened its first foreign factory, in Malaysia, in 1970. The company continued to introduce innovative products through that decade, such as the launch of the first auto-reverse cassette player, solving an inconvenience of car cassette players. In 1976, Clarion, which had continued to develop home audio systems for the domestic market, branched out into the professional sector, introducing a business-class karaoke system. Another important Clarion innovation, a graphic equalizer for car stereo systems, debuted in 1978.

Clarion had by then begun to adapt new microchip technology into its car stereo designs, adding integrated circuit components for suppressing noise on the FM and AM bands in the late 1970s. In 1980, the company went a step further and opened its own semiconductor development center at its Tohoku factory. This enabled the company to pioneer Spread Spectrum (SS) communications technologies in the mid-1980s. The company also released the first car DAT player in 1984.

Clarion's international growth took off in the 1980s, starting with the opening of a factory in France in 1983. The company moved to boost its North American presence as well, launching construction of a facility in Mexico in 1983. The company began producing parts in Mexico in 1986. The following year, Clarion also opened a plant in the United States. By the end of the decade, the company had added manufacturing capacity in Taiwan as well, where production began in 1989. The following year, Clarion added a new feather to its cap with the acquisition of the United States' McIntosh, a highly respected name in developing audiophile systems.

Clarion remained at the forefront of car audio technology—and became a pioneer in a newly emerged automotive communications category. In 1987, the company became the first to add compact disc compatibility to its car audio systems. In 1992, the company debuted its first voice-activated automotive navigation system, the NAC-200. In that year, also, Clarion became one of the first to provide integrated audio and mobile telephone systems. A year later, the company's SS-based wireless modems were approved for use by the Japanese government.

New Technologies for a New Century

Through the 1990s and into the 2000s, Clarion continued to build up its worldwide presence, opening manufacturing plants in Hong Kong and China in 1995, launching production in Taiwan, Germany, and in 1997, in Hungary as well. The increased capacity helped the company keep up with production of its increasingly diversified product line.

A major force behind this diversification was the company's continued commitment to innovation. In 1996, the company debuted its Vehicle Information & Communication System (VICS)-compatible car navigation systems. That year, the company also received clearance to market its wireless modems in the United States. In the meantime, Clarion teamed up with Microsoft to produce the so-called "AutoPC," which debuted in 1998. The AutoPC was the first in the world to offer drivers a voice-activated on-board computer capable of performing a variety of functions. Although sales of the AutoPC, which was plagued by a number of bugs, proved disappointing, its release allowed Clarion to remain at the cutting-edge of technology as the automotive market shifted away from traditional audio systems to full-fledged entertainment and information systems combining audio, television, and video/DVD capabilities with navigation and telephony functions.

After adding DVD capacity in 1999, the company continued to boost its integration of technologies, launching a second-generation AutoPC in 2001. The following year, the company became the first to add in Dolby Pro Logic capability. This expanded audio functionality was complemented by the development of a dual-audio system that provided two different audio streams for the cabin and for headphone listening. The company also began marketing a new receiver capable of receiving satellite radio transmissions in 2002.

The emergence of MP3 and other hard-drive based digital audio compression technologies encouraged Clarion's innovative side. In 2004, the company debuted a new ''Music Catcher'' system, capable of transferring up to six CDs to an onboard hard-drive, eliminating the need for CD changer systems. Clarion, which sold its McIntosh subsidiary to H&D Holdings in 2004, had proved itself a primary driver of the global automotive entertainment and communications market.

Principal Subsidiaries

Clarion (GB) Ltd.; Clarion (HK) Co. Ltd.; Clarion (HK) Industries Co. Ltd.; Clarion (Malaysia) Sdn Bhd; Clarion (Taiwan) Manufacturing Co. Ltd.; Clarion Asia Pte Ltd. (Singapore); Clarion Australia Pty. Ltd.; Clarion Canada Inc.; Clarion Corporation of America; Clarion Deutschland GmbH; Clarion Europe Gmbh (Germany); Clarion France SA; Clarion Manufacturing Corporation of America; Clarion Manufacturing Corporation of the Philippines; Clarion Nederland; Clarion Orient Co. Ltd.(Hong Kong); Clarion Spain SA; Clarion Svenska AB; Clarion-Miutsuwa Phils. Inc. (Philippines); Dongguan Clarion Orient Electronics Co. Ltd. (China); Electronica Clarion SA de CV (Mexico); McIntosh Laboratory Inc.

Principal Competitors

Aiwa Corporation; Kenwood Corporation; Pioneer Corporation.

Further Reading

Armstrong, Julie, ''Suppliers Enjoy Sharp Uptick,'' *Automotive News,* April 19, 2004, p. 17.

''Clarion Inks Long-Term Partnership with ESS Technology,'' *DVD News,* August 5, 2002.

''Clarion's Golden Jubilee of Sound,'' *Daily Record,* December 19, 2003, p. 3.

Hinchcliffe, Mark, ''Clarion Leads Charge in Touchy Music,'' *Courier-Mail,* April 14, 2004, p. C03.

Kirkwood, Roger, ''Speech-Enabled Cars from Clarion,'' *PC Magazine,* June 2002, p. 196.

Pollard, Dave, ''Car Stereo That Catches Music,'' *Sunday Times,* April 18, 2004, p. 11.

—M.L. Cohen

SAINT-GOBAIN

Compagnie de Saint-Gobain

Les Miroirs, 18 Avenue d'Alsace
92096 La Defense Cedex
France
Telephone: (+33) 1 47 62 30 00
Fax: (+33) 1 47 78 45 03
Web site: http://www.saint-gobain.com

Public Company
Incorporated: 1665 as Compagnie des Glaces
Employees: 172,357
Sales: EUR 29.59 billion ($37.14 billion) (2003)
Stock Exchanges: Euronext Paris London Frankfurt
   Zurich Euronext Brussels
Ticker Symbol: SGO
NAIC: 327211 Flat Glass Manufacturing

Founded in 1665 as the royal glassmakers to Louis XIV, Compagnie de Saint-Gobain is a multinational group of over 1,000 companies in 46 countries worldwide. Saint-Gobain operates as one of the top 100 industrial corporations in the world, supplying the glass for 50 percent of all cars in Europe, manufacturing 30 billion bottles, flasks, and jars each year, and supplying insulation for one-fifth of all homes in the United States. The company's subsidiaries fall into three main divisions: housing, glass, and high performance materials. Its Housing division, responsible for 51 percent of sales in 2003, manufactures and supplies a variety of building materials, including roofing, mortars, wall facings, and pipe. The Glass unit, accounting for 38 percent of sales, provides containers, flat glass, insulation, and reinforcements. The firm's High Performance Materials segment includes its ceramics, plastics, and abrasives businesses. From its original base of flat glass manufacture in the 17th century using traditional methods, the company rapidly began to organize production on an industrial basis, establishing a strong European presence during the 19th century. It diversified into the chemical sector as well as other glass-based products. It has operated in Brazil since the 1930s and in the United States since 1974. Following an attempted takeover bid by a much smaller French glass concern in 1969, Saint-Gobain merged with Pont-á-Mousson—founded in 1854—which makes products for the construction industry and is famous for its cast-iron pipes. The merger made Saint-Gobain the world's leading manufacturer of ductile cast-iron piping for water supply systems.

Early History

Saint-Gobain is the only survivor of a group of private manufacturers founded in 1665 as part of the economic revival of France planned by Jean Baptiste Colbert, chief minister of Louis XIV. The letters patent which created the Compagnie des Glaces granted the company a monopoly on production and sale of glass in France. The original name of the company was Dunoyer, after the individual to whom these privileges were accorded. A group of Venetian glass-workers was persuaded to come to Paris, and production began in the Faubourg Saint-Antoine. However, disputes and difficulties arose with the Venetian authorities and workers, and they returned to Venice after two years. The company then formed an association with Richard Lucas de Nehou, proprietor of a glassworks at Tourlaville, near Cherbourg. Glass produced there was sent to Paris for the finishing process of grinding and polishing. Around 1680, Richard's nephew Louis was responsible for an invention that transformed the manufacture of glass and remained in use until 1920; glass could now be rolled out on a flat surface, allowing much larger sheets to be produced. After Colbert's death in 1683, his successor, whose name was Louvois, allowed the establishment of rival companies and restricted the original company to the production of blown glass. This led to the establishment in 1692 of a new factory at the village of Saint-Gobain, which was located nearer Paris and was designed for the new process.

Following the death of Louvois, the newly created companies were united with Dunoyer under the name of Plastrier, but problems continued and by 1702 Plastrier was declared bankrupt. Rescue came in the surprising form of the Geneva bank of Antoine Saladin. After complex negotiations, Saladin purchased the company, now to be called Dagincourt. The influence of the Swiss bank was to be felt throughout the 18th century.

The company now possessed a more entrepreneurial spirit and was able to exploit the new technique of rolled glass, benefiting from 18th-century prosperity and the numerous new uses for glass, especially mirrors. Beginning in 1740, technical expertise was sought to supplement the aristocratic element always prevalent in the company. Various rationalizations and reforms took place from 1755 to 1760 in response to the expansion of the market.

The company ceased glassblowing in 1763, and the ovens were improved. At the village of Saint-Gobain itself, a separate workers' enclave was established in 1775, partly as a solution to rivalry between the workers and other villagers.

The French Revolution of 1789 and its aftermath caused serious disruption at the company, and it took 40 years to restore sales to the level of the best years of the Ancien Régime. In 1806, the first attempts at diversification took place, with the implementation of the Leblanc process for producing soda ash, an important ingredient in glass and later used in many other industrial materials. This activity was transferred to new works at Chauny in 1822. The Tourlaville glass works closed in 1824, and production was concentrated at Saint-Gobain. In 1830, the company was incorporated as a *société anonyme*. The revolution had ended its monopoly, and there was a threat of competition from English glassworks—Ravenhead had been started by ex-Saint-Gobain workers—and several new French glass factories established during the 1820s, notably Saint-Quirin. The distribution of shares in the new company still reflected an aristocratic bias not suited to the world of 19th-century industry. Nevertheless, rationalization was taking place during this period, led by directors recruited from among technical university graduates. The process of mechanization had begun at the turn of the century.

With the boom in public building, the middle of the 19th century was a turning point for Saint-Gobain, heralding a golden age under the long presidency of the Duc de Broglie from 1866 to 1901.

Foreign ventures began with the lease of a factory at Stolberg in Germany in 1857, and in the following year a merger with its principal French rival Saint-Quirin gave Saint-Gobain a second presence in Germany—the glassworks built in 1853 at Mannheim, which was also to be the site of a French workers' city. Two other younger French rivals, Commentry and Prémontré, had been acquired jointly before the merger. These moves were prompted by the growing threat of competition from Belgium, as well as the expanding English glassworks. Broglie's predecessor as president, Antoine-Pierre Hély D'Oissel, recruited Hector Biver, an Englishman who had also worked in Belgium. Following its 1858 merger, the company became the Société Anonyme de la Manufactures des Glaces et Produits Chimiques de Saint-Gobain, Chauny et Cirey. On the chemical side, the company benefited from the presence of the famous chemist Joseph Louis Gay-Lussac, who had been president from 1844 to 1850 and who perfected his method of sulfuric acid production at Chauny. Considerable effort was devoted to improving the social and educational conditions of the workers, with the provision of schools, chapels, orphanages, savings and pension schemes, and even philharmonic and shooting societies. The image of aristocratic incompetence was largely dispelled during the second half of the 19th century.

Entering the Modern Era

After 200 years, a fundamental shift occurred as a result of the merger with the firm of Perret-Olivier in 1874. The company consequently comprised nine chemical works compared with eleven, including three overseas, for glass: the turnover was almost equal in both sectors. Continuing strong Belgian and U.K. competition in the glass industry was now joined by market entrants from the United States and Germany, reducing Saint-Gobain's share of an expanding industry. Pittsburgh Plate Glass, founded in 1883, attained the size of Saint-Gobain in only six years. The company responded by improving production methods and constructing further production sites in Europe: at Pisa, Italy, in 1889, and at Franiére, Belgium, between 1898 and 1900. Subsidiaries were acquired in Holland, Spain, and Germany. Turnover increased from FRF 18 million in 1890 to FRF 47 million in 1913. Saint-Gobain was now Europe's leading glass producer, with 26.8 percent of the market, followed by Belgium with 23.3 percent and Pilkington with 22 percent. Engineers played a growing role in a centralized administration in this period, but provisions continued to be made for the workers: at Pisa there was a children's home, dispensary, and school, and training in housework was provided.

The early 1900s also saw the introduction of highly significant technical developments in glassmaking, including the Bicheroux and Fourcault processes, which allowed continuous sheets to be produced. A joint venture undertaken with Pilkington to exploit the American Window Glass process, although not a technical success, helped in the forging of a commercial treaty between the glassmakers of Belgium, France, and the United Kingdom which lasted until World War II. The end of the 19th century also saw a radical change in the chemical division, where new processes resulted in the conversion of plants to superphosphate fertilizer production, for which Saint-Gobain was to remain famous in France until the abandonment of all its chemical interests in 1970.

The presence of French aristocrats and Genevan families still exerted considerable influence on the company, but with the quotation on the French Bourse in 1907 came greater dispersion of capital. From 1893, a new administrator, the archeologist and diplomat Melchior de Vogue, accelerated reform, giving more power to the divisions and creating the new posts of secretary-general and inspector of finances. He was president from 1901 to 1916. New headquarters were constructed in Paris between 1899 and 1902. With the support of shareholders, moves were made toward a more open management, but capital ventures continued to be financed on an internal basis.

At the beginning of the 20th century, key factors in the company's development were the growth of U.S. competition, further technical developments in glassmaking, and extensions

Key Dates:

1665: The company gets its start as the royal glassmakers to Louis XIV.
1874: The company merges with Perret-Olivier.
1970: Saint-Gobain and Pont-á-Mousson merge.
1978: The firm reorganizes into ten production branches.
1986: The company is re-privatized.
1990: U.S.-based Norton is acquired.
1994: Saint-Gobain sells its paper, pulp, and packaging unit.
1995: The company joins with Ball Corp. to form Ball-Foster Glass.
1996: The Poliet group is added to the firm's holdings.
2004: Dahl International is acquired.

of the way glass was used. In addition to new types of continuous processes and improved furnaces, there were innovations in grinding and polishing techniques and, perhaps most significant, the discovery of tempering to produce security glass and allow its shaping. This discovery opened the way for expansion into the automobile market as well as the structural and artistic markets. Security glass was developed and patented by Saint-Gobain, and manufacturing on a production line for Citroën began in 1929. A new factory had been opened in 1920 at Chantereine to exploit the new processes.

International relations were important in the late 1920s; various accords led to stabilization of the industry between manufacturers in the United States, the United Kingdom, and France. Saint-Gobain chose the Pittsburgh process for window glass as technically superior to that of its competitors. Surprisingly, glass bottles and flagons were still being manufactured at this time by the traditional glassblowing method, usually by small family enterprises scattered throughout France, Spain, and Italy. Saint-Gobain gradually absorbed these firms, as the increasing pace of mechanization rendered them uncompetitive. The 1930s witnessed perhaps the most important strategic move in the recent history of the company: diversification into glass fiber. Known by 18th-century English nobles, whose wigs had to be fireproof because of candles, glass fiber was also said to have been used in the Empress Josephine's coronation dress. Saint-Gobain, convinced by its U.S. contacts of the potential market for this product, obtained the necessary licenses, formed a new company, Isover, and acquired Balzaretti-Modigliani in Italy. However, production did not begin on an industrial scale until after World War II. Considerable research into improvements followed, which led to the intervention of the TEL and SUPERTEL processes for insulating materials, licensed by Saint-Gobain throughout the world.

Meanwhile the chemical side of the business had continued to decline, partly because of unsuccessful diversifications in this area. Of various diversifications attempted, including petroleum refining, one proved to be a long-term success: cellulose production. This began in 1920 and was the only process surviving from this period. An association with Papeteries Navarre in 1924 led to the formation of Cellulose du Pin and construction of a works at Facture in the Landes in 1928. It was planned at

first to produce fibers for paper-based artificial textiles, but their decline after the war led to a switch to Kraft paper and bags.

The rest of the chemical side continued to be dangerously exposed. Saint-Gobain had refused offers from Solvay for a merger in 1927 and 1928 which would have created a Franco-Belgian group on a par with ICI or I.G. Farben. Another proposal, from Kuhlmann for a French chemical union, was also turned down. These negative responses may have sprung from the desire by management to cling to the old regime. Management reforms in the 1920s and 1930s had been only tentative, and it was not until the presidency of Pierre Hély D'Oissel from 1936 to 1953 that fundamental changes in management and structure were initiated, heralding the new models of management of the 1950s and 1960s.

Postwar Changes

The period from 1950 which led up to the merger of the two very dissimilar firms of Saint-Gobain and Pont-á-Mousson in 1970 was characterized by the growing power of the state in the French economy, which began during World War II under the Vichy regime. Senior officials of government were closely involved in the management of a planned economy and saw much of French industry as archaic and fragmented. The glass industry continued to flourish, and Saint-Gobain acquired a stake in its famous Belgian rival, Glaceries de Saint-Roch. Overseas expansion in glass fiber was dramatic, and the development of a presence in Brazil beginning in 1960 supplemented solid bases in Belgium, Germany, Italy, Switzerland, and Spain. The TEL process was proving successful in the United States and led to the acquisition of interests in the CertainTeed Corporation and the conversion of three old factories, which gave the company 10 percent to 15 percent of the U.S. market. However, another U.S. venture went wrong. A new subsidiary, American Saint-Gobain, founded in 1959, having already acquired four glassworks, then designed a new one in Greenland, Tennessee, intended to exploit the latest techniques in grinding and polishing. Disastrously, this factory did not open until 1962, after the invention of float glass by Pilkington. This revolutionary technique obviated the need for lengthy finishing processes. To compound the problem, the United States reacted strongly to the French invasion by an increase in tariffs of 30 percent.

Although the invention of float glass effectively killed off American Saint-Gobain, the parent company did not take the new process seriously until 1965, when it had to be acquired on much less favorable terms than were available just after the invention was introduced in the 1950s. Saint-Gobain, however, made up for lost time by rapidly modernizing all of its factories, starting with those overseas, thus helping amortize the old installations.

The 1960s also witnessed unsatisfactory alliances during the period when the company was making its last attempts to revive its chemical operations, notably through the creation of Péchiney-Saint-Gobain to develop organic chemicals, in particular the new plastics materials. Due to the instability of this sector, a government commission recommended a fundamental regrouping. However, before these recommendations could be acted upon, Rhône-Poulenc preempted them by acquiring Péchiney-Saint-Gobain. Péchiney itself did not want the chemical interests, and Saint-Gobain could not afford to buy them.

Merger Negotiations in the 1960s

During this period the company raised capital to fund various ill-fated ventures. The increasing deficit caused further recourse to the banks, much against the Saint-Gobain tradition. At the end of 1968 came a major turning point: the dramatic offensive by Boussois Souchon Neuvesel (BSN) with a public offer for exchange to acquire 30 percent of Saint-Gobain, following tentative negotiations, which Saint-Gobain had rebuffed. BSN, a small but ambitious glass producer with an annual turnover of just under FRF 600 million, had set its sights on a company with consolidated funds of more than FRF 5 billion. BSN had chosen the moment when Saint-Gobain was suffering from the effects of the chemical restructuring as well as internal management struggles; these difficulties were reflected in the low price of the shares at the time. The offensive was a technical failure, securing only 7 percent of Saint-Gobain's capital, one million shares out of the minimum 3.4 million required. A vigorous rescue bid had to be mounted by a consortium of banks led by the Compagnie de Suez, and 40 percent of the shares changed hands during the battle. This shift left the company badly shaken and with diminished funds. As a direct consequence of this affair, the bankers took the initiative in arranging the merger with Pont-á-Mousson, which they saw as a means of securing Saint-Gobain against further attacks of this nature. Arnaud de Vogué, president since 1952, was initially reluctant but eventually recognized the end of the grand liberal regime of Saint-Gobain and the beginning of a new era.

One-third the size of Saint-Gobain, Pont-á-Mousson, founded in the 1850s, had begun to detach itself from its coal and metallurgical interests during the 1960s. Originally founded by local coal merchants in the Lorraine after the discovery of new iron-ore deposits, the little town of Pont-á-Mousson between Metz and Nancy was chosen as the site of the first blast furnace in 1860. The company began to pursue a strategy of vertical integration, with the control of mines, ironworks, and end products, a policy continued right up until the 1960s. In 1866, it made the key decision to specialize in the production of cast-iron pipes. The invention in Brazil in 1915 of an improved technique of casting pipes using centrifugal force led to the company's establishing production in that country in 1937. After World War II, a new importance was given to cast iron by the ductile iron process discovered by researchers at International Nickel in Canada during the 1940s. Pont-á-Mousson quickly obtained a license from a U.K. subsidiary of International Nickel and began production in 1950. Even so, the old type of cast-iron pipe remained in production until the end of the 1960s.

In contrast to Saint-Gobain, the dominant personalities in the history of Pont-á-Mousson were engineers, notably Camille Cavallier, sole administrator from 1900 to 1917 and president from 1917 to 1926. In 1970, following the merger, a provisional organizational structure was adopted based on the Pont-á-Mousson model, and it was Pont-á-Mousson's director, Roger Martin, who succeeded Arnaud de Vogué as the head of the new group. A gradual process of rationalization then took place involving decentralization, the establishment of a management structure, and the creation of product-based departments. In 1978, following a convention of all 41 directors, more fundamental reorganization of the new group led to the replacement of the six market departments by ten production-oriented branches. The 1970s also witnessed the jettisoning of the remaining chemical and petroleum investments, as well as the iron and steel interests inherited with Pont-á-Mousson. A brief flirtation with the products for nuclear reactors in 1972 was abandoned for political reasons. In glass fiber, the U.S. presence was reinforced by control of CertainTeed, and in France a new factory for insulation products was built at Orange. The energy crisis helped here: between 1973 and 1975, Saint-Gobain doubled its European production of glass fiber. Significant investments were also made in float glass, with Saint-Gobain building ten out of the 17 new plants constructed in Europe during 1976.

The new strength of the combined companies was illustrated by their ability to weather the crises of this period, including heavy losses in brassware and machinery during 1977 and 1978, as well as a sudden downturn in the insulation market in 1981, resulting in massive overproduction.

The 1980s–90s

After the 1978 reorganization, a search for further diversification led to the decision to enter the information technology sector. A joint subsidiary, Eurotechnique, was set up with National Semiconductor to produce electronic components, a partnership established with Cii-HB, and 30 percent of the capital of Olivetti acquired. However, before this venture could get off the ground, Saint-Gobain was nationalized by the new government of 1981 and forced to liquidate these holdings between 1982 and 1983. Yet Saint-Gobain was the only nationalized company to retain its top management, which continued to pursue its vigorous investment strategy and maintain a high level of industrial activity. The result was increased debt countered by such austerity measures as plant rationalization. The group had to be slimmed down further with approaching reprivatization in 1986. The effect of these policies was spectacular; global profits increased by a factor of seven in six years.

The company made several important acquisitions in the early 1990s. In 1990, Saint-Gobain acquired the U.S. company Norton, which was the world's leader in abrasives. The company paid $1.9 billion for Norton, one of the biggest French takeovers of an American company. The deal with Saint-Gobain rescued Norton from a hostile takeover by a British conglomerate, and Norton was a valuable asset. Norton was the only world producer of all three leading kinds of industrial abrasives—grinding wheels for machining metals, coated abrasives for polishing wood and glass, and "super-abrasives" with a diamond or boron nitride base. Norton had a strong reputation for quality, and its purchase gave Saint-Gobain a firm presence in the North American market. Saint-Gobain also acquired two German glassmakers in 1991, GIAG and Oberland. By 1992, Saint-Gobain had become the world's leading manufacturer of glass.

However, sales began to slump by 1992, and net income fell precipitously. Despite sales of over FRF 70 billion each year from 1991 through 1993, the company was beset by a downturn in the industrial cycle that it could do little to control. Demand for its products was low across Europe, and the company's activities in Asia were not vigorous enough to offset the lull in its home economy. In 1993, Saint-Gobain's profits plunged 45 percent. The company struggled to rein in costs and reduce its debt. The next year, Saint-Gobain took a major step to strengthen its core business by selling off its paper, pulp and packaging unit. The company raised FRF 5.63 billion ($1.07 billion) by selling its paper subsidiary La Cellulose du Pin to an Irish company, Jefferson Smurfit Group plc. Saint-Gobain had been involved in the paper industry for 70 years, but the company's chairman, Jean-Louis Beffa, called La Cellulose du Pin ''too small and too French'' to be a global player like the rest of Saint-Gobain's divisions. The loss of the paper business was expected to cut Saint-Gobain's sales by 10 percent, but the injection of cash was badly needed.

The next year, the recession in Europe seemed to be ending. Sales volume rose, although prices were still slack. Saint-Gobain did very well in North America in 1994, which improved the company's overall performance, and Saint-Gobain announced that it was ready to resume acquisitions now that sales and profits were back to manageable levels. In June 1995, the company announced a complex deal with two companies that would effectively make Saint-Gobain the largest glass-packaging manufacturer in the world. Saint-Gobain spent $1 billion for management control of a joint venture with Ball Corp., an American manufacturer. The joint venture bought up Ball Glass Container Corporation and another U.S. glass container manufacturer, Foster Forbes, giving Saint-Gobain control of 22 U.S. plants. The deal put Saint-Gobain second only to Owens-Illinois in the U.S. glass-packaging market. Saint-Gobain was already the leader in the European glass-packaging market, and it was important to the company to expand into the North American market. The deal with Ball Corporation seemed indicative of the company's future plans—to increase Saint-Gobain's presence in markets around the world.

Late 1990s and Beyond

Expansion played a significant role in Saint-Gobain's strategy in the years leading up to the 21st century. In fact, Saint-Gobain's feverish acquisition pace continued over the next several years. In 1996, the company acquired Poliet SA, a French specialty distribution firm. Ceramic companies from Germany and France were added to its holdings in 1997 along with an abrasives manufacturer based in the United Kingdom. Saint-Gobain strengthened its U.S. presence in 1998 by purchasing Bird Corp., a roofing materials manufacturer, and CALMAR, a supplier of plastic pump sprayers. The company announced its $620 million deal to buy Furon, a U.S. engineered products concern, the following year.

Growth continued in 2000 with the addition of U.K.-based Meyer International, Germany's Raab Karcher, and U.S. polymers firm Chemfab. In 2002, it purchased the remaining 25 percent of subsidiary Lapeyre SA that it didn't already own. While the company continued to make key acquisitions, it faced challenges due to slowing global economies. At the same time, it announced that it would have to book a $49.4 million charge to cover asbestos litigation risks in the United States. Saint-Gobain's financial performance for 2002 remained steady; however, the revelation that it could be subjected to years of expensive lawsuits sent its shares plummeting by 30 percent the day the company announced the charge in July. By March of the following year, it faced 114,000 claims.

For a short while, Saint-Gobain slowed its acquisition pace as a result of potential asbestos-related problems. By 2004, its financial results were positive as it secured a small increase in sales and operating income. Management was optimistic that the company would be able to resume its growth strategy. Early that year it acquired Dahl International AB, a Scandinavian distributor of heating and plumbing supplies, for $450.5 million.

Overall, Saint-Gobain continued to focus on its core businesses in three main business groups—Glass, Housing, and High Performance Materials. It looked for ways to strengthen its technology and marketing skills of each division and stepped up its distribution efforts. The company continued to plan for international expansion through an aggressive acquisition policy. As one of the oldest companies in the world, Saint-Gobain's involvement in global industries was far-reaching. By the early 2000s, it had supplied over 80 capitals and 1,000 major cities with water supply ducts, had provided the glass for the Louvre pyramid, and manufactured the crystals used in airport security detectors. While the threat of costly asbestos litigation remained a nagging concern, Saint-Gobain appeared poised to continue as a leading industrial concern for years to come.

Principal Divisions

Housing; Glass; High Performance Materials.

Principal Competitors

CRH plc; Lafarge S.A.; Owens Corning.

Further Reading

''Compagnie de Saint-Gobain,'' *Industry Week*, June 7, 1999.

Comes, Frank J., ''The Yuppie Who's Rewriting the Socialist Agenda,'' *Business Week*, May 13, 1985, p. 46.

''France's Saint-Gobain Says It Expects Drop in Net Profit for 1993,'' *Wall Street Journal*, April 2, 1993, p. A4B.

Hamon, Maurice, *Saint-Gobain (1665–1990): The Making of a French Multinational*, Editions Jean-Claude Lattès, 1990.

Johnson, Jo, ''Asbestos Fear Hits French Group,'' *Financial Times*, July 27, 2002, p. 8.

Kamm, Thomas, ''Transaction Gives Saint-Gobain New Growth Potential,'' *Wall Street Journal*, August 23, 1994, p. 4B.

——, ''Gobain in Deal to Establish a Bottle Giant,'' *Wall Street Journal*, June 28, 1995, p. 10A.

Milne, Richard, ''Downgrade Risk for Saint-Gobain,'' *Financial Times*, March 10, 2004.

''More Asbestos Claims for Saint-Gobain,'' *Le Figaro*, April 25, 2003.

''Results of Saint-Gobain Buyout Bid for Poliet,'' *Figaro*, April 21, 1999.

''Saint-Gobain: Expanding Empire,'' *Business Latin America*, July 21, 2003.

''Saint-Gobain SA: Unit to Buy Dahl International in $450.5 Million Transaction,'' *Wall Street Journal*, March 8, 2004.

''St-Gobain Sees Stable 1996 Net Result,'' *Reuters News*, September 20, 1996.

Truell, Peter, ''Scandals Crimp Business for French Firms,'' *Wall Street Journal*, October 20, 1994, p. 10A.

Westervelt, Robert, ''Saint-Gobain Pays $620 Million to Acquire Furon,'' *Chemical Week*, September 29, 1999, p. 18.

—Peter W. Miller
—updates: A. Woodward and Christina M. Stansell

Constar International Inc.

1 Crown Way
Philadelphia, Pennsylvania 19154-4599
U.S.A.
Telephone: (215) 552-3700
Fax: (215) 552-3707
Web site: http://www.constar.net

Public Company
Incorporated: 1927 as Chattanooga Glass Company
Employees: 1,990
Sales: $742.3 million (2003)
Stock Exchanges: NASDAQ
Ticker Symbol: CNST
NAIC: 326160 Plastics Bottle Manufacturing

Based in Philadelphia, Pennsylvania, Constar International Inc. is a major global manufacturer of polyethylene terephthalate (PET) plastic containers for the food and beverage industries. The publicly traded company is especially strong in the soft drink and water container segment, or conventional PET, and is looking to grow its custom PET business, which includes containers for hot-fill beverages, food, juices, teas, sport drinks, new age beverages, beer, and flavored alcoholic beverages. The company possesses a number of advanced packaging technologies needed to make custom PET bottles, such as OxBar O , an oxygen-scavenging technology that helps protect oxygen-sensitive products. Major customers include PepsiCo, Coca-Cola, and ConAgra. Constar maintains 15 plants in the United States and four in Europe.

Lineage Dating to 1927

Constar's corporate ancestry started in 1927 with the establishment of Chattanooga Glass Co. in Chattanooga, Tennessee, which was licensed to produce green-glass bottles for Coca-Cola bottlers. Chattanooga Glass became a subsidiary of Dorsey Corp., which diversified into the trailer truck business and added a restaurant chain. Dorsey went public in 1969. In 1970 the company became involved in plastic containers when it acquired Atlanta-based Sewell Plastics Inc., which provided the basis for Constar's current business. The company was founded in 1963 by Charles K. Sewell, who stayed on to run the operation that produced blow-mold polyethylene containers for milk and food products. Dorsey added to its new plastics division in 1971 by acquiring Polyco Inc., a company that made polyethylene containers for industrial and household chemicals and other nonfood products.

Despite these acquisitions, however, Dorsey was still very much a glass company that took a less-than-ambitious approach to future growth. According to a 1983 *Fortune* magazine article, "At the helm was Chairman J. Frank Harrison, who just happened also to be the largest shareholder of Coca-Cola Bottling Co. Consolidated of Charlotte, North Carolina. Harrison, says a former colleague, 'ran the company like the absentee owner of a Coke franchise.' The Board of directors was heavy with retired executives as mature and vitreous as the glass industry they grew up with." The company's plants used obsolete, inefficient furnaces, which played a significant role in Dorsey's declining revenues. By 1975—when sales had fallen to $155 million, 60 percent of which came from the glass division—the board finally took action and recruited an executive from outside the company. It chose Jack Pollock, the president of Dart Industries' subsidiary Thatcher Glass, which had been founded by his father. Pollock assumed the role of executive vice-president under Harrison in preparation for an eventual promotion to the top job, but he wasted no time in making his presence felt. He modernized the plants, set a mandatory retirement age for both employees and board members, and landed new customers in Schlitz and Seagram, taking advantage of contacts made during his time at Thatcher. More important to the growth of Dorsey, however, would be his willingness to listen to Charles Sewell, who urged him to embrace the new PET technology.

1973 Patent of the PET Soda Bottle

The PET soda bottle was invented by Nathaniel C. Wyeth, the older brother of painter Andrew Wyeth. After studying engineering at the University of Pennsylvania, he went to work for the Du Pont Corporation. It was in 1967 that he wondered aloud why no one had thought to use plastic for soda bottles, and was quickly told by a colleague that the carbonation would cause

Company Perspectives:

Constar is a packaging solutions leader, designing and manufacturing innovative methods for customers to address their production and marketing challenges.

the bottles to expand and ultimately explode. To test this explanation, Wyeth poured ginger ale into an empty plastic detergent bottle and left it in his refrigerator overnight. As his colleague predicted, the bottle had ballooned in size. Over the next five years Wyeth experimented with thousands of polymers in a determined effort to produce clear, light, and stable plastic soda bottles. Finally in 1973 he perfected a process and filed for a patent on PET soda bottles. By 1977 the Federal Drug Administration had approved the two-liter PET Bottle and a machine was developed to mass-produce it. The plastic bottle was clearly superior to its glass counterpart: 11 times lighter, unbreakable, and able to hold a carbonated beverage for three months without a loss of flavor or gas. Moreover, plastic bottles were much cheaper to ship and eliminated a major safety problem for soft drink companies and bottlers, which suffered some 20,000 injuries each year from breaking and exploding glass bottles.

Because of Sewell's lobbying, Dorsey became one of the few glass companies to recognize the inevitable move toward plastic soda bottles and took steps to join the revolution rather than be one of its victims. Sewell recognized that Dorsey had to move quickly if it was to become established in the marketplace before corporate giants like Owen's Illinois, Continental Group, and Amoco weighed in. At Pollock's behest the Dorsey board approved Sewell's request to purchase two-liter, PET bottle-making machines. While the larger competitors took time to build large, dedicated two-liter plants, Sewell installed a new machine in each of the division's 12 plants spread across the Sunbelt. In this way, the company was able to quickly enter the marketplace, spread the overhead costs, and was in a position to better serve local markets. Dorsey could offer a better price and service, and as a result, by 1980, it was the category leader with 28 percent of the business.

Dorsey's glass business was now an afterthought compared with the success of the Sewell division. Intent on selling off the glass division, Pollock made efforts to revitalize the operation, but even then it took more than a year to sell Chattanooga Glass to a management-led investment group for $40 million a piece, just two-thirds of book value. Unfortunately for Dorsey, the plastic division suffered a severe setback in the meantime. Sewell tried to move too quickly into the one-liter and half-liter soda bottle categories, but the one-liter size proved unpopular with consumers, leading to a rash of canceled orders. In addition, the half-liter bottle proved more difficult to perfect than expected.

Pollock grew disenchanted with Charles Sewell, whose strong suit was not administration. In November 1982, according to *Fortune,* "Pollock showed up unannounced at Sewell Plastics headquarters, demoted Charles, and placed corporate planner Bud Ahern at Sewell's helm. Charles, who is described by a friend as 'ungodly proud,' walked out of the company that afternoon." Under new leadership, the Sewell subsidiary intro-

duced controls and more layers of management, and also opened its own research and development laboratory to develop packaging for food, beer, wine, and hard liquor. But plastic liquor and wine bottles failed to catch on with consumers, and overcapacity in the plastic beverage-bottle industry led to steep price cuts, dimming the company's prospects. Dorsey also had to deal with a hostile takeover attempt by its largest shareholder, the Far Hills, New Jersey-based investment firm of Shamrock Associates. Owning an 8 percent stake in Dorsey, Shamrock made a buyout offer that was rejected, leading Shamrock to increase its stake to more than 20 percent. Dorsey's management dug in to resist and went to court to head off Shamrock's "creeping tender." By October 1984 Shamrock had accumulated 24.7 percent of Dorsey voting stock and made a tender offer for another 29 percent, which if successful would have given it a controlling interest. To the surprise of many outside observers, a month later the two parties reached a settlement, with Dorsey buying out Shamrock. A few months later, the Dorsey board of directors adopted provisions to thwart any future takeover attempts.

The market for plastic bottles stabilized, as no new capacity came on line and some plants closed. In July 1984 Dorsey signed a major agreement with Ball Corporation to jointly develop plastic containers for such items as catsup, mayonnaise, salad dressings, and peanut butter. Although these were positive developments, Sewell still suffered from out-of-control operating costs, which could prove fatal in a commodity business like plastic. To address this problem, Pollock brought in Charles F. Casey, a friend and former colleague at Dorsey who had just retired a rich man after selling a glass company he headed. Casey and a Sewell vice-president named Robert Nickels worked together to upgrade the cost accounting system and introduce computerized production and design systems. Once the new capabilities were in place, they brought customers to the plant to work with company engineers and designers to develop more serviceable products.

Adopting the Constar Name in 1987

Casey replaced Pollock as Dorsey's president in 1987. Pollock and Casey now decided to sell off the trailer division (the restaurant chain would be divested later), and in April 1987 shareholders voted to change the company's name to Constar International Inc., reflecting the change in the company's focus. A year later, in April 1988, Casey succeeded Pollock as Constar's chairman and CEO. Pollock retired but stayed on as a director. In 1992 the Sewell plastics, Inc. subsidiary became Constar Plastics Inc. Under Casey, Constar became more interested in producing rigid plastic containers for food packaging, both in the United States and overseas. To ward off criticism about the environmental impact of plastics, Constar formed a partnership with New Jersey-based Wellman Corporation, a major waste plastics recycling company. Constar contracted to buy Wellman's used polyethylene bottles and began to increase the amount of recycled plastic it used. In addition, Constar and Wellman formed Wellstar Europe, to buy European rigid plastic container companies. A plastic manufacturer teamed up with a recycler was a strong combination in environmentally-minded Europe.

In October 1992 Constar was acquired by Philadelphia-based Crown Cork & Seal Company in a $515 million tender

Key Dates:

1927: The company is founded and becomes known as Dorsey Corp.
1963: Sewell Plastics Inc. is founded.
1970: Dorsey Corp. acquires Sewell.
1987: Dorsey changes its name to Constar International Inc.
1992: Crown Cork & Seal acquires Constar.
2002: Crown Cork spins off Constar in a stock offering.

offer. The previous year, Constar posted sales of $548 million, operating 24 plants in the United States and Canada. Its new parent company was a $3.8 billion manufacturer of metal containers, crowns, closures, and packaging machinery. Casey retired from an active role in the running of Constar, although he became a member on Crown Cork's board. At the time of the transaction, Casey maintained that the sale to Crown Cork would strengthen Constar's ability to service the many packaging needs of its customers.

At the time of the Constar acquisition, Crown Cork was enjoying its 100th anniversary. The company was founded in 1892 by William Painter who revolutionized the beverage business by inventing the "crown cork" to seal bottles. His original company was called CrownHCork & Seal Company and was located in Baltimore. Several years later Painter brought out a foot-powered machine that could fill and cap 24 bottles a minute, a development that led to expansion around the world. By the time he died in 1906 the business was known as Crown Cork & Seal Company. In 1936 the company entered the can business, acquiring Acme Can Company of Philadelphia. Twenty years later, as a result of poor diversification efforts, the company was on the verge of bankruptcy when John F. Connelly, a former Crown Cork supplier, took over as president and turned around the company. A year later corporate headquarters was moved to Philadelphia. During the 1960s Crown Cork wisely moved into the soft drink can business, and in the 1970s Connelly was also prescient in avoiding conglomerating like his competition, instead focusing on international growth. The acquisition of Constar helped to round out Crown Cork's packaging business.

Constar soon discovered that its interests and those of its parent company did not always coincide. Crown Cork quickly cannibalized the Constar operation by transferring some of its machinery to European can-making plants to make plastic bottles as well, a move that was intended to better serve customers that used both cans and plastic bottles. Constar efforts at expansion were stunted because the subsidiary found itself competing for cash with the steel food can and aluminum beverage can units. Because Crown Cork had taken on an excessive amount of debt, money became even tighter in the second half of the 1990s. Moreover, the parent company was burdened by costs associated with asbestos litigation. Constar was picking up a good deal of momentum in the bottled water business, but Crown Cork forced the company to concentrate more of its efforts on the soft drink market, primarily because the aluminum can unit was losing market share in the area.

To many industry observers, Constar appeared to have the most growth potential of Crown Cork's businesses. In 2001 Constar generated $745.8 million, or about 10 percent of Crown Cork's $7.2 billion in sales. In 2002 Crown Cork decided to spin off the subsidiary in an initial public offering (IPO) of stock in an effort to pay down some of the parent company's $4.8 billion in debt. According to one analyst, Eric Bosshard with Midwest Research, "This was probably not plan A. . . . It's unfortunate they are going to have to cut some muscle in order to stabilize the portfolio." Also unfortunate was the timing, given that the stock market was in a prolonged slump and not overly receptive to IPOs. Casey came out of retirement to help, assuming the chairmanship of Constar to get the company on its feet once it was independent. After some delays and amendments—in response to concerns that the offering was priced too high for a company involved in a very competitive business faced with rapid technological change—Crown Cork finally completed the spin-off in November 2002. Shares were priced at $12 each, far below the original range of $14 to $16. In the end, Crown Cork sold about 90 percent of Constar, raising some $550 million.

On a temporary basis, Constar set up shop in Crown Cork's Philadelphia headquarters and began to operate as an independent company once again. It was now free to pursue a number of opportunities, from increased emphasis on bottled water to what was considered the new frontier in the industry, and in some cases represented old goals, replacing the glass bottles used for teas, juices, beer, and flavored alcoholic drinks. The challenge was to design bottles able to withstand temperatures as high as 185 degrees without a loss of shape, while also finding a way to prevent the infiltration of oxygen through the plastic and spoiling the drink. The future also looked promising because it was estimated that the plastic food and beverage container market was expected to grow by 11 percent over the next few years. To achieve growth in the marketplace, Constar needed adequate funding, but it was weighed down by debt incurred in the spin-off. The company carried a debt-to-capital ratio in excess of 60 percent. By September 2003—when the price of its stock traded below $6, less than half of its IPO price—Constar was forced to take decisive measures to improve its situation. It closed two plants and hired investment banks Citigroup and Deutsche Bank to present ideas on how to better handle its debt load. Constar was not the only plastic container company feeling the pinch, however. The entire industry faced an overcapacity problem, which would be relieved to some extent by the Constar plant closings. In April 2004, Casey, having fulfilled his commitment to help launch an independent Constar, turned over the chairmanship to John F. Neafsey, president of JN Associates, an investment consulting firm. Along with CEO Michael J. Hoffman, he faced the difficult task of helping Constar chart a course to stability and growth.

Principal Subsidiaries

Constar, Inc.; Constar Plastics, LLC; Constar Foreign Holdings, Inc.

Principal Competitors

Ball Corporation; Bemis Company, Inc.; Plastipak Holdings, Inc.

Further Reading

''Bottles and Trailers Right Ticket for the Long Haul at Dorsey Corp.,'' *Barron's,* September 2, 1968, p. 18.

Boyer, Edward, ''Turning Glass to Plastic to Gold,'' *Fortune,* April 4, 1983, p. 172.

Brubaker, Harold, ''New Philadelphia-Based Container Firm Finds Rough Going in Competitive Market,'' *Philadelphia Inquirer,* September 5, 2003.

''Engineer's Art: Nathaniel Wyeth Sculpted Plastic into a Better Soda Bottle,'' *Technology Review,* January-February 2002, p. 96.

Koselka, Rita, ''Casey at the Bottling Plant,'' *Forbes,* August 6, 1990, p. 88.

—Ed Dinger

Cortefiel S.A.

Avda del Llano Castellano 51, Ap
Madrid E-28034
Spain
Telephone: (+34) 91 387 34 00
Fax: (+34) 91 387 38 09
Web site: http://www.cortefiel.es

Public Company
Incorporated: 1980; 1993 as Grupo Cortefiel
Employees: 9,767
Sales: EUR 921.25 million ($994.56 million) (2003)
Stock Exchanges: Madrid
Ticker Symbol: CTF
NAIC: 448140 Family Clothing Stores

Spain's Cortefiel S.A. is one of the leading clothing retailers in that country, holding the number three spot behind Inditex (Zara) and Mango. The company is also placed among the top clothing retailers in the European market. One of the first to pursue a brand diversification strategy in Spain, Cortefiel operates under a range of strong brands. These include Cortefiel, with 212 stores; youth-oriented Springfield, with 351 company-owned stores as well as nearly 80 additional franchises and corner boutiques; 18 higher-end Milano stores; 140 Women's Secret lingerie stores; 11 Pedro del Hierro shops; and, in a joint-venture with Germany's Douglas perfume stores, 47 Douglas-branded shops in Spain. Altogether, Cortefiel's operations encompass more than 830 company-owned stores, an additional 150 franchised locations, and strong a number of "corner" shops in department stores and other locations. In 2004, Cortefiel acquired the Werdin chain of men's jeans retail stores in Germany. Most of Cortefiel's activities remain in Spain, which represents some 70 percent of the group's retail empire; however, in the late 1990s and early 2000s the company pursued an ambitious international expansion, adding company-owned stores in Portugal, France, Belgium, Germany, Poland, and Hungary. The company's franchised operations give it a presence in nearly 30 international markets, including Canada, Mexico, Peru, Chile, Malta, Ireland, Slovenia, Serbia, Greece,

Ukraine, Russia, Indonesia, Malasia, Israel, Lebanon, Saudi Arabia, Jordan, Qatar, Kuwait, UAE, Oman, Singapore, Thailand, Australia, and the Philippines. In 2004, the company reached a new agreement to introduce up to 200 franchised stores in China as well. Supporting the group's retail sales operations is a manufacturing base of two factories in Spain, three in Morocco, and one factory in Hungary. These plants produce about 15 percent of the company's total requirements; the remainder is outsourced to a global network of third-party manufacturers in Asia, North Africa, and South America, as well as in Spain, where the company's contracts with some 50 cooperative companies produce 40 percent of the group's clothing. Listed on the Madrid Stock Exchange, Cortefiel remains controlled at more than 54 percent by the founding Hinojosa/Garcia families. The company is led by chairman and CEO Gonzalo Hinojosa, who joined Cortefiel in 1970.

Origins and Growth

Cortefiel originated as a small haberdasher's shop in Madrid in 1880. Toward the turn of the 20th century, the shop began producing its own men's suits and accessories. Sales of the family-owned company's clothing remained limited to its Madrid store into the 1920s.

In the 1930s, the Cortefiel company decided to take the next step and develop a full-scale manufacturing wing. In 1933, the company launched the mass-production of its men suits. By the beginning of the 1940s, Cortefiel had already become the top producer of clothing in Spain. In 1950, the company officially launched the Cortefiel retail brand and over the next couple of decades added a small number of new stores, although that number did not top 25 stores before the mid-1970s.

In the meantime, Cortefiel developed into a major supplier of clothing to other Spanish retailers, an activity started in the 1950s. The company also began exporting its clothing to other European markets, then to the United States in the 1960s.

In the 1970s, however, the company came under pressure from the shift in the global textiles market to the cheaper labor markets in the Far East. The growth of the Spanish economy had led to concurrent wage rises. As a result, Cortefiel began to

---

Key Dates:

1880: The company begins trading as a haberdashery in Madrid, Spain, then begins manufacturing men's suits by the turn of the century.

1933: The company begins mass production of men's suits and other clothing, becoming Spain's leading clothing manufacturer.

1950: Cortefiel retail format and brand is launched; the company begins supplying clothing to foreign market.

1960: Export of clothing to the U.S. market begins.

1975: The company changes its strategy to emphasize retailing over manufacturing.

1986: Dacosa joint venture is formed to open Don Algodon women's clothing stores.

1994: Cortefiel goes public on the Bolsa de Madrid and begins an international expansion strategy.

2002: The company begins a new aggressive store expansion, adding 150 stores over two years.

---

lose its competitive edge against a growing number of Asian and South American clothing producers.

Returning to Retail in the Mid-1970s

In 1975, Cortefiel decided to adopt a new business strategy by reducing its reliance on its manufacturing operations in favor of its retail side. Cortefiel increasingly shifted its own textile needs to a range of contract manufacturers, mirroring an overall industry trend. By the 1990s, reliance on the third-party contract manufacturing market had already begun to impose itself as the dominant business model in the retail clothing sector. Nonetheless, Cortefiel retained a small manufacturing base, with two plants in Spain, three in Morocco, and a sixth plant in Hungary.

From 1976, Cortefiel began adding new stores. Over the next two decades, the number of Cortefiel stores more than quadrupled, topping 112 stores by 1994. In the early 1980s, the company pioneered a new marketing technique in Spain, launching its Club Cortefield loyalty card, which provided customers with credit card services on their purchases.

Cortefiel also pioneered another retailing trend for the Spanish market, that of branded retail diversification. The company began developing new retail formats and clothing collections designed to broaden its consumer base. The group launched its first new retail format, Milano, in 1984. The first Milano store, which opened in Barcelona, offered a line of men's couture products, including suits and accessories appropriate for office wear. The Milano concept was later broadened to include a full range of men's clothing and accessories.

The Milano format catered to older men. Cortefiel moved to broaden its range by launching its next new retail format, Springfield, in 1988. The Springfield stores catered to younger men and featured a full collection of more casual fashions. Springfield turned into Cortefiel's biggest success, and by 1994 the company had opened 85 stores throughout Spain as well as in Portugal. A decade later, there were more than 350 Springfield stores in Cortefiel's growing retail empire.

International Retailer in the 1990s

Cortefiel filled another retail segment in 1986 with the formation of the 50–50 joint venture Dacosa, which began opening a network of Don Algodon franchised stores throughout Spain. The Don Algodon store enabled Cortefiel to extend its range into the young women's knitwear and outerwear segments. The chain flourished, building up a network of some 115 stores before Cortefiel sold its stake in the joint venture in 2002.

The launch of Women's Secret in 1993 brought Cortefiel into the women's lingerie category. The format quickly grew into a segment leader. In the meantime, the company extended its reach into the higher-end fashion market, launching a new chain of Pedro del Hierro stores in partnership with the Spanish designer. That chain reached 16 stores and over 80 corner boutiques by the early 2000s.

Cortefiel also became the first international partner in the expansion plans of famed British retailer Marks & Spencer. In 1989, the two companies reached a franchise agreement whereby Cortefiel was to lead the introduction of the Marks & Spencer brand into Spain. The partnership, in which Cortefiel held a 20 percent stake compared to Marks & Spencer's 80 percent, opened five stores by the mid-1990s. In the later part of that decade, however, Marks & Spencer's financial difficulties led it to end its attempt at international penetration.

In the meantime, Cortefiel had become determined to extend its own operations into the international market. Backing that plan, the company went public in 1994, listing on the Madrid Stock Exchange. The Springfield brand, already present in Portugal, proved to be the company's most successful international format, and the company added France to its regions of operation in the early 1990s. In 1994, the company formed a partnership in order to move into Germany, Austria, and Switzerland as well. Other markets followed, including Belgium, Hungary, and Poland.

Cortefiel developed a franchise network in order to introduce the Springfield brand, as well as its other formats, into other countries. Toward this end, the company entered a far wider range of international markets in the 1990s, with franchised stores in Cyprus, Malta, Greece, Luxembourg, Slovenia, Mexico, Chile, Canada, Saudi Arabia, Jordan, the United Arab Emirates, Qatar, Oman, and Lebanon.

The Milano chain, too, which had grown to 18 stores by the turn of the century, included a growing number of foreign locations, including stores in Lisbon and Oporto in Portugal; Paris, Versailles, Lyon, and Nantes in France; and Antwerp in Belgium.

Challenges and Opportunities in the Late 1990s and Beyond

In 1997, Cortefiel expanded its retail empire again, reaching an agreement with Germany's Douglas, the leading perfume retailer in Europe, to open a network of Douglas shops in Spain and Portugal. Cortefiel moved quickly, rolling out 40 Douglas shops in Spain and another seven stores in Portugal by the early 2000s.

By 1998, however, Cortefiel appeared to be running out of steam as its growth slowed in the second half of the decade. The company's biggest difficulties came from its reliance on its main Cortefiel brand, which still accounted for more than 55 percent of its revenue and which had slipped to less than 3 percent in sales growth. The company's difficulties continued into the 2000s with the unsuccessful launch of its first e-commerce sites. Additional problems came from Cortefiel's 50 percent stake in the struggling Don Algodon chain, leading the company to sell back its half to that company's founder in 2001. Meanwhile, the Cortefiel increased its presence in Germany, acquiring the 74-store chain of Werdin jeans shops in 2000. Yet that market quickly softened, adding to Cortefiel's difficulties.

With its sales growth stagnating—in part because of increased competition from the likes of Spanish rival Zara and the entry into Spain of other European retailers, including H&M—Cortefiel attempted to regain its momentum by launching a hostile takeover offer for Adolofo Dominguez SA, a smaller Spanish retailer, in 2001. However, the company failed to convince a majority of its rival's shareholders to accept the offer.

Instead, Cortefiel moved to regain its momentum through organic growth. In 2002, the company launched a new and more aggressive expansion program, adding more than 90 stores that year and another 63 stores in 2003. It also reached an agreement with Aldeasa, which specialized in operating retail stores at Spain's airports, to introduce Cortefiel's brands in its shops. The agreement also called for the two companies to investigate the possibility of extending their partnership to the international market.

In the meantime, Cortefiel continued its own expansion, adding sites in Poland and Ireland and extending its franchise empire to include Yugoslavia and Israel. The company's expansion drive had also restored its sales growth, as revenues neared EUR 925 million ($994 million) at the end of 2003. Further growth seemed already assured, particularly through a franchise agreement to open as many as 200 Springfield stores in China before the end of the decade. This and other strategic moves appeared to promise that Cortefiel would retain its place among the leading European retailers.

Principal Subsidiaries

Algamar, S.A.; Bizarro e Milho, Lda. (Portugal); BMML, Confecçoes, Lda. (Portugal); Bruxeland S.P.R.L. (Belgium); Casual Wear Española, S.A.; Classe Affaires, S.A.S. (France); Comercial Española del Vestido, S.A.; Confecciones Sur, S.A.; Confemo—Confecçoes e Moda Portfolio company; Confespanha, Lda. (Portugal); Coralí, S.A.; Corom, S.A. (Morocco); Cortefiel Commercial, S.A. (Switzerland); Cortefiel France, S.A.; Creasel, S.L.; de Espanha, Lda. (Portugal); Dr. E. Rudnick, S.A. (Morocco); Eurofiel Confección, S.A.; Fifty Factory, S.L. (Spain); Hijos de Primitivo Muñoz, S.A.; Milano Difusión, S.A.; Milano France, S.A.S. (France); Quiral Belgique, S.A. (Belgium); Quiral Luxembourg, S.A. (Luxembourg); Quiral, S.A.; Quirós, S.A.; S.B.C. France, S.A.S. (France); SPF Polska Sp. Z o. o. (Poland); Springfield Bekleidung Vertriebs, GmbH (Germany); Springfield France, S.A.S.; Springfield Handelsgesellschaft GmbH. (Austria); Springfield Hungary Trading, Lt. (Hungary); Springfield Sportswear GmbH & Co. KG (Germany); Tulipan Confection, S.A. (Hungary); Werdin Beteiligungs, GmbH (Germany); Werdin GmbH & Co. KG. (Germany); Women'Secret France, S.A.S. (France); Women's Secret GmbH & Co. KG. (Germany); Women's Secret Hungary, Lt (Hungary); Women's Secret, S.A.

Principal Competitors

Royal Vendex KBB N.V.; Benetton Group S.p.A.; Vivarte; Gruppo Coin S.p.A.; Kiabi S.A.; La Redoute; Charles Vogele Holding AG; Peek und Cloppenburg KG; Somfy International S.A; Inditex SA; Mango SA.

Further Reading

Alarcon, Jose, "Cut-back Cortefiel Sees Sales and Profits Return," *TDCTrade.com*, August 22, 2003.
Burney, Ellen, and Barker, Barbara, "Growing Paul . . . Expansion Mode," *WWD*, May 10, 2004, p. 15.
Burns, Tom, "Cortefiel Bids for Spanish Rival," *Financial Times*, March 15, 2001, p. 30.
"Cortefiel," *Marketing Week*, March 22, 2001, p. 32.
Elkin, Mike, "Cortefiel Pulls Hostile Bid for Rival," *Daily Deal*, April 17, 2001.

—M.L. Cohen

Covanta Energy Corporation

40 Lane Road
Fairfield, New Jersey 07004
U.S.A.
Telephone: (973) 882-9000
Toll Free: (866) 268-2682
Fax: (973) 882-7234
Web site: http://www.covantaenergy.com

Wholly Owned Subsidiary of Danielson Holding
*   Corporation*
Incorporated: 1939
Employees: 2,400
Sales: $790.5 million (2003)
NAIC: 561790 Other Services to Buildings and
    Dwellings; 221119 Other Electric Power Generation

Covanta Energy Corporation develops and operates waste-to-energy (WTE) power projects and also owns and operates independent power facilities across the United States and in Asia and Europe. Overall, Covanta facilities generate over 2,000 megawatts (MW) of electricity. Its WTE facilities convert over 30,000 tons of municipal solid waste into renewable energy each day. The company—known as Ogden Corporation until 2001—adopted is current moniker after selling off its entertainment and aviation assets to focus on its energy operations. Covanta filed for Chapter 11 bankruptcy protection in 2002 and was acquired by Danielson Holding Corporation in March 2004.

Origins

The original activities of Ogden Corporation bore little resemblance to the company that existed at the start of the new century. In its first half-century of existence, Ogden Corporation was, successively, a public utility holding company, an investment company, a manufacturing company operating through diverse subsidiaries, and a major service company. Ogden Corporation began its history as a public utility holding company in 1939. In 1948, the company registered with the Securities and Exchange Commission (SEC) as an investment company. Ogden acquired W.A. Case & Son Manufacturing Company in 1952, an action that decisively altered the status of the corporation, as the SEC ruled that Ogden had ceased to be an investment company. Thereafter, Ogden operated as a manufacturing company and followed the emerging trend to create conglomerates. In the following decades, Ogden became what one observer called a mini-conglomerate, accumulating such diverse holdings as the Suffolk Downs Race Track, Better Built Machinery, and Wilson Foods.

Diversification and Restructuring in the 1970s–80s

Ogden's most significant corporate acquisition may have been the purchase of Luria Brothers, a scrap processor, in 1955. This transaction brought Ralph E. Ablon into the employ of Ogden Corporation. Ablon had begun his career with Luria Brothers in 1939. In 1948, he was named executive vice-president; he became president of Luria Brothers after its purchase in 1955. Seven years later, Ablon became chairman and chief executive officer of Ogden Corporation. He presided over the company during decades of expansion as a conglomerate, then re-structured the company in the 1980s. His son Richard succeeded him as chief executive officer in 1991, while the senior Ablon remained chairman.

The weaknesses of the conglomerate as a form of business organization had become apparent by the end of the 1970s. Large corporations had accumulated more businesses than they could understand or effectively manage. The 1980s saw widespread reorganizations in American corporations as managers sought to regain a clear sense of identity and a coherent strategy for the future. Ralph Ablon believed that the economy would shift toward a service orientation, and in 1981 he set forth plans for a major reorganization of Ogden Corporation that would fully embrace the service economy. As he later explained, "We looked at what kind of world we would live in and the ideal company for the balance of the century. We discovered that everything we had didn't fit and we had almost nothing we needed to become a total services company." Ablon began the transformation of Ogden with the purchase of Allied Maintenance Corporation, a well-established firm that provided Ogden with a firm base for its expansion into the service sector. Between 1981 and 1987, Ogden virtually re-created itself. In 1987, only 5 percent of income came from businesses that Ogden had owned in 1981. By 1989, Ogden enjoyed annual sales of more than $1 billion.

Ogden's restructuring eliminated many capital-intensive op- erations that could damage the company in slow economic times. Its new service orientation provided a measure of secu- rity even in uncertain economic situations. In the wake of the Wall Street crash of 1987, one financial analyst praised Ogden for its management and stability. "They represent the highest quality in terms of balance sheet, market liquidity, cash avail- ability and earnings stability." Ogden continued to benefit from that stability during the recession of the early 1990s.

Ogden's decision to focus on the service sector still provided an enormous range of action. Ogden Entertainment provided a good example of the diversity of Ogden activity, providing any combination of "concession food service, merchandise, main- tenance, janitorial [service], security, parking, total facility management services and concert promotions" to its cus- tomers. Ogden Entertainment Services counted among its cli- ents dozens of stadiums, convention centers, and other enter- tainment venues in North and South America. Clients included Rich Stadium in Buffalo, New York, the Capital Centre Arena in Landover, Maryland, the Rosemont Horizon, near Chicago, Illinois, the Anaheim Stadium in Anaheim, California, and the Sports Palace in Mexico City. In addition, in 1991 Ogden Entertainment was awarded a contract to manage a soccer sta- dium in London.

Ogden Industrial Services offered a variety of personnel, maintenance, and warehouse services to clients that included many Fortune 500 companies such as IBM, Exxon, and Dow Chemical. The company also worked in conjunction with Ogden projects to provide services to its waste-to-energy plants. Ogden Industrial, like other Ogden subsidiaries, benefited from the desire of other companies to cut overhead expenses and made its profit by offering services more cheaply than compa- nies could afford to provide them for themselves. Among other enterprises, Ogden employees, for example, ran a waste-acid treatment plant for Kemira, Inc. As an independent contractor, Ogden could develop procedures that were not restricted by work rules stipulated in union contracts with Kemira. For exam- ple, a lower-paid maintenance employee could perform minor plumbing or mechanical repairs without calling in a more ex- pensive tradesman. While contracting saved money for the customer and provided an additional source of income for Ogden, it caused unease among union members, who feared the threat to high-paying jobs and the possibility that contracting could become a tool to weaken unions. Responding to such concerns in 1987, an Ogden spokesman observed that contrac-

ting "is going to become even more widespread, because it is the only solution to saving what is left of America's smokestack industries."

Entering the Waste-to-Energy Market in the 1980s

Ogden Projects, through the activities of its subsidiary Ogden Martin Services, emerged as a leader in the waste-to- energy market. Ogden based its involvement on two develop- ments of the 1970s: rising energy costs and the decreasing availability of landfill space. The Environmental Protection Agency calculated that in 1971 the United States generated 113 megatons of municipal solid waste. Advocates of commercial re-use began to argue that waste should be viewed as an eco- nomic resource. Waste included materials that could be recy- cled or burned for fuel. The process of utilizing these resources was known as resource recovery. Scarcity provided opportunity for investment and profit. Citing "long term increases in refuse generation and disposal costs, decreased availability for all land uses, and greater demand for energy and material resources," Lisa M. Bithell, writing in the *Journal of Resource Manage- ment and Technology* in 1983, predicted that "centralized re- source recovery will continue to play an important role in resource management and solid waste disposal."

Interest in waste-to-energy facilities, however, developed slowly in the United States. After European companies had spent decades working on recovery systems, some American engineers began to experiment with new technologies. Klaus S. Feindler, then president of Beaumont Environmental, criticized American efforts in 1983. Writing in the *Journal of Resource Management and Technology,* he pointed out that the western European market neared saturation in waste recovery facilities. He calculated that one facility per million of population existed in western Europe while barely 0.2 facilities per million existed in the United States, noting that this combination of an open American market and experienced European companies pro- vided an opportunity for both groups. American preoccupation with experimental systems indicated "a lack of appreciation for the simpler and proven European technology, perhaps because of a preoccupation with space age technology." Ogden, com- mitted to approaches that contained costs, did not make that mistake. In 1983, Ogden acquired the North American rights to the Martin GmbH system of incineration, the most widely used technology.

Ogden Projects completed its first waste-to-energy plant in 1986. In 1992, the company operated 21 plants and had eight additional plants either under construction or awarded. Its 21 plants had the capacity to process 20,675 tons of waste per day. These figures included the acquisition of Blount Energy Resource Corporation, a transaction that brought two operational plants to Ogden. Ogden's rapid growth reflected its reputation for helping local governments address a pressing problem. Herbert Florsdorf, executive director of the Lancaster County (Pennsylvania) Solid Waste Management Authority, expressed relief when Ogden opened its Lancaster County facility in 1991. "Last year," he told Ogden officials, "when we looked at our landfill, we saw 12 acres of potential environmental problems, a risk to our future. Now we see 12 acres of resources." While the company was best known for waste-to-energy operations, Ogden offered a full range of waste disposal services, including recycling.

Not all of Ogden's new operations met with success. In 1986, Ogden began to market a new service to deal with hazardous waste. The group, Ogden Environmental Services, used mobile units to clean up hazardous waste on-site. The company hoped to eliminate the expense and political controversy involved in programs that required extensive transportation of dangerous materials. The enterprise, which offered technology that was useful for a wide range of problems, drew an enthusiastic response from the investment community. John Kaweske, manager of the Financial Industrial Income Fund, told *Barron's* that prospects for the new technology were excellent. He rated this effort alongside the waste-to-energy business as a reason to look favorably on the long-term prospects of Ogden Corporation. Counter to all expectations, in 1990 the unit endured a loss of almost $4 million on revenues of $6 million. Ralph Ablon ruefully told *Business Week* in 1989: "Companies with hazardous waste problems are disinclined to spend money, and they will find ways to avoid it." In 1991, Ogden discontinued the on-site remediation business.

Ogden renamed that troubled subsidiary Ogden Waste Treatment Services and developed an approach closer to the model that had succeeded so well in its waste-to-energy operations. The new strategy emphasized permanent facilities "targeting permanent regional hazardous waste treatment and disposal facilities." Such plants encouraged long-term relationships with municipalities. Ogden hoped to become identified as a valued problem solver in this field. The company planned a large thermal treatment plant in Houston and hoped that the new effort would allow this part of its business to prosper.

During the early 1990s, Ogden continued to strengthen its position in environmental services. In 1991, the company acquired complete control over ERC Environmental and Energy Services, which became Ogden Environmental and Energy Services. This purchase was one of the first important actions taken by R. Richard Ablon after he became chief executive officer. The acquisition of this successful consulting and engineering concern supported the position of Ogden's waste-to-energy

operations and paved the way for further expansion. In 1991, Ogden Environmental and Energy Services undertook a major environmental testing operation for the Department of Defense, analyzing conditions at naval bases in the Pacific. Ogden hoped that this contract would lead to further business in the Pacific.

During this time period, prospects for Ogden remained good. While some of its subsidiaries, such as Ogden Aviation Services, were dependent on a single industry for their success, the ability to offer a wide range of essential services allowed Ogden Services Corporation to provide a stable base for corporate planning. The future of Ogden Projects depended in part on the development of environmental legislation in the United States. Ogden paid close attention to environmental concerns, and the research expertise of Ogden Environmental and Energy Services meant that Ogden was well positioned to anticipate future environmental needs and business opportunities.

Changes in the 1990s and Beyond

Throughout most of the 1990s, Ogden continued to make strategic purchases and secure lucrative contracts that strengthened its position as one of the largest service companies in the world. It was involved in a host of diverse activities. In 1993, it opened Arrowhead Pond—home to the NHL's Mighty Ducks. The Ogden aviation arm expanded as well, moving into Latin America by offering ground service in Chile, Venezuela, Peru, and Brazil. The company landed a contract to manage the observation deck at the World Trade Center in New York City in 1995 and also acquired a 50 percent interest in Metropolitan Entertainment Inc. and Firehole Entertainment Corporation.

Ogden began to redefine its business scope in the mid-1990s and reorganized itself into three main business segments: aviation, energy services, and entertainment. While the company shuttered unrelated businesses, it continued to expand its core units. In 1999, Wet'n Wild Inc. and several other water parks were purchased.

During this process, Ogden's stock price faltered because it continued to be viewed as a conglomerate. The company finally decided in early 1999 to split its entertainment and aviation business into one publicly traded company while its energy holdings would be spun off. By September, however, plans had changed. Ablon resigned and was replaced by Scott Mackin. Under Mackin's direction, the company announced it would sell its entertainment and aviation holdings in order to focus solely on its energy business.

Ogden entered the new century with additional changes on the horizon. Aramark Corporation purchased its entertainment division and its theme and waterparks were sold to Alfa Holdings SA. Its aviation ground and fueling business, along with its energy engineering operations, were also divested. To mark its transformation into a pure play energy company, Ogden changed its name to Covanta Energy Corporation in 2001.

Despite its restructuring over the past several years, Covanta posted losses from 1999 through 2002. Its exposure to the faltering energy market in California left it struggling to shore up profits. The company's financial situation went from bad to worse when it defaulted on a $4.6 million interest payment in March 2002. In April, Covanta was forced to file for Chapter 11 bankruptcy protection. Its geothermal assets were sold in December 2003.

The company toyed with several reorganization plans but eventually accepted a buyout bid from Danielson Holding Co. The $30 million deal, which included Covanta's energy and water-related businesses, was completed in March 2004. Covanta emerged from bankruptcy that month. Covanta CEO Anthony J. Orlando commented on the transaction in a March 2004 company press release. "We are very pleased to have concluded Covanta's reorganization and are now focused on the continued success of our waste-to-energy business. The plan approved by the court maximizes creditor recovery and affords the company a solid capital structure. In addition, it enables us to embark on a dynamic partnership with the Danielson team." Orlando went on to claim, "By combining our complementary skill sets, we will position Covanta to do what it does best—provide our clients with world class, reliable service." Indeed, Covanta management was optimistic that the problems of the past were well behind it. Only time would tell, however, if Covanta would achieve success in the years to come.

Principal Subsidiaries

8309 Tujunga Avenue Corporation; AMOR 14 Corporation; Bal-Sam India Holdings Ltd.; Burney Mountain Power; Covanta Acquisition, Inc.; Covanta Alexandria/Arlington, Inc.; Covanta Babylon, Inc.; Covanta Bangladesh Operating Ltd.; Covanta Bessemer, Inc.; Covanta Bristol, Inc.; Covanta Chinese Investments Ltd.; Covanta Cunningham Environmental Support, Inc.; Covanta Energy Americas, Inc.; Covanta Energy Asia Pacific Ltd.; Covanta Energy Construction, Inc.; Covanta Energy Europe Ltd.; Covanta Energy Group, Inc.; Covanta Energy International, Inc.; Covanta Geothermal Operations, Inc.; Covanta Waste to Energy Asia Investments; Covanta Water Holdings, Inc.

Principal Competitors

The AES Corporation; Calpine Corporation; Wheelabrator Technologies Inc.

Further Reading

Alter, H., "The Future of Solid Waste Management in the U.S.," *Waste Management & Research* (1991).

Auerbach, Jonathan, "Ogden Corp. Plans Divestitures," *Wall Street Journal*, November 10, 1995, p. B10.

Bithell, Lisa M., "Status of the Resource Recovery Industry," *Journal of Resource Management and Technology*, April 1983.

Brennan, Terry, "Judge OKs Danielson Buy of Covanta," *Daily Deal*, March 5, 2004.

Cochran, Thomas, "Cleaning up with Ogden," *Barron's*, November 28, 1988.

Cook, James, "Garbage into Gold," *Forbes*, January 22, 1990.

"Covanta Energy Files for Bankruptcy Protection," *Global Power Report*, April 4, 2002, p. 4.

"Danielson Holding Corporation Acquires Covanta Energy Corporation," *PR Newswire*, March 10, 2004.

Feindler, Klaus S., "European Energy and Resource Recovery Systems," *Journal of Resource Management and Technology*, April 1983.

"It Ain't Glamorous, But the Money Sure Is Good," *Business Week*, August 28, 1989.

Parker, Marcia, "Ogden Hits Goal in Self-Imposed Diet," *Pensions & Investment Age*, November 11, 1987.

"Purchase of Firehole Is Part of Company's New Plan," *Wall Street Journal*, October 18, 1995.

Sullivan, Allanna, "Odgen to Break up Three Business Lines into 2 Traded Firms," *Wall Street Journal*, March 12, 1999, p. B4.

Welsh, Jonathan, "Ogden Announces Change in Strategy," *Wall Street Journal*, September 20, 1999, p. B9.

—Joseph Bator
—update: Christina M. Stansell

CRH plc

Belgard Castle
Clondalkin 22
Ireland
Telephone: (+14) 041 000
Fax: (+14) 041 007
Web site: http://www.crh.ie; http://www.crh.com

Public Company
Incorporated: 1926 as Roadstone Ltd.; 1970 as Cement
    Roadstone Holdings
Employees: 54,239
Sales: EUR 11.08 billion ($13.29 billion) (2003)
Stock Exchanges: Irish London
Ticker Symbol: CRHPLC
NAIC: 327310 Cement Manufacturing; 212321
    Construction Sand and Gravel Mining; 324121
    Asphalt Paving Mixture and Block Manufacturing;
    327390 Other Concrete Product Manufacturing

CRH plc has emerged as a leader in the fast-consolidating global building materials market. The Dublin, Ireland-based company has long pursued an active acquisition program, spending as much as EUR 1 billion in a single year and typically targeting small and mid-sized businesses in order to build up an international network of companies. Most of CRH's acquisitions continue to operate under their former names and management, while taking advantage of their parent company's strong market position and international infrastructure. CRH operates in nearly 2,000 sites in 23 countries, with a particularly strong presence in the United States—operating under the primary Oldcastle Materials umbrella—and in Europe. CRH handles a broad spectrum of building materials, including primary materials—including cement, ready-mixed concrete, aggregates and asphalt—and value-added materials such as precast concrete products, bricks, insulation, glass, and related products. CRH is also present in the distribution segment, operating its own networks of builders merchants and consumer-oriented do-it-yourself stores in various markets, including the Benelux countries, Switzerland, and Spain, as well as in the United States. The strategy behind CRH's acquisition program has long focused on achieving a balanced geographic and product-mix portfolio. The company's four primary divisions—Europe Materials, Europe Products & Distribution, Americas Materials, and Americas Products & Distribution—each represent roughly 25 percent of total group sales and operating profits, although the company's Americas businesses, especially its North American operations, remain the group's sales and profits leader. CRH posted sales of more than EUR 11 billion ($13 billion) in 2004. The group is led by chairman Pat Malloy and CEO Liam O'Mahoney and is listed on the Irish and London stock exchanges.

Merging Irish Roadstone Leaders in the 1970s

CRH started out in the 1930s as an aggregates business founded by brothers Tom and Donald Roach. Their company became Roadstone Ltd. in 1949, and for the next two decades remained one of only two authorized cement producers in Ireland. The other licensed producer was the far larger Irish Cement, which was in fact owned by Danish interests. In 1970, however, a merger—described as "acrimonious" was pushed through, combining Roadstone and Irish Cement into a new company, Cement Roadstone Holdings, later known as CRH. The new company included operations in cement, aggregates, asphalt, and concrete products. Nearly all of the group's sales, which stood at the equivalent of EUR 26 million in 1970, were generated in Ireland.

CRH, led by Tom Roach, went public in 1973. The public offering was made in part to fuel the group's expansion objectives. Although the group enjoyed a near-monopoly hold on much of Ireland's primary building materials sector, the country's small population left little room for growth, while the focus on a single market left the company vulnerable to economic downturns. CRH therefore looked to the international market for its future expansion.

The company's first international move came that same year with the purchase of Van Neerbos, in the Netherlands. The acquisition added concrete products operations, as well as a distribution operation. Other acquisitions followed throughout the 1970s, including a move into the United Kingdom, and into

Scotland in particular, with the purchase of the builders merchants group Henderson in 1978.

The year 1978 also marked CRH's entry into the United States, where it acquired Utah-based concrete products group Amcor. That acquisition formed the basis of the company's U.S. division, which took on the name of Oldcastle Building Products. Nonetheless, the company had already adopted its expansion policy of maintaining its acquisitions' names and management in order to take advantage of each company's local affiliations.

CRH's expansion in the 1970s had transformed the company from a small-sized operation into a fast-growing building products and distribution group with sales topping the equivalent of EUR 325 million at the start of the next decade. By the end of the 1980s, however, CRH was to transform itself yet again, with operations in seven countries and sales passing the equivalent of EUR 1.3 billion. Importantly, the company had also diversified its product mix, which included cement, asphalt and other basic construction and road-building materials, and an increasing range of finished products such as concrete products, bricks, glass, and the like.

Geographic distribution had been ensured in part by the continued build-up of the group's U.S. holdings, which included the 1985 purchase of Callanan Industries, which produced aggregates and asphalt, in New York State. The Callanan acquisition proved a cornerstone of CRH's later dominance of the New York and Northeastern building materials markets. In another international expansion, the company moved into Spain in 1988, acquiring Beton Catalan Group. The company continued to develop its European interests, adding new subsidiaries in the Netherlands and the United Kingdom, as well as in Germany. Meanwhile, CRH had also built up a number of strong regional distribution networks, such as in the United Kingdom, where it renamed its building merchants network as Keyline in 1988.

Rapid Expansion in the 1990s

CRH's expansion also included an ever-increasing range of products, such as its entry into the U.S. glassmaking market with the purchase of 13 plants for a total cost of $135 million in 1990. The company also stepped up its U.S. masonry presence with the purchase of three companies that year, including Betco Block & Products Inc, based in Bethesda, Maryland. By then, the company's record already included some 60 acquisitions.

CRH's geographic and operational diversity helped shield it from the worst effects of the economic recession of the early 1990s. By 1993, the company was able to return to its expansion effort, starting with the purchase that year of Pennsylvania-based Pennsy Supply. The United States retained the group's growth focus, with further acquisitions in 1994 including Balf Co. in Connecticut, Lebanon Rock in Pennsylvania, and additional quarry and asphalt operations in New York.

The arrival of Don Godson as company CEO in 1995 signaled the start of accelerated expansion for the company. CRH's acquisition strategy became still more ambitious, backed up by 12 (and later 14) acquisition teams which scouted the group's markets for potential takeover targets. CRH nonetheless maintained its preference for acquiring small- and mid-sized, privately owned, and usually family-run and profitable businesses, rather than costly headline-making mega-acquisitions. CRH took a patient approach to purchases, often spending years wooing owners of businesses it wished to acquire.

In 1995, CRH made its first entry into Poland, buying Holding Cement Polski, which later gained majority control of Cementownia Ozarow, one of the country's major cement producers. That acquisition also marked the first CRH cement manufacturing operation outside of Ireland. By the end of the decade, CRH numbered more than a dozen operations in Poland.

Meanwhile, the company stepped up its spending, paying, for example, $87 million to acquire the Jack B. Parson Companies, which operated quarries in Idaho, Utah, and Nevada, in 1996. The company also purchased Ritangela and Brooks Products, based in New York, and Foster & Southeastern, based in Massachusetts, that year.

The company's purchases were now growing larger. In July 1996, CRH paid more than $120 million to acquire Allied Building Products, which specialized in roofing and cladding products. Then, in September 1996, the company made its largest acquisition to date, paying nearly $329 million to acquire Tilcon, a major road construction specialist in the Northeast. The Tilcon acquisition established CRH as that region's leading building materials supplier.

International Building Materials Leader in the 2000s

CRH continued adding to its U.S. road-building business, extending into the Midwest and the mideastern region and adding such companies as CPM, Trenwyth Industries, Akron Brick and Block, and New York Trap Rock. The company also moved into France, buying up a building materials distribution network, and deepened its presence in the Netherlands, with purchases including a brick manufacturer, additional do-it-yourself stores, and a maker of skylights and ventilation systems. In 1998, the company boosted its French business with the purchases of Rabnoi SA, a builders merchant company, and majority control of drainage systems and concrete vault manufacturing group Prefaest SA.

Key Dates:

1930s: Tom and Donald Roach found a cement production business, one of only two licensed cement producers in Ireland.

1936: Irish Cement, the other licensed cement producer, is formed.

1949: The Roach company takes on the name of Roadstone Ltd.

1970: Roadstone and Irish Cement merge to form Cement Roadstone Holdings (CRH).

1973: CRH enters the Netherlands with the acquisition of Van Neerbos.

1978: The company enters the U.S. market with purchase of Amcor and forms a U.S. holding company, Oldcastle Building Products.

1985: Callanan Industries of New York is acquired.

1987: The company enters Spain with the purchase of Beton Catalan Group.

1993: Pennsy Supply of Pennsylvania is acquired.

1995: The company enters Poland with the purchase of 75 percent of Cementownia Ozarow.

1996: CRH purchases Tilcon for EUR 329 million.

1999: The company sells Keyline, UK builders merchants, to Travis Perkins and enters Finland through the purchase of Finnsementti; Thompson-McCully Cos, based in Michigan, is acquired.

2000: Shelly Co. of Ohio is acquired for $362 million.

2003: CRH acquires the Netherlands' Cementbouw, its largest acquisition to date, for EUR 639 million.

2004: The company enters Portugal with the EUR 200 million purchase of cement producer Secil.

By then, the company's sales were nearing the equivalent of EUR 4 billion. In 1999, CRH decided to focus on its materials and products operations in the United Kingdom, selling its Keyline distribution business to Travis Perkins. CRH then found a new market when it bought up Finland's only cement producer, Finnsementti Oy, together with Lohja Rudus Oy, that country's top producer of aggregates and ready-mix concrete. At the same time, CRH boosted its U.S. presence with the $422 million purchase of Michigan's Thompson-McCully Cos.

CRH's spending on acquisitions in 1999 topped EUR 1.5 billion ($1.3 billion), double the year before, as the company continued to build scale. Don Goodson retired the following year, replaced by Liam O'Mahoney as the company's chief executive. O'Mahoney maintained his predecessor's acquisition policies, describing the group's scouting and purchasing process to The Financial Times with the statement, ''We try to make ourselves user friendly to crusty owner-entrepreneurs. We support the hidden talent in a family business where the rake of a son was going to take over.''

As it entered the 2000s, CRH's revenues neared EUR 7 billion. By the end of 2001, the group's continued purchases had boosted it past EUR 10 billion. In that year, the company completed a EUR 1.1 billion rights issue, providing it with the ammunition for further growth. The company entered Switzer-

land that year with the EUR 425 million purchase of that country's Jura Group, adding cement, concrete and aggregates operations, as well as a regional distribution network. The company also entered Israel, acquiring a major stake in Nesher Israel Cement Works, the only cement producer in that country. In the United Staes, CRH paid $362 million in order to acquire Ohio's Shelly Group.

In 2002, the company stepped up its presence in Germany, paying EUR 214 million to acquire EHL Group, a maker of paving materials and products. The company in the meantime completed a spree of 25 acquisitions in the United States, including Mount Hope Rock Products, based in New Jersey, for $144 million. At this time, CRH, through Oldcastle, had become the leading U.S. asphalt producer and a top producer of aggregates and ready-mix concrete as well. The company also claimed regional leadership in a number of product categories, including glass, brick, and precast concrete products.

CRH's largest acquisition to date came in July 2003 when it agreed to pay EUR 693 million in order to acquire the Netherlands' Cementbouw. The acquisition, which included Cementbouw's own building materials production, as well as its market-leading do-it-yourself stores, gave CRH a dominant position in the Netherlands building materials market. The Cementbouw purchase, however, was only part of a company record of more than EUR 1.6 billion in purchases that year.

With revenues topping EUR 11 billion, CRH had carefully constructed an international empire of building materials, building products, and distribution outlets. CRH showed little sign of slowing down as it approached the mid-decade mark; by May 2004, the company had spent more than EUR 600 billion on new acquisitions, including the EUR 200 million purchase of a 49 percent stake in cement producer Secil, signaling the company's entry into the Portuguese market. CRH appeared to have cemented its place among the world's top building materials groups.

Principal Subsidiaries

Allied Building Products Corporation (United States); B-Complex S.A. (Poland); Beton Catalan Group (Spain); Béton Moulé Industriel sa (France); Betonelement A/S (Denmark); Callanan Industries, Inc. (United States); Cementbouw Detailhandel bv (Netherlands); Cementownia Rejowiec S.A. (Poland); CRH America, Inc.; CRH Fencing Ltd.(United Kingdom); CRH Klinkier Sp. z o.o. (Poland); CRH Sudamericana S.A. (Argentina); Douterloigne nv (Belgium); EHL AG (Germany); Farrans Ltd. (United Kingdom); Finnsementti Oy (Finland); Grupa Ozarów S.A. (Poland); Heda sa (France); Ibstock Brick Ltd. (United Kingdom); Irish Cement Ltd.; JURA-Holding (Switzerland); Oldcastle Building Products Canada, Inc.; Oldcastle Materials Southeast; Oldcastle Materials, Inc. (United States); Oldcastle, Inc. (United States); Pennsy Supply, Inc. (United States); Premac Spol. s r.o. (Slovakia); Premier Cement Ltd. (United Kingdom); Premier Periclase Ltd. ; R.J. Maxwell & Son, Scott (United Kingdom); Roadstone-Wood Group; The Shelly Company (United States); Tilcon Capaldi, Inc. (United States); Van Neerbos Bouwmarkten bv (Netherlands); Van Neerbos Bouwmarkten nv (Netherlands); Vidrios Dell Orto, S.A. (79.95, Chile); EcoTherm GmbH (Germany).

Principal Competitors

IFI; Lafarge S.A.; Cementos Apasco S.A. de C.V.; Glacier Northwest Inc.; HeidelbergCement AG; Fomento de Construcciones y Contratas S.A.; HBG, Hollandsche Beton Groep N.V.; Cemex S.A. de C.V.; Grupo Ferrovial S.A.

Further Reading

Batchelor, Charles, "CRH Acquisitions Hit Euros 1.5bn," *Financial Times*, January 16, 2001, p. 26.

Blackwell, David, Peter Smith, and Lucy Smy, "CRH Expands European Empire with Euros 693m Deal," *Financial Times*, July 30, 2003, p. 21.

Cole, Robert, "Global Acquisitions Help to Cement CRH's Houdini-like Escape," *Times* (London), January 8, 2004, p. 28.

Craig, Carole, Frederick Studemann, "Home Truths for Ireland," *International Management*, May 1993, p. 32.

Guthrie, Jonathan, "Poetry Lover with His Own Quarry," *Financial Times*, August 29, 1998, p. 20.

Lavery, Brian, "Building Materials Company Ireland Loves to Hate," *New York Times*, September 5, 2002, p. W1.

Mortished, Carl, "Continent a Growth Blackspot for CRH," *Times* (London), March 3, 1999, p. 23.

O'Halloran, Barry, "CRH Makes 'Positive' Start to Year," *Irish Times*, May 6, 2004, p. 19.

Phillips, Richard, "Big in the Material World," *Independent on Sunday*, September 8, 1996, p. 6.

Waples, John, "Irish Combine Strides ahead with Small Steps," *Sunday Times*, March 30, 1997, p. 10.

—M.L. Cohen

DAIMLERCHRYSLER

DaimlerChrysler AG

Epplestrasse 225
70546 Stuttgart
Germany
Telephone: (+49) 711 17 0
Toll Free: (800) 736-5030
Fax: (+49) 711 17 94022
Web site: http://www.daimlerchrysler.com

Public Company
Incorporated: 1998
Employees: 362,063
Sales: EUR 136.4 billion ($171.8 billion) (2003)
Stock Exchanges: New York Euronext Paris Frankfurt
   Tokyo Zurich
Ticker Symbol: DCX
NAIC: 336111 Automobile Manufacturing; 336411
   Aircraft Manufacturing; 421110 Automobile and
   Other Motor Vehicle Wholesalers; 522220 Sales
   Financing; 532112 Passenger Cars Leasing

DaimlerChrysler AG—the third-largest car maker in the world—is the product of the November 1998 merger of Daimler-Benz AG of Germany and Chrysler Corporation of the United States. Vehicles built by the resultant powerhouse include Mercedes-Benz luxury passenger cars; a microcompact car sold under the name Smart; Chrysler, Jeep, and Dodge cars, pickup trucks, minivans, and sport utility vehicles; and commercial vehicles, including vans, trucks, and buses, under the brand names Mercedes-Benz, Freightliner, Sterling, Setra, and Western Star Trucks. The company's revenue stream is heavily weighted toward the United States and Europe—the Mercedes Car Group and the Chrysler Group divisions account for the majority of company sales. The company has been plagued with problems in recent years related partly to its investment in Mitsubishi Motors. Its troubled Chrysler division experienced a $637 million loss in 2003 due to restructuring costs and slowing U.S. sales. In addition to its vehicle manufacturing operations, DaimlerChrysler is a leading provider of information technology services in Germany and offers a variety of financial services—including

vehicle sales and leasing financing, dealer financing, and insurance services—primarily in North America and Europe. The European Aeronautic Defence and Space Company (EADS), which is 33 percent-owned by DaimlerChrysler, operates as the world's second-largest aerospace and defense company.

The History of Daimler-Benz AG

The roots of Daimler-Benz go back to the mid-1880s and two engineers, Carl Benz and Gottlieb Daimler, who are cited by most authorities as the most important contributors to the development of the internal combustion engine. Despite the fact that they were both concerned with the same idea at virtually the same time, and they lived within 60 miles of each other, the two apparently never even met. They certainly never envisioned the 1926 merger of their two companies.

Although Benz drove his first car in 1885 and Daimler ran his in 1886, neither was actually the first to create gasoline-powered vehicles. They were, however, the first to persist long enough to make them viable as transportation. At this time the obstacles to motorized vehicles were enormous: gasoline was considered dangerously explosive, roads were poor, and few people could afford an automobile in any case. Nevertheless, Benz dedicated himself to revolutionizing the world's transportation with the internal combustion engine.

Early in 1885 Benz—who had formed Benz & Companies in Mannheim in 1883—sat in a car and circled a track next to his small factory, while his workers and his wife stood nearby. The car had three wheels and a top speed of ten mph. This engineering triumph was only slightly marred by Benz's first public demonstration, which took place shortly afterward, in which he forgot to steer the car and smashed into the brick wall around his own home. Despite this inauspicious debut, Benz's cars quickly became known for their quality of materials and construction. By 1888 Benz had 50 employees building his three-wheeled car. Two years later, he began making a four-wheeled vehicle.

Daimler's convictions about the internal combustion engine were as intense as Benz's. Originally a gunsmith, Daimler later trained as an engineer, studying in Germany, England, Belgium, and France. After working for a number of German and British firms, he became technical director for the Gasmotorenfabrik Deutz. Disillusioned by the company's limited vision, he and researcher Wilhelm Maybach resigned in 1882 to set up their own experimental engine workshop near Stuttgart. They tested their first engine on a wooden bicycle. Later, they put engines into a four-wheeled vehicle and a boat. Daimler sold the French rights to his engines to Panhard-Levassor (which later fought him for the use of his name). In 1896 he granted a patent license to the British Daimler company, which eventually became independent of the German Daimler-Motoren-Gesellschaft, which was incorporated in 1890.

The story of how Daimler found a new brand name for its cars has become legendary. In 1900 Austro-Hungarian Consul-General and businessman Emil Jellinek approached the company with a suggestion. He offered to underwrite the production of a new high-performance car. In return, he asked that the vehicle be named after his daughter—Mercedes. Daimler's Mercedes continued to make automotive history. In 1906 the young engineer Ferdinand Porsche took the place of Daimler's oldest son, Paul, as chief engineer at the company's Austrian factory. (Paul Daimler returned to the main plant in Stuttgart.) In the five years Porsche was with Daimler, he produced 65 designs, which made him one of the most influential and prolific automotive designers ever. Approximately the same time, in 1909, the Mercedes star emblem was registered; it has embellished the radiators of all the company's cars since 1921.

In 1924 the Daimler and Benz companies began coordinating designs and production, but maintained their own brand names. They merged completely in 1926 as Daimler-Benz Aktiengesellschaft and began producing cars under the name Mercedes-Benz. The merger undoubtedly saved the two companies from bankruptcy in the poverty and inflation of post-World War I Germany.

The company continued to grow throughout the 1930s. The most consistently successful participant in automobile racing history, Mercedes-Benz scored international victories that added to its reputation. The company's racing success was also used as propaganda by the Third Reich in the years before World War II. The Mercedes-Benz became Adolph Hitler's parade transportation. Whenever he was photographed in a vehicle, it was a Mercedes. In 1939 the state took over the German auto industry, and during the war Daimler-Benz developed and produced trucks, tanks, and aircraft engines for the

Luftwaffe—using, in large part, the slave labor of prisoners. The company's importance to the German war machine made Daimler-Benz a primary target for Allied bombing raids. Two weeks of air strikes in September 1944 destroyed 70 percent or more of the company's plants. Although little was left of the company, workers returned to resume their old jobs after the war. To the surprise of many people, the factories recovered and the company again became one of the most successful auto manufacturers in the world.

Much of Daimler-Benz's growth in the 1950s occurred under the direction of stockholder Friedrich Flick. A convicted war criminal, Flick lost 80 percent of his steel fortune at the end of World War II. Yet he still had enough money to purchase a little more than 37 percent interest in Daimler-Benz between 1954 and 1957. By 1959 his $20 million investment was worth $200 million, and he had become Germany's second ranking industrialist. Flick's holdings allowed him to push the company in 1958 to buy 80 percent of competitor Auto Union GmbH and its Audi line, to gain a smaller car for the Daimler product line. The acquisition made Daimler-Benz the fifth largest automobile manufacturer in the world and the largest outside the United States.

The acquisition probably lessened the competitive impact of the new U.S. compact cars introduced in the 1950s; moreover, Daimler-Benz faced a lesser threat than other European automakers because the Mercedes appealed to the market segment made up of wealthy, status-conscious customers, and its appeal grew steadily. By 1960 Daimler-Benz already had 83,000 employees in seven West German plants. Additional plants were located in Argentina, Brazil, and India, and the company had established assembly lines in Mexico, South Africa, Belgium, and Ireland. In 1966 Auto Union was sold to Volkswagenwerk AG.

Daimler-Benz's conservative outlook was evident in its strategy of gradual growth, concentration on areas of expertise, foresight, and willingness to sacrifice short-term sales and earnings for long-term benefits. This conservatism helped soften the effect of the recession and gasoline shortages that had severely affected other automakers in the 1970s. While many manufacturers were closing facilities and cutting workers' hours, Daimler-Benz registered record sales gains. Chairman Joachim Zahn, a lawyer, said the company had foreseen the challenging era the auto industry was about to confront. Between 1973 and 1975, Zahn had set aside some $250 million as preparation for bad times. While other automakers spent time and money on model changes, Daimler-Benz had invested in engines powered by inexpensive diesel fuel. These vehicles comprised 45 percent of its output by the mid-1970s. The company was not without problems during these years, as high labor costs and the increasing value of the deutsche mark were making Mercedes-Benz automobiles more expensive than ever. Rather than reducing costs or cutting corners, however, the company began to speak of its cars as investments.

Although primarily known for its passenger cars, Daimler-Benz's commercial truck line was its largest source of profits for many years. The company profited from the oil price increase of the late 1970s, when demand for its commercial vehicles rose dramatically in the Middle East. Most of the company's trucks were made outside of Germany, unlike its cars. Later, the commercial line led the company into one risk

Key Dates:

1883: Carl Benz forms Benz & Companies in Mannheim.

1890: Daimler-Motoren-Gesellschaft is incorporated.

1924: Walter P. Chrysler introduces the Chrysler Six model.

1926: Daimler and Benz are merged to form Daimler-Benz AG, which begins producing cars under the name Mercedes-Benz.

1928: Chrysler acquires Dodge Corporation.

1944: Most of Daimler-Benz's plants are destroyed in Allied bombing raids.

1979: Through passage of the Chrysler Loan Guarantee Bill, the U.S. government guarantees $1.2 billion in loans to Chrysler.

1984: Chrysler introduces the first minivan.

1987: Chrysler acquires American Motors Corporation.

1993: Daimler-Benz becomes the first German firm listed on the New York Stock Exchange.

1995: Jürgen Schrempp takes over as Daimler-Benz's chairman and CEO; company posts losses of nearly $4 billion, the largest in German history.

1998: Daimler-Benz and Chrysler merge to form DaimlerChrysler AG.

2001: Dieter Zetsche launches a major restructuring effort at the Chrysler division.

that was stalled by unfortunate timing. In 1981 Daimler-Benz purchased the U.S.-based Freightliner Corporation, a manufacturer of heavy trucks, just as sales ground to a halt in the face of a U.S. recession.

Some risk-taking was inevitable, of course; usually it paid off. Daimler-Benz increased its car production from 350,000 to 540,000 units a year between 1975 and 1983. Most of the increase was due to the introduction in 1983 of its 190 model, a smaller version of its sedan. Despite some concern that the 190 would cannibalize sales of its larger cars, the 190 expanded Daimler-Benz's customer base, and the updated image of the new model attracted younger customers, lowering the average age of a Mercedes owner from 45 to 40.

As a manufacturer of luxury automobiles, Daimler-Benz was less vulnerable than most automakers to shifts in demand during the early 1980s. Most Mercedes-Benz customers were wealthy enough to rise above concerns about finance rates, inflation, recession, gasoline prices, or tax breaks. Another traditional safeguard for Daimler-Benz was its longstanding policy of making only as many cars as it could expect to sell, especially during a recession. The result was usually a backlog of demand when a recession ended. In addition, since the company's sales were good even when the market was poor, Daimler-Benz never had to cater to demands from dealers.

However, during the mid-1980s Daimler-Benz was confronted with a dramatic increase in competition for the luxury car market, the fastest-growing segment of the automobile business. Along with this market competition was the increasing speed and sophistication of competitors' automotive research. For exam-

ple, pioneering Daimler-Benz engineers spent 18 years developing anti-skid brakes to enable drivers to keep control of their vehicles during sudden stops. A few months after the company introduced the breakthrough in the United States, Lincoln brought out a similar system as standard equipment.

Competition and the high price of research and development were two of the factors precipitating the sudden moves Daimler-Benz made between February 1985 and February 1986. Industry analysts were surprised when the company acquired, in quick succession, three large conglomerates: Motoren- und Turbinen-Union, which made aircraft engines and diesel motors for tanks and ships;

Dornier, a privately held manufacturer of spacecraft systems, commuter planes, and medical equipment; and AEG, a high-technology manufacturer of electronic equipment such as turbines, robotics, and data processing, as well as household appliances. Many industry watchers were dubious about the diversification of a company that was already doing so well. Profits had increased every year but one between 1970 and 1985, and increased more than 50 percent in 1985 alone. Some analysts also questioned the speed of Daimler-Benz's purchases, as well as management's ability to hold such a large and diverse enterprise together.

Yet Chairman Werner Breitschwerdt maintained full confidence in the moves. By bringing the technical and research expertise of the new subsidiaries to Daimler-Benz, Breitschwerdt hoped to significantly expand the company's research base. The prospects were highly promising for the automotive division, whose engineers were already interested in developing ''intelligent cars.'' In this area, the radar technology of AEG and the materials expertise of Dornier would be extremely useful.

The Deutsche Bank (which owned 28 percent of Daimler-Benz) became increasingly troubled, however, by Breitschwerdt's apparent lack of a clear program for integrating the company's $5.5 billion in recent acquisitions, and in July 1987 Breitschwerdt announced his resignation. Despite the major reservations of several board members, but with Deutsche Bank's full approval, Edzard Reuter, the company's chief strategic planner, was appointed to succeed Breitschwerdt. These upheavals seemed to have little impact on Daimler-Benz's performance; it still emerged as the largest industrial concern in Germany.

In 1989 Daimler-Benz InterServices AG (Debis) was created to handle data processing, financial and insurance services, and real estate management for the Daimler group. The following year, the dismantling of the Berlin Wall had both positive and negative repercussions for Daimler-Benz; although the recently acquired aeronautical and defense businesses were hurt, the resulting unification provided a welcome jump in demand for Daimler-Benz's automotive division.

By the early 1990s the German economy took a turn for the worse, and the consequences of Daimler-Benz's mid-1980s spending spree began to take their toll. For the first time in its history, Daimler-Benz was forced to eliminate jobs (14,000 of them, through early retirement and attrition) in its automotive division as Mercedes sales plunged and Daimler's overall profit dropped 25 percent in 1992.

First quarter figures for 1993 reflected Germany's widening recession, with Daimler-Benz's net income plummeting by 96 percent to $12.4 million on sales of $13.1 billion, while Mercedes' sales (65 percent of the group's) fell 24 percent for the period. Yet with long-term goals in mind, Daimler-Benz announced hidden reserves of $2.45 billion in an effort to become the first German firm listed on the New York Stock Exchange. The disclosure by Daimler-Benz, which had been prevented from admittance in the past by discrepancies between German and U.S. accounting procedures, was the first of several compliances offered to satisfy U.S. regulators. By midyear, using stringent U.S. accounting procedures, Daimler-Benz reported sales of $69.6 billion and its first loss since the end of World War II. Yet the company's financial maneuvering earlier in the year had paid off: in October 1993, Daimler-Benz triumphantly listed its stock on the Big Board of the New York Stock Exchange.

Mercedes-Benz, meanwhile, was busy with both internal and external expansion. A new lower-priced C-Class Mercedes (known as the Baby-Benz) was introduced in 1993 to appeal to younger buyers in the United States and Europe. Other big moves in 1993 included Debis's construction of new headquarters in Berlin, rewarded by $5.1 billion in sales, nearly double those of 1990. Also in 1993, the company's aerospace arm, Deutsche Aerospace AG (DASA), acquired a controlling 51 percent stake in Fokker, a Dutch airplane manufacturer. Daimler-Benz finished 1993 with overall revenue of $70 billion and losses of $1.3 billion, including an $88.3 million deficit from DASA, which continued to hemorrhage for the next several years.

In 1994 Mercedes-Benz initiated a sweeping reorganization that included manufacturing more car parts outside Germany, appealing to younger buyers through radically different U.S. advertising, and developing more of the smaller, C-Class Mercedes or Baby-Benz models, as well as sport utility vehicles and minivans.

While Mercedes streamlined operations, Daimler-Benz's workforce reductions from 1992 to 1994 now totaled 20 percent of its 350,000 worldwide employees (bringing with it a $2.5 billion restructuring charge). Believing it had weathered the worst of its recessionary storms, Daimler-Benz climbed back to profitability in 1994 with earnings of $750 million, due in part to a sharp increase in both buying and selling outside Germany. Yet 1995 brought a series of highs and lows beginning with a changing of the guard: Edzard Reuter was forced out as CEO and was succeeded by former protege Jürgen E. Schrempp, former chairman of DASA.

Among Schrempp's first moves was to stem the flow of red ink. Arranging a 50/50 merger with the Swedish-Swiss ABB Asea Brown Boveri Ltd. in exchange for $900 million in cash from Daimler-Benz, the new venture, ABB Daimler-Benz Transportation (ADtranz), would become the world's largest international rail systems provider, generating sales in the neighborhood of $4.5 billion annually. With the climb of the deutsche mark in 1995, Daimler-Benz was saddled with higher labor costs and serious setbacks as the dollar remained weak. Anointed as the Daimler-Benz group's savior, Mercedes-Benz, which earned $1.3 billion in 1994, was held up as a model to its ailing parent. Always Daimler-Benz's cash cow, Mercedes had just agreed to a

$1.2 billion joint venture with Nanfang South China Motor Corporation to build minivans and engines in China, as well as a second $50 million venture with Yangzhou Motor Coach Manufacturing Company to build touring buses and commercial undercarriages. Nevertheless, the still-troubled DASA and Daimler-Benz Industrie posted huge losses in 1995, in part because of writeoffs, leading the company deeply into the red: a nearly $4 billion loss, the largest in German industrial history.

Fokker proved a major burden for Daimler-Benz, causing Schrempp to cut off funding in January 1996, leading to the aircraft maker's bankruptcy. That same month, Schrempp tackled another headache when he distributed the remnants of the troubled AEG electronics subsidiary into other divisions. The revitalization of the Mercedes-Benz unit continued in 1996 with the introduction of the SLK, a convertible roadster sold for about $40,000 and aimed at younger buyers. That same year, three others models were launched: C-Class and E-Class station wagons and a V-Class minivan. In early 1997 the A-Class made its debut with the launch of the A140, a 141-inch-long compact sporting a small 82-horsepower engine located underneath the floor, and selling for as little as $17,000—expensive for a compact but cheap for a Mercedes.

Spearheading the risky effort to transform Mercedes-Benz into a full-range carmaker aiming to sell 1.2 million cars a year was the unit's chief executive, Helmut Werner. The key to his strategy was to find market niches in which buyers were willing to pay more for a Mercedes-Benz because of its reputation for luxury and quality. His plan appeared to be working as Mercedes' worldwide passenger car sales increased from about 500,000 in 1993 to nearly 650,000 in 1996. In January 1997, however, Werner resigned in a power struggle with Schrempp. Werner's departure was in anticipation of a sweeping reorganization, which Schrempp launched in April 1997. As part of a dismantling of the holding company structure adopted by Daimler-Benz during its 1980s diversification, Mercedes-Benz AG, which had operated since the 1980s as a subsidiary with its own board of directors, was merged into its parent. Daimler-Benz was then organized into several divisions: passenger cars, commercial vehicles, aerospace (DASA), and services (Debis). The new structure also included three units directly managed by Daimler-Benz: rail systems (the ADtranz joint venture), Motoren- und Turbinen-Union (the diesel engine and gas turbine maker), and TEMIC TELEFUNKEN microelectronic (a specialist in automotive electronic systems). The reorganization significantly flattened the management structure, eliminating hundreds of management positions.

By early 1998 Schrempp's restructuring efforts had reduced the company's work force by 63,000 and had seen the divestment of a dozen unprofitable businesses. Then, in November 1998, Daimler-Benz merged with Chrysler Corporation, which, like Daimler, had endured tough times in the 1970s and 1980s and emerged in the mid-1990s as one of the top car companies in the world.

History of Chrysler

The story of the Chrysler Corporation began in 1920, when the company's founder, Walter Percy Chrysler, resigned his position as president of Buick and vice-president of General

Motors (GM) over policy differences with GM's founder, William C. Durant. Chrysler was soon asked by a group of New York bankers to restore the Maxwell Motor Corporation to solvency; in the process, he designed a new Maxwell model, the Chrysler Six. First exhibited in 1924, the car was an immediate success, and before year's end the company sold 32,000 cars at a profit of more than $4 million. In 1925 Chrysler renamed the company Chrysler Corporation.

The enthusiasm with which the Chrysler Six was met encouraged Walter Chrysler to design four additional models for the coming year: the 50, 60, 70, and Imperial 80. These model numbers referred to the maximum velocity that the cars could reach on a level stretch of road. Until that time, Ford's Model T had enjoyed the reputation of the fastest car, achieving a modest 35 mph. Alarmed by Chrysler's technological breakthrough, Ford closed its doors for nine months and emerged with a replacement for the Model T. By 1927, however, the Chrysler Corporation had firmly established itself with a sale of 192,000 cars, becoming the fifth largest company in the industry.

Walter Chrysler realized that to exploit his firm's manufacturing capacities to their fullest, he would have to build his own plants. Since he could not afford the estimated $75 million to achieve this, he approached the New York banking firm of Dillon Read and Company. Dillon Read had bought the Dodge Corporation of Detroit from the widows of the Dodge brothers and was happy to reach an agreement with the now highly regarded Walter Chrysler. In July 1928, Dodge became a division of the Chrysler Corporation; overnight, the size of the company increased fivefold. Soon thereafter, the company introduced the low-priced Plymouth and the DeSoto.

Walter Chrysler, carefully avoiding the dangers associated with rapid growth, discontinued his policy of manufacturing as many parts as possible for his cars. Although he paid more for components than other car makers, he was able to maintain greater flexibility in models and designs. This proved to be extremely important in an age of rapid technological advance. Indeed, Walter Chrysler's farsightedness helped the company to survive the Great Depression far better than most in the industry, and his strategy of spending money on research, no matter how bleak the prospects, may have been responsible for his firm's sound financial standing until well into the 1940s.

Along with the rest of Detroit's motor industry, Chrysler converted to war production during World War II. The manufacture of its Chrysler, Dodge, and Plymouth cars was put on hold while the corporation specialized in defense hardware such as small arms ammunition and submarine nets. But chief among its war products were B-29 bomber engines and anti-aircraft guns and tanks.

The corporation's problems started in the immediate postwar period. The ambition and spirit that drove the company to constant innovation and experimentation in the early days had been lost. The auto market had exhausted fundamental engineering breakthroughs, and American tastes had changed. It seemed that the public was more excited by the sleeker, less traditional, and sometimes less reliable models being produced by Chrysler's rivals. In short, the car industry was becoming a marketer's game, and Chrysler's management was not playing.

In 1950, L.L. Colbert, a lawyer hired by Walter Chrysler in 1929, became the corporation's president. By this time, some major overhauling was necessary, and Colbert hired the management consulting firm of McKinsey and Company. Three reforms were instituted: Chrysler developed international markets for its cars, its management was centralized, and the role of the engineering department was redefined.

Colbert's reforms did little to revive the company's flagging fortunes, and two years later there was another change of management. Lynn Townsend, the new corporate head, proved to be more effective. He consolidated the Chrysler and Plymouth car divisions, closed some unproductive plants, and generally tightened operations; he also reduced the workforce and installed an IBM computer system to replace 700 members of the clerical staff. Most important, he enhanced sales by improving the quality of the Chrysler automobile, introducing the best warranty the industry had yet seen and instituting a more aggressive marketing policy. In less than five years, Townsend had revitalized the corporation.

Success led to expansion: an aerospace division was formed, and Chrysler became the prime contractor for the Saturn booster rocket. By the end of the 1960s, Townsend's international strategy yielded plants in 18 foreign countries. Before the decade was over, however, the domestic market was undergoing major changes. Inflation was taking its toll on U.S. auto manufacturers, imports of foreign vehicles had substantially increased, and the price of crude oil had risen drastically. Chrysler's troubles were compounded by internal factors: the company was more concerned with competing against Ford and GM than in adapting itself to the rapidly changing market; it did not produce enough of its popular compact cars to meet consumer demand; and it had an overstock of larger vehicles.

The corporation reported a $4 million loss in 1969 and was operating at only 68 percent of its capacity; the previous year, it had earned profits of $122 million. Car prices were substantially reduced, but this did little to solve the underlying problems. John J. Riccardo, an accountant, succeeded to the presidency and immediately set about reducing expenses. Salaries, work force, and budget were all cut, and the company experimented with the marketing of foreign-made cars.

Unfortunately, Chrysler seemed incapable of reading the public mood: it narrowed and shortened Dodge and Chrysler models to bring prices down, but sales also tumbled; it continued to make Imperials long after Cadillacs and Lincolns had demonstrated their superiority in the luxury market; and it greeted the 1973–74 Arab oil embargo with a large inventory of gas-guzzlers. Losses in 1974 totaled a massive $52 million, and the next year's deficit was five times that amount.

The company experienced a brief respite in 1976 and 1977. Its trucks were in demand and foreign subsidiaries turned in good results, but domestic car sales remained a problem. Riccardo further consolidated North American operations and increased manufacturing capacity for compact cars. By the time Chrysler became a significant contender in that market, however, American car buyers were showing a distinct preference for the reliable and relatively inexpensive Japanese compacts. The days of U.S. manufacturing hegemony appeared to be over.

A loss of $205 million in 1978 led many industry watchers to wonder if Chrysler's rollercoaster finances could rebound from this latest big dip. The syndicate of banks (with Manufacturers Hanover Trust in the vanguard), which for years had been pouring money into Chrysler, panicked. Incredibly, many of the smaller banks had agreed to virtually unlimited lines of credit on the assumption that the company would never need to use them.

However, complex and highly charged negotiations eventually saved Chrysler from bankruptcy. The federal government agreed to guarantee loans up to $1.5 billion, provided Chrysler raised $2 billion on its own. Politicians could not justify such a massive bailout, however, without changes in Chrysler's management. Riccardo, who had diligently fought against heavy odds, had to go.

It was left to the charismatic Lee Iacocca, who took over in 1978, to preside over Chrysler's comeback. An ex-Ford man with a flair for marketing and public relations, Iacocca took Chrysler's problems to the people, explaining that the company's failure would mean the loss of hundreds of thousands of jobs and could seriously damage the economy of the state of Michigan. Despite popular mythology and the near-adulation of Iacocca in some quarters, many observers suggested that Riccardo was in large part responsible for forging the agreement that gave Chrysler a new lease on life. In any event, the Chrysler Loan Guarantee Bill passed the U.S. Congress on December 27, 1979 and guaranteed $1.2 billion in loans to Chrysler.

During the early 1980s, Iacocca's skills as a superb television salesman were of crucial importance as Chrysler lost nearly $1.8 billion in 1980—the largest loss ever for a U.S. company—and another $475 million in 1981, before returning to the black in 1982. In August 1983 Chrysler was able to pay off the government loan guarantees seven years early, with the government making a $350 million profit on its investment. Chrysler's road to recovery was a difficult one, demanding the closure of several plants and the reduction of the company's workforce. Once restructured, Chrysler scrapped its plans to diversify and divested the Gulfstream Aerospace unit it had purchased five years earlier, selling it to a New York investment firm for $825 million in early 1990. Two other units in the company's Chrysler Technologies subsidiary—Electrospace Systems and Airborne Systems—were slated for divestiture as well, which underscored Iacocca's intent to create a leaner, more sharply focused company. Meanwhile, there were two key developments in the 1980s that helped form the foundation for the 1990s resurgence: the introduction of the minivan in 1984 and the acquisition three years later of American Motors Corporation and its Jeep brand for $1.2 billion.

Reorganized as such, Chrysler entered the 1990s braced for a full recovery, but the economy did not cooperate. The decline in automotive sales during the fourth quarter of 1989—the company's first fourth quarter decline since 1982—portended a more crippling slump to come, as an economic recession gripped businesses of all types, both domestically and abroad. Net income in 1990 slipped to $68 million, then plunged to a $795 million loss the following year, $411 million of which was attributable to losses incurred by the company's automotive operations. Mired in an economic downturn, Chrysler appeared destined for more of the same, rather than headed toward recovery as Iacocca had hoped, but part of the reason for 1991's losses also led to the company's first step toward genuine recovery.

Partly to blame for the $795 million loss in 1991 were the high preproduction and introduction costs associated with Chrysler's new Jeep Grand Cherokee and increased production costs at the company's St. Louis minivan plant. These two types of vehicles—minivans and sport utility vehicles—represented the key to Chrysler's recovery. The popularity of these vehicles, coupled with significant price advantages over Japanese models, fueled Chrysler's resurgence. In 1992, Chrysler turned its $795 million loss the year before into a $723 million gain. It was a signal achievement, accomplished in Iacocca's last year as CEO. Taking over during 1992 was Robert Eaton, who was hired away from GM, where he was head of European operations. Chrysler then went on to enjoy its most successful year ever, with 1994 earnings of $3.7 billion on revenues of $52.2 billion.

The good news at Chrysler continued into the late 1990s, after the company managed to fend off a $22 billion buyout proposed by billionaire investor Kirk Kerkorian in 1995. The long prosperity and low gasoline prices of the middle to late 1990s created a huge demand for large vehicles, and Chrysler was producing hot models in each of the hottest segments: the Dodge Ram pickup truck; the Town & Country minivan; and several sport utility vehicles—the Jeep Grand Cherokee, the Jeep Wrangler, and the Dodge Durango. Questions about the quality of Chrysler products continued to pop up, but the company's share of the U.S. auto market reached as high as 16.7 percent in 1996, the highest level since 1968. In 1996, the year Chrysler moved into new headquarters in Auburn Hills, Michigan, sales reached $61.4 billion.

The Creation and Early Years of DaimlerChrysler

Daimler-Benz Chief Executive Jürgen Schrempp had concluded as early as 1996 that his company's automotive operations needed a partner to compete in the increasingly globalized marketplace. Chrysler's Eaton was drawing the same conclusion in 1997 based on two factors emerging around the same time: the Asian economic crisis, which was cutting into demand, and worldwide excess auto manufacturing capacity, which was looming and would inevitably lead to industry consolidation. With annual global overcapacity as high as 18.2 million vehicles predicted for the early 21st century, it became clearer that Daimler-Benz and Chrysler could survive as merely regional players if they continued to go it alone.

After several months of negotiations, Daimler-Benz and Chrysler reached a merger agreement in May 1998 to create DaimlerChrysler AG in a $37 billion deal. The deal was consummated in November 1998, forming an auto behemoth with total revenues of $130 billion, factories in 34 countries on four continents, and combined annual unit sales of 4.4 million cars and trucks. The two companies fit well together geographically, Daimler strong in Europe and Chrysler in North America, and in terms of product lines, with Daimler's luxurious and high-quality passenger cars and Chrysler's line of low-production-cost trucks, minivans, and sport utility vehicles. Although this was ostensibly a merger of equals—the company set up co-headquarters in Stuttgart and Auburn Hills, naming Eaton and Schrempp co-chairmen—it soon became clear that the Germans were taking over the Americans. DaimlerChrysler was set up as a German firm for tax and accounting purposes, and the early 2000 departures of Thomas Stallkamp, the initial head of DaimlerChrysler's U.S. operations, and Eaton (who was originally slated to remain until as late as November 2001) left Schrempp in clear command of the company.

During 1999 DaimlerChrysler concentrated on squeezing out $1.4 billion in annual cost savings from the integration of procurement and other functional departments. The company organized its automotive businesses into three divisions: Mercedes-Benz Passenger Cars/smart, the Chrysler Group, and Commercial Vehicles. In November 1999 DaimlerChrysler announced that it would begin phasing out the aging Plymouth brand. The Debis services division was merged with Chrysler's services arm to form DaimlerChrysler Services, while DASA was renamed DaimlerChrysler Aerospace. Late in 1999 the company reached an agreement to merge DaimlerChrysler Aerospace with two other European aerospace firms, the French Aerospatiale Matra and the Spanish CASA, to form the European Aeronautic Defence and Space Company (EADS). DaimlerChrysler would hold a 30 percent stake in EADS, which would be the largest aerospace firm in Europe and the third largest in the world.

In early 2000, DaimlerChrysler set the lofty goal of becoming the number one automaker in the world within three years. The company's most pressing needs were to bolster its presence in Asia, where less than 4 percent of the company's overall revenue was generated, and to gain a larger share of the small car market in Europe. Filling both of these bills was DaimlerChrysler's purchase of a 34 percent stake in Mitsubishi Motors Corporation for $2 billion, a deal announced in late March. The company later increased its interest in Mitsubishi when it purchased a 3.3 percent stake from Volvo. In another key early 2000 development, DaimlerChrysler agreed to join with GM and Ford to create an Internet-based global business-to-business supplier exchange named Covisint.

DaimlerChrysler's lofty goal would remain unrealized however, as the company faced a host of challenges. The Chrysler Group division was plagued by high costs and weak sales which ultimately cost James P. Holden his CEO position. Buoyed by its strong sales in the mid-1990s, Chrysler had spent heavily on product development in the late 1990s and bolstered its work force while costs were skyrocketing. By the second half of 2000 Chrysler lost $1.8 billion while spending over $5 billion. Dieter Zetsche was tapped to reorganize the faltering U.S. division. He launched a major restructuring effort in February 2001 that included cutting $2 billion in costs, making additional cuts in supplier costs, slashing 20 percent of its workforce, and making changes to Chrysler's product line that included the elimination of the Jeep Cherokee (the Grand Cherokee remained in the product line) and the launch of the Jeep Liberty.

At the same time, global economies began to weaken in the aftermath of the September 11, 2001, terrorist attacks. To entice customers, car makers began offering buyer incentives that began to wreak havoc on profits. Industry analysts began to speculate that the 1998 merger may have been a mistake— Schrempp's proclamation that the deal would create the most

profitable car maker in world had indeed fallen short. In fact, the company's market capitalization was $38 billion in September 2003. Before the union Daimler's market cap had been $47 billion.

Meanwhile, the company's Mercedes division plugged along launching the E-Class sedan, the SLK roadster, and the Maybach luxury vehicle. In 2003, Chrysler launched the Crossfire, a roadster developed with Mercedes components, and the Pacifica, a SUV/minivan. It also began to heavily market its powerful Hemi engine, which could be purchased for the Dodge Ram pickup and its passenger cars. In early 2004, Chrysler's 300C sedan and the Dodge Magnum sports wagon made their debut.

Competition remained fierce in the auto industry prompting DaimlerChrysler to make several changes in its strategy. In December 2003, the company sold its MTU Aero Engines business. That year the firm acquired a 43 percent stake in Mitsubishi Fuso Truck and Bus Corporation hoping to cash in on Asia's growing truck market. Perhaps its most drastic move, however, came in April 2004 when DaimlerChrysler's supervisory board voted against providing funds to bailout Mitsubishi Motors, which by now was struggling under losses and a huge debt load. Mitsubishi played a crucial role in Schrempp's Asian expansion strategy and it developed the platforms for Chrysler's compact and midsize cars. The failure to provide funds put a strain on the business relationship between the two and threatened to result in huge problems for Chrysler, which had cut back on engineering capacity as it relied on Mitsubishi to develop its small and mid-sized cars.

At the same time, DaimlerChrysler moved ahead in the Chinese market—without Mitsubishi and without another partner, Hyundai. To bolster is presence in the region, DaimlerChrysler restructured its joint venture with Beijing Automotive Industry Holding Co. Ltd. and set plans in motion to tie up with Chinese Fujian Motor Industry Group and the Taiwanese China Motor Corporation to launch several cars in the Chinese market by 2005. Rumors circulated that DaimlerChrysler's relationship with Hyundai was faltering as a result, and in 2004 the company signaled that it would sell its interest in the South Korean automaker.

By 2004, Schrempp's DaimlerChrysler was a far cry from what the 1998 merger promised to deliver. The company's financial record was lackluster, bogged down by Chrysler's $637 million loss in 2003. DaimlerChrysler remained the world's number three car maker, leaving the 2000 goal—to become the number one auto company in the world— unfulfilled. Whether the merger would provide the hoped-for results remained to be seen.

Principal Subsidiaries

DaimlerChrysler Motors Company LLC (United States); Mercedes-Benz U.S. International Inc. (United States); smart GmbH; DaimlerChrysler South Africa Pty. Ltd.; DaimlerChrysler Canada Inc.; DaimlerChrysler de Mexico S.A. de C.V.; EvoBus GmbH; Mercedes-Benz Espana S.A. (Spain); Detroit Diesel Corporation (United States); Freightliner LLC (United States); Mercedes-Benz Mexico S.A. de C.V.; DaimlerChrysler do Brasil Ltda. (Brazil); DaimlerChrysler Argentina S.A.; P.T.

DaimlerChrysler Indonesia (95%); MTU Friedrichshafen GmbH (88.4%); Mitsubishi Fuso Truck and Bus Corporation (Japan; 43%); Mercedes-Benz USA LLC; DaimlerChrysler France S.A.S.; DaimlerChrysler Belgium Luxembourg S.A.; DaimlerChrysler Nederland B.V. (Netherlands); DaimlerChrysler UK Ltd.; DaimlerChrysler Italia S.p.A. (Italy); Daimler-Chrysler Schweiz AG (Switzerland); DaimlerChrysler Japan Co. Ltd.; DaimlerChrysler Australia/Pacific Pty. Ltd.; Daimler-Chrysler Bank AG; DaimlerChrysler Services Leasing GmbH; DaimlerChrysler Services North America LLC (United States); debis Financial Services Inc. (United States); European Aeronautic Defence and Space Company (EADS) N.V. (Netherlands; 33%); Mitsubishi Motors Corporation (Japan; 37%); Hyundai Motor Co. (Korea; 10.5%).

Principal Divisions

Mercedes Car Group; Chrysler Group; Commercial Vehicles; Services; Other Activities.

Principal Competitors

Ford Motor Company; General Motors Corporation; Toyota Motor Corporation; Volkswagen AG.

Further Reading

Abodaher, David, *Iacocca,* New York: Macmillan, 1982.

"Backbiting at Daimler," *Business Week,* August 7, 1995, p. 45.

Ball, Jeffrey, and Scott Miller, "DaimlerChrysler Aims to Be No. 1 Auto Maker," *Wall Street Journal,* January 14, 2000, pp. A2, A6.

Breer, Carl, *The Birth of Chrysler Corporation and Its Engineering Legacy,* Warrendale, Penn.: Society of Automotive Engineers, 1995.

"Can Motown Get Out of This Funk?," *Business Week,* June 23, 2003.

"Daimler's Designated Driver," *Business Week,* November 27, 2000.

Gardner, Greg, "Chrysler: The Cat with Nine Lives," *Ward's Auto World,* May 1996, p. 67.

——, "The Cloud Over Chrysler," *Ward's Auto World,* June 1996, pp. 25–28.

"Gentlemen, Start Your Engines," *Fortune,* June 8, 1998, pp. 138 + .

Gordon, Maynard M., *The Iacocca Management Technique,* New York: Dodd Mead, 1985.

Gregor, Neil, *Daimler-Benz in the Third Reich,* New Haven, Conn.: Yale University Press, 1998.

Iacocca, Lee, with William Novak, *Iacocca: An Autobiography,* New York: Bantam, 1984.

Kimes, Beverly Rae, *The Star and the Laurel: The Centennial History of Daimler, Mercedes, and Benz, 1886–1986,* Montvale, N.J.: Mercedes Benz of North America, 1986.

Langworth, Richard M., and Jan P. Norbye, *The Complete History of Chrysler Corporation, 1924–1985,* New York: Beekman House, 1985.

Moritz, Michael, and Barrett Seaman, *Going for Broke: The Chrysler Story, Garden City,* N.Y.: Doubleday, 1981.

Palmer, Jay, "Shake-Up Artist: Daimler-Benz Chairman Jurgen Schrempp Has Knocked the Dust Off Mercedes," *Barron's,* March 23, 1998.

Reed, Stanley, "Backbiting at Daimler," *Business Week,* August 7, 1995, p. 45.

Reich, Robert B., and John D. Donahue, *New Deals: The Chrysler Revival and the American System,* New York: Times Books, 1985.

"A Shaky Automotive Ménage à Trois; Now, Daimler Is Backing Away from Mitsubishi," *Business Week,* May 10, 2004.

"Stalled: Was the Daimler-Chrysler Merger a Mistake?," *Business Week,* September 29, 2003.

Taylor, Alex III, "Can the Germans Rescue Chrysler?," *Fortune,* April 30, 2001.

——, "For Schrempp, It Was a Cruel April," *Fortune,* May 17, 2004.

——, "The Germans Take Charge," *Fortune,* January 11, 1999, pp. 92–94, 96.

——, "Iacocca's Last Stand at Chrysler," *Fortune,* April 20, 1992, p. 63.

Templeman, John, "The New Mercedes," *Business Week,* August 26, 1996, pp. 34 + .

——, "Upheaval at Daimler," *Business Week,* February 5, 1996, pp. 14 + .

Vlasic, Bill, et al., "The First Global Car Colossus," *Business Week,* May 18, 1998, pp. 40 + .

Washington, Frank S., "Merger? What Merger?," *Ward's Auto World,* November 1999, pp. 66–67.

Zellner, Wendy, "Chrysler's Next Generation: An Heir Apparent and New, Upscale Cars," *Business Week,* December 19, 1998, p. 52.

—updates: Taryn Benbow Pfalzgraf,
David E. Salamie, Jeffrey L. Covell, and
Christina M. Stansell

Diamond of California

1050 South Diamond Street
Stockton, California 95205-1727
U.S.A.
Telephone: (209) 467-6000
Fax: (209) 461-7309
Web site: http://www.diamondwalnut.com

Cooperative
Incorporated: 1980
Employees: 1,200
Sales: $300.2 million (2003)
NAIC: 115114 Postharvest Crop Activities (Except Cotton Ginning)

Diamond of California is one of California's largest grower cooperatives and the leading supplier of in-shell and culinary walnuts. Its other products include pecans, almonds, hazelnuts, Brazil nuts, Spanish peanuts, macadamia nuts, and pine nuts. Formed in 1912 by a handful of walnut farmers, Diamond was an amalgamation of five agricultural cooperatives—Diamond Walnut Growers, Sun-Maid Growers of California, Sunsweet Growers, Valley Fig Growers, and Hazelnut Growers of Oregon—who pooled their distribution and marketing resources. The group split in 2000, and Diamond of California began operating on its own.

History of Diamond Walnut and Sunsweet

Much of Diamond's history involves the coming together of individual growers to form cooperatives, which in turn formed larger cooperatives. The first of the cooperative members to confederate were Diamond Walnut and Sunsweet, both of which were already over 50 years old when they joined forces in 1974.

Diamond Walnut was organized in 1912 by citrus and walnut grower Charles Teague, who had also been a founder of another highly successful agricultural cooperative, Sunkist Growers. The company was originally known as the California Walnut Growers Association (CWGA) and sought to stabilize

walnut prices. Success came early to CWGA, aided somewhat by the outbreak of World War I, which eliminated competition from imported French walnuts. In 1918, CWGA became the first producer of walnuts to pack shelled nutmeats in airtight metal cans, and, in 1925, it began using its trademark diamond-shaped logo, stamping it on the shell of every walnut that it sold.

The outbreak of World War II posed a threat to CWGA by cutting it off from its export markets, but domestic demand helped take up the slack. The federal government purchased 1.5 million pounds of walnuts as part of its Lend-Lease program; in addition, the military used the protein-rich nutmeats as a dietary substitute to compensate for the general scarcity of meat. The supply of walnuts quickly overtook demand after the end of the war, and this oversupply required more aggressive marketing in the postwar period. In 1956, CWGA changed its name to Diamond Walnut Growers to associate itself more closely with its trademark.

Sunsweet traces its history back to 1917, when some California fruit growers formed a cooperative named California Prune and Apricot Growers in an effort to raise and stabilize what had been disastrously low prices for their commodities. Immediately, the cooperative began nationwide advertising and marketing under the brand name Sunsweet. Although the company lost members during the boom times of the 1920s, as general confidence in market conditions prompted a desire for independence, it regained many members during the Great Depression when companies sought safety in numbers. In 1934, the cooperative joined with fruit juice company Duffy-Mott to produce and market Sunsweet prune juice.

Already smarting from the worldwide depression, California Prune and Apricot took another heavy blow in 1933 when the German government banned imported fruit. Exports to Germany had accounted for as much as half of California's annual prune sales since before World War I. The company sought to improve sales with improved packaging and high profile domestic advertising campaigns, and, once the United States entered World War II, the demand for dried fruit products rose again. However, as with its future associates in the walnut industry, chronic oversupply and depressed commodity prices burdened California Prune and Apricot in the postwar period.

1922, CARC changed its name to Sun-Maid Growers to link itself more explicitly with its famous logo.

Shortly thereafter, however, the Sun-Maid cooperative declared bankruptcy and was nearly dissolved. It recovered only to face financial disaster again during the depths of the Great Depression. After World War II, when both the federal and California governments acted to stabilize the raisin market, Sun-Maid once again became a steady and profitable organization. Despite its troubles, the Sun-Maid remained a popular trademark with consumers and perhaps the most famous logo in the dried fruit industry.

Sun-Maid's alliance with Diamond/Sunsweet and Valley Fig Growers produced a company with nearly $500 million in annual sales, and revenues grew sharply in the years immediately following the formation of Sun-Diamond despite a national recession and general crop oversupply. The new company owed much of its success to energetic marketing; under Frank Light's direction, Sun-Diamond significantly increased its annual advertising budget to $14 million. It also put considerable emphasis on developing new products, such as raisin bread and English muffins sold under the Sun-Maid name, and new applications for waste parts, such as distilling substandard raisins and prune pits into alcohol or selling them as cattle feed.

Sun-Diamond continued to expand, adding a relatively small cooperative, Hazelnut Growers of Oregon, to its ranks in 1984. It had also become a Fortune 500 company early in the decade. At the same time, however, sales began to slow, from $522 million in 1983 to $487 million in 1985, and low commodity prices continued to plague the company. Sun-Diamond also fell victim to international trade battles, as protective and retaliatory tariffs imposed by the European community cut into its export business.

Adding to these difficulties, Sun-Diamond found itself in a financial dilemma in 1985, when internal audits discovered a series of accounting errors worth $43 million. In August of that year, an accounting review found that Diamond Walnut had over-reported its profits for fiscal 1985 by $4.7 million, distributing more money to its member growers than it should have. Further review revealed that an inventory of unfinished walnuts sitting in Diamond Walnut's storage sheds had been overvalued by $11 million. Finally, in November, Sun-Maid discovered that it had over-reported its pool proceeds by $27.3 million and had paid its members accordingly.

The loss of members' equity that followed these errors and their discovery hit Sun-Maid particularly hard. The venerable raisin cooperative suffered a mass defection, as 29 percent of its member growers chose not to renew their membership contracts after the financial disclosures. These growers accounted for about one-third of Sun-Maid's crop, forcing the company to buy processed raisins from independent growers to make up for the shortfall. Diamond Walnut suffered far less—only 50 of its 2,700 growers defected—in part because fewer of its members had their contracts up for renewal but also because daunting conditions in the walnut market made it risky to abandon the economies of scale that a large cooperative offered.

Frank Light's tenure ended late in 1985, and the company entered a period of restructuring as the cooperatives evaluated

Company Perspectives:

The company is owned by approximately 1,900 family farmers from California who take great pride in the nuts they grow. Since 1912, they have led the industry in production and quality standards. This attention to detail shines through in every package that bears the Diamond symbol—signifying the best-tasting and highest-quality products grown anywhere. From our growers' orchards to your table, Diamond brings flavor and nutrition to every bite!

As a response, the company increased its membership in 1959 and in 1960 changed its name to Sunsweet Growers.

By the mid-1970s, both Diamond Walnut and Sunsweet had become preeminent in their respective domains. Diamond Walnut processed and marketed just over half of California's walnut crop, while Sunsweet handled about one third of the state's prune crop. Both companies felt that combined marketing would be of further benefit, and in 1974 they banded together to form Diamond/Sunsweet. The two companies did not merge assets and liabilities but did combine their marketing operations. Diamond Walnut president and general manager A.L. Buffington became CEO of the separate cooperatives, and headquarters were established in Stockton, California.

Sun-Maid Growers Joins Diamond and Sunsweet in 1980

Such combinations between agricultural cooperatives were seen as necessary in a time of increasing competition from overseas, as well as from other large cooperatives in the United States, and Diamond/Sunsweet would soon show that it felt even further growth would be necessary for it to maintain its competitive edge. Seeking an alliance that would strengthen the marketing punch of its famous Sun-Maid raisins, Sun-Maid Growers of California began courting Diamond/Sunsweet. In 1980, its sales, distribution, and administrative functions were combined with those of Diamond and Sunsweet. Sun-Maid president Frank Light became president and CEO of Sun-Diamond Growers of California. Valley Fig Growers, a cooperative of California fig growers, also joined the alliance at this time. As with the Diamond/Sunsweet alliance, the member companies pooled their marketing operations but retained autonomy over their own assets and liabilities, although the agreement substantially centralized executive power by making Light CEO of all four member cooperatives, as well as of the new concern.

Sun-Maid had a long history not unlike that of its new allies. It was formed in 1912 under the name California Associated Raisin Company (CARC) to pool advertising resources and attempt to bring price stability to a market that had suffered from highly variable commodity prices. CARC debuted with a spectacular marketing gimmick, sending a train pulling sixty raisin-laden freight cars to Chicago, with each car displaying a banner with the slogan, "Raisins Grown by 6,000 California Growers." In 1915, the company introduced its longtime brand name and also its trademark, a smiling young woman wearing a red bonnet and backlit by a yellow sunburst, the Sun-Maid. In

Key Dates:

1912: The California Walnut Growers Association (CWGA) is organized by Charles Teague.
1917: California Prune and Apricot Growers is formed as a cooperative.
1925: CWGA begins using its trademark diamond-shaped logo.
1956: CWGA changes its name to Diamond Walnut Growers.
1960: California Prune changes its name to Sunsweet Growers.
1974: Diamond Walnut and Sunsweet band together to form Diamond/Sunsweet.
1980: Sun-Maid Growers of California joins the company and forms Sun-Diamond Growers of California.
2000: Diamond of California begins operations independent of Sun-Maid.

their needs and considered revised designs for the agency agreement that defined their relationship. By 1987, the process was complete and a leaner, stronger Sun-Diamond emerged. This was the Sun-Diamond that existed throughout the remainder of the 1980s and early 1990s under the leadership of its president, Larry Busboom, as a service organization rather than a management organization. Greater autonomy was returned to the cooperatives, and each had its own marketing team. Sun-Diamond provided a consolidated sales and distribution network for the cooperatives' consumer product line and earned a position of prominence in the agricultural commodity field. It showed healthy sales growth in the early 1990s, topping $600 million in both 1991 and 1992.

In addition, the efficacy of the concept behind Sun-Diamond was proven. The collective safety and the economies of scale that it created seem essential in an industry in which variable commodity prices, competition from overseas and large domestic concerns, and the vagaries of international trade could all have considerable impact on one's ability to do business. Perhaps even more important, the impact of consolidated representation for the leading brands in the business was a powerful tool for success.

Changes in the 1990s and Beyond

Distinct challenges in the 1990s would eventually bring about major changes for Sun-Diamond. During 1991, workers at Diamond Walnut walked out in protest and launched a boycott of the company. They claimed that during the mid-1980s they had accepted a 30 to 40 percent pay cut in an attempt to remedy the company's faltering financial record. When Diamond returned to profitability in 1991, its workers were not rewarded—instead the company asked for additional concessions from union representatives. As such, the employees initiated a very public boycott of Diamond Walnuts. By 1994, Fannie May and Fannie Farmer Candies, Godiva Chocolates, Dreyers Ice Cream, Nabisco, and Quaker Oats refused to buy from Diamond Walnuts.

Sun-Diamond took another blow in 1996 when it was indicted for giving illegal gifts to U.S. Agriculture Secretary Mike Espy. The company was convicted in September of that year and faced a ban that would prohibit Sun-Diamond and its affiliates from selling products to the military, federal prisons, and school lunch programs for three years. Espy was eventually acquitted, however, and the U.S. Circuit Court of Appeals for the District of Columbia reversed its conviction against Sun-Diamond in 1999.

By the time Michael Mendes took over as CEO and president in 1997, Sun-Diamond was in need of a face lift. Under his leadership, the company began to make significant changes. In 1998, it broadened its product line and began selling a full line of culinary and in-shell nuts. In 1999, Diamond Nut Company was formed to oversee the retail of mixed in-the-shell nuts. Overall, the company's product line grew from 30 items in 1997 to over 55 by 2000.

Under the leadership of Mendes, Diamond of California gained its independence from Sun Growers in 2000. The marketing partnership born in 1980 was dissolved in August of that year, leaving Diamond on its own. A March 2000 *Modesto Bee* article claimed, "With its new sales and marketing structure, Diamond is more focused on retail sales and can move more quickly as opportunities arise." Indeed, Mendes's strategies appeared to be paying off as both revenues and profits climbed.

As part of its split from Sun Growers, Diamond acquired Berner Nut Company in 2000. It also began bolstering its international business, adding Diamond Europe GmbH and Diamond of California UK Ltd. to its arsenal. In 2002, it launched a glazed snack nut line. By 2003, Diamond's nut sales had increased by 35 percent since 1998. According to the company, one in every two walnuts sold in the U.S. was a Diamond of California walnut.

In early 2004, Emerald of California was introduced as a new snack line that included different flavored almonds, walnuts, peanuts, and cashews. The company doubled its advertising budget to promote the new products, hoping to cash in on the $27 billion snack market. New product development and brand expansion promised to be at the forefront of the company's strategy in the years to come. With a longstanding history of success behind it, Diamond appeared to be well positioned for continued growth well into the future.

Principal Subsidiaries

Diamond Nut Company; Diamond Europe GmbH (Germany); Diamond of California UK Ltd.

Principal Competitors

Blue Diamond Growers; Dole Food Company Inc.; Tejon Ranch Company.

Further Reading

Estrada, Richard T., "California Walnut Harvestor Tries New Approach to Reach Broader Market," *Modesto Bee*, April 18, 2000.

Fujii, Reed, "Stockton, Calif.-Based Walnut Processor Expects Acquisition to Raise Revenues," *Record*, September 13, 2000.

Greenberger, Robert S., "Top Court Rules for Sun-Diamond over Smaltz," *Wall Street Journal*, April 28, 1999.

Ingersoll, Bruce, "Sun-Diamond Growers Is Indicted in Case Involving Gifts to Espy," *Wall Street Journal*, June 14, 1996, p. B2.

Keppel, Bruce, "Sun-Diamond Co-op: Harvest of Discontent," *Los Angeles Times*, May 11, 1986.

Moran, Tim, "Stockton, Calif.-Based Walnut Cooperative Posts Increased Revenues," *Modesto Bee*, March 9, 2000.

Morrill, David, "Diamond Expanding Snacks Line," *Oakland Tribune*, January 20, 2004.

Reyes, Sonia, "Diamond Shells Out $10M to Uproot Rival Planters," *Brandweek*, April 19, 2004.

"Stockton, Calif.-Based Walnut Grower Changes Name, Focus," *Sacramento Bee*, April 19, 2000.

"U.S. Seeks to Cut Off Fruit Growers' Co-Op Over Gifts to Espy," *Wall Street Journal*, December 16, 1996, p. B10.

"What Makes Sun-Diamond Grow," *Business Week*, August 9, 1982.

—Douglas Sun
—update: Christina M. Stansell

Dick Corporation

1900 State Route 51
Large, Pennsylvania 15025
U.S.A.
Telephone: (412) 384-1000
Fax: (412) 384-1150

Private Company
Founded: 1922
Employees: 3,500
Sales: $1.1 billion (2002)
NAIC: 236220 Commercial and Institutional Building
Construction.

Dick Corporation, based outside of Pittsburgh, Pennsylvania, is a major contractor, construction manager, and design builder, active throughout the United States as well as the Caribbean and the Pacific Rim. Dick's business is organized under four divisions—General Contracting, Building, Heavy/Industrial, Construction Management—and includes two subsidiaries, Dick Corporation of Puerto Rico and Dick Pacific. The company is owned and by the third generation of the Dick family. Brothers David E. Dick and Douglas P. Dick serve as co-chairmen.

1920s Origins

The founder of Dick Corporation, Noble J. Dick, was born in 1899 in Homer City, a coal town 45 miles east of Pittsburgh. His father did some farming and coal mining but mostly supported his family through construction work. After dropping out of high school Dick left home at the age of 17 and moved to Clariton, Pennsylvania, where he married two years later and found work as a laborer. He worked for a short time at a U.S. Steel mill and a Westinghouse manufacturing plant before he realized that he wanted to work for himself. Using the building skills he learned from his father, Dick soon landed his first job: building a neighbor's garage for less than $100. He briefly formed a construction business with his brother-in-law to build homes and do renovations, then in 1922 went solo again, launching Dick Corporation.

As Noble Dick grew his construction business, he also developed a flamboyant persona. He was partial to wearing different shades of green suits and a Stetson hat. At the same time, Dick was also hard working and driven to succeed, character traits that appeared in later generations of his family, who ultimately grew the company into a $1 billion concern. In addition to construction, Dick also ran a Pittsburgh-area bus line for 20 years and helped start Three Rivers Bank.

In 1942, Noble's son Dorsey went to work for his father. His brother Perry would soon follow suit. In 1970, Noble began to cut back on his involvement in the day-to-day activities of the construction business, gradually turning over control to his sons. It was at this stage that Dick Corporation began to grow beyond its regional base to become a national construction company, a move very much borne out of necessity. The company had evolved beyond home building to school construction and took on large projects constructing Pittsburgh steel mills in the 1960s and early 1970s. In 1971, 80 percent of Dick Corporation's business came from building steel mills.

With the decline of the steel industry in the 1970s, however, Dick Corporation faced a turning point in its history. It could either contract or expand. The decision was made to expand, meaning that Dick Corporation had to become a national player. The most promising opportunity was working for the United States Postal Service, which was launching a program to build bulk-mail facilities across the country. The Dick family believed that because the work was repetitive the company would be able to gain valuable experience and procedures for handling this type of major project. Moreover, it would lend a national scope to the company's resume. In the mid-1970s, Dick Corporation was successful in winning contracts from the U.S. Corps of Engineers to build five bulk mail facilities in Pittsburgh, Atlanta, Denver, Memphis, and Jacksonville, Florida. Dick Corporation was then able to leverage this experience in order to win other contracts around the country, working for both the public and private sectors and different market segments.

The power industry, which was enjoying significant growth at the time, became an important source of new contracts. Dick Corp was able to transfer the expertise it gained from pouring the stiff concrete foundations that were part of the construction of large steel mills to the similar needs of power plants. Other important projects during this period included a power plant in Florida, an amusement park, the Federal Express headquarters in Memphis, and a U.S. Steel pipe mill in Texas. Although Dick Corporation was increasingly looking beyond the Pittsburgh area for important new jobs, it continued to be involved in some major projects at home, including a library at the University of Pittsburgh, Mellon Arena, the Beaver Valley Nuclear Power Station, and the Pittsburgh International Airport.

Third Generation Joins Firm in 1970s

A third generation of the Dick family went to work for the construction company in the 1970s. Dorsey's son David joined in 1971 after earning a business degree from Robert Morris College. He was followed in 1973 by his brother Douglas, who earned a business degree from Nathaniel Hawthorne College. David and Douglas would go on to lead the company; their brother Michael also came into the business. He worked as a bricklayer for 15 years and eventually became the firm's lead estimator before dying of cancer at the age of 54 in 2001. David and Douglas Dick forged a strong working relationship after witnessing the falling out of their father and uncle during the 1970s. David Dick told the *Pittsburgh Business Times* in a 2002 interview, "We watched two brothers try and destroy each other." In 1979, Dorsey became chairman of the family business, and Perry, at the age of 61, left to start his own regional construction company, P.J. Dick Inc. He would pass away ten years later.

Noble Dick died in 1983, leaving the company he founded in the hands of Dorsey, who maintained he was simply the caretaker of what his father had started. He was far more reserved than his father but proved just as effective in leading the company. He established the marketing plan that helped take Dick Corporation into different markets, and in the mid-1980s he reorganized the company along horizontal rather than vertical lines. Three business units serving as three separate profit centers were established to serve specific markets. Later in the 1980s, Dick Corporation began offering construction management services. Starting in the early 1980s, Dorsey began grooming David and Douglas to succeed him at the helm of Dick Corporation. That day came in 1992 when Dorsey Dick died.

David and Douglas Dick, mindful of the rupture between their father and uncle, took care to work closely together. Nearly every day, they took time to eat lunch together to discuss business. They also delineated their roles, with David, who held the title of CEO, handling operational duties and Douglas taking responsibly for legal and financial matters. Nevertheless, there was a good deal of overlap in their duties. They took over Dick Corporation at a time when the construction business was flat. Although annual revenues at this point were in the $350 million

range, the brothers worked out a strategic plan to grow Dick Corporation into a $1 billion company. To achieve this goal, the firm had to expand within the United States as well as overseas. Over the next few years, it landed major contracts building casinos in Las Vegas and took on construction projects in Puerto Rico and elsewhere in the Caribbean. In 1999, Dick Corporation, which had increased annual revenues to $600 million, revised its structure to help the company reach the $1 billion mark. An international division was formed with the hope of one day doing work in Central and South America and the Middle East. Dick Corporation was also very much attracted to the quickly emerging market in India. Domestically, Dick Corporation split its operation into East and West divisions. In looking to use its record in Las Vegas as a springboard for new work in the western United States, it was felt that the company needed an office located closer to those projects. In addition, the company's bridge and highway and power and industrial units were combined into a new Heavy/Industrial Division.

Organizational Changes in the 1990s

Although organizational changes played a role in taking Dick Corporation past $1 billion in revenues, a more important factor was the 1999 acquisition of Honolulu-based Fletcher Pacific Construction Co. Ltd., the largest construction firm in Hawaii. Fletcher was founded in 1939 and was owned by a New Zealand parent company, Fletcher Challenge Ltd., which now wanted to consolidate its construction, pulp, and forestry businesses in the New Zealand markets. Fletcher Pacific generated some $260 million in annual revenues and maintained operations in Guam and Saipan. Major clients included the state of Hawaii, the Department of the Navy, The Federal Bureau of Prisons, Hyatt Corp., Marriott International, Toyota Motors, Sears Roebuck & Co., First Hawaiian Bank, Neiman Marcus, Wal-Mart, and Nike. Fletcher Pacific was not without its share of suitors, with 19 companies expressing an interest, but Dick Corporation had an inside track because the two companies had worked well together on several joint ventures in Hawaii. They also shared a similar corporate culture as well as the same software and comparable training programs. Not only did the addition of Fletcher, which was renamed Dick Pacific, add a significant amount of revenues to Dick Corporation, it served as a base for further expansion further into the Pacific Rim. It also added some flexibility in the use of Dick Corporation's labor, with Pacific Dick's personnel able to move from Hawaii to the West Coast depending on the company's needs at a given time. Former Fletcher Pacific CEO Denny Watts was retained to run the unit and given a great deal of autonomy. Once a month, he flew to Pittsburgh to take part in a management meeting.

Dick Corporation enjoyed tremendous growth in the final years of the 1990s and into the new century. It cracked the $1 billion mark ahead of schedule and outgrew its suburban headquarters. In 2001, the company began construction on a new 90,000-square-foot mixed-use facility located along the Monongahela River in Homestead, but several events took place that hurt the company on several levels. First, the company's reputation for safety was tarnished when in February 2001 an employee was killed and two others injured by a steel truss that collapsed during the construction of the David L. Lawrence Convention Center in Pittsburgh. A subsequent in-

> **Key Dates:**
>
> **1922:** Noble J. Dick founds the company.
> **1979:** Dorsey Dick is named chairman.
> **1983:** Noble Dick dies.
> **1992:** Dorsey Dick dies, leaving sons David and Douglas in charge.
> **2002:** The first non-family member is named CEO.

vestigation of the U.S. Occupational Safety and Health Administration cited Dick Corporation and the firm that fabricated the truss for safety violations, fining each $19,000. The amount was later reduced to $12,000. The coroner of Allegheny County, in the meantime, recommended that Dick Corporation face involuntary manslaughter charges, a matter which hung over the company for more than year until the district attorney's office finally declined to press charges against corporate officials, maintaining that the matter belonged in civil rather than criminal court.

Challenges in the 2000s

During this time, Dick also faced serious fiscal problems. A natural down cycle in the construction industry was exacerbated by a recession that would only grow worse with the terrorist attacks of September 11, 2001. Dick Corporation also found itself a victim of the Enron scandal, which erupted as Dick Corporation was building a $400 million power plant project near Joliet, Illinois, for an Enron subsidiary, Nepco. When Nepco went bankrupt in June 2002, Dick Corporation had to go to court in an attempt to recover some of the $50 million for work performed for the project's owner, NRG Energy Inc., a Minnesota-based power company that was having troubles of its own and was on the verge of bankruptcy.

Dick Corporation soon found itself in the unfamiliar position of being late in paying its bills and the subject of rumors which claimed that the firm was on the verge of declaring bankruptcy and about to initiate large-scale layoffs. The Dick brothers decided that it was time to bring in someone to take charge of the company and make the changes necessary to keep the business viable. Rather than looking to executives who had dedicated their careers to Dick Corporation, they named Pacific Dick's Denny Watts as the first non-family member to head the company. Not only had Watts performed well at Pacific Dick, he was enough of an outsider to make some difficult but necessary decisions in restructuring the company. There were modest layoffs, 15 in August 2002 and another 34 in October, which Watts attributed to a restructuring effort that streamlined operations and reduced headcount. He also look for ways to cut overhead, which had grown so high that the company had difficulty making money. Thus, after the construction of Dick Corporation's new $10 million headquarters in Homestead was completed, the building was not occupied but instead put up for sale. Watts' larger goal was to move away from risky ventures, such as design work for the power plant industry and international projects, and to solicit more military and government

work on the East Coast, perhaps connected to Homeland Security.

In January 2003, Watts brought in more outside help to run Dick Corporation, hiring Stephen D'Angelo to serve as chief administration and restructuring officer. A former CFO at Bekins Van Lines, D'Angelo was a principal at Impact Consulting Group, a specialist in financial turnaround. Company spokesperson Janet Love denied that D'Angelo was brought in to ready the company for sale, maintaining, rather, that he would be "looking for efficiencies in process implementation." Within a matter of weeks, two senior Dick Corporation executives resigned and four other senior executives, including Janet Love, were laid off. The company also announced that it was reducing the number of divisions from eight to six but had no intention of exiting or selling off any of those businesses, especially the highway unit (although it did close the Chicago office).

In 2003, Watts was able to secure a new line of credit, hoping that this would sustain Dick Corporation in the near term and allow it to tackle a $1.5 billion backlog of work. Then, unexpectedly, in July 2003, Watts resigned to "pursue other interests and opportunities outside the region." He agreed to stay on for three months under a consulting arrangement. D'Angelo remained with the company and was named president. Over the next several months Dick Corporation found a buyer for its unoccupied headquarters and in 2004 sent out query letters to highway contractors to determine if there were any interested buyers for its highway division. Beyond these moves, the company's future remained uncertain.

Principal Subsidiaries

Dick Corporation of Puerto Rico; Dick Pacific.

Principal Divisions

General Contracting; Building; Heavy/Industrial; Construction Management.

Principal Competitors

Jacobs Engineering Group Inc.; Peter Kiewit Sons', Inc.; The Turner Corporation.

Further Reading

Elliott, Suzanne, "Construction Work Spans Three Generations," *Pittsburgh Business Times*, July 2, 2002, p. 21.
——, "New CEO Readies Strategy for Beleaguered Dick Corp.," *Pittsburgh Business Times*, September 6, 2002, p. 1.
——, "Banking On It," *Pittsburgh Business Times*, May 2, 2003, p. 1.
Fisher, David W., "Flying with Eagles," *SMPS Marketer*, February 2000, p. 4.
Fitzpatrick, Dan, "Baptism by Fire," *Pittsburgh Post-Gazette*, September 15, 2002, p. E2.
Zapinksi, Ken, "Master Builder," *Pittsburgh Post-Gazette*, October 19, 1997, p. E5.

—Ed Dinger

Elektra Entertainment Group

75 Rockefeller Plaza
New York, New York 10019-7284
U.S.A.
Telephone: (212) 707-3000
Fax: (212) 956-7284

Division of Atlantic Records Group
Founded: 1950
Sales: $65 million (1998)
Employees: 110
NAIC: 541990 All Other Professional, Scientific and
  Technical Services

Elektra Entertainment Group is a division of Atlantic Records Group, a business unit of Warner Music Group, the largest privately held music company in the world. Both maintain their headquarters at 75 Rockefeller Plaza in New York City. Elektra is comprised of a number of labels, including Asylum, EastWest, and the flagship Elektra imprint. Elektra has recorded such legendary artists as the Doors, the Eagles, Joni Mitchell, Linda Ronstadt, and Jackson Browne. In more recent years, Elektra's roster of artists has included Metallica, Tracy Chapman, Phish, and Bjork.

Origins in the Postwar Era

The man behind the creation of the independent Elektra record label that grew into today's Elektra Entertainment Group was Jac Holzman. He was born in 1931, the eldest son of a well-to-do family residing in New York City's Upper East Side. His father, a Harvard Medical School graduate, was a highly successful doctor who, according to his son, was domineering and quick to dismiss him as a failure. Holzman ran away from home a number of times, and at the age of 12 actually made it to Trenton, New Jersey, before he was found in a hotel and brought back to the family's Manhattan apartment, where the one saving grace was top-of-the-line phonograph equipment. To escape his unhappy home life, Holzman became obsessed with music and electronic equipment. His grandmother headed the National Council of Jewish Women and did political com-

mentary on a local station. He often accompanied her and developed an interest in radio, even trying his hand at building crystal radio sets. His father indulged his passion to some extent, buying him as a 15th birthday present a semi-professional disc recorder, equipment which Holzman then used to record bar mitzvahs and weddings. Despite his father's judgment that the boy failed to measure up to his exacting standards for a firstborn son, Holzman managed to graduate from high school by the age of 16 and start his university studies in Annapolis, Maryland, at St. John's College. What especially appealed to Holzman about the school was its electronics lab, in reality a Quonset hut supplied with an array of army surplus equipment. At St. John's, he also came to appreciate folk music, which would become a staple of the Elektra label years later. During his first two years in college, the idea of starting his own independent record label began to take root in Holzman's mind. The concept came to fruition in the fall of 1950, at the start of his junior year, when he attended a recital at school featuring soprano Georgianna Bannister, who performed a number of poems set to music composed by John Gruen. Impulsively, he asked Bannister and Gruen if they would record the songs on his nonexistent record label, and they accepted.

Holzman quickly cobbled together a record label. He took $300 from his bar mitzvah bank account and convinced a classmate, an ex-serviceman named Paul Rickolt, to match that amount. For the label's name, Holzman drew on his classwork, settling on the Greek demi-goddess Electra, who was associated with the artistic muses. Holzman ultimately used the Germanic spelling ''Elektra'' for the name of his record label. He then substituted the Es with sideways Ms as an inexpensive way to create a distinctive look for the company name that could also serve as a logo. According to company lore, Holzman made his first entry in the Elektra ledgers on October 10, 1950. To establish an off-campus mailing address, he then bartered a free copy of his first album for the right to make use of Wally's Tobacco Shop in Annapolis. Recording for the album was conducted during a three-hour session in a New York studio in December 1950, and the resulting tapes were taken to RCA Records to be mastered and custom-pressed. Unfortunately, surface noise all but drowned out the music. Holzman personally oversaw the next attempt, and in March 1951 the fledgling

Company Perspectives:

The ruby is a stone of telepathy. Prized as talisman and divinatory tool it dispels nightmares when placed under a pillow and guards against storms if touched to the four outside corners of a house. The Alumina of its blood line projects rather than receives energy; a double refraction that according to arcane lore harmonically vibrates to the note E. An E for Elektra: She of the seven Pleiades daughter of the Oceanus mother of the Harpies. The bright and brilliant one: A muse transformed four decades ago to celebrate music that most mind-reading of the arts. A record's label is hardly as important as the artisans who give it reason for being: yet with few exceptions, it helps to bridge the chasm between creative impulse and realization offering continuity with an oversoul and family tree all its own. An emotional geography spread over time, place and sheer chance it stands like a great center of trade at the crossroads of inspiration and commerce merging in a marketplace of ideas. Our Town: Folks move in, folks move out, humming and hymning life's soundtracks.

label's first effort, *New Songs* (EKLP-1), was delivered to Holzman's dormitory. The 500 records were stored in an empty room, which became Elektra's de facto shipping department. To sell the album, Holzman turned to a so-called national distributor, Jay Wesley Smith, who agreed to take 100 copies if he would also receive an additional 50 for promotional uses. Although *New Songs* was well received by obscure musical publications, Smith sold few copies. Those that he did sell came out of his free promotional copies. The 100 that he ''bought'' were all returned for credit, so that Elektra in its first outing took back more records than it actually sold.

Despite this inauspicious start, Holzman left college (at the urging of a dean who suggested he take a year off ''to get his bearings'') and moved back to New York to follow his dream. He found a cheap walk-up in Greenwich Village and for a while helped to make ends meet by installing sound systems, mostly for family friends. He then started his own record store, taking over the lease of a local sheet music store, which he renamed the Record Loft, although it was actually a street-level shop. A large portion of his stock was devoted to folk music, prompting a number of area ''folkies'' to visit the store to browse and chat. One of these customers was George Pickow, who was married to a Kentucky folk singer, Jean Ritchie. After listening to her, Holzman decided to make her Elektra's second recording artist. Unlike EKLP-1, Ritchie's collection of Appalachian mountain ballads, not only received excellent reviews, it also sold well, perhaps as many as 2,000 copies. More importantly, the success of the record validated Holzman's decision to launch his own record label. Because it was inexpensive to produce, Holzman concentrated on recording folk music.

Early 1950s Expansion

In 1952 and 1953, Holzman recorded nine more folk albums, then in 1954 released his first blues album. No longer a pipe dream or a hobby, Elektra now required all of Holzman's attention, and in 1954 he closed the Record Loft and moved

Elektra's offices from the shop's backroom to new accommodations at 361 Bleecker Street. A year later, he bought out Rickolt's interest for $1000, but the business remained very much a shoestring affair, the sales of one record barely able to finance the production of the next. Holzman turned to a St. John's classmate, Leonard Ripley, who came from wealth, and over the course of the next two years Ripley invested some $10,000 in the business. Although Ripley was now a partner in Elektra, the accounting, such as it was, and other business matters remained the sole responsibility of Holzman, who at this stage was paying himself about $11 a week. In spite of Ripley's financial help, Elektra continued to operate on a tight budget, a money-losing proposition that lacked the resources to achieve any level of significant growth.

In 1956, Holzman refined a concept that proved to be instrumental in turning Elektra into a profitable business: the sampler. For some time, record companies had been providing radio stations with compilations of their artists, and in 1954 Elektra itself produced a ten-inch sampler for radio play. Holzman's new idea was to create sampler albums for the retail market, selling at the bargain price of $2. Because the sampler helped to spur sales of their individual albums, Elektra artists now agreed to waive royalty payments on the use of a limited number of songs in samplers. Record dealers also agreed to a short discount for similar reasons: the cheap price led to greater sampler sales, which in turn led to increased sales for fully discounted individual albums. As a result, a sampler could make a profit for Elektra ranging from $10,000 to $20,000, while at the same time effectively promoting the label's other titles. In 1956, Elektra moved into the black ink for the first time.

In 1958, Holzman was able to buy back a 100 percent interest in Elektra and moved to larger offices on West 14th Street, on the northern border of Greenwich Village. It was here that Holzman built his first studio. As the company moved into the 1960s, its catalog was still very much dominated by folk music. Holzman also eased away from production responsibilities, now devoting most of his time to the signing and management of new artists. Although he generally had a strong sense of the world of popular music, Holzman made a significant mistake in 1962 when he decided that the New York folk scene had played itself out and moved to Los Angeles to establish a West Coast office for Elektra. In the early sixties, Bob Dylan suddenly burst onto the New York folk scene, debuting with a highly acclaimed first album. Dylan was a natural fit for Elektra, but Holzman on the West Coast had missed out on the singer-songwriter's emergence in Greenwich Village. He promptly shuttered the Los Angeles office and returned to New York.

In 1963, after moving Elektra's offices uptown to the Rockefeller Center neighborhood, Holzman proved that he had not lost his touch for innovation when he started up a classical music label, Nonesuch. One night, while he waited with his wife for friends to join them at a restaurant located across the street from Carnegie Hall, Holzman thought back to his college days when he faced the difficult choice of picking one of two classical albums to purchase because he lacked the money to buy both. Classical albums in the United States cost in the $5 range in 1963, leading Holzman to daydream about bringing out a line of specialty records priced as cheaply as paperback books. He wrote out the basic business plan on a paper tablecloth and

```
┌─────────────────────────────────────────────┐
│                 Key Dates:                    │
│                                               │
│ 1950:  Jac Holzman founds Elektra records.    │
│ 1956:  The company releases the first sampler │
│        album for retail sale.                 │
│ 1963:  Nonesuch label is launched.            │
│ 1970:  Holzman sells Elektra to Warner        │
│        Communications.                        │
│ 1983:  Bob Krasnow becomes head of the        │
│        company.                               │
│ 1994:  Sylvia Rhone replaces Krasnow.         │
│ 2004:  Elektra becomes part of Atlantic       │
│        Records Group; Rhone and other         │
│        Elektra executives are replaced by     │
│        a management team headed by new        │
│        Atlantic chairman Jason Flom.          │
└─────────────────────────────────────────────┘
```

the next day took a jet to Europe. In London and Paris, he met with various record companies, offering a $500 advance plus royalties for each album that the European labels had no intention of attempting to market themselves in the United States. He quickly signed several properties and targeted more sources for future material. Holzman was so convinced that his idea would work, and fearful that larger rivals would emulate his idea and bring their financial muscle to bear before he could secure more material to build a larger catalog, that he grew secretive, giving his new venture the name of Nonesuch because, as he stated, "if we were ever asked we could truthfully say there was no such project." Indeed, the idea proved popular, and Nonesuch quickly became a cash cow for Elektra.

New Leadership in the 1970s

Elektra moved into popular rock and roll music in the 1960s. In May 1966, Holzman first saw the Doors, signed them, and a year later the company had its first number one single on the pop charts, "Light My Fire." The album was also highly popular and over the course of the next three decades would sell in excess of 45 million copies. On the strength of its success with the Doors, Elektra once again established a Los Angeles office. However, the days of being able to launch an independent record label in your dorm room were long past, and Holzman took note of the changing conditions. For instance, Atlantic Records, the rise of which mirrored that of Elektra, was bought by Warner Brothers in 1967. Holzman ultimately sold Elektra to Warner Communications in 1970. He stayed on to run the label, in the next couple of years signing such notable talents as Carly Simon and Harry Chapin, but in 1973, at the age of 42, Holzman, believing that he was starting to repeat himself, decided to retire, turning over the reins of Elektra to others.

In 1974, under the Warner umbrella, former agent and manager of Crosby, Stills & Nash, David Geffen, merged his Asylum label with Elektra. Without Holzman, Elektra lost its bohemian edge, growing into a more traditional record label. It added such pop acts as Tony Orlando & Dawn and the Cars, heavy rockers like Queen, and branched into punk as well as country music. In 1983, the company took on new leadership in the form of Bob Krasnow. The former sales rep for Decca Records and manager/producer for Captain Beefheart, Krasnow had launched his own independent record label in 1968 called Blue Thumb Records, which he once told Holzman he planned

to grow into the next Elektra. Instead, he moved on, eventually becoming vice-president of talent for Warner before taking charge of Elektra on January 1, 1983. Over the course of the next 11 years, Krasnow was to transform the Elektra, Asylum, and Nonesuch labels into a true entertainment group, adding a classical music division as well as a video company. At the same time, he returned Elektra to its roots, moving the company's headquarters to Rockefeller Center.

After a long run of success, Elektra began to experience some difficulties in the early 1990s. By 1994, the company's market share among U.S. labels dipped to just 2.8 percent, with revenue under $200 million. In the same year, Krasnow quit during a management shakeup at Warner in which Atlantic co-chairman Doug Morris was put in charge of all Warner music labels. According to press reports, Krasnow balked at the idea of reporting to Morris. In any case, he was replaced by Sylvia Rhone, the first African American woman to head a major music company. She was given the mission of building Elektra's sales to the $300 million level in three years.

Raised in the Harlem section of New York City, Rhone graduated from the University of Pennsylvania's Wharton School with a BS in economics. She became a trainee at Bankers Trust Company in New York, but after a year quit in order to make a career in the music industry. She got her foot in the door by taking a secretarial position at Buddah Records but quickly advanced to the position of national promotion coordinator. After serving in that same capacity for small independent label Bareback Records, in 1976 she moved to ABC Records, where she became regional promotion manager, a position she later held at Ariola Records. In 1980, she moved to Elektra and for three years served as northeast regional promotion manager in charge of special markets. For two years, she then became director of marketing. As a result of this varied experience, she was well prepared in 1986 to become vice-president and general manager of Atlantic's Black Music Operations. Some 18 months later, she was named senior vice-president for the label. She was instrumental in the rapid growth of the Black Music Division: from March 1988 to May 1990, revenues increased by 400 percent.

Taking over Elektra, Rhone was just as successful as she had been at Atlantic. In just two years, she was able to reach the $300 million goal for Elektra. According to *Billboard,* in November 1996, Elektra commanded 5.47 percent of album sales, making it the sixth-largest label in the United States. Of particular achievement was the revitalization of the career of singer-songwriter Tracy Chapman and the emergence of rock group Phish. In addition, Elektra's heavy metal act Metallica would become the biggest selling band of the 1990s.

New Ownership in the 1990s

With the rise of digital technology and the Internet, the music business as a whole was presented with a host of challenges in the new century, and the industry braced itself for a period of what promised to be revolutionary changes. A number of restructurings ensued, and in March 2004 Elektra was recast, along with the Atlantic and Lava record labels, as part of a single entity called Atlantic Records Group. Rhone and other senior executives were ousted in favor of a management team headed by new Atlantic chairman Jason Flom, Lava's founder, who was known for developing such 1980s acts as Twisted Sister and Skid Row and in the 1990s signed artists Tori Amos, Matchbox Twenty, and Kid Rock. The mandate of the new Atlantic group was to devote less resources to promotion and return to its core mission—to identify and develop new talent. Elektra's Rhone was clearly a survivor and would likely find a new position in the industry. So too, Elektra, after more than 50 years in operation, would likely continue to find a way to build upon its storied legacy.

Principal Competitors

BMG Entertainment; Sony Music Entertainment Inc.; Universal Music Group.

Further Reading

Davis, Andrea, ''Rap-sody & Blue,'' *Executive Female*, May-June 1990, p. 44.

Holzman, Jac, *Follow the Music: The Life and High Times of Elektra Records in the Great Years of American Pop Culture*, Santa Monica, California: FirstMedia Books, 1998, 441 p.

Jeffrey, Don, ''Exec Shift Rocks Warner Family,'' *Billboard*, July 23, 1994, p. 1.

——, ''Sylvia Rhone Leads Elektra's Turnaround,'' *Billboard*, November 9, 1996, p. 1.

—Ed Dinger

Esselte

U.S. Headquarters:
44 Commerce Road
Stamford, Connecticut
U.S.A.
Telephone: (203) 355-9000
Fax: (203) 355-9071
Web site: http://www.esselte.com

Private Company
Incorporated: 1913 as SLT
Employees: 6,500
Sales: $1.2 billion (2003)
NAIC: 422120 Stationery and Office Supplies
Wholesalers; 333313 Office Machinery Manufacturing

Esselte is the world's leading office supply manufacturer with customers in 120 countries across the globe. The company has over 30,000 items in its product arsenal including file folders and ring binders, staplers and desk accessories, printers and labels, and computer accessories. These products—found under the DYMO, Esselte, Leitz, Pendaflex, and Oxford brand names—are sold to wholesalers, office supply stores, and mass retailers. J.W. Childs Associates L.P., a private equity investment firm, acquired the company in 2002.

Esselte was born out of the 1913 union of 13 Swedish printing businesses, some of which had been in operation since the 1600s. The merger consolidated the operations of all 13 companies into an entity known as the SLT group, creating one of the largest graphics firms in the region. SLT grew substantially over the next 50 years, adding a variety of different operations to its holdings through strategic acquisitions. By the 1950s, the company printed stationary, playing cards, maps, forms, share certificates, and bonds, and was also involved in book binding and paper manufacturing.

It soon became apparent however, that SLT's unwieldy group of companies was not operating efficiently. Thus, it launched a major restructuring effort in the early 1960s in an attempt to streamline operations. It sold off unprofitable businesses combined similar divisions. The reorganization proved successful, and in August 1970 the company, now organized as a top office supplies concern, adopted the name Esselte AB.

Rapid Growth in the 1970s–80s

As a result of the restructuring process, Esselte found itself in an enviable position. With annual sales of over $300 million, almost no debt, and cash to spend, the company embarked on an international expansion plan that would eventually catapult it into the top spot in the industry. Under the direction of managing director Sven Wallgren, Esselte made its first key move by acquiring Benson's International Systems Ltd., the world's largest producer of ring binder mechanisms, in 1975.

The shopping spree continued. Esselte gained a foothold in the U.S. and Canadian markets in 1976 when it bought Oxford Pendaflex Corporation, a company with $60 million in annual sales, best known for its suspension filing systems. Two years later, Esselte moved to take over DYMO Industries Inc., a California-based embossing company, whose products Esselte already distributed abroad. DYMO resisted the acquisition, seeking a white knight in Daylin Inc. Esselte won out in the end, however, topping Daylin's bid by 40 cents per share. The $43.5 million purchase brought with it DYMO's well-known label makers and tapes, Ideal accounting books, and the Meto barcoding business. As Esselte made the deal under the auspices of the Pendaflex subsidiary, Pendaflex absorbed DYMO's business.

By the early 1980s, over half of Esselte's revenues stemmed from operations outside of Sweden. A September 1981 *Financial Times* article summed up Wallgren's acquisition strategy as consisting of two principles: "acquisitions should possess a strongly defined market or technical characteristic and secondly that they should have greater growth and profit potential than the parent company." In keeping with this logic, the company added Letraset Ltd., a large graphic design and technical drawings products supplier, to its holdings in 1981. Overall, the company bought more than 150 companies over the next ten years.

In 1984, Esselte combined Pendaflex and three other holdings to create U.S. subsidiary Esselte Business Systems Inc. (EBS), which it then positioned to take on a significant share of the $35

Company Perspectives:

We strive to make it easier for people to organize the modern workplace. We work close to our customers and help them conduct a profitable business. They get easy-to-sell products with strong brands. They also get a reliable partner with a superior service level and with local and global presence.

---

billion office supplies market in the United States and Europe. Esselte took EBS public—selling 3.3 million shares at $13.50 per share—and EBS began to grow by acquisition, purchasing looseleaf binder and supplies manufacturer Boorum & Pease in 1985. By 1987, EBS accounted for 60 percent of Esselte AB's sales and nearly 80 percent of its earnings. Esselte announced the following year that it would focus solely on its EBS unit and its Information Systems and Media (ISM) business. The latter included office equipment importing operations and its entertainment holdings that included pay television ventures.

Changes in the 1990s

During the late 1980s, Esselte entered the retail outlet market through a series of acquisitions including Einersen of Norway. This move into the retail sector proved ill-considered as the company began competing with many of its customers. Esselte's fortunes began to change as a recession slowed its customers' spending. Profits fell and sales in its key markets faltered. In 1990 its major shareholder, Mobilia, declared bankruptcy. By now, Esselte was plagued by many of the same problems it had faced in the 1960s when it was forced to undergo a major overhaul. Hans Larsson, Esselte's CEO at the time, insisted the company restructure in order to shore up profits. In May 1990 Larsson's management team agreed and set plans in motion to sell off its commercial real estate, printing, and publishing businesses. The firm also bought back the shares of EBS it didn't already own, making it a wholly-owned subsidiary. Despite these efforts, pre-tax profits fell by 75 percent that year.

Cost cutting measures and job cuts continued in 1991. During a management shakeup, Larsson was ousted, and Bo Lundquist was named CEO. He reorganized the company into three main business segments—Esselte Office Products, Esselte Information Systems, and Esselte Retail and Equipment. One year later Esselte was split into two separate companies. Esselte would remain involved in office products with the following divisions: Esselte DYMO; Esselte Pendaflex; Esselte Bensons; Esselte Letraset; and Esselte Meto. The second company, Scribona, included Esselte's Nordic information systems arm.

The trimmed-down Esselte had five major goals after the demerger. Lundquist outlined these initiatives in his annual speech to shareholders in 1994. According to the CEO, Esselte's focus at this time was on strengthening its market positions; securing cost savings by streamlining operations, enhancing efficiency, an capitalizing on synergies; looking for new product opportunities that were made possible by advances in new media and electronics; maintaining an aggressive product launch schedule; and strengthening the company's overall financial performance. Lundquist reiterated this strategy in a 1994 interview with the *Wall Street Journal*. "Regarding Esselte's greatest growth opportunities over the next three to five years," he summed up, "We will have a concentration to office products, pure niche product coming from the electronic development and from the new information technology. And this is our core, and we are large, and will still be in the retail sales and equipment. We have not any other plans to go into new businesses."

Esselte's restructuring efforts over the past several years appeared to be paying off. As profits began to rise, the company resumed its expansion strategy. At this time Esselte looked to expand geographically, looking toward the Asian, Eastern European, and South American markets as potential new growth areas. The company bolstered its existing product line in 1996 with the acquisition of U.S. computer products manufacturer Curtis Manufacturing Company. It also bought Karl Bene & Company, Austria's largest office supply company.

The Late 1990s and Beyond

Lundquist resigned in 1997, leaving Jan Kvarnström at the helm. Esselte once again revamped its operations under new leadership. It adopted a holding company structure with three independent subsidiaries—Esselte Office Products Inc., Meto, and Nielsen & Bainbridge. The latter was divested in 1998, positioning Esselte to focus on its office products business and Meto subsidiaries.

Esselte's office products arm purchased L. Leitz International GmbH for $337.7 million in 1998. By adding Germany's largest office supply manufacturer to its arsenal, Esselte secured a position as the world's leading manufacturer in the office supplies industry. The two companies fit well together, and Esselte gained a stronger foothold in markets where its performance had traditionally been weak. Leitz's past investment in automation and technology was also considered a benefit and was expected to add cost savings to Esselte's existing operations. The company also acquired U.S. printer label manufacturer CoStar that year.

Meto was sold to shareholders in 1999 in a move that pared Esselte down to its Office Products business. Kvarnström moved into the chairman position that year, and Anders Igel was named CEO. By now, Esselte had undergone an intense transformation, changing from a large conglomerate into a streamlined office products supplier. The dramatic changes positioned it to face the challenges of the new millennium which included a severe recession and weak economies that affected most of the company's markets. The firm continued to take action in order to maintain profitability. It divested its Monti printing business in 2000 and its Letraset graphics and Tarifold filing system holdings in 2001. That year it also restructured its Curtis operations.

Perhaps the most significant move in the company's history came in 2002 when J.W. Childs Associates L.P., a Boston buyout firm, made a $550 million cash offer for Esselte. This type of transaction, a public-to-private-buyout, was gaining popularity in Europe. Before 1999, the value of such deals in Europe hovered around EUR 300 million. By 2001, the value of this type

Key Dates:

1913: Thirteen Swedish businesses join together to form SLT.
1964: The company launches a major restructuring effort to streamline operations.
1970: SLT changes its name to Esselte AB.
1976: Oxford Pendaflex Corporation is acquired.
1978: Esselte purchases DYMO Industries Inc.
1981: Letraset Ltd. is added to the company's holdings.
1992: Company operations are split into two companies.
2002: J.W. Childs Associates L.P. acquires Esselte.

of buyout had reached EUR 6 billion. J.W. Child's purchase was expected to boost profitability in Esselte, and this prompted company board members to recommend the offer. Esselte's largest shareholder, Ratos, agreed to sell its interest to J.W. Childs in May 2002. The transaction was completed in July. Magnus Nicolin was named Esselte's new president and CEO.

As a private company, Esselte had the financial wherewithal to pursue an aggressive growth strategy that included geographic expansion, acquisition, and investment in current brands. Nicolin commented on Esselte's new parent in a May 2003 Office Products International article. "JW Childs is a strong owner and is more committed to the company's growth," he claimed. "It has the desire to add value and support new initiatives." Holding JW Childs to its word, Esselte made several key moves after the change in ownership.

In August 2002 the company revamped its sales and marketing operations in Europe and created the Esselte Sales Group Europe division to provide enhanced customer services, support, and trade marketing. It completed a management realignment in 2003 and set several initiatives in place that increased productivity and operational efficiency and improved waste reduction. Acquisition activity also resumed with the purchase of the consumer products division of Centis Inc. in March 2003. The deal included JM, Duo Tang, Century Craft, and Centis Canada, which were integrated into Esselte's Filing Americas division.

The company's key brands at this time were Pendaflex, DYMO, Esselte, and Leitz. It added the Xyron brand to product line in October 2003. In early 2004, Esselte bought Universal Trade Stationers, leading to the creation of its first office in Ireland. It also purchased EJA CZ of the Czech Republic. In May 2004 it completed a EURO 150 million bond offering.

In the coming years, Esselte planned to strengthen its brands through product innovation, marketing and investment, and by expanding its customer base. Additional growth in China, one of the fastest-growing countries in the world, and in the Eastern European region was at the forefront of Esselte's expansion strategy. J.W. Childs' cash infusion came at a crucial moment in Esselte's history and left it well positioned in the industry. Esselte had indeed experienced a wave of changes over the past decade but it appeared as though it was on track for growth in the years to come as the world's largest office supply manufacturer.

Principal Subsidiaries

Esselte Sverige AB (Sweden); Esselte UK Ltd.; Esselte Leitz GmbH & Co. KG (Germany); Esselte de Mexico S.A. de C.V.; Esselte S.A. (France); Esselte Canada Inc.; Esselte S.r.l. (Italy); Esselte Australia Pty Ltd.; Esselte Ltd. (Hong Kong).

Principal Operating Units

Filing Americas; Filing Europe; Sales Group Europe; DYMO; Workspace; Esselte Asia Pacific.

Principal Competitors

Avery Dennison Corporation; MeadWestvaco Corporation; Smead Manufacturing Company.

Further Reading

"After the Storm, The Struggle - Esselte," *Financial Times*, December 6, 1990.
"CEO Interview Esselte AB," *Wall Street Transcript*, November 14, 1994.
"Daylin Inc Abandons Battle with Esselte AB of Sweden for Control of Dymo," *New York Times Abstracts*, May 25, 1978.
"Esselte: A Name Most Offices Keep on File," *Newsday*, February 16, 1987.
"Esselte Accepts Private Equity Firm's Euro 330m Bid," *eFinancial News*, May 27, 2002.
"Esselte Announces Aggressive Growth Strategy After Acquisition by J.W. Childs," *Waymaker*, July 12, 2002.
"Esselte Appoints Igel to Top Job," *Financial Times*, September 17, 1999.
"Esselte to Sell Property, Entertainment, and Print Divisions," *Financial Times*, April 11, 1990.
Eyriey, Nick, "Hungry for Growth," *Office Products International*, May 2003.
"Esselte" *Financial Times*, September 2, 1981, p. 22.
Koshetz, Herbert, "Oxford Pendaflex Corp Pres and Chief Exec Officer William I Thompson Says Co. . . . ," *New York Times Abstracts*, April 13, 1976.
Latour, Almar, "Esselte Unit Agrees to Acquire Leitz," *Wall Street Journal Europe*, August 4, 1998.
"Lundquist Has Two Years to Make Esselte Profitable," *Veckans Affarer*, November 27, 1991, p. 66.
McIvor, Greg, "New Esselte Chief to Split Group Into Three," *Financial Times*, April 30, 1997, p. 34.
Moore, Stephen D., "Sweden's Esselte Plans to Cut Work Force a Further 7.5%," *Wall Street Journal Europe*, June 26, 1991.
"Profile: Esselte Issued Private Bonds in Europe," *Private Placement Letter*, June 14 2004.
"Ratos Sells its Esselte Holding," *Waymaker*, June 7, 2002.

—Christina M. Stansell

Fatburger Corporation

1218 Third Street Promenade
Santa Monica, California 90401-1308
U.S.A.
Telephone: (310) 319-1850
Fax: (310) 319-1863
Web site: http://www.fatburger.com

Private Company
Incorporated: 1990
Employees: 500
Sales: $20 million (2003 est.)
NAIC: 722211 Limited-Service Restaurants

Fatburger Corporation, based in Santa Monica, California, operates and franchises more than 50 hamburger restaurants located in Arizona, California, Colorado, Florida, Nevada, and Washington State. About half are company owned. Although Fatburger—"The Last Great Hamburger Stand"—has been around for over 50 years, and maintains something of a cult following in Los Angeles among celebrities and everyday people, attempts since 1980 to grow the chain have been met with limited success. Now owned by a management group led by chief executive officer Keith Warlick, the company is pursuing an ambitious plan to place Fatburger hamburger stands across the country. Fatburger units maintain a retro 1950s setting, featuring jazz, rhythm and blues, and classic soul on the jukebox. In fact, a "fat" burger is '50s' slang for "supreme," as in Fat Cat and Fat Times. Fatburger offers casual dining but not fast food and generally avoids drive-thru operations. Burgers ranging from a two-ounce Baby Fat burger to the signature five-ounce Fatburger and the half-pound Kingburger—are handmade from fresh, 100 percent lean USDA ground beef and then cooked to order on an open grill. An abundance of condiments, garnishes, and extras are available, including eggs. In addition, Fatburger makes its onion rings from real onions and milkshakes from hand-scooped ice cream. Other offerings on the menu include chili dogs, grilled chicken sandwiches, and bacon and egg sandwiches.

First Fatburger Stand Opens in 1952

Fatburger was founded in 1952 in Los Angeles by African-Americans Lovey Yancey and Charles Simpson. According to company lore, their friends so enjoyed the hamburgers Yancey served them in her kitchen, often during the course of late-night jam sessions, that they encouraged her to open her own hamburger stand. She and Simpson decided to go into business together, and, despite a lack of money, they worked out a rudimentary business plan. They coined "Mr. Fatburger" as the name of the restaurant, determined the menu, and found a site at 31st Street and Western Avenue in Los Angeles. Simpson was then able to construct the first building at no cost. He worked for Martin Sheavy Construction Company, whose owner made a habit of dividing leftover building materials with his crews after a job was completed. With these materials and the free labor of his co-workers, Simpson was able to construct the first stand after working hours. When this walk-up restaurant, offering just three stools, opened, Yancey and a helper worked the day shift, while Simpson, after a day of working construction, with the help of his sister, Josie, took the night shift.

The first burger stand proved so successful that Simpson and Yancey opened three more sites. When they decided to part ways, they split the business. Simpson and his wife ran their Mr. Fatburger stands, while Yancey dropped the "Mr." and looked to expand her Fatburger business beyond Los Angeles's inner city. In 1973, she opened a store in Beverly Hills, and then in 1980 she began to grow the business through local franchising of the Fatburger concept. By the end of 1985, the chain had 32 units, four of which were company owned, and was named the number five fastest growing burger franchise chain by *Entrepreneur* magazine in its annual Franchise 500 list, trailing only McDonald's, Burger King, Wendy's, and Jack in the Box. There was talk in the press about expanding Fatburger beyond Los Angeles to Orange County and San Diego, and the possibility of moving into Ann Arbor, Michigan, and New York. Overseas licensing was also being discussed. Although the chain during this phase would grow to 40 units, many of the locations proved ill-suited to the business, and a number were forced to close. It was also during the 1980s that CEO Keith Warlick first went to work with Fatburger, learning the culture of the chain from Yancey herself.

Founder Sells in 1990

In 1990, Yancey sold out to a group of investors led by Island Trading Co., a New York investment firm connected to Island Records founder Chris Blackwell. Fatburger Corporation was formed to effect the purchase. Yancey continued to operate two of the restaurants, while Warlick joined the new owners as they began to restructure the business and establish new procedures for franchising, which resumed two years later. Before then, however, Fatburger opened a company-owned store in Las Vegas in 1990 on the strip. A second unit opened in Las Vegas in 1992, a move that caused some disagreement within management. Warlick, a supporter of Las Vegas expansion, chose to leave the company at this point. His belief in the Las Vegas market would be justified, however, when these stores became the top grossing units in the chain. He would return to Fatburger in 1995 and a year later emerged as the president, serving under chief executive officer Glen Hutloff. Also during the first half of the 1990s, Fatburger took steps to distinguish itself from fast food competitors like McDonald's and Burger King. Big board menus with pictures were removed, and while orders were made at the counter, the food was brought to customers' tables. In addition, chairs and tables designed to promote turnover were replaced by comfortable booths. Hutloff told *Food & Beverage Marketing* in 1997, "We want to be a chain that doesn't feel like a chain. . . . We want to feel like a neighborhood place." As a result, Fatburger was positioning itself into a challenging niche, neither a fast-food operation nor full-service diner.

By the end of 1997, Fatburger had 29 units, of which 12 were corporate units, but management held ambitious dreams of much greater growth. To help in its efforts to move into suburban areas like Santa Clarita Valley and Orange County, the chain introduced a smaller version of its signature Fatburger, the Baby Fat, which featured a two-ounce patty. The smaller sandwich was intended for children and allowed the chain to attract more families. At this stage, management was talking about growing to 250 units within five years. Fatburger had also established a relationship with basketball-star-turned-entrepreneur Earvin "Magic" Johnson, hoping to piggyback on his move into some 15 cities over the course of the next three years. In the short-term, Hutloff was targeting Atlanta, Houston, and Detroit.

As was often the case with Fatburger, these plans for expansion failed to materialize, although the chain managed to move into two new markets: Arizona and Washington state. In 1999, Texas-based Restaurant Teams International, Inc. announced that it had an agreement to buy Fatburger Corporation for $8 million. RTIN professed even bigger plans for the chain, announcing that it intended to develop nearly 500 franchised Fatburger restaurants over the next five years. A year later, however, the sale was still not completed. Then, in October 2001, Magic Johnson stepped in, after keeping his eye on the chain for the past few years. His Johnson Development Corpo-

ration in partnership with GE Capital Franchise Finances bought Fatburger. Other investors included the former president of Motown Records, Jheryl Busby, and Darren Star, the creator and executive producer of the HBO television series *Sex and the City*. Warlick was also a major shareholder and became the president and chief executive officer of the company.

Fatburgers' new expansion plan called for 100 new restaurants, 80 percent of them franchises, to be rolled out in five years. Possible new markets—with an emphasis on areas where Johnson Development Corporation already had a presence—included Michigan, Indiana, Ohio, Illinois, Pennsylvania, Colorado, Texas, Georgia, New York, and the Carolinas. Franchisees were expected to commit to opening at least ten restaurants in a new market. Franchisees for a single-unit were required to possess a net worth of $250,000 (not including their house and car) and to have on hand a minimum of $150,000 in cash. Franchisees agreed to pay a 5 percent royalty on net sales, earmarked for corporate services, and 2 percent that would go into a national advertising fund. In addition, they were required to spend 1 percent of their net sales on local marketing efforts.

Magic Johnson's involvement with Fatburger created a great deal of excitement about the chain, finally realizing its potential. One of his friends, TV personality Montel Williams, was quick to assemble an investment group, FB Colorado Inc., to acquire the Colorado territory. Johnson had introduced Williams to Fatburgers some years earlier, and he now claimed to visit a Los Angeles Fatburger restaurant roughly twice a week to eat a double Fatburger with cheese, bacon, and chili. Williams had started out his television career in Colorado, often visited the state, and was preparing to buy a house there, making it a natural location for his Fatburger operation. In December 2002, he opened his first Fatburger restaurant in Aurora City Place.

Magic Johnson Sells Controlling Interest in 2003

By the time the Colorado Fatburger opened, however, Magic Johnson had already taken steps to lessen his involvement with the chain, selling a majority interest for an undisclosed amount of money in 2003 to an investment group led by Warlick. Johnson and his partners did, nevertheless, retain a minority, non-voting interest. According to the Los Angeles *Daily News,* "Friction between the management and Johnson's investment team led them to part ways. . . . The ambitious plans never materialized, with the chain adding only three restaurants while Johnson Development held it. Ken Lombard, president of Johnson Development, admitted, 'We just found too many times we weren't in agreement with where we had to go.'" According to the *Daily News,* "Delays in selecting real estate contributed to the slow roll-out, but [Warlick] said deals were in place to open 84 stores in 17 states." Expressing his frustration, Warlick said, "We can't afford to wait 100 years to exploit a hot 50-year-old concept." Johnson Development considered buying out Warlick, but in the end decided instead to accept his offer. Much of the difference between the two parties Warlick related to brand loyalty: "We prefer to control our own brand. . . . Magic Johnson is a brand itself, and with celebrity groups, their interest is controlling their brand." However, according to the *Daily News,* "Industry watchers conjectured that financial reasons played into Johnson's decision to sell. . . . 'I can only think there's one reason to sell: It's not generating the kind of return

Key Dates:

1952: First Mr. Fatburger hamburger stand opens.
1973: A Beverly Hills Unit opens.
1980: Franchising begins.
1990: Fatburger Corporation is formed to affect buyout.
2001: Magic Johnson group acquires a controlling interest.
2003: Management-led investment group acquires a controlling interest.

on (Johnson's) investment he's accustomed to,' said Richard Martin, managing editor of the *Nation's Restaurant News.* 'When you have people threatening to sue McDonald's over obesity, it's not the best time to be called Fatburger.' ''

Warlick made it clear that he had no intention of changing the Fatburger name or formula. Warlick vowed, "We're not going into the salad business, we're staying with what got us here in the first place." Although Fatburger would clearly miss the financial muscle of Magic Johnson, it had a new backer in Portland, Oregon-based Fog Cutter Capital Group Inc., which provided the cash needed to complete the buyout and pledged additional financing to build Fatburger's infrastructure and support management's expansion plans.

There was clear evidence that Fatburger was indeed making a strong effort to establish a national presence. In 2003, the chain moved into Florida, and in 2004 entered the market in Pittsburgh, Pennsylvania, as well as in Georgia, Louisiana, and New Jersey, within the New York City metropolitan area. Moreover, the chain had commitments for the openings of 200 stores in 22 new markets by 2008. This expansion notwithstanding, it remained to be seen whether the long-held promise of Fatburger would finally be realized, more than a half-century after it was founded as a three-stool hamburger stand.

Principal Competitors

Burger King Corporation; In-N-Out Burgers, Inc.; McDonald's Corporation.

Further Reading

Christopher, Cheryl V., "The Secret 'Recipe' of the Fatburger," *Los Angeles Sentinel*, April 7, 1994, p. A12.
"Fat's Where It's At," *Food & Beverage Marketing*, April 1997, p. 9.
Hopkins, Brent, "Magic Gobbles up Fatburger Fast-Food Chain," *Daily News* (Los Angeles), October 2, 2001, p. N1.
——, " 'Magic' Johnson Sells Stake in California-Based Burger Chain," *Daily News* (Los Angeles), August 20, 2003.
Martin, Richard, "The Legacy of Lovie Yancey," *Nation's Restaurant News*, January 13, 1986, p. 61.

—Ed Dinger

The Food Emporium

20 Livingstone Avenue
Dobbs Ferry, New York 10522
U.S.A.
Telephone: (914) 826-2300
Fax: (914) 826-2378
Web site: http://www.thefoodemporium.com

Wholly Owned Subsidiary of The Great Atlantic &
Pacific Tea Company Inc.
Founded: 1919
Employees: 4,000
Sales: $720 million (1999 est.)
NAIC: 445110 Supermarkets and Other Grocery (Except
Convenience) Stores

Based in Dobbs Ferry, New York, The Food Emporium is a subsidiary of The Great Atlantic & Pacific Tea Company (A&P), operating approximately 36 upscale supermarkets located in New York, New Jersey, and Connecticut, with almost half found in Manhattan and all within the greater New York City area. Food Emporium stocks a wide variety of gourmet and other expensive grocery item, as well as staples, and features such specialty shops as its Corner Deli, Seafood Cove, Corner Bakery, and Floral Shoppe. The chain also employs in-house chefs to perform cooking demonstrations. An innovative format when launched in the late 1970s, Food Emporium has since found its niche populated by many others. The brand is associated with high quality among consumers in its market, but perhaps the chain's greatest strength lies in its choice Manhattan locations.

1919 Origins

Food Emporium's history can be traced to 1919, when Louis Daitch founded a dairy. Over the years, he opened shops in the New York City area selling butter and eggs. Following World War II, his Daitch Crystal Dairies, a public company trading on the American Stock Exchange, enjoyed tremendous growth in the new supermarket format, emerging in the 1950s as a significant chain. In 1955, Daitch and its 34 stores located in New York City, Long Island, and Connecticut merged with Shopwell Foods' chain of 18 Westchester County supermarkets. Shopwell was founded by Sigmund Rosengarten, who came to the supermarket business as a butcher. Along with other shareholders of the private company, he received stock in the merged company. The supermarket chain, known under variations of the Daitch and Shopwell names, underwent a period of significant expansion. Within a year, seven new stores were opened and nine more were added by acquiring the Diamond K chain.

Daitch's supermarket chain peaked in 1962 with 103 stores, but the company's growth was not focused. It attempted to launch a chain of convenience stores called Shop-Quik and in 1970 opened Shopwell Plaza in Westport, Connecticut, a shopping center that included Daitch's attempt at running a package liquor store. In 1973, Daitch changed its name to Shopwell Inc., now headed by Rosengarten's son Martin Rosengarten, who was aided by his own sons, Jay and Glenn. A year later, the company entered the Vermont and Massachusetts markets, where it opened seven stores. The venture did not work out, however, and in 1976 the company sold off these units, taking a $800,000 loss.

Following their failure in New England, the Rosengartens took stock of their situation. First, they concluded that for Shopwell to succeed it needed to focus on being a regional chain. The company reached a turning point during a 1979 management meeting. The participants made a chart with the names of the three Rosengartens at the top and 33 vice-presidents listed below them. When asked to whom they reported, the vice-presidents pointed at one another, but no one pointed to the three in charge. The chart became known in company lore as the "spaghetti chart." Shopwell was clearly in need of massive reorganization. The number of vice-presidents was reduced to just 12, and Martin Rosengarten turned over active control of the chain to his sons, who were both in their thirties. They began to close stores located in unprofitable areas and allowed other leases to expire, so that the chain was reduced to 65 units. The company also conducted some market research, which revealed the unpleasant truth that Shopwell stores had no discernable image. Their customers patronized Shopwell stores simply because of their convenient locations.

Food Emporium Format Launched in 1979

During the course of trimming the size of the chain, the Rosengartens noticed that the remaining stores were mostly located in upper income neighborhoods, such as Manhattan's Upper East Side and in Westchester County. Not only did it make sense to cater to the higher-income customer, the Rosengartens also recognized that no supermarkets in the area were doing much upscale marketing, leaving the business to smaller shops like Zabar's and Balducci's. From these insights came the idea of the Food Emporium format, which would mix regular and specialty items on the same shelves, rather than following the lead of other supermarkets, which at best offered a small gourmet corner. Elsewhere in the country the concept was already being refined, pioneered by Byerly Foods in Minneapolis in 1973. Grand Union was already in the process of developing specialty supermarkets in the New York market, making Shopwell's decision to launch the Food Emporium format in 1979 a timely one.

According to press reports, Martin Rosengarten did not support the Food Emporium idea. Nevertheless, his sons pressed on, converting six Shopwell stores to the new format. The transition was not without difficulty, however. Making the switch was more than just putting ties on clerks. The Rosengartens had to change the way they bought for the store, eschewing bulk buying to receive the best price in favor of scouring the country for specific products that their customers might want. As a result, the brothers had to educate themselves about food and then educate their employees. The stores also needed more workers than the average supermarket, driving up labor costs, but this was offset by the higher margins the stores received on specialty items. While typical supermarkets devoted about 72 percent of shelf space to dairy goods, frozen food, bakery items, and canned and packaged goods, Food Emporium allocated just 60 percent, reserving the rest of its stock for the higher-margin specialty items. Although many of the converted stores were smaller than typical supermarkets, the significant increase in traffic resulted in margins three times the norm.

By the end of 1983, Shopwell had converted 17 of its 55 stores to the Food Emporium format. Another seven would be converted over the next two years, but the conversions proved costly. It took about 18 months for a Food Emporium to attain profitability, rather than the industry average of around eight months. Shopwell also tried moving into the economy sector of the supermarket trade, an effort that failed. A One Stop Shop cash-and-carry store opened in 1984 and closed that same year. As a result of these and other factors, Shopwell lost $3.4 million in 1985 on sales of $464 million, and the Rosengarten brothers in 1986 (their father retired the year before) announced they were looking to sell the company. Insiders and their families, along with other major shareholders, accounted for 38 percent of Shopwell's stock; this group agreed not buy or sell shares or to enter into any voting arrangements until June 30, 1986, allowing management to locate a suitable buyer, which accord-

ing to press accounts was far from certain. *Crain's New York Business* quoted John A. Catsimatidis, CEO of the Red Apple supermarket chain, as saying, "We looked at it and walked away. . . . They've got beautiful stores, but there's too much debt." According to *Crain's*, Shopwell had $38.7 million in current liabilities, $40.5 million in long-term debt, and assets of $39.8 million. While the Food Emporium stores may have been expensive to start and required some outlay of cash before they turned profitable, the older Shopwell stores were a serious burden. According to *Crain's*, "One industry consultant [said], 'The Shopwell stores are just sad, small stores,' while the industry trend even in urban markets is toward relatively large, new stores." Moreover, the Shopwell stores faced the expiration of 30- and 40-year leases and an increase in rents from $5 a square foot to over $50. Although margins were slim and the cost of doing business in New York City was higher, in the words of *Crain's*, "Still, a few in the supermarket business think the Rosengartens' Shopwell sale isn't sincere. 'They really don't want to sell,' says Mr. Catsimatidis of Red Apple. 'It's a horse and pony show to satisfy the bank'."

New Ownership in the Mid-1980s

Despite the skepticism of rival supermarket executives, the Rosengarten did negotiate a sale of Shopwell, agreeing to accept $64 million from the Great Atlantic & Pacific Tea Company, which acquired 91.5 percent of Shopwell's common shares in 1986. A&P picked up 25 Shopwell stores, three Value Center Stores, two distribution centers, and a dairy, but clearly the reason why it acquired the company was to add the Food Emporium format to its portfolio. A&P had been in business since 1859, when George Huntington Hartford and George Gilman opened their first retail tea shop in Manhattan. In 1912, A&P launched a chain of cash-and-carry "economy" grocery stores, out of which grew a massive supermarket chain by the 1950s. Nevertheless, the company endured some difficult times adjusting to changing conditions, especially during the 1970s when the chain became too spread out and lost some $500 million. A&P mounted a comeback during the 1980s, closing more than 2,500 stores and choosing to concentrate its efforts in the East. The company expanded its Super Fresh chain and in 1985 acquired Dominion Foods to strengthen its position in Canada. A&P was in the process of developing a format similar to Food Emporium called Food Bazaar but elected instead to scrap that idea in favor of buying Shopwell and growing the Food Emporium chain.

Glen Rosengarten went to work for A&P at its Montvale, New Jersey, headquarters but did not stay long, as the relationship between the Rosengartens and A&P quickly soured. Early in 1987, A&P filed a lawsuit accusing the Rosengarten brothers and ten other Shopwell executives of overstating the value of the company, which it said led A&P to overpay by $9.4 million. Shopwell executives countered by suing A&P for $8 million in damages resulting from the breach of employment contracts and consulting agreements. Neither suit amounted to much, and each side went its own way.

The Food Emporium chain was tucked into A&P's Metro New York division. In the year following the purchase of Shopwell, A&P opened two Food Emporium stores, one of which was a Food Bazaar that was under development and reconfigured and another that Shopwell was developing. The first Food Emporium built from scratch by A&P, as part of a $450 million capital spending program to expand all of its formats, opened in New Canaan, Connecticut, in the fall of 1987. A handful of other stores located in New York City and Connecticut would follow over the next few years. In 1990, A&P attempted to transfer the Food Emporium format outside the New York City area, opening two stores in Canada under the Dominion Food Emporium banner and two in Milwaukee as Kohl's Food Emporium. There was some talk at the time of exporting the Food Emporium name to upscale neighborhoods in other major cities, such as Chicago, Philadelphia, and Washington, D.C., but nothing ever materialized, and the Food Emporium format remained focused in New York City.

The size of the Food Emporium chain grew by just a dozen units over the next 20 years. In 1997, Food Emporium moved across the Hudson River to Fort Lee, New Jersey, but no more New Jersey units would follow. The excitement that accompanied the launch of the Food Emporium chain had long since waned. The stores had carved out a local customer base, but there was no reason to believe that the Food Emporium concept was original enough to warrant large scale expansion, nor was it likely that the chain's corporate parent would commit the kind of money necessary to fund such growth. By the turn of the 21st century, A&P was once again struggling and even turned to an industry outsider, Elizabeth Culligan, a Nabisco veteran with experience in the pharmaceutical industry, to serve as president and chief operating officer and help turn it around. Although she was able to return the company to profitability within 15 months, A&P suffered a severe setback, and less than two years after taking the job she resigned ''to pursue other interests.'' Her successors struggled to return the company to health and were forced to close stores and retreat from several markets. As a result, the future of the Food Emporium chain was somewhat uncertain.

Principal Competitors

D'Agostino Supermarkets, Inc.; Gristede's Foods, Inc.; Pathmark.

Further Reading

Alson, Amy, ''Shopwell Faces Big Task Selling Debt-Laden Stores,'' *Crain's New York Business*, May 5, 1986, p. 3.
Bernstein, Aaron, ''Truffles, Anyone?'' *Forbes*, April 25, 1983, p. 132.
''Daitch Crystal Dairies, Inc. to Ring up Large Profits,'' *Barron's National Business and Fiancial Weekly*, January 28, 1957, p. 23.
Hollie, Pamela G., ''The New Gourmet Shopwell,'' *New York Times*, October 16, 1983.

—Ed Dinger

Ford Motor Company

One American Road
Dearborn, Michigan 48126-2798
U.S.A.
Telephone: (313) 322-3000
Toll Free: (800) 555-5259
Fax: (313) 845-6073
Web site: http://www.ford.com

Public Company
Incorporated: 1919
Employees: 327,531
Sales: $164.1 billion (2003)
Stock Exchanges: New York Pacific Euronext Paris
    Swiss London
Ticker Symbol: F
NAIC: 336111 Automobile Manufacturing; 336112 Light
    Truck and Utility Vehicle Manufacturing; 33612
    Heavy Duty Truck Manufacturing; 33621 Motor
    Vehicle Body Manufacturing; 532112 Passenger Car
    Leasing; 524126 Direct Property and Casualty
    Insurance Carriers

As the second-largest automobile company in the world, Ford Motor Company represents a $164 billion multinational business empire. Known primarily as a manufacturer of automobiles, Ford also operates Ford Credit, which generates more than $3 billion in income, and owns The Hertz Corporation, the largest automobile rental company in the world. The company manufactures vehicles under the names Ford, Lincoln, Mercury, Jaguar, Volvo, Land Rover, and Aston Martin. Ford also maintains controlling interest in Mazda Motor Corporation. Ford's financial stability was shaken in early years of the new millennium as a result of slowing sales, quality issues, and a debacle involving Firestone tires.

Origins of an American Legend

Henry Ford, the founder of the Ford Motor Company, was born on a farm near Dearborn, Michigan, in 1863. He had a talent for engineering, which he pursued as a hobby from boyhood, but it was not until 1890 that he commenced his engineering career as an employee of the Detroit Edison Company. In his spare time, Ford constructed experimental gasoline engines and in 1892 completed his first gasoline buggy. Dissatisfied with the buggy's weight, he sold it in 1896 to help fund the construction of a new car. Ford's superiors at the electric company felt his hobby distracted him from his regular occupation and, despite his promotion to chief engineer, he was forced to quit in 1899.

Shortly afterwards, with financial backing from private investors, Ford established the Detroit Automobile Company. He later withdrew from the venture after a disagreement with business associates over the numbers and prices of cars to be produced. Ford advocated a business strategy which combined a lower profit margin on each car with greater production volumes. In this way, he hoped to gain a larger market share and maintain profitability.

Independently in a small shed in Detroit, Henry Ford developed two four-cylinder, 80-horsepower race cars, called the 999 and the Arrow. These cars won several races and helped to create a new market for Ford automobiles. With $28,000 of capital raised from friends and neighbors, Henry Ford established a new shop on June 16, 1903. In this facility, a converted wagon factory on Mack Avenue in Detroit, the Ford Motor Company began production of a two-cylinder, eight-horsepower design called the Model A. The company produced 1,708 of these models in the first year of operation.

The Ford Motor Company was sued by the Licensed Association of Automobile Manufacturers, an industrial syndicate which held patent rights for road locomotives with internal combustion engines. Ford responded by taking the matter to the courts, arguing that the patent, granted to George B. Selden in 1895, was invalid. During the long process of adjudication, Ford continued to manufacture cars and relocated to a larger plant on Piquette and Beaubien Streets. A Canadian plant was established in Walkerville, Ontario, on August 17, 1904.

Henry Ford and his engineers designed several automobiles, each one designated by a letter of the alphabet; these included

Company Perspectives:

Our vision is to become the world's leading consumer company for automotive products and services. We are a global family with a proud heritage passionately committed to providing personal mobility for people around the world.

the small, four-cylinder Model N (which sold for $500), and the more luxurious six-cylinder Model K (which sold poorly for $2,500). The failure of the Model K, coupled with Henry Ford's persistence in developing inexpensive cars for mass production, caused a dispute between Ford and his associate Alexander Malcolmson. The latter, who helped to establish the company in 1903, resigned and his share of the company was acquired by Henry Ford. Ford's holdings then amounted to 58.5 percent. In a further consolidation of his control, Ford replaced John S. Gray, a Detroit banker, as president of the company in 1906.

In October 1908, despite the continuing litigation with the Selden syndicate, Ford introduced the durable and practical Model T. Demand for this car was so great that Ford was forced to enlarge its production facilities. Over 10,000 Model Ts were produced in 1909. Able to vote down business associates who favored more conventional methods of production, Henry Ford applied his assembly line concept of manufacturing to the Model T.

In developing the assembly line, Ford noted that the average worker performed several tasks in the production of each component, and used a variety of tools in the process. He improved efficiency by having each worker specialize in one task with one tool. The component on which the employee worked was conveyed to him on a moving belt, and after allowing a set time for the task to be performed, the component was moved on to the next operation. Slower workers thus needed to increase their work rate in order to maintain production at the rate determined by the speed of the belts.

Ford's battle with the Selden group led to a decision by the Supreme Court in 1911, eight years after the initial suit. The Court ruled that the Selden patent was invalid. The decision freed many automobile manufacturers from costly licensing obligations; it also enabled others to enter the business.

When the United States became involved in World War I (April 1917), the Ford Motor Company placed its resources at the disposal of the government. For the duration of the war, Ford Motor produced large quantities of automobiles, trucks, and ambulances, as well as Liberty airplane motors, Whippet tanks, Eagle submarine chasers, and munitions. In 1918, Henry Ford officially retired from the company, naming his son Edsel president and ceding to him a controlling interest. But, in fact, Henry continued to direct company strategy and spent much of his time developing a farm tractor called the Fordson. He also published a conservative weekly journal, the *Dearborn Independent*. Edsel, who was more reserved and pragmatic than his father, concerned himself with routine operations.

At the end of the war Henry and Edsel Ford disagreed with fellow stockholders over the planned expenditure of several million dollars for a large new manufacturing complex at River Rouge, near Detroit. The Fords eventually resolved the conflict by buying out all the other shareholders. Their company was re-registered as a Delaware corporation in July 1919. The River Rouge facility, built shortly afterward, was a large integrated manufacturing and assembly complex which included a steel mill of substantial capacity.

Cash-Strapped in the 1920s

Between January 1 and April 19, 1921, the Ford Motor Company had $58 million in financial obligations due, and only $20 million available to meet them. Convinced that Ford Motor would be forced into bankruptcy, representatives of several large financial houses offered to extend loans to the company, on the condition that the Fords yield financial control. When the offer was refused, the bankers retreated, certain that they would soon be called upon to repossess the company.

With little time available, Henry Ford transferred as many automobiles as possible to his dealerships, who were instructed to pay in cash. Almost immediately, this generated $25 million. Next, Ford purchased the Detroit, Toledo & Ironton railroad, the primary medium of transportation for his company's supplies. By rearranging the railroad's schedules, Ford was able to reduce by one-third the time that automotive components spent in transit. This allowed him to reduce inventories by one-third, thereby releasing $28 million. With additional income from other sources, and reduction in production costs, Ford had $87 million in cash by April 1, $27 million more than he needed to pay off the company debts.

The Ford Motor Company's only relationship with banks after this crisis was as a depositor. Moreover, despite poor financial management, Ford maintained such strong profitability that it offered to lend money on the New York markets, in competition with banks. With large quantities of cash still available, Ford acquired the financially troubled Lincoln Motor Company in 1922.

Edsel Ford was more enthusiastic about the development of the aircraft industry than his father, and in 1925 persuaded his fellow shareholders (all family members) to purchase the Stout Metal Airplane Company. His close friend William Stout, who was retained as vice-president and general manager of the company, developed a popular three-engine passenger aircraft known as the Ford Trimotor. Nearly 200 of these aircraft were built during its production run.

After 18 years producing the Model T, the Ford Motor Company faced its first serious threat from a competitor. In 1926, General Motors Corporation introduced its Chevrolet automobile, a more stylish and powerful car. Sales of the Model T dropped sharply. After months of experimenting with a six-cylinder model, Ford decided to discontinue the Model T in favor of the new Model A. On May 31, 1926, Ford plants across the country were closed for six months while assembly lines were retooled.

That year Ford voluntarily reduced its work week to five days, declaring that workers should also benefit from the success of the company. Ford was also one of the first companies to limit the work day to eight hours, and to establish a minimum

Key Dates:

1903: Henry Ford sets up shop in a converted wagon factory.
1908: Ford's Model T is introduced.
1922: Lincoln Motor Company is acquired.
1945: Henry Ford II is appointed company president.
1963: Ford Mustang is released.
1985: Ford Taurus is introduced.
1989: Jaguar Cars Ltd. is acquired.
1999: Swedish automaker Volvo is acquired in a $6.45 billion deal.
2001: The company takes a $2.1 billion charge to cover the cost of replacing Firestone tires on its vehicles; William Clay Ford, Jr., is named CEO.

wage of $5 per day. At Henry Ford's own admission, these policies were instituted more to improve productivity than to appease dissatisfied (and unrepresented) workers.

The British Ford Company was formed in 1928 and shortly thereafter the German Ford Company was founded. Henry Ford recognized the Soviet Union as a market with great potential, and like a number of other American industrialists, he fostered a relationship with officials in the Soviet government. Later, Ford participated in the construction of an automobile factory at Nishni-Novgogrod.

The economic crisis of October 1929, which led to the Great Depression, forced many companies to close. Ford Motor managed to remain in business, despite losses of as much as $68 million per year. By 1932, economic conditions became so difficult that the Ford minimum wage was reduced to $4 per day. But for its Model A, which sold 4.5 million units between 1927 and 1931, Ford's situation would have been much worse.

The economy of Detroit was heavily dependent on large, locally based industrial manufacturers and when companies less successful than Ford were forced to suspend operations, a banking crisis developed. The Ford Motor Company, and Edsel Ford personally, extended about $12 million in loans to these banks in an effort to maintain their solvency. But these efforts failed and the banks were forced to close in February 1933. Ford lost over $32 million in deposits and several million more in bank securities. The principal Ford bank, Guardian National, was subsequently reorganized by Ford interests as the Manufacturers National Bank of Detroit. Ford's largest business rival, General Motors, having suffered a similar crisis, emerged with control over the National Bank of Detroit.

The implementation of President Roosevelt's New Deal made conditions more favorable to the organization of labor unions. But Henry Ford, who had supported President Hoover in the election, advised his workers to resist union organization, and in 1935 raised the company's minimum wage to $6 per day.

In 1937, the United Automobile Workers (UAW) union began a campaign to organize Ford workers by sponsoring the employee occupation of a Ford plant in Kansas City. The conflict was resolved when Ford officials agreed to meet with

union representatives. That same year, there was trouble at the River Rouge complex. Several men distributing UAW pamphlets at the gates were severely beaten by unidentified assailants, believed to have been agents of the Ford security office. Following an investigation by the National Labor Relations Board, Ford was cited for numerous unfair labor practices. The finding was contested, but eventually upheld when the Supreme Court refused to hear the case.

The War Years

In 1940, Henry Ford, who opposed American involvement in World War II, canceled a contract (arranged by Edsel) to build 6,000 Rolls-Royce Merlin aircraft engines for the British Royal Air Force, and 3,000 more for the U.S. Army. In time, however, public opinion led Ford to change his mind. Plans were made for the construction of a large new government-sponsored facility to manufacture aircraft at Willow Run, west of Dearborn.

Unionization activities climaxed in April 1941 when Ford employees went on strike. The NLRB called an employee election, under the terms of the Wagner Act, to establish a union representation for Ford workers. When the ballots were tabulated in June, the UAW drew 70 percent of the votes. Henry Ford, an avowed opponent of labor unions, suddenly altered his stand. He agreed to a contract with union representatives which met all worker demands.

The company devoted its resources to the construction of the Willow Run Aircraft plant. Eight months later, in December 1941, the Japanese bombing of Pearl Harbor resulted in a declaration of war by the United States against Japan, Germany, and Italy. Willow Run was completed the following May. It was the largest manufacturing facility in the world, occupying 2.5 million square feet of floor space, with an assembly line three miles long. Adjacent to the plant were hangars, covering 1.2 million square feet, and a large airfield. The airplanes produced at this facility were four-engine B-24E Liberator bombers, the Consolidated Aircraft version of the Boeing B-24. Production of aircraft got off to a slow start, but after adjustments the rate of production was raised to one plane per hour, 24 hours a day. During the war, other Ford Motor plants produced a variety of engines, as well as trucks, jeeps,—4 tanks,—10 tank destroyers, and transport gliders. The company also manufactured large quantities of tires, despite the removal of its tire plant to the Soviet Union.

Edsel Ford died unexpectedly in May 1943 at the age of 49. At the time of his death, Edsel was recognized as a far better manager than his father. Indeed, Henry Ford was often criticized for repeatedly undermining his son's efforts to improve the company, and the managerial crisis which occurred after Edsel's death is directly attributable to Henry Ford's persistent failure to prepare capable managers for future leadership of the company.

Edsel had been responsible for much of the company's wartime mobilization and his absence was deeply felt by his aging father, who was forced to resume the company presidency. In need of assistance, Henry Ford sought a special discharge from the Navy for Edsel's son Henry II. The navy complied, citing the special needs of Ford management during wartime. Henry Ford vigorously prepared his grandson to succeed him. By the end of the war, when the Willow Run plant was turned over to the government, Ford had produced 8,600 B-24E bombers and over 57,000 aircraft engines.

In September 1945, Henry Ford II, aged 28, was named president of the Ford Motor Company. The inexperienced man could not have started at a worse time. No longer supported by government contracts, the company began to lose money at a rate of $10 million per month. The source of the problem was Henry Ford I's financial management policy, specifically designed to perplex the Internal Revenue Service and discourage audits. The severe economic conditions after the war made Ford's finances an albatross.

Unable to bring the company's finances under control, Henry II hired Ernest R. Breech, a General Motors executive and past chairperson of Bendix, in 1946. Breech was placed in charge of two groups—a managerial group and a financial one. The first one was comprised of several managers hired away from General Motors, and the second group was made up of ten talented financial experts who had served with the Air Force Office of Statistical Control. The Air Force group included Robert S. McNamara, J. Edward Lundy, Arjay Miller, and Charles Tex Thornton; they spent several years reconstructing the company's system of financial management.

Henry Ford I, who had retained the title of chairperson since 1945, died in April 1947 at the age of 83. Henry II and Ernest Breech were then able to implement their own strategies for recovery, and these included the adoption of the proven General Motors management structure, and the decision to establish the Ford Motor Company in foreign markets. In its first year under Breech, the company registered a profit and it continued to gain strength in the late 1940s and early 1950s. Breech's top priority was strict adherence to a financial plan with strong profit margins; unfortunately, this proved to be at the expense of developing automobiles for an increasingly complex market.

Over the previous two decades, the Ford Motor Company had been a notable pioneer and achiever in the industry, and it was the first company to cast a V-8 engine block (1932). Ford had produced its 25 millionth automobile in 1937 and the following year its Lincoln Division introduced the Mercury line, which proved highly successful in the growing market for medium-priced automobiles. Ford's good image had been further enhanced by its contributions to the Allied effort in World War II; even Josef Stalin had kind words for the enterprising American company.

Before he died, Henry Ford I had created two classes of Ford stock. The B Class was reserved for family members and constituted the controlling 40 percent voting interest. The ordinary common shares were to be retained by the company until January 1956, when they were to be offered to the public for the first time.

Two years after Henry I's death, in 1949, the company unveiled a number of new automatic styles. But while the cars were practical, and to a degree fashionable, the company no longer appeared to be a pioneer; indeed it gained a reputation, not wholly justified, as being an imitator of General Motors.

Regaining its initiative, the Ford Motor Company decided to introduce a new model to fill a gap in the market between the Ford and Lincoln-Mercury lines. In 1958, the much heralded 410 horsepower Edsel made its debut. It was a terrible flop. Ford's market researchers had been very wrong; there was no gap in the market for the Edsel to fill. After just two years, production of the ill-fated car ceased—110,847 units had been produced, at a loss of some $250 million.

The 1960s–70s

The 1960s saw many changes at Ford: dissatisfied with his secondary role in the company decision-making, Henry Ford stripped Breech of his power, replacing him with Robert McNamara. But McNamara left the Ford Motor Company in 1961 to serve as Secretary of Defense in the Kennedy administration. Many of McNamara's duties were taken over by Arjay Miller, who succeeded the interim president, John Dykstra, in 1963.

The Ford Motor Company purchased the Philco Corporation in 1961 and established a tractor division in 1962. The following year, Ford introduced its highly successful Mustang; more than 500,000 of these cars were sold in 18 months. The man most responsible for developing the Mustang was a protege of Robert McNamara named Lee Iacocca.

In another move intended to assert his authority over management, Henry Ford II dismissed Arjay Miller in 1968 and named Semon E. Knudsen as president. Knudsen, a former executive vice-president at General Motors known for his aggressive personality, found himself in constant conflict with Henry Ford, and after 19 months he was replaced by Lee Iacocca. Iacocca was a popular figure, highly talented in marketing and sales, but like Knudsen, he frequently disagreed with Henry Ford.

Ford Motor Company subsidiaries in Europe entered a period of strong growth and high profitability in the early 1970s, and these subsidiaries produced components for the Pinto, a sub-compact introduced in the United States in 1971. Pinto models from 1971 to 1976 and similarly configured Bobcats from 1975 to 1976 drew a great deal of attention after several incidents in which the car's gas tank exploded in rear-end collisions. The unfavorable publicity from news reports damaged Ford's public image, as did wrongful death litigation.

In April 1977, Henry Ford II reduced Iacocca's power by creating a new executive triumvirate. Iacocca was a member of this, along with Ford himself and Philip Caldwell. But a year later, Ford added his brother William Clay Ford to the group and relegated Iacocca to a subordinate position; then within a few months, Ford suddenly fired Iacocca and installed Caldwell as president. Henry Ford was battling stockholder allegations of financial misconduct and bribery at the time and his dismissal of Iacocca made him more unpopular than ever. Iacocca went on to head Chrysler Corporation.

Henry Ford made a critical decision and a very misguided one. He cancelled development of a small car which had been proposed by Iacocca and which was intended to succeed the aging Pinto. Thus, as the Japanese compacts became increasingly popular in the United States, Ford found itself quite unable to compete. Adding to its woes, Ford, along with other

U.S. car manufacturers, was obligated by Congressional legislation (particularly the Clean Air Act) to develop automobiles which would emit less pollutants. Henry Ford relinquished his position as chief executive officer to Philip Caldwell in October 1979. The following March, Ford retired and gave the chair to Caldwell, while retaining his seat on the board of directors.

Ford Motor Company encountered severe economic losses as a result of a reduction in market share, as well as the high costs incurred by labor contracts and the development of automobiles that met the new federal standards. In 1980, the company lost $1.54 billion, despite strong profits from the truck division and European operations. Ford lost a further $1.06 billion in 1981 and $658 million in 1982 while trying to effect a recovery; its market share fell from 3.6 percent in 1978 to 16.6 percent in 1981.

Company officials studied Japanese methods of industrial management, and worked more closely with Toyo Kogyo, the Japanese manufacturer of Mazda automobiles (Ford gained a 25 percent share of Toyo Kogyo in November 1979, when a Ford subsidiary merged with the company). Ford imported Mazda cars and trucks, and in many ways treated Toyo Kogyo as a small car division until the Escort, its successor to the Pinto, reached the showrooms. This new compact was modeled after the Ford (Europe) Erika; another version of it, the Lynx, was produced by Ford's Lincoln-Mercury division.

Caldwell transferred the talented manager Harold Poling from the European division to the United States in an attempt to apply successful European formulas to the American operation. In the restructuring that followed, several plants were closed and more than 100,000 workers were dismissed. Ford's weakness in the market was a major concern of the unions; consequently, the company inaugurated a policy of employee involvement in plant operations and was able to secure more favorable labor contracts. Productivity improved dramatically.

In 1984, with costs reduced, Ford started to repurchase 30 million shares (about 10 percent of the company's stock). Its production of cars in Mexico was increased, and through its interest in Kia Motors, output was stepped up in South Korea. The following year, Ford introduced the Taurus (another version, the Sable, was produced by its Mercury division), a modern full-size automobile which had taken five years to develop at a cost of $3 billion. The Taurus proved highly successful and won several design and safety awards.

Sales and profits reached record levels in 1984, and in 1986 Ford surpassed General Motors in income for the first time since 1924. In addition, Ford's market share increased to just under 20 percent. Ford Motor purchased several companies in the mid-1980s, including the First Nationwide Financial Corporation and the New Holland tractor division of Sperry, which was later merged with Ford Tractor. Ford also purchased a 30 percent share of Otosan, the automotive subsidiary of the Turkish KoX Group. The attempted acquisition of the Italian car maker Alfa Romeo in 1986 failed, due to a rival bid from Fiat.

Challenging Early 1990s

The diversification into financial services that began in the mid-1980s continued in earnest throughout the rest of the dec-

ade, as each of the major U.S. car manufacturers sought to insulate themselves against the cyclical nature of their business. Ford spent $5.5 billion acquiring assets for its financial services group during the latter half of the decade, including a $3.4 billion purchase in 1989 of The Associates, a Dallas-based finance company. That acquisition, completed the same year Ford purchased the venerable British car manufacturer Jaguar Cars Ltd. for $2.5 billion, made Ford the country's second largest provider of diversified financial services, ranking only behind Citicorp. With plans to eventually derive 30 percent of the company's profits from financial service-related business, Ford entered the 1990s with $115 billion worth of banking-related assets, a portfolio that provided the company's only bright moments during the otherwise deleterious early 1990s.

An economic recession crippled U.S. car manufacturers during the early 1990s, and Ford bore the brunt of the financial malaise that stretched around the globe. Domestically, car sales faltered abroad, particularly in Great Britain and Australia, Ford's sales plummeted. In 1991, Ford's worldwide automotive operations lost an enormous $3.2 billion after recording a $99 million profit the year before. In the United States, automotive losses reached an equally staggering $2.2 billion on the heels of a $17 million loss in 1990. The losses struck a serious blow to Ford, which as recently as 1989 had generated $3.3 billion in net income; however, the financial results of 1991 would have been worse without the company's strategic diversification into financial services. For the year, Ford's financial services group registered a record $927 million in earnings, up from the previous year's total of $761 million, which left the company with a $2.25 billion loss for the year, an inauspicious record in Ford's nearly 90-year history.

The financial disaster of 1991, however, was just a prelude to more pernicious losses the following year, as the global recession reached its greatest intensity. In 1992, with revenue swelling to slightly more than $100 billion, Ford posted a $7.38 billion loss. Although 1992 represented one of the bleakest years in Ford's history, the worst was over, and as the economic climate improved, the company emerged with renewed vitality. Against the backdrop of successive financial losses, Ford had increased its presence in the truck and minivan market niche, which represented the fastest-growing segment of the broadly defined automotive market. Roughly 200,000 minivans and sports utility vehicles were sold in the United States a decade earlier and now, as consumers once again returned to car dealers' showrooms, more than 2.3 million opted for minivans and light trucks, a trend that bolstered Ford's financial position and predicated its return to a profitable future.

During this time, the gap separating Japanese and American car manufacturers' production standards had narrowed considerably, with the U.S. manufacturers emerging from the early 1990s in a more enviable position—Ford included. As the technological and managerial race between U.S. car manufacturers and their Japanese counterparts tightened, the importance of prudent product development and effective distribution networks increased. Toward this end, Ford reorganized its production and distribution operations in mid-1994 to better respond to the changing economic structure of the numerous countries in which Ford operated facilities. Regional trading areas, rather than nation states, would represent the primary focus of Ford's future efforts, a direction the company moved toward with its worldwide reorganization in 1994.

Ford's notable achievements during the latter half of the 1990s were philosophical in nature, as the company attempted to replace the corporate culture of its past with a new way of thinking for the future. The proponent of Ford's new vision was Lebanese-born, Melbourne, Australia-raised Jacques Nasser, who was named president and chief executive officer in January 1998, concurrent with the appointment of William Clay Ford, Jr., great-grandson of the founder, as chairman. Two years before his historic promotion—at age 51, Nasser became the youngest, non-family chief executive in the company's history—Nasser was named president of Ford's worldwide automotive operations, and he did not like what he saw. The company had the lowest profits from total vehicle sales of any U.S. automaker, an alarming statistic that Nasser began to improve by slashing costs. His cost-cutting efforts earned Nasser the nickname Jac the Knife, but once he was named Ford's chief executive in 1998, the characterization of his influence took on an added dimension. Nasser's aim was to replace the corporate culture of decades past with an entrepreneurial style that placed a much more intense emphasis on the customer. He continued making his trademark cuts in costs, realizing $5 billion in savings between 1997 and 1999, but he also worked toward instilling a new ethos at Ford.

As part of the new movement espoused by Nasser, the company's Lincoln-Mercury division was relocated from Detroit to Irvine, California, an unprecedented move for a major U.S. automaker. Nasser wanted the division to attract younger customers—Lincoln's typical customer was 63 years old, Mercury's was 56 years old—and to be closer to suppliers and to emerging auto trends. Nasser wanted the division to breathe new life into itself away from the scrutiny of company headquarters, to benefit from a more entrepreneurial-driven perspective.

The changes at Lincoln-Mercury typified the profound currents of change sweeping through Ford at the century's end. Much remained to be done to achieve Nasser's vision of a fundamentally revamped Ford, but by the end of the 1990s there were impressive signs of progress. The company ended the decade as the most profitable automaker in the world. Its stock price increased 130 percent between 1996 and 1999, outpacing the increases recorded by its rivals. Analysts predicted great things for Ford, thanks in large part to the company's increased ownership stake in Mazda Motor Corporation (from 25 percent to 33.4 percent in 1996) and its $6.45 billion acquisition of Swedish auto maker Volvo in 1999.

The New Millennium

However, Ford faced major challenges in the early years of the new millennium. While it continued to lay the groundwork for future growth by spinning off its Visteon unit, acquiring BMW's Land Rover SUV business, and purchasing the remaining shares of Hertz that it did not already own, it was dealt a significant blow when Bridgestone recalled over 6.5 million Firestone brand tires—tires used as original equipment on Ford's popular Explorer model, the Mercury Mountaineer, the Ranger, and some of its F-150 pickups. In the largest recall in automotive history, Ford was forced to call back over 300,000

vehicles and replace over 13 million Firestone tires at a cost of $3 billion in 2001 alone. To make matters worse, several deaths had been linked to faulty tires on the Ford Explorer, and some alleged that Ford had known about the problem all along and had failed to act.

As a result of the tire debacle and several other product recalls, Ford was ranked last in the industry in terms of quality according to J.D. Power & Associates. In 2001, the company posted a loss of $5.45 billion. Nasser was ousted in late that year, leaving William Clay Ford, Jr., at the helm. The task set before him was monumental; he faced faltering employee morale, major quality issues, sluggish sales, and intense price wars.

In early 2002, Ford launched a major restructuring effort that included the closure of five plants, the elimination of 35,000 jobs, over $9 billion in cost cutting measures, and the shuttering of several car lines including the Mercury Cougar and the Lincoln Continental. Included in the plan were efforts to boost the morale of employees. In a speech quoted in a November 2002 *Fortune* article, CEO Ford reminded his work force "We've come back from adversity many times in our history. We're going to do it again. On the eve of our 100th anniversary, the stage is set for a dramatic return to greatness. We started the job; now let's finish it."

The company forged ahead in 2002 cutting its losses to $559 million. Market share continued to fall, however, hovering at 21 percent versus the 25 percent it held in 1998. In response, Ford sold some non-core assets and ramped up new product development, launching the Ford Focus C-MAX in Europe, the Jaguar XJ, the Volvo S40, a new Ford F-150, the Ford Freestar, and the Mercury Monterey in 2003. Ford anticipated launching 40 new products in 2004 including the new Mustang and the Escape Hybrid, the first gasoline/electric SUV. Overall, the company planned to have 150 new products in the marketplace by mid-decade.

While a turnaround at the Ford Credit subsidiary bolstered the company's income, automotive operations, especially the international arm, continued to struggle. James J. Padilla, elected chief operating officer in 2004, and William Clay Ford, Jr., indeed faced a long road ahead. Restoring Ford's image and getting the company back on a successful financial path would no doubt be their focus in the years to come.

Principal Subsidiaries

Ford Brasil Ltda.; Ford Capital B.V. (Netherlands); Ford Motor Company (Belgium) N.V.; Ford Espana S.A.; Ford European Holdings, Inc.; Ford Holdings LLC; Volvo Car Holding Germany GmbH; Ford Motor Land Development Corporation; The Hertz Corporation; Ford Global Technologies, LLC; Ford International Capital Corporation; Jaguar Ltd.; Ford Italia S.p.A.; Ford Mexico Holdings, Inc.; Ford Motor Company of Canada, Ltd.; Land Rover Holdings; Ford Motor Company of Southern Africa (Pty) Ltd.; Ford Motor Company of Australia Ltd.; Ford Deutschland Holding, GmbH; Ford Motor Credit Company; Ford Credit Canada Ltd.; Ford Motor Service Company; Ford Motor Vehicle Assurance Company; Ford Trading Company, LLC; Groupe FMC France SAS; Volvo Cars of North America, LLC.

Principal Competitors

DaimlerChrysler AG; General Motors Corporation; Toyota Motor Corporation.

Further Reading

Beynon, Huw, *Working for Ford,* London: Penguin, 1984.

"Carload of Trouble," *Business Week,* March 27, 2000, p. 56.

Connelly, Mary, "Ford's Biggest Job: Lift Lincoln," *Automotive News,* July 31, 2000, p. 23.

"A Crisis of Confidence," *Business Week,* September 18, 2000, p. 40.

Dubashi, Jagannath, "Ford: Looking Beyond the Shadows," *FW,* February 6, 1990, p. 23.

"Ford: Will Slow and Steady Win the Race?," *Business Week,* May 10, 2004, p. 43.

Gelderman, Barbara, *Henry Ford: The Wayward Capitalist,* New York: Dial Press, 1981.

Gross, Ken, "Ford: Big, Bigger, Biggest," *Automotive Industries,* July 2000, p. 64.

Keatley, Robert, "Ford Reorganizes to Stay Competitive and Reach New Markets in the World," *Wall Street Journal,* July 22, 1994, p. A4.

Kerwin, Kathleen, "One of Ford's Engines is Humming," *Business Week,* July 21, 2003, p. 26.

Kerwin, Kathleen, and Joann Muller, "Bill Takes the Wheel," *Business Week,* November 12, 2001, p. 50.

Lewis, David L., *The Public Image of Henry Ford: An American Folk Hero and His Company,* Detroit: Wayne State University Press, 1976.

Meyer, Stephen, *The Five Dollar Day: Labor Management and Social Control in the Ford Motor Company 1908–1921,* Albany: State University of New York Press, 1981.

Moreau, Dan, "Instant Prosperity: Behind Ford's Fast Turnaround," *Kiplinger's Personal Finance Magazine,* July 1993, p. 28.

Morris, Betsy, "Can Ford Save Ford?," *Fortune,* November 18, 2002, p. 52.

"Nasser: Ford Be Nimble," *Business Week,* September 27, 1999, p. 42.

Nye, David E., *Henry Ford: Ignorant Idealist,* Port Washington: Kennikat Press, 1979.

Reiff, Rick, "Slowing Traffic Ahead," *Forbes,* April 30, 1990, p. 82.

"Remaking Ford," *Business Week,* October 11, 1999, p. 132.

Sorge, Marjorie, "1999 Executive of the Year," *Automotive Industries,* February 1999, p. 54.

Taylor III, Alex, "Getting Ford in Gear," *Fortune,* May 12, 2003, p. 102.

——, "The Fiasco at Ford," *Fortune,* February 4, 2002, p. 111.

——, "Why Ford's Chairman Has Kept Mostly Mum," *Fortune,* October 2, 2000, p. 43.

Thomas, Charles M., "Ford Loses a Record $2.3 Billion," *Automotive News,* February 17, 1992, p. 4.

Zesiger, Sue, "Ford's Hip Transplant," *Fortune,* May 10, 1999, p. 82.

——, "Mr. Ford and Mr. Nasser Learn to Share: The Lords of Ford," *Fortune,* October 12, 1998, p. 34.

—updates: Jeffrey L. Covell and Christina M. Stansell

Fred Meyer Stores, Inc.

3800 Southeast 22nd Avenue
Portland, Oregon 97202
U.S.A.
Telephone: (503) 232-8844
Toll Free: (800) 858-9202
Fax: (503) 797-5609
Web site: http://www.fredmeyerstores.com

Wholly Owned Subsidiary of The Kroger Co.
Incorporated: 1923
Employees: 92,000
Sales: $14.9 billion (1998)
NAIC: 452110 Department Stores; 452910 Warehouse
   Clubs and Superstores

Fred Meyer Stores, Inc. operates the third-largest group of supercenters in the United States. It has approximately 130 stores, ranging from 130,000 to 200,000 square feet in size, that provide over 225,000 food, apparel, and general merchandise products to shoppers in the Northwest. Fred Meyer significantly increased its holdings in 1997 and 1998 by acquiring Smith's Food & Drug Centers Inc., Quality Food Centers Inc., and Food 4 Less Holdings Inc. The company and its subsidiaries, including Fred Meyer Jewelers, were purchased by The Kroger Co. in 1999. The $13.5 billion deal secured Kroger's position as the largest grocery chain in the United States.

Entrepreneurial Beginnings

The history of Fred Meyer, Inc. revolves around its founder, Fred G. Meyer, who guided the company until his death in 1978. In 1908, 22-year-old Frederick Grubmeyer, son of a Brooklyn grocer, moved to Portland and began selling coffee to workers at the farms and lumber camps that surrounded the burgeoning town of Portland. The horse-drawn route prospered, but young Grubmeyer, who eventually changed his name to Fred G. Meyer, wanted more. In a few years, he moved to Alaska to seek other business opportunities. Alaska was overrun with would-be entrepreneurs, however, and Meyer returned to Portland and founded the Java Coffee Company, selling coffee, tea, and spices from a storefront in the market district.

The Java Coffee Company, later renamed the Mission Tea Company, prospered, while many neighboring businesses succumbed to the uncertain economics of the time. Meyer snapped up their properties and soon was landlord, and sometimes operator, of several specialty food operations.

In the early 1920s, the center of commercial activity moved uptown, and Meyer moved with it, consolidating his several specialty businesses into a single location that became the flagship store for the Fred Meyer chain. The store, which opened in 1922, had 20 employees, with Meyer serving as buyer and manager. Its seven departments included meat, delicatessen, coffee, lunch, homemade mayonnaise, grocery, and tobacco. In 1923, Fred Meyer incorporated his business in Oregon, and a second store was opened that featured grocery and dairy products.

Fred Meyer continued expanding throughout the 1920s. Across the street from the parent store, he opened a packaged food store selling sugar, dry beans, rice, macaroni, spaghetti, coffee, and dried fruits. Then, in 1928, he opened what many regard as the world's first self-service drugstore. The store's lower labor costs meant lower prices, and Meyer's reputation as a value merchandiser was established.

The company prospered despite the stock market crash of 1929 and the ensuing Great Depression. Meyer opened four new stores between 1929 and 1932: a toiletry store, a department store in the outlying Portland neighborhood of Hollywood, and his first stores outside Portland, in the towns of Salem and Astoria, Oregon. The Hollywood store marked Meyer's recognition of the growing importance of the car in retailing. Finding that customers were often double-parking in front of his downtown stores and getting ticketed in the process, Meyer would pay the tickets. Meyer did an informal survey and found that many customers lived in the Hollywood section of Portland, about five miles from downtown. This led to the opening of the Hollywood store, which included an off-street parking lot and an automobile lubrication and oil service.

Throughout the 1930s, Meyer ran a series of aggressive promotions that highlighted the company's low prices. Meyer saw these entertaining promotions as ways of getting customers into stores during cash-starved times. He rented movie theaters and gave children free admission if they brought three My-Te-

Fine store-brand labels. He had newspapers add peppermint to their ink, giving his candy ads a sweet smell.

These and other promotions helped make Fred Meyer a major player in Portland, but the company was not without competition. Drugstores banded together to stop the company from obtaining a prescription license. Retailers threatened to drop lines if manufacturers sold to Fred Meyer. An anonymously sponsored radio show spent all its time lambasting the quality of Fred Meyer goods. However, all of these tactics were to no avail.

Expanding the Product Line in 1930s

Fred Meyer began adding new products in the early 1930s, and the stores began selling men's and women's wear in 1933. Automotive departments, housewares, and other nonfood products followed in succeeding years. The middle of the decade saw the opening of a central bakery, a candy kitchen, an ice cream plant, and a photo-finishing plant. These facilities paved the way for house brands such as Vita Bee bread, Hocus Pocus desserts, and Fifth Avenue candies. Fred Meyer capped the decade with large new stores in northeast and southeast Portland.

As with other retailers, Fred Meyer was challenged by World War II. Demand was high but supplies were low, and many employees were called to service. After the war, a more modern Fred Meyer began to emerge. Old stores were renovated and standardized, and new Fred Meyer stores were built from the ground up instead of being housed in existing space. A new management team, still working directly under Meyer, began adding departments such as home improvement, nutrition centers, fine jewelry, audio, and photo services and products. Some experiments, such as carpet and draperies, major appliances, furniture, and automotive service did not meet expectations and were eventually dropped.

The 1950s saw Fred Meyer opening a stream of successful outlets in suburban Portland. These stores were larger than previous Fred Meyer outlets, at 45,000 to 70,000 square feet. Meyer often led or kept pace with developers and was able to spot prime retail space on major suburban thoroughfares before suburban traffic patterns were apparent.

Major Acquisitions: Late 1950s to Mid-1960s

The mid-1950s also saw the construction of Fred Meyer's first modern distribution facility at Swan Island, Oregon. Also located at Swan Island was a new dairy plant and a central kitchen for the company's in-house food operation, Eve's Buffet Restaurant. In 1959, the company made its first major acquisition. For stock worth close to $1 million, Fred Meyer acquired four Marketime drug stores in Seattle, Washington.

In 1960, when there were 20 Fred Meyer stores with combined annual sales of $56 million, the company went public. Meyer then made a series of large acquisitions. In 1964, the company acquired Roundup Wholesale Grocery Company of Spokane, Washington, including 14 Sigman supermarkets in Washington and Oregon and three B & B Stores in Montana. The following year, Fred Meyer purchased seven Market Basket stores in Seattle and one in Yakima, Washington.

In 1966, management again upgraded the look of Fred Meyer stores. Tiled aisles and carpeted apparel departments replaced concrete floors. Displays were made more colorful, and new marketing ideas were introduced throughout the store. By year's end, earnings had reached $1.56 million on sales of $170.8 million.

Fred Meyer also continued to develop a vertical management organization. The heads of each of up to 11 departments per store would eventually report to corporate vice-presidents in charge of those departments rather than to an individual store manager. Individual departments became as strong as specialty stores and operated as such, complete with their own checkouts.

Although business was booming, not every venture went as planned. In 1968, Fred Meyer sold the Market Basket stores it had bought three years earlier, as the small stores did not fit in with other operations. This move meant a $225,000 writeoff against 1968 profits. Nevertheless, sales and income continued to grow.

Meyer, by now in his early 80s, continued to rule the company. A younger management team was beginning to take at least some of the reins of power, however. In 1969, Jack Crocker, a 20-year employee of the company, became president of Fred Meyer, Inc., with Meyer as chairman. Crocker's presidency coincided with Fred Meyer's opening of its Levi jeans centers.

Difficult 1970s

While profits continued to increase, the early 1970s were a difficult time for Fred Meyer's management. In 1971, Meyer suffered a stroke that left him weakened but still alert. In November of the same year, Crocker tendered his resignation, effective January 1, 1972. In March 1972, the Fred Meyer board elected Cyril K. Green to replace Crocker as president and Oran W. Robertson as first vice-president of the company.

The new management team continued relentless expansion. The main focus was on additions to existing stores, but plans also called for three new stores in 1972 and one in 1973. Acquisitions were also part of the plan. In 1973, Fred Meyer acquired five Valu-Mart stores in Oregon from Seattle-based Weisfield's Inc., ending the year with 52 stores and a thriving business in the Pacific Northwest.

In 1975, the company ventured into finance, buying a local savings and loan with deposits of $3.8 million. The idea was to install S&L in each of his full-service stores. The S&Ls would make money through banking and by bringing more customers and money into the stores. Although many in the banking industry were skeptical, Fred Meyer Savings and Loan Association grew rapidly, bringing in small depositors who probably had not saved at all before opening their Fred Meyer accounts.

Key Dates:

1923: Fred Meyer Inc. is incorporated in Oregon.
1928: Meyer opens what many regard as the world's first self-service drug store.
1959: The company acquires four Marketime drug stores.
1960: Fred Meyer goes public.
1964: Roundup Wholesale Grocery Co. is purchased.
1981: Fred Meyer is acquired by KKR in a leveraged buyout.
1986: The company goes public for a second time.
1997: Fred Meyer adds Smith's Food & Drug Centers Inc. to its holdings.
1998: The company buys Quality Food Centers Inc. and Food 4 Less Holdings Inc.
1999: The Kroger Co. acquires Fred Meyer in a $13.5 billion deal.

The company drew on its retailing experience to build the bank, offering free loaves of bread and steaks for customers opening accounts. The Fred Meyer Savings and Loans also stayed open longer hours than their competitors.

In 1975, Fred Meyer bought three Baza'r outlets and nine more department stores from Weisfield's Inc. of Seattle, including two Valu-Mart stores and six Leslie's stores located in Seattle, Spokane, and Yakima, Washington, and Anchorage, Alaska. All were to be merged into Fred Meyer operations.

In 1976, Fred Meyer retired from the day-to-day affairs of the company and became chairman of the executive committee. Oran B. Robertson was named chairman of the board and chief executive officer. Cyril K. Green remained president, and Virgil Campbell became executive vice-president.

In 1978, Meyer died. The success of Fred Meyer, Inc. was a testament to his hard work, intuition, and intelligence. His stores dominated the Northwest and continued to expand. Their net profit margin of 1.9 percent was better than those of big national chains, such as Winn-Dixie Stores (1.7 percent), Lucky Stores (1.5 percent), and Safeway (0.9 percent).

Meyer's death inspired many testimonials, but it also set the stage for a power struggle among the four executors of his will; Meyer owned 29.1 percent of the company's outstanding stock. On one side was Oran B. Robertson, chairman and CEO. Opposing him was G. Gerry Pratt, a Meyer protégé, and chairman and chief executive of Fred Meyer Savings and Loan. Other executors included a Fred Meyer vice-president and Warne H. Nunn, Pratt's friend and longtime local power company executive.

The struggle over Fred Meyer's will was further complicated by Pratt's troubles at Fred Meyer S&L. Pratt, a former journalist and talk-show host, was hired by Meyer in 1972. Two years later, he was made head of Fred Meyer S&L. With Pratt's innovative flair, the Fred Meyer S&L grew fast, but when the cost of money skyrocketed in 1979, the S&L was overextended and lost $1 million. The savings and loan's loss ended nearly 20 years of quarterly profit increases. In May 1980, chairman and CEO Oran

B. Robertson fired Pratt and replaced the Fred Meyer S&L board with Fred Meyer executives. Pratt responded with a lawsuit that was later settled. Fred Meyer sold its savings and loan.

Going Private Then Public: The 1980s

With the death of Meyer, outside investors began showing an interest in the company. In September 1980, the investment firm of Kohlberg Kravis Roberts & Co. (KKR) offered to buy the entire organization for $45 a share—more than $300 million. Ultimately KKR successfully negotiated a leveraged buyout in December 1981 with the Fred Meyer management as equity participants for $55 per share, or $435 million. This took Fred Meyer stock out of circulation and made the company private once again. In the meantime, the company had sold Roundup Wholesale to West Coast Grocery. The leveraged buyout split Fred Meyer into two companies. The retail operations continued as Fred Meyer, Inc., and the real estate assets were transferred to a separate partnership, Fred Meyer Real Estate Properties Ltd., which leased properties back to Fred Meyer, Inc. Occupancy expenses rose dramatically due to the spinoff of real estate holdings, and initially the company operated in the red.

Despite higher occupancy expenses and the cost of debt normally associated with leveraged buyouts, Fred Meyer continued to expand aggressively. Over the next five years, it built 11 new stores and acquired the Grand Central chain, which had stores in several Rocky Mountain states. The company sold Grand Central's New Mexico and Nevada stores but kept its 21 stores in Utah and Idaho, remodeling 15 of them. Furthermore, it cut costs by consolidating departmental checkouts.

Overall, during the time the company was private, Fred Meyer grew from 64 to 93 stores. Net income increased from $5.2 million in fiscal 1982 to $22.5 million in fiscal 1986. Sales jumped from $1.1 billion to $1.7 billion over the same period.

Management attempted and failed to bring Fred Meyer public again in 1983. By 1986, management felt investors were ready to buy Fred Meyer stock. In the fall of 1986, the company issued 6.75 million shares of common stock, 4.5 million new shares and 2.25 million from existing shareholders, at $14.25 per share.

Through the late 1980s, Fred Meyer continued its expansion, adding several new stores yearly as well as replacing and expanding existing stores. The Pacific Northwest had become a more competitive market with the entrance of discounters—such as Dayton Hudson's Target stores and the grocery chains Food 4 Less and Cub Foods—but most analysts believed Fred Meyer's one-stop shopping centers gave it a unique niche in the market.

In 1988, under the leadership of newly hired CEO Frederick Stevens, the company began a major overhaul of its stores and management organization. Fred Meyer also unveiled a new prototype store with a flexible design to facilitate layout changes without expensive remodeling; the first store in the new format opened in 1989. In 1990 and 1991, the company opened eight large new stores, closed ten small stores, and remodeled several other stores. The closings and remodelings led the company to take a $49.3 million restructuring charge in 1990 ($8.3 million of which was reversed in 1991); consequently, Fred Meyer posted a loss of $6.8 million in 1990. In January 1991, Stevens resigned unexpectedly; in August of that same year, Robert G. Miller took over the CEO spot, after most recently serving as executive vice-president of retail operations for the Albertson's supermarket chain.

Expansion and Reorganization: Mid-1990s and Beyond

As the 1990s progressed, Fred Meyer continued to fine-tune its store formats and locations in order to fend off increasing competition that cut into sales and earnings. The rise of category-killers was particularly troubling, especially in the areas of hardware and home electronics. In response, Fred Meyer reduced the amount of space devoted to lumber and building materials and began to phase out computer hardware. In 1993, Fred Meyer altered its growth strategy, deciding to concentrate on adding stores in areas where the chain was already strong; in some cases smaller-than-typical Fred Meyer stores were subsequently opened in smaller markets within these areas. A byproduct of this strategy was the chain's 1994 exit from the northern California market, into which it had only just begun to expand. The company incurred a $15.98 million charge as a result, leading to a profit of only $7.2 million for the fiscal year. Results for 1994 were also affected by an 88-day strike which centered on the number of part-time employees at the company. Sales increased at a more healthy rate in fiscal 1995 and 1996, buoyed by a surge in sales in Fred Meyer's nonfood departments.

The mid-1990s saw the company make its most dramatic moves outside the realm of one-stop shopping supercenters. Fred Meyer had entered the fine jewelry business in 1973. Over the next two decades, it had built up a chain of about three dozen Fred Meyer Jewelers standalone stores, which were located within malls, and it had also included Fred Meyer Jewelers departments in nearly 100 of its supercenters. In 1995, the company acquired 22 mall jewelry stores located on the West Coast, then the following year purchased 49 Merksamer Jewelers mall stores spread throughout 11 states. In the summer of 1997, Fred Meyer further bolstered its jewelry operations with the acquisition of Fox Jewelry Company and its 44 Fox Jewelry stores located in malls in six Midwest states—Michigan, Wisconsin, Indiana, Illinois, Iowa, and Ohio. With the addition of Fox Jewelry, which had been founded in 1917 with a store in Grand Rapids, Michigan, Fred Meyer became the fourth-largest fine jewelry chain in the country.

An even larger acquisition the summer of 1997 brought Fred Meyer an enhanced presence in food retailing. In a $2 billion deal, Fred Meyer purchased Smith's Food & Drug Centers, Inc., a leading regional supermarket and drug store chain with more than 150 stores in the southwestern and mountain states of Arizona, Idaho, New Mexico, Nevada, Texas, Utah, and Wyoming, making for an ideal geographic fit. Founded in 1948 and headquartered in Salt Lake City, Smith's large stores combined full-line supermarkets with drug and pharmacy departments and operated under the names Smith's, Smitty's Supermarket, and PriceRite Grocery Warehouse. Smith's reported sales of $2.89 billion for 1996.

Fred Meyer's growth continued in 1998. In March, Quality Food Centers Inc. (QFC) was added to the company's arsenal. QFC operated 89 supermarkets in the Seattle area and had been expanding by making strategic acquisitions over the past several years, much like Fred Meyer. The company purchased a second retailer that month, Food 4 Less Holdings Inc., an operator of 264 Ralphs stores in California and 80 Food 4 Less warehouses. Overall, Fred Meyer's merger activity catapulted it into the upper echelon of retailers with $15 billion in annual sales.

During the remainder of the 1990s, it was expected that the company would need to concentrate on issues of integration, including administrative, purchasing, information systems, distribution, and manufacturing functions. The management team charged with this responsibility was Ronald W. Burkle, CEO of Smith's, who was named chairman of Fred Meyer, and Miller, who remained president and CEO. Consolidation in the industry continued, however, and by this time Fred Meyer had become a very attractive acquisition target.

Sure enough, in October 1998, The Kroger Co. made a 13.5 billion play for Fred Meyer. Kroger stood to gain handsomely from the deal. The transaction would secure its spot as the leading supermarket chain in the United States, a position for which competitors Albertson's and Wal-Mart Stores were vying. Kroger gained several new retailing formats—including jewelry stores, warehouses, and department stores—and strengthened its foothold in the western United States. The company also expected the combined operations would secure cost savings of $75 million in the first year of operation, $150 million in the second year, and $225 million in the third year. The Federal Trade Commission gave its nod for the union after Kroger agreed to divest eight of its stores. Fred Meyer and its subsidiaries were integrated into Kroger in May 1999.

Kroger president David B. Dillon assured consumers that little would change at its stores in a May 1999 *Portland Oregonian* article. "Customers will continue to see the neighborhood chain they are familiar with today," he commented. "The combined company will have 18 food-store divisions, each with the authority to establish operating, merchandising, and pricing strategies in response to the demographic, economic and competitive conditions in each market."

As part of Kroger's growing list of holdings, the company operated as Fred Meyer Stores, Inc., the third-largest supercenter operator in the United States. In the early years of the new century, it continued to focus on pleasing its customers by offering a variety of national brand and private label products. It also kept pace with consumer demand, making necessary adjustments to its product mix. One example was the addition of Naturally Preferred, a line of natural and organic items that was found in the Natural Choice departments of its stores. In March 2003, Fred Meyer began offering its customers *Naturally Preferred* magazine, which included information and coupons. While Fred Meyer had certainly come a long way from its roots in the 1920s, its focus on customer satisfaction and low prices was sure to remain in effect for years to come.

Principal Competitors

Albertson's Inc.; Safeway Inc.; Wal-Mart Stores Inc.

Further Reading

Dubashi, Jagannath, "Fred Meyer: One-Stop Shopping, One-Stop Investing," *Financial World*, September 28, 1993, p. 18.

Duff, Mike, "Fred Meyer: New Standard for One-Stop Shopping?," *Supermarket Business*, December 1990, pp. 43–46, 48, 77.

Hill, Jim, "Kroger Completes Fred Meyer Deal," *Portland Oregonian*, May 28, 1999, p. B1.

"Hypermarket Concept Is Old Hat in Pacific NW," *Discount Store News*, December 19, 1988, p. 99.

Lipin, Steven, "Fred Meyer Agrees to Buy Smith's Food," *Wall Street Journal*, May 12, 1997, p. A3.

Orgel, David, "Fred Meyer's Food Focus," *Supermarket News*, April 18, 1994, pp. 1, 10, 12.

Rose, Michael, "Fred Meyer's New Profile," *Business Journal-Portland*, January 3, 1997, pp. 11–12.

Sahm, Phil, "Fred Meyer, Kroger Merger Approved," *Salt Lake Tribune*, May 28, 1999, p. B1.

Schwartz, Donna Boyle, "Grand Design," *HFN-The Weekly Newspaper for the Home Furnishing Network*, December 4, 1995, p. 1.

Zwiebach, Elliot, "Fred Meyer Fuels Five-Year Plan," *Supermarket News*, July 25, 1994, p. 12.

——, "Fred Meyer Grows Natural/Organic Offering," *Supermarket News*, November 3, 2003, p. 26.

—Jordan Wankoff
—updates: David E. Salamie and
Christina M. Stansell

Garan, Inc.

350 Fifth Avenue
New York, New York 10018
U.S.A.
Telephone: (212) 563-2000
Toll Free: (800) 759-4219
Fax: (212) 971-2250
Web site: http://www.garanimals.com

Wholly Owned Subsidiary of Berkshire Hathaway Inc.
Incorporated: 1957
Employees: 5,100
Sales: $257.20 million (2001)
NAIC: 315291 Infants' Cut and Sew Apparel
Manufacturing; 315223 Men's and Boys' Cut and
Sew Shirt (Except Work Shirt) Manufacturing;
315232 Women's and Girls' Cut and Sew Blouse and
Shirt Manufacturing; 315233 Women's and Girls' Cut
and Sew Dress Manufacturing

Garan, Inc., is engaged in the design, manufacture, and sale of men's, women's, and children's apparel under the Garanimals, Garan, Bobbie Brooks, and private label names. Most of Garan's output is sold to mass merchandisers, major national chain stores, department stores, and specialty stores. Wal-Mart Stores Inc. accounts for over 85 percent of company sales, while nearly 10 percent of sales stem from the company's relationship with JC Penney Company Inc. Garan was acquired by Warren Buffet's Berkshire Hathaway Inc. in 2002.

Eight Years of Growing Profits: 1957–65

Garan was incorporated in 1957 as a merger of seven companies, the first of which was incorporated in New York in 1941 as Myrna Knitwear, Inc. Its name originated from management coining "Guarantee" as the name for a new T-shirt but instead deciding to use the first part of the word as the corporate title. Company headquarters were located in Manhattan's garment district. Sales rose to $9.1 million in fiscal 1960 (the year ended September 30, 1960) from $3.2 million in 1957, when net income was only $47,000.

By 1961, the year the company went public, Garan was the nation's leading manufacturer of men's and boys' knitted sport shirts. It also made men's and boys' woven sports shirts, polo shirts, and boys' knitted pajamas. Knitted products were being made from cotton, acrylics, polyester and cotton blends, and textralized nylon yarn. Woven products were being made from cotton and rayon and from cotton, acetate, and polyester blends. The materials were being purchased from a number of textile manufacturers.

More than 90 percent of Garan's sales volume of $8.8 million in 1961 came from its sports shirts, which retailed for between $1.95 and $2.95. About two-thirds of its output was being sold under private labels, with the remainder selling under the Garan name. Accounts included Macy's, JC Penney, Woolworth's, and Sears, Roebuck. A new plant in Lambert, Mississippi, began manufacturing higher-priced Ban-Lon shirts from Garan's own knitted fabric in 1961, and another factory, in Clinton, Kentucky, also began operations that year.

Garan's first public offering, at $6.50 per share on the American Stock Exchange, raised $700,000 for the company and enabled it to finance its own receivables without factoring (hiring someone else to collect its bills). Almost two-thirds of the shares, the value of which rose as high as nearly $21 per share in 1961, remained in the hands of the officers and directors of the company, headed by the president and chairman of the board, Samuel Dorsky, and the executive vice-president and secretary, Seymour Lichtenstein, who soon advanced to president. The company's property in 1962 consisted of six leased factories in Kentucky, Mississippi, Pennsylvania, and Tennessee, and a warehouse in Tennessee. Net sales rose to $12 million that year, and net income increased to $464,703 from the previous fiscal year's $328,894. The company then declared a dividend for the first time.

Sales and net income for 1963 reached new levels of $15.1 million and $547,000, respectively. A 76,000-square-foot facility for the production of woven sports shirts opened in Kosciusko, Mississippi, in 1963, replacing two smaller units, and the company began selling Acrilon (as well as Ban-Lon) shirts for boys under its own Rhodes label. The following year, Garan opened another 76,000-square-foot plant for knitted garments in Starksville, Mississippi, and a 35,000-square-foot factory for woven sports shirts in Carthage, Mississippi. The Lambert facility was doubled in size. Plans were begun to devote part of the existing Adamsville, Tennessee, facility to popular-priced, man-tailored women's blouses.

In 1965, a new factory opened in Philadelphia, Mississippi, for the manufacture of boys' jeans and slacks. Garan's net sales reached nearly $23 million that year, and its net profit increased for the eighth year in a row. Long-term debt was only $1.9 million. All nine of the company's plants were situated in the South. JC Penney and Sears were taking about two-thirds of total production. The company's Rhodes label, sold through department stores, was being promoted only modestly, and its own Garan label, directed at discounters and chain stores, required minimal advertising.

The going got rougher for Garan in the next few years. Profits fell for the first time in 1966 because of inventory write-offs in velour, high in-house costs for a computer system subsequently phased out, and the costs of decentralizing company-wide operations to a divisional basis. Net income passed the $1 million mark in 1967, and doubled in 1968, but fell to $920,000 in 1969 as the company's Ban-Lon sweaters and shirts met with increased competition. In 1970, sales fell from $45.1 million to $43.8 million, although net income rose slightly.

A Wider Mix of Products in the 1970s

By 1972, Garan was back in stride, having topped $2 million in net income the previous year. Heightened productivity, tighter cost controls, fewer markdowns, and a wider mix of products were credited for the company's turnaround. Of its eleven factories, seven were located in Mississippi and one each was located in California, Kentucky, Louisiana, and Tennessee. The company started making men's pants in 1969, jeans for girls in 1971, and children's apparel in 1972. It also introduced a "Jugs" line of pants and knit shirts for girls 15 years and older. Shirts now represented only 46 percent of Garan's varied production. Roughly three-quarters of its merchandise bore the labels of its customers, and the balance was being sold under the Garan label.

By the mid-1970s, Garan was a broad-based producer of knitted and woven apparel for girls, infants, and men as well as boys. Branded children's apparel was introduced in 1972 under the Garanimals label, a system of coordinating tops and bottoms with color-keyed mix-and-match animal tags and hangers. Two years later, the company opened a new plant devoted exclusively to turning out knitted tops and woven bottoms for infants and toddlers. Garan also restored men's knit sport shirts as a meaningful part of its apparel mix. A licensing division established in 1975 began distributing sweatshirts, sweaters, knit shirts, and T-shirts bearing designs of professional sports leagues and teams.

There were 23 Garan plants at the end of 1977, a year in which net sales reached $122.8 million and net income rose to $7.7 million, both records. The Garanimals label accounted for 30 percent of sales volume. Sears and JC Penney remained the largest of Garan's more than 2,000 accounts. Long-term debt was only $1.9 million. About 44 percent of the company's shares of common stock was closely held.

Garan averaged an excellent annual return on equity of more than 17 percent between 1979 and 1983. During this period, it added the Garan Mountain Lion brand name, which along with Garanimals accounted for more than half of company sales in 1983 and also enjoyed higher profit margins than the firm's private labels. Licensed sweatshirts and T-shirts continued to be marketed through mass merchandisers, department stores, and other customers. Sales of children's clothing represented about 70 percent of the 1983 sales total. Branded and licensed apparel accounted for about two-thirds of sales, and private label and licensed business to Sears and JC Penney accounted for the rest.

Garan Advantage, a line of discounted men's sportswear with the same tagging system as Garanimals, was introduced in 1982. Garan Man, a sportswear line of knit and woven shirts, casual slacks, and pullover and cardigan sweaters, was unveiled the following year. Also in 1983, the company introduced Garan By Marita for women. Garan net sales reached a record $176.9 million in 1984, and net income rose to a record $22.8 million. At the end of 1985, there were 20 company plants distributed throughout seven states: Alabama, Arkansas, Kentucky, Louisiana, Mississippi, Oklahoma, and Tennessee. A manufacturing facility was established in Costa Rica in 1984, and two facilities were opened in El Salvador during fiscal 1985. Long-term debt that year came to $9.9 million. By the mid-1980s, Seymour Lichtenstein had succeeded Dorsky, who remained a director, as chairman and chief executive officer, and Jerald Kamiel had succeeded Lichtenstein as president and chief operating officer.

Fiscal 1985 began a tailspin for Garan: sales fell to $105 million in 1986 and earnings dropped to a low of $2.2 million the following year. A number of factors were blamed, including cheap imports, the demise of the preppy look, and the miniskirt disasters. The company cut back on branded products, which accounted for only 47 percent of sales in 1988, compared with 75 percent in 1986. It introduced Bobbie Brooks, an in-house label for Wal-Mart Stores' women's clothing, and began a licensed menswear line featuring the insignia of professional sports teams. Company plants were retooled for lower costs and greater efficiency. Sales and profits improved, reaching $145.3 million and nearly $10 million, respectively, in 1990.

Relying on Wal-Mart in the 1990s

By 1992, burgeoning Wal-Mart was accounting for 45 percent of Garan's annual sales. A licensing agreement in 1990 gave Garan the right to carry the insignias of various colleges and universities on sweatshirts and knit shirts. In 1991, it became one of the few apparel companies allowed to use characters from Disney movies. After a strong first quarter in fiscal 1992, Garan, holding $30 million in cash with virtually no debt, declared a $1.20-per-share annual dividend on top of the quarterly payout. During 1988–92, the company earned an annual average of almost 18 percent on equity.

Key Dates:

1957: Garan is incorporated as a merger of seven companies.
1961: The company goes public.
1972: Branded children's apparel is introduced under the Garanimals label.
1975: A licensing division is established to distribute clothing bearing the designs of professional sports teams.
1991: Garan becomes one of the few apparel companies allowed to use characters from Disney movies on its products.
2002: Garan is acquired by Berkshire Hathaway Inc.

Net sales came to a record $189.6 million in 1993, when net income totaled $16.8 million. The following year was not as good, with sales of $173 million and income of $9.4 million. For fiscal 1995, results were even more disappointing: only $143.3 million in sales and $5.5 million in income. The company's market value, once nearly $190 million, dipped to less than $90 million. Some analysts blamed the company's heavy dependence on Wal-Mart (accounting for 63 percent of sales during fiscal 1995). Oversaturation in licensing, rising raw material costs, and cut-throat pricing were also cited as reasons for the firm's poor performance. During 1995, Garan became the exclusive licensee of the Everlast trademark for men's, boys', and girls' activewear, and of the trademark Hang Ten for boys' sportswear.

During fiscal 1995, children's apparel accounted for 72 percent of Garan's net sales, with women's apparel accounting for 18 percent and men's apparel accounting for 10 percent. Sales of sports and colleges licensed apparel accounted for about 12 percent of sales and Garan's own label accounted for about 6 percent. The Bobbie Brooks label accounted for another 7 percent, and Disney characters, scenes, and logos accounted for about 8 percent. In addition to Wal-Mart, JC Penney was an important customer that provided 20 percent of Garan's sales. Some 3,500 or so clients took the rest of the company's output.

Garan maintained 18 manufacturing plants in 1995 in the following locations: Haleyville, Jemison, and Rainesville, Alabama; Ozark, Arkansas; Clinton, Kentucky; Church Point, Kaplan, and Marksville, Louisiana; Carthage, Corinth, Eupora, Lambert, Philadelphia, and Starksville, Mississippi; Adamsville, Tennessee; San Jose, Costa Rica; and two in San Salvador, El Salvador. All were leased in whole or in part except for the plants in Clinton, Haleyville, and San Jose. The company was also leasing its headquarters and showroom in New York City's Empire State Building. Seymour Lichtenstein owned 12 percent of Garan in 1995 and heirs of Samuel Drosky owned another 12 percent. Other officers and directors owned 16 percent. The long-term debt was $3.2 million in March 1995. Dividends had been paid every year since 1962.

Changes in the Late 1990s and Beyond

Competition remained fierce in the apparel industry well into the late 1990s and beyond. Garan continued to rely heavily on its relationship with Wal-Mart and its other large customers to shore up sales and profits. In 1998, *Apparel Industry Magazine* named Garan as one of the top eight most successful apparel manufacturers in the industry based on profits, a sure sign that management's efforts were paying off. Indeed, the company forged ahead creating a strategy focused on remaining competitive in the early years of the 21st century. Sales in 2001 reached $257 million, an increase of 8.9 percent over the previous year. Net earnings rose as well, climbing from $17 million in 2000 to $22.6 million in 2001. The company decided to phase out its professional sports team and college and university licensed activewear that year.

During this time, Garan management began laying the groundwork for a major change that would secure a financially sound future for the company. In 2002, the firm struck a deal with Warren Buffett, chairman of Berkshire Hathaway Inc. Known for his business savvy, Buffett had amassed billions over the years by acquiring shares of various companies. "Because he controls, through his company Berkshire Hathaway, one of the most liquid sources of capital on earth, Buffett has recently been able to step up and buy huge chunks of American businesses, especially in the hard-hit sectors like telecom, utilities, and energy," reported a November 2002 *Fortune* magazine article.

Berkshire Hathaway's holdings were diverse, proof that Buffett's interests ran across the board. The aforementioned article described the company, stating, "It is a conglomerate with sizable operations in insurance. It holds large stakes in giant American companies such as Coke, Gillette, and American Express. Berkshire also controls a significant utility and gas pipeline business, and it owns an amazing cornucopia of mundane operations—things like furniture retailers, jewelry shops, and shoe factories." As such, industry observers were not shocked Berkshire Hathaway announced its acquisition of Garan in the summer of 2002.

Buffett made a $60 per share cash offer for the firm, believing it would fit nicely into Berkshire Hathaway's apparel division along with Fruit of the Loom Co., the underwear manufacturer purchased earlier in the year. Garan management agreed, and the acquisition was completed in September. The company remained intact with headquarters in New York. Seymour Lichtenstein remained at the helm, confident Garan would succeed in the years to come as a Berkshire Hathaway subsidiary.

Principal Subsidiaries

Garan Central America Corporation; Garan Export Corporation; Garan Manufacturing Corporation; Garan Services Corporation; Garan de El Salvador, S.A. de C.V.; Confecciones Cuscatlecas, S.A. de C.V. (El Salvador); Servicios de Corte y Confeccion, S.A. de C.V. (El Salvador); Servicios de Manufacturas, S.A. de C.V. (El Salvador); Servicios Industriales Diversos, S.A. de C.V. (El Salvador); Servicios Profesionales de Manufactura, S.A. de C.V. (El Salvador); Producciones Manufacturas, S.A. de C.V. (El Salvador); Garan de Honduras, S.A. de C.V.; Garan San Jose, S.A. de C.V. (Honduras); Garan Buena Vista, S.A. de C.V. (Honduras).

Principal Competitors

Happy Kids Inc.; OshKosh B'Gosh Inc.; VF Corporation.

Further Reading

"Berkshire Hathaway to Purchase Garan for $273.1 Million," *Wall Street Journal*, July 3, 2002, p. D2.

Brammer, Rhonda, "Threads and Chips," *Barron's*, October 23, 1995, p. 30.

Campanella, Frank W., "Garan Fashions Gains with Expanded Output," *Barron's*, June 5, 1972, pp. 28–31.

Furman, Phyllis, "Apparel Firm Rides Wal-Mart Juggernaut," *Crain's New York Business*, May 4–10, 1992, p. 3.

"Garan, Apparel Maker, to Sew up Record Sales, Earnings This Year," *Barron's*, January 23, 1978, pp. 31–32.

"Garan Fashions Handsome Growth from Stress on Private Label Line," *Barron's*, March 1, 1965, p. 19.

"Garan to Button Down Higher Net on Steady Expansion of Facilities," *Barron's*, April 6, 1964, pp. 32, 59.

Johanson, Amelia, "Where Pretty and Practical Are Child's Play," *Plain Dealer*, May 13, 1999.

Lawrence, Calvin, Jr., "Garan's New Look Wows Wall Street," *USA Today*, May 23, 1989, p. 3B.

"New Streamlined Facilities Help Garan Style Operating Advances," *Barron's*, July 16, 1962, p. 18.

Rolland, Louis J., "Garan Grows," *Financial World*, November 22, 1961, p. 24.

Serwer, Andy, "The Oracle of Everything," *Fortune*, November 11, 2002.

Sparr, Susan L., "Garan Gears up with EDI," *Bobbin*, July 1988, p. 102.

"Study Reveals Top U.S. Apparel Companies," *Business Wire*, August 4, 1998.

Taylor, John, "Berkshire Hathaway Acquires Maker of Garanimals Clothing," *Omaha World-Herald*, July 4, 2002.

—Robert Halasz
—update: Christina M. Stansell

GEMPLUS

Gemplus International S.A.

Aerogolf Center, 1
Hohenhof
Senningerberg
L-2633
Luxembourg
Telephone: 352 26 34 61 00
Fax: 352 26 34 61 61
Web site: http://www.gemplus.com

Public Company
Incorporated: 1988
Employees: 5,000
Sales: EUR 749 million ($941.90 million) (2003)
Stock Exchanges: Euronext Paris NASDAQ
Ticker Symbol: GEMP
NAIC: 334413 Semiconductor and Related Device
    Manufacturing

Gemplus International S.A. is the world's leading manufacturer of smart cards—microchip-embedded cards used for a wide range of functions, including debit cards for the banking industry, SIM (Subscriber Identity Module) cards for mobile telephones and set-top television terminals, and a variety of other functions. Gemplus, one of the smart card industry's pioneers, holds an approximate one-third share of the global market, producing more than half a million cards per year. The company has shipped more than four billion cards since its formation in 1988. Gemplus is a truly international company—registered in Luxembourg, the group's corporate headquarters are in Geneva, its manufacturing headquarters are near Marseilles, and its information technology headquarters is located in the Silicon Valley. The company is led by American-born CEO Alex Mandl, listed on both the Euronext Paris and NASDAQ stock exchanges, and its largest shareholder, at 25 percent, is U.S.-based fund group Texas Pacific. In addition, Gemplus operates in 37 countries, with 11 production plants and four research and development centers, as well as 17 "personalization" plants enabling it to tailor its software and technology to specific customer needs. Hit hard by the slump in the telecom-

munications sector—which previously accounted for more than 70 percent of the company's revenues—Gemplus has been showing the first signs of a recovery, posting profits again at the beginning of 2004. The company is working to reduce its reliance on the telecommunications industry with a push to gain a strong share of the financial smart card market. In 2003, the company posted sales of EUR 749 million ($941 million).

Smart Card Pioneer in the 1980s

The first proposals for the creation of "smart cards"—that is, credit cards embedded with microchips that could be programmed for use in a variety of applications—appeared in the early 1980s, and a number of companies began developing their own version of the cards. Gemplus founder Marc Lassus became one of the early proponents of the new technology. Lassus, who had earned his PhD in solid-state physics at Lyons University, had been working at Motorola in the early 1980s when France's Bull approached that company about the idea of developing a smart card. Later in the 1980s, Lassus joined Thomson Microelectronics, then still controlled by the French government.

Lassus became the manager of Thomson's integrated circuits division, where he led a team of engineers in the development of a new smart card design. Yet Thomson's management remained skeptical about the potential of the smart card, and after an outside consultant hired to look into the feasibility of the project proclaimed that there was no future in the technology, the project was shelved.

Lassus's opportunity came in 1988, when Thomson was merged with SGS, forming STMicroelectronics. As part of the merger, Thomson prepared to lay off a number of its engineers. Lassus decided to leave Thomson to pursue the smart card idea, setting up Gemplus with seed money provided by Thomson. At the same time, the proposed layoffs at Thomson provided Lassus with a pool of highly trained engineers to back the Gemplus project—with Thomson underwriting each hire by Gemplus by as much as $10,000 per employee.

Gemplus found its first customer by the end of 1988, when France Telecom placed an order for one million microchip-embedded telephone cards. The use of the cards, which contained a fixed value encoded in the chip, enabled France Telecom to begin eliminating coin-based—and theft-prone—public telephones. The company then set up its first plant to manufacture the card, opening in Gemenos, near Marseilles. Gemplus already displayed confidence in its future, building a plant capable of producing ten times the amount of the France Telecom order.

Gemplus signed up a new major customer in 1989, when Sky TV contracted the company to produce smart cards for its set top-based pay-television system. That contract also helped demonstrate the flexibility of the new technology. The following year, another major customer signed on, as Deutsche Telekom placed an order for 16 million smart cards.

The company's relationship with both France Telecom and Deutsche Telekom placed it in a strong position for its next major development—that of winning the order to produce the SIM (Subscriber Identity Module) for the newly agreed-upon, European-wide GSM mobile telephone protocol. The company became the SIM supplier for the mobile telephone networks in France, Denmark, Norway, Finland, and Sweden. In support of those contracts, Gemplus built a new production facility, in La Ciotat, France, which provided the company with clean room technology for the production of the SIM modules. That plant opened in 1991.

The European market greeted the emergence of the smart card enthusiastically, and Gemplus began signing up more and more customers, with a wider array of applications. One example of the flexibility of the new technology was provided by the company's contract with British Gas in 1991 for a smart card for use with the utility's gas meters. The company also signed on its first bank customers, Cilme and Moneta/Cariplo in Italy, and FISC in Taiwan, which were followed by the award of a license to produce bank cards for the French banking system in 1992.

The U.S. market proved slower to accept the new technology, although the company had established an office in Washington, D.C. in 1989. In 1991, however, the company managed to sign on the state of Wyoming, which turned to Gemplus for the production of its WYO healthcare cards. Nonetheless, Gemplus's growth in the United States was hampered by the slow growth of the country's mobile telephone sector and the banking industry's reluctance to switch from magnetic strip-based credit card technology.

Industry Leader in the 1990s

Gemplus began to take off in the 1990s, as sales grew from the equivalent of just $89 million in 1992 to more than $300

million by 1995. The company supported its growth by opening new sales offices in Italy, the United Kingdom, Germany, and Italy by 1992, adding new sales offices in Spain and in Chile and Argentina in 1993, then entering Canada, Japan, Australia, China, and Venezuela in 1994. By 1996, the company had added sales offices in Hong Kong, Brazil, Russia, and Poland, among other markets. Gemplus also opened its first production facility outside of France, in Filderstadt, Germany, in 1992.

By 1995, Gemplus had produced more than half a million phone cards and more than 120 million mobile phone SIM cards, establishing itself as a clear leader in the bustling smart card market. In that year, Gemplus backed up its organic growth with its first acquisition, of the U.S. and European smart card production and personalization facilities of DataCard Corporation. The following year, the company set up a joint venture in Tianjin, China, where it launched production of telephone cards, as well as a new production plant in Mexico. In the meantime, the company had taken on a new financial backer, in the form of Germany's Quandt family, which acquired a significant stake in Gemplus in 1994.

Marc Lassus stepped down as Gemplus's CEO in 1997, taking on the chairman's role, and concentrating his own efforts on targeting new acquisitions, such as the purchase of Austria's SkiData in 1997. The company opened a new research and development facility for the North American market, in Montreal, that year, ahead of the transfer of its IT headquarters to Silicon Valley, specifically Redwood City, California, in 1998.

Gemplus rolled out a steady stream of new products and technologies into the late 1990s as well, such as its GemClub re-programmable loyalty program support cards; a dual mode SIM card compatible with both AMPS and GSM mobile telephone networks; the GemCore smart card reader; the GemSAFE network services security platform; as well as the company's participation in the creation of an open-platform, Java-based smart card in partnership with Visa International, Sun Microsystems, and others.

Gemplus's sales gained strongly at the end of the decade, rising from EUR 583 million in 1998 to nearly EUR 670 million in 1999—and topping the EUR 1 billion mark by 2000. Aiding the company's expansion was its acquisition of Euritis, which provided smart card security systems and software, and the opening of Gemplus's production plant in Singapore, both in 1999. The company also announced strategic partnerships that year with Microsoft and Dell to build smart card readers and software into computer systems.

With sales of more than EUR 1.3 billion at the end of 2000, Gemplus remained the global smart card leader, controlling more than one-third of the world market. In that year, the company launched its own venture capital fund, GemVentures, to provide investment capital for start-up companies working in the smart card field. Meanwhile, Gemplus itself took on a new major investor, when Texas Pacific Group, which paid in $500 million—then the largest private equity investment in Europe—to take a 26 percent share in Gemplus.

The Texas Pacific investment enabled Gemplus to go on a brief acquisition spree, in part for the company to make the transition from a reliance on smart card manufacturing to the

Key Dates:

1988: Marc Lassus and other engineers from Thomson Microelectronics found Gemplus in order to develop smart card technology.

1989: Gemplus receives a contract for one million cards from France Telecom and builds its first factory in Gemenos, France; the company opens a sales office in the United States.

1990: The company receives a contract to produce SIM cards for GSM mobile telephone protocol.

1991: The company builds a new plant in France featuring clean room technology for SIM production.

1992: The company opens a production facility in Germany, its first outside of France.

1995: DataCard Corporation is acquired.

1996: The company opens a new plant in Mexico; a joint venture is formed in China to produce telephone cards.

1997: SkiData of Austria is acquired.

1999: The company acquires Euritis, a specialist in smart card security systems and software.

2000: Texas Pacific becomes a major shareholder with a $500 million investment; the company acquires ODS Landys & Gyr, SLP InfoWare, and Celocom; the company goes public on the Paris and NASDAQ exchanges.

2002: Marc Lassus is forced to resign from the board of directors; the company begins restructuring, shedding more than 2,000 jobs.

2004: Gemplus reports a return to profitability in the first quarter.

development of new smart card technology, software, and related systems. The company bought up Celocom, which provided electronic transaction security systems; SLP Infoware, a software specialist; and ODS Landys & Gyr, which had been the smart card operations of Landys & Gyr Communications.

By the end of the year, Gemplus completed its initial public offering (IPO), listing on the Euronext Paris and NASDAQ exchanges, in large part to enable its initial investors, including Marc Lassus, to cash in on part of their investment. As part of the IPO process, Gemplus provided Lassus with some EUR 70 million to purchase stock options ahead of the public offering—a move that came back to haunt Lassus later.

Rebuilding for the 2000s

Gemplus entered the 2000s with high hopes—a number of observers began forecasting that the company's sales could reach as high as $10 billion before the end of the decade. Yet Gemplus, which saw 70 percent of its sales generated from the telecommunications market, and especially the market for mobile telephones, crashed headlong into the global telecoms slump in 2001. The company's sales began dropping, a trend worsened by the slowdown in mobile telephone purchases in an increasingly saturated market. Gemplus's concentration on growth, rather than developing mature corporate practices, dur-

ing its first decade now came to haunt it, as its profits—and share price—fell.

Gemplus entered a period of revolving-door CEOs, going through four chief executives over as many years. The company's difficulties led main shareholder Texas Pacific into direct conflict with Marc Lassus. When the Quandt family sided with Texas Pacific, Lassus was finally forced to sell off his shareholding in the company and resign from its board of directors in 2002. Texas Pacific was then free to bring in its choice for chief executive, the American Alex Mandl. That appointment led to accusations that the company was attempting to shift its focus of operations to the United States, and was even accompanied by allegations of corporate espionage. In the meantime, Gemplus sales continued to collapse, dropping back to less than EUR 790 million—with net losses of more than EUR 320 million.

Mandl helped lead Gemplus through a restructuring, which dropped its worldwide headcount by more than 2,000 employees by the end of 2003. The company won a number of important contracts that year as well, including the supply of 15 million smart cards to Halifax Bank of Scotland, and ten million SIM cards for China Unicom. Gemplus also received certification that year to provide smart cards for the SCOSTA National Driving License and Vehicle Registration program in India, opening the company to that vast potential of the more than one-billion-strong population.

By the beginning of 2004, the tide appeared to be turning for Gemplus, as the company reported a return to quarterly profits. Sales, which had dropped down to below EUR 750 million in 2003, also were showing signs of renewed growth as the telecommunications sector, and the high technology market in general, began to rebound. Despite its difficulties at the beginning of the decade, Gemplus had managed to hold onto its global leadership position, and promised to remain a leading smart card player in the new century.

Principal Subsidiaries

Gemplus Corporation (United States); Gemplus S.C.A. (France); Gemplus GmbH (Germany): Gemplus Ltd. (United Kingdom); Gemplus Bank Note Ltda. (Brazil); Gemplus Industriales S.A. de C.V. (Mexico).

Principal Competitors

SchlumbergerSema SA; Axalto; Giesecke & Devrient GmbH; Oberthur Card Systems.

Further Reading

Balaban, Dan, "Exec's Exit Signals Changes at Gemplus," *Card Technology,* February 2004, p. 8.

——, "Gemplus Looks Past Cards," *Card Technology,* April 2001, p. 32.

"Dealing a Smartcard to Swipe the Board," *Financial Times,* October 7, 1999 p. 10.

"Gemplus Founder Loses Out in Power Struggle," *Cardline,* December 27, 2002, p. 1.

"Gemplus Led the 2002 Smart Card Market," *Cardline,* May 2, 2003, p. 1.

''Gemplus's Financial Life Turns Around in the First Quarter,'' *Cardline,* April 30, 2004, p. 1.

Hohler, Alice, ''Gemplus Gears Up for International Market,'' *Financial News,* June 1, 2003.

Matlack, Carol, ''A Global Clash at France's Gemplus,'' *Business Week,* December 21, 2001

''A New CEO Faces Old Rifts at Gemplus,'' *Card Technology,* October 2002, p. 6.

Ratner, Juliana, ''Gemplus Founder Expected to Quit Board,'' *Financial Times,* December 5, 2002, p. 30.

Reinhardt, Andy, ''Gemplus Wants Its Gleam Back,'' *Business Week,* March 10, 2003, p. 28.

—M.L. Cohen

General Motors Corporation

300 Renaissance Center
Detroit, Michigan 48265-3000
U.S.A.
Telephone: (313) 556-5000
Fax: (248) 696-7300
Web site: http://www.gm.com

Public Company
Incorporated: 1916
Employees: 326,000
Sales: $185.5 billion (2003)
Stock Exchanges: New York Toronto Frankfurt Euronext
    Paris London
Ticker Symbol: GM
NAIC: 336111 Automobile Manufacturing; 336112 Light
    Truck and Utility Vehicle Manufacturing; 336211
    Motor Vehicle Body Manufacturing; 336350 Motor
    Vehicle Transmission and Power Train Parts
    Manufacturing; 336510 Railroad Rolling Stock
    Manufacturing; 421110 Automobile and Other Motor
    Vehicle Wholesalers; 441110 New Car Dealers;
    522220 Sales Financing; 522291 Consumer Lending;
    522292 Real Estate Credit; 524126 Direct Property
    and Casualty Insurance Carriers; 532112 Passenger
    Cars Leasing

General Motors Corporation (GM) is the world's largest full-line vehicle manufacturer and marketer. Its arsenal of brands includes Chevrolet, Pontiac, GMC, Buick, Cadillac, Saturn, Hummer, and Saab. Opel, Vauxhall, and Holden comprise GM's international nameplates. Through its system of global alliances, GM holds stakes in Isuzu Motors Ltd., Fuji Heavy Industries Ltd., Suzuki Motor Corporation, Fiat Auto, and GM Daewoo Auto & Technology. Other principal businesses include General Motors Acceptance Corporation and its subsidiaries, providers of financing and insurance to GM customers and dealers. In the early 2000s, struggling under the weight of escalating healthcare and pension costs, GM sought to shed some of its less profitable activities. Toward that end, among other moves, the company sold its stake in Hughes Electronics, phased out production of the Oldsmobile, and discontinued the Chevrolet Camero and Pontiac Firebird. Facing a tough economic climate, GM has nevertheless retained its position as the world's leading automaker.

19th-Century Origins

The beginning of General Motors Corporation can be traced back to 1892, when R.E. Olds collected all of his savings to convert his father's naval and industrial engine factory into the Olds Motor Vehicle Company to build horseless carriages. For several years, however, the Oldsmobile (as the product came to be known) did not get beyond the experimental stage. In 1895 the first model, a four-seater with a petrol engine that could produce five horsepower and reach 18.6 mph, went for its trial run.

Olds proved himself not only an innovative engineer but also a good businessman and was very successful with his first model, of which relatively few were built. As a result of his success, he founded the first American factory in Detroit devoted exclusively to the production of automobiles. The first car was a luxury model costing $1,200, but the second model was introduced at a list price of $650 and was very successful. At the turn of the century, Olds had sold more than 1,400 cars.

Also during this time, the Cadillac Automobile Company was established in Detroit, founded by Henry Leland, who built car engines with experience gained in the Oldsmobile factory, where he worked until 1901. By the end of 1902 the first Cadillac had been produced—a car distinguished by its luxurious finish. In the following year, tiller steering was replaced by the steering wheel, the reduction gearbox was introduced, and some cars were fitted with celluloid windscreens. Oldsmobile also reached its projected target of manufacturing 4,000 cars in one year. A third player, engineer David Buick, founded his own factory in Detroit during this time as well.

By 1903, a time of market instability, so many different manufacturers were operating that the financially weakest disappeared and some of the remaining companies were forced to form a consortium. William Durant, a director of the Buick

Company Perspectives:

General Motors' enjoys a long tradition of accountability, integrity, and transparency that has helped establish our reputation as a leader in corporate responsibility. We place a high value on communicating clear, consistent, and truthful information about our performance to our employees, suppliers, dealers, investors, and customers.

Motor Company, was the man behind the merger. The nephew of a Michigan governor, and a self-made millionaire, Durant believed that the only way for the automobile companies to operate at a profit was to avoid the duplication that occurred when many firms manufactured the same product. General Motors Corporation was thus formed, bringing together Oldsmobile and Buick in 1903, and joined by Cadillac and Oakland (renamed Pontiac) in 1909. Positive financial results were immediately seen from the merger, although the establishment of the company drew little attention.

Other early members of the GM family were Ewing, Marquette, Welch, Scripps-Booth, Sheridan, and Elmore, together with Rapid and Reliance trucks. GM's other U.S. automotive division, Chevrolet, became part of the corporation in 1918. Only Buick, Oldsmobile, Cadillac, and Oakland continued making cars for more than a short time after their acquisition by GM. By 1920 more than 30 companies had been acquired through the purchase of all or part of their stock. Two were forerunners of major GM subsidiaries, the McLaughlin Motor Company of Canada (which later became General Motors of Canada Limited) and the Fisher Body Company, in which GM initially acquired a 60 percent interest.

By 1911 the company set up a central staff of specialists to coordinate work in the various units and factories. An experimental or "testing" laboratory also was established to serve as an additional protection against costly factory mistakes. GM's system of administration, research, and development became one of the largest and most complex in private industry.

About the same time that GM was establishing itself in Detroit, an engineering breakthrough was taking place in Dayton, Ohio: the electric self-starter, designed by Charles F. Kettering. GM introduced Kettering's invention in its 1912 Cadillacs, and with the phasing out of the dangerous and unpredictable hand crank, motoring became much more popular. Kettering's Dayton Engineering Laboratories were merged into GM during 1920 and the laboratories were relocated in Detroit in 1925. Kettering later became the scientific director of GM, in charge of its research and engineering programs.

During World War I GM turned its facilities to the production of war materials. With no previous experience in manufacturing military hardware, the U.S. automobile industry completed a retooling from civilian to war production within 18 months. Between 1917 and 1919, 90 percent of GM's truck production was for the war effort. Cadillac supplied army staff cars, V-8 engines for artillery tractors, and trench mortar shells, while Buick built Liberty airplane motors, tanks, trucks, ambulances, and automotive parts.

It was at this time that Alfred Sloan, Jr., who went on to guide GM as president and chairman until 1956, first became associated with the company. In 24 years, Sloan had built a $50,000 investment in the Hyatt Roller Bearing Company to assets of about $3.5 million. When Hyatt became part of GM, Sloan joined the corporate management, becoming president in 1923. Overseas expansion soon commenced, with the 1925 purchase of U.K. automaker Vauxhall Motors and the 1931 acquisition of Germany's Adam Opel.

The Depression and World War II Era

GM suffered greatly under the effects of the Great Depression, but it emerged with a new, aggressive management. Coordinated policy control replaced the undirected efforts of the prior years. As its principal architect, Sloan was credited with creating not only an organization that saved GM, but a new management policy that was adopted by countless other businesses. Fundamentally, the policy involved coordination of the enterprise under top management, direction of policy through top-level committees, and delegation of operational responsibility throughout the organization. Within this framework management staffs conducted analysis of market trends, advised policy committees, and coordinated administration. For a company comprised of many varied divisions, such a system of organization was crucial to its success.

By 1941 GM accounted for 44 percent of the total U.S. automotive sales, compared with 12 percent in 1921. In preparation for America's entry into World War II, GM retooled its factories. After Japan struck at Pearl Harbor in 1941, the industrial skills that GM had developed were applied with great effectiveness. From 1940 to 1945 the company produced defense material valued at a total of $12.3 billion. Decentralized and highly flexible local managerial responsibility made possible the almost overnight conversion from civilian production to wartime production. GM's contribution included the manufacture of every conceivable product from the smallest ball bearing to large tanks, naval ships, fighting planes, bombers, guns, cannons, and projectiles. The company manufactured 1,300 airplanes and one-fourth of all U.S. aircraft engines.

Postwar Expansion

Car manufacturing resumed after the war, and postwar expansion resulted in increased production. The decade of the 1950s was characterized by automotive sales records and innovations in styling and engineering. The public interest in automatic gears convinced GM to concentrate their research in this field; by 1950, all of the models built in the United States were available with an automatic gearbox. Car body developments proceeded at the same time and resulted in better sight lines and improved aerodynamics.

During the Korean war, part of the company's production capacity was diverted into providing supplies for the United Nations forces (although to a smaller extent than during World War II). The reallocation reached 19 percent and then leveled off at about 5 percent from 1956 onward. Between 1951 and 1955 the five divisions of GM—Buick, Chevrolet, Pontiac, Oldsmobile, and Cadillac—all began to feature a new V-8 engine with a higher compression ratio. Furthermore, the electrical supply was

Key Dates:

1892: R.E. Olds founds the Olds Motor Vehicle Company.
1895: The first Oldsmobile model is taken on its trial run.
1900: David Buick founds a factory in Detroit.
1902: Henry Leland produces the first Cadillac.
1903: William Durant forms General Motors Corporation, bringing together Oldsmobile and Buick.
1909: Cadillac and Oakland (renamed Pontiac) join GM.
1912: GM introduces the electric self-starter in its Cadillacs.
1918: Chevrolet becomes part of GM.
1923: Alfred Sloan, Jr., is named president.
1925: U.K. automaker Vauxhall Motors is acquired.
1931: Germany's Adam Opel is acquired.
1940: GM begins producing defense materials.
1950: All U.S. models are available with an automatic gearbox.
1971: GM acquires a 34 percent stake in Isuzu Motors.
1984: GM acquires Electronic Data Systems.
1986: Hughes Aircraft is acquired.
1990: Company acquires a 50 percent stake in Swedish carmaker Saab Automobile AB; Saturn Corporation is created as a subsidiary.
1996: EDS is spun off.
1999: GM acquires a 20 percent stake in Fuji Heavy Industries, maker of Subaru cars.
2000: GM gains a 20 percent stake in Fiat S.p.A.'s Fiat Auto S.p.A. unit and takes full control of Saab.
2002: A majority interest in Daewoo Motor Company—later known as GM Daewoo Auto & Technology—is acquired.
2003: The company sells its stake in Hughes Electronics to News Corporation.

changed from six to the more reliable 12 volts. Power-assisted steering and brakes appeared on all car models and the window dimensions were increased to further enhance visibility. Interior comfort was improved by the installation of the first air conditioning systems. Also during this period GM completely redesigned its classic sedans and introduced front seat safety belts.

The period between 1950 and 1956 was particularly prosperous in the United States, with a rise in demand for a second car in the family. Americans, however, were beginning to show real interest in smaller European cars. By 1956, a year of decreasing sales, Ford Motor Company, Chrysler Corporation, and GM had lost some 15 percent in sales while imports were virtually doubling their market penetration. The longer Detroit's automobiles grew, the more popular imports became. In 1957 the United States imported more cars than it exported, and despite a recession, imports accounted for more than 8 percent of U.S. car sales. Although GM promised that help was on its way in the form of smaller compact cars, the new models failed to generate much excitement; the company's market share slipped to just 42 percent of 1959's new car sales.

The 1960s were difficult years in Detroit. The 1967 riot in the neighborhoods surrounding GM's facilities forced management to recognize the urban poverty that had for so long been in their midst, and they began to employ more workers from minority groups. Much of the new hiring was made possible by the expansionist policies of the Kennedy and Johnson administrations. GM prospered and diversified; its interests now included home appliances, insurance, locomotives, electronics, ball bearings, banking, and financing. By the late 1960s after-tax profits for the industry in general reached a 13 percent return on investment, and GM's return increased from 16.5 percent to 25.8 percent.

Remaining Competitive in the 1970s–80s

Like the rest of the industry, GM had ignored, in large part, the importance of air pollution control. However, new, costly federal regulations were mandated, and GM had to invest in developing devices to control pollution. By the early 1970s, this issue was temporarily overshadowed by the impact of the oil embargo. GM's luxury, gas-guzzling car sales were down by 35 percent in 1974, but the company's compacts and subcompacts rose steadily to attain a 40 percent market share. Ford, Chrysler, and GM had been caught unaware by a vast shift in consumer demand, and GM suffered the greatest losses. The company spent $2.25 billion in 1974 and 1975 to meet local, state, and federal regulations on pollution control. By the end of 1977 that figure had doubled.

Under the leadership of President F. James McDonald and Chairman Roger Smith, GM reported earnings declines from 1985 to 1992. The only respite came from an accounting change in 1987, which effected an earnings increase. McDonald and Smith attempted to place these losses in perspective by arguing that they were necessary if GM was to develop a strong and secure position on the worldwide market. Since the start of the 1980s, GM had spent more than $60 billion redesigning most of its cars and modernizing the plants that produce them. The company also acquired two major corporations, Hughes Aircraft, in 1986, and Electronic Data Systems (EDS), in 1984. Though expensive, the EDS purchase provided GM with better, more centralized communications and backup systems, as well as a vital profit center. GM also purchased a 50 percent stake in Saab Automobile AB, a Swedish maker of premium cars, in 1990. That same year Saturn Corporation was created as a subsidiary to produce compact cars in a Japanese-influenced factory in Tennessee; Saturns became popular because of their quality and the no-haggle method employed to sell them.

GM's market share dropped steadily from 1982 to 1992. In 1987 Ford's profits exceeded GM's for the first time in 60 years. From 1990 to 1992, the corporation suffered successive and devastating annual losses totaling almost $30 billion. Problems were myriad. Manufacturing costs exceeded competitors' due to high labor costs, overcapacity, and complicated production procedures. GM faced competition from 25 companies, and its market share fell from almost 50 percent to about 35 percent.

The 1990s: Regaining Ground

In 1992 Jack Smith, Jr., advanced to GM's chief executive office. He had earned respect as the engineer of GM Europe's late 1980s turnaround, and he quickly applied those strategies to the parent, focusing on North American Operations (NAO).

During 1993, Smith simplified the NAO, cut the corporate staff, pared product offerings, and began to divest GM's parts operations. He was also hailed for his negotiations with the United Auto Workers (UAW). In 1993 he pledged $3.9 billion in jobless benefits, which raised the blue-collar payroll costs about 16 percent over three years. At the same time the contract gave Smith the ability to cut 65,000 blue-collar jobs by 1996 in conjunction with the closure of nearly 24 plants. Salaried positions were not exempted from Smith's job-cutting plan; staffing at the corporate central office was slashed from 13,500 to 2,300 in 1992.

In the early 1990s GM began to recapture the automotive vanguard from Japanese carmakers, with entries in the van, truck, and utility vehicle markets and the launch of Saturn. GM also gained an advantage in the domestic market because the weak dollar caused the price of imported cars to increase much faster than domestics. Market conditions along with Smith's strategies effected a stunning reversal in 1993, when GM recorded net income of $2.47 billion on sales of $138.22 billion. Riding the booming economy, the company recorded record profits of $6.88 billion on record sales of $163.86 billion in 1995. Despite the improved financial performance, GM's share of the U.S. car market continued its steady decline, falling to slightly more than 31 percent by 1995. The company's North American operations continued to be criticized by observers for its inability to produce innovative models, the glacial speed of its new product development, and the inefficiencies inherent in running six separate car divisions and a GMC truck division.

The mid-to-late 1990s saw a number of important initiatives in GM's non-automaking operations. In 1994 the renamed Hughes Electronics unit introduced Direct TV, a satellite-based direct-to-home broadcast service. The 1995 sale of the company's National Car Rental business was followed by the spin-off of EDS the following year. One year later, Hughes Electronics was revamped through the sale of its defense electronics operations to Raytheon Company and the merging of its automotive electronics activities (Delco Electronics) into GM's auto parts subsidiary, Delphi Automotive Systems. Hughes began concentrating on digital entertainment, information, and communications services and made a key acquisition in 1999 when it paid $1.3 billion for the direct-to-home satellite business of Primestar. In early 2000 Hughes would make a further divestment of a then noncore unit, selling its satellite manufacturing operations to the Boeing Company for about $3.75 billion. Delphi, meanwhile, would be completely separated from GM through a May 1999 spinoff to shareholders.

GM remained profitable through the end of the decade, but its U.S. market share dipped below 30 percent by 1999; at times GM's share was less than that of the combined share of all Asian automakers, an unprecedented development. While continuing to attempt to reverse the now three-decades-long fall, GM began looking for future growth from Asia, where early 21st-century growth in car sales was expected to surpass both North America and Europe. Instead of attempting to directly sell its own models, GM began assembling a network of alliances with key Asian automakers for its push into that emerging continent, aiming to increase its market share across Asia from its late 1990s level of 4 to 10 percent by 2005. The company already had a 34 percent stake in Isuzu Motors Ltd., which it

had bought in 1971, and a 3 percent stake in Suzuki Motor Corporation, obtained in 1981. In 1998 GM increased its stake in Suzuki to 10 percent and agreed to build cars with the Japanese automaker. The following year GM increased its stake in Isuzu to 49 percent; acquired a 20 percent stake in Fuji Heavy Industries Ltd., maker of Subaru all-wheel-drive vehicles; and entered into an alliance with Honda Motor Co., Ltd. involving Honda producing low-emissions gasoline engines for GM and Isuzu producing diesel engines for Honda.

2000 and Beyond

In May 2000 GM, Fuji, and Suzuki agreed to develop compact cars for the European market. Another deal involving Europe was reached in early 2000, when GM agreed to acquire a 20 percent stake in the Fiat Auto S.p.A. unit of Fiat S.p.A., the number six automaker in the world, in exchange for Fiat taking a 5.1 percent stake in GM. Through this deal, GM aimed to grab a larger share of the market for the small vehicles popular in Europe and Latin America but shunned in the United States. In mid-2000 GM and Fiat jointly bid to acquire troubled South Korean carmaker Daewoo Motor Company but were outbid by Ford. Also in 2000, GM acquired the 50 percent of Saab Automobile that it did not already own.

Closer to home, GM began building a factory in Lansing, Michigan, its first new plant in 15 years. In another key early 2000 development, the company agreed to join with Daimler-Chrysler AG and Ford to create an Internet-based global business-to-business supplier exchange, Covisint LLC, that would be open to all suppliers and automakers. This would create the world's largest virtual marketplace. Although the Federal Trade Commission (FTC) quickly opened a preliminary antitrust inquiry into the plan, clearance was eventually gained and the Covisint venture went forward.

In June 2000 G. Richard Wagoner was promoted from president to CEO, with Smith remaining chairman. At the age of 47, Wagoner became the youngest CEO in GM history and faced the daunting task of running what was still considered by many observers to be an excessively bureaucratic and overly complex organization, which was extremely resistant to change and seemingly unable to anticipate most market trends.

The focus on strengthening its foothold in the Asian market continued into 2001. Ford suddenly announced that it was dropping its offer for Daewoo, leaving GM wide open to relaunch its bid. Negotiations began that year and were finalized in 2002. GM ended up acquiring a majority interest in Daewoo Motor, renaming it GM Daewoo Auto & Technology. At the same time, the company purchased an additional 10 percent of Suzuki, increasing its stake to 20 percent, and signed a deal with AvtoVAZ to build sports utility vehicles (SUVs) for the Russian market.

GM chalked up a solid performance during this period. While its competitors struggled with recalls, and quality and merger integration issues, the automaker appeared to have overcome the problems of its past. An April 2002 *Fortune* article noted that ''some of what's driving GM is very basic: improvements in quality and productivity, the pruning of unprofitable vehicles, and frankly, weakness at its crosstown rivals Ford and

Chrysler.'' GM's market share rose in 2001 and by early 2002 had reached 30.9 percent in the U.S. market. Chevrolet had also started to outsell Ford. This was due in part to the successful zero percent financing plans it introduced after the terrorist attacks in September 2001. The financing plan was advertised under the ''Keep America Rolling'' slogan. Sales of GM cars increased by 31 percent one month after its launch.

The company did face one major hurdle however—its $76 billion pension fund. Deals struck with the UAW in past years left GM forced to pay out costly health and retirement benefits. The company was the largest purchaser of health care in the United States, spending nearly $5 billion on healthcare alone in 2003. Word spread quickly that GM's pension fund was underfunded by nearly $18 billion at the start of 2003. The company was able to generate cash for the fund by selling off its Hughes Electronics stake to News Corporation in 2003 for approximately $3.1 billion. It also jettisoned its armored vehicles business in a $1.1 billion deal. The sale of its noncore assets, global debt offerings, and income from its automotive operations allowed to the company to fully fund its U.S. salaried and hourly employee pension plans by the end of 2003. Its automotive earnings, however, felt the crunch. Overall, the company's net income for 2003 reached $3.8 billion. The majority of earnings stemmed from its GMAC and Asian operations.

Smith retired in May 2003, leaving Wagoner at the helm. GM's management team continued to focus on controlling costs while phasing out car lines—including Oldsmobile, the Camero, and the Firebird—and launching such new products as the Cadillac CTS, the Hummer H2, and the Opel Vectra in Europe. GM faced a challenging road ahead. Rising healthcare costs, intense competition, and having to shore up its North American auto sales were just some of its obstacles. GM was, however, in the top position in its industry and was no stranger to adversity.

Principal Subsidiaries

General Motors Acceptance Corporation; General Motors Investment Management Corporation; GMAC Commercial Finance LLC; Saturn Corporation; Holden, Ltd. (Australia); General Motors do Brasil Ltda. (Brazil); General Motors of Canada, Ltd.; Adam Opel AG (Germany); General Motors de Mexico, S.A. de C.V.; Saab Automobile AB (Sweden); Saab Cars Holding Corporation; Vauxhall Motors Limited (United Kingdom).

Principal Operating Units

GM Automotive; Financing and Insurance Operations.

Principal Competitors

AmeriCredit Corporation; Bayerische Motoren Werke AG; Credit Acceptance Corporation; DaimlerChrysler AG; Ford Motor Company; Ford Motor Credit Company; General Electric Capital Corporation; General Electric Company; Honda Motor Co., Ltd.; Hyundai Motor Company; Mazda Motor Corporation; Mitsubishi Motors Corporation; Nissan Motor Co., Ltd.; PSA Peugeot Citron S.A.; Renault S.A.; Suzuki Motor Corporation; Toyota Motor Corporation; Volkswagen AG.

Further Reading

Bary, Andrew, ''How to Fix GM,'' *Barron's,* July 5, 1999, pp. 18–19.

Cray, Ed, *Chrome Colossus: General Motors and Its Time,* New York: McGraw-Hill, 1980.

Dassbach, Carl H.A., *Global Enterprises and the World Economy: Ford, General Motors, and IBM; the Emergence of the Transnational Enterprise,* New York: Garland, 1989.

De Lorean, John Z., *On a Clear Day You Can See General Motors,* London: Sidgwick and Jackson, 1980.

Geyelin, Milo, ''Lasting Impact: How an Internal Memo Written 26 Years Ago Is Costing GM Dearly,'' *Wall Street Journal,* September 29, 1999, pp. A1+.

Hamper, Ben, *Rivethead: Tales from the Assembly Line,* New York: Warner Books, 1992.

Jacobs, Timothy, *A History of General Motors,* New York: Smithmark, 1992.

Keller, Maryann, *Collision: GM, Toyota, Volkswagen, and the Race to Own the 21st Century,* New York: Currency Doubleday, 1993.

——, *Rude Awakening: General Motors in the 1980s,* New York: Morrow, 1989.

——, *Rude Awakening: The Rise, Fall and Struggle for Recovery of General Motors,* New York: HarperCollins, 1990.

Kerwin, Kathleen, ''For GM, Once Again, Little Ventured, Little Gained,'' *Business Week,* March 27, 2000, pp. 42–43.

Kerwin, Kathleen, and Joann Muller, ''Reviving GM,'' *Business Week,* February 1, 1999, pp. 114+.

Kuhn, Arthur J., *GM Passes Ford, 1918–1938: Designing the General Motors Performance-Control System,* University Park: Pennsylvania State University Press, 1986.

Madsen, Axel, *The Deal Maker: How William C. Durant Made General Motors,* New York: Wiley, 1999.

May, George S., *R.E. Olds, Auto Industry Pioneer,* Grand Rapids, Mich.: Eerdmans, 1977.

Meredith, Robyn, ''Can GM Return to the Passing Lane?,'' *New York Times,* November 7, 1999, Sec. 3, p. 1.

Miller, Scott, ''Open No Quick Fix for GM's 'Mr. Fix It','' *Wall Street Journal,* June 13, 2000, p. A22.

Osterland, Andrew, ''Al and Me: Why General Motors Will Finally Get Serious About Downsizing,'' *Financial World,* December 16, 1996, pp. 39–41.

Palmer, Jay, ''Reviving GM,'' *Barron's,* June 22, 1998, pp. 31–35.

Pollack, Andrew, ''Paper Trail GM After It Loses Injury Suit,'' *New York Times,* July 12, 1999, p. A12.

Ramsey, Douglas K., *The Corporate Warriors: Six Classic Cases in American Business,* Boston: Houghton Mifflin, 1987.

''Rick Wagoner's Game Plan,'' *Business Week,* February 10, 2003, p. 52.

Rothschild, Emma, *Paradise Lost: The Decline of the Auto-Industrial Age,* New York: Random House, 1973.

Shirouzu, Norihiko, ''GM Cracks Japan's Market with Its Wallet, Not Its Cars: Network of Alliances Aids Asia Expansion by Filling Gaps in Product Line,'' *Wall Street Journal,* January 26, 2000, p. A17.

Simison, Robert L., Fara Warner, and Gregory L. White, ''Big Three Car Makers Plan Net Exchange,'' *Wall Street Journal,* February 28, 2000, pp. A3, A16.

Simison, Robert L., Gregory L. White, and Deborah Ball, ''GM's Linkup with Fiat Opens Final Act of Consolidation Drama for Industry,'' *Wall Street Journal,* March 14, 2000, pp. A3, A8.

Sloan, Alfred, Jr., *My Years with General Motors,* New York: Doubleday, 1964.

Smith, Roger B., *Building on 75 Years of Excellence: The General Motors Story,* New York: Newcomen Society of the United States, 1984.

Taylor, Alex, III, ''Finally GM is Looking Good,'' *Fortune,* April 1, 2002, p. 68.

——, "GM's $11 Billion Turnaround," *Fortune,* October 17, 1994, pp. 54–56+.

——, "GM Gets Its Act Together," *Fortune,* April 5, 2004, p. 136.

——, "GM: Some Gain, Much Pain," *Fortune,* May 29, 1995, pp. 78–80, 84.

——, "GM: Time to Get in Gear," *Fortune,* April 28, 1997, pp. 94–96+.

——, "GM: Why They Might Break Up America's Biggest Company," *Fortune,* April 29, 1996, pp. 78–82, 84.

——, "Is Jack Smith the Man to Fix GM?," *Fortune,* August 3, 1998, pp. 86+.

Weisberger, Bernard A., *The Dream Maker: William C. Durant, Founder of General Motors,* Boston: Little Brown, 1979.

Welch, David, "Has GM Outrun its Pension Problems?," *Business Week,* January 19, 2004, p. 70.

White, Gregory L., "As GM Courts the Net, Struggling Saturn Line Exposes Rusty Spots," *Wall Street Journal,* July 11, 2000, pp. A1, A10.

Zachary, Katherine, "Shopping Spree: GM Plunks Down Hard Cash to Add Strength in Asia," *Ward's Auto World,* February 29, 2000.

Zesiger, Sue, "GM's Big Decision: Status Quo," *Fortune,* February 21, 2000, pp. 101–02, 104.

—April Dougal Gasbarre
—updates: David E. Salamie and
Christina M. Stansell

Godiva Chocolatier, Inc.

355 Lexington Avenue, Floor 16
New York, New York 10017
U.S.A.
Telephone: (212) 681-2600
Toll Free: (800) 946-3482
Fax: (212) 984-5901
Web site: http://www.godiva.com

Wholly Owned Subsidiary of Campbell Soup Company
Incorporated: 1926
Employees: 100
Sales: $35 million (2003 est.)
NAIC: 311330 Confectionery Manufacturing from Purchased Chocolate; 445292 Confectionery and Nut Stores

Godiva Chocolatier, Inc., is a leading manufacturer of premium-quality chocolates, cookies, ice cream, cocoa, and flavored coffees. Its products are sold at about 250 company-owned stores in North America and in major cities worldwide, as well at sales counters in several thousand upscale department and specialty stores like Marshall Field's and Barnes & Noble. Godiva also sells its chocolates through direct-mail catalogs and via the Internet. Founded in Belgium, the firm has been owned since the 1960s by Campbell Soup Company and is now headquartered in the United States.

Beginnings

Godiva Chocolatier traces its roots to 1926, when Pierre Draps started making chocolates in Brussels, Belgium, for sale to local shops. His son Joseph began working for the family business at the age of 14 and shortly after World War II took control of it. When he decided to open a shop of his own, he sought a distinctive name to give it and turned to his wife for ideas. She suggested Godiva, after the legendary countess who had protested high taxes by riding nude through Coventry, England, and Draps chose it for the new endeavor.

His shop in Brussels' Grande Place was a success, and over the next decade several other outlets were opened around Bel-

gium. Joseph Draps was both a talented chocolate-maker and a skilled businessman, and under his guidance the firm built the Godiva brand into a leader in the super-premium chocolate category through the use of sophisticated advertising and elegant packaging, as well as by limiting distribution to select locations.

Godiva's signature offering was a creamy ''ganache,'' or hazelnut praline filling, that was inserted into a molded shell of high quality chocolate. Over the years, Draps built up a repertoire of distinctive products, many of which had been introduced to commemorate specific events. His best-known creation was the Comtesse, which celebrated Lady Godiva herself and was made from dark or milk chocolate with a chocolate cream center. Another was the Autant, a hand-decorated chocolate leaf made from coffee and chocolate creams covered in milk chocolate, which had been made to commemorate the 1939 premiere of the film *Gone With the Wind*. Other popular offerings included the Fabiola, introduced in 1958 to celebrate the engagement of Queen Fabiola to King Baudouin I of Belgium, and the Golf Ball, which honored Draps' golf-playing friendship with Belgium's King Leopold III. Godiva would later be named the official purveyor of chocolate to the Belgian Royal Court.

In 1958, the first Godiva shop outside Belgium opened in Paris, and in 1966 the company's offerings reached America with distribution to select chains of luxury department stores. At the same time, the Draps family sold a two-thirds stake in the firm to Pepperidge Farm, a unit of Campbell Soup Company. Later, Campbell would acquire the remainder.

In 1972, the company opened its first American location on Fifth Avenue in New York City, near the shops of Tiffany and Cartier. As in its European boutiques, Godiva's products were displayed like jewels in refrigerated brass and glass cases.

Rapid Growth Beginning in the Late 1970s

In 1978, the company named a new president, Albert J. Pechenik, and under his leadership sales leapt from approximately $4 million to more than $22 million in four years. Godiva's profile was raised by advertising in tony publications such *Gourmet* magazine and *Architectural Digest*, along with such moves as partnering with designer Bill Blass, who created a signature line of chocolates for the firm. Marketing materials were improved as well, and department stores were encouraged to set up separate Godiva counters. During this period, the firm's chain of stores was also expanded, with shops opened in such countries as Japan for the first time.

The customer at a Godiva boutique, as the firm termed its outlets, was treated like a buyer at a fine jewelry store. Once a selection of chocolate pieces had been made from the display case and weighed, the candy was placed in a golden box, tied with imported golden string, and then put into a golden bag for transport. In addition to chocolates by the pound (then priced at $17.50), special items like chocolate-filled Limoges china bowls and Wedgwood dishes were also sold. Other extravagant offerings included model kits of Porsche, Rolls Royce, and Mercedes automobiles, which could be ''glucd'' together by melting an included extra piece of chocolate. The company's products were frequently purchased for gifts, and 70 percent of Godiva's sales were made during the holiday season, which stretched from November to Valentine's Day.

The company had by now set up a second headquarters in New York and an American production facility in Reading, Pennsylvania, though European customers were still supplied by a plant in Belgium. Some debated the relative merits of Godiva chocolates from Belgium versus those made in the United States, but the company dismissed such concerns, noting that it used the same supplier for its raw chocolate but created unique recipes for different markets, factoring in regional preferences for sweetness and flavorings. Additionally, laws in some states limiting alcohol content required that American recipes omit certain liqueur-based flavoring agents that were preferred in Europe.

In the summer of 1982, Albert Pechenik resigned as president to form a chocolate company of his own, Gourmet Resources International, and his position was taken by Thomas H. Fey. A disgruntled Pechenik later charged that his former employer was trying to undermine his new operation, but Godiva countered that it was simply being competitive.

The company continued to grow during the mid-1980s by such actions as boosting its retail presence in the UK and adding a chocolate gift registry. By 1988, Godiva was operating 56 stores in the United States alone and taking in revenues of approximately $100 million worldwide, with the bulk of earnings continuing to be derived from sales to department stores and other specialty retailers. The company had also begun issuing catalogs for mail-order sales, though this made up only a small portion of its business. The price of Godiva's 50-plus varieties of solids, cremes, mints, caramels and cordials now stood at approximately $22 per pound, almost twice what lower-end competitors such as Fanny Farmer charged.

As the U.S. economy hit a serious downturn at the end of the 1980s and sales of luxury goods fell off, Godiva found its sales in decline. In May 1991, seasoned marketer David L. Albright was named to replace Thomas Fey as the company's president. Albright, formerly vice-president of Pepperidge Farm's biscuit division, refocused Godiva on its core product line of shell-molded chocolates, while also inaugurating a new $5 million advertising campaign. A primary goal of the ads was to increase sales beyond the holiday season by depicting the firm's chocolates as personal indulgences rather than primarily as gift items.

New Products in the 1990s

Brand-building efforts continued during 1993 with the introduction of the Café Godiva line of gourmet coffees and a chocolate liqueur made in conjunction with Seagram's, as well as a number of new single-serving chocolate treats and a line of biscotti cookies. To boost sales in department stores, Godiva also began offering them new refrigerated cases that better displayed the company's pre-packaged boxes of chocolates.

In 1994, following a successful test at its Chicago boutique, Godiva began a chain-wide redesign of its stores, which now numbered more than 110. Abandoning the jewelry-store look of pink marble and black lacquer, a new Art Nouveau-inspired combination of bleached wood floors, creamy white marble, and richly-finished cherry wood cabinets was introduced. At the same time, the shops were made more welcoming, with the layout changed to encourage browsing while prices were displayed in public view. New, affordable treat items were introduced including Bouches, single-serving chocolates priced below $3. In 1995, the company gained Kosher certification, with most of its chocolates now manufactured in accordance with Jewish dietary laws.

While these changes were taking place, Godiva also revamped its direct-marketing unit, which had never heretofore turned a profit. Catalogs were redesigned and other elements of the operation were restructured, which helped produce profits as well as a sales increase of 15 percent in 1995 and 20 percent in 1996. The mail-order division, which still accounted for less than 10 percent of the firm's total earnings, targeted both corporate accounts as well as the general public. A survey done via Godiva's Web site, which had been launched in 1995, found that a typical customer was a woman who earned $60,000 per year.

The year 1996 saw the company redesign its Web site and experiment with the idea of creating small retail kiosks in shopping malls. Over the next year, three such kiosks were opened, while Godiva's chain of U.S. stores, also located primarily in malls, grew to 131. A new line of coffee products was introduced for use by office service companies during the year as well.

Key Dates:

1926: Draps family begins making chocolate in Brussels, Belgium.
1940s: Joseph Draps opens the first Godiva shop.
1958: Draps opens a Paris shop, his first outside of Belgium.
1966: A majority stake in Godiva is acquired by Campbell Soup Co.; U.S. sales begin.
1968: Godiva is named the official chocolatier to the Royal Court of Belgium.
1972: Godiva's first U.S. shop opens on Fifth Avenue in New York City.
1993: Coffees, cookies, liqueur are introduced.
1994: The company starts a chain-wide redesign of its stores.
1997: Valentine's Day Chocolate & Diamonds promotional giveaway debuts.
1999: Godiva ice cream is introduced.
2003: Norman Love's G Collection of chocolates is added.

In 1997, Godiva launched a new promotional campaign to boost sales for Valentine's Day. The company placed three certificates redeemable for one-carat diamond rings valued at $10,000 in boxes of its Love in Bloom chocolate collection, which retailed for $18 or more per box. The successful giveaway brought the company significant media attention, and it was reprised and expanded each year thereafter.

In the fall of 1998, president Craig Rydin, who had been running the company since 1996, was moved up in the Campbell organization, and his place taken by Archbold van Beuren. At this time Godiva was also introducing a new line of cookies (known in the industry as biscuits), which included such flavors as Hazelnut Belgique and Chocolate-Dipped Pirouette.

In 1999, Godiva introduced a line of ultra-premium ice cream in conjunction with Dreyer's/Edy's Grand Ice Cream, which initially consisted of six flavors. A 12.5 ounce container retailed for $3.19, making it more expensive than established premium brands such as Ben & Jerry's. Within six months of its introduction in March 1999, the line had come to account for 7 percent of the super-premium category's sales, with annual revenues projected to reach $20 million or more. The year had also seen the most lavish Chocolates & Diamonds Valentine's promotion to date, featuring prizes of 100 diamond earring sets and a 7.2 carat diamond ring valued at $125,000, courtesy of DeBeers.

During the late 1990s, the company experienced a drop in sales to Asia due to an economic downturn in that region, but its business in Japan and Hong Kong continued to grow, and distribution there was expanded despite the financial crisis. By the latter half of 2000, Godiva chocolates were being sold in 37 countries at 232 company-owned stores and at more than 2,500 counters in specialty and department stores such as Marshall Field's and Barnes & Noble. To help its customers find the nearest location, the company introduced a free service to users of cell phones and wireless handheld devices which offered downloadable maps.

2000 and Beyond

The fall of 2000 saw the firm introduce Palets D'Or, dark chocolate pieces whose smooth centers featured such flavors as tea, lemon, and red wine. Godiva also took advantage of the promotional opportunity afforded by Miramax Films' hit *Chocolat,* giving holders of tickets to the movie free samples and sponsoring a contest which offered the winner a trip for two to Brussels.

In January 2001, Godiva began its 75th anniversary year by announcing that the annual Valentine's Day giveaway would include a 7.5 carat diamond ring and 75 diamond bracelets worth $3,500 each. During the year, the company also introduced a number of new chocolates, including the Romaine, Noix Macadamia, Nippon, and Creole pieces, each of which contained a unique combination of chocolate, praline, and other flavors.

In 2003, the company's Valentine's Day promotion shifted away from diamonds to feature 50 five-day trips for two to a Marriott resort in Arizona, with a pair of ''his and hers'' BMW Z4 automobiles as the Grand Prize. That same year also saw the Starbucks coffee chain begin test-marketing Godiva products at 50 of its stores in New York, Chicago, and Seattle. In the fall, Godiva introduced new items for the holiday gift season, including the G Collection of hand-decorated chocolates created by pastry chef Norman Love, which retailed for close to $100 per pound. Other offerings included a new collection of deluxe caramels and a limited-edition music box filled with chocolates, which was produced in conjunction with Steinway & Sons.

More than three-quarters of a century after the Draps family first started making chocolates in Belgium, Godiva Chocolatier, Inc. had evolved into the preeminent luxury chocolate company in the world. The combination of innovative, high-quality products, finely tuned marketing, and the powerful backing of Campbell Soup had helped make the name Godiva synonymous with indulgence and pleasure.

Principal Subsidiaries

Godiva Brands, Inc.; Godiva Belgium N.V. QSA (Belgium); Godiva Chocolatier (Asia) Ltd. (Hong Kong); Godiva Chocolatier of Canada Ltd. (Canada); Godiva France S.A. (France); Godiva Japan Inc. (Japan); Godiva U.K. Ltd. (United Kingdom)

Principal Competitors

Russell Stover Candies, Inc.; The Ghirardelli Chocolate Company; Hershey Foods Corporation; Nestlé S.A.; Mars, Inc.; Cadbury Schweppes plc.

Further Reading

Crownover, Catherine, ''Godiva Kiosk Riding into the Avenues,'' *Florida Times-Union,* June 2, 1997, p. 3.
Franks, Sara Hope, ''Godiva: Better in Belgium?,'' *Washington Post,* September 14, 1994, p. E1.
''Ganache with Panache,'' *Business Times Singapore,* November 17, 2001.

"Godiva History and FAQ," March 1, 2004. Available from http://www.godiva.com/about/faq.asp.

"Godiva's Naked Ambition," *South China Morning Post*, September 24, 2000.

Ng, Eric, "Chocolate-Maker Bucks Trend by Opening Two New Branches," *South China Morning Post*, May 5, 1999.

Pepper, Jon, "Sweet Success in Sales Automation," *Working Woman*, April 1, 1989, p. 59.

Philippidis, Alex, "Godiva Chocolatier Provides a Tempting Taste of Things to Come," *Westchester County Business Journal*, October 24, 1994, p. 2.

Pokela, Barbara, "How Sweet it Is—Minneapolis Godiva Store Wants to Cash in on Candy," *Star-Tribune Newspaper of the Twin Cities*, June 20, 1988, p. 3D.

Ramirez, Anthony, "Marketing Executive Is New Head of Godiva," *New York Times*, May 3, 1991, p. 4.

Warner, Fara, "Upscale Chocolate's Not Hot, So Godiva Does a Makeover," *Brandweek*, July 4, 1994, p. 21.

Weidlich, Thom, "Chocolate Shakeup," *Direct*, December 1, 1996, p. 1.

—Frank Uhle

Goody's Family Clothing, Inc.

400 Goody's Lane
Knoxville, Tennessee 37922
U.S.A.
Telephone: (865) 966-2000
Fax: (865) 777-4220
Web site: http://www.goodysonline.com

Public Company
Incorporated: 1954
Employees: 10,000
Sales: $1.23 billion (2004)
Stock Exchanges: NASDAQ
Ticker Symbol: GDYS
NAIC: 44814 Family Clothing Stores

Goody's Family Clothing, Inc., is a value-priced chain with over 335 locations in Alabama, Arkansas, Florida, Georgia, Indiana, Illinois, Louisiana, Kentucky, Mississippi, Missouri, North Carolina, Ohio, Oklahoma, South Carolina, Tennessee, Texas, Virginia, and West Virginia. Found mainly in strip malls, Goody's stores offer a variety of apparel and accessories for the women, men, and children. Goody's struggled in the early years of the 21st century, in part due to weak sales and intense competition. A plan to sell the company to a private equity group fell through in 2002.

Origins and Development: 1953–90

The company that would become Goody's started as a 2,000-square-foot small discount apparel store opened in 1953 by Mike Goodfriend and his family. The first "Goodfriend" store, located in Athens, Tennessee, was modest and family-oriented. A big "G" over the door was the simple logo, and the merchandise consisted of irregulars, last year's styles, and closeouts piled on tables and packed onto hanging racks. The lighting was poor, the customer service sketchy, but the lure of good clothes at great prices kept people coming. The bargain store grew slowly over the next 20 years. When outlet and factory stores began to come into their own in the mid-70s, Goodfriend was in a very competitive niche, but stores continued offering seconds and discontinueds at discount prices. The chain had expanded to 12 stores by

1972 and had annual revenue of $12 million. Goodfriend was squeezed by the proliferation of national outlet stores and discounters and knew something had to change to keep his stores in the game. He looked to his son, Bob, for help.

In 1972, Bob—Robert M. Goodfriend—joined the team. With a background in retailing, Bob brought outside experience to the family-run operation. He considered the market and decided to take a middle road, a path different from that of discounters or department stores. He redirected the company to offer well-recognized, fashion names and up-to-the-minute trends at moderate prices. Everything reoriented not around the family seeking a discount but around the average family looking for today's stylish clothes at good prices. The store no longer purchased closeouts, irregulars, last year's goods, or factory seconds.

Acknowledging this adjustment of direction, the store was renamed "Goody's," after a college nickname of Bob's. By 1979, the chain had 21 stores, and Bob took over the reins of leadership completely as president and CEO.

New corporate headquarters were designed in 1990, when the company left the small town of Athens to relocate to Knoxville. Designed by award-winning architectural firm McCarty Holsaple McCarty, Inc., the headquarters not only contained an office complex but a completely customized 344,000-square-foot clothing distribution center. The state-of-the-art center made it possible to receive new fashions in one day and have them on trucks and out to stores the next, making for a minimal time lag in getting the latest fashions to the consumer. The distribution center could process 350,000 garments safely in one day and it was computer-linked to each of the chains. Whatever was happening in the stores—sellouts, poor movers, runs on special items—was reported back to the main office. Acquisition strategy as well as distribution time lines could be adjusted. Clothes sales were also tracked by color and size for a very precise measure of how business was running from day to day.

1990s: Public Offering and Boardroom Battles

By 1991, prospering under a reign of technological advantage, Goody's had seen a decade of meteoric growth. The company closed the year with 91 stores and $273 million in annual sales. It was time to make a public launch. Goody's held its initial public offering in October of that year. It elected a very conservative board of directors and successfully expanded its base of capital.

Three years later, the company had doubled its 1990 sales figures and growth to 171 stores. Goody's was also gradually remodeling its interiors, doing away with tables and updating to clean, brightly lit interiors with wide aisles and clearly marked departments. The image went from discount house to department store, and the prices stayed 10 to 30 percent down from regular department store prices.

Just when things were looking their best, the conservative board of directors began to clash with Goody's management, which wanted to pursue a more aggressive purchasing policy and keep the stores more up to date and better stocked. In a bitter feud, chief operating officer Henry Call and merchandising executive Tom Kelly left the store in 1992. Bob Goodfriend, despite the fact that his dream had developed much of what Goody's had become and that he was one of the members of the original family who started the chain, was forcibly ousted from the board. His absence lasted for three months, during which he sued the company and eventually won $1.24 million in legal settlement and fees. The store's margin of pre-tax earnings dropped from 5.6 percent of sales. Although Henry Call and Tom Kelly came back on board in 1995 as president and executive vice-president, respectively, and Goodfriend was accepted back on the board as chairman, the store has not yet returned to its pre-schism profitability margin. In 1996, it stood at only 3.4 percent. Climbing back up to 5.6 percent profitability is a continuing goal for the company and is reiterated in much of its internal literature.

Part of Goody's strategy to improve that profit percentage began in 1993, when it was decided to create Goody's own private label merchandise. Establishing a private label was seen to give Goody's long-range control over its inventory. Brand name fashions manufactured by other companies were always "outside" variables. However, by developing its own fashions, Goody's management felt that it could more directly please and serve its customers. The first of these private labels was Ivy Crew for men, a stylish, golf-inspired collection that became a popular suite of apparel for the store. Estimates in the late 1990s saw that the Ivy Crew label accounted for 18 percent of the total sales in the men's department.

New Help and a New Slogan for 1995

Contracting year by year with overseas manufacturers in Southeast Asia and Central America, Goody's has expanded its private labels into all of its clothing departments. It hired John Okvath in 1995, an old hand in the Asian rag market, to oversee product development. It also hired people away from The Limited and BIKE Athletic who were well-seasoned in overseas garment development. The expansion of the private label program was viewed by senior management as Goody's "ace in the hole" for future profit creation. While maintaining a commitment to national brand name fashions, Goody's was encouraging in its customers a taste for its own house labels.

One of the recurring elements in the story of Goody's is the store's striving to keep a friendly, family look and compete with the slick finish-outs of its department store competitors. As a part of this effort to stay in tune with its market, in the spring of 1995 Goody's came out with a new slogan—"Goody's feels like you." The logo was redesigned and the whole atmosphere of the stores was redone in shades of upbeat, feel-good, country casual. An in-house brochure recapped the marketing policy as follows: "Customers like the prices, and they like the selection. But most important, they feel good about themselves when they wear the clothing they buy at Goody's." The "Customer First" training initiative helped to carry out the theme by teaching store associates to smile and respond to customers immediately. Goody's also followed up on its progress by bringing people from the sales floor to headquarters periodically for "round-table" meetings that debriefed associates on the customer experience and gathered grass-roots comments about improvement.

In 1995, the company opened 13 new stores and saw gross sales of $696.7 million. With better sales, aggressive promotion, remodeled looks, and Goodfriend, Call, and Kelly firmly back on board, Goody's stock rose 150 percent.

Enjoying a calmer political atmosphere, Goody's headed into 1996, a year when the company opened 20 new stores and closed only one. Now with a newly picked management team, the corporation redirected its policies away from slashing prices quickly on slow-moving apparel and more towards holding a stable, mid-priced lineup. The company also began to invest more heavily in inventory. The new corporate policy also encouraged a move out of the "country"—the suburbs where many of the chains were located—and into metropolitan areas. In 1996, Goody's opened six stores in Atlanta and three in Charlotte. Sales were up 17 percent over 1995, to $819.1 million, and the stores ended the year with no long-term debt.

Goody's business was seasonal in nature, with the peak seasons being traditional family-oriented times. Goody's made its money during the periods before Christmas, Easter, and the reopening of school in September—these weeks accounting for 35 percent of the company's annual sales from 1993 to 1996, a trend expected to continue. In late 1996, the company also took a new direction by offering gifts and accessories, an approach which was evaluated as profitable and successful.

With the addition of non-clothing items, Goody's standard merchandise fit in nine carefully tracked categories, and the labels in each category fluctuated slightly from year to year as the corporation determined which popular brands would fit into its pricing structure.

In 1997, Goody's planned to improve its profit margin by reducing dependence on denim, a low-cost leader for the store that brought in almost a quarter of all sales across all departments, and increasing its stock of house-label merchandise and high-margin garments, such as women's career clothing. It also continued to lease, not own or build, its stores, in order to avoid long-term debt. Goody's looked for a very specific sort of

Key Dates:

1953: Mike Goodfriend and his family open a small discount apparel store.
1972: Robert M. Goodfriend joins the company.
1991: Goody's goes public.
1993: By now, the company has doubled its 1990 sales figures and expands to 171 stores.
1995: The company launches the "Goody's Feels Like You" slogan.
2001: The Goody's Good Friend Bus Tour is created.
2003: Goody's acquires the Duck Head brand.

location—nice strip centers with popular anchor stores in areas where its customers, the $30,000 to $50,000 annual income families, lived. It planned a minimum of 20 new stores to open in 1997, and its goal was to reach $1 billion in sales by the close of 1998.

Part of the strategy to increase sales was sharp advertising. Goody's slogans "take a good look" and "Goody's feels like you" were splashed across all of their materials. Goody's advertising was headed by Mary Beth Fox, who joined the company in 1992 as a graphic designer. The company's point-of-sale, signs, print ads, and other sales materials were all designed and distributed in-house.

Not only did Goody's aggressively promote itself through ads in the local paper and direct mail, but the company also had strong corporate giving and community service programs. Local stores were often the drop-off points for canned goods and clothing to benefit the needy. Goody's also supported the Children's Miracle Network and mobile medical clinics in its communities. The store strived to foster a friendly, family image.

"We're in a position today not to keep pace, but to set the pace for our competitors," said chairman of the board Bob Goodfriend in 1997. "We have the right products, we have a great group of associates, and we have good locations. If we stay focused on our customers and concentrate hard on the day-to-day basics of the business, it's a winning combination."

Goody's rising stock figures seemed to suggest that analysts agreed. The stock was purchased by several large brokers to season mutual fund markets. Nevertheless, Goody's was in keen competition with a host of rivals that were larger and more established. Department store chains and factory outlet stores provided ongoing competition for the mid-priced family apparel chain.

Overcoming Challenges in the Late 1990s and Beyond

Goody's fortunes took a turn for the worse in 1998. Even though it achieved its $1 billion sales goal, expanded into Texas, and launched several new private-label offerings, profits began to show signs of weakness. Warm weather in the third and forth quarters forced profits down by 17 percent in 1998 and earnings continued to fall the following year.

During 2000, comparable stores sales—sales from locations open for at least a year—dropped by 4.8 percent. Call resigned

that year, leaving Bob Goodfriend at the helm with president Lana Cain Krauter. During this period, Goody's management team launched a restructuring of the company in order to shore up sales. Faith Popcorn, a trend consultant, was hired to revamp Goody's image. A June 2001 *Knoxville News-Sentinel* article printed part of Goodfriend's speech at the annual shareholders meeting that summed up the company's strategic direction. "As most of you know," Goodfriend claimed, "we are repositioning Goody's. Changes are being made virtually in all areas of our company. The goal of our restructuring is two-fold. First and foremost, of course, is to encourage shoppers, women in particular, to see Goody's as their first and best option for buying clothing for themselves and their families." Goodfriend also addressed the issue of competition. "There's no question that this battle for our target female consumer is a pretty difficult one. Our competition is equally interested in winning that same battle."

While the company worked to recover sales and profits, its operating environment remained extremely challenging. The terrorist attacks in 2001 depressed an already weak economy and unseasonable weather was wreaking havoc on sales and inventory levels. Goodfriend launched the Goody's Good Friend Bus Tour that year. He traveled by bus to stores around the country in order to talk to employees and customers about changes they would like to see at Goody's. Despite company efforts, Goody's reported a loss of $20.2 million in 2001—the worst financial performance in its history.

As a result, expansion was scaled back from 18 new store openings in 2001 to just two in 2002. A series of job cuts were launched and six stores were closed. Krauter resigned in 2002, one month after Goody's revealed that a private equity group had offered to buy the company for $6.50 to $7.50 per share. Several shareholders opposed the deal, claiming the buyout undervalued the company and that management had failed to negotiate a higher price. In November, Goody's announced that negotiations had ended and that it had terminated its plans to sell the company.

Goody's management remained optimistic despite sluggish sales. Profits rebounded in 2002 and continued to climb in 2003. The company faced a minor setback that year when it was forced to pay $11 million in damages to Tommy Hilfiger after a judge ruled that Goody's had sold counterfeit Hilfiger T-shirts and was guilty of trademark infringement.

Goody's acquired the Duck Head brand for $4 million in 2003. The brand was expected to bring in over $60 million in sales in its first year. It also began eyeing Iowa, Pennsylvania, and Kansas as potential expansion areas. Along with women's fashions, it focused on increasing its lines of expanded sizes for both men and women. Goody's continued to face intense competition while it worked to bolster comparable store sales. With a solid strategy in place, it appeared to be well positioned to battle future challenges.

Principal Subsidiaries

SYDOOG, Inc.; GOFAMCLO, Inc.; GFCFS, LLC; Trebor of TN, Inc.; GOODY'S MS, LP; GOODY'S IN, LP; GFCTX, LP; GFCGA, LP; GFCTN, LP; Goody's Giftco, LLC.

Principal Competitors

J.C. Penney Company Inc.; Target Corporation; The TJX Companies Inc.

Further Reading

Brewer, Bill, ''Goody's Hires Consultant to Help Reverse Slumping Sales,'' *Knoxville News-Sentinel*, June 14, 2001, p. C1.

——, ''Goody's Posts $20.2 Million Loss for 2001,'' *Knoxville News-Sentinel*, March 21, 2002, p. C1.

——, ''Goody's President Resigns,'' *Knoxville News-Sentinel*, October 17, 2002, p. C1.

Blackmon, Douglas A., ''Lower-Scale Chains May Be Worth a Look as Retail Stocks Slump,'' *Wall Street Journal*, June 25, 1997, p. S1.

Geisel, Amy, ''Goody's Dances to the Beat of Its Customers,'' *Knoxville News-Sentinel*, July 29, 1998, p. B1.

——, ''Goody's Said to Be 'Clicking on All Cylinders.' '' *Knoxville News Sentinel*, June 15, 1997, pp. D1–D3.

Nolan, Amy, ''Goody's Ends Talks,'' *Knoxville News-Sentinel*, November 2, 2002, p. A1.

Owens, Jennifer, ''Goody's Net Soars to $5M in 1st Quarter,'' *Women's Wear Daily*, June 19, 1997.

''Retailers' Earnings Exceed Expectations,'' *Reuters*, May 14, 1997.

Seay, Steve, ''Goody's Feathers Nest with Duck Head,'' *DNR*, June 21, 2004, p. 44.

Yeldell, Cynthia, ''Goody's Credits Inventory Control for Higher Profits,'' *Knoxville News-Sentinel*, March 20, 2003, p. C1.

——, ''Goody's May Grow Into 2 More States,'' *Knoxville News-Sentinel*, June 19, 2003, p. C1.

—Lisa Calhoun
—update: Christina M. Stansell

GP Strategies Corporation

777 Westchester Avenue, 4th Floor
White Plains, New York 10604
U.S.A.
Telephone: (914) 249-9700
Fax: (914) 249-9745
Web site: http://www.gpstrategies.com

Public Company
Incorporated: 1959
Employees: 1,692
Sales: $168.7 million (2003)
Stock Exchanges: New York
Ticker Symbol: GPX
NAIC: 541611 Administrative Management and General
     Management Consulting Services; 611699 All Other
     Miscellaneous Schools and Instruction

GP Strategies Corporation, formerly National Patent Development Corporation (NPD), is primarily a holding company, a legal entity separate and distinct from its various operating subsidiaries. Its principal operating subsidiaries are the General Physics Corporation and MXL Industries. General Physics specializes in management consulting, or performance improvement, offering training, consulting, and technical services to companies in various manufacturing fields, to government agencies, and to utilities. General Physics began as a training and support firm with expertise in nuclear power. Its clients now include leading auto makers such as General Motors, Ford Motor Co., and Daimler Chrysler, steel makers Inland Steel, USX, and AK Steel, pharmaceutical firms such as Pfizer Corporation and Johnson & Johnson, computer and communications firms including IBM and AT&T, and consumer manufacturing companies such as Pepsi Cola and Anheuser Busch. General Physics also find the U.S. Army, the U.S. Navy, and the U.S. Postal Service among its clients. GP Strategies' other principal operating unit is the wholly owned subsidiary MXL Industries, Inc. MXL specializes in the manufacture of specialized molded and coated plastic goods, including optical products, shields, and face masks. MXL sells its products in countries around the

globe and is known for its proprietary anti-scratch and anti-fog coatings. GP Strategies also has significant investments in several companies in diverse industries. It owns a stake in Millennium Cell Inc., a company that researches and develops fuel cell technology. It also has investments in Valera Pharmaceuticals, involved in cancer drug development, and Five Star Products, Inc., which makes home improvement and decorating items. In 2002, GP Strategies announced it was considering a spin-off of MXL Industries and some other holdings into a separate, publicly owned company to be called National Patent Development Corp. The spin-off was still pending as of May 2004.

Behind the Iron Curtain in the 1960s–70s

In 1959, three New York City lawyers, Jerome Feldman, Martin M. Pollak, and Jess Larson began National Patent Development Corporation as a scouting service for dormant patents. Their idea originated in 1958 after Feldman and Pollak heard about a new resin plasticizer developed and put on hold by a company unsure about the product's marketability. The partners believed the resin offered a superior base material for the manufacture of lipstick, and they offered to arrange a licensing agreement. Although the partners found a major cosmetics manufacturer, problems arose when each company told them to get their fee from the other.

While the deal ultimately fell through, Feldman and Pollak saw profit potential in the patent exchange business and decided to form a company that could act, under contract, as a middleman. They found a third partner in Jess Larson, an attorney with considerable government experience, having formerly served as Administrator of the General Services Administration, War Assets Administrator, and Brigadier General in the Air Force Reserve. Larson also saw the possibility of reaping substantial profits developing new commercial products from forgotten patents.

From the beginning, NPD focused on screening and buying patents on various devices, technologies, and materials, then licensing them to other companies or trying to market the products themselves. To screen the thousands of patents lying idle in corporate files, the partners formed a consulting board consisting of patent lawyers, scientists, and engineers.

National Patent began gaining momentum in 1961, a year before the Cuban Missile Crisis, after Feldman and Pollak wrote a letter to then-Soviet Premier Nikita Khrushchev asking for rights to Soviet inventions. Surprisingly, despite Cold War tensions, the Soviets were willing to deal to obtain American dollars and invited them to visit. After three weeks in Russia, NPD experts screened Soviet developments by conferring with some 250 Russian scientists and technicians and won patent rights to market 14 innovations in the United States. National Patent then signed an agreement with Amtorg, the U.S.-based Soviet trade wing.

While some Soviet-acquired innovations proved profitable, others flopped. A surgical stapling device that replaced needle-and-thread suturing earned enough for Feldman to start a medical instrument business. That venture—U.S. Surgical—was later sold off and grew into a multi-million dollar corporation. Unfortunately, most products were far less successful, including an electric eye pad touted as inducing a blissful nap.

Using their Kremlin link, NPD made inquiries in other communist bloc countries. In Czechoslovakia, they met Otto Wichterle, polymer chemist at the Czechoslovak Academy of Sciences. Wichterle devised a novel application for a new plastic compound called Hema, which turned soft and pliable when infused with a liquid. Hema was originally intended for making artificial veins and body organs, but Wichterle found that spinning a droplet of Hema in a thimble-size dish could produce a soft contact lens.

In the West, contact lenses were still produced of hard plastic. By purchasing the spinning technology and the rights to make and market Hema, NPD found its first important product. Nevertheless, for two years the company experimented with the compound, prevented by scarce capital from marketing its new product. Then, in 1966, NPD concluded a licensing agreement with Bausch & Lomb of Rochester, New York, a major player in the optical business that well aware of the potential market for soft lenses. The agreement gave Bausch & Lomb exclusive license to the new lens material and Wichterle's spinning and manufacturing technology. In return, NPD would receive a licensing fee plus half of all Bausch & Lomb's domestic lens profits.

After the Bausch & Lomb agreement, Feldman searched for other uses for Hema, which had been trademarked as Hydron.

While National Patent licensed the rights to Hydron for contact lenses, it retained rights to use the compound for other applications and to produce new products. The company's labs produced a range of new Hydron-based products, including nail polish, burn-wound dressings, dental root-canal fillers, artificial breasts, and algae-resistant boat paint.

Most promising of all was a reactive chemical that showed potential for dissolving tooth decay, thus replacing drilling. Feldman found the compound at Tufts University, bought the patent rights, and offered the product to Warner-Lambert, which anticipated a use for the product as a plaque-removal agent in mouthwash. NPD's stock shot up from less than $10 in 1971 to $67 a share in 1972, one year after the Food & Drug Administration (FDA) approved Bausch & Lomb's new soft lens.

NPD shareholders' rising expectations proved false when the company's fortunes turned sour. Bausch & Lomb royalties proved disappointing, prompting National Patent to file suit in a protracted legal battle that threatened to end NPD's royalties entirely. Then Warner-Lambert announced that trial tests on schoolchildren showed their new mouthwash to be a failure as a plaque remover. NPD's stock collapsed to just $4 a share in 1973. Responding to these disappointments, Feldman diversified the company into gardening supplies, sporting equipment, solar energy, medical instruments, and contact lenses, planning to make NPD more independent. He also recruited a Russian professor to train company chemists in the production of interferons, a group of proteins produced by the body's immune system to help combat disease. This erratic strategy proved a dismal failure, causing a decade of poor earnings and a blighted reputation for the company. Feldman later recalled this period as the "dark years."

Through the 1970s, National Patent's fortunes rested on a $14 million settlement from Bausch & Lomb. Charles Allen, a world-class dealmaker and founder of Allen & Co., also figured prominently in the company's survival. Allen took Feldman as a client, arranged private infusions of cash, and bought NPD stock even when times appeared bleakest. He soon controlled one of the largest interests in NPD after the combined holdings of Feldman and Pollak. In spite of Allen's help, NPD continued to be plagued by marketing mishaps and technological failures. For example, a malfunction in an intravenous control system forced an expensive recall, and the company fell more than a year behind schedule in developing and marketing a solar energy cell. As a result, Feldman cut corporate staff and sold off NPD's medical equipment and solar energy ventures.

Pollak had better luck with American Hydron, NPD's contact lens subsidiary. Established in 1979 as International Hydron Corporation to manufacture and sell contact lenses in the United States, the subsidiary produced its first earnings in 1982. A year later, industry leader Bausch & Lomb considered American Hydron its major competitor in the sale of daily-wear soft contacts. Pollak's clever marketing strategy—offering Mercedes-Benzes, videocassette recorders, and gold coins to optometrists who placed large orders—caused the subsidiary's second-year shipments to double.

Despite intense competition, American Hydron fared well in producing high-quality lenses at a low cost. By the end of 1983, the subsidiary unveiled a new, compact, spincast system that could make lenses similar to Bausch & Lomb's most popular line. American Hydron also began testing collagen, a protein produced from cowhide, in an attempt to displace Hydron in low-cost lens production. By 1987, American Hydron was producing contact lenses using three distinct methods—lathing, cast molding, and spincasting, each having its own production and marketing advantages. While lens lathing was labor intensive, it proved superior for specialty lenses and low production. Cast molding maintained high optical lens quality but was more efficient in large-volume production. Spincasting was particularly suited for large-volume manufacture with low labor costs.

At the same time, NPD's Interferon Sciences, Inc. (ISI) subsidiary was moving toward marketing a host of interferon-based treatments for viral diseases. Production problems stemming from inefficiencies in extracting interferon from leukocytes, or white blood cells, were helped by the company's Czech connection. Pollak was vice-chairman of the Czechoslovak-U.S. Economic Council, a bilateral organization formed to promote trade between the two countries. This role introduced him to council chairman Fred Kuhlmann, vice-president of Anheuser-Busch, the St. Louis-based brewery that used Czechoslovakian hops to make beer. Anheuser's advanced fermentation technology for cultivating yeast cells proved to be the solution to the interferon production problem. Through the innovative process of "transformation," DNA molecules containing the genetic code for interferon could be extracted from human white blood cells and inserted into yeast cells, thereby producing interferon on a large scale.

Mutual interest in this process led both companies to embark on a joint production enterprise. ISI would alter individual yeast cells for use by Anheuser to produce billions of offspring. In return for the option of making new interferon products, Anheuser would provide ISI $6 million for research and development. This money aided Interferon Sciences' clinical trials of an interferon ointment for treating genital herpes—which afflicted an estimated 20 million in the United States alone—and allowed the company to begin testing a treatment for genital warts.

Holding Company in the 1980s

Feldman's typical business strategy was to spin off new technological ventures into separate companies while retaining most of their stock. By doing so, he transformed NPD into a holding company benefited by the rising asset value of satellite

companies taken public. In 1981, Feldman spun off ISI into a public company while retaining 75 percent of the shares. Two years later, he spun off NPS Waste Technologies, an innovator in particle-glass filtering mechanisms for radioactive waste.

By 1987, NPD essentially operated through various subsidiaries and affiliates as a manufacturer and distributor of a wide array of products and services. The company's operations consisted primarily of four business segments, as well as various research and development programs that were not yet commercially viable. The company's Ophthalmic Products Group produced and marketed soft contact lenses and accessories. The Medical Science Group produced and distributed first aid products, surgical dressings, and various other hospital and medical products primarily through three subsidiaries, Acme Cotton Products, Chaston Medical & Surgical Products, and Abbey Medical, Inc. In addition to its interferon subsidiary, the Medical Group included dental products, such as the Caridex (R) Caries Removal System. An FDA-approved product that showed promise in removing tooth decay without the need for drilling, Caridex was the same failed dental plaque remover that had shown false promise a decade earlier.

NPD's Consumer and Service Group distributed home and garden products, as well as produced paint, paint specialties, coated and molded plastic products, and electronic components through several subsidiaries: J. Levin & Co., Inc., E. Rabinowe & Co., Inc., acquired in 1985, and Interstate Paint Distributors Inc., acquired in 1986. The Physical Science Group provided training, operations, engineering, and maintenance services to the electrical power industry and the U.S. Navy. In addition, this group also developed, manufactured, and marketed products and services used in the clean up of low-level radioactive material from waste water at utility-operated nuclear power plants.

In 1987, NPD sold its interest in both International Hydron and Abbey Medical, Inc., a renter and seller of durable medical equipment. In 1989, the Medical Group introduced a new quick-opening adhesive bandage, STAT STRIP, to the hospital and medical markets. Interferon Sciences (ISI) received FDA approval of its Alferon N Injection, an alpha interferon product derived from human leukocytes developed for the treatment of recurring genital warts in patients 18 years or older. This achievement essentially transformed ISI from a research and development firm into an operating pharmaceutical company. An agreement was made with the Purdue Fredrick Company, a privately owned multinational drug company, to market Alferon N Injections in the United States and abroad. In addition, ISI acquired the worldwide rights from Amarillo Cell Culture for the oral administration of natural interferon, apparently effective in boosting the immune system. In addition, NPD's consumer and service group, collectively known as the Five Star Group, acquired State Leed, a distributor of various paint items. Together these companies, comprising J. Levin, E. Rabinowe, and Interstate Paint Distributors, had become the largest U.S. distributor of paint specialties, including interior and exterior stains, brushes, rollers, and caulking compounds.

Complex Interests in the 1990s

By 1995, NPD had developed into three primary business segments: Physical Science, Distribution, and Optical Plastics.

The company also had investments in Hydro Med Sciences (HMS), a health care business, and GTS Duratek, Inc., an environmental technology firm, as well as continuing investments in ISI.

The Physical Science Group consisted of SGLG, Inc. (formerly GPS Technologies), of which NPD had a 91 percent controlling interest, and General Physics Corporation, approximately 51 percent owned. General Physics provided numerous services, including personnel training and engineering, environmental, and technical support, to commercial nuclear and power utilities, the U.S. Departments of Defense and Energy, Fortune 500 companies, and other commercial and governmental clients. SGLG was a holding company with a 35 percent interest in GSE Systems, a company specializing in simulator software. In 1995, General Physics acquired Cygna Energy Services, a provider of design engineering, materials management, and safety analysis services to the nuclear power industry. General Physics also acquired all of the assets of SGLG, Inc. for approximately $34 million. In response to federal cutbacks in the Departments of Defense and Energy, General Physics began focusing on expanding its management and technical training services as well as specialized engineering services to manufacturers and federal agencies.

Five Star operated as a wholesale distributor of home decorating, hardware, and finishing products. Through the mid-1990s, Five Star remained the largest distributor in the United States of paint products and accessories, caulking compounds, and other items, despite intense competition from considerably larger hardware franchises, including Servistar and True Value.

The Optical Plastics Group operated through NPD's wholly owned subsidiary MXL Industries, a producer of molded and coated optical and non-optical products. MXL also made state-of-the-art injection molding tools, using polycarbonate resin to make shields, face masks, and lenses for over 55 clients in the safety, recreation, and military industries.

NPD's Hydro Med Sciences subsidiary manufactured medical devices, drugs, and cosmetic polymer products. HMS was established to explore the application of HydronR polymers for biomedical purposes. Since the 1970s, HMS was involved in the development of human and veterinary drugs and dental and medical devices. The company developed the Syncro-Mate BR implant for the synchronized breeding of bovine heifers, the first veterinary implant drug to be approved by the FDA. HMS also produced a water-soluble HydronR polymer for commercial applications in cosmetic products, including body lotions, moisturizers, and sunscreens.

ISI, a biopharmaceutical company, continued to be involved principally in the production and sale of Alferon N Injections. In 1995, the product still represented the only FDA-approved drug based on a natural source for the treatment of certain types of genital warts. ISI also explored new applications for its injectable, topical, and oral formulations of natural alpha interferon for the treatment of HIV, hepatitis C, hepatitis B, multiple sclerosis, cancers, and other diseases. In the biomedical industry, various alpha interferon drugs have been approved for 17 different medical uses in more than 60 countries. As a group, sales of these biopharmaceuticals approached $2 billion in 1994. Gaining approval to sell the product in Mexico in the mid-1990s, ISI also sought regulatory approval to market Alferon N Injections in Austria, Canada, Hong Kong, Israel, Singapore, and the United Kingdom.

ISI's other products under development included Alferon N Gel and Alferon LDO. Alferon N Gel, a topical application, had potential for treating cervical dysplasia, recurrent genital herpes, other viral diseases, and cancers. Alferon LDO constituted a low oral dose of liquid alpha interferon, possibly proving beneficial in treating HIV and other viral diseases. These products were undergoing clinical trials during the mid-1990s.

NPD organized its American Drug Company (ADC) subsidiary in 1993 to distribute general pharmaceuticals and medical products in Russia and the Commonwealth of Independent States (CIS), countries which formerly composed the defunct Soviet Union. ADC was formed from NPD Trading (USA), Inc., which had been set up in 1990 to provide consulting services to Western businesses in Russia and Eastern Europe. NPD Trading would continue to operate as a subsidiary of the newly formed ADC, providing a broad range of business services to many American and Western corporations. Through NPD Trading, ADC's various activities involved developing and assisting Western businesses to create trading, manufacturing, and investment opportunities in Russia, the Czech and Slovak Republics, and other countries in Eastern Europe and the CIS. ADC also focused on marketing American-made pharmaceuticals and health care products—antibiotic ointments, pain-relief medication, vitamins, bandages, prescription injectable anti-cancer drugs, antibiotics, and other prescription drugs—under its own label in Russia and the CIS. To distribute these products, ADC initiated marketing ventures with hospitals, pharmacies, and clinics throughout Russia and the CIS.

NPD's interests in environmental technology centered on GTS Duratek, Inc. As of March 1, 1995, NPD decreased its holdings of Duratek's outstanding shares of common stock from 61 to 40 percent. Incorporated in Delaware in December 1982, Duratek's operations comprised two principal groups. The Technology Group converted radioactive and hazardous waste to glass by means of in-furnace vitrification processes, as well as specializing in removing radioactive and hazardous contaminants from waste water through a filtration and ion process. The Services Group provided consulting, engineering, and training services, as well as technical personnel, assistance with nuclear power outages and operations, and Department of Energy environmental restoration projects. As of 1995, major customers for these services included Duke Power Company, Vermont Yankee Nuclear Power Corporation, New York Power Authority, Tennessee Valley Authority, GPU Nuclear Corporation, PECO Energy Company, and FERMCO.

New Directions in the 2000s

Through the mid-1990s, NPD had operated in a host of different areas, with little tying together its various products and services. Feldman was interested in new technology, whatever the industry, and he was not always successful in picking winners. For instance, two of National Patent's earliest products, surgical staples and soft contact lenses, had very different fortunes. Feldman sold his interest in the company that became U.S. Surgical for $2 million in 1964, and it went on to have a market capitalization of $2.2 billion by the end of the century. On the other hand, NPD had retained its soft contact lens business until 1987, when it was worth only about $155 million. Despite many promising products, NPD had often sold at the wrong time or held on too long, with the consequence that the company had never really hit it big. Beginning in 1996, National Patent went in a new direction, consolidating its business and changing its name.

In late 1996, NPD announced that it was buying up the remaining 48 percent of its engineering consulting subsidiary General Physics. General Physics had expanded its service offerings in the mid-1990s through acquisitions, and it had grown from a specialist in nuclear engineering to a consulting firm with expertise in materials management, seismic engineering, systems engineering, and safety analysis, with clients across the globe. It acquired a training and consulting company that gave it a significant slice of the automotive industry training market. In 1998, National Patent Development Corp. announced that it was changing its name to GP Strategies, Inc. This new name emphasized the importance to the parent company of its General Physics subsidiary. A few months later, the company moved its stock from the American Exchange to the more prestigious New York Stock Exchange. As GP Strategies, the company was very different from the old National Patent. Feldman described his company to the *Westchester County Business Journal* (April 22, 2002) as "the largest customized technical company in America, offering businesses and entrepreneurs help in building their companies." There was no mention here of new or developing technology. While GP Strategies continued to own MXL Industries, Hydromed, Five Star, and various other assorted subsidiaries and investments, it focused on General Physics, which had more than 2,000 employees in 75 offices worldwide by the late 1990s. General Physics continued to grow by acquisition, buying up a Seattle, Washington, management consulting firm, Deltapoint, in 1998. That year it also paid $24 million for the learning technologies business of Systemhouse, a subsidiary of MCI Corp. This became part of General Physics' Information Technologies group.

The company looked much more focused in the late 1990s, but it still had its troubles. It lost money in 1998 and 1999 on its investment in ISI when the FDA failed to approve a key product. ISI was essentially washed out at that point. Founder Feldman was nearing 70, and he decided to sell GP Strategies. The buyer was to be VS&A Communications Partners III, a publishing and communications company. However, VS&A withdrew its offer shortly after it was made. GP Strategies had revised its revenue projection for the fourth quarter due to poor performance at its new learning technologies group, and VS&A backed out. GP Strategies took a huge charge in 2000 because of the problems with the learning technologies group and posted a loss of $34.3 million for the year.

For 2001, sales were flat, though the company was back in the black. The business magazine *Forbes* (July 23, 2001) noted that investors were interested in GP Strategies at that point principally because it owned a 20 percent interest in Millennium Cell, the fuel cell development company. Millennium Cell went public in 2001, and GP Strategies' stake in the company was valued at as much as GP Strategies itself. The next year, GP Strategies announced that it was filing preliminary papers that would allow it to spin off some of its assets into a separate, publicly owned company to be called National Patent Development Corp. The new company would include the optical plastics business of MXL and its subsidiaries, plus Five Star and some other assets. General Physics would continue to focus on business and information training and technology.

The deal was slow to come to fruition. In the meantime, GP Strategies increased its stake in GSE, the simulation company it had owned in part since the early 1990s. This business was to go with General Physics when the spin-off took place. Jerome Feldman remained CEO of the company into 2004, and he still owned more than 20 percent of its shares.

Principal Subsidiaries

General Physics Corporation; Five Star Group, Inc.; MXL Industries, Inc.

Principal Competitors

McKinsey & Company; Accenture Ltd.; BearingPoint Inc.

Further Reading

Curan, John J., "National Patent Rises Again," *Fortune*, August 8, 1983, pp. 98–102.

Doba, Jinida, "MXL Industries Getting a Buyer," *Plastics News*, October 25, 1999, p. 3.

Fisher, Daniel, "Death Grip," *Forbes*, July 23, 2001, p. 89.

Glenn, David J., "Searching the World," *Westchester County Business Journal*, April 22, 2002, p. 18.

Marcial, Gene G., and Jeffery M. Laderman, "Why National Patent Is Feeling No Pain," *Business Week*, January 13, 1986.

"National Patent Development Corp: Soft Lenses Now Mean Hard Profits for This Fallen Angel," *Financial World*, February 1, 1976, p. 3.

"Russian Grab Bag," *Newsweek*, July 31, 1961, pp. 60–63.

"Strategic Move," *Computer Reseller News*, June 15, 1998, p. 57.

"The Riches in Dormant Patents," *Business Week*, April 15, 1961, p. 96.

—Bruce Montgomery
—update: A. Woodward

Grupo Eroski

Barrio San Agustin s/n
Elorrio
E-48230
Spain
Telephone: (+34) 94 621 12 11
Fax: (+34) 94 621 12 22
Web site: http://www.eroski.es

Cooperative Company
Incorporated: 1969
Employees: 29,013
Sales: EUR 5.2 billion ($5.5 billion)(2003)
NAIC: 445110 Supermarkets and Other Grocery (Except
   Convenience) Stores; 311811 Retail Bakeries; 445210
   Meat Markets; 445230 Fruit and Vegetable Markets;
   445292 Confectionary and Nut Stores; 445299 All
   Other Specialty Food Stores; 448150 Clothing
   Accessories Stores; 452910 Warehouse Clubs and
   Superstores; 452990 All Other General Merchandise
   Stores; 561510 Travel Agencies; 722110 Full-Service
   Restaurants

Grupo Eroski is the distribution arm and the largest part of Spain's powerful cooperative group Mondragon Corporacion Cooperativa. Eroski is also Spain's second-largest retail distribution group, trailing only France's Carrefour. Eroski operates more than 800 supermarkets throughout Spain. Since the pullout of partner Consum—which left with more than 400 supermarkets as well as the group's former Consum and Charter banners—Eroski has restructured its operations around three core banners. The group's nearly 70 large-scale hypermarkets remain under the Eroski banner, while the company's more than 500 supermarkets have been rebranded under the Eroski Center name. More than 250 smaller, urban stores have now adopted the Eroski City banner, reinforcing the Eroski name as a whole. In addition, Eroski oversees 305 franchised stores and 28 wholesale cash & carry centers. In a move to diversify its distribution base, Eroski has built a network of 176 Eroski Travel Agencies and nearly 150 perfume stores under the If

name. The company also operates 28 gasoline stations as part of its retail network and plans to extend that operation, placing fuel pumps at all of its stores. At the same time, Eroski has begun building an Internet presence, launching e-commerce enabled retail and travel agency sites. While most of Eroski's sales remain in Spain, the cooperative has made some moves into the south of France. It has also entered a strategic partnership with France's Intermarche, providing for international purchasing and logistics cooperation and creating Europe's third-largest supermarket entity. Eroski operates along an employee-consumer ownership model, producing more than EUR 5.2 billion per year in revenue. Despite the departure of Consum, Eroski remains committed to leading the consolidation of the Spanish retail food distribution sector and has added such regional supermarket players as Udama (Aragon and Andalusia), Supera (Madrid and elsewhere), Vergonsa (Galicia), and Mercat (Balearic Islands).

Cooperative Origins in the 1950s

The Basque region suffered more than other parts of Spain following that country's civil war. The region's resistance to Franco-led forces left it subject to reprisals following the establishment of the dictatorship following the war. The Franco government adopted a discriminatory policy against the region, banning the Basque language, among other repressive acts. At the same time, the Basque region became discriminated against economically as well, and into the 1950s it continued to struggle to rebuild following the devastation brought on by the civil war. Low levels of government investment brought about a high level of poverty throughout the region.

This situation, however, provided fertile ground for the development of a strong cooperative movement and especially the rise of the Mondragon Corporacion Cooperativa (MCC) as one of Spain's industrial and economic forces. The MCC was founded by Father José Maria Arizmendiarrietta, who had come to the small town of Mondragon in 1941. Arizmendiarrietta, who had been sentenced to death during the Spanish Civil War but had managed to escape, originally worked to provide social welfare programs and opportunities to the local population, organizing sporting, cultural, and educational events. In 1943, he founded a school that later evolved into the University of Mondragon. The new school provided essential education and training for a new generation that were to transform Mondragon itself into a regional economic center.

By the mid-1950s, the region possessed a strong, talented pool of young and enthusiastic workers. Led by Arizmendiarrietta, the decision was made to develop a home-grown industrial base in the region. In 1956, the MCC backed the founding of Talleres Ulgor, which began producing stoves and heaters. That company grew strongly and was later transformed into Fagor Electrodomesticos, one of Europe's leading manufacturers of home appliances.

Inspired by the work of Robert Owen, considered to be the founder of the European cooperative movement in the mid- and late 19th century, Arizmendiarrietta now began promoting the creation of a series of local worker cooperatives in the Mondragon valley and surrounding areas, starting with the San Jose Consumers' Cooperative, founded in 1958 in Mondragon itself. By the end of 1959, there were already four worker cooperatives in operation, and these joined together to create their own bank, the Caja Laboral. This unusual move was later credited for providing the backbone for MCC's national and international expansion and for the emergence of Eroski as one of Spain's top retailers.

By the end of the 1960s, the Basque region boasted more than 40 cooperatives, including a growing number of consumer cooperatives, working either under or in association with MCC. By then, however, the shift in traditional food retailing that had already swept through the United States and through much of Western Europe, bringing modern self-service supermarket formats and centralized buying practices, had begun to make itself felt in Spain as well. In the new environment, the small-scale cooperatives were forced to recognize that they would be increasingly hard pressed to compete in the emerging modern retail market.

In 1969, ten of the smaller consumer cooperatives in the region decided to join together and create a new, more powerful cooperative entity, originally called Comerco. By the following year, however, the organization had found a new name, Eroski. Backed by the Caja Laboral, Eroski began expanding through-

out the Basque region, opening a number of supermarkets and adding a number of existing cooperatives as well. During the economic crisis of the 1970s, the group adopted a new ownership model, becoming a hybrid worker-consumer cooperative. This change enabled the company not only to survive the difficult economic period but to thrive.

By the end of the 1970s, Eroski had already claimed the position as the clear leader in the Basque region supermarket sector. The company began pioneering new store formats, notably by importing the "hypermarket" department store and supermarket hybrid. While the company's hypermarkets offered both food and non-food items for sale, Eroski also launched its first non-food stores in 1975 as well. The rise of the Eroski name in the region led it to launch its own Eroski line of foods in 1978, a move that was backed by the opening of a new research and development facility in Elorrio, the following year.

National Expansion in the 1990s

Eroski continued to grow throughout the 1980s, while remaining focused on its Basque regional base. Yet the cooperative's success, and its worker-consumer ownership structure, attracted interest from cooperative groups from other parts of Spain. In the mid-1980s, representatives from a Valencia region cooperative came to visit with MCC in order to study aspects of Eroski's success, then returned with backing from MCC in order to found their own worker-consumer cooperative, named Consum. Others followed suit, such as the S. Coop chain.

Consum quickly grew into the leading food retailer in the Valencia region. With this confirmation that the Eroski formula could be exported to other regions—and was therefore not dependent on the highly close-knit nature of the Basque community—Eroski began plans to expand itself to a national level.

A new factor intervened to ensure Eroski's success. The supermarket sector began a new transformation in the 1990s, as the rising competition among Spanish retailers was joined by the appearance of a new wave of competition from foreign retail groups. The entry into Spain by such European retail powerhouses as Carrefour and Auchan of France and Ahold of the Netherlands placed the country's highly fragmented national supermarket sector under a new level of competitive pressure.

The arrival of new competition led Spain's cooperatives to cooperate with each other. In 1990, Eroski formed an alliance with the S. Coop chain and the Consum Coop group, launching Eroski onto the national scene. That alliance provided the basis for the expansion of the Eroski-branded chain of hypermarkets, which topped 60 by the end of the 1990s. At the same time, Eroski rebranded its own supermarket operations under the Consum and Charter names, which enabled Eroski to become part of a nationally operating, widely recognized brand.

By the mid-1990s, the Spanish retail food distribution, like its European counterparts, had entered an era of heightened competition and consolidation. While the Spanish market remained highly fragmented, increasing numbers of smaller, regional chains and independent supermarkets found themselves unable to compete against the juggernaut of the multinational giants. Consolidation became the sole means of survival for many of Spain's supermarket groups, including Eroski.

Key Dates:

Key Dates:

1958: San Jose Consumers Cooperative in Mondragon, part of the Mondragon Corporacion Cooperativa (MCC), is founded.
1959: Four MCC coops found their own bank, Caja Laboral.
1969: Ten local food coops join together to form Comerco.
1970: Commerco becomes Eroski, the distribution arm of MCC.
1975: Eroski begins opening hypermarkets and selling non-food items.
1978: The company launches its own in-store brand.
1979: Eroski opens its own research and development laboratory for new products.
1990: A partnership with Valencia-based Consum is formed.
1997: Eroski merges with Unide, Mercat, and Vegonsa.
1998: The company creates a new private label brand, Consumer.
1999: Cenco, Disbor, and Aundia are acquired.
2000: Supera is acquired.
2002: Eroski forms an international partnership with Les Mousquetaires (Intermarche).
2004: Consum pulls out of its partnership with Eroski, which then rebrands its stores under the Eroski, Eroski Center, and Eroski City names.

Eroski began a drive to gain scale and to emerge as a truly national retail player in the second half of the 1990s. The company launched a massive growth strategy, more than doubling in size in just five years. At the same time, the company looked beyond its cooperative base, adding an increasing number of new supermarkets, many of which were placed under a franchise model.

A decisive turning point for Eroski came in 1997, when it agreed to a three-way merger with Madrid-based Group Unide, the Galicia region's Vegonsa, and Group Mercat, then the largest supermarket group on the Baleares Island chain. The merged group became a national powerhouse, second only to Carrefour. Eroski nonetheless remained committed to its cooperative model.

Following the merger, Eroski began rolling out a new branding strategy. While the group retained the Eroski name for its hypermarkets, it decided to adopt partner Consum's name for its national supermarket network. Backing up its national aspirations, Eroski launched its own private label brand, Consumer, in 1998. In 1999, the company began rolling out a new, smaller convenience store format for the city center market, which adopted partner Consum's Charter brand format.

International Connections in the 2000s

Eroski continued to build its network at the turn of the 21st century. In 1999, the company acquired three supermarket chains: Cenco, based in Castile and Leon; Disbor, serving the Catalan region; and Aundia, based in the Navarrese. The following year, the company added the Supera! chain as well. By 2001, Eroski had gained more than 500 new stores in just five years.

Eroski had also added new business lines during that period, launching its own travel agency service, Eroski Travel Agencies, which neared 200 branches by 2004. Another retail format, the If perfume store, proved popular with the consumer public, and by the early 2000s Eroski operated almost 150 stores. The company had also begun rolling out its own network of service stations, beginning with its hypermarket chain. As it approached the middle of the decade, Eroski already operated more than 30 service stations, with plans to add fuel pumps to all of its supermarkets.

By 2002, Eroski's more than EUR 4.5 billion in sales gave it a solid second-place position in Spain, with a market share of more than 12.5 percent. Eroski had also surpassed MCC's industrial operations by then, becoming the largest part of the cooperative and forcing it to revise its own long-term strategy.

In the meantime, the European retail sector turned towards new developments. The lowering of trade barriers, the introduction of the single European currency, and the prospect of an enlargement of the European Community in 2004 promised increased cross-border competition. At the same time, European retailers braced themselves for the entry of a new—and daunting—competitor, Wal-Mart, which threatened to repeat its U.S. success in Europe.

These factors encouraged Eroski to begin looking for a partner in order to give it a stronger presence throughout the international market. In 2002, Eroski signed an agreement with France's Les Mousquetaires, which operated the InterMarche retail group, the third largest in Europe with annual sales of more than EUR 26 billion. The deal gave the partnership the second place among Europe's retailers. At the same time, Eroski strengthened its relationship with Italy's Co-op Italia, that country's largest food retailer.

Eroski suffered a setback at the beginning of 2004, when long-time partner Consum announced its intention to pull out of the partnership. The move meant the loss of some 450 Consum and Charter stores owned by Consum, as well as the Consum and Charter brand names. Despite having lost some one-third of its total retail park, Eroski quickly discovered a new opportunity in the end of the relationship. By April 2004, Eroski announced a restructuring of its retail network. The group's 62 hypermarkets retained the Eroski name, while its supermarkets were rebranded as Eroski Center and the smaller convenience stores as Eroski City. This move helped reinforce the Eroski name as a national brand.

Eroski continued to look for growth opportunities, while remaining committed for the time being at least to its domestic market. The announcement of Ahold in 2004 that it intended to sell its 160 stores in Spain represented a new opportunity for Eroski to gain scale, as the company acknowledged its interest in bidding. From a small local coop, Eroski has grown into one of Europe's top 50 retailers.

Principal Competitors

Centros Comercial Carrefour S.A.; Distribuidora Internacional de Alimentacion S.A.; Mercadona S.A. Tavernes Blanques; Alcampo S.A.; Ahold Supermercados S.A; Caprabo S.A.; Superdiplo S.A.

Further Reading

Bruce, Anna, ''Playing at Leapfrog,'' *Grocer*, February 3, 2001, p. 40.

''Consum Decides to Go It Alone,'' *FoodAndDrinkEurope.com*, February 6, 2004.

Dowdy, Clare, ''Eroski Holds Its Own with Wagstaffs' Help,'' *Design Week*, July 30, 1999, p. 6.

''Eroski to Change Supermarket Banner,'' *FoodAndDrinkEurope.com*, April 7, 2004.

''Intermache/Eroski Purchasing Partnership,'' *European Report*, October 9, 2000.

Thompson, David, ''Mondragon Retail Strategy: Eroski Partnership Path,'' *Cooperative Grocer*, November-December 2002.

—M.L. Cohen

Guardian

Guardian Financial Services

Royal Exchange
London EC3V 3LS
United Kingdom
Telephone: (+071) 283 7101
Fax: (+071) 621 2599
Web site: http://www.guardianfs.co.uk

Business Segment of AEGON NV
Incorporated: 1968
Employees: 17,500
Total Assets: £22 billion ($36.5 billion) (1998 est.)
NAIC: 524113 Direct Life Insurance Carriers; 524114
    Direct Health and Medical Insurance Carriers; 524126
    Direct Property and Casualty Insurance Carriers

Once one of the largest composite insurers in the United Kingdom, Guardian Financial Services, known previously as Guardian Royal Exchange plc, provided life and non-life insurance services as well as financial and investment services to customers in the United Kingdom and abroad. The company struggled in the 1990s, in part due to intense competition brought on by industry consolidation. Unable to remain independent, Guardian was purchased by Sun Life and Provincial Holdings, a subsidiary of the French insurance group AXA, in 1999. AXA then sold Guardian's life and pensions business to the Dutch insurance concern AEGON NV. In 2004, Guardian's remaining holdings were administered by AEGON UK Services.

Early History

Guardian Royal Exchange was created in 1968 from the merger of two venerable insurance institutions, Royal Exchange Assurance and the Guardian Assurance Company. Royal Exchange was founded in 1720 and was one of the first two insurance companies to receive legal status by Royal Charter. Originally established for marine business, the company expanded within a year to include fire and life insurance as well, thereby becoming Britain's first composite insurer.

Royal Exchange expanded rapidly, both in domestic and foreign business and was a well-established firm by the time of the Guardian's creation in 1821. Guardian, founded as a fire and life insurer, also grew quickly throughout Britain and in foreign markets. The company achieved composite status in 1893, when it was granted new powers of underwriting and investment by Act of Parliament. In 1902, the name was changed from Guardian Fire & Life to Guardian Assurance to reflect the company's new interests in theft and burglary insurance, employers' liability, and general accident. The Royal Exchange, too, had expanded its cover, moving into personal accident (1898), employers' liability and fidelity guarantee (1899), burglary insurance (1900), and accident insurance. In 1917, the company added auto insurance to its portfolio by merging with the motor insurer Car and General.

Both the Royal Exchange and the Guardian built up profitable overseas businesses, first through foreign agents and later through branch offices. In the years 1890 to 1912, for example, the Royal Exchange opened branches in the United States, Canada, South Africa, New Zealand, India, Egypt, and South America, as well as establishing a substantial presence in continental Europe.

Guardian Assurance and the Royal Exchange, then, both prospered during the 19th century, no small achievement at a time when the insurance industry—mostly unregulated and highly speculative—was notoriously volatile. The two companies emerged in the 20th century with respectable reputations for sound, conservative business practices.

Over the years, both companies fueled their expansion as much by strategic mergers and amalgamations as by organic growth. Such insurance alliances were generally viewed favorably in the industry, as a broader financial base tended to be a stronger one and therefore of most benefit to policy holders. After World War II, insurance mergers became even more common and popular, and it was thus considered sensible strategy that the Royal Exchange and Guardian Assurance should merge, a move undertaken in 1968. Finalizing the merger was a long and complicated process. The integration of two work forces, the harmonization of different working practices and procedures, and the monumental task of converting all documents and records to the same system all required years to complete.

Success and Struggles in the Early 1990s

The result was the Guardian Royal Exchange, Britain's fifth largest composite insurer. The company's business embraced three primary areas: non-life insurance, life insurance, and corporate investment. Taken as a whole, Guardian's non-life insurance business, dominated by personal, motor, and household business, was the company's most lucrative. Indeed, Guardian's U.K. business in this category was significant, accounting for some 43 percent of the company's premium income. In the 1990s, Guardian sought to strengthen its non-life portfolio through acquisitions and additions. In 1993, the company purchased the health care and personal lines insurance business of Orion Insurance, establishing the U.K. subsidiaries Orion Healthcare Ltd. and Orion Personal Insurances Ltd. The acquisition, particularly its health care aspect, filled a void in Guardian's insurance range. Both new enterprises were relatively small but had successful records. Guardian did not intend them to compete with the major insurers in their field but hoped rather to establish and slowly build up a niche market for the two. The new business quickly accounted for a significant proportion of Guardian's non-life U.K. insurance business.

Guardian also moved into the direct telesales market with the establishment of Guardian Direct in 1993. Direct sales of car and household insurance policies were increasingly popular in the United Kingdom, and Guardian hoped to reap its share of the profits from this new and rapidly expanding market.

Guardian's overseas operations in non-life insurance was less successful. In Germany, where the group operated Albingia, conditions were difficult for a number of years, due largely to the recession and to significant increases in claims rising from household burglaries, car theft, and arson. Guardian attempted to offset such vicissitudes with several measures designed to improve its position—restructuring its portfolio, insisting on rigorous underwriting policies, and exercising strict financial control of costs—but had met with limited success in most overseas operations in the early 1990s.

The picture was somewhat brighter in the U.S. market, however, where Guardian was set on expansion. In 1993, the company acquired another non-standard motor insurer, American Ambassador Casualty Company, to complement the operations of a similar existing American subsidy, Globe American. Both companies offered car insurance to the "non-standard" driver—older drivers, drivers with poor records, and drivers of specialty vehicles. While Guardian historically approached the U.S. market with caution, American Ambassador had a healthy record of profit-making over the years, and the company was quietly confident that its acquisition would continue to perform well.

Guardian had non-life insurance operations in many other countries as well, including Canada, Ireland (where it was the country's largest motor insurer), South Africa, France, Holland, Portugal, and several Asian countries, where the company planned further expansion.

Guardian's position in the life insurance market was generally viewed as less secure than its niche in non-life markets. This was due in part to less favorable conditions in the market industry-wide. The selling of life insurance products was heavily linked to the mortgage market, which had been severely depressed in the recession of the early 1990s.

Guardian's corporate investment was largely in equities and properties in the United Kingdom and Germany. Over the years, this was generally a profitable area for Guardian, but it was, of course, a field subject to much fluctuation. Guardian included realized and unrealized investment gains in its profit figures for the first time in 1993, two years before such reporting was due to become compulsory for the insurers. The volatility of the corporate investment market was such that the new reporting could be a welcome boost to Guardian's figures, as it was in 1993, or a disquieting loss, as in the first six months of 1994.

In the early 1990s, Guardian was beset by a string of misfortunes, some shared by the insurance industry as a whole and others uniquely the company's own. The year 1990 was a particularly disastrous one for all the big insurers in the United Kingdom. Years of progressively ruthless competition among the insurance companies, fighting desperately to retain their market shares, had resulted in pricing and underwriting decisions that proved unrealistic and unsustainable. This state of affairs, coinciding as it did with the recession and a higher than usual incidence of claims (many resulting from the natural disasters that hit the country at this time) had a devastating effect on the industry. Guardian itself plunged to a record loss, the company's first operating loss since the group's formation.

Guardian acted quickly to redeem the loss, instituting what the company termed "remedial" measures, including a rigorous review and overhaul of its underwriting policies, careful conservation of capital, strict control of expenses, and a sharpened focus of what kind of business the company meant to attract and to retain. A corporate philosophy of attracting as wide a range of business as possible, and doing whatever necessary to keep it, had led Guardian and the other big insurers to an unwise—and ultimately calamitous—competition. Guardian's new policy led to decisions to jettison some aspects of its business in order to concentrate on higher quality, higher profit business. Premiums were raised even at the risk of losing customers.

Guardian's strategies were successful, as the company climbed from a loss of some £210 million in 1991 to a 1992 profit of £3 million. The company was one of only two of the big composite insurers to return to profitability and in so doing performed significantly better than financial analysts had predicted: Guardian "deserves credit for playing itself back into the game," the *Financial Times* allowed. Guardian's 1993 pretax profit figures were still more impressive, reaching one of the highest levels in Guardian's history, even discounting the new inclusion of investment gains.

Other troubles plagued the company, however, as Guardian found itself at the center of several controversies. Guardian's propriety was first called into question in 1987, when the company's chief tax accountant, Charles Robertson, fired for alleged misconduct, protested to an industrial tribunal. Robertson claimed that the true cause of his dismissal was his investigation of irregular transactions between Guardian and some of its overseas subsidiaries and his insistence that he must inform the Inland Revenue of these transactions. The tribunal found in Robertson's favor and recommended (it did not have the power to order) his reinstatement. The company refused and later gave Robertson a settlement of £91,000 in compensation.

Guardian was also widely excoriated for its dubious connection with businessman Vinodchandra Manubhai Patel, a star salesman of the company in the 1980s whose ambitious forays into property investment were financed by loans (some £80 million worth) from Guardian. Patel's bankruptcy in 1991 led to allegations that Guardian had acted, if not actually improperly, then certainly unwisely.

Further scandal was aroused by allegations that "tied agents" (those not directly employed by Guardian but engaged in selling Guardian insurance products) had "mis-sold" insurance policies in 1990 and 1991, prompting an investigation by the Life Assurance and Unit Trust Regulatory Organisation and garnering a great deal of bad publicity for the company. Guardian also found itself the target of legal actions in 1993 brought by several ex-agents who alleged that the company had failed to pay them the commissions to which they were entitled on policies they sold in the late 1980s. Guardian maintained that the trouble was due largely to a new computer system installed at that time.

It was perhaps in response to such setbacks—both to its finances and its image—that Guardian modified its name. Known as Guardian Royal Exchange since the 1968 merger of Guardian Assurance and Royal Exchange Assurance, the company sought a new image to boost public awareness and confidence. A team of corporate identity consultants, working in great secrecy for some seven months, finally unveiled the new image in 1993. While officially remaining Guardian Royal Exchange, the company would be known henceforth simply as Guardian, represented by the new logo of an owl that symbolized the company's attributes of stability, dignity, and awareness.

Succumbing to Industry Consolidation in the Late 1990s

Some analysts suggested, however, that it would take more than a new name and logo to fully resuscitate Guardian's fortunes. Though one of the United Kingdom's largest corporate insurers, Guardian was frequently viewed as one of the weakest, particularly in the area of life insurance. In response, the company brought in a new management team for its life insurance business in 1992. Guardian's expansion policies were also criticized, particularly its purchase in the late 1980s of an Italian motor insurer; Guardian sold the company a year after buying it, at a loss of some £68 million. Nevertheless, many of Guardian's efforts to counteract the industry-wide disasters of 1990 were met with approval, especially its unexpected turnaround from dramatic loss to decent profit in the early 1990s. Acquisitions such as the Orion companies were cautiously welcomed as sound strategy.

Guardian made several key purchases in the late 1990s in an attempt to strengthen its operations. In 1996, the company added RAC Insurance Services to its holdings. Two years later, it acquired PPP Healthcare Group Plc in a $711.4 million deal. The purchase of PPP—the U.K.'s second-largest privately held health insurer—was expected to result in significant increases in Guardian's earnings as well as provide annual cost savings.

Despite Guardian's efforts, it soon became apparent that it was unable to compete in the rapidly consolidating insurance industry. It became the U.K.'s smallest composite insurer as its competitors grew quickly through a series of large mergers. General Accident teamed up with Commercial Union, Royal Insurance joined with Sun Alliance, and Zurich purchased BAT Industries' financial services business to form Allied Zurich. Critics claimed that Guardian had been slow in its actions, had failed to capitalize on opportunities, written very little new business, and had not been effective in cutting costs. Indeed, Guardian's market share had fallen dramatically and management was forced to make a difficult decision about its future. "We will consider all options--including a complete bid, or a break-up," declared CEO John Robins in a December 1998 *Financial Times* article. "We have got to be able to stand up in front of our shareholders and say: 'This is the best way forward.'"

In May 1999, Guardian was acquired by Sun Life and Provincial Holdings plc, a subsidiary of the French insurance group AXA, in a $5.76 billion deal. Sun Life and Provincial—its name was changed to AXA UK plc in 2000—integrated Guardian's U.K. and Irish non-life business into its U.K. operations. Albingia, Guardian's German subsidiary, was purchased by AXA Colonia. The rest of Guardian however, was sold off to companies unrelated to AXA. Liberty Mutual Group purchased Guardian's U.S. business for $1.47 billion. The Guardian businesses became wholly owned subsidiaries operating under the names Peerless Insurance Cos. and Indiana Insurance Cos.

AEGON UK plc, a subsidiary of AEGON NV, acquired Guardian's life insurance and pensions business from AXA for $1.2 billion in October 1999. The business fit with AEGON's Scottish Equitable and Scottish Equitable Asset Management subsidiaries and gave it a stronger foothold in the U.K.'s pensions and savings market. These businesses ended up forming AEGON's Guardian Financial Services division. While the Guardian brand name lived on through the AEGON purchase, Guardian Royal Exchange had fallen victim to industry consolidation and ceased to exist as a company.

Principal Competitors

Royal & Sun Alliance Insurance Group plc; Aviva plc; Zurich Financial Services.

Further Reading

Bagnall, Sarah, ''GRE Investment Fall Wipes out Trading Profit,'' *Times* (London), August 26, 1994, p. 23.

''Composites Face Up to Direct Challenge,'' *Lloyds List*, February 28, 1994.

Cook, Lindsay, ''Guardian Goes Astray,'' *Times* (London), August 27, 1994, p. 23.

''Guardian Royal to Buy Insurer in Deal Valued at $711.4 Million,'' *Wall Street Journal*, December 18, 1997, p. 12.

''GRE Buys US Motor Insurer for Dollars 100m,'' *Financial Times*, November 16, 1993.

''GRE Could Pay Pounds 30m in Fraud Aftermath,'' *Daily Mail*, August 20, 1993.

''GRE Counts the Cost of Funding One Man's Empire,'' *Independent*, March 5, 1993.

''GRE Gives Up Struggle to Go It Alone,'' *Sunday Times*, November 29, 1998.

''GRE in Dramatic Swing Back to Profit,'' *Lloyds List*, March 4, 1993.

''GRE Settles with Sacked Whistleblower,'' *Accountancy*, December 1988, p. 8.

''GRE to Launch Direct Insurance Operation,'' *Financial Times*, August 25, 1993.

''GRE Will Come Back to Earth with a Bump,'' *Evening Standard*, December 30, 1992.

''Guarded Confidence,'' *Times* (London), August 26, 1994, p. 25.

''Guardian Royal Jumps to Pounds 751m,'' *Financial Times*, February 23, 1994.

Howard, Lisa S., ''Aegon Acquires U.K. Insurer,'' *National Underwriter Life & Health*, August 16, 1999, p. 38.

——, ''Axa to Acquire U.K. Insurer for $5.6 Billion,'' *National Underwriter Life & Health*, February 8, 1999, p. 8.

''Insurer Faces Pay-Out Claims,'' *Financial Times*, November 5, 1993.

''The Lex Column: Guardian Royal,'' *Financial Times*, August 27, 1993.

''Options Weighed as GRE Hangs in the Balance,'' *Financial Times*, December 5, 1998, p. 20.

''Retrenchment at GRE Pays Off,'' *Financial Times*, March 4, 1993.

''Sacked Accountant Denied Reinstatement,'' *Accountancy*, February 1988, p. 8.

Taylor, Catherine, ''Guardian Unlikely to Receive Sweet Offer,'' *Wall Street Journal Europe*, December 8, 1998.

Thomson, I.D., *Guardian Royal Exchange Worldwide: A Brief History of the Guardian Royal Exchange Companies' Contribution to the Development of International Insurance*, London: Guardian Royal Exchange, n.d., 86 p.

''UK Turnaround Drives Sharp Recovery at GRE,'' *Times* (London), August 27, 1993.

''Whistleblower to Sue over Pension,'' *Accountancy*, June 1989, p. 8.

—Robin DuBlanc
—update: Christina M. Stansell

Hellenic Petroleum SA

17th km., Athens-Corinth National Road
GR-193 00 Aspropyrgos
Attikí
Greece
Telephone: (+30) 210-55-33-000
Fax: (+30) 210-55-39-298
Web site: http://www.hellenic-petroleum.gr

Public Company
Incorporated: 1988
Employees: 520
Sales: EUR 4.67 billion ($5.6 billion)(2003)
Stock Exchanges: Athens
Ticker Symbol: ELPE
NAIC: 424720 Petroleum and Petroleum Products
Merchant Wholesalers (Except Bulk Stations and
Terminals); 424710 Petroleum Bulk Stations and
Terminals

Hellenic Petroleum SA is the largest company in Greece and the leading petroleum refiner both in that country and in nearby Macedonia. Hellenic Petroleum holds a 56 percent share of the market in Greece, where it operates two refineries, in Aspropyrgos and Thessaloniki. The acquisition of Petrola Hellas in 2003 helped consolidate the company's domestic position. In Macedonia, the company's refinery in Skopje controls 72 percent of that country's market. Petroleum refining contributes nearly 77 percent to Hellenic Petroleum's turnover, which topped EUR 5.29 billion in 2003. The second-largest activity of Hellenic Petroleum is its Petroleum Marketing division, which operates nearly 1,500 service stations throughout Greece as well as in Georgia, Albania, the former Yugoslav Republic of Macedonia, Cyprus—since its 2002 acquisition of the former BP Cyprus network—and Montenegro, where the company owns 54.34 percent of Yugopetrol Ad Kotor. Together, Hellenic Petroleum's marketing activities contribute more than 17 percent to the company's total turnover. Other operations include the operation of Greece's only petrochemicals complex, an activity that adds more than 9 percent to sales; Exploration and Production,

which includes the exclusive license for the discovery and exploitation of oil reserves in Greece, adds 3.3 percent to sales. The company is also active in Engineering: its subsidiary Asprofos SA is the largest engineering company in Southeastern Europe. Formerly known as the government-owned Public Petrol Corporation (DEP), Hellenic Petroleum was privatized in 1998 through a public offering. The Greek government retains more than 58 percent of Hellenic Petroleum's stock.

State-Owned Petroleum Company in the 1970s

Like most countries in the 20th century, Greece hoped to discover and exploit petroleum deposits within its borders. For most of the century, however, the Greek government turned to foreign companies for the exploratory phase. The search for petroleum began as early as 1903, when the country awarded a drilling concession to the London Oil Development Co. for the island of Zakynthos. London Oil went on to drill two wells on the island. When these turned out to be dry, however, the company abandoned the effort. Others were to follow over the next decades, but no oil was discovered.

A renewed effort began in 1938, this time led by A.W. Chellis, a Greek-American. Chellis went on to spend more than two decades hunting for Greek oil, starting in western Thrace. Later, Chellis began exploring the Peloponnese Islands before making a new attempt to find petroleum in Zakynthos in the late 1950s.

The Greek government stepped into the exploration effort in the following decade. In 1960, the government, through the Ministry of Industry, joined with consultants from France's Petroleum Institute and Greece's own Geology and Subsoil Research Institute on a new and massive program to find oil reserves in Greece. The team took a more systematic approach, conducting geological and geophysical research operations and drilling extensively through the country. The team's operations focused on the Greek mainland, with particular emphasis on the regions of Thessaloniki, Epirus, Evyrtania, Central Macedonia, and the Ionian Islands.

These drillings, too, remained without result. As the decade progressed, the government stepped up its efforts to locate new fuel reserves. Part of the country's motivation was the large-scale infrastructure and industrial development that were helping to transform the country from a relatively non-industrialized state at the end of World War II. Yet Greece's only native basic fuel source were its lignite coal deposits, which were unsuited for much of the country's industrial and transportation needs. Greece was forced to turn to imports to meet its growing fuel demands. A refinery was built in Aspropyrgos and began refining fuel from imported crude petroleum.

In the 1960s, concessions were awarded to a wide array of internationally operating companies, including British Petroleum, Esso, Safor, and RAP-Ilios. These companies and others began exploration operations on the Ionian Peloponnese and Dodecanaese Islands, as well as such areas as Thrace and Aitoloakarnania.

The development of new technologies permitting offshore exploration provided a new boost to the Greek effort, and in 1969 the government awarded a new range of concessions for its coastal waters to a range of companies, including Chevron, Texaco, Da Oil, An-Car Oil, C&K Petroleum, and Oceanic. While these companies searched the sea, the government continued to award concessions for mainland exploration, notably to Anshutz, which began exploring the regions around Tehssaloniki, Kassandra, and Epanomi in 1971. By 1974, however, the company withdrew from that unsuccessful effort.

The ocean at last provided the country with the discovery of its first exploitable oil fields. Between 1973 and 1974, petroleum deposits were discovered in the Thasos region, at two offshore sites known as Prinos and South Kavala. These discoveries led the Greek government to establish its own oil company, Public Petroleum Corporation (or DEP, after its Greek name) in 1975. Under the law establishing DEP, the Greek government took control of all petroleum exploration, drilling, and refining, including the importation of crude oil for refining. At the same time as it created DEP, the Greek government took over the operation of the Aspropyrgos refinery as well. That refinery operated under the name Hellenic Aspropygos Refinereies SA, or ELDA.

DEP's production ramped up in the early 1980s, and by the middle of that decade production had reached 25,000 barrels per day. Yet by the late 1980s, production had already begun to dwindle, as the Prinos and South Kavala sites proved to offer only limited reserves. By the late 1990s, the sites produced just

14,000 barrels per day of crude oil. DEP now took oversight of further exploration operations, much of which was conceded to third parties.

Vertically Integrated Regional Player in the 21st Century

In the meantime, DEP took on a more central role in Greece's energy industry. The company took over the operations of DEP-EKY, created as the government-controlled exploration and production entity. DEP also took over the operations of another state-created company, Public Gas Corporation, or DEPA, which targeted the natural gas exploration and production market.

As part of its entry into the European Union, the Greek government was forced to deregulate the domestic petroleum market in the early 1990s. In preparation for deregulation, and for its own coming privatization, DEP took steps to increase its level of vertical integration. In the early 1990s, DEP took over the government's EKO service station network, which had been acquired from Esso at the beginning of the previous decade. The takeover of EKO also gave DEP control of EKO's refinery in Thessaloniki. With its acquisition of control of the ELDA refinery in Aspropygos, DEP now entered refining of its own and imported crude oil.

DEP's vertical integration continued into the 1990s, with the creation of VPI and the construction of a polyethylene plant as part of DEP's move into the petrochemicals market. DEP then became the only petrochemicals company in Greece. In 1996, as its domestic oil supplies approached depletion, DEP awarded a new round of four exploration concessions to Enterprise Oil, Union Texas Petroleum, MOL, and Triton Energy. DEP itself, through subsidiary DEP-EKY, took part in the consortiums backing the Enterprise and Triton concessions.

These moves helped prepare DEP for its privatization in 1998. In that year, the Greek government sold a first block of 23 percent of the company with a listing on the Greek and London stock exchanges. DEP then changed its name to Hellenic Petroleum SA. At that time, Hellenic Petroleum shifted 85 percent of its stake in DEPA to the Greek government in order to refocus itself purely on the petroleum market. Also, Hellenic Petroleum restructured parts of its operations, merging ELDA and EKO into a single company, EKO-ELDA. In that same year, the newly created EKO-ELDA expanded with the acquisition of G. Mamidakis, which specialized in petroleum marketing, and of Petrolina, active in the liquified petroleum gas (LPG) market.

Hellenic Petroleum next began to target expansion beyond the domestic market. In 1999, the company made its first step into the wider Balkans region, setting up a joint-venture, ELPET Valkaniki, which then acquired a 54 percent stake in the Okta Ad Skopje facility in the Former Yugoslav Republic of Macedonia. The company also moved into Albania that year, acquiring 75 percent in petroleum marketer Global SA. Following that purchase, the company set up a new subsidiary in Albania, Elda Petroleum Albania.

The Greek government continued to reduce its stake in Hellenic Petroleum, launching a new public offering of the company's shares in 2000. By the following year, however, the

Key Dates:

1902: The first attempt is made to drill for oil in Greece.
1960: The Greek government sets up an oil exploration department in cooperation with France's Petroleum Institute and Greece's Geology and Subsoil Research Institute.
1969: The first offshore exploration concessions are awarded.
1973: Oil reserves are discovered at Prinos and South Kavala sites in Thasos offshore field.
1975: The Greek government establishes the Public Petroleum Corporation (DEP) to oversea oil industry development.
1998: DEP is privatized, changes its name to Hellenic Petroleum, and lists on the Athens and London stock exchanges.
2000: Hellenic Petroleum acquires a majority control of Global SA in Albania.
2003: Hellenic Petroleum acquires BP Cyprus and merges with Petrola Hellas.

government announced its interest in selling off as much as 23 percent of its remaining holdings to a strategic partner. When no appropriate bidder appeared, the government called off the offer. Instead, it continued to reduce its stake in Hellenic Petroleum, selling a 16.5 percent stake to the Latsis Group for $383 million. By 2003, the Greek government shareholding in Hellenic Petroleum had dropped below 58 percent.

In 2002, Hellenic Petroleum strengthened its Balkan-region interests with the acquisition of a 54 percent stake in Montenegro's Yugopetrol Ad Kotor. The following year, the company purchased BP Cyprus Ltd., providing Hellenic Petroleum with an entry into that market through a network of 70 service station, as well as related fuels businesses, including an LPB storage and bottling plant and a 65 percent share of a Superlube lubricants blending plant.

Back at home, Hellenic Petroleum moved to consolidate its dominant position in the domestic market through the acquisition of Petrola Hellas in 2003. That company had set up its own petroleum refining operations in the late 1960 and had grown into the country's second-largest refiner with a 23 percent market share—with the Latsis Group serving as its main shareholder.

Hellenic Petroleum continued building on its plans to become a major regional player. By the beginning of 2004, the company had entered the Bulgarian market as well, setting up a local subsidiary of EKO-ELDA, and opening 11 service stations for a cost of EUR 22 million. In early 2004, the company announced its intention to spend another EUR 23 million in order to build 14 new service stations by the end of the year. Hellenic Petroleum in the meantime announced its intention to look abroad for new strategic partners, as a new block of some 8 percent of the company was slated to come up for sale in July 2004. Hellenic Petroleum had established itself as the dominant oil company at home and was well on its way to becoming a major regional player as well.

Principal Subsidiaries

Eko-Elda A.B.E.E.; Asprofos S.A.; Hellenic Petroleum International A.G.; Diaxon A.B.E.E.; Hellenic Petroleum—Poseidon Shipping Company; Elpet-Balkaniki S.A. (63%); Global Petroleum Albania S.A./Elda Petroleum Sh.P.K. (99.96%); Athens Airport Fuel Pipeline S.A. (34%); B. Of Hellenic Petroleum International A.G. Jugopetrol Ad Kotor (54.35%); Hellenic Petroleum Cyprus Ltd; C. Of Eko-Elda A.B.E.E.; Eko Georgia Ltd (94.8%); Ekota Ko S.A. (49%); Eko—Yu—Ad—Beograd; Eko—Elda Bulgaria Ead; D. Of Elpet-Balkaniki S.A.; Okta Crude Oil Refinery A.D./Okta Trade (69.5%).

Principal Divisions

Petroleum Refining; Petroleum Marketing; Petrochemicals; Exploration and Production; Engineering.

Principal Competitors

Petrom S.A.; Misr Petroleum Company; SOCAR; Kramds NJSC; ENI S.p.A.; Consolidated Contractors Company; Koç Holding A/S.

Further Reading

''Bulgaria Industry: Hellenic Petroleum to Build New Petrol Stations,'' *Country ViewsWire*, March 19, 2004.

''Greece's Hellenic Petroleum Shifts E&P Focus Abroad While Shrinking Its Upstream Role Domestically,'' *Oil and Gas Journal*, March 27, 2000, p. 27.

''Greek Refiners to Merge,'' *International Petroleum Finance*, June 2003, p. 13.

''Hellenic Petroleum Seeks to Expand in Balkans Market,'' *Europe Intelligence Wire*, October 18, 2002.

''Industry Restructuring—BP Is Selling Its Retail Network of 70 Service Stations and Other Inland Fuels Businesses in Cyprus to Hellenic Petroleum,'' *Petroleum Intelligence Weekly*, October 21, 2002, p. 6.

''New CEO of Hellenic Petroleum Sees Room for New Strategic Investor,'' *Europe Intelligence Wire*, April 22, 2004.

''Petrola, Hellenic Petroleum Merger Deal Progresses as Scheduled,'' *Europe Intelligence Wire*, June 24, 2003.

''Synergies in Oil Firm Merger to Total Up to 300 Mln Euros,'' *Europe Intelligence Wire*, June 5, 2003.

—M.L. Cohen

Hensley & Company

4201 North 45th Avenue
Phoenix, Arizona 85031
U.S.A.
Telephone: (602) 264-1635
Fax: (602) 247-7094
Web site: http://www.hensley.com

Private Company
Incorporated: 1955
Employees: 600
Sales: $162.4 million (2002)
NAIC: 424810 Beer and Ale Merchant Wholesalers

Hensley & Company is one of the largest beer distributors in the United States. Hensley & Company's operates exclusively as a wholesaler for Anheuser-Busch Companies, Inc., controlling the largest contiguous Anheuser-Busch territory in the country. The company maintains a fleet of more than 400 trucks that rely on three warehouse facilities in Arizona. The facilities are located in Phoenix, Tempe, and Prescott Valley.

Origins

Hensley & Company's founder, Jim Hensley, gave his company a single-minded focus from its inception: the distribution of products made by St. Louis, Missouri-based Anheuser-Busch Companies, Inc. Before entering the wholesale business, Hensley fought in World War II, serving as a bombardier on B-17 aircraft. He flew a dozen missions before being shot down over the English Channel. After his return to the United States, Hensley worked briefly in the beer and liquor industry. In 1955, he reached an agreement with Anheuser-Busch to distribute the brewer's products in the Phoenix area, forming Hensley & Company to act as an exclusive Anheuser-Busch wholesaler.

Anheuser-Busch celebrated its 103rd anniversary the year Hensley wed his professional career to the massive brewer. His close association with the company, whose future success would largely determine the success of Hensley & Company, began at a favorable juncture in the brewer's development. Anheuser-Busch towered as a brewing giant before Hensley began distributing the company's products, producing more than five million barrels of beer each year during the early 1950s. Rather than exhibiting any complacency, however, the company was intent on building upon its well-established prosperity, demonstrating an aggressiveness with respect to expansion that worked in Hensley's favor. In 1951, Anheuser-Busch opened a brewery in Newark, New Jersey, a moment of significance because it represented the first time a brewer opened a brewery outside its home city. The opening of the Newark facility led to the establishment of an Anheuser-Busch brewery in Los Angeles in 1954, one year before Hensley formed his company. The opening of the Los Angeles facility, capable of producing one million barrels of beer per year, was an extension of Anheuser-Busch's national, expansionist mindset first demonstrated by the opening of the Newark brewery. For Hensley, the opening of the Los Angeles brewery, which most likely factored heavily in his decision to form Hensley & Company, provided his company with a supply of beer to distribute. For the remainder of the 20th century, Hensley & Company received the bulk of its Anheuser-Busch products from southern California.

The year Hensley formed his company also marked the beginning of Anheuser-Busch's renewed interest in its wholesalers. In 1955, August A. Busch, Jr., embarked on a lengthy tour of the country one year before being named chairman of the brewing company. In a tour akin to a whistle-stop political campaign, he used the railroad to visit Anheuser-Busch wholesalers, endeavoring to strengthen the relationship between the brewing company and its distributors. August A. Busch was intent on making Anheuser-Busch the country's leading brewing company, a distinction it had lost several years earlier. In 1957, a year after August Busch, Jr., was elected chairman, Anheuser-Busch regained its leadership position, ranking as the country's largest brewing concern in terms of annual production and annual sales. The company did not relinquish its lead for the remainder of the 20th century.

Hensley & Company started as a modestly sized business, operating as a locally oriented company that gradually developed into a regional powerhouse. Hensley hired 15 employees during his first year of business, selling 73,000 cases of Anheuser-Busch beer products during his first year in operation. The amount of beer distributed by the company was a small

Company Perspectives:

While Hensley's business is to sell fresh Anheuser-Busch beers and provide excellent customer service, its philosophy is to do much more. As a longstanding member of Phoenix and its surrounding communities, the company expends great effort to sell responsibly—and promote responsibility. At the forefront of finding, supporting and implementing effective awareness efforts—such as designated drivers, cab rides home, server training for those who work in bars and restaurants—the company continues its development of awareness and education programs. It is a nationally-recognized leader in campaigns to reduce alcohol abuse, underage drinking and drunk driving.

fraction of the annual total Hensley & Company recorded later in its history, but it was a beginning for Hensley. His stature within the ranks of Anheuser-Busch wholesalers rose as the territory he controlled increased according to a gradual, methodical process whereby his tiny operation grew into one of the most vital facets of Anheuser-Busch's sprawling operations.

Hensley was one of a legion of distributors used by Anheuser-Busch, but his close attention to managing his business distinguished Hensley & Company within the Anheuser-Busch organization. In 1970, 15 years after establishing the company, Hensley established Anheuser-Busch's first controlled-environment warehouse, or CEW, a facility designed to keep beer cool while in storage. Hensley & Company's CEW set a precedent after test marketing in Phoenix revealed that chilling the beer while in storage increased sales by 7 percent. Anheuser-Busch executives looked at the market study and ordered that all its beer be stored in warehouses tailored after Hensley & Company's Phoenix facility.

By the end of the 1980s, more than 30 years had passed since Hensley established his distributorship. In the intervening years, Hensley & Company had grown dramatically, ranking by the end of the decade as the largest beer distributor in Arizona. In 1955, the company sold 73,000 cases of beer. By 1989, the company was selling one million cases of beer every month. The volume of business was aided by recessed rail tracks at Hensley & Company's warehouses, which enabled forklifts to offload the beer from trains arriving from southern California. Hensley, whose daughter Cindy had married U.S. Senator John McCain, presided as president and chief executive officer, occupying an influential position within Arizona and within the Anheuser-Busch organization. His decision to keep Hensley & Company private left industry observers limited to guesswork about the company's financial stature, but the business press estimated that Hensley's distributorship generated approximately $100 million in annual sales. Roughly 70 percent of the company's business at this point was derived from sales to chains of supermarket and convenience stores. For the rest of its business, the company relied on sales to bars, restaurants, and hotels.

Reorganization in 1994 Breeds Success

As Hensley & Company entered the 1990s, it faced a critical juncture in its history. The nearly 40-year-old wholesaling business built by Hensley was a major force in the western United

States, its long-standing and solid relationship with Anheuser-Busch underpinning a seemingly sturdy organization. To industry observers, the privately held Hensley & Company appeared to occupy solid ground, but company officials began to grow concerned during the early years of the decade. "It was a tough time in our industry," a Hensley & Company executive reflected in a July 2, 1999 interview with *The Business Journal—Serving Phoenix & the Valley of the Sun*. "There was an inability to increase our price and we were still recovering from a doubling of the excise tax," the executive continued. "We were in the middle of a downsizing by corporate America. A lot was going on at the time."

As the mid-1990s neared, Hensley & Co was forced to redefine itself. Recessive economic conditions during the early 1990s coupled with a substantial increase in excise taxes conspired to stagnate Hensley & Co's financial growth, but the company also faced a more daunting threat as retailers were presented with the opportunity to receive beer shipments directly from the manufacturer. The advent of direct shipping portended the eradication of wholesalers from the supply chain, or at the very least a major change in the wholesalers' relationship with both manufacturers and retailers. The prospect of direct shipping in markets such as California prompted Anheuser-Busch to look at its wholesale system from a new perspective, which, in turn, also forced Hensley & Company to rethink the way it operated. A Hensley & Company executive, in a September 15, 2002 interview with *Beverage World*, recalled the central issue discussed in the early 1990s. "We asked ourselves: 'Do we just put beer on a truck and deliver it to the back of a store, or do we add value beyond that?' At that time we looked inward and decided that we had to become an indispensable entity."

Hensley & Company's crucible occurred at roughly the same time another momentous change occurred. In 1994, Hensley relinquished day-to-day control over the company, vacating his post as president but remaining chairman of the company he founded 39 years earlier. The plans for Hensley & Company's recovery were developed while Hensley presided as president, but the responsibility for the execution of the plan fell to his successor, Robert Delgado. Delgado joined Hensley & Company a year after his graduation from Bowling Green University in 1974. When he was hired as a staff accountant, Delgado foresaw his stay at Hensley & Company as only temporary, but promotions followed, seeing him rise to controller, vice-president, senior vice-president, and executive vice-president. By the mid-1980s, Delgado was being groomed as the company's future leader, and he accepted the post just as Hensley & Company was preparing to adopt a new identity.

The changes enacted added new dimensions to Hensley & Company's role as a wholesaler, and they ran counter to the corporate trend sweeping throughout the country. While other companies embraced the idea of reducing their payrolls, Hensley & Company, its profits declining, expanded its workforce by 30 percent to increase its level of service to retailers. "It was a gutsy, gutsy move," Delgado remembered in a July 2, 1999 interview with *The Business Journal—Serving Phoenix & the Valley of the Sun*. "And it hurt for a few years," he added, "but it was the way to go."

Organizational changes were made concurrently as the company divided its sales group into 13 teams, each led by a team

Key Dates:

1955:   Hensley & Company is formed.
1970:   Hensley & Company establishes Anheuser-Busch's first controlled environment warehouse.
1989:   Hensley & Company's annual sales reach $100 million.
1994:   Hensley & Company's workforce is increased to provide better service to retailers.
2000:   Hensley & Company acquires Mile-Hi Distributing.

leader who governed from ten to 20 team members. In the fall of 1994, the company also began using computer software and hardware to enhance its service to retailers, using a system named Margin Minder that provided data related to retailers' needs at an exponentially faster rate. From the mid-1990s forward, Hensley & Company began to offer its customers increased attention and service, which enabled it to increase its market share by ten percentage points by the end of the 1990s.

Hensley & Company in the 21st Century

As Hensley & Company entered the 21st century, it ranked as the fifth-largest beer distributor in the United States. The company that sold 73,000 cases of beer in its first year of business sold more than 20 million cases during its 45th anniversary year, when it controlled the largest contiguous Anheuser-Busch territory in the country.

The new decade began on a sad note for Hensley & Company. In June 2000, Jim Hensley died. His daughter, Cindy Hensley McCain, was appointed chairman, while Delgado increased his influence over the company by adding the title of vice-chairman to his posts as president and chief executive officer. At roughly the same time this transfer of power took place, Hensley & Company completed the first acquisition in its history, purchasing Mile-Hi Distributing. Owned by the Fornara family since the 1930s, Mile-Hi operated as an Anheuser-Busch distributor based in Prescott, Arizona. The acquisition increased

Hensley & Company's sales by 5 percent, adding 900,000 cases of beer to the company's business.

As Hensley & Company approached its 50th anniversary, it held sway as one of the largest beer distributors in the country, enjoying more than a 60 percent share in its markets and dominating the distribution business in Arizona. In the years ahead, the company was expected to maintain its dominance, with its legacy of success fueling optimism for the future.

Principal Operating Units

Hensley—Phoenix; Hensley—Tempe; Hensley—Prescott.

Principal Competitors

Pearce Beverage Company; Phoenix Distributing Company; Alliance Beverage Distributing Company.

Further Reading

Davis, Tim, "Dream Teams: An A-B Wholesaler Moves Data Access to the Front Lines," *Beverage World*, August 1995, p. 35.

Foote, Andrea, "Tier Value: All Three Tiers—Supplier, Wholesaler and Retailer—Benefit When Hensley Stakes the Leading Edge," *Beverage World*, September 15, 2002, p. 37.

Gilbertson, Dawn, "Phoenix-Based Hensley Acquires Another Distributor for Anheuser-Busch," *Knight Ridder/Tribune Business News*, June 21, 2000.

Jensen, Tom, "Hensley Taps Profitable Niche as State's Top Beer Distributor," *Business Journal—Serving Phoenix & the Valley of the Sun*, November 6, 1989, p. 21.

Schwartz, David, "Top Draft Choice," *Business Journal—Serving Phoenix & the Valley of the Sun*, April 21, 2000, p. 17B.

——, "Top Draft Choice: Temporary Job Leads to Fulfilling Career," *Business Journal—Serving Phoenix & the Valley of the Sun*, July 2, 1999, p. 21.

Wagner, Eileen Brill, "Cindy McCain Named Hensley Board Chair," *Business Journal—Serving Phoenix & the Valley of the Sun*, December 8, 2000, p. 4.

—Jeffrey L. Covell

on tv & online

HSN

1 HSN Drive
St. Petersburg, Florida 33729
U.S.A.
Telephone: (727) 872-1000
Fax: (727) 872-6615
Web site: http://www.hsn.com

Wholly Owned Subsidiary of IAC/InterActiveCorp.
Incorporated: 1982
Employees: 4,500
Sales: $2.2 billion (2003)
NAIC: 454110 Electronic Shopping and Mail-Order
Houses

HSN, formerly known as Home Shopping Network, Inc., is the second-largest shop-at-home television network in the United States, behind QVC. HSN sells thousands of unique products through its shows, which are broadcast 24 hours a day via cable, satellite, and network television. Its main product areas are electronics, fashion and jewelry, health and beauty, and home and entertainment. HSN reaches some 81 million households in the United States. It also runs home shopping subsidiaries in Germany, Italy, Japan, and China. HSN also runs an Internet subsidiary, HSN.com. The company benefits from a stable of celebrity designers and pitchmen, including chef Wolfgang Puck, actress Suzanne Somers, singer Patti Labelle, and jewelry designer Cathy Waterman. HSN sells many goods designed exclusively for it, as well as products from popular brands such as Sony, Hoover, and Gateway. The company runs four order fulfillment centers in the United States, and one each in Germany, Japan, and China. The company is owned by IAC/InterActiveCorp., a publicly traded firm that includes several e-commerce divisions. IAC is run by Barry Diller, one of the leading media dealmakers in the United States and formerly the head of Fox Television Network.

Origins in the 1970s

The idea for the Home Shopping Network originated in the 1970s when Lowell W. Paxson, who owned an AM radio station in Clearwater, Florida, began to lose listeners to FM alternatives. Paxson also lost advertisers. He decided to try selling merchandise directly over the air, switching from an easy-listening music format to an at-home radio shopping service called The Bargaineers. To finance the new format, Paxson turned to Roy M. Speer, a lawyer and real estate developer. Speer would later become Home Shopping's chairman.

Almost immediately after the switch in format, the station's revenues swelled so much that Paxson was eager to try out his home shopping idea on television. Speer liked the idea of expanding to television but wanted to proceed slowly, investing $500,000 for a 60 percent stake and set out to make sure that viewers would not be disappointed before he gave the go-ahead in July 1982.

Speer and Paxson called their local TV program the Home Shopping Club (HSC). Within three months, it was turning a profit. After two more Tampa Bay-area cable companies decided to carry HSC, Speer and Paxson began to explore markets in Fort Lauderdale and Miami. By 1985, HSC was so successful that it went national, calling itself the Home Shopping Network. Speer based his decision to expand on the belief that the profiles of Tampa Bay customers would be the same for people all over the United States.

Speer commissioned the development of a computer system that would have the capacity to respond to customers' needs immediately. He acquired a large number of phone lines and hired many operators, all in an effort to make a return customer of that first-time buyer. Within three months, Home Shopping had become the world's first network to broadcast live 24 hours a day, and its number of employees had grown from 300 to 1,280. Speer's approach was successful; in just one year he was able to take the company public.

Public Offering in the Mid-1980s

In February 1986, Merrill Lynch underwrote the Home Shopping Network's initial public offering at $18 a share. An investment banker who helped with the offering commented on Speer's wisdom in pricing Home Shopping's stock so low, because it was still perceived as a risky company in an untried

Company Perspectives:

HSN, an operating business of IAC/InterActiveCorp (NAS-DAQ: IAC), originated the electronic retailing industry in 1977. The idea materialized on a small AM radio station in Florida and has since grown into a global MultiChannel retailer with worldwide consolidated sales of $2.2 billion in 2003 and a growing customer base of over 5 million.

industry. At that time, Home Shopping was still in the process of trying to convince cable operators to carry its show over other alternative programming. Home Shopping stock became the fastest rising new issue of 1986, registering a 137 percent gain by the end of the day. Since the initial offering, Home Shopping stock went on to split twice, the first time at three for one and the second time at two for one.

The Home Shopping Club had developed three formats: Home Shopping Network 1 (HSN 1), Home Shopping Network 2 (HSN 2), and Home Shopping Spree. HSN 1 was available live, 24 hours a day, seven days a week, and was produced exclusively for cable. HSN 2, which offered upscale merchandise, was also available live, 24 hours a day, seven days a week, but was marketed to both broadcast and cable television. Home Shopping Spree offered limited-time or 24-hour programming to broadcast stations.

Opinions varied on the reasons for the rapid rise in popularity of HSN 1 and HSN 2 stations. Perhaps viewers were attracted to the fact that they automatically became members the first time they placed an order and that they received a $5 credit applicable to the next purchase. Another reason may have been that the shows' hosts gave no warning as to what items would appear on the TV screen and when. As viewers could only purchase items for as long as the products appeared on their screens, anywhere from two to ten minutes, the typical member would watch the program for several hours each day in an effort to find the best deals on products they wanted.

The hosts of the program, almost all of whom had a background in retail sales, soon became popular personalities and were given nicknames by their adoring fans. As Home Shopping's success grew, competing stations began popping up, causing host as well as viewer defections. Competition continued to grow, with many stations in the industry, including Home Shopping, turning to celebrity endorsements and hosts. Another, more conventional, way that Home Shopping ensured that customers kept coming back was by allowing the return of any purchase if for any reason a member was not satisfied.

As Home Shopping grew, so did the companies that supported it. Home Shopping was one of United Parcel Service's largest accounts, and many suppliers owed their success to Home Shopping. A new product could be introduced to the nation on the network, and within minutes thousands of items could be sold. While some of the merchandise sold over Home Shopping came from closeouts, overstocks, or overruns, the company's purchasing clout was evident in the fact that at least 60 percent of the company's sales in 1987 consisted of products made specifically for Home Shopping and sold to them for rock-bottom prices.

Not everything, however, was on the upswing in 1987. In that year alone, more than 15 television shop-at-home programs went off the air. Stock market analysts began to question how long Home Shopping could sustain its rapid growth rate. Some believed that members would eventually reach their credit card limits, while others thought the company was paying too much for its acquisitions of UHF television stations and burdening itself with excessive debt. Still others speculated that the company would lose market share to its ever-growing number of competitors who offered improvements on Home Shopping's unpredictable format, such as the plan JC Penney and Sears announced for Telaction, which would allow customers to use their phone to select items from their screens.

In one year, between March 1987 and March 1988, Home Shopping stock experienced a market slip of 18.95 percent, compared to a 6.76 percent drop in the Dow Jones Industrial Average. The company lost no time in reacting, however; as early as 1987, it was looking around for better ways to harness its market. In January 1987, Home Shopping announced plans to build a new telecommunications center and corporate headquarters in St. Petersburg, Florida. By September, the company had started using the UHF television stations it had been acquiring, and the network began broadcasting from its new 180,000-square-foot telecommunications facility, hoping to beat down its competitors with better reception. In September 1987, Home Shopping announced its plans for a major corporate restructuring, with HSN Inc. becoming a holding company for the various subsidiaries conducting its businesses.

Distinctions such as fast delivery and guaranteed products, the ability to process orders rapidly and reduce labor costs, and the higher quality of television reception provided by its own TV stations enabled HSN to preserve its market share, as well as distance itself from all but one of its competitors. It also reported good annual sales gains, passing the $1 billion mark in 1990. However, these distinctions still had not succeeded in recapturing wary investors. There was worry about the stability of the home shopping industry in the face of recession years. HSN stock, nevertheless, moved to the New York Stock Exchange from the smaller American Stock Exchange in 1990, and the company began a stock repurchase program.

New Owners in the 1990s

HSN had grown quickly, but it remained in second place behind the home shopping industry leader, QVC. In late 1992, a complicated set of mergers and acquisitions began, which almost resulted in a combination of the two leading companies. In December 1992, Liberty Media Corporation bought a 23-percent stake in HSN by acquiring shares from chairman Roy Speer. Liberty offered to buy the remaining stake in the company a few months later but then dropped its bid when allegations surfaced before a Florida grand jury about improprieties at the company and investigations into Speer and co-founder Lowell Paxon. Speer resigned his chairmanship of HSN soon after. Liberty Media also owned a stake in QVC. QVC was headed by media mogul Barry Diller, the former chairman of the Fox network. Diller invested some $25 million in QVC and led it through some unsuccessful takeover attempts. In July 1993, Diller's QVC offered a $1.3 billion stock swap to gain control of HSN. By November, however, HSN and QVC ended

Key Dates:

1977: Clearwater, Florida, radio station debuts home shopping concept.
1982: Home Shopping Club moves to television.
1986: Home Shopping Network makes a public stock offering.
1990: The company's stock moves to the New York Stock Exchange.
1993: Liberty Media Corporation acquires a stake in company.
1995: Barry Diller becomes chairman of HSN after its merger with Silver King.
1998: HSN purchases Universal TV.
2003: HSN's parent changes its name to IAC/InterActive-Corp.

their merger discussions when QVC decided to pursue the acquisition of Paramount Communications Inc.

In the meantime, HSN went into 1994 with global aspirations. The company prepared to partner with Tele-Communications Inc. to launch an international teleshopping service. In late 1993, HSN established an international division, headed by Michael W.D. McMullen, to explore international television opportunities. Known as Home Shopping International, the service countered the international activities of rival QVC, which earlier had established shopping services in the United Kingdom and Mexico. HSN launched its first international venture—a home shopping company in Japan—in February 1994. Cable television was not widely available in Japan, but it was available to the wealthy, so HSN planned to develop a home shopping program for more upscale viewers. HSN intended to export products to the Japanese market but also stated a commitment to developing businesses there, especially for apparel and other products that might depend on local appeal.

About this time, HSN and Prodigy Services Company began working together on an online store to debut in the fall of 1994. Selling housewares, electronics, fashions, jewelry, and products for personal-computer users, the service was the first to use full-color photos rather than drawings of merchandise. In addition to the shopping aspects, the service also provided a bulletin board for contacting HSN hosts and celebrity guests. HSN also established HSN Interactive, a new division headed by Jeff Gentry.

Beginning in May 1994, HSN worked on expanding its viewer base. The company again entered into an agreement with Tele-Communications Inc. that added 500,000 viewers to its Home Shopping Club in the form of new Tele-Communications Inc. subscribers. The federal government's Cable Act of 1992 ensured that 4.8 million other homes also would be covered through the agreement, since the rules specified that cable operators must carry all broadcasters with signals in the areas. In addition, HSN renewed contracts with ten cable operators with seven million subscribers, including Continental Cablevision, a system with three million subscribers. HSN added 16 million subscribers through agreements with five additional cable television companies that would carry Home Shopping Network programming the following month.

In order to compete financially with the revenues generated by commercials aired on other home shopping networks, HSN initiated a division to produce infomercials and distribute them globally in July 1994. HSN Direct, located at the HSN headquarters in St. Petersburg, Florida, aired its infomercials on cable networks and through broadcast services—excluding HSN's home shopping vehicles, which were not formatted for long commercials. HSN embarked upon a joint venture to produce the infomercials. Headed by Kevin Harrington, a past vice-president at National Media and co-owner of the venture, HSN Direct positioned Home Shopping Network to sell to a European audience. Harrington was responsible for developing the infomercial in Europe through Quantum International, a company he formed in 1988. He expected HSN to create infomercials for housewares, exercise equipment, and other products—especially merchandise produced by manufacturers unaware of the infomercial potential of their goods or for products with a history of success on HSN.

New Directions in the Mid-1990s

From 1994 to 1995, HSN underwent a transformation. The network redesigned sets, changed the format of programs, and improved the merchandise that it offered. Nevertheless, it remained unprofitable and posted millions of dollars in losses. The company came under new leadership in 1995 when it was finally captured by media entrepreneur Barry Diller. Diller resigned from QVC in early 1995 after the failure of his ventures to buy Paramount and CBS. He then spent $10 million to buy a 20-percent controlling stake in a small string of television stations called Silver King Communications. In a complex transaction valued at $1.3 billion, Silver King then bought HSN. Diller came to HSN with a proven track record. He had successfully managed Paramount Pictures and engineered the creation of the Fox network. Under his direction, QVC, the competing home shopping network, flourished. Diller demonstrated a knack for interesting high-profile investors in his projects, such as John Malone, owner of 39 percent of Silver King, and billionaire David Geffen. Diller's arrival as chairman of HSN created excitement and anticipation within the industry. Analysts expected Diller to continue to improve programming at HSN and to develop the true value of the company. For example, observers assumed that Diller, well-connected with high-profile designers and celebrities, would utilize his contacts to enhance HSN's offerings and contacts.

However, Diller's interests were varied, and the company moved in some unexpected ways. In a stock-for-stock transaction during the summer of 1997, HSN gained control of Ticketmaster, a broker of entertainment tickets. Valued at about $209 million, the merger created opportunities for both companies. HSN greatly expanded its distribution system. HSN's network provided Ticketmaster with a massive venue through which to market concert, theater, and other entertainment event tickets. Founder Paul Allen sold his controlling interest in Ticketmaster in exchange for 11 percent of HSN. He also became a member of HSN's board, as did Frederic Rosen and William Savoy.

Expansion continued after the merger, especially on an international level. Earlier, with Sumitomo Corporation, a large

Japanese trading company, HSN brought televised home shopping to Japan through 30-minute programs broadcast in Tokyo, Osaka, and nearby regions beginning in 1996. Similarly, Jupiter Programming and HSN introduced the SHOP channel in Japan in November 1997. After success in Japan, HSN developed a shopping channel for Germany in conjunction with Quelle, a European catalog company, and Kirch Media Interests of Germany.

Then, with Spanish-language broadcaster Univision, HSN initiated a Spanish-language shopping channel in 1997 for full operations in 1998. Univision secured U.S. distribution, and HSN controlled operations of the channel target for seven million Hispanic households in the United States. Since HSN recognized more than 500 million Spanish-speaking consumers worldwide, the company planned to expand the shopping channel into Latin America and Spain, both of which had millions of existing or cable-ready households.

In November 1997, Diller sold an HSN network in Baltimore, Maryland—WHSW—in order to set the groundwork for his Silver King Communications' planned joint venture with the Universal Television Group and USA Networks. Diller negotiated with the parent company of Universal Studios—Seagram—to join HSN with the television unit of Universal Studios. In exchange for more than $1 million and a 45 percent share of HSN, Seagram, Universal TV's owner, sold its USA Networks and its domestic television business. Diller purchased the lion's share of Universal TV Studios operations in the United States, including production and distribution of such hit television programs as *Law and Order* and *Xena: Warrior Princess,* in a billion-dollar deal. Though Universal Studios retained part ownership in the newly formed company, HSN gained the domestic and some of the international activities of the USA Network (a popular cable station) and the Sci-Fi Network. In addition to the merger on the domestic scene, HSN and Universal worked together on a venture for international television. Diller remained as chairman of the new company. Executives from Universal TV and its parent company, Seagram, joined USA Networks board; Diller assumed a seat as a director of Seagram. Shareholders approved HSN's purchase of Universal TV for $4 billion, changing the company's name to USA Networks Inc. This became the holding company for Home Shopping Network and other entities.

Changing Landscape in the 2000s

When USA Networks completed its transaction with Seagram for Universal TV Studios in 1998, the *Wall Street Journal* (February 13, 1998) reported, "Some entertainment executives were puzzled when the deal was announced" and others were unsure what Diller's role at Universal would be. *Fortune* magazine (May 3, 2004) later claimed that Diller had at first envisioned USA Networks as his second Fox. Yet shortly after buying the Universal properties, Diller began making other deals that brought the company away from traditional television and into new media. In 1999, USA Networks planned to buy Lycos Inc., an Internet search engine portal. USA Networks planned to spend $3.8 billion on 60 percent of Lycos, which at the time was the number three company among Internet search engines. This deal did not come off, though it did apparently lead to the resignation of James Held, who had been chief

executive of HSN since 1995. Held was credited with improving the fortunes of the company over the previous few years, when it took market share from QVC. Held had also handled HSN's expansion into German and Japanese home shopping shows, and pushed HSN into expanding its Spanish-language shows in the United States. Mark Bozek took over Held's job. USA Networks did manage to buy a stake in another Internet company, Citysearch, which soon became part of a new company merged with Ticketmaster, called Ticketmaster Online-Citysearch, or TMCS. Parent company USA Networks also bought a hotel reservation company which became Hotels.com and a stake in the Internet travel reservation company Expedia.

Home Shopping Network continued to do what it did best—sell things on TV. While not quite catching up with QVC, Home Shopping Network in the late 1990s was a solid money maker. *Broadcasting & Cable* (April 3, 2000) reported that over 1999, HSN made on average $2,500 per minute, 24 hours a day, seven days a week. The network improved the quality of its offerings, and by 2000 the largest percentage of its sales was in electronics exclusively made for HSN. HSN had other successful exclusive deals, such as selling the video of the hit movie *Titanic* three months before it was available in stores. HSN made $6 million on the *Titanic* videos alone. HSN also swiped a popular show from rival QVC in 2000, broadcasting live from ABC's *Monday Night Football* to retail football-related goods through its exclusive "NFL Shop." Home Shopping Network changed its name officially to just its initials, HSN, in 2000. HSN made an Internet purchase of its own that year, buying up a Web site that sold home craft goods, Craftopia.com. It also did cross-marketing with the ABC network, selling jewelry on HSN worn by characters on ABC's popular soap opera *All My Children.*

The Internet bubble lost its air over 2000 and 2001, with many promising web companies folding or seeing their stock prices plummet. USA Network's Diller had built up a complex of Internet firms, making HSN an odd fit with the parent company. In May 2001, USA Network sold back to Vivendi Universal the entertainment properties it had given up (as Seagram) in 1998. A few months later, Diller announced he was ready to sell HSN. The parent company changed its name to USA Interactive, which at that point consisted principally of the shopping channel, Ticketmaster, Expedia, and Hotels.com. The *Wall Street Journal* (November 15, 2002) reported that Diller was frustrated with trying to market USA Networks to investors. Its businesses were confusing. Though it looked like a "new media" company with its online businesses, most of its revenues came from solid old HSN.

However, HSN did not do very well over 2002. It grew only 3.2 percent in what was a dismal year for many retailers. Yet QVC showed an 11 percent growth rate over the same period.

HSN did not find an immediate buyer. In 2003, Tom McInerney took over as the company's new chief executive. McInerney questioned why QVC consistently did better than HSN and ultimately told *Fortune* in the article cited above that the rival had "better execution," meaning QVC simply sold better goods and offered better service. By 2003, HSN had half the sales and a third of the profits of QVC. McInerney resisted his boss Barry Diller's request that he acquire companies in order to promote growth at HSN. McInerney's focus on better service, however, did apparently improve results, and HSN sales grew strongly in 2003. On December 6, 2003, HSN set a one-day sales record of $30 million. Its previous one-day sales record was $16.9 million, set in 2002, so this represented a huge jump. HSN took significant steps to improve its customer service in late 2003. These included signing an agreement with the carrier service UPS to deliver HSN packages on average two days faster than previously. The company also felt that it benefited from some of its exclusive sales agreements, such as the Wolfgang Puck line of cookware, Adrien Arpel beauty items, and a desktop computer system available only on HSN from Gateway Computers.

Sales for 2003 came to $2.2 billion. That year, HSN's parent company again changed its name, settling on IAC/InterActiveCorp. HSN seemed to be doing better, yet it was still an odd match with the rest of the parent company's holdings. The fate of the parent company seemed to hinge on shakeouts in the online sales industry, which in the early 2000s was still very much in flux. Diller had already said he wanted to sell HSN, and to many analysts this still seemed likely. IAC had been anointed one of the ''four horsemen'' of the Internet, along with bookseller Amazon.com, the auction site eBay, and the portal Yahoo. HSN was clearly a different kind of animal. Yet Diller was unpredictable and a veteran of many convoluted business combinations. Thus, it was uncertain in 2004 what might lie ahead for HSN.

Principal Subsidiaries

HSN.com; Craftopia.com; Home Shopping Europe (Germany); Home Shopping Europe (Italy); SHOP Channel (Japan); TVSN Ltd. (China).

Principal Competitors

QVC, Inc.; ValueVision Media, Inc.; Summit America Television, Inc.

Further Reading

Angwin, Julia, ''USA Interactive Is a Hard Sell to Investors,'' *Wall Street Journal*, November 15, 2002, pp. C1, C5.

Applefeld, Catherine, ''HSN Founder Buys MOR Music TV; Nashville Firm Aims to Build Alternative Distribution,'' *Billboard*, August 5, 1995, p. 6.

Botton, Sari, ''Merger Mania Hits TV Shopping,'' *HFD—The Weekly Home Furnishings Newspaper*, July 26, 1993, p. 10.

Brodesser, Claude, ''Diller Does Station Deal,'' *MEDIAWEEK*, November 17, 1997, p. 6.

Brown, Rich, ''Home Shopping Network Launches Infomercial Unit,'' *Broadcasting & Cable*, July 18, 1994, p. 22.

——, ''It's Everywhere: HSN Gets on the Internet,'' *Broadcasting & Cable*, September 12, 1994, p. 33.

Colman, Price, ''Diller Consolidates Position with HSN Deal,'' *Broadcasting & Cable*, September 2, 1996, p. 48.

Dickson, Martin, ''QVC, Home Shopping Axe Merger,'' *Financial Post*, November 6, 1993, p. 12.

Dolbow, Sandra, ''Shop 'til Ya Drop,'' *Brandweek*, August 7, 2000, p. 4.

Edelson, Sharon, ''Barry Diller Returns to Home Shopping,'' *WWD*, November 28, 1995, p. 2.

——, ''HSN, BET Slate Shopping Program Targeting Blacks,'' *WWD*, July 20, 1994, p. 17.

——, ''HSN, TCI and Sumitomo Sign Pact for Japan Home Shopping Venture,'' *WWD*, February 25, 1994, p. 2.

Egan, Jack, ''Barry Diller Wheels and Deals,'' *U.S. News & World Report*, November 3, 1997, p. 62.

Fitzpatrick, Eileen, ''Ticketmaster, HSN Deal Opens Options for Both,'' *Billboard*, May 31, 1997, p. 6.

Flint, Joe, and Martin Peers, ''HSN to Hawk ABC 'Soap Opera' Jewelry,'' *Wall Street Journal*, August 6, 2001, p. B8.

Gunther, Marc, ''Once Again, It's Diller Time,'' *Fortune*, November 24, 1997, p. 37.

Harris, Kathryn, ''Is Diller Scheming or Just Dreaming?,'' *Fortune*, December 25, 1995, p. 164.

Hass, Nancy, ''Liberty Media: No Need to Shop Around,'' *Financial World*, May 25, 1993, p. 13.

Higgins, John M., ''Diller Shopping HSN,'' *Broadcasting & Cable*, January 13, 2002, p. 48.

——, ''HSN Takeover Underwhelms Wall Street,'' *Multichannel News*, September 2, 1996, p. 3.

''Home Shopping Network, Inc.: A History of Growth,'' Home Shopping Network, Inc., corporate typescript, 1988.

''Home Shopping Network Owner HSN Completed Purchase of Paul Allen's Controlling Interest in Ticketmaster,'' *Communications Daily*, July 21, 1997, p. 8.

''Home Shopping Network Will Launch Japanese Channel in Joint Venture with Jupiter Programming,'' *Communications Daily*, November 20, 1996, p. 7.

''HSN Enters Pact to Furnish Intel, Microsoft with Software,'' *WWD*, May 9, 1995, p. 11.

''HSN to Be a Unit of Silver King,'' *WWD*, August 27, 1996, p. 8.

James, Ellen L., ''So What's a Billion to Roy Speer?'' *Venture*, May 1987.

Kohl, Christian, ''Diller Spree Nets Stake in Teuton Shopping Web,'' *Daily Variety Gotham*, June 10, 2002, p. 7.

Lippman, John, ''Home Shopping's Held Steps Down as CEO, Chairman,'' *Wall Street Journal*, March 8, 1999, p. B14.

McAdams, Deborah D., ''Not Just Cubic Zirconium,'' *Broadcasting & Cable*, April 3, 2000, p. 36.

McLean, Bethany, ''Diller.com,'' *Fortune*, May 3, 2004, p. 86.

''Merger of Home Shopping Network,'' *Communications Daily*, December 20, 1996, p. 7.

Moin, David, ''Macy and HSN: A TV Marriage in the Making,'' *WWD*, June 8, 1993, p. 1.

Prior, Molly, ''HSN Acquires Craftopia.com,'' *DSN Retailing Today*, February 19, 2001,. P. 6.

''Seagram Joins with Diller's HSN in $4.075-Billion Deal,'' *Communications Daily*, October 21, 1997, p. 1.

Shapiro, Eben, ''Seagram Completes a Spinoff to HSN of Majority of Its Television Business,'' *Wall Street Journal*, February 13, 1998, p. A5.

''Ted Turner Is at It Again: The Atlanta-based Entrepreneur Is Eyeing the Home Shopping Network,'' *Broadcasting & Cable*, April 4, 1994, p. 56.

Zimmerman, Ann, ''Top Designers Shill on TV,'' *Wall Street Journal*, December 3, 2002, pp. B1, B5.

—Maya Sahafi
—updates: Charity Anne Dorgan and A. Woodward

Huhtamäki Oyj

Lansituulentie 7
Espoo
FIN-02100
Finland
Telephone: 358 9 686 881
Fax: 358 9 660 622
Web site: http://www.huhtamaki.com

Public Company
Incorporated: 1920 as Huhtamäki Industries
Employees: 15,500
Sales: EUR 2.1 billion ($2.3 billion)
Stock Exchanges: Helsinki
Ticker Symbol: HUHIV
NAIC: 322215 Non-Folding Sanitary Food Container
Manufacturing; 322221 Coated and Laminated
Packaging Paper and Plastics Film Manufacturing;
322222 Coated and Laminated Paper Manufacturing;
322223 Plastics, Foil, and Coated Paper Bag
Manufacturing; 322224 Uncoated Paper and Multiwall
Bag Manufacturing; 322231 Die-Cut Paper and
Paperboard Office Supplies Manufacturing; 322299
All Other Converted Paper Product Manufacturing

Finland's Huhtamäki Oyj is the world's leading producer of molded fiber-based and rigid packaging products for the consumer foods and foodservices markets, and is one of the world's leading manufacturers of paper cups and plates. Huhtamäki's turn-of-the century transformation—the company's formerly highly diversified operations included the Leaf candy company, among others—was accomplished in large part through the acquisition of a number of noted packaging players, including The Netherlands' Van Leer Royal Packaging Industries and the United States' Sealright, among others. Consumer Goods account for the largest part of the group's revenues, accounting for 67 percent of Huhtamäki's sales of EUR 2.1 billion ($2.5 billion) in 2003. In addition to standard consumer foods packaging products, the company works closely with food industry customers to develop and produce innovative packaging products, such as plastic baby food containers for Danone in 2004. Included in the group's Consumer Goods division are its sales of paper and plastic cups and plates under the Chinet (Americas), Bibo (Europe), and Lily (Oceania) brand names. The Foodservice sector adds the remaining 33 percent to the company's total revenues. Customers include nearly all of the major fast-food customers, as well as other institutional customers such as caterers. A globally operating company with manufacturing and distribution facilities in 36 countries, Huhtamäki remains headquartered in Finland and has been listed on the Helsinki Stock Exchange since 1960. Europe remains the group's largest market, at 56 percent of sales, while the Americas account for 29 percent and Asia, Oceania, and Africa combine for 15 percent of sales. The company is led by Chairman and CEO Timo Peltola.

Cooking Up a Conglomerate in the 1920s

Huhtamäki Oyj traced its origins to the village of Kokkola, in Western Finland, where Vilhelm Huhtamäki operated a bakery and confectioner's shop. Huhtamäki had been somewhat of a world traveler, having worked in the United States, as well as in Norway and Sweden, a trait inherited by his eldest son, Heikki, who became a confectioner's apprentice in St. Petersburg in 1917. Born in 1900, Heikki Huhtamäki became caught up in the Bolshevik Revolution, and eventually crossed the continent through Siberia and to Japan, before ultimately returning to Finland. There, Heikki Huhtamäki published a book about his adventures, then set up his own confectionery business, backed by his industrialist father-in-law, in 1920.

Huhtamäki, as the company came to be called, quickly grew into one of the leading candy companies in Finland. The company's success in the candy market led it to diversify into other areas beginning in the 1930s. At first, Huhtamäki remained close to its original business, expanding into other food categories. By the 1940s, however, the company had evolved into a holding company for an increasingly varied range of companies, including clothing, advertising, and, in later decades, electronics and heavy engineering. Pharmaceuticals, under the Leiras name, was also an important area of operation for the company, which later came to specialize on the production of contraceptives and anticancer agents.

By the late 1980s, Huhtamäki oversaw a widely diversified array of some 20 separate businesses, each operating under its own name. Candy and Confectionery remained a major part of the group's businesses, particularly with the acquisition of the United States' Leaf Candy Company, as well as two other U.S. candy makers, in 1983. Into the early 1990s, confectionery continued to account for as much as 60 percent of Huhtamäki's sales. Through Leaf, Huhtamäki had succeeded in building a position for itself among the global top ten confectionery companies, with particular strength in the non-chocolate and chewing gum categories.

The arrival of Timo Peltola as CEO in 1989 signaled the start of a new era for Huhtamäki. Peltola set out to refocus the company as a global leader in a narrower array of industries. The company began selling off its holdings, and by the early 1990s had refocused itself around a triple core of confectionery under Leaf, pharmaceuticals under Leiras, and packaging under the group's Polarpak division.

Huhtamäki's entry into the packaging market began as an offshoot of its confectionery and foods business, as the company built up packaging operations in order to support its growing array of food and nonfood products. Into the early 1960s, however, Huhtamäki's packaging division, which produced both paper and metal-based packaging for the company's products, remained dedicated to serving the company's in-house needs.

The transformation of that in-house function into a full-fledged business began with the acquisition of the Mensa canning plant, which specialized in producing paper food containers, based in Hämeenlinna, in Finland, in 1960. Two years later, Huhtamäki separated its metal packaging and paper packaging operations into a new company, Pakkaus Oy. Huhtamäki soon after chose to phase out its metal packaging business, however. Instead, the company decided to focus on the younger thermoformed plastics market, selling off its metal packaging business and creating the Polarpak business in 1965. Polarpak also took over the company's paper-based packaging operations, which traded under the brand name Bibo, among others. By the 1970s, Polarpak had emerged as the leading producer of paper cups in Europe. The production of cups and containers for the ice cream industry became another company specialty.

The company also became active in other industrial packaging-related areas. Such was the case of its Pyrkijä subsidiary, which brought the company into the production of large, blow-molded plastic containers in 1972. The company exited that market in 1984, however.

The internationalization of Huhtamäki's packaging business began in the early 1980s, starting with the creation of a German sales subsidiary, Polar Cup GmbH, in 1979 but especially with the purchase of the United Kingdom's DRG Cups & Containers in 1982. In that year, also, Huhtamäki moved into France, buying up a local distributor to the foodservice industry in order to create Polar Cup France.

Huhtamäki made an initial attempt to crack the U.S. market in the early 1980s as well, with an offer to acquire Maryland Cup Corporation, then the leading paper cup maker in the country. That bid failed, however; instead, the company turned to the Asian market, setting up a joint venture, Polarcup Singapore, in 1983. Back in Europe, Huhtamäki continued its geographical spread with the purchase of Spain's Pallarès Group in 1985. That company was then renamed as Polarcup Spain. In that year, the company made a brief foray into the market for aluminum aerosol cans, through Printal, but exited that operation in 1988. In 1986, Huhtamäki regrouped its consumer-oriented packaging businesses under a single name, Polarcup.

Global Niche Leadership in the New Century

Huhtumaki continued to expand its packaging holdings into the late 1980s, buying up Germany's Bellaplast in 1987, then turning to Australia and New Zealand with the purchase of Lilypak in 1988. The Lily brand name then became one of the company's core brands. In 1991, the company added new operations in The Netherlands and the United Kingdom through the purchase of Sweetheart International. Two years later, Huhtamäki added the rigid plastics operations of France's Carnaud Metalbox, giving it new production facilities in the United Kingdom, Portugal, Italy, and France.

By 1994, packaging had emerged as the second largest—although least known—part of Huhtamäki's business, accounting for nearly one-third of its revenues. In 1996, Huhtamäki took the decision to restructure the company entirely around its packaging operations, a move that placed Huhtamäki in direct operational control of its business since the 1930s. In that year, the company sold off its Leiras pharmaceutical business to Germany's Schering AG. That sale was quickly followed by the breakup of the Leaf candy business into two halves, consisting of Leaf's North American operations on one side, and its European and Asian business on the other. The former was then sold to Hershey in the United States, while The Netherlands' CSM acquired the latter.

With a war chest approaching EUR 1 billion, Huhtamäki now set out to remake itself as a global packaging leader. The company began an extended acquisition campaign that more than tripled its revenues and made it a clear-cut leader in several niche categories. The company's first acquisitions came in 1997, with the purchases of Pacific World Packaging, active in Australia and Hong Kong; Monservizio Bibo, based in Italy; and Turkey's Gûven Plastik.

The following year, Huhtamäki at last made its packaging entry into the United States, buying up that country's Sealright Inc. for $202 million. The purchase added Sealright's dominance for the North American ice cream packaging market to Huhtamäki's own leading positions in Europe and Asia, making it the world's top ice cream packaging company. That year, also, the company acquired Tetra Corporation, another U.S.

Key Dates:

1920: Heikki Huhtamäki founds a confectionery company in Kokkola, Finland; the company later diversifies into other food products, and develops in-house packaging operations.

1960: Huhtamäki acquires Mensa, a Finnish paper food container producer as a step toward full-fledged packaging operations; Huhtamäki lists on the Helsinki Stock Exchange.

1962: The company forms a dedicated packaging business, Pakkaus Oy.

1965: The company forms Polarpak and begins production of thermoform plastics, which leads to its exit from the metal packaging market.

1972: The company begins production of blow-molded plastic containers (exits in 1984).

1979: Internationalization begins with the creation of a German subsidiary.

1982: The company acquires DRG Cups & Containers in the United Kingdom; Polarcup France is established.

1985: The company acquires Pallares of Spain, which becomes Polarcup Spain.

1988: The company acquires Lilypak with operations in Australia and New Zealand.

1989: The company begins to sell off some holdings to focus on pharmaceuticals, confectionery, and packaging.

1991: The United Kingdom's Sweetheart International is acquired.

1996: The company sells pharmaceutical and candy companies to focus on packaging products.

1999: The company acquires Van Leer Packaging, becoming one of the world's leading packaging groups, and changes its name to Huhtamäki Van Leer.

2000: The sell-off of nonconsumer goods packaging operations is initiated.

2001: The company sells off Van Leer's industrial packaging operations and is renamed Huhtumäki.

company. The company next turned to Brazil, buying up that country's Brasholanda.

In the meantime, Huhtamäki made a leap into the big leagues with the 1999 purchase of Royal Packaging Industries Van Leer. Based in The Netherlands, Van Leer had been founded as a steel drum maker in 1919 before going on to become one of the world's leading consumer and industrial packaging producers. The addition of Van Leer, which cost Huhtamäki nearly EUR 1 billion, gave Huhtamäki control of the U.S.-based Chinet brand, and placed it as one of the top two leading producers of molded fiber packaging in the world.

The company took on a new name in 1999 as Huhtamäki Van Leer—by 2001, however, the company simplified its name again to Huhtamäki Oyj. Meanwhile, Huhtamäki made a series

of bolt-on acquisitions to solidify its hold in the local, regional, and global markets. In the United States, the company bought Packaging Resources Inc. and the Malvern Flexibles operations of Graphic Packaging in 2000, while in South Africa that year the company acquired Mono Containers. The company began its sell-off of Van Leer's nonconsumer business that year, a process completed in 2001 with the sale of its industrial packaging business to the United States' Grief. Following the group's name change, it also decided to bring all of its operations under the single Huhtamäki banner.

Huhtamäki ended its acquisition drive that year, and instead began concentrating on integrating its operations and in developing new packaging types and technologies. That effort paid off with the début of a new self-venting film for ready meal packaging products at the end of 2003. The company also launched a new plastics-based baby food container, introduced first to the French market through Danone's Bledina baby foods brand. The company had not given up on external growth, however. In 2004, the company opened a new flexible packaging plant in Vietnam, which began producing packaging products for the domestic market there. Huhtamäki had successfully transformed itself from its confectionery to a place among the packaging industry's global leaders.

Principal Subsidiaries

Huhtamäki (Norway) Holdings A/S; Huhtamäki (NZ) Holdings Ltd; Huhtamäki (Vietnam) Ltd; Huhtamäki Americas, Inc.; Huhtamäki Anglo Holding; Huhtamäki Argentina S.A.; Huhtamäki Australia Limited; Huhtamäki do Brasil Ltda.; Huhtamäki Egypt Ltd; Huhtamäki Finance B.V.; Huhtamäki Holdings France SNC; Huhtamäki Holdings Pty Ltd (Australia); Huhtamäki Hungary Kft; Huhtamäki Istanbul Ambalaj Sanayi A.S. (Turkey); Huhtamäki Portugal SGPS, Lda; Huhtamäki S.p.A (Italy); Huhtamäki Singapore Pte. Ltd; Huhtamäki South Africa (Pty) Ltd.; Huhtamäki Sweden Holding AB; Laminor S.A. (Brazil); Pacific World Packaging (International) Ltd. (Hong Kong); Partner Polarcup Oy.

Principal Competitors

Nippon Unipac Holding; Tetra Laval Group; Tetra Pak Schweiz AG; M-real Corporation; Fort James Corporation; Nampak Ltd.; Daiwa Can Co.; American Greetings Corporation.

Further Reading

Brown-Humes, Christopher, "Huhtamäki Sells Off Industrial Division," *Financial Times,* October 31, 2000, p. 34.

George, Nicholas, "Finnish Group to Focus on Growth," *Financial Times,* May 24, 2000, p. 33.

"Huhtamäki Gets All Steamed Up," *Packaging Today International,* December 2003, p. 13.

"Huhtamäki Opens Flexible Packaging Facility in Vietnam," *Plastics in Packaging UK,* May 10, 2004.

"Huhtamäki's US Operations to Adopt Single Name," *Packaging Magazine,* June 7, 2001.

—M.L. Cohen

Making a Difference in Healthcare™

IDX Systems Corporation

40 IDX Drive
Burlington, Vermont 05402-1070
U.S.A.
Telephone: (802) 862-1022
Toll Free: (888) 439-6584
Fax: (802) 862-6848
Web site: http://www.idx.com

Public Company
Incorporated: 1969
Employees: 2,048
Sales: $399.2 million
Stock Exchanges: NASDAQ
Ticker Symbol: IDXC
NAIC: 541512 Computer Systems Design Services;
   511210 Software Publishers

IDX Systems Corporation is a leading healthcare information technology company that offers software, hardware, and related services to the likes of academic medical centers, hospitals, clinics, and management service organizations. The company's products include electronic medical record software and information systems that address functions like billing, scheduling, and patient registration. According to IDX, some 138,000 physicians use the company's practice management software to provide more efficient care to their patients. In addition to its headquarters in Burlington, Vermont, IDX has regional offices in Arlington, Virginia; Atlanta; Boston; Chicago; Dallas; Deerfield Beach, Florida; Louisville, Kentucky; San Diego; San Francisco; Seattle; and London.

Establishing a Foothold: 1969–79

Robert Hoehl and Richard E. Tarrant founded IDX on June 2, 1969 in Burlington, Vermont. Then known as Burlington Data Processing Inc. (BDP), the company initially managed accounting, billing, and payroll for other firms. Hoehl and Tarrant, who both played basketball for Saint Michael's College in Vermont and then went to work for IBM as marketing representatives, used $12,500 to start their own enterprise.

BDP quickly became involved in the healthcare industry. In its June 1998 issue, *Business Digest* revisited a 1985 article about Hoehl and Tarrant that included comments from Dr. Henry Tufo, one of BDP's first customers. Tufo recalled how Hoehl and Tarrant outbid a number of national firms to build an information system for the new University Health Center during the 1970s. At the time, the field of medicine was evolving from a so-called cottage industry into one characterized by physician groups.

Joking that their low bid may have stemmed from a relative lack of industry experience at the time, Tufo praised the entrepreneurs, calling Hoehl "the best practical computer mind I've ever run into" and stating that Tarrant "understands his business and has the talent to sell ice cream to the Eskimos."

In 1970, BDP rolled out what it described as the first open item physician billing system. The following year the company declared that the healthcare industry would be its specialty and it embarked on a path of steady growth that continued into the late 1970s. In 1978, an important development occurred when BDP merged with Interpretive Data Systems, a Boston firm with similar capabilities.

Formed in 1974 by Paul Egerman and Terry Ragon, Interpretive Data Systems developed medical software that operated on Digital Equipment Corporation (DEC) mini-computers. Prior to merging with BDP, Interpretive Data Systems recorded several noteworthy accomplishments. In 1975, the company developed the National Timesharing Center in Boston, and the following year it installed the first physician billing system that operated on mini-computers. As a result of the merger between BDP and Interpretive Data Systems, a new enterprise called Interpretive Data Systems Inc. (IDS) was formed. That same year, an IDS office was established in Boston and the IDS Systems Group was created to serve small physician group practices.

Initial Growth and Expansion: 1980–94

Computer workstations with graphical capabilities appeared in growing numbers across all industries during the 1980s, and healthcare was no exception. In 1980, IDS rolled out an interfacing standard for labs and pharmacies called HL7. The following year, the company began offering comprehensive software systems for large healthcare organizations. It also was in

189

Company Perspectives:

IDX Systems Corporation uses information technology to maximize value in the delivery of healthcare by improving the quality of patient service, enhancing medical outcomes, and reducing the cost of care. Supporting those objectives is a broad range of complementary, functionally rich, and highly integrated products that are proven across care settings and organizational models.

1981 that IDS moved into new headquarters in Burlington, Vermont, at 1500 Shelburne Road.

A period of regional expansion took place during the early 1980s, as IDS continued to grow by serving new markets and introducing new products. The company installed its first hospital information system in 1984. More milestones were reached the following year when IDS introduced an integrated system for ambulatory care, hospitals, and managed care, as well as an integrated electronic medical record (EMR) application. Initially named IDX Electronic Medical Record, the application would eventually become the company's Clinical Repository System (CRS).

By late 1985, IDS had sales of $20 million and employed approximately 200 people. In addition to its Vermont headquarters, the company had established offices in Dallas, Chicago, Philadelphia, and San Francisco. At this time, IDS's sales force was broken down into separate groups that concentrated on specific vertical segments like billing or scheduling applications. By the end of the 1980s, the company, now known as IDX Corporation, had moved into a new headquarters facility at 1400 Shelburne Road in Burlington.

IDX began the 1990s with 425 employees. In 1991 the company began marketing a radiology information system called IDXrad. Formerly named DECrad, the system was originally created by the Radiology Information System Consortium and Digital Equipment Corporation. In 1992, IDX Corporation changed its name to IDX Systems Corporation. The following year, the company made its applications capable of running on both IBM and Digital platforms. It also continued to expand, opening a new office in San Diego. A new Atlanta office was established in 1994, when IDX celebrated 25 years of operations.

During its silver anniversary year, IDX paid $23 million for a 14-story building in Boston at 116 Huntington Avenue. Built in 1991, 60 percent of the building was already occupied by other clients. The purchase enabled IDX to move some 200 workers from Brookline, Massachusetts, to the new location in 1995.

Going Public in 1995

IDX recorded revenues of $128.1 million in 1995 and employed 1,095 workers. In November of that year, the company went public. Dr. Henry Tufo, who had been among the company's first clients some 25 years before, was named chief operating officer in 1995. In the June 1998 issue of *Business Digest*, Richard Tarrant commented on how going public affected IDX. "Going public helped us focus," he explained. "One

of the best parts—and I never would have expected this about going public—was that, while I had heard all the bad things about dealing with Wall Street and stockholders—the pressures, quarterly numbers, all the stuff that's hard—what nobody ever said is that they will ask great questions. Wall Street analysts ask great questions. They are very smart people. They focus on an industry. They study the competition. They really make you answer the tough questions. It's had a side benefit that I never would have expected."

By this time in IDX's history, the company had shifted its focus from individual products that addressed specific functions like billing or scheduling for doctors' offices to broader systems and methodologies. These changes mirrored the maturation of healthcare from a fragmented industry to one that included so-called integrated delivery networks comprised of clinics, hospitals, home healthcare agencies, and managed care companies. Along these lines, IDX's sales force was no longer broken down into different groups that focused on different vertical markets.

IDX was experiencing rapid growth during the mid-1990s. In addition to its Vermont headquarters and an international site in the United Kingdom, the company had offices in San Francisco; San Diego; Seattle; Louisville, Kentucky; Deerfield Beach, Florida; Dallas; Chicago; Boston; Arlington, Virginia; and Atlanta.

As IDX evolved from a small firm to a large public enterprise, Tarrant found it challenging to switch to a new style of management. In the same *Business Digest* article, he said: "An entrepreneur kind of manages everything him- or herself, knows where everything is, can do everything. Entrepreneurs can do a job better than someone they're going to hire, but they need someone to help them. I pride myself on having made the transition to professional management, where the people who report to me are better at what they do than I could ever be. I couldn't do any of their jobs. In fact, I don't even manage day-to-day stuff. That's the chief operating officer's stuff. As the CEO, I'm responsible for strategy, direction, Wall Street, the investors and waving the flag when we're dealing with big customers. You know, a lot of times, with a CEO, if you just show up, it means something."

Sales reached $251.4 million in 1997. That year, the company acquired PHAMIS Inc., a Seattle-based hospital information systems company founded by Drs. Mark Wheeler and Malcolm Gleser. With its LastWord patient record system, PHAMIS bolstered IDX's capabilities to serve integrated healthcare systems that included hospitals and clinics.

At this point in IDX's history, the company's growth frequently included the acquisition of other firms. One of the biggest challenges for Tarrant was not coming up with resources to acquire other technology companies, but figuring out which ones to acquire and how to combine them in meaningful ways. Acquisitions in 1998 included Laureate Enterprises Inc., a project and process consulting services firm for LastWord users, as well as Trego Systems Inc., a company that had developed a contract management system for integrated delivery networks.

In 1998, IDX released a Web-based practice management system called IDXsite. The company also established a new

Key Dates:

1969: Robert Hoehl and Richard E. Tarrant establish Burlington Data Processing Inc. (BDP).
1970: BDP rolls out an open item physician billing system.
1971: The company declares healthcare as its specialty.
1978: BDP merges with Interpretive Data Systems, a Boston firm with similar capabilities, forming Interpretive Data Systems Inc. (IDS).
1981: IDS moves to new headquarters in Burlington, Vermont.
1989: The company, now known as IDX Corporation, moves into a new headquarters facility in Burlington.
1992: IDX Corporation changes its name to IDX Systems Corporation.
1995: IDX goes public.
2001: IDX is selected to spearhead a $9.2 million, three-year project for the U.S. Commerce Department's National Institute of Standards and Technology (NIST) Advanced Technology Program.
2003: President and Chief Operating Officer James Crook, Jr., is named CEO; net income skyrockets to $58 million on sales of $399.2 million.

business unit called The Huntington Group (THG) to serve as its consulting arm. THG provided a variety of technology and application-related consulting services in areas like systems integration and information-driven operational redesign. Revenues reached $321.7 million in 1998, about 15 percent of which was devoted to research and development initiatives. IDX employed 2,000 people, 650 of whom worked at IDX's Vermont headquarters, which was made up of two buildings with 143,000 square feet of space.

Late in the year, the company announced a $28.6 million expansion plan for its Vermont campus. Scheduled for completion in 2003, the plans included a five-story, 240,000-square-foot building and a parking garage capable of accommodating 1,400 cars. The expansion plan, which was supported by nearly $9 million in state tax incentives, meant the addition of nearly 1,400 new IDX jobs over four years. In addition, the plan held the potential to create more than 1,000 jobs within the surrounding community and nearly 1,000 new homes. By this time, IDX had evolved into the third-largest player in its industry. While the company's competitors served more hospitals, IDX had made significant inroads with clinics and physician practices and served about 75 percent of U.S. medical schools.

IDX capped off the 1990s by celebrating 30 years of operations. However, the company posted an $8 million loss on sales of $341 million in 1999. Also in that year, James H. Crook Jr. was named president and chief operating officer, responsible for an employee base that had grown to approximately 3,000 people.

Two acquisitions were made in 1999. These included EDiX Corporation, a medical transcription service provider serving hospitals and large medical groups, and ChannelHealth, a Web-based service provider for the healthcare market. As part of the latter acquisition, ChannelHealth became an IDX subsidiary, enabling the company to offer more Web-based products and services to physicians and their patients.

In December 1999, IDX announced that it had formed a strategic partnership with ProxyMed Inc., a provider of network-based connectivity services for the healthcare industry. The partnership allowed clients to engage in various types of transactions, including online insurance claims processing.

Challenges and Achievements in the New Century

The call for automation was a boon for healthcare information technology companies in the 1980s and 1990s. However, the dawn of the 21st century found many of these firms struggling amidst Y2K-related problems, Medicare reimbursement cuts, and subsequent delays and cutbacks in spending by healthcare providers. IDX was no exception. In 2000, the company withstood a $36 million loss on revenues of $341.9 million and cut roughly 250 jobs. IDX also sought to save $10 million by eliminating under-performing products for hospital-owned physician groups, as well as some of its offerings for the managed care market.

Despite this grim news, IDX agreed to lease 40 percent of Seattle's newest office building in April of 2000. Named IDX Tower at Fourth and Madison, the 40-story structure spanned 810,000 square feet. Approximately 1,500 IDX employees were to move from an office at 1001 Fourth Avenue to the new building when it was completed in 2003. IDX also pressed on with the expansion of its Burlington campus.

In July 2000, IDX agreed to sell ChannelHealth Inc. to Libertyville, Illinois-based Allscripts Inc., a developer of software that physicians used to submit patient prescription information to pharmacies. According to the Associated Press, the deal was worth $250 million in stock, making IDX Allscripts' largest shareholder. The sale was beneficial to both sides. Allscripts gained access to IDX's large base of physician customers and expanded its sales channel, while IDX rid itself of the money-losing ChannelHealth.

In 2001, sales climbed to $379.9 million and employees numbered 4,200. However, the company registered a loss of $8.6 million amidst weak economic conditions. IDX also restructured in 2001, putting less emphasis on its Enterprise Solutions Division, which had accounted for some 40 percent of revenues in 2001.

While sales had steadily improved during 2001, IDX was negatively affected by the terrorist attacks against the United States on September 11, 2001. In their wake, the company was forced to eliminate 200 jobs. In a September 28, 2001, Associated Press story, Richard Tarrant said: "The real issue here is that after September 11, meetings stopped, work stopped. We have a counseling program going on for people who want to talk about air travel. There are some people who will not get on airplanes. . . . We're giving them time to reconcile that or see if there are other positions they can fill."

One positive development in 2001 came midway through the year, when IDX and Stentor Inc., a medical image distribution firm based in Silicon Valley, joined forces to offer clients a medical image and information management system. Based on a hosted, or application service provider model, the system would allow healthcare providers to bypass the hefty costs normally required to implement picture and archive communications systems (PACS), which enable doctors and clinical staff to transmit, view, and store X-rays via computer. The partnership involved the integration of Stentor's iSite system with IDX's Imaging Suite and ConnectR products. In its issue for June 7, 2001, *Market News Publishing* said the proposed system would be ''an integrated solution for image and information management, without redundancy of data or function. The resulting solution is an entirely Web-based system covering most aspects of the radiology enterprise—from registration and scheduling through the patient scanning process to diagnostic interpretation and reporting, onto archive storage and image/report distribution to referring physicians.''

Another significant achievement came in December 2001, when IDX was selected to spearhead a three-year project for the U.S. Commerce Department's National Institute of Standards and Technology (NIST) Advanced Technology Program. Worth $9.2 million, IDX explained that the project would ''fund the development of software infrastructure aimed at improving healthcare quality and reducing medical errors by enabling the creation, distribution and application of computable clinical practice guidelines (or CPGs—best practice benchmarks that provide clinicians with patient-specific recommendations at the point of care).''

By early 2002, conditions were again improving at IDX, as the company continued to cut costs. That year, sales reached $460.1 million, the company posted net income of nearly $10.0 million, and IDX's employee ranks swelled to 4,900. IDX also unveiled its Carecast enterprise clinical information system, which was based on the company's pioneering LastWord system that had been developed many years before.

In October, IDX announced that President and Chief Operating Officer James Crook, Jr., would assume the role of CEO in January 2003, replacing Richard Tarrant, who would become chairman. Robert Hoehl, who had been serving as IDX's chairman, became vice-chairman. At this time, IDX systems were in place at some 3,200 locations.

In June 2003, IDX sold EDiX to Franklin, Tennessee-based Total eMed, a medical transcription services provider. The company's employee base then fell to 2,100 workers. By late 2003, things were going well for IDX. The company served a customer base of 138,000 physicians and its solutions were installed at 3,300 sites across the United States, Canada, and the United Kingdom. Tarrant told the Associated Press that IDX had made corrections to change the company's course from the previous three years, including the addition of new management personnel and a comprehensive product suite that included IDX Flowcast, IDX Groupcast, IDX Carecast, IDX Imagecast, and EdiX. Although sales fell to $399.2 million in 2003, IDX's net income skyrocketed to $58 million—up from $10 million the previous year. One encouraging development was a contract to provide a clinical information system to Britain's national health system. According to IDX CEO Jim Crook, the project gave the company its first real foothold for international expansion.

Two key leadership appointments were made at IDX in early 2004. First, Thomas W. Butts was named president and chief operating officer. In addition, Stephen C. Gorman was named president and general manager of IDX Groupcast. As IDX headed toward the mid-2000s, the future appeared to be bright. In a February 12, 2004, Associated Press story, CEO Jim Crook provided an optimistic outlook, stating: ''Today, we're performing better, delivering better results for our customers than we have last year and three years ago, and next year we'll be delivering better results than we are today.''

Principal Competitors

Cerner Corporation; Eclipsys Corporation; McKesson Corporation.

Further Reading

Graff, Christopher, ''Republican Richard Tarrant Will Not Be Candidate for U.S. Senate,'' *Associated Press,* February 9, 2004.

''IDX Gets New CEO,'' *Associated Press,* October 8, 2002.

''IDX Planning to Hire 1,000,'' *Boston Globe,* November 7, 1998.

''Integrated Research, IDX Systems Expand Partnership,'' *AsiaPulse News,* December 4, 2003.

Lindauer Simmon, Virginia, ''IDX Revisited,'' *Business Digest,* June 1998.

McCormack, John, ''Ringing out the Century with a Whimper,'' *Health Data Management,* June 1999.

Miller, James P., ''Libertyville, Ill., Online Prescriptions Firm to Purchase Software Company,'' *Knight Ridder/Tribune Business News,* July 14, 2000.

''Newest 40-Story Building Will Be Called IDX Tower,'' *Puget Sound Business Journal,* April 14, 2000.

''ProxyMed and IDX Sign Key E-commerce Customer,'' *South Florida Business Journal,* December 3, 1999.

''Software Firm's Expansion Seen Having Big Impact,'' *Associated Press,* March 22, 1999.

—Paul R. Greenland

Industria de Diseño Textil S.A.

Edificio Inditex, Avda de la Dip
Arteijo A Coruna
E-15142
Spain
Telephone: (+34) 981 18 54 00
Fax: (+34) 981 18 54 54
Web site: http://www.inditex.com

Public Company
Incorporated: 1963
Employees: 39,760
Sales: EUR 4.59 billion ($5.09 billion)(2003)
Stock Exchanges: Madrid
Ticker Symbol: ITX
NAIC: 315230 Women's and Girls' Cut and Sew Apparel
   Manufacturing; 315220 Men's and Boys' Cut and
   Sew Apparel Manufacturing; 315291 Infants' Cut and
   Sew Apparel Manufacturing; 424310 Piece Goods,
   Notions, and Other Dry Goods Merchant Wholesalers;
   424340 Footwear Merchant Wholesalers; 448140
   Family Clothing Stores; 448210 Shoe Stores; 522291
   Consumer Lending; 531210 Offices of Real Estate
   Agents and Brokers; 551112 Offices of Other Holding
   Companies

Industria de Diseño Textil S.A., also known as The Inditex Group, is one of the world's leading and fastest-growing producer and retailer of clothing fashions. Based in the small Spanish town of A Coruna, Inditex operates more than 2,000 stores worldwide under seven retail formats. The most well-known of these is the Zara chain of more than 600 clothing stores, the company's flagship, accounting for some three-quarters of the group's sales. Other retail formats include the youth-oriented Pull and Bear, the higher-end Massimo Dutti, Bershka, Stradivarius, the lingerie chain Oysho, and Zara's Home, launched in 2003 to feature home furnishings and accessories. The company has pursued an extremely aggressive expansion program, more than doubling its number of stores since 1999. In 2003 alone, the company added more than 360 stores and expects to open a similar number in 2004. Setting Inditex apart from competitors such as the Gap and H&M is its extremely short design-to-store turnaround times. The company renews its collection every two weeks, producing some 12,000 items each year from its 16 factories in Spain and elsewhere. By eliminating advertising spending, the company has avoided outsourcing its production to third-party producers, reducing its turnaround times while also maintaining a low pricing policy. Inditex is led by founder, chairman, and majority shareholder Amancio Ortega Gaona. The company, which posted sales of nearly EUR 4.6 billion ($5.1 billion) in 2003, is listed on the Bolsa de Madrid.

Kitchen Table Designs in the 1960s

Amancio Ortega Gaono got his start in the clothing business at the age of 13, when he went to work for a local A Coruna shirtmaker delivering the shop's goods, which included lingerie and dressing gowns. Ortega worked his way up to become an assistant manager, then shop manager, by the early 1960s. These positions gave Ortega experience not only in dealing directly with customers but also in purchasing fabrics and other materials for the shop's line of apparel.

Working out of his sister's home, Ortega began developing his own designs. One day in the early 1960s, he hit upon the formula that was to become central to the operations of Inditex: that of reproducing popular fashions using less expensive materials in order to sell high-demand clothing items at lower prices. Ortega left his job and set up in business with just 5,000 pesetas (the equivalent of $25). Legend has it that Ortega's first project was to remake a popular but expensive dressing gown. Ortega cut the pattern himself, then, with the help of his brother and sister, began producing the dressing gown at his sister's kitchen table.

Ortega's first customer was his former employer at the shirtmaker's shop. Before long, Ortega began supplying the dressing gown, as well as a growing range of housecoats and lingerie, to other clothing shops in A Coruna. By 1963, Ortega had saved up enough to open his first factory.

From manufacturing, Ortega soon turned to retail, launching an initial format for his housecoats and lingerie in the early

Company Perspectives:

The Inditex Group is made up of almost a hundred companies dealing with activities related to textile design, production and distribution. Its unique management methods, based on innovation and flexibility, and its successes, have turned Inditex into one of the world's largest fashion Groups. Its vision of fashion—creativity and quality design together with a rapid response to market demands—have allowed for fast international expansion and an excellent response to its sales concept.

1970s. In 1975, however, Ortega, then 39 years old, hit upon the formula that was to bring him his biggest success. In that year, Ortega opened a new retail store called Zara, which featured low-priced lookalike products of popular, higher-end clothing fashions.

The store proved a success, and the following year Ortega incorporated his business under the name Goasam and began opening more Zara stores in Spain. Despite the stores' growing popularity, Ortega himself remained decidedly behind the scenes, avoiding the spotlight and developing a reputation for himself as a recluse—no photographs of Ortega were made publicly available until 2001.

Computing Success in the 1980s

By the early 1980s, Ortega had begun formulating a new type of design and distribution model. The clothing industry followed design and production processes that required long lead times, often up to six months, between the initial design of a garment and its delivery to retailers. This model effectively limited manufacturers and distributors to just two or three collections per year. Predicting consumer tastes ahead of time presented inherent difficulties, and producers and distributors faced the constant risk of becoming saddled with unsold inventory.

Ortega sought a means of breaking the model by creating what he called "instant fashions" that allowed him to quickly respond to shifts in consumer tastes and to newly emerging trends. Ortega's dream remained unfulfilled, however, until he met up with José Maria Castellano. A computer expert, Castellano had worked in Aegon Espana's information technology department before becoming chief financial officer for a Spanish subsidiary of ConAgra. Castellano joined Ortega in 1984 and set to work developing a distribution model that revolutionized the global clothing industry.

Under Castellano's computerized system, the company reduced its design to distribution process to just 10 to 15 days. Rather than placing the design burden on a single designer, the company developed its own in-house team of designers—more than 200 by the turn of the 21st century—who began developing clothes based on popular fashions, while at the same time producing the company's own designs. In this way, the team was able to respond almost immediately to emerging consumer trends as well as to the demands of the company's own customers—for instance, by adding new colors or patterns to existing designs. State-of-the-art production and warehousing procedures, as well as the installation of computerized inventory systems linking stores to the company's growing number of factories, enabled the company to avoid taking on the risk and capital outlay of developing and maintaining a large back inventory.

The leaner, more responsive company—which adopted the name of Industria de Diseño Textil S.A., or Inditex, in 1985—captured the attention of Spanish shoppers. By the end of the decade, the company had opened more than 80 Zara stores in Spain. The company's instant fashion model, which completely rotated its retail stock every two weeks, also encouraged customers to return often to its stores, with delivery day becoming known as "Z-day" in some markets. The knowledge that clothing items would not be available for very long also encouraged shoppers to make their purchases more quickly.

The success of the Zara model in Spain led Inditex to the international market at the end of the 1980s. In 1988, the company opened its first foreign store in Oporto, Portugal. The following year, Inditex moved into the United States. Success in that market remained elusive, however, and at the beginning of the 2000s, the company had opened just six U.S. stores. A more receptive market for the Zara format existed in France, which Inditex entered in 1990. The company quickly began adding new stores in major city centers throughout the country.

Through the 1990s, Inditex added a steady stream of new markets. The company entered Mexico in 1992, Greece in 1993, Belgium and Sweden in 1994, Malta in 1995, and Cyprus in 1996. In the late 1990s, Inditex stepped up the pace of its international expansion, adding Israel, Norway, Turkey, and Japan (the latter in a joint-venture with a local partner) in 1997, then, in 1998, moved into Argentina, the United Kingdom, and Venezuela. While the bulk of the group's stores remained company owned, in certain markets, such as the Middle East, starting in 1998, Inditex's expansion took place through franchise agreements with local distributors. By 2000, Inditex had added another dozen or so countries to its range of operations, including Germany, the Netherlands, and Eastern European markets including Poland.

Multiple Retail Formats in the New Century

At the same time as Inditex pursued its geographic expansion, it also began expanding beyond its flagship Zara retail format. The company launched the Kiddy's Class children's wear format as a subgroup of the main Zara concept in the early 1990s. In 1991, the company added an entirely new retail format, Pull & Bear, which began providing "urban" fashions. By the beginning of the 2000s, the Pull & Bear chain had grown to 300 stores in nearly 20 countries; it also produced its own offshoot format, Often, targeting the 20- to 45-year-old men's segment, in 2003.

Inditex went upscale in 1991 when it bought 65 percent of the Massimo Dutti group. Inditex took full control of Massimo Dutti in 1995 and began building it into a chain of nearly 300 stores in 23 countries. While Massimo Dutti appealed to a more sophisticated men's and women's fashions market, the company targeted the young female market in 1998 with the

Key Dates:

1963: Amancio Ortega Gaona begins producing house-coats and lingerie in his sister's home in A Coruna, Spain, then later opens his own factory and retail stores.

1975: Ortega launches a new retail format, Zara, which produces low-priced copies of popular fashions.

1984: José Marie Castellano joins the company as CEO and develops a computerized systems for "instant fashions" concept.

1985: The company becomes Industria de Diseño Textil S.A., or the Inditex Group.

1988: The company expands internationally with the opening of a store in Oporto, Portugal.

1989: The company enters the U.S. market.

1990: Inditex enters the French market.

1991: Pull & Bear retail format is launched and 65% of Massimo Dutti is acquired.

1995: The company acquires full control of Massimo Dutti.

1998: The Bershka retail format is introduced.

2001: Inditex goes public on the Bolsa de Madrid.

2004: The company tops 2,000 stores worldwide with plans to open more than 350 new stores during the year.

creation of a new format, Bershka. That retail chain quickly evolved into a network of more than 200 stores operating in 11 countries.

Inditex continued adding new formats at the turn of the 21st century. In 1999, the company acquired Stradivarius, a youth fashion chain present in nine countries. In 2001, Inditex added its lingerie format, Oysho. In 2003, Inditex moved beyond the garment trade for the first time, launching its own home furnishings concept, Zara's Home.

Meanwhile, Inditex had begun a corporate evolution as well. As Ortega approached retirement, and no members of his immediate family appeared likely to succeed him in the business, the company looked to the public market to ensure its future. In 2001, Inditex listed its stock on the Bolsa de Madrid, one of the most successful initial public offerings of the year. Ortega's sale

of more than 20 percent of his holding in Inditex made him Spain's wealthiest man, with a fortune estimated to be worth more than EUR 4.6 billion.

Inditex moved to a new corporate headquarters in Arteixo, outside of A Coruna in 2000. In 2002, the company began construction on a state-of-the-art logistics center in Zaragoza. At the same time, Inditex continued adding to its array of international markets, opening stores in Luxembourg, Iceland, Ireland, Jordan, and Puerto Rico in 2001; Switzerland, Finland, El Salvador, and Singapore in 2002; and Hong Kong in 2003. By mid-2004, Inditex's global operation spanned more than 2,000 stores, and its sales had neared EUR 4.6 billion ($5.1 billion), making it one of the world's leading clothing retailers.

Principal Divisions

Bershka; Massimo Dutti; Zara; Kiddy's Class; Oysho; Pull & Bear; Stradivarius; Zara Home.

Principal Competitors

The Gap Inc.; Hennes & Mauritz AB; Benetton Group S.p.A.; Vivarte; Gruppo Coin S.p.A.; Kiabi S.A.; La Redoute; Charles Vogele Holding AG; Peek und Cloppenburg KG; Somfy International S.A.; Cortefiel SA; Mango S.A.

Further Reading

Barker, Barbara, "Inside the Inditex Empire," *WWD*, July 30, 2002, p. 10.

——, "Spanish Clothing Manufacturer Inditex Enters New Territory with Zara Home," *HFN: The Weekly Newspaper for the Home Furnishing Network*, June 16, 2003, p. 4.

Crawford, Leslie, "Spanish Recluse Tailors New Way to Do Business," *Financial Times*, April 28, 2001, p. 16.

Heller, Richard, "Galician Beauty," *Forbes*, May 28, 2001, p. 98.

Kassam, Isabelle, "Pounds 7bn Empire Born on a Kitchen Table," *Sun*, May 26, 2001, p. 56.

Levitt, Joshua, "Expansion Plan Hits Inditex's Profit Margin," *Financial Times*, December 12, 2003, p. 26.

"The Mark of Zara," *Business Week*, May 29, 2000, p. 98.

Murphy, Robert, "Inditex See Net Rise 2 Percent," *WWD*, March 25, 2004, p. 3.

Walker, Jane, "Made to Measure," *Time International*, May 21, 2001, p. 56.

—M.L. Cohen

Initial Security

Initial Security

3355 Cherry Ridge, Suite 200
San Antonio, Texas 78230
U.S.A.
Telephone: (210) 349-6321
Toll Free: (800) 683-7771
Fax: (210) 349-0213
Web site: http://www.initialsecurity.com

Wholly Owned Subsidiary of Rentokil Group plc
Founded: 1928
Employees: 8,000
Gross Billings: $261.9 million
NAIC: 561612 Security Guards and Patrol Services

Initial Security, a San Antonio-based subsidiary of British business-to-business service company Rentokil Initial PLC, offers a range of security services: investigation, patrol services, security officers, special event security, strike coverage, and consulting services. The company employs a proprietary 24-hour personnel management system called SystemsWatch, which protects a site by merging an automated check-in system with a real-time personnel database and service records. In this way, Initial Security can improve site safety and service as well as provide accurate billing to customers. At the heart of the system are mandatory check-in times that must be met by on-site officers. Should they fail to check in, the personnel database can quickly locate the closest back-up officer to be dispatched to the site. The timekeeping function of SystemsWatch is then leveraged on the accounting side to provide customers with a detailed listing of times and types of services provided. Initial Security employs 14,000 security officers in North America, working out of 60 U.S. and Canadian branch offices. The company also has 22,000 security officers working internationally.

1928 Origins

The roots of Initial Security started in 1928 when 18-year-old Stanley Sylvester Smith opened a one-man private detective agency in San Antonio, setting up shop in the recently opened Milam Building (the first air-conditioned building in the world).

Despite his youth, Smith had learned the business from another investigator and decided to strike out on his own. Over the years, he developed a steady clientele by forging a solid reputation for competence and honesty. Because many of his assignments required legwork in other parts of the country, he developed alliances with investigators across America. Eventually this network of independent private detectives expanded overseas, leading to the creation of the World Secret Service Association in 1950. Smith became the organization's second president, serving from 1951 to 1952, and 20 years later his contribution to the industry would be recognized when he was named president emeritus of what was now called the World Association of Detectives.

In 1956, a second generation of the Smith family, Stanley's son Sterling, joined the agency. It was Sterling who steered the company toward security services. In 1960, he began to concentrate on the business of providing guard and mobile patrol service in San Antonio, a move that would result in the company adopting the name of Stanley Smith Security. Several years later, in 1968, the company reached a major turning point when it was hired to provide security for San Antonio's World's Fair, officially know as the Texas World Exposition HemisFair.

The idea for a ''Fair of the Americas'' was hatched ten years earlier by a downtown haberdasher named Jerome K. Harris and became part of an effort to commemorate the 250th anniversary of San Antonio's founding. With a Texan in the White House, Lyndon Johnson, the HemisFair received the kind of international backing necessary to make the idea a reality. Although San Antonio's public officials and business leaders were excited about the benefits to the city in hosting a world's fair, they shared a considerable number of security concerns, which fell on the shoulders of Sterling Smith, the head of security. It was a turbulent time in America's history: the Vietnam War was at its height and the civil rights movement had experienced a good deal of violence. Two days before the HemisFair was to open on April 6, civil rights leader Martin Luther King, Jr. was assassinated. Then, on inaugural day, Lady Bird Johnson, representing the president, and Texas Governor John Connally received death threats, requiring extra security measures. After the fair had been open for just two months, Senator Robert Kennedy, an outspoken critic of the Vietnam war, was assassinated.

Company Perspectives:

Our methods are meticulous, but our philosophy is simple: we do it right the first time. Don't wait until something happens to protect your company.

World's Fair of 1968 Leads to Expansion

Stanley Smith Security was involved in the HemisFair from the outset. The event was built on the site of an old city housing development, and the firm was hired to provide security during this phase and was then contracted by construction companies for security support while structures were built and sites developed. Sterling Smith was then named security director for the run of the fair, and the family firm was hired by most of the private pavilions to provide security. As a result of its strong record during the fair, Stanley Smith Security was able to utilize the contacts it made, especially with construction companies, when the fair closed. As these builders began work on projects in other Texas cities, they contacted the company about providing security services in these new locations. As a result, Stanley Smith Security began to open branch offices to service their customers' needs, expanding to Austin, Corpus Christi, and Rio Grande Valley. Later, the company entered the major markets of Houston and Dallas. Four central offices located in four Texas cities were then established to support the business across the state. Stanley Smith Security would also expand south of the border into Mexico, providing ''total security'' services to a major Mexican corporation, which led to a Monterrey-based joint venture with this company to offer security services to the Mexican market.

It was the entry into alarm systems that formed the basis for the company's total security platform, a move that resulted from another major occurrence in the 1960s: the passage of the Bank Act of 1968. Because banks were now required to install security systems and procedures, Stanley Smith Security recognized there was a growing market for alarm systems and decided to become involved in this sector. The company solicited business from some 200 South Texas banks, and about half signed on. This success led to the company's next step, entering the armored car business. A subsidiary to build armor cars was established in Mexico to provide vehicles for both the Mexican and U.S. markets.

With so many security operations in place, Stanley Smith Security looked to become a multi-regional operator in the United States. Much of this expansion was achieved through acquisitions and resulted in major offices being established in such cities as Chicago and Washington, DC. To enjoy further growth, however, the company needed a major supply of funding. After considering the options the Smiths elected to sell the family business to Seattle-based Loomis Armored Car.

Loomis was founded in the 1880s by Leo B. Loomis at a time when armored cars were 50 years in the future. Loomis, armed with a pistol, started out by transporting gold from Alaska mines by dogsled. With the money he earned from the gold rush, he moved to Portland, Oregon, and in 1925 established the Loomis Armored Car Service. The business spread throughout the West, eventually relocated its headquarters to Seattle, added courier services for banking and commercial customers in 1960, and in 1968 went public. Loomis now diversified into the electronic protection sector, establishing a local burglar and fire alarm system for commercial and residential customers. The company also became involved in guard and patrol services, a business that the 1975 acquisition of Stanley Smith Security would greatly enhance.

Selling the company to Loomis was also of strategic value for Stanley Smith Security. Although the company's founder now retired at the age of 65, his son Sterling stayed on to run the business, which retained the family name. With financing from its corporate parent, the company was able to complete a number of acquisitions to achieve further growth. Ownership would change hands in 1979 when Loomis was acquired by Mayne Nickless, an Australian transport company that had diversified into health services and security services. With the backing of its new owners, Stanley Smith Security accelerated its pace of acquisitions and grew even larger. It also took advantage of Mayne Nickless's operations in Canada, where the Australians were already heavily involved in transportation but also operated a small guard service business. This formed a platform for Stanley Smith Security's entry into the Canadian market. While the company was expanding, it was also in some ways contracting: The increased focus on guard services led to the divestiture of other security services.

New Leadership in the 1990s and Beyond

In 1988, the Smith family's connection to the business came to an end when Sterling Smith decided to launch his own company, Sterling Smith Cecurity. Five years later, a third generation of the family became involved in the security field when Sterling's daughter, Julie Smith, joined her father's firm. In 1998, she too would strike out on her own, opting to name her San Antonio company Smith Legacy Security, a tribute to the heritage established by her father and grandfather. Stanley Smith lived until September 7, 2001, dying at the age of 91.

Mayne Nickless did not fare well in the U.S. armored car business, and after a decade of disappointing results sold off Loomis in 1989. Stanley Smith Security, on the other hand, was retained for several more years, but in the mid-1990s became expendable as Mayne Nickless decided to concentrate on its core transportation and logistics businesses. In September 1995, it sold Stanley Smith Security and Barnes Security Services of Canada to Rentokil Group PLC for $51.5 million.

A pest-control business, Rentokil was founded in 1924 by Harold Maxwell Lefroy, a professor of Entomology at Imperial College in London. A few years earlier, Lefroy was enlisted by the government to find a way to eliminate the death watch beetles that infested Westminster Hall, which was uncomfortably close to England's House of Parliament. He developed some wormwood fluids that proved successful, and as a result he received a number of inquiries from people asking if he could provide them with some of his chemical formulations. He and an assistant, Elizabeth Eades, started up a small factory and went into business. He coined the name of the business, Ento-Kill by merging an abbreviation of the Greek word for insect, ''entomon,'' with ''kill.'' Unfortunately for Lefroy, his line of work was highly dangerous: a year later he was killed by poisonous fumes while conducting an experiment. His assistant managed to carry on the business until it was well established. In 1957, Entokill was acquired by British Ratin, a company that specialized in the extermination of rats and mice. The names of the two brands were combined to create the name of the resulting company, Rentokil Group. Starting in the 1970s, the company began to expand geographically and diversify into such areas as health care, office cleaning, plant care, and office machinery maintenance. In 1993, Rentokil became involved in the security business with the acquisition of Securiguard plc. The acquisitions of Stanley Smith Security and Barnes Security extended the business into the North American market.

Rentokil's management decided that the Rentokil name was not suitable for some of its new business lines, including security, and turned to another brand name—"Initial"—it had picked up in the 1996 acquisition of British Electric Traction (BET). This brand started out associated with a London towel rental service launched by American A.P. Bigelow in 1903. Each towel was marked with the customer's initials, hence Bigelow named the business "Initial Towel Supply Company." BET bought a stake in the company in the 1930s, which would proved highly valuable because Initial, in the years following World War II, expanded into Europe, the United States, and Australia. BET bought more of the company and in 1985 acquired a 100 percent interest. BET was a major competitor of Rentokil in the business support services sector and its acquisition, the largest in Rentokil's history, was a major step in growing the company. Among the areas strengthened by the addition of BET, to the benefit of subsidiary Stanley Smith Security, was electronic security.

One of the Rentokil businesses designated to assume the Initial brand was Stanley Smith Security, which on January 1, 1998 officially changed its name to Initial Security, severing its final tie to founder Stanley Smith. Under its new name and new corporate sponsorship, the company expanded steadily over the next several years, completing a number of major acquisitions. In 1999, the company acquired four Houston-based security companies that collectively comprised thirteen branches, with operations spread across Texas, Louisiana, Arkansas, and Tennessee. In 2000, Initial Security bought southern Illinois-based Barton Protective Services, adding to the company's Midwest business, which was further strengthened in 2002 by the acquisition of Industrial Security Specialists Inc., serving the Chicago and Milwaukee markets. In 2003, Initial Security again looked to Chicago, adding the assets of NTC Electronics Inc., a company that designed and installed electronic security systems and which became the foundation for a new division, Initial Electronics. In 2003, Initial Security added the Seattle firm Amerisex and also grew its Canadian business, acquiring Vancouver-based security firm The Inner-Tec Group.

By 2004, Initial Security was one of the top five security firms in the United States. As a result of its spate of acquisitions in 2003, the company reorganized the way the business was divided among regions, splitting the Central Region into two entities, Central and East Central. Responsibilities of senior management were also refined and new executives brought on board as Initial Security positioned itself for even greater growth in the future.

Principal Divisions

Initial Electronics.

Principal Competitors

Allied Security, Inc.; Guardsmark, Inc.; The Wackenhut Corporation.

Further Reading

Freymann, Carlos, "The Fair That Changed San Antonio," *San Antonio Business Journal*, April 4, 2003.
"Loomis Branches Out in Major Way: Armored Car to Protection Services," *Barron's National Business and Financial Weekly*, March 9, 1970, p. 31.
"Obituary: Stanley S. Smith," *W.A.D. News*, October-November-December 2001, p. 20.
Silva, Tricia L., "Smith Legacy Establishing a Secure Niche," *San Antonio Business Journal*, October 23, 1998.

—Ed Dinger

Intercorp Excelle Foods Inc.

1880 Ormont Drive
Toronto, Ontario M9L 2V4
Canada
Telephone: (416) 744-2124
Toll Free: (888) 473-6337
Fax: (416) 744-4369
Web site: http://www.renees.com

Private Company
Incorporated: 1985
Employees: 100 (est.)
Sales: $25 million (2003 est.)
NAIC: 311941 Mayonnaise, Dressing, and Other
    Prepared Sauce Manufacturing

Based in Toronto, Canada, Intercorp Excelle Foods Inc. is a family-owned and operated manufacturer and distributor of more than 300 kinds of salad dressing, dips, meat and steak sauces, marinades, and mayonnaise to the retail and food service markets. Products lines include Renee's Gourmet Originals salad dressings, Renee's Naturally Light Dressings & Marinades, Renee's Grillin' Sauces, Renee's Sizzlin' Sauces, Renee's Gourmet Dips, and the Canadian marketing rights to A-1 Steak Sauce. Intercorp also produces private label products for customers in both Canada and the United States. The company is making a concerted effort to expand its presence in the United States.

Origins

The basis of what would become Intercorp were the combined talents and experience of a married couple, Renee and Arnold Unger, who lived in the Toronto area community of Downview. While Renee's gift for cooking provided the spark for the business, she was also a natural entrepreneur who had a role model in her mother, Faye Mendelson, owner and operator of a Toronto store called The Adorable Hat Shop. After Renee's father died when she was 12, her mother continued to run the shop, despite having no financial need after inheriting her husband's real estate holdings. Renee spent time at the shop watching her mother conduct business, and she also displayed a

strong aptitude for math. She even studied math at college for two years before transferring to a teacher's college. After teaching elementary school for a few years, she quit to start a company with her sister-in-law, importing clothes and jewelry. Her husband also displayed an entrepreneurial spirit, with an emphasis on selling. From 1970 to 1973, he ran his own marketing firm, Global Incentives, working with such major clients as General Foods, Carnation, and Heinz. After selling the business, he became involved in the building industry, but by 1984 he was in trouble and forced to declare bankruptcy.

By Renee Unger's own account, she had a vivid sense of taste. She told *The Toronto Star* in 2000, ''I see things in colours. If a taste is flat, I see brown; lively, I see spikes of dancing colour. It's like music.'' She was known to prepare spectacular, multi-course dinners. For Christmas 1984, she and Arnold gave out homemade food baskets as gifts to their friends. He made the baskets and she provided the homemade dressings, which proved so popular among their set that soon Renee was beset by requests for her dressings whenever friends hosted dinner partners. The couple sensed a business opportunity, one they desperately needed after Arnold's business failure. After some study, and learning the basics of the food industry, they became convinced that there was an emerging market for low-fat, low-cholesterol salad dressings made from fresh ingredients without preservatives.

Incorporation in the 1980s

The Ungers invested $50,000 of their own money and procured a $30,000 credit line from Toronto Dominion Bank and launched Intercorp in 1985. A major hurdle to overcome from the outset was the limited shelf life of Renee's dressings, which could only stay fresh for two weeks. Working with an area food laboratory, they were able to modify the recipes to produce a product that with refrigeration could stay fresh for six months. Refrigerated dressings, moreover, was a market at the time that offered less competition and provided a greater chance for new products to succeed. The couple also researched the name of the product line and engaged a company to design the packaging. The Ungers then began to share their products with gourmet grocery stores, which loved the dressings but were worried that

Company Perspectives:

A Passion for Quality—We believe that in order to produce quality you have to start with quality. Our products are made with premium quality, fresh ingredients, such as fresh garlic, fresh buttermilk, eggs and real cheese—never any preservatives or MSG. We offer only the best-tasting products for you and your family.

the new company might not be able to fill orders. To address this concern, the Ungers, who at this stage were labeling their product in their garage, arranged a co-packing agreement with an established manufacturer.

The Ungers hoped to achieve revenues from $200,000 to $250,000 in their first year, but when their initial line of four salad dressings (Caesar, Greek, blue cheese, and poppy seed) began shipping in the spring of 1985, they were disappointed to generate sales of just $1,300. June brought only modest improvement to $3,900. They hired professional brokers who had relationships with buyers and began to make inroads with retailers while also making sure that the products were properly displayed. Sales now began to take off. Moreover, once small stores agreed to carry Renee's dressings, it was easier to approach larger chains. By the end of Intercorp's first full year in business, May 1986, sales far exceeded the Ungers' expectations, reaching $600,000, and greater prosperity was on the horizon. In March 1986, Intercorp participated in a trade promotion called "Ontario Week," held at Macy's department store in New York City. Macy's was won over and began to stock Renee's dressings. Back in Ontario, most of the area supermarkets also agreed to stock the product line, which would soon grow to ten in all. Preparations for moving into sauces were also in place. The first major supermarket chain to sign on was Mr. Grocer, followed by IFA, A&P, and Loblaws. By the end of the second year, the company generated nearly $2 million in sales.

Having quickly established itself in the marketplace, Intercorp was able to drop the co-packing arrangement and establish its own manufacturing operation. Arnold was responsible for outfitting the plant, and he also used his building background to construct trade show booths in which Renee conducted hundreds of demonstrations. Arnold also proved to be a relentless salesman. Renee told the *Toronto Star* in a company profile, "Arnie won't take no for any answer. If you turn me down four times, I'll go away. Not Arnie. Turn him down 20 times and he'll be back." With hard work and persistence came recognition and greater opportunities. In 1988, the president of Loblaws, Dave Nichol, asked Renee if she could replicate an unknown dressing from the Orient he had in a jar. He was satisfied with the result and entered into a private labeling agreement for what would be called Memories of Szechwan. It was Intercorp's entry into private-label products and the first in a line of "Memories" sauces produced for the Loblaw chain. Over the years, the private label customers among supermarket chains would include Sobey's (Our Compliments), A&P (Masterchoice), Western Canada Safeway stores, and Shaw's in the United States. Restaurant clients would include The Keg, Pat and Mario's, Mr. Sub, and East Side Mario's.

The business was so successful and respected in the food industry that in 1989 the Ungers were courted by major corporations wanting to buy them out. Best Foods, known for Hellmann's mayonnaise, engaged in a bidding war with Kraft Foods, which finally offered $9 million. Although pleased by the attention, the Ungers declined the offer, opting to remain independent. By this time, the Ungers were having problems with their marriage. They separated in 1989 and eventually divorced. Selling the company would have provided an easy exit strategy, but they decided instead to carry on working together, primarily for the sake of their daughters, who were already very much committed to the business. Both Lori and Alysse Unger were involved with Intercorp since its inception. Lori joined the company on a full-time basis in 1990 after earning a marketing degree from Toronto's Ryerson University. Alysee also participated in the founding of the company. She would study Food Science as well as business and become involved in the development of salad dressings and sauces as well as one day heading New Business Development and spearheading the company's push into the United States. In addition, her husband, Andrew LuePann, worked at Intercorp, joining the company in 1993 and becoming director of national sales. (The couple met on the job.) A third daughter, Karen, practiced as a criminal attorney before eventually becoming a director of the company. Their parents, despite the breakup of their marriage, found a way to continue working together despite the awkwardness, with Renee acting as president and Arnold as CEO. Renee was now free to emerge as an executive on her own abilities in an industry that was dominated by men. According to a profile in *Western Grocer*, "When Renee walked into a boardroom they barely gave her a second glance. 'They would talk directly to Arnie,' she says. 'Even when I asked a question they would turn to Arnie and answer.' Determined to gain respect of the boys' club, she learned all she could about every aspect of the industry, from the manufacturing machinery to the fine points of money management." Renee Unger told The *Toronto Star* that her frustration with her role in the business was a major factor in the breakup of her marriage: "The wife was supposed to be in the backseat. I didn't like it." She would go on to win a number of business awards, including being named "Woman Entrepreneur of the Year, 1998" by the Women in Food Industry Management organization, and became a role model for many women executives and entrepreneurs. While contentious at times, the relationship between the former spouses sometimes worked to the benefit of the business. Arnold would push Renee to introduce new products, and she would hold off until satisfied with a recipe. "I have to yell and scream (to get new products)," he told the *Toronto Star* in December 2000. "She cries, 'We're too big, Arnie.' I say, if we don't grow, we'll die." In the words of the newspaper, "Their creative differences—her perfectionism, his gung-ho salesmanship—seem to contribute equally to the company's success."

Challenges and Growth in the 1990s and Beyond

In 1993, Intercorp won a major contract providing coleslaw dressing to Kentucky Fried Chicken in Canada. In the same year, as the company moved into a new plant, Intercorp also faced its greatest period of challenge. A $1 million cost overrun in construction adversely impacted cash flow. Sales continued to grow but margins were thin and the company had trouble keeping up on its payments to suppliers and other vendors. Although the banks provided the necessary funds, they also kept close tabs on Intercorp. To help them better manage their finances and make the difficult cost-cutting decisions, the Ungers hired Fred Burke in 1994 to serve as chief operating officer, described by Renee Unger as "the proverbial Mr. Slash-and-Burn." He came to the company with several years of experience in the food industry, holding positions at Robinhood Multifoods, Inc. and Effem Foods Ltd. After a period of belt tightening, Intercorp returned to fiscal health by 1996.

In October 1997, the Ungers were able to take the company public; it began trading on the NASDAQ at $5 per share. Over the next few years, Intercorp made progress on a number of fronts. In June 1998, the company launched a new line of sauces and marinades. It also landed a pair of supply agreements later in the year. Intercorp became the exclusive supplier of dressings for Mr. Sub, a 500-unit sandwich shop chain, and the Westfair Foods supermarket chain in Western Canada. The company's line of Naturally Light Sauces were named the Best New Condiment in the Canadian Grand Prix New Products Awards in May 1999. To achieve further growth, Intercorp also looked to make acquisitions, hiring PricewaterhouseCoopers to assist in the effort. In August 1999, the company acquired the rights to "A-1 Steak Sauce" for the Canadian marketplace from Campbell Soup Company. A-1, the roots of which could be traced back to England 1835, had been sold in the North America for nearly 100 years. Intercorp picked up all of A-1's assets, including inventory, formulas, and manufacturing equipment. Renee Unger tinkered with the recipe, taking out the preservatives, so that

in addition to the "original" sauce, Intercorp would also come out with its own "zesty" version, resulting in a 40 percent increase in sales within a year.

Intercorp scouted for more acquisitions and was especially interested in buying a "synergistic" firm or possibly a plant in the United States. Increasingly, the company looked to the vast American market. Although by the start of the 2000s, Intercorp had made some inroads—its product lines selling in New York State, North Carolina, and Minnesota—the Ungers proceeded cautiously. Arnold Unger told *Profit* in 2001, "To take on the United States all at once will destroy us. We couldn't handle all that business initially."

Despite achieving steady growth over the years, Intercorp never received much respect from investors. The company's stock dipped below $1, was relegated to trading on an over-the-counter basis, and in late 2001 the Ungers bought back the outstanding shares, taking the company private once again. Although its refrigerated products dominated the Canadian market, the future of the company clearly hinged on its ability to succeed in the United States, where it was hoped that its preservative-free products would find a receptive clientele among the country's more health-conscious consumers.

Principal Competitors

Kraft Foods Inc.; Lancaster Colony Corporation; Unilever plc.

Further Reading

Baillie, Susanne, "Fridge over Trouble Waters," *Profit*, February 1, 2001, p. 58.

Kidd, Kenneth, "Metro Pair's Salad Dressings Are Conquering New York," *Toronto Star*, September 18, 1986, p. E1.

Peters, Carly, "Breaking the Barriers," *Western Grocer*, March–April 2004, p. 46.

Steed, Judy, "She Came, She Saw, She Conquered—Tastefully," *Toronto Star*, November 26, 2000, p. WB01.

—Ed Dinger

Itron, Inc.

2818 North Sullivan Road
Spokane, Washington 99216
U.S.A.
Telephone: (509) 924-9900
Toll Free: (800) 635-5461
Fax: (509) 891-3355
Web site: http://www.itron.com

Public Company
Incorporated: 1977
Employees: 1,434
Sales: $317.0 million (2003)
Stock Exchanges: NASDAQ
Ticker Symbol: ITRI
NAIC: 334519 Other Measuring and Controlling Device
   Manufacturing; 334290 Other Communication
   Equipment Manufacturing; 423430 Computer and
   Computer Peripheral Equipment and Software

Itron, Inc., provides products and services to utility companies, helping its customers to collect, manage, and analyze data gathered from electricity, water, and gas meters. The company designs and manufactures devices that automate meter reading. Itron also offers a range of software and services that provide sophisticated analysis of energy usage and distribution. Itron serves more than 2,000 utilities in more than 40 countries.

Origins

The path of technological progress that charted Itron's development began in 1977 in a garage in northern Idaho. There, a small group engineers started developing computers and software designed to read utility meters and worked on technology that would replace the manual and paper-intensive meter-reading methods employed by virtually every utility company during the late 1970s. Instead of registering meter information on paper, meter readers with an Itron device could enter the information electronically, a leap in technology that made the meter reader's job less cumbersome and one that delivered its

greatest rewards at the utility's central offices. No longer forced to wade through thousands of sheets of paper to determine customers' consumption of water, gas, and electricity, the utility company could efficiently organize its data electronically, yielding significant reductions in labor-related costs while substantially enhancing the accessibility and manipulation of the data collected. This new, revolutionary method of collecting meter information became known as Electronic Meter Reading, or EMR, a method of manually collecting, entering, and storing meter-reading data into a handheld computer.

Itron's pioneering engineers achieved success within several years after their first meeting in the Idaho garage. By the beginning of the 1980s, the small company was ready to ship its first EMR systems, a package consisting of handheld computers and software. Over the course of the ensuing decade, the company brokered deals with one utility after another, gradually building its business as the acceptance of EMR equipment became widespread. By the end of the 1980s, Itron had developed into a roughly $50 million-in-sales company, its business entirely dependent on the use of EMR solutions by the utility industry.

By the end of the 1980s, Itron engineers were looking to lessen the company's dependence on EMR. Reviving the pioneering spirit prevalent in the northern Idaho garage roughly a decade earlier, the engineers of Spokane, Washington-based Itron were working on the next technological leap in meter reading. The objective pursued involved eliminating the need for the visual inspection of meters, an advancement that promised to deliver great increases in efficiency and substantial savings in labor costs. Itron engineers focused their efforts on automating the meter-reading process by equipping an electric, gas, or water meter with a meter module. Once in place, the module could transmit the data to a collection system, rendering visual inspection obsolete. The process the engineers were working on became known as Automatic Meter Reading, or AMR, a technology that held great promise for Itron's future growth,

Itron introduced its first AMR systems to the market in 1991, a debut that had the double-edged effect of raising expectations and setting the company up for failure if these expectations were not met. After the unveiling of Itron's AMR meter modules, the company continued to manufacture and market EMR

Company Perspectives:

Our idea is pretty simple: In today's increasingly competitive marketplace, energy and water providers that are able to leverage the value of information will enjoy a significant competitive advantage over those that do not. Itron delivers value to its clients by collecting data and transforming it into valuable knowledge. Our clients use this knowledge to run their businesses more efficiently, optimize energy and water delivery, strengthen their connection to their customers, manage competition and customer choice, enable new business development and increase shareholder value.

systems, but AMR equipment quickly became the driving force propelling the company's growth. Between 1992 and 1995, the company's sales more than doubled, swelling from $67.8 million to $155.3 million, with much of the growth generated from the sale of encoder, receiver, transmitter (ERT) modules. Itron dominated the emerging AMR market during the first half of the 1990s, taking an almost monopolistic lead over its competitors. In December 1995, less than five years after it first offered AMR capabilities, Itron manufactured its five millionth ERT, delivering the module to Philadelphia Gas Works. An industry research firm, Chartwell Inc., estimated that Itron's five million ERTs in service represented 80 percent of the market share of AMR installations in North America.

When Itron shipped its five-millionth ERT, Philadelphia Gas Works was only one of more than 1,275 utilities located in more than 40 countries that counted itself as an Itron customer. The company's customers were supplied by manufacturing facilities in Spokane and Minnesota, as well as subsidiaries in the United Kingdom, France, and Australia. The company had grown enormously in the 18 years separating its start in a Idaho garage and the symbolic delivery to Philadelphia Gas Works, but its standing as the largest supplier of AMR systems in the world did not breed complacency. Beginning in the mid-1990s, Itron augmented its own research and development activities with the technologies developed by other companies, executing an acquisition program that added to the complexity of its business. Itron evolved from a company trying to aid utilities in reading meters into one that provided comprehensive solutions to utilities, helping them to better manage, gauge, and distribute their energy resources.

Acquistion Campaign Begins in 1995

One of the first significant acquisitions in Itron's history occurred in the fall of 1995. Itron's AMR systems utilized radio-based technology to transmit data, a capability that the company wanted to complement with telephone-based technology, which was particularly useful in rural areas, where deploying a radio network was not cost-effective. Instead of developing the technology itself, Itron acquired the company that pioneered the technology, purchasing Metscan, Inc., a firm with more than 50,000 AMR devices installed in more than 40 major North American utilities.

Itron's next strike on the acquisition front took place within months of the Metscan acquisition. In the spring of 1996, the

company announced it had agreed to acquire Raleigh, North Carolina-based Utility Translation Systems, Inc. (UTI). UTI, which supplied software to more than 70 percent of the major electric utilities and a substantial number of gas utilities in the United States, excelled at linking large commercial and industrial customers to utilities' computing systems. The company's single most important achievement was solving the protocol problem for communicating with the complex meters installed at the buildings used by large commercial and industrial energy users. By virtue of this success, UTI's software was capable of communicating with virtually all commercial and industrial gas and electric meters.

As Itron neared its 20th anniversary, the company held a commanding lead in its market. Its EMR systems, which accounted for 25 percent of the company's revenues at the end of 1996, were installed at 80 percent of the largest 25 utilities in North America. Itron's AMR systems, which accounted for 75 percent of sales, were installed at 269 utilities. In 1996, the company shipped nearly 3.5 million AMR meter modules, widening its lead as world's largest supplier of AMR systems. The company's progress was encouraging, but a source of greater encouragement could be found in what the company had yet to achieve. Itron's dominance of the AMR market represented only a fraction of the market's potential. The company estimated there were 268 million meters in North America during the mid-1990s. Of this total, only 12 million, or 5 percent, had installed AMR technology. Outside North America, Itron officials estimated there were roughly 800 million meters in existence, with only a fraction possessing AMR technology.

Despite Itron's commanding market share and the enormous growth potential of the AMR market, the company's financial results were less than scintillating. In 1996, the company's revenues increased to $177.6 million, but it lost $1.5 million. The company was plagued by delays in orders for its products, excess manufacturing capacity, and the high costs incurred by product development. Itron exuded sufficient strength to win the support of industry pundits and investors, however. Observers were convinced that Itron was a company destined for great things. One analyst, in an interview with the *Puget Sound Business Journal,* offered his perception of Itron. "The company has a huge customer base, and excellent reputation among conservative utilities, and has added key financial and marketing talent," the analyst noted. "Once utilities more fully embrace AMR systems, we believe Itron will be the leader in a very large market."

Itron pressed ahead with enhancing its capabilities in the face of declining profitability. In May 1997, the company augmented the capabilities gained with the acquisition of Metscan by announcing its had agreed to acquire Boise, Idaho-based Design Concepts Inc. in an all-stock acquisition valued at $16.7 million. Design Concepts, with 1996 revenues of $2 million, supplied telephone-based devices for remote meter reading for nearly 100 electric utilities worldwide. Unlike Metscan, Design Concepts' systems provided outage detection and power quality monitoring capabilities, adding to the menu of services Itron was able to offer to utilities.

Roughly one year after the Design Concepts acquisition, Itron could no longer wait for market conditions to improve its anemic financial performance. In July 1998, the company announced it was eliminating 100 workers from its payroll, a 10 percent reduction in its workforce. The announcement, which coincided with the acknowledgment of a $1.1 million loss for the company's second fiscal quarter, was prompted by a prolonged slowdown in orders for Itron's AMR equipment. "We continue to win most of the AMR business out there," Mima Scarpelli, Itron's Vice-President of Investor Relations, said to *Knight Ridder/Tribune Business News* in a July 23, 1998 interview. "It's just that the AMR business is very slow," she explained, voicing the company's frustration about its lackluster financial performance. Half of the job cuts affected employees in Spokane, while approximately 25 Minnesota-based employees lost their jobs. The remaining reductions affected various U.S. and foreign offices.

Although the layoffs announced in mid-1998 projected a negative image of Itron's fortunes, the reductions marked the beginning of the company's road to recovery. Beginning with its moves to streamline its operations, Itron began to take the shape of a company capable of producing a profit and living up to the high expectations that had followed it since its introduction of AMR technology in 1991. The individual credited for Itron's transformation into a moneymaker arrived at the company a year after Itron trimmed its workforce in July 1998, taking the changes begun and shaping them into a blueprint for financial success.

Turnaround Begins in 1999

Michael Chesser was appointed Itron's president and chief executive officer in May 1999, replacing Johnny Humphreys, who had held identical posts since 1987. Chesser possessed a wealth of experience in the utility industry, having spent 23 years at Baltimore Gas and Electric, where he held various executive positions. After his tenure at Baltimore Gas, Chesser served as president and chief operating officer of Atlantic Energy, Inc., holding the posts from 1994 to 1998.

Chesser made sweeping changes that steered Itron toward profitability. The company's manufacturing operations were consolidated, with activities from plants in Washington and Idaho organized into one facility in Waseca, Minnesota. Chesser cut back on the company's European operations and its

research and development activities, while trimming the company's workforce by 200. After making the reductions aimed at increasing efficiency and cutting costs, Chesser reorganized Itron into what the company referred to as "customer-focused business units." The reorganization, according to Scarpelli in a March 23, 2001 interview with *Puget Sound Business Journal*, "really gave us a better feel for each individual market. In the past," she added, "we spent a lot of time focusing on really big orders—home runs. But over the past year we really got back to basics and focused on hitting just singles and doubles." By the end of 2000, there was evidence that the changes initiated by Chesser had worked. The company generated $184 million in sales for the year and, most significantly, it posted a profit of nearly $5 million.

By the time the financial results for 2000 were made public, Chesser had already vacated his leadership posts at Itron. In April 2000, just three months after being named Itron's chairman of the board, Chesser left the company to become president and chief executive officer of GPU Energy. S. Edward White, an Itron executive vice-president, was appointed chairman and LeRoy Nosbaum, the company's chief operating officer, was promoted to president and chief operating officer.

Acquisitions in the 21st Century

As Itron plotted its course under new leadership, the company continued to acquire companies that expanded the capabilities it was able to offer to utilities. In 2002, Itron acquired three companies, beginning with the announcement made in March that it had purchased Linesoft Corporation for $41.4 million. Based in Spokane, Linesoft provided software and consulting services to more than 130 utilities, generating $14 million in sales in 2001. In September, Itron announced it had agreed to acquire eMobile Data Corporation for $6.2 million. A publicly traded Canadian company, eMobile provided wireless, Web-based workforce management products for the utility industry. The company's most important product, Service-Link, enabled utilities to streamline and automate many of the processes associated with field service. The deal to acquire eMobile was completed in October, the same month Itron acquired Regional Economic Research, Inc., a San Diego, California-based company that provided forecasting services and software products designed to improve scheduling, risk management, and system operation.

Itron's acquisitive activities intensified in 2003, as the company achieved great strides in increasing its stature. In March, the company completed the acquisition of Silicon Energy Corporation for $71.2 million, an investment that gave Itron entry in the energy-services market. Silicon specialized in energy and asset management, providing customers with energy consumption data and tools. The company's next purchase was by far the biggest acquisition in its 26-year history. In July, Itron announced it had agreed to acquire the electricity metering business belonging to Schlumberger Limited, one of the largest oil-field services companies in the world. According to the terms of the agreement, Itron agreed to pay $255 million for Schlumberger's electricity metering business, which was based in Oconee, South Carolina, and served roughly 3,400 utility customers. The company served customers in the United States, Canada, Mexico, and the Caribbean and sold electricity meters in Taiwan.

The deal to acquire Schlumberger's electricity meter business was expected to close in 2004. As Itron prepared for its future, considerable attention was begin paid to integrating the Schlumberger acquisition into its fold. After years of recording disappointing financial results, the company was enjoying financial success in the early years of the decade, recording consistent growth that fueled justifiable optimism for the future. As Itron pressed forward with plans to dominate as a provider of comprehensive products and services to the utility industry, its financial totals for 2003 offered a source of encouragement. That year, the company reported an 11 percent increase in revenues to $317 million and a net income of $10.5 million, a gain of nearly $3 million over the previous year. The company's shipments of AMR equipment increased 10 percent, led by a 44 percent increase in water unit shipments. In the years ahead, Itron hoped to continue the trend established early in the decade and to position itself as the premier competitor in its field.

Principal Subsidiaries

Itron Connecticut Finance, Inc.; Itron Spectrum Holdings, Inc.; Itron International, Inc.; Itron Finance, Inc.; EMD Holding, Inc.; Itron S.A. (France); Itron France SARL; Itron Ltd. (United Kingdom); SLCN Ltd.; Itron Australasia Party Ltd.; Itron Australasia Technologies Pty. Ltd. (Australia); Itron Australasia Holdings Pty. Ltd. (Australia); Itron Canada, Inc.; Itron B.C. Corporation (Canada); Itron Guam, Inc.; Itron de Mexico, S.A. de C.V.; Electricity Metering Distribucion, S.A. DE C.V.; Electricity Metering Servicios, S.A. DE C.V.; Silicon Energy Corporation (BVI), Ltd.; SLCN Netherlands B.V. (Netherlands).

Principal Competitors

ABB Ltd.; Nexus Telocation Systems Ltd.; AREVA Group.

Further Reading

Caldwell, Bert, ''Boise, Idaho's Design Concepts, Itron Strike Deal,'' *Knight Ridder/Tribune Business News*, May 2, 1997.
——, ''Itron of Spokane, Wash., Posts Loss, Plans Cutback,'' *Knight Ridder/Tribune Business News*, July 23, 1998.
——, ''Itron Posts Loss Totaling $3.3 Million,'' *Knight Ridder/Tribune Business News*, April 16, 1997.
''Itron Acquires Silicon Energy,'' *Public Utilities Fortnightly*, April 15, 2003, p. S6.
''Itron Inc.,'' *Puget Sound Business Journal*, December 6, 1996, p. 30.
''Itron Looks for Turnaround,'' *Puget Sound Business Journal*, March 21, 1997, p. 4.
Neurath, Peter, ''Itron Rebuts Allegations by Forbes,'' *Puget Sound Business Journal*, October 24, 1997, p. 10.

—Jeffrey L. Covell

JLM Couture, Inc.

225 West 37th Street, Fifth Floor
New York, New York 10018
U.S.A.
Telephone: (212) 921-7058
Fax: (212) 921-7608
Web site: http://www.jlmcouture.com

Public Company
Incorporated: 1986 as Jim Hjelm's Private Collection,
    Ltd.
Employees: 70
Sales: $26 million (2003)
Stock Exchanges: NASDAQ
NAIC: 315999 Other Apparel Accessories and Other
    Apparel Manufacturing

JLM Couture, Inc., is a New York City-based publicly trade company devoted to the business of designing, manufacturing, and distributing bridal gowns, bridesmaid gowns, and veils. JLM's main lines are Jim Hjelm, Lazaro, and Alvina Valenta. High-end apparel from these lines range in retail price from $1,000 to $6,000 for bridal gowns, and $180 to $300 for bridesmaid gowns. The company also offers a less expensive label, "Visions," which uses less costly fabrics for bridal gowns and retail from $800 to $1,200. Manufacturing is done at two company-owned plants as well as through independent contractors. JLM primarily sells its gowns in bridal boutiques and bridal departments in department stores and women's clothing stores. Advertising is purchased in such magazines as *Modern Bride, Martha Stewart, Weddings,* and *Elegant Bride.* In addition, JLM generates sales through the distribution of its own bridal and bridemaids catalogs and by promoting its products on five Internet sites.

From Star Designer to Company Founder: 1960s–80s

Originally named Jim Hjelm's Private Collection, Ltd., JLM was founded by long-time bridal gown designer Jim Hjelm. He was born and raised in Worcester, Massachusetts, where at an early age he became interested in fashion design. As a child, he designed wardrobes for the comic book character Brenda Starr and grew up with the dream of one day designing for the theater or film industry. However, after attending the New England School of Design, he was simply eager to find work. After a job-hunting trip in 1960 to New York City proved unsuccessful, a friend told him about an opening in Boston at the House of Bianchi, a major bridal house. He got the job and, essentially by accident, became a bridal gown designer. He stayed at Bianchi for two years and learned the basics: patterns, laces, and the construction of wedding gowns. He also began to develop his own flare for the traditional wedding gown design.

In 1962, Hjelm took a position with a rival bridal house, Priscilla of Boston, where he would work for 19 years. It was here that he learned the business side of the bridal gown industry and developed a reputation as a topnotch designer of both bridal gowns and party dresses, gaining luster for designing clothes for the daughters of American presidents: Lucy Baines Johnson and Julie and Trisha Nixon. Hjelm regarded the Johnson wedding as one of his most enjoyable and rewarding experiences. He stayed a full week in the White House, working out of the Lincoln bedroom, producing the wedding gown and 11 bridesmaids' gowns. In 1980, Hjelm finally moved to New York, becoming a designer for Galina-Bouquet, Inc. From his new boss, Steve Lawrence, Hjelm learned, in his owns words, "how to be a little tough." His name at this point had enough value that Galina often featured him in the company's ads, which added further to his name recognition. After several years at Galina, and 25 years in the bridal industry, Hjelm felt he was ready to launch his own label. In 1985, he found a business partner in Joseph L. Murphy, an accountant by training who was the boyfriend of a showroom model. They turned to families and friends to raise the money needed to launch the company, which was incorporated in April 1986 and then taken public in 1987 by First Devonshire of Spokane, Washington, priced at $1 a share. Thus, Jim Hjelm's Private Collection became the only publicly held bridal house in the industry.

The company got off to a smooth start, which was not surprising to Hjelm, who had a bankable name and all the

206

requisite contacts after a quarter-century in the business. He later told the press, "I knew we would be successful. It wasn't scary at all." He also discovered the joys of working for himself and the freedom to add his own touches. "When you work for somebody else," he told *WWD* in 1987, "you have to stay with the look of the house. When you have your own firm, you wear ten hats: production, boss, designer." At this stage, Hjelm both designed and ran the company, while Murphy served on the board as secretary-treasurer and devoted the bulk of his time to his own start-up, a public relations firm. He would become more active in the running of the bridal company when he took the position as chief financial officer.

Jim Hjelm's first collection under his own name premiered for the spring 1988 season. He pursued his preference for traditional wedding gown design, especially "heirloom" dresses featuring nets, silks, and antique-like laces. This approach, by his own admission, was in keeping with his background: "It's my Bostonian upbringing and working with Priscilla all those years. When you're a snob, it's very difficult." As long as his conservative taste was shared by brides, the company prospered, but in the early 1990s trends would change, and he would have to adapt. In the meantime, the company made a number of moves. In October 1990, it acquired Exclusives for the Bride, Inc. A year later, trademarks and inventories were bought from Samir & Associates Inc., a two-year-old company which designed and marketed special occasion women's apparel. These assets then formed the basis of a wholly owned subsidiary named Samir of New York, Inc. The goal was to spur the growth of the undercapitalized firm and allow Hjelm to expand beyond the bridal business.

New Leadership and New Lines in the 1990s

In 1991, Hjelm began to face some serious challenges. The poor economy proved especially harmful to its line of expensive bridal gowns, which were priced in the $2,000 range. The average price for a wedding gown, however, was around $800, a trend recognized by ready-to-wear manufactures such as Armani, Anne Klein, and Donna Karan. To offset the drop in demand for its high-end gowns, Hjelm introduced the JH Collection line of gowns that used synthetic fibers and retailed at the $750 price point. According to a 1994 *Crain's New York Business* article, "Making matters worse, prices for beaded lace skyrocketed and theft of the company's merchandise increased dramatically. When workers were denied their request for a pay raise, they slowed production by a third in protest." A 1997 *Crain's* profile offered another summary of this period for the company: "After a whirlwind romance, Jim Hjelm Private Collection Ltd. cashed in on Wall Street's infatuation with new issues. . . . But by the early Nineties, the company looked more like an old maid than a blushing bride. With just $7.1 million in sales in 1992, the fledgling wedding dress manufacturer was stuck in a time warp, its entire product line made up of dated

traditional styles." Jim Hjelm tried to answer the problem of declining sales of traditional gowns by forming a Contemporary Classic division to produce gowns with simpler styling, less lace and bead work, and less ornamentation overall. To take charge of the line, a young designer named Lezaro Perez, who had developed a strong reputation in the contemporary category, was brought it. The gowns would then be marketed under his name. The creation of the new division did not, however, address the underlying problems at the company.

The board of directors decided that it was time for Jim Hjelm to relinquish his management responsibilities and concentrate on design. In January 1993, Murphy was installed as president and he began to implement a three-pronged strategy to turn around the company's fortunes: cut costs, increase sales by diversifying the line, and find a new customer base. Part of cutting costs involved theft, known as "shrinkage" in retail parlance. According to *Crain's,* "Mr. Murphy took aggressive steps to stop shrinkage, including sprinting out of his own welcome party to track down two crates of dresses that had disappeared." In April 1993, the company launched a new line of less expensive dresses under the "New Traditions" label. A few months later, in July 1994, the Exclusives subsidiary was sold off.

Hjelm took an important step in 1994 when it created a new line called Occasions Collection, which grew out of a focus group the company sponsored in November 1993. According to *Forbes,* Murphy heard one woman complain, "I have ten ugly bridesmaids' gowns hanging in my closet that I don't have the heart to throw away." Her sentiment was repeated by others. After months of "going to weddings, calling up friends and checking out bridal boutiques," Murphy became convinced that there was a market for fashionable bridemaids' dresses that were designed to be worn beyond the wedding ceremony and reception. He told the company's designer for bridesmaids' dresses "to throw away the old book." Puffy sleeves and hoop-like skirts were eschewed in favor of a more fitted look and contemporary silhouettes. Cotton-candy shading gave way to muted pastels and metallic earth tones. Because the dresses could be worn to functions others than weddings, Murphy choose the Occasions name.

Although revenues fell from $7.1 million in fiscal 1992 to $6 million in fiscal 1993, Murphy, through his cost-cutting measures, was able to squeeze out a profit of four cents per share in 1993, compared to a loss of eight cents in 1992. In fiscal 1994, Hjelm experienced a further erosion in sales, dipping to $5.8 million, and the company essentially broken even, recording a loss of $2,700. More importantly, the company had turned the corner, as the product mix found a new balance between high-end traditional wedding dresses and less expensive bridal lines. The success of Murphy's initiatives were revealed in fiscal 1995, when the company enjoyed a 35 percent increase in sales, to $7.9 million, and a net profit of $63,586, or five cents a share. Earnings would have been even greater, but Murphy elected to plow profits into additional marketing to expand the Occasions line as well as the new Visions line, a collection of moderately priced wedding dresses designed by Jim Hjelm. These promotional expenses, however, were not expected to remain at such a high level. The investment clearly paid off in fiscal 1996, as Hjelm saw its revenues balloon by 61 percent to $12.6 million, due primarily to growth in the Occasions, Visions, and Lazaro lines. Net income improved to $471,000, or 29 cents per share.

Late 1990s and Beyond

Hjelm may have been enjoying success with its less expensive lines, but it was far from abandoning the high end of the market. In May 1997, Hjelm acquired Alvina Valenta Couture Collection, an upscale designer of wedding gown apparel. The addition of Valenta was important on at least two levels. It provided entry into an important new styling category in the bridal apparel business, falling in between the traditional and contemporary-classic sectors. Moreover, Hjelm added the asset of Alvina's talented designer Victoria McMillan, who had been designing the line since 1989. Because the company was now comprised of a number of labels, only one of which was Jim Hjelm, in July 1997 the business was renamed, JLM Couture Inc., which management believed more readily identified it as holding company for a number of bridal-related designer brand names.

JLM was enjoying success at both ends of the markets. The Occasions line was so successful that rivals began to emulate the line, not only copying styles but also the company's advertising. With young talents like Perez and McMillan designing expensive bridal gowns for the company, JLM quickly moved up the ranks of the upper end of the bridal gown business, from inside the top 20 to number three. JLM also began to turns its attention to the European market. In 1999, it established a sales office in England to begin to penetrate this new market with the Occasions and Lazaro bridesmaids gowns. From 2001 to 2003, European sales would contribute about 3 percent of JLM's total sales. Revenues grew at a steady pace over the next few years, topping $18 million in fiscal 1999 and $20 million in 2000, the same year that the company launched two new bridesmaid divisions: Lazaro Ensembles and Jim Hjelm Just Separates. Revenues reached $24.7 million in fiscal 2002 and profits surpassed $1.1 million. In 2003, JLM experienced a modest improvement in sales, reaching $26 million, due in large part to a national slowdown in the industry. Income dropped to $808,000, caused primarily by the cancellation of stock options and the renewal of certain leases. Nevertheless, JLM was well positioned for on-growing growth. When the company went public in the 1980s, a major risk factor was its dependence on Jim Hjelm. Now, with the name change to JLM Couture and the addition of designers Lazaro and McMillan, the business was preparing for the day when its founder would no longer be the driving force.

Principal Subsidiaries

JLM Europe Ltd.

Principal Competitors

Bar-Jay Fashions Inc.; House of Bianchi; Priscilla Of Boston Inc.

Further Reading

Griffin, Linda Gillan, ''Jim Hjelm: The Man Behind 30 Years of Brides,'' *Houston Chronicle*, January 27, 1994, p. 1.

Kamen, Robin, ''Gown Maker Recovers with Less Pricey Lines,'' *Crain's New York Business*, May 2, 1994, p. 35.

Kroll, Luisa, ''What Would Queen Victoria Have Said,'' *Forbes*, October 20, 1997, p. 266.

Michals, Debra, ''Jim Hjelm: On His Own,'' *WWD*, September 28, 1987, p. S12.

—Ed Dinger

JM JohnsManville

Johns Manville Corporation

<table>
<tr><td>

717 17th Street
Denver, Colorado 80202
U.S.A.
Telephone: (303) 978-2000
Toll Free: (800) 654-3103
Fax: (303) 978-2318
Web site: http://www.jm.com

Wholly Owned Subsidiary of Berkshire Hathaway Inc.
Incorporated: 1901 as H.W. Johns-Manville Corporation
Employees: 10,400
Sales: $2 billion (2003)
NAIC: 324122 Asphalt Shingle and Coating Materials
    Manufacturing; 339991 Gasket, Packing, and Sealing
    Device Manufacturing

</td></tr>
</table>

Johns Manville Corporation (JM) operates as a leading manufacturer and marketer of insulation products for buildings and equipment, roofing systems, and various engineered products, including fibers, fabric and nonwoven mats, and filtration media. The company has 55 manufacturing facilities in North America, Europe, and China. Until the mid-1980s, JM mined and sold asbestos for use in insulation, building, aerospace, automotive, and other industries. The company divested itself of its interests in all asbestos-related businesses but remained involved in substantial litigation brought by asbestos workers with claims based on the effects of working with the material. As such, JM underwent significant restructuring in the 1990s and was acquired by Berkshire Hathaway Inc. in 2001.

Origins

In 1858, at the age of 21, Henry Ward Johns founded the H.W. Johns Manufacturing Company in New York City. The company specialized in the manufacture of asbestos textiles, roofing, and insulation materials. Over the next 40 years, until his death in 1898 of dust phthisis pneumonitis, believed to be asbestosis, Johns discovered a number of the applications of asbestos, which became known as the mineral of a thousand uses. In 1886, Charles B. Manville founded the Manville Covering Company in Milwaukee, Wisconsin, and managed the

company until 1900. In 1901, H.W. Johns and Manville merged to create H.W. Johns-Manville (JM), a corporation engaged primarily in the mining, manufacturing, and supply of asbestos fibers and products to industry and the government.

The management of JM was relatively stable over the years. The Manville family remained active in the management of the company through most of the twentieth century. From 1921 to 1923, Thomas F. Manville headed the company as president, treasurer, and a member of the board. In 1924, he became chairman; H.E. Manville was elected president and T.F. Manville, Jr. joined the board of directors. By 1928, H.E. Manville and Thomas Manville, Jr. sat on the board, while T.F. Merseles served as the company's president. In 1930, H.E. Manville was named chairman of the executive committee and L.H. Brown became president. This hierarchy continued until 1939.

In 1927, JM became a publicly held corporation. During the 1920s and 1930s, JM acquired several mining and manufacturing operations in the United States and Canada. Purchases included the Celite Company of California, miners and processors of diatomaceous earth—diatomite is a filtering agent—in 1928 and, in 1930, the Stevens Sound Proofing Company of Chicago, owners of patents for sound insulation.

Asbestos Problems Begin in the Late 1920s

As early as 1929, JM was defending itself against lawsuits for asbestos-related deaths. Asbestosis is a nonmalignant scarring of the lungs caused solely by exposure to asbestos. The incidence of the disease seems to be related to the duration and intensity of exposure. It may take decades for evidence of the disease to appear. Mesothelioma is a form of cancer associated with asbestos that affects the linings of the chest or abdominal cavities and that usually kills its victims within a year of its appearance. The legal issues in asbestos cases centered on the following two questions. When did the health hazards of working with asbestos become foreseeable? When warnings were issued, did they adequately communicate the danger?

From the beginning, JM claimed that employees were contributorily negligent because they knew or should have known the dangers associated with asbestos and taken precautions. Manville used this defense, often successfully, in cases filed

Company Perspectives:

John Manville has four core values that are central to the company and that underlie everything we do. The corporate commitments by which we live are people, safety, ethics, and environmental leadership.

during the next four decades. In addition, Manville continued to argue into the 1980s that until 1964 there was no known reason to warn insulation workers of the dangers of working with asbestos. Plaintiffs countered that warning labels should have been in use as early as the 1950s.

In 1930, Dr. A.J. Lanza of the Metropolitan Life Insurance Company began a four-year study, *Effects of Inhalation of Asbestos Dust upon the Lungs of Asbestos Workers.* Based on his findings, in late 1933 Lanza recommended that JM perform dust counts at its plants. Vandiver Brown, who served as Manville's vice-president, corporate secretary, and chief attorney, wrote Lanza to request changes in his report. Specifically, Brown requested that he downplay the negative implications of asbestos exposure. In his book, *Outrageous Misconduct: The Asbestos Industry on Trial,* Paul Brodeur described a memo Brown wrote in 1935 to company colleagues in which he noted a speaker who said, ''The strongest bulwark against future disaster for the industry is the enactment of properly drawn occupational-disease legislation, which would eliminate the jury as well as eliminate the shyster lawyer and the quack doctor since fees would be strictly limited by the law.'' Later that year, Brown wrote that the company's best interests would be served by having asbestosis receive minimal publicity. Brown's correspondence would be entered as evidence in trials almost a half century later by plaintiffs who, in efforts to win punitive as well as compensatory damages against the company, contended that JM deliberately downplayed the effects of exposure.

British studies concurrent with Lanza's encouraged Parliament to pass legislation to protect asbestos workers in 1931. In the United States, three years passed before asbestosis was considered for classification as a disease under workmen's compensation laws.

Beginning in 1936, JM and nine other asbestos companies funded a study of the effects of asbestos on animals. Dr. LeRoy U. Gardner reported significant changes in the lungs of guinea pigs within a year after exposure to asbestos dust. Gardner died in 1946 before formally reporting his findings.

In 1939, L.H. Brown became president of JM, a position he held until 1948, and H.E. Manville stepped down as chairman. The year 1940 was significant as the first year in which the name Manville did not appear in the list of company officers. In 1941, H.E. Manville, Jr. joined the board of directors, a post he held into the 1960s.

Growth Continues in the Prewar and Postwar Eras

At the start of World War II, JM was among the world's leading suppliers of asbestos, and 1939 through 1945 were strong years for JM financially. During those years, tens of

thousands of workers in U.S. government shipyards and other installations used thousands of tons of asbestos in building ships and airplanes. In 1943, the Navy Department and the U.S. Maritime Commission published a study that outlined the risks to insulation workers of high asbestos dust levels. *Minimum Requirements for Safety and Industrial Health in Contract Shipyards* reported that asbestosis could arise from breathing asbestos in any job that created dust. Many of the workers and seaman exposed to asbestos during this period would bring suit against JM years later.

In 1947, JM signed the first in a series of policies with the Travelers Insurance Company, the company's insurers for the next 30 years. The extent of the insurers' liability in the asbestos suits would be debated and litigated well into the 1990s.

In 1948, L.H. Brown became chairman of the board, while R.W. Lea was named president. Three years later, L.M. Cassidy, formerly vice-president of sales, assumed the position of chairman; a second vice-president, A.R. Fisher, became president and a third, C.F. Rassweiler, was named vice-chairman. These men controlled the company until 1957.

From 1950 through 1970, JM's sales grew at an average annual rate of 4 percent. While sales of asbestos and other raw materials represented only 13 percent of JM's volume, they contributed between 30 percent and 40 percent of earnings.

In 1951, John A. McKinney joined the company as a patent lawyer; he was to become president 25 years later. By 1952, the staff included Fred L. Pundsack, Chester E. Shepperly, Monroe Harris, and Chester J. Sulewski, all of whom, along with McKinney, figured prominently in the bankruptcy court protection program some 30 years later. In 1958, JM acquired L-O-F Glass Fibers Company, which then became known as the Manville Sales Corporation. Francis H. May, Jr. of Libbey-Owens-Ford Glass Company joined Manville and became Executive Vice-president for Finance and Administration. Fisher was named chairman as well as president.

During the 1950s, JM workers who came into contact with insulation on job sites began filing workmen's compensation claims against the company. The company's first-hand knowledge of the dangers of asbestos would become a factor in future suits in which it would be a defendant.

In 1960, Clinton Brown Burnett became president of JM, a post he held for a decade. Burnett headed the company during a period of rising production costs and price declines. In response, he trimmed operations by closing plants and assembly lines. He led the company through cautious diversification into fiberglass, carpeting, and gypsum, opened a building materials research and development center in New Jersey, and expanded vigorously overseas.

Addressing Challenges in the 1960s

During the 1960s, asbestos received increasing attention from the medical community. In 1963, Dr. I.J. Selikoff of Mount Sinai Medical Center in New York reported to the American Medical Association the findings of his study of the effects of asbestos on workers. Selikoff estimated that 100,000 U.S. workers and their family members would die of diseases

Key Dates:

1858: Henry Ward Johns establishes the H.W. Johns Manufacturing Co.
1886: Charles B. Manville founds the Manville Covering Co.
1901: The two companies merge to form H.W. Johns-Manville (JM).
1930: Dr. A.J. Lanza begins a four-year study, *Effects of Inhalation of Asbestos Dust upon the Lungs of Asbestos Workers.*
1964: For the first time, JM agrees to place warning labels on its asbestos products.
1973: The company and its co-defendants are found guilty of contributory negligence in asbestos-related litigation.
1981: The company reorganizes its corporate structure, creating a new parent company, Manville Corporation, and five subsidiaries.
1982: Asbestos litigation prompts the company to file for protection under Chapter 11.
1988: Manville emerges from Chapter 11.
1996: The company changes its name to Schuller Co.
1997: The firm reverts back to Johns Manville Corporation (JM)
2001: Berkshire Hathaway Inc. acquires JM.

associated with asbestos in the twentieth century. That study, coupled with the news coverage that followed, brought the problem to the public's attention. In 1964, for the first time, JM agreed to place warning labels on its products. The labels read, "Inhalation of asbestos in excessive quantities over long periods of time may be harmful."

By 1969, Burnett, now 62, and the board of directors were looking for solutions to two problems: JM's slow growth over the preceding ten years and the lack of an heir apparent to succeed the president when he retired. William C. Stolk, a director since 1951, recommended W. Richard Goodwin, a 45-year-old management consultant with a doctorate in experimental psychology, for help in solving the first problem and, potentially, the second. Goodwin began counseling JM in June 1968. He joined the company as Vice-president for Corporate Planning in April 1969 and was named president in December 1970. Burnett became chairman of the board, only to retire about a month later. He left Goodwin with a solid company, having $145 million in working capital, no long-term debt, and a leading position in environmental control, building materials, and asbestos.

Goodwin immediately implemented the changes he had recommended during his consultancy. He formed a three-man management team, composed of himself and JM veterans Francis May and John B. Jobe, Executive Vice-president for Operations. May and Jobe ran the company while Goodwin concentrated on growth. He led the company into real estate development, recreation, irrigation systems, and construction. Sales rose 91 percent from 1970 to 1975; profits rose 115 percent between 1970 and 1974, and earnings in 1976 set a

company record. In 1974, JM's international division, with 22 plants and four mines in 12 countries and sales offices worldwide, generated 32 percent of corporate net profit on 14 percent of gross sales.

In 1973, Manville and its co-defendants lost their final appeal in *Clarence Borel v. Fibreboard Paper Products Company, et al.* The case would be a turning point in asbestos litigation, for the jury found the defendants guilty of contributory negligence. It also awarded the plaintiff damages based on the contention that the companies knew of the dangers inherent in working with the product. In upholding the verdict, the U.S. Appeals Court wrote what was described in *Strategic Management* as a scorching indictment of the defendants.

One of Goodwin's major contributions to JM was his decision to move the company from Madison Avenue in New York. Goodwin selected the Ken-Caryl cattle ranch, 15 miles from downtown Denver, Colorado, as the site for the new headquarters. When completed, the new building was described in *Business Week* as "ultramodern. . . . [The building] juts out like a landlocked ocean liner in a mountain canyon." The building was a tangible reminder that JM's style had changed drastically.

Goodwin never worked at the new location. Just two weeks prior to its completion, he was summoned to New York to meet with the board of directors. On September 1, 1976, Goodwin, Francis May, and other aides flew in and were met by John A. McKinney, a senior vice-president and the company's top legal officer by this time. The next evening, William F. May, John P. Schroeder, and Charles J. Zwick, members of the board of directors, met with Goodwin. Schroeder explained that they represented the nine outside directors on JM's 12-member board and that they all wanted his resignation. Goodwin was surprised but acquiesced. The terms of his separation agreement prevented him from ever discussing his departure or the reasons for it. Industry observers speculated that Goodwin's management style was too casual or flamboyant for the conservative board and that once he got the company moving in the right direction, the directors replaced him. The next morning, John A. McKinney, who did not know in advance that the board sought to remove Goodwin, was appointed the new president of JM. *Fortune* quoted McKinney as saying, "It happened so fast, I almost missed it."

1970s: Focusing on Profits under McKinney

Under Goodwin, JM had stressed growth; under McKinney, JM stressed profits. During his first year as president, McKinney eliminated unprofitable diversification and expanded asbestos and fiberglass capacity. One of his early acts as president was to elevate Fred L. Pundsack, a 24-year JM veteran, to Executive Vice-president of Operations, on equal footing with Francis May. Pundsack's directive was to maximize profits.

McKinney quickly earned a reputation as a tough negotiator. In 1977, Quebec threatened to nationalize the company's Jeffrey mine, the world's largest asbestos mine. McKinney put JM's $77 million expansion plan on hold and took a hard line with Premier René Lévesque. Lévesque withdrew his proposal, and JM resumed its expansion plans. Later in the year, JM's fiberglass production suffered from a 102-day strike at its Defiance, Ohio, plant. The strike cost the company $7.5 million in lost revenues. McKinney stood his ground, and in October workers accepted the same offer they had rejected in September, by a two-to-one margin. In May 1977, McKinney was named chairman of the board and chief executive officer. Pundsack became president and chief operating officer.

In 1977, JM estimated that the $16 million available through primary coverage to settle outstanding asbestos suits would be depleted within two years. New case filings rose from 159 in 1976 to 792 in 1978. Cases were being settled at a faster pace as well, with an average cost to the company of $21,000, of which $15,400 was awarded to the plaintiff and the balance going for legal fees. As Travelers was unable to predict the scope and number of future suits, it refused to renew its policy for the 1977 fiscal year. JM was forced to insure itself.

By 1979, McKinney was spending half of his time on the asbestos problem. He continued to be a tough negotiator. In May 1979, a writer for *Fortune* stated, ''Asbestos litigation is almost a separate business at JM.'' The company was a co-defendant in about 1,500 lawsuits brought by insulation workers who handled JM's products while working for other companies in construction or in the shipyards. At McKinney's insistence, JM sued the government to force it to indemnify the company against the suits from shipyard workers, as many of the claimants had worked with asbestos insulation during World War II and the Korean War in defense-related capacities.

In January 1979, JM completed its acquisition of Olinkraft Inc., a $447 million forest-products company, for about $600 million. W. Thomas Stephens, who was to have a lead role in JM's later bankruptcy reorganization, moved to JM from Olinkraft. Olinkraft, now operating as Manville Forest Products Corporation, owned 600,000 acres of timberlands in Louisiana, Arkansas, and Texas. It owned or leased another 100,000 acres in Brazil. Unexpectedly high start-up costs for Olinkraft, combined with a currency devaluation and tax increases in Brazil, caused JM's net income to fall 20 percent in the fourth quarter of 1979. Although its stock price fell 40 percent, Manville surpassed the $2 billion mark in sales for the first time.

Revenues in 1980 were on a par with those in 1979, with earnings dropping sharply in a weak construction market. The company remained heavily involved with asbestos. McKinney noted that asbestos and Manville were virtually synonymous and told *Forbes* in May 1980, ''The day asbestos isn't good business for us, we'll get out of it.'' At the same time, he felt that Olinkraft, once past its initial problems, would shape the future of JM. In 1980, McKinney reported that the company remained optimistic in the face of mounting lawsuits, as the firm had been victorious in the majority of the cases that had thus far proceeded to trial.

Restructuring and Bankruptcy: 1980s

Effective October 30, 1981, JM's shareholders approved a reorganized corporate structure consisting of a new parent company, Manville Corporation, and five wholly separate operating subsidiaries: Manville Building Materials Corporation, Manville Forest Products Corporation, Manville International Corporation, Manville Products Corporation, and Johns-Manville

Corporation. Johns-Manville shareholders retained their stock, which was converted to Manville Corporation stock on a share-for-share basis.

As of December 31, 1981, Manville was a defendant or co-defendant in approximately 9,300 asbestos suits brought by 12,800 individuals. Juries were making large awards in punitive damages, which were not covered by insurance. By 1982, settlements approximated $40,000 per case, including legal fees. Manville's consultants estimated that over the course of the next 20 years the company could be liable for 32,000 cases in addition to the 16,500 that had already been filed. Possible litigation costs were estimated at $2 billion, twice the company's assets at the time. By 1985, 19,750 claims had been filed against the company. In addition, Manville was alleged to be liable for asbestos-removal property-damage claims. Manville repeatedly filed appeals to postpone payments in suits it had lost. McKinney continued to assert that the government must pay a portion of the claims arising from exposure in the shipyards and other government jobs.

On August 26, 1982, in light of the asbestos litigation and posted losses in the first and second quarters of the year, Manville filed for protection under Chapter 11 of the U.S. Bankruptcy Code. While under bankruptcy court protection, Manville's earnings for the first nine months from continuing operations improved from $10 million to $59 million. Legal expenses, however, increased apace: legal costs rose from $1 million for a period of nine months in 1982 and 1983 to $11 million for the same period a year later.

After a dozen court-granted postponements, Manville proposed its reorganization plan on November 21, 1983. The plan was produced unilaterally, since attempts at a negotiated settlement with asbestos victims' representatives had failed. At that time, Manville proposed to split itself into two companies: the first would handle the business and the second would possess few assets yet all of the liability for the asbestos claims. Manville would be insulated from any and all claims. All cash, after operating expenses, would be funneled to the second company. Suits would be settled by the company out of court. Concurrently, Manville left the asbestos business, selling its last plant in 1985.

Leon Silverman, court-appointed attorney for unknown future asbestos claimants, helped orchestrate the final reorganization plan, filed on February 14, 1986. This plan resembled the earlier proposal with these amendments: the second company became two trusts, one for personal injury—the health fund—and the other for property-damage claims. The trusts would be funded through cash, future earnings, stock, bonds, and insurance payments worth at least $2.5 billion. Initially, the health-fund trust was to receive $1 billion. Beginning in 1992, Manville would have to pay the health fund $75 million a year. The property-damage trust was to be funded initially with $125 million, with additional funds available. Furthermore, plaintiffs retained the right to a jury trial if they disagreed with the determination made by the trusts. The plan seemed to satisfy the claimants but at considerable expense to Manville common stock owners, who saw their investment becoming virtually worthless under the plan. On neither side was there agreement that the trusts were viable solutions. Michael L. Goldberg, attorney for 700 asbestos claimants, estimated in 1988 that the trusts would be almost $200 million short by 1992.

In 1986, McKinney resigned and Josh T. Hulce, who had been president since 1984, abruptly quit. George Dillon, a Manville director for 17 years, became chairman and W. Thomas Stephens was tapped to become president and chief executive officer. Stephens, formerly an industrial engineer with Olinkraft and Manville's chief financial officer during the preceding three years, was credited with playing a pivotal role in bringing Manville out of bankruptcy. One of Stephens's first moves as president was to establish small meetings with Manville employees, who, like the public and the stockholders, had lost faith in the company. Stephens reassured them that Manville would continue to operate much as it had in the past. He intended to concentrate on its core businesses and generate enough cash flow over the next years to fund the trust. Profits doubled in 1987 to a record $164 million.

Late 1980s Turnaround

In 1988, Manville emerged from bankruptcy. The Chapter 11 filing forced Manville to reexamine the way it conducted its business. Extensive in-house restructuring resulted in a policy of encouraging more decision-making from the company's various components. Incentive programs were also instituted.

After three full years of trimming operations, Manville was again a healthy company with new product lines. It moved out of its headquarters into smaller spaces in Denver and reinvested the concomitant savings in plant upgrading. In the November 1988 issue of *Business Month,* Stephens stated, ''Two back-to-back years of record performance should send out a signal pretty loud and clear that we're stronger than ever.''

One of Manville's subsidiaries, Atlanta-based Riverwood International, was a rising star in the paper industry stock market. A producer of lumber, containerboard, and clay-coated paperboard for the beverage and food industries, Riverwood made 50 to 60 percent of the paper beer cartons in the United States. The company also manufactured 20 to 30 percent of all paper containers made for soft drinks. Riverwood became a public company in June 1992 when it sold 12.1 million shares of stocks. Manville, however, still controlled 80 percent of the company.

By 1990, almost 130,000 claims had been filed and the Manville Personal Injury Settlement Trust ran out of funds. The dearth of cash was due to the rapid pace of claims settlement, many of which were delayed during Manville's bankruptcy. The Fund trustees, headed by Director Marianna Smith, proposed three cost-cutting measures. First, the Fund would refuse to pay post-judgment interest whenever plaintiffs contested their trust settlements. Second, settlements and court-order judgments would be paid in installments rather than in lump sums. Third, the Trust would declare that funds were not subject to attachment or levy by the court. Attorneys for the plaintiffs argued that the Fund trustees did not have the authority to implement such restrictions and called for Manville to liquidate the Trust's 24 million shares, worth approximately $1 billion. Although the company accelerated a $50 million payment to the trust, it was revealed that the claims that had been settled would not be paid for almost 20 years, long after many of the claimants

had died. In July 1990, the court imposed a payments freeze while the company tried to determine how to handle the situation. In September 1990, Manville agreed to add up to $520 million to the asbestos fund during the next seven years.

Manville suffered great public relations setbacks as a result of the asbestos lawsuits. In an annual *Fortune* magazine poll of America's most admired companies, Manville finished last for five consecutive years, from 1987 to 1991. In an effort to regain the public's trust, Manville began to regularly monitor the health of its employees with a computer tracking system. In addition, Manville placed cautionary labels on any of its products that had been found to contain possible carcinogens. This procedure hurt sales, particularly in Japan, where packages with cancer warnings were initially refused entry into the country.

Manville spent the majority of the 1990s restructuring in an attempt to revamp its image. During 1991, the firm adopted a holding company structure with two main business units. Manville Sales Corporation—renamed Schuller International Group Inc. in 1992—oversaw its fiberglass operations and Manville Forest Products operated the company's forest products business.

In 1993, Schuller entered into an agreement with Owens Corning Fiberglass in which Schuller acquired its commercial and industrial roofing business, while selling its residential roofing business to Owens Corning. The company also acquired Steinachglas, a German glass mat producer.

The firm appeared to be digging out of its asbestos problems by the mid-1990s. The Bankruptcy Act of 1994 included a provision that stated Schuller was permanently shielded from any asbestos liability, which started to put many investors' minds at ease. At the same time, a new settlement method for the Trust was approved by the District Court of New York in 1995. Schuller launched an initial public offering of $400 million senior notes in late 1994. The proceeds were filtered back to the Trust.

During this time period, the firm sold off its interests in Riverwood International Corporation and Stillwater Mining Company. Fueled by these sales, the company began making strategic acquisitions. It added Nord Bitumi, Dibiten USA, Web Dynamics, and NRG Barriers to its arsenal in 1996, bought Ergon Nonwovens the following year, and Exeltherm and Tasso AB in 1998. It also began building new manufacturing facilities in the United States and expanded into Poland and China.

Manville changed its name to Schuller Corporation in 1996. The new name did not stick, however, and shareholders agreed to revert back to Johns Manville Corporation in 1997. As CEO Jerry Henry—who replaced Stephens in 1996—commented in an April 1997 *Wall Street Journal* article, ''People were asking me what this Schuller company was.'' He added, ''Wouldn't we be better off with a name with so much more recognition?'' While many industry analysts balked at the decision to take a name that was practically synonymous with asbestos, Henry stood firmly behind the corporate moniker believing JM would be more successful with its original name.

As JM pushed forward with its growth plans, the Trust announced in 1999 that it wanted to sell its shares in order to fund the $250 million it was paying in claims each year. In June

2000, Hicks, Muse, Tate & Furst Inc. and Bear Stearns Cos. agreed to acquire JM for $2.4 billion. The slowing economy and weak earnings forced the parties to call off the deal in early December. Later that month, Berkshire Hathaway Inc. offered $1.96 billion for JM. The purchase, completed in 2001, was Berkshire's fourth materials acquisition in just over a year. Berkshire's legendary chairman and CEO, Warren Buffet, was known for his attraction to market leaders, and by now JM had strong footing in the commercial and industrial fiberglass insulation and roofing systems industries. To Buffet, JM was a perfect fit.

Under its new parent, JM was afforded the financially stability to continue its growth strategy. In 2001, it added Slovakian fiberglass manufacturing concern Skloplast a.s. to its holdings. The company remained focused on bolstering its product lines while at the same time maintaining high levels of customer satisfaction. The Berkshire Hathaway purchase put JM on solid ground, leaving it to focus on a successful future in the years to come.

Principal Competitors

Lafarge S.A.; Owens Corning; Saint-Gobain plc.

Further Reading

Adler, Stacy, "Judge Sets a Deadline for Manville Trust Reform," *Business Insurance*, July 16, 1990.
——, "Manville Proposes Steps to Preserve Claims Fund Cash," *Business Insurance*, January 22, 1990.
——, "Manville Trust Officials Defend Management," *Business Insurance*, June 18, 1990.
Brodeur, Paul, *Outrageous Misconduct: The Asbestos Industry on Trial*, New York, Pantheon Books, 1985.
Conklin, J.C., "Johns Manville Can't Find a Buyer, Seeks Other Options," *Wall Street Journal*, April 21, 1999.
Crespo, Mariana, "Albatross," *Financial World*, April 11, 1995, p. 36.
Dillon, George C., "Does It Pay to Do the Right Thing?," *Across the Board*, July-August 1991.
Galen, Michele, "Back in Jeopardy at Manville," *Business Week*, June 25, 1990.
Gerlin, Andrea, "Schuller Has a New Attitude but Faces Old Tensions," *Wall Street Journal*, September 11, 1996, p. B6.
Green, William, "Resurrection," *Forbes*, November 3, 1997, p. 68.
Lee, Louise, "Company Thinks Old Reputation May Be Better Than None at All," *Wall Street Journal*, April 1, 1997, p. B1.
McNaughton, David, "Manville Corp. Unit Prospers in the Paper Industry," *Denver Post*, February 17, 1993.
Pearce, John A., II, and Richard B. Robinson, Jr., *Case 18: Manville Corporation (1987), Strategic Management: Strategy Formulation and Implementation*, Homewood, Ill.: Irwin, 1988.
Roach, John D.C., "Reshaping Corporate America," *Management Accounting*, March 1990.
Scannell, Kara, "Johns Manville Abandons Buyout after Failing to Agree on Terms," *Wall Street Journal*, December 11, 2000, p. A23.
Solomon, Stephen, "The Asbestos Fallout at Johns-Manville," *Fortune*, May 7, 1979.
Spurgeon, Devon, "Berkshire to Buy Manville for $1.96 Billion," *Wall Street Journal*, December 21, 2000, p. A3.
Zepser, Andy, "The Asbestos Curse," *Barron's*, October 14, 1991.
Zirin, James D., "Wining the Asbestos Game," *Barron's*, November 19, 2001, p.40.

—Lynn M. Kalanik
—updates: Mary McNulty and Christina M. Stansell

JURYS DOYLE
HOTEL GROUP plc

Jurys Doyle Hotel Group plc

146 Pembroke Road, Ballsbridge
Dublin
Ireland
Telephone: (+353) 1 607 0070
Fax: (+353) 1 660 5728
Web site: http://www.jurysdoyle.com

Public Company
Incorporated: 1924 as Jurys Hotel
Employees: 4,000
Sales: EUR 253.77 million ($303 million)(2003)
Stock Exchanges: Irish London
Ticker Symbol: JDH
NAIC: 721110 Hotels (Except Casino Hotels) and
    Motels

Jurys Doyle Hotel Group plc is Ireland's leading hotel group with a fast-growing international component as well. The company operates more than 30 hotels in Ireland, the United Kingdom, and in the United States. The company's Irish home base includes 13 hotels in Dublin, Limerick, Cork, and Galway. Ireland accounts for just under half of the group's revenues. The company's fastest-growing segment is in the United Kingdom, where it operates 15 hotels in London, Manchester, Birmingham, Newcastle, Edinburgh, and Glasgow, as well as in Belfast. Jurys Doyle is also present in the United States with three hotels. Since the early 2000s, the company has been shifting its portfolio to emphasize its higher-margin four-star and five-star properties and has been selling off its lower-margin three-star properties. Jurys Doyle hotels are marketed under two core brands, the four-star Jurys Hotel brand, and the mid-priced Jurys Inn brand. The group's five-star hotels operate under their own names and include The Berkeley Court, The Westbury, and The Towers in Dublin. The company has put into place a strong development program, with six new hotels slated to add 1,500 more rooms by mid-2005. The new openings will boost the company's total number of rooms to nearly 8,000. Quoted on the Irish and London Stock Exchanges, Jurys Doyle posted sales of EUR 253.77 million ($303 million) in 2003. The company is led by CEO Pat McCann.

19th Century Beginnings

William Jurys, a former commercial traveler, set up an inn catering to the commercial sector on Dublin's College Green in 1839. The inn grew and by mid-century had become known as the Commercial and Family Hotel. In 1866, Jurys became part of the partnership that built the city's Shelbourne Hotel. After that hotel opened, Jurys sold his original business to a cousin, Henry James Jurys. Over the next two decades, Henry Jurys further expanded the College Green hotel site. Henry Jurys died, but the hotel remained in the Jurys family, becoming known as Jurys Hotel—one of several Dublin locales featured in James Joyce's *Ulysses*—until it was requisitioned by the British forces during Ireland's War of Independence in 1918.

In 1924, after the hotel had been vacant for some two years, a group of Dublin businessmen bought the property, founding Jurys Hotel Ltd. That company bought a second property in Dublin, on Moira Street. Later, in 1963, the company unveiled a new 80-room wing for the original College Green property. The boom in the Irish tourist market during that decade encouraged the company to add two new hotels in the west of Ireland; one opened in Westport in 1970 and the other in Sligo in 1971.

Yet even as the company's new hotels opened, the tourist market appeared to fizzle out. Confronted with high maintenance costs for its aging Dublin hotels, softer than expected traffic at its western sites, and rising competition—notably from the PV Doyle Group, founded in 1964—Jurys now faced an uncertain future.

In response, the company decided to disband, selling off its properties, including the original Jurys Hotel, in order to reform as a new company, Jurys Hotel Group Ltd. That company was specifically founded in order to acquire three new hotels in Dublin's Ballsbridge, and in Cork and Limerick from the Irish and Interncontinentals Hotels group. Nearly all of the company's former shareholders participated in the operation. At the same time, the company took on a number of new investors.

International Growth in the 1990s

The company next renamed its new properties under the Jurys Hotel brand, with the Jurys Hotel Ballsbridge serving as

Company Perspectives:

At Jurys Doyle, we are dedicated to providing good quality hotel products that are appropriate to our customers needs in a friendly, professional and flexible environment.

the company's flagship. The company grew strongly into the early 1980s, expanding its Cork hotel in 1980 and again in 1986. The boom in Ireland's tourist trade prompted the group to begin seeking further expansion. In order to fuel its new growth plans, the company went public in 1986, listing on the Irish Stock Exchange. The public offering was accompanied by the opening of a new major hotel, The Towers, in Dublin.

The 1990s marked a new era for Jurys as it grew into one of Ireland's leading hotel groups, then captured the top position at the end of the decade. Acquisitions formed a good part of the company's growth, starting with its first acquisition, in 1990, of the Ardree Hotel in Waterford. Yet Jurys had also set its sights on developing an international hotel portfolio, with its natural target being the United Kingdom. In 1990, the company made its first entry into the United Kingdom, buying a Glasgow hotel from the Stakis Group. A new acquisition, in 1993, added the group's first London hotel, the Onslow, which was subsequently renamed the Jurys Kensington.

By then, Jurys had developed a new hotel brand, the mid-priced Jurys Inn, the first two of which were opened in Galway and Christchurch, in Dublin, in 1993. A third Inn opened in Cork in 1994. By mid-decade, the formula had proved a success, and the company began a larger rollout, targeting especially the United Kingdom from 1996. In 1995, the company had begun listing on the London Stock Exchange.

In the meantime, Jurys had been adding a number of other hotel properties, which were brought in under the Jurys Hotels brand. These included Bristol's Unicorn in 1994 and the Cardiff International in 1995. The company also bought the prestigious London-based Custom House, which was redeveloped as the Jurys Great Russell Street Hotel in 1999.

That year marked the next major moment in Jurys history when the company agreed to purchase Irish rival Doyle Hotel Group in a cash and shares deal worth IRP194.5 million. Since its founding in 1964, the Doyle Group had grown into one of Ireland's major hotel groups, with properties in Ireland and the United Kingdom, but also with a small holding in the United States.

Founded by builder Pascal Vincent Doyle, that company had opened its first hotel, The Montrose, in Dublin in 1964. By the end of the 1960s, Doyle had already added three more hotels. In 1972, Doyle opened The Burlington, which became the largest hotel in Ireland, and in 1977 the company added its five-star Berkeley Court in Dublin. Another five-star hotel, The Westbury, also located in Dublin, was added in 1984. Doyle also sought growth beyond Ireland, and in the early 1980s added two hotels, The Normandy and The Courtyard by Marriot Northwest in Washington, D.C. In 1997, Doyle added a third Washington, D.C, site, buying the Dupont Plaza, where it built The Washington Hotel which opened in 1999.

Key Dates:

1839: William Jurys opens his commercial lodgings in Dublin, Ireland.

1866: After Jurys becomes a partner in a new Shelbourne Hotel, he sells his original hotel to his cousin Henry James Jurys, who expands the property, then called Commercial and Family Hotel, and later the Jurys Hotel.

1918: Jurys Hotel is requisitioned by the British army during Ireland's War of Independence.

1924: Jurys Hotel is acquired by a group of businessmen.

1963: The hotel adds a new 80-room wing.

1964: Developer Pascal Vincent Doyle opens his first hotel, The Montrose, in Dublin.

1966: Doyle opens two more hotels in Dublin.

1969: Doyle adds a fourth Dublin hotel.

1970: Jurys adds a new hotel in Westport.

1971: Jurys opens a new hotel in Sligo.

1972: Jurys sells off its properties and reforms as a new company in order to acquire three hotels in Dublin, Cork, and Limerick; Doyle opens Burlington Hotel.

1977: Doyle opens five-star Berkeley Court Hotel.

1984: Doyle moves into London with the acquisition of Clifton Ford Hotel; he also acquires two hotels in Washington, D.C.

1986: Jurys goes public on the Irish Stock Exchange.

1991: Jurys enters the United Kingdom with the purchase of a hotel in Glasgow.

1997: Doyle acquires Dupont Plaza in Washington, D.C., and begins construction on The Washington Hotel (opened in 1999).

1999: Jurys acquires Doyle and becomes Jurys Doyle Hotel Group, the largest in Ireland.

2002: The company begins selling off three-star properties to focus on four- and five-star hotels.

Critical Mass for the 2000s

The merger with Doyle doubled Jurys in size, boosting its portfolio to 32 hotels, with a total of nearly 5,500 rooms. The deal had also transformed the company, which became the Jurys Doyle Hotel Group, into a truly international company, with more than half of its properties located outside of Ireland.

As one observer stated, the deal enabled the company to achieve "critical mass," at least in terms of generating higher levels of institutional investments in order to fuel its growth strategy. Those plans called for the group to expand onto the European continent, with its most likely targets to come in the Eastern European markets, where the entry threshold was lower than in such major markets as Paris or Berlin. The company also hoped to expand beyond its Washington, DC, core in the United States, with plans to add new properties along the eastern seaboard.

In the meantime, the company set to work restructuring its existing portfolio, a process led by new CEO Pat McCann, who joined the company in 2000. Jurys Doyle began renovating and expanding a number of its existing properties, such as the 69-

bedroom addition to its London-based Jurys Clifton. The company also added a number of new sites, including two Chamberlain hotels in Birmingham in 2001.

In 2002, the company began a shift toward higher-margin properties, beginning a sell-off of many of its three-star locations in favor of refocusing its hotels portfolio around four- and five-star properties. At the same time, Jurys Doyle continued its expansion into the United Kingdom, where the company had targeted some 60 cities as potential future markets, opening the Jurys Inn Croydon in London in 2002 and the Jurys Inn Newcastle and Jurys Inn Glasgow in 2003.

By then, Jurys Doyle had already boosted its number of rooms to nearly 6,500, and its revenues had climbed to EUR 257 million ($303 million). The company had also begun a new expansion drive, with six new properties in development at the beginning of 2004, two of which, the Jurys Inn Leeds and the Jurys Inn Chelsea opened in London in February and March of that year. Other properties slated for opening included a new hotel in Dublin's Parnell Street, a hotel serving London Heathrow, and an entry into Southampton slated for 2005.

Jurys Doyle also looked forward to its first extension beyond Washington, D.C., in the United States, as it prepared for the opening of the new four-star Jurys Boston Hotel, scheduled to be in operation before the summer of 2004. The new openings were expected to add 1,500 bedrooms to the group's portfolio. Jurys Doyle had evolved into Ireland's leading hotel group, with plans to become a major European hotels player in the new century.

Principal Subsidiaries

Thornhill Inc; P.V. Doyle Holdings Ltd.; Koyland Ltd.; Back Bay Investments Ltd.; United Kingdom Hotel Investments Ltd.; P.V. Doyle Hotels Ltd.; Belfcard Ltd.; Jurys Doyle Hotel Management (UK) Ltd.; Jurys Doyle London Hotels Ltd.; Chamberlain Hotels Ltd. (United Kingdom); Jurys Doyle Hotel Group (UK) Ltd.; Jurys Doyle US Holdings, Inc; Jurys Washington, LLC (United States); Jyle B.V. (Netherlands); Jurys Doyle Hotels (Europe) SA (Luxembourg).

Principal Competitors

Loews Corporation; Radisson Hotels and Resorts; Compass Group plc; Marriott International Inc.; ACCOR S.A.; SABMiller plc; Hilton Group plc; Virgin Group Ltd.

Further Reading

Bergsman, Steve, "Doyle Dominates Dublin Market," *Hotel & Motel Management*, June 5, 1995, p. 4.

Creaton, Siobhan, "Good News at Inns for Jurys Doyle," *Irish Times*, April 22, 2004, p. 19.

Hensdill, Cherie, "Jurys Doyle Achieves Critical Mass," *Hotels*, October 2000, p. 18.

"Jurys Boss Banks on Three-star Inns to Give Group a Five-star Future," *Irish Times*, January 10, 2003, p. 61.

"Jurys Hotel Group Acquires Doyle Hotel Group," *Hotel-online.com*, April 1999.

"Jurys to Buy Its Inns at Christchurch and Galway," *Irish Times*, April 28, 2004, p. 42.

McAffrey, Una, "Jurys Slips in Tough Trading Conditions," *The Irish Times*, September 10, 2003, p. 16.

McCabe, Eileen, "Jurys to Open London Inn," *Times*, October 17, 1996, p. 33.

McHugh, Fiona, "Doyle Hotels Set for Pounds 225m Float," *Sunday Times*, May 17, 1998, p. 1.

Walsh, Dominic, "Jurys Close to Finalising Doyle Deal," *Times*, November 19, 1998, p. 35.

—M.L. Cohen

Knight Transportation, Inc.

5601 West Buckeye Road
Phoenix, Arizona 85043
U.S.A.
Telephone: (602) 269-2000
Fax: (602) 269-8409
Web site: http://www.knighttransportation.com

Public Company
Incorporated: 1989
Employees: 3,005
Sales: $340.06 million (2003)
Stock Exchanges: NASDAQ
Ticker Symbol: KNGT
NAIC: 484121 General Freight Trucking, Long-Distance,
  Truckload

Knight Transportation, Inc., is a trucking company focused on short-to-medium lengths of transporting freight. The average length of a Knight Transportation haul is 532 miles. The company operates regional terminals that serve as hubs for freight routes within 750 miles of the facility. The company maintains terminals in Phoenix, Arizona; Salt Lake City, Utah; Portland, Oregon; Denver, Colorado; Kansas City, Kansas; Katy, Texas; Indianapolis, Indiana; Charlotte, North Carolina; Gulfport, Mississippi; Memphis, Tennessee; Atlanta, Georgia; and Las Vegas, Nevada. The company hauls general commodities, including consumer goods, packaged foods, paper products, and beverage containers, as well as import and export products. Knight Transportation is praised for the loyalty of its drivers and its efficient operation. The company ranks as one of the fastest growing companies in its industry.

Origins

Knight Transportation, from its conception to its widely hailed success as one of the fastest-growing corporations in the United States, was led, and majority-owned, by four members of the Knight family. The central figures in the family-run business that drew excited praise from the business press were brothers Randy Knight and Gary Knight and their cousins, also brothers, Keith Knight and Kevin Knight. The four Knights cemented their kinship early in their lives, choosing the same profession and the same employer. After completing high school, Randy, Gary, Keith, and Kevin joined a trucking company named Swift Transportation Co., a firm that factored as a major player in the industry during Knight Transportation's celebrated rise.

All of the four Knight family members were groomed as future executives of Swift Transportation, a company managed by the Moyes family. Randy Knight, who figured as the impetus for Knight Transportation's formation, rose to the rank of vice-president at Swift Transportation, spending 16 years at the company before leaving in 1985. Randy Knight's departure was prompted by his perception that his professional progression at Swift Transportation was limited. He was not a member of the Moyes family, which, according to his thinking, barred his advancement beyond the position of vice-president. Randy Knight left Swift Transportation in 1985 and started a company named Total Warehousing Inc., but his entrepreneurial talents would find their greatest expression with the formation of Knight Transportation. Randy Knight was forced to wait for his destiny, however. The eldest member of the founding Knight Transportation contingent, Randy Knight was bound by a five-year noncompete agreement he signed with Swift Transportation. When he left in 1985, the clock started ticking toward the end of his noncompete agreement, when he was legally able to start his own trucking enterprise.

Randy Knight acted as swiftly as he could after he left the Moyes-run company. He incorporated Knight Transportation in 1989, an event that served as a prelude to the actual operation of the company as a commercial enterprise. With him at the inception of the company were Gary Knight, appointed Knight Transportation's president, Kevin Knight, named chief executive officer, and Keith Knight, an executive vice-president who managed the company's sales operation in Los Angeles. Each of the four Knights contributed $50,000 to get the company up and running, an investment that was coupled with a $10 million

Company Perspectives:

Our operating strategy is to achieve a high level of asset utilization within a highly disciplined operating system while maintaining strict controls over our cost structure. To achieve these goals, we operate primarily in high-density, predictable traffic lanes in select geographic regions, and attempt to develop and expand our customer base around each of our terminal facilities. This operating strategy allows us to take advantage of the large amount of freight traffic transported in regional markets, realize the operating efficiencies associated with regional hauls, and offer more flexible service to our customers than rail, intermodal, and smaller regional competitors. In addition, shorter hauls provide an attractive alternative to drivers in the truckload sector by reducing the amount of time spent away from home. We believe this improves driver retention, decreases recruitment and training costs, and reduces insurance claims and other costs. We operate a modern fleet to accelerate revenue growth and enhance our operating efficiencies. We employ technology in a cost-effective manner where it assists us in controlling operating costs and enhancing revenue. Our goal is to increase our market presence significantly, both in existing operating regions and in other areas where we believe the freight environment meets our operating strategy, while seeking to achieve industry-leading operating margins and returns on investment.

line of credit from Mercedes-Benz of North America. On July 19, 1990, Knight Transportation officially became operational, hauling its first three loads from Phoenix, Arizona, to Los Angeles and back. By the end of its first week in business, Knight Transportation had hauled 15 loads.

Combined, the four Knight family members had more than 80 years of experience in the trucking industry when they started Knight Transportation. They intended to use their experience to make the company one of the major competitors in the industry. The Knights cast their company as a regional trucking concern focused on offering short- to medium-length hauls, the largest segment of the trucking market; approximately 75 percent of all truckload freight moved less than 500 miles. To succeed, the Knights emphasized fostering driver loyalty and they placed a premium on the efficient execution of coordinating the movement of their customers' freight. Every trucking operator claimed to strive for efficient operation, but the Knights made good on their claim, excelling at managing the movement of freight. "Face it," an analyst remarked in a March 26, 2001 interview with *Investor's Business Daily,* "these are asset-intensive businesses, so the key to success or failure is asset utilization. Knight [Transportation] doesn't let a tractor sit under a trailer to be loaded or unloaded for any period of time."

The four Knight family members gradually expanded their business during the early 1990s. The company was able to recruit drivers by paying them well and by offering what few other trucking employers offered their drivers: frequent oppor-

tunities to spend time with family. Thanks to the company's ability to neatly choreograph the complex web of routes that sustained its operations, its drivers typically spent three nights a week at home, while drivers for other short-haul trucking concerns typically spent two nights a week at home or less. (The industry average for all types of trucking firms was one night every two to three weeks.) Drivers were eager to work for the family-owned and -managed firm, enabling the company to record impressive financial growth during its first years in operation. In 1991, its first full year in operation, Knight Transportation generated $13.4 million in revenue. Within the next two years, Knight Transportation's sales volume nearly doubled, reaching $26.4 million in 1993, when the company's fleet consisted of more than 200 trucks.

Expansion After 1994 Public Offering

The company's success during its first three years in operation was based on its development of markets in Arizona and California. The Knight family's objective from the outset, however, was to make Knight Transportation one of the leading companies in the industry, a goal to be achieved only if the company expanded beyond its core markets. To facilitate the company's maturation into a national force, the Knights took the company public in 1994, filing with Securities and Exchange Commission for a $22 million initial public offering (IPO) of stock. The company completed its IPO in October 1994, enabling it to develop ambitious expansion plans. Looking ahead, Randy Knight wanted to expand into Nevada, Utah, Colorado, New Mexico, Texas, and the Pacific Northwest. To support this geographic march, he placed orders in 1994 to increase the size of the company's fleet by 40 percent, including the purchase of 83 tractors and 225 trailers by the end of 1995.

Aside from the financial advantages of becoming a publicly traded company, Knight Transportation also strengthened its bond with its drivers through the IPO. The company initiated a stock-option program concurrent with its conversion to public ownership, which made Knight Transportation one of only two trucking companies in the country to offer its drivers stock options. The allegiance of the company's drivers, which had been remarkably strong before the implementation of the program, became legendary throughout the industry after stock options were granted as perquisites for driving a Knight Transportation truck. The loyalty of the company's drivers had a salubrious effect on all aspects of the company's operations, figuring as one of the chief reasons the company earned praise from critics and peers. In 1996, *Forbes* magazine placed Knight Transportation on its annual list of the "200 Best Small Companies in the United States." Typically, annual driver turnover in the trucking industry neared 100 percent, but at Knight Transportation the turnover rate averaged 50 percent. The company, by this point, ranked as the fastest growing and most profitable publicly traded trucking firm in the country. Between 1991 and 1996, the company's revenue increased at an annual compound rate of 43 percent, a growth rate eclipsed by its increases in profits. During the same five-year period, Knight Transportation's earnings grew at an annual compound rate of 61 percent.

The physical expansion aided by the company's IPO in late 1994 began to chart its progress as *Forbes* and other onlookers took note of its success. Knight Transportation's geographic reach was extended by establishing regional terminals that served as hubs to support the company's expanding fleet of trucks and trailers. In February 1996, the company opened a terminal in Katy, Texas, which was followed two months later by the establishment of a terminal in Indianapolis, Indiana, its first terminal east of the Mississippi River. By mid-1996, the company maintained a fleet of 500 trucks, more than twice the number in operation three years earlier. In addition to these vehicles, the company was supported by trucks owned by its drivers, who contracted with Knight Transportation as independent contractors. The company began contracting with owner-operators in 1994, when it initiated its independent contractor program. By the end of 1996, when sales totaled $77.5 million, the company relied on 158 trucks that were owned and operated by independent contractors.

The company's expansion in the late 1990s was fueled by opening additional regional terminals and by taking advantage of a new mode of expansion—acquiring other trucking companies. By pursuing both avenues of expansion, the company's financial stature swelled during the late 1990s and, particularly, in the first years of the 21st century. In 1998, after generating $99.4 million in revenue the previous year, Knight Transportation eclipsed a financial milestone, recording $125 million in revenue, the same year it eclipsed another milestone by employing more than 1,000 workers for the first time in its history. In 1999, the company set out to increase these totals substantially, initiating an expansion program that added new regional terminals and the assets of other trucking concerns to its fold. The company established a terminal in Charlotte, North Carolina, and a terminal in Salt Lake City, Utah. On the acquisition front, the company completed its first major deal, purchasing Action Delivery Service Inc. and its affiliated company, Action Warehouse Services Inc. Based in Corsicana, Texas, Action operated as a privately held carrier serving customers in Texas and the south-central United States. The company maintained a fleet of 50 tractors and 130 trailers, registering $5.6 million in revenue in 1998.

Knight Transportation pressed ahead with its growth plans as the company entered a new decade with a change in leadership. In July 1999, Randy Knight retired as chairman of the board. Kevin Knight took on the responsibilities of chairman while holding on to his post as chief executive officer. Under Kevin Knight's stewardship, the company struck again on the acquisition front in 2000, purchasing the trucking operation of Gulfport, Mississippi-based John Fayard Fast Freight Inc., which operated as Fastway Systems.

Rapid Growth in the 21st Century

During the first years of the 21st century, Knight Transportation focused on increasing its physical presence. The company opened a number of new terminals, transforming it into a genuine, national competitor. A new terminal in Kansas City, Kansas was opened in 2001, fleshing out the company's presence in the Midwest. For the seventh consecutive year, *Forbes* magazine selected Knight Transportation as one of the ''200 Best Small Companies in the United States'' in 2001, a year in which the company's trucks logged more than 240 million miles. In 2002, after recording 11 consecutive years of revenue growth ranging between 20 percent and 30 percent, Knight Transportation added two new terminals to its growing list of regional hubs. In March, the company entered the Pacific Northwest for the first time, establishing a terminal in Portland, Oregon. In July, Knight Transportation opened a terminal in Memphis, Tennessee.

As Knight Transportation neared its 15th anniversary, the company exuded enviable vitality. It ranked as the fastest growing trucking company in the nation, boasting an impressive record of financial growth. In 2003, the company posted $35.5 million in net income, nearly three times the total recorded five years earlier. Revenues, which stood at $125 million in 1998, had swelled to $340 million, making Knight Transportation, as its founders had envisioned, one of the industry's major competitors. As the company prepared for the future, there were few observers who doubted the ability of the Knight family to continue its record of success. To maintain its electric rate of growth, the company pressed forward with expansion, opening terminals in Atlanta, Georgia, and Denver, Colorado, in 2003. In February 2004, the company established a regional hub in Las Vegas, Nevada, with plans calling for the opening of two additional terminals by the end of the year. With a national network of regional terminals in place, Knight Transportation promised to figure prominently in the trucking industry's future.

Principal Subsidiaries

Knight Management Services, Inc.; Knight Transportation South Central, L.P.; KTTE Holdings, Inc.; QKTE Holdings, Inc.; Quad K Leasing, Inc.

Principal Competitors

Heartland Express, Inc.; Schneider National, Inc.; Swift Transportation Co., Inc.

Further Reading

''The Arizona Republic AZ Inc., Column,'' *Knight Ridder/Tribune Business News*, April 21, 2000.

''The Arizona Republic AZ Inc., Column,'' *Knight Ridder/Tribune Business News,* April 1, 1999.

Elliot, Alan R., ''Market Woes Aside, Sales Keep On Trucking,'' *Investor's Business Daily,* March 26, 2001, p. A10.

''Kings of the Road,'' *Business Journal—Serving Phoenix & the Valley of the Sun,* December 14, 2001, p. 27.

Luebke, Cathy, ''Knight Transportation Files for $22 Million IPO,'' *Business Journal—Serving Phoenix & the Valley of the Sun,* September 9, 1994, p. 7.

Much, Marilyn, ''In This Business Only the Strong(est) Survive,'' *Investor's Business Daily,* April 17, 2003, p. A08.

Shinkle, Kirk, ''Knight Transportation Inc.; Phoenix, Ariz., Trucker Hits High Gear, Avoids Market Potholes,'' *Investor's Business Daily,* December 28, 2001, p. A08.

Upbin, Bruce, ''Happy Drivers, Happy Customers,'' *Forbes,* November 4, 1996, p. 165.

—Jeffrey L. Covell

Koenig & Bauer AG

Friedrich-Koenig-Strasse 4
D-97080 Würzburg
Germany
Telephone: (+49) 931 909-0
Fax: (+49) 931 909-4101
Web site: http://www.kba-print.com

Public Company
Incorporated: 1817 as Schnellpressenfabrik Koenig & Bauer
Employees: 7,054
Sales: EUR 1.23 billion ($1.55 billion) (2003)
Stock Exchanges: Frankfurt
Ticker Symbol: SKB
NAIC: 333293 Printing Machinery and Equipment Manufacturing

Koenig & Bauer AG (KBA) sees itself as the world's third-largest manufacturer of printing machines. The company makes web presses for printing newspapers, books, booklets, and directories, as well as publication rotogravure, and is the world's largest manufacturer of securities and banknote printing machines. KBA also produces presses for conventional and digital offset printing and supplements its range of printing presses with peripheral systems for paper logistics and counterfeit-proofing. Headquartered in Wurzburg, Germany, the KBA group has production subsidiaries in Germany, Austria, and the United States and a network of sales offices and service stations stretching from Sweden to Italy, from Singapore to Australia, from Russia to China, and from the United States to Brazil. The Bolza-Schünemann family owns roughly 41 percent of KBA.

A Steam-Powered Printing Press in the Early 19th Century

For three centuries, printing businesses relied on the Gutenberg hand press invented in the late 15th century. Operating the heavy presses that put out about 240 sheets per hour was physi-cally exhausting. In 1803, Friedrich Gottlob Koenig, a 27-year-old German printer who had studied mathematics, physics, and mechanics at Leipzig University became obsessed with the idea of creating a steam-powered printing press. Looking for funding, he traveled throughout Europe but was only greeted with deep-seated skepticism and rejections. In November 1806, he traveled to England and finally found a sponsor for his idea in Thomas Bensley, the country's most prominent book printer. With the help of Andreas Friedrich Bauer, a German precision instrument maker whom Koenig had met in London, he was able to make his idea a reality. In April 1811, the machine, for which Koenig had received a patent a year earlier, was first presented at a printing trade show in London. However, the 400-sheet output of the all-metal steam-engine-driven press was not enough to convince English printing houses to spend the considerable amount it cost to manufacture. Looking for a way to significantly increase the machine's output, Koenig came up with the idea to replace the flat platen used in the Gutenberg press by a rotating cylinder that was able to move the paper sheets rapidly under pressure over the flat type form. Using this principle, Koenig was able to double the output of his machine, which operated smoothly and created high-quality impressions. When John Walter, publisher of the daily newspaper *The Times,* saw the new press in action in December 1812, he ordered two of them. Put together secretly in a different building to avoid an uproar among his workforce, Walter's machines printed the entire circulation of *The Times* overnight on November 28, 1814. Koenig's cylinder press, the output of which was further increased to 1,100 sheets per hour, initiated the industrial revolution in printing. Another improvement of his machine was a model that was able to print on both sides of the paper in one step.

When Koenig and Bauer set out to sell their new type of machines outside of England, they met resistance from their business partner Bensley. Finally, the three men agreed to part. Koenig and Bauer went back to Germany and purchased a secularized monastery in Oberzell near Wurzburg, Bavaria. On August 9, 1817, the two partners, who had become close friends, also established their new company, Schnellpres-senfabrik Koenig & Bauer. While the shipping of tools, machinery, and iron and coal from England took a few months, Friedrich Koenig traveled Germany in search of new customers.

Company Perspectives:

Our customers inspire our policies. Our workforce is our greatest asset. Our innovations secure our future. Our commitment is to quality. Our duty is to society. Our Objectives: To expand the frontiers of technology according to our motto 'Innovation is timeless.' To become the technological leader in prime markets. To expand our global market position in sheet-fed offset, web offset, newspaper and digital offset. To offer systems competence through in-house know-how or strategic partnerships. To maintain a consistently high quality both in our products and services. To offer practical solutions for individual production requirements. To intensify our customer care. To maintain a high level of staff motivation and qualification. To enhance shareholder value. To protect the environment by enhancing press and production ecology. To fulfill our social and cultural obligations.

The first ones were Berlin-based publishers Decker and Spener, who received the two presses they ordered in 1822.

Soon after the first machine-printed newspaper in continental Europe had come out in early 1823, Germany's top printing establishments became interested in the new technology. While they all received their steam-powered presses made in Oberzell by retrained iron and steel workers, Koenig was already on the road again, this time looking for business outside of Germany. After a demonstration of his machine at a trade show in Paris, Koenig brought in orders from Denmark, Switzerland, the Netherlands, Spain, and France. The first order from Spain was sent by mule over the Pyrénées mountains. In 1828, Koenig established a paper mill as a side business in another former monastery in Bavaria. Two years later, when business was soaring, the July Revolution in Paris brought export business with France as well as domestic orders to a sudden halt. The paper mill became the young company's sole source of income, and its workforce was cut back from 120 to 14. Three years later, Friedrich Koenig died just before his 54th birthday, and Andreas Bauer became the company's managing director.

While the company's orders began to increase as Germany's economy slowly recovered in the second half of the 1830s, the growing demand for printing machines created a number of competitors. Oddly, most of them sprang from Koenig & Bauer. Bauer was a brilliant engineer but lacked Koenig's business sense, strategic thinking, and imagination. His resistance to trying out new designs and manufacturing procedures proposed by some of the company's younger staff led to the establishment of new enterprises by former Koenig & Bauer employees. One of them was Friedrich Koenig's nephew, Fritz Helbig, who set up a printing press factory in Vienna, Austria, in 1836. When the new competition began to threaten Koenig & Bauer's market leadership, Bauer created a new type of circular motion press and sold 24 of them in the year after the new machine was first presented to the public in 1840. However, Bauer resisted the idea of expansion until his death in February 1860. By that time, two other main players in the German printing machine industry, which together with Koenig & Bauer were to become the world's leading manufacturers in the business, had been established. In 1844, another nephew of Friedrich Koenig, Carl Reichenbach, founded a printing press factory that later became one of Koenig & Bauer's main competitors, MAN Roland. The other one, Heidelberger Druckmaschinen, was founded by Andreas Hamm after he left a partnership with former Koenig & Bauer employee Andreas Albert.

Innovation and Expansion after 1860

After Andreas Bauer's death, Friedrich Koenig's two sons, Wilhelm and Friedrich, Jr., took over the management of the company. Friedrich, Jr., was a great organizer while Wilhelm took care of the technical side of the enterprise. They were greatly supported by their young mother Fanny Koenig, who did the business correspondence and helped with calculations and negotiations. Fanny Koenig was the driving force behind a number of social benefit programs for Koenig & Bauer workers—such as a sickness benefit fund, a company savings bank, an employee training center, and housing for workers—which were introduced in the 1860s. In 1873, a factory ordinance was introduced that defined workers' and managers' rights and obligations and a democratically elected factory council consisting of managers as well as workers was established that defined the rules of conduct and discussed and solved important work-related issues.

In 1886, the older son of Friedrich Koenig, Jr., Edgar Koenig, joined the company. However, he died at the age of 38. Albrecht Bolza, the son of Friedrich Koenig's daughter Luise, entered the family business in 1896, followed by the younger son of Friedrich Koenig Jr., Constantin Koenig. After Wilhelm Koenig's death in 1894, Bolza stepped in to help Friedrich Koenig, Jr., manage the company. With domestic and export business thriving again, demand outgrew the capacity of the factory in Oberzell by the late 1860s. A brand-new production hall was built nearby Würzburg in 1872. Another new factory, including Germany's largest manufacturing hall that stretched out over 740 feet was built in 1900. One year later, the monastery in Oberzell was sold. In 1905, the firm was transformed into a limited liability company with Alfred Bolza as managing director. In 1913, Koenig & Bauer acquired a 40 percent stake in Vienna-based Schnellpressenfabrik L. Kaiser's Söhne, the company which one of Friedrich Koenig's nephews had founded.

In the last quarter of the 19th century, Koenig & Bauer introduced a number of important innovations which formed the foundation of the company's success for decades to come. In 1875, the company started making so-called web-fed presses, or web presses. First introduced in the United States, the new presses printed on paper from rolls instead of paper sheets. In 1886, Wilhelm Koenig invented a web press that was able to cut the paper fed from a roll into sheets before they were printed. The machine also allowed for a variety of sheet sizes. Two years later, he constructed the first web press that was able to print in four colors. In 1890, Koenig & Bauer launched another novelty—a web press with two integrated printing units, a twin web press. In the early 1890s, Wilhelm Koenig laid the groundwork for two other of Koenig & Bauer's important product lines. He began to design presses for printing luxury color products and for printing securities and bank notes.

In the first decade of the 20th century, Koenig & Bauer focused on catering to the growing number of publishers that

Key Dates:

1817: Cylinder printing press manufacturer Schnellpressenfabrik Koenig & Bauer is established.
1828: The company sets up a paper mill.
1876: Koenig & Bauer's first web-fed rotary press is delivered to a Magdeburg newspaper.
1901: A new factory in Würzburg replaces the old one in the Oberzell monastery.
1913: Austrian Schnellpressenfabrik L. Kaiser's Söhne in Vienna is acquired.
1923: The company builds its first collective press for colored bank notes.
1936: Koenig & Bauer constructs the first "Rembrandt" sheet-fed rotogravure press.
1945: The company's production facilities in Würzburg are destroyed during bombings.
1952: The company enters a strategic partnership with Swiss security printing specialist Gualtiero Giori.
1959: Hans Bolza formally adopts engineer Hans-Bernhard Schünemann.
1964: A new factory is built in Trennfeld.
1978: Koenig & Bauer acquires a major share in Albert-Frankenthal GA.
1985: The company goes public.
1995: Koenig & Bauer merges with Albert-Frankenthal.
1998: The company merges with KBA-Planeta to form Koenig & Bauer AG (KBA).
2001: KBA takes over Swiss security printing specialist De La Rue Giori; the Bolza-Schünemann family gives up its absolute share majority; KBA shares are listed on the MDax.
2003: The company acquires specialty printing machine makers Bauer + Kunzi and Metronic.

were putting out richly illustrated books and magazines. The company developed a variety of publication presses, including stitching or ribbon fold units. At the same time, Koenig & Bauer began to make flat-bed presses and took on the development of rotogravure machines. In 1910, the company introduced an innovative security press with very high accuracy, the "Iris" press, followed by the first matrix-molding press, "Gigant," and a new type of plate-casting machine three years later. The first Koenig & Bauer rotogravure press left the factory in 1912.

Era of Destruction and Rebirth Begins in 1914

When World War I began in 1914, Koenig & Bauer was cut off from markets abroad and domestic demand for printing machines also came to a sudden halt. During the war, the company manufactured a cornucopia of necessary goods, from grinding machines and agricultural machinery, delivery vehicles, and wheel hubs and axles to horseshoes and cooking equipment. Germany's currency became catastrophically devalued in the early 1920s. Causing a short boom in demand for money-printing machines on one the hand, galloping inflation rapidly pushed up costs and wages on the other. To gain some advantage from this dire situation, Koenig & Bauer even issued its own emergency currency, which soon gained acceptance in

the Würzburg region. Meanwhile, the managing director of the company's Austrian subsidiary, a retired army officer who was fluent in several languages, brought in a number of orders from Eastern and Northern Europe. In November 1920, when one American dollar was worth 4.2 billion German paper marks, the German government got the situation under control with the introduction of a new currency. Through a close cooperation with the German Government Printing Office, Koenig & Bauer strengthened its leading position as a manufacturer of security presses. During the mid-1920s, orders from abroad picked up again. The company delivered large rotogravure press installations to customers in the United States and Canada and installed Europe's largest newspaper web press in Norway. However, the short-lived economic boom was stopped by the Great Depression, initiated by the New York Stock Exchange crash in late October 1929. High import duties shut down the export markets in France and Spain, while domestic demand began to dry up due to decreasing investment activities in the printing industry.

In 1931, Alfred Bolza's son Hans took over as Koenig & Bauer's managing director. The 41-year-old Hans, who had changed his course of studies from physics and mathematics to engineering after his older brother Benno suddenly died, led the company during the chaotic political and economic climate in Germany during the 1930s. By 1932, roughly one-third of German workers were looking for a job. One year later, Adolf Hitler became the country's new chancellor and immediately established a totalitarian regime. Once again, the demand for printing presses slipped into a steady decline. At first, the company's efforts to counteract this trend, including increased investment in trade show presentations, product innovation, reducing the number of models in certain product lines, and job sharing among workers to avoid layoffs, seemed to work. However, as Germany increasingly isolated itself from the rest of the world, demand for the country's products declined. At the same time, the Nazi Party began to suppress publishers that were not in line with its narrow ideology, diminishing the demand for printing presses even further. In 1936, Hitler launched his plan to prepare the country for yet another war, and the National Socialist government seized control of the economy. Koenig & Bauer gave in to the mounting political pressure and began to manufacture war goods. In 1937, the company acquired a Würzburg-based competitor, Schnellpressenfabrik Bohn + Herber. One year later, when Austria was occupied by Nazi Germany, Koenig & Bauer's Austrian subsidiary was unable to bring in business from abroad. During World War II, Koenig & Bauer's remaining workforce repaired damaged machine tools for the German roller-bearing industry in nearby Schweinfurt. In March 1945, just before the war ended, the company's main production facilities in Würzburg were destroyed by Allied bombs.

Under the postwar Allied military administration, Koenig & Bauer's business had to be reconstructed from scratch. While rebuilding its two production plants in Würzburg, the company's engineers took on any kind of mechanical repair work. While bartering flourished during the postwar period, the flood of decrees issued by the military occupation forces had to be put in print, causing the demand for printing presses to pick up once again. The introduction of the new Deutsche Mark in the three western German zones in 1948, the foundation of the Federal Republic of Germany in 1949, and the signing of the Paris agreements in 1954, which granted West Germany its political independence, marked the end of the immediate postwar period. It was followed by an economic boom that became known as the German Economic Miracle. As the world recovered from the devastation of the war, Koenig & Bauer began to receive a steady flow of orders, some of them from countries that had gained political independence after the war or did not suffer significant war damage, such as Portugal, Egypt, Iran, Pakistan, and Ghana. Customers from countries in the newly formed Eastern Bloc that were not able to pay for their orders in an acceptable currency traded other goods for printing presses. In this way, Koenig & Bauer received trainloads of Yugoslavian prunes, Cuban sugar, and Argentinean oranges in return for printing presses. However, the company's main customer base evolved in Western Europe, the United States, and Canada. In 1959, Hans Bolza, who had lost his two sons in the war, formally adopted Hans-Bernhard Schünemann, his best printing-press design engineer, who had joined the company in 1951.

During the 1960s, Koenig & Bauer was able to regain its leading position in printing press technology through a number of important innovations. Among them were the Rotafolio sheet-fed four-color letterpress with an output of 8,000 sheets per hour and the newspaper web press Koebau-Courier, both of which became long-term bestsellers. In addition, Koenig & Bauer began to develop special printing presses for telephone directories. With export business thriving, the company established a number of sales offices abroad in Canada, France, England, and Italy. After the Austrian government had expropriated Koenig & Bauer's subsidiary there, the company was able to regain a controlling stake in Schnellpressenfabrik Mödling. Production capacity in Germany was further expanded with the erection of a brand-new factory in Trennfeld near Würzburg in 1964. Three years later, in the company's 150th anniversary year, the German Post Office issued a stamp honoring Friedrich Koenig's invention of the cylinder printing press.

Becoming a Global Leader after 1967

In the last three decades of the 20th century, Koenig & Bauer evolved from an export-oriented German family business into an international family of businesses that became one of the world's major players in the printing machine industry. This transformation was led by Hans B. Bolza-Schünemann, who succeeded Hans Bolza as CEO in 1971. However, his first major task was crisis management. When offset printing, a technology that used films of text and images instead of lead plates and was therefore much cheaper, rapidly replaced letterpress printing within just five years, Koenig & Bauer invested huge sums to develop their own range of offset printing presses. This investment, combined with the cost of building new production lines, significantly drained the company's financial resources. Only with the help of foreign investors was Bolza-Schünemann able to rescue the company from bankruptcy and from being taken over by a competitor at a time of increasing industry consolidation. In 1985, Koenig & Bauer went public, although the Bolza-Schünemann family still held a controlling interest in the company.

Koenig & Bauer's growth through acquisition began in the late 1970s. In December 1978, one year after the company had regained a majority stake in its Austrian subsidiary, Koenig & Bauer bought a 49.9 percent share in Albert-Frankenthal AG.

Founded in 1873 in Frankenthal by a former Koenig & Bauer employee, the state-owned company was the worldwide leading manufacturer of publication rotogravure presses, a product line that perfectly complemented Koenig & Bauer's. In 1988, Koenig & Bauer increased its shareholding in Albert-Frankenthal to 74.99 percent and took over the remaining shares from the Rhineland-Palatinate Ministry of Finance two years later. From then on, the company presented itself to the public as the Koenig & Bauer-Albert group—in short KBA. Finally, in 1995 Koenig & Bauer merged with Albert-Frankenthal into Koenig & Bauer-Albert AG (KBA).

In 1979, Koenig & Bauer took the first step towards establishing a foothold in the United States with the acquisition of Indianapolis-based Egenolf & Rasdall, a company that specialized in the rigging and repair of printing presses. Renamed Koenig & Bauer/Egenolf Machine Inc., the company was used as a sales and service support center for Koenig & Bauer customers in the United States. Nine years later, the company bought a 20 percent stake in Dallas, Texas-based Publishers Equipment Corporation (PEC). In 1990, Koenig & Bauer took over the U.S. manufacturer of web-fed gravure presses and folders Motter Printing Press Company, located in York, Pennsylvania. Koenig & Bauer renamed the company KBA-Motter Corp. and transferred all of their U.S. activities to its facilities, while the association with Koenig & Bauer/Egenolf was discontinued.

In the same year that the Berlin Wall fell, 1989, an East German printing machine manufacturer, Planeta Druckmaschinenwerke, was founded near Dresden. In 1991, Koenig & Bauer acquired a majority holding in the company, which had already become a leading international producer of high-tech sheet-fed offset presses and had acquired Royal Zenith Corp. in the United States in 1990. Planeta Druckmaschinenwerke was renamed KBA-Planeta AG. In 1994, Koenig & Bauer bought the remaining shares in KBA-Planeta and merged with it to create Koenig & Bauer AG (KBA) four years later. Besides these major acquisitions Koenig & Bauer conquered other new markets, such as Japan and Russia, through licensing agreements with local manufacturers. The acquisitions of Albert-Frankenthal and Planeta catapulted Koenig & Bauer into the top global league of printing press manufacturers. However, the integration of the company's new subsidiaries took a considerable amount of cash and effort. Albert-Frankenthal, Planeta, and Motter posted losses which in turn resulted in net losses for the KBA group well into the 1990s.

In 1995, Hans B. Bolza-Schünemann was succeeded by his long-time right-hand man and CFO Reinhart Siewert as CEO. Under his leadership, KBA launched a rigid reorganization, rationalization, and cost-cutting program. However, not until 1997 did Planeta finally come out of the red. While this was mainly due to a vastly oversized workforce and huge reorganization cost, another reason for the company's slow recovery was the fact that a growing number of competitors in the industry were offering ever-lower prices in order to lure a decreasing number of customers. In 1996, after a complaint by U.S. printing press maker Rockwell International about unfairly low-priced competition from Germany and Japan, the U.S. Department of Commerce threatened Koenig & Bauer with a heavy 46 percent anti-dumping import duty. However, the company successfully defended itself, and the case was finally settled six years later. The combination of global overcapacities and stagnating markets in Western Europe, the United States, and Asia resulted in a steep 30 percent drop in price levels. The worldwide printing press industry, including Koenig & Bauer, went through waves of crises during the 1990s and into the early years of the 21st century.

In 2000, the Koenig & Bauer group's turnover passed the EUR 1 billion mark for the first time. In 2001, the Bolza-Schünemann family gave up its majority stake in the company. To increase KBA's capital base, the company transformed its preferred shares into ordinary shares with voting rights, which increased the number of free-floating shares from one-third to almost 60 percent. In mid-2001, KBA shares were listed on the German MDax stock market index. In the same year, the company acquired its long-time business partner, Swiss security-printing specialist De La Rue Giori. Two years later, KBA took over two other German business partners: metal-decorating press manufacturer Bauer + Kunzi and Metronic, a producer of UV offset systems for printing CDs, CDRs, DVDs, and plastic cards. These acquisitions followed the company's group strategy to venture into promising niche markets. Other areas for potential future growth were "74 Karat" digital offset presses for short runs of color publications and the "Rapida" line of super-large sheet-fed offset presses. In mid-2003, Hans B. Bolza-Schünemann's oldest son Albrecht, who had managed the restructuring of the Planeta division in the 1990s, took over as Koenig & Bauer's CEO. His younger brother Claus Bolza-Schünemann was appointed deputy president.

Principal Subsidiaries

KBA-Mödling AG (Austria); KBA North America Inc. (United States); KBA Berlin GmbH; Metronic AG (73.9%); Bauer + Kunzi; KBA (UK) Ltd.; KBA-France SAS; KBA-Italia SpA; KBA Asia Pacific Sdn. Bhd. (Singapore); KBA Australasia Pty Ltd (Australia); KBA (HK) Co. Ltd. (China; 51%); KBA RUS (Russia); KBA-Le Mont-sur-Lausanne SA (Switzerland); Holland Graphic Occasions (HGO) (Netherlands); KBA Printing Machinery (Shanghai) Co., Ltd. (China); KBA Nordic A/S (Denmark; 50.2%); KBA Leasing GmbH.

Principal Competitors

Heidelberger Druckmaschinen AG; MAN Roland Druckmaschinen AG; Tokyo Kikai Seisakusho (TKS); Goss International Corporation; Komori Corporation; Mitsubishi Heavy Industries, Ltd.

Further Reading

"Competition in Web Arena Hits Orders for KBA," *Print Week*, May 31, 2002, p. 5.

1817–1992: 175 Years Koenig & Bauer, Wurzburg, Germany: Koenig & Bauer AG, 1992, 160 p.

"K&B Reports Lower Sales, Steady Profits," *Editor and Publisher*, June 25, 1994, p. 97.

"KBA Presses Feds—Dump Sales Review," *Editor & Publisher*, January 7, 2002, p. 19.

"KBA Takes Control of Karat," *American Printer*, May 2001, p. 12.

"Koenig & Bauer," *Editor & Publisher*, November 26, 1994, p. 29.

"125 Jahre Werkberufsschule Koenig & Bauer," *Süddeutsche Zeitung*, July 6, 1993.

"Suppliers Struggle but Prospects Rise," *Print Week*, November 20, 2003, p. 05.

—Evelyn Hauser

L.S. Starrett Company

121 Crescent Street
Athol, Massachusetts 01331-1915
U.S.A.
Telephone: (978) 249-3551
Fax: (978) 249-8495
Web site: http://www.starrett.com

Public Company
Incorporated: 1900
Employees: 2,800
Sales: $175.7 million (2003)
Stock Exchanges: New York
Ticker Symbol: SCX
NAIC: 333515 Cutting Tool and Machine Tool
    Accessory Manufacturing; 332212 Hand and Edge
    Tool Manufacturing; 332213 Saw Blade and Handsaw
    Manufacturing; 334513 Instruments and Related
    Product Manufacturing for Measuring, Displaying,
    and Controlling Industrial Process Variables; 334519
    Other Measuring and Controlling Device
    Manufacturing

Founded in 1880, the L.S. Starrett Company manufactures more than 5,000 industrial, professional, and consumer products. However, the company is perhaps best known for its precision hand tools, some of which are considered virtual works of art. Starrett is also a leading manufacturer of saw blades and makes many tools for the metalworking industry. Its products range from huge machines and measuring devices designed for industrial use to smaller equipment made for the do-it-yourself handyman market. Starrett sells its products across the United States and in more than 100 foreign countries. It maintains manufacturing facilities in Ohio, Pennsylvania, and North and South Carolina. It also operates factories in Brazil, Scotland, England, Germany, Australia, and China. Its customers are primarily found in the marine, automotive, aviation, farm equipment, and appliance industries. Its single largest customer is Sears Roebuck and Co., which accounts for more than 10 percent of sales. Although Starrett is a public company,

the conservatively managed business remains, after more than 100 years, a family-run operation. Starrett family members and current and past company employees hold about 40 percent of the company's stock.

Getting a Start in the 1880s

The founder, Laroy Sunderland Starrett, one of 12 children of a Maine farmer, rented a 600-acre Newburyport, Massachusetts, farm in 1861. Mechanically inclined, he also patented a number of inventions, including a meat chopper, a washing machine, and a butter working machine. In 1868, Starrett became general agent and superintendent of the Athol Machine Co. of Athol, Massachusetts, incorporated with the purpose of manufacturing his inventions. He eventually took out about 100 patents.

Among Starrett's inventions were a number of hand tools useful in the building trades. The first of these devices, patented in 1879, was a combination square that contained a steel rule with a sliding head. With the aid of the head, it could be used as a square or mitre, a bevel, or a plumb bob. Starrett established a shop on Athol's Crescent Street in 1880 to manufacture the popular hand tool. Ambitiously seeking out new markets for his inventions, he made his name known worldwide by establishing agencies in London and Paris in 1882. Also during the 1880s, Starrett manufactured steel rules and tapes, micrometers, calipers, and dividers.

As business increased, Starrett established a larger factory on the other side of Crescent Street. In 1894, the compound was expanded to span Millers River, and it occupied some 60,000 square feet in 1901. A year later, a new building of more than twice the floor space was erected on an adjoining site. The enterprise was incorporated in 1900, with Starrett as president and treasurer; along with him, four other members constituted the stockholders and directors. By 1906, Starrett was employing about 1,000 workers in the Athol factory and a caliper-manufacturing plant in Springfield, Massachusetts.

L.S. Starrett Co. reported assets of $8.6 million in 1918. By the time its founder died in 1922, the Athol factory was being hailed as the largest plant in the world wholly devoted to making fine mechanical tools. These products included micrometer gauges of more than 30 different styles and nearly 200 types of calipers and dividers. In addition, L.S. Starrett maintained offices and stores in New York, Chicago, and London, and special agencies in England, Germany, France, Belgium, Italy, Switzerland, Sweden, Denmark, Austria, Argentina, Australia, and Japan.

Ups and Downs in the Mid-20th Century

When L.S. Starrett was reincorporated in 1929, its assets had fallen to $4.8 million and the number of employees to about 720. In 1934, as the nation was slowly emerging from the depths of the Great Depression, assets were down to $3.8 million and employment to 402. However, following deficits in both 1932 and 1933, the company had earned a net income of $190,134 on sales of over $1.3 million, a distinct improvement over the $734,110 in sales registered in 1932 and $856,845 in 1933. At the end of the year, Starrett was able to resume dividends, which had not been paid in 1932 or 1933. In 1935, Starrett acquired the Last Word indicator business of Henry A. Lowe Co. in Cleveland, Ohio, and moved its equipment to the Athol factory. Throughout the remainder of the decade, Starrett gradually recovered from the Depression despite damage to the company's facilities from river floods in 1936 and 1938.

In fiscal year 1941 (ending June 30, 1940) L.S. Starrett's net income was $740,978 on record sales of more than $3.6 million. The number of employees had grown to 1,300 and the number of stockholders to 1,742. During World War II, Starrett increased its output eightfold, operating around the clock. Net sales advanced to a peak of $12.9 million in fiscal 1943. During this period of prosperity, Arthur H. Starrett, the founder's grandson, assumed the presidency. Starrett took control of the company in 1946, only to watch postwar sales slump to $6.9 million in 1950. As a result, net income declined from $1.4 million in 1943 to $486,129 in 1950, and by 1950 employment fell to 1,135 from the 1943 high of 2,034.

The advent of the Korean War in the early 1950s created a new surge in business for Starrett that the company was able to sustain after the 1953 armistice. In fiscal year 1957—Starrett's best year of the decade—the company earned $1.5 million on net sales of $16.2 million. Shortly thereafter, Starrett began a modest program of acquisitions. In 1959, the company purchased Bristol Engineering & Manufacturing Co. based in Rehoboth, Massachusetts. Further, Starrett acquired Rhode Island Tool Co. of Providence for shares of common stock in 1962. That same year, Starrett acquired Webber Gage Co. of Cleveland, Ohio, for 20,000 shares of stock and $840,000 in cash. The acquisition of Webber, a manufacturer of precision gage blocks and certain types of optical measuring tools, enabled Starrett to begin manufacturing extremely high precision products.

Meanwhile, Transue & Williams Steel Forging Corporation of Alliance, Ohio, a maker of forgings and stampings for the automotive, truck, and tractor industries, was buying significant amounts of Starrett stock. Together with stock purchases by Russell McPhail, chairman of Transue & Williams, and his McPhail Candy Corporation, these holdings represented about 30 percent of Starrett's outstanding stock in 1964, with a value of $6.8 million. At the 1963 annual meeting, McPhail unsuccessfully proposed a cumulative-voting proposal that would have made it easier for him and other minority stockholders to win seats on the company's board of directors. This challenge to Starrett's family management ended in October 1964, when the company purchased and retired the McPhail-Transue & Williams stock holdings for $31 a share, or about $6.8 million.

In the 1960s, Starrett's fortunes were favorably tied to war once again as the conflict in Vietnam escalated throughout the decade. Net sales, only $12.8 million in fiscal 1959, surged to $33.1 million in 1968, while net income grew from $886,588 to $4.2 million during this period. By the end of the decade, the company had major branches in Chicago; Cleveland; Los Angeles; Providence, Rhode Island; and Springfield, New Jersey, and a warehouse in Toronto. Further, Starrett established subsidiaries in Brazil and Scotland in 1958 to manufacture products for foreign markets, and a Canadian subsidiary was established in 1962. Starrett also owned Herramientas de Precision—a Mexican subsidiary—from 1972 to 1985.

During this period, Starrett was also making its presence known in nonmilitary markets. While it would seem that hand-operated tools should have been rendered obsolete with the advent of power machinery and automation, the reality was that a growing number of do-it-yourself property owners were in the market for affordable and easy-to-use hand tools for repair and maintenance. At the other end of the spectrum, the increasing complexity of modern industry stimulated demand for all kinds of specialized hardware, some of which Starrett was manufacturing.

Holding Its Own in the 1970s–80s

In fiscal 1970, Starrett bought Herman Stone Co., a Dayton, Ohio, producer of granite slabs for measuring tables, for $308,000 worth of stock. It was made a division of Starrett and moved to Mount Airy, North Carolina, in 1972. During the 1970s, Starrett's net sales grew from $28.7 million in 1971 to $92.9 million in 1979, while net income rose from $2.7 million to $10.8 million over that period. By this time, Starrett tools and instruments were being sold in over 100 countries through a network of industrial distributors. By far, the largest consumer of Starrett's products was the metalworking industry—which constituted about 65 percent of the company's revenue—but other important costumers were automotive, aviation, marine, and farm equipment shops, as well as tradesmen such as builders, carpenters, plumbers, and electricians.

Douglas R. Starrett, who had joined the company as an apprentice tool-and-die maker in 1941, succeeded his father as president in 1962. By 1985, the Starrett headquarters was a little-changed four-story brick factory and the company's inventory of small metal parts was piled haphazardly into wooden boxes. Despite its outmoded appearance, Starrett's profit mar-

Key Dates:

1880: L.S. Starrett opens his own shop in Athol, Massachusetts.
1900: The company incorporates.
1935: The company acquires the indicator business of Henry A. Lowe Co.
1958: The company founds subsidiaries in Brazil and Scotland.
1962: Starrett acquires Webber Gage Co. and Rhode Island Tool Co.
1986: Evans Rule Co. is acquired.
1996: Starrett opens its first Chinese subsidiary.
2001: The company recalls defective measuring devices.
2002: A federal investigation is launched relating to the 2001 recall; Starrett's stock plummets.
2004: The company closes several of its warehouses and its plants in Skipton, England, and Alum Bank, Pennsylvania, moving the business offshore to the Dominican Republic.

gin of 10.7 percent was three times that of the rest of the machine-tool industry. Even in the face of Japanese competition and its own high prices, Starrett's tools were selling because they were so finely made. Ground to within two-thousandths of an inch and sometimes triple-plated, these tools were valued by machinists as the equivalent of works of art.

Half the company's shares were being held by present and retired employees under a retirement-benefits plan adopted in 1946. In fact, the Starrett family held only slightly more than 2 percent of the stock. However, after the employee stock-ownership plan purchased 400,000 shares in the Starrett treasury in 1984, the company bought 341,514 shares from stockholders at $30 a share to avoid dilution of the existing shareholders' voting power. As added protection against any future takeover attempts of the company, Starrett adopted a "poison pill" defense in 1990.

After a sharp slide in fiscal 1983 due to a severe recession, Starrett's sales resumed steady growth later in the decade, reaching $169.9 million in 1988, when net income came to $15.8 million. In 1986, the company bought Evans Rule Co. of North Charleston, South Carolina, for between $20 million and $30 million. A subsidiary of Masco Corporation, Evans was producing measuring tapes and associated items. Interviewed for *New England Business* in 1987, Douglas Starrett reaffirmed his company's commitment to manufacturing. "We could have reduced ourselves to a selling organization," he said, citing companies that had abandoned domestic manufacturing in favor of foreign-made goods. While expressing confidence that Starrett could compete with Japanese and German competitors, Starrett admitted that he was troubled by potential low-wage rivals from China, Taiwan, or South Korea, subsidized production overseas, and product dumping in U.S. markets.

During the 1980s, L.S. Starrett began manufacturing coordinate measuring machines, which combine the functions of several tools and allow for faster and more efficient measuring. A new division for this purpose was established in Mount Airy. To complement this investment, Starrett acquired in 1990 Sigma Optical, a British firm designing and manufacturing optical measuring projectors, and established a new division for this purpose in Farmington Hills, Michigan.

Globalizing Operations in the 1990s

As Starrett entered the 1990s, net sales, which had reached a peak of $201.6 million during fiscal 1990, fell to $174.8 million three years later. Net earnings dropped from $18.8 million to $8.7 million over this period. In the 1993 annual report, Douglas Starrett deemed 1990 "the year of the largest federal tax increase in history" and went on to say that "because of that tax increase, the economy has gone downhill ever since." Sales increased slightly to $180.2 million and earnings to $9 million in fiscal 1994.

Among the products being manufactured by Starrett in the 1990s were precision tools, tape measures, levels, electronic gages, dial indicators, gage blocks, digital readout measuring tools, granite surface plants, optical measuring projectors, coordinate measuring machines, vices, M1 lubricant, hacksaw blades, hole saws, band saw blades, jigsaw blades, reciprocating saw blades, and precision ground flat stock. Subsidiaries in Brazil and Scotland were making hacksaw and band saw blades and a limited line of precision tools and measuring tapes. These foreign operations accounted for 26 percent of the company's sales in 1994. One retailer, Sears, accounted for about 11 percent of the company's sales. Starrett's Brazilian subsidiary owned and occupied a facility in Itu, Brazil. The Scottish subsidiary owned a manufacturing plant in Jedburgh, Scotland, and also leased manufacturing space in Skipton, England. The Canadian subsidiary owned and occupied a building in Toronto.

The company was described by *Barron's* (August 11, 1997) as "nicely profitable" from the mid-1980s through the mid-1990s. Starrett's business was cyclical, and the company endured troughs like the drop in earnings in 1993. On the whole, however, the company did well during this period. In the middle years of the 1990s, its earnings rose solidly, so that Starrett paid out $1.28 per share in 1994 and raised the payout to $2.45 by 1996. The company's Brazilian subsidiary did particularly well during this period. With business there very strong in the mid-1990s, more than half of the company's total profits came from overseas operations. In 1996, Starrett opened a small factory in Suzhou, China, an area where the company expected business to grow. The Chinese facility only employed 24 people in its first few years of operation, but it gave Starrett a foothold in Asia.

The late 1990s were boom years for the U.S. economy in general, as evidenced by the galloping stock market. Yet the industrial manufacturing sector of the economy was a different story. By 1999, the industrial manufacturing sector was shrinking both in the United States and abroad, and Starrett felt the effects. While 1998 had been a record year for the company, with sales of $262 million, 1999 saw an 11 percent drop in sales to $232 million, and an even steeper drop, of 27 percent, in earnings. In January 1999, the Brazilian government devalued its currency by 40 percent, cutting deeply into Starrett's profits from its vigorous Brazilian subsidiary. Manufacturing cutbacks in the United Kingdom forced the company's Scottish subsidiary to lower prices in order to remain competitive. Starrett's chairman Douglas R. Starrett claimed that the company had done well in 1999 despite the dip in sales and profits; it had not laid off employees and had performed reasonably in spite of the sharp blow to its Brazilian business. The company had continued to invest in its facilities and equipment, spending some $20 million over 1999.

Struggles in the 2000s

Douglas R. Starrett expected the company to do well in 2000 despite a worsening world industrial picture. However, the company faced increasing pressure as ever larger numbers of its customers and competitors moved their businesses abroad to low-wage countries. Starrett began laying off employees in 2000. In 2001, revenue fell to $183.1 million, down more than 7 percent from a year earlier. The company saw its future as increasingly dependent on overseas operations. Douglas R. Starrett's son, Douglas A. Starrett, who had been president of the company since 1994, had been responsible for pushing the company into more global markets. In 2001, the younger Starrett became chairman and CEO, and his father, at the age of 81, finally retired. The elder Starrett promised to stay on as his son's assistant, but he died within two months after retiring. The company then faced new troubles.

Starrett brought out a new generation of measuring devices in the late 1990s called Rapid Check. The new devices turned out to be plagued with problems that made them unreliable, and in March 2001 the company began replacing them at no charge to its customers. Starrett claimed it had been aware of the problem and had been dealing with it properly, yet in 2002 a former subcontractor alerted investigators with the U.S. Defense Department, and federal agents raided Starrett's Mt. Airy, North Carolina plant, evidently looking for evidence of fraud concerning the Rapid Check devices. Starrett's stock price plunged in the wake of this event, while the company sought to prevent documents related to the allegations from being released publicly. A resident of Athol characterized the drama to a reporter from the Worcester, Massachusetts, *Telegram & Gazette* as "the first time in a hundred years anything serious has happened up there."

The federal investigation yielded nothing damaging, and it was terminated in December 2003 with no charges filed. Yet sales were flat for 2002, and the company ended the fiscal year with a net loss of $380,000. From mid-2002 on, Starrett lost money quarter after quarter. The company struggled to reduce its inventory in order to hang on to cash that might be needed in the future. Between 2000 and 2004, Starrett cut some 800 jobs worldwide. In 2004, the company closed a warehouse in Cleveland and proposed shutting its remaining three warehouses as well as the plant in Mt. Airy. Starrett closed its plant in Skipton, England, that year. It also closed its plant in Alum Bank, Pennsylvania, moving the business offshore to the Dominican Republic. The company was in a money-losing slide, which it blamed principally on the movement of both its customers and competitors overseas.

Principal Subsidiaries

Starrett Industria e Comercio Ltda. (Brazil); L.S. Starrett Co. (Australia); L.S. Starrett Co. Ltd. (Scotland); Starrett GmbH (Germany); Starrett Tools (Shanghai) Co. Ltd. (China); Starrett Tools (Suzhou) Co. Ltd. (China).

Principal Competitors

The Stanley Works; General Tools Manufacturing Company; Robert Bosch Tools Corporation.

Further Reading

Baldwin, William, "The Antique Shop in Athol," *Forbes*, November 4, 1985, pp. 54, 58.

Bodor, Jim, "Athol Stands with Starrett," *Telegram & Gazette* (Worcester, Mass.), November 17, 2002, p. E1.

Brammer, Rhonda, "Tempting Trio," *Barron's*, August 11, 1997, p. 38.

Chesto, Jon, "Athol-Based Tool Maker to Shut Penn., U.K. Units," *Boston Herald*, February 7, 2004, p. 29.

Crane, Ellery Bicknell, ed., *History of Worcester County Massachusetts*, Vol. 2, New York and Chicago: Lewis Historical Publishing Co., 1924, pp. 79–80, 829, 845–46.

Donker, Peter P., "Starrett Had Some Setbacks in '99, but Predicts Healthy Growth in 2000," *Telegram & Gazette* (Worcester, Mass.), September 16, 1999, p. E1.

"Douglas R. Starrett Dies at 81," *Industrial Distribution*, December 2001, p. 17.

Esposito, Andi, " 'D. R.' Starrett Hands the Reins to 'D. A.,' " *Telegram & Gazette* (Worcester, Mass.), September 20, 2001, p. E1.

Lazo, Shirley A., "Road Warrior," *Barron's*, June 9, 2003, p. 36.

McLaughlin, Mark, "The Tales of Two Survivors," *New England Business*, September 21, 1987, pp. 11, 13, 15–16.

Mitman, Carl W., "Laroy S. Starrett," *Dictionary of American Biography*, Vol. 17, New York: Scribner's, 1943, pp. 535–36.

"Over 100 Years of Measuring History," *Industrial Distribution*, January 1996, p. 74.

Pasztor, Andy, "U.S. Is Investigating Allegations L.S. Starrett Defrauded Customers," *Wall Street Journal*, September 12, 2002, p. A3.

The Starrett Story, Athol, Mass.: L.S. Starrett Co., 1991.

Wilson-Youngquist, Sherry, "Contractor Faults Starrett Instruments," *Winston-Salem Journal*, September 13, 2002, p. B2.

——, "Federal Agents Seize Computers at Plant," *Winston-Salem Journal*, September 6, 2002, p. B1.

Vasilash, Gary S., "Best of Both Worlds," *Automotive Manufacturing & Production*, December 2000, p. 58.

—Robert Halasz
—update: A. Woodward

LANE BRYANT

Lane Bryant, Inc.

8655 East Broad Street
Reynoldsburg, Ohio 43068
U.S.A.
Telephone: (614) 577-4000
Fax: (614) 577-4219
Web site: http://www.lanebryant.com

Wholly Owned Subsidiary of Charming Shoppes, Inc.
Incorporated: 1914
Employees: 10,000
Sales: $903.6 million (2004)
NAIC: 448120 Women's Clothing Stores; 448150
Clothing Accessories Stores

Lane Bryant, Inc., is the largest plus-size retailer in the United States. It sells its modestly priced, mostly private-label apparel through a chain of about 700 retail stores and an innovative web site. Half of American women wear a size 14 or larger; Lane Bryant specializes in the style-conscious, 25- to 45-year-old segment of the market. Lane Bryant, Inc. is not affiliated with Lane Bryant catalog (Brylane, Inc.), which was spun off as a separate business in 1993.

Immigrant Origins

The story of Lane Bryant begins with Lena Bryant, a Lithuanian immigrant who immigrated to New York City in 1895. After she arrived, she found that her family had arranged her marriage to the gentleman who had paid her passage. She refused, and the 16-year-old took a job sewing lingerie in a factory to support herself. She developed her skills and increased her weekly salary from one dollar to $15 over the course of several years, recalls *Figure* magazine.

Around 1898, she stopped working as a seamstress after she married a jeweler from Russia, David Bryant. Unfortunately, he died a few months after the birth of their son. She then began working out of her apartment, tailoring lingerie for new brides and expectant mothers.

By 1904, Bryant was successful enough to open her own shop on Fifth Avenue at 120th Street. In the process of obtain-

ing a loan from Oriental Bank, her first name was misspelled, giving birth to "Lane Bryant."

Bryant soon turned to producing dresses as well as undergarments for pregnant women, who had a difficult time finding stylish clothes that fit well. Bryant designed a maternity tea dress, called "Number 5" after its place on the order form. According to *Figure*, no newspaper would run advertisements for her maternity dresses—it was against the mores of the day for "ladies in waiting" to appear in public. When Bryant finally managed to have a small ad run in the *New York Herald*, she sold out of maternity dresses the day it appeared.

Bryant married Albert Malsin, an engineer and fellow Lithuanian, in 1909. They soon had three children together. Within a few years, the pair launched their own survey of female proportions, obtaining data on 200,000 women from an insurance company and measuring 4,500 of Bryant's customers themselves.

The Flapper Era was just around the corner, and the fashion world was already focused on the slender, athletic "Gibson Girl." Bryant and Malsin found, however, that "women of ample figure" made up more than half the female population, providing an ample, underserved customer base.

Branching Out in 1915

The company was incorporated on June 12, 1914, according to the Ohio secretary of state's office. The first branch store opened in Chicago in 1915. Other stores in Detroit and Brooklyn soon followed.

The mail-order catalog brought in more than $1 million in sales in 1917. A turning point for the company, reported *Figure*, occurred in 1923, when plus-size clothes outsold maternitywear for the first time. Total revenues were up to $5 million by this time. Bryant soon added shoes, hosiery, and bathing suits for plus sizes.

According to *Figure*, Lena Bryant was a pioneer in progressive human relations, among the first to offer employees complete benefit packages including health insurance and profit sharing. The company was left to her sons after her death in

Company Perspectives:

Fashion comes first for Lane Bryant and the Lane Bryant customer, who is influenced by the same fashion trends as every other woman in the U.S. Size is only a technical specification of the garment. Lane Bryant continually provides its customer with fashionable apparel that has been inspired by the international fashion designers and global vendors. Customers appreciate both classic silhouettes as well as up-to-the-minute fashion direction. Lane Bryant recognizes that its customer's increasing demand for fashion reflects a growing sense of confidence and self-acceptance. By listening to and taking direction from its customer, Lane Bryant strives to celebrate women's individual sense of style reflected in the diverse range of fashion offerings, uplifting, compelling store environments, energetic, knowledgeable customer service and through marketing, advertising and promotional programs that present positive images for all women.

1951. Her son Raphael B. Malsin had become CEO in 1940 and would remain in that role until 1972. Another son, Arthur Malsin, would be chairman of the board until the company's acquisition by The Limited in 1982.

In 1961, Lane Bryant launched a discount chain called Town and Country. It had stores in Pennsylvania, Maryland, Virginia, and West Virginia. The unit was closed in 1977. Plus-size clothing had grown to a $2 billion market by this time; there were an estimated 150 manufacturers competing in the category.

Lane Bryant began the 1980s with 200 stores in 33 states, plus another 29 Smart Size stores in six states. The company also owned Coward Shoe and Farr's Shoe stores, two small regional chains, and the Olof Daughters footwear importer. Sales for the fiscal year ended January 31, 1981 were $400.4 million, up 5 percent from fiscal 1980.

Perceiving a lack of interest in plus fashions from the national fashion press, Lane Bryant began a short-lived publishing venture, *It's Me* magazine, in August 1981. LB for Short, the company's first catalog for petites, was launched in January 1982. Lane Bryant already catered to tall women; petites, another underserved market segment, were defined as being 5 feet 3 inches or less in height. They accounted for 37 million U.S. women at the time.

Acquisition by The Limited in 1982

The Limited Stores Inc. acquired Lane Bryant, Inc. for $105 million in May 1982. The Limited, based in Columbus, Ohio, operated 440 retail clothing stores oriented toward women aged 16 to 35 and had annual sales of $365 million. Lane Bryant had earlier agreed to be acquired by the Wertheim & Company investment group for $88 million, but changed its mind after market reaction (its shares were then traded on the New York Stock Exchange) indicated that offer to be undervalued. Lane Bryant updated its fashions after its acquisition by The Limited, which was known for the trendy clothes of its other stores, including Victoria's Secret and its namesake The Limited chain.

In the mid-1980s, the plus-size clothing market in the United States was estimated to be worth $8 to $10 billion and was the

fashion industry's fastest-growing segment. This caught the attention of other manufacturers, giving Lane Bryant some competition. According to one estimate, the number of manufacturers in the category had grown to 1,000.

Lane Bryant was opening about 200 new stores a year in the late 1980s. It had closed its Fifth Avenue at 40th Street store in 1986, however, after losing its lease. Lane Bryant headquarters moved from New York City to a new $110 million complex in Columbus, Ohio in the spring of 1990.

After The Limited acquired Lane Bryant, the catalog business was renamed Brylane, Inc. and came to include the mail-order divisions of other Limited acquisitions, including Roaman's (1982) and Lerner (1985). In 1993, Brylane was spun off as a privately held company; it was acquired five years later by Redcats, the home shopping unit of Pinault-Printemps-Redoute.

Mid-1990s Makeover

In 1995, reported the *Los Angeles Times,* new marketers were brought in to update Lane Bryant's image, particularly among younger women. Annual sales were up to $915 million by 1996, producing a $60 million operating profit. Sales stalled in the late 1990s, but Lane Bryant was able to revive them by offering sexier, more close-fitting clothing, accompanied by head-turning advertising. Lane Bryant placed its first ads in fashion magazines *Vogue* and *Harper's Bazaar* in 1996. The company was soon advertising in *Glamour* and *Marie Claire* as well.

Lane Bryant launched a web site in March 1997. At first, the company did not actually sell clothes online, but offered coupons and conducted surveys to boost in-store sales and to learn more about its customers. E-commerce started on the web site in March 2003.

The company's first fashion show was held in New York City in 1997. Two years later, taking a page from the Victoria's Secret catalog, Lane Bryant simulcast the show live on the Internet as well as on the JumboTron in Times Square. This was followed by what was billed as the first plus-size lingerie fashion show in February 2000. Lingerie accounted for about 20 percent of revenues, reported the *Los Angeles Times.*

At the time, plus-size models and actresses were gaining more exposure in magazines and on television. Lane Bryant counted among its spokesmodels Camryn Manheim, from ABC's ''The Practice,'' and the curvaceous and notorious Anna Nicole Smith. In 2001, Chris Noth reprised his role as *Sex and the City*'s Mr. Big for TV ads displaying the desirability of Lane Bryant's plus-size clientele. According to the *New York Times,* Lane Bryant was spending $2.5 million a year on advertising and public relations.

It was apparent the makeover worked, noted the *Wall Street Journal,* which reported Lane Bryant was one of The Limited's hottest brands. Same-store sales were up and profits were up even though the number of stores had been cut to less than 700. Sales were $934 million in 1999.

Charming Acquisition in 2001

Charming Shoppes, Inc. of Bensalem, Pennsylvania acquired Lane Bryant from The Limited in August 2001 in a deal

Key Dates:

1904: Dressmaker Lena Bryant opens a Fifth Avenue shop.
1914: The company is originally incorporated.
1915: A branch opens in Chicago.
1917: Mail-order revenues top $1 million.
1982: Lane Bryant becomes a division of The Limited, Inc.
1993: The Brylane catalog business is spun off.
1995: Lane Bryant begins a rebranding exercise.
2001: Charming Shoppes acquires Lane Bryant for $335 million.
2004: A new flagship store opens near Fifth Avenue.

worth $335 million, $280 million of it in cash. Charming operated other plus-size chains, including Fashion Bug and Catherine's Plus Sizes, which together had yearly sales of $1.6 billion and 1,770 stores. Charming had first entered the plus-size business in 1982.

Charming began to aggressively expand Lane Bryant, particularly in strip malls (most of its 650 existing stores were in enclosed malls), where most of its other stores were located. The plus-size category was the fastest-growing segment of the clothing business, prompting new competition from the likes of Old Navy (Gap Inc.) and Tommy Hilfiger Corp.

Lane Bryant achieved an industry first when it installed 3-D virtual model technology on its web site. The feature, developed with My Virtual Model, Inc. and introduced in the fall of 2001, allowed customers to create a 3-D model in their own likeness and try out outfits on it. In 2003, Lane Bryant hosted a modeling contest whose winner's likeness formed the basis of one of the virtual models on the web site.

In August 2003, Lane Bryant launched *Figure*, a magazine for plus-size women. Catherine's and Fashion Bug stores also carried it, as did book and grocery chains.

Lorna Nagler was named president of Lane Bryant in January 2004, replacing Diane Missel. Nagler was formerly president of sister company Catherine's Plus Sizes. After a 10-year absence from its original home base of Midtown Manhattan, Lane Bryant opened a new flagship store at 7 West 34th Street in April 2004.

Principal Competitors

Dress Barn Woman; sizeappeal.com; Torrid; United Retail Group Inc. (Avenue).

Further Reading

Barmash, Isadore, "Lane Bryant and Ohio Chain in $100 Million Merger," *New York Times*, April 29, 1982, p. D4.

——, "Purchase of Lane Bryant Set," *New York Times*, April 8, 1982, p. D6.
"Bigger Variety Expands Plus Business," *DSN Retailing Today*, April 8, 2002, p. A10.
"Charming Shoppes Buys Limited's Lane Bryant," *Morning Call* (Allentown, Pa.), July 11, 2001, p. A9.
Clark, Evan, "Lane Bryant Returns to Manhattan," *WWD*, April 14, 2004, p. 17.
Cowan, Kevin, "Plus-Size Gals 'Figure' into New Mag," *News Sentinel* (Knoxville), October 23, 2003, p. E4.
Cowie, Denise, "The Plus-Size World Expands; Fashions Fitting for Big Women," *Record* (Bergen County, N.J.), October 27, 1996, p. Y26.
Cuneo, Alice Z., "Chris Hansen: Exec VP-Marketing, The Limited's Lane Bryant Chain; Changing the Shape of Apparel Market," *Advertising Age*, February 7, 2000, p. S10.
Diluna, Amy, "Bold and Beautiful: Lane Bryant's Contest Winner Talks—and Walks—Tough," *New York Daily News*, February 9, 2003, p. 9.
Glanton, Eileen, "If You've Got It, Flaunt It," *Forbes*, March 5, 2001, p. 145.
Goldman, Abigail, "Chain Sees Big Business in Larger Sizes; Lane Bryant Has Been Remaking Its Image to Capture More of the Market Catering to 'Realistic Body Sizes,'" *Los Angeles Times*, June 25, 1999, p. 1.
Jenkins, Maureen, "A Plus for Plus Sizes; Catalog Sells Delta Burke's Clothing for Fuller Figures," *Chicago Sun-Times*, Features Sec., July 23, 1997, p. 37.
Kane, Courtney, "A Male Sex Symbol Enjoys the Company of Larger Women in a New Campaign for Lane Bryant," *New York Times*, February 1, 2001, p. C8.
Kraft, Courtney, "The 100th Anniversary of Lane Bryant," *Figure*, Summer 2004, pp. 40–41, 114.
"Lane Bryant's Canadian Suitor," *New York Times*, September 30, 1980, p. D1.
"Limited Inc. Offices Will Leave NY," *Newsday*, Bus. Sec., January 31, 1990, p. 41.
Nowak, Ann, "A Cut Above: Stores Discover Life After Size 16," *Newsday*, January 19, 1987, p. 8.
Quick, Rebecca, "Fashion's New Frontier: Racy Lingerie for the Larger-Size Woman—Lane Bryant, with Inspiration from Victoria's Secret, Adds Gauzy Chemises, Teddies," *Wall Street Journal*, February 3, 2000, p. B1.
Steinhauer, Jennifer, "The Limited May Sell Off Subsidiaries," *New York Times*, September 4, 1997, p. D1.
"Stores Try Publishing Their Own Magazines," *Business Week*, July 27, 1981, p. 34.
Teitelbaum, Richard S., "Cheryl Nido Turpin, 42," *Fortune*, June 4, 1990, p. 266.
Wall, Joan Slattery, "Get 'Em in the Door," *SBN Columbus* (Ohio), April 1, 1999, p. 7.
——, "Keep 'Em Coming Back," *SBN Columbus* (Ohio), April 1, 1999, p. 8.
White, Erin, "Charming Shoppes Turns Bigger Sizes into Bigger Business—Lane Bryant Acquisition Adds 60% More Revenue As Aggressive Expansion Plans Ensue," *Wall Street Journal*, September 5, 2001, p. B4.
Yen, Hope, "Clothes Retailer Thinking Big; Women's Plus-Sizes a Growing Market for Charming Shoppes," *Journal-Gazette* (Ft. Wayne, Ind.), August 23, 2001, p. 6B.

—Frederick C. Ingram

Lee Enterprises Inc.

201 Harrison Street
Davenport, Iowa 52801-1939
U.S.A.
Telephone: (563) 383-2100
Fax: (563) 323-9609
Web site: http://www.lee.net

Public Company
Incorporated: 1890 as the *Ottumwa Daily Courier*
Employees: 6,700
Sales: $656.7 million (2003)
Stock Exchanges: New York
Ticker Symbol: LEE
NAIC: 511110 Newspaper Publishers

Lee Enterprises Inc. is a leading newspaper publisher of daily newspapers in mid-size markets found in the Pacific Northwest, Midwest, and Northeastern United States. It owns and has stakes in approximately 45 newspapers that have a combined circulation of 1.1 million daily and 1.2 million Sunday. The company also publishes nearly 200 weekly newspapers, shoppers, and classified and specialty publications, and maintains Web sites for many of its papers. Lee sold off its broadcast holdings in 2000 in order to focus on its core printing and publishing operations.

Early History

The founder of the publishing venture that would become Lee Enterprises, A.W. Lee, was shaped by his conservative midwestern upbringing. Soon after marrying, Lee's parents moved from Philadelphia to Iowa City and became pioneer farmers. His mother abandoned her Quaker roots, and his father left behind a family that was well placed in society. Lee was exposed to both a strict upbringing and the newspaper business during his childhood. Besides working as a bookkeeper for the *Muscatine Journal,* Lee's father, John B. Lee, enjoyed writing and kept a detailed diary of the family's affairs. Even after his childhood, Lee would be exposed to his father's stern business ethics and attention to detail while working under him as a bookkeeper.

Before Lee took a job with his father at the *Muscatine Journal,* he distinguished himself at the age of 13 by being the youngest student ever admitted to the State University of Iowa. While he excelled at mathematics, Lee knew at that early age that he wanted to pursue a career related to writing and editing. He was an admirer of the writings of Ralph Waldo Emerson and always carried small pocket books of Emerson's essays wherever he went. Lee subscribed to Emerson's motto "trust thyself," which meant that individuals could improve their lives if they believed strongly in what they were doing and what they wanted to achieve.

A few years after graduating from college, Lee succeeded his father as head bookkeeper at the *Muscatine Journal.* However, because he wanted to write, he left that secure position to work for the *Chicago Times.* Following a two-year stint as a writer and part-time editor, he returned to Iowa. After getting together $16,000, which was most of his savings combined with money invested by family and friends, the 32-year-old Lee bought the *Ottumwa Daily Courier* in 1890. He then began to shape it into what he believed a newspaper should be: a medium that served the local community and had a duty, as well as a right, to provide the most reliable and most provocative news available. Above all, Lee believed his newspaper should conform to a high ethical standard that would instill confidence in its readers. Lee's writing and editing skills, combined with his training as a bookkeeper, contributed to his success in this new venture during the 1890s. Furthermore, his emphasis on integrity and journalistic responsibility, which is documented in company annals, became a hallmark of the *Daily Courier.* During the 1890s, Lee's two sons died, and to that misfortune was attributed his noted determination to help young men achieve success in his company.

Expansion Begins in the Late 1890s

Encouraged by the growth of the *Daily Courier,* Lee began seeking a way to expand his publishing operations near the turn of the century. In 1899, he purchased the *Davenport Times,* whose name he changed to the *Daily Times,* thus initiating a newspaper syndicate. He sent an associate and long-time *Muscatine Journal* employee, E.P. Adler, to help run the new con-

Company Perspectives:

Our company is focused on five key operating priorities: Grow revenue creatively and rapidly; Improve readership and circulation; Emphasize strong local news; Build our online future; Exercise careful cost controls.

cern. Lee had considered a number of potential acquisitions but selected the *Davenport Times* because of its solid reputation, untapped readership potential, and advertising opportunities. It was soon clear that Lee's perception of the publication's potential was correct, as readership and revenues climbed.

Recognizing the potential to improve and then profit from other holdings, Lee bought his old hometown newspaper, the *Muscatine Journal,* from his brother-in-law in 1903. In 1907, he picked up the *Hannibal Courier-Post,* a newspaper in nearby Missouri, and the *La Crosse Tribune* in Wisconsin, which was just north of Lee's Iowa operations. Lee achieved gains with those papers similar to those he had enjoyed with the *Daily Times.* His recipe for success was relatively straightforward: find a newspaper with promise in a small- to medium-sized town, increase its circulation and advertising sales, and hire an astute manager to operate it. An important element of Lee's strategy was management autonomy. The management team of each of his papers was allowed to run the organization almost as though it was their own business. Lee believed that each publication should be financially independent and should not rely on resources from his other holdings to support it.

Shortly after launching his aggressive acquisition program, Lee died as a result of heart failure during a 1907 vacation in Europe. Because he had hired capable and independent managers, however, the company was in good hands. Adler was selected to head the Lee Syndicate, as it had become known, and co-worker Jim Powell became his vice-president. Adler, once described as ''a fire-eating and adventurous but resourceful pioneer,'' complemented Powell's more cautious nature. Adler's colorful life was evidenced in 1917 when several men attempted to kidnap him from a hotel, stuff him in a trunk, and hold him for $40,000 ransom. Adler was able to fend off the kidnappers as they beat him and captured one of them with the help of passersby. All of his attackers were eventually convicted, and one hanged himself in jail. Immediately after the renowned event, Adler sent this telling radiogram message to his family: ''Have suddenly become famous. Slightly injured. Nothing serious. Home tonight. Don't worry.—Dad.''

Adler ran Lee Syndicate until 1947. During that period he perpetuated A.W. Lee's legacy of ethical reporting and community service. In addition, he sustained efforts to expand the company by acquiring other newspapers and improving their performance. In 1915, he purchased the *Democrat,* a Davenport, Iowa, newspaper. By 1930, he had added five newspapers to the Lee fold, including publications in Nebraska and Illinois. The firm was organized as a holding company in 1928 under the name Lee Syndicate Company before postponing its acquisition activity during the Depression years. When it did resume expansion efforts, Adler took the company in a new direction.

Diversification and Reorganization: 1930s–60s

In 1937, Lee purchased its first broadcasting unit, KGLO, a radio station in Mason City, Iowa. In 1941, it purchased interests in a Nebraska station, and in 1944 Lee bought WTAD, of Quincy, Illinois. Lee's extension into the broadcasting industry was led by Lee P. Loomis, who had started with Lee in 1902 as a farm-to-farm subscription solicitor. Loomis was a nephew of A.W. Lee and had worked his way up to become publisher of one of Lee's newspapers. Adler had disagreed with Loomis about whether or not the company should get into radio but relented under the condition that the investments begin to show a profit within two years. Despite several hurdles, Loomis achieved profitability in radio. Lee's radio holdings were eventually jettisoned, however, in response to Federal Communication Commission requirements regarding simultaneous ownership of radio and newspaper concerns.

Adler died in 1949 after 42 years of leadership, and Loomis assumed the presidency. In 1950, all of Lee's holding were linked under a new corporate umbrella, Lee Enterprises, Incorporated. The company was reorganized, and some of its newspapers were consolidated. In 1953, Lee's first television station, KHQA-TV, began broadcasting to Hannibal and Quincy, Illinois. One year later, Lee started KGLO-TV in Mason City, Iowa. Loomis viewed the jump into television as a means of capturing the advertising market share that was shifting away from newspapers. He also continued to emphasize growth of Lee's core publications divisions. Just before retiring in 1960, Loomis oversaw the buyout of six Montana newspapers for $6 million. Also in 1960, all of Lee's holdings were officially consolidated under Lee Enterprises Inc.

Loomis passed the baton to Philip Adler, the son of E.P. Adler. The younger Adler had worked as a reporter, editor, and then publisher for Lee since 1926 and had also served as editor on both his high school and college newspapers during the 1920s. Like those before him, E.P. Adler maintained the company's emphasis on integrity and honesty. Earlier in his career, Adler was tested by a series of investigative pieces he wrote about a local businessman. Several readers canceled their subscriptions in protest, but Adler stuck to his story. After the businessman fled town with much of their money, most of those subscribers renewed. In addition to a strong code of ethics, Adler also worked to improve the quality of Lee's newspapers. He ended the practice of running many syndicated columns and press releases, for example, and instead encouraged his publishers to generate copy in-house.

Adler served as president of Lee for ten years, during which he continued to increase its operations and holdings. In 1960, for example, KEYC-TV of Mankato, Minnesota, began broadcasting. In 1967, the company moved all of its newspaper and broadcasting divisions to a new corporate headquarters in Davenport, and in 1969 Lee made its first public stock offering to raise cash for a new round of acquisitions. Shortly thereafter, Lee bought the *Journal Times* in Racine, Wisconsin, and the *Corvallis Gazette-Times* of Corvallis, Oregon. It also completed the acquisition of a few newspapers in which it held a partial interest. By the time Adler retired in 1970, Lee was a diversified radio, television, and newspaper company active in ten midwestern and western states.

David K. Gottlieb succeeded Adler. Gottlieb started working for Lee in 1936 and worked his way up through the ranks to vice-president of the entire company by 1967. He served only three years before he died unexpectedly of a heart attack in 1973. His most important contribution to Lee during that period was the initiation of a joint venture with Nippon Paint Co., Ltd, of Japan. In 1972, the two companies formed NAPP Systems Inc. to manufacture an advanced printing device for sale to the publishing industry. NAPP's innovative printing plates significantly sped up the plate-making process and reduced the number of people required to accomplish a specific task by as much as 50 percent. Also under Gottlieb's leadership, Lee purchased WSAZ-TV, an NBC affiliate in North Carolina, and WMDR-FM in Illinois.

Continued Growth: 1970s–90s

Lloyd G. Schermer became president of Lee in 1973. The 46-year-old Schermer started with Lee in 1954 after receiving his masters degree in business administration from Harvard University. He moved from an advertising position to publisher of a Lee newspaper by 1961. Schermer was an avid outdoorsman and, like all of the Lee presidents before him, played a very active leadership role in local and regional volunteer programs. Schermer also emphasized reporting and broadcasting integrity as an integral tenet of the Lee Enterprises philosophy, and he sustained the steady expansion and acquisition activity that had made Lee a regional media contender. The first Lee purchase under Schermer's direction was KGMB-TV of Honolulu, Hawaii, in 1976. Lee also picked up KOIN-TV in Portland, Oregon, in 1977, and purchased the *Bismarck Tribune* (North Dakota) in 1978. In 1979, and 1980, moreover, the company acquired newspapers in Illinois and Minnesota. Acquisitions of TV stations in New Mexico, Arizona, and Nebraska followed in 1985 and 1986.

In addition to expanding Lee's holdings, Schermer drew on his Harvard-taught management techniques to whip the company's organizational structure into shape and boost its operating efficiency. Like A.W. Lee and his successors, Schermer believed in a relatively high level of autonomy for Lee's division managers, who knew better than central management how to serve their local markets. However, Schermer brought a new

emphasis on productivity to the company. Augmenting his technical style was a penchant for taking calculated risks. Schermer came from a family of entrepreneurs and was not afraid to test new waters at Lee. In 1983, for example, Schermer initiated Call-It Co. as a subsidiary of Lee. Research and development of the innovative venture, which was inspired by Schermer's interest in the ballooning market for telecommunications services, continued into the early 1990s.

In 1986, Schermer became chief executive officer of the company and Richard D. Gottlieb, son of David Gottlieb, took over as president. The two ran the company together, with Schermer slowly transferring supervision of day-to-day management duties to Gottlieb. Gottlieb had been with the company since 1964 and worked his way up to vice-president of newspapers by 1980. Known for his human relations and managerial skills, Gottlieb maintained the management style and growth strategy that had become a legacy of Lee enterprises. In 1990, he oversaw the acquisition of the *Rapid City Journal* (Iowa) and helped to complete the 100 percent purchase of NAPP Systems Inc. for $100 million.

By 1990, the year of its 100th anniversary, Lee was operating 19 newspapers in small- to medium-sized towns and six television stations broadcasting to 13 states. It also owned and operated in excess of 30 specialty publications, most of which were magazine-like weeklies in the upper Midwest that carried classified advertisements. In addition, the company operated four printing facilities, NAPP Systems Inc., and Voice Response, Inc. (Call-It Co.). Despite heavy borrowing to feed its capital-intensive expansion program, the company was financially healthy and had succeeded in minimizing its debt load. Indeed, by 1990 Lee Enterprises was raking in $287 million annually and capturing $44 million per year in net income. As a result of its 1990 acquisitions, moreover, Lee's revenues leapt to $346 million.

Despite Lee's financial successes, the newspaper industry, as well as most other media sectors, encountered setbacks during the economic recession of the late 1980s and early 1990s. As the economy slumped, advertising revenues sagged. Furthermore, the newspaper industry, which accounted for the bulk of Lee's sales, was struggling under the pressure of increased competition from electronic media. Fortunately, Lee was able to endure the downturn unscathed, unlike many of its industry peers. Its stability was largely a result of geography: most of its holdings were located in the economically healthy upper Midwest. Nevertheless, Lee's net income slipped to $31.5 million in 1991 before buoying back up to about $39 million in 1992.

As Lee slowly added new radio and television holdings to its portfolio during the early 1990s, its balance sheet began to reflect the economic recovery. Sales swelled to $373 million in 1993 as net income rose to about $41 million. Furthermore, the company anticipated receipts of about $400 million during 1994 based on surging sales early in the year. Under Gottlieb's direction, Lee was beginning to eye new markets for growth, such as farm magazines, book publishing, and electronic multi-media opportunities. In addition, Lee's NAPP subsidiary had developed and was selling a breakthrough photosensitive polymer printing plate that was receiving widespread market acceptance.

Success in the Late 1990s and Beyond

Lee's growth strategy continued in the late 1990s and into the new century. The firm acquired the Pacific Northwest Publishing Group in 1997, which strengthened its foothold in Oregon and the surrounding Northwest region. Other dailies and weeklies were added the company's arsenal in the following years, including the *Ravalli Republic,* the *Beatrice Daily Sun,* the *Columbus Telegram,* and the *Fremont Tribune.* At this time, the company opted to focus solely on its core publishing and printing operations. As such, it sold most of its broadcasting holdings to Emmis Communications Corp. in 2000 in a $560 million deal.

Long-time newspaper executive Mary Junck was at the helm of Lee as president and CEO by 2001. She was named chairman in 2002 after Gottlieb retired. Eager to make use of the funds stemming from its broadcasting sell-off, Junck made it clear that the firm was looking to purchase daily newspapers in lucrative markets with circulations from 30,000 to 125,000. She orchestrated the largest deal in company history in 2002 when she announced the $694 million acquisition of Howard Publishing Inc. Overall, Lee added 16 daily newspapers to its holdings as a result of the buyout and became the 12th largest newspaper company in the United States. It acquired Iowa's daily *Sioux City Journal* later that year. By early 2003, Lee's revenue had climbed by 58.9 percent and its daily circulation was up by 75 percent to 1.13 million.

The company's achievements over the past several years left it in an enviable position among its competitors. Lee was reporting increases in sales and profits when many in the industry were suffering due to a weak economy and slowing advertising revenues. To ensure success in the years to come, Junck set forth five key operating priorities that included growing revenue creatively and rapidly, improving leadership and circulation, emphasizing local news, building an online future, and exercising careful cost controls. Employees at company headquarters carried cards with these priorities printed on them. As it focused on the future, Lee continued to draw on many of the principles established by its founder to achieve prosperity and to serve as a responsible leader in the newspaper industry.

Principal Subsidiaries

Lee Procurement Solutions Company; Lee Publications Inc.; Sioux City Newspapers; Journal Star Printing Company; Lee Consolidated Holdings Company; Accudata Inc.; LINT Company; Target Marketing Systems Inc.; K. Falls Basin Publishing Inc.; Madison Newspapers Inc. (50%); INN Partners L.C. (81%).

Principal Competitors

Community Newspaper Holdings Inc.; Gannett Co. Inc.; Journal Communications Inc.

Further Reading

Bielema, Ross, "Times Makes an Effort to Recycle," *Quad-City Times,* December 28, 1992.

Byrne, Harlan S., "Newspaper Tiger," *Barron's,* April 11, 1994.

Cross, Wilbur, *Lee's Legacy of Leadership,* Essex, Conn.: Greenwich Publishing Group, 1990.

Fitzgerald, Mark, "All a Matter of Priorities," *Editor & Publisher,* February 10, 2003, p. 10.

Johnson, Charles S., "Lee Publishers, Governor Deny Making Sales-Tax Deal," *Missoulian,* May 25, 1993, p. B1.

"Lee Closes Purchase of Oregon Newspaper Group," *Wisconsin State Journal,* September 10, 1997.

"Lee Enterprises Reports Earnings Slump," *Billings Gazette,* July 25, 1991, p. C7.

Marcial, Gene G., "Newspapers with Lots of Black Ink," *Business Week,* February 11, 1991, p. 70.

"Missoulian Editor Joins New Venture," *Missoulian,* May 7, 1994, p. B1.

"Montana Magazine Purchased by Lee Enterprises," *Missoulian,* May 1, 1994, p. B2.

Richgels, Jeff, "Burgess to Leave Journal," *Madison Capital Times,* April 1, 1993.

Rondy, John, "Racine's Journal Times Takes the Flexographic Press Plunge," *Business Journal-Milwaukee,* February 12, 1994, p. 6A.

Steinberg, Brian, "Lee Thinks Small to Achieve Big Things," *Wall Street Journal,* March 27, 2002, B5.

Weber, Joseph, "Small-Town Papers, Big-Time Profits," *Business Week,* July 1, 2002, p. 94.

—Dave Mote
—update: Christina M. Stansell

Liebherr-International AG

rue de l'industrie 45
CH-1630 Bulle
Switzerland
Telephone: (+41) 26 913-3111
Fax: (+41) 26 912-3485
Web site: http://www.liebherr.com

Private Company
Incorporated: 1949
Employees: 20,900
Sales: EUR 4.07 billion ($4.5 billion) (2002)
NAIC: 333923 Overhead Traveling Crane, Hoist, and
Monorail System Manufacturing; 333120 Construction
Machinery Manufacturing; 333131 Mining Machinery
and Equipment Manufacturing; 335311 Power,
Distribution, and Specialty Transformer Manufactur-
ing; 335313 Switchgear and Switchboard Apparatus
Manufacturing; 335312 Motor and Generator Manu-
facturing; 336413 Other Aircraft Parts and Auxiliary
Equipment Manufacturing; 335222 Household Refrig-
erator and Home Freezer Manufacturing; 333512
Machine Tool (Metal Cutting Types) Manufacturing;
721110 Hotels (Except Casino Hotels) and Motels

Liebherr-International AG is the Swiss holding company of the Liebherr Group, one of the world's leading manufacturers of construction and mining machinery. Liebherr products are developed and manufactured at 25 production plants in 11 countries in Europe, North and South America, and Asia. The company's Earth-moving Machinery division makes excavators, crawlers, loaders, and mining trucks, which account for about 30 percent of sales. Liebherr's Construction Machinery division makes a broad variety of construction cranes, as well as pipe-laying machines, concrete mixing plants, and ready-mix concrete trucks. The company's broad range of cranes includes stationary tower cranes, mobile cranes, and crawler cranes, which in addition to construction purposes are also used for cargo handling in harbors, on ships, and in logistics centers. Cranes account for about one-third of Liebherr's revenues. The company also makes aviation equipment, diesel motors, and gear-cutting machines, offers a line of household refrigerators and freezers, and runs six top-class hotels in Ireland, Austria, and Germany. Roughly 70 percent of the company's sales come from Western Europe. About half of Liebherr's total workforce is in Germany, where the company was founded. Liebherr-International AG is owned by the Liebherr family and managed by two children of the company founder, Hans Liebherr.

New Construction Crane Meets a Need in the 1950s

Hans Liebherr grew up in Kirchdorf, a small southern German town on the Iller river. At the time he lost his father in World War I, Liebherr was only two years old. At age 13, he started an apprenticeship in his stepfather's small construction business. During World War II, Liebherr served in the engineering corps of the German army, specifically in a unit that built bridges for the German troops in Russia. There he gained valuable insights into common challenges connected with construction projects. At the end of the war, Germany lay in ruins, and it was evident that the rebuilding of the country would occupy the nation for many years.

The currency reform in western Germany in 1948 marked the beginning of what was later called the German Economic Miracle. Back home from the war, Liebherr—now in his mid-30s—started working on the prototype of a construction crane that he envisioned would be needed by smaller construction firms in the postwar reconstruction years. The new kind of crane he had in mind would be easy to set up and transport, have a far better performance than the models available at that time, and still be affordable for smaller businesses. In a little wooden shed that he had set up, Liebherr, together with the local blacksmith and a few other men, built the 30-foot tower crane he had envisioned. After he was granted a German patent for his invention in August 1949, he exhibited his crane at the Frankfurt Trade Fair. The crane stirred a great deal of interest, but Liebherr received not one order.

Liebherr, however, believed in his idea and started building a number of his cranes. A few weeks later, orders started coming in. Liebherr's first crane model, the TK 10, could extend from 4.5 to 16 meters and carry from 650 kilograms to 2,000 kilograms in weight. It was folded up for transportation and could be set up within two to three hours. Conventional construction cranes were much bigger than the TK 10, and it took several days to set them up. In 1950, the business took off quickly. Liebherr modified the TK 10 and constructed a number of models with different performance parameters to meet the needs of various construction projects. Because all these models were built in series, Liebherr was able to sell them at very reasonable prices. All of his cranes could be folded up and transported as one unit.

Within a few weeks, the small workshop was turned into a small factory. Soon Liebherr employed 110 people who built about one crane per day. In his first year of business, Liebherr sold 160 cranes, generating DM 2.2 million in sales. In 1952, Liebherr introduced a new model, the TK 28, which was equipped with an adjustable arm. The necessary gears were made by outside suppliers according to Liebherr's specifications. In the year of its introduction, 267 TK 28 cranes were sold.

Conquering New Markets in 1954

Cranes remained Liebherr's major product during the 1950s, 1960s, and 1970s. However, only a few years after he successfully established himself in one market, Liebherr ventured into new ones. After his innovations in the way construction materials were hauled at construction sites, he took on how dirt was dug out of the ground. The excavators of the early 1950s were extremely big, heavy, and slow. Thick steel cables running through pulleys maneuvered the bucket and digging arm, a technology that was inefficient in terms of precision and the application of leverage. Liebherr wanted to improve the performance of excavators by utilizing hydraulic power—which was already used to tilt the bed of dump trucks—to drive the bucket into the ground and pull it out. In eight months, Liebherr invented his first hydraulic excavator, which was much lighter had a much larger bucket than other machines of its kind. The new invention, which again revolutionized the construction industry, was a huge success. Soon Liebherr's excavators became a second leg for the company to stand on.

This, however, was not enough for Liebherr. The production of construction machinery was complemented by concrete mixers. At the same time, the company ventured into a completely

new field when it started making household refrigerators in the mid-1950s. New plants were set up in Biberach, Bad Schussenried, Kempten, and Ochsenhausen for these new activities. By the end of the 1950s, Liebherr had grown to an enterprise of considerable size. The company employed roughly 2,400 people and generated DM 77 million in sales.

Liebherr's know-how in hydraulic technology led the company into another market. In the 1970s, the company started making aircraft equipment for the European Airbus, including the nose-wheel and modules for the air-conditioning system. The Airbus business was worth more than $500 million. Another area where the company had gained special know-how was gear manufacturing. Early on, Liebherr had adopted a policy to outsource as little as possible in order in keep control over the production of major components that went into the company's products. Among those components were gear boxes and motors for Liebherr's cranes and excavators, for which the company's engineering division developed even the machinery to make them. Over time, the company became a supplier of hydraulic gear-making automates to major automobile manufacturers as well as to competitors such as the American heavy machinery manufacturer Caterpillar.

Finally, Liebherr started setting up whole plants for other companies. For a client in Algeria, Liebherr built a complete plant for the production of excavators worth $500 million and even trained the personnel there. Among the company's biggest projects was the installation of a transmission assembly line for a truck plant in Russia worth about $225 million. In addition to these activities, Liebherr ventured into a completely unrelated field. One of Liebherr's strategies was to set up new production facilities in rural areas where, in his opinion, work and business ethics were better and labor cost cheaper. When a new crane plant was set up in the Irish countryside in 1958, Hans Liebherr realized that there was no place where visitors could spend the night, so he initiated the construction of two modern hotels nearby. Eventually, the number of hotels run by Liebherr increased to six.

Building a Global Enterprise in the 1960s–70s

Not only did Hans Liebherr build a diversified enterprise almost from the very beginning, but he also expanded into new geographical markets early on. The erection of the crane plant in Killarney, Ireland, marked the beginning of the company's international expansion. During the 1950s, Liebherr production subsidiaries were established in France, Switzerland, and the United Kingdom. In the 1960s, the company set up its first production plant in Austria. In the following decades, Austria emerged as Liebherr's second most important location besides Germany. The first plant for excavators and bearings was followed by production facilities for crawler-excavators and pipe-laying machines, refrigerators and freezers, harbor cranes and offshore cranes for ships and floating drilling platforms, as well as the construction of two high class hotels. A new factory for mobile cranes that were mounted onto a chassis and could therefore be moved rapidly between construction sites opened in Ehingen, Germany, in 1969. Early orders for them were received from England as well as from the Soviet Union.

In the 1970s, Liebherr expanded even further, setting up new sales offices and production plants overseas in Brazil, Canada, and South Africa. However, Hans Liebherr's main focus was to gain a foothold in the United States, which was not an easy task. In 1970, Liebherr set up a brand-new excavator plant near Newport News, Virginia. The most difficult task, however, was to find dealers in the country who were willing to start offering their clients products from a European newcomer that was competing with the well-known American manufacturers. What made it even harder was the fact that the most profitable part of a U.S.-dealer's business was selling replacement parts and offering repair services to their customer base. However, since there had been no Liebherr products on the market, it would be a while until that kind of business could be expected.

Another problem was the decision to modify the company's excavators to match American taste. The undercarriage was extended—as were the fuel tanks—and had a more robust design. However, as the construction industry slipped into recession in the mid-1970s, sales of heavy-duty machinery declined sharply in the United States. Suddenly, Liebherr had a backlog of excavators made for the American market that could not be sold in Europe, where the company tried to keep up with the high demand. To use the free capacity in its Virginia plant, the company started making cranes there and received a $15 million order from the U.S. Navy. However, the deal turned out to be costly for Liebherr, since the company had to make changes in the crane design on an already very low bid to meet the desired requirements. All in all, the crane production cost the company the profits it had made with excavators in 1979, and the manufacture of cranes in Virginia was ceased soon afterwards.

Despite initial difficulties, Liebherr managed to sign up 50 dealers in the United States by the end of the 1970s and had gained a market share of between 3 and 4 percent. By that time, the Liebherr group of companies employed 15,000 people in ten countries and brought in $1.1 billion in sales. The enterprise had grown from a mid-sized, family-owned business into a multinational corporation, ranking number 431 on *Fortune* magazine's list of the largest industrial companies outside the United States.

Financial Conservatism, Decentralization, and Transfer of Ownership in the 1980s

Up until the 1990s, Liebherr was firmly under the company founder's control. Hans Liebherr's management style was legendary. His success was built on his unshakable belief in frugality and delegation of responsibility. In 1980, Hans Liebherr told *Fortune* reporter Robert Ball that he believed that owing money to other people was gambling. He was aware that his enterprise could have grown faster with the help of bank loans but adhered strictly to his maxim that money could only be spent after it was earned. Liebherr flew economy class and drove a seven-year-old Mercedes. Besides financial conservatism, Liebherr believed in decentralization. Every new subsidiary's top management was fully responsible for its operation. Fewer than 20 people worked at the group's headquarters.

Hans Liebherr relied on two methods for steering his enterprise: monthly reports and unannounced visits. All of the 26 subsidiaries filled in a one-page report at the end of each month that contained the most important financial and operational figures. One of Liebherr's foremost concerns was that administrative cost did not run out of hand. To complement this information, he regularly visited each of the production plants in Germany, Austria, France, and Switzerland. Without any warning, he often walked into the production halls and spoke with the workers and foremen there before talking to any manager.

In the early 1970s, Hans Liebherr moved his residence from Germany to Switzerland in order to avoid the hefty German inheritance tax. Then Hans Liebherr transferred stock ownership in his enterprise to his children. The company was split in two parts: a German holding company for all business activities in Germany and another holding company based in Switzerland for all the other subsidiaries. Hans, Jr., Markus, and Hubert Liebherr received equal shares in the German holding company. Willi and Isolde Liebherr were co-owners of the Swiss holding company. However, despite the transfer of ownership, Hans Liebherr remained in control of his enterprise through a power of attorney with each of his children. In 1983, the company's headquarters were moved to Switzerland after the establishment of the new Swiss-based management holding company Liebherr-International AG.

After Hans Liebherr's daughter and four sons had finished their education in their late 20s and early 30s, they all started working as full-time executives at their father's business. The company founder's oldest son, Hans, Jr., studied engineering and economics. Willi Liebherr became a mechanical engineer, while his younger brother Markus studied engineering with an agricultural focus. Hubert, the youngest of the Liebherr brothers, became a construction engineer, and their sister Isolde studied business administration. Hubert Liebherr managed an excavator plant in Algeria, Isolde was responsible for the hotels, and the other Liebherr siblings had management positions in production or marketing. However, around 1990, Hubert Liebherr gave his share in the family business back to his father.

Second Liebherr Generation Takes Over in 1990

When company founder Hans Liebherr died in 1993, at age 78, his industrial enterprise generated roughly $2.5 billion in sales annually. Now it was time for the second Liebherr generation to take over management of the family enterprise. Hans, Jr. took over responsibility for the crane and concrete mixing business, Willi for earth moving equipment, and Isolde for the refrigerator production and hotels. Markus Liebherr, however, had changed his life plans and gave most of his shares in the company back to his brothers and sister. Hans, Jr., Willi, and Isolde met every other week to discuss the basic decisions concerning investment, product development, and finances.

Hans Liebherr had left behind a financially healthy business. Due to his conservative financial policy, the company was free of long-term debt. All investment projects were financed out of the company's cash-flow. In the 1990s, after profiting from the construction boom brought about by the reunification of East and West Germany, the Liebherr group increasingly focused on the emerging markets in Asia, North America, and the Far East. In 1995, Liebherr helped establish a manufacturing plant for truck gears in Tatarstan for the Russian truck maker Kamaz. In 1997, the company acquired Axel Friedmann Verkehrstechnik, a manufacturer of air conditioning systems for high-speed trains, adding a new branch to the group's portfolio. The new business division profited from Liebherr's know-how in air-conditioning technology for airplanes. In the same year, the company founded Liebherr-Mietpartner, a new subsidiary that established a network of over 70 rental centers for construction equipment throughout Germany. Also in the 1990s, Liebherr acquired North American dump truck manufacturer Wiseda, an important step into the U.S. market for mining equipment. In 1999, a new Liebherr refrigerator plant was set up in Plovdiv, Bulgaria, which started putting out low-priced models for the European market in 2000. New production lines in Asia included a crane plant in Thailand and four manufacturing joint ventures in China.

In 1999, Hans, Jr. stepped down from his active involvement in the family business but remained on its supervisory board. Willi was named the Liebherr group's chairman and Isolde became vice-chairman. Some observers interpreted this as a sign that one of Willi's six sons and daughters might follow their father in running the company. Three years later, Liebherr's organizational structure was changed when four business divisions—earthmoving machinery, construction machinery, refrigerators/freezers, and aviation equipment—replaced the former management holdings in Germany and Austria. The first three were managed from Germany, while Liebherr's headquarters for aviation equipment was moved to Toulouse, France, the European aviation industry's center. The mobile and maritime crane plants in Ehingen, Germany, and Nenzing, Austria, however, reported directly to the group holding in Switzerland.

Relentless diversification, globalization, and investment in modernization and product innovation helped Liebherr sustain a comparatively favorable position in terms of sales and profits. Sluggish growth and decreasing sales in Germany and Western Europe were offset by the growing demand in emerging markets such as Asia and the Far East. The sharp decline in demand for construction equipment in Germany, and a drop in orders for aviation equipment after the terrorist attacks in the United States on September 11, 2001, were partly offset by an increasing number of orders for mobile harbor and offshore cranes. How-

ever, after an average sales growth of 12 percent from 1997 until 2001, the company's revenues dropped slightly in 2002.

Despite a difficult global economic climate Liebherr had an optimistic outlook on the group's future and invested in a number of new ventures. In 2002, the company announced a new business venture with German truck maker MAN Nutzfahrzeuge to jointly develop and manufacture a new diesel motor which was slated to be introduced in 2005. Also in 2002, Liebherr launched an investment project to expand the wellness sections of Liebherr's two upscale hotels in Austria to accommodate the trend towards health-tourism. In 2003, the company broke ground for a new production plant for maritime cranes in Rostock, a harbor city on the German Baltic coast, and invested in an excavator plant in China. The year 2003 also saw the launch of Liebherr's new heavy-duty crane for the erection and maintenance of offshore wind-power systems. With the third Liebherr generation attending college, Willi and Isolde Liebherr believed that the company would be able to grow from its own resources—without the help of outside investors—and to withstand growing pressures from accelerating global consolidation and competition. That was the way it had grown to its current size: as a family-owned business.

Principal Divisions

Earth-Moving Machinery; Construction Machinery.

Principal Subsidiaries

Liebherr-Holding GmbH; Liebherr-Werk Nenzing GmbH (Austria); Liebherr-Aerospace Toulouse SAS (France); Liebherr Machines Bulle S.A. (Switzerland); Liebherr Mining Eqipment Co. (United States); Liebherr Industrias Metálicas, S.A. (Spain); Liebherr Container Cranes Ltd. (Ireland); Liebherr Sunderland Works Ltd. (United Kingdom); Embraer-Liebherr Equipamentos do Brasil S.A.; Liebherr Brasil Ltda.; Xuzhuo Liebherr Concrete Machinery Co. Ltd. (China); Liebherr (Thailand) Co., Ltd.

Principal Competitors

AB Electrolux; BSH Bosch und Siemens Hausgeräte GmbH; Caterpillar Inc.; Demag Holding; Cummins, Inc.; Kobelco Construction Machinery America Inc.; Komatsu Ltd., Hitachi, Ltd.; Potain S.A.S.; O&K Orenstein & Koppel GmbH; Whirlpool Corporation.

Further Reading

Ball, Robert, "It's Tough Digging in the U.S.," *Fortune*, August 11, 1980, p. 142.

Davies, John, "In-house output begins," *Financial Times*, February 4, 1985, Section III, p. 6.

"Disarming Talent," *Economist*, July 30, 1988, p. 70.

"Geschichte am Haken," *bd baumaschinendienst*, 4 + 5/2000, 15 p.

"Hans Liebherr," *Frankfurter Allgemeine Zeitung*, October 12, 1993, p. 22.

Heller, Michael, "Die Liebherrs widerstehen den Verlockungen des vielen Geldes," *Frankfurter Allgemeine Zeitung*, April 13, 1995, p. 23.

Marsh, Peter, "Investment Helps Lift Sales," *Financial Times*, October 7, 1999, p. 5.

——, "Liebherr Plans DM50bn Refrigerator Plant," *Financial Times*, October 2, 1998, p. 25.

——, "Senior Members of Liebherr Family Move Places," *Financial Times*, August 11, 1999, p. 13.

"Quick Loading," *World Mining Equipment*, January-February 1996, p. 22.

Ruemmele, Martin, "Liebherr erweitert Gesundheitshotel," *Wirtschaftsblatt*, January 24, 2002, p. 1.

——, "Liebherr Nenzing wird eigene Konzernsparte," *Wirtschaftsblatt*, June 12, 2002, p. 21.

—Evelyn Hauser

LSI Logic Corporation

1621 Barber Lane
Milpitas, California 95035
U.S.A.
Telephone: (408) 433-8000
Toll Free: (866) 574-5741
Fax: (408) 954-3220
Web site: http://www.lsilogic.com

Public Company
Incorporated: 1980 as LSI Logic, Inc.
Employees: 4,700
Sales: $1.7 billion (2003)
Stock Exchanges: New York
Ticker Symbol: LSI
NAIC: 334413 Semiconductor and Related Device
    Manufacturing; 334419 Other Computer Peripheral
    Equipment Manufacturing

LSI Logic Corporation is a leading global designer and manufacturer of custom semiconductors. The company's principal products are Application Specific Integrated Circuits, or ASICs, as well as Application Specific Standard Products, or ASSPs. LSI Logic competes in three main market areas: consumer products, communications, and storage components. The company planned to spin off a fourth business area, storage systems, as the public company Engenio Information Technologies, Inc., in 2004. LSI Logic was a defining force in the customized semiconductor market through the mid-1990s. The company adapted to changing market conditions by developing a strong market in standardized semiconductor products as well. LSI Logic operates subsidiaries in Japan, Hong Kong, and the United Kingdom, and a manufacturing facility in Gresham, Oregon. Wilfred J. Corrigan founded the company in 1980. Corrigan still headed the company in 2004.

Gaining a Foothold in the 1980s

During the early 1980s, the global semiconductor industry was neither a fertile nor a hospitable market for U.S. companies to enter. Japanese manufacturers had gained an early and sizeable lead over the rest of world, controlling 70 percent of the worldwide market for 64K DRAM chips—key components in computers, video games, and telecommunications systems and the most widely sought products on the market. The few U.S. semiconductor manufacturers mustering any appreciable opposition against the Japanese during the period were large corporations based in California's Silicon Valley. These manufacturers—even those with sufficient financial clout—struggled to catch up in an expensive high-technology race, especially against the Japanese, who held considerable market share and ample funding for the expensive endeavor of designing and producing memory chips.

Such was the climate pervading the semiconductor industry during the formation of LSI Logic. Despite the overwhelming odds against a small entrepreneurial company successfully competing in a market where much larger corporations were floundering, Wilfred J. Corrigan, the founder of LSI Logic, was intent on carving a niche in the industry and in defying what he later called the ''conventional wisdom that the semiconductor industry was only for major corporations.'' To accomplish this formidable task, Corrigan positioned LSI Logic in a small segment of the semiconductor industry, focusing on a branch that offered tremendous growth potential and the opportunity for a small, fledgling enterprise to survive. By doing this, Corrigan gave LSI Logic a viable niche in which to begin business. No matter the strength of his idea, however, Corrigan needed money to get his venture started. The money would need to come from investors willing to take a high-risk gamble with their dollars on the slim hope that a small company could effectively compete in the combative semiconductor industry. Much, then, would depend on Corrigan's ability to convince the financial community that his company was worth investing in, a task made even more difficult by his recent, less-than-illustrious track record as the leader of another company involved in the semiconductor industry. The high risk of financing such a small, entrepreneurial company, combined with Corrigan's unfavorable record in the years leading up to his new venture with LSI Logic, presented investors with an opportunity they presumably would avoid.

Roughly six years prior to LSI Logic's formation, Corrigan, son of a Liverpool, England, dockworker and a graduate in

Company Perspectives:

For more than 20 years, we've been providing innovative solutions to customers worldwide. As the foremost global supplier of custom, high-performance semiconductors, we partner with trend-setting customers to build complete systems on a single chip. Customers take advantage of our unique CoreWare methodology to increase performance, lower system costs and accelerate bringing their products to market. Also, because of our leadership in connectivity solutions and interface I/O, OEMs continue to look to us for standard product solutions in SCSI and Fibre Channel technology.

chemical engineering from the Imperial College of Science, had gained control over a prominent semiconductor company, Fairchild Camera and Instrument Company. Serving as Fairchild's chairman, chief executive, and president, Corrigan led the company through an over ambitious and disastrous diversification into video games and digital watches while losing market share and falling behind in the technological race in the semiconductor business. Against this backdrop of disappointing results, Corrigan gained the reputation as a somewhat dictatorial leader who liked to show the opening scene of the movie *Patton* during sales meetings. Corrigan's troubled tenure as Fairchild's top executive ended approximately five years after it began, precipitated by Fairchild's acquisition by another company, Schlumberger Ltd., in 1979. Less than a year later, Corrigan left Fairchild to embark on a short stint as a private investor, then began effecting plans to launch his own business, LSI Logic.

With LSI Logic, Corrigan planned to enter a small segment of the semiconductor industry that produced relatively small batches of semi-finished microelectronic chips, which were then customized for each customer. As opposed to the major segment of the semiconductor industry contested by large manufacturers in Silicon Valley and in Japan, the customized chip industry produced chips that enabled its customers to differentiate their products from those of their competitors, while the major semiconductor companies manufactured standard chips in bulk. Corrigan intended to focus on one technique in the customized chip business known as gate arrays, in which the basic logic elements, or "gates," were laid out on a chip and then connected in a particular customized order during the last stages of production.

During the early 1980s, this field of the semiconductor industry was quite small, yet Corrigan believed the demand for customized chips, or application-specific integrated circuits (ASICs), would grow immensely in the coming decade. Corrigan convinced a group of venture capitalists, based chiefly in the Bay Area, to provide his company with the $6 million necessary to begin business. The company was incorporated in November 1980 and began operating in early 1981 using leased facilities in Santa Clara, California. Corrigan occupied the same executive positions he had held at Fairchild, serving as LSI Logic's chairman, chief executive officer, and president, ready to steward the company in a market that represented under $100 million at the time but was expected to become a $1 billion industry by 1986.

Although Corrigan held the same senior management titles at LSI Logic as he had at Fairchild, there the similarities ended. At LSI Logic, Corrigan shed the unsavory image he had developed at Fairchild and astutely led his small company through its formative first years. In August 1981, less than a year after beginning business, LSI Logic entered what company officials described as the "first fully cooperative semiconductor development program involving U.S. and Japanese companies" when it formed a joint venture with Toshiba Corporation to develop a line of advanced semi-custom circuits. The joint venture represented a connection that would grow stronger and deeper as the company sought to take the lead in a burgeoning market. To secure a commanding position in the market, however, LSI Logic needed ample funding for developmental programs intrinsic to success in a high-technology business. Corrigan was repeatedly able to obtain the necessary capital for development, which consequently enabled LSI Logic to expand and capture market share in a field other semiconductor companies were slow to enter. Another major infusion of capital arrived in March 1982, this time totaling more than $16 million, the bulk of which came from the same venture capitalists that had provided the money to get LSI Logic started. A group of investment bankers in the United Kingdom and First Interstate Bank supplied the rest of the money, which was used for capital equipment purchases and plant expansion.

Despite the arrival of the needed funding, the year-end finances were disappointing. By the end of 1982, LSI Logic had collected $5 million in sales, but recorded a loss of $3.7 million, making Corrigan's plan of reaping profits in the customized chip market still a dream. The following year, however, the company recorded the first of many prodigious leaps in its sales volume when revenues shot up seven-fold to $35 million. Perhaps more encouraging, LSI Logic also demonstrated its profitability, registering $12.5 million in net income for the year—an enormous sum given the company's revenue total. During the next few years, however, LSI Logic's profit total fell considerably short of the sales-to-profit ratio recorded in 1983; revenues rose vigorously throughout the decade, but profits remained comparatively low.

As before, the drive to become the leader in its market required the infusion of capital, something LSI Logic needed in 1981, 1982, and again in 1983. In May 1983, while LSI Logic was recording its first year of undeniable financial strength, Corrigan orchestrated his company's first public offering, which the Japanese investors readily accepted. Japanese investors acquired a considerable portion of LSI Logic's stock, demonstrating a willingness to invest in the company. Corrigan then allowed Japanese investors to take part in LSI Logic's growth the following year with the formation of LSI Logic's Japanese affiliate, Nihon LSI Logic Corporation. The venture financing of Nihon LSI Logic was completed in April 1984 through a private offering in Japan that raised $20 million and ceded a group of 28 Japanese investors a 33 percent stake in the newly formed affiliate. Corrigan raised an additional $20 million by employing the same strategy two months later through a private placement for LSI Logic's British subsidiary, LSI Logic Ltd.

Global Growth in the Mid-1980s

The creation of Nihon LSI Logic and the strengthening of the British subsidiary, LSI Logic Ltd., which had been in existence since 1982, were part of Corrigan's strategy to expand internationally. Corrigan envisioned the establishment of largely autonomous operations in three major markets: Japan, the United States, and Europe. Corrigan referred to this blueprint for expansion as his "global triad strategy," a plan that would firmly root LSI Logic's presence in three critical regions and, according to Corrigan, insulate each autonomous division from downturns peculiar to each continent while enabling each part of the "triad" to take advantage of changing market conditions in its region.

By the beginning of 1985, Corrigan could claim overwhelming success in one market of his global triad strategy, when LSI Logic ranked as the number one company in the U.S. market for ASICs. LSI Logic controlled 40 percent of the market by this time and its sales volume reflected its quick rise in the industry. Sales had soared from the $35 million generated in 1983 to $84.4 million by 1984, then shot past the $100 million mark the following year, reaching $140 million. The company's net income, in contrast, did not record a commensurate meteoric rise, falling, in fact, from $15.4 million in 1984 to $10.1 million in 1985. In comparison to other U.S. semiconductor companies, however, LSI Logic at least remained profitable, a rare occurrence among other domestic rivals who were suffering debilitating losses from unrelenting Japanese competition.

To actualize his global triad strategy and help invigorate lagging profits, Corrigan moved resolutely toward the eye of storm, increasing LSI Logic's presence where the most powerful semiconductor companies existed—in Japan. In 1985, LSI Logic extended its joint development program through a multi-year agreement with Toshiba. During that same year, LSI Logic entered into a joint venture with Kawasaki Steel—Japan's third largest steel manufacturer—to build a $100 million wafer fabrication plant near Tokyo.

By 1986, LSI Logic controlled 45 percent of the U.S. ASIC market and 25 percent of the worldwide market. Although the company had secured an enviable position in the customized chip market, the increasing growth of the industry's sales volume had drawn numerous competitors attracted by the enormous growth potential in the business. By the mid-1980s, LSI Logic was competing in a crowded field and one that, as the decade progressed, became increasingly unprofitable. Much attention had been paid to revenue growth in the customized chip market, but little could be said of parallel profit growth, a phenomenon borne out in the annual revenue and net income totals recorded by LSI Logic, an industry leader. LSI Logic could claim enviable victories in revenue growth, market share, and consistent ad-

vancement in technological sophistication, but these victories came with a price: alarmingly low profits. In 1986, LSI Logic generated nearly $200 million in revenues, yet recorded a paltry $3.8 million in net income. Two years later, revenues surged to $379 million, while the company's net income climbed to $23.8 million, which was a considerable increase to be sure, but it was merely a prelude to two years of consecutive losses totaling nearly $60 million. By 1991, after halting its two-year net income slide into the red, LSI Logic, still an industry leader, was a $700 million company with net income amounting to $8.3 million, or $4 million less than it had earned when it was a $35 million company in 1982. Significant changes were needed to lift LSI Logic's profitability, but the company's transformation was costly, leading to another year of what industry pundits termed LSI Logic's "profitless prosperity."

Shifting Focus in the Early 1990s

In 1992, the company instituted sweeping cost-cutting measures to reduce overhead expenses and to embark on a new path toward increased profitability. Employment was trimmed by 1,000, falling to 4,500; a test and assembly plant in Braunschweig, Germany, was closed; and several operations deemed inconsistent with the company's new future were eliminated. The company-wide downsizing program reduced LSI Logic's operating expenses as a percentage of revenues from 36 percent to 27 percent, but it also resulted in an enormous $102 million restructuring charge and a $110 million loss for the year, making 1992 the third of the previous four years that LSI Logic lost money.

The changes effected in 1992 sought to propel the company back into the black and end its near decade-long inability to produce profits commensurate with its leading position in the customized chip market. Reducing overhead was not sufficient by itself to eliminate LSI Logic's problems. To more resolutely transform the company's fortunes, Corrigan also implemented LSI Logic's CoreWare program in 1992. This program offered customers access to a library of system-level building blocks and design tools. The company had always distinguished itself with its ability to provide a high level of customer service through computer software and other means, one of the chief reasons Corrigan believed back in 1980 that a small company could fare better in the customized chip market than a large company. CoreWare represented a significant leap in LSI Logic's ability to provide responsive service and, perhaps most importantly, CoreWare represented a sophisticated service that would yield higher profit margins, something the company desperately needed.

With the changes implemented in 1992, including its centerpiece CoreWare program, LSI Logic moved forward, invigorated and redirected toward a more positive future. By the end of the company's first fiscal quarter in 1995, it had recorded increases in its revenues for ten consecutive quarters. The company had also recorded consecutive quarterly improvements in its net income total during the same time span, a feat without rival in the company's history. In the first quarter of 1995 alone, LSI Logic recorded $45.3 million net income, twice the amount it had generated during its most profitable year before the implementation of its cost-cutting measures and the CoreWare program. With this encouraging financial growth fueling optimism,

Corrigan and the management of LSI Logic planned for a future beyond the mid-1990s that promised to be decidedly more profitable than the company's past.

Ups and Downs in the Late 1990s

Revenue at LSI Logic exceeded $1 billion in 1995, and the company seemed to have secured its place in the industry. That year, LSI became the sole owner of its Japanese affiliate, Nihon Semiconductor, and that company changed its name to LSI Logic Japan Semiconductor, Inc. LSI broke ground on a U.S. manufacturing facility that year as well, building a plant in Gresham, Oregon. Yet revenue fell slightly the next year, and the company continued to face challenges. Though it led the market in ASICs, it nevertheless felt the heat from strong competitors such as computer giant IBM Corp. and Lucent Technologies, Inc. LSI continued to bring out new products, but it had to spend huge amounts on research and development. By 1998, research and development spending equaled 20 cents for every dollar in revenue the company pulled in. LSI seemed a bit lost in the late 1990s, with *Electronic Business* (September 1999) characterizing the period leading up to 1999 as "three miserable years." In 1998, LSI made a major acquisition that had industry analysts scratching their heads. It put in an offer for part of Symbios Inc., a Colorado-based chip maker that had recently changed hands several times. LSI put in a bid for Symbios's chip business in January 1998, but parent company Hyundai instead offered Symbios to Adaptec, Inc. When that deal fell through, LSI returned to the table and bought all of Symbios—not just the chip business—for $804 million, substantially more than Adaptec had put down in its failed offer. The expensive transaction led LSI to post a loss of $126 million for 1998.

Nevertheless, by 1999, LSI Logic looked to be in a much better position. Whereas it had made its reputation by making customized chips, LSI began to move into standardized devices, or ASSPs (Application Specific Standard Products). Wilfred Corrigan had long insisted on rigorous design protocol which meant that all LSI's products could work together. *Electronic Business*, in the article cited above, described the company's evolution from making customized products to making a broader product line of standardized chips: "it became like a kid with an erector set, assembling the most appropriate pieces for each customer from its library." By 1999, application-specific, or custom, products made up only a quarter of LSI's sales. In addition, a growing portion of its sales came from what it called system-on-a-chip, or SOC, devices. This was an evolving market that put processors, memory, and logic on a single chip. The SOC allowed manufacturers of products like digital cameras and cell phones to pack more features into smaller, lighter machines. It also let manufacturers upgrade and refine their products more quickly. The SOC market was expected to grow rapidly in the late 1990s through the early 2000s, and LSI confidently predicted that revenue would reach $2 billion by the end of 1999. This represented a 40 percent leap over 1998, but LSI pulled it off.

New Purchases and Product Lines: 2000 and Beyond

The company now began a series of acquisitions. Between 1998 and 2003, LSI picked up more than a dozen companies, giving it ever broader product lines. It paid $106 million for SEEQ Technology, Inc. in 1999, a California firm that was a leading designer of data communications devices specifically for the networking market. The next year, LSI picked up another California company, DataPath Systems. The deal was a stock swap valued at around $420 million. In 2001, LSI bought the RAID (Redundant Array of Independent Disks) business of American Megatrends, Inc., a Georgia computer engineering firm. These and other acquisitions helped LSI Logic consolidate its product offerings into four main markets, consumer goods, communications, storage components, and storage systems.

LSI Logic greatly expanded its product line just in time for the semiconductor industry to contract. In 2000, two top executives at LSI, including John Daane, considered the likely successor to founder Wilfred Corrigan, resigned in order to take jobs at other firms. Corrigan was in his early sixties, and the company lacked a plan for carrying on without him. LSI's stock plunged on the news. The stock price had also slid several months earlier, on news that the company would not meet its second quarter sales estimates. By the last month of 2000, it was clear that the semiconductor market as a whole was skidding. The year 2000 had been a profitable one for LSI, despite the second quarter bobble. Sales hit $2.74 billion, and profits had risen as much as 140 percent. The company had done well selling to the communications market, taking 50 percent of its sales in this area. Yet by December, orders slowed to a trickle, and Corrigan predicted much slower sales growth for his company in the next few years. Corrigan also predicted in an interview with *Electronic News* (March 26, 2001) that storage would now be the most important market for LSI. It had picked up a lot of its storage systems business when it bought Symbios in 1998, and it eventually consolidated all its storage business into a subsidiary company called LSI Logic Storage Systems, Inc.

Corrigan had been through many ups and downs in the semiconductor industry, and by late 2002 he told *Electronic Engineering Times* (October 28, 2002) that the market was about to rebound. LSI had a new product, RapidChip, that the company hoped would give it inroads to new customers. Nevertheless, the first quarter of 2003 did not go well, with a 10 percent revenue decrease compared to a year earlier. LSI began to cut costs. It cut hundreds of jobs and planned to sell its manufacturing plants in Colorado Springs and in Tsukuba, Japan. In mid-2004, LSI announced plans to spin off its storage systems subsidiary. This firm changed its name to Engenio Information Technologies, Inc. in May, 2004. It was to go public on the New York Stock Exchange, with LSI Logic retaining a majority of the shares.

Principal Subsidiaries

Engenio Information Technologies, Inc.; LSI Logic Europe Ltd.

Principal Competitors

IBM-Microelectronics; Broadcom Corporation; Agere Systems, Inc.

Further Reading

"Cash Backing for LSI," *Electronics Weekly*, March 31, 1982, p. 4.

"Fourth Quarter Better for Most, But Not All," *Electronic Buyers' News*, February 1, 1999, p. 8.

Fuller, Brian, "LSI Chairman Sees Modest Chip Rebound, Sudden Plateau," *Electronic Engineering Times*, October 28, 2002, p. 35.

Gibson, Paul, "Liverpudlian Logic," *Electronic Business*, September 1999, p. 79.

"LSI Corp.," *Business Week*, August 24, 1981, p. 42L.

"LSI Files IPO Papers for Storage Systems Subsidiary," *Electronic News*, March 8, 2004.

"LSI Logic Cuts 580 Jobs on Sour Q1," *Electronic News*, April 28, 2003.

"LSI Logic to Build Fast Chip in Venture with 2 Other Firms," *Wall Street Journal*, March 27, 1990, p. 4B.

"LSI to Buy All of Chip Venture," *Wall Street Journal*, January 27, 1995, p. 7A.

McCarthy, Vance, "LSI Logic Steps away from Chip Consortium," *PC Week*, January 13, 1992, p. 120.

Murphy, Tom, "LSI Sees Storage as Key to Future," *Electronic News*, March 26, 2001, p. 28.

Pasha, Shaheen, "Cisco Sparks Technology Purge, as LSI Logic, Nvidia Also Sink," *Wall Street Journal*, November 8, 2002, p. C3.

Pollack, Andrew, "A Computer Chip Maker in the Black," *New York Times*, November 5, 1985, p. 1D.

——, "Big Goals and Hurdles for New Chip Maker," *New York Times*, July 13, 1989, p. 1D.

"Profit Is Reported as Cost Cuts Offset a Decline in Revenue," *Wall Street Journal*, January 29, 2004, p. B3.

Ristelhueber, Robert, "LSI Logic Is Turning Around Its 'Nonprofit Personality,'" *Electronic Business*, October 1993, p. 29.

——, "Profitless Prosperity Hits the Gate Array Market, *Electronic Business*, March 1993, pp. 108–09.

Russel, W. Sabin, "Ex-FC&I Chairman Starts Array Firm," *Electronic News*, January 19, 1981, p. 8.

Serant, Claire, "Wariness Grips Wall Street as Tech Stocks Slide," *Electronic Buyers' News*, July 31, 2000, p. 16.

Tharp, Mike, "LSI Logic Corp. Does as the Japanese Do," *Wall Street Journal*, April 17, 1986, p. 6.

Thurm, Scott, "LSI Logic Loses Pair of Top Executives to High-Tech Firms, as Stock Falls 20%," *Wall Street Journal*, November 22, 2000, p. B10.

"Try It in Japan," *Forbes*, June 18, 1984, p. 176.

Wade, Will, "LSI, Motorola Execs: It's Worse Than We Thought," *Electronic Engineering Times*, February 26, 2001, p. 1.

"Wall Street's Lapse in LSI Logic," *Business Week*, March 18, 1996, p. 4.

Wilson, John W., "Selling Chips to the Japanese: LSI Logic Has an Ace up Its Sleeve," *Business Week*, January 28, 1985, pp. 133–34.

—Jeffrey L. Covell
—update: A. Woodward

Luigino's, Inc.

525 Lake Avenue South
Duluth, Minnesota 55802
U.S.A.
Telephone: (218) 723-5555
Fax: (218) 624-7019
Web site: http://www.michelinas.com

Private Company
Incorporated: 1990
Employees: 1,385
Sales: $295.6 million (2002)
NAIC: 311412 Frozen Specialty Food Manufacturing

Luigino's, Inc., a privately held company based in Duluth, Minnesota, is one of North America's leading manufacturers of frozen entrees, primarily in the value category. The company offers more than 200 different Italian, Oriental, Mexican, and children's single-serve entrees, and a limited number of family-size entrees. Brands include Authentico, Budget Gourmet, Homestyle Bowls, Lean Gourmet, Michelina's, Oven Baked Pizzas, Signature, Yu Sing, and Zap'ems. Luigino's is owned by the family of its founder and chairman, legendary entrepreneur Luigino "Jeno" F. Paulucci.

Paulucci: A Child of the Depression

Jeno Paulucci was born in 1918 in Aurora, Minnesota, to Ettore and Michelina Paulucci, who had immigrated six years earlier to America. He faced a hard life growing up in Hibbing, Minnesota. Not only was he ostracized by the mostly Scandinavian community, his family was poor even before the onset of the Great Depression. His father, a miner, was able to work only occasionally. His mother tried to make ends meet by running a grocery store out of their home. Young Paulucci began contributing to the family's finances at a young age, using a homemade wagon to gather stray coal along the railroad tracks to heat the house, unloading boxcars for a dollar, and early on showing some flair for retailing by selling ore samples to tourists who came to view the open mine pits of northeast Minnesota's Iron Range. He also helped his mother in her grocery business and

sold the wine they made in their basement. By the age of ten, he was hawking fruits and vegetables at a local market. A year later, the stock market crashed, and the country lapsed into a deep economic depression, making it even more difficult for the Paulucci family to scrape by. At one point, Jeno Paulucci was desperate enough to join a relief line, but during the long wait to receive his handout, he came to a turning point in his life, recalling, "I couldn't stomach it so I just stepped out of the line and never returned."

Paulucci became a tireless worker. At the age of 14, he found a job at the market in Hibbing, working before and after school and on Saturday's, toiling from 5 a.m. to midnight. Two years later, he graduated to the position of barker, the youngest on Duluth's produce row. In one legendary incident, the young barker was faced with the challenge of selling 18 crates of brown bananas, which had been accidentally sprayed with ammonia but were otherwise fine. Paulucci's response was to turn the problem to his advantage by creating a clever pitch: "Get your Argentine bananas. You'll never see bananas like this again." As a result, he sold the damaged goods for a profit. Not only was he the youngest, but Paulucci also became the loudest barker in the market, and was so vociferous that the city passed an ordinance banning fruit stand barking. When he was 17 he went to work as a salesman for a groceries wholesaler but was so successful that he made more money than his boss and was fired.

During the depression, Paulucci gained some higher education, attending Hibbing State Junior College, and for a time he worked as a wholesale grocery salesman. When the United States entered World War II, Palucci joined the military and served in the Pacific, where he noticed how much his fellow Americans enjoyed Chinese food. Upon his discharge and return home he was unimpressed by the canned Chinese food that was available at the time. He also discovered that some Minnesota Japanese residents were growing bean spouts, a basic ingredient of Chinese dishes. In 1947, Paulucci, not quite 30 years old, decided to use his mother's guidance for seasonings to enhance taste and entered the canned Chinese food business. After a bank turned him down, resulting in a lifelong enmity towards bankers, he was able to borrow $2,500 from a friend to launch his business, which he called Chun King, his idea of a

Chinese-sounding city. It would be the start of his career as an entrepreneur and make his fortune. Over the next 20 years, he worked typically long days that began before dawn and ended after dusk, slowly expanding his business across the country from its Minnesota base. As usual, he made his own breaks. Realizing that celery was a principal ingredient in chow mein, he paid a visit to Florida farms, where he discovered that celery was trimmed evenly to fit into crates for shipping. He was able to contract for the cut-off celery trimmings at a major price break, which made him the low-cost producer of chow mein in the market and gave him the money to advertise his product. With this edge, along with a gift for promotion, he was able by the mid-1960s to build Chun King into the top seller in its category. R.J. Reynolds Tobacco offered him $40 million for the company, but Paulucci turned it down. In 1967, however, R.J. Reynolds met his price, $63 million in cash, and this time Paulucci accepted. He also became the first chairman of R.J. Reynolds Foods, Inc., but did not fit in well at a traditional corporation. One day he came to work at his usual pre-dawn hour only to have a guard turn him away because he arrived two hours before the building was to open.

Jeno's Launched in the 1960s

Paulucci returned to Duluth to run a food business he owned, which he decided to name Jeno's, Inc. During his time at Chun King, he had developed an egg-roll making machine, and now to put these machines to good use he created the pizza roll, which along with frozen pizza would became a staple of the company. As had been the case with Chun King, Paulucci successfully anticipated the mood of American consumers and sensed a business opening. At the time, there were only local and regional brands for frozen pizzas, but he thought he could make Jeno's the top-selling brand and take it national. By 1972 he succeeded, making Jeno's America's market leader in frozen pizza. However, with success came competition, and the frozen pizza operations of major corporations like Pillsbury, Purex, and Quaker Oats carved out major slices of market share. By the early 1980s, Jeno's was losing money, due in large part to the high freight costs of shipping from Minnesota. During its last full year in Duluth, the company lost $16 million on sales of $170 million. In 1981, Paulucci closed down the Duluth plant, one of the city's largest employers, and moved Jeno's operations to Ohio. For this act, at a time when the city's fortunes were already depressed, he was vilified in Minnesota. Paulucci vowed to replace all the lost jobs to Duluth, and over the next several years would make several attempts to keep his pledge.

Paulucci Returns to Duluth in 1990 to Start Luigino's

Paulucci sold Jeno's to Pillsbury for $150 million in 1985, and over the next few years he was involved in launching several restaurant concepts and a pizza delivery chain that failed to take hold, as well as an ambitious Florida real estate development project that became the Central Florida City Heathrow. Then, in 1990, at the age of 72, Paulucci decided to return to the frozen foods business and created Luigino's, Inc. (Jeno Palucci's full first name was Luigino), which he established in Duluth to help keep his word about bringing jobs back to the city. It was an audacious move, given that the frozen entree sector was already crowded with such heavyweight corporate competition as ConAgra's Healthy Choice brand, H.J. Heinz's Weight Watchers, and Nestlé's Stouffer's. Sensing that his larger rivals would also carry higher overhead costs, Paulucci believed he could find a niche in value-priced, single-serve pasta entrees.

After fulfilling the term of his non-competition contract with Pillsbury, Paulucci, rather than using a head hunter, contacted a number of people who had worked for him previously, many of whom came out of retirement. All told, 29 ex-employees signed on, together totaling an estimated 758 years of experience working for Paulucci. To fund the start-up, Paulucci invested $8 million of his own money, which was augmented by $2.2 million in industrial revenue bonds; $1.5 million in loans from the Minnesota Power Economic Development Fund, the Minnesota Small Cities Program, and St. Louis County; and $250,000 from Duluth's 1200 Fund, named after the number of jobs lost when Jeno's closed.

Paulucci reopened the old Jeno's plant with 100 workers and launched his first line of Italian entrees under the Michelina's label, named after his mother. Luigino's also produced frozen sauces for commercial and military use. From the start, the business was nationally oriented, yet Paulucci elected not to advertise, which generally cost manufacturers from 5 percent to 10 percent of revenues. He relied instead on a lower price point to drive sales. He also saved money by accepting only large orders, a minimum of 600 cases, to lower warehouse costs. He also kept staffing lean and even negotiated discounts on utilities. In addition, Paulucci traded on his reputation and connections to avoid slotting fees for supermarket space. What marketing money he did budget went primarily to promotional allowances for retailers, in store displays, and sample giveaways. As a result of keeping a tight rein on costs, Luigino's was able to price its products at 50 to 75 cents less than the competition. In the Midwest, the items retailed at $1.39 and in the New York City market for $1.69. On special, Michelina's entrees were priced as low as 99 cents. Because of a downturn in the economy, the inexpensive price proved even more enticing to consumers, whose acceptance of Michelina's quickly established Luigino's as a force to be reckoned with in the frozen entree business. In its first full year in business, Luigino's recorded sales of $50 million and two years later reached the neighborhood of $200 million.

In addition to going national from the start, Paulucci also talked early on about taking Luigino's public. Although he was devoted to building his businesses, he never became overly attached to them and was always ready to sell when the time was right. However, talk of a stock offering lessened over the years, while at the same time Paulucci vigorously expanded the company's product lines. Not only did the Michelina's label add dozens of Italian dishes and an "Internationals" line with such

Key Dates:

1947:   Jeno Paulucci starts Chun King.
1967:   Paulucci sells Chun King, then starts Jeno's Inc.
1985:   Paulucci sells Jeno's.
1990:   Paulucci launches Luigino's.
2002:   Ronald Bubar replaces Paulucci as CEO.

dishes as Swedish meatballs and beef stroganoff, Luigino's launched a Chinese food line, Yu Sing. The competition answered Luigino's success by imitation, resulting in new budget lines and lower price points. Part of Paulucci's counter-response was to introduce 30-ounce, family-sized entrees that retailed for between $1.99 and $2.99.

Well established in the marketplace in the second half of the 1990s, Luigino's augmented internal growth of product lines with expansion into Canada, the creation of a vending division, and the acquisition of businesses. In 1999, Luigino's bought Minneapolis-based Paradise Kitchen and its six varieties of Howlin' Coyote brand Southwestern-style frozen chili, as well as three types of shelf-stable salsa. In 2001, Luigino's absorbed a major competitor when it acquired The All American Gourmet Co., along with the Budget Gourmet and Budget Gourmet Value Classics brands of frozen entrees from Heinz Frozen Food Co. Luigino's completed another major deal in 2002 with the purchase of Arden International Kitchens, an industrial kitchen based in Lakeville, Minnesota. Originally the central kitchen for Minneapolis area restaurants, it was later expanded to make frozen entrees for foodservice and supermarket customers and in 1994 was acquired by Schreiber Foods of Green Bay, Wisconsin, a major packager of private label cheese products. The frozen entree business did not prove to be a good fit for Schreiber, which was operating at just 50 percent capacity,

but was an excellent opportunity for Luigino's to increase it production. In addition to packaging frozen private-label lasagna, stromboli, and other items, Arden would now use its excess capacity to make products for the Michelina's and Budget Gourmet labels.

In January 2000, Paulucci, now over 80 years in age, stepped down as Luigino's chief executive officer, turning over the post to the company's president and CEO Ronald O. Bubar, who had worked with Paulucci at Jeno's, where from 1980 to 1985 he served as executive vice-president of operations. He then went to work for Pillsbury in a similar capacity before joining Paulucci at Luigino's, where he initially served as a consultant. He then became executive vice-president of operations and in 1996 was appointed president and chief operating officer. Paulucci stayed on as Luigino's chairman and remained highly active in the business despite his advancing years. As he had done with earlier successful companies, he might very well sell off Luigino's, but it was unlikely, as long as his health held up, that the erstwhile produce barker would ever quit working.

Principal Competitors

Celentano Brothers; ConAgra Foods, Inc.; Nestlé USA, Inc.

Further Reading

Brissett, Jane, "Jeno's Homecoming," *Corporate Report—Minnesota*, June 1991, p. 48.
Meyer, Ann, "Jeno's Back in Business," *Prepared Foods*, January 1991, p. 15.
Rudnitsky, Howard, "What Makes Jeno Run," *Forbes*, p. 56.
Serwer, Andrew E., "Head to Head With Giants—And Winning," *Fortune*, June 13, 1994, p. 154.
Wojahn, Ellen, "Little Big Man," *Inc.*, June 1986, p. 77.

—Ed Dinger

Lydall, Inc.

1 Colonial Road
Manchester, Connecticut 06045
U.S.A.
Telephone: (860) 646-1233
Toll Free: (800) 365-9325
Fax: (860) 646-8847
Web site: http://www.lydall.com

Public Company
Incorporated: 1913 as Colonial Board Company
Employees: 1,241
Sales: $271.38 million (2003)
Stock Exchanges: New York
Ticker Symbol: LDL
NAIC: 325222 Noncellulosic Organic Fiber
    Manufacturing; 322130 Paperboard Mills; 322221
    Coated and Laminated Packaging Paper and Plastics
    Film Manufacturing

Lydall, Inc. designs and produces specialty engineered products that withstand heat, reduce noise, and act as filters for a variety of industrial applications. The bulk of Lydall's business is derived from the automotive industry, for which the company makes heat shields, thermal and acoustical barriers, and insulation products. The company's two largest customers are automobile manufacturers DaimlerChrysler AG and Ford Motor Company. Lydall's products also are used in other industrial applications, such as in furnaces and kilns, and as filtration devices in industrial settings. More than one-third of the company's annual revenue is derived from overseas sales. Lydall operates three manufacturing facilities in Europe and maintains sales offices in Asia. Domestically, the company owns production plants in New Hampshire, New York, Connecticut, Virginia, North Carolina, Florida, and Pennsylvania. Through Lydall Transport Ltd., the company provides trucking and logistics services throughout the United States and Canada.

Origins

Lydall traced its corporate roots to 1913, when a company named Colonial Board Company was founded. More than a half-century passed before the Lydall name first appeared, however, a moment that arrived when Colonial Board merged with another company in 1969, creating Lydall, Inc. The 1969 merger paved the way for several important additions made in the following decade that gave Lydall its modern-day business foundation. There was one important development that occurred before the 1970s, however. In 1951, Norfould, Inc. was organized as part of Colonial Board Company, a company that represented the predecessor to Lydall Transport, Ltd., the logistics services arm of Lydall's operations in the 21st century. Considering that much of what constituted Lydall in its second century of business was developed following the 1969 merger, the 1970s marked the beginning of Lydall's second era of existence and the beginning of it modern corporate history.

Lydall's involvement in the manufacture of engineered fiber materials and composites eventually became organized in two business segments the company labeled "filtration/separation" and "thermal/acoustical." The first of these two business groups was bolstered significantly by the formation of a fiber process division in 1970. Located in Rochester, New Hampshire, the division manufactured high-performance, engineered filtration and specialty separation media. In 1977, when Lydall merged with Logistics Industries, the company completed an acquisition that strengthened the other pillar supporting its existence. Lydall acquired a plant in Hamptonville, North Carolina, that was jointly operated by Chatham Manufacturing and Scott Paper Company. The plant, which was known as Lydall Westex before becoming part of the company's thermal/acoustical group, manufactured integrated automotive test shields and acoustical barrier systems.

The two additions to the company's operations in the 1970s helped establish Lydall's future foundation, although, at the time, the company was involved in a variety of businesses. A third significant addition arrived in 1986, when the company acquired a plant from the Hammermill Paper Company. Located in Green Island, New York, the facility initially was

---

Company Perspectives:

Lydall participates in progressive markets providing healthy growth opportunities for the Company. The increasingly technical and sophisticated demands of the automotive, semiconductor, consumer liquid-and air-filtration, bioprocessing/biomedical, and commercial building markets in which we concentrate present both challenges and opportunities. Lydall looks forward to meeting the challenges and maximizing the opportunities. Our resolve is strengthened by our commitment to greater investment in new-product development and sales and marketing efforts.

---

known as Lydall Manning before becoming the Green Island Operation of Lydall Industrial Thermal Solutions. The plant, which began operating in 1846, was used by Lydall to produce industrial thermal and flame barriers and electrical insulating materials. Not long after acquiring the Green Island plant, Lydall's management decided to restructure the company, aiming to narrow its strategic focus. In 1988, a number of elastomer product businesses and a partial ownership stake in a defense electronics business were divested. The following year, Lydall moved from the American Stock Exchange to the New York Stock Exchange.

Lydall in the 1990s

The 1990s brought significant change and significant growth to Lydall. For the first time in its history, the company established a presence overseas. In 1991, when Lydall's sales volume amounted to $135 million, the company acquired a facility in Brittany, France, using the plant to manufacture high efficiency air filtration media. The acquisition became part of the company's filtration/separation group, functioning as the Saint-Rivalain operation within Lydall's corporate structure. Several years later, the company expanded domestically, adding another production facility to its thermal/acoustical group. In 1994, Lydall acquired a plant in Columbus, Ohio, capable of fabricating automotive thermal and acoustical insulation products.

The Columbus production plant symbolized an important aspect of Lydall's future. Although the plant itself would not be part of the company's future, it was devoted to serving the automotive market, a market of increasing importance to Lydall in the late 1990s and early 21st century. The company's thermal and acoustical products were used by parts suppliers, thermal insulation fabricators, air-bag manufacturers, and by automobile manufacturers. Ford Motor Company, for example, accounted for nearly one-fifth of Lydall's annual sales during the latter half of the 1990s. The company made several investments in strengthening its automotive business during the late 1990s, completing acquisitions that broadened the geographic presence of the company and expanded its thermal/acoustical group. The acquisitions were completed in 1998, a year that also brought sweeping change throughout the Lydall organization.

Lydall's 85th anniversary coincided with the significant overseas expansion and the appointment of a new leader. After acquiring what the company referred to as the St. Johnsbury

Operation—a facility geared for the production of automotive heat shields—Lydall followed up on its foray into France seven years earlier when it acquired a German firm, which was renamed Lydall Gerhardi, that produced numerous metal heat shields and acoustical components that were distributed to manufacturers competing in the automotive market. The addition of the Gerhardi operation greatly aided Lydall's efforts to become a global manufacturer of automotive thermal and acoustical components. The acquisition, completed in December 1998, occurred the same month the company promoted its chief operating officer, Christopher Skomorowski, to the post of chief executive officer.

Under Skomorowski's leadership, an extensive restructuring program was started. Like the company's reorganization 11 years earlier, assets deemed outside the company's strategic scope were divested. Lydall shed non-core and underperforming properties, focusing its efforts exclusively on its filtration/separation and thermal/acoustical business segments. At the same time, the company announced the formulation of an acquisition program. The restructuring efforts, begun in 1999 shortly after Skomorowski's promotion, sharpened in focus in the fall of 2000 when the company announced it was abandoning its decentralized structure in favor of a group structure built around the filtration/separation and thermal/acoustical business segments. The sweeping restructuring program, which included the adoption of a new corporate logo meant to convey the company's two-pronged strategic focus, was completed in early 2001.

In the wake of the nearly two-year-long restructuring program, Lydall completed two important deals, both concluded in October 2001. In the first half of the month, the company announced that its subsidiary, Lydall Distribution Services, Inc., had formed a partnership with the Virginia Port Authority to establish a new paper distribution facility at The Port of Virginia's Newport News Marine Terminal. The addition of the 100,000-square-foot facility was hailed by Bill Franks, president of Lydall Distribution Services. "We look forward to offering a total distribution solution for all types of paper products to our customers and to attracting new customers to The Port of Virginia," Franks remarked in an October 11, 2001 interview with *Internet Wire.* "The center will give us the opportunity to expand the breadth of our services as well as to enhance the services of Virginia ports and to be a part of the continuing expansion of business within the Commonwealth." The new facility operated as the Lydall Paper Distribution Center under the management of Lydall Distribution Services.

Roughly two weeks after the announcement of the partnership with the Virginia Port Authority, Skomorowski made good on his promise to expand through acquisitions. In late October 2001, Lydall announced it had acquired Affinity Industries, Inc. for $21.7 million. Based in Ossipee, New Hampshire, Affinity designed and manufactured high-precision specialty temperature-control equipment. The equipment was used in industrial processes involved in semiconductor, medical, laser pharmaceutical, and telecommunications applications. The $18 million-in-sales company represented Lydall's first attempt to expand its industrial thermal business. "Two years ago," Skomorowski said in an October 22, 2001 interview with *Internet Wire,* "we announced a concentrated, systematic ap-

Key Dates:

1913: The Colonial Board Company is formed.
1951: The predecessor to Lydall Transport, Ltd. is formed as part of the Colonial Board Company.
1969: The Colonial Board Company merges with another company, creating Lydall, Inc.
1970: Lydall's fiber process division is formed.
1977: Lydall acquires a plant in Hamptonville, North Carolina.
1991: Lydall acquires a plant in Brittany, France, its first foreign property.
1998: A German company, renamed Lydall Gerhardi, is acquired.
2001: Lydall acquires Affinity Industries, Inc.
2003: David Freeman is appointed chief executive officer.

proach to growing Lydall through strategic acquisitions. The acquisition of Affinity is the initial product of extensive research and analysis under that program and represents the first step in our strategy to broaden our industrial thermal focus in value segments of high growth markets.''

Skomorowski's commitment to growth manifested itself a year after the Affinity acquisition, as the company bolstered its presence overseas. In December 2002, the company announced its intention to construct a 90,000-square-foot production plant in St. Nazaire, France, its second plant in France and its third in Europe. The $16-million facility, which was expected to be completed in 2004, was established to manufacture engineered thermal and acoustical components for automotive applications. From the St. Nazaire plant, Lydall intended to serve automobile manufacturers Renault-Nissan and Peugeot/Citroen, as well as other European manufacturers. Commenting on the new plant in a December 19, 2002 interview with *Internet Wire*, Skomorowski said: ''The French expansion initiative that we are announcing today represents a continuation of Lydall's strategy to further globalize our automotive business and to expand its base of customers and vehicle platforms.''

New Management in the 21st Century

Despite the expansion achieved in 2001 and 2002, Lydall's financial totals lagged behind the figures recorded in the late 1990s. In 2002, the company generated $253.5 million in sales, a $30 million increase from the previous year's total but significantly less than the $318 million recorded in 1999. Recessive economic conditions largely were to blame, according to Lydall officials, as anemic market conditions negatively affected the automotive industry, which accounted for 47 percent of Lydall's business in 2002. The purchase of Affinity and the expansion in France positioned the company to reap the benefits of a more robust economy, however. To take full advantage of more prosperous times once they arrived, the company's board of directors decided to appoint a new chief executive officer. In July 2003, Skomorowski returned to his post as chief operating officer, making room for the appointment of David Freeman as Lydall's new chief executive officer. In a statement released in

the July 1, 2003 issue of *Internet Wire*, Lydall's chairman, Roger Widmann, explained that the change was made to strengthen the senior management of the company in anticipation of significant growth ahead. ''David [Freeman] and Chris [Skomorowski] have been working closely together during the past several months,'' Widmann said, ''and the board believes that having them work as a team will give the company the management and leadership to achieve the best growth.''

Freeman, who joined Lydall as a director in 1998 after spending 25 years as an executive at Loctite Corp., hoped to achieve considerable growth during his command. Shortly after his appointment as chief executive officer, Freeman announced he expected to double the company's sales by 2008, projecting a pace of growth unprecedented in Lydall's history. Freeman expected much of the company's forecasted growth to be realized from existing operations, not from acquisitions.

In late 2003, Freeman announced a major restructuring program. According to the details of the plan, Lydall's group structure, which called for separate leaders for each of its divisions, was to be removed and replaced with two councils: a manufacturing council headed by Freeman and a sales and marketing council headed by Skomorowski. ''Effective January 1, 2004,'' Freeman announced in the December 15, 2003 issue of *Internet Wire*, ''we are streamlining our organization into a corporate structure which will enable us to manage Lydall as a cohesive whole. We seek to reduce overhead redundancies, move closer to our customers and markets, leverage our manufacturing knowledge, and solidify a Lydall corporate culture.''

As Lydall prepared for its future, much of the company's efforts were directed toward implementing the new organizational structure envisioned by Freeman. In January 2004, the company announced it was closing its Columbus plant and integrating the facility's operations into other plants. The closure was expected to be concluded by the end of 2004.

Principal Subsidiaries

Lydall Thermal/Acoustical, Inc.; Lydall Filtration/Separation, Inc.; Lydall FSC, Ltd.; Lydall Transport, Ltd.; Lydall Finance, Inc.; Lydall International, Inc.; Lydall France S.A.S.; Lydall Deutschland Holding GmbH (Germany) Charter Medical, Ltd.; Lydall Thermal/Acoustical Sales, LLC; Lydall Industrial Thermal Solutions, Inc.; Trident II, Inc.; Lydall Distribution Services, Inc.; Lydall Filtration/Separation S.A.S. (France); Lydall Thermique/Acoustique S.A.S. (France); Lydall Gerhardi GmbH & Co. KG (Germany).

Principal Competitors

Johns Manville Corporation; The Morgan Crucible Company PLC; Pall Corporation.

Further Reading

''Announcement from Lydall, Inc. Freeman Appointed CEO of Lydall,'' *Internet Wire*, July 1, 2003.
Jaffe, Thomas, ''The Lid's Off Lydall,'' *Forbes*, March 16, 1992, p. 173.
''Lydall Acquires Affinity Industries,'' *Industrial Heating*, January 2002, p. 26.

''Lydall Announces Acquisition of Affinity Industries Inc.,'' *Internet Wire*, October 22, 2001.

''Lydall Announces Consolidation of Its Columbus, Ohio, Automotive Business into Other Lydall Facilities,'' *Internet Wire*, January 19, 2004, p. 39.

''Lydall Announces Partnership with Virginia Port Authority,'' *Internet Wire*, October 11, 2001.

''Lydall Announces $16 Million European Expansion,'' *Internet Wire*, December 19, 2002.

''Lydall Inc.,'' *CDA—Investnet Insiders' Chronicle*, June 15, 1998, p. 3.

''Manchester, Conn.-Based Filtration Product Manufacturer Taps Chief Executive,'' *Knight Ridder/Tribune Business News*, July 2, 2003.

—Jeffrey L. Covell

Matsushita Electric Industrial Co., Ltd.

1006 Kadoma
Kadoma, Osaka 571-8501
Japan
Telephone: (06) 6908-1121
Fax: (06) 6908-2351
Web site: http://www.matsushita.co.jp

Public Company
Incorporated: 1935 as Matsushita Denki Sangyo
Employees: 288,324
Sales: $61.7 billion (2003)
Stock Exchanges: Tokyo New York
Ticker Symbol: MC
NAIC: 334310 Audio and Video Equipment
   Manufacturing; 334290 Other Communication
   Equipment Manufacturing; 334413 Semiconductor and
   Related Device Manufacturing; 335211 Electric
   Houseware and Fan Manufacturing

The Matsushita Electric Industrial Co., Ltd. is one of the largest consumer electronics firms in the world. Although the company's name is virtually unknown outside of Japan, the brand names under which Matsushita sells its products are household words. Panasonic, Technics, Quasar, and JVC are all manufactured by Matsushita. The company operates four main business segments: AVC Networks, Home Appliances, Industrial Equipment, and Components and Devices. Its product line ranges from color televisions and DVDs to washing machines, industrial robots, and semiconductors. In Japan, Matsushita is as well known as its brand names. The company's founder, Konosuke Matsushita, is hailed as the patriarch of the Japanese consumer electronics industry.

Early History

Konosuke Matsushita was born in 1895, the son of a modest farmer who lost his family's savings speculating on commodity futures when Matsushita was only nine years old. At that age, Matsushita was forced to take a job in a bicycle shop to help his family survive. When he heard some years later that the city of Osaka had installed an electric railway system, Matsushita realized that great opportunities lay ahead for the Japanese electronics industry. He spent a few years working for a light bulb factory in Osaka, and by age 23 had accumulated enough business experience to found his own company to manufacture electric plugs, with his wife and brother-in-law Toshio Iue (who later founded Sanyo Electric).

Although Japan became a major international power during the 1920s, its domestic economy developed unevenly. Matsushita's small company prospered by keeping prices low and by incorporating new technological advances into its products. For this, Matsushita became very popular with consumers. He was also popular with his workers, whom he regarded as important partners with a right to participate in decisions.

After diversifying production to include bicycle lights and electric heaters, Matsushita moved boldly to secure a position as a direct supplier to Japan's large, complex retailing networks, which were historically dominated by larger, more established companies. Matsushita introduced radio sets and dry batteries in 1931 and electric motors in 1934; by creating fierce competition through discounts, the company was able to build large market shares in these selected markets. By 1935 the company had grown to several times its original size. On December 15 of that year, it was incorporated as Matsushita Denki Sangyo (Electrical Industrial).

Japan at this time was undergoing a severe political transformation as a right-wing militarist clique rose to power. The group won support from many industrialists, including Konosuke Matsushita, because it advocated the establishment of a Japanese-led pan-Asian economic community promising great profits for Japanese companies. As a leading manufacturer of electrical devices, Matsushita benefited greatly from the government's massive armament program. It soon gained markets in Japanese-controlled Taiwan, Korea, and Manchuria, and prospered during the beginning of World War II.

After the Battle of Midway, it was clear not only that Japan would lose the war, but also that the Greater East Asia Co-Prosperity Sphere promised by the militarists would never come

to pass. Matsushita, locked in an uneasy partnership with the
government, saw its fortunes deteriorate with Japan's.

Postwar Growth

After the war it seemed that the company's greatest task was
to maintain sales in a country so thoroughly decimated by the
war that the economy relied on barter. But first the company had
to deal with the American occupation authority, which not only
set price controls but also attacked Konosuke Matsushita for his
support of the Japanese war effort and demanded that he resign
his chairmanship. The labor unions, which the occupation authority sought to preserve, strongly supported Matsushita and
threatened to strike if he resigned. Hoping to avoid wider labor
unrest, the authority relented.

In 1951 Matsushita traveled to America for the first time to
study the "rich America" he planned to make his most profitable
market. An astute businessman, Matsushita recognized that his
product lines must first prove themselves in their local market.
His company successfully introduced washing machines, televisions, and refrigerators in Japan in 1953, and vacuum cleaners
the following year. Concerned with maintaining measured and
well-planned growth, Matsushita also became the first Japanese
businessman to introduce five-year business plans.

When anti-monopoly laws were relaxed after the Korean
War, Matsushita was permitted to make its first major corporate
acquisition in 1954, a 50 percent share of the financially troubled
Japan Victor Company (JVC). It was, for Matsushita, merely an
investment; JVC was to remain not only independently managed, but also Matsushita's competitor in several areas.

Matsushita moved "upmarket" early, around 1957, by introducing a line of high-quality FM radio receivers, tape recorders, and a stereo sound system developed by JVC. In 1958
the company succeeded in relaying a color television signal, and
soon afterward entered the television market—an especially
important market as Japanese consumers became increasingly
prosperous.

Until now, Matsushita had focused on the foreign market in
its growth strategies, but the company began actively working
to build a solid domestic market share, confident that its sales in
Japan would grow with the economy. Using the brand name
National, the company established a retail network to sell Matsushita products. With income generated by domestic sales,
Matsushita was able to finance an ambitious global strategy
independent of the trading houses that controlled the retail system in Japan. As a result, Matsushita brand names became well
known in Europe and the United States.

Cheap labor and good labor relations kept Matsushita's costs
low and helped the company to build a strong following in

North America. Yet, as the Japanese economy continued to
grow, unemployment fell and wages rose. Predicting that rising
labor costs would one day compromise its price competitiveness, Matsushita was one of the first companies to set up
factories in less developed countries such as Taiwan and Singapore, where wages were lower and the local currency was more
stable against the dollar.

In May 1974 Matsushita purchased the Quasar television
division of Motorola for $100 million, hoping to gain U.S.
market share by capitalizing on Quasar's well-known name.
Quasar had begun to lose market share to more popular imports,
so Matsushita made heavy capital investments to improve production efficiency. Efficiency was raised, but market share
remained stagnant.

Success with VHS in the 1970s

In the early 1970s Matsushita became deeply involved in the
development of a commercial home videocassette recording system, or VCR. Matsushita seemed close to an acceptable design
when Akio Tanii, then head of the VCR group, saw what he
believed was a far superior design under development at JVC.
Tanii convinced Matsushita to delay the introduction of a VCR
until JVC's Video Home System, or VHS, could be perfected
and adopted. This meant allowing Sony, the company's largest
competitor, to enjoy a one-year monopoly on the market.

Sony refused to share its Betamax VCR technology with
other manufacturers. But Matsushita knew that despite its VCR
monopoly, Sony had a limited VCR production capacity. He
gambled that there would be enough pent-up demand when JVC
and Matsushita entered the market for the two companies to
establish VHS as the industry standard. To help this prediction
come true, Matsushita made licensing agreements with RCA,
General Electric, Philips (which had abandoned its own VCR
design), NEC, Toshiba, and Sanyo, all of whom introduced
VHS-compatible machines. Sony's Betamax lost so much market share so quickly that Sony's chairman, Akio Morita, was
compelled to ask for a compromise. Konosuke Matsushita refused, telling him that such a desperate display was both unac-
ceptable and dishonorable. Eventually even Sony began to
manufacture VHS machines.

By the mid-1980s Japan's consumer market was saturated.
Tanii, who had been chosen to succeed the company's popular
president, Toshihiko Yamashita, advocated entrance into new
markets: semiconductors, factory automation, business machines, and audiovisual devices. He noted Matsushita's inability
to attract the best engineers graduating from universities and
began an effort to build a talented research and development
team. He also saw that Matsushita's older, "obsolete" engineers
would become under-utilized, and recommended transforming
them into expert salesmen capable of selling these new technologies, if not creating them. Finally, he complained that Matsushita's 600 subsidiaries and group companies were too poorly
coordinated to work with each other efficiently and decided that
contacts within the company should be improved in order to
develop technologies more quickly and economically.

In 1989 Konosuke Matsushita died at the age of 94. He had
seen his company rise from a small manufacturer of electric

Key Dates:

1935: Konosuke Matsushita's company incorporates as Matsushita Denki Sangyo.
1953: The company begins selling washing machines, televisions, and refrigerators in Japan.
1954: A 50 percent share of JVC is acquired.
1974: The Quasar television division of Motorola is purchased.
1989: Founder Konosuke dies.
1990: MCA Inc. is acquired in a $6.1 billion deal.
1995: The company sells an 80 percent interest in MCA.
2000: Kunio Nakamura is named president and launches a major restructuring effort.

sockets to one of the world's premier consumer goods manufacturers. Matsushita had retired from active management of the company in 1973 and had spent his later years writing books on business philosophy—his basic philosophy, ''Peace and Happiness Through Prosperity,'' was the focus of some 50 books.

At this time, Matsushita was under contract to manufacture a number of computers for IBM, which was historically weak in the consumer market, and expressed interest in acquiring Fujitsu, which traditionally attracted the most talented software engineers. A closer relationship with either company would strengthen Matsushita's sales in the more dynamic and profitable corporate and institutional markets. In the end, however, Matsushita looked to the United States for growth in new markets.

Matsushita was poised to remain a major consumer goods manufacturer, protected by its strong presence in the Japanese market both from competition at home and from currency fluctuations and trade protectionism abroad. The company's expansion into industrial electronics was also highly profitable. In fiscal 1989, industrial electronics represented 35 percent of sales by Matsushita's major operating units. Tanii's initiatives positioned the company for growth. He did much to dispel the notion that Matsushita was merely an imitator of more original companies, but continued to look for ways to transform the company.

Changes in the 1990s and Beyond

Intense competition forced Matsushita to put its strategy into action in the early 1990s when a wave of merger activity hit both the electronics and entertainment industry. Competitor Sony Corp. acquired Columbia Pictures Entertainment Inc., and Time Inc. and Warner Communications Inc. joined forces. Matsushita began looking for its own deal and in November 1990 began negotiations with MCA Inc., a Hollywood studios company. MCA eyed the deal as crucial to its growth strategy, especially since its peers had grown significantly over the past several years through mergers of their own. After hammering out the terms of the deal, Matsushita agreed to pay $6.13 billion—$66 per share—for MCA.

The company faced challenges in the following years due in part to high costs related to the merger and falling demand for its low-margin audio and video products. To make matters worse, Japan's economy was faltering. Akio Tanii stepped down in 1993 and was replaced by Yoichi Morishita, who immediately began to restructure the company. It was apparent that the benefits of the MCA merger had failed to reach fruition and in 1995, Matsushita sold 80 percent of MCA to Seagram in a $5.7 billion deal. The company reported a $531.1 million loss in fiscal 1996 as a result of the sale.

A July 1998 *Business Week* article summed up Morishita's actions, reporting, ''He has reduced the company's emphasis on low-margin consumer electronics, from 50% to 35% of sales, and moved into more lucrative areas of digital technology.'' The article continued, ''Already a leader in digital cellular phones, Matsushita is grabbing Sony's market share in digital cameras and maintaining dominance in digital video discs (DVD). Most importantly, it is enhancing its growth potential by becoming a key supplier of parts for the next generation of mobile phones, DVDs, and digital TVs.'' Profits continued to fall over the next several years, however, as the Asian economic crisis took hold. Undeterred, the company continued to forge ahead, acquiring stakes in mobile phone venture Symbian and Mobile Broadcasting, a digital satellite firm.

Matsushita entered the new millennium with additional changes on the horizon. Kunio Nakamura took over as president in 2000 and Morishita became chairman. As part of its revitalization strategy the company slashed jobs, shut down unprofitable factories, and looked to develop new products while phasing out poor performing items. Management focused on revitalizing the Panasonic brand and began to heavily market DVD recorders, flat-panel and plasma televisions, and cell phones, especially Internet-ready handsets. Its operations were organized into four business segments: AVC Networks, Home Appliances, Industrial Equipment, and Components and Devices.

While the company posted its largest-ever loss in fiscal 2002, its sales and earnings began an upward climb during the following year. Nakamura—named Forbes Global Businessman of the Year in 2004—was confident that Matsushita was on track to remain one of the largest consumer electronics manufacturers in the world. Intense competition with Sony was sure to continue in the years to come. With a focus on new product development and a solid management team in place, Matsushita appeared to be ready to meet its challenges head on.

Principal Subsidiaries

Matsushita Battery Industrial Co., Ltd.; Matsushita Electronic Components Co., Ltd.; Panasonic Factory Solutions Co., Ltd.; Matsushita Industrial Equipment Co., Ltd.; Panasonic Communications Co., Ltd.; Panasonic Mobile Communications Co., Ltd.; Matsushita Ecology Systems Co., Ltd.; Matsushita Kotobuki Electronics Industries, Ltd.; Victor Company of Japan, Ltd.

Principal Competitors

Hitachi Ltd.; Samsung Corporation; Sony Corporation.

Further Reading

Chowdhury, Neel, ''Matsushita's Legacy Lives On,'' *Fortune,* March 31, 1997, p. 111.

Fulford, Benjamin, "The Tortoise Jumps the Hare," *Forbes Global,* January 12, 2004, p. 30.

Gross, Neil, "Matsushita's Urgent Quest for Leadership," *Business Week,* March 8, 1993, p. 52.

Grover, Ronald, and Susan Duffy, "Even for Michael Ovitz, $8 Billion Is a Big Deal," *Business Week,* October 15, 1990, p. 114.

Grover, Ronald, and Judith H. Dobryznski, "Lights, Camera Action," *Business Week,* December 10, 1990, p. 27.

"Japan: Will It Lose Its Competitive Edge?," *Business Week,* April 27, 1992, p. 50.

Kunii, Irene M., "A Bold Mechanic for a Creaky Machine," *Business Week,* June 31, 2000, p. 30.

——, "Matsushita: The Electric Giant Wakes Up," *Business Week,* July 20, 1998.

"Matsushita: Back to the Glory Days," *Business Week,* July 21, 2003, p. 24.

"Matsushita Electric Industrial Co.," *Wall Street Journal,* May 24, 1996, p. B4.

—update: Christina M. Stansell

Matsuzakaya Company Ltd.

3-16-1 Sakae
Naka-ku
Nagoya 460-8430
Japan
Telephone: (+052) 251 1111
Fax: (+052) 264 7140
Web site: http://www.matsuzakaya.co.jp

Public Company
Incorporated: 1910 as Ito Gofuku Company Limited
Employees: 5,516
Sales: $3.26 billion (2003)
Stock Exchanges: Tokyo Osaka Nagoya
Ticker Symbol: MSUZ F
NAIC: 452110 Department Stores

Matsuzakaya Company Ltd. is Japan's oldest department store with roots that can be traced back to the 17th century. The Nagoya-based chain operates ten department stores in central Japan and one in Paris. Matsuzakaya ranks fifth among Japanese department stores in terms of sales, and its business centers on the retailing of clothes, accessories, housewares, and personal products. Matsuzakaya is also involved in wholesale textiles, furniture manufacturing, and supermarkets. In response to intense competition and falling sales, the company launched a major restructuring effort in the late 1990s. Several stores were closed, including outlets in Hong Kong, Osaka, and Yokkaichi.

Early History

In 1611, Yudo Ito opened a kimono and clothing store in Nagoya in central Japan. His family were members of the samurai, or warrior, class in feudal Japan, and it was taken for granted that Yudo would carry on the family name and tradition. Instead, he chose the life of a merchant and used part of the family estate to go into business. The store was moderately successful and became renowned in Nagoya and the surrounding areas for its high-quality clothes. It stayed in the Ito family for many generations.

In 1768, the Ito family decided to expand further afield. It purchased a clothing store called Matsuzakaya—meaning "pine hill store"—in the Ueno district of Tokyo, which was known as a busy shopping area. At the time, Tokyo—then known as Edo—was Japan's most important city and one of the world's major metropolitan areas, with a population exceeding one million. The Ueno store was destroyed in 1858 in a fire that swept through Tokyo but was subsequently rebuilt.

New stores were opened and continued to be operated and owned by the Itos as a family business. In 1910, the 33-year-old Morimatsu Ito, a 15th-generation descendant of Yudo Ito, decided that the time was ripe for expansion. He formed a company called Ito Gofuku Co. Ltd.—"Gofuku" can be translated as drapery or clothing—with capital of ¥500,000. Leading up to the establishment of this company, the Nagoya and Tokyo stores had been expanded and a new store built in Kyoto. A large advertising campaign in major newspapers preceded their opening. An inauguration sale was held in the Nagoya store, with 40,000 people passing through the store's gates during the sale. The store was the largest in Nagoya at the time and flourished in the rapidly growing economy. Japan had defeated China and Russia in 1896 and 1904 respectively and was reaping the benefits of these victories. An affluent upper-middle class was appearing in Japanese society as new businesses flourished. The Ito Gofuku store in Nagoya catered to these customers, selling Western clothes, tobacco, jewelry, and footwear as well as the traditional Japanese clothing that had been the foundation of the family's business for many years. In 1914, the Nagoya store established a food department specializing in imported items and delicacies. In 1913, a restaurant was introduced in the Ueno store, and in 1917 the store was illuminated by electric lighting, as was the Nagoya store shortly afterwards. In 1916, senior managers of the company traveled to the United States to view its prestigious department stores and the current fashion trends. The following year saw the further expansion of the Ueno Matsuzakaya store to a floor space of 5,940 square meters and the addition of elevators. By 1920, the company's capital exceeded ¥5 million, a tenfold increase in ten years. The company's store in Kyoto was expanded further in 1922 and new items, such as imported glassware, were sold at all three stores.

Key Dates:

1611: Yudo Ito opens a kimono and clothing store in Nagoya in central Japan.

1768: The Ito family purchases a clothing store called Matsuzakaya.

1910: The company incorporates as Ito Gofuku Co. Ltd.

1925: Ito Gofuku changes its name to Matsuzakaya Co. Ltd.

1946: A postwar shareholders meeting is held and plans to rebuild company stores are announced.

1966: A new store in Osaka attracts 30,000 people opening day.

1978: A store opens in Paris.

1980: The first Matsuzakaya store is launched in the United States.

1999: U.S. operations are shuttered as part of a company-wide restructuring effort.

In 1923, the Kanto region of Tokyo suffered its worst earthquake in recent memory, and the resulting fire destroyed or damaged large areas of the city. The destruction was compounded by the fact that most houses were constructed from wood and that most households used gas lamps, which were easily upset in an earthquake. The Matsuzakaya store in Ueno was totally destroyed and its staff of 150 temporarily relocated to the company's other stores. Within months, however, a new store had been constructed and was open for business by early 1924.

In the same year, Ito Gofuku acquired a building in the Ginza, a shopping and entertainment district in Tokyo, and opened a second Matsuzakaya store for the Japanese capital. A store had also been opened in Japan's second largest city, Osaka, in 1923. The opening was preceded by extensive publicity and canvassing by company employees. In 1924, the company's Nagoya flagship store was renovated to become a six-story structure illuminated by neon lighting at night. To unite the company's stores under a brand name, all Ito Gofuku stores became known as Matsuzakaya, and the company changed its name to Matsuzakaya Company Ltd. in 1925. Company revenues increased rapidly as the stores were expanded and demand for imported Western items boomed.

In 1929, Matsuzakaya's Ueno store was rebuilt and opened to the public with much fanfare. The store was spectacular for its time, with 26,000 square meters of floor space, eight elevators, heating and air conditioning, and its own post office and hairdresser. The store also contained a zoo on the roof of the six-story building and was hailed as the most prestigious department store in Japan at the time. Fashion shows were regularly held at the store, and it was known as the best place to shop for the latest fashions. The expansion and investment in all Matsuzakaya stores continued in the 1930s as the Japanese economy grew at a fast pace. A new store was opened in the city of Shizuoka in 1932, and in 1937 the Nagoya store was expanded to 30,000 square meters, surpassing the Ueno store. In the same year, Matsuzakaya's Nagoya store hosted the New Japan Cultural Exhibition.

With the start of World War II, Matsuzakaya's fortunes declined. The supply of luxury consumer goods from the West slowed greatly after 1940, and the military government's policy was to stimulate the economy and labor force to help the war effort. This led to falling sales for the company, and the military government asked the store to help publicize and take part in energy-saving and recycling initiatives. By 1944, it was clear to many Japanese that the country would lose the war. In this atmosphere, Matsuzakaya began the retailing of gold, silver, platinum, and jewels to nervous investors. By 1945, Japan had lost the war and the U.S. Air Force had inflicted destruction on major Japanese cities with its nightly B-29 attacks. Matsuzakaya's Ginza and Nagoya stores were destroyed in air raids in March and the Osaka and Ueno stores were damaged. During the war, Matsuzakaya had optimistically invested in various parts of Asia occupied by Japanese forces. These investments included a hotel in Kuala Lumpur and a store in Peking. These were confiscated after Japan's defeat and the cost to the company totaled ¥8 million.

Postwar Growth

In the years following World War II, Matsuzakaya, along with most other Japanese businesses, was in a state of disarray. The Japanese were, however, quick to rebuild their country, and corporate Japan began to reorganize itself with the aid of subsidies from the U.S. government, which effectively controlled Japan until 1951. The occupying forces asked most large Japanese companies to aid in the relief effort. Matsuzakaya's contribution was the conversion of its Osaka store, which had escaped the air raids largely undamaged, into a Red Cross center to tend to the sick and wounded. In early 1946, the first postwar shareholders' meeting was held and plans to rebuild the company's stores were announced. This was followed by the reopening later in the year of the Ginza, Nagoya, and Shizuoka stores. The Ueno store was refurbished, with a cinema built on the top floor of the seven-story structure. In 1948, the company launched a promotion campaign in which it claimed to be "binding together lifestyle and culture" in Japan. The late 1940s, however, were a time of rationing in Japan, and it was not until 1949 that Matsuzakaya's sales reached the level of prewar years. The year 1949 marked a turning point in the Japanese economy overall, with living standards finally reaching prewar levels.

In 1950, Matsuzakaya celebrated its 40th anniversary of incorporation and in the following year the 340th anniversary of Yudo Ito's first store. The year 1952 saw the expansion and refurbishment of Matsuzakaya's Ginza store and the next year that of the Nagoya store. The Ueno store followed in 1957. The work on these stores laid the foundation for their present-day position as landmark department stores in Tokyo and Nagoya.

By 1960, the world economy, and Japan's in particular, was booming. The 1960s were years of strong growth for Matsuzakaya at a time when new retail empires such as Ito-Yokado and Daiei were building up large chains of supermarkets. These were hugely successful in catering to the day-to-day shopping needs of the consumer, while Matsuzakaya offered upmarket goods. There was now less emphasis on food and more on luxury goods. In 1964, Japan's economic recovery was in full swing and the country played host to the Olympic Games. The Matsuzakaya Ginza store mounted several exhibitions connected with the games, and a salon, a pool hall, and a boutique devoted to Nina Ricci clothes were added to the store. This was complemented by the addition of a Henry Poole men's suit boutique in each store in 1964. The boutiques were staffed by tailors hired from the United Kingdom to cut suits in the style worn by English gentlemen. In 1965, the accounting operations of the company were computerized with the introduction of an IBM mainframe. The following year saw investment in staff training with the establishment of a training scheme for all employees and a training school in Nagoya for the company's managers. In 1966, a new store was completed in Osaka with a floor space of 67,000 square meters. The store was built on Osaka Bay and attracted 30,000 customers on its opening day. In 1968, Matsuzakaya set itself a sales target of ¥100 billion to be achieved by the company's 60th anniversary in 1970. The company exceeded this figure with sales of ¥103 billion in that year.

By 1971, Matsuzakaya, along with Daimaru Co. Ltd., had become the leading department store in Japan in terms of reputation and prestige. The company completely refurbished its Nagoya store in 1971, and once again this became Matsuzakaya's largest store. With floor space of 71,000 square meters and ten floors above ground and two underground, it was one of the largest department stores in the country. In addition, a new store was opened in Nagoya, located near the main railway station. The 1970s saw the continued expansion of the Matsuzakaya chain into other Japanese cities such as Okasaki in 1971 and Kuzuka in 1972. A Paris branch was added in 1978. The original customer base of Matsuzakaya's first overseas department store was the Japanese expatriate community in Paris, but the store soon became popular with native Parisians. In 1980, Mayor Bradley of Los Angeles officially opened the first Matsuzakaya in the United States. Again, the targeted customer base was the large Japanese community in Los Angeles.

The 1980s saw Japanese consumers spending more and more on luxury items as the huge and affluent middle class reaped the rewards of Japan's booming economy. Women's fashions from France and Italy became especially popular, with an extremely lucrative and competitive market. Matsuzakaya and the other big department stores such as Mitsukoshi Co. Ltd. and Isetan Co. Ltd. devoted several floors of their large city stores to women's fashion and saw large profits from the sales in this department.

A 17th-generation Ito, Jirozaemon Ito, headed the company at this time, although the Ito family no longer held a significant number of shares. A development for the company in the late 1980s and early 1990s was the establishment of retailing via communications satellite tie-ups with Prestel of the United Kingdom and Teletel of France. Although Japanese department stores had a record year in 1991 in terms of earnings, Matsuzakaya included, the slowing of growth in the Japanese economy made the company more cautious about future investment plans.

Problems in the Mid-1990s and Beyond

Increases in sales and profits were hard to come by for most operators in Japan's retail sector in the mid-1990s due to the continued weakening of the economy throughout Asia. An April 1998 *Chain Store Age* article summed up conditions in the industry, declaring, ''For some retailers, the currency crisis resulted in a worse case scenario—shutting doors on former shop-'til-you-drop streets and centers. The moderate reaction for some merchants has been to cut back on expansion, while still others are forging ahead despite what they feel are short-term challenges.''

At this time, Matsuzakaya took several strategic actions to combat falling sales. By 1998, the company was in the midst of a major restructuring effort. It announced the closure of its Hong Kong store that year. A round of job cuts were launched in 1999, and the firm announced it would not recruit any graduates for employment in 2000. (Matsuzakaya had been recruiting since the early 1950s.) Its store in Los Angeles, California, was shut down. Certain operations were streamlined, and remaining stores were organized into three main business segments: Nagoya, Osaka, and Tokyo.

While the company worked to shore up sales and profits, it became entangled in a scandal when one of its executives was arrested for making payments to a corporate racketeer. This type of criminal, known in Japan as *sokaiya,* extorted funds from major businesses by threatening to disrupt annual or shareholder meetings. Despite the bad press, Matsuzakaya moved ahead with its turnaround efforts, determined to overcome this challenge.

Problems, however, continued in the early years of the 21st century. The company posted a loss in 2000 as result of intense competition and restructuring charges related to an early retirement program. It closed its unprofitable store in Yokkaichi in 2001. ''Recent changes in the business environment, including the introduction of international accounting standards and cutthroat competition beyond the traditional boundary of business sectors, has made it difficult for loss-making stores to continue to exist,'' explained president Kunihiko Okada in a February 2001 *Japan Weekly Monitor* article. Indeed, stagnant personal consumption had halted Matsuzakaya's growth altogether. The company closed down its 81-year-old Osaka store in 2004.

Matsuzakaya struggled as its peers appeared to be overcoming the problems facing the retail industry. In fiscal 2004, the company was alone in reporting a drop in pretax profits. Foreign companies, supermarkets, and specialty retailers were cutting into Matsuzakaya's market share, putting the firm in a precarious position. Japan's oldest department store company was quickly becoming one of its weakest and smallest, leaving industry analysts speculating about its future.

Principal Subsidiaries

Elmo Co., Ltd. (40%); Central Park Building Co., Ltd. (29%); Nagoya Underground Parking Lots Co., Ltd. (36.6%); Aichi Xerox Co., Ltd. (39%); Seikosha Co., Ltd.; Matsuzakaya Membership Association Co., Ltd.; Sakae Printing Co., Ltd.; Rec Resort Co., Ltd. (80%); Sakae Linen Supply Co., Ltd. (33.3%); Toto Transportation Co., Ltd. (66.7%); Showa Transportation Co., Ltd. (66.6%); Shizuoka Itaku Co., Ltd.; Yokohama Matsuzakaya Co., Ltd. (51.1%); Sanmen Shoji Co., Ltd. (68.6%); Matsuzaka Service Co., Ltd.; Tokiwa shokai Ltd.; Japan Rifex Co., Ltd.; Shoei Foods Co., Ltd. (48.7%); Rec Finance Co., Ltd. (31%); Funazu Kogei Co., Ltd. (44.7%); Matsuzakaya Store Co., Ltd.

Principal Competitors

The Daimaru Inc.; Mitsukoshi Ltd.; Takashimaya Company Ltd.

Further Reading

"Asia's Crisis: The Retail Toll," *Chain Store Age Executive with Shopping Center Age*, April 1, 1998, p. 52.

"Department Stores Hit Hard by Tightfisted Shoppers," *Nikkei Weekly*, October 28, 2002.

"Japanese Retailer Matsuzakaya to Close Hong Kong Department Store," *Agence France-Presse*, March 3, 1998.

"Matsuzakaya Boosts Profits and Sales for 4th Year," *Jiji Press English News Service*, May 7, 1991.

"Matsuzakaya Group Pretax Profit Drops 55% on Falling Purchases," *Asian Wall Street Journal*, May 10, 1994.

"Matsuzakaya Group Pretax Profit Plummeted 67% in Latest Year," *Asian Wall Street Journal*, May 12, 1993.

"Matsuzakaya to Close Two Osaka Stores by 1st Half of '04," *Asia Pulse*, October 22, 2003.

"Matsuzakaya to Cut 700 Jobs, Restructure," *Japan Weekly Monitor*, February 8, 1999.

"Police Raid Matsuzakaya over Alleged Pay-Off to Racketeer," *Agence France-Presse*, October 21, 1997.

Yabe, Makiko, and Yoshiyuki Shuto, "Japan—Gloomy Times Here," *Asahi Shimbun*, March 20, 1999.

—Dylan Tanner
—update: Christina M. Stansell

Mauna Loa Macadamia Nut Corporation

2445 McCabe Way, Suite 250
Irvine, California 92614-4293
U.S.A.
Telephone: (949) 851-1994
Fax: (949) 851-1993
Web site: http://www.maunaloa.com

Private Company
Incorporated: 1976
Employees: 295
Sales: $15.4 million (2003)
NAIC: 311911 Roasted Nuts and Peanut Butter
   Manufacturing

With it corporate headquarters located in Irvine, California, and its processing facility in Hilo, Hawaii, Mauna Loa Macadamia Nut Corporation is the largest processor and marketer of macadamia nut products in the world. The private company, named after the largest active volcano in the world, markets nuts from 10,000 acres of orchards planted on the Big Island of Hawaii on the slopes of Mauna Loa volcano. Macadamia trees are highly fragile, their shallow roots putting them at risk to high winds. To provide a windbreak, pines trees usually ring the macadamia trees. They are also bred to be suitable to all microclimates of the Big Island, offering something of a hedge if overly wet or dry conditions prevail during the course of a year. Because macadamia seedlings are so genetically unstable, commercial nut-bearing trees are created by grafting onto rootstock in a nursery, where they are kept for two years. The trees are then transferred to an orchard, but a dozen years will pass before they are producing at commercial levels. Mature nuts fall off the trees naturally and are harvested five times a season, which lasts from mid-August to March. In contrast to the trees, the macadamia nut is the hardest nut in the world, requiring 300 pounds per square inch of pressure to crack the shell. Further, the nut requires an extensive drying, separation, and dry roasting process, which leads in large part to the product's high price. In addition to selling salted and unsalted dry roast macadamias and honey-roasted macadamias, Mauna Loa also offer a number of confec-

tions relying on macadamias, including a variety of chocolate covered macadamias, candy-coated macadamias, nut and fruit mixes, macadamia candy bars, and macadamia cookies.

Macadamia Tree Named in 1857

The macadamia tree was not native to Hawaii. Rather, it originated in Australia, and in 1857 was named after Dr. John Macadam, a chemistry professor at the University of Melbourne and a member of Australia's Parliament who apparently had nothing to do with the plants. His friends, Baron Ferdinand von Muller, head of Melbourne's Botanic Gardens, along with Walter Hill, the superintendent of Brisbane's Botanic Gardens, were the first to classify the tree botanically, having discovered it on an expedition. The honor of providing a name fell upon von Muller, who elected to pay tribute to his friend Macadam. Hill removed the kernels from the shells in order to plant and cultivate the trees. He believed the nuts were likely poisonous, according to some aborigines at least, and was shocked to discover a young assistant happily snacking on some. When the boy seemed to suffer no ill effects, Hill tried the kernels, found them delicious, and became an enthusiast.

The man responsible for introducing the macadamia tree to Hawaii was William H. Purvis, who was a manager of a sugar plantation on the Big Island. While visiting Australia, he was so taken by the beauty of the macadamia tree that he brought back seeds to Hawaii and in 1881 planted them to adorn his house, uninterested in their nuts. Brothers E.W. and R.A. Jordan in 1892 were also successful in planting seeds at their home in Nu-Uanu. Macadamia trees thrived in the Hawaiian climate, but for the next thirty years they were valued mostly for their appearance, although residents of Hawaii had in the meantime learned to appreciate the flavorful macadamia nut. It was Massachusetts-born Ernest Van Tassel who commercialized the macadamia nut, having first tasted it at a cocktail party in 1916 after coming to Hawaii for his failing health. Because his health improved, he looked for a way to show his gratitude, and he decided to plant a macadamia orchard for the purpose of sharing the delicacy with other people and perhaps establishing a new industry on the islands. With seeds from the Purvis and Jordan trees, he leased 25 acres of government land near Honolulu to plant them, and in 1922 he created Hawaiian Macadamia Nut Co., Ltd.

Company Perspectives:

Hawaii's perfect growing conditions, and Mauna Loa's matchless attention to quality at every step of processing, has earned Mauna Loa Macadamia Nut Corporation its premium reputation as the leader in macadamias.

Van Tassel was not experienced in agriculture, and his initial efforts at commercializing macadamia nut production proved unsuccessful because seedlings from the same tree produced nuts that differed wildly in terms of quality and yield. With the help of the University of Hawaii, a method of grafting was developed and over the course of 20 years nine strains of the macadamia were developed that were able to produce a consistently high quality nut. In the meantime, Van Tassel was able to begin commercial processing of macadamia nuts on a limited basis in 1934 under the brand name Van's Macadamia Nuts. Also in the 1930s, Ellen Dye Candies and the Alexander Young Hotel candy shop began to sell chocolate-covered macadamia nuts, and by the end of the decade Hawaiian Candies & Nuts Ltd. was marketing macadamias under the Menehune Mac label.

The consortium of corporations known as the ''Big Five,'' which had dominated the Hawaiian economy for more than 100 years, took note of the macadamia nut's emergence and began to become involved. Castle & Cooke, best known as the owners of the Dole Pineapple Co., planted the orchard that would form the foundation of Mauna Loa Macadamia Nut Corp. in 1946 on the Big Island near Kea'au. In 1948, Castle & Cooke organized the Royal Hawaiian Macadamia Nut Company, but it was not until 1954 that trees began to bear fruit, and another two years would pass before the first commercial crop was available. Full production would not be achieved on the company's holdings until 1965, at which point a state-of-the-art processing plant was built near Hilo. The plant was ahead of its time in that it was designed to supply its own power by burning macadamia shells.

Mauna Loa Created in 1976

Another major Big Five company to become involved in macadamia nuts was C. Brewer and Company Ltd., which formed subsidiary Royal Iolani. Long involved in running sugar plantations, C. Brewer began divesting its sugar operations in the early 1970s, when sugar became an unprofitable commodity, and looked elsewhere for opportunities. In 1973, it bought Castle & Cooke's macadamia nut orchard and processing plant, which was doing about $4 million in annual business. Royal Iolani changed its name to Mauna Loa Macadamia Nut Corp in 1976 and began marketing its nuts under the Mauna Loa label. It was also in 1976 that C. Brewer began to convert five sugar plantations to macadamia cultivation, turning over 1,000 acres each year. In the late 1970s, Mauna Loa found a way to fund its expansion by selling off its nut orchards to private investors in small parcels. As part of the deal, Mauna Loa would buy the nuts produced under a long-term contract.

With the loss of sugar as a strong cash crop, many Hawaii agriculturalists believed that macadamia nuts held the most potential to make up the loss in business. However, macadamia nuts remained very much a delicacy enjoyed while staying in Hawaii or on the airplane during the flight to the islands. In large part, people on the mainland bought macadamia nuts as a way to relive their Hawaiian vacation. Although Mauna Loa was by far the largest producer of macadamia nuts, it faced serious challenges from other Hawaiian growers as well as from nuts grown in South America and elsewhere. The result was a glut of macadamias and concern that the market was simply not large enough for the gourmet nut. In the early 1980s, Mauna Loa began to advertise on the mainland (advertising ceased in 1988) and in 1984 moved its marketing division to Los Angeles in order to make further inroads in the mainland market, where it established regional distribution centers in New York, Atlanta, Chicago, and Los Angeles. In addition, Mauna Loa looked to the Japanese market, signing a distribution contract with Suntory, Ltd. Another answer was to find a way to add value to the product. In 1985, Mauna Loa opened a 10,000-square-foot chocolate factory. In this way, the company could increase the value of substandard nuts by making candy out of them. In addition, this strategy served to expand the appeal of macadamias. Mauna Loa also continued its program of selling small orchards to real estate syndicates, in many cases to visiting investors, as a way to fund its diversification efforts and plans to continue converting old sugar land to macadamia cultivation. In 1985, the company launched a ten-year program to sell off orchards in 30-acre parcels. At the same time, it purchased much of the land it had been leasing as a way to accumulate additional orchard land to sell to investors. Buyers had the option of signing a farm management contract, but no formal agreement was necessary in order to sell the nuts to Mauna Loa, which was always in the market to acquire the harvests.

In the mid-1980s, C. Brewer's corporate parent, IU International Corporation, decided to spin-off the Hawaiian company. C. Brewers' chief executive officer, John ''Doc'' Buyers, who had turned around the business ten years earlier, making it something of a cash cow for IU, was given the opportunity to head the spin-off. However, because IU suffered severe losses in 1985 and was burdened by an inordinate amount of debt, it was unable to afford the spin-off. Rather than take his chances with new owners, Buyers assembled a group of investors, formed a company called Buyco, Inc., and bought C. Brewer, including Mauna Loa. The sale of macadamia orchards was a key component in the financing, as Buyers sold shares in a master limited partnership, Mauna Loa Macadamia Partners, which packaged more than 2,400 acres of macadamia nut orchards. The offering raised about $35 million of the approximate $207 million purchase price for C. Brewer. Moreover, Buyco retained a management contract to farm, process, and sell the nuts produced by the orchards.

Sluggish Growth in the 1990s and New Owners in 2000

In the 1990s, Mauna Loa was far from aggressive in growing the business. The company increased its output of macadamia nuts and allowed the market for the product to essentially grow at its own pace. The company overcame some problems, such as a lawsuit from mainland buyers who charged that Mauna Loa and Mac Farm International Inc. conspired to fix the price of macadamia nuts. Another concern was a tree disease, Macadamia Quick Decline (MQD), which cost Mauna Loa some 25,000 trees over the course of a five-year period. A more positive development was the signing of a distribution agreement with the Planters Division of Nabisco Foods Group for the sale of Mauna Loa nuts on the U.S. mainland. In 1994, that relationship was severed when Mauna Loa formed a mainland marketing and sales division, headed by Scott C. Wallace. In 1998, Wallace was named president and chief operating officer for the company, working out of Irvine, California, a move that began the transition of the corporate office from Hawaii to Irvine.

In September 2000, Mauna Loa changed ownership as part of a restructuring of C. Brewer, which Buyers now wanted to reposition as an agricultural services company in alliance with the local biotechnology industry. Mauna Loa was sold to the Shansby Group, a San Francisco private equity group founded in 1987 by J. Gary Shansby, a former CEO who was responsible for growing Shaklee Corporation from a small family business to a Fortune 500 company. Along with partner Charles H. Esserman, Shansby invested in a number of brand consumer products, including The Famous Amos Chocolate Chip Cookie Co., Terra Chips, and La Victoria Foods.

Under the Shansby Group, Mauna Loa made a number of changes. Scott Wallace was named CEO and the headquarters relocated to Irvine. Mauna Loa resumed advertising on the mainland, which led to a major increase in sales. The company also expanded its product offerings, so that in spite of a significant macadamia nut shortage in the early 2000s, Mauna Loa enjoyed an annual growth rate in the 40 percent range. To make up for the lack of nuts, the company became adept at quickly launching products that did not rely on the entire kernel, such as trail mixes, cookies, caramel corn, toffee, and brittle. After decades in business, Mauna Loa was finally coming of age in its marketing approach. It now leveraged the strength of the Mauna Loa brand name, which management believed connoted more than just macadamia nuts and could be associated in the consumer mind with anything tropical. Not only would the company continue to expand its slate of confectionary products, it might acquire other food business in order to create a premium products company centered on the Mauna Loa name.

Principal Competitors

Hawaiian Host Inc; Mac Farms of Hawaii Inc.; Kraft Foods Inc.

Further Reading

Furlong, Tom, "Macadamias Helping to Bring Hawaii out of Its Shells as an Exporter," *Los Angeles Times*, May 29, 1988, p. 5.

Koepke, Bill, Stephen W. Knox, and Richard Ha, "Putting Down Roots," *Hawaii Business*, November 1985, p. 66.

MacNeil, Karen, "The Noblest of Nuts," *St. Petersburg Times*, October 12, 1989, p. 1D.

Porrazzo, Kimberly A., "Custom Packages Lure Buyers," *OC Metro*, March 18, 2004, p. 32.

Rodrigo, Christine, "Hawaii's Mac Nut Crop Threatened by Disease," *Pacific Business*, July 8, 1991, p. 34.

—Ed Dinger

MEDITECH
Medical Information Technology, Inc.

Medical Information Technology Inc.

MEDITECH Circle
Westwood, Massachusetts 02090-1542
U.S.A.
Telephone: (781) 821-3000
Fax: (781) 821-2199
Web site: http://www.meditech.com

Private Company
Incorporated: 1969
Employees: 2,000
Sales: $271 million (2003)
NAIC: 511210 Software Publishers; 541511 Custom Computer Programming Services

Headquartered in Westwood, Massachusetts, Medical Information Technology Inc. (MEDITECH) is a leading developer of healthcare information system (HCIS) software. Serving more than 1,800 healthcare organizations worldwide from five company-owned facilities in Massachusetts, MEDITECH's principal geographic markets include the United States, Canada, the United Kingdom, and South Africa. In addition to its primary market of acute care hospitals, MEDITECH also serves home healthcare agencies, large healthcare systems, physician offices, and clinics. MEDITECH's HCIS is available on two platforms: a client/server-based Microsoft Windows setup, or the company's proprietary MAGIC operating system. Striving to address virtually every portion of the healthcare spectrum, the company's HCIS modules help clients handle such functions as billing, payroll, decision support, materials management, and staffing and scheduling. On the clinical side, MEDITECH's system manages health information in such patient care areas as registration, radiology, ambulatory, pharmacy, laboratory, emergency, operating room, medical records, and physician practice management. The MEDITECH HCIS also includes information technology management functions related to patient and staff Internet access, as well as data archiving and integrated communications. In making its software systems available to clients, MEDITECH maintains partnerships with IBM, Dell, Patient Care Technologies Inc., and LSS Data Systems, among others.

MEDITECH also offers flexible lease financing options to its customers via Captech Funding Corporation.

Making MUMPS: 1966–69

MEDITECH's origins are rooted in a programming language called MUMPS, which is short for Massachusetts General Hospital Utility Multi-Programming System. Later known as M, the language was developed in 1966 at Massachusetts General Hospital's Lab of Computer Science (LCS). The LCS was established by Guy Octo Barnett, a Harvard-trained cardiologist hired to oversee Massachusetts General's Hospital Computer Project.

The Hospital Computer Project involved an early PDP1 computer with one of the very first time-sharing systems. Instead of monitor screens, the computer initially output data onto paper via a KSR teletype. According to Dr. Robert A. Greenes, in the *Journal of the American Medical Informatics Assocation,* "Octo headed a very dynamic laboratory in those days of the late 1960s, with new projects underway to automate much of the hospital's activities, including ADT, the clinical laboratory, pharmacy, radiology, and other functions." Greenes further explained, "The design and programming of this system represents one of the first comprehensive hospital information systems using modular definition as the specification paradigm."

The development of MUMPS was funded through a contract with the National Institute of Health, and by a grant from the National Center for Health Services Research and Development. With Barnett serving as the principal investigator, Greenes contributed some of the programming language. However, the lion's share of the code was developed by two project engineers: A. Neil Pappalardo and Curtis Marble. When MUMPS became commercially available in 1969, Greenes established Automated Health Systems and Pappalardo founded MEDITECH in Cambridge, Massachusetts.

Pioneering Medical Informatics: 1969–89

On the company's web site Pappalardo later summarized the manner in which his new enterprise blazed a trail into the emerging world of healthcare informatics, remarking: "In the

Company Perspectives:

MEDITECH's mission is to provide software that enables physicians, nurses, and other clinicians to orchestrate and deliver patient care in a safe, effective, and efficient manner. Our software is integrated in a manner that fully optimizes the financial and business potential of the health care enterprise. Our mission mandates that information is available whenever and wherever clinicians need it by ensuring access to a full electronic record that includes data from across the continuum. We will continue to take advantage of new technologies that allow for caregiver mobility and integration of evidence into the practice, with the end goal of enabling effective patient management.

beginning, we had no great and far reaching plan. Each event, every decision, a success here, a mistake there, would take us another step forward.''

Early developments at MEDITECH included the company's first customer, the Hyannis, Massachusetts-based Cape Cod Hospital, as well as the MEDITECH Interpretive Information System Language (MIIS), which was introduced in 1970. Although they were closed a few years later, in 1972 the company opened two regional offices in the western United States and one in the Midwest. The following year, MEDITECH developed an information system for the New York City Criminal Justice Department.

During the early 1970s, MEDITECH assembled what would later prove one of the industry's most stable management teams, in terms of permanence and longevity. The company's very first employee, Larry Polimeno, eventually became vice-chairman. Other early employees included eventual Senior Sales and Marketing Vice-President Ed Pisinski; Howard Messing, who rose to the position of president and chief operating officer; and one-day CFO Barbara Manzolillo. Roberta Grigg, who later served as senior vice-president of MEDITECH's international operations before retiring in 2001, was another staffer who joined the company at this time.

During the second half of the 1970s, MEDITECH furthered the evolution of its technology. In 1976 the company released the first MIIS Standard and started development on financial and patient care modules for its HCIS. A number of pioneering installations followed, including the first MIIS LIS at Seattle's Swedish Hospital in 1977; a redundant dual-processor system at Hartford, Connecticut-based Mt. Sinai in 1978; and the installation of MIIS Standard on an IBM Series 1 Minicomputer in 1979. That same year, a new facility was erected in Cambridge, Massachusetts, and a new client was gained when the Hong Kong Telephone Company installed MEDITECH's MIIS Inquiry System.

As MEDITECH's customer base grew, so did the need for users to meet and share information. This was evident when some 70 users convened in Boston in 1981. Two years later, a handful of MEDITECH users met to talk about issues regarding the HCIS and decided that a formal, standing users group was needed. This led to the formation of the Medical Users Software

Exchange (MUSE). According to the group, MUSE supported ''healthcare organizations using MEDITECH developed software and technologies, by providing a user-driven networking environment conducive to learning—where ideas are exchanged and information is shared so that our members can continually improve organizational performance.'' Led by volunteers, MUSE began hosting an international conference every spring, as well as a number of U.S. regional fall conferences.

Following the addition of real-time billing and accounts receivable functionality in 1981, the Magic operating system was introduced in 1982. By 1984, MEDITECH was supporting the VAX family of computers produced by Digital Equipment Corporation (DEC). That year, revenues totaled approximately $20 million. Other noteworthy developments on the technology front included the introduction of color windows and graphics in 1986, as well as the development of PCI in 1988, a forerunner of its Computerized Patient Record offering.

In tandem with these developments, MEDITECH was experiencing commensurate growth and expansion during the 1980s. Internationally, this was marked by the firm's entrance into the Canadian market in 1980, the achievement of ''preferred vendor'' status by governments in both Labrador and Newfoundland in 1986, and expansion in Saudi Arabia in 1987. Domestically, the company acquired a facility formerly known as the Underwood Building and opened its new headquarters in Westwood, Massachusetts, in 1983. MEDITECH's employee base reached 226 in 1985, exceeded 300 the following year, and reached 400 by 1988. MEDITECH celebrated 20 years in business in 1989 and reached another milestone by opening a new facility in Norwood, Massachusetts.

Advancing Healthcare Technology: 1990 and Beyond

In August 1990, MEDITECH purchased a three-story facility to accommodate its growing enterprise. Located on 55 acres, the historic Prowse Farm in Canton, Massachusetts, was acquired for $30 million. Formerly the world headquarters of Motorola subsidiary Codex Corporation, the site was home to a 250,000-square-foot office building made of glass and brick, which included a tropical atrium and mahogany floors. In addition to flexible conference and training facilities, the building provided more office space for MEDITECH's 700-employee work force, which had grown by 200 people in only 12 months.

Other noteworthy developments during this time included MEDITECH's expansion into the United Kingdom in 1990, and the introduction of handheld computing technology at Arkansas Children's Hospital the following year. Key leadership changes took place in 1993 when Pappalardo became MEDITECH's chairman, and Polimeno assumed the role of president. Howard Messing was named executive vice-president in 1994, when MEDITECH celebrated 25 years of operations and employed 1,159 people.

By late 1994, MEDITECH's revenues totaled $100 million, and its systems were in use by approximately 12 percent of all U.S. hospitals, or 640 institutions. That year, healthcare giant Columbia/HCA had installed the company's software in 60 of its 311 hospitals, with plans for 100 percent adoption over the next two years. At this time, MEDITECH software was saving

---

Key Dates:

1966: A. Neil Pappalardo helps develop the MUMPS programming language at Massachusetts General Hospital's computer lab.

1969: Pappalardo founds Medical Information Technology Inc. (MEDITECH) when the MUMPS language becomes commercially available.

1976: The company releases the first MIIS Standard and starts development on financial and patient care modules for its healthcare information system.

1979: A new facility is erected in Cambridge, Massachusetts.

1981: MEDITECH offers real-time billing and accounts receivable functionality.

1983: The company purchases its headquarters facility in Westwood, Massachusetts.

1989: MEDITECH opens a facility in Norwood, Massachusetts.

1993: Pappalardo becomes chairman, and Larry Polimeno is named president.

1997: MEDITECH's software is in place at 1,100 sites throughout the world.

1999: MEDITECH celebrates 30 years of operations.

2002: MEDITECH begins supporting both Citrix and Windows XP.

---

doctors time by putting such patient data as lab results and vital signs at their fingertips faster and from more locations, including the office, hospital, and home.

In the mid-1990s, while many healthcare organizations still relied on mainframe computer systems to manage information, some were transitioning to client/server configurations. MEDITECH made preparations to pilot-test its system at one hospital in a purely client/server setup. In the January 5, 1995, issue of *Hospitals & Health Networks*, MEDITECH Chief of Technical Research Chris Anschuetz commented on the new configuration: "You are now making use of all the computing power that's sitting on everybody's desktop, and all that computing power is linked in one big happy network. That one network is capable of doing a lot more than it would if it were depending on central hosts to do all the computing."

MEDITECH's revenues reached $167.8 million in 1996, with more than 20 percent devoted to research and development initiatives. That year, the company launched its Web site, provided Internet e-mail to its 1,600 employees, and established a corporate technology division. MEDITECH also completed HCIS installations at 244 additional hospitals.

At this time, MEDITECH's proprietary Magic-based operating system ran only on computers built by Data General and DEC. This situation stemmed from the fact that, early on, both computer companies were willing to adapt their computer systems to the specific needs of the healthcare industry. In addition, they were both located in Massachusetts, in close geographic proximity to MEDITECH's headquarters.

MEDITECH's HCIS had earned a solid reputation for reliability by the mid-1990s, and the company reported that 98 percent of its customers had never replaced the MEDITECH HCIS with one from another firm. Even so, some industry analysts identified lack of compatibility with other computer systems as a limiting factor. For this reason, MEDITECH made its move toward an open, client/server architecture a top priority.

In its May 1997 issue, *Health Data Management* revealed that MEDITECH's HCIS software was in place at 1,100 sites throughout the world. A company announcement in March of the following year listed the addition of seven new customers. These included five organizations in the hospital/medical center category, as well as the Pennington Biomedical Research Center in Baton Rouge, Louisiana, and the Institute for Rehabilitation and Research in Houston Texas.

Growth continued at MEDITECH in 1997. With 1,840 employees company-wide, the enterprise acquired a new building in Lowder Brook, Massachusetts, and began serving customers in Puerto Rico. Several new offerings were released the following year, including electronic medical record (EMR), long-term care and patient education products, and an electronic documentation system called MEDITECH Patient Care System (PCS).

MEDITECH was evaluating the feasibility of making its HCIS operate on a wider variety of hardware in 1999, beyond systems made by Data General and DEC. Other developments that year included an image-enabled automated patient information system and picture archiving communications system, as well as the Web-based Patient Education Suite. The latter product allowed healthcare organizations to provide patients with access to password-protected health content, including information about diagnosis and treatment for a variety of conditions. It also allowed hospitals to conduct patient satisfaction surveys, showcase staff members, and provide details about upcoming events.

MEDITECH ended the 1990s by celebrating 30 years of operations and earning revenues of $225.6 million. By this time, more than 100 of the company's customers were using its HCIS via a client/server configuration. Still, challenges to MEDITECH and its industry as a whole cropped up in the form of slowed sales, particularly as competition ensued to gain the business of hospitals that were at the same time seeking to contain ever-spiraling healthcare costs. Analysts considered the market flat and predicted increasing struggles for the healthcare information technology sector.

Nevertheless, MEDITECH began the 21st century by successfully dealing with the Y2K issue and signing its 1,500th customer. Revenues fell to $216.9 million that year, but improved to $223.8 million in 2001. At that time, MEDITECH reorganized into three divisions: New Application Development, Implementation, and Client Services. That year, Dell and IBM partnered with the company as new hardware providers, and MEDITECH introduced its Magic EDM Ambulatory Care Suite. Another important technical milestone came in 2002, when MEDITECH began supporting both Citrix and Windows XP.

Several important developments took place at MEDITECH in 2003. On the leadership front, Polimeno was promoted to vice-chairman and Messing was named president and COO. That year, the company was reporting a 23 percent market share and sales of $270.8 million, up from $256.2 million in 2002. MEDITECH appeared to be positioned for growth as it continued to compete in the medical informatics industry it pioneered some 35 years before.

Principal Divisions

New Application Development; Implementation; Client Services.

Principal Competitors

Cerner Corporation; Epic Systems Corporation; IDX Systems Corporation.

Further Reading

Bergman, Rhonda, "Romancing the Server," *H&HN: Hospitals & Health Networks*, January 5, 1995.

Greenes, R.A., et. al., "A System for Clinical Data Management," *Fall Joint Computer Conference*, Las Vegas, 1969.

——, "Design and Implementation of a Clinical Data Management System," *Computers and Biomedical Research*, Vol. 2, No. 5; October 1969.

Greenes, Robert A., M.D., Ph.D., "Presentation of the Morris F. Collen Award to G. Octo Barnett, MD," *Journal of the American Medical Informatics Association*, March 4, 1997.

Jones, Del, "Columbia/HCA System Speeds Test Result Delivery," *USA Today*, November 11, 1994.

McCormack, John, "Ringing Out the Century with a Whimper," *Health Data Management*, June 1999.

"Medical Information Technology Purchases Maresfield Farm," *Business Wire*, August 30, 1990.

"MEDITECH," *Health Management Technology*, March 1998.

"MEDITECH Banking on Client/Server," *Health Data Management*, May 1997.

"New Products & Services," *Health Management Technology*, December 1999.

Vennochi, Joan, "Codex Sells Prowse Farm at a Loss," *Boston Globe*, August 31, 1990.

"Why One Software Vendor May Offer More Options," *Health Data Management*, February 1999.

—Paul R. Greenland

Meiji Seika Kaisha Ltd.

4-16, Kyobashi 2-chome
Chuo-ku
Tokyo 104-8002
Japan
Telephone: (03) 3272-6511
Fax: (03) 3271-3528
Web site: http://www.meiji.co.jp

Public Company
Incorporated: 1916
Employees: 4,418
Sales: $2.94 billion (2003)
Stock Exchanges: Tokyo Osaka Nagoya Fukuoka
    Sapporo
Ticker Symbol: 2202
NAIC: 325412 Pharmaceutical Preparation
    Manufacturing; 311320 Chocolate and Confectionery
    Manufacturing from Cacao Beans; 311330
    Confectionery Manufacturing from Purchased
    Chocolate; 311423 Dried and Dehydrated Food
    Manufacturing; 311919 Other Snack Food
    Manufacturing; 325320 Pesticide and Other
    Agricultural Chemical Manufacturing; 424210 Drugs
    and Druggists' Sundries Merchant Wholesalers;
    424410 General Line Grocery Merchant Wholesalers;
    424450 Confectionery Merchant Wholesalers

Founded in 1916 as a manufacturer of biscuits and caramels, Meiji Seika Kaisha Ltd. is one of Japan's leading confectioners. The company manufactures a wide variety of products, ranging from chocolate and snack foods to antibiotics and agricultural chemicals. It is one of the few companies in Japan allowed to sell contraceptive pills. Meiji operates three main business segments—Food, Pharmaceutical, and Healthcare. Japan's sluggish economy in the early years of the new millennium forced Meiji to restructure its operations and launch several cost-cutting efforts. During 2003, the company featured English soccer star David Beckham in advertising campaigns in an attempt to bolster sales of its flagship chocolate products.

Diversification Leading to Growth

Meiji sought to establish a competitive advantage right from the start by being the first company to introduce chocolate snacks, bars, and candies, all of which quickly became a standard part of the Japanese diet. These products soon were followed by other snack and health-related items.

In 1936, the company diversified into the production of canned vegetables and fruit. The technology used in this expansion was later applied to the manufacture and packaging of a variety of related food products, including cocoa, juices, and carbonated drinks, powdered mixes, and high-protein health foods.

Meiji entered the pharmaceutical market when it began to produce penicillin in 1946. This diversification was a logical outgrowth of the company's experience in using fermentation in food production. Successful introductions of other antibiotic products, geriatric and cancer drugs, and diagnostic reagents provided high levels of return on Meiji's extensive research and manufacturing investments and served as the basis for later development of animal feed additives, germicides, and herbicides both for export and for domestic use. Meiji grew to become one of the largest antibiotic producers in the world; pharmaceuticals accounted for approximately 30 percent of the company's total sales in 2003.

Beginning in the late 1960s, Meiji turned its attention abroad, establishing its first U.S. subsidiary, Meiji Seika (U.S.A.), for the import and export of food and confectionery products in 1969. Another American subsidiary, Stauffer-Meiji, was established in 1985 and began manufacturing cookies and crackers from its Pennsylvania headquarters in 1986.

Additional marketing and sales affiliates for food and confectionery items were formed in Singapore in 1974, Europe and Colombia in 1984, and Taiwan in 1986. A joint venture with United Biscuits in 1971 brought that British company's McVitie biscuits to Japan in exchange for Meiji's confectionery expertise. The next year Meiji began to import chocolate manufacturing technology from Switzerland's Interfood Ltd. (now Jacobs Suchard A.G.).

In 1973, Meiji established the Dong-Myung Industrial Company Ltd. in Korea to produce and market its pharmaceutical

Company Perspectives:

Our corporate principle is to help people lead happier and more fulfilling lives by emphasizing the taste experience and zest in life.

Key Dates:

1916: The company is established.
1936: The company diversifies into the production of canned vegetables and fruit.
1946: Meiji enters the pharmaceutical market.
1969: Meiji Seika U.S.A. is created to oversee the import and export of food and confectionery products.
1985: U.S. subsidiary Stauffer-Meiji is established.
2001: The company launches its healthcare division.
2003: Meiji launches a major restructuring effort; a product recall costs the company more than 2 billion yen, contributing to the worst financial performance recorded in company history.
2004: Meiji announces the acquisition of the animal drug business of Daiichi Pharmaceutical Co.

products. These drugs were subsequently introduced in more than 60 countries through affiliates formed in Indonesia in 1974, Thailand in 1979, and Brazil in 1983—the location of another affiliate created nine years earlier to manufacture and sell the company's veterinary products.

Success in the 1980s–90s

By the 1980s, Meiji's confectionery technology was in high demand. Two joint ventures, one in the United States in 1988 and the other with the French-based Beghin Say S.A. in 1989, were established to manufacture and market the artificial sweetener fructooligo saccharide, which Meiji had introduced in Japan in 1984.

By this time, under the management of Chairman Takeshi Nakagawa, Meiji operated 12 plants, 9 research laboratories, 93 branch offices, 45 subsidiaries, 3 overseas offices, and 102 sales offices worldwide. While continuing to focus on confectionery products, food, and pharmaceuticals, the company also had begun to develop more health-oriented food products, new drugs, enzymes, edible fungi, and agricultural chemicals.

Meiji's skill in applying technological advancements to new product development proved to be a key factor in its growth. Swings in the value of the yen, intensified consumer demand and changing tastes, and increasing competition from both domestic and foreign firms continued to challenge the company's major business areas in the early 1990s. As the competitive environment forced Meiji to reduce product prices in order to hold onto its market share, the company continued to institute operating and production efficiencies and cost-reduction measures to ensure a high level of productivity and performance.

Meiji's strategy and its focus on creating new drugs used for diseases related to the central nervous system and the cardiovascular system appeared to pay off in the 1990s. As competition remained fierce, sales and profits were on the rise throughout much of the decade. At the same time, the company continued to bolster its overseas business. It licensed its Meiact antibiotic to several European firms as well as U.S.-based TAP Holdings Inc. in 1997 and strengthened its presence in Indonesia and China through joint ventures. In 1999 the Japanese government approved the use of certain contraceptive pills, which allowed Meiji to market them for the first time. By 1999, the firm's recurring profits had reached record levels.

Overcoming Challenges in the New Millennium

Meiji entered the new millennium on solid ground. The company launched its Healthcare division in 2001 in an attempt to cash in on significant growth opportunities in the health food and sport supplement industry. After the 2001 terrorist attacks, the company stock rose due to its stockpile of drugs that could

be used in the event of an anthrax outbreak. During 2002, the company announced that it would strengthen its research and development efforts for drugs used to fight against infectious diseases. It also entered the water purification market.

The company's bottom line began to falter that year, due in part to sluggish sales brought on by a faltering Japanese economy. A major restructuring effort was launched in 2003 that included plant closures and job cuts. Meiji was dealt a major blow when it was forced to recall products that included a certain flavoring additive that had not received approval under Japan's Food Sanitation Law. The recall ended up costing the company more than 2 billion yen. As such, Meiji recorded its worst financial performance in its history in the first half of 2003.

Under the leadership of newly elected president Naotada Sato, the company set several strategic initiatives in place to help bolster sales. English soccer star David Beckham was featured in an advertising campaign for its flagship chocolate products. It also signed a deal with Proctor & Gamble Far East Inc. to market the potato chips under the Pringles brand name in Japan. In September Meiji introduced karadanavi, a line of nutritional supplements and health food products. The firm announced that it would acquire the animal drug business of Daiichi Pharmaceutical Co. in early 2004. A change in Japanese law that year allowed Meiji to hire temporary staff for its production facilities.

While Meiji continued to face intense competition, the company's executive team was confident that its restructuring efforts would pay off. By focusing on growth opportunities within its Healthcare segment, Meiji hoped to offset sluggish sales in its Food and Pharmaceuticals divisions. With a longstanding history of success behind it, Meiji Seika Kaisha appeared to be well positioned to handle future challenges.

Principal Subsidiaries

Meiji Trading Corporation (90%); Donan Shokuhin Co. Ltd.; Zao Shokuhin Kaisha Ltd.; Ronde Corporation; Meiji Sangyo Co. Ltd. (85%); Meiji Chewing Gum Co. Ltd. (51%); Okayamaken Shokuhin Co. Ltd. (94%); Shikoku Meiji Co. Ltd.

(84%); Taiyo Shokuhin Co. Ltd.; Fuji-Amide Chemical Co. Ltd. (90%); Kitasato Pharmaceutical Industry Co. Ltd. (60%); Meiji Kaihatsu Co. Ltd.; Meiji Sports Plaza Ltd.; Meiji Seika Singapore Pte. Ltd.; D.F. Stauffer Biscuit Co. Ltd. (United States; 92.23%); Laguna Cookie Co. Inc. (United States); P.T. Meiji Indonesian Pharmaceutical Industries (83.86%); Thai Meiji Pharmaceutical Co. Ltd. (Thailand; 93.53%); Tedec-Meiji Farma S.A. (Spain; 20%); Meiji Seika Europe B.V. (Netherlands).

Principal Competitors

Ezaki Glico Co. Ltd.; Nestlé S.A.; Yamanouchi Pharmaceutical Co. Ltd.

Further Reading

"Confectioner Meiji Seika Logs Record Profit," *Jiji Press,* May 19, 1999.

"Japan Meiji Seika to Sell Pringles Potato Chips in Japan," *Japanese News Digest,* April 1, 2003.

"Meiji Licenses Cephalosporin Antibiotic to U.S. Firm," *Japan Chemical Week,* December 22, 1997, p. 12.

"Meiji Seika Aiming to Score Higher Sales with Beckham Again," *Nikkei Report,* June 21, 2003.

"Meiji Seika Enters Water-Purifying Market," *Nikkei Report,* October 26, 2002.

"Meiji Seika Needs More Restructuring for Growth," *Nikkei Report,* October 23, 2003.

"Meiji Seika to Boost Sales Abroad, Focused on Drugs," *Japan Chemical Week,* March 28, 1997, p. 7.

"Meiji Seika to Concentrate on Infectious Diseases," *Pharma Japan,* January 21, 2002, p. 7.

"Meiji Seika to Get Animal Drugs Biz Rights from Daiichi Pharm Group," *Jiji Press,* January 4, 2004.

Messer, Ian, "Slow Growth Seen for Contraceptive Pill Mkt in Japan," *Dow Jones International News,* June 3, 1999.

"Quiet, Stubborn Chief Heads Meiji Seika," *Nikkei Weekly,* June 30, 2003.

—update: Christina M. Stansell

MERCER

Mercer International Inc.

14900 Interurban Avenue South, Suite 282
Seattle, Washington 98168
U.S.A.
Telephone: (206) 674-4639
Fax: (206) 674-4629
Web site: http://www.mercerinternational.com

Public Company
Incorporated: 1968 as Pacific West Realty Trust
Employees: 1,022
Sales: $244.6 million (2003)
Stock Exchanges: NASDAQ
Ticker Symbol: MERCS
NAIC: 322121 Paper (Except Newsprint) Mills

Mercer International Inc. maintains its legal address in Seattle, Washington, although its CEO, Jimmy S.H. Lee, resides in Zurich, Switzerland, and the company's business of pulp and paper manufacturing is conducted in Germany. Controversy has often surrounded Mercer in the 20 years since Lee and his business associates gained control of a real estate investment trust, converted it into an operational company, and became involved in a number of activities, including iron ore royalties and insurance. After spinning off some financial assets in the mid-1990s, Mercer has concentrated on the pulp and business, primarily located in the former territory of East Germany, which is advantageously located close to many European customers. The company owns two paper mills that produce specialty papers and printing and writing papers, a pulp mill with a capacity to produce 300,000 tons of market kraft pulp, and a 63.6 percent share in another kraft pulp mill, a state-of-the-art Greenfield project with a capacity in excess of 550,000 tons.

1968 Origins

The corporate entity that evolved into Mercer was launched in 1968 as a real estate investment vehicle, organized under the laws of the state of Washington and named Pacific West Realty Trust. The company formed a limited partnership that attracted more than 450 Washington state investors, whose $4.7 million was invested in strip malls, a nursing home, and other western Washington assets. Many of these types of limited partnerships were used during this period as tax shelters, a practice which was shut down by the passage of the Tax Reform Act of 1986. Interest and depreciation deductions were greatly reduced so that taxpayers could not generate paper losses in order to lower their tax liabilities. Many of these limited partnerships were rolled up by syndicators who converted them into stock. In the case of Pacific West, investors in 1988 eagerly accepted a chance to trade their limited partnership positions for stock, thereby gaining a way to cash out. The stock company that entered the picture was called Asiamerica Equities Ltd., which according to the *Seattle Times,* "was owned by Stone Mark Capital, a previously empty shell company on the Vancouver Stock Exchange" whose "principals were in Hong Kong." Asiamerica offered $3.5 million in stock for Pacific West's land, buildings, and other assets, which were transferred to Asiamerica. According to the *Seattle Times,* however, the stock was not conveyed to the limited partners.

Asiamerica was founded by Mercer's current CEO Jimmy S.H. Lee. Press reports reveal that he was born into a wealthy Korean family and came to Canada by way of Hong Kong. After graduating from the University of British Columbia with a degree in chemical engineering in 1981, he then worked for two years as a process engineer for FMC Canada Ltd. In 1984, Lee and associates, including English-born Michael Smith, founded Asiamerica with assets of $3 million. The company looked for opportunities to acquire undervalued assets in any number of industries. Early on, by way of a subsidiary, it began quietly acquiring shares to control a Montreal-based mining company called Nalcap Holdings Ltd., which each year generated more than $10 million in royalties from Labrador iron ore deposits and western petroleum leases. Doing business under the name of Javelin International Ltd. a dozen years earlier, Nalcap had become notorious after its chairman, John C. Doyle, was convicted of some 400 fraud charges and fled to Panama. By court order, Doyle's shares in the company were frozen. Also vying for control of Nalcap was another controversial figure, J. Bob Carter, president of Vancouver-based Kelvin Energy Ltd. The *Toronto Star* described Carter as "a grade eight dropout, a former barroom bouncer, high-steel rigger and undercover drug

Company Perspectives:

Mercer International Inc. owns and operates market pulp and paper businesses in the southern German states of Saxony and Thuringia in the former East Germany.

agent. He wears cowboy boots, sucks on half-dead cigars and swears a lot.'' Carter also had on his resume two criminal convictions on sex-related charges involving prostitutes. ''I'm an outcast now and I will continue to be an outcast,'' he admitted. ''I might as well be a rich one.'' On the other hand, Lee, according to the newspaper, ''wears stylish oversized suits with padded shoulders, and cultivates a refined and sophisticated air.'' Regardless of the contrast, both men were more than willing to negotiate on the quiet with Doyle to purchase his Nalcap shares at below-market prices. Moreover, Lee formed a joint venture with Australian businessman Ron Brierly, who owned a pivotal 10 percent stake in Nalcap, which gave Asiamerica tentative control of the company. However, Carter was then able to convince Brierly to make a handshake deal to sell his shares to him instead. Brierly backed out of this agreement when pressed by Lee, and the entire matter landed in court in 1988. Although he would ultimately prevail, the reticent Lee received much unwelcome publicity for the way he and his associates did business. It would not be the last time Lee's group came under scrutiny.

Mercer Name Adopted in 1991

Gaining Nalcap's royalty stream laid the foundation for Mercer. The acquisition of Pacific West in 1988 not only added real estate assets but also provided the corporate entity that would later emerge as Mercer. Asiamerica's assets were merged with Pacific West, which then took on the Asiamerica name. Because Asiamerica failed to pay Pacific West's limited partners the stock owed to them for turning over their real estate assets, Lee found his company in court once again. The matter would finally be settled in 1991 when Asiamerica agreed to settle the class action suit by repaying $3.4 million plus legal fees of another $500,000. Also in 1991, the company was able to take another major step by gaining control of Constitution Insurance Co. of Canada, a deal that brought with it a $63 million investment portfolio. As a result, Asiamerica's revenues grew to $70.1 million in 1991, a three-fold improvement over the previous year. At the end of 1991, Asiamerica decided to change its name to Mercer International to reflect the company's move away from investment and to de-emphasize its Asian roots.

Mercer was now very much interested in becoming involved in international environmental services, especially in Europe. Lee was attracted to the recently reunified Germany, especially the Saxony/Sachsen Anhalt areas of the former communist state of East German, which was undergoing privatization and offering a number of incentives to investors. In 1991, Mercer acquired a 70 percent interest in Spezialreinigung Meissen GmbH, an environmental services company. In early 1992, Mercer formed a joint venture with Canada Energy Services Ltd., an environmental engineering and industrial cleaning company

operating in Europe and North America. Mercer was particularly interested in becoming involved in the North American hospital waste disposal business.

With a focus still on environmental services, Mercer gained a foothold in the paper industry in 1993 with the acquisition of Dresden Paper AG, a state-owned paper recycling company. Mercer was able to buy Dresden Paper, whose assets were valued at $76.8 million, for just $660,000 plus the guarantee of 490 jobs and the investment of $49 million over the next three years to upgrade the facilities. Moreover, the state agreed to forgive $80 million in debt owed by Dresden Paper and pledged as much as $41 million to help the company meet short-term financial requirements. Mercer's investment would also be financed with state-subsidized low-interest loans, and the company was in line to receive a rebate of 31 percent of its investment as a cash payment.

As Mercer began to convert Dresden Paper into a specialized maker of grease paper, tissue paper, and wallpaper, it also lined up its next deal in Germany and further committed the company to the paper industry while moving it away from environmental services, which did not prove to have as much promise as many had thought. To gain access to raw material, and forward its new goal of becoming a leading supplier of specialty pulp and paper in Europe, in 1994 Mercer acquired another state-owned business, Sellstoff & Papierfabrik Rosenthal GmbH, a 160,000-ton sulfite paper mill producing chlorine-free pulp and ethanol. Under the terms of this sale, Mercer committed to keeping at least 350 people employed until 1998 and investing $45 million in capital improvements. In return, the state forgave $76 million in debt, pledged nearly $44 million in cash contributions, and offered other rebates and tax incentives. Also in 1994, Mercer acquired a 70 percent interest in another German pulp operation, Bundesanstalt fur Vereinigungsbedingte Sonderaufgaben.

By now, Mercer was essentially being operated out of Zurich, where Lee chose to reside. As the company's focus on the pulp and paper industry increased, revenues on the financial services side steadily declined, falling from $56.5 million in 1992 to $23.7 million in 1994, while during the same period pulp and paper revenues grew by nearly 300 percent. At this point, it was decided that it was in the best interest of the company to split the pulp and paper business from financial services, and the assets of the later were spun-off as Arbatax International Inc. They included the iron ore royalties, insurance assets, and real estate investments. Mercer, as a result, became a pure-play pulp and paper manufacturer.

Focus on Specialty Paper in the Late 1990s and Beyond

Aside from removing non-pulp and paper assets from Mercer, management also began in late 1997 to restructure its remaining business to focus on specialty papers, especially wallpaper based paper production. During 1998, Mercer sold a packaging paper mill in Greiz and a carton paper mill in Raschau. In addition, a packaging paper mill and a corrugating base paper mill in Trebsen and a printing paper mill and recycled paper facility in Hainsberg were divested in 2000. The Rosenthal mill completed an important capital project in 1999 when it was converted from the production of sulfite pulp to

Key Dates:

1968: The company is formed as Pacific West Realty Trust.
1988: Pacific West is acquired by Asiamerica Equities and assumes Asiamerica name.
1992: Mercer International name is adopted.
1993: Company purchases Dresden Papier AG.
1996: Non-paper assets are spun off.
2001: Mercer acquires Landqart AG.

that of kraft pulp, making it the only kraft chemical facility operating in Germany. In December 2001, Mercer paid approximately $2.7 million to acquire Landqart AG, a Swiss manufacturer of security and specialized printing papers, used to print such documents as banknotes, customs forms, and passports. The following year, Mercer also began construction on a new 552,000-ton kraft-pulp facility near the town of Stendal. This project was originally scheduled to begin in 1999, but three years were required to complete the financing. When operational by the end of 2004, the plant would nearly triple the company's pulp capacity and make Mercer into one of the largest pulp producers in the world.

Although Mercer appeared to have a promising future, it was not performing that well. Then, in 2003, the company once again became associated with controversy when its chief financial officer resigned after becoming involved in a criminal investigation unrelated to the company. Some of the company's investors, in particular Greenlight Capital LLC, a New York hedge fund and the largest institutional investor, with a stake of nearly 15 percent, expressed severe reservations about the way Mercer was being managed. According to the *Puget Sound Business Journal*, Greenlight officials claimed that Mercer's board was in "disarray." They had been concerned about the business during the previous year, and the resignation of the CFO was simply the final straw. As a result, Greenlight launched a proxy fight with the intention of placing two nominees on Mercer's board of trustees. If elected, they would have the ability to change the way the board operated. Although he would not elaborate, Lee said he suspected that Greenlight had a hidden agenda in the proxy fight. Within a matter of weeks, however, Greenlight, Mercer, and three other significant shareholders worked out a deal to add two outside trustees, and the proxy solicitation was terminated.

Free to focus on growing its pulp and paper business, Mercer was able to raise new funding to complete the Stendal project and look for acquisition candidates. The company was especially interested in opportunities in other former Soviet Bloc countries, such as Poland, which were attempting to gain a more prominent role in the European economy.

Principal Subsidiaries

Dresden Papier GmbH; Papierfabrik Fahrbrucke GmbH; Spezialpapierfabrik Blankenstein GmbH; Zellstoff-und Papierfabrik Rosenthal Gmbh & Co KG.

Principal Competitors

International Paper Company; Norske Skogindustrier ASA; Svenska Cellulosa Aktiebolaget SCA.

Further Reading

Bayless, Alan, "Going South," *Barron's*, September 19, 1994, p. 22.
Erb, George, "Mercer International Faces Proxy Fight by N.Y. Firm," *Puget Sound Business Journal*, July 11, 2003, p. 6.
Marsh, Peter, "Pulp Friction for Korean Entrepreneur," *Financial Times*, May 1, 2002, p. 28.
Thomas, Bridget, "Saved!," *World Paper*, May 1994, p. 24.
Virgin, Bill, "Papermaker Is All over the Map," *Seattle Post-Intelligencer*, March 6, 2004, p. C6.
Westell, Dan, and Patricia Lush," *Globe and Mail*, June 18, 1992, p. B7.

—Ed Dinger

Millea Holdings Inc.

West Tower, Otemachi First Square
5-1-1 Otemachi
Chiyoda-ku, Tokyo 100-0004
Japan
Telephone: (+03) 6212-3341
Fax: (+03) 6212-3343
Web site: http://www.millea.co.jp

Public Company
Incorporated: 1879 as Tokio Marine Insurance Company;
    1914 as Nihon Dosan Fire Insurance Co. Ltd.
Employees: 6,700
Total Assets: $92.2 billion (2003)
Stock Exchanges: Tokyo Osaka NASDAQ
Ticker Symbol: MLEA
NAIC: 524126 Direct Property and Casualty Insurance
    Carriers; 551112 Offices of Other Holding Companies

Millea Holdings Inc. was created in 2002 when The Tokio Marine and Fire Insurance Co.—Japan's largest property and casualty insurance company—and The Nichido Fire and Marine Insurance Co. Ltd. joined forces. Millea Holdings oversees the operations of both companies, providing its customers with marine, fire, property and casualty, personal accident, and auto insurance. In order to streamline operations and maximize efficiency, management plans to eventually merge Tokio Marine and Nichido Fire together to form Tokio Marine & Nichido Fire Insurance Co. Ltd. Intense competition in its domestic market has Millea Holdings focused heavily on expanding internationally.

Early History

Tokio Marine Insurance Company was founded in 1879. Its beginnings were closely tied to the onset of Japanese westernization in the mid-19th century. In 1639, the Tokugawa government came into power and isolated Japan from the rest of the world for more than two centuries. During this period of seclusion, no Japanese was allowed to travel abroad, and trade with foreign nations was strictly regulated. Even in the absence of contact with the West, primitive types of insurance were developed for internal trade. In 1859, however, the Japanese ports were reopened, and Japan was again in touch with the West. Foreign insurance companies immediately established agencies in these ports to protect the risks of foreign shippers. In 1868, the embattled Tokugawa regime collapsed, and the Meiji restoration government took power. Its first acts were to restore full communication with the West and adopt Western economic structures. Many young industries were financed by the Meiji government, including insurance firms, which were modeled after western companies.

In 1878, representatives of the government, financiers who had been feudal lords, and Eiichi Shibusawa agreed on the need for a marine insurance company. Shibusawa was a leader in the development of modern industries in Japan. On Shibusawa's commission, the plan for Tokio Marine was drafted by Katsunori Masuda, one of the few Japanese experts on insurance at that time. Masuda proposed an initial capital investment of ¥500,000 and branch offices or agencies in all the major port cities. On August 1, 1879, the Tokio Marine Insurance Company was born, funded by both the government and private investors.

Tokio Marine received its early impetus from the rapidly expanding insurance needs of the westernizing Japanese economy rather than from a single visionary leader. Mochiaki Hachisuka became the firm's first president. Almost immediately, however, he was called to serve in the Foreign Ministry and was succeeded by Munenari Date. Date led the new company until 1883, when he too resigned to fill a government post. Mochimasa Ikeda, the third president, served until 1896. All three presidents had been feudal lords before the Meiji government took over; they championed the Western example but knew little themselves about the business of insurance. During these early years, the firm was held together by Masuda, who became general manager.

Originally, Tokio Marine insured only cargo. Even with this limited product line, however, its business grew quickly. Mitsubishi and Mitsui, both trading companies, not only patronized the new insurance firm but also acted as agents in Japanese cities where Tokio Marine could not yet establish branch offices. Wholesalers around the country also served as agents, and

Company Perspectives:

The Millea Group is committed to the continuous enhancement of corporate value with customer trust as the base of all its activities. By providing customers with the highest quality products and services, we will spread safety and security to all around us.

soon an extensive network was established with minimal solicitation on the part of Tokio Marine. By carefully selecting risks among ships with first-class ratings, the firm's early leaders assured its secure beginning.

Overcoming Problems in the Late 1800s and Early 1900s

In the early 1880s, however, the young firm was beset by extensive losses. In 1881, four insured cargoes were sunk, capped in 1882 by the loss of the Gulf of Panama, a ship whose cargo was worth ¥86,000. These claims would have exhausted the reserves—funds kept in reserve for the payment of claims and usually not booked as profit—as well as investments of Tokio Marine if the Meiji government had not again offered a grant in 1883. At this time, the government also expanded the firm's charter to permit the writing of hull insurance.

The years leading up to World War I were punctuated by the Sino-Japanese War of 1894–95 and the Russo-Japanese War of 1904–05. After an economic crisis in 1890, both wars briefly stimulated the newly industrialized but unstable Japanese economy, resulting in the inception and growth of many new businesses. In the insurance industry, several new companies were started and failed. Following the Sino-Japanese War, 19 nonlife insurances firms were formed, but only six survived beyond 1910. In order to regulate the speculation in this field, the government enacted the Insurance Business Law in 1900. The statute tightened methods of accounting and prohibited companies from concurrently writing life and nonlife insurance.

Tokio Marine suffered during the 1890s from the too rapid expansion of its own business as well as increasing competition from new businesses. Building on its newly solidified capital base, the company looked to foreign markets, establishing agencies in Liverpool, London, and Glasgow in 1891, and in San Francisco in 1893. The British operations rapidly raised the level of premium income from hull insurance, a line that was not expanding as quickly as expected in Japan. In 1890, domestic hull insurance generated barely ¥11,000. In the first half of 1891, overseas hull insurance brought in ¥82,000, and by the second half of the same year that amount had more than doubled. In the first half of 1892, foreign agencies generated ¥290,000 in hull insurance, leaving cargo insurance income far behind.

The rapid increase in premiums, however, was followed by a multitude of claims. In 1892, overseas losses were beginning to climb, amounting to ¥226,000; by the second half of 1893, losses had reached ¥667,000, with overseas premiums only ¥775,000 for the same term. At the same time, Tokio Marine was faced with stiffening competition at home. Two new marine companies were formed in 1893: The Nippon Kairiku

Insurance Company and the Imperial Marine Insurance Company. In the early 1890s, Tokio Marine lost the cargo business of rice, grain, and fertilizer wholesalers to Nippon.

Tokio Marine responded to the overseas crisis by closing the San Francisco agency in 1897 and the London office in 1898 and by negotiating with brokerage firms to act as their agents. Domestically, the firm took the opposite approach and countered its competition by assuming responsibility for its own promotion rather than relying on agents from other companies. To weather the two financial crises, Tokio Marine was forced to draw on its capital, effecting a reduction of ¥375,000. Accepting responsibility for the company's performance, Mochimasa Ikeda resigned in 1896 and was succeeded by Heigoro Shota. Shota resigned almost immediately to become general manager of the Mitsubishi shipyards, and Michinari Suenobu was appointed to succeed him. Despite corporate and financial upheaval, Tokio Marine opened a branch office in Osaka in 1896.

Tokio Marine benefited greatly from the economic revival during the war with Russia. In 1903, the firm's overall profit was less than ¥100,000; by 1910, it exceeded ¥1 million and reserves were comparable to those of longer-standing British companies. The first decade of the 20th century also saw the consolidation of Japan's commercial enterprises into large family-run financial blocs called *zaibatsu,* a structure that characterized the Japanese economy until after World War II. Fiscal retrenchment inevitably followed the prosperous wartime years; in this environment, the *zaibatsu* were thought to be more secure. Tokio Marine became part of the Mitsubishi *zaibatsu.* In these years of mergers and reaffiliations, the company formed its first subsidiary. In 1907, it cooperated with the Meiji Fire Insurance Company to form Tomei Fire and Marine Insurance Company, a firm that reinsured the preferred risks of both companies—a reinsurer does not write policies directly but contracts with the primary insurer to share the risk for large or preferred risks, thus backing the insurer's ability to settle claims.

Growth in the World War I Era

In the years leading to World War I, the nonlife insurance industry expanded both in size and in product lines. Marine insurance grew with the expanded marine business during the war with Russia, while competition in fire insurance markets increased. Many new companies were formed to handle the growing needs. In addition, new types of insurance expanded the scope of the industry.

The performance of Tokio Marine during these years reflected the general industry expansion. The directors had learned from the firm's financial setbacks in the 1890s and, with prudent retrenchment, prospered during the lean years after the war with Russia. In 1912, Tokio Marine reentered the U.S. market, establishing an agency for marine insurance in New York, with subagencies soon following in San Francisco and four other U.S. port cities. In 1913, the company applied for permission to add six new lines of insurance: inland transit, fire, personal accident, credit, theft, and automobile. In 1914, approval was granted for transit, fire, and automobile. Tokio Marine thus became the first Japanese firm to offer auto insurance.

Expansion continued and escalated during World War I. With the outbreak of war, trade and industry grew rapidly. From

---

Key Dates:

1879: Tokio Marine Insurance Company is founded.
1907: The company forms its first subsidiary, the Tomei Fire and Marine Insurance Company.
1914: Tokio Marine becomes the first Japanese firm to offer automobile insurance; Nihon Dosan Fire Insurance Co. Ltd. is established.
1918: The company changes its name to The Tokio Marine and Fire Insurance Company Ltd.
1946: Nihon Dosan adopts the name The Nichido Fire and Marine Insurance Co. Ltd.
1956: Tokio Marine renews direct underwriting operations in England and the United States.
1981: Tokio Marine becomes the first Japanese nonlife insurance company to begin operations in Italy.
1989: Tokio Marine operates as the world's largest property and casualty insurance company.
2002: Millea Holdings Inc. is created to oversee the operations of Tokio Marine and Nichido Fire.

1914 to 1918, exports tripled, and industrial production increased fivefold from 1914 to 1919. The need for nonlife insurance concomitantly grew as well, and Tokio Marine strengthened its position by acquiring control of several other insurance companies. In 1915, it purchased the Meiji Fire Insurance Company, in 1916 became part-owner of Fukuju Fire, and in 1917 acquired stock in Hokoku Fire. In addition, when Mitsubishi, one of its long-standing customers, moved to create its own insurance company, Tokio Marine became a large shareholder in the new firm. From 1908 to 1918, Tokio Marine's assets increased 12-fold. In 1918, the firm began to write fire insurance in the United States. At the same time it changed its name to The Tokio Marine and Fire Insurance Company Ltd. to reflect its expanded business.

In 1920, Japan's postwar economy slid into a depression that lasted most of the decade and prefigured the global depression of the 1930s. Shipping and trading were particularly affected, and the nonlife insurance business suffered accordingly. Tokio Marine and other major companies weathered the crisis, but many smaller companies could not stay afloat on their own. Tokio Marine spearheaded a move toward consolidation of the insurance market. To protect themselves, the smaller, less secure companies became affiliated with those that were larger and more stable. Reinsurance pools and tariff agreements were also used to regulate the market and to establish consistent conditions for determining premium rates. Tokio Marine was instrumental in organizing one of these pools, the Hull Insurers' Union, in December 1927.

The years of financial crisis were exacerbated in 1923 by the Great Kanto Earthquake, which killed 100,000 people and destroyed property valued at over ¥10 billion. Aggregate net assets of all nonlife firms amounted only to ¥235 million; a serious attempt at payment of all claims would have wiped them out. Prime Minister Gonnohyoe Yamamoto, however, publicly called for settlement of claims, and popular pressure exploded in 1924 in seven mass rallies supporting the prime minister's appeal. Ken-

kichi Kagami, then a managing director of Tokio Marine, led a coalition of insurance companies into an agreement with the government whereby the government and the nonlife insurance companies shared the financial burden of the earthquake, even though in some cases the companies were not liable. Because most claims were for settlement on fire policies, an area Tokio Marine had only recently entered, its payments were not debilitating.

Although the 1920s continued to be years of economic decline, Tokio Marine operated with a surplus and was able to expand its presence overseas. In 1921, it established the Standard Insurance Company of New York, its first subsidiary in the United States, to handle the growing fire insurance business. The company also began to expand in other parts of the world. In 1926, it concluded an operating agreement with Cornhill Insurance Company, a British firm. According to the terms of this agreement, the two firms shared liability on all policies, with Tokio Marine managing operations in Japan, China, and Southeast Asia, and Cornhill handling them in Europe, Africa, and Australia.

At home, the 1920s were years of corporate consolidation for Tokio Marine. The firm had lost business when Mitsubishi formed its own insurance company, and to forestall further losses the executives of Mitsubishi Marine and Tokio Marine coordinated their operations in 1925. At that time, Michinari Suenobu, chairman of Tokio Marine's board but also an executive at Mitsubishi, resigned and was succeeded by Kenkichi Kagami, Tokio Marine's managing director. Kagami, who had been board chairman at Meiji Fire since 1922, was concurrently made chairman of Mitsubishi's board. Under Kagami, the three firms cooperated and exchanged personnel. In 1933, they began to exchange capital as well. Tokio Marine also purchased numerous smaller subsidiaries during the 1920s.

Surviving World War II

In 1929, the collapse of the U.S. stock market initiated a global depression. Japan began to recover in 1932 after it went off the gold standard and adopted an inflationary policy. Nonlife insurance firms profited in this inflationary environment and developed smoothly in the early 1930s. In 1937, however, war broke out with China. Japan's relations with Britain and the United States deteriorated when its friendships with Italy and Germany deepened in the turbulent years before World War II.

To prepare for economic withdrawal from much of the Western world and to finance the war with China, the Japanese government instituted strict economic controls of the insurance industry in 1937. Nonlife insurance firms were required to reinsure domestically, rather than in London, a center for reinsurance. When war broke out in Europe in 1939, the requirement became a need. Two Japanese syndicates were established for domestic reinsurance in 1938 and 1939. To enlarge reinsurance capacity, the Toa Fire & Marine Reinsurance Company was established in 1940, with 42 domestic insurance companies as shareholders. Because Tokio Marine was now required to reinsure with the government-approved companies or syndicates, Tomei Fire's function became meaningless and it merged with Toyo Marine and Fire, another Tokio Marine subsidiary. Tokio Marine suspended or shut down all operations in England in 1941, when the British government froze all Japanese assets.

In 1939, Kenkichi Kagami died. At his death, the three affiliated companies—Mitsubishi Marine, Meiji Fire, and Tokio Marine—decided to elect separate presidents. Sakae Suzuki became president of Tokio Marine. The three companies, however, increased the exchange of officers to maintain coordination. In 1941, the Japanese government decreed the need for mergers of financial institutions in order to raise funds for the war effort. At the government's insistence, the three closely affiliated companies were dissolved as separate entities in 1944, and a single firm under Tokio Marine's name emerged in their place. Suzuki became chairman of the new Tokio Marine, and Shunzo Kameyama, president of the old Mitsubishi Marine, became president.

Although operations abroad ceased during World War II, domestic operations sustained a measure of growth, at least initially. As Japanese occupation of foreign soil expanded, the market for nonlife insurance also grew, particularly in Manchuria. In 1943, attacks on Japan increased, and the need for war-risk insurance climbed. Air raids became more frequent, and underwriters wrote more policies. Payments also escalated. Following the major air raid on Tokyo in March 1945, the numbers of policies and payments reached their peak. Between January 1942 and September 1945, income from war-risk policies issued by Japanese companies reached ¥500 million, while payments amounted to ¥46 billion. In early August 1945, the United States dropped atom bombs on Hiroshima and Nagasaki, and, on August 15, Japan surrendered. The Japanese fleet and all major cities had been completely destroyed. With no risks left to insure, Tokio Marine and other nonlife insurance companies simply ceased to function. Chairman Suzuki resigned in 1945, and Kameyama was appointed in his place.

Occupation forces arrived in Japan on August 30, 1945 under General Douglas MacArthur, Supreme Commander for the Allied Powers (SCAP). Under the SCAP administration, economic controls were inaugurated that reversed the trend of Japanese business, and American-style antitrust legislation was passed. One of SCAP's first directives dissolved the *zaibatsu*. Over the next few years, companies had to divest themselves of stock held in other businesses in their respective *zaibatsu*. Top management personnel who had held their positions during the war were dismissed.

The following years, 1946 and 1947, were the most difficult years in Tokio Marine's history. First its office building then its replacement offices were requisitioned by SCAP. The company ended up in a suburb of Tokyo until 1950. Under the Restriction of Securities Decree of November 1946, Tokio Marine was forced to divest itself of stock amounting to ¥96 million, which represented more than 76 percent of its total holdings. At Tokio Marine, Kameyama was forced to resign as chairman, Issaku Yatsui as president, as well as other top managers and directors. Tukujiro Tanaka became the new president, but the post of chairman was not filled. By 1948, Tokio Marine had complied with most of SCAP's directives.

Marine business, in general, had declined after the war, and the firm concentrated on fire insurance. It introduced fire-prevention techniques to the Japanese insurance market. By 1947, with government support, the shipping industry began to show signs of recovery and the company's marine business grew substantially between 1949 and 1954. In 1950, the company moved back to central Tokyo. The following year, it became an early proponent of office automation and in 1953 purchased IBM automation equipment.

Postwar Expansion

The company gradually reopened communications in foreign markets. In 1950, it signed reinsurance treaties with London companies. In 1953, it resumed overseas training of personnel. In 1956, it renewed direct underwriting operations in England and the United States. These domestic and foreign successes revived Tokio Marine's profitability. In 1949, the firm resumed dividend payments and by 1956 had almost recovered its prewar position in the industry. In the period from 1949 to 1954, total assets increased more than fivefold and working assets sevenfold. In 1957, the position of chairman of the board was reestablished, and President Tanaka was appointed to fill the post. He was succeeded by Mikio Takagi as president.

The 15 years from 1955 to 1970 were years of spectacular growth for both the Japanese economy and for Tokio Marine. From a nation devastated by World War II, by 1968 Japan rose to become second only to the United States in gross national product. The 1960s were especially profitable for Tokio Marine. In 1964, its direct premiums totaled ¥39.3 billion, with total assets of ¥86.5 billion. By 1973, direct premiums had climbed to ¥238.5 billion, with total assets of ¥491 billion. Although both marine and fire insurance coverage did well, much of the new business came from auto insurance. In 1956, Japan adopted compulsory auto insurance. Although premium income from compulsory insurance could not be counted as profit, supplemental voluntary auto insurance also increased. By 1967, Tokio Marine's combined auto insurance exceeded 50 percent of the company's total business. In 1966, Tanaka was succeeded by Kenzo Mizusawa as chairman. Genzaemon Yamamoto became president.

Tokio Marine introduced several other lines of insurance during the 1960s. Compulsory auto insurance had given the Japanese public a new awareness of the advantages of personal insurance, and Tokio Marine added new lines of personal coverage to its largely corporate business. Several types of personal accident insurance were offered: householders' and storekeepers' comprehensive, traffic personal accident, long-term comprehensive, and earthquake insurance for individual citizens. Its corporate lines continued to develop as well. The firm added aviation insurance, nuclear-energy liability, movables comprehensive, and employees' housing-loan credit insurance.

Between 1964 and 1975, Tokio Marine increased to 19 the number of foreign countries in which it did business. In the United States, Tokio Marine affiliated with the Continental Insurance Company and directed more of its efforts toward nonmarine business. In both European and U.S. markets, the company did an increasing amount of reinsurance. Yamamoto became chairman in 1972, and Minori Kikuchi followed him as president.

In the early 1970s, the rapid growth of the previous decade slowed dramatically. The growth in premium income of nonlife insurance companies in Japan dropped from 40 percent in 1970 to 12.8 percent in 1971. The economic slump was exacerbated by the oil crisis of 1973. To counteract the domestic downturn, Tokio Marine focused even more intently on overseas expansion and plotted a strategy of internationalization in the mid-1970s. Net overseas premium income increased from ¥14 billion in 1969 to ¥49.7 billion in 1978. In 1978, Kikuchi advanced to the chairmanship, and Fumio Watanabe followed him as president.

The 1980s were years of stable financial growth for Tokio Marine, especially from investment income. In 1980, the company purchased three subsidiaries from the Equitable Life Insurance Society of the United States. One year later, it became the first Japanese nonlife insurance company to begin operations in Italy. Investment income soared as the firm invested extensively in high-yield foreign securities. Auto-premium income also continued to climb, bolstered by a premium rate hike in 1983. In 1984, President Watanabe became chairman, and Haruo Takeda succeeded him as president. In 1985, Tokio Marine reported a record ¥25 billion net profit. In 1989, the firm purchased a 10 percent stake in Delaware Management Holdings, the fifth-largest independent money-management firm in the United States, in order to train itself in the management of pension funds. By 1989, Tokio Marine was the world's largest property and casualty insurance company. In 1990, Takeda advanced to the chairmanship, and Shunzi Kono became president.

Changes in the 1990s and Beyond

The last decade of the 20th century proved to be challenging for Tokio Marine. Indeed, by the early 1990s, both Japan's banking sector and its insurance industry were experiencing difficulties brought on by a wave of bad or non-performing loans and a faltering stock market. During the prosperous years of the 1980s, many banks and insurance companies, including Tokio Marine, invested significantly in both real estate and stocks. This investment strategy came back to haunt many companies, however, when the Japanese property market collapsed in the early 1990s.

While better off than many of its peers in the insurance industry, Tokio Marine was forced to contend with its exposure to poor investments. In 1996, the company wrote off $122 million in bad loans as its non-underwriting profits fell by 53.7 percent over the previous year. At the same time, Japan's economy was weakening, its banks were in financial disarray, and interest rates were reaching record lows.

In an attempt to bolster its financial market, Japan began laying the groundwork for deregulation in its finance and insurance sectors, believing that looser regulations and new competition would remedy the problems facing these industries. In 1996, Tokio Marine was given the nod to enter its competitors' markets. That year, the company branched out into the life insurance sector by forming subsidiary Tokio Marine Life. Throughout the remainder of the 1990s, the firm worked diligently to develop new products and services that would give it an edge during the liberalization process. In 1998, it formed investment banking, pension, and trust joint ventures. It teamed up with Charles Schwab the following year to offer its customers securities.

At the same time, Japan's insurance sector began to experience increased merger and consolidation activity as Tokio Marine's competitors began carving out deals and forming alliances. In 2001, Sumitomo Marine & Fire Insurance Co. and Mitsui Marine & Fire Insurance Co. merged to form Mitsui Sumitomo Insurance Co. Yasuda Fire & Marine Insurance Co. and Nissan Fire & Marine Insurance Co. joined together the following year, creating Sompo Japan Insurance Inc. Tokio Marine kept pace with its peers, announcing its own deal in 2002 with The Nichido Fire and Marine Insurance Co. Ltd.

Nichido Fire had been in business since 1914, operating under the name Nihon Dosan Fire Insurance Co. Ltd. In 1944, the company moved its headquarters to Tokyo and merged with Toho Fire. Two years later, it adopted the Nichido Fire name. Throughout its history, Nichido Fire focused on direct sales in both the wholesale and retail field. It branched out into life insurance in 1996 and by 2000 was operating as a leading nonlife insurance company.

In April 2002, Tokio Marine and Nichido Fire were united under a newly formed holding company, Millea Holdings Inc. The Kyoei Mutual Fire & Marine Insurance Company and Asahi Mutual Life Insurance Company originally planned to become part of Millea as well but later cancelled their merger plans. Undeterred, Tokio Marine and Nichido Fire went ahead with their plans and blended their management teams under one corporate umbrella. Millea hoped to integrate the operations of Tokio Marine and Nichido Fire together to form Tokio Marine & Nichido Fire Insurance Co. Ltd. by late 2004. In Millea's 2003 annual report, president Kunio Ishihara summed up the company's intentions, declaring, "The main reason behind the merger decision was an urgent need to stay in step with the quickening pace of change in our operating environment in order to increase the corporate value of the Millea Group."

In its early years of operation, Millea focused on growing its international holdings. In December 2002, Millea Asia was created to oversee expansion in Asian insurance markets. In early 2004, the Chinese government allowed Tokio Marine to sell nonlife insurance policies to individuals and companies in China. Millea's domestic market remained highly competitive, a sure sign that international development would continue well into the future. Given the strength of Tokio Marine and Nichido Fire's backgrounds, Millea Holdings appeared to be well positioned for growth in the years to come.

Principal Subsidiaries

Tokio Marine Capital; Tokio Millennium Re; Tokio Marine Risk Consulting; Tokio Marine Asset Management; Tokio Marine Medical Service; Tokio Marine Financial Solutions; International Assistance; Millea Agency; Tokio Marine Nichido Better Life Service; Sino Life Insurance Co.; IFFCO-TOKIO General Insurance Co. Ltd.; The Tokio Marine and Fire Insurance Co. Singapore Pte. Ltd.; Newa Insurance Co. Ltd.; Tokio Marine Insurans Malaysia Bhd.; Tokio Marine Malayan Insurance Co. Ltd.; ; Vietnam International Assurance Co.; The Sri Muang Insurance Co. Ltd.; Millea Life Insurance Thailand Public Co. Ltd.; The Tokio Marine and Fire Insurance Company Hong Kong Ltd.

Principal Operating Units

Tokio Marine & Fire; Nichido Fire & Marine; Tokio Marine & Nichido Life; Tokio Marine & Nichido Financial Life; Tokio Marine & Nichido Career Service; Millea Real Estate Risk Management; Millea Asia.

Principal Competitors

Aioi Insurance Co. Ltd.; Mitsui Sumitomo Insurance Co. Ltd.; Sompo Japan Insurance Inc.

Further Reading

Ion, Edward, "Millea Will Try to Stabilise via Diversification and Acquisition," *Insurance Day*, November 29, 2002.

"Japan's Non-Life Insurers Look Towards the Rest of Asia," *Insurance Day*, March 25, 2004.

"Life Industry Ploughs Ahead Amidst Growing Challenges," *Asia Insurance Review*, April 20, 2004.

"Millea: A Leader to the Last," *Asia Insurance Review*, April 20, 2004.

"Nonlife Insurers' Earnings Improve in FY '94," *Japan Economic Newswire*, May 24, 1995.

"Nonlife Insurers Face Shake-up," *Nikkei Weekly*, August 26, 2002.

Sato, Makoto, "Merger Momentum Hits Insurers," *Nikkei Weekly*, October 25, 1999.

Smith, Charles, "Millea Insurance Units to Merge," *Daily Deal*, March 29, 2003.

Terazono, Emiko, "Write-Offs Hold Japan's Insurers Back," *Financial Times*, May 24, 1996.

The Tokio Marine $1 Fire Insurance: The First Century, 1879–1979, Tokyo: Tokio Marine & Fire Insurance Co., Ltd., 1980.

"Tokio Marine, Nichido Eye Merger," *Nikkei Weekly*, January 27, 2003.

"Tokio Marine, Nichido Fire Launch Millea Holdings," *Japan Economic Newswire*, April 1, 2002.

—Lynn M. Voskuil
—update: Christina M. Stansell

Miramax Film Corporation

375 Greenwich Street
New York, New York 10013
U.S.A.
Telephone: (212) 941-3800
Fax: (212) 941-3949
Web site: http://www.miramax.com

Wholly Owned Subsidiary of the Walt Disney Company
Incorporated: 1979
Employees: 425
Operating Revenues: $50 million (2000 est.)
NAIC: 512110 Motion Picture and Video Production

Miramax Film Corporation is one of the top independent motion picture studios in the world, with a long list of hits that includes *sex, lies, and videotape, Pulp Fiction, The English Patient, Shakespeare In Love,* and *Chicago.* The company also operates Dimension Films to release genre pictures such as *Scary Movie* and *Scream,* as well as family fare such as the *Spy Kids* series. Other divisions include Miramax Television, which produces such programs as *Project Greenlight,* and Talk Miramax Books. Purchased in 1993 by the Walt Disney Company, the firm is run by founders and co-chairmen Harvey and Bob Weinstein.

Beginnings

Miramax was founded in 1979 by Harvey and Bob Weinstein, the sons of a New York City diamond cutter. Harvey, born in 1952, and Bob, born in 1954, became fans of foreign films in their teens after seeing Francois Truffaut's French New Wave classic *The 400 Blows,* and for Harvey in particular the experience stirred a lifelong passion for the uncompromising movies of independent filmmakers who worked outside the Hollywood system.

After graduating from high school in 1969, Harvey entered the State University of New York at Buffalo, where he and a friend, Corky Burger, formed Harvey & Corky Presents, a rock concert promotion firm. In 1973, he dropped out of school to focus on the business, and not long afterwards he and his brother Bob took over the run-down Century theater in Buffalo, where they presented concerts by the likes of The Grateful Dead and showed triple bills of offbeat movies.

In 1979, Harvey sold his stake in the concert business, and he and Bob moved back to New York City with plans to start a movie distribution company. Taking the names of their mother, Miriam, and late father, Max, they christened the new endeavor Miramax Films. The company started out by releasing low-budget titles that played at fringe theaters in big cities or at drive-ins but not in mainstream movie houses. The Weinsteins would typically pay a fee to get exclusive U.S. distribution rights for a foreign-produced title, then would do what they could to promote it and get it into theaters. Miramax took a percentage of the gross ticket sales, with the copyright owners later receiving royalties after the firm's expenses had been met. Early releases included *Goodbye, Emmanuelle,* a French pornographic movie, British concert documentaries featuring Paul McCartney and the rock band Genesis, and a cheaply made horror film, *The Burning,* which Harvey produced and Bob co-scripted.

During the first several years, the Weinsteins lived mostly hand-to-mouth, operating the business out of Harvey's Broadway apartment, but 1982 saw Miramax have its first hit with a film called *The Secret Policeman's Other Ball.* Based on more than four hours of Amnesty International benefit concert footage, which they had purchased for $180,000, it included performances by Sting, Phil Collins, and the Monty Python troupe. To promote it, a TV ad campaign was concocted that featured Monty Python's Graham Chapman in women's underwear, decrying the film's ''lewd, lascivious'' content. When one station refused to air it, primarily because of an American flag in the background, the Weinsteins capitalized on the ''banned'' ad to stir up a healthy dose of publicity for the film, and it went on to gross $6 million in the United States. Though not much by Hollywood standards, this was tremendous business for a film that generally played at ''midnight movie'' screenings or on college campuses, and the brothers earned a tidy profit.

Over the next several years, Miramax began to shift its focus to the art-film category with more sophisticated releases such as the Brazilian import *Erendira.* In 1984, the Weinsteins returned to production, co-writing and co-directing *Playing For Keeps,* a teen comedy with a mostly unknown cast. Its production was fraught with difficulties, and it made little impact when released two years later, losing the brothers and their outside backers a considerable sum.

Breakthrough in 1988–89

Miramax's fortunes improved again in 1988 when the company released the Errol Morris documentary *The Thin Blue Line.* The film, which helped free a man wrongly convicted of murder in Texas, proved a major success on the art-film circuit. The following March the company celebrated an important milestone when its release *Pelle the Conqueror* won the Best Foreign Film Oscar at the Academy Awards. Taking advantage of their firm's higher visibility, the Weinsteins sold a $3.5 million stake in Miramax to British bank Midland Montague and also secured a $10 million loan from Chase Manhattan. The money was quickly put to use to buy distribution rights to three new films, a British drama called *My Left Foot,* a sentimental Italian film called *Cinema Paradisio,* and the Sundance Film Festival hit *sex, lies and videotape.* All three did well, with *sex, lies* proving the company's biggest success to date, grossing $25 million and playing dates in both art-house and general-audience multiplex theaters.

Miramax was now again involved with an original production, this time in partnership with British firm Palace Pictures. The film, *Scandal,* was rated X by the Motion Picture Association of America's Classification and Rating Administration, but after cuts this was lowered to an R rating. Subsequent releases *The Cook, The Thief, His Wife and Her Lover* and *Tie Me Up! Tie Me Down!* were also rated X, but were released unrated to strong art-house business. For the latter title, Miramax had appealed the X rating and then sued the movie ratings board, after which the case went all the way to New York's Supreme Court, where the company lost. The controversy helped sell

tickets, and Harvey Weinstein reportedly joked that he considered his legal bills to be advertising costs.

Driven by the company's new growth, a satellite office was opened in Los Angeles in 1989, and in early 1990 Miramax's headquarters were moved to Robert DeNiro's Tribeca Film Center in the south end of Manhattan. The firm now had 50 employees. During 1991, Miramax put more films in theaters than any major studio, nearly 40, though few reached the multiplexes. The year's biggest title was the Madonna documentary *Truth or Dare,* which took in $15 million, and revenues hit $74 million, with profits of $4.35 million.

In early 1992, Miramax launched international sales and home video units, with a new theatrical film division called Dimension Films formed in the summer. It would be run by Bob Weinstein, whose taste ran more toward horror and science fiction films than the imports and independents favored by Harvey.

At this time, Miramax was experiencing an extended dry spell at the box office, and reports began to surface that the company was missing payments to filmmakers, at least one of whom took their case to court. Strapped for cash, the Weinsteins made preparations for a public stock offering, but then called it off at the last minute. Miramax was now the subject of a small wave of negative media coverage, some of which centered on the Weinstein brothers' reputations for uncontrolled outbursts of temper. Other stories focused on Harvey Weinstein's propensity for cutting films to appeal to American audiences, which had earned him the nickname "Harvey Scissorhands" among some filmmakers.

Rumored to be approaching bankruptcy, the firm's luck turned around with a film that most of its competitors had passed on. *The Crying Game,* about a British soldier kidnapped by the IRA in Northern Ireland, was sold with an advertising tagline as old as the hills—"don't reveal the ending." Miramax had spent just $4 million for the American rights, but the film went on to take in $63 million at the box office. In early 1993, it was nominated for 6 Oscars out of a total of 12 for the studio—more nominations than any other company except giant Warner Brothers—and won two. The company had for some time been aggressively courting Oscar nominations with such methods as sending "screener" videotapes to all eligible Motion Picture Academy voters.

Sale to Walt Disney in 1993

With the difficulties of the previous year still fresh in their minds, the Weinsteins continued to look for the greater stability that outside funding would bring. After sitting down for talks with Paramount, they surprised industry observers by selling Miramax to the Walt Disney Company in 1993 for a figure estimated at $60 million plus assumption of the company's debt. The brothers would continue to have almost full autonomy, as well as receiving a share of the firm's profits. Though many felt that the family-oriented Disney would not be supportive of the Weinsteins' brand of film fare, the brothers were apparently comfortable with top brass Michael Eisner and Jeffrey Katzenberg, and Disney itself had already formed the adult imprints Touchstone and Hollywood Pictures. After the sale, the firm would continue to be based in New York, and its films would be distributed by Disney's powerful Buena Vista subsidiary.

With Disney's backing, Miramax went on a buying spree, purchasing a larger number of films than it had ever done before, though not all would see release to theaters. The company also signed production deals with several leading actors and directors and soon struck box office paydirt with an $8 million title that had been shelved by Columbia Tri-Star. Quentin Tarantino's *Pulp Fiction,* which featured stars-in-decline John Travolta and Bruce Willis, along with relative unknowns Samuel L. Jackson and Uma Thurman, became one of the "must-see" titles of the year and grossed $108 million, the highest ever for an independent film. At the same time, Dimension was finding success with *The Crow,* a modestly budgeted martial arts film that grossed more than $51 million. Miramax had also recently formed book and record divisions and released its first Woody Allen title, *Bullets Over Broadway.*

In 1995, the company found itself in the midst of controversy with *Priest,* the story of a gay member of the Catholic clergy, as well as the NC-17 rated *Kids,* about sexually active, drug-abusing teenagers. When Disney balked at releasing the latter, the Weinsteins bought back the $3.5 million film and released it unrated via a separate company they had formed. Box office gross for the year hit $185 million, with successful titles including *Muriel's Wedding, Smoke,* and the sentimental Italian import *Il Postino (The Postman).*

Although the *Kids* controversy had caused a rift between the Weinsteins and parent Disney, in May of 1996 the brothers signed a new, enhanced seven-year agreement to stay on at Miramax. The deal gave them significant profit incentives, and Disney pledged to invest heavily in the Dimension operation. In 1996, the company released 37 films, with its biggest successes including Dimension's *Scream,* which raked in a division record $100 million and later spawned several sequels, and *The English Patient,* which won Miramax its first Best Picture Academy Award in the spring of 1997, along with eight additional Oscars. The year 1996 had also seen the successful releases of *Trainspotting* and Billy Bob Thornton's *Sling Blade,* among others.

In May 1997, Miramax bought the rights to make sequels to the *Total Recall* and *Rambo* films for $3.6 million from bankrupt studio Carolco Pictures. The company was taking on more and more of the attributes of a major studio and released two $30 million movies during the year, *Cop Land* with Sylvester Stallone and *Mimic,* a Dimension horror entry. The firm was now producing approximately a third of its releases, up from just 10 percent when Disney first acquired it.

Talk Media Formed in 1998

The year 1998 saw the company unveil a new venture called Miramax/Talk Media. It would be headed by former New Yorker Magazine editor Tina Brown, who would coordinate a variety of film, television, and book projects and publish a monthly magazine called *Talk* in conjunction with Hearst Magazines. The company was now riding a wave of film hits, including the Matt Damon/Ben Affleck vehicle *Good Will Hunting,* which took in $138 million, Robert Begnini's Holo-

caust "comedy" *Life Is Beautiful,* and the $24 million *Shakespeare In Love,* co-financed with Universal, which grossed $100 million and won the Best Picture Oscar. The firm released 42 films for the year, including Dimension's *Halloween: H20,* which was the unit's first-ever summer hit. By now, Miramax's staff had grown to 300.

In the fall of 1999, Tina Brown's *Talk* magazine debuted. It was not an instant success, and after the first few issues several top editors left and changes were made to its layout. The company's recently formed television division was also having troubles, with its debut program, *Wasteland,* cancelled after three episodes. Meanwhile, the Dimension unit, which was now pulling in 40 percent of Miramax's box office take, was expanded to encompass family-oriented titles. Also in 1999, Miramax entered the live theater business, co-producing Tom Stoppard's play *The Real Thing* on Broadway. Estimated profits, reflecting the absence of a big hit, dropped by half from a year earlier to $67 million.

In May 2000, the Weinstein brothers signed a new seven-year contract extension with Disney, which reportedly boosted the budget level at which they could "greenlight" films, while guaranteeing them a percentage of the profits from Miramax's film library. They were now making more co-production deals with outside studios, including Columbia, Universal, and MGM. In the summer of 2000, Dimension scored its biggest success to date with *Scary Movie,* which did $157 million at the box office, while Miramax hit with the romantic *Chocolat* to the tune of $71 million.

During 2001, Miramax had success with titles like *Bridget Jones' Diary, The Others,* and French import *The Closet,* but almost two-thirds of the firm's profits came from Dimension, via hits like *Scary Movie 2* and *Spy Kids.* The company was also having success with its direct-to-video releases, which equaled in number those put into theaters. Titles like *The Crow: Salvation* and *Mimic 2* were among the top five films in the category in 2001, with combined revenues of more than $9 million.

In January 2002, with advertising sales in decline following the September 11, 2001 terrorist attacks, Miramax and Hearst suspended publication of Tina Brown's *Talk* magazine after reportedly losing upwards of $27 million. The company later bought out her contract for an estimated $1 million. Though the firm was having art-house success with the drama *In The Bedroom,* the $35 million *Shipping News* got poor reviews and bombed, and in March the company announced it was laying off 75 of its workforce of 500.

December 2002 saw the release of several major titles, including Martin Scorsese's epic *Gangs of New York* and a starstudded film adaptation of Broadway musical hit *Chicago.* *Gangs,* which Miramax claimed had cost just under $100 million and others estimated at $120 million, had been long in coming, with its scheduled December 2001 opening postponed first seven months, then twelve. Its cast included teen heartthrob Leonardo DiCaprio, and when Steven Spielberg's upbeat *Catch Me If You Can,* in which DiCaprio also starred, came out a week later, it effectively stole the long, violent *Gangs'* thunder. The Scorsese film went on to gross just $77 million at the U.S. box office, but its failure was tempered by the overwhelming success of *Chicago,* which took in $170 million domestically and went on to win the Best Picture Oscar.

In 2003, Dimension hit with *Spy Kids 3-D,* which grossed more than $111 million, while Miramax's *Kill Bill Volume 1* sold $69 million worth of tickets. The latter, Quentin Tarantino's fourth film for the company, had been cut into two parts at Harvey Weinstein's insistence. At year's end, the $80 million Civil War epic *Cold Mountain* proved a relative disappointment with a gross of $95 million.

Early 2004 saw Miramax without a Best Picture Oscar contender for the first time in several years, though its 15 nominations were still the most of any studio. In the spring *Kill Bill Volume 2* did strong business, but the firm found itself once again in the midst of controversy over Michael Moore's summer release *Fahrenheit 9/11.* Citing the film's anti-Bush administration stance, Disney announced it would not distribute the title.

After a quarter-century in business, Miramax Film Corporation had evolved from a small independent distributor into a "mini-major," producing films whose budgets occasionally approached or even, allegedly, exceeded $100 million. At the same time, it continued to release a wide range of smaller films, including many independently produced and foreign art-house titles like those with which it had first found success.

Principal Subsidiaries

Dimension Films; Miramax International; Miramax Television; Talk Miramax Books.

Principal Competitors

Sony Pictures Classics; United Artists Corporation; Paramount Classics; Fine Line Features; Lions Gate Entertainment; Newmarket Films.

Further Reading

Auletta, Ken, "Beauty and the Beast—Harvey Weinstein Has Made Some Great Movies, And a Lot of Enemies," *New Yorker,* December 16, 2002, p. 65.

Bernstein, Richard, "Miramax Films Goes up against the Big Guns," *New York Times,* March 20, 1991, p. 11.

Biskind, Peter. *Down and Dirty Pictures—Miramax, Sundance and the Rise of Independent Film.* New York: Simon & Schuster, 2004.

Carvell, Tim, "Dimension Films' Successful Scare Tactics—Studio-Sized Returns on Indie-Sized Budgets," *Fortune,* December 29, 1997, p. 27.

——, "The Talented Messrs. Weinstein," *Fortune,* March 6, 2000, p. 169.

"Dimension Jazz Pumps Miramax," *Hollywood Reporter,* January 7, 2004, p. 62.

Dunkley, Cathy, "Weinsteins Re-up at Disney," *Hollywood Reporter,* May 9, 2000, p. 74.

Grove, Martin A., "Hollywood Report: Miramax Enters New Dimension in Features," *Hollywood Reporter,* June 19, 1992, p. 12.

Grover, Ronald, "Crying All the Way to the Oscars," *Business Week,* March 15, 1993, p. 38.

Gubernick, Lisa, "We Don't Want to Be Walt Disney," *Forbes,* October 16, 1989, p. 109.

Holson, Laura M., "Miramax Films Cuts 75 Jobs After Some Recent Setbacks," *New York Times,* March 16, 2002, p. 1.

Honeycutt, Kirk, and Galloway, Stephen, "Weinsteins, Dis Renewal Something to Crow About," *Hollywood Reporter,* May 10, 1996, p. 1.

Horn, John, "Miramax Films Emerges as Top Independent," *Associated Press,* January 25, 1990.

King, Thomas R., and Turner, Richard, "Disney Agrees to Buy the Distributor of 'Crying Game' at Possibly $60 Million," *Wall Street Journal,* May 3, 1993, p. B13.

Landler, Mark, "How Miramax Sets Its Sights on Oscar," *New York Times,* March 23, 1997, p. H17.

Lyons, Daniel, "The Odd Couple—How Did the Disney-Miramax Marriage Work out So Well?," *Forbes,* March 22, 1999, p. 52.

——, "The Other Side of Miramax," *The Wall Street Journal,* April 22, 2002, p. B1.

"The Mighty Weinsteins," *Hollywood Reporter,* January 7, 1999, p. 13.

Rose, Matthew, and Bruce Orwall, "Talk Collapses Just as Strategy Was Taking Root," *Wall Street Journal,* January 21, 2002, p. B1.

Rutenberg, Jim, "Disney Is Blocking Distribution of Film That Criticizes Bush," *New York Times,* May 5, 2004, p. 1A.

Sharkey, Betsy, "The Brothers Miramax," *New York Times,* April 24, 1994, p. 1.

"Tag-Teaming the Boxoffice," *Hollywood Reporter,* September 6, 2001, p. 10.

—Frank Uhle

Nippon Express Company, Ltd.

Higashi-shimbashi 1-9-3
Minato-ku
Tokyo 105-8322
Japan
Telephone: (03) 6251-1111
Web site: http://www.nittsu.co.jp

Public Company
Incorporated: 1937
Employees: 40,081
Sales: ¥1.25 trillion ($13.99 billion) (2003)
Stock Exchanges: Tokyo
Ticker Symbol: 9062
NAIC: 484121 General Freight Trucking, Long-Distance, Truckload; 484122 General Freight Trucking, Long-Distance, Less Than Truckload; 484230 Specialized Freight (Except Used Goods) Trucking, Long-Distance; 483111 Deep Sea Freight Transportation; 484110 General Freight Trucking, Local; 493110 General Warehousing and Storage; 541614 Process, Physical Distribution, and Logistics Consulting Services; 481112 Scheduled Freight Air Transportation; 492110 Couriers

Nippon Express Company, Ltd., is one of Japan's largest transportation companies, with nearly 1,170 service centers in Japan and 288 centers in 33 countries across the globe. Nittsu, as it is familiarly called, is involved in a wide variety of transportation-related services, including motor freight transport and forwarding, railway forwarding, marine transport, air freight forwarding, and warehousing. Nippon Express is also familiar to Japanese householders for the ''Pelican'' parcel delivery service. While the name ''Nippon Express'' was first used in 1937, the company's direct antecedents date from the 19th century, and it can trace the origins of its express courier business back centuries before that. Several other strands of business, such as tourism and marine transportation, figured in the company's distant past, then disappeared, only to reappear in the late 20th century.

Early History to World War II

Messenger services existed in Japan from the seventh century A.D. However, the service did not conspicuously evolve until the period when, for two and a half centuries (1600 to 1867), Japan was ruled by shoguns of the house of Tokugawa. The shogun, officially the emperor's deputy, effectively governed with the aid of a handful of counselors and a quasi-feudal network of samurai. After many centuries of civil war, the relative peace of the Tokugawa period encouraged a surge of economic growth. Because the country's ruling class was centered on the shogun's capital of Edo (now Tokyo), whereas the commercial center was Osaka, more than 200 miles away, the growth of commerce stimulated the rapid development of transportation systems.

The first Tokugawa shogun, Ieyasu, set up a system of staged or relay courier services: men and horses were kept on hand at staging posts, or occasionally requisitioned from convenient villages, for the use of members of the nobility and those carrying their property and mail. A number of commercial horseback express messenger services flourished. These services multiplied between about 1800 and 1867, the last years of the Tokugawa regime, which were, like its first years, associated with a resurgence of commercial growth.

The shoguns kept Japan isolated from the outside world, but the country was becoming irresistible to the West, both as a trading partner and as a port of call where ships could take on fuel and provisions. In 1854, Commodore Matthew Perry of the United States secured the first of a series of treaties which were to open up Japan to international commerce. Contact with the outside world contributed to the destabilization of the Tokugawa regime, which fell in 1868, when the Meiji Restoration assigned to the emperor the administrative power that the shoguns had once wielded.

The Meiji government undertook a radical modernization of the Japanese economy. The Postal Service Law of 1871 inaugurated a national mail system. The messenger services found themselves unable to compete with the government's 3,000 offices, which soon offered a telegraph service alongside the conventional post.

Sosuke Sasaki was the manager of Izumiya, the most powerful of the express messenger companies; he was also a trade representative. Aware of the nature of modern postal services, he bowed to the inevitable. After consultation between Sasaki and Hisoka Maejima, the minister for the postal service, it was agreed that the express messenger services would cede their business to the official mail and would switch instead to bulk freight transportation. They would be rewarded with an exclusive contract for the government's own haulage requirements.

Accordingly, in 1872 the former courier suppliers joined to form the Riku-un Moto Kaisha, or General Land Transportation Company, under the presidency of former Izumiya head Jinbei Yoshimura and the vice-presidency of Sosuke Sasaki. The new enterprise, launched with capital of ¥50,000, was Japan's first joint-stock transportation company and was to form the backbone of the company later known as Nippon Express. Riku-un Moto Kaisha operated through a number of small Riku-un Kaisha ("land transportation") companies, each corresponding to one of the old relay stages. This organizational structure was overhauled in 1875, when the small Riku-un Kaisha companies were abolished and the parent company, with its 2,000 employees, was renamed Naikoku Tsu-un Kabushiki Kaisha, the Domestic Express Company.

As Riku-un Moto Kaisha, the company had started a horse-drawn freight carting service between Tokyo and Odawara in 1874. Shortly afterwards, the route was extended to Kyoto and Atsuta. At the end of the 1870s, the service started to carry passengers as well as freight. Although the road service was temporarily supplanted by the coming of railways in the late 19th century, in the late 20th century road freight was once again the most important component of Nippon Express's business.

The year of the company's inauguration, 1872, had also seen the opening of Japan's first railway service. In 1873, the trains began to accept freight, and by 1875 Naikoku Tsu-un Kaisha was handling rail freight, transporting it between sender and station at one end and between station and recipient at the other. With the expansion of the railway network over the following two decades, railway cargo became a major source of revenue.

As Naikoku Tsu-un Kaisha, the company began to operate river freight transport services in 1876. The following year, a paddle steamer was acquired, the first to be used for civil purposes in Japan. River transportation declined in importance with the appearance of motorized road transport and the expansion of the railways. Once again, however, the wheel came full circle: in 1990, containerized shipping and other marine transport earned Nippon Express almost ¥120 billion.

Naikoku Tsu-un Kaisha entered the motorized road transport business in 1911 with the purchase of four trucks for the carriage of imperial mail. Their white-liveried drivers confined their activities to the driving of the trucks; loading and unloading them was too menial a task.

The spread of railways and motor vehicles at a time of rapid industrialization and trade attracted new entrants into the express transportation business. By 1910, there were 5,000 competitors; by 1919, the number had almost doubled. This made for an overcrowded market at a time when Japan, in common with most of the developed world, was suffering from the severe economic slump that followed World War I. In 1923, an earthquake devastated Tokyo, after which scarce funds had to go into reconstruction, with further adverse economic effects. The Japanese economy's response to the doldrums of the 1920s was to rationalize. In harmony with this tendency, the government decided to reduce the number of competitors in the transportation business. In 1928, Naikoku Tsu-un Kaisha merged with its two main competitors, Nihon Un-so Kaisha and Meiji Un-so Kaisha.

The resulting joint-stock company, named Kokusai Tsu-un, or International Express, engaged in both domestic and international freighting and was the immediate predecessor of Nippon Express. At war with China during the late 1930s, the Japanese government was actively managing the economy in the national interest; under the new Express Business Law and the Nippon Express Co. Ltd. Law, Kokusai Tsu-un was dissolved and its business taken over by Nippon Express, which came into being on October 1, 1937, and was 53 percent government-owned.

Postwar Growth

After World War II, the Allied forces occupying Japan considered that too much of the country's economic power was concentrated in too few hands. Among other initiatives, they threatened to break up Nippon Express, whose market strength was contrary to the provisions of the Law for Decentralization of Excessive Economic Power. In the end, however, the company was not abolished but, beginning in February 1950, became a private enterprise.

During the postwar years, Nippon Express embarked on a series of measures that equipped it to share in and to contribute to Japan's economic boom. These measures changed both the way the company was run and the nature of its business. Nippon Express was among the earliest companies to adopt a decentralized management structure, delegating a high degree of financial autonomy to its divisions. It also gradually reduced its focus on the handling of rail freight, hitherto its most important activity, and diversified into other forms of transport and into completely new business areas.

One of the earliest diversifications came in 1949, when the company began to engage in international air freight forwarding, acting as cargo sales agent for various international airlines. This new enterprise received the stamp of International Air Transport Association approval in 1953. Air transportation proved a profitable area. In 1990, the magazine *Business Japan* interviewed Nippon Express's vice-president Kiyosumi Hosokawa, who was also chairman of the International Air Express Association of

Key Dates:

1872: Riku-un Moto Kaisha (General Land Transportation Co.) is created.
1875: The company is renamed Naikoku Tsu-un Kabushiki Kaisha (Domestic Express Co.).
1928: The firm merges with its two main competitors to form Kokusai Tsu-un Kabushiki Kaisha (International Express Co.).
1937: Kokusai Tsu-un is dissolved, and its business is taken over by Nippon Express Co. Ltd.
1950: The company is privatized.
1962: A U.S.-based subsidiary is created.
1973: The company buys its first container vessel.
1990: Nippon Express groups its businesses under three regional supervisory bodies in order to streamline operations.
1998: The firm launches a major restructuring in response to Japan's economic climate.
2004: Nippon Express becomes the first major transportation concern to win a governmental license to launch a special mail deliveries service in Japan.

Japan and the International Airfreight Forwarders' Association of Japan. He stated that the air freight business could look back on three decades of steady growth, interrupted only by the two oil crises. He added that "the air freight growth rate is far higher than Japan's economic growth rate."

Another landmark year was 1955, when Nippon Express became an authorized travel agent. In doing so, it was returning to a business in which it had dabbled 80 years before, as a sideline to its horse-drawn haulage service. Sosuke Sasaki had founded an association of inns approved for use by his messengers. Soon the company had begun to act as a travel agency, offering a room-booking service to the public, a side of the business that had atrophied with the coming of the railways. This time, however, the emphasis was on arranging package tours of Japan and on assisting the Japanese with foreign travel. In the two decades from their launch in 1968, more than three million people would buy the "Look" packages catering to Japanese tourists abroad.

Expansion and Diversification: 1950s–80s

The late 1950s and the 1960s were a time of phenomenal expansion for the Japanese economy. Between 1960 and 1970, a year-on-year growth rate of about 13 percent was sustained. Foreign trade, too, was increasing dramatically: during the same years, imports multiplied in value by a factor of four and exports by a factor of five. In order to be able to play its part in the internationalization of Japanese industry, Nippon Express embarked on the construction of a network of overseas offices that eventually spanned five continents. The process began in 1958 with the inauguration of a representative office in New York. The year 1962 saw the establishment of a New York subsidiary, which by 1991 had a chain of 97 U.S. offices with 1,808 employees.

During the 1960s, the marine transportation industry was revolutionized by the advent of containerization. Since the early

years of the 20th century, road and rail freight had been packed in large, tough boxes, which rendered loading and unloading more efficient and reduced the risk of loss or damage. In the 1960s, container ships that were able to use the same type of box began to be built. The adoption of standard-size containers, which could be loaded on ship, truck, or train, facilitated intermodal transport, allowing the forwarder to combine different modes of transport to get the most cost-effective package. For example, in shipping to Brazil from Japan, Nippon Express sent containers by sea to Seattle, then trucked the containers to Miami before transferring the goods to airplanes for the last stage of the journey.

Nippon Express was quick to see the advantages of containerization. As well as using the scheduled services of other shipping companies to carry its containers around the coasts of Japan, Nippon Express acquired ships of its own. In 1973, it bought its first container vessel, the Acacia Maru, and launched a cargo service between Tokyo and Tomakomai.

International container services, too, became an important source of business for Nippon Express, attracting both Japanese and overseas customers. Germany was one of the most important markets for Far Eastern container traffic; in 1991, Nippon Express (Deutschland) reported that it obtained half its revenue from Japanese companies and half from German companies buying from and selling into Japan. In the 1990s, sea transportation by container vessel became one of Nippon Express's most rapidly growing services.

During the 1970s, Nippon Express became a highly diversified business. Plant transportation and installation was one new venture. As early as 1966, the company had become involved with the transportation and installation of petrochemical equipment, which had begun in 1966 with its participation in the construction of a Peru oil refinery. The year 1977 marked the start of Nippon Express's involvement in a major petrochemical construction project in Iran. This project was cut short by Iran's internal upheavals a few years later.

The 1970s and 1980s were a period of continued expansion for Nippon Express's overseas activities. Subsidiaries opened in Singapore in 1973, the Netherlands in 1977, Hong Kong and Brazil in 1979, the United Kingdom and West Germany in 1981, Saudi Arabia, Belgium, and Canada in 1983, Malaysia in 1984, Australia and France in 1985, and Italy in 1986.

Also during the 1970s and 1980s, a new market known as *takuhaibin*—parcel delivery service—was opening up in Japan. Domestic or international door-to-door delivery of documents and small packages was provided, with a guaranteed delivery deadline. This service was originally a U.S. import, introduced by DHL Corporation, which established DHL Japan in 1979. Once launched in Japan, it was a runaway success, both with consumers and with the business community that needed to exchange items such as contracts and product samples with minimal delay. The profile of Japan's industrial output was changing to include less heavy industry and more high-technology products; for carrying such fragile, relatively low-volume loads, the express parcel service was ideal.

Nippon Express was soon a leader in the parcel delivery market, with its Pelican services aimed at deliveries to the private individual and Arrow services for company-to-company deliveries. In 1990, Nippon Express was second only to Yamato in the Japanese parcel delivery market, and whereas this was 41 percent of Yamato's business, it represented only 28 percent of Nippon Express's.

Success Continues in the Early 1990s

Nippon Express had one outstanding advantage both in parcel deliveries and other types of international transportation. Whereas other carriers set up links with foreign companies, Nippon Express had its own overseas representation. This consisted in 1990 of 31 overseas affiliates and 16 representative offices. It had 366,000 square meters of overseas warehouse space in addition to its two million square meters inside Japan.

To manage this vast network in the most efficient way possible, and speed the decision-making process, in 1990 the company grouped its overseas branches and affiliates under three regional supervisory bodies. Nippon Express U.S.A., Inc. was responsible for North and South America, Nippon Express (U.K.) Ltd. took charge of Europe, and Nippon Express (H.K.) Co., Ltd. covered Southeast Asia and Oceania.

Nippon Express appeared to be set to maintain the competitive edge that its extensive international network afforded it. September 1990 saw it entering the Mexican freight market ahead of its Japanese competitors with the launch of Nippon Express de Mexico. In April 1991, it opened a new trucking service between Singapore and Malaysia.

A key component of Nippon Express's integration was the efficient communication of information. Through the late 1980s, the company was engaged in establishing an online data network to connect all its offices, enabling it to track individual cargo items across the world. Its communications expertise enabled it to engage in several new specializations such as just-in-time (JIT) deliveries. JIT is a manufacturing method whereby parts are brought to the shop floor from a remote warehouse at the moment they are needed in order to minimize on-site stock holding. In 1989, Nippon Express's U.S. information networks enabled it to start NEX Transport Inc. to supply JIT services to Japanese automobile manufacturers operating in Ohio.

The company continued to invest in new ventures at home and overseas. In December 1990, it announced that it would set up an air cargo company, the Japan Universal System Transport Co. Ltd., as a joint venture with Japan Airlines Co. Ltd. and the Yamato Transport Co. Ltd. In March 1991, Nippon Express made public another new venture, the Dalian Nittsu Container Manufacturing Company, which would manufacture shipping containers in Dalian, China.

In an economy that was a byword for dynamism, Nippon Express was one of the most successful and fastest growing companies of all. In June 1991, *Tokyo Business Today* ranked it Japan's 127th most profitable company, a position to which it had climbed from 164th the year before, with a 50 percent growth in declared income. The Japanese economy had its difficulties, however. A labor shortage was pushing up costs, and in August 1990 Nippon Express and other leaders of the transportation industry applied to the Japanese Ministry of Transport for permission to raise tariffs for regular delivery

routes for the first time in five years. At the same time, chartered delivery prices were raised. Such price adjustments enabled the company to sustain its profitability despite the rising costs.

Automation was one response to a labor shortage, and in March 1991 the company announced that it was about to install a new information network to manage its two million railway containers. Also in 1991, it announced plans to invest ¥540 million in modernizing its international telecommunications network.

In June 1991, Shoichiro Hamanaka succeeded Takeshi Nagaoka as president. Hamanaka, who had been with the company since 1954, had previously been in charge of the Sendai branch and of the general affairs and labor management divisions.

Looking to the future, Nippon Express now saw that it faced the threat of increased competition in its domestic distribution business, which the Japanese government was taking steps to deregulate. To deal with this competition, it planned to rely on accurate market research and an ever-improving quality of service to its customers. Overseas, it prepared for the coming unification of the European market and the opening up of Eastern Europe by developing its European trucking network and improving its warehousing facilities. By increasing its representation in China and building a Chinese transport network, Nippon Express readied itself for the expansion in trade that was expected to ensue from the reversion of Hong Kong to Chinese rule in 1997.

Mid-1990s and Beyond

By the mid-1990s, Japan's economy had bottomed out, forcing Nippon Express to revamp its strategy in order to shore up profits. The firm immediately began to cut costs and streamline operations, but the slowdown in sales as a result of Japan's financial crisis took its toll on the company's bottom line. The Kobe earthquake in 1995 made matters worse, affecting Nippon Express's revenues by an estimated ¥8 billion.

During 1998, the company launched a major business restructuring. In order to gain a larger share of the home-delivery service market, the firm converted 125 of its cargo collection centers to handle home-delivery requests. Over 20 branch offices were also refurbished to allow for home-delivery. Nippon Express created several new divisions as part of the restructuring, including a unit to focus on offering logistics services to handle customers' outsourcing needs and a new business designed to market the company's inventory-management system. Despite the company's efforts, sales and profits fell for the second straight year in 1999.

Masahiko Okabe, named company president in 1999, commented on industry conditions in a November 1999 *Nikkei Weekly* interview. He pointed to a major problem transportation companies were contending with—competitive pricing. "Transportation charges have fallen sharply since the end of the boom economy in the early 1990s. Over the past decade, trucking charges for raw materials and heavy goods have declined around 10 percent and charges for international air and sea shipments around 25 percent. They are continuing to fall under pressure from customers for lower charges." As Japan's economy remained stagnant, Nippon Express and its competitors were forced to remain sensitive to rising consumer demands. As such, Nippon Express looked for ways to add value to its transportation services in order to keep its customer's distribution expenses at a minimum.

During the early years of the new century, a changing distribution industry and heightened competition forced the company to focus on new distribution services including third-party logistics (3PL), e-commerce distribution, and transportation for the recycling industry. Nippon Express also worked to strengthen its international businesses. A new 3PL subsidiary, NEX Global Logistics, was launched in the United States in 2000, and the firm also began offering domestic air and truck service in certain U.S. cities in 2003. In addition, Nippon Express secured a new Chinese license that enabled it to provide seamless mixed cargo transportation, both by land and sea, between Japan and China. The license enabled the company to deliver cargo faster than many of its competitors by allowing it to avoid certain customs restrictions.

Japan allowed private firms to begin handling mail delivery in 2003. By early 2004, Nippon Express had become the first major transportation concern to win a license from the Ministry of Public Management, Home Affairs, Posts and Telecommunications. The license gave the firm rights to launch a special mail deliveries service in Japan.

A turnaround in Japan's economy appeared unlikely in the immediate future. With that fact in mind, Nippon Express understood that it had its work cut out for it. Nevertheless, management remained optimistic. The company was dedicated to providing a wide range of logistics services in a cost-friendly fashion, as well as expanding its information systems and bolstering its international and small package business. While only time would tell if the company's restructuring efforts would pay off, Nippon Express appeared to be on track to remain a leading name in transportation for years to come.

Principal Subsidiaries

Nittsu Shoji Co., Ltd.; Nittsu Real Estate Co., Ltd.; Nippon Shipping Co., Ltd.; Nippon Truck Co., Ltd.; Bingo Express Co., Ltd.; Nippon Express U.S.A., Inc.; Nippon Express (Deutschland) GmbH; Nippon Express H.K. Co., Ltd.

Principal Competitors

Nippon Yusen Kabushiki Kaisha (NYK Line); Yamato Transport Co. Ltd.

Further Reading

"Courier/Small Package Service in the Spotlight," *Quarterly Survey, Japanese Finance and Industry*, Industrial Bank of Japan, 1987.

Eller, David, "Resolved: The Nittsu Enigma," *Containerisation International*, January 1988.

"Exploiting New Fields Seen as Key to Recovery," *Daily Yomiuri*, September 9, 1999.

Flynn, Matthew, "Nippon Express in Profit and Revenue Falls," *Lloyd's List*, May 27, 1999, p. 2.

Fujimura, Masanori, "Int'l Air Deliveries Continue Sharp Growth," *Business Japan*, June 1990.

General Information on Nippon Express, Tokyo: Nippon Express Co. Ltd, 1987.

"Goods Distributors Looking for Route out of Slump," *Nikkei Weekly*, November 29, 1999, p. 5.

"Here Come the Just-in-Time Japanese Truckers," *Economist*, December 5, 1987.

Mino, Hokaji, "Courier, Shipping Services Meet the Needs of the Times," *Business Japan*, June 1988.

"Nippon Express Group's Profits Decline in FY '93," *Japan Economic Newswire*, May 20, 1994.

"Nippon Express Profit Seen Suffering from Quake," *Japan Economic Newswire*, March 15, 1995.

"Nippon Express Sets Sights on Seamless Transport," *Nikkei Weekly*, January 14, 2003.

"Nippon Express Targets Rival's Home-Delivery Share," *Nikkei Weekly*, May 11, 1998, p. 5.

Putzger, Ian, "Nippon Express Launches 3PL Subsidiary," *Journal of Commerce*, March 28, 2000, p. 10.

"Transporters, Trading Firms Moving into Inland China," *Nikkei Weekly*, February 23, 2004.

—Alison Classe
—update: Christina M. Stansell

Nobleza Piccardo SAICF

Cerrito 268
Buenos Aires, C.F. 1010AAF
Argentina
Telephone: (+54) (11) 4370 6784
Fax: (+54) (11) 4370 6059
Web site: http://www.noblezapiccardo.com

Public Company
Incorporated: 1913 as Compania Nacional de Tabacos
   S.A.
Employees: 1,700
Sales: ARS 353.66 million ($104.95 million) (2002)
Stock Exchanges: Over the Counter
Ticker Symbols: NBZP F
NAIC: 312221 Cigarette Manufacturing

Nobleza Piccardo SAICF is the smaller of Argentina's two cigarette manufacturers but has the longer pedigree. Using roughly equal amounts of imported and Argentine tobacco, it manufactures and distributes 14 brands, including Lucky Strike and Camel, which are produced and marketed under license. Although Nobleza Piccardo is a public company, almost all shares are held by giant British American Tobacco plc, a British-based company with operations in over 100 countries.

Piccardo and Nacional: 1898–1933

Juan Piccardo and Juan Oneto founded Manufactura de Tabacos Piccardo y Cia. in 1898 by purchasing a hand-operated cigarette machine and installing it in a downtown Buenos Aires building. Their first cigarette was called 43 for reasons now obscure but said to relate to a market rally on the Buenos Aires Stock Exchange that became a symbol of optimism. Like most—perhaps all—Argentine cigarettes at the time, 43 was made from dark tobacco. The company followed with Casino and later with other brands, many of them—such as Reina Victoria (Queen Victoria)—intended to denote quality and prestige; nevertheless, in some parts of Argentina, their cigarettes were sold in mini-packs for only two centavos. Before long the company was able to move to a factory at another Buenos Aires location.

Publicity-savvy Piccardo donated a French-built airplane to the Argentine army in 1912 and presented another the following year to an Argentinian who had just established a record flight over water. This was only the beginning of the company's dedication to sporting exploits, with a special emphasis on motor racing. Piccardo also enhanced its image by making donations to public health, education, parks, and recreation. One of Oneto's good deeds was to stake Aristotle Onassis to a business importing tobacco from the Near East in 1929. Far from the shipping tycoon he would become, Onassis was then a refugee from Turkey selling nuts on the streets of Buenos Aires. In gratitude, he later gave Oneto a tapestry with the numerals "43" stitched in the center.

The cigarette manufacturing business was highly fragmented when, in 1911–12, the recently formed, London-based Argentine Tobacco Co., Ltd. purchased 19 manufacturers and combined them into a single operation, Compania Argentina de Tabacos Ltda. British American Tobacco Company Ltd. (BAT) was already a worldwide organization planning to expand to South America. It reacted to the news by incorporating Compania Nacional de Tabacos S.A. in Buenos Aires in 1913. This company was then used to purchase Bozetti & Co., one of the few surviving independent tobacco businesses with its own Buenos Aires factory. Bozetti marketed its products under the Misterio brand name. Nacional also formed a subsidiary for the purpose of acquiring cheaper local brands that it could manufacture and market along with Misterio and established BAT brands. It purchased rival Argentina de Tabacos in 1919 and opened operations in Cordoba, Mendoza, Rosario, and Tucuman between 1918 and 1922.

Nacional's sales reached three million packs in 1919, but four years later its flagship brand, Pour La Noblesse, sold 14 million packs alone. This was a traditional cigarette made of dark tobacco, as were other company favorites such as Parisiennes, Embajadores, and Senadores, but "blond" cigarettes made of American bright tobacco were also gaining popularity. In 1925, Nacional initiated production of Virginia tobacco in Argentina, and in 1927 it began manufacturing its first blends with imported tobaccos. Among the brands it was producing and marketing now were Jockey Club and Player's, along with cheaper standbys like Cuyanos and Flor de Ceibo. It introduced

---

Company Perspectives:

At Nobleza Piccardo we share the ability to create and innovate, and are constantly seeking new success opportunities. The passion for our business is another of the characteristics of our employees, who show a firm commitment towards the Company and work hard to turn Nobleza Piccardo into the leading tobacco company in the Argentine market.

---

no less than six brands in 1927; two dark ones and four blonds. Besides its multiplicity of brands, a vital factor in Nacional's success was its ability to deliver them reliably to its dealers by means of 400 vans. This fleet had to be renewed every two years because of the appalling condition of Argentina's roads.

The advent of the Great Depression meant a period of stagnation for Nacional. In 1932, BAT had to write off loans that Nacional and its subsidiaries had incurred for advertising expenses. The company's brands were being undercut by cheap 20 centavo packs brought out by two rivals. Seeking to improve its profit margin, Nacional converted to direct selling, establishing a pooling arrangement with two other cigarette manufacturers— one of them Piccardo. The enterprise was renamed Compania Nobleza de Tabacos—a name taken from Pour La Noblesse— in 1933 because an executive order had banned the word ''Nacional'' in corporate names.

Narrowing the Playing Field: 1940s to the Mid-1970s

Six firms accounted for 70 percent of all tobacco manufactured in Argentina in 1942. Argentine tobacco accounted for almost 60 percent of the tobacco used, and low-priced cigarettes were almost exclusively of Argentine tobacco. The tobacco of choice at the time was still the dark type by a margin of more than four to one. Nobleza opened a second manufacturing plant, in Zuviria, Salta, which was closer to the tobacco-growing parts of Argentina, in 1945. Piccardo, in 1960, introduced the first filtered Argentine cigarettes: versions of 43, Gloster, and Florida. Nobleza introduced the first king-size Argentine cigarette, a version of Jockey Club, in 1962. This brand was the most popular one in Argentina and held one-quarter of the cigarette market in 1967; by 1976, when it was still the leading brand, it was available in five versions. Nobleza followed up this success by introducing the first 100-millimeter cigarette (1969), the first slim-size one (1972), and the first 120-millimeter cigarette (1976). Piccardo introduced 43/70, a blend of dark and blond tobacco, in 1969.

Only five cigarette manufacturers remained in Argentina in 1966. Nobleza was well out in front, with 43 percent of the market. Piccardo—which, with a 14 percent market share, was in fourth place—was publicly traded but also partly owned by Liggett & Myers, a leading U.S.-based cigarette firm. During 1966–67, Philip Morris International Inc. acquired Massalin & Celasco, and a Dutch firm purchased the two others. By 1972, Piccardo had moved up to third place. L&M was its best seller, but it also manufactured two more of the top ten brands. The company had processing plants in Salta and Tucuman and was exporting reduced-price tobacco lots to France. In the mid-1970s, all Argentine cigarette companies were losing money because the government would not allow them to raise prices in order to keep up with inflation.

Nobleza Piccardo: Late 1970s to the Mid-2000s

After Liggett & Myers decided to withdraw from the international portion of its business, Piccardo merged with Nobleza in 1978 to form Nobleza Piccardo, receiving 30 percent of the combined shares of the merged company to Nobleza's 70 percent. Since Nobleza held 43 percent of the cigarette market at the time and Piccardo 20 percent, the merged company was now by far the leader in its field, with two Buenos Aires factories, four processing plants, and 13 sales offices. By this time, the tobacco companies had been allowed to raise their prices, and in 1980 Nobleza Piccardo ranked sixth in sales among all Argentine companies. Taxes imposed on its product, however, absorbed two-thirds of the company's revenues and represented a sum of almost $1 billion.

Nobleza Piccardo bought the recently vacated General Motors auto-manufacturing factory in suburban San Martin in 1979 to replace its existing ones in Buenos Aires. This plant opened in 1981, the year Nobleza Piccardo was licensed to introduce Lucky Strike and Camel to the Argentine market. However, the company was facing strong competition in the form of Massalin Particulares S.A., the firm formed in 1979 by the merger of Massalin y Celasco with the two other cigarette manufacturers. Backed by heavy advertising for Philip Morris's brands, which included Marlboro, Massalin Particulares held 42 percent of the market in 1982 compared to Nobleza Piccardo's 58 percent. Jockey Club, in king-size form, was by far the leading brand, followed by king-size 43/70 and Jockey Club in its 100-millimeter version. Another development of this period was the virtual disappearance of dark cigarettes; by 1983, blonds held three-quarters of the market and blends more than fourth-fifths of the remaining quarter.

Nobleza Piccardo introduced Derby in 1988 and purchased the printing firm of S.A. Alejandro Bianchi y Cia. Ltda. the following year. Bianchi and another printing subsidiary, Grafica San Juan S.A., were merged into the parent company the following year. By 1992, Nobleza Piccardo had fallen behind Massalin Particulares in market share but was still the top tobacco exporter. In 1995, Nobleza Piccardo deployed the highest-speed cigarette-manufacturing machines in the industry, capable of turning out 11,000 cigarettes per minute. The following year, the company introduced Kent Super Lights. Camel was growing faster than other brands in Argentina thanks to the popular Joe Camel cigarette character and an advertising campaign that also featured his Hard Pack blues band, whose members wore identical wraparound sunglasses. Nobleza Piccardo also introduced many extensions of existing brands, such as low tar and nicotine versions and hard boxes to supplement soft packs.

Nobleza Piccardo was spending about $125 million a year on advertising in the late 1990s. In 1998, it established its own distribution network in all chief Argentine cities, replacing its wholesalers at a cost of about $20 million. In 2000, BAT spent $33 million to buy most of the remaining Nobleza Piccardo outstanding shares, raising its ownership of common stock to almost 96 percent. By this time the company had fallen well back of Massalin Particulares, which now held 63 percent of reported cigarette sales. Not reported but a definite threat to profits was the black market that thrived because of heavy taxes on cigarettes. Illegal sales were estimated at 16 to 20 percent of the market.

Key Dates:

1898: The Piccardo company is founded in Buenos Aires.

1913: Compania Nacional de Tabacos, a British American Tobacco subidiary, is incorporated.

1925: Nacional initiates begins production of Virginia tobacco in Argentina.

1933: Nacional is renamed Compania Nobleza de Tabacos.

1960: Piccardo introduces filtered cigarettes to the Argentine market.

1967: Nobleza's Jockey Club accounts for one-quarter of all cigarette sales.

1978: Nobleza and Piccardo merge to form Nobleza Piccardo.

1980: Nobleza Piccardo ranks sixth in sales among all Argentine companies.

1992: Nobleza Piccardo has fallen behind rival Masalin Particulares S.A. in market share.

2000: British American Tobacco buys most of the remaining outstanding shares of Nobleza Piccardo stock.

2002: The firm remains marginally profitable despite Argentina's deep economic crisis and continued loss of market share.

The economic crisis that resulted in Argentina failing to make payments on its debts in 2001 resulted in a devaluation of the peso in early 2002. Economic activity fell precipitously in 2002, with Nobleza Piccardo's net profit falling by 93 percent. The company attributed its drop in earnings to sustaining its price levels in spite of higher costs. Seemingly as an economy measure, Nobleza Piccardo sold its leaf purchasing and processing operation to Standard Tobacco Argentina late in 2002 for $5 million. The sale included the threshing plant of El Carril in the province of Salta and the company's six purchasing stations at El Carril and Alvarado, Salta; Perico, Jujuy; Villa Alberdi, Tucuman; Leandro N. Alem, Misiones; and Goya, Corrientes. Three redistribution centers in the provinces of Santa Fe, Cordoba, and Bahia Blanca remained. It was agreed that Standard would henceforth acquire and process Nobleza Piccardo's tobacco leaf. However, the company continued to own its own warehouses, near the Salta airport. Tobacco bought by the company was delivered there and then shipped to San Martin, where Nobleza Piccardo continued to make its own blends. Also in 2002, the company introduced Viceroy and reintroduced Pall Mall to the Argentine market.

Nobleza Piccardo had gross sales (in terms of prices at the end of 2001) of ARS 1.11 billion ($329.38 million) in 2002 and net sales (gross sales less taxes) of ARS 353.66 million ($104.94 million). This represented a further erosion of the firm's share of the cigarette market; it was now being outsold two to one by Masalin Particulares. Net profit came to only ARS 1.07 million ($296,736) in this year of grave economic crisis. Nobleza Piccardo's brands included Lucky Strike, Camel, Derby, Parisiennes, Kool, Barclay, 43/70, Gitanes Blondes, Jockey Club, Pall Mall, and Player's.

Nobleza Piccardo monitored the manufacturing processes at its San Martin factory by computer and used laser rays to ensure uniform ventilation of its "lights" (lower tar and nicotine cigarettes) and its rolling and packaging machines. Capacity had increased to 14,000 cigarettes per minute, and the packing machinery was capable of turning out at least 530 packs per minute. The company employed satellite tracking for its road-transport distribution, a voice-response system to reply to questions from its suppliers, satellite communications between its office and installations, pen-computing and laptop technology for all members of its sales team, and toll-free numbers for consumer comments on its products. It became the first Argentine tobacco company to launch a Web site in 2002. For 2003, Nobleza Piccardo planned to invest ARS 50 million (about $15 million) in marketing, software, and technology needed to modernize its plant. Since the factory was operating at only 50 percent of installed capacity, the company had plans to export production to countries who found the firm's cigarettes, priced in devalued pesos, newly attractive.

Principal Competitors

Massalin Particulares, S.A.

Further Reading

"Argentina: El regreso a lo natural," *Mercado*, February 12, 1981, pp. 35–36.

"Argentina: Nobleza Piccardo Invests Pesos $50 Mil.," *South American Business Information* (Business and Company ASAP database), November 7, 2002.

"Argentina: Trends in the Tobacco Industry," South American *Business Information* (Business and Company ASAP database), August 24, 1999.

Bickers, Christopher, "Nobleza-Piccardo: 100 Years of 43," *World Tobacco*, July 1998, pp. 30–31.

——, "Peso Devaluation Offers Leaf Export Openings" and "Standard Buys Nobleza's Leaf Operation," *World Tobacco*, March 2002, pp. 20, 22.

"Un camino para dos," *Mercado*, August 3, 1978, pp. 56–58.

Catania, Monica, and Carlos Carballo, *La actividad tabacalera en Argentina a partir de la decada de 1970*, San Martin, Buenos Aires: Centro de Estudios Labores, 1985, pp. 22–23, 51.

Cox, Harold, *The Global Cigarette.* New York and Oxford: Oxford University Press, 2000, pp. 128–31, 252–54.

"El deporte favorito de Piccardo," *Mercado*, November 17, 1977, pp. 71–72.

Friedland, Jonathan, "Under Siege in the U.S., Joe Camel Pops Up Alive, Well in Argentina," *Wall Street Journal*, September 10, 1996, p. B1.

"Jockey tiene algo nuevo que decir," *Mercado*, February 19, 1976, pp. 29–30.

Moyano, Julio, ed., *The Argentine Economy*, Buenos Aires: J. Moyano Comunicacciones, pp. 508–09.

"Nobleza: Life after Processing," *World Tobacco*, September 2002, p. 69.

"Piccardo aumenta su nivel," *Mercado*, August 3, 1972, pp. 32–35.

"Piccardo: trescientos pesos bastaron," May 3, 1973, pp. 29–30.

El tabaco en la Republica Argentina, Buenos Aires: Instituto Agrario Argentina, 1944.

—Robert Halasz

Noranda Inc.

181 Bay Street, Suite 200
Toronto, Ontario M5J 2T3
Canada
Telephone: (416) 982-7111
Fax: (416) 982-7423
Web site: http://www.noranda.com

Public Company
Incorporated: 1922 as Noranda Mines Ltd.
Employees: 15,000
Sales: $4.65 billion (2003)
Stock Exchanges: New York Toronto
Ticker Symbol: NRD
NAIC: 212231 Lead Ore and Zinc Ore Mining; 212234
　　Copper Ore and Nickel Ore Mining; 212221 Gold Ore
　　Mining; 212222 Silver Ore Mining

Noranda Inc. is one of the largest mining and metals companies in the world with operations in 18 countries. Production of copper and nickel accounts for the majority of Noranda's revenues—the company also mines aluminum, zinc, and precious metals. Noranda restructured in the late 1990s by selling off its forest products and oil and gas businesses in order to focus on its core metals and mining assets.

Origins and Development: 1920s–50s

The history of Noranda begins with the story of a prospector named Edmund Horne, and a hunch. During the early 1920s, at a time when northern Canada was unchartered—the area was mostly wilderness, and prospectors preferred to stay on the familiar grounds of Ontario—Horne was drawn to the Rouyn district in northeastern Quebec. He visited Rouyn repeatedly, because he believed it "didn't seem sensible that all the good geology should quit at the Ontario border!" Horne could reach Rouyn only by way of a chain of lakes and rivers.

His enthusiasm was contagious, and soon a group of 12 men had raised C$225 to finance further explorations. The effort paid off when word of Horne's first strike made it to S.C.

Thomson and H.W. Chadbourne, two United States mining engineers with a syndicate of investors interested in exploring Canadian mines. In February 1922, the syndicate bought an option on Horne's mining claims in Ontario and Quebec and exercised it. Noranda Mines Ltd. was incorporated in 1922 to acquire the U.S. syndicate's mining claims.

The next task was to make the area more accessible to miners. Roads were cut through the forests, and travel often required skis and sleds. Some equipment arrived by barge and ski-equipped plane, both of which could travel the lakes and rivers with relative ease. The mine began producing gold, copper ore, sulfur, and iron, and Noranda convinced the Canadian government to lay roads, railways, and power lines. Eventually, Noranda Mines Ltd. constructed a mill and a smelter, and a city began to take shape in what was once untamed wilderness.

Not satisfied with this initial success, Noranda Mines began to acquire other holdings. In 1927, it bought 80 percent of the stock in Waite-Ackerman-Montgomery Mines, which changed its name six years later to Waite Amulet Mines Ltd. Also that year, Noranda acquired a majority interest in Aldermac Mines Ltd., of Rouyn.

Because it believed strongly that Canadian ore should be processed in Canadian plants, Noranda Mines eventually acquired or built several processing companies. Canadian Copper Refiners, Ltd., a company in which Noranda Mines held majority interest, was constructed in eastern Canada in 1929 as a joint effort of Noranda Mines, London's British Metal Corporation, and Nichols Copper Company of New York City. The following year, Noranda Mines purchased a rod and wire mill just east of the copper refinery and bought a substantial interest in Canada Wire & Cable Company, Ltd., of Leaside, Ontario.

In the early 1930s, Noranda Power Company, Ltd., a new subsidiary, was formed. In 1934, this company took over the parent firm's power rights and leases on the Victoria River, only to transfer the rights to the government's National Electricity Syndicate under a new agreement four years later.

The 1930s set the stage for a decades-long tradition of growth through acquisitions, as Noranda made its climb to the ranks of Canada's largest companies. In 1935, the firm bought a substantial interest in Pamour Porcupine Mines, Ltd., located in the Porcupine district of Ontario. A few years later, it also acquired a 63.75 percent interest in Compania Minera La India for its gold mines in Nicaragua. In 1939, Noranda bought the controlling interest in Aunor Gold Mines, Ltd., which was formed earlier that year to take over additional Porcupine property. The late 1930s also saw the creation of Noranda Exploration Company, Ltd., a subsidiary formed in 1938 to undertake exploration work in Quebec.

By 1936, output of metals in the province of Quebec totaled well over C$30.6 million, thanks to the development sparked by Noranda Mines. From 1926 to 1936, Noranda stimulated the nation's economy by pouring into it approximately C$71 million in supplies, transportation, salaries, and taxes. By the end of World War II, the area's mineral production had climbed to C$150 million annually.

Perhaps due to the events of World War II, however, the 1940s and even the 1950s saw less corporate activity than earlier decades. Still, the company made two major acquisitions, including Castle Tretheway Mines Ltd.'s Omega Gold Mines, which Noranda Mines bought jointly with Anglo-Huronian Ltd. in 1944. Four years later, Noranda Mines and a subsidiary, Waite Amulet Mines, bought more than 500,000 shares of Mining Corporation of Canada Ltd. In 1956, Noranda acquired a sizable interest in Bouzan Mines Ltd.

Growth Continues in the 1960s–70s

By the early 1960s, the company began to see a flurry of activity, beginning with the acquisition of Western Copper Mills Ltd., located near Vancouver, in 1963. The new acquisition joined with Noranda Copper & Brass Ltd., a Noranda Mines subsidiary, to form Noranda Copper Mills Ltd. Also that year, the company acquired the remaining shares of Mining Corporation of Canada, which continued the firm's exploration efforts. In addition, Anglo-Huronian, Bouzan Mines, Kerr-Addison Gold Mines, and Prospectors Airways—all Noranda affiliates—merged to form Kerr-Addison Mines Ltd.

In December 1964, Noranda Mines made its most important acquisition when it merged with Geco Mines Ltd. The new company retained the name Noranda Mines Ltd. Based in Manitouwadge, in northwestern Ontario, Geco was a major producer of copper, silver, and zinc. The following year, Canada Wire & Cable, in which Noranda Mines had an interest since 1964, became a wholly owned subsidiary. In 1966, the firm also bought 80 percent of Norcast Manufacturing Ltd., which then purchased shares in Wolverine Die Cast Group. Also that year, Noranda Mines formed Noranda Manufacturing, Ltd., a holding

company for its various manufacturing subsidiaries. Noranda Mines also acquired a controlling interest in Pacific Coast Company in 1967.

By 1968, Noranda Mines had become a widely held mining company with most of its activities centered in Quebec. Employees numbered 5,000. It was also in 1968 that 37-year-old Alfred Powis became president of Noranda Mines. Formerly a financial analyst in Montreal with Sun Life Assurance Company of Canada, Powis joined Noranda Mines in 1955 as an assistant to the firm's treasurer. Under Powis's leadership, the company began its evolution from a regionally based mining firm to an industry leader with subsidiaries involved in energy and forestry, in addition to mining.

It seems that Powis's aggressive tactics, including a chain of takeovers, were key contributors to the company's success. Powis's success did not come overnight, however. The company first had to weather the impact of several large investments made in the late 1960s.

In the early 1970s, the mining industry, as a whole, was depressed. Consequently, Noranda Mines had limited earnings from 1966 to 1972, increasing in that period by only 21 percent. In addition, gross capital employed rose from C$500 million in 1967 to C$1.5 billion in 1973. The rate of return on that capital dropped from 16 percent in 1966 to only 9 percent in 1972. Powis worked through the cyclical, industry-wide recession, and finally, in 1973, investments began to pay off; Noranda's sales climbed 75 percent to C$121 million, a company record.

Additional investments made in the early 1970s included Tara Exploration and Development Ltd., which owned lead and zinc properties in Ireland, and Belledune Fertilizer Ltd., acquired from Albright & Wilson Ltd. in 1972. The year 1974 saw even more acquisitions, including a 55 percent stake in Fraser Companies Ltd. and Alberta Sulphate Ltd., and 38.5 percent of Frialco, a Cayman Island firm with controlling interest in Friguia, a bauxite mining company in the Republic of Guinea. In addition, Noranda Sales Corporation of Canada Ltd., a subsidiary, bought in the spring of 1971 a 50 percent interest in Rudolf Wolff & Company, a British trading firm dealing with metals and other commodities.

The mining industry, known for caution, watched Powis march on this unusual acquisition path, then witnessed Noranda sales climb from C$60 million in 1972 to C$155 million two years later. It was during this era that a *Canadian Business* contributor referred to Powis as "the Houdini of the Canadian mining industry."

Diversification in the Late 1970s–80s

In 1976, however, earnings dropped to C$47 million. Demand for the two biggest contributors to the company's sales—copper and zinc—began to lag. The automobile industry was replacing zinc die castings with plastics. Copper, too, was being supplanted by various substitutes, from aluminum for power lines to glass fibers for communication cables.

In addition, many of the firm's earlier investments had been financed with short-term loans, which seemed like a good idea when business was booming. Although Powis acknowledged that money was tight at Noranda Mines in 1977, he defended his decision to load up on short-term debt, telling *Canadian Business,* ''We put restraints on at the end of 1974 when we could see that things were getting grim. Those clamps have stayed on.'' Powis also indicated he was prepared for the tight zinc market.

To help wait out the cyclical downturn in the mining industry, the company diversified, concentrating on other business segments, such as manufacturing and forestry. As Powis stated in the July 22, 1974, issue of *Iron Age,* the future of Noranda would be ''where our nose takes us. . . . We originally got into manufacturing so we could have a home for our products.'' In addition, the company invested millions of dollars in efforts to convert some old saw mills into profitable lumber plants. That marked its entry into the forestry industry.

In 1981, Powis lost a long-running, highly publicized battle with Brascan, Ltd., a Toronto holding company owned by Edward and Peter Bronfman. Brascan became Noranda Mine's largest stockholder, and Powis, who became accountable to the Bronfmans, stayed on as chief executive officer. Brascan added C$500 million to Noranda Mines's bankroll and set the company back on its acquisition path.

In 1981, Noranda Mines first picked up Maclaren Power and Paper Company, a newsprint, pulp, and wood-products enterprise located in Buckingham, Quebec. The following year, it bought 49.8 percent of MacMillan Bloedel, Canada's largest paper company. The minority shareholding was sufficient to give Noranda Mines control of the company. While the acquisitions were intended to decrease the company's concentration on the lagging copper market, the expansion of the early 1980s initially resulted in decreased profits: in 1980 the firm had record earnings of C$408 million, while in 1983 it lost C$117 million due to interest payments on the acquisitions and expansion loans, which totaled C$169 million in 1983.

Powis and Adam Zimmerman, president of Noranda Mines, shared an optimism that began to pay off in the mid-1980s.

Sales of zinc, fine paper, and other products began to recover, and, just as Noranda Mines finished a C$300 million addition to its aluminum smelter, demand for the element skyrocketed. Diversification was paying off, and to reflect its expanded activities the company changed its name from Noranda Mines Ltd. to Noranda Inc. in 1984.

In 1986—after a C$253,900 loss caused by strikes and other labor problems in 1985—the firm's net income stood at C$43,300 and total revenue was C$3.55 billion. In 1987, as various labor strikes were resolved, company officials predicted the firm would see its highest earnings since 1980. Also in 1987, the company was restructured, dividing its various business segments into four subsidiaries: Noranda Energy, Noranda Forest, Noranda Minerals, and Noranda Manufacturing.

In October 1989, after a heated battle between Powis and former protege William James—who had left Noranda and become chairman of Falconbridge, Ltd., a rival mining company—Noranda bought 50 percent of Falconbridge. Ownership of the multibillion dollar company was shared by Trelleborg A.B., a Sweden-based conglomerate. The move not only gave Noranda half of Falconbridge but also ownership of Kidd Creek, a Timmons, Ontario, copper and zinc mine that Noranda had long coveted.

Challenges in the Late 1980s and Early 1990s

Although most of Noranda's assets were located in North America, Noranda marketed its products globally. The firm's goal was to be a premier diversified natural resources company. Under the leadership of President David Kerr, the company remained committed to a sensitive environmental policy, a pledge necessary for any business to be well received in the 21st century. Nevertheless, the company's professions of environmental responsibility and the public's perception of its efforts often diverged. Noranda's Forest division was a frequent target of criticism. While environmental groups decried clear-cutting, Noranda Forest officials often cited re-seeding programs that planted twice as many seedlings as were cut. Although the company was unable to meet environmentalists' demands in some areas, Noranda Forest was compelled to meet consumer demands for recycled paper.

Noranda Forest Recycled Papers was established in 1989 and operated at a mill with a 50-year history of recycled paper production. The mill was the first to receive the Canadian Standards Association's Environmental Choice designation for its inclusion of more than 50 percent recycled paper and 5 percent postconsumer fiber in its fine paper. The operation was very successful, and Noranda raised the postconsumer content of its recycled paper to 10 percent in line with 1991 federal guidelines.

Noranda made halting progress in its handling of labor relations in the 1990s. When officials at a subsidiary, Brenda Mines Ltd. in British Columbia, realized that the mine's ore vein would be exhausted within three years, the company took steps to ensure a more stable transition for its workers. With the cooperation of the Canadian government's department of Employment and Immigration, the provincial Ministry of Advanced Education Training and Technology, representatives of management, and hourly and salaried employees, a job placement center was created to help employees recognize and prepare for new job prospects. The program earned an award from the Canadian Mental Health Association for "excellence in addressing the personal issues" related to the closure.

The Brenda Mines scenario, however, did not necessarily characterize labor relations in the late 1980s and early 1990s. A 94-day strike at the Noranda Aluminum smelter in New Madrid, Missouri, capped a 20-year adversarial relationship at that Noranda division. A ten-month strike that started in July of 1990 at Brunswick Mining and Smelting's huge zinc/lead mine near Bathurst, New Brunswick, threatened to shut down that division. Noranda executives admitted that management-labor relations were never lower, but agreements in 1991 at both subsidiaries focused on more open communications at all levels.

The lingering recession of the early 1990s hit Noranda hard in 1991, when it posted a C$133 million loss for the year. Although the mining and metals and oil and gas groups posted net gains, a C$75 million loss in the forest division cut into those profits. The balance of the losses was blamed on overproduction and the high level of the Canadian dollar relative to the U.S. dollar. The poor financial performance inspired management throughout the conglomerate to focus on cash conservation, cost containment, and asset sales. In 1991, the Canada Wire and Cable division was sold to Alcatel Cable for more than C$400 million.

Changes in the Mid-1990s and Beyond

In the early 1990s, Noranda's Alfred Powis and David Kerr were cautiously optimistic about the conglomerate's future. Encouraging forecasts of persistently low interest rates and a weakening of the Canadian dollar had been offset by lingering low levels of demand for Noranda's products. The company's leadership hoped to merely ride out the financial storm.

For the next several years, Noranda sold off certain unprofitable assets, including holdings in Hemlo Gold, Minnova Inc., MacMillan Bloedel, Central Canada Potash, Norandex Inc., and a 9 percent stake in Noranda Forest Inc. It also looked to make key investments that would pay off in the future. In 1994, it acquired 31.9 million shares of Falconbridge in order to become its largest shareholder. In addition, Noranda purchased the remaining shares of Brunswick Mining and Smelting Corp. that it did not already own. The deal bolstered Noranda's zinc holdings and strengthened its leading position in the industry.

While diversification had played an important role in the firm's business strategy since 1980s, Noranda began to backpedal in 1997 in order to focus on its core metals and mining businesses, and in 1998 divested its forest products and oil and gas businesses—Norcen Energy, Noranda Forest, and Canadian Hunter. A much leaner company, Noranda was left to shore up profits within its metals and mining operations.

It made several strategic moves that included the purchase of several Chilean companies that eventually formed Noranda Chile S.A., a subsidiary that operated the Altotnorte copper smelter in northern Chile. The company also continued to increase its stake in Falconbridge. In 1999, it acquired a stake in the Altamira copper and zinc mine in Peru. Construction on the

mine—one of the largest mining projects in the world—was completed in 2001.

The early years of the 21st century were marked by low selling prices and a labor strike at the company's Horne copper smelter. Debt was also on the rise due mainly to expensive mining projects that were in the works. During 2002, the company reported a loss of $447 million. That year the company cut costs by shuttering its Gaspe, Quebec, copper smelter and the Warsaw, Kentucky, wheel plant. The firm also aligned various operations of Noranda and Falconbridge in an attempt to recover profits. It announced that its main focus for future growth would be in the copper and nickel mining industries.

Things began to turn around for Noranda in 2003. The labor strike was resolved and profitability was restored at its Canadian copper operations. Strong demand from China also signaled that prices for Noranda's products would rise. Overall, the company secured net income of $34 million for the year. By early 2004, rumors began to circulate that Noranda's major shareholder, Brascan Corp., was looking for a buyer. Because it would most likely fetch a price of approximately $4.5 billion, potential Noranda suitors would surely come from the pool of industry giants—such as BHP Billiton or Rio Tinto plc. Although consolidation was sweeping through the industry, a deal had yet to be announced by June 2004. While it appeared as though a change might be on the horizon for Noranda, its name in the mining world would no doubt continue to be a mainstay for years to come.

Principal Subsidiaries

Geco Mine; Brunswick Mining; Canadian Electrolytic Zinc Ltd. (95.2%); Mattabi Mines Ltd. (60%); Micro Metallics Corporation; Noranda Mining and Exploration Inc.; Noranda Group Pty. Ltd.; Noranda Sales Corporation Ltd.; Noranda Sales Corporation of Canada Ltd.; Noranda Sales, Inc.; Novicourt Inc. (61%); RudolfWolff & Co. Ltd.; American Racing Equipment, Inc.; Noranda Metallurgy Inc.; Noranda Aluminum, Inc.; Noranda Copper Smelting and Refining; Norandex Inc.; Wire Rope Industries Ltd. (85%); James Maclearen Industries; Noranda Advanced Materials; J.P. Levesque & Sons, Inc.; Northwood Panelborard Company; Heath Steele; Mines Gaspe; Matagami; Fundicion Refimet S.A. (24.8%); Falconbridge Limited (46%); Brunswick Smelting; CCR Refinery; CEZinc; Home Smelter; New Madrid Smelter; Falcondo Mine, Smelter and Refinery (85%); Kidd Creek Operations; Battle Mountain Complex; Golden Giant Mine; Holloway Joint Venture (85%); Kori Kollo (88%); James Maclaren Industries Inc.; Norbord Industries Inc.

Principal Competitors

Corporación Nacional del Cobre de Chile; Inco Ltd.; Teck Cominco Ltd.

Further Reading

Antoniak, Jane, "Profile: Green Giant," *CA Magazine*, March 1991.

Beizer, James, "Metal Mining Troubles Loom Large in Canada," *Iron Age*, July 22, 1974.

Daly, John, "The Final Victory: Falconbridge May Prove to Be Too Expensive," *Maclean's*, October 9, 1989.

Damsell, Keith, "Noranda Spinoffs Are Hot on Debut," *Financial Post*, December 9, 1998.

Francis, Diane, "Alfred Powis as Corporate Superman," *Maclean's*, November 27, 1989.

Lamphier, Gary, "Noranda Offers $225-million to Buy Rest of Brunswick Unit," *Globe and Mail*, July 25, 1995.

"New Strategic Plan for Noranda," *Skillings Mining Review*, November 22, 1997, p. 7.

"Noranda Gets Buyout Interest Amid Consolidation in Mining," *Wall Street Journal*, June 17, 2004, p. C4.

"Rationale for Restructuring," *Mergers & Acquisitions in Canada*, December 1, 1997.

Roberts, Leslie, *Noranda*, Toronto: Clarke-Irwin, 1956.

"Wedding Bells Ring out All Over," *Courier-Mail*, June 18, 2004.

Young, Jim, "Noranda Meets New Fine Paper Postconsumer Waste Standards," *Pulp & Paper*, March 1991.

Zuehlke, Mark, "The Right Way to Handle a Closure," *Canadian Business*, August 1991.

—Kim M. Magon
—updates: April Dougal and Christina M. Stansell

180s, L.L.C.

701 East Pratt Street
Suite 180
Baltimore, Maryland 21202
U.S.A.
Telephone: (410) 534-6320
Toll Free: (877) 725-4386
Fax: (410) 534-6321
Web site: http://www.180s.com

Private Company
Incorporated: 1997 as Big Bang Products, L.L.C.
Employees: 122
Sales: $47 million (2003)
NAIC: 315999 Other Apparel Accessories and Other
    Apparel Manufacturing; 339999 All Other
    Miscellaneous Manufacturing

180s, L.L.C., is known for its distinctive, highly engineered ear warmers, called Arctic 180s, which wrap around the back of the neck. The company produces other innovative products, including sunglasses and Exhale gloves, and has two other main brands: Gorgonz Performance Work Gear and From the Blue (fashion-oriented ear warmers for women). "Nothing that we do is gadgetry," company cofounder Brian Le Gette told the *Baltimore Sun,* "We try to reinvent the wheel on products that are already out there." The company's products are distributed in more than 18,000 locations around the world. 180s has sold more than 17 million ear warmers. The company is a vigorous defender of its more than 100 patents and patents pending. *Inc.* magazine has recognized the company as the Fastest Growing Inner-City Company in America and one of the country's fastest growing private companies overall. Company headquarters and the 180s Performance Lab are housed in a futuristic building on Baltimore's Inner Harbor. 180s also has offices in Canada and France.

Wharton Origins

The story of 180s began in 1993, as Ron L. Wilson II and Brian Le Gette, two new graduate students at the University of Pennsylvania's Wharton School of Business, discussed possible business ventures over a beer. According to the *Baltimore Sun,* after sifting through schemes such as selling cheese steaks in China, Wilson revisited an idea he had had while trudging through the snow as an undergraduate at Virginia Polytechnic University: building a better ear warmer.

Traditional earmuffs, with polyester fur earpieces and a cheap plastic band over the top of the head, were bulky, and could interfere with one's hairstyle and headwear. They did not stay on very well and, most important, they did not look cool. Their design, recalled the *Oregonian,* dated back to the 1870s, when a Maine farmhand created "The Greenwood Champion Ear Protector." Their inventor, Chester Greenwood, started a company in Farmington, Maine that was producing 400,000 pairs a year before his death in 1937. Although materials were updated over the years from the original haywire and beaver pelt, earmuffs had changed little since the 1950s. The original fur "ear protectors" were replaced by synthetic fleece products and, reported the *San Diego Tribune,* even L.L. Bean, Maine's giant catalog retailer, dropped them from its extensive winterwear collection in the mid-1980s.

Having picked up some engineering background as undergraduates, Wilson and Le Gette spent two years coming up with a revolutionary ear warmer design. They developed a sleeker, sportier version that wrapped around the back of the neck. Advanced, microfiber materials kept weight and bulk to a minimum while allowing the user to hear through them. Designed with active people in mind, they stayed in place during sports, and folded up easily. The pair began pitching their ear warmers on the University of Pennsylvania campus in fall 1994, reported *Inc.*

The new ear warmers, a 180-degree departure from the competition, were dubbed "Arctic 180s." *Entrepreneur Magazine* reported Wilson and Le Gette spent $50,000 to produce their first big batch of 5,000 ear warmers. "We were down to our last $100," Wilson told the *Oregonian.* Le Gette described to *Entrepreneur* their 1996 debut on the QVC television shopping network: "By minute four we hadn't sold anything, but by minute eight and a half, we were sold out." The 15-minute segment ended with 3,000 on back order. QVC soon ordered another shipment of 25,000; according to *Inc.,* 600,000 were sold through this channel by 1997. *Inc.* reported that Le Gette

Company Perspectives:

At 180s, we see what's out there, turn it on its head, un-cover its blind spots, and pull a wholly new performance wear solution from the wreckage. And it's not just uniquely differ-ent, its uniquely better. Jumpstarted in 1995 with the sole mission of pushing performance wear beyond all previous boundaries, 180s was created for athletes who are pushing themselves, in the most unforgiving environments. Sound like fun? Then you're one of us.

and Wilson were originally talked into trying out TV retailing by two classmates who had landed internships at QVC.

Wilson and Le Gette funded development of the prototype with $7,500 in credit card charges. They then raised $100,000 from 18 fellow MBA students, who were future investment bankers after all. Within a couple of years, family and friends raised the kitty to $2 million.

Incorporating in Maryland in 1997

The pair moved the business to a shared Chicago apartment in 1995. Two years later, they relocated to Canton, a suburb of Baltimore. Their new two-story, 10,670-square-foot building had started life in 1875 as a pencil factory and had also been used as a parking garage and a base for counterfeiters.

The company hired its first five employees in 1997. Le Gette and Wilson served as co-presidents and co-CEOs of the venture, which was incorporated in Maryland on September 26, 1997 as Big Bang Products, L.L.C.. A holding company, Gray Matter Holdings, L.L.C., was incorporated on February 10, 1998.

Sales reached $340,000 in 1998, when the product was distributed only through TV and catalogs. According to the *Sun,* after the company's bank balance fell to $1,000, Big Bang focused on getting products into department stores with the help of hired marketing experts. This was a turning point for the company, which would double its sales every year for the next several years.

New York's Paragon Sports became the first retail store to carry 180s, reported the *Sun.* Macy's, Eddie Bauer, Dick's, Nordstrom, Galyan's, and others soon followed. The ear warm-ers sold for $20 to $30.

Gray Matter began breaking even in 1999, and profit growth was soon in the double digits. By 2000, Gray Matter's sales were up to $10 million, a 750 percent increase in one year. The product line-up had expanded to include the recently added Snap-2-It folding beach mat/towel and the Aggressor, a radio-controlled airplane launched as a kite. The Gorgonz Group, Inc. was created on March 29, 1999 to focus on work-oriented accessories and industrial design. Big Bang opened an office in Paris during 2000.

Chief financial officer Gib Mason joined Big Bang in 1999. After his arrival, the company started a mentoring program for inner city students, dubbed "Little Bang."

The company's workforce numbered 31 employees in 2001. Sales grew to $32.6 million in 2002, when the company had 85 employees. More than 15,000 retail outlets distributed Big Bang products in the United States. They were also available in more than 40 other countries, and branch offices had been set up in Canada and France.

Ernst and Young named Big Bang "Entrepreneur of the Year" in 2002. Big Bang had introduced 35 different products over the years, though only ten items remained in the catalog. These included redesigned lightweight, scratchproof sunglasses, or "eyegear," whose earpieces folded over the front of the lenses to protect them. Another newer product was the Kelsyus floating beach chair.

Big Bang also updated the 180s with new fabrics, including leopard print and the like for fashion-conscious females. Women were enthusiastic consumers of the product; a separate line for them called From the Blue was launched in the winter of 2003–04.

Between 1998 and 2002, reported the *Baltimore Sun,* reve-nues increased 9,669 percent. This led to being named the fastest growing private company in the inner city by *Inc.* maga-zine and the Initiative for a Competitive Inner City. The value of the original $2 million investment was estimated to have in-creased tenfold, reported the *Baltimore Sun.*

New Name, New HQ in 2003

Growth left Big Bang desperate for more office and ware-house space. In April 2003 the company signed a seven-year lease on 50,000 square feet of offices in the Hall of Exploration at the Columbus Center, a former marine science museum on Baltimore's Inner Harbor. The company began shifting employ-ees into the new space, which would include a retail outlet, in December 2003. Big Bang Products was renamed 180s, L.L.C. in early 2003, and sales reached $47 million that year. The *Baltimore Sun* quoted a SportScanINFO study giving 180s a 4.1 percent share of the winter headwear market. By October 2003, the company had shipped 15 million units, reported the *Balti-more Business Journal.*

The distinctive 180s ear warmers were seen on high-profile figures, including, reported the *Sun,* three Supreme Court jus-tices who had worn them to the presidential inauguration of George W. Bush. Big Bang relied on guerilla marketing tech-niques and gave away lots of product to create awareness quickly. The company distributed ear warmers and sunglasses to movie stars at the Sundance Film Festival. Eventual product placements included Matt Damon wearing 180s in the comedy *Stuck on You.* Big Bang also sponsored the 2000 Bud Light Beach Volleyball Series, dispensing 1,000 Snap-2-It beach mats to division winners, and donated half of a 1,000-unit order of sunglasses to U.S. Marines in Afghanistan. The company show-cased its 2004 lineup at Baltimore's Shamrock 5K Run, which drew 4,000 participants.

180s continued to look for products to reinvent. According to its research, nine out of ten glove wearers complained of cold fingers. 180s debuted its innovative Exhale gloves in September 2003. With the Exhale Heating System O , users could distrib-ute heat from their breath throughout the glove, particularly the

Key Dates:

1994: Two Wharton MBA students develop the wrap-around ear warmer.
1996: 180s debuts on QVC.
1997: Big Bang moves to Baltimore.
1999: The company breaks even.
2003: Big Bang is renamed 180s, L.L.C.; Exhale gloves are introduced.

fingertips, without having to take the gloves off. *Fortune* called them one of the six best outdoor products of the year.

New products in development included ear warmers with built-in headphones supplied by JVC Company of America. 180s also sold headphones designed to fit into the ear warmers separately, for about $20 a pair.

The company owned about 100 patents and patents pending and aggressively pursued purveyors of knock-offs. By 2004, 180s had filed more than 100 copyright infringement lawsuits.

Principal Subsidiaries

180s of Canada Corporation; 180s Europe SARL (France).

Principal Divisions

180s; From the Blue; Gorgonz.

Principal Competitors

adidas A.G.; Columbia Sportswear Company; Earbags of Sweden; Luxottica Group; Nike, Inc.; Oakley, Inc.

Further Reading

"Big Bang's Good Move to Harbor," *Baltimore Business Journal,* Opinion Sec., April 28, 2003.
Dash, Julekha, "Making Headgear Profitable," *Baltimore Business Journal,* October 3, 2003.
——, "180s Set for Move to Inner Harbor," *Baltimore Business Journal,* December 19, 2003.
Dresser, Michael, and June Arney, "Earmuff Maker Leases Harbor Tourism Site in Baltimore," *Baltimore Sun,* April 17, 2003.
Fieser, Ezra, "Columbus Center Gets New Tenant, at Long Last," *Daily Record* (Baltimore), April 17, 2003.
Green, Abigail, "Knowing What It Takes to Be an Entrepreneur," *UMBC Generations* (Baltimore), Fall 2003.
Fenn, Donna, "Innovative Minds: The B-School Boys," *Inc.,* September 2002.
Hopkins, Jamie Smith, "180s Reinvents Its Way to Top of Inner-City List; Growth: A New Baltimore Company That Makes 'Performance Wear' Is Ranked First in the National Inner City 100," *Baltimore Sun,* April 6, 2004, p. 1D.
Kercheval, Nancy, "Baltimore-Based 180s Named by Inc. Magazine As 9th Fastest Growing Privately Held Company," *Daily Record* (Baltimore), January 24, 2004.
Kim, Ann S., "Earmuffs? Ear Warmers? A Rose Is a Rose," *San Diego Union-Tribune,* January 19, 2003, p. E12.
Laermer, Richard, "Arctic 180s Can Be Music to Cold Ears," *PR Week* (U.S.A.), January 13, 2003, p. 28.
McInery, Vivian, "Trend Spotter: Winter Warmth; Earmuffs' The Next Generation Is Here," *Oregonian* (Portland), December 22, 2002, p. L7.
Parks, Ann, "180s Inc. Gets Aggressive with Infringement Suits," *Daily Record* (Baltimore), January 28, 2004.
Walker, Andrea K., "Big Bang Keeps on Growing; Niche: From the Sale of 1,000 Ear Warmers, the Founders of Canton-Based Big Bang Products Have Built a $40 Million Business by Reinventing Everyday Products and Selling Them," *Baltimore Sun,* July 8, 2002, p. 10C.
Williams, Geoff, "Star Lite," *Entrepreneur Magazine,* March 1, 2001.
Wilmot-Weidman, Kimberly, "Launching Pad: Big Bang Products Used QVC to Get Off the Ground," *Baltimore Business Journal,* August 18, 2000.

—Frederick C. Ingram

OTTAKAR'S

Ottakar's plc

St. John's House, 72 St. John's
London
SW11 1PT
United Kingdom
Telephone: 44 20 7978 7700
Fax: 44 20 7978 7711
Web site: http://www.ottakars.co.uk

Public Company
Incorporated: 1987
Employees: 1,360
Sales: £153.7 million ($246 million) (2004)
Stock Exchanges: London
Ticker Symbol: OKR
NAIC: 451211 Book Stores

Ottakar's plc is one of the United Kingdom's largest and fastest-growing retail booksellers. London-based Ottakar's is also one of the country's few truly nationally operating booksellers, with a network of more than 120 shops across the United Kingdom, including a strong presence in Scotland. The company boasts a highly flexible bookshop concept that enables it to adapt its store sizes and features to individual local markets. As such, the company is able to retail successfully in catchment areas of as low as 32,000 people, with store sizes ranging from as small as 2,000 square feet to as much as 20,000 square feet. Ottakar's has successfully adapted retail bookstore sales techniques from the United States, introducing family-friendly bookstores to the United Kingdom, featuring in-store reading areas, coffee bars, and space for events such as readings and book signings. The company's larger stores also feature stationers corners and the company-developed Launch Pad concept of books and educational materials geared toward the 5-year-old to 12-year-old set. Ottakar's—the name comes from the title of a Tintin comic book—also has distinguished itself through its hiring policy, giving it a very stable, highly knowledgeable sales staff. Founder James Heanage remains the company's managing director and one of its largest shareholders. Ottakar's has been listed on the London Stock Exchange since 1998. In its 2004 fiscal year the company recorded sales of nearly £154 million ($246 million).

Adman's Brainstorm in the 1980s

James Heanage began his professional career in the advertising industry, working first for D'Arcy MacManus, before joining Ogilvy & Mather in the early 1980s. There, Heanage became the account director for the prestigious Guinness account. Yet Heanage remained unsatisfied. As he told the *Sunday Times,* "I knew that if I didn't like the Guinness account, I would never like advertising." Instead, Heanage began looking for new business opportunities, adding: "I had always thought I would work for myself eventually. I was always anti-establishment—if you believe you can do something better than the person above you, there are few alternatives. I was not good at working for anyone else."

Heanage started searching for a potential outlet for his entrepreneurial plans. Among the ideas he considered were the creation of a video player rental service for ski resorts and restaurants with bookstores. Heanage's work with Ogilvy & Mather eventually helped him spot a new niche, however. While conducting consumer panel studies, Heanage discovered a gap in the United Kingdom's retail book market.

Into the mid-1980s, that market was dominated in large part by traditional, small-scale, and independent booksellers. While a number of national chains had begun to develop—such as WH Smith, Waterstone's, and Dillons—these chains tended to target only the largest urban markets. Book shopping remained an intimidating proposition for many British consumers. Yet Heanage recognized the potential for adapting new bookselling formats then being tested in the United States—which included added reading areas and coffee bars to encourage customers—that were transforming the book shopping experience into a more informal, family-oriented activity.

Heanage began devising a business model for his proposed company. One of the features of Heanage's model was to target smaller market locations, where rents were low and his own stores would face less competition from the larger chains. Heanage also sought a more restricted, specialist orientation to his shops. As he told the *Sunday Times:* "Our idea was to use new technology to target customers within a specific area with a range of books that matched their interests, thus bringing a higher stock turnaround and profit."

Heanage settled on the name Ottakar's for his company, after the title of one his favorite books, *King Ottakar's Revenge,* part of the Tintin comic book series. Heanage next found a business partner in Donaldson Lufkin Jenrette investment banker Philip Dunne, who went on to become the company's chairman. Heanage and Dunne both took out second mortgages on their homes in order to launch Ottakar's, then went in search of additional venture capital, eventually convincing Baronsmead to put up £1.5 million.

By 1987, Heanage and Dunne had succeeded in finding locations in Brighton and Banbury for their first two stores. The new stores opened in 1988, but found mixed results. If the Banbury site proved successful from the start, the Brighton store was another story, and the company was forced to shut that store down after less than two years. Heanage himself described the Brighton shop as "an unmitigated disaster." Yet Heanage remained undeterred, as he told *The Sunday Times:* "We got the wrong site in Brighton. You can make a bad idea work in a good location, but not a good idea in a bad location. But I was confident that only the location was wrong because the idea was successful in Banbury and it was clear one part of the equation worked."

Ottakar's opened its third site in Salisbury in 1989, and with the success of that shop, was able to shut down the Brighton store and move ahead with building a national chain. Nonetheless, for the time being, Ottakar's remained a loss-making enterprise, lacking the critical mass that would enable it to sell books profitably.

The turning point for the company came in 1990, when Baronsmead agreed to put up an addition £1 million, which Ottakar's used to acquire the small six-store chain of the Town Booksellers group, which was active mostly in the West Country. With eight stores now converted to the Ottakar's concept, the company turned its first profit by 1992.

In that year, the company found new financial backing when venture capital specialist Foreign & Colonial paid in £1 million, in exchange for a majority share of Ottakar's. Backing from Foreign & Colonial enabled the company to step up its expansion. In that year, it made an unsuccessful attempt to acquire the Hammicks bookstore chain, then already a prominent bookseller in the southeast. Instead, Ottakar's continued adding new

stores, and by 1995, the company had already achieved sales of more than £9 million. The company continued adding new stores, some through acquisition, such as its purchase of four Bells Bookshops in 1998. That acquisition brought the company's total number of shops to nearly 50, for sales of more than £36 million.

National Bookseller for the New Century

By then, however, Foreign & Colonial had begun to seek to cash in on its investment. While Heanage set his own goals on a public offering, for a time the company appeared a possible candidate for being bought up by a larger rival, specifically the United States' Barnes & Noble, then seeking an entry into the United Kingdom.

The two sides failed to reach an agreement, however, and Ottakar's did indeed go public in 1999. The initial public offering was a great success; launched at 153p per share, the stock price shot up to 204p by the end of its first day's trading, and soon after soared to 270p per share. The listing also gave Ottakar's the distinction of being the only pure-play bookseller to be listed on the London Stock Exchange.

Ottakar's turned toward the new century with ambitious expansion plans. The company continued to expand its store chain, entering the Scottish market with a store in Glasgow in 1999. Yet Ottakar's also sought a piece of the Internet action, launching an ambitious e-commerce site as well. At the same time, the company believed it had discovered a new consumer niche—that of the 5- to 12-year-old "post-Early Learning" segment—and developed a new retail format, Launch Pad, combining books and other educational toys, games, and materials. The company began rolling out the Launch Pad concept as in-store boutiques in its larger stores, while also developing an independent retail format for the concept.

By 1999, however, it became clear that the company's expansion plans had been too ambitious. As Heanage admitted to the *Bookseller:* "The most obvious failure of 1999 was opening some shops that didn't work initially and one that hasn't worked at all. Until then we had exercised enormous care in the selection of every single site. But the pressure of what was going on meant that we didn't research them quite as we should have." With its store expansion sputtering, and its e-commerce site performing well below expectations, the company found itself struggling to retain profits. By the end of that year, Heanage was forced to issue a profit warning—sending the company's stock price plunging to just 66p per share.

The fall in the company's share price left it dangerously vulnerable to a potential hostile takeover. Luckily for the company, however, no takeover ever came. Instead, Heanage devised a new strategy to carry the company into the next century. Ottakar's pulled the plug on its e-commerce site—which Heanage claimed had been set up in the first place due to pressure from the company's investors—and instead launched a new intranet focused on using online capacity to streamline its supply chain side. The company also scaled back its plans for the Launch Pad format, restricting it to an in-store boutique concept.

By 2000, Heanage and his management team had succeeded in returning Ottakar's to growth and profits. The company now

Key Dates:

1987: James Heanage develops a business model for a chain of bookstores in England, and forms Ottakar's together with Philip Dunne.

1988: The first two stores open in Brighton and Banbury.

1989: The third store opens in Salisbury.

1990: The company closes the Brighton shop; the six-store Town Booksellers group is acquired.

1992: Ottakar's turns a profit; new capital backing is received from Foreign & Colonial.

1998: The company acquires four Bells Bookstores and goes public on the London Stock Exchange.

1999: The company launches an e-commerce web site and Launch Pad concept, but is forced to issue a profit warning at the end of the year.

2002: Eight James Thin bookstores in Scotland are acquired.

2003: Ottakar's acquires 24 Hammicks bookstores in southern England, boosting the company into the top three U.K. booksellers.

2004: The company announces the potential for as many as 300 Ottakar's shops; the first store in Ireland opens.

sought to continue its store expansion, in part through targeting other bookstore chains. In 2001, the company was rumored to be in talks to acquire the troubled Waterstone's bookstore chain from HMV, although no deal materialized.

Instead, the company maintained an organic growth track for the time being, raising its store numbers past 75 by the end of 2001, and seeing its revenues near £100 million for the first time. At last, in 2002, the company turned to Scotland, acquiring the eight specialist book shops of the struggling James Thin company, which had been placed in receivership earlier that year. With its store network now at 86 stores, Ottakar's began a crucial shift away from its former reliance on book wholesalers to making its first direct purchases within Britain's publishing industry.

A new turning point for Ottakar's came in 2003, when the company announced that it had agreed to acquire 24 of the 25 Hammicks bookstores operating in southeastern England. The deal, dubbed "transforming" by the *Bookseller,* gave Ottakar's a nationally operating chain of more than 120 stores, with revenues nearing £154 million by the end of the company's 2004 fiscal year.

Buoyed by its new industry clout, Ottakar's set its sights on further expansion, with Heanage announcing in early 2004 the potential for as many as 300 Ottakar's shops in the United Kingdom over time. The company also began its first moves outside of its home base, opening its first store in Ireland that year. Meanwhile, the company had been experimenting with releasing its own line of branded products, including exclusive book titles, but also calendars, gift cards, stationery, and the like. Under Heanage's guidance, Ottakar's had built itself a solid position among the United Kingdom's retail bookstore leaders.

Principal Competitors

WH Smith plc; HMV Group plc; Surridge Dawson Ltd.; Martin Retail Group Ltd.; Waterstone's Booksellers Ltd.; Eason and Son Ltd.; Blackwell Ltd.; Borders UK Ltd.; TOG Ltd.; Remainders Ltd.; Ian Allan Group Ltd.

Further Reading

Aldrick, Philip, "Ottakar's a Success Tale," *Daily Telegraph (London, England),* March 26, 2004.

Blackwell, David, "Ottakar's Looks to New Chapter of Growth," *Financial Times,* September 25, 2002, p. 28.

Bury, Liz, "Ottakar's Pushes Back the Boundaries," *Bookseller,* September 27, 2002, p. 8.

Bury, Liz, and Richard Lewis, "Ottakar's Claims Hammicks: Transforming Deal Sets Out Ottakar's Challenge to Titans Waterstone's and WH Smith," *Bookseller,* May 2, 2003, p. 5.

Fraser, Ian, "Books with Coffee to Create a Marriage Made in Heaven," *Sunday Herald (Glasgow, Scotland),* September 29, 2002, p. 5.

Lewis, Richard, "Thins Helps Ottakar's Grow," *Bookseller,* April 4, 2003, p. 7.

"Ottakar's Flexes Its Format," *Bookseller,* April 2, 2004, p. 7.

"Ottakar's Gets Real," *Bookseller,* April 9, 2004, p. 7.

"The Return to Grace," *Bookseller,* May 17, 2002, p. 28.

Steiner, Rupert, "Disillusioned Ad Man Turned Over New Leaf As a Bookseller," *Sunday Times,* January 17, 1999, p. 10.

Waller, Phil, and Martin Faint, "Ottakar's Turning Exciting New Page," *Birmingham Post (England),* May 13, 2004, p. 21.

—M.L. Cohen

PGG

Pendleton Grain Growers Inc.

1000 S.W. Dorion Avenue
Pendleton, Oregon 97802-2938
U.S.A.
Telephone: (541) 276-7611
Toll Free: (800) 422-7611
Fax: (541) 276-4839
Web site: http://www.pggcountry.com

Cooperative
Incorporated: 1930
Employees: 205
Sales: $71.67 million (2003)
NAIC: 422510 Grain and Bean Wholesalers; 422910
Farm Supplies Wholesalers; 444220 Nursery and
Garden Centers; 421710 Hardware Wholesalers;
444130 Hardware Stores; 422720 Petroleum and
Petroleum Products Wholesalers (Except Bulk
Stations and Terminals); 424910 Agricultural
Chemicals Merchant Wholesalers

Pendleton Grain Growers Inc. is an agricultural cooperative formed in 1929 in response to an initiative by the Federal Farm Board. Its Grain Division provides marketing, storage, transportation of grain and other commodities, and grain storage facilities at approximately 30 locations in Umatilla, Union, and Wallowa counties in Oregon. PGG's five stores in its Retail Division sell hardware, fencing, feed, lawn and garden, pump and irrigation products, and livestock supplies.

1930s: Steady Growth Through Collaborative Action

In the late 1920s and early 1930s, in response to sliding wheat prices, hard economic times, and the Agricultural Marketing Act of 1929, the Federal Farm Board introduced a system designed to empower farmers to own their own businesses and marketing facilities. This form of farm relief employed a hierarchy of cooperatives: The Farmers National Grain Corporation (FNGC) worked with the North Pacific Grain Growers (NPGG) as its regional arm and purchasing agent in the Northwest. The

NPGG purchased wheat in turn from a network of 30 local Oregon-based cooperatives.

Pendleton Grain Growers (PGG), one such local cooperative, was organized in late 1929 by a group of about 70 farmers in Umatilla County, Oregon. According to PGG's first president and manager from 1934 to 1970, James Hill, Jr., in *PGG: The Growth of a Cooperative*, "The existing grain marketing structure was unstable. Some trade practices were questionable, and the farmer was at the mercy of the trade." With speculation causing daily price swings, PGG formed "to protect the farmer against these surges and also raise the price of wheat."

Those who joined the new cooperative signed up 500,000 bushels of wheat for initial production. They purchased stock in PGG at $30 a share, with one share allowed for each 1,000 bushels they produced. Farmers put 10 percent of their stock purchase down in cash and signed a note for the balance. PGG used this money and notes to buy stock in NPGG. The new cooperative incorporated in early 1930 and elected its first board of directors. It had 71 members, who put up a total of $2,248.50 in cash, pledging another $20,416.50.

PGG's members had a vision that included bulk handling of grain, using the Columbia River to transport grain, developing a feed mill, and building bulk grain storage facilities. Bit by bit, they began to put this vision into practice: buying and selling grain; acting as an agent for grain stabilization advances for farmers from federal funds; making loans for seed and sacks; providing a dependable, low-cost source of supplies. The cooperative's directors asked the Federal Farm Board to seek guarantees that farmers would not be asked for a margin if wheat prices fell below the loan value on crops. It provided competition in grain buying sufficient to begin to raise the price of wheat. By the end of its first year of operation, PGG had made a profit of close to $5,000 and paid an 8 percent cash dividend on subscribed stock. In its second year, the cooperative earned a net profit of almost $7,500.

According to a retrospective view expressed in PGG's 20th annual report, "The obvious trend was to bulk facilities.... As rapidly as our financial status would allow, we bought, built and acquired facilities with which to handle our growers' crops."

Company Perspectives:

This is a co-operative business; our shareholders are also our customers. Customers who choose to do business with us provide our reason for existence; we will treat everyone as though they are the owner of the business. Employee involvement is our way of life. We are a team and must treat each other with trust and respect. Management's role is to mentor. We will provide training opportunities to every employee and provide an open and approachable presence in the workplace. Listening will be our greatest skill. Our health is beyond value; we will always take the time and give the extra effort to be safe. Profits are the ultimate measure of how efficiently we perform our mission. Our goal is to share profits between our shareholders and our employees.

During the 1930s, the cooperative engaged in acquisitions, new ventures, and mergers that enabled it to realize this objective. In 1931, PGG negotiated a contract with FNGC to handle all grain buying at Pendleton through the local cooperative's offices. In 1932, it merged with Helix Grain Growers Inc., another local cooperative, and thus increased its capital stock to almost $100,000; in 1936, it merged with Athena Grain Growers. In 1934, PGG leased a warehouse as the cooperative's first storage facility and joined with other local cooperatives to organize Pacific Supply Cooperative (PSC) as a means of pooling petroleum purchases to obtain lower gas prices. It also took out a loan from Spokane Bank for Cooperatives for funds to build its first grain elevator, a 220,000-bushel bulk facility, which it readied for the 1935 crop. In 1936, in a big step forward, PGG obtained a lease on additional grain elevators and sack warehouses owned by the Farmers National Warehouse Corporation (later the Farm Credit Administration), and in 1938, it purchased a second grain elevator from the Farmers National Warehouse Corporation.

PGG also began to acquire ancillary businesses in the 1930s. In 1934, it merged with Umatilla Oil Company, and in 1935, it bought Pendleton Flour and Feed Mill. Owning the petroleum business offered the advantage of smoothing out the grain business's surges in income. In 1938, as farmers were selling horses and mules in a switch to diesel crawler tractors, PGG bought an International Harvester machinery franchise. According to PGG's 1949 annual report, the move into the machinery business was intended to "save the farmer on his purchases, and in order to establish standards of service." It also helped the cooperative's "other lines such as grain and petroleum because [the cooperative] had more and frequent contacts with a larger number of farmers." Along with its petroleum, sack warehouse, and grain elevator ventures, the machinery business began making money for the cooperative, which by 1935 had earned about $11,500 for the year.

1940s–50s: Expanding Facilities and Diversification

Spring 1940 saw another step forward for PGG with the opening of its Columbia River terminal at Umatilla. According to Hill in *PGG: The Growth of a Cooperative*, "Our hope was to develop sufficient river traffic to be a factor on rail rates." By fall, 350,000 bushels of grain had been shipped by barge from

the new terminal, which was already too small. In 1941, the cooperative initiated its Feed and Seed Division with the opening of its first seed cleaning plant, which handled wheat and winter peas. The year 1942 was the cooperative's best financially with net profits of close to $200,000.

PGG's growth slowed during World War II, although earnings remained good; the cooperative made no new plans but carried out plans already begun. It built new grain elevators and expanded old ones, as well as expanding its seed cleaning plant. A rail spur serving the Umatilla terminal debuted in 1943, accommodating the move to river transportation of grain and the use of the cooperative's network of elevators. According to Hill in *PGG: The Growth of a Cooperative*, "Via river, barge and truck, grain transportation literally moved into our farmer's barnyard ... Before we started moving grain on the river, farmers had to haul their grain to rail points. Then the light turned on—go build elevators in the heart of the grain area and tie them into our main operation. . . . These highway plants were possible only because of the Umatilla elevator and the use of barges and bulk grain trucks which we used to haul grain from the elevators to the river."

Up until the war ended, the cooperative focused on gradually developing its major lines of business—grain, warehousing, petroleum, machinery, and feed and seed. After the war, it spent time improving its facilities and enhancing its work force. In the mid-1940s, PGG's membership increased to 680 stockholders. In 1947, the best year in cooperative's history to that point, the cooperative doubled the amount of wheat it moved by river to two million bushels. In response to a need for more long-term capital to expand facilities, stockholders voted to issue $500,000 in debenture bonds at interest of four percent.

In the second half of the 1940s PGG expanded its feed business as part of a move toward diversification. The Feed and Seed division, which had taken on the Purina line, made plans to expand its cleaning plant for wheat, oats, and barley. In 1949, the cooperative took over the Hermiston Farm Bureau Cooperative, organized in 1926 as a purchasing cooperative for feed. PGG also made organizational changes, shifting the business's capital structure by giving up the cooperative's income tax exemption and moving into a new administration and farm machinery building in 1951.

Beginning in the early 1950s and continuing for the next decade and a half, agriculture as an industry lost its profitability throughout the nation. Farmers produced more volume, but earnings reached a plateau. The main growth in Umatilla County during this period occurred in livestock. In 1952, in an attempt to control the livestock feeding industry in its area, and create outlets for its members' booming grain production, the Hermiston feed mill increased production to 250 tons a month; by 1958, it was producing 100 tons a day. In the mid-1950s, while farmers elsewhere were forced to liquidate crops at 30 to 60 cents below loan levels, PGG enjoyed a net profit—$441,000 in 1954. The co-op had 14 elevators with a total capacity of four million bushels and still needed additional storage space.

PGG formed the Federated Livestock Corporation in 1955 and offered 4,500 shares at $100 a piece. With the Northwest importing more meat than it raised, and the Pacific Coast producing only 6 percent of the nation's meat (for 10 percent of the U.S. population), members reasoned that raising livestock would be a sound new investment. The business dissolved, however, in 1963 after years of losses. Even so, Federated Livestock helped increase the volume of the Hermiston feed mill and doubled the income from livestock marketing in Umatilla County. By 1959, the feed mill was running seven days a week around the clock and using almost a million bushels of local grain annually. In response to the need for larger facilities, Feedville USA began operations in 1960.

1960s–80s: The Struggle for Additional Capital

The 1960s witnessed another change of direction for PGG. Losses for the cooperative as a whole in the early 1960s led to management's appeal to local farmers to patronize their own business. The need for a larger capital base became evident in the second half of the 1960s in response to national firms taking over local business outlets. In a report on PGG completed by Oregon State University, experts opined that "the [co-op's] key problem is inadequate member investment to support the volume of business. . . . Members' share of ownership is too low relative to the amount of service the business provides."

Don Cook, who had been with PGG since 1950, succeeded Jim Hill as general manager of the co-op in 1970. Cook implemented the board's decision not to develop any major new service. Profits, which had sometimes been elusive, began to improve in the early 1970s, and by 1972, the cooperative has its best financial year in its history.

PGG continued to focus and consolidate throughout the early seventies. In 1973, it joined a trucking cooperative, Northwest Agricultural Cooperative Association. In 1974, it opened a new seed cleaning plant and acquired Farmers Mutual Warehouse Company, a new grain storage facility, and a new bulk plant. It also closed its Athena feed store and relocated its hardware store. Profits rose steadily—from 1.5 million in 1973 to almost $2 million in 1974, about one-quarter of which came from affiliated cooperatives.

In the second half of the 1970s, PGG created a new division, its retail division, which included hardware, feed stores, petroleum products, the Pendleton tire center, and its Twin City and Athena branches. It joined CENEX, a regional farm supply cooperative, in 1977, the same year CENEX merged with Pacific Supply Cooperative. Still the co-op continued to struggle with the problem of accumulating sufficient capital. Despite having more than 2,000 members as it entered its 50th year, PGG's long-term debt was $6 million.

The 1980s were challenging for PGG, given the high interest rates, competitive supply markets, and increased expenses of the times. In order to cut back on its borrowing, PGG closed its machinery division in 1981 and consolidated its tire shop and irrigation department into its remodeled hardware and feed stores in Pendleton. To handle larger volumes of grain faster, the co-op improved its grain elevators, increasing its storage capacity to 12.3 million bushels. PGG also decided to undertake construction of an additional warehouse at McKennon Station to properly store chemicals whose use in agriculture was expanding dramatically.

By mid-decade, most farm commodities were selling below the cost of production, and the value of farm land and farmer's net worth were both declining. PGG continued to upgrade its grain handling capability by developing increased storage capacity, but while the additional grain storage generated a large volume of income for the coop, the borrowed capital used to make the additions increased its debt. PGG's retail stores also showed a definite turnaround beginning in 1985; still, profits for the division were poor. Toward the end of the decade, sales increased in the co-op's petrol business, and Feedville showed profits after several years of losses. By 1987, PGG enjoyed record earnings of $2.3 million.

The 1990s and Beyond

However, the next four years were hard ones for PGG because of a dry weather cycle that lasted until 1991. This cycle contributed to very weak wheat harvests and reduced dry land fertilizer rates. In addition, the co-op suffered the loss of storage revenue once the government's stock surplus came to an end. PGG looked again to its retail division to offset its losses, and beginning in 1988, it remodeled one retail store, built a second new one, and built a second petroleum facility. In 1994, it formed PGG/HSC Feed Company LLC with Harvest States Cooperative to operate Feedville. After Ed Balsiger replaced Don Cook as general manager in 1991, the co-op oversaw an environmental cleanup project at the McKennon Station that it completed in 1993.

Albert Gosiak, who joined PGG in 1995 as chief financial officer, took over leadership of the cooperative in 1998, becoming president and CEO. Gosiak would preside over an era of change and challenge at PGG. First, in 1996, the so-called Freedom to Farm Act was passed by Congress. While farmers were now allowed to produce as many crops as they chose, the minimum price for those crops would no longer be guaranteed by the government. Production and prices rapidly escalated. Shortly thereafter, foreign markets, particularly in Asia and Russia, collapsed. As PGG members and others in the Pacific Northwest exported some 90 percent of their wheat to foreign markets, a surplus ensued, driving wheat prices down dramatically. By the close of the 1990s, the U.S. government had stepped in to offer the industry some relief, but their solution sparked competition that adversely affected the growers in Pendleton, Oregon. PGG's future seemed shaky. In an interview for *Oregon Business,* Gosiak admitted that ''In 1999 we did not know if the company was going to make it. All we had to rely on was each other. We started by creating a vision, values and mission statement, and we started to make big changes.''

Among the big changes were job cuts and store closings. The co-op sought to shutter some of its non-core activities (tire and hardware retail outlets, for example), while combining other divisions in order to realize operating efficiencies. Finally, management slashed its administrative and operating expenses; managers even accepted salary cuts in order to help turn the co-op around.

As PGG entered the 2000s, the economic climate remained difficult. Overseas sales continued to slump, and another long local drought cycle negatively affected all of PGG's holdings in 2002. After all of its cutbacks, however, the co-op had a little room to explore different opportunities for generating income. For example, it began supplying Washington's grape growers with trellis equipment. By 2003, management was cautiously optimistic about the co-op's future. PGG had weathered tough times and seemed prepared in spirit to do so again; the real challenge, according to Gosiak, would be in adapting to meet the needs of its members, whose ever larger and more technologically advanced farms would ''demand better prices and a higher level of service.''

Further Reading

''Grain Growers Are Organized, Saturday Meet,'' *Oregonian,* December 23, 1929, p. 1.
Green Stacy, ''Up and Down on the Farm,'' *Oregon Business,* September 2001, p. 34.
Rupp, Virgil, *PGG: The Growth of a Cooperative,* Pendleton, Ore.: PGG, 1996.

—Carrie Rothburd

The Providence Service Corporation

5524 East 4th Street
Tucson, Arizona 85711
U.S.A.
Telephone: (520) 747-6600
Toll Free: (800) 489-0064
Fax: (520) 747 9787
Web site: http://www.provcorp.com

Public Company
Incorporated: 1997
Employees: 1,721
Sales: $59.27 million (2003)
Stock Exchanges: NASDAQ
Ticker Symbol: PRSC
NAIC: 624110 Child and Youth Services; 624190 Other Individual and Family Services

The Providence Service Corporation provides and manages government-sponsored social services, offering community-based services as an alternative to programs involving institutional care. Providence provides care to individuals who are eligible for government assistance, collecting its revenues from contracts with state and local governments, government intermediaries, and not-for-profit organizations. The company does not own or operate any hospitals, institutions, or similar facilities. Instead, it employs social workers, mental health professionals, and counselors who offer their services in the client's home or community. Providence operates in 18 states, serving nearly 13,000 clients.

1980s Origins

Providence was started by three individuals well versed the provision of social services and health care. The group was led by Fletcher J. McCusker, who founded his first company, Century Healthcare, in 1983. McCusker led Century Healthcare, a mental health care company, for nearly a decade, presiding over its development until 1992, when it was acquired by Columbia Healthcare. Next, McCusker served as the chief executive officer of Introspect Healthcare Corporation, a company that operated as a behavioral health provider. McCusker led Introspect from September 1992 until July 1995, when he left the organization to become the executive vice-president of Youth Services International, Inc. Youth Services operated as publicly traded company that provided private institutional care for at-risk youth.

It was during his tenure at Youth Services that McCusker came up with the idea of Providence. Part of his job responsibilities at Youth Services required McCusker to broker deals with agencies that dispensed state funds for social services. He negotiated with these state payer entities and, if successful in his discussions, signed contracts with them. More often than not, McCusker was successful. He developed working relationships with agencies in 38 states, which kept him in contact with what government entities desired in terms of social-service practices. In the course of his discussions with the agencies, he was asked frequently to develop community-based programs as an alternative to the conventional institutionally based programs that forced at-risk juveniles to receive care outside their home communities. McCusker wanted to respond to what the agencies wanted, but at institutionally oriented Youth Services he was unable to develop a community-based program to replace the prevailing out-of-state programs. McCusker decided to start his own company and answer the need he perceived to be unfulfilled. He left Youth Services in December 1996, less than a year and a half after joining the company, and founded Providence.

To assist him in running Providence, McCusker, a Tucson, Arizona, native, turned to two individuals with a wealth of experience in Arizona's health care industry, William B. Dover and Mary J. Shea. In his lengthy professional career, Dover held numerous executive positions, including serving as director of the Arizona Department of Health, a title he held for one year beginning in 1986. Between 1988 and 1991, Dover worked as the assistant director for the Arizona Department of Behavioral Health before starting his own company, Dover Consulting, which specialized in juvenile justice, child welfare, and child and adult mental health. In 1993, he served as vice-president for program development of Arizona Health Care Contract Management Services, Inc. In 1995, Dover began a two-year stint as executive director of Desert Hills, an in-patient facility serving

---

children and adolescents in Tucson. Dover left Desert Hills in January 1997 and joined McCusker's fledgling Providence the following month, hired as the company's president. Mary Shea joined Providence in February 1997 as well, when she was appointed president of the company's Arizona operation. Before joining Providence, Shea served as a supervisor for the State of Arizona and Arizona Center for Clinical Management, working in that capacity from 1990 to 1995. In October 1995, Shea joined Introspect, three months after McCusker vacated his post as chief executive officer. She served as the director of case management at Introspect, leaving the company to join McCusker and Dover at Providence.

McCusker organized Providence to reflect the essence of the company's motto "human services without walls." Providence did not own any facilities, a condition of its strategy to provide services in the client's own environment, rather than in hospitals, institutions, or correctional facilities. The company employed a staff of counselors, social workers, and mental health professionals who provided individual and family counseling in a client's own home. Providence's clients were eligible for government assistance for a variety of reasons, including emotional/educational disabilities, income level, or a court order. The company's paying customers included public schools, state-level agencies in charge of Medicaid programs for the poor, and government departments such as those dealing with welfare, child welfare, and justice. Providence's contracts with these entities typically stipulated an hourly fee for the services provided by the company.

McCusker's close contact with state and local government agencies during his stint at Youth Services enabled him to sense the first stirrings of what would become a national trend. This trend—the search for alternative ways of providing government-sponsored social services—was propelled by economic considerations rather than purely out of concern for the welfare of the individuals who benefited from government-funded programs. It was a trend whose development was fueled by the privatization of the government's social-service business, a process that took time and, consequently, held Providence's financial growth in check. When McCusker set about organizing Providence in December 1996, social-service agencies were just beginning to respond to government initiatives geared toward privatization, spawning McCusker's visionary perspective on the development of the government-sponsored social services. Because of McCusker's pioneering role in the industry, Providence did not experience widespread demand for its services until the trend

toward non-institutional care and social-service privatization became a national policy.

Although McCusker was early into the game, his perception of the coming demand for alternative social services was correct. Within 30 days of its inception, Providence secured its first contract, legitimizing the company's "human services without walls" strategy. During its first year, Providence accumulated 1,333 clients, all located in Arizona. The company added to its client roster exponentially and greatly extended its geographic reach as the alternative-care trend developed into a movement and as the range of its services increased. To a lesser extent, the company grew by acquiring other companies, a means of expansion first explored in February 1997, the same month William Dover and Mary Shea arrived to assist McCusker.

Acquisitions in the Late 1990s

The acquisitions completed during Providence's formative years were not large in scope, but the additions did enable the company to add new services and new markets. The company acquired smaller versions of itself, completing its first "tuck-in" acquisition on February 5, 1997. On that date, Providence purchased Parents and Children Together, Inc. (PACT), an acquisition that provided the basis of Providence's business. A Tucson-based provider of home-based and school-based services to troubled youths and their families, PACT gave McCusker his first asset with which to build Providence into a going enterprise. PACT represented the genesis of Providence's home- and community-based services, the source of its only revenue during its first several years in business and reason the company was able to secure more than 1,300 clients in Arizona during its first year of business.

Following the acquisition of PACT, Providence completed its first geographic leap, establishing a presence outside Arizona for the first time. At the end of November 1997, the company acquired Family Preservation Services, Inc. for $3.1 million, a purchase price that was reduced to $2.2 million in 1999. Although the acquisition of Family Preservation represented a modest capital outlay, the strategic importance of the acquisition was considerable. Family Preservation offered home-based counseling for children, operating six locations in Virginia. The deal also included the acquisition of the rights to a management agreement with Family Preservation Services of South Carolina, Inc., a not-for-profit social-service organization. Together, the acquisitions gave Providence a foothold in the eastern United States, a region that played a major role in sustaining the company's operations in the coming years. The company used its six locations in Virginia as a springboard for expansion into other states, eventually adding Family Preservation offices in Maine, Florida, North Carolina, and West Virginia.

The two acquisitions completed in 1997 were fundamentally important to Providence's transformation from an idea by McCusker into a financially viable business. The addition of PACT and Family Preservation gave Providence a foundation to build upon, something the company did during the late 1990s, as it relied on organic means of expansion to fuel its growth. New services and new markets were added to the company's operations, providing a modest rate of growth. At the end of Providence's fiscal year in June 1998, revenues totaled $8.5 million.

Key Dates:

1996: Fletcher J. McCusker forms Providence.
1997: Providence acquires Parents and Children Together, Inc., and Family Preservation Services, Inc.
2002: Providence acquires Camelot Care Corporation.
2003: Providence completes its initial public offering of stock.
2004: Providence acquires Dockside Services, Inc., and Pottsville Behavioral Counseling Group.

The following year, the company registered a $5 million increase, generating $12.5 million in sales. Not long after releasing its annual financial statement for 1999, Providence began to benefit from increased national demand for alternative methods of providing social services, an interest that was noted by McCusker. In a November 11, 2003 interview with *The Wall Street Transcript,* McCusker explained the discernible change in the mindset of those agencies charged with allotting government funds. "Texas and other states that were very hard on the criminal element with mandatory sentences and those kinds of things made it hard for us to get in and even make our pitch because they were perfectly satisfied with the institutional alternative. In about 2000 though," McCusker continued, "when state budgets began to experience deficits, even the unenlightened states began to approach us."

As it entered the 21st century, Providence began to experience a surge in growth that stemmed from the financial benefits of "human services without walls." In his interview with *The Wall Street Transcript,* McCusker expressed his understanding of why Providence was succeeding, even if the reason for the company's success was not at the heart of its mission. "Demand is now being driven more by the economics than by any program value," he explained. "We believe we can also demonstrate that our clients function better and do better in community-based programs compared to the institutional alternative. Instinctively, you can see that someone who is treated in their own home is going to have a better long-term outcome than someone that's in an institution, but they're still coming to us because of the pure economics. If you look at our growth, it's really been since 2000 that we've taken off in terms of the number of contracts and the number of states that we currently work with."

As Providence pressed ahead in a climate increasingly receptive to its market approach, the company was able to leverage its financial success toward becoming a more sophisticated, mature corporation. In March 2002, the company completed a $10.3 million acquisition, purchasing Camelot Care Corporation. The acquisition of Camelot served as Providence's entry into providing foster care services. Camelot provided foster care services in Tennessee, Illinois, Indiana, Nebraska, Ohio, and Florida to roughly 1,700 children when it became part of Providence's operations.

Providence in the 21st Century

Profitability and fast-paced revenue growth described Providence's progress during the early 2000s. After recording a net loss totaling more than $2.6 million during its first three years of business, the company posted its first annual profit in 2001, registering $394,000 in net income. The following year, Providence generated $1.3 million in net income. After this rise in profits, coupled with sales growth that saw Providence post $27.7 million in revenue for the fiscal year ended in June 2002, the business press took note of the company's achievements. In the fall of 2002, *Inc.* magazine selected Providence as one of the 500 fastest growing, privately held companies in the United States. It was an honor Providence ensured it would not receive the following year. In early 2003, McCusker began to make plans for Providence's initial public offering (IPO) of stock.

After delays in meeting reporting obligations mandated by the Securities and Exchange Commission (SEC), Providence filed for its IPO in June 2003. The Company wanted to offer as much as $60 million worth of stock, intending to use this revenue to pay down $17.3 million in long-term debt and to continue expanding its services and its geographic reach. Providence completed its IPO in August 2003, selling 4.3 million shares at $12 per share. After paying for expenses incurred while completing the IPO, the company raised approximately $30 million.

In the wake of its IPO, Providence stood positioned to expand in earnest. Financially, the company exuded a level of strength unprecedented in its existence. At the end of 2003 (Providence changed its fiscal year to coincide with the calendar year), the company recorded a 42 percent increase in revenue to $59.3 million, while its net income, excluding expenses related to the IPO, totaled $3.3 million. As the company prepared for the future, it was expected to augment its organic expansion by completing acquisitions of companies similar to itself, although McCusker did not expect acquisitions to be the driving force of the company's expansion strategy. "There's not a whole lot of providers out there like us," he said in an August 19, 2003 interview with *Knight Ridder/Tribune Business News.* Nevertheless, Providence completed two acquisitions in the first half of 2004, perhaps indicating a more active posture on the acquisition front than McCusker articulated. In January, the company acquired Dockside Services, Inc., an Indiana-based provider of services to children, youth, and families. In May, Providence acquired Pottsville Behavioral Counseling Group, a Pennsylvania-based provider of screening and assessment services to children and adolescents.

Principal Subsidiaries

Family Preservation Services, Inc.; Camelot Community Care, Inc.; Pottsville Behavioral Counseling Group; Parents and Children Together, Inc.; Cypress Management Services, Inc.

Principal Competitors

Maximus, Inc.; National Mentor, Inc.; Cornell Companies, Inc.; Res-Care, Inc.; Psychiatric Solutions, Inc.; The Devereaux Foundation.

Further Reading

"Fletcher J. McCusker, The Providence Service Organization," *Wall Street Transcript,* November 11, 2003, p. 32.

Higuera, Jonathan J., ''Two Tucson, Ariz., Firms Are among Nation's Fastest-Growing Companies,'' *Knight Ridder/Tribune Business News*, October 16, 2002.

Jacobs, Shella, ''Tucson, Ariz., Counseling Firm Sells $51.6 Million Worth of Stock,'' *Knight Ridder/Tribune Business News*, August 19, 2003.

Jaurez, Macario, Jr., ''Tucson, Ariz., Social Services Firm Wants to Go Public,'' *Knight Ridder/Tribune Business News*, June 21, 2003.

—Jeffrey L. Covell

Publishers Clearing House

382 Channel Drive
Port Washington, New York 11050
U.S.A.
Telephone: (516) 883-5432
Fax: (516) 767-4567
Web site: http://www.pch.com

Private Company
Incorporated: 1953
Employees: 800
Sales: $345 million (1997 est.)
NAIC: 454110 Electronic Shoppng and Mail-Order
    Houses; 541860 Direct Mail Advertising

Publishers Clearing House (PCH) is one of the largest magazine subscription agencies in the United States. The company is known as a "stampsheet" marketer for the perforated stamps consumers stick on their subscription forms. Publishers Clearing House is best known for its dramatic sweepstakes, a marketing campaign that offers millions of dollars in prizes every year. In the mid-1990s, PCH claimed to be reaching 75 percent of U.S. households with at least one mailing per year. However, the company's fortunes fell after a series of lawsuits for deceptive business practices targeted it and its competitors in the late 1990s and early 2000s. While its major competitor ceased offering sweepstakes, PCH continues to run its sweepstakes, best known for the ostentatious Prize Patrol that disburses the winnings. PCH also sells consumer goods through direct mail and through its Web site. Items include videos, music, books, jewelry, health and beauty products, and collectibles. The company operates as a limited partnership, and members of the founding Mertz family still retain a majority interest.

Origins and Development

During the 1950s, salespeople, usually college students going door to door, were the largest source of subscriptions for magazine publishers, other than their own direct-mail efforts. Harold Mertz was manager of some of the crews of foot soldiers who trudged through residential neighborhoods to drum up business.

In 1953, however, he founded Publishers Clearing House in the basement of his Port Washington, Long Island, home to sell magazine subscriptions through the cheaper method of mail promotion. His simple, but revolutionary, idea was to increase the chance of making a sale by offering a selection of 20 magazines, rather than just one, in a single mailing.

Mertz's first mail package was a simple white envelope containing a folder depicting several magazines, an offer, and a reply form. In 1967, however, the company borrowed an idea that Reader's Digest initiated in 1962 and began making sweepstakes promotions, offering prizes to entrants who filled out a numbered entry blank and mailed it to the company. "We started giving out bunches of singles, fives and ten-dollar bills as prizes," a former PCH executive recalled in 1996. "It barely made a ripple, so we went up to $5,000."

Since the numbers were preselected, Publishers Clearing House could promote the sweepstakes truthfully with the words, "You may already be a winner!" According to a 1980 *Advertising Age* article, direct-mail marketers had discovered that they could increase sales 50 percent more through sweepstakes than by any other promotional technique. Cash, automobiles, and vacation trips were said to be the most appealing and popular awards. As a sweepstakes, rather than a lottery, the contest was open to all entrants whether or not they chose to be customers. At first PCH did not feel obligated to award prizes if no winning entry was received, but later a second random drawing came to be held from entries submitted if no one turned in the winning number for the top prize.

Publishers Clearing House had its chosen field to itself until 1980, when a consortium of Time Inc., McCall's Corp., and Meredith Corp. formed rival American Family Publishers. Still based in Port Washington, where it now had 100,000 square feet of office and warehouse space, PCH was representing nearly every major publisher in the United States and was promoting some 395 magazines. Its mailings were going to 40 to 60 million households a year, with the addresses obtained from other direct-mail sources to take in people who bought by mail, who had spent more than a specified amount in the last few months, and who paid their bills promptly. PCH also had its own mailing list of recent customers.

PCH normally conducted two major mailings a year at this time: one around the Christmas/New Year's period and a second in early July, each closely timed to television commercials telling viewers to be looking for the mailing. Between 50 to 110 magazine subscriptions were being offered in any given mailing. A typical sweepstakes mailing contained up to eight separate printed pieces. One of these was a sheet of gummed stamps offering the various magazine subscriptions at discounted rates. Also essential were the order vehicle (generally, a return card) and the sweepstakes offer, often a four-color brochure. Occasionally, the mailing also contained product coupons.

Refining the Concept: 1981–93

Publishers Clearing House's annual sales were about $50 million in 1981, when Robin Smith, a former Doubleday executive, became its president and chief executive officer. Annual revenues passed the $100 million mark in 1988. After American Family Publishers raised its biggest prize from $200,000 to $10 million in 1985, PCH had to follow suit. In 1987, the company added a ''Catalog Clearing House'' sweepstakes that included inserts promoting 36 products from a selected group of catalogers. It was mailed to more than 1.5 million households and offered $10 million in prizes. PCH processed the orders, collected the payments, and sent the orders to the catalogers with an invoice representing the difference between the product price and its advertising and acquisition costs. During the late 1980s, PCH also expanded its product line to include books (mostly children's and how-to books) and audio and visual items.

By late 1991, Publishers Clearing House had 700 full-time employees at its 14-acre complex, plus another 700 part-timers hired during promotional drives. The staff included about 12 copywriters and four art directors. One of the company's brightest ideas—a tag listing a recipient's sweepstakes numbers that could be hung from a television dial—had resulted in a 5 percent increase in entries returned. By then, PCH had distributed more than $50 million in prizes to more than two million people, including $13 million in fiscal 1991.

The grand prize of $10 million was being delivered since 1988, along with flowers, champagne, and balloons, by a Prize Patrol clad in blue blazers—and a cameraman. Advertising Director David C. Sayer, who said he personally had handed out more than $30 million in his years with the company and now headed the patrol, told a reporter, ''The best part of my job is seeing how people react. One woman didn't believe me at first, and while I kept trying to tell her that she had just won $1 million, she just kept doing her laundry.''

By this time, Publishers Clearing House was receiving subscription requests from eight million people each year through its 25 annual mailings, which included millionaire-of-the month mailings, fast 50s ($50,000) for early entrants, and car giveaways. It was compiling its database by processing 450 million names from its own list and those rented from others, and it was dropping people who, after a certain period, failed to turn in entries or turned them in without ordering products. Mailings were aimed primarily at the middle-aged, middle-class consumer and disproportionately outside ''the more skeptical and cynical Northeast,'' as Sayer put it. Prime prospects—those who ordered frequently—might receive 30, even 40, mailings a year.

The need to ''mail smarter'' had grown more urgent because the price of a typical sweepstakes mailing had increased to between 40 and 50 cents. The stampsheets alone cost seven cents, but, said Smith, ''Every time we think about getting rid of them, testing always proves they are worth the money.'' PCH planners also had found, over the years, that given its middle-American target audience, cold cash, rather than exotic prizes like a private airplane or a thoroughbred racehorse, were the grabbers. Vice-president Tom Owens told a *Washington Post* reporter in 1993, ''You talk to winners, all they want to do is pay their bills and do very mundane things.''

The 1992 year-end package arrived with a new ''snap-pack'' on the front of the envelope, which had to be peeled open to find the finalist notification label to paste onto the finalist notification certificate—in other words, the entry form. According to Owens, the rationale behind the ''snap-pack'' was to make the recipient react at once in the critical first step of opening the mailing. The pasting regulations were described as ''involving devices.'' As Owens explained, ''The longer you have someone looking at what you're trying to sell, the better the odds are they'll make a purchase.''

PCH's share of the subscription price ranged from 74 to 90 percent. These subscriptions were being offered at deep discounts, and PCH insisted on a magazine's lowest advertised price. Publishers, therefore, collected little money directly, but the increase in circulation allowed them to charge advertisers more money. PCH also was endearing itself to publishers by paying the magazine's share up front, and besides, as one magazine circulation manager said, ''If we mail one million names and get no response, we still have to pay for the mailing. If Publishers Clearing House does the mailing, we don't pay for anything.'' On the debit side, however, subscribers obtained from stampsheet agents like PCH had a low percentage of renewals.

Problems in the 1990s

By 1994, Publishers Clearing House and its sweepstakes rivals were running into three problems: contest fatigue, increased government oversight, and private lawsuits and other bad publicity. Despite relentless promotion of its sweepstakes, including expenses of more than $20 million a year for advertising, response rates for PCH mailings were said to have dropped by 7 to 12 percent, and perhaps more, in 1994. Sales volume from the mid-1995 mailings of PCH and American Family Publishers was reported to be down 22 percent. A PCH executive acknowledged that the company had cut back some of its mailings because of paper and postage increases but said these cost reductions were only in the 5 percent range and hence could not fully account for the drop in orders. The company, however, also had cut its advertising expenditures by 7 percent in 1994.

Government officials seemed to be casting a jaundiced eye at Publishers Clearing House's promotions. The Federal Trade Commission's expert on sweepstakes said the odds of winning could be one in 100 million or worse. Being labeled a "finalist," he declared, generally merely meant that the contestant had sent in a previous entry. It was also noted that the $10 million prize was not given in a lump sum, but over 30 years, with $2.5 million not paid out until the final year. Million-dollar winners received only $50,000 in the first year.

In 1994, PCH agreed to pay $490,000 to 14 states to settle allegations that it used deceptive advertising in its annual sweepstakes. The company agreed to stop using the word "finalist" on most solicitations and to employ the phrase "final round" only in the last weeks of the promotions. Some states had reported that all persons receiving sweepstakes entries were identified as finalists. PCH also agreed to explain to consumers that if they were dropped from the mailing list they could write the company to be reincluded in the sweeps and then entitled to all entry mailings produced for the next 12 months.

A lawsuit was filed in 1992 after New York City sanitation workers found several thousand Publishers Clearing House envelopes discarded by a roadside and "literally blowing in the wind." PCH settled the suit by agreeing to enter the names and addresses of everyone who had received mailings between February and October 1992 for the January 1993 $10 million contest and April 1993 $1 million contest whether they had returned their entries or not. The company said it had discontinued its use of outside processors, one of which it blamed for improperly handling the discarded entries.

Disgruntled contestants were a fact of life for all sweepstakes agencies, but Publishers Clearing House could have done without the page-one *Detroit News* story in April 1997, in which Stephen Worhatch complained he had waited in vain for the Prize Patrol in response to a PCH letter asking him and his wife—bed-ridden with multiple sclerosis—to draw a map to their West Bloomfield home so that the patrol could deliver a check for the first installment of a $10 million prize. A company executive pointed out that the fine print in the entry form said the patrol "would come to your house if you were selected the winner." He added that the map request was merely "a fun way to get them interested . . . in the spirit of fun and entertainment."

Another disappointed Michigan contestant, Raymond Workmon, sued PCH in federal court for breach of contract and violation of the state consumer protection law. He was turned down for the second time by an appeals court in 1997, which declared, "Although Workmon believed he had won, his belief was not reasonable. . . . If Workmon read the entire certificate, he would have known, or reasonably should have known, he was not automatically the winner." An attorney for the company said that it was only the third time in 20 years that a contestant had sued PCH and that all three had lost.

By January 1996, PCH had awarded more than $92 million in prizes since instituting its sweepstakes. The $10 million prize winner that month was presented in a 30-second spot aired shortly after the completion of the Super Bowl. Camera crews from *Dateline News* and *Extra* were present, giving the event even more publicity. Like a majority of sweepstakes winners, the lucky recipient, Mary Ann Brandt of Phoenix, had not ordered a magazine with her entry and had been selected in the alternate drawing from entrants after the holder of the first randomly assigned number had failed to return his or her entry.

Publishers Clearing House's offerings in 1997 included not only magazines but such items as a Cal Ripken, Jr., commemorative baseball, a Star Trek Communicator pin, a "6 in 1" hose nozzle, a reversible lint brush, and a collection of five mercury dimes. The company began selling subscriptions through its Web site in 1996. This site offered sweepstakes promotions (including Internet-only offers), discounted subscriptions to 300 magazines, and general merchandise.

More Legal Woes in the Late 1990s and Early 2000s

By the late 1990s, only about 12 percent of total U.S. magazine subscription sales came from the stampsheet purveyors, including principally PCH and its main rival, American Family Enterprises. PCH was thought to have revenue of $345 million by 1997, and this year was the last before the start of a rough patch, defined by numerous lawsuits and a steep drop in subscription orders. The troubles were actually sparked by American Family but spread to PCH as well. PCH had settled a significant lawsuit as recently as 1994, but state attorneys general were not done with the company. In 1997, an American Family sweepstakes contestant, 88-year-old Richard Lusk, flew from his home in California to Tampa, Florida, in the belief that he had won an $11 million prize. Unfortunately, Lusk had not perceived the fine print, which stated only that he *might* be a winner. His odds of winning were actually in the range of 150 million to one. The incident got wide media coverage and started a new round of state lawsuits against both American Family and PCH.

The bad publicity had an immediate effect on subscription orders. Magazine industry sources claimed that orders were down by between 30 and 50 percent by late 1998. PCH officials admitted that orders had fallen off but would not confirm a figure. A PCH executive told *Advertising Age* (October 19, 1998) that subscription volume was down, but "certainly nowhere near the neighborhood of 40 percent." This seemed to argue for 30 percent, by any measure a significant loss. The bad publicity seemed to be the primary reason for the slacking of orders, but other factors may have been at work as well. Some magazine industry analysts suggested that consumers were tired of the whole sweepstakes phenomenon and needed something new. Another factor may have been the widespread legalization of state-run lotteries. Consumers may have been less likely to fill out a laborious magazine sweepstakes form when they could easily buy a lotto ticket for a cash prize equal to or better than what the PCH contest offered.

The lawsuits continued to pile up. Magazine industry sources reported a 30 percent drop off in PCH subscription sales for 1998 and flat sales for 1999. The fall off in magazine sales also presumably led to a decline in sales of PCH's merchandise. In August 1999, PCH settled a federal suit against it, agreeing to pay $5.5 million to cover claims of some 40 million consumers. Two months later, its main competitor, American Family, announced it was filing for bankruptcy, unable to handle the expenses of litigation. PCH ended 1999 with the vaunted relaunch of its Web site. The company hoped this would be a new way to entice consumers to buy its magazine subscriptions and goods. Yet in early 2000, the company announced it had taken a drastic cost-cutting measure, laying off about a quarter of its employees. Later that year, PCH settled another raft of lawsuits, paying $18 million to 24 states and the District of Columbia. The settlement came with a new set of rules, such as that PCH would no longer use "involvement devices" such as the 1992 "snap-pack" or other game pieces that seemed to offer an increased chance to win. The company also agreed to stop contacting its so-called "high activity" customers—people who mailed in with extreme frequency to increase their chance of winning.

PCH continued to run its sweepstakes, including the offer of a large prize at the annual football Super Bowl. Its competitor American Family declared it would exit the sweepstakes business in 2000, leaving PCH alone on the field. In 2001, PCH settled an additional round of lawsuits, paying $34 million to 26 states. The company agreed to another set of rules governing its contests and also set up a "special compliance counsel" for continuing liaison with the states. By this time, it had settled with all fifty states and the District of Columbia, so the litigation seemed to be at an end. The company had released no financial information after the late 1990s. PCH continued seemingly much as usual after it put its litigation problems behind it. The company celebrated its 50th anniversary in 2003, with festivities in Port Washington. In 2004, the company's Prize Patrol delivered a $25,000 check to a retired Wichita couple who had been married for more than 50 years. The husband was 91 years old and hoped to put the money away for a rainy day.

Principal Competitors

Synapse Group, Inc.; Cross Media Marketing Corporation.

Further Reading

Alberta, Paul M., "PCH Blind-Sided by Latest Lawsuits," *Direct*, March 15, 1999, p. 22.
Berglund, Elizabeth, "Winning the Publishers Clearing House Printing Sweepstakes," *American Printer and Lithographer*, September 1980, pp. 47–48, 50–51.
Bounds, Wendy, "Subscriptions Drop off as Sweepstakes Soften Sell," *Wall Street Journal*, October 19, 1998, p. B1.
Conlon, Thomas J., "Sweepstakes Rank as Tops," *Advertising Age*, October 6, 1980, pp. 54–55.
DeHaven, Judy, "Sweepstakes 'Winner' Feels Deceived," *Detroit News*, April 18, 1997, pp. 1A, 7A.
DeMarrais, Kevin, "Sweepstakes-Sponsor American Family Enterprises Files for Bankruptcy," *Knight Ridder/Tribune Business News*, November 1, 1999, p.OKRB99040E3.
Egol, Len, "Stamps of Approval," *Folio's Publishing News*, November 15, 1991, pp. 43–44.
Freedman, Eric, "PCH Superprize Claimant Loses Again," *Folio*, March 1, 1997, p. 22.
Gattuso, Greg, "PCH Agrees to Modify Copy," *Direct Marketing*, October 1994, p. 6.
Jaffe, Greg, "Sweepstakes Industry May Not Be a Winner!," *Wall Street Journal*, February 18, 1998, p. B1.
Kahn, Joseph P., "Super Bowl Is at Six," *Boston Globe*, January 28, 1996, pp. 1, 16.
Kelly, Keith J., "Mags Stamped by Dramatic Drop," *Advertising Age*, October 30, 1995, pp. 1, 4.
Krol, Carol, "Dismal Year for Sweepstakes Doesn't Signal a Demise," *Advertising Age*, October 19, 1998, p. S24.
"The Law: Sweeping Up," *Promo*, October 2000.
Lehman, R.J., "Raising the Stakes on Circulation," *Folio*, October 2000, p. 12.
Levere, Jane L., "Publishers Look to New Medium to Rekindle Sales in Older One," *New York Times*, December 1, 1997, p. D11.
Meier, Barry, "You're All Finalists!," *New York Times*, January 27, 1996, pp. 33, 35.
Miller, Paul, "Strong Response for Catalog Clearing House Sweeps," *Catalog Age*, January 1987, p. 11.
"PCH Reaches $34 Million Sweepstakes Settlement with 26 States," *Direct Marketing*, September 2001, p. 6.
Rothenberg, Randall, "Read This and Win $10 Million!!," *New York Times*, January 31, 1989, pp. D1, D21.
Saslow, Linda, "It's Sweepstakes Time, and It's a Frenzy," *New York Times (Long Island Weekly)*, January 20, 1991, pp. 1, 4.
Schnuer, Jenna, "Are the Stampsheets Licked?," *Folio*, May 15, 1995, p. 17.
Span, Paula, "Sweep Dreams, America!," *Washington Post*, January 28, 1993, pp. C1, C8.
Walzer, Robert, "PCH Cleans House, Goes Virtual in Profit Play," *Long Island Business News*, February 18, 2000, p. 4A.
——, "Prize Patrol Lumbering Along," *Long Island Business News*, October 22, 1999, p. 1A.
Wells, Melanie, "This Loot's for You," *Advertising Age*, February 6, 1996, p. 42.

—Robert Halasz
—update: A. Woodward

The Rank Group plc

6 Connaught Place
London W2 2EZ
United Kingdom
Telephone: (207) 706-1111
Fax: (207) 262-9886
Web site: http://www.rank.com

Public Company
Incorporated: 1937 as Odeon Theatres Holdings Ltd.
Employees: 24,003
Sales: £1.93 billion ($3.43 billion)(2003)
Stock Exchanges: London NASDAQ
Ticker Symbol: RNK RANKY
NAIC: 72112 Casino Hotels; 713210 Casinos; 713290
     Other Gambling Industries

The Rank Group plc operates as a leading international gaming, leisure, and entertainment group. Rank is structured with three main business groups—Gaming; Hard Rock Cafes, Hotels, and Casinos; and Deluxe Film and Media Services. The company oversees Mecca Bingo clubs in the United Kingdom and Spain, Grosvenor Casinos in the United Kingdom and Belgium, Hard Rock Casinos in London and Manchester, and three online interactive gaming Web sites through Blue Square. Rank's holdings also include the Hard Rock brand of cafes and hotels, along with Deluxe Film and Media Services, which provides film and DVD production and distribution throughout the United States, Canada, Australia, and Europe. Rank launched a major restructuring in the late 1990s that included the divestiture of Odeon Cinemas and Pinewood Studios—two companies that date back to its roots in the 1930s.

Early History in the 1930s

The overall picture of Rank remains rather confusing until one understands that its history falls into two very distinct parts. When Joseph Arthur Rank—later dubbed Lord Rank—founded the conglomerate in 1935, he quickly assembled the dominant motion picture combine in Great Britain, with inter-

ests in everything from the manufacture of cameras to Lawrence Olivier's interpretation of *Henry V.* Twenty years later, the nation's film business was suffering, so Rank made a deal with a little-known American company to market the company's products everywhere outside of the western hemisphere. That company was Xerox, and since then the only real task for the managers at Rank has been to decide how to intelligently utilize the endless profits generated by its partnership. Continually seeking to diversify in order to lessen its fiscal dependence on Rank Xerox, the Rank Organisation followed a wobbly course of expansion into a variety of areas without managing to correct its fundamental, if hardly fatal, imbalance, although it began to do so only when it sold part of its stake in Rank Xerox in 1995.

The story of Rank's emergence as the leading film magnate in Great Britain is complex and closely bound up with the history of British film as a whole. Joseph Arthur Rank was born in 1888 to a wealthy Yorkshire flour miller. His father was the founder of today's Ranks Hovis McDougall, one of Britain's leading food companies. The younger Rank first became interested in film as a means to spread the truths of the Methodist religion, to which he was deeply devoted. Working with a group called the Religious Film Society, he paid for the 1934 production of *Mastership,* and shortly thereafter joined a like-minded millionaire, Lady Yule, in founding Pinewood Studios. Rank soon decided to leave religion in the pulpit. Taking advantage of his growing connections in the film world, he began to produce and distribute popular entertainment. The board of directors of Pinewood included members from the boards of the British and Dominion Film Corporation and British National Films Ltd., two of the country's leading production houses. British and Dominion also had an agreement with United Artists (UA), the American film company, whereby the latter distributed Dominion films in Great Britain. From this nucleus of financiers and filmmakers would grown one-third of Rank's empire—the production division.

In March 1936, Rank and four other men formed the General Cinema Finance Company (GCFC) with enough capital to allow its subsequent acquisition of General Film Distributors Ltd. (GFD), the basis of Rank's future distribution business. GFD's board included members of the British and Dominion board, which formed an important link between GFD and United Artists. (Rank was a lover of intricate corporate strategy.) Also in 1936, Rank and a group of American and British investors brought a controlling interest in one of the American ''majors,'' Universal Pictures. As a result, GFD became the distribution arm of Universal in Britain. Another thread in Rank's densely woven corporate cable was represented by A.H. Giannini, a member of the new Universal board of directors who also happened to be the president and chairman of United Artists. In this way, Rank tightened his links with the critically important Hollywood industry and its vast American market.

Having solidified his interests in production and distribution, Rank needed only a circuit of theaters to complete a vertically integrated film combine. As of 1936, the two leading circuits in Great Britain were Gaumont-British and ABPC (Associated British Pictures Corporation), but Odeon Theatres Ltd. was a rising power. In May 1937, Odeon had purchased a rival company's theaters to secure its position as the third major circuit, with some 250 cinemas in the country. Odeon was already half-owned by United Artists, making it a kind of second cousin to Rank's growing interests. Also closely allied to UA was the important London Film Productions Ltd., managed by Alexander Korda and the owner of large new studios at Denham. Toward the end of 1938, Rank began putting together these many pieces. In December, he merged his Pinewood Studios with the extensive complex at Denham (creating D & P Studios), and in the following year GCFC added to its production capacity with the purchase of the Amalgamated studios at Elstree. Finally, and most significantly, Rank acquired an interest in Odeon Theatres by subscribing (via GCFC) to its issue of debentures.

Odeon Theatres was soon in grave financial difficulties. The holding company which controlled it, Odeon Cinema Holdings Ltd., turned to Rank for assistance, and he soon became a 50 percent owner along with United Artists (because of certain peculiarities in the company's rules, Rank was able to outvote his partner despite their equal stakes). At about the same time, GCFC was able to buy the holding company that ran the Gaumont-British theaters, giving Rank effective control over approximately 619 cinemas, or one-fifth of the total in Britain. Through a complicated series of holding companies, all of the above-named entities and some 80 subsidiaries were ultimately owned by Manorfield Investments Ltd., a private corporation in turn owned by Arthur Rank and his wife. This tidy arrangement allowed Rank to exert personal control over a vast segment of the British film industry, with commanding positions in all three

of the industry's basic components—production, distribution, and exhibition. His dominance is perhaps best illustrated by the fact that of 63 new films made in Britain in 1948, more than half were produced by Rank's empire.

Many of Rank's acquisitions were made possible by the slump that overtook the business in 1938. Inspired by the success of Alexander Korda's 1933 hit, *The Private Life of Henry VIII,* English producers convinced themselves that they could compete with Hollywood in the high-budget blockbuster market. They were wrong, and the failure of numerous costly films during the next few years drove many companies to the brink of bankruptcy. Rank took advantage of the buyer's market to complete the integrated group of holdings outlined above, purchasing for about £1.7 million assets later estimated to have had a market value of £50 million.

Battling Monopoly Accusations in the 1940s

Such conspicuous success attracted its share of resistance. After its 1941 buyout of Gaumont-British, the Rank Organisation had grown sufficiently large to merit the accusation of monopoly. In 1944, the government's Palache Report made several recommendations about how best to curb the growth of the combines while encouraging a healthy degree of independent production. Rank agreed to seek government approval before he bought more theaters, but as he already held a commanding lead over his nearest rivals, the agreement did little to change the industry's excessive concentration.

The government did, however, manage indirectly to bring about the decline of Rank's power. In an effort to redress the growing imbalance in U.S.-British trade, the Labor government instituted in 1947 the so-called Dalton duty, a prohibitively high tax on all foreign films distributed in the country. In retaliation, Hollywood refused to release any films at all in Great Britain, at which point the latter's film industry, led by the highly patriotic Rank, offered to step up production to fill the gap. The year 1948 marked the zenith of British production, with Rank showing the way. However, in March the government abruptly reversed itself and lifted the duty, precipitating an avalanche of high-quality American imports. More hastily produced British films were destroyed at the box office, none more so than Rank's. For the fiscal year ending June 1949, the group lost a painful £3.35 million.

The year 1948 signaled the beginning of a long decline for the British film industry in general, and for Rank in particular. Despite his still-dominant position in all three aspects of the business, Rank could hardly continue to suffer the huge losses incurred after the 1948 debacle. Yet even after cutting his production drastically, Rank faced a complex of more formidable problems. The war years had actually boosted theater attendance, as war-weary British citizens sought escape. By 1950, however, relative prosperity encouraged a raft of new leisure resources, none more important than the automobile and the emerging television industry. The cumulative effect of these and other changes was a fall in theater attendance during the postwar years from 1.6 billion tickets sold in 1946 to only 400 million in 1963. The golden age of cinema had passed, and those producers who survived did so by moving quickly into other fields. Rank and his managing director, John Davis,

Key Dates:

1936: Joseph Arthur Rank and four other men establish the General Cinema Finance Co.
1938: Pinewood Studios merges with Denham to form D & P Studios.
1941: Rank buys out Gaumont-British.
1956: Rank agrees to manufacture and sell xerographic machines.
1969: Sales at Rank Xerox reach $276 million.
1990: Rank acquires Mecca Leisure Group.
1995: The company sells a 40 percent stake in Rank Xerox.
1999: Rank launches a major restructuring effort designed to focus on three major divisions—Gaming; Hard Rock Cafes, Hotels, and Casinos; and Deluxe Film and Media Services.
2000: Odeon Cinemas and Pinewood Studios are sold.
2003: Blue Square Ltd. is acquired.

proceeded to do just that, searching for allied industries in which to make use of the company's expertise and financial muscle. They really found only one such nugget in 20 years of prospecting, but it turned out to be a big one.

Diversification in the 1950s–60s

Rank's search for alternatives to the film business led him and Davis in two distinct directions, accounting for the oddly bifurcated nature of Rank's portfolio. On the one hand, Davis tried to exploit the enemy, as it were, by expanding Rank interests into competing leisure and entertainment fields. He first closed down many of the large Odeon theaters; total Rank holdings fell from a postwar peak of 507 cinemas to around 350 by the end of the 1950s. The vacant theaters were either used as real estate for development by one of Rank's newly formed construction companies or were converted into bowling alleys, dance halls, or bingo parlors. The company also took a stab at the burgeoning record business in the late 1950s and began investing in the new American-style motels and service areas needed alongside Britain's new system of highways. Most promising of all, Rank bought a piece of the television industry, taking a 37.5 percent interest in the Southern Television Corporation, which served several million homes by the end of the decade.

However, none of these projects proved more than briefly successful. Bowling alleys and large dance halls were largely passé by the early 1960s, the Rank record business failed utterly Rank's motels and restaurants were not well situated, and even the television station failed to take off as Rank and Davis had expected. Rank had better luck in the other half of its diversification drive—precision industries and electronics.

Always involved in film producing and processing, Rank was well positioned to expand into new applications of similar technology. Among other companies, it acquired Taylor Hobson, a manufacturer of lenses and precision measuring instruments, and Cintel, an image processing concern. Soon thereafter, Rank began to make and sell television sets in its own retail outlets. The electronics program was much more success-

ful than Rank's leisure ventures, but the company's future did not fully reveal itself until Rank Xerox began its spectacular rise in the early 1960s.

The connection between the two companies dates back ten years earlier, when Rank began making lenses for a new American manufacturer of copying machines called the Haloid Company. Its president, Joseph Wilson, had bought the rights to a dry-copy technique that could be used with nearly any type of paper—a great improvement over the later generation of copiers, which required specially treated paper and liquid toner. To take advantage of his find, called "xerography," Wilson needed a large amount of money and worldwide marketing strength. The Rank Organisation had both, and in 1956 an agreement was formed whereby Rank undertook to manufacture and sell (or lease) xerographic machines everywhere except in the Americas. A new company was formed, eventually to be called Rank Xerox (RX), of which Rank owned 48.8 percent of the equity but only one-third of the profit above a certain minimum. Xerox controlled and managed the joint venture while Rank supplied some cash, the manufacturing facilities, and a distribution network. In 1956, it was far from certain that this venture would turn into anything more than another good idea, and John Davis in particular must be credited with the foresight and courage needed to make the initial investment. Two other leaders in the field, IBM and Gestettner, had already declined to put their money on the line.

By the early 1960s, Rank had entered the era of Rank Xerox. RX's sales soared from $7 million in 1962 to $276 million in 1969. Its success was so great that the Rank Organisation's other activities became of "academic interest only," as one financial analyst commented at the time. In 1965, the two divisions contributed equally to total Rank profit, but three years later RX profits were four times those generated by the rest of Rank (£33 million to £8.4 million). This treadmill continued to spin for quite a few years. While Rank muddled its way in and out of investments in both the leisure and technology fields, making a few pounds here and there, its Xerox associate churned out profits as if they too could be duplicated at the press of a button. By 1982, this tail-wags-dog situation had reached the point where the rest of Rank's many businesses contributed only 7 percent to the company's overall profit, while RX brought in 93 percent. Davis, Rank CEO from 1962 to 1977, seemed somewhat embarrassed by the reduction of his once-mighty empire to the role of coupon-clipper, and for that reason strove to establish the company in other areas. The results were not good. In 1971, Rank made $17 million on non-Xerox assets of about $204 million. Eleven years later, it garnered only $7 million on assets worth twice that much. While RX forged ahead, Rank fell behind.

In the meantime, the world copier market caught up with Xerox. By the end of the 1970s, heavy Japanese competition cut into RX's profit and its market share. The combination of ineffective Rank management and a cooling RX sent investors into a panic. In 1976, institutional investors with large holdings in Rank pushed through a rules change enabling them to exercise closer control over the troubled company. By 1983, brokers were speculating that the organization might be taken over by corporate raiders and its substantial assets sold off to those who could manage them more profitably.

By 1988, however, Rank seemed to have rebounded under the management of its new CEO, Michael Gifford. All but one of its divisions reported a healthy increase in profits in 1988, and the balance of earnings between Rank and RX was closer to a 50–50 split. The holidays and recreation division had become the company's largest, and its collection of resorts and travel interests netted a robust £58 million on sales of £276 million in 1988.

Late 1980s Investments

Under Gifford's direction, Rank made additional investments and acquisitions in its core leisure, recreation, and holidays operations during the next several years. In 1988, Rank entered into a partnership with MCA to build the $600 million Universal Studios Florida theme park in Orlando. Rank invested £115 million for a 50 percent interest in the project, which opened in 1990 and by 1994 was attracting seven million visitors a year and generating £11.4 million in profits for Rank. In 1995, MCA and Rank began work on a $2 billion expansion that would include a second theme park called Islands of Adventure, scheduled to open in 1999.

In 1990, Rank offered to acquire Mecca Leisure Group for £512 million ($819 million). Mecca's management initially rejected the offer, then suddenly accepted it two months later. Mecca's holdings—hotels, theme parks, 85 bingo parlors, and 11 Hard Rock Cafes—fit in well with Rank's operations. Under Rank, some of these operations were expanded, such as the Hard Rock Cafes—that chain grew to 15 units by 1995—while others were closed or sold off, such as the hotels, the last of which Rank sold in 1994.

With these additions, Rank's revenue surged from £1.33 billion in 1990 to £2.11 billion in 1991. Over the next few years, revenue increased only slightly to £2.2 billion in 1994. Surprisingly, the increase in revenue did not reduce the firm's dependence on its Rank Xerox stake. The amount of profits owing to RX surpassed 50 percent once again by the mid-1990s. Rank made a move to lessen the role of RX in the company's future. In January 1995, it sold to Xerox 40 percent of its interest in RX for £620 million. Rank intended to use the funds to invest in leisure and recreation businesses.

This was perhaps a fitting time for a leadership transition at Rank since it was Gifford who had consistently focused on leisure and recreation during his reign at Rank and now had reduced its stake in its most important holding outside this area. Gifford announced in 1995 that he would retire in 1996, and Rank began the search for a new leader.

The question for Rank—now operating as the Rank Group Plc—at this point in its history was whether it would invest its Rank Xerox money wisely, since what the firm did with its excess money had often been its downfall in the past. Signs indicated that Rank would increasingly concentrate on the leisure, recreation, and entertainment industries through the rest of the 1990s and that perhaps it would sell its entire stake in Rank Xerox to provide additional funding for expansion.

Restructuring in the Late 1990s and Beyond

Sure enough, Rank launched a costly acquisition program in 1996 fueled by a strategic divestiture program that included the sale of its remaining interest in Rank Xerox. The company purchased Duplico, a video duplicator, and Tom Cobleigh, a chain of UK-based pubs and restaurants. In 1997, Rank bought the Hard Rock Cafes and brand rights that it did not already own in the Caribbean and Argentina. Parkdean Holidays was added to the company's arsenal the following year.

By 1999, however, it was apparent that Rank was suffering under a major debt load. Its acquisition activity over the past several years had failed to produce positive financial results. As such, Rank tapped betting and gaming industry executive Mike Smith to oversee the company's turnaround. Named CEO in April 1999, Smith immediately began a major streamlining effort designed to restore profits and reshape the company into an international entertainment and leisure group. The firm began to focus solely on its Gaming, Hard Rock, and Deluxe Film and Media Services divisions and started to divest its holdings that were considered unrelated to its core businesses. In 2000, Rank sold off its nightclubs, its Holidays division, Odeon Cinemas, and Pinewood Studios. It also sold its 50 percent interest in Florida-based Universal Studios Escape and the Tom Cobleigh chain.

At the same time, the company looked to bolster its remaining divisions. Rank made several purchases to strengthen its film and media services unit, adding Electric Switch and Pioneer Video Manufacturing Inc. to its portfolio. London's Park Tower Casino was acquired in 2000. Other gaming ventures included the creation of online casinos and the 2003 purchase of Blue Square Ltd., a leading Internet and telephone betting concern. The company also planned to expand its Hard Rock segment. In 2003, the Hard Rock division formed a joint venture with Sol Melia SA to develop Hard Rock Hotels in Europe and the Americas.

While the long term effects of Smith's restructuring efforts were not yet known, Rank stood well positioned to benefit from future deregulation in the U.K. gaming industry slated to take effect in 2005. A February 2004 *Financial Times* article reported, ''Changes to the gambling laws are expected to lead to growth in casino gaming because many of the restrictions that have prohibited operators from opening premises and attracting customers will be scrapped.'' According to Rank's 2003 annual report, deregulation could lead anywhere from an 82 to 98 percent increase in the number of casinos in the United Kingdom. In 2003, the company had 36 U.K. casino licenses and 121 bingo clubs, giving it a distinct advantage over its competitors if and when the new gaming laws took effect.

Principal Subsidiaries

Rank Group Finance plc; Rank Leisure Holdings plc; Grosvenor Casinos Ltd.; Mecca Bingo Ltd.; Rank Leisure Machine Services Ltd.; Rank Group Gaming Division Ltd.; Hard Rock Café International (U.S.) Inc.; Hard Rock International Ltd.; Hard Rock Canada Inc.; Deluxe Laboratories Ltd.; Deluxe Laboratories Inc. (United States); Deluxe Toronto Ltd.; Deluxe Media Services Inc. (United States); Deluxe Global Media Services LLC (United States; 80%); Rank America Inc.

Principal Divisions

Gaming; Hard Rock Cafes, Hotels, and Casinos; Deluxe Film and Media Services.

Principal Competitors

DOCdata N.V.; Hilton Group plc; Planet Hollywood International Inc.

Further Reading

Armes, Roy, *A Critical History of the British Cinema*, New York: Oxford University Press, 1978, 374 p.

Daneshkhu, Scheherazade, "From Hard Times to Hard Rock," *Financial Times*, September 27, 1995, p. 23.

Ferry, Jeffrey, "Rank Returns to Its Roots," *Forbes*, August 6, 1990, pp. 60–61.

Garrahan, Matthew, "Rank Set to Take a Punt on Hard Rock Casinos," *Financial Times*, February 28, 2004, p. 2.

Grow, Brian, "Where the Hard Rock Is Going Soft," *Business Week Online*, October 29, 2003.

Laurance, Ben, "Embattled Empire Strikes Back," *Observer*, August 8, 1999, p. 7.

"Rank Feels the Pressure," *Leisure & Hospitality Business*, August 22, 2002.

"Rank Refocus Is Clearer as Disposals Continue," *LeisureWeek*, March 9, 2000.

Robinson, Elizabeth, "Rank's New Head Raises Hopes of Changes," *Financial Times*, January 30, 1999, p. 21.

Smith, Terry, "The Good, the Bad, and the Ugly," *Management Today*, September 1995, pp. 54–60.

"Struggling Back into the First Rank Is a Big Challenge," *Financial Times*, September 30, 2000, p. 18.

Wendlandt, Astrid, "Rank Sells Its Games and Slot Machines Divisions for Pounds 30m," *Financial Times*, October 31, 2003, p. 26.

—Jonathan Martin
—updates: David E. Salamie and Christina M. Stansell

Ravensburger◢

Ravensburger AG

Marktstrasse 22-26
D-88188 Ravensburg
Germany
Telephone: (+49) 751 86-0
Fax: (+49) 751 86-1289
Web site: http://www.ravensburger.com

Private Company
Incorporated: 1893 as Otto Maier, Verlagsbuchhandlung
Employees: 1,441
Sales: EUR 258 million ($324 million) (2003)
NAIC: 339932 Game, Toy, and Children's Vehicle
   Manufacturing; 511130 Book Publishers

Ravensburger AG is a publisher based in Ravensburg, Germany, that educates and entertains the whole family with its broad variety of puzzles, games, books, TV shows, and arts and crafts kits. The company is Europe's leading manufacturer of jigsaw puzzles, which are manufactured in Germany and the Czech Republic and marketed throughout the continent by the company's subsidiaries in major Western European countries. Ravensburger is also a leading manufacturer of brand name board games, and the Ravensburger brand is known by over 90 percent of German consumers. The company's game and toy manufacturing arm accounts for roughly 80 percent of total sales and about half of the company's revenues are generated around Christmas. Ravensburger's book publishing arm publishes educational and entertaining books for children, from toddlers to teenagers. The company's products are exported to more than 50 countries around the world. Other Ravensburger subsidiaries produce programming for German television stations, help brand name companies with event planning and promotion, and run the company's amusement park. Ravensburger is owned by fewer than a dozen members of the founding Maier family.

Bookstore Owner Becomes a Publisher in 1884

As a publishing enterprise, Ravensburger evolved from the Dorn'sche Buchhandlung, a bookstore in the southern German town Ravensburg near the Bodensee lake. Since 1845, the bookstore had been partly owned and run by bookseller, journalist, and publisher Carl Maier. After his sudden death in 1867, his wife Julie inherited his share in the bookstore. In 1876, after completing apprenticeships with booksellers in Berlin, Graz, and Zurich, Carl Maier's oldest son Otto Robert—then 24 years old—became co-owner of the Dorn'sche Buchhandlung. Besides managing the bookstore in Ravensburg, he soon developed a special interest in the publishing activities the store ran as a side business. Accommodating the bookstore's customers, Dorn'sche Buchhandlung published maps and booklets focusing on the geography, biology, and history of the region, how-to literature for craftspeople, textbooks for schoolchildren, sheet music of church hymns, and a few board games. In 1883, Otto Robert Maier signed his first publishing contract with two architects to produce a collection of patterns for gravestones to be used by local stonemasons. One year later, Maier signed a local teacher and author to create eight *Gesellschaftsspiele*—games for adults—which were then released by Dorn'sche Buchhandlung.

In 1884, Maier published his first commissioned board game for the whole family: *Reise um die Erde* ("A Trip Around The World"). The game was modeled after the popular novel by Jules Verne, *Around the World in 80 Days,* which had been published nine years earlier. By the time the game was published, there was already a thriving market for a broad variety of games for children, teenagers, and adults in Germany. *Reise um die Erde,* in which players could follow the adventurer Phineas Fogg on his trip around the world, became a bestseller and remained in Maier's catalogue for 30 years. Besides the use of a popular theme, the game's success was credited primarily to its lavish color and graphics, its detailed tin figurines, and the high-quality durable board. A handful of suppliers—specialty printers, book binders, figurine and dice makers—delivered the different parts for this and other popular games that followed. They were then assembled, put into boxes, and shipped from Maier's bookstore.

While these games gave the young publisher a chance to follow his strong interests and talent in art and creative design, the financial backbone of his enterprise grew out of a different line of publications. In 1885, Maier published a collection of patterns for stonemasons and gravestone designers. At the time, construction and related activities were booming in the newly founded German Empire, and the fashion of the time was to embellish new buildings with style elements from earlier eras. Therefore, patterns and other how-to literature related to such architectural styles were in great demand by architects, stone engravers, locksmiths, and painters. Targeting regional craftspeople, Maier published patterns that they could easily use. In order to avoid high cash advances, Maier asked the authors he signed to deliver their work in regular installments, which were then published as one volume of a larger collection. This method generated a steady cash flow that made Maier's publications easier to finance and more affordable for his customers. It also allowed him to pay the authors and printers for the next installment out of the revenues the last one generated. Within 30 years, Maier had published about 90 such pattern collections, each of which comprised between 5 and 15 bound volumes.

In 1891, Maier became the sole owner of Dorn'sche Buchhandlung. Two years later, he sold the bookstore and decided to devote his time and energy exclusively to publishing. In 1892, his publishing business Otto Maier, Verlagsbuchhandlung was officially registered in Ravensburg. By then, Maier had married, become a father, and moved in with his in-laws, who were lawyers. By 1899, he had moved his business to another building in Ravensburg's center, moved his family to a newly built residence, published a number of short stories for young readers written by a local minister, and authored a number of games and patterns under the pseudonyms "Otto Robert" and "C. Hoffmann."

Expansion in Germany and Europe after 1900

Between 1880 and 1915, the number of game publishers exploded. In 1900, Otto Robert Maier registered *Ravensburger Spiele* ("Ravensburger Games") as a trademark. Realizing that his business could succeed only if his products were sold throughout Germany, Maier hired Jacob Dietler, an experienced bookseller, as a traveling salesman. By 1902, Maier's product catalogue included about 100 games and roughly 50 hardcover books for teenage readers, arts and crafts sets, picture books for children, language guides in pocket book format, as well as technical, legal, and medical publications. Besides visiting bookstores, Dietler's task was to offer Maier's products to toy and stationery stores. At the same time, the company founder systematically employed all the marketing tools available to him to reach potential customers, including brochures, advertisements, and press releases. Maier also realized that he had to adjust the cost of his products to his customers' financial resources. Therefore, his cut-out books, picture books, and games were available in different editions, either hardcover or paperback, with accessories of varying cost.

The next logical step to expand his business was to move beyond Germany's borders. In 1912, Maier started offering some of his games in nine different European languages. However, the beginning of World War I interrupted this endeavor. By that time, Maier's enterprise employed 19 people and generated a quarter million goldmarks. Maier's oldest and youngest sons Otto and Eugen had to serve in the German army during the war, while his son Karl helped manage the business. After returning from the battlefield in 1918, Otto and Eugen also became involved in the family business. Three years later, Otto Maier became a co-owner and managing director. By that time, the German economy began to feel the impact of the increasing inflation that quickly picked up speed in the early 1920s. Selling books and games became much easier because people were eager to spend their money as soon as they received it. On the other hand, suppliers delayed their shipments. To become more independent, the Maiers hired an experienced book binder and two printers to work on the company's premises. The company's cash was used to purchase another building in the Ravensburg city center, right next to the one the publishing house already occupied. In 1924, the company founder retired. His oldest son, Otto, became the company's new executive director, while Karl and Eugen became shareholders. Otto Robert Maier died in December 1925.

Second Generation Takes over in 1925

Besides his duties as executive director, Otto Maier oversaw the development of the book publishing business. His brother Karl took on the management of the arts and crafts collection and technical books, while his brother Eugen devoted himself to the development of new games and children's books, as well as to the improvement of the internal workflow of the company. When the worldwide economic depression hit Germany in the early 1930s, the company could not avoid layoffs and shortened hours but limited the scope of the crisis by launching its own public works program—the renovation of one of its inner-city buildings.

After 1933, when Adolf Hitler's National Socialist Party (Nazi) came to power, the company focused on specialized books for the construction trade, for artists and craftspeople such as carpenters, arts and crafts kits for children and teens, and on arts and crafts books. Activities such as woodworking and model plane assembly for boys or weaving and sewing for girls were greatly encouraged and widely taught at school and in the various youth organizations the Nazis had formed. A book series for artists covered various instructional guides for oil and water color painting, painting of miniatures, pastel and charcoal drawing, lithography, woodcut and linoleum printmaking, letter art types, and technical drawing. Maier's non-political product range saved the company from being shut down—a fate suffered by many other German publishing houses. However, a

Key Dates:

1884: Otto Maier begins publishing board games and books.

1885: Maier published a collection of patterns for stonemasons.

1893: The publishing business Otto Maier, Verlagsbuchhandlung is officially registered.

1912: Otto Maier launches foreign versions of its board games.

1923: The company establishes its own production department.

1945: Otto Maier Verlag survives World War II undamaged and receives a publishing license.

1946: The company's graphic design department is formed.

1959: The game Memory is launched.

1960: The game Malefiz ("Barricade") is introduced.

1964: Ravensburger puzzles are launched.

1977: The book and game publishing arms become two separate subsidiaries.

1981: The company's legal form is changed to a limited liability corporation.

1984: A television production subsidiary, Ravensburger Film + TV, GmbH, is formed.

1988: The company becomes a family-owned corporation.

1993: Management Holding company Ravensburger AG is established.

1998: Ravensburger acquires French game manufacturer Jeux Nathan.

2001: The company launches a massive product innovation program.

number of Jewish authors the publisher had worked with fled the country to escape the wave of increasingly violent anti-Semitism. At the onset of World War II in 1939, Maier employed 65 people. Many of them, including Eugen Maier, were inducted into the military. As more and more German cities became the target of bombings, securing the company's assets became the most important task of the remaining workers. It was successfully accomplished. Luckily, none of the company's buildings in Ravensburg had been demolished during the war. Machinery and equipment, office furniture, even some of Maier's inventory survived. However, the war took a much greater toll: Eugen Maier died on May 8, 1945, the day when the war officially ended in Europe.

Trade Magazine Publishing after World War II

The company's luck continued in the chaotic years following the war. Only a few days after French soldiers had marched into Ravensburg in late April 1945, they went shopping at Otto Maier Verlag, standing in line to buy one of their favorite games with instructions in French instead of simply confiscating them. At the same time, the company's offices had been crammed with old printed material, none of which were seized for use by the Allied military government. In the following weeks, Otto Maier's employees lived from the cash flow generated by selling old inventory over the counter to a steady stream of "pilgrims" who came to Ravensburg to snatch some of their favorite games or books from "the good old days." Only six months after the war had ended, Otto Maier Verlag received an official permit from the French authorities to resume operations. Despite the red tape—every publication had to be approved by the military government—the company was ready to write a new chapter of its history.

Realizing that the reconstruction of the country would be the foremost task for many years to come, Otto Maier set his sights on publishing a new professional book for bricklayers. In November 1945, a man named Tress visited Maier in Ravensburg and proposed publishing a trade journal for the construction industry. Although the company had never published a periodical, Otto Maier agreed to work with Tress. In May 1946, he received the license to publish the journal, which was named *BAUEN UND WOHNEN* ("Construction and Residences"). The first issue, which was 24 pages long, was published soon after and the print run of 15,500 copies sold out. Between 1946 and 1951, Otto Maier Verlag published between 6 and 12 issues a year with print runs between 8,000 and 15,500. After the currency reform in 1948, sales of the journal dropped significantly. In addition, another such publication with almost the identical title evolved in neighboring Switzerland in 1947, and the legal battle between the two over rights to the name of the journal went on until 1951. With other editorial, production, and advertising issues mounting, Otto Maier decided to drop the project. In the following year, he suddenly died after a surgery. He was 62 years old.

Renewed Success with Games in the Late 1950s

The cash from publishing *BAUEN UND WOHNEN* helped Otto Maier Verlag enormously in getting its traditional branches back on their feet after the war. By 1948, the company's workforce had reached prewar levels. Two years later, three traveling salesmen were back on the road again. Around the same time, the company began to present its products at the major annual book and toy trade shows in Frankfurt/Main and Nuremberg. After Otto Maier's death, his brother Karl became the company's executive director. He oversaw the expansion of its printing department, the creation of a sales department, the reorganization of the company's accounting division, and the reallocation of management responsibilities among the third generation of the Maier family. Otto Maier's son Otto Julius joined the company's technical book department and gradually acquainted himself with all aspects of the family business. Eugen Maier's son Peter took an interest in the company's books for children and youth and in finding new game ideas. In 1955, Willi Baumann, an experienced traveling book salesman, joined the company. He brought not only a growing number of orders but also invaluable insight into the marketplace. Determined to help launch Otto Maier Verlag to a new level of success, he tried to influence business decisions regarding the company's product lines, pressured for predictable publication dates, and finally took on the management of the company's sales department in 1959. In the same year, Peter Maier's sister Dorothee joined the company to learn the book selling and publishing trade. After finishing her training, she took over the editorial management of Otto Maier Verlag's book publishing arm in 1962. Also in that year, Peter Maier, who had successfully established a graphic design department, left the company to pursue projects of his own. Four years later, he gave up his share in Otto Maier Verlag.

Meanwhile, the company's markets underwent fundamental changes during the 1950s. The demand for the publisher's books for the trades decreased as mechanization made its way into the construction industry. Improved technologies brought about changes in the arts and crafts market, where instructional literature and old-fashioned cut-out books were replaced by kits with pre-fabricated parts. Within only a few years, the company's sales dropped sharply, while much of its cash was invested in acquiring a large piece of land in Ravensburg's business district and in expanding the in-house printing department. However, big German and Swiss toy retail chains started asking the company for new board games. At that time, Ravensburger's reputation among Germany's toy retailers was synonymous with high quality. When the diminished cash flow was just about to cause a severe financial crisis, a number of successful board games helped turn around the company's fate once again. A soccer board game created by a popular German sports reporter was launched in 1957 and became a bestseller. One year later, following the demand from toy retailers, the company brought out a kit for amateur magicians, which was also well received. In 1959, Otto Maier Verlag published Memory, a game by Swiss inventor Heinrich Hurter. One year later, the company introduced another game by German inventor Werner Schöppner, which Karl Maier named *Malefiz*. Memory and *Malefiz,* which became known as "Barricade" in non-German speaking countries, turner out to be huge sellers that helped establish the company among Europe's leading makers of board games. By the early 1960s, games contributed more to Otto Maier Verlag's total sales than books. In 1963, Otto Julius Maier became a personally liable shareholder in the company, which employed roughly 280 people and generated DM 10 million in sales in 1964.

Puzzles, Electronic Gaming, and More: Mid-1960s–Early 2000s

Throughout the second half of the 20th century, Otto Maier Verlag managed to stay on top of the German board game market. The company also continued to publish educational book series for children and teenagers. However, the major boost in sales during that time period came from another novelty the publisher put out in 1964 for the first time: jigsaw puzzles. Made out of thin wood, and later from cardboard, the puzzles became Otto Maier Verlag's new signature product. Since there was no need for any instructions in foreign languages, exporting the puzzles was no problem. In the mid-1960s, the company began to set up subsidiaries in many Western European countries, including Switzerland, Austria, France, and the United Kingdom. During the 1970s, the company's business soared. In 1977, the games and book departments were transformed into legally independent subsidiaries, Ravensburger Spieleverlag GmbH and Ravensburger Buchverlag Otto Maier GmbH. By 1978, the company's workforce had grown to roughly 800, including 27 traveling salesmen, and sales had grown more than tenfold

within 14 years, passing the DM 100 million mark for the first time. In 1979, Karl Maier died at age 85.

In the 1980s, electronic media such as television, video, and computer games began to change the way people spent their leisure time. Ravensburger ventured into the evolving market in different ways. The company founded a television production subsidiary, Ravensburger Film & TV GmbH, that created and produced animated and entertaining shows for children and families.

A venture into interactive media in the mid-1990s, including "educational entertainment" CD-ROMs and computer programs, was abandoned in 2002. Besides the new electronic media, Ravensburger wanted to profit from two other trends: event marketing and amusement parks. In 1993, the company established Ravensburger Freizeit- und Promotion-Service GmbH, a marketing, event planning, and promotion service for large manufacturers of brand-name products and for operators of leisure facilities for children. Five years later, the company's amusement park Ravensburger Spieleland opened its doors. A number of acquisitions and high-risk investments in the late 1990s caused a sudden financial meltdown of the company's capital and resulted in several million euros of net losses in 1999 and 2000. After streamlining the company's operations and cutting the group's activities back to its core markets, Ravensburger was back in the black again in 2001.

The process of creating a company that was able to function without the involvement of family members began in 1981, when its legal form was changed from a company with personally liable family shareholders into a limited liability corporation. In 1988, the company was transformed into the legal form of a joint stock company. Five years later, a holding company named Ravensburger AG was established as an organizational umbrella for the group's various activities. In 1995, Otto Julius Maier retired from the management of the Ravensburger group and became president of its advisory board. His cousin, Dorothee Hess-Maier, succeeded him as executive director until she retired in 2000, while the day-to-day business was managed by two experienced executives from outside the family. The Ravensburger group was hoping to succeed in a domestic toy market that was stagnating at the same time that competition from large international toy manufacturers and retail chains was increasing. Toward this goal, the company began manufacturing new products such as "intelligent" board games with integrated electronic modules, three-dimensional puzzles, toys for toddlers, electronic games for young men under 20, and stuffed animals modeled after popular cartoon characters under license agreements.

Principal Subsidiaries

Ravensburger Spieleverlag GmbH; Ravensburger Buchverlag Otto Maier GmbH; Ravensburger Freizeit- und Promotion-Service GmbH; Ravensburger Spieleland AG; F.X. Schmid Vereinigte Münchener Spielkartenfabriken GmbH & Co. KG; Ravensburger S.p.A. (Italy); Ravensburger Gesellschaft m.b.H. (Austria); Carlit + Ravensburger AG (Switzerland); Jeux Ravensburger S.A. (France); Ravensburger B.U. (Netherlands); Ravensburger Karton s.r.o. Policka (Czech Republic); Ravensburger Ltd. (United Kingdom); Ravensburger F.X. Schmid USA Inc.

Principal Competitors

Hasbro, Inc.; Schmidt Spiel + Freizeit GmbH; AMIGO Spiel + Freizeit GmbH; Carlsen Verlag GmbH; Friedrich Oettinger Verlag, Loewe Verlag GmbH.

Further Reading

1883–1983: Hundert Jahre Verlangsarbeit Otto Maier Verlag Ravensburg, Ravensburg, Germany: Otto Maier Verlag Ravensburg, 1983.

''Eine fast antikapitalistische Verlegerin,'' *Financial Times* (Deutschland), November 20, 2002, p. 37.

Goldschmitt, Wolf H., ''Moorhuhn und Teletubbies verdrängen Malefiz & Co.,'' *Welt*, December 13, 2000.

Iwersen, Sönke, ''Ravensburger entdeckt Kleinkinder als Zielgruppe,'' *Stuttgarter Zeitung*, June 4, 2003, p. 13.

Simonian, Haig, ''Gegen die Spielregeln verstoßen und gewinnen,'' *Financial Times* (Deutschland), May 8, 2002, p. 38.

—Evelyn Hauser

Raving Brands, Inc.

1935 Peachtree Road
Atlanta, Georgia 30309
U.S.A.
Telephone: (404) 355-5400
Fax: (404) 603-8070
Web site: http://www.ravingbrands.com

Private Company
Incorporated: 2003 as Wow! Brands, Inc.
Employees: 78
Sales: NA
NAIC: 722211 Limited-Service Restaurants

Raving Brands, Inc., is an Atlanta-based private company with a portfolio of five fun and irreverent franchise restaurant concepts in the fast-casual category. Planet Smoothie, with 136 franchises, is the third largest fresh fruit smoothie company in the United States. The chain offers four categories of smoothies: Booster, Fat Burner, Wellness, and Workout. Vitamin and other supplements, called Blasts, are also available to customize the drinks. In addition, Planet Smoothie offers a range of sandwiches, wraps, paninis, and salads. Raving Brands' fast-growing Moe's Southwest Grill takes a fresh and healthy approach to southwest cuisine while adopting a lighthearted attitude. Menu items include Joey Bag of Donuts, Homewrecker, The Ugly Naked Guy, I Said Posse, Puff the Magic Dragon, and Moo Moo Mr. Cow. Another Raving Brands concept is Mama Fu's Noodle House, which offers healthy wok-cooked Korean, Thai, Vietnamese, Chinese, and Japanese food. As with other Raving Brands restaurants, Mama Fu attempts to create a high energy and fun atmosphere. Doc Green's Gourmet Salads, Raving Brands' latest concept, specializes in healthy and fresh made-to-order salads, casseroles, and sandwiches. PJ's Coffee is Raving Brands' only acquired concept. In addition to franchising Starbucks-like PJ's Coffee outlets, Raving Brands has launched PJ's Coffee and Wine Bars to create a hybrid category to set the franchise apart from Starbucks and other coffee house chains.

1980s Origins

After graduating from the University of North Carolina at Chapel Hill, Raving Brands founder, Martin Sprock, spent five years in commercial real estate with Portman, Barry and Carter during the 1980s. He became involved in the restaurant business when his favorite bar, Clarence Foster's, closed. He team up with the bar's founder and reopened the business at a new location. Sprock went on to build or buy a number of other bars and nightclubs in the Southeast, creating a profitable business. But in the early 1990s he decided to sell off his interests and start over, eschewing the nightlife for healthy family-oriented food and beverage restaurant concepts.

Sprock's first idea was to take advantage of the rising popularity of the smoothie, a concept that had been pioneered by the Orange Julius chain, which had begun selling juice drinks with a smoothie consistency back in the 1920s. The term smoothie did not come into popular usage until the 1980s. The drinks were mostly sold at health clubs and so-called juice bars on the West Coast. Sprock saw an opening to sell nutritional smoothies in the Southeast and in 1995 opened a store in Atlanta he called Planet Smoothie. He quickly began to build a chain of Planet Smoothie stores and within two years had 25 partnered locations in Atlanta and another 20 spread across the Southeast. Reflecting his playful attitude were the names Sprock gave to his smoothie concoctions: Werewolf, Frozen Goat, Two Piece Bikini, and Mr. Mongo. Like other smoothie chains emerging across the country, Planet Smoothie viewed its drinks as meal replacements, but most consumers still required the "chew factor," which led to the introduction of wraps in the Atlanta stores in the fall of 1997.

Planet Smoothie began to franchise in mid-1998 and by the end of 1999 topped the 100-unit mark. Generally the chain targeted strip mall locations but began looking to shopping mall food courts as well as less traditional sites such as airports and office buildings. In Atlanta Planet Smoothie worked a co-branding arrangement with Exxon, establishing outposts in three convenience store gas stations. The chain's menu evolved in the meantime, with a number of new wraps offered. Store design also was upgraded, with menu boards simplified, and a more fun, hip, and lighthearted décor was introduced, more in

Company Perspectives:

Atlanta-based Raving Brands features a franchisee-centric portfolio of fun, healthy and fresh restaurant concepts.

keeping with the image Sprock wanted to convey. Colors that mirrored the fruits used in the drinks—reds, oranges, yellows, and greens—were now employed.

Although Sprock talked about opening 250 Planet Smoothies operations in 2000 and 1,000 total units by 2002, the smoothie market was quickly becoming saturated. Competition not only included other smoothie chains—such as Jamba Juice, Smoothie King, Freshens Smoothies, and Juice Works—but also ice cream chains Baskin Robbins and Dairy Queen and local restaurants, health food stores, and health clubs. To better compete, Planet Smoothie refined its menu in 2000, adding blended soups. The chain was also very successful in establishing Planet Smoothie as a fun brand. Nevertheless, accelerated growth did not materialize and the chain stalled around the 135-unit level. An attempt to launch a health and nutrition web site called Planet Living was shelved in the aftermath of the dot-com bubble bursting.

Moe's Southwest Grill Debuts in 2000

Sprock now looked for a new restaurant concept to franchise, one that would embody the same values as Planet Smoothie—merging a zany outlook and eclectic environment with healthy fast food. In addition, he wanted any new franchise concepts to have the ability to coexist, so that if joined they could offer customers a choice of healthy food at one location. He settled on Mexican food and launched Moe's Southwest Grill, which Sprock described as "a Mexican Subway." According to the *Atlanta Business Chronicle*, "Moe's was based in small part on [Atlanta] local favorite Willy's Mexicana Grille. Sprock even offered to go into business with Willy's founders." Moe's was intended to be a cut above the typical Mexican burrito shop, offering a wholesome ambience as well as fresh food. Everything was to be made from scratch and no freezers or microwaves were to be found on the premises. Like Planet Smoothie, Moe's coined colorful names for menu items and created a fun atmosphere. When customers entered they were greeted by an employee calling out "Welcome to Moe's." The first store opened in December 2000 in the Buckhead section of Atlanta in the Peach Shopping Center. Moe's was not the only fresh Mexican food chain that was attempting to crack the market, but the Moe's concept took hold and soon became the fastest growing chain in the category.

Sprock's next franchising concept came by way of acquisition and was again inspired by personal experience. He told the *Atlanta Business Chronicle* that his wife got tired of drinking $3.50 cups of "trendy" coffee. In 2002 he acquired New Orleans-based PJ's Coffee and Tea Co., a 25-shop chain. PJ stood for the chain's founder, Phyllis Jordan. She moved from Des Moines, Iowa, to New Orleans in 1977, escaping an unsatisfactory job as a social worker to open a store that sold whole coffee beans and loose tea. She soon began to sell prepared drinks as well. It was not until 1984 that she opened her second

store, and five years later, in 1989, she began to franchise PJ's. After selling the chain to Sprock she stayed on as an adviser on product development. Included in the sale was a coffee roasting and packaging plant in New Orleans, which was underutilized. According to Jordan the plant could roast three times as many coffee beans, which meant the chain was well positioned to support significant growth. Not only did Sprock and the PJ's management team plan to aggressively franchise the coffee shops, with the goal of becoming the second largest in the category behind only the Starbucks chain, but also to begin selling wine in some of the shops. This idea would ultimately lead to the introduction of PJ's Coffee and Wine Bar. The belief was that wine would complement the chain's quality coffee and increase evening traffic. Because more than half of the income would come from coffee and tea sales, PJ's would still be classified as a restaurant.

Forming Raving Brands in 2003

Sprock was in the vanguard in the emergence of the healthy, made-to-order food fast-casual restaurant sectors, one of the hottest trends in the industry. One reason offered for this shift was that consumers had become more health-conscious and customers appreciated watching their food prepared; fast-food restaurants, on the other hand, failed to keep pace. University of Central Florida restaurant professor Chris Muller further speculated to the *Orlando Sentinel* in a 2004 article on what accounted for the sudden rise in the category: "9-11 was a catalyst in the industry—a bolt of lightning that really shook things up. . . . Because so many people were out of work and returned to the restaurant industry, all of a sudden we had a pop of new ideas. The growth of fast-casual restaurants has energized the business. We're seeing new Mexican, Asian, and other concepts like we never have before." To house his budding empire of fast-casual franchise concepts, in 2003 Sprock formed a holding company named Wow! Brands, which soon was renamed Raving Brands.

In 2003 Raving Brands conducted a four-month trial in an Orlando Planet Smoothie store, which was converted into a Planet Smoothie Café concept. A number of items were added to the menu to help differentiate the smoothie chain. The trial proved successful enough that management elected to move forward on franchising the café idea. The food items, branded as Planet Smoothie Eats, included such breakfast fare as energy bowls, egg beaters, and cereal; lunch items like veggie wraps and lemongrass chicken panini; and a children's menu that offered soy-based peanut butter and jelly sandwiches and fruit rollups.

It was also in 2003 that Raving Brands launched yet another new fast-casual healthy food concept, exploring Pan-Asian cuisine: Mama Fu's Noodle House. The name was coined by Sprock who reportedly thought "Fu" was a fun word and that the addition of "Mama" provided southern connotations. Like Moe's, the new concept relied heavily on a funky atmosphere: bright colors and 1980s music. Employees greeted diners with "Come to Mama." The first Mama Fu Restaurant was opened in Buckhead in June 2003. Due in large part to the success of Moe's, Raving Brands was able to quickly pitch Mama Fu to franchisers. By the end of 2003 the company had commitments for 175 Mama Fu restaurants across the country. Former Wendy's International executive John Casey, for instance, signed a deal to open 44 franchises in Florida. In 2004 Mama Fu planned to open additional restaurants in the Atlanta area and more than 50 altogether. Initially the chain looked to target southeastern markets—Georgia, Florida, North Carolina, and South Carolina—with hopes of moving into such growth markets as Houston, Los Angeles, and Washington, D.C.

Far from content, Sprock launched yet another healthy, fast-casual concept in 2004: Doc Green's Gourmet Salad stores. The source for this idea came from Sprock's own frustration in finding a good salad. He told the *Atlanta Business Chronicle* in January 2004, "Sometimes you want to eat something a little lighter, but those wimpy fast-food salads or '70s-style salad buffet troughs aren't appetizing at all. . . . We know we can do a better job in the salad business." A Doc Green's corporate store was opened in Atlanta in 2004, offering made-to-order salads with a range of salad greens, lettuces, and vegetables, as well as such toppings as chicken, fish, crumbled cheese, nuts, and a number of dressings. In addition, Doc Green's offered soups, panini sandwiches, and other bistro items. Like other Raving Brands restaurants, Doc Green's relied on vibrant colors and popular music on the sound system.

In 2004 Raving Brands planned to open ten Doc Green's, 50 Planet Smoothies, 150 Moe's, 50 Mama Fu's, and 25 PJ's. The goal was to have 1,000 units between the five concepts in the near future. But even the idea of such a mini-empire did not satisfy Sprock and Raving Brands. He continued to look for new fast-casual concepts. Very likely his next move would be into the seafood category. He told the *Atlanta Business Chronicle* in 2003, "It's something I've thought about, and it hasn't really been done well before. . . . And maybe if nobody else (meaning possible franchisers) likes the idea, I might go ahead and do it myself."

Principal Subsidiaries

Moe's Southwestern Grill, LLC; Mama Fu's Noodle House, Inc.; Planet Smoothie Franchises LLC; PJ's USA, Inc.; Doc Green's Gourmet Salads Inc.

Principal Competitors

Jamba Juice Company; Smoothie King Franchises, Inc.; Chipotle Mexican Grill, Inc.; Fresh Enterprises, Inc.; Santa Barbara Restaurant Group.

Further Reading

Butler, Elizabeth, "PJ's Coffee and Tea Co. Pours into New Markets," *New Orleans City Business,* January 26, 2004, p. 1.

Credeur, Mary Jane, "Chain Sees Green in Salad," *Atlanta Business Chronicle,* January 23, 2004, p. A3.

Gibson, Richard, "In Search of the Next Hot Dog," *Wall Street Journal,* August 6, 1999, p. B1.

Meitner, Sarah Hale, "Ethnic Fast-Casual to Spice Up Fare Offerings in Orlando, Fla., Area," *Orlando Sentinel,* January 12, 2004.

Mello, Marina, "He Hopes You'll Buy an 'Ugly Naked Guy,' " *Atlanta Business Chronicle,* December 8, 2000, p. A3.

Strauss, Karyn, "Planet Smoothie Orbits New Growth Strategy," *Nation's Restaurant News,* November 22, 1999, p. 8.

——, "Smoothie Indies Face Rocky Road As Chains Slurp Up Market Share," *Nation's Restaurant News,* June 14, 1999, p. 8.

—Ed Dinger

REVLON

Revlon Inc.

237 Park Avenue
New York, New York 10017
U.S.A.
Telephone: (212) 527-4000
Toll Free: (800) 473-8566
Fax: (212) 527-4995
Web site: http://www.revlon.com

Public Company
Incorporated: 1933 as Revlon Products Corporation
Employees: 6,100
Sales: $1.29 billion (2003)
Stock Exchanges: New York
Ticker Symbol: REV
NAIC: 32562 Toilet Preparation Manufacturing

Revlon Inc. operates as one of the world's leading cosmetics companies and markets its products in over 100 countries under such familiar brands as Revlon, ColorStay, Age Defying, Almay, and Skinlights. Revlon also sells skin care products (Ultima II, Vitamin C Absolutes, Eterna 27), fragrances (Charlie), and personal care products (High Dimension, Flex, Mitchum, Colorsilk). Ronald Perelman, who gained control of the company in a nasty hostile takeover in 1985, owns approximately 83 percent of Revlon.

A Nail Polish Company Is Founded in 1932

Revlon's first beauty item was nail enamel. Opaque and long-lasting, it was an improvement over the more transparent, dye-based products of other manufacturers. Revlon's nail polish owed its superiority to the use of pigments, which also allowed a wider color range than the light red, medium red, and dark red then available. Initially, the revolutionary "cream enamel" came from the tiny Elka company, in Newark, New Jersey, a polish supplier to beauty salons for whom Charles Revson began to work as a sales representative in 1931. Charles Revson and his older brother Joseph distributed Elka nail polish as Revson Brothers. Within a year, however, Charles Revson

decided to open his own nail polish company, going into partnership with his brother and a nail polish supplier named Charles R. Lachman, who contributed the "l" to the Revlon name. Revlon was formed on March 1, 1932.

Revson had a keen fashion instinct, honed by his seven years of sales experience at the Pickwick Dress Company in New York. Coupling this with his experience at Elka, he noted that the permanent wave boom was making beauty salons more popular and that demand for manicures was rising in tandem. He therefore targeted beauty salons as a market niche—a fortunate choice whose importance would grow.

Within its first nine months, the company boasted sales of $4,055. There was a sharp rise in sales to $11,246 in 1933, the year the company incorporated as Revlon Products Corporation. At the end of 1934, the company had grossed $68,000. By 1937, sales multiplied more than 40 times. In that year, Revson decided to enlarge his market by retailing his nail polish through department stores and selected drugstores. This gave him access to more affluent customers as well as those with a moderate amount of money to spend on beauty products. Formulating a maxim he followed for the rest of his life, Revson steered clear of cut-rate stores, selling his product only at premium prices.

Advertising helped Revson stick to this rule. Its use was a fateful step for the industry; never again would major cosmetics companies attempt to sell beauty items without it. Revson began by labeling his nail enamels with evocative names such as Fatal Apple and Kissing Pink, which served both to describe a particular color while offering the promise of novelty at the same time. The company's first commercial advertisement appeared in *The New Yorker* in 1935. Aimed carefully at the upper-income clientele Revson was trying to attract, the advertisement came with a price tag of $335, constituting Revlon's entire advertising budget for the year.

By 1940, Revlon had a whole line of manicure products. Lipstick, Revlon's next major item, appeared in 1940. A perfectionist by nature, Revson made sure that its quality was the best he could produce. Its introduction was marked by a full-color advertising campaign stressing the importance of cosmetics as a fashion accessory and featuring the novel idea of "matching lips and fingertips." The campaign's success showed in the 1940 sales figures; reaching $2.8 million, they more than doubled those of 1939.

World War II brought shortages of glass bottles and metal lipstick cases. Paper had to be substituted. Also in short supply were aromatic oils, fixatives, and packaging materials, which had previously been imported from Italy, Ethiopia, and France. Since the shortages affected the entire industry, secrecy was replaced by mutual cooperation, new synthetics and domestic sources of supply were shared, and a new U.S. aromatics industry was born.

During wartime, patriotic activities replaced expansion. In addition to cosmetics, Revlon turned out first-aid kits, dye markers for the navy, and hand grenades for the army. Characteristically, Revson's military products were the best his company could produce. His attention to detail was rewarded in 1944 with an army-navy production award for excellence.

By the end of the war, Revlon listed itself as one of America's top five cosmetic houses. Expanding its capabilities, the company bought Graef & Schmidt, a cutlery manufacturer seized by the government in 1943 because of German business ties. Costing $301,125, this acquisition made it possible for Revlon to produce its own manicure and pedicure instruments, instead of buying them from outside supply sources.

Postwar Promotions and Growth

Postwar sales strategy, too, was influenced by increases in spending and department store credit sales. Returning interest in dress sparked the company's twice-yearly nail enamel and lipstick promotions, which were crafted in anticipation of the season's clothing fashions. Each promotion featured a descriptive color name to tempt the buyer, full-color spreads in fashion magazines, color cards showing the range of colors in the promotion, and display cards reproducing or enlarging consumer ads. Packaging was designed specifically for each line.

The Fire and Ice promotion for fall 1952 was one of the most successful. Its features included the cooperation of *Vogue* magazine, which planned its November issue around the lipstick and nail enamel, "push" money given to demonstrators in stores without Revlon sales staff to insure full retail coverage, and radio endorsements written into scripts for performers such as Bob Hope and Red Skelton. These efforts produced excellent publicity and helped to raise 1952 net sales to almost $25.5 million.

The company received its next boost from its 1955 sole sponsorship of the CBS television show *The $64,000 Question*. Though initially reluctant to go ahead with this project, Revson was persuaded by the success of rival Hazel Bishop, whose

sponsorship of *This is Your Life* was providing serious competition for Revlon's lipsticks. Attracting a weekly audience of 55 million people, *The $64,000 Question* topped the ratings within four weeks of its debut. Revlon's advertising budget for the year, $7.5 million, proved Charles Revson's adage that publicity had to be heavy to sell cosmetics; as a result of the television show, sales of some products increased 500 percent, and net sales for 1955 grew to $51.6 million, from $33.6 million one year previously.

In November 1955, an allegation of wiretapping was filed against Revlon by Hazel Bishop. In testimony given in a hearing before the New York State Legislative Committee to Study Illegal Interception of Communications, the charge was denied by Revlon controller William Heller, who nevertheless admitted "monitoring" employees' telephones for training purposes. Underscoring the denial of Hazel Bishop's charges, a Revlon attorney added a denunciation of wiretapping for industrial espionage and promised cooperation in efforts to stop it.

Also in November 1955, Revlon reorganized as Revlon, Inc. A month later, in December 1955, the company went public. Initially offered at $12 per share, Revlon stock reached $30 within weeks, and the company was listed on the New York Stock Exchange at the end of 1956.

Meanwhile, the success of *The $64,000 Question* soon spurred a spinoff called *The $64,000 Challenge*. The two shows helped to raise the company's net sales figures to $95 million in 1958 and to $110 million in 1959. The three-year bonanza came to an end, however, in 1959, amid charges that both shows had been rigged. At the resulting congressional hearings, the shows' producers and the Revsons blamed each other. Nevertheless, the committee's verdict cleared Revlon of any blame in this matter.

A Segmented Product Line in the 1960s

As the 1960s began, Charles Revson became aware that his company was in danger of locking itself into a narrow, upper-middle-class image that could restrict sales. To avoid this, he borrowed a technique from General Motors and segmented his product line into six principal cosmetics houses, each with its own price range, advertising program, and image. Princess Marcella Borghese aimed for international flair, Revlon was the popular-priced house, Etherea was the hypoallergenic line, Natural Wonder served youthful consumers, Moon Drops catered to dry skins, and Ultima II offered the most expensive products. Top-priced lines were sold only in department stores, while others were available in other outlets. This strategy allowed the company to cover a wide market area without in-house conflict.

Early attempts to diversify into other fields were unsuccessful. For instance, Knomark, a shoe-polish company bought in 1957, sold its shoe-polish lines in 1969. Other poorly chosen acquisitions, such as Ty-D-Bol, the maker of toilet cleansers, and a 27 percent interest in the Schick electric shaver company were also soon discarded. Evan Picone, a women's sportswear manufacturer which came with a price tag of $12 million in 1962, was sold back to one of the original partners four years later for $1 million.

The company's first successful acquisition came in January 1966, when Revson bought U.S. Vitamin & Pharmaceutical

Key Dates:

1932: Brothers Charles and Joseph Revson and Charles R. Lachman establish Revlon.

1935: The company's first ad appears in *The New Yorker* magazine.

1940: Lipstick is added the company's product line.

1955: The company changes its name to Revlon Inc. and goes public.

1966: U.S. Vitamin & Pharmaceutical Corporation is acquired.

1970: Mitchum Co. is purchased.

1973: The Charlie fragrance is launched.

1985: Revlon is sold to Pantry Pride, a subsidiary of Ronald Perelman's MacAndrews & Forbes Holdings, and becomes a private company.

1994: ColorStay lipstick is introduced.

1996: Revlon makes an initial public offering of stock.

2000: The company's professional products line is sold.

Corporation in exchange for $67 million in Revlon stock. The buyout brought Revlon a company with annual sales of $20 million, most of them coming from a drug used to treat diabetes. Within a year, U.S. Vitamin proved its worth with its acquisitions of Laboratorios Grossman, a Mexican pharmaceutical company, as well as comparable concerns in Argentina and Chile. In 1971, Revson traded U.S. Vitamin's diabetes drug and $20 million cash for a group of drugs Ciba-Geigy was required to divest for antitrust reasons. Another U.S. Vitamin acquisition was Nysco Laboratories and its Nyscap process for timed-release medication. This, in turn, led to the introduction of vasodilation drugs. Fully disposable injectables, introduced in 1968, also came from U.S. Vitamin.

The company had begun to market its products overseas at the end of the 1950s. By 1962, when Revlon debuted in Japan, there were subsidiaries in France, Italy, Argentina, Mexico, and Asia. Revlon's entrance into the Japanese market was typical of its international sales strategy. Instead of adapting its ads and using Japanese models, Revlon chose to use its basic U.S. advertising and models. Japanese women loved the American look, and the success of this bold approach was reflected in the 1962 sales figures, which were almost $164 million.

By 1967, expanding worldwide markets produced sales of $281 million, showing a 5.7 percent increase over the figure of almost $266 for 1966. Planning further expansion, Revlon spent $12.5 million on improvements to existing facilities plus a new cosmetics and fragrance manufacturing plant in Phoenix, Arizona.

During the 1960s, the company consisted of four divisions: International, Professional Products, Princess Marcella Borghese, and U.S.V. Pharmaceutical. In 1968, Revson decided to add two more divisions: Cosmetics and Fragrances, headed by Joseph Anderer, and the Revlon Development Corporation, which was headed by Evan William Mandel and concerned chiefly with long-range planning concepts and strategies for marketing opportunities.

Acquisitions and Restructuring in the 1970s

The 1970s began with annual sales of about $314 million. The Cosmetics and Fragrances division, its six lines separately aimed, advertised, and marketed, was the industry leader in all franchised retail outlets. Revlon fragrances, such as Norell and Intimate for women and Braggi and Pub for men, had also become familiar to U.S. consumers. Revlon also had a new line of wig-maintenance products called Wig Wonder.

An important 1970 acquisition was the Mitchum Company of Tennessee, makers of antiperspirants and other toiletries. Mitchum joined the Thayer Laboratories subsidiary, formerly Knomark. Mitchum-Thayer division's widely publicized products required a 1971 advertising budget of $4 million.

In 1973, Revlon introduced Charlie, a fragrance designed for the working woman's budget. Geared to the under-30 market, Charlie models in Ralph Lauren clothes personified the independent woman of the 1970s. Charlie was an instant success, helping to raise Revlon's net sales figures to $506 million for 1973 and to almost $606 million the following year.

High profits notwithstanding, 1974 was a difficult year. Charles Revson was diagnosed with pancreatic cancer. Determined to leave a worthy successor, he picked Michel Bergerac, a president of International Telephone and Telegraph's European operations. Terms of Bergerac's contract included a $1.5 million signing bonus, an annual salary of $325,000 for five years, bonuses, and options on 70,000 shares.

Company profitability was Bergerac's chief interest. Impressed with Revson's experienced management team, he induced them to stay by introducing the Performance Incentive Profit Sharing Plan, which allotted each executive points based on profit objectives achieved for the years 1974 to 1976. He also cut company spending with tighter inventory controls and instituted an annual savings of $71.5 million by the elimination of 500 jobs. Bergerac installed a management-information system requiring that all managers report monthly on problems, sales, and competition.

Through acquisitions, Bergerac tried to reduce Revlon's dependence on the increasingly crowded cosmetics market. His first major purchase came in 1975. Coburn Optical Industries was an Oklahoma-based manufacturer of ophthalmic and optical processing equipment and supplies which cost 833,333 Revlon common shares. Barnes-Hind, the largest U.S. marketer of hard contact lens solutions, was bought in 1976 and strengthened Revlon's share of the eye-care market. Other acquisitions included the Lewis-Howe Company, makers of Tums antacid, acquired in 1978, and Armour Pharmaceutical Company, makers of thyroid medicines, acquired in 1977. These health-care operations helped sales figures to pass the $1 billion mark in 1977, bringing total sales to $1.7 billion in 1979.

By the late 1970s, company pharmaceutical research and development had extended into plasma research and new drugs for the treatment of osteoporosis and hypertension. The markets for soft contact lenses and their rinsing solutions were also growing. Bergerac compounded a successful 1979 by buying Technicon Corporation, a leading maker of diagnostic and laboratory instruments for both domestic and international markets, in 1980.

During the mid-1970s, Bergerac also organized the six cosmetics lines into three groups for easier administration. Revlon, Moon Drops, Natural Wonder, and Charlie now belonged to group one. Group two was comprised of Flex hair-care products and other toiletries, while group three included Princess Marcella Borghese and Ultima II, the prestige cosmetic brands sold in upscale department stores. The domestic cosmetics operations also included the government sales division, carrying almost all the beauty lines through military exchanges and commissaries in the United States and overseas. By the mid-1980s, Revlon's health-care companies, rather than Revlon's beauty concerns, were innovating and expanding. Reluctant to initiate beauty-product development or department store promotions, Revlon lost ground to Estée Lauder, a privately held company whose marketing strategy of high prices with accompanying gifts had earned it almost universal center-aisle department store space. This caused Revlon's share to drop from 20 percent to 10 percent of department store cosmetics sales.

Drugstore and supermarket sales were also suffering; Natural Wonder, a low-priced line, lost 24 percent of its supermarket volume in 1983 alone, and competitor Noxell's inexpensive Cover Girl line was claiming more drugstore sales. Comparisons of profits from total operations told the story: $358 million in 1980 sank to $337 million in 1981, which fell to $234 million by 1982.

1985 Takeover

By 1984, industry analysts believed that Revlon would be worth more if it were broken up and sold. Within a year, this opinion was borne out by a takeover bid from the much smaller Pantry Pride, a subsidiary of Ronald Perelman's MacAndrews & Forbes Holdings. In defense, Bergerac accepted a $900 million offer for the cosmetics businesses from Adler and Shaykin, a New York investment company. The rest of Revlon was to go to Forstmann Little & Company, a management buyout corporation, for about $1.4 billion. These sales, however, were disallowed by a Delaware judge, who ruled that the deal was not in Revlon's shareholders' best interests. On November 5, 1985, at a price of $58 per share, totaling $2.7 billion, Revlon was sold to Pantry Pride, becoming a private company and giving the name of Revlon Group to the former Pantry Pride. The highly leveraged buyout—engineered with the help of junk bond king Michael P. Milken—saddled Revlon with a huge $2.9 billion debt load, which was an albatross around the company's neck for years to come.

Perelman immediately began to divest the company of the healthcare businesses. By 1987, only National Health Laboratories remained. By the end of 1988, Perelman had recovered $1.5 billion of his borrowed funds, partly by selling the eyecare businesses to the British firm of Pilkington for $574 million.

Divested companies were replaced with others geared to the Perelman objective—restoring the luster to the original beauty business. Costing about $300 million, Max Factor joined the Revlon lineup in 1987, along with its Halston perfume and its Almay toiletries. Other newcomers were Yves Saint Laurent

fragrances and cosmetics; Charles of the Ritz, Germaine Monteil, and Alexandre de Markoff followed soon after. In 1989, Perelman spent another $170 million to acquire Betrix, a German makeup and fragrance maker.

Other innovations of the 1980s meshed with national trends. The concern of a burgeoning older population with health and fitness led to wider company research on skin-care products as well as on makeup. International concerns for animal rights found a response in Perelman's Revlon, which abandoned the Draize test in 1989 after closing its animal testing center in 1986. Revlon also sought to improve the company image when it signed supermodels Cindy Crawford and Claudia Schiffer for its advertising in the late 1980s and early 1990s.

During the late 1980s, fears of an approaching recession made bankers generally wary of highly leveraged transactions, and Revlon's junk bonds began to lose value. Internal problems stemmed partly from the department store market, where an attempt by Revlon to economize by grouping its Ritz, Monteil, and Borghese prestige brands at one counter failed. Other problems included the introduction of No Sweat, a deodorant which, despite its $12 million introductory advertising budget, failed to garner market share; the reformulation of Flex, a popular shampoo which lost market share when Revlon introduced a new formula with new packaging and a higher price; and a 2 percent shrinkage in the fragrance market that affected the entire industry.

Turning the Corner in Mid-1990s

By 1990, Revlon held only 11 percent of the U.S. mass-market cosmetics market. Losses were mounting year after year thanks in large part to the money that had to be spent each year to service the debt. In 1991 alone, $131.6 million went toward debt service, contributing to an operating loss of $241.7 million ($226.9 million of which stemmed from extraordinary restructuring charges). Perelman was forced to sell still more assets to keep Revlon from defaulting on its loans.

In addition to selling 80 percent of National Health Laboratories by 1992, Perelman had to also sell off some assets from the core cosmetics area. In 1991, Max Factor and Betrix were sold to Procter & Gamble for $1.14 billion in cash. Sold off the following year were the high-end Halston and Princess Marcella Borghese brands. Unfortunately for Perelman, such moves were not enough to gain the confidence of Wall Street. In 1992, Perelman tried to sell 11 million shares of Revlon stock in an initial public offering (IPO) at about $18 to $20 per share. The IPO failed, a victim of a sluggish stock market, poor Revlon earnings, and the huge debt that continued to weigh down the cosmetics giant.

To shore up sagging sales, Revlon CEO Jerry Levin boosted Revlon's advertising budget by 25 percent in 1992 to $200 million. Much of this money was spent on television advertising, with less spent on print ads and in-store promotions than in the past. While the Revlon line was promoted in this fashion and through mass-market retailers, the company's only remaining premium brand, Ultima II, was shifted down from upscale stores to JC Penney and Dillard's department stores. Early indications were positive for these moves as overall market share for the Revlon Group hit 14.7 percent in 1992. By 1993, the company was finally able to report operating income—$51.5 million—although debt service remained high at $114.4 million.

Meanwhile, the company started to develop successful new products. The ColorStay line of longlasting cosmetics was introduced in 1994 with the debut of ColorStay lipsticks, which soon captured the top spot in its category. The Age Defying line of cosmetics for women over 35 soon followed and also proved popular. By 1995, overall market share had reached 19.4 percent and what *Advertising Age* called the "reborn cosmetics juggernaut" unseated Maybelline from the number one position in cosmetics. Net sales were improving steadily from $1.59 billion in 1993 to $1.73 billion in 1994 to $1.94 billion in 1995. In addition, while debt service remained high ($137.7 million in 1995), it was finally exceeded by operating income ($145.1 million).

Backed by what was clearly a remarkable, though long-in-coming turnaround, Perelman felt confident enough to try another initial public offering in early 1996. This time he succeeded, and Revlon once again became a public company, although Perelman retained 99.7 percent of the voting stock. About 15 percent of overall shares were sold in the initial public offering, raising about $150 million.

Financial Woes in the Late 1990s and Beyond

Revlon's turnaround was short-lived, however, and by the late 1990s the company was plagued with problems. Losses began to pile up, due in part to intense competition, dwindling shelf space in stores, inventory overstock, and problems overseas. Saddled by over $2 billion in debts, Perelman announced that he was looking for a buyer for Revlon. He was unable to strike a deal, however, and instead began selling off parts of the company. He sold Revlon's professional products business and its Plusbelle line in 2000 and divested the Colorama brand the following year.

CEO Jeff Nugent resigned in 2002, leaving Coca-Cola executive Jack Stahl at the helm of Revlon. Losses continued to mount as the new CEO and his team worked to save Revlon from bankruptcy. Overall, sales had fallen by 40 percent since 1998 as competitors stole market share. To make matters worse, cosmetic sales at drugstores, supermarkets, and discount stores had slowed significantly over the past several years. Perelman set plans in motion to bail out the company, offering a cash infusion of $150 million in 2003 to help eliminate some of the firm's debt.

In an attempt to bolster Revlon's sales, the company launched an expensive marketing campaign featuring Hollywood stars Halle Berry and Julianne Moore. Market share for Revlon and Almay increased slightly, and the company posted a 16 percent increase in sales as a result. While the company focused on strengthening its brands, restoring growth, building stronger relationships with its retail partners, and revamping the organization as a whole, Stahl continued to have his work cut out for him. A November 2003 *Business Week* article stated, "Today, the company isn't making a dime—and Stahl can't get away with that for long. Sales may be rising, but only because of a pricey ad blitz that some outside Revlon think is unsustainable." Indeed, without the financial backing of Perelman and potential debt-for-equity transactions that would reduce Revlon's debt, the company faced a long road of financial difficulties.

In late 2003, the company launched Destination Model, a business plan designed to get profits back on track. The model's strategies were based on improving promotional and advertising success, reducing manufacturing and supply chain costs, and developing successful new products while effectively managing current products. Despite its financial position, Revlon management remained optimistic about its future. Regardless of what happened in the years to come, Revlon's brands would no doubt continue to be recognized across the globe.

Principal Subsidiaries

Almay, Inc.; Charles of the Ritz Group Ltd.; Charles Revson Inc.; Cosmetics & More Inc.; North America Revsale Inc.; PPI Two Corporation; Revlon Consumer Corporation; Revlon Consumer Products Corporation; Revlon Development Corporation; Revlon Government Sales, Inc.; Revlon International Corporation; Revlon Products Corporation; Revlon Real Estate Corporation; RIROS Corporation; RIROS Group Inc.; RIT Inc.

Principal Competitors

L'Oréal SA; The Proctor & Gamble Company; Unilever NV.

Further Reading

Bary, Andrew, "Kissed Off?," *Barron's*, November 18, 2002, p. 20.

Berman, Phyllis, "Revlon without Revson," *Forbes*, June 26, 1978.

Cole, Robert J., "High-Stakes Drama at Revlon," *New York Times*, November 11, 1985.

Doherty, Jacqueline, "Revlon, Once Perelman's Jewel, May Prove Less Than Marvelous and More Like Marvel," *Barron's*, October 11, 1999.

Holland, Kelly, "A Whole New Look for Revlon?," *Business Week*, April 19, 1999, p. 46.

Khermouch, Gerry, "Putting a Pretty Face on Revlon," *Business Week*, November 3, 2003, p. 92.

Light, Larry, and Laura Zinn, "Painting a New Face on Revlon," *Business Week*, April 6, 1992, pp. 26–27.

Light, Larry, and Monica Roman, "Why Perelman Faces Life without Makeup," *Business Week*, April 1, 1991, pp. 71–72.

Morgenson, Gretchen, "The Perils of Perelman," *Forbes*, December 10, 1990, pp. 218–22.

Nelson, Emily, "Forget Supermodels—Revlon's New Face Gets Lipstick on Her Teeth," *Wall Street Journal*, March 30, 2001, p. B1.

Ono, Yumiko, "Revlon Swings to Profit on Sales of Makeup Line," *Wall Street Journal*, July 31, 1996, p. B8(E), p. B5(W).

Ramirez, Anthony, "The Raider Who Runs Revlon," *Fortune*, September 14, 1987.

"Revlon's Formula: Smart Words, Quality, and Freud," *Business Week*, August 12, 1950.

Sloan, Pat, "Revlon Redistributes to Win Wider Appeal," *Advertising Age*, August 19, 1991, p. 12.

——, "Cosmetics Competitors Try to Slap Down Revlon," *Advertising Age*, December 4, 1995, p. 38.

Sparks, Debra, "Fading Beauty," *Business Week*, December 13, 1999, p. 156.

Spiro, Leah Nathans, and Ronald Grover, ''The Operator: An Inside Look at Ron Perelman's $5 Billion Empire,'' *Business Week*, August 21, 1995.

Tobias, Andrew, *Fire and Ice: The Story of Charles Revson—The Man Who Built the Revlon Empire*, New York: William Morrow & Company, 1976, 282 p.

Zinn, Laura, Sunita Wadekar Bhargava, and Elizabeth A. Lesly, ''The New Ron Perelman Has an Old Problem,'' *Business Week*, June 14, 1993, pp. 94–95.

—Gillian Wolf
—updates: David E. Salamie and
Christina M. Stansell

Rush Enterprises, Inc.

555 IH 35 South
New Braunfels, Texas 78130
U.S.A.
Telephone: (830) 626-5200
Toll Free: (800) 973-7874
Fax: (830) 626-5318
Web site: http://www.rushenterprises.com

Public Company
Incorporated: 1995
Employees: 1,880
Sales: $815.3 million (2003)
Stock Exchanges: NASDAQ
Ticker Symbol: RUSHB
NAIC: 441200 Other Motor Vehicle Dealers

Based in New Braunfels, Texas, Rush Enterprises, Inc., is a full-service retailer of heavy and medium-duty trucks and construction equipment. The company's business is conducted through four divisions. Rush Truck Center Division operates a network of nearly 40 centers, located mostly in the Sunbelt, which specialize in the sales of Peterbilt Class 8 heavy duty trucks. All told, Rush Enterprises accounts for more than 20 percent of all Peterbilt trucks sold in the United States, making it Peterbilt's largest dealer. The Truck Center Division also sells Class 7 Peterbilt trucks, Peterbilt refuse chassis and cement mixer chassis, and some medium-duty trucks from General Motors Corporation and Nissan Motor Co. It also sells used trucks and provides truck parts and services. Rush Equipment Center, headquartered in Houston, Texas, sells new and used construction equipment, including a complete line of John Deere construction equipment, such as backhoe loaders, crawler-dozers, four-wheel drive loaders, and hydraulic excavators. In addition, the division offers parts and service. Rush Leasing and Rental Division provides leasing and rental options for customers of both the truck and construction equipment divisions. Rush Financial and Insurance Division offers truck and construction equipment customers with financing options as well as insurance. Although Rush Enterprises is publicly traded, its chairman, W. Marvin Rush, and his family own approximately 39 percent of the company.

Origins: 1950s–70s

In the early 1950s, when he was just 14 years old, Marvin Rush got his start in business in the Houston area by selling sodas for five cents each. From his profits, he bought his first car, complete with radio. When the radio broke, he took it to a shop where televisions were also repaired. There, as he often would in his life, he spotted a business opportunity. Because many people were starting to trade in their first television sets for the newer and larger units that were coming onto the market—as television was just beginning to become an standard household item—Marvin Rush decided to visit area television stores and buy their trade-ins. He spruced them up and resold them at a profit. In addition, he offered financing to customers who could not afford the purchase price up front—a practice he would refine years later as a truck dealer.

Even before graduating from high school, Rush turned from selling used televisions to selling used cars. He then took on a partner to become involved in the bus business. After selling out to his partner, he bought his first truck dealership in Houston in 1965, launching Rush Enterprises. He had a franchise agreement with General Motors to sell mid-sized GMC trucks, which had a very limited market and placed Marvin Rush in fiscal jeopardy. The money was in big rig trucks, a fact that prompted Rush to search around for a new franchise. He found it in the relatively new Peterbilt Motors Company, which mostly sold to the West Coast, and he was able to secure a franchise in Houston. He now began to prosper in the truck sales business and soon opened sales operations in Fort Worth and San Antonio. He then acquired a number of assets to complement his truck business, including Houston's World Wide Tires and some leasing and finance companies.

When he turned 40, Rush made a drastic change of course that almost led to his financial ruin. He sold all his businesses, with the exception of the San Antonio truck dealership and World Wide Tires, and in the late 1970s moved to Hawaii. He bought up a number of tire stores on the islands, but with the advent of a recession he found himself in a precarious position. He slashed prices, a move that merely bought him time, given that Hawaii had a limited number of potential customers. Rush was only days away from filing for Chapter 11 bankruptcy protection, the prospect of which he found morally repugnant, when the Frost National Bank agreed to help him stay in business until he could find a buyer for his tire stores.

Rush Returns to Mainland in 1982

Saddled with debt, Rush returned to the mainland in 1982. His only assets were World Wide Tires, the San Antonio Peterbilt dealership, and his original Houston GMC dealership. The next three years were spent getting back on his feet and paying off the banks. He then began to build up Rush Enterprises again, buying back his Houston Peterbilt dealership as well as one in Lufkin, Texas, and once more added complementary businesses. Rush also made personal investments in other areas, buying a freight company, two Texas car dealerships, and heading an investment group that took control of TexStar National Bank. By 1990, he was joined by his sons, Robin Rush and W.M. "Rusty" Rush.

Rush asked his sons in 1992 whether they should sell Rush Enterprises, and they convinced him to expand the business instead, establishing a lofty goal of becoming a $1 billion company by the end of the decade. Rush sold off many of his personal holdings in order to focus on Rush Enterprises, as the company went into growth mode. It acquired truck dealerships in Laredo, Texas; Shreveport, Louisiana; Oklahoma City and Tulsa, Oklahoma; and Fontana, Pico Rivera, and Sun Valley, California. Rush Enterprises also added a finance company, an insurance agency, and began accumulating leasing companies.

Rush recognized that truck sales was a highly fragmented industry that was going through some significant changes and recognized an opening to become a major consolidator. He told the *San Antonio Business Journal* in 1997 that his desire to consolidate was "driven by our customers' customers to bring this industry into the 21st Century. . . . They have to deliver within a two-hour window. They need a support system." As a result of adding businesses, revenues grew at a rapid clip. By 1995, Rush Enterprises was the largest Peterbilt truck dealer in North America, accounting for 14 percent of all sales. At this stage, the company operated eight full-service and six parts and services truck centers. Total revenues reached $269 million in 1995, a 30 percent increase over the year before.

To fuel further growth, Rush Enterprises elected to go public in June 1996, becoming the largest American car or large-truck dealership to take that step. With New York's Ladenburg, Thalmann & Co. Inc. serving as lead underwriter, the offering was oversubscribed and all shares sold in one day, netting Rush

Enterprises $32 million. The company earmarked $10 million to buy additional Peterbilt dealerships, improve existing truck centers, and pay down debt. In addition, the company planned to spend $3 million of the proceeds to open a full-service dealership in the Texas Rio Grande Valley area and a southern California parts and service facility.

Rush Enterprises appeared poised to become a major consolidator among truck dealership, many of which were mom-and-pop operations that would welcome an exit option, but in some ways the company became a victim of its own success. In a short period of time, five new-car dealership groups went public and other truck dealers talked about following suit. Dealerships took notice of the trend and increased their asking price. In the ten months following its initial public offering, Rush Enterprises completed just one acquisition, paying approximately $7.9 million for Denver Peterbilt, Inc., adding two full-service Peterbilt dealerships in Denver and Greeley, Colorado. Rush told *Automotive News* in April 1997 that dealers "are having visions of grandeur. . . . Going public has raised the bar. Dealers are reading all that hype on the auto side."

Rather than overpay to add dealerships, Rush decided instead to look for a complementary industry ripe for consolidation. He found it in construction equipment. In July 1997, the company formed a new construction equipment division, Rush Equipment Centers. Following the example of the truck division, Rush Equipment was designed to combine sales and rentals of new and used heavy-duty construction equipment, backed by support services. By October, the new division established a foundation by acquiring a Houston John Deere dealership from C. Jim Stewart & Stevenson, Inc. in a deal worth $25.1 million. The goal was to grow the business to the $300 million to $400 million level in annual sales by the year 2000, but the reality would fall far short of the company's ambitions. (Construction equipment sales were less than $35 million in 2000.)

Further Diversification in the Late 1990s

Rush Enterprises sought further diversification, and a hedge against softening in the truck industry, by branching out into another area. In February 1998, it formed a retail center division, Rush Retail Centers, in preparation of the $10.5 million purchase of D&D Farm and Ranch Supermarket, Inc. D&D was a retail farm and ranch superstore located in Sequin, Texas, outside of San Antonio. The plan was to introduce the D&D format to other metropolitan markets. Stores would be opened in the Houston and Dallas-Fort Worth areas, and in 2000 Rush Enterprises supplemented D&D's business by acquiring Smith Bros. Catalogs, a western apparel and gear marketer. D&D gained access to Smith Bros.' database of more than 120,000 catalog and Internet customers. It hoped to add D&D products to Smith Bros. catalogs, which it could also mail to D&D customers.

In the late 1990s, Rush continued to add to its slate of construction equipment and Peterbilt truck dealerships. In September 1998, it added Klooster Equipment for $13.1 million in cash, then in August 1999 it bought Calvert Equipment Inc., a John Deer construction equipment dealership, in a deal worth $11.1 million. Rush Enterprises added five Peterbilt truck dealerships in Arizona and New Mexico in October 1999 through the

---

Key Dates:

1965: The company is founded when Marvin Bush acquires his first truck dealership.
1995: Rush Enterprises is incorporated.
1996: The company is taken public.
1997: A construction equipment division is formed.
2000: Rush is named Peterbilt's North American Dealer of the Year.

---

acquisition of Phoenix-based Southwest Peterbilt Inc., paying nearly $24 million. Subsequently, Rush Enterprises spent another $4.5 million to acquire Norm Pressley's Truck Center, adding three more Peterbilt truck dealerships located in San Diego, Escondido, and El Centro, California. In the meantime, the relationship between Rush Enterprises and Peterbilt's parent corporation, Paccar Inc., was strengthened when the Bellevue, Washington, company bought a 14 percent interest in the business from Marvin Rush, whose own interest was reduced to 39 percent.

Rush Enterprises capped a period of strong truck sales through the late 1990s by being named Peterbilt's North American Dealer of the Year in 2000, an honor that provided cold comfort because of a dramatic drop in truck sales early in the year. As was often the case, the truck market was the first to show signs of a troubled economy. Exacerbating the problem was rising fuel prices that, despite strong demand for freight services, forced larger carriers to cut back on plans to expand their fleets and forced smaller trucking companies out of business. Rising interest rates, a tight labor market, and overproduction also contributed to an oversupply of trucks. Because of its efforts at diversification and its strong service operation, Rush Enterprises was much better positioned than most competitors to weather the storm. The company was still able to post record revenues of $805.4 million in 2000, while realizing a profit of $3.3 million. A year later, the decrease in truck sales, as well as a drop off in demand for construction equipment, led to an overall decline in revenues to $691.5 million, the numbers mitigated somewhat by a significant increase in sales from truck parts and service. The company still managed to hold the line on profits, with net income falling slightly to $3.2 million.

Rush Enterprises was able to take advantage of tough times by making opportune acquisitions. In August 2001, it paid approximately $2.5 million in cash for El Paso Great Basin Trucks Inc., picking up two Peterbilt truck dealerships in El Paso and Las Cruces, Texas. As a result, Rush Enterprises was now the sole provider of Peterbilt new truck, parts, and service at every major United States-Mexico border cross. The transaction left Rush Enterprises with 34 truck locations in seven states. Later in 2001, Rush Enterprises strengthened its truck refitting business by paying another $4.2 million in cash to acquire Oklahoma City-based Perfection Equipment, Inc.

Rush Enterprises and other truck dealerships enjoyed a brief spurt in truck sales in 2002, following a two-year slump, because new cleaner-running, and more expensive, diesel engines were scheduled to come on the market in October of that year as part of a federal mandate to cut nitrogen oxide emissions. The new trucks were expected to run hotter, resulting in an earlier need for overhauls and higher maintenance costs. However, truck dealers were well aware that new truck sales would quickly dry up once the cleaner-running trucks came on the market, and carriers held off purchasing until they could determine how well the new engines performed.

Again, Rush Enterprises was better off than most, but management did decide it would be wise to concentrate on its core business. In 2002, it sold off its D&D farm-and-ranch supply business, which was losing money. The company also sold its Michigan John Deere construction equipment dealerships, preferring to focus on the Sunbelt area for its Rush Equipment Center Division. At the same time, the Rush Truck Center Division continued to expand. In a deal that closed in 2003, it paid $5.4 million to acquire Orange County Truck and Trailers, Inc., adding three central Florida Peterbilt dealerships. Later in 2003, Rush Enterprises completed another acquisition, paying $1.4 million for Peterbilt of Mobile Inc., picking up a Peterbilt dealership located in Mobile, Alabama. Rush Enterprises now had 39 truck locations in nine states. As Rush Enterprises entered 2004, management believed that the truck business was in the initial stages of a sharp upswing. If so, the company was well positioned to take full advantage of improved conditions.

Principal Divisions

Rush Truck Center Division; Rush Equipment Center; Rush Leasing and Rental Division; Rush Financial and Insurance Division.

Principal Competitors

American TruckSource, Inc.; Coast Counties Truck and Equipment Co., Inc.

Further Reading

Kisiel, Ralph, "High Prices Slow Rush's Expansion Plans," *Automotive News*, April 14, 1997, p. 19.
——, "Peterbilt Dealer Goes Public," *Automotive News*, June 17, 1996, p. 1.
Lowe, Sandra, "CEO Steering Rush onto the Fast Track," *San Antonio Business Journal*, February 7, 1997, p. 1.
Weiss, Sebastian, and James Aldridge, "Heavy-Duty Truck Market Hits the Skids," *San Antonio Business Journal*, May 5, 2000, p. 1.
Weiss, Sebastian, "Rush Enterprises Set to Expand," *San Antonio Business Journal*, January 26, 1998.

—Ed Dinger

Sbarro, Inc.

401 Broadhollow
Melville, New Jersey 11747
U.S.A.
Telephone: (631) 715-4100
Fax: (631) 715-4192
Web site: http://www.sbarro.com

Private Company
Incorporated: 1977
Employees: 5,600
Sales: $332.3 million (2003)
NAIC: 722211 Limited-Service Restaurants; 722212
   Cafeterias; 533110 Lessors of Nonfinancial Intangible
   Assets (Except Copyrighted Works)

Sbarro, Inc., owns, operates, and franchises an international chain of family-oriented Italian restaurants under the "Sbarro" and "Sbarro The Italian Eatery" names. Most of these are buffet and cafeteria-style restaurants located in food courts in shopping malls. Others are found in airports, toll-road rest areas, sports arenas, hospitals, universities, casinos, and downtown locations. The Sbarro menu offers pizza, pasta, hot and cold Italian entrees, salads, sandwiches, cheesecake, and other desserts at a modest price with fast service. As of December 2003, there were 915 Sbarro restaurants, located in 46 states, the District of Columbia, Puerto Rico, and in 26 countries across the globe. A total of 528 of these were company-owned and operated; the others were franchised. Members of the founding family took the company private in 1999.

Early History

In 1956, Gennaro Sbarro (pronounced zah-BAHR-ro) and his wife Carmela emigrated from Naples, Italy, to Brooklyn with their three young sons, Joe, Mario, and Anthony. The Sbarros wanted to open a salumeria—a gourmet Italian delicatessen—like the one they had back in Italy. To earn the money to do so, Carmela worked as a seamstress and Gennaro, Joe, and Mario worked in various delis in the city.

In 1959, the Sbarros opened their salumeria in the Bensonhurst section of Brooklyn, offering sandwiches, pasta dishes, and homemade cheesecake. The deli was a hit, and by 1964 the family had opened three more. Working behind the counters, the Sbarros noticed fewer customers were "taking out" their purchases. Instead, they were eating the deli food before they left the store. "Customers were standing at the counter eating pasta," Mario Sbarro told *Business Week* in 1987. "We knew we were on the threshold of something different." Responding to customers' needs, the Sbarros put in some chairs and tables and started offering hot food, such as pizza and lasagna.

Expansion in the 1970s–80s

By the early 1970s, the Sbarros found themselves owning four popular restaurants. At that point the family had to decide how to expand but keep standards high. Gennaro Sbarro did not want to franchise his operation. Instead, he opened 12 new restaurants in the New York area, and had all the food made daily at the original deli. Eventually Sbarro and his sons established a formula that gave productive managers 15 percent of a restaurant's net profits but kept the ownership of the restaurants in the family. Under the growth plan, Carmela still produced all the cheesecakes, while other ingredients were all purchased through one wholesaler. In 1977, the family incorporated its various food and restaurant businesses as Sbarro, Inc.

As the Sbarros were developing their growth strategy, real estate developers were building shopping centers at a furious pace to serve the expanding suburban customer base. In the 20 years from 1970 to 1990, the number of shopping centers nationally grew from about 10,000 to 37,000, according to the International Council of Shopping Centers. Shopping at malls became a leisure-time activity, and mall developers incorporated food courts into their plans to keep customers within the facility. For the Sbarros, food courts appeared to offer the perfect opportunity to combine their dine-in focus with quick service while reaching a dependable flow of customers, and they took it.

Under the food court concept, shoppers were able to select their meal from a variety of restaurants and take the food to an

Company Perspectives:

The Sbarro brand, currently operating and franchising in nearly 1,000 units worldwide, has become synonymous with fresh and inventive Italian food. The company's prevailing mission, to satisfy customers, has been the dynamic spirit behind three generations of fine cuisine, and continues to drive our entire organization.

open, common dining area. Sbarro's food court restaurants were small, occupying about 500 to 1,000 square feet, and contained only enough space for kitchen and service areas. The menu was more limited than at the larger, sit-down units, and there were fewer staff, usually between 6 and 30 employees. The decor of all Sbarro units incorporated the green, white, and orange of the Italian flag, and many had replicas of cheeses, salamis, and prosciutto hams hanging from the ceiling, harking back to the company's origin as a delicatessen.

At the time of Gennaro Sbarro's death in 1984, the company had 97 stores grossing $20 million. Mario headed the company as chairman and CEO. Tony became president and chief operating officer, and Joe was named senior executive vice-president. Carmela was vice-president and continued to make her cheesecakes. The following year Mario opened 36 more restaurants and took Sbarro public, raising $8 million on the American Stock Exchange for 30 percent of the equity. Mario used the money to pay down bank loans made to finance the expansion and to develop the franchising side of the business.

By mid-1987, Sbarro had grown to 157 company-owned restaurants and 63 franchises, with units in the United States, Puerto Rico, and Canada. *Business Week* ranked Sbarro 21st on its list of America's 100 hot-growth companies, and the company agreed to let Marriott Corporation open 20 franchises on selected highways, testing the Sbarro concept beyond the shopping mall. Sales for the year rose 70 percent over 1986, to $58.5 million, and profits jumped 43 percent, to $4.8 million.

The company was opening between 65 and 70 restaurants a year. Wanting to increase the number of franchise operations, Mario started a program in 1989 offering managers with three years' seniority the opportunity to buy their own franchise with 100 percent company financing. During the first year, four managers took advantage of the program. Company revenues for 1989 reached $149 million, a 27 percent increase over 1988, and profits reached $14.5 million.

The Early 1990s

In 1990 the first Sbarro restaurant opened in Europe, in the London suburb of Woking. The move was made through a joint venture with a British partner, Forte plc (formerly Trusthouse Forte), and was part of Mario's plan to achieve systemwide sales of $500 million.

The company was growing by nearly 16 percent a year but was still operating much as it had 20 years earlier. When a problem arose at any outlet, the manager could pick up the phone and call Tony. The brothers needed better information systems and operating controls for the more than 300 restaurants the company owned if they were to reach their goal. They hired several computer specialists familiar with the restaurant industry to set up new information systems. To improve operations, they established a new regional and district structure and brought in 20 managers from such larger chains as McDonald's and Roy Rogers.

Problems quickly developed as resentment grew among longtime Sbarro managers and employees toward new forms and rigid rules. Sales per restaurant began to drop. Earnings for the first quarter in 1992 were one-third lower than expected. The Sbarros realized they had made a mistake going outside and not promoting their own employees. "Many of our own people had the qualifications to do the job," Mario told Robert La Franco in a 1994 *Forbes* article. "It was a case of 'the grass always looks greener.' "

Mario and his brothers corrected the situation; during the second quarter of 1992 they fired 14 of the new managers and began promoting Sbarro managers to district and regional positions. By the fall, sales and earnings were improving. The company ended the year with 587 restaurants (131 of them franchises) and revenues up 13.2 percent to $237.5 million.

Employees at Sbarro units prepared the food fresh daily, according to special recipes developed by the family. John Bowen, one of Sbarro's early franchisees, explained in a June 1995 article in *Inc.*, "I lean upon the operations manual. They are successful procedures. If you are going to make a cake—in our case, a pizza—and you don't follow that recipe, it's going to turn out a little different every time." Restaurants bought pastries locally, but in 1996, Carmela Sbarro was still overseeing the preparation of the company's cheesecakes in the kitchen of the original Sbarro's in Brooklyn.

During 1993 and 1994, Sbarro continued to open new restaurants and franchises, though at a slower rate of about 10 percent a year. Sales from company-owned restaurants increased by more than 11 percent annually, well ahead of the average for the pizza restaurant industry. In 1993 the company began paying quarterly cash dividends, which increased approximately 20 percent each year. By the end of 1994, Sbarro had 729 restaurants. Of these, 162 were franchised. Host Marriott Services Corp., with 19 units, and Concession Air, with 11 units, were among Sbarro's biggest franchisees, with units at airports and at travel plazas on toll roads. In September 1994, Sbarro moved its stock listing to the New York Stock Exchange.

Pizza, sold primarily in individual slices, accounted for about half of Sbarro's sales. The pizza restaurant industry, structured into several tiers, was highly competitive. In the mid-1990s, three giant chains led the industry. Pizza Hut, with 9,566 restaurants in the United States and 2,989 international units, had sales of $6.9 billion in 1994. Domino's Pizza (5,100 domestic restaurants and 860 overseas) reported sales of $2.5 billion. Little Caesar had sales of $2 billion from its 4,600 locations in the United States, Canada, Puerto Rico, Guam, and the Czech and Slovak Republics.

The second tier of pizza chains included Papa John's International (730 restaurants in 21 states), with reported sales of

Key Dates:

1959: The Sbarros open their first salumeria.
1977: The family incorporates its various food and restaurant businesses as Sbarro, Inc.
1985: Thirty-six new restaurants are opened; the company goes public.
1990: A Sbarro location opens in Europe.
1999: Sbarro family members purchase 100 percent of the company.
2003: The company reports the largest loss in its history.

$297.6 million for 1994; Sbarro, with $296 million; and Show-Biz Pizza Time (327 units) with $267.8 million. Round Table, a private company with 560 locations, was believed to have sales in that range, and Pizza Inn reported sales of about $218 million from its 485 restaurants. Chains with 1994 sales between $100 and $200 million comprised a third tier, and included Uno Restaurant Corporation, Shakey's Pizza, and Bertucci's Brick Oven Pizzeria.

In 1994 the $20 billion pizza business grew at a rate of 2 percent, below the overall restaurant industry's rate of 4.1 percent. That figure was skewed by relatively flat sales for the big three companies; the gourmet and casual dining segments grew faster, as evidenced by Sbarro's growth. Pizza operators, however, were taking steps to expand their business in the face of competition. For some it meant more international operations; others added new menu offerings such as buffalo wings, stuffed crust or deep dish pizza, roasted chicken, and pastas. Some chains beefed up delivery services and moved into nontraditional locations. Little Caesar, for example, opened pizza restaurants with some seating in 561 Kmart stores and began delivery service.

The Mid-1990s

In the mid-1990s Sbarro, too, was looking at ways to remain competitive. During 1995 the company explored new growth opportunities through joint ventures with other restaurateurs. The first of these, Boulder Creek Steaks & Saloon, a steakhouse, had two restaurants opened by early 1996. The second, BICE Med Grille, was a moderately priced, casual-dining restaurant featuring Italian and Mediterranean food. The third new opportunity was a family restaurant concept, Umberto's of New Hyde Park Pizzeria. This offered both sit-down and takeout service, and featured pizza and other Italian-style food. The initial locations of these two ventures opened in April 1996, with more planned for later that year.

Within its existing units, the company began testing a buffet format in 45 of its restaurants. Sbarro also expanded abroad, with franchise restaurants opening in Israel, Lebanon, and Saudi Arabia in 1995. As in the United States, overseas Sbarros were located primarily in malls and airports. In England they were also found at service areas along major motorways. At home, company-operated restaurants continued moving into locations other than shopping malls, such as the Balboa Naval Hospital in San Diego, Florida State University in Tallahassee, St. Joseph's Hospital in Towson, Maryland, and Hofstra University Student Union, in New York City. Sbarro also operated restaurants in

downtown areas of major U.S. cities, including New York, Boston, Chicago, and Philadelphia. By the end of 1995 the company had 771 restaurants in 14 countries on six continents. Of these, 200 were franchised. Company revenue grew 7 percent to $319.2 million for the year. Sales systemwide, including franchised units, increased 8 percent to $416.3 million.

Despite the growth in sales, the company had a rough 1995 financially, with net income down. After taking various steps to control costs, profits for the last half of the year were greater than those of 1994. In December 1995, the company announced plans to close 40 underperforming locations and to open about 80 new units during 1996, half of which would be company-operated. In the mid-1990s Sbarro was strong financially. It paid quarterly cash dividends of $.19 per share in 1995; in March 1996, the company increased quarterly dividends to $.23 per share. The company also was debt free, paying for its expansion with cash from existing operations.

Changes in the Late 1990s and Beyond

The company's financial position remained strong going into the late 1990s, but the rapid growth it had experienced in years past began to slow. At this time, Mario Sbarro began to set plans in motion to regain full control of his family's company. Sure enough, in early 1998 the Sbarro family made a $380 million play for its namesake, hoping to reclaim the shares it did not already own by taking the company private. Several shareholders balked at the idea and eventually Mario Sbarro and his family members withdrew their bid in June. The family came to the table once more in November with a cash offer valued at 3.5 percent less than their first attempt. The privatization process was eventually completed in September 1999—the family acquired the remaining 65.6 percent of Sbarro at $28.85 per share in a deal valued at approximately $389.5 million.

As a private company, Sbarro entered the new millennium intent on bolstering it holdings through joint ventures as well as increasing its restaurant count. The company grew in size from 800 units in 1999, to more than 900 by 2001. By this time Sbarro had added several new concepts to its arsenal as a result of joint venture activity over the past several years. These included Mama Sbarro, which operated as a quick and table service casual-dining restaurant; an Italian table service restaurant named Salute; and Baja Grill and Waves, two quick service Mexican-style restaurants. Sbarro also focused on international expansion, opening its 30th unit in Russia in 2003. Future plans included branching out into the African and Chinese markets.

Meanwhile, the company began to launch a new brand campaign in an attempt to revitalize its image. In a November 2003 *Nation's Restaurant News* article, a company spokesperson commented, ''We have not been doing a good job in explaining to our guests what goes on behind the scenes of the product that [they're] eating. No one knows that we make our dough from scratch in every single restaurant around the world, that we buy the industry's best flour, that we buy the industry's best cheese.'' Sbarro looked to industry veteran Michael P. O'Donnell to head up these new management initiatives. O'Donnell was named president and CEO of Sbarro in 2003 and became the first nonfamily member to oversee company operations. Mario Sbarro remained chairman.

The new leader had his work cut out for him. Indeed, Sbarro reported the largest loss in its history—$17.2 million—in 2003 as revenues fell. The company pointed to the downturn in the economy, international tensions, the closure of restaurants, and higher ingredient prices as culprits in the earnings decline. Management remained optimistic, however, and pledged to turn around its namesake Sbarro restaurants while continuing to look for profitable new concepts in which to invest. The company believed its strategy would result in higher profits and revenues in the long run, and that Sbarro was on track for growth and success in the years to come.

Principal Competitors

Noble Roman's Inc.; Pizza Hut Inc.; Pizza Inn Inc.

Further Reading

Brumback, Nancy, "Market Report: Pizza, Foreign Service," *Restaurant Business,* August 10, 1995, pp. 122–41.

Burns, Greg, "All Together Now: 'Make That to Go,' " *Business Week,* January 8, 1996.

——, "Restaurants: Bye-Bye to Fat Times?," *Business Week,* January 9, 1995.

Garrett, Echo Montgomery, "Franchise Inc.: The Many Faces of Franchising," *Inc.,* June 1995, pp. 98–106.

Glazer, Fern, "Sbarro Continues Global Expansion, Rises to Challenge in Moscow," *Nation's Restaurant News,* November 10, 2003, p. 80.

Hamstra, Mark, "Sbarro Makes Bid to Take Chain Private," *Nation's Restaurant News,* February 2, 1998, p. 3.

La Franco, Robert, "Promote from Within," *Forbes,* February 28, 1994, pp. 86–87.

Matsumoto, Janice, "Saving Sbarro," *Restaurants & Institutions,* October 1, 1998, p. 22.

McCoy, Frank, "Sbarro's Juicy Slice of the Fast-Food Market," *Business Week,* September 7, 1987, pp. 72–73.

Pressler, Margaret Webb, and Steven Pearlstein, "Growing Out of Business: The Shakeout Has Just Begun in the Overbuilt Retail Industry," *Washington Post,* February 22, 1996, pp. A1, A8.

"Sbarro Inc. Is Now Closely Held," *Wall Street Journal,* September 30, 1999, p. B20.

"Sbarro Shares Fall After Family Withdraws Offer," *New York Times,* June 19, 1998, p. D3.

"Sbarro Taps O'Donnell As First Nonkin CEO, Pres," *Nation's Restaurant News,* September 29, 2003, p. 64.

"Sbarro to Shutter 40 Units by March," *Nation's Restaurant News,* January 1, 1996, p. 2.

Slovak, Julianne, "Corporate Performance: Companies to Watch," *Fortune,* May 7, 1990, p. 114.

Stark, Ellen, "Small-Stock Outlook: Sbarro," *Money,* March 1995, p. 62.

Therrien, Lois, "The Upstarts Teaching McDonald's a Thing or Two," *Business Week,* October 21, 1991, p. 122.

Wax, Alan J., "Sbarro's Largest-Ever Loss," *Newsday,* March 31, 2004, p. A32.

—Ellen D. Wernick
—update: Christina M. Stansell

Scientific Games Corporation

750 Lexington Avenue, 25th Floor
New York, New York 10022
U.S.A.
Telephone: (212) 754-2233
Toll Free: (800) 367-9345
Fax: (212) 754-2372
Web site: http://www.scientificgames.com

Public Company
Incorporated: 1979 as Autotote Systems, Inc.
Employees: 3,430
Sales: $560.9 million (2003)
Stock Exchanges: NASDAQ
Ticker Symbol: SGMS
NAIC: 541512 Computer Systems Design Services; 713290 Other Gambling Industries; 713990 All Other Amusement and Recreation Industries

Scientific Games Corporation, formerly known as Autotote, operates as the global leader in lottery and pari-mutuel technology. It provides wagering equipment, online and instant ticket lottery systems, video gaming machines, and pre-paid phone cards. The company holds a 64 percent share of the instant ticket market in the United States, controls 27 percent of U.S. online gambling, and over 65 percent of the North American pari-mutuel market. Scientific Games' pari-mutuel division supplies technology and equipment for wagering conducted at thoroughbred, harness, and greyhound race tracks, jai alai frontons, and off-track betting facilities.

Autotote Before 1992

Autotote Corporation began as Autotote Systems, a firm established in 1979 by Thomas H. Lee, a Boston venture capitalist and specialist in leveraged buyouts who purchased Autotote Limited from ATL Limited of Sydney, Australia. Based in Newark, Delaware, Autotote Systems designed, engineered, manufactured, marketed, and operated computerized pari-mutuel wagering systems in the form of totalizators, or tote

boards, which calculate and display odds and potential payouts for racetrack bettors. The company maintained a warehouse and manufacturing facilities as well as its offices in Newark. It also had manufacturing facilities in Hatfield, Pennsylvania, and a sales office in Konstanz, West Germany. Net sales rose from $5.4 million in fiscal 1980 (the period from the firm's inception in May 1979 to June 30, 1980) to $10.2 million in fiscal 1982. Net income increased from $124,000 to $970,000 over this period.

Autotote Systems had revenues of $36.2 million in fiscal 1989 and was supplying wagering equipment to some of the largest racing associations in the United States and more than 50 racetracks abroad when it merged in 1989 with United Tote, Inc. By this means, United Tote, though smaller than Autotote, acquired all of Autotote's outstanding shares for $87.8 million in cash and securities. Together, the two companies commanded almost half of the $92-million-a-year U.S. market for the manufacturing and servicing of totalizators. United Tote's owners thought they would run the business, but Autotote's owners conceived the transaction as a back-door method of taking their company public. Since Lee and his partners held the largest share in the combined company—36 percent—the president of Autotote, James H. Pierce, became president of United Tote.

The deal quickly unraveled when, despite assurance by lawyers from four major firms that there would be no problem with the merger, the U.S. Department of Justice filed suit against United Tote for violation of antitrust law. While the suit was in the courts, it became impossible to integrate the operations of the two firms except to discuss essential financial information. Moreover, one of the lenders who had made a bridge loan to finance the cash portion of the deal refused to refinance it when it ran into legal difficulties, and no other lender would step in to complete the transaction. Largely because of legal costs, increased interest payments, depreciation, and amortization expenses from the acquisition as well as delays in international sales, United Tote posted a loss of $2.7 million in fiscal 1990 (the year ended October 31, 1990) on revenues of $69.2 million.

A federal court decision in 1991 forced the dissolution of United Tote. Autotote Corp., founded in 1992, retained operations accounting for about 59 percent of the consolidated company's revenues, consisting of the principal totalizator unit and a Nevada sports/race-wagering business. A. Lorne Weil, a director and consultant to Autotote Systems since 1982, became chief executive officer of Autotote Corp., which assumed about $50 million of the consolidated company's long-term debt.

Expanded Operations: 1992–95

In fiscal 1992, Autotote had revenues of $48.4 million—two-thirds in the United States—and net income of $5.7 million. It was providing about 60 percent of the tote boards in the United States, receiving a percentage (about 0.5 percent) of the sum of wagers placed. Moreover, Autotote had become the leader in the field not only in on-track but also inter-track betting. In 1992, it won a contract to provide on-site betting parlors for all three major California racetracks, so that between races at one track patrons could bet on races being held at the other two. The company was also poised to introduce a new system, called Probe, that was the first fully integrated system not only for pari-mutuel betting but also video lotteries, keno, nonracing-sports betting, and any other form of legal betting involved with odds.

In 1993, Autotote was selected to operate Connecticut's off-track betting (OTB) system, which was being privatized. The company, which was already providing systems for keeping track of the Connecticut OTB bets, now took over operation of the betting parlors as well, paying the state a flat fee of about $20 million and making annual payments based on total dollars wagered. In the spring of 1995, it opened a $9 million, Las Vegas-style New Haven emporium called Sports Haven, where patrons could view and bet on races throughout North America and also patronize a bar wrapped around a cylindrical aquarium stocked with exotic sharks, dine at an upscale restaurant, dance the night away at a discotheque, or shop for sports memorabilia.

Autotote also was adding to its significant level of operations abroad. It signed a contract in 1992 to supply 10,000 lottery terminals to an Italian lottery based on horse racing. In June 1993, Autotote acquired the ETAG Group of Switzerland, a leading supplier of European computerized wagering systems, for $10.5 million, and in September of that year it completed its acquisition of Tele Control GmbH, an Austrian company providing lottery systems in Germany, Austria, the Netherlands, and Switzerland, and wagering systems for racetracks in Germany and Austria. In fiscal 1993, the company had net income of $9.5 million on revenues of $84.9 million.

In 1994, Autotote acquired Marvin H. Sugarman Productions Inc. and its affiliate, Racing Technology Inc., for 500,000 shares of common stock. Sugarman Productions was the largest

simulcaster of live horse and greyhound racing events to OTB patrons in North America. In January 1995, Autotote acquired certain assets of IDB Communications Group Inc.'s broadcast division for $13.5 million in cash and subleases for satellite transponders, or channels. A spokesman for Autotote said the transaction would allow it to telecast simultaneously races from more than 60 horse and dog tracks in North America.

Heavy Losses: 1994–96

By this time, however, Autotote was clearly sailing into troubled waters. Although its revenues climbed to $149 million in fiscal 1994, it lost $22.2 million and doubled its long-term debt to $144 million. As factors contributing to the loss, management cited charges of about $3.8 million resulting from closing the Newark manufacturing facility and discontinuing certain product lines, a $4.3 million writeoff of certain assets principally related to domestic and overseas projects, costs of $2.8 million attributed to a strike by employees of a subsidiary, and an extraordinary noncash writeoff of $4.2 million associated with the company's repayment of its prior senior bank credit facility, as well as payments for the acquisitions made in 1993 and 1994.

Autotote's stock fell from a year-long high of $26.50 a share to a low of $4.50 in February 1995, when the company admitted it was not in compliance with its credit covenants. Nine banks refused to lend the company additional funds for violation of these covenants in lending agreements. Several shareholders filed a class-action suit in federal court, charging that Autotote's officers and directors had violated certain securities laws. A settlement in 1996 for $11.8 million in cash and preferred stock did not require any admission of guilt on the company's part.

Thomas DeFazio was appointed chief financial officer of Autotote in May 1995 and president and chief operating officer later in the year. He restored the company's relations with its creditors and launched a restructuring program expected to save the company some $15 million by closing its North American lottery headquarters and its plant in Ballymahon, Ireland. In October, DeFazio persuaded Autotote's subordinated debtholders to accept company shares instead of $2.2 million in interest payments that it could not meet.

Nevertheless, Autotote lost $49.9 million in fiscal 1995 on revenues of $153 million. The company attributed $11.6 million of the loss to a restructuring charge taken for the closing of the support facility for lottery operations in Owings Mills, Maryland, and the scaling back of certain international activities, including the closing of the Irish plant. The company also wrote off $6.6 million in investments and assets, including $2.7 million attributable to its Mexican video-gaming-machine contracts and $2.6 million attributable to European wagering terminals. Its long-term debt swelled to $166 million.

During fiscal 1996, Autotote reduced its long-term debt by $6 million and cut its loss to a still substantial $34.2 million on revenues of $176.2 million. Its costs included a $6.6 million litigation-settlements charge. Autotote's stock dropped below $1 a share at one point during the year. In October 1996, the company sold its Autotote CBS Inc. sports-wagering subsidiary, which had provided systems to 107 of the 113 Nevada casinos and to the leading operator of sports-wagering facilities in Mexico. Three months later, Autotote signed a letter of intent to sell its European lottery business, Tele Control, to Scientific Games Holding Corp. for a price estimated at between $25 million and $30 million, using the proceeds to pay off bank debt.

In 1996, Autotote's pari-mutuel wagering systems processed approximately two-thirds of the estimated $20 billion total racing-industry handle (betting volume). Its wagering systems and/or related equipment were installed at more than 100 racetracks in North America, including 10 of the 15 largest, and in more than 800 OTB betting parlors. These company systems were also in use in many of the largest racetracks and OTB parlors in Europe—including all French, German, and Austrian racetracks—Latin America, the Far East, and New Zealand, as well as in eight Atlantic City casinos. In addition, Autotote had installed about 1,300 video-gaming machines in racetracks in West Virginia and Manitoba, Canada.

Autotote was also simulcasting live horse and greyhound racing events to approximately 50 racetracks and more than 850 OTB parlors throughout North America and to Atlantic City casinos. In its simulcasting operations, the company leased satellite transponders and owned decoders used to unscramble the transmission signal. Prior to its decision to sell its lottery operations abroad, Autotote was providing terminals for a nationwide Italian lottery based on horse racing and, with a European partner, designing and installing computer-based lottery systems in six German states. It had also been selling central processing systems and/or terminals for lotteries in Austria, Switzerland, the Netherlands, and Israel. In the United States, Autotote was operating the Connecticut Lottery and providing services to the Massachusetts State Lottery.

Of Autotote's revenues in 1996, services accounted for 78 percent and sales contracts for wagering equipment and software for the remaining 22 percent. The pari-mutuel group (including wagering and simulcasting systems, the Connecticut OTB, video gaming, and casino/sports wagering) accounted for 73 percent of revenues and lottery operations for the remaining 27 percent. The company's long-term debt was $159.7 million at the end of fiscal 1996. Officers and directors held about 26 percent of Autotote's common stock, with director Thomas H. Lee controlling nearly 13 percent.

Changes in the Late 1990s and Beyond

Autotote continued to improve its financial record in 1997. Several U.S. subsidiaries were sold to pay down debt. It placed a seven-year $110 bond offering in July, which provided additional relief for the company's debt load. The firm also completed the divestiture of its European lottery operations that year, leaving it to focus on its pari-mutuel and North American lottery holdings.

By 1998, business appeared to be back on track. Autotote secured its largest contract in company history that year when it teamed up with Sisal Sport Italia Spa. As part of the deal, the company was slated to provide up to 20,000 Extrema terminals to the Italian lottery operator. It also landed a seven-year contract to provide services to the Montana State Lottery that year. Additional lottery contracts were obtained over the next several years in Vermont, New Hampshire, Iowa, and Maine.

Sales reached $211 million in 1999, and the company reported a small profit compared to a loss of $15.9 million in the previous year. Despite another revenue gain in 2000, Autotote found itself once again posting another loss. Company management believed it was time to make a bold move. As such, the firm made a $310 million play for competitor Scientific Games Holding Corp. William Mallory, CEO of Scientific Games, and Autotote chairman and CEO Lorne Weil believed a merger would greatly benefit the two companies. "In a world where 'bigger is better' is no longer just a saying, the merger with Autotote gives the newly combined company the breadth and scale to develop and deliver products that will drive the future success of the lottery industry," Mallory declared in a 2000 *Atlanta Journal* article. Weil agreed, and in a company press release he added that as a result of the merger Autotote would be the "largest provider of service, systems and products to both the pari-mutuel gaming and instant ticket lottery industries as well as the only fully integrated lottery service provider in the world." Shareholders approved the deal and during the integration process in 2001, Autotote changed its name to Scientific Games Corporation.

The newly merged company acquired a 65 percent stake in Serigrafica Chilena S.A. in June 2002, which strengthened its position in the Latin American phone card and instant-win lottery ticket market. It bolstered its holdings in 2003 by acquiring MDI Entertainment Inc. and IGT OnLine Entertainment Systems Inc.

In just two short years, it appeared that the union of Autotote and Scientific Games was paying off. Sales reached $560.9 million in 2003 while net income remained steady at $52.1 million. With the problems of the past behind it, the company was poised for future growth. As a leading force in the lottery and pari-mutuel industries, Scientific Games looked as if it was on track for growth in the years to come.

Principal Subsidiaries

Scientific Games Management Corporation; Scientific Games Holdings Corporation; Scientific Games (Greece), Inc.; Scientific Games Acquisition, Inc.; Scientific Games International Holdings Ltd. (United Kingdom); Scientific Games International GmbH (Austria); Scientific Games UK Holdings Ltd.; Scientific

Games International Ltd. (United Kingdom); Scientific Connections SDN BHD (Malaysia); Knightway Promotions Ltd. (United Kingdom); Scientific Connections Ltd. (United Kingdom); Scientific Games Finance Corporation; Scientific Games International, Inc.; MDI Entertainment, LLC; Scientific Games Royalty Corporation; Scientific Games Canada, Inc.; Scientific Connections India Private Limited (India; 99.9%); Scientific Games del Peru, S.R.L. (99.9%); Autotote Systems, Inc.; Autotote International, Inc.; Autotote Canada, Inc.; NASRIN Services LLC; SG Racing, Inc.; TRACKPLAY LLC (70%); Autotote Electronics and Computer Services and Trading LLC (Turkey; 99.9%); Autotote Enterprises, Inc.; Autotote Keno Corporation; Autotote Europe GmbH (Germany); Scientific Games Racing SAS (France; 99.96%); Autotote Panama, Inc.; Autotote Nederland B.V. (Netherlands); Autotote Gaming, Inc.; Autotote Dominicana, Inc.; Autotote Interactive, Inc.; Scientific Games Online Entertainment Systems, Inc.; Scientific Games Chile Ltda.; Scientific Games Worldwide Ltd. (Ireland).

Principal Competitors

Alliance Gaming Corporation; International Game Technology; Youbet.com Inc.

Further Reading

"Autotote Selling off European Lottery Business," *New York Times*, January 15, 1997, p. D4.

Benson, Barbara, "Exec's Focused Course Improves Firm's Odds," *Crain's New York Business*, November 13, 1995, p. 15.

Berman, Phyllis, "Home on the Range," *Forbes*, November 9, 1992, pp. 113–14, 116, 118, 120.

Marcial, Gene G., "Big Bets on Scientific," *Business Week*, February 4, 2002, p. 103.

Schuch, Beverly, "Autotote CEO," *CNNfn*, October 9, 1998.

"Scientific Games' Buyout Not Expected to Cost Georgia Jobs," *Atlanta Journal*, May 20, 2000, p. F3.

"Scientific Games' Shareholders Approve Acquisition by Autotote Corporation," *PR Newswire*, August 9, 2000.

Siklos, Richard, "Autotote Gambles on High-Tech High-Rollers," *Financial Post*, May 25, 1995, p. 5.

Simmons, Jacqueline, "Autotote Corp. Appoints New Finance Officer," *Wall Street Journal*, March 24, 1995, p. B4.

Temes, Judy, "Autotote Off and Running with Financing from DLJ," *Crain's New York Business*, August 18, 1997.

Welling, Kathryn M., "No-Name Stocks," *Barron's*, December 14, 1992, p. 15.

—Robert Halasz
—update: Christina M. Stansell

SHIMANO®

Shimano Inc.

3-77 Oimatsu-cho
Sakai, Osaka 590-8577
Japan
Telephone: (+81) 72-223-3210
Toll Free: (800) 833-5540
Fax: (+81) 72-223-3258
Web site: http://corporate.shimano.com/

Public Company
Incorporated: 1940 as Shimano Iron Works Co., Ltd.
Employees: 5,500
Sales: ¥143.65 billion (2003)
Stock Exchanges: Tokyo
Ticker Symbol: 7309
NAIC: 336991 Motorcycle, Bicycle, and Parts
   Manufacturing; 33992 Sporting and Athletic Goods
   Manufacturing

Shimano Inc. is a leading producer of bicycle parts and fishing equipment. It is the world's largest manufacturer of such bicycle components as gear wheels, derailleurs, and brakes, with a 70 percent market share. In the late 1990s, Shimano began selling equipment for golf as well as snowboarding and other sports. Headquartered near Osaka, Japan, Shimano has 24 sites in 17 countries around the world. The company is known for its efficiency as well as innovation.

Origins and Growth of Shimano

Shimano dates back to 1921, when Shozaburo Shimano founded Shimano Iron Works in Sakai City, near Osaka. The town was a legendary blacksmithing center known for its swords and gun barrels. Rather than follow his father into farming, Shozaburo had apprenticed at an iron works after high school. Later, he started his own company, and the first product it made was a single-speed bicycle freewheel. In ten years, Shimano was exporting freewheels to China.

The business was incorporated as a limited corporation in January 1940 under the name Shimano Iron Works Co., Ltd. In 1951, it was renamed Shimano Industrial Co., Ltd.

Shimano began making its famous derailleurs in 1956. Also called external speed changers, these were the mechanisms that moved the bicycle chain from gear to gear on ten-speed bikes and the like. The next year, the company began producing an internal, three-speed gearing mechanism that was enclosed in the hub of the rear wheel. This internal speed changer was introduced to the U.S. market a few years later and soon became the standard for three-speed bikes. In 1960, Shimano installed a cold forge that enabled stronger products to be made in a more efficient fashion.

Shozaburo Shimano eventually turned over management of the business to his three sons. Though the company made brakes and other components, Shimano refused to produce complete bicycles. "Our founder said, 'never ever compete with a customer,'" remarked one of Shimano's sons to the *Straits Times*. A U.S. subsidiary, Shimano American Corporation, was set up in January 1965. Shimano launched into the bike-crazy European market in the same year.

Tackling New Challenges in the 1970s

In 1970, Shimano built what was then the largest bicycle plant, located in Yamaguchi Prefecture, Japan. Later in the decade, according to *Design Week*, Shimano began hiring engineers to create a unified look among component systems as well as elevating their performance. A European unit, Shimano (Europa) GmbH, was established in Düsseldorf in 1972 with just two employees. The company's shares began trading on the Osaka Securities Exchange the same year and were also listed on the Tokyo Stock Exchange in 1973.

Shimano's first manufacturing plant abroad was set up in 1973 in Singapore. Opening a sales office in California in 1974, the company was well placed to ride the booming bike market in the United States during the 1970s.

Shimano's path to success was not without its bumps. As Yoshizo Shimano later told the *Asian Wall Street Journal,* the company made a huge investment designing, developing, and testing a series of aerodynamic bicycle components in the late 1970s. They were well ahead of their time and took several years to catch on.

Shimano had also begun to diversify into tackle for fishing, another sport whose tools required precision mechanisms.

Company Perspectives:

At Shimano, we're in the business of producing bicycle components and sport fishing equipment, recreational tools whose value is determined by how well they perform in the hands of the people who use them. Our business philosophy is based on developing products that help people to interact with nature through the outdoor activities they love. In our rapidly growing urban society it is sometimes easy to forget the importance of harmonious balance between people and nature. Protecting that balance will assure the world's children the very same natural experience we enjoy today. We will be firm with our resolve towards the realization of our corporate ideal—making ourselves closer to people while bringing people closer to nature.

However, it did not become a major force in this industry until the late 1970s. Shimano's Bantam reels were introduced in 1978, followed by X-line rods in 1981.

Ahead of the Pack in the 1980s

Shimano continued to refine its biking products, creating new market leaders. The AX line of components for bicycle racing came out in 1980, followed two years later by a series for mountain bikes dubbed Deore XT. The Shimano Index System allowed cyclists to dial in to specific gears by numbers. Annual sales exceeded ¥50 billion in the mid-1980s. At this time, Shimano employed 1,500 people around the world.

Shimano beat its European competitors to the mountain biking craze, observed the *Far East Economic Review*. The company developed a thumb-shifting mechanism specifically for mountain bikes and produced tougher versions of its brakes and steering controls to stand up to knobby tire abuse. By the late 1980s, Shimano was considered the standard for mountain bike components.

The range of Shimano's cycling offerings expanded throughout the 1980s. New shifting systems continued to be developed, such as the Rapidfire Remote (1989) for mountain bikes. The company began selling a line of bike shoes in 1988.

In 1988, Shimano set up a UK subsidiary that focused on fishing tackle sales. In the same year, Shimano shifted some of its fishing reel production to Singapore, which, due to the rise of the yen, was producing about ¥4 billion ($26 million) worth of bike parts a year. In 1989, Shimano established three subsidiaries in the Netherlands that sold an array of products.

Sales were ¥84 billion in 1989. Exports of Japanese bicycles and components as a whole grew furiously in the late 1980s, reported the Asahi News Service, reaching ¥115.4 billion ($848.7 million) in 1990. By now, one-third of Shimano's production went to Europe.

Global Expansion Continues in the 1990s

Shimano opened a plant in Malaysia in 1990. In the same year, the company bought an interest in Alfred Thun S.p.A. This was renamed Shimano Italia S.p.A. after the rest of the stock was acquired. A fishing equipment unit was also set up in Italy in 1990. In addition, Shimano was expanding its Singapore operations. The company also set up subsidiaries in Belgium and Indonesia in the early 1990s. The parent company's name was changed to Shimano, Inc. in 1991.

The proprietary SPD (Shimano Pedaling Dynamics) line of quick-release "clipless" pedals called was introduced in 1990. Evolution of the fishing tackle line soon saw the introduction of the Stella reel and the SHIP (Smooth and Hi-Power) system.

In 1995, Shimano rolled out its Nexus line of seven- and four-speed internal hubs for cruiser bicycles, which were growing in popularity in the United States due to their retro styling and simplicity of operation. Shimano was also developing an in-hub gear system that could be locked to prevent theft. It was introduced to the Japanese market in 1997.

Competition in Asia increased towards the end of the decade as European manufacturers entered this market. Bicycles had long been a staple form of transportation in China, and, as its economy grew, so did the demand for high-end bikes. The *Far Eastern Economic Review* had observed that most of China's 320 million bicycles did not have gears in the early 1990s. However, this was changing rapidly, and Shimano claimed a 50 percent market share on gears there.

After reports of cyclists being injured by broken cranks, Shimano recalled more than 2.5 million of them in 1997. It was the largest recall in the bike industry to date, reported the *Los Angeles Times,* and cost the company $15 million or more. Due to the popularity of Shimano's mountain bikes, the affected parts had been installed in about 50 different brands over the previous three years.

Shimano acquired G. Loomis Inc. in 1997 as it launched an Action Sports Division offering products for growing new sports such as snowboarding. Shimano set up a Golf Division in 1999 and continued to develop new products in other areas, such as a wobble-free fishing rod.

2000 and Beyond

Shimano became more visible than ever on the global stage as longtime user Lance Armstrong began his winning streak at the Tour de France in 1999. While overseas production accounted for 30 percent of production in 2000, exports accounted for more than 80 percent of revenues of ¥141 billion. As the Japanese bike market stalled, the *Nikkei Weekly* reported Shimano was shifting the focus of its overseas plants to supplying local bike manufacturers rather than producing parts to export back to Japan. Shimano was investing ¥1 billion to boost production at its Shanghai plant by 60 percent and was adding a three-speed gear line there to meet new demand.

In 2001, the company set up a ¥5 billion factory in the Czech Republic to meet booming bike demand in Eastern Europe, as well as building a plant in mainland China. A Taiwanese unit was established in 2002, and a second, ¥2 billion ($17 million) factory opened in the People's Republic of China in 2003. Shimano also opened a ¥500 million ($4 million) fishing rod production facility on the site of its Kunshan, China, bike parts

Key Dates:
1921: Shimano Iron Works is established.
1940: The company is incorporated.
1951: The company is renamed Shimano Industrial Co., Ltd.
1956: Shimano begins producing derailleurs.
1960: A cold forge is installed.
1965: A unit is opened in the United States.
1970: A Fishing Tackle Division is created.
1972: A European unit opens, and the company is listed on the Osaka Stock Exchange.
1973: A manufacturing plant abroad opens in Singapore.
1991: The company's name is changed to Shimano Inc.
1997: An Action Sports Division is established; Shimano recalls 2.5 million cranks.
1999: A Golf Division is created.
2001: Factories are set up in China and the Czech Republic.

complex. The company was aiming to increase overseas production to half of total production by 2004, reported *Asia Pulse.*

After extensive design and testing, an automatic gear shifter for bicycles was announced in late 2003. The device used magnets and other sensors to determine a bike's speed and make shift adjustments accordingly. Shimano was hoping to sell 50,000 units a year at ¥200,000 ($1800) each. Yoshizo Shimano told the *Financial Times* that the motivation for the idea was to allow bike commuters to concentrate on traffic by freeing them from the distraction of selecting gears.

Shimano continued to innovate as a manufacturer of fishing gear as well. In late 2001, it introduced the Dendomaru 3000SP, an electric reel with an LCD screen displaying the length of line cast as well as other data to give novices feedback on their technique. A few years later, Shimano developed an underwater fish detector in partnership with Furuno Electric Co., a maker of navigation instruments.

Sales were growing at the rate of 6 or 7 percent a year, reaching ¥143.7 billion in 2003. Net income grew more than 50 percent to ¥12.3 billion. As it proceeded into the first decade of the 21st century, the company had an estimated 70 percent share of the world market for bike parts.

Principal Subsidiaries

Dunphy Holding Pty. Ltd. (Australia); G. Loomis Products, Inc. (United States); P.T. Shimano Batam (Indonesia); Shimano American Corporation; Shimano Australia Pty. Ltd.; Shimano Belgium N.V.; Shimano Benelux B.V. (Netherlands); Shimano Canada Ltd.; Shimano Components (Malaysia) Sdn. Bhd.; Shimano Czech Republic s.r.o.; Shimano Eurasia ooo (Russia); Shimano (Europa) GmbH (Germany); Shimano Europe Holding B.V. (Netherlands); Shimano Europe Fishing Holding B.V. (Netherlands); Shimano France Composants Cycles S.A.S.; Shimano Italia S.p.A.; Shimano Italy Fishing S.r.l.; Shimano (Kunshan) Bicycle Components Co., Ltd. (China); Shimano (Kunshan) Fishing Tackle Co., Ltd. (China); Shimano (Mersing)

Sdn. Bhd. (Malaysia); Shimano (Shanghai) Bicycle Components Co., Ltd. (China); Shimano (Singapore) Pte. Ltd.; Shimano Taiwan Co., Ltd.; Shimano U.K. Ltd.; Wooyun Co., Ltd. (Korea).

Principal Divisions

Action Sports; Cycling; Fishing; Golf.

Principal Competitors

Campagnolo s.r.l.; Daiwa Seiko Inc.; Falcon Cycle Parts; SR Suntour Inc.; SRAM Corporation; Sun Race Sturmey-Archer Inc.

Further Reading

Dickerson, Marla, "Shimano to Recall 2.5 Million Bicycle Cranks," *Los Angeles Times*, July 10, 1997, p. D2.

Foremski, Tom, "Fishing Gear Maker Floats a Helpful Idea," *Financial Times* (London), February 3, 1999, p. 5.

Friedland, Jonathan, "Components of Success: Japanese Bicycle-Parts Maker Shimano Eyes China," *Far Easter Economic Review*, November 18, 1993, p. 66.

"Japan's Exports of Bicycle Parts Show Rapid Growth," *Asahi News Service*, April 9, 1991.

"Japan's Shimano to Invest US$17.1 Mln in New Chinese Subsidiary," *Asia Pulse*, March 11, 2003.

Kanabayashi, Masayoshi, "Japan's Shimano Prospers Amid Gloom with Line of High-Tech Bicycle Gear," *Wall Street Journal*, January 13, 1994, p. A6.

Kwan Weng Kin, "How Shimano Pedalled Its Way to Success," *Straits Times* (Singapore), August 3, 2003.

"LCD on Fishing Reel Dispenses Tips for Novice Anglers," *Nikkei Weekly* (Japan), December 3, 2001.

Marsh, Peter, "New Products Crucial to Success," *Financial Times* (London), Survey—Manufacturing Excellence, May 21, 2001, p. 2.

Mitchell, Colin, "A New Line in Fishing Rods," *Guardian* (Manchester), The Guardian Online Page, October 22, 1998, p. 6.

"Motorized Reels Hook More Anglers," *Nikkei Weekly* (Japan), February 21, 2000, p. 16.

"Not a Single Worker Retrenched Since 1973," *Straits Times*, April 26, 1998.

"Shimano Acquires EGS Patents (Shimano Rachete les Brevets d'EGS)," *La Tribune*, July 13, 2000, p. 21.

"Shimano Aims to Lift Chinese Sales of High-End Bike Parts," *Nikkei Report*, April 23, 2004.

"Shimano Develops Automatic Bicycle Gear-Shifter," *Nikkei Report*, November 14, 2003.

"Shimano Group Profit Pedaling Toward All-Time High," *Dow Jones International News*, July 2, 1999.

"Shimano On Course to Raise Gear Production Overseas," *Nikkei Weekly* (Japan), September 4, 2000.

"Shimano Steps up Activities in Asean," *Business Times Singapore*, December 11, 1990, p 28.

"Substitute Teacher; Firms Turn Tutor for Schoolkids," *Asahi Shimbun*, March 14, 2002.

Thisdell, Dan, "From Its Humble Start in a Swordmaking Centre, Shimano, the Japanese Manufacturer of Bicycle Components, Has Become a Hallmark of Quality," *Management Today*, March 6, 1990, p. 74.

Vickers, Graham, "Graham Vickers Explains How a Japanese Cycle Component Maker Is Having a Growing Impact on the High Quality Bicycle Market," *Design Week*, April 19, 1987, p. 19.

Voigt, Kevin, "Your Life—The Interview: Pedal Power," *Asian Wall Street Journal*, November 28, 2003, p. P3.

—Frederick C. Ingram

Siegel & Gale

437 Madison Avenue
New York, New York 10022
U.S.A. ·
Telephone: (212) 817-6650
Fax: (212) 817-6680
Web site: http//www.siegelgale.com

Wholly Owned Subsidiary of Omnicom Group Inc.
Incorporated: 1969
Employees: 130
Sales: $30 million (2002)
NAIC: 541618 Other Management Consulting Services

New York City-based Siegel & Gale is a subsidiary of Omnicom Group Inc., the world's largest advertising conglomerate. As part of Omnicom's Diversified Agency Services Group, Siegel provides a wide range of brand marketing services, such as strategic positioning, brand training for employees and vendors, and tailored relationship programs. The company has also made a specialty of helping corporations to simplify their communications and improve verbal and visual expressions across all media. In recent years, Siegel has become very active in interactive services, including online branding, Web design, and Web strategy consulting. With more than 30 years of experience in its field, Siegel boasts an impression roster of clients, including Citibank, the American Red Cross, Jiffy Lube, Disney, the National Basketball Association, and the Securities and Exchange Commission.

Alan Siegel Learns the Advertising Business in the 1960s

The driving force behind the founding and success of Siegel & Gale is its longtime chairman, Alan Michael Siegel. He was born in 1938 in New York City in sight of Yankee Stadium, the son of a photograph engraver who worked in the advertising industry. Although he would follow in his father's footsteps in many ways, he took a circuitous route in the journey. He graduated from Cornell University in 1960 with a degree in Industrial Aid Relations and Economics but had no certain career path and was not pleased with his job prospects. He returned to school to study law at New York University School of Law, then two years later dropped out to serve a two-year stint as a first lieutenant in the Army. Stationed in West Germany, Siegel developed an interest in photography, learning the trade from an elderly German who worked on the military base. This newfound enthusiasm for the visual arts led Siegel, after his discharge from the Army, to study with professionals Alexey Brodovitch, renowned photographer for Harper's Bazaar, and Austrian-born Lisett Model. To support himself, Siegel took a position with the Batten, Barton, Durstine and Osborn (BBDO) advertising agency, becoming part of the firm's training program. He learned the full range of the advertising business—marketing, media, project management, new product development, creative, cognitive research—which served as valuable preparation for the day he would strike out on his own. After completing his traineeship, Siegel worked for a man named Bruce Crawford, who 40 years later, as the chairman of Omnicom, would acquire Siegel & Gale. In 1967, Siegel went to work for the public relations firm of Ruder Finn, becoming an account executive, and two years later accepted a position with Sandgren & Murtha Inc., a New York marketing and design consultancy, where he again served as an account executive but was promised a partnership down the line. Because Siegel was just 30 years old, however, the firm backed away from the idea. Rather than wait to become a partner at Sandren, Siegel decided to start his own business.

In 1969, Siegel developed a business plan for a corporate logo design shop. He hired a designer named Robert Gale, who subsequently took equity in the company, which assumed the name Siegel & Gale. At first, the company operated out of Alan Siegel's apartment. In his words, ''The concept behind new firm was strategic thinking plus top-flight design. At the time nobody was combining the two.'' The first customer was tire manufacturer Uniroyal, which was interested in creating a brand identity for stores it owned in Colombia and Venezuela. The relationship was later expanded to include the company's global brand identity. Another early client was the mailing solutions firm Pitney Bowes. Siegel moved out of its founder's apartment to a half-residential, half-commercial building. By the end of the first year, the company consisted of five employees. Revenues totaled about $120,000.

Diversification in the 1970s–80s

After four years, Gale decided he wanted to spend more time on architectural graphics. Siegel bought him out but retained the Siegel & Gale name because of its brand recognition and established reputation in the corporate identity field. It was during the 1970s that the firm began to diversify beyond logo and branding work, setting up a unit devoted to the simplification of business and government documents. Alan Siegel told *Interactive PR* in a 1997 online interview, "Working with many banks in the mid '70s, I was surprised at how atrocious the bank applications and legal agreements were. . . . I was amazed that the insurance companies, the banks, leasing companies, were still using documents that were draconian in every sense. They were intimidating looking. They were unreadable. We were working for Citibank, and I approached them about simplifying the documents they used in their retail marketing. We simplified their consumer loan note, which was absolutely impenetrable. We changed the content to reflect the way the bank actually behaved, as opposed to how lawyers wanted to treat a transaction." Simplification in communications became a preoccupation for Alan Siegel, who spent several years traveling the country lecturing on the subject, in the process building up this pioneering business within Siegel & Gale. The firm worked with a number of financial services companies, helping them to retool their forms and documents. Ultimately, Siegel & Gale funded, and Alan Siegel co-founded, a graduate program at Carnegie Mellon University to teach students document simplification. While many of the graduates went to work for technology companies, some of the most gifted were recruited to work for Siegel.

The firm diversified even further during the 1980s. It went beyond the traditional idea of creating a corporate identity and began to develop "corporate voice" programs that helped companies to create a distinct and consistent personality when interacting with customers. Moreover, Siegel began to offer integrated marketing campaigns. In addition to creating brand strategies, the firm, well established in the United States, was now looking to expand overseas in order to implement these plans on a global basis. In 1984, Siegel was generating around $6 million in annual revenues, only 5 percent of which came from overseas work. It was at this point that advertising giant Saatchi and Saatchi was assembling a global network of marketing services and targeted Siegel as a company it would like in its fold. Alan Siegel recognized that the design business was going global, appreciated Saatchi's aggressive spirit, and decided that by aligning with a deep-pocketed corporate parent his firm would have the resources to expand in a way that would prove

impossible by going it alone. Thus, Alan Siegel agreed to sell the business to Saatchi for $13.5 million, although he continued to head the company and enjoyed virtual autonomy.

Struggles with Saatchi: 1980s–90s

The relationship with Saatchi, however, never proved as beneficial as hoped. On the positive side, Siegel was able to expand internationally by latching onto local Saatchi operations; the firm was also able in some cases to land Saatchi customers, and revenues grew at a steady pace, with international sales accounting for half of all sales by 1988. At the same time, however, Siegel's growth was in many respects stunted. Saatchi went through some difficult financial times and was unable to provide the kind of capital that was necessary for Siegel to make acquisitions, invest in needed equipment, and open offices in new locations. Furthermore, opportunities to create synergy with other parts of the Saatchi empire were limited. In fact, Siegel's interests were often in conflict with those of other Saatchi units, some of which competed with the firm over the same business. "Early on," Alan Siegel told *Brand Strategy,* "we realized that it wasn't as productive a relationship as we had hoped." In 1990, Alan Siegel attempted to buy back the firm, but Saatchi rejected the offer and Siegel & Gale was forced to continued to operate under the auspices of a ponderous corporate parent that was focused on advertising and far less interested in growing Siegel than did was the entrepreneurial leader and his team.

During the 1990s, Siegel became increasingly involved in incorporating the Internet into its business. Work with document simplification had introduced the company to the power and possibilities of personal computers interacting with consumers. In the mid-1990s, Siegel launched its interactive media practice, one of the first companies to do so. Well before the Internet reached critical mass with the public, Siegel was already exploring the impact of the Internet and e-commerce on branding, especially for well-established businesses. It designed early Web sites for American Express, Kodak, Ernst & Young, and IBM. While highly enthusiastic about the Web, Siegel still chose to view it as just another tool, albeit a powerful one, serving the firm's traditional goal of defining and building brands.

In the meantime, Siegel's corporate parent changed its name to Cordiant (with the help of Siegel) and was forced to sell off a number of units. It appeared in the fall of 1996 that Cordiant might spin-off Siegel in a stock offering, taking advantage of Siegel's expertise in interactive marketing and a boom in this field, to raise some much needed cash. In the end, however, the offering did not come to pass. Finally, in 1998, events transpired that would allow Alan Siegel an opportunity to regain the firm's freedom. Cordiant was broken into two companies, with Siegel assigned to the Saatchi & Saatchi entity, which its management decided to position as a pure advertising company, eschewing the idea of emphasizing or associating their services around brand identity. As a consequence, Siegel became an ill-fitting part and Saatchi was receptive to a buyout offer. Alan Siegel put together a $33.8 million package and in June 1998 bought back the firm.

Key Dates:

1969: Siegel & Gale is founded.
1985: The company is sold to Saatchi & Saatchi.
1998: Alan Siegel buys back the company.
2000: The company's name is altered to Siegelgale.
2003: Following the sale of the company to Omnicom, its name reverts to Siegel & Gale.

Independence Regained in the New Century

Independent once again, Siegel continued to become increasing involved in its Internet and e-commerce services. Unlike its dot-com counterparts of this era, however, Siegel was not burning through seed money and had been profitable for many years. In 2000, the firm decided to apply the lessons it learned working on clients to perform a makeover on itself. To emphasize the importance of its e-commerce practice, it renamed itself Siegelgale so that the firm's Internet address and official name would be the same. Although there was no intention of abandoning more traditional branding work, the firm anticipated that in time the majority of its business would be done on the e-commerce side. Moreover, a company spokesperson told *Design Week* that Siegelgale "predicts e-strategies will come to dominate the shaping of brands and believes a new breed of branding communications company is needed to exploit the full potential." To support its commitment to e-commerce and goal of becoming a dominant player in the market, the firm launched a $6 million in-house developed advertising campaign, including print advertisements, radio commercial, airport posters, and online advertisements. The intent was to bring attention to the firm's many e-commerce clients, the likes of which included dot-coms such as Lycos, old-line corporations such as American Express, as well as "click and mortar" hybrids such as Toys "R" Us. Later in 2000, Siegelgale expanded its e-services by launching a Broadband and Wireless Group to develop branding initiatives for the new wireless devices that would be entering the marketplace. As had been the case with the Internet several years earlier, the firm had already had been involved in the area before establishing this specialized unit.

With the bursting of the dot-com bubble, emphasizing its e-commerce credentials quickly lost its luster for Siegelgale. At least it was not among the many dot-com casualties, but the slumping economy of the early years of the new century took its toll on the firm. In 2002, the London office was downsized and a year later was eliminated entirely, with the work for international clients turned over to the New York office. Although Alan Siegel was pleased with the firm's freedom, he was practical enough to realize the company's limitations as an independent company competing in a world of massive, global media concerns. In an August 2001 interview with *Brand Strategy,* he admitted that the eventual realignment of the firm with a large advertising agency was "a distinct possibility." Nearly two years later, in May 2003, that possibility became reality when Omnicom Group acquired Siegelgale for an undisclosed amount of money, part of a buying spree to build up its Diversified Agency Services Group. Alan Siegel stayed on as chairman of the company, which subsequently reverted to its original name of Siegel & Gale.

Principal Competitors

Corporate Branding, LLC; FutureBrand Worldwide; The Richards Group, Inc.

Further Reading

Bernstein, Robert, "Brand Man," *Brandweek*, November 27, 2000, p. IQ14.
Elliott, Stuart, "Siegel & Gale, a Brand and Image Makeover Consultant, Decides to Practice What It Preaches," *New York Times*, February 9, 2000, p. C8.
Grieves, Robert T., "Rewrite Man," *Forbes*, September 19, 1988, p. 198.
Mortimer, Ruth, "The Frank Yank, Who Shoots From the Hip," *Brand Strategy*, August 2001, p. 3.
"Online Interview: Alan Siegel," *Interactive PR*, February 3, 1997.

—Ed Dinger

Simplicity Manufacturing, Inc.

500 North Spring Street
Port Washington, Wisconsin 53074-1752
U.S.A.
Telephone: (262) 377-5450
Fax: (262) 377-8202
Web site: http://www.simplicitymfg.com

Private Company
Incorporated: 1922 as Simplicity Manufacturing
   Company
Employees: 500
Sales: $350 (2003 est.)
NAIC: 333112 Lawn and Garden Tractor and Home
   Lawn and Garden Equipment Manufacturing

Wisconsin-based Simplicity Manufacturing, Inc., makes lawn mowers, riding mowers, garden tractors, and a variety of attachments. The company is also known for its Giant-Vac leaf blowers, trail vacuums, debris handlers, and collection systems, as well as for chipper shredders, tillers, and field and brusher mowers. The wide range of snowthrowers and attachments it manufactures rounds out the company's products and provides some seasonal diversity to the business. With manufacturing facilities in Georgia and New York, the company is majority owned by Kohlberg & Co., a New York state private investment firm. Employees also own a share of Simplicity through an Employee Stock Ownership Trust. In 2004 Simplicity agreed to be acquired by Briggs & Stratton Corporation, a large manufacturer of gasoline-powered engines for outdoor equipment.

The Early Years

The roots of Simplicity can be traced back to Milwaukee, Wisconsin, where in 1872 the Western Malleable and Gray Iron Manufacturing Company was established to produce gray iron castings. With the advent of the automobile, the company began to make gasoline-powered engines, marketed under the "Simplicity" trade name. Western was bought by businessman L.M. Turner in 1911 and moved to the shores of Lake Michigan, to Port Washington, Wisconsin, where the company, now called Turner Manufacturing, continued to produce internal combus-

tion engines as well as two models of farm tractors. Unfortunately, Henry Ford entered the tractor market after World War I, cut prices, and drove several firms out of business, including Turner Manufacturing, which went under in 1920. Turner's sales manager, William J. Niderkorn, acquired some of the assets of his former employer including the Simplicity name. In 1922 he founded Simplicity Manufacturing in Port Washington.

Simplicity's first product was a portable cylinder-boring machine used to rebuild car and truck engines. It was a popular enough product that the company was able to carry on through the first several years of the Great Depression, but in 1936 the market collapsed when Detroit automakers began to rebuild engines, selling them at low prices directly to car and truck owners. Forced to find a new product, Simplicity, in 1937, entered the garden tractor market with a two-wheel walking tractor that was sold by Montgomery Ward and Company. It was the popularity of this product that laid the foundation for Simplicity's long-term success. Not only did the company make money selling the walker, but the machine was versatile and could be fitted with a wide range of attachments produced by Simplicity, including a cultivator, plow, and sickle bar mower. In 1939 a "sulky attachment" (essentially two wheels and a simple seat) was introduced, converting the walker into a rudimentary riding garden tractor.

Postwar Growth

World War II intervened, temporarily putting a halt to Simplicity's growth in the lawn and garden market, as the government limited the number of tractors the company could produce. As part of its war effort, the company manufactured electric fence controllers, a product it had recently introduced, and external surface grinders. Simplicity elected to focus its resources on the garden tractor business in 1945 and enjoyed steady growth in the postwar years that saw large number of war veterans getting married and raising families in the suburbs sprouting up across the country, many of whom would now be in the market for garden and lawn equipment.

A major step in the company's evolution took place in 1955 when Simplicity began to offer a snow throwing attachment to its walker. This advance led to the 1961 launch of a single purpose, walk-behind, 23-inch rotary snowthrower using a 3.5 horsepower motor. The Snow-Away retailed for $285. Other major developments also took place during this period. In 1955 the company introduced the Simplicity Roticul, a single-purpose, walk-behind rotary tiller. Two years later Simplicity brought out the Wonder-Boy, the first rear-engine riding mower. This model featured a full floating mower deck and relied on a joy stick for steering. In 1959 the company produced the 700 Wonder-Boy, its first four-wheel riding tractor. As Simplicity entered the 1960s, it was generating close to $9 million in annual revenues and posting profits in the $500,000 range. It was also a public company by now, and its common shares traded over the counter.

Simplicity continued its steady pace of growth. In 1963 it began to manufacture its first lawn tractor. Then, in 1965, it underwent a change in ownership. A major farm equipment manufacturer, Allis-Chalmers Corporation, sought to acquire Simplicity to gain entrance into the suburban market for lawn and garden equipment. At first, the transaction was challenged by the government, which questioned whether it violated fair trade laws. As part of its attempt to address concerns that it controlled too much of the market, thus stifling competition, Allis-Chalmers opened a plant in South Carolina to manufacture garden tractors under its own name. Six years later, after the Nixon administration repealed the fair trade laws, Allis-Chalmers closed the South Carolina plant and moved all of its garden tractor production to the Port Washington plant. Under new ownership, Simplicity also began to look more at foreign markets. In 1969 it opened an office in Brussels, Belgium, to handle its European business.

1970s–80s: New Products and Directions

Simplicity continued to expand its product offerings and make improvement to existing lines during the 1970s. In 1971 the company began selling its first commercial industrial tractor. A year later it introduced a new garden tractor, the three-speed PowrMax. The PowrMax, being larger than a traditional garden tractor yet smaller than a farm tractor, set the standard for a new category in the industry: the compact tractor. In 1973 a more robust engine, featuring 19.5 horsepower, was added to the PowrMax. The tractor was so popular that the government acquired a number for use on military bases. Some of the PowrMax models would eventually, in the early 2000s, become virtual collector's pieces, fetching double the price originally paid for them. Simplicity also reached a milestone during the 1970s, turning out its one-millionth power unit in 1975. On the snowthrower side of the business during this period, Simplicity introduced a new single-stage snowthrower in 1978.

More changes in ownership took place during the 1980s. In 1983 three Simplicity executives—Warner C. Frazier, president; Nicholas P. Trunzo, vice-president of operations; and Carl Charles, vice-president of finance—teamed up with Wesray Cor-

poration, a private investment firm, to buy the business from Allis-Chalmers. Wesray, formed just two years earlier, was headed by a former Secretary of the United States Treasury, William E. Simon, and had already completed a number of acquisitions, including Gibson Greeting Cards and Wear-Ever Aluminum. A subsidiary, Wesray Equipment, was formed to serve as the new parent company for Simplicity. At this point in its history, Simplicity was logging annual sales of $70 million and employing a work force of 500. The relationship with Wesray, however, would prove to be short-lived. In 1985, just two years later, Wesray sold its interest to an Employee Stock Ownership Trust (ESOT). Papers filed in this transaction indicated that in fiscal 1985 Simplicity sales had grown to $90 million.

Simplicity faced some challenges in the late 1980s. A drought during the summer of 1988 hurt sales of lawn and garden equipment, and was followed by a dry winter, which adversely impacted the sale of snowthrowers. As a result, sales that had increased to $100 million in 1988 receded to $90 million in 1989. Of greater long-term significance was the maturation of the lawn mower and snowthrower markets. The sales of outdoor power equipment had peaked in the early 1970s, and there were dozens of American companies involved in the business, as well as Japanese heavyweights like Honda. Simplicity was, to some extent, a victim of its own success; the better the company built its products, the longer they lasted and the less often customers would reward Simplicity with repeat business.

As a way to generate growth, Simplicity looked for opportunities beyond the consumer market. In 1989 it acquired Middlesworth Engineering and Manufacturing Inc., a Greentown, Indiana, maker of industrial mowers, which had patented an advanced steering mechanism. Some of Simplicity's dealers had begun selling turf maintenance machinery and suggested Simplicity try that market as well. The company was able to modify the Middlesworth products to create a line of six professional lawn cutters. Simplicity quickly surpassed Middlesworth annual sales in the $500,000 range. Simplicity also invested money in the development of a new snowthrower that relied on tracks rather than wheels for propulsion, but the track supplier proved to be unreliable, hampering the introduction of this winter product line.

Acquisitions in the 1990s

In the early 1990s, Simplicity was able to take advantage of changes in a law that prohibited yard waste from landfills, introducing to the market an attachment that would fit on most of the company's mower decks to mulch grass clippings. Patented shredder blades could also shred fallen leaves. Simplicity entered the stand-alone chipper shredder business when it acquired Tornado Products Company in 1992. The line, which featured patented triangular hammers to boost shredding power, was later supplemented with an electric-powered unit as well as larger commercial versions. Walk-behind chipper vacuums were then added in 1994.

Simplicity again experienced another change in ownership during the 1990s. In 1994 an affiliate of private investment firm Kohlberg & Co., based in Mount Kisco, New York, bought a 70 percent interest from the ESOT. It appeared that the company would change hands yet again in 1997. A sale appeared immi-

Key Dates:

1922: Company founded by William J. Niederkorn.
1937: Simplicity builds first walking tractor.
1957: Wonder-Boy riding mower introduced.
1961: Sno-Away Snowthrower introduced.
1965: Allis-Chalmers Corporation acquires business.
1985: Employee Stock Ownership Trust buys company.
1994: Kohlberg & Co. acquires controlling stake.
2002: Snapper, Inc. acquired.
2004: Briggs & Stratton acquires Simplicity.

nent to Questor Partners Fund L.P., a Detroit-area buyout firm that had recently acquired Ryder TRS Inc. and Schwinn Cycling & Fitness Inc. However, that deal ultimately fell through, and Simplicity was taken off the block.

To maintain its steady growth in the late 1990s Simplicity introduced several innovations. In 1998 the company invested more than $1 million in new technology to increase productivity. A laser-cutting machine, costing more than $1 million, was installed, capable of cutting through steel sheets as large as four by eight feet and three-quarters of an inch thick. Simplicity also invested in a 165-ton hydraulic press with quick die-change capabilities to bend the cut steel into the necessary parts for tractor frames or lawnmower decks. Previously, parts had to be cut with a traditional punch press, which was both time consuming and expensive because a die had to be fashioned for each individual part and that die would cost in the $10,000 range. The laser cutter could be programmed to cut steel in any number of shapes without need for a die. Moreover, it could be set to continue work unmanned over weekends. The punch press continued in use for larger production runs where it was much faster than the laser, but the laser was ideally suited for a variety of smaller jobs. Simplicity also invested in robotics, introducing welding robots in the mid-1990s. In the end, the addition of new technology was intended to increase efficiency rather than capacity, given that the lawn-and-garden industry was a cyclical business and management was careful not to overextend itself.

In February 1999, a new president was brought in: Jim Weir, who had been groomed to succeed Warner Frazier as chief executive officer. A Wisconsin native, Weir went to the University of Wisconsin to study mechanical engineering but graduated in 1966 with a business degree instead. After going to work for the Arthur Anderson firm in Milwaukee, he was drafted during the Vietnam War and spent two years stateside. After returning to Arthur Anderson, he went to work for Briggs & Stratton, the top manufacturer of lawn mower engines. One of Briggs' major customers was Simplicity. Wier started out in the finance department and rose to the rank of executive vice-president of operations, overseeing four divisions, a position he held for ten years. During his time at Briggs he was involved in some difficult labor negotiations and was believed to be instrumental in the cutting of jobs in Milwaukee, a reputation which would follow him to Simplicity.

When Wier arrived, Simplicity began to initiate a plan to move into the fast-growing lawn-and-garden equipment market,

serving such customers as municipal parks and landscaping companies. It was also interested in growing its European business, and developed a riding mower more suited to the lush grass found on the Continent. Rather than discharging the grass out the side of the mower, the new units discharged from the back. However, Simplicity's efforts were soon placed in jeopardy when management and the Machinists union were unable to reach agreement on a new labor contract. In October 1999 some 350 union workers walked off the job. With Frazier, who had a good reputation with the union, set to retire at the end of the year, labor leaders expressed concern that Wier, given his history at Briggs, was more likely to take a hard line on the negotiations. Health care, rather than higher wages, proved to be the sticking point for workers, while management insisted on a five-year contract, rather than three, to give Simplicity a better chance to grow the business without labor distractions. Finally, after more than six weeks on strike, the union workers agreed to a new five-year contract that addressed the major concerns of both parties.

2000 and Beyond

Before Warner stepped down as CEO on January 1, 2000 (he stayed on as chairman), Simplicity announced that it had agreed to purchase Ferris Industries, a Munnsville, New York-based company that produced professional turf care machinery. Like Simplicity, Ferris had started out in an unrelated field, launched in 1909 to make milking machines. It did not become involved in the manufacture of commercial walk-behind and riding mowers until 1985 but quickly gained a solid reputation for innovation, in particular for its revolutionary suspension system. For Simplicity, the addition of Ferris helped fill out its product line in the fast growing commercial mower market. In 2000 Simplicity completed another purchase, picking up Giant-Vac Manufacturing Inc., a Connecticut company that added leaf blowers to a product mix that was increasingly being steered towards the commercial sector, for sale through independent dealers rather than mass-market retail chains.

An even more important acquisition would take place in October when Simplicity agreed to a $73.3 million purchase (later adjusted to $55.8 million) of Georgia-based Snapper Inc., a lawn equipment manufacturer which Simplicity had been pursuing for several years. Snapper, founded in 1890 to make saws, was owned by Metromedia International Group Inc, which after a change in leadership elected to put the business up for sale. Simplicity finished second in the bidding, but when a deal with the high bidder failed to materialize, Simplicity was quick to step in and buy the Snapper assets. In addition to doubling its size, becoming a company with annual sales in the $350 million range, Simplicity gained the valuable Snapper brand name, and in addition to supplementing its current lines of lawn and garden equipments, it gained a line of walk-behind lawnmowers that it previously did not sell. Moreover, it expanded the company's reach into the southern states.

Then, in June 2004, Simplicity announced that it would be acquired by Briggs & Stratton for some $225 million in cash. Expected to be completed in 2005, the deal would make Simplicity a part of its new parent's Power Products Group, though the company planned to maintain its current management team and manufacturing facilities. "We're pleased with the acquisition,'' said CEO Wier, the former Briggs & Stratton executive, adding, ''We believe Briggs & Stratton has the financial resources and support to allow us to continue our current growth strategy.''

Principal Subsidiaries

Ferris Industries; Giant-Vac, Inc.; Snapper, Inc.

Principal Competitors

The Black & Decker Corporation; Deere & Company; Honda Motor Co., Ltd.; The Toro Company.

Further Reading

Content, Thomas, ''Port Washington, Wis., Manufacturer to Double Sales with Acquisition,'' *Milwaukee Journal Sentinel,* October 24, 2002.

Gallun, Alby, ''Advances Help Simplicity Mow Labor Costs,'' *Business Journal-Milwaukee,* June 15, 2000, p. 22.

——, ''For Simplicity's Sake: Newcomer Wier Tries to Master Retail Side of Lawn Mower Industry,'' *Business Journal-Milwaukee,* March 19, 1999, p. 3.

Kurschner, Dale, ''Simplicity's Shifting Gears in Unpredictable Weather,'' *Business Journal-Milwaukee,* October 30, 1989, p. 8.

—Ed Dinger

⌖ LUXAIR

Société Luxembourgeoise de Navigation Aérienne S.A.

Aéroport de Luxembourg
L-2987 Luxembourg
Luxembourg
Telephone: (+352) 4798-1
Toll Free: 1-888-4-LUXAIR
Fax: (+352) 4798-4170
Web site: http://www.luxair.lu

Private Company
Incorporated: January 9, 1948 as Luxembourg Airlines
    Company
Employees: 2,137
Sales: EUR 289.1 million ($363.0 million) (2003)
NAIC: 452990 All Other General Merchandise Stores;
    481111 Scheduled Passenger Air Transportation;
    481211 Nonscheduled Chartered Passenger Air
    Transportation; 481212 Nonscheduled Chartered
    Freight Air Transportation; 49211 Couriers; 561520
    Tour Operators; 541614 Process, Physical
    Distribution, and Logistics Consulting Services;
    722211 Limited-Service Restaurants; 722320 Caterers

Société Luxembourgeoise de Navigation Aérienne S.A. (Luxair) is the national airline of the Grand Duchy of Luxembourg. Every year, more than a million passengers fly the airline, which connects 60 destinations across Europe and beyond. Regional jets made up Luxair's fleet of 16 aircraft in 2003; the airline also had four medium-haul Boeing 737s and three Fokker F50 turboprops.

Luxair's network of 60 destinations stretches north to Stockholm, southeast to Egypt, and southwest to the Canary Islands. While the airline's traditional strength has been its convenience for business travelers, Luxair also operates charters for tourists. The company's tour division carried 173,000 passengers in 2002. Luxembourg State is the company's largest shareholder, owning 23.1 percent. Luxair itself owns one of the largest air cargo centers in Europe, as well as a stake in Cargolux, Europe's largest all-freight carrier. In addition to the airline and ground handling, Luxair operates shops and restaurants at the airport at Findel, Luxembourg, and provides catering of in-flight meals.

Taking Wing in the "Golden Sixties"

Construction of Luxembourg's airport, located at Findel, began in 1937 but was not completed until 1946. Luxair traces its origins to the Luxembourg Airlines Company, founded on January 9, 1948. In 1961, this was reorganized and became "LUXAIR—Société Luxembourgeoise de Navigation Aérienne S.A." Luxair began operating a single leased Fokker Friendship F27 turboprop between Luxembourg and Paris in April 1962. Routes to Frankfurt and Amsterdam soon followed.

Based at Luxembourg's Findel Airport, the airline carried 12,000 passengers during 1962. The new airline aimed to offer its clientele of business passengers great service and excellent connections to larger intercontinental airlines, recounted *Le Mensuel d'Agéfi Luxembourg,* a regional business monthly.

Luxair benefited from the growth of European economies during the "Golden Sixties," which led to increased business and pleasure travel. Two more Friendships and a larger Vickers Viscount were added by 1967. The popularity of Luxair's charter flights to the Mediterranean led to the formation of LUXAIRTOURS in 1968.

Flying Jets in the 1970s

Another important factor in Luxair's development was its diversification. In March 1970, Luxair, along with the Salen Shipping Group (Sweden), Loftleidir (Icelandair) and private local investors, established Cargolux Airlines S.A., one of Europe's first cargo airlines. Luxair also operated duty-free shops and established food services subsidiaries (AIRREST S.A. and Catering Services S.A.) responsible for in-flight meals on Luxair and client airlines as well as restaurant concessions at the Findel Airport.

Luxair began operating its first jet aircraft, the French-made Caravelle airliner, in 1970. By 1972, the annual passenger count was up to 240,000. Boeing 737s, which would be the mainstay of the fleet, were first added in 1977. The company gradually replaced its Friendships with Fokker F50s and Embraer Brasilia turboprop aircraft.

1980s Emphasis on Cargo

Luxembourg was liberal with its fifth freedom rights, allowing foreign airlines to pick up local passengers for flights to other international destinations. Icelandair had built a thriving United States to Europe business using Luxembourg as a hub, while other governments aggressively protected their own national carriers' shares of the transatlantic trade.

Luxembourg Airport's runway was extended to four kilometers in 1986, making it the longest in Europe. This reflected the duchy's new emphasis on air cargo, reported Britain's *Financial Times*. Luxair raised its stake in Cargolux from 10 percent to 24.5 percent in late 1987. In 1989, Luxair joined Lufthansa Commercial Holding to create a freight handling operation, Eurocargo S.A. This would form the basis for Luxair CargoCenter six years later.

In the late 1980s, Luxair was carrying 500,000 passengers a year. In 1989, the airline was relatively early to join the Amadeus computer reservations system, becoming its fifteenth partner carrier.

Luxair ended the 1980s with 1,050 employees. The fleet consisted of one Boeing 747 jumbo jet, three 737s, five Fokker turboprops, and one of the Embraer Brasilias.

Network Expands in the 1990s

Major European destinations such as Frankfurt, London, Paris, and Amsterdam were the first layer of Luxair's network. The airline had also been adding second tier locations, including Berlin, Madrid, Hamburg, and Nice. There were also long-range charter flights booked under the auspices of Luxair Tours, which was selling 150,000 vacation packages a year.

Luxair was one of the few airlines not to post losses during the Gulf War, due to additional military troop and cargo flights. The airline completed a LUF 7 billion fleet renewal program in 1992. Towards the end of the year, the German carrier Lufthansa acquired a 13 percent stake in Luxair. Lufthansa and Luxair were both already shareholders in the Cargolux freight airline.

Turnover was LUF 7.29 billion in 1995; the airline carried about 730,000 passengers during the year. The Luxair CargoCenter at Luxembourg Airport opened in 1996. Luxair financed its LUF 3 billion cost itself. Luxair raised its stake in Cargolux from 24.5 percent to 30.5 percent in January 1997.

Luxair's first ERJ-145 Embraer Regional Jets entered the fleet in August 1998. Dubbed "Eurojets" by Luxair, these small (50-passenger), efficient aircraft were suited for the continent's short hops and preferred by passengers who found them more comfortable than turboprops.

Regional destinations Bologna, Florence, Dublin, London (City Airport), Stuttgart, and Stockholm were added in 1998, reported *Air Transport World*. Luxair had marketing arrangements with Lufthansa, Air France, and Austrian Airlines, and VLM Airlines; a deal with United Airlines was signed in May 1999. Icelandair stopped operating transatlantic flights through Luxembourg in January 1999, after 50 years of operations there, in order to develop Reykjavik as a hub. This led Luxair to offer a 767 service to New York beginning in March 1999, using a Boeing 767 leased from City Bird, a Brussells-based commuter airline. However, the route was not profitable and was soon dropped. Luxair also flew to resorts in the Canary Islands and Egypt. Within a few years, losses curtailed Luxair's plans to add more long flights and prompted the carrier to focus on its core short- and medium-haul European routes.

Luxair carried more than one million passengers in 1999. According to *Air Transport World*, the airline was pursuing a quick growth strategy to ensure its survival in a consolidating marketplace. The company aspired to develop a route network beyond its traditional home in west central Europe. The company was pitching the relatively uncrowded airport of Luxembourg as a quicker alternative to larger ones.

Celebration and Tragedy in 2002

By the time of Luxair's 40th anniversary in 2002, the airline was the third-largest employer in Luxembourg, with nearly 2,100 employees. Revenue was EUR 318 million, up nearly 6 percent. Net profits rose 46 percent to EUR 29.6 million.

In the same year Luxair celebrated 40 years of successful flight, Luxembourg suffered the worst air disaster in its history when one of Luxair's Fokker 50 turboprops crashed while attempting to land in the fog at Findel on November 6, 2002. The wreck, which killed 20 people, was ultimately attributed to pilot error.

Luxair had a 70 percent market share at Findel Airport, reported *Le Mensuel d'Agéfi Luxembourg*. The airport was undergoing a EUR 324 million ($320 million) modernization.

Luxair had a new rival in cargo handling at Luxembourg Airport, CS-Lux, which was acquired by Swissport Cargo Services in October 2002. Soon after, it expanded into a new market, opening the ground handling service Luxair Cargo Deutschland GmbH (LCDG) at Frankfurt Airport in July 2003.

Key Dates:

1948: Luxembourg Airlines Company is formed.
1961: The airline is reorganized as LUXAIR—Société Luxembourgeoise de Navigation Aérienne.
1968: LUXAIRTOURS is formed.
1970: The first jet airliner, a Caravelle, enters the company's fleet.
1977: Boeing 737s are added to the fleet.
1989: Luxair and Lufthansa form Eurocargo freight handling venture.
1996: Luxair CargoCenter opens.
1998: Embraer ERJ-145 regional jets enter fleet.
1999: Annual passenger count exceeds one million.
2002: Luxair's 40th anniversary is marred by a crash.
2003: Luxair enters the freight handling market at Frankfurt Airport.

The company was expanding its Luxembourg facility, which employed 1,000 people, in 2004. Swiss-based freight forwarder Panalpina acquired a 12.1 percent stake in Luxair in late 2002.

A Luxembourg-London City Airport codeshare arrangement with VLM Airlines ended in July 2003. The partnership had begun five years earlier. Tourist and business traffic were both down in 2003, when Luxair carried 1.1 million passengers. Turnover was EUR 289.1 million ($363 million) for the year.

Principal Subsidiaries

Air Pub S.à.r.l.; Airrest S.A. (99%); Luxair Cargo Deutschland GmbH (Germany); Luxair Commuter S.A. (99%); Luxair Deutschland GmbH (Germany); Luxair Executive SA (51%); Luxair Finance S.A.H.; Luxair France S.A.

Principal Divisions

Airline; Tour Operating; Cargo Handling; Passenger Handling; Airport Shops; Catering Services.

Principal Competitors

KLM; Martinair; SN Brussels Airlines; Virgin Express; VLM Airlines.

Further Reading

Cooper, Richard, "Luxair Orders EMB-145s—Regional Jets to Replace Fokker 50s and Brasilias," *Airclaims*, October 9, 1997.
Crols, Bart, "Luxair to Increase Flights, Set up Two New Bases," *Reuters News*, November 23, 2001.
Daly, Kieran, "Bitter Dispute at Luxair Blocks Safety Data Programme," *Air Transport Intelligence*, December 16, 2003.
De Wulf, Herman, "Losses Prompt Luxair to Re-Focus on Europe," *Flight International*, March 6, 2001, p. 25.
——, "Luxair Kills Sabena's Luxembourg Pilot-Pool Plan," *Flight International*, January 25, 1995, p. 8.
——, "Luxair Looks to Tie-Up with Sabena," *Flight International*, July 31, 2001, p. 23.
Evans-Pritchard, Ambrose, "Twenty Killed as Commuter Plane Crashes in Fog," *Daily Telegraph* (London), November 7, 2002, p. 18.
"Fliegender Wechsel Bei Der Luxair," *Luxemburger Wort*, October 3, 2000, p. 25.
"Gulf War Had Positive Effect on Luxair," *Aviation Daily*, May 21, 1992, p. 3.
"Happy Birthday Luxair," *Le Mensuel d'Agéfi Luxembourg*, June 1, 2002.
"Luxair," *Airliner* (Frankfurt, Germany), April 2000, p. 22.
"Luxair Can Survive Among the European Giants, Says Managing Director," *Trends*, June 10, 1993, p. 56.
Luxair Corporate Communications, *Annual Report 2003*, Luxembourg: Luxair S.A., 2004.
"Luxair Joins Amadeus as 15th Partner Carrier," *Aviation Daily*, November 20, 1989, p. 336.
"Luxair to Increase Its Stake in Cargolux," *Reuters News*, December 3, 1987.
Nelms, Douglas W., "Reaching Out," *Air Transport World*, August 1, 1999, p. 86.
Penney, Stewart, "Flandre Air Takes Luxair's Last Brasilias," *Air Transport Intelligence*, October 8, 1998.
"Swissport Acquires Luxembourg-Based CS-Lux and Gains Access to One of Europe's Key Air Cargo Hubs," *Hugin*, October 15, 2002.

—Frederick C. Ingram

SPSS Inc.

233 South Wacker Drive, 11th Floor
Chicago, Illinois 60606-6307
U.S.A.
Telephone: (312) 651-3000
Toll Free: (800) 525-4980
Fax: (312) 651-3668
Web site: http://www.spss.com

Public Company
Incorporated: 1968
Employees: 1,263
Sales: $211 million (2003)
Stock Exchanges: NASDAQ
Ticker Symbol: SPSS
NAIC: 511210 Software Publishers

Based in Chicago, SPSS Inc. is a leading global manufacturer of software used in data analysis, reporting, and modeling. Its products include CustomerCentric Data Analysis, Clementine Advance Analysis, Quantime, In2itive, SurveyCraft, and student versions of the company's SPSS Base and SYSTAT products. From more than 40 offices throughout the world, SPSS serves more than 250,000 customers in a wide range of fields including academia, banking, consumer packaged goods, finance, government, healthcare, insurance, retail, telecommunications, and market research. These clients use the company's applications to detect and hinder fraud, increase revenue, reduce costs, and operate more efficiently.

A Product is Born in the Late 1960s

The history of SPSS can be traced back to 1967, when Norman H. Nie, then a 22-year-old Ph.D. candidate at Stanford University, decided to develop his own solution after becoming "frustrated trying to use a computer to analyze data describing the political culture of five nations," according to the September 22, 2003, issue of the *Chicago Tribune*.

The application Nie was trying to use was created for biologists, not social scientists. With that in mind, Nie took detailed notes about what he needed in a software application and en-

listed the help of Dale H. Bent, a fellow doctoral candidate whose background was in operations research, to design a file structure. Hadlai "Tex" Hull, who had recently received his MBA from Stanford, was tapped to write the code, and by 1968 the Statistical Package for the Social Sciences (SPSS) was born.

Nie and Hull left Stanford to pursue careers at the University of Chicago, and they brought their SPSS program along with them. However, their main focus was on academics and research—not on developing or selling software. Hull became head of the university's Computation Center. Nie joined its National Opinion Research Center and eventually was named chairman of the political science department.

Nie became a top authority on social science data and statistical analysis. His specialty was working with voting patterns, and he went on to author a well-known book on American politics called *The Changing American Voter*. Through the years, Nie would receive national awards for his books, and by the early 2000s he had become professor emeritus in the University of Chicago's political science department, as well as a research professor in political science at Stanford University's Graduate School of Business.

With help from a university librarian and the University of Chicago's support, Nie and Hull began selling SPSS to academicians at other universities. As they concentrated on their academic careers, SPSS grew by itself. The data analysis application became increasingly popular and by 1974 was earning revenues of $200,000 per year—without any marketing or promotional effort at all.

As the company Web site later explained: "The early success of SPSS was directly related to the quality and availability of the documentation that accompanied the software. McGraw-Hill published the first SPSS user's manual in 1970. Once the manual was available in college bookstores, demand for the program took off. Nie, Bent, and Hull received a royalty from sales of the manual but nothing from distribution of the program. In Nie's words, 'It was like Gillette selling razors at cost and getting its profits from the blades'."

SPSS became so successful that the IRS took notice in 1971, indicating that it considered SPSS a small software company.

This determination in turn called into question the University of Chicago's status as a tax-exempt organization. Mainly for that reason, Nie and Hull incorporated their operation in 1975, and SPSS officially became an independent company. Dale Bent, who had played a role in the design of SPSS at Stanford, opted to accept an academic position at the University of Alberta in his native Canada instead of becoming involved with the new Chicago-based enterprise.

For several years, SPSS remained a part-time endeavor for Nie and Hull. "Initially, this was an ego trip," Hull explained in a September 2003 article in the *Chicago Tribune*. He noted: "It was fun to do, and it was neat when people knew your name at computer conferences. But there was no money in it."

While a competitor called SAS Institute was making strides during the late 1970s by partnering with the likes of IBM, SPSS remained focused on its base of academic users. The company sought to keep its software easy to use for those who were not computer savvy, and even paid fellow academicians to make upgrades. According to SPSS, the portable nature of its software enabled colleges and universities to use it on a variety of mainframe computer systems, including Burroughs large systems, the Control Data 6000 series, Digital Equipment Corporation (DEC) large systems, GE/Honeywell large systems, and the Univac 1108.

SPSS eventually was adopted by government and business users as well. In the mid-1970s SPSS software was employed by NASA to calculate the mean time between Space Shuttle part failures. The National Forest Service used SPSS to track bear encounters and injury reports in national parks. Within the business sector, SPSS became a tool for consumer marketing research and gained popularity among Anheuser-Busch, Procter & Gamble, and other consumer products companies.

According to company lore, while attending a company picnic in 1980, Nie and Hull looked about and were impressed with the growing number of people who were involved with SPSS and depending on the firm for their livelihood. The partners made the important decision to take the enterprise to a new level.

1980s: The PC Age

By the mid-1980s, the analysis software that Nie developed years before had achieved widespread adoption among university researchers. With the introduction of SPSS/PC+ in 1984, SPSS became the first software firm in its class to make applica-

tions available on individual PCs, as opposed to only large mainframes. That year, sales reached approximately $18 million.

In 1985, Nie appointed a seasoned software industry executive, John Grillos, as president and chief operating officer at SPSS. Focused on expanding the company's reach, Grillos oversaw new marketing initiatives for SPSS software. Shortly after Grillos joined the company, the work force at SPSS had grown from 160 to 220, and the company was realizing $25 million in annual sales. SPSS had evolved into a leader in its industry segment, competing mainly with North Carolina-based SAS Institute. The company next introduced SPSS/PC+ Graphics. Resulting from a partnership with Microsoft, the software gave users the ability to display data with presentation quality graphics via an interface with Microsoft's Chart tool.

In the fall of 1986, Pansophic Systems Inc., a systems software company based in Oak Brook, Illinois, agreed to acquire SPSS for $32 million. SPSS released new versions of its SPSS-X mainframe software, which retailed for anywhere between $3,000 and $10,000, and SPSS-PC+, which retailed for about $795. In addition, the company unveiled a forecasting program called SPSS-X Trends, priced between $1,500 and $3,000. These products pushed 1988 revenues to $33 million. In addition to higher sales volume, SPSS had extended its geographic presence, making its products available in some 90 countries. SPSS ended the 1980s by signing an agreement with JV Dialogue to market its software in the Soviet Union.

1990s: The Windows Age

Jack Noonan was named the company's SPSS president and CEO in 1992, when sales reached approximately $38 million. Noonan arrived at SPSS with considerable experience in the industry. Prior to joining SPSS, Noonan had served as president and CEO of database software developer Microrim Corporation from 1990 to 1991. Before that, he was vice-president of the Candle Corporation's Product Group, which produced IBM mainframe system software, from 1985 to 1990. While Noonan assumed his new responsibilities, Nie continued as chairman of SPSS, and Hull remained actively involved in developing the company's software.

Among Noonan's first initiatives was the founding of a sales team that would push into new markets, including the government and business sectors. Among the products the company introduced at this time was the first statistical software compatible with Microsoft Windows.

The mid-1990s brought some concerted efforts at expansion. In May 1993, SPSS reincorporated in Delaware under the same name and made an initial public offering of stock on the NASDAQ exchange. Also during this time, the company made an acquisition (of SYSTAT Inc.), and released software compatible with Microsoft Windows 95.

SPSS's acquisition efforts continued at a rapid pace in 1996, when revenues reached $84 million. That year, the company acquired BMDP Statistical Software Inc., Jandel Scientific Software, and Clear Software. Its SPSS 6.1 for Windows package received favorable reviews from the likes of *PC Week*, which called it "easy to use and significantly faster than other recently released Windows packages," despite low marks for having poor menu labels and a boring on-line tutorial. In addition, the

Key Dates:

1968: Norman H. Nie, Dale H. Bent, and Hadlai "Tex" Hull develop a software program and begin selling it from the University of Chicago.

1971: The IRS determines that SPSS is not just a program but a software company, jeopardizing the University of Chicago's status as a tax-exempt organization.

1974: SPSS has sales of $200,000, with no marketing or promotional efforts.

1975: Nie and Hull incorporate SPSS in Illinois.

1984: SPSS becomes the first in its class to make applications available on individual PCs, as opposed to only large mainframes; sales reach approximately $18 million.

1986: Pansophic Systems Inc. signs a letter of intent to acquire SPSS for $32 million.

1993: SPSS is reincorporated in Delaware and is taken public on the NASDAQ exchange.

1994: SPSS embarks upon an expansion strategy and acquires eight companies in the coming five years.

1997: SPSS adds to its offerings new products for the business intelligence software market.

2003: Company eyes audio and video mining as a new market niche.

company released Neural Connection, a decision support application that incorporated neural network technology to help users find order in chaotic data sets.

Late 1990s and Beyond

During the late 1990s and early 2000s, SPSS wanted to become a bigger player within the business intelligence software market, which was experiencing strong growth. Along with its competitors, SPSS sought to provide universal products capable of warehousing large corporate databases and performing data mining functions like linear regression and multivariate analysis. In the past, such data operations had required the involvement of professional statisticians. However, modern software applications were delivering this analytic power to everyday professionals.

Noonan led SPSS toward this goal. According to the company, SPSS introduced "technologies such as data mining, a business intelligence suite for the IBM eServer iSeries, Web analytics, sophisticated analytical components, a Web interface for online analytical processing (OLAP) technology and text mining. These technologies were introduced by SPSS Inc. to better capitalize on the expanding need for understanding ever-increasing volumes of data, and to support the company's mission to drive the widespread use of data in decision-making."

Many of the new technologies introduced by SPSS were obtained when it acquired other software companies. In 1997, when revenues reached $110.6 million, the company acquired Quantime Ltd., a market research software company, as well as In2itive Technologies Corp. Other acquisitions followed when data mining software company Integral Solutions Ltd. was ob-

tained in 1998 for $7.1 million. The acquisition gave SPSS ownership of the highly sophisticated Clementine data analysis software.

Sales reached $121 million in 1998, and the company launched SPSS Data Entry, a new survey design and collection application for Windows 95 and NT. The company ended the 1990s by acquiring Vento Software Inc. and forming an agreement with Harcourt College Publishers to bundle its software with statistics and marketing research textbooks.

SPSS entered the new millennium by earning a host of honors. Besides a place on *Forbes'* 200 Best Small Companies list, *Working Mother* recognized the firm on its 100 Best Companies for Working Mothers list. Several software industry publications, including *Software Magazine*, also included SPSS in different "best of" industry rankings.

In 2001, SPSS' revenues totaled $176.6 million. However, a weakening domestic economy and declines in foreign currency impacted earnings. In response, SPSS cut 90 jobs that April, amounting to 7 percent of its work force. The jobs were mainly sales positions and included 10 positions in the company's Chicago office.

Several important developments occurred in 2001. In February, SPSS acquired ShowCase Corporation, a manufacturer of middle market business intelligence software. In May, it released a version of its Data Entry software specifically designed for Sun Solaris and Linux platforms. At about the same time, the company launched its new CustomerCentric Solutions division to market its CustomerCentric customer relationship management software in high-service, custom deals exceeding $1 million.

In July, SPSS forged a strategic alliance with e-business software company Siebel Systems Inc. when it became a Strategic Software Partner in the Siebel Alliance Program. The alliance essentially involved efforts to integrate Siebel's eBusiness Applications with SPSS programs like Clementine and CustomerCentric.

In October 2001, SPSS forged a strategic alliance with America Online's Digital Marketing Services (DMS) subsidiary. According to Standard & Poor's, the alliance was worth $42 million over four years. DMS explained that under the alliance, SPSS "acquired the exclusive rights to distribute a survey sample generated through OpinionPlace.com."

In 2002, sales reached $209.3 million and employees numbered 1,263. That year, SPSS finalized a deal initiated in 2001 to acquire NetGenesis Corporation in a stock swap valued at $44.6 million. NetGenesis produced analytical applications for Web data, and was expected to add $15 million-$20 million to SPSS' annual revenues.

Commenting on the acquisition in the October 29, 2001, issue of *Canadian Corporate News*, Noonan said: "We are making investments that enable us to strengthen and develop our core competencies so that we emerge from this economic downturn as a stronger organization. Current market conditions are providing us with unique opportunities to accomplish this objective. Our merger with NetGenesis is a perfect example.

Where before we could only dream of adding NetGenesis web-oriented capability to our multi-channel analytical CRM framework, today we are making it a reality.''

SPSS also acquired text mining software manufacturer Lexiquest SA in 2002, along with Netexs LLC, which had developed a Web interface for OLAP technology. The following year, SPSS acquired DataDistilleries BV, a Netherlands-based applications developer, founded in 1995 at the Dutch National Research Center for Mathematics and Computer Science.

The early 2000s at SPSS were characterized by a focus on so-called predictive analytics, which, according to company literature ''connects data to effective action by drawing reliable conclusions about current conditions and future events.'' In 2003, SPSS introduced Predictive Web Analytics, a new product that combined the Clementine data-mining program with its NetGenesis Web analysis software. With prices starting at $135,000, the new program made it possible for users to see patterns in Web data and design more effective, relevant Web sites. An automated predictive analytics application for marketers called PredictiveMarketing also debuted that year, and the company held an informational summit in Stockholm to promote the technology and the products.

Looking toward the future, SPSS had its eye on audio and video mining as a new niche. As Noonan explained in the September 22, 2003, issue of the *Chicago Tribune*, ''Market research firms are especially interested in video mining. When you get feedback from focus groups, it is data and text, but if you could add in the body language, what their eyes do, that adds a lot to what's not said.'' The company had several products in the pipeline, but it also faced financial and legal challenges. While sales remained good, earnings declined. Moreover, allegations heard in U.S. District Court that the company had deceived stockholders by issuing misleading financial information, caused SPSS stock prices to slip, and a late filing with the Securities Exchange Commission raised some red flags at NASDAQ. Nevertheless, management remained optimistic about restoring earnings and stockholder confidence to prior levels, given, in particular, new leadership in the sales department and new markets for predictive analytics.

Principal Subsidiaries

SPSS UK Ltd.; SPSS GmbH Software (Germany); SPSS Schweiz AG (Switzerland); SPSS France SA; SPSS Argentina SA; SPSS Finland Oy; SPSS Hong Kong Ltd.; SPSS Mexico SA de CV; SPSS Japan Inc.

Principal Competitors

Cognos Inc.; Computer Associates International Inc.; IBM Corporation; Microsoft Corporation; Oracle Corporation; PeopleSoft Inc.; SAS Institute Inc.; Siebel Systems Inc.

Further Reading

''Acquisition: SPSS Buys ISL In Order to Boost Data-Mining Wares,'' *InfoWorld*, January 11, 1999.

Barry, Theresa, ''SPSS Enriches Data Analysis Programs,'' *Datamation*, December 1, 1987.

Callaghan, Dennis, ''Analytic Detective Work,'' *eWeek*, September 1, 2003.

——, ''SPSS Broadens CRM Scope,'' *eWeek*, May 14, 2001.

——, ''SPSS SAS Take Predictive Paths,'' *eWeek*, May 26, 2003.

Coffee, Peter, ''SPSS 6.1 for Windows Strikes a Balance,'' *PC Week*, September 12, 1994.

Copple, Brandon, ''Data Miner,'' *Forbes*, June 14, 1999.

Costlow, Terry, ''SPSS Software to Soviets,'' *Electronic Engineering Times*, July 10, 1989.

Goodman, JoEllen, ''First Big Acquisition Rounds Out Pansophic Software Line,'' *Crain's Chicago Business*, November 10, 1986.

Nelson, Don, ''High-Tech Entrepreneurs Honored,'' *Crain's Chicago Business*, November 21, 1988.

Oloroso, Arsenio, Jr., ''For SPSS, So Much to Buy, So Little Cash,'' *Crain's Chicago Business*, November 30, 1998.

''Pansophic Buys SPSS for $32 Million,'' *Crain's Chicago Business*, November 3, 1986.

Rose, Barbara E., ''Chicago-Based Software Firm Cuts 90 Jobs,'' *Chicago Tribune*, April 24, 2001.

''SPSS Inc. and Siebel Systems Announce Strategic Alliance,'' *Canadian Corporate News*, July 25, 2001.

''SPSS Inc. to Acquire NetGenesis Corp.,'' *Canadian Corporate News*, October 29, 2001.

''SPSS Launches New Data Entry Program,'' *Wall Street & Technology*, February 1998.

''SPSS Ships Data Entry 3.0 for Linux and Sun Solaris Systems,'' *EDP Weekly's IT Monitor*, May 7, 2001.

''SPSS Takes to Road to Give Public Sector Professionals a Leg Up On Their Data,'' *EDP Weekly's IT Monitor*, May 14, 2001.

''SPSS Uses Harcourt College Publishers to Introduce its Software to Students,'' *Electronic Education Report*, August 18, 1999.

Stinson, Craig, ''SPSS's Neural Connection: PC Statistics Meet Gray Matter,'' *PC Magazine*, March 26, 1996.

Stoll, Marilyn, ''Presentation Graphics, Statistical Software Linked,'' *PC Week*, March 25, 1986.

Van, John, ''Chicago-Based Statistical Software Firm Hits $200 Million in Annual Sales,'' *Chicago Tribune*, September 22, 2003.

Watt, Peggy, ''SPSS Teams Up With Chart: Pairing Combines Graphics with Statistical Functions,'' *Computerworld*, March 10, 1986.

Whiting, Rick, ''SPSS Broadens Web Reach with NetGenesis Deal,'' *InformationWeek*, November 5, 2001.

—Paul R. Greenland

Stater Bros. Holdings Inc.

21700 Barton Road
Colton, California 92324
U.S.A.
Telephone: (909) 783-5000
Fax: (909) 783 3930
Web site: http://www.staterbros.com

Private Company
Incorporated: 1989
Employees: 13,500
Sales: $2.75 billion (2003)
NAIC: 445110 Supermarkets and Other Grocery (Except
 Convenience Stores)

Based in Colton, California, Stater Bros. Holdings Inc. owns and operates some 158 supermarkets concentrated in Riverdale and San Bernardino counties, the so-called Inland Empire. In addition, it has some stores on Kern, Los Angeles, Orange, and San Diego counties. The chain, the largest locally owned in southern California, is known for its strict adherence to an appearance and dress code, which requires that store-level employees wear white shirts or blouses and have closely trimmed hair. In addition, beards are banned, and mustaches must be closely trimmed. From the start of its history, Stater Bros. has been built on the principle of low shelf prices combined with outstanding customer service. In 2003, *Consumer Reports* ranked Stater Bros. Markets as the best place to buy groceries in southern California; nationally, the chain ranked ninth. Stater Bros. is a private company owned by La Cadena Investments, a general partnership majority owned by the chain's chairman, chief executive officer, and president, Jack H. Brown.

1930s Origins

Stater Bros. was founded by twin brothers Cleo and Leo Stater in 1936. At the time, 24-year-old Cleo, a high school dropout, was working at a small grocery store in Yucaipa, California, earning ten cents a hour to man the cash register, stack the shelves, work the meat counter, and sweep the floor. The owner, W.A. Davis, told the young man that he was willing

to sell the store to Cleo and Leo for $10,000. Because they did not have the money, he would further accommodate them by accepting just $600 down and the balance through $300 monthly payments. With their cars serving as collateral, he brothers were only able to borrow $300. Cleo decided to take a chance, and he approached rival grocery store owner, as well as the richest and meanest man in town, D.M. Holsinger, to ask for a loan. Years later Stater recalled, "He just looked at me and said, 'If [Davis] is crazy enough to sell you his store, then I'm going to be crazy enough to give you the money.' " The brothers opened for business in August 1936.

According to Jack Brown, the area east of Los Angeles was not an attractive market at the time: "The L.A. chains didn't want to serve this area. This was cement plant country and a railroad town—very blue collar. So the Stater brothers developed their own niche." Frugality, on a number of levels, also became a watchword for the brothers. In the midst of the Great Depression of the 1930s, it was difficult to meet the monthly $300 payments. As a result, they agreed to avoid credit and pay for everything with cash. In this way, they would buy only what they truly needed. At the same time, they were committed to providing their primarily working-class customers with the lowest possible prices, leading to the company's motto: "The low price leader in your hometown." This approach quickly proved successful, as the Staters began to expand their operation in San Bernardino County. In 1937, they opened a grocery store in Redlands, followed in the next two years by stores in Bloomington, Colton, and Fontana.

The Staters' careers were interrupted in the 1940s by America's entry into World War II. While they were serving as Army Air Corps pilots, their parents, Clarence and Mary, were forced to step in to run the business. As a matter of necessity, in order to keep all the stores in operation, they sold half-interests to each store manager, a move that made sense at the time but would later cause legal problems. Upon their discharge from the service, the Stater twins returned to the business and were joined by another brother, Lavoy.

During the postwar years of the late 1940s, as the Baby Boom generation was born and their parents moved en masse to new suburban housing developments, grocers began to open larger formats, ''super'' markets, which were actually modest in size compared to most contemporary stores. Stater Bros. first entry into this new era of grocery retailing came in April 1948 when they opened a 12,500-square-foot supermarket in Riverside. Above the store was an apartment where some of the Stater family lived. This state-of-the-art store featured air conditioning, fluorescent lighting, and music playing over the public address system. According to Cleo Stater's recollection, ''We opened that store, stocked it and we sold practically everything in there the first day. That gave us the idea that we had to start expanding fast, which we did. For about two or three years, we were making a 100% return on our investment.'' With this steady cash flow, the brothers were able to grow without taking on debt. Each new store essentially funded the next, which was paid for by the time it was opened.

Although the Staters lacked contemporary research data and software programs, deciding where to locate a new store was not entirely a matter of guesswork—and was not, in fact, that far removed from current retail strategies. Because Cleo was a licensed pilot, they were able to fly over their market area and look for major clusters of houses. They then bought property as close as possible to these areas. Nevertheless, it was a risky approach to expansion: a few bad decisions could have easily led to ruin.

Innovations and New Owners: 1950s to the Mid-1980s

In other ways, Stater Bros. was also ahead of its time. During the 1950s, nine of their stores featured coffee shops to offer dining to their customers. One of the two San Bernardino stores included a restaurant on a second floor balcony overlooking the shoppers. In 1951, the company headquarters was moved to a Colton, where a 9,000-square-foot office and warehouse facility was opened. All of the produce and meat were now distributed from this central location, as were many of the items purchased in bulk. For a while, the facility even operated a bakery that supplied the chains' coffee shops and restaurants. It was in 1952 that Stater Bros. found itself in trouble with the government over its practice of having equal partnership in all of its stores and was sued for antitrust violations. Although Stater Bros. won, it elected to incorporate the chain. In 1958, Stater Bros. incorporated, and all but five of the partnerships were dissolved, and the store managers were bought out with either cash or stock. It was not until 1964 that all of the stores were brought into the fold.

In the 1960s, Stater Bros. grew with the communities it served: Orange, San Bernardino, and Riverside counties. All three were among the fastest growing urban counties in the United States. Because all of the chain's growth was internal, the company formed a construction division in 1960 to plan and build new supermarkets and other facilities. A year later, Stater Bros. opened a new 37,000-square-foot warehouse in Colton,

but business was so strong that just two years later an additional 115,000 square feet was added.

By the end of 1967, the chain operated 32 supermarkets located in 20 cities. (Also of note, the restaurant division was closed in July 1967.) Net sales over the previous five years had grown from $51.5 million to nearly $77 million. At this stage, the chain did not own a dairy or bakery operation but was involved in a growing private label business, offering such products as coffee, cheese, salad oils, and soaps. A year later, in July 1968, ownership of the chain passed out of family hands. Deciding it was time to exit the grocery business, the brothers sold the chain to Long Beach-based Petrolane, Inc. for stock and approximately $32 million.

Petrolane started out as a single-product company, liquefied petroleum gas, launched after World War II. By the early 1960s, management had concluded that Petrolane was in essence a marketing company and was capable of selling virtually any product within its area of operation. The company began to diversify, adding petroleum services as well as becoming involved in consumer products such as Mark C. Bloome tire stores and the Stater Bros. supermarket chain. Petrolane invested in the opening of new supermarkets, and by 1970 Stater Bros. became the second-largest contributor to the Petrolane balance sheet, trailing only the LP-gas division. At the close of 1970, the chain was 38 units strong and on the verge of reaching the $100 million mark in annual revenues. Three years later, the chain comprised 49 stores. By the end of the 1970s, there were 83 Stater Bros. stores and sales were in the $450 million range. Although Petrolane was quick to invest in new store openings, it was slow in introducing technology to the operation, which hurt profitability. It was not until 1977 that the company's accounts payable system was computerized, the first step in modernizing the chain. Scanning was introduced in 1979.

Stater Bros. entered the next decade with a strong push, opening ten new stores in 1980. Despite the expanding store base, however, the chain experienced a tailing off in profits. To help address this problem, in 1981 Petrolane recruited Jack Brown, who had a record as a turnaround artist, to serve as the president of Stater Bros. Locally born in 1938, Brown had worked his way up in the grocery business. At the age of eight, he lost his father, a San Bernardino County chief deputy sheriff who died from illness, and to help the family pay the bills he went to work at the age of 13 as a box boy at a San Bernardino grocery, Berk's MarketSpot. There, the owner, Mr. Berk, became something of a substitute father to Brown and taught him the business. After college, Brown made a career in supermarkets. When he was just 28, he became Vice-President of Sales and Merchandising for a San Bernardino chain, Sage's Complete Markets, then moved to Indiana, where he spent nine years as a corporate vice-president of a Midwest chain. He returned to California to become president of Pasadena's Pantry Markets and later assumed the presidency of American Community Stores in Omaha, Nebraska. According to Brown, he three times refused to take the Stater Bros. job before Petrolane made an offer he thought was too good to refuse.

Brown's relationship with Petrolane would be short lived, however. In 1983, Petrolane decided to sell most of its non-energy assets, including the Stater Bros. supermarket chain.

Brown and two other executives led an investor group that paid $110 million to acquire the business. The man with the bulk of the money was Bernard Garrett, who made his fortune from a Jerico, New York, electronics company, Instruments Systems Corp. In 1979, he set up a Los Angeles management firm to handle family investments. Garrett, who owned a 51 percent stake, became chairman of the board, while Brown stayed on as CEO and his management group controlled the remaining 49 percent interest.

From Private to Public and Back Again: Mid- to Late 1980s

From the start, the new owners of Stater Bros. talked about eventually taking the chain public. In 1985, the company took steps to prepare for an initial offering of stock, forming a holding company to make the offering and house the subsidiaries. Kidder Peabody was contracted to serve as the lead underwriter. Brown began to conduct road shows later in the year to attract investors. However, one night while he was in Minnesota, according to Brown, he received a phone call from Kidder informing him that Garrett had been involved in some leveraged buyouts that had ended up in bankruptcy court and that one of the directors had once been involved in a bankruptcy. None of this information had been disclosed in the offering's preliminary prospectus.

To rectify this situation, the director was quickly removed, the prospectus amended, and the offering was completed in November at $10 a share. Initial estimates had ranged from $12.50 to $14.50. The intrigue, however, was just beginning. Early in 1986, Garrett called for an emergency board meeting where he announced that he had conducted an investigation of Brown which revealed wrongdoing. Brown was quickly suspended by a board dominated by people chosen by Garrett, and guards were dispatched to bar Brown from his office while the locks were changed. A subsequent suit filed by the company charged that Brown had ordered the chain's inventory to be arbitrarily reduced by $600,000, thereby reducing profits as a way to depress the price of the company's stock when it hit the market. In this way, Brown could allegedly buy shares on the cheap.

Brown vehemently denied the allegations, maintaining that the inventory decision was aboveboard, and he countered that Garrett, who now owned about 38 percent of the company, was trying to oust the management partnership that controlled about 40 percent. Brown was backed by both the community and the work force. In a highly unusual move, members of the Teamsters and United Food and Commercial Workers not only staged noisy demonstration in support of Brown, their union bought stock in an attempt to help Brown win an upcoming proxy fight for control of the business. Brown was admired by Stater Bros. employees in part because he was known to keep a box cutting knife on his desk to remind him of his own working-class roots. Moreover, during a strike against other supermarkets the previous year, he refused to lock out the Teamsters. After a five-month fight for control of Stater Bros., Brown emerged victorious, and Garrett was bought out. Craig Corporation, a Compton-based electronic distributor, helped to provide the financing. Craig and Brown's group, La Cadena Investments, then took the business private again in 1987. In 1993, La Cadena bought out's Craig's 50 percent share and became the sole shareholder.

Continued Success in the 1990s and Beyond

By the 1990s, Stater Bros. was generating more than $1 billion in annual revenues, but as one of only a handful of locally owned and relatively small grocery chains it faced a challenging retail environment. Smith's Food & Drug, a Salt Lake-based chain, moved into the southern California market early in the decade. The Utah outfit was expected to offer stiff competition for Stater Bros., but by 1996 Smith's decided to pull out. Given the opportunity to acquire some of the stores, Stater Bros. declined, preferring instead to open stores in locations of its own choosing, concentrating on areas where the chain was already strong. During much of the 1990s, the chain added only a handful of new stores—four in fiscal 1992, two in 1993, and three in 1994—while just four replacement stores were replaced. In 1996, Stater Bros. launched a $20 million renovation project that would enlarge and modernize 83 of the chain's 110 stores, the most aggressive program of its kind for the chain since Brown took over. In addition, Stater Bros. earmarked $15 million to open three larger format stores.

By a stroke of good fortune, Stater Bros. increased by 43 stores in 1999 when it became the beneficiary of a merger between supermarket chains Albertson's Inc. and American Stores Co., parent of the Lucky grocery chain. Because the $11.7 billion merger caused concern among state and federal regulators about the impact on competition in the southern California grocery industry, the two companies were ordered to divest a significant number of stores before the merger could be completed. As a result, Stater Bros. was able to acquire 33 Albertson's and ten Lucky supermarkets, many of which were located in areas where Stater Bros. was hoping to expand. Brown called it a "one-in-a-lifetime occurrence" for the company. At a cost of $147.2 million, Stater Bros. virtually doubled its presence in Los Angeles County and Orange County. All told, the Stater Bros. chain of supermarkets grew to 155.

Although it was the largest locally owned independent chain, Stater Bros. hardly measured up in size to the national chains like Kroger, Ralphs, and Albertson's that had a strong presence in the southern California market. When Brown met with executives from the Big 3 chains in 2002 to discuss a strategy for upcoming contract talks with union employees, he was placed in a difficult position. The Big 3 wanted concessions on health, pension, and salary benefits and were determined to take a hard line. Because the southern California market represented a small percentage of their national business, they could ill afford to wait out a strike or initiate a lockout. The only private company involved, Stater Bros. operated entirely in southern California and could not afford a major loss of business. Brown was also advised that his employees had taken a vote, and 100 percent voted not to strike Stater Bros. In turn, he pledged not to lock out the union and took the unusual—and in the opinion of many, brilliant—step of accepting up front whatever agreement the union and the Big 3 eventually settled on. Thus, when talks broke down in the fall of 2003, leading to a supermarket strike that began on October 11, Stater Bros. was able to pick up an unprecedented amount of additional business. Not only was it a temporary windfall for the company, it was expected that at the end of the strike a large percentage of the new shoppers would remain Stater Bros. customers.

In 2004, Stater Bros. gained approval to build a new $200 million general office and distribution center on part of the former Norton Air Force Base in San Bernardino County. The new state-of-the-art distribution center would consolidate the operations of eight facilities and the resulting efficiencies were expected to save the chain millions of dollars. A number of communities in state and out of state attempted to attract Stater Bros., but in the end the native son and the local supermarket chain decided to stay home.

Principal Subsidiaries

Stater Bros. Markets; Stater Bros. Development, Inc.

Principal Competitors

Albertson's, Inc.; Ralphs Grocery Company; The Vons Companies, Inc.

Further Reading

Ascenzi, Joseph, "Cleo Stater Co-Founder of Grocery Chain Started What Has Become a Regional Power," *Business Press*, April 20, 1998, p. 14.

Coupe, Kevin, "Stater Bros.: Relentlessly Mainstream, Relentlessly Successful," *Progressive Grocer*, May 1996, p. 76.

Greenberg, David, "Stater Bros. Stays Out of Cities, Makes Peace with Union," *San Diego Business Journal*, January 19, 2004, p. 8.

Hammond, Teena, "Jack Brown the Inland Empire's Home-Grown Grocer," *Business Press*, September 16, 1996, p. 16.

Pitchford, Phil, "Stater Bros. Grocery Chain to Build Headquarters in San Bernardino," *Press-Enterprise*, March 13, 2004.

Simmons, Tim, "Jack Brown," *Supermarket News*, August 26, 1991, p. 2.

Tracy, Eleanor Tracy, "Man Bites Dog: Unions Back Boss," *Fortune*, May 26, 1986, p. 40.

Weinstein, Steve, "Stater Bros.' Jack Brown," *Progressive Grocer*, May 1987, p. 109.

—Ed Dinger

Stone & Webster, Inc.

100 Technology Drive
Stoughton, Massachusetts 02072
U.S.A.
Telephone: (617) 589-5111
Fax: (617) 589-2156
Web site: http://www.shawgrp.com/stonewebster

Wholly Owned Subsidiary of Shaw Group Inc.
Incorporated: 1889 as The Massachusetts Electrical
    Engineering Company
Employees: 5,000
Operating Revenues: $1.16 billion(1999)
NAIC: 541330 Engineering Services; 541690 Other
    Scientific and Technical Consulting Services; 213112
    Support Activities for Oil and Gas Fuel Exploration

Stone & Webster, Inc., one of the nation's engineering giants, has since 1889 offered its customers in the United States and the world engineering, design, construction, consulting, and environmental services to build electric power plants, petrochemical plants and refineries, factories, infrastructure, and civil works projects. Stone & Webster helped build substantial portions of the nation's power production infrastructure, including coal, oil, natural gas, nuclear, and hydroelectric plants constituting around 20 percent of U.S. generating capacity. The company played a significant role in the nation's defense efforts during World War I and II and afterwards, helping develop the A-Bomb, constructing large shipyards, and creating alternate means of production of strategic materials such as synthetic rubber. Much of the world's capacity in petrochemical and plastics development was also developed as a result of Stone & Webster efforts. After a sudden decline in fortunes in the late 1990s, the company declared bankruptcy in 2000 and was bought by the Baton Rouge, Louisiana-based engineering firm the Shaw Group. Stone & Webster continues to be a leader in power plant construction, engineering, and plant management, as well as in hazardous waste management and environmental services.

Origins in the 19th Century

The company's founders were two electrical engineering graduates from the Massachusetts Institute of Technology (MIT), Charles A. Stone and Edwin S. Webster, who started their own firm, the Massachusetts Electrical Engineering Company, a year after their graduation. Electrical engineering was a new field in the 1880s—Thomas Edison had patented the incandescent lamp only a decade earlier—and Stone and Webster opened their doors in spite of discouraging advice from respected mentors such as Professor Charles Cross, who told them that "there might be enough electrical consulting work to support one of you, but not both."

From the company's start in Boston in 1889, however, there was work for both, work which initially involved small jobs such as testing equipment and performing feasibility studies. Stone and Webster soon developed original testing systems and expanded their test activities to encompass the complete range of electrical equipment.

A year after the company that became known as Stone & Webster opened for business, it obtained its first significant contract, with the S.D. Warren Company in Maine, to design and install a direct current generating plant associated with a dam, along with a transmission line to the Warren paper mill a mile distant. In this task and those that followed, the new engineering company hired part-time university students, beginning a relationship with the Boston academic community which would continue into the 1990s.

By the early 1900s, Stone & Webster had diversified rapidly, involving itself in engineering, building, constructing, and managing power plants, and developing a name for its ability to build and operate integrated systems fueled either by coal or hydroelectric generation. Initial start-up operations were handled by the company's plant betterment division, which created and used an early form of quality control. In addition to its plant operations, the company also installed and managed lighting systems and electric-powered street railway systems.

By 1906, a number of major engineering projects were in process in six states, with several others being planned. To handle the load, Stone & Webster formed its first subsidiary, Stone & Webster Engineering Corporation, which managed all engineering, construction, and purchasing activities. Corporation activities underwent rapid growth, and by 1910 some 14 percent of the nation's total electrical generating capacity had been designed, engineered, and built by Stone & Webster.

Military and Power Projects in the 1920s–30s

After the onset of World War I, Stone & Webster took on a variety of military assignments, including designing and building new arsenals, military bases, airfields, and camp facilities, as well as the massive Hog Island Shipyard at Philadelphia, which employed 35,000 workers and had more launching ways than the three largest British shipyards combined. Once open, Hog Island completed 82 ships in two and one-half years.

In the post-armistice years and into the next decade, the company continued to grow and expand in the United States as well as abroad, constructing increasingly larger power plants and stations and transmission lines, as well as laboratories, factories, sugar refineries, warehouses, and a variety of other facilities. By 1920, the company also began building what at that time was the world's longest continuous tunnel, an 18.2 mile water tunnel which doubled the supply of Catskill water to Manhattan.

That year, Stone & Webster also managed 59 utility companies in 18 states and held a financial interest in many of them. As the decade moved on, growing national energy needs resulted in a need for increased availability of financing, and Stone & Webster responded in 1927 by merging with a 41-year-old investment banking organization to create a new investment subsidiary. During the next three years, the subsidiary participated as a principal in originating and underwriting more than a billion dollars in security issues and participating in the sale of nearly one-quarter of all new offerings syndicated in the United States.

In 1929, Stone & Webster decided for the first time to offer its stock to the public at $100 a share. However, in the words of former company President William F. Allen, Jr., in an address to the Newcomen Society, "That was not, perhaps, the greatest piece of timing." Only a few months later, the stock market crashed, eventually bringing the value of Stone & Webster stock to the low teens during the worst years of the Depression.

The 1930s were particularly challenging years for Stone & Webster. While the momentum in construction built by long-term contracts signed in the boom years of the late 1920s carried the company through 1931, new business became increasingly difficult to secure. During the early part of the decade, the company built, among other projects, the Rock Island Dam (the first to cross Washington's Columbia River), the 50-story RCA building in New York City, and a natural gas pipeline in Texas and New Mexico; however, by 1934 the company had far fewer contracts and was forced to reduce its staff.

Moreover, with the 1930 acquisition of Engineers Public Service, a utility holding company, Stone & Webster had itself become a utility holding company. When the Public Utilities Holding Company Act was passed just five years later, Stone & Webster was forced to choose between remaining a holding company or focusing on the engineering and construction business. The company opted to divest itself of its utility holdings. Through the mid-1930s, Stone & Webster continued to be active in appraisals and studies for major clients and in designing and constructing plants. As the decade drew to a close, the chemical industry began to undergo a rapid expansion, and Stone & Webster established a petroleum division.

War Efforts

America's entry into World War II brought a dramatic increase in demand for all types of engineering and construction, and Stone & Webster became intensely involved in the war effort. According to former Stone & Webster president Allen, "Few elements of war production were not impacted in a significant way by Stone & Webster." Typical Stone & Webster wartime assignments included the design and construction of cartridge case plants, a complete steel foundry, a plant to produce bombsights and other equipment, a plant furnishing fire-control instruments, a facility producing aircraft superchargers, and three TNT-production plants, in addition to meeting demands for infrastructure and power facilities. The company was also called upon to engage in more creative projects. For example, since the Japanese invasion of Southeast Asia had eliminated virtually all of the world's access to natural rubber, Stone & Webster was asked to develop a production process for synthetic rubber technology, and the company subsequently designed or built all U.S. plants for the production of butyl rubber.

Perhaps the most creative Stone & Webster wartime effort was its involvement in the Manhattan Project, which devised the atomic bomb. Beginning in early 1942, company efforts resulted in the establishment of a completely separate engineering organization employing 800 engineers and draftsmen in order to examine ways to obtain large quantities of fissionable uranium-235. Stone & Webster also built an electromagnetic separation plant and constructed a city in Oak Ridge, Tennessee, that ultimately housed 75,000 workers. These extensive efforts were undertaken despite the complexities that often follow a change in organizational leadership, for in 1941, after 52 years, founder Charles Stone passed away; five years later, partner Edwin Webster retired from his position as chairman of the board.

Postwar Growth and the Nuclear Power Industry

Immediately after the end of the war, demand for Stone & Webster services rose rapidly among U.S. public utilities. Under the leadership of Texan George Clifford, the company began to build interstate gas pipelines and compressor stations and also became the largest single stockholder in the Tennessee Gas Transmission Company (Tenneco). Unique solutions were found to problems related to the need to store natural gas under extreme pressure in stainless steel containers underground. The company built the world's largest turbine manufacturing plant and also continued to concentrate heavily on power generation. In 1949, Stone & Webster accounted for some 16 percent of the steam electric generating capacity in the United States.

The company was also retained on tasks that helped shift the nation's economy from a defense to a civilian basis, such as estimating the costs of deactivation and stand-by maintenance of defense plants and shipyards, providing technical advice and services on Japanese reparations, evaluating the mobile equipment that remained in overseas theaters, and continuing work at Oak Ridge.

During the 1950s and 1960s, Stone & Webster was perhaps the most significant engineering company to be involved in the nation's developing nuclear power industry. Chosen after a competition with 90 other companies to build the nation's first nuclear power plant in Shippingport, Pennsylvania, Stone & Webster was subsequently selected to design and supervise the construction of a large accelerator at the Brookhaven National Laboratory, design the neutron shield tank for the nuclear-powered merchant ship *N.S. Savannah,* and engineer and construct a prototype atomic energy power plant for the U.S. Army.

The steady demand for electric power generation also meant an increase in construction contracts for more conventional power plants. By the early 1950s, Stone & Webster had built 27 separate hydroelectric plants constituting 5 percent of U.S. capacity, steam power plants aggregating six million kilowatts in capacity, and some 6,000 miles of power transmission lines.

During this time, the company also obtained a variety of chemical process contracts in the United States, Canada, Japan, and other countries to meet the worldwide demand for plastics. Under the ''process'' category, the company designed ethylene plants, oil refineries, artificial gas producing plants, paper mills, specialized processing and purification facilities, extraction plants, and breweries. From 1950 through 1970, for example, the company designed 22 petrochemical plants in Japan alone.

As the 1960s drew on, however, Stone & Webster's petrochemical and plastics activity began to slow as U.S. refinery capacity caught up with customer demand and declined accordingly. To smooth the impact of these fluctuations, the company diversified its process interests, developing, for example, a more extensive relationship with the paper industry. During the decade, the company designed the first commercial mill to make pulp from hardwood trees.

Slowing business activity also resulted in some conceptual restructuring within the company, including an effort to standardize designs in areas of proven success and placing a greater emphasis on the use of project work teams that combined staff with differing specialized skills. The increased emphasis on teaming fit well with Stone & Webster's need to address problems that developed in the energy supply sector in the mid- to late 1960s and was used in the design of synthetic natural gas plants, a liquified natural gas distribution center, and demonstration projects in coal and oil gasification.

During the 1970s, major world events—including the two OPEC (Organization of Petroleum Exporting Countries) oil embargoes, uncertainty in the chemical process industry with respect to feedstock supplies, increasing opposition to the use of nuclear power, and a growing public awareness of environmental issues—brought difficulties as well as new business opportunities for Stone & Webster.

The high prices that followed the embargoes, for example, constrained energy demand and thus reduced the need for new electric generating capacity. Utilities looked into every possible alternative to meet demand, short of constructing major new baseload stations, resulting in ''one of the severest drop-offs in building in the history of the engineering-construction industry,'' according to former Stone & Webster president William Allen in *Public Utilities Fortnightly* (July 20, 1989). An equally severe, simultaneous downturn in international construction compounded the problem.

Challenges in the 1970s–80s

Stone & Webster's difficulties with constructing conventional power plants were matched by its problems in nuclear construction. By the late 1970s, the company had attained a central role in the nuclear power industry—a significant portion of all nuclear energy in the United States was being generated at plants designed and generated by Stone & Webster. In 1975, the company had been selected to construct the Clinch River Breeder Reactor. However, increasing public opposition to the construction of nuclear plants, lengthy delays brought by challenges before Public Utility Commissions, and corresponding increases in plant construction costs, capped by the incident at Three Mile Island in 1979, brought about a moratorium on the construction of large nuclear plants and the cancellation of many existing orders.

The company began to respond to these challenges during the remainder of the 1970s and into the early 1980s. Stone & Webster met its clients' reluctance to build by improving engineering and construction efficiencies through the use of computer-assisted design and innovative working agreements with contractors and the building trades unions, as well as by providing services that kept plants operating safely, efficiently, and for a longer time than originally intended.

To further survive in this complex business environment, Stone & Webster began to more intensely solicit government and international business, increase its activity in the area of environmental protection and alternative energy production, continue its activity in extending the lives of existing power plants, and develop other areas of diversification as long as they did not distract from the company's core business—engineering. Stone & Webster also began to phase out those parts of the company that were unrelated to its core activities and no longer considered financially viable, such as its securities subsidiary.

In the 1990s, Stone & Webster faced a business environment in which its core activities of power plant and petrochemical plant construction were lagging, and new areas targeted for growth had not yet fulfilled their potential. As a result, company stock performance was sluggish, and in 1992 a stockholder group headed by corporate gadfly Bob Monks attacked Stone & Webster management, asserting that the company had not exploited its assets to keep its stock price high and inquiring as to growth plans the company intended to institute in order to raise stock value. Over the two years that followed, Monks brought suit in federal court and also took action before the Securities and Exchange Commission (SEC) on issues related to Stone & Webster's performance, but both the court and the SEC rejected his assertions.

In 1994, the company registered a net loss of $7.8 million despite revenues of over $818 million. Recognizing that a need existed to improve its financial picture, Stone & Webster opted for a further change in its traditional marketing strategy. The company centered its hopes for future growth on a broader expansion of its core businesses into global markets, a cutback in its dependence on power generation, and the expansion of its environmental and transportation efforts.

According to then president and CEO Bruce Coles, Stone & Webster's engineering and construction efforts were projected to move from 80 percent in the power market to between 30 and 50 percent by the year 2000. Government contracts in transportation and the environment were expected to constitute another 17 to 25 percent of revenues, with 16 to 25 percent from process activities, and 8 to 15 percent from the industrial sector. Coles estimated that some 40 percent of Stone & Webster's business would take place overseas by 2000.

In the mid-1990s, new Stone & Webster environmental services contracts included an exclusive licensing arrangement with Texaco entered into in 1994 to help develop and market the High Rate Bioreactor (HRB), which used bacteria to detoxify industrial and municipal wastes. Stone & Webster was also involved in the U.S. Department of Energy's nuclear cleanup

efforts at Hanford, Washington, and Rocky Flats, Colorado; water and sewer cleanup programs that included the cleanup of New York and Boston harbors; the development of a land-based sludge disposal system for New York City; and the expansion of the wastewater treatment system at Disney World in Florida.

Stone & Webster's infrastructure and transportation activities during this time included the engineering and design of railway and other large transit systems, including part of the Washington, D.C. metro; major airport improvements in Denver and Miami; bridge construction, such as the eight mile-long bridge linking Prince Edward Island to the Canadian mainland; and roadway upgrading, including work on the New Jersey Turnpike. Moreover, the company's advanced computer applications efforts included the use of three-dimensional models; expert systems which monitored, diagnosed, and recommended solutions in areas from equipment vibration to chemical plant processing; and advanced controls that continuously monitored all plant operations.

Changes in Leadership in the Late 1990s

Despite its challenges, Stone & Webster appeared to retain considerable strengths on which to draw. Once the impact of strategies responsive to the business environment of the 1990s had been put in place, company officials and outside observers seemed reasonably optimistic about the company's prospects as it moved on into its second century. However, righting the company was difficult, and after a quick turnover of leadership in the mid-1990s, Stone & Webster found itself floundering. CEO Coles had spent his entire career moving up the ladder at Stone & Webster. Three months after being named chairman in 1995, Coles resigned, citing only personal reasons for his abrupt departure. Coles was succeeded by H. Kerner Smith, who became president and CEO in 1996 and chairman in 1997. Smith had been the chief executive of several global engineering firms. He had been president and CEO of Riley Consolidated, Inc., a manufacturer of power plants, and had served as managing director of the German engineering giant Deutsche Babcock AG. Smith was also well known as an advocate of the so-called independent power movement, which sought to restructure the electric utility industry. Well aware of the problems at Stone & Webster, Smith vowed to turn the company around. Smith's hiring was taken as a positive sign by dissident shareholders, who included not only Bob Monks but Frank Cilluffo, a company director who owned 11.5 percent of the company's shares. Early in 1996, Cilluffo dropped a proxy resolution which had demanded that the company sell off some non-essential assets, apparently because he was cheered by the hiring of Smith. Shareholders seemed mollified by mid-1997, when the company projected a 15 percent increase in earnings per share. The company's stock price rose to over $40 in May 1997, financial performance was on the upswing, and H. Kerner Smith was credited with having changed the direction of Stone & Webster.

There was little sign that anything was wrong at the company in the late 1990s. Stone & Webster announced it was selling some buildings in Boston in 1997 but claimed that this was only because the company had an excess of real estate. The chief financial officer, who was retiring as the sale took place, assured a *Boston Globe* reporter (June 10, 1997) that despite rumors that the company was struggling, it was, in fact, ''very strong financially.'' Stone & Webster also moved its corporate headquarters out of New York City and back to Boston, and sold or subleased office space in New York and New Jersey. Whatever was actually the case in 1997, by 1999 Stone & Webster had serious cash flow problems. Company executives later charged that chairman Smith had consistently underbid on projects in order to win business, putting Stone & Webster on shaky ground. A lawsuit filed in 2001 revealed that by late 1999 Stone & Webster was desperate for cash and had been forced to cancel some everyday expenses, such as newspaper delivery to corporate headquarters. While problems had evidently been building up for some time, in was only in May 2000 that the company revealed that a cost overrun at a domestic project it would not name had led to what it called ''liquidity problems.'' The company's stock price plummeted by more than 50 percent in one day, as Stone & Webster declared it would have to restate its 1999 financial results. Chairman Smith soon resigned, as did the president and chief operating officer. The company declared bankruptcy and was up for sale. The Jacobs Engineering Group seemed the likely buyer, with a bid for $150 million. However, Jacobs was swept aside by the Shaw Group, a Baton Rouge supplier of fabricated piping and other equipment for both the power and the oil and gas industries. Shaw took on Stone & Webster for $163 million, assuming about $450 million in liabilities as well as assets valued at roughly $600 million.

The sudden bankruptcy of the venerable company elicited ire and consternation. The Shaw Group filed suit against former chairman Smith, who was due a severance package estimated at more than $10 million. Allegations swirled that Smith had tried to hide the weakening condition of the company in order to provoke a sale. Shaw shepherded its new subsidiary through bankruptcy proceedings that lasted for three years. The acquisition of Stone & Webster had doubled Shaw's size, and the subsidiary seemed to do well under its new owner. Stone & Webster picked up contracts for work around the globe. In 2002, it won a contract for managing a construction project for gas works for the Abu Dhabi Marine Operating Company in the United Arab Emirates. It secured work on a power project in the United States and began other projects in the Middle East, Turkey, and China in the early 2000s. The company finally emerged from bankruptcy in late 2003. Under the Shaw Group, Stone & Webster was part of a global leader with revenue of over $3.3 billion. The Stone & Webster subsidiary retained 5,000 employees, working on construction and engineering projects, hazardous waste management, and environmental services across the world.

Principal Subsidiaries

Stone & Webster Engineering, Ltd. (United Kingdom); Stone & Webster Engineering Corporation; Stone & Webster Management Consultants, Inc.; Stone & Webster Abu Dhabi UAE, Inc.; Stone & Webster Asia Corporation.

Principal Competitors

Jacobs Engineering Group, Inc.; Tetra Tech, Inc.; URS Corporation.

Further Reading

Allen, William F., Jr., ''Evolution in an Industry—As Seen by an Engineer,'' *Public Utilities Fortnightly*, July 20, 1989, p. 15.

——, *Stone & Webster: A Century of Service*, Exton, Penn.: Newcomen Society of the United States, 1989.

Bailey, Steve, ''Shareholder Uprising Ends for Boston's Stone & Webster,'' *Boston Globe*, March 31, 1996.

——, ''The Boston Globe Downtown Column,'' *Boston Globe*, January 4, 2001.

Biswas, Soma, ''S&W Wins Approval to End Ch. 11 Case,'' *Daily Deal*, November 3, 2003.

Guarisco, Tom, ''New Digs for Shaw: Stock Price Is Down, but Prospects Remain Strong for Growing Company,'' *Greater Baton Rouge Business Report*, January 15, 2002, p. 31.

Hadjian, Ani, ''Stone & Webster's Unhappy Pen Pal,'' *Fortune*, October 30, 1995, p. 22.

Keller, David Neal, *Stone & Webster: 1889–1989*, New York: Stone & Webster, 1989.

Kerber, Ross, ''Boston-Based Engineering Firm Seeks Buyers as Financial Slide Continues,'' *Knight Ridder/Tribune Business News*, May 7, 2000.

Kerber, Ross, ''Boston Construction Firm's Value Halved after Fire Sale Announced,'' *Knight Ridder/Tribune Business News*, May 1, 2000.

Kindleberger, Richard, ''Stone & Webster to Sell or Lease Boston Office Space,'' *Boston Globe*, June 10, 1997, p. NA.

Lobsenz, George, ''Shaw Group Beats Jacobs, Acquires Stone & Webster,'' *Energy Daily*, July 18, 2000, p. 3.

Marcial, Gene G., ''Monks the Gadfly Lands On Stone & Webster,'' *Business Week*, January 10, 1994, p. 57.

Savitz, Eric J., ''Rebuilding America: It's the Kicker in Stone and Webster's Future,'' *Barron's*, May 11, 1992, p. 15.

Seewald, Nancy, ''Shaw Reorganizes S&W Business,'' *Chemical Week*, September 6, 2000, p. 39.

—Bob Swierczek
—update: A. Woodward

TAPEMARK

Tapemark Company Inc.

150 Marie Avenue East
West St. Paul, Minnesota 55118
U.S.A.
Telephone: (651) 450-8410
Toll Free: (800) 535-1998
Fax: (651) 450-8403
Web site: http://www.tapemark.com

Private Company
Incorporated: 1952
Employees: 245
Sales: $71 million (2003, est.)
NAIC: 322221 Coated and Laminated Packaging Paper
and Plastics Film Manufacturing; 322299 All Other
Converted Paper Product Manufacturing; 325412
Pharmaceutical Preparation Manufacturing; 339113
Surgical Appliance and Supplies Manufacturing

Tapemark Company Inc. converts paper into specialized printed, coated and adhesive products for industrial and consumer uses. The development of the company's product line over the years has been driven by advancements in adhesive and printing technology. In the early 1950s, Tapemark attracted its first customers with the ability to print on self-wound tape. A decade later, with the development of pressure sensitive adhesives, the company began printing color labels for consumer products. In the 1980s, Tapemark's expertise in handling difficult materials found applications in the manufacture of medical devices and electronics components. The company's capabilities now include precision die cutting, custom coating, laminating, packaging, and 16-color flexographic roll printing, as well as the ability to work with a client to engineer a product meeting specific demands and specifications. Tapemark does not market its products under its own name. Instead, most of its business involves supplying custom components to original equipment manufacturers in the diagnostics, medical device, consumer products, and electronics markets. All of Tapemark's manufacturing is done at five facilities in West Saint Paul, Minnesota. The company sells its products through a nationwide network of sales representatives. Company founder Robert Klas, Sr., still chairs the company and his son Robert Klas, Jr., acts as president. While Tapemark's industrial clients appreciate its manufacturing capabilities, the company is best known locally as the sponsor of the annual Tapemark Charity Pro-Am golf tournament, which raises money to help people with developmental disabilities.

1950s Origins

Tapemark was founded in 1952 when Robert C. Klas, Sr., bought the experimental division of a larger stamping and imprinting company, Northwestern Stamp Works. Klas had grown up in a small southern Minnesota town, attended Hamline University in St. Paul, and began working as a sales representative for Northwestern Stamp Works shortly after graduation. When he bought the Tapemark division, its primary technology was the ability to print on self-wound tape. Tapemark could print a text or logo on the nonsticky back of the tape and then wind the tape up onto itself into a roll. When the roll was unwound, the sticky side came loose without pulling the printing off the tape below. One of the early applications for this technology was the tape used to wrap bananas in grocery stores. Klas printed the Red Owl logo on the tape and sold it to Red Owl grocery stores.

For more than a decade, Klas operated out of the second floor of a small building in St. Paul. He rode the streetcar across the Twin Cities during the day to drum up orders from clients, then ran the orders on the press in the evening. Tapemark's original location was inconvenient because all materials had to be brought up to the second floor using a pulley. In 1965, increasing sales allowed Klas to build a new facility in the suburb of West St. Paul. By this point, most of Tapemark's business growth was in the area of label printing. The paper company Avery Dennison had recently developed a technology known as pressure sensitive adhesives. This was the type of adhesive that came with a liner that was pulled off to uncover a sticky surface that would adhere when pressed onto a material. The adhesive did not need to be moistened to function, and it was often more convenient than using glue to affix a product label. Pressure-sensitive adhesives stuck particularly well to plastic. As the use of plastic packaging became more prevalent, pressure-sensitive adhesives began to be more widely used to label consumer products. The pressure-sensitive segment grew rapidly starting in the mid-1960s and

Company Perspectives:

Tapemark is driven and supported by a set of simple, yet fundamental, values that contribute to a rewarding, productive and trusting environment for our employees and customers. These values are evident every day in our pride of workmanship, quality and service: Excellence—Responsibility—Integrity—Community—Knowledge—Attitude. Guided by our mission, we believe that Tapemark has maintained a strong reputation throughout the industry, among our employees and within our community: One Tapemark. Delivering the Promise . . . To provide our customers with innovative solutions to complex converting challenges through strategic collaboration, integrated capabilities, emerging technologies and value-added service. To encourage our employees to achieve their full career and personal potential, offering opportunities for feedback, growth and rewards. To support our community through individual leadership and corporate sponsorship of significant events and charitable donations.

into the 1970s. Tapemark grew along with the pressure-sensitive business, becoming an expert in printing, cutting, and converting the material into labels.

An important Tapemark tradition was started in 1972 when the company sponsored its first golf tournament. Tapemark's manufacturing facility happened to be located close to the Southview Country Club golf course. Southview had hosted the Peters Open, sponsored by a local meat company, for 13 years. However, the meat company had recently fallen into the hands of new owners who were not interested in sponsoring a golf tournament. Southview contacted Klas, an avid golfer, about taking over the tournament. Klas, who had a daughter with mild mental retardation and another with learning disabilities, came up with the idea of using the tournament to raise funds to support social service agencies for the developmentally disabled. Tapemark's sales manager Pat Cody, Sr., was skeptical of the idea at first but eventually took a lead role in developing the tournament. The first Tapemark Pro-Am raised $9,000 for the St. Paul Association for Retarded Children (later known as Arc), starting a tradition that was still going three decades later. Tapemark paid for all expenses at the golf tournaments—including lunches, advertising, salaries, and a banquet—and gave all proceeds to charity.

Entering New Markets in the 1970s–80s

Tapemark became involved in decorative automotive striping in the 1970s. St. Paul-based manufacturer 3M made the basic striping material and Tapemark converted it into multicolored strips ready to be pressed onto a vehicle. The conversion process involved laying several colors together in a precise alignment to create the desired pinstripe pattern. The finished product was sold to body shops and Detroit automakers. Tapemark operated 3M's automotive striping warehouse in St. Paul and eventually bought the building.

By 1978, Tapemark had built two facilities on its West St. Paul campus and purchased a third building. The company had close to 200 employees and about $8 million in annual sales, making it one of the larger label manufacturers in the nation. Revenues grew as plastic packing became widespread and more manufacturers switched from the traditional heat-glue labels to pressure-sensitive labels. The converting industry, as Tapemark's segment was known, was growing about four times as quickly as the printing industry as a whole since pressure-sensitive products were replacing older types of labels. Most of Tapemark's business came from pharmaceutical and cosmetic companies, who bought labels for shampoo bottles, antiperspirant containers, and similar consumer products. Tapemark also made the labels for Tonka Toys. When Tonka moved production to Mexico, Tapemark opened a facility in the southwestern United States at the company's request and continued a close relationship with Tonka for many years. Other Tapemark customers included Pillsbury, General Mills, 3M, and Delco Batteries. Klas, who developed a reputation as a workaholic by putting in 12-hour days, emphasized the importance of the label for selling any product.

Tapemark began distributing automatic labeling machines in 1978 in order to give its customers the equipment they needed to efficiently apply labels to containers. Tapemark was also starting to manufacture products for medical purposes. Years of printing on sticky, multilayer paper stocks had given Tapemark a reputation for being good at handling difficult materials. Because of this, medical concerns came to Tapemark in the later 1970s to see if the company would apply its expertise to the medical field. Some of Tapemark's first products in this segment were a plastic sheet used to suppress pain and the electrodes that were affixed to skin for electrocardiograms. In 1980, Tapemark began providing custom medical devices to domestic and international original equipment manufacturers. The company was branching out beyond the label printing business not only into the medical field but also into areas like personal care products, meat packaging, and promotional products.

In 1981, Tapemark bought a building in Woodville, Wisconsin, and renovated it to serve as the location for the manufacture of medical products. After a few years, the medical products division was moved back to St. Paul and Woodville became the center for the automotive striping business. The facility was expanded three times and became an early example of just-in-time manufacturing. If an order came in at 11 a.m., it was sent out by the end of the afternoon. According to Tapemark, the facility operated for ten years without a back order. Visitors came to the tiny Wisconsin town from far away to see how Tapemark's facility was set up.

Tapemark's sales grew to around $17 million in 1984. As Tapemark's activity in the medical field increased, the company registered with the U.S. Food and Drug Administration in 1986 as a device contract manufacturer. Three years later, Tapemark was also certified as a drug contract manufacturer, which allowed it to incorporate medications in products such as wound dressings and patches. Klas's son Robert C. Klas, Jr., who had left a career in banking to join the company in the early 1980s, became president of Tapemark in 1990.

Tapemark branched out to the industrial and electronics markets in 1988. This new business area developed naturally from the company's work with medical products, since electronic products required a similar controlled manufacturing

Key Dates:

1952: Robert Klas, Sr., buys Tapemark from a larger St. Paul printing company.
1965: Tapemark builds a new manufacturing facility in West St. Paul.
1972: The first Tapemark Charity Pro-Am golf tournament is held.
1980: Tapemark starts providing medical devices to larger manufacturers.
1988: Tapemark begins making products for the industrial and electronics markets.
1990: Robert Klas, Jr., becomes president of Tapemark.
1992: A fourth facility is added to the West St. Paul site.
1997: Tapemark moves into custom coating.
2003: Tapemark purchases a fifth facility in West St. Paul.

environment in order to keep dust particles and contaminants off sensitive components. One of Tapemark's first products in the electronics field was the so-called ''slack tab'' used to control videotape slack. During the videotape cassette craze of the late 1980s, Tapemark made millions of these tiny tabs.

Even though all manufacturing was done in West St. Paul, Tapemark found that it was useful to have sales representatives close to its clients around the United States. The company developed a sales network by hiring people around the country who operated out of their homes or an independent office. All sales representatives were Tapemark employees, but many were located far afield. At certain times, Tapemark had representatives in Europe and, during the high point of electronics production, in Singapore.

Continued Expansion in the 1990s and Beyond

As sales continued to grow, Tapemark added a fourth facility to its West St. Paul campus in 1992. This building incorporated a state-of-the-art clean room manufacturing facility for sensitive electronics and medical products. Soon after this facility was completed, the automotive striping business in Woodville was sold to Tapemark employees. Tapemark's community involvement also evolved: the Tapemark Pro-Am added a women's golf tournament in 1995. The men's tournament had raised around $2.6 million since 1972.

In 1997, Tapemark added custom coating to its range of capabilities. Now the company could buy plain paper and add a specific adhesive or other coating to it. The expansion into custom coating, when combined with Tapemark's existing expertise in printing, die cutting, and packing, made the company more vertically integrated. That year Tapemark was also certified to ISO 9001, the international quality management standard, and EN46001, the specific standard for the medical device industry. These certifications increased the company's market penetration, since some countries required ISO certification before a product could be marketed.

Over the years, Tapemark had tried to retain a productive work force by paying attention to the work-life needs of its employees. This became even more of a challenge in the late 1990s as the number of immigrants in the work force increased. Tapemark began offering on-site English classes for workers from Southeast Asia and Africa to enable them to learn the language needed to understand company policies and safety procedures. This helped the company keep the employees it needed to staff round-the-clock shifts.

Tapemark celebrated its 50th anniversary in 2002. That year the company certified its processes to ISO 13485, the medical device standard that was replacing EN46001. Even though the U.S. economy was going through a troubled period, Tapemark was prospering. Larger manufacturers were nervous about investing in new employees themselves, so they gave more manufacturing business to Tapemark. Tapemark invested more than $10 million in new die cut equipment in 2003 and hired many new employees, although they were temporary employees for the time being. The company also registered with the FDA as a food contract manufacturer, allowing it to make products classified as food such as breath fresheners on a strip or other edible films. In order to make room for expansion in new and current markets, Tapemark bought a fifth facility in West St. Paul in 2003.

In 2004, Tapemark began to offer chipless ID, a form of radio frequency identification, to its clients. This increased the company's existing capabilities for ensuring the security and authenticity of its products. Tapemark's major business areas now were the medical, consumer products, and pharmaceutical fields. In the medical and pharmaceutical sectors, Tapemark manufactured items such as diagnostic home test kits, transdermal drug delivery systems, suture strips, cosmetic cleansing pads, and hydrogel face masks. The company also made electronic products such as disk drive components, vibration dampers, and radio frequency interference shields. As always, Tapemark could also supply printed packaging and labeling for these products. The Tapemark Charity Pro-Am, meanwhile, was expecting in 2004 to surpass $5 million raised for charity over the decades.

Principal Divisions

Diagnostics; Medical; Consumer Products; Electronics/Industrial; Security.

Principal Competitors

Corium International, Inc.; 3M Corporation.

Further Reading

Ehrlich, Jennifer, ''Companies Offer Classes in English at Workplace,'' *St. Paul Pioneer Press*, May 14, 1999, p. 4E.
Greenberg, Herb, ''TapeMark Man Charged by Life,'' *St. Paul Dispatch*, July 7, 1978, p. 36.
Meyers, Mike, ''As Economy Improves, Companies Are Cautious,'' *Star Tribune*, November 9, 2003, p. 1A.
Shefchik, Rick, ''Vital Links: The Tapemark Charity Pro-Am Has a High Profile among the State's Sporting Events,'' *St. Paul Pioneer Press*, June 25, 1992, p. 1D.
Wells, Jim, ''Taped Together: After 32 Years, Tapemark Company and Southview Country Club Have Become Synonymous with a Golf Tournament,'' *Saint Paul Pioneer Press*, June 4, 2003, p. D8.

—Sarah Ruth Lorenz

TAROM S.A.

Otopeni Airport, Soseaua Bucuresti
Ploiesti Km 16.5
Ploiesti
Romania
Telephone: (+40) 21 201 4700
Fax: (+40) 21 201 4761
Web site: http://www.tarom.ro

State-Owned Company
Incorporated: 1954 as TAROM—Transporturile Aeriene
    Române
Employees: 2,608
Sales: $245 million (2004 est.)
NAIC: 481111 Scheduled Passenger Air Transportation;
    481112 Scheduled Freight Air Transportation; 481212
    Nonscheduled Chartered Freight Air Transportation;
    481211 Nonscheduled Chartered Passenger Air
    Transportation; 488119 Other Airport Operations;
    488190 Other Support Activities for Air
    Transportation

TAROM S.A. is the national airline of Romania. It is majority owned (92.63 percent) by the government's Ministry of Transportation, which has long held plans to partially privatize the carrier. Other shareholders are ROMATSA (Romanian Air Traffic; 5.42 percent), the "Muntenia" Private Financial Investment Fund (1.43 percent), and the Romanian Civil Aviation Authority (0.52 percent). The airline flies to about three dozen scheduled destinations, provides charter flights, and operates a fleet of 16 aircraft. TAROM'S offerings focus on Europe and the Middle East. The airline brings in intercontinental traffic with its code share partners, which include Alitalia, Air France, Aeroflot, Austrian Airlines, CSA Czech Airlines, Lot Polish Airlines, Malev, Syrian Arab Airlines, Iberia, and Cimber.

Origins

Transporturile Aeriene Române, or TAROM, was founded on September 18, 1954, when the state of Romania bought out the Soviet Union's 50 percent stake in TARS (Transporuri Aeriene Romana Sovietica). TARS had been formed in 1946 to take over the interests of LARES, a state-owned airline that had operated in Romania before World War II.

Romania's airline business dated back to the French-Romanian Company for Air Navigation (CFRNA), formed in 1920. Using POTEZ aircraft from France, CFRNA was billed as the world's first transcontinental airline, with a route extending from Bucharest to Paris via Strasbourg, Prague, Vienna, and Budapest.

CFRNA was renamed CIDNA, "The International Air Navigation Company" in 1927. LARES was established within three years, and merged with SARTA (The Romanian Air Transport Society Ltd.) in 1937.

TAROM expanded its route network throughout Europe in the 1960s, and in 1966 conducted its first transatlantic flight. Use of British-made BAC One-Elevens powered by Rolls-Royce engines gave TAROM a selling point in London, which was a three-hour flight from Bucharest. Scheduled flights to New York and Beijing began in 1974. Resorts on the Black Sea and Carpathian Mountains attracted tourists from both sides of the Iron Curtain.

Traffic Drops in 1980s

Tourism to Romania fell dramatically from a mid-1970s peak to new lows in the 1980s. Besides scaring away foreign tourists, the communist regime of dictator Nicolae Ceausescu also made it nearly impossible for Romanian citizens to travel outside the country. Nevertheless, TAROM managed a profit of $78 million in 1988, one company official told the *Chicago Tribune*. The airline was carrying more than three million passengers a year.

TAROM ended the 1980s with 65 planes, most of them Soviet in origin and fewer than half of them airworthy. Twin-engine Antonov An-24 turboprops and the four-engine Ilyushin Il-18s were its workhorses. The airline had 4,000 employees, reported *Aviation Week & Space Technology*.

The overthrow and execution of Ceausescu in December 1989 marked the end of an era for TAROM as well as for

Company Perspectives:

Passenger satisfaction and comfort is the ultimate goal of any air carrier. At TAROM, special attention was paid to the quality of services and products. Punctuality and reliability are being enhanced in order to satisfy the passengers' expectations and requirements. Thus, complex measures were set in place, among which it is worth mentioning the improvement of the quality and the variety of food choices on all international flights.

Key Dates:

1954: TAROM is founded.
1974: Flights to New York and Beijing begin.
1989: The fall of communist dictator Nicolae Ceausescu results in huge jump in demand for air transportation in Romania.
1991: TAROM is reorganized as a joint stock company.
1999: The company's passenger count exceeds one million.
2003: Long-haul flight operations cease.
2004: The company celebrates its 50th anniversary.

Romania. The airline was now at liberty to acquire more planes from the West. Tourist traffic also boomed. TAROM's charter business increased dramatically after the fall of Communism in Romania. The lifting of travel restrictions contributed to an overall 45 percent traffic increase in one year as Romanians were freed to take trips outside the country. They were especially eager to take trips to former Soviet Bloc territories, especially Moldavia, as well as venturing into the Free World.

Revamping in the 1990s

TAROM was reorganized as a joint stock company in 1991. The next year, the airline launched a catering joint venture, ABELA ROCAS, in cooperation with Casrom, the Otopeni Airport, and Albert Abela Corporation. TAROM also partnered with Lufthansa, TV-Rom International, and Anarom to form the Lufthansa-Tarom Airport Service (LUTAS) at Bucharest Airport. Avicon, established by Austrian Airlines and Swissair, was brought in to raise TAROM's level of service to Western standards.

TAROM began the 1990s with a mixed fleet of Soviet-made Ilyushin, Tupolev, and Antonov aircraft, as well as a handful of 1970s era Boeing 707s and 14 BAC One-Elevens produced in Romania under license. These older aircraft were soon to be banned from most Western countries due to pollution, noise, and safety issues. In this period, TAROM leased out some of its aircraft to other airlines to raise much-needed hard currency. TAROM later developed a specialty in third-party maintenance for ATR 42s and Boeing 737s.

The airline underwent a massive fleet renewal program in the 1990s. Three Airbus A310s were bought in 1992 (one of these crashed upon takeoff in March 1995). TAROM also took advantage of a depressed airliner market to order Boeing 737s.

While domestic fares were regulated and subsidized by the government, international routes provided the cash revenue that the airline needed to stay in business. (Not all long-haul flights were profitable, however.) TAROM's network of 39 destinations stretched as far as New York and Singapore, as well as coverage of the Middle East.

There was new competition in the mid-1990s from both established Western carriers expanding eastward and a few start-up airlines in Romania itself. One of them, DAC-Air, took over some of TAROM's domestic and regional routes using Dash 8 turboprops and Canadair regional jets in May 1996. TAROM acquired a holding in privately owned DAC in exchange for routes and use of its facilities and technologies.

Nevertheless, TAROM was losing money—$24 million in 1996. It had more than 3,300 employees, and the need to thin its staff would be a contentious issue throughout the late 1990s and beyond, resulting in tense negotiations with the unions and high turnover in the CEO position. The company also needed to cut back on the number of different types of aircraft it operated, then nine.

Passenger count exceeded one million in 1999, a new record. By this time, TAROM had added service to Chicago and Montreal. Bucharest was turning into something of a hub for travelers to the Middle East, which TAROM was serving with several new destinations. In addition, more European cities were added to the network. TAROM had marketing arrangements with Swissair, Alitalia, Austrian Airlines, and TWA.

Building Partnerships after 2000

The fleet was augmented in 2000 with the $100 million acquisition of six ATR 42 turboprops for regional and domestic flights. The airline also studied the possibility of using regional jets to bolster its feeder network. TAROM cancelled an order for four Boeing 737s in 2001. It placed another order for four medium-range Airbus A318s, worth $219.6 million, two years later.

To make visiting Romania easier for U.S. tourists, in 2002 the Romanian Tourism Ministry designated Austrian Airlines as its preferred carrier for travel from America, which TAROM no longer served directly. Other code share partners (Alitalia, Air France, Aeroflot, CSA Czech Airlines, Lot Polish Airlines, Malev, Syrian Arab Airlines, Iberia, and Cimber) helped bring in intercontinental traffic.

The airline cancelled its own long-haul flights in 2003. Those to Beijing were suspended in April due to the SARS epidemic; services to New York ceased in November. TAROM then sold the two Airbus 310 aircraft it had used to fly these routes for eleven years.

The idea of privatization, floated in the early 1990s, was still being discussed ten years later as the carrier continued to lose money. TAROM was planning to narrow losses from $14.5 million to $6 million in its fiftieth anniversary year, 2004, when turnover was expected to be $245 million. The company was aiming to post a profit by 2005 to attract investors in its planned privatization. According to Dow Jones Newswires, Central and

Eastern Europe was expected to see the greatest growth in air traffic during the decade, thanks in part to impending membership of countries in the region to the European Union.

Principal Competitors

British Airways plc; CSA Czech Airlines; KLM Royal Dutch Airlines; LOT Polish Airlines; SAS AB; Deutsche Lufthansa AG.

Further Reading

"Airline Branches Out in China," *China Daily*, December 10, 1999, p. 5.

Bale, Peter, "Power Struggle at Romania's TAROM Airline," *Reuters News*, May 20, 1996.

Cameron, Doug, "TAROM Heads over Two," *Airline Business*, January 1998.

Cretzan, Cristi, "Romanian Airline Tarom's Airbus Deal Puzzles Boeing," *Dow Jones International News*, July 8, 2003.

——, "Romanian Airline Tarom Seeks Global Alliance," *Dow Jones International News*, February 6, 2003.

Dalton, Joyce, "Tarom Builds on Rich Romanian Airline History," *Travel Weekly*, September 18, 1995, p. 30.

Dascalu, Adrian, "Romanian TAROM Airline Relaunch Restructure Plan," *Reuters News*, August 28, 1997.

Dunn, Graham, "Tarom Knuckles Down to Privatisation," *Air Transport Intelligence*, February 21, 2000.

Hofmann, Kurt, "Politics Influence Tarom A318 Plan," *Flight International*, August 5, 2003, p. 10.

Kaminski, David, "Romania Studies Regional Jet Feeder Airline for Tarom," *Air Transport Intelligence*, April 10, 2003.

——, "Tarom Puts Long-Haul Fleet Up for Sale," *Air Transport Intelligence*, December 1, 2003.

Koring, Paul, "Letter from Romania: Taking a Flight Back to Yesterday," *Globe and Mail* (Toronto), June 9, 1990, p. D6.

Lisella, Maria, "A New Welcome: Romania Reaches out to North America with a New Preferred Airline and Improved Infrastructure," *Travel Agent*, July 22, 2002, p. 42.

Longworth, R.C., "Doing Business in Romania: How State Airline Stayed Aloft, Despite Ceausescu," *Chicago Tribune*, January 3, 1990, Bus. Sec., p. 1.

O'Keefe, Emer, "The Long Night Flight on TAROM Brings Cheap Thrills, 'Little Gems'," *Chicago Tribune*, March 13, 1994, Travel Sec., p. 14.

Rodina, Mihaela, "Romanian Airline Flies into Turbulence," *Agence France-Presse*, May 26, 1996.

"Romanian Airline's Dilemma," *East European Markets*, February 2, 1996.

"Romanian Aviation after Ceausescu: Tarom Faces Long, Costly Rebuilding Process but Airbus A310s Will Help," *Aviation Week & Space Technology*, September 3, 1990, p. 167.

Shibata, Kyohei, "Airline Privatisation in Eastern Europe and Ex-USSR," *Logistics & Transportation Review*, June 1994, pp. 167+.

Shifrin, Carole A., "Romanian Startup Opts for Bombardier," *Aviation Week & Space Technology*, February 5, 1996.

"TAROM Chief Details Steps to Improve Services," *BBC Summary of World Broadcasts*, November 10, 1994.

"Tarom Prepares to Go Private," *Flight International*, September 23, 1992.

"Tarom Sets Record Numbers with Added Service," *Travel Weekly*, February 28, 2000, p. 18f.

"Too Little, Too Late?" *Airfinance Journal*, September 1997, p. 55.

—Frederick C. Ingram

Titan Cement Company S.A.

22A Halkidos and Doxara Str
Athens GR-111 43
Greece
Telephone: (+30) 210 259 1111
Fax: (+30) 210 259 1205
Web site: http://www.titan-cement.com

Public Company
Incorporated: 1902
Employees: 4,909
Sales: EUR 1.04 billion ($1.23 billion) (2003)
Stock Exchanges: Athens
Ticker Symbol: TITK
NAIC: 327310 Cement Manufacturing

Titan Cement Company S.A. is Greece's leading cement producer—the 100-year-old company is also that country's only domestic producer of cement and cement products. The company's four Greek cement plants produce more than six million tons per year, and command a 40 percent market share at home. Since the beginning of the 1990s, Titan also has made a push to become a diversified and vertically integrated company, adding ready-mix concrete production, aggregates, and cement products including cement blocks and mortar. Titan also owns a producer of china tableware in Greece, Ionia S.A. Together, these activities represent some 40 percent of the company's total sales of more than EUR 1 billion ($1.2 billion) for 2003. Meanwhile, Titan has matched the diversification of its products with a geographic expansion. Since the early 1990s, Titan has entered a number of foreign markets, most notably the United States, where the company controls Tarmac America Titan also is present in the former Yugoslav Republic of Macedonia, and in Serbia, Bulgaria, and Egypt. In all, the company operates 11 cement plants with a total production capacity of 16 million tons per year. This operation is supported by a network of seven cement distribution facilities in the United States, France, the United Kingdom, Egypt, and Italy. Titan also produces more than 4.5 million tons of ready-mix concrete at 67 distribution centers; and the company operates ten quarries, three mines, and

a mortar production facility. Titan Cement has been listed on the Athens Stock Exchange since 1912, but remains controlled at 51 percent by the founding Canellopoulos family.

Cementing Greece's Industrialization in the 20th Century

The beginnings of industrialization in Greece at the turn of the 20th century brought with it an increasing demand for building materials, and most important, for cement. At the time there were no native cement producers, and the country depended on imports for its cement needs. In 1902, however, brothers Nicholaos and Angelos Canellopoulos launched their own cement production business in the town of Elefsis. That plant became not only the first cement plant in Greece, but in the region as well.

The Canellopoulos' company prospered, and by 1912 went public, changing its name to the Titan Cement Company S.A. After becoming hooked up to Greece's developing electrical grid in 1924, Titan was able to step up its production, and by 1930 the company had begun exporting cement for the first time, becoming an important supplier for the region. Titan also distinguished itself by a high degree of commitment to social welfare. As such, the company began providing accident insurance as early as 1922, and in 1927 Titan scaled back its employees' workday from 12 to 8 hours.

World War II interrupted the company's export operations, but by 1948, Titan cement once again found its way onto the international market. Nonetheless, the high cost of transporting cement, and the product's comparatively low value, ensured that the cement sector remained a more or less local industry. This factor helped Titan maintain its position as Greece's leading cement company.

Titan began upgrading its production in the early 1960s. In 1961, the company refitted its Elefsis plant, becoming the first in Greece to install environmentally friendly electrostatic filters. The following year, the company debuted a second plant, bringing its production to Thessaloniki. That plant was followed shortly by a third site, this time in Drepano, in the Peloponese island chain, which began production in 1966.

Company Perspectives:

GOVERNING OBJECTIVE We aim to be an independent multinational vertically integrated cement producer, combining entrepreneurial spirit and operating excellence with respect for people, society and the environment.

Titan continued enhancing its production capacity into the 1970s, building a fourth plant in Kamari in 1976. That facility enabled Titan to claim a larger share of the crucial Athens market. By then, Titan's annual cement production had already topped five million tons. The company also had launched an early move to become a vertically integrated operation. That effort began in 1971 with the acquisition of a number of ready-mix concrete producers. At the same time, the company began formulating a new environmental regeneration policy of planting trees at its former quarry sites. In support of that program, the company started up its own tree nursery in 1977.

Vertically Integrated, International Operator in the New Century

International expansion took on new importance for Titan as it turned toward the 1980s. In 1979, the company launched exports to the Eastern Mediterranean market, using cost-efficient floating terminals to transport its cement products. Toward the end of the decade, Titan's international expansion became still more ambitious, as the company began targeting the distribution markets in western Europe and the United States. In support of that strategy, Titan opened a series of distribution terminals in France and the United Kingdom, as well as in the United States.

Titan's two-pronged growth strategy—of vertical integration and international expansion—crystallized in the 1990s. The company began making a series of acquisitions of ready-mix producers and also picked up a number of new quarries, starting in 1991. The following year, the company made a major commitment to growth in the United States when it bought up a 59.1 percent stake in Roanoke Cement, based in Virginia, from Tarmac PLC. The remaining shares were held by Tarmac's U.S. subsidiary.

Titan added to its product lineup at mid-decade, launching production of intermix dry mortar in 1997. That operation helped complete Titan's vertical integration, extending it beyond cement to ready-mix concrete, aggregates, and mortar, as well as quarry operations. These diversified products grew to represent some 40 percent of Titan's total sales by the turn of the new century.

Titan sought to step up its international operations at the same time. The company targeted the nearby Balkan region especially, placing bids on a number of nationally controlled cement producers in Albania, Bulgaria, and in the former Yugoslav Republic of Macedonia as they came up for privatization. Yet the company's expansion hopes were dashed as it found itself outbid by its larger competitors on a number of prime Balkan region cement producers.

At last, in 1998, Titan found its foothold in the Balkans, when it succeeded in its bid for the 48.6 percent stake in Plevenski

Key Dates:

1902: Brothers Nicholaos and Angelos Canellopoulos found the first cement production plant in Elefsina, Greece.

1912: The company goes public on the Athens stock exchange as Titan Cement Company.

1924: Titan connects to the electrical grid, increasing production.

1930: Titan begins its first exports of cement, which end during World War II.

1948: Titan returns to cement exports.

1962: A second cement plant is built in Thessaloniki.

1966: A third cement plant is built in Drepano, Peloponese Islands.

1971: Production of ready-mix concrete begins.

1976: A fourth cement plant is built in Kamari, near Athens.

1979: Titan begins exporting to the Eastern Mediterranean region using floating terminals.

1988: Titan opens distribution centers in the United States and Europe.

1991: Titan launches a new vertical integration strategy, adding quarries and ready-mix concrete plants.

1992: Titan acquires 59 percent of Roanoke Cement in Virginia, in the United States.

1997: Titan begins production of intermix dry mortar as part of a vertical integration strategy.

2000: Titan acquires Tarmac America, including the remaining stake in Roanoke Cement.

2003: Titan completes a EUR 350 million investment program, including expansion of the Thessaloniki plant.

Cement put up for sale by the Bulgarian government. Titan later stepped up its stake in Plevenski to 98 percent. The addition of the Bulgarian plant added 400,000 tons per year to Titan's production capacity, raising it above six million tons per year. Soon after, the company joined with Holcim, of Switzerland, to acquire 95 percent control of Cementarnica Usje, in Macedonia.

Titan next turned to Egypt, forming a joint venture with France's Lafarge to acquire a 76 percent stake in Beni Suef Cement Company. The following year, the joint venture increased its holding in Beni Suef to 95 percent. In that year, Titan returned to its expansion in the United States, buying up Tarmac America for $636 million from Tarmac PLC's new parent Anglo American. Following the acquisition, Titan began refocusing Tarmac America on its cement and ready-mix concrete operations, selling off Tarmac America's non-cement businesses, such as its sand and gravel, building products, and others, helping to reduce the purchase price by nearly $300 million.

Titan went back to Egypt for its next expansion in 2002, joining Lafarge again to acquire an 88 percent stake in Alexandria Portland Cement Co. The company went on its own to Serbia, buying a 70 percent stake in a cement operation in Kosjeric. The addition of the Serbian operation added 600,000 tons per year of capacity to Titan's total, a figure expected to top

800,000 tons after a $26 million investment by Titan. Titan continued its acquisition drive, buying up fly ash producer Separation Technologies in the United States.

As it moved into the 2000s, Titan engaged on an extensive investment program. Much of the company's spending went toward upgrading its newly acquired Balkan region operations. In all the company earmarked some EUR 352 million on expanding its production capacity, including nearly EUR 80 million spent on expanding its plant in Thessaloniki. After 100 years in operation, Titan Cement remained one of the top 20 titans of the global cement industry and the largest in its Greek home.

Principal Subsidiaries

A.D. Cementarnica Usje (FYR of Macedonia); Achaiki Maritime Co. S.A; Aeolian Maritime Co. S.A; Alexandria Portland Cement Company (Egypt); Beni Suef Cement Company (Egypt); Cementara Kosjeric Ad (Serbia); Fintitan Srl (Italy); Interbeton Building Materials S.A.; Intertitan Trading International S.A. (France); Kimolos Maritime Co. S.A.; Naftitan Maritime Co. S.A.; Polikos Maritime Co. S.A.; Roanoke Cement Plant (United States); Titan America LLC (United States); Titan Atlantic Cement S.A. (United States); Titan Cement U.K. Ltd.; Titan International Trading Co. S.A.

Principal Competitors

IFI; Lafarge S.A.; CRH PLC; Heidelberg Cement AG; HBG, Hollandsche Beton Groep N.V.; Fomento de Construcciones y Contratas S.A.; Grupo Ferrovial S.A.; Holderbank Financiere Glaris Ltd.; Italmobiliare S.p.A.; Rinker Group Ltd.; Société des Ciments Francais S.A.

Further Reading

Dinsmore, Christopher, ''Greek Cement Company Announces Completion of Production Asset Sale,'' *Knight Ridder/Tribune Business News,* January 3, 2001.

Hope, Kerin, ''Recipe for a Strong Mix,'' *Financial Times,* June 1, 1998, p. 5.

Maxwell-Cook, Paul, ''Titan's Latest Modernisation Project,'' *World Cement,* April 2003, p. 19.

Parker, Akweli, ''Greek Firm to Buy Tarmac,'' *Virginian Pilot,* August 29, 2000, p. D1.

''Titan Acquires 70% of Serb Cement Manufacturer Kosjeric,'' *European Report,* February 13, 2002.

''Titan Cement Completes Buy of Tarmac America,'' *Pit & Quarry,* December 2000, p. 18.

—M.L. Cohen

Tofutti Brands, Inc.

50 Jackson Drive
Cranford, New Jersey 07016
U.S.A.
Telephone: (908) 272-2400
Fax: (908) 272-9492
Web site: http://www.tofutti.com

Public Company
Incorporated: 1981 as Tofu Time, Inc.
Employees: 11
Sales: $17.5 million (2002)
Stock Exchanges: American
Ticker Symbol: TOF
NAIC: 311520 Ice Cream and Frozen Dessert Manufacturing

Tofutti Brands, Inc., sells soy-based, dairy-free frozen desserts and other food products throughout the United States and in more than a dozen other countries, including England, Japan, and Israel. The firm targets consumers who avoid or are allergic to milk, as well as observant Jews who do not consume dairy products and meat at the same meal. The company's product line includes hard-pack and soft-serve Tofutti and sugar free Tofutti, a variety of frozen sandwiches and novelties such as Tofutti Cuties and Tofutti Monkey Bars, and other soy-based products like Better Than Cream Cheese, Sour Supreme imitation sour cream, soy nuts, soy cheese, cookies, candy bars, and frozen pizza and blintzes. Tofutti also markets Egg Watchers, a whole egg replacement product. More than half of the publicly traded company's stock is owned by founder and CEO David Mintz.

Beginnings

The ice cream-like frozen dessert called Tofutti was invented by David Mintz, a caterer in Brooklyn, New York. The offspring of a family of bakers, Mintz had originally worked as a furrier before running a take-out shop in Brighton Beach, which he called Mintz's Buffet. It had become popular after he staffed his kitchen with elderly women who excelled at creating delicacies like noodle pudding, stuffed cabbage, and rugalach, and he later opened a second location in Manhattan to provide dishes for 20 restaurants and 12 catering halls.

Because Mintz's customers were largely Jewish, his kitchens served kosher food. One requirement that particularly challenged his cooks' creativity was the kosher prohibition against serving dairy and meat together. This meant that such things as butter, cheese, milk, and ice cream could not be consumed at most meals. Although butter could be replaced by margarine, Mintz got requests for dairy-free versions of many items that were not so easily duplicated. After reading an article about the nutritional benefits of tofu, the protein-rich food made from coagulated soybean milk that was found in Asian cooking, he began to experiment with it starting in the late 1970s. He soon found ways to use it in cookies, cakes, tuna casserole, and even beef stroganoff, where it stood in for sour cream.

The carefully formulated imitations were readily accepted by his patrons, and Mintz continued to seek additional uses for tofu, with his ultimate goal being a mock ice cream. After many failed attempts, including one in which an experimental batch exploded and left chunks of goo all over his roof, he arrived at a blend of water, corn sweetener, corn oil, soy powder, and flavorings that had the proper consistency when frozen and tasted surprisingly close to real ice cream. He had a hard time coming up a name for the new product, until one night at four a.m. the word popped into his head: ''Tofutti.'' In 1981, Mintz formed a marketing company, Tofu Time, and began to sell a soft-serve version of his creation in the New York City area.

The public response was favorable, and Tofutti soon became a popular treat with people who wanted to avoid dairy products. In addition to those who kept kosher, it also appealed to strict ''vegan'' vegetarians, persons who were lactose intolerant and could not digest milk, and those who wished to avoid the saturated fat and cholesterol with which ice cream is laden. Tofutti was not strictly a health food, however, and in fact had more calories than ice cream. It also contained fat, though not the undesirable saturated kind found in dairy products. Its actual tofu content was small, and early versions had in fact not contained it at all but used isolated soy protein, a relatively flavorless soybean derivative that was easier to work with and had a longer shelf life. Mintz got complaints, however, and eventually added tofu to the recipe, though it still contained a sizable amount of isolated soy protein.

Company Perspectives:

If nondairy is your thing, we are the right place for you. Tofutti Brands, Inc. exclusively develops a wide variety of soy based nondairy, kosher parve products. All products are cholesterol, nondairy, lactose and milk free.

Public Stock Offering in 1983 Helps Spur Growth

To help expand operations, Tofu Time made a public offering of 500,000 shares of stock in December 1983. In the spring of 1984, a hard-pack version of Tofutti was perfected and offered for sale in two-and-a-half-gallon containers, with pints added later as well. For the fiscal year ending in July of 1984, the company's annual sales topped $2.36 million, up from $329,000 the year before.

At this time, Tofutti was still largely sold in the New York metropolitan area in ice cream shops and via company-owned pushcarts, but a distribution agreement with premium ice cream maker Haagen Dazs quickly brought it into stores and supermarkets in a number of eastern states. Other deals were worked out to bring the product to much of the rest of the United States as well.

In December 1984, Tofu Time, which now had 30 employees, moved its headquarters from Brooklyn to a 30,000-square-foot freezer warehouse facility in Rahway, New Jersey. The new location was closer to the dairies that were contracted out to produce its products and also near Haagen Dazs. Tofutti, which sold for about the same price as premium ice cream, was now offered in a wide range of flavors.

During the latter half of 1984 and into 1985, sales grew rapidly as the rest of the country discovered Tofutti. With distribution reaching more than 18,000 stores across the United States, annual sales jumped more than seven-fold to $17.4 million and profits hit $2 million. The company's stock was subsequently moved to the American Stock Exchange. Tofu Time also opened a store on Columbus Avenue in New York, which led to the firm's first international sales contract when a group of Japanese tourists who tasted the soy-based product for the first time sought out Mintz to let them open Tofutti shops in Japan. Other agreements were made to introduce the product in countries like Canada, Finland, and Australia.

By now, as many as 30 different competitors had arisen, including Ice Bean, which had actually been marketed since the late 1970s, Tofu Dream, Tofree, and Gloria Vanderbilt's Glace. Their introduction served to blunt the impact of Tofutti, as did increasing media scrutiny of the frozen soy dessert fad, which brought to light the relatively high calorie count of products that the public perceived to be diet or health foods.

Sales Plummet in Late 1980s

Though the company fought to stay on top with such measures as forcing one competitor to change a too-similar package design, sales began to fall off. In 1986, Haagen Dazs ended its distribution of Tofutti, leaving the firm scrambling to get its products into stores. New distribution deals were lined up with Steve's Homemade Ice Cream, Inc. for 12 western and southern states and Calip Dairies/T&W Suffolk, Inc. in the Northeast region, among others. Seeking a more seasoned hand to run the operation, Mintz turned to 43-year-old Francis I. Mullin III, former president of Del Monte Franchise Beverages U.S.A., who was appointed president in August. During the year, the company also changed its name to Tofutti Brands, Inc. and announced that it had received a patent on the formula for Tofutti. Fiscal 1986 sales declined to $11.6 million, and the firm reported a loss of $658,000.

Mullin's first move was to reorganize the firm into four units: domestic sales, foreign sales, licensing, and franchised stores.

At that time, 95 percent of revenues were being generated domestically, but Mullin wanted to boost exports and foreign marketing deals dramatically and also generate more sales through franchising Tofutti stores and licensing formulas to other companies to use in their own product lines.

The year 1987 saw the introduction of Lite Lite Tofutti, a 98 percent fat-free version which halved the calorie count to just 90 per four-ounce serving. It was rolled out in several markets in a cross-promotion with Diet Coke. In March, the first franchise store opened in Teaneck, New Jersey. It offered 16 flavors of Tofutti and a variety of baked goods such as imitation cheesecake, which the firm had begun distributing in the New York City area. The company was also actively cutting costs by streamlining its warehousing and shipping methods and decreasing its workforce by 25 percent.

In the summer of 1987, the firm reached agreements with new partners who would handle Tofutti distribution in Canada and Australia. In December, Tofutti bought back its franchise outlet in New Jersey and announced plans to open a second company-owned store in New York City. Sales for the year dropped to $7.7 million, with a loss of slightly more than $2 million.

In 1988, another cross-promotion was launched with Diet Coke and Lean Cuisine, and Tofutti established a toll-free nutrition hot line, which customers could call with questions about cholesterol, lactose, and the company's products. Annual sales rebounded to $9.5 million, though a net loss of $652,000 was recorded.

New Products in the 1990s

In 1989, the company added a new product line, Egg Watchers, which were cholesterol-free egg replacement products made from processed egg whites. A package which yielded the equivalent of eight eggs retailed for just over $2, about twice the cost of fresh eggs. Other new items included Tofutti Cuties and Tofutti Fruttis, which resembled ice cream sandwiches and bars, and soy-based Better Than Creamcheese. In the summer of 1989, Francis Mullin gave up the job of president to Mintz, though he remained on the firm's board of directors. The company also moved its headquarters from Rahway to a smaller facility in Cranford, New Jersey.

In early 1992, Tofutti added a new line of fruit-juice-sweetened non-dairy frozen desserts called Land of the Free. Sold in vanilla-apple and three berry flavors, pints were priced at under $3. Sales for the year declined to just over $4 million, but

Key Dates:

1981: David Mintz forms Tofu Time, Inc. to market soy-based, kosher foods.
1983: Tofu Time offers stock for public sale to expand sales of Tofutti.
1984: Distribution through Haagen Dazs begins; sales hit $2.3 million.
1985: Sales jump to $17.5 million; Tofu Time stock moves to AMEX.
1986: Tofutti is patented, and the company changes its name to Tofutti Brands, Inc.
1987: One-fourth of Tofutti's workforce is laid off; the company moves to smaller quarters.
1992: Revenues drop to $4 million, but the firm records its first profit in seven years.
1990s: Cream cheese, sour cream, cookies, and egg replacement products are added.
2002: Rebounding sales top $17.5 million.

earnings of $56,000 gave the company its first annual profit in seven years.

In 1993, Tofutti re-signed with Haagen Dazs for East Coast distribution to supermarkets, convenience stores, and restaurants, as well as to food service operators. The company also added a low-fat yogurt substitute called Better Than Yogurt in a variety of flavors, a sour cream substitute called Sour Supreme, and contracted with Papetti's Hygrade Egg Products, Inc. to produce and distribute its Egg Watchers line.

The year 1994 saw the firm introduce Tofutti to the United Kingdom, where it offered the Tofutti Supreme and Lite Lite varieties in a number of flavors. Products were imported from the United States at first, but manufacturing was later set up in the United Kingdom. Sales inched upward to the $5 million range during the middle of the decade as the company expanded its U.K. lineup to include a new fat-free chocolate fudge product along with Better Than Cream Cheese and Egg Watchers.

In 1997, Tofutti brought out several varieties of nondairy cookies and fig bars, added new flavors to the Better Than Cream Cheese and Sour Supreme lines, and introduced Dairy Free Ice Cream Cakes. By this time, the U.K. subsidiary was also exporting products to France.

In 1998, the company added a line of Soy Lavasch Flatbreads in a variety of flavors, imitation cream cheese filled crepes, a soy beverage, honey-sweetened Tofutti desserts, and a Tofutti Italian Style Cannoli, among other items. Sales were growing and rose to just under $9 million with earnings of $560,000 for the year.

New products for 1999 and 2000 included frozen novelty Tofutti Too-Toos and Tofutti Monkey Bars, as well as imitation cheese slices, soy nuts, soy protein powder, and frozen veggie

burgers, pizza, bagels, and potato pancakes. The company's fortunes were continuing to improve, with sales for 2000 topping $13.3 million and profits reaching $956,000. Distribution now extended to 15 countries.

In late 2000 and early 2001, Tofutti bought back nearly 300,000 shares of the 6.1 million it then had outstanding. The firm's best-selling product at this time was Tofutti Cuties, bite-sized frozen novelties which had recently ranked 18th out of 124 ice cream sandwiches sampled in a taste test conducted by A.C. Nielsen.

In 2002, growth continued, though higher raw material, freight, and packaging costs, as well as "slotting fees" paid to supermarkets to insure product display, cut into earnings. Sales for the year topped $17.5 million, and earnings approached $940,000. The company's stock price was also rising, and rebounded to nearly $3.50 per share by the spring of 2004.

Approaching a quarter-century in business, Tofutti Brands, Inc. was making a strong comeback after years of rebuilding. The company had an established brand name and a loyal base of customers with special dietary needs for whom it was happy to supply a variety of soy-based desserts, snacks, and other food items.

Principal Subsidiaries

Tofutti UK Ltd.

Principal Competitors

Turtle Mountain, Inc.; The Hain Celestial Group, Inc.; The Whole Soy Company; Double Rainbow; Galaxy Nutritional Foods, Inc.

Further Reading

Alson, Amy, "This Slick Executive Says He'll Save Tofutti," *Crain's New York Business*, November 10, 1986, p. 1.

Belsky, Gary, "Tofutti Trims to Fatten up Lean Earnings," *Crain's New York Business*, August 31, 1987, p. 7.

Bennett, Bev, "Imitation Ice Cream Is Hot—Tofutti Creator's Success Recipe Is Down Cold," *Chicago Sun-Times*, July 27, 1989, p. 16.

Eftimiades, Maria, "Tofu Innovator Dreams of New Creations," *New York Times*, February 19, 1989, p. 14.

Geist, William E., "About New York: High Hopes for Pushcart Sales of Frozen Tofu," *New York Times*, June 20, 1984, p. B3.

Hall, Trish, "Tofu Products May Be In, But Its Fans Wonder If There's Tofu in the Products," *Wall Street Journal*, February 27, 1985.

" 'Sleeping Giant' Tofutti Wakes up in the U.K.," *Grocer*, November 12, 1994, p. 45.

Snow, Jane, "Shoppers with a Sweet Tooth Warm up to Tofu Frozen Desserts," *Seattle Times*, June 12, 1985, p. E14.

Stepneski, Ron, "Tofutti Maker Moves Its Headquarters to Rahway," *Record, Northern New Jersey*, January 4, 1985, p. B12.

Winerip, Michael, "Our Towns: Tofu Wars—Battling For the Suburban Palate," *New York Times*, November 15, 1985, p. B3.

—Frank Uhle

Townsends, Inc.

919 North Market Street, Suite 420
Wilmington, Delaware 19801
U.S.A.
Telephone: (302) 777-6650
Fax: (302) 777-6660
Web site: http://www.townsends.com

Private Company
Incorporated: 1937
Employees: 3,000
Sales: $350 million (2003 est.)
NAIC: 311615 Poultry Processing

Townsends, Inc., is a private, family-owned, Wilmington, Delaware-based poultry company that processes nearly 625 million pounds of chicken each year. The company is one of the top three producers of boneless breast meat. About 80 percent of Townsends' boneless breasts, parts, whole birds, and roasters are sold domestically to poultry distributors, retail chains, and food service institutions. The rest is exported, primarily to Japan, Hong Kong, and Singapore. The first broiler company to become fully integrated, Townsends in recent years has chosen, in the face of consolidation in the poultry industry, to sell off some operations and pursue niche opportunities in value-added products. The company's Speedy Bird product line offers pan-fried and fully cooked chicken products. Organic chicken is sold under the Pristine Cuisine label, and the Ruby Dragon brand covers chicken products that target the Asian market. In addition to Delaware, Townsends maintains operations in Arkansas and North Carolina. The company is headed by the third generation of the Townsend family, P. Coleman Townsend.

Company Founding in the 1890s

Townsends' founder, John Gillis Townsend, Jr., was a transplanted Delawarean. He was born in 1871 on a farm in Maryland, close to Selbyville, Delaware. When in 1894 he moved his wife and two children to Selbyville, using a mule-drawn cart, he began a remarkable association with his adopted state, which combined highly successful careers in both business and politics. As an entrepreneur, he started out in the lumber business, but soon became involved in fresh produce, eventually earning the moniker the "Strawberry King." In the early 1900s Selbyville was one of America's top strawberry producers. Townsend also opened the first tomato cannery in the state's Delmarva region, and became involved in ice plants and banks. In addition, Townsend joined forces with T. Coleman Dupont in 1911 to create the Du Pont Highway, which opened up remote southern Delaware to increased commerce.

Townsend launched his political career in 1901 when he was elected to the Delaware state house of representatives, serving one term. Then in 1916, he ran for the governorship of Delaware as a Republican and won. As governor from 1917 to 1921, Townsend was credited with the passage of legislation involving women's rights, school reform, modern road construction, and social services. In 1928 Townsend was elected to the U.S. Senate from Delaware, serving two terms, from 1929 to 1941. While in the Senate he played an important role in crafting legislation to help the country recover from the Great Depression, with his ideas on banking contributing to some New Deal reforms, including the creation of the Federal Deposit Insurance Corporation. He also played a key role in the passage of legislation regarding silver purchases and the protection of farm patents. After being defeated in his reelection bid in 1940, Townsend again offered his services to the nation following World War II, when he was named as an alternate delegate to the first United Nations Assembly, held in London. He also would serve as a trustee for numerous colleges and universities and was a member of the Mount Rushmore National Memorial Commission. He lived well into his 90s, passing away in 1964.

Townsend Becoming Involved in Poultry in the 1930s

During and between stints in public life, Townsend nurtured his business empire. Increasingly he was aided by his son, Preston Townsend. After leaving the governorship, Townsend concentrated on fruit trees and by the mid-1920s he had more than 5,000 acres in production, making him the second largest orchard owner in America. His attention shifted again in the early 1930s, when he and Preston recognized a business opportunity in the emerging poultry industry in Delmarva. Many farmers at this time had decided to raise chickens because it was more reliable than other forms of agriculture. It could be pursued year-round and not be subject to the vagaries of the weather. The Townsends decided to become involved in the chicken business and incorporated a company to pursue it in 1937.

Chickens had been introduced in the United States by European settlers and were raised on almost every farm, mostly for family consumption. Excess products were sold in town or exchanged for goods at the general store. Chickens were also commonly kept by people in town, but it was not until the post-Civil War era that a large-scale poultry industry began to develop. Even then, raising chickens was considered women's work. As the poultry industry began to flourish, however, men began to become more involved and took control. The industry experienced significant changes in the 1920s. Poultry science programs were instituted at American colleges, as the small-farm chicken enterprises run by women and children gave way to large organizations. Hatcheries gained wide use in the 1920s, as did research facilities funded by the major feed companies: Ralston Purina, Quaker Oats, and General Mills' predecessor, Larrowe Milling. In 1934 Kimber Farms was established in Fremont, California, to engage in genetic research to develop chickens for desirable traits, such as the ability to lay a large number of eggs. Vaccines also were developed to cope with the results of not only the chickens' compromised immune systems caused by genetic hybridization, but also the spread of disease caused by the increasingly more crowded conditions under which chickens were kept. Battery cages arranged in rows and tiers became standard in the 1940s, as did the practice of using confinement sheds for broiler chickens. These practices were in many ways a response to the increased demand for poultry and eggs that would be the result of red meat rationing during World War II. Many dairy barns were then converted to the factory system to meet the new market for fresh eggs and broiler chickens after the war.

Townsends built its first hatchery in Millsboro, Delaware, in 1938. The chicks produced from the hatchery were then supplied to farmers who were contracted to raise them on a profit-sharing basis. As with many industries, poultry, in the postwar years, moved toward vertical integration. Well-known poultry giants Tyson and Perdue began to acquire all sectors of production: breeder and commercial flocks, eggs, hatcheries, grain, feed mills, medications, slaughter, processing, and delivery. But it was Townsends that in 1957, with the opening of a poultry-processing plant, became the first broiler company to realize full vertical integration, controlling the process from grain to the delivery of the finished product.

Townsends did not yet confine itself to the poultry industry, however. In the 1950s the company also focused a great deal of attention on its agricultural interests. To the surprise of many, Townsends cut down its orchards during this period, converting the land for use in cultivating corn, soybeans, and feed grain that could be used by the company's growing poultry operation. In 1951 it built a soybean extraction plant, used to process the crop for use in the poultry business as well as an ingredient for use in salad oil, which became an important product line for Townsends.

Townsends' poultry business took on increasing importance over the years. In the late 1970s the company built a state-of-the-art hatchery, followed in 1982 with the opening of a modern feed mill, and a soybean oil refinery in 1985. At this point, a third generation of the Townsend family, P. Coleman Townsend, stepped in to head the company and lead it into the future. A 1969 graduate from the University of Delaware with a degree in Agricultural Science, he was now in his late 30s and well prepared to take over as chief executive. By the mid-1980s Delaware's chicken country was producing nearly $340 million worth of broilers each year, but Townsends, under Coleman Townsend's leadership, moved into other major poultry producing areas in the United States. In 1986 the company acquired operations in Siler City and Pittsboro, North Carolina, and in Batesville, Arkansas. Both operations would be supported by local farmers working on a contract basis. In North Carolina, Townsends would operate two breeder farms, a hatchery, feed mill, and a compost facility. The Arkansas operation grew to include four farms, a feed mill, hatchery, and a poultry-processing plant.

As it entered the 1990s Townsends ranked as the ninth largest poultry company in the United States, and one of the largest producers of boneless breast meat. The company found a healthy balance between its North American business and overseas sales, which were especially strong in Japan. Because white meat was the preference of customers in the United States and Canada, there was an excess of dark meat, which fortunately was favored by other countries. Much of the company's growth over the years was the result of the rising level of chicken consumption, but that trend leveled off in the early 1990s. Although a recession hurt the industry, consumers still preferred the more expensive cut-up chickens, rather than whole fryers, which accounted for just a small amount of Townsends' business. The market was strong enough for broiler parts that in 1992 the company opened a new state-of-the-art tray packaging plant in Delaware, capable of weighing and applying price tags on trays of boiler parts for distribution to East Coast supermarkets. The introduction of high-tech innovations to the poultry industry, while a boon on one hand, also proved to be a problem with the company's less educated workforce. To help address this issue, the company launched a program to assist employees in receiving a high school education.

Challenging Conditions in the 1990s

Townsends faced other challenges in the 1990s, primarily the result of consolidation in the industry. It found it increasingly difficult to compete with other vertically integrated poultry companies like Tyson and Perdue. As a way to diversify, Townsends toyed with the idea of pursuing aquiculture, hoping

Key Dates:

1894: John Gillis Townsend moves to Delaware and launches a lumber business.
1916: Townsend is elected governor of Delaware.
1938: Townsend becomes involved in the poultry industry.
1957: Townsends, Inc. becomes the first fully integrated poultry company.
1986: Poultry operations in Arkansas and North Carolina are acquired.
2000: Facilities are sold as part of an effort to reposition the company in the processed chicken market.

to transfer the company's success in creating a vertically integrated operation for chicken to the hatching, growing, and processing of striped bass and other fish. It was a long-term vision, however, that was never realized.

To better compete in the poultry industry, Townsends began the process of repositioning itself as a value-added chicken processor rather than a vertically integrated operator. One attempt at making this change came in 1996 with the acquisition of Grace Culinary Systems, a Laurel, Maryland, prepared foods manufacturer, supplying traditional foodservice accounts, supermarkets, and mass merchandisers with several lines of premium, cooked, and chilled packaged foods. It also offered some items vacuum sealed for in-package cooking. Grace Culinary was renamed Townsend Culinary. The business became the source of undesirable publicity, however. In June 1998 the plant was hit with a class action lawsuit filed by the Equal Employment Opportunity Commission, which charged that a number of immigrant women employees were asked by supervisors to perform sexual favors or risk losing their jobs. Many of the violations occurred before Townsends acquired the company, but the conduct continued under new ownership. Two years later, in June 2000, the company reached a settlement, agreeing

to pay $1 million, split among 22 defendants. Less than a month later, Townsends sold off the business.

In 2000 Townsends sold off other assets as well, including a chicken processing plant and a soybean processing plant. The buyer was Little Rock, Arkansas-based Mountaire Farms. Although both facilities were located in Delaware, company officials made it clear that Townsends had no intention of leaving the state. The move was part of a strategy to cope with changing industry conditions. Consolidation in the industry coupled with a significant oversupply of chickens was resulting in low prices and depressed profits. Townsends earmarked the money received from selling the plants for further expansion into the prepared chicken market. Nevertheless, the company intended to keep its chicken processing plants in North Carolina and Arkansas. To support the North Carolina operation, Townsends bought a feed mill in the state. But the Pittsboro, North Carolina, poultry plant would be troubled by wastewater discharge problems that fouled nearby creeks and resulted in state fines. In 2004 Townsend restructured its North Carolina operation, moving 200 jobs from Pittsboro to the Siler City plant to shift some production to the Siler plant in an effort to lower the amount of waste produced at the Pittsboro facility. In addition, Townsends cut 225 of the 1,500 jobs at Pittsboro as part of the company's plan to allocate more resources to better grow its processed foodservice business.

Principal Competitors

ConAgra Foods, Inc.; Gold Kist Inc.; Tyson Foods, Inc.

Further Reading

Carter, Richard B., ''Clearing New Ground: The Life of Governor John G. Townsend Jr.,'' privately printed, 2001.

Rainey, Doug, ''Townsends Finds Niches in Broiler Industry,'' *Delaware Business Review,* August 31, 1992, p. 8.

Thorton, Gary, ''Turbulent 2002 Leads to Rationalization,'' *Watt Poultry USA,* January 2003.

—Ed Dinger

TPG N.V.

PO Box 13000
1100 KG Amsterdam
Netherlands
Telephone: (+31) 20 500 6000
Fax: (+31) 20 500 7000
Web site: http://www.tpg.com

Public Company
Incorporated: 1752 as Statenpost
Employees: 163,028
Sales: EUR 11.8 billion ($14.9 billion) (2003)
Stock Exchanges: Amsterdam Frankfurt London New
    York
Ticker Symbol: TPG
NAIC: 492210 Delivery Service; 491110 Postal Delivery
    Services

The Netherlands' TPG N.V., formerly known as TNT Post Group, operates as the world's first publicly traded postal system. The company has three main divisions—mail, express, and logistics—and provides a wide range of collection, storage, sorting, transport, and distribution services. Its postal arm, Royal TPG Post, oversees mail networks in nine European countries. TNT Express covers 32 countries while TNT Logistics manages contracts in 36 countries with over 500 warehouses. TPG was formed in 1998 by the breakup of the former Dutch postal and telecommunications monopoly, PTT Nederland.

Birth of a Postal System in the Mid-18th Century

The formation of the Netherlands' post office system coincided with the evolution of that country from a collection of loosely federated cities into a single national entity. Prior to the mid-18th century, each of the various cities operated its own postal services. The federalization of the region—which at one time included much of Belgium—into a more cohesive gathering of states under Stadhouder Willem III also encouraged the consolidation of the region's postal facilities. In the first half of the 18th century, ownership of postal services was transferred from a city level to a state level. In 1752, the Netherlands officially established a new postal service, called the Statenpost, which granted regional monopoly status to each of the state-run post offices.

The new entity placed the Dutch mail services on a more equal footing with the postal systems of other countries. It was not until the end of the 18th century that the Dutch postal services were reformed into a single, national system, modeling its organization after the system developed by the French. This system, officially established in 1799, provided the foundation of what would soon become known as the PTT Post.

The Dutch postal service inherited a variety of postal tariffs and collection and delivery methods. In 1807, however, the Post was placed under the administration of the Ministry of Finance. This body passed the country's first Postal Act, a series of regulations providing for a more standardized collection, carrying, and delivery system, while also establishing a single rate system—based on distance and weight—for the entire country. Yet the Post was still not conceived of as a public service; instead, it was expected to operate more along the lines of a tax collection service, providing funds for the national treasury.

A shift in the vision of the Netherlands' postal services came in the mid-19th century. The passage of the Postal Act of 1850 established the postal delivery as a service in the public interest. While remaining under the finance ministry, the Post shed its role as tax collector to become a public service. The Postal Act of 1850 further codified the postal service's domestic monopoly and created a simplified postal rate structure.

Two years later, the Post marked its entry into the modern era of postal services delivery when it issued its first postage stamp. That same year also saw the institution of a nationally organized network of postal service facilities—now, every town received its own post office and a system was established for the collection and delivery of letters. The postman quickly became a national fixture, delivering mail as many as three times a day. The postal service rapidly extended its network of post offices. New services, including delivery of postcards and packages, were introduced. By the 1870s, the Post's network of post offices covered most of the country.

A new communication technology would soon join the postal service. By the mid-1850s, the Netherlands had begun to install its first telegraph transmission networks. In 1852, the country formally organized its telegraph utility, the Rijkstelegraaf, under the Ministry of the Interior, which assumed responsibility for installing a roadside network of telegraph poles and cables. Use of the telegraph as a communication means remained relatively limited, however.

The postal system and the telegraph service, which was soon to add the newly invented telephone, operated as separate government agencies until the 1880s. Given the limited growth of the telegraph in the Netherlands, it was decided that the two services should be joined into one agency under a single ministry in 1886. With the addition of telephone services, this agency would become known as the PTT (for Post, Telegraph, and Telephone) and remain a state-run monopoly for more than 100 years.

Transition and Modernization: 1890s–1950s

The combination of postal services with the country's telegraph and telephone systems was never wholeheartedly performed. Even though the two services were available through the same offices—the network of post offices created by the postal service—operations remained more or less separate, with each branch retaining its own personnel, budget, finances, and infrastructure.

The worldwide depression of the 1930s forced the PTT to modernize. Where mail previously had been sorted by hand, the government agency introduced mechanized systems, notably the Marchand Transorma, a machine capable of sorting mail to 400 different destinations, placed into service in 1931. A more efficient sorting system enabled the PTT to cut back on the number of its delivery rounds—instead of the three deliveries per day, PTT postmen now performed only two. This cutback produced still more economies, encouraging the PTT later to cut back the number of daily deliveries to one.

The economic climate presented another opportunity for the PTT, as the government allowed the agency to operate more and more as a commercial enterprise. Unlike other government agencies, which were provided for in the national budget, the PTT was given a more corporate status, enabling the company to make the necessary capital investments and take write-offs on its balance sheets, rather than to depend on government approval for each investment. The PTT was also given its own press and publicity departments, enabling the agency to compete for consumer attention. While most of Europe's postal services and telephone companies remained under government control, the PTT's relative independence allowed it to present a more modern appearance to consumers, who were treated with original postal stamp designs.

The Nazi takeover of the Netherlands during World War II interrupted the PTT's independent activities, as the German occupier seized control of the country's communications systems. With the Allied liberation, the PTT was faced with rebuilding its telephone infrastructure. By the end of the 1940s, however, the agency was presenting heavy losses. In this way, the PTT was no different from most of its government-run counterparts in other countries.

The agency performed its first analysis of postal usage, identifying national traffic trends and postal processing rates. This analysis led to more cost-cutting steps, including the scaling back of the post office network, in which many of the smallest offices were closed and the number of daily deliveries was reduced, as a single daily delivery became standard. At the same time, the agency began raising its postage and telephone rates. Telephone services provided a means to maintain a positive balance sheet when the telephone quickly imposed itself as a mainstay in the postwar home. Yet the PTT's postal arm continued to represent a financial burden, in part because its personnel were considered civil servants and granted all of the benefits of this status.

Restructuring Leads to Privatization: 1960s–80s

By the late 1960s, the PTT was faced with the need for still more cost-cutting measures. The decision was made to reorganize operations, in particular to consolidate sorting, culling, canceling, and other handling activities into larger-scale facilities. The process of concentration began in the 1960s and continued through the 1970s, with the opening of 18 "mail interchange" processing facilities. Advancements in automating, sorting, and handling systems enabled fewer processing centers to process increasingly larger volumes of mail. An important improvement in the PTT's mail system came with the introduction of the postal code (known as the ZIP code in the United States) in 1977. The four-digit, two-letter postal code system allowed automated equipment to sort mail down to the individual delivery round, whereas the previous system could only automate sorting to a citywide level. This improvement finally enabled the PTT to reduce its delivery schedule to a single delivery per day. The number of processing facilities could also be reduced, down to 12. The great volumes of mail being processed in these facilities enabled the PTT to operate at a profit.

Innovation also was coming to the telephone industry—soon to become known as the telecommunications industry. The use of telex equipment and facsimile machines, joined later by electronic messaging systems and Internet-based voice and video communication technology, as well as portable telephone systems freed of dependence on a physical telephone wiring system, threatened a drastic transformation of traditional communication systems. While the telephony industry was facing a time of great change, the postal world was changing as well: the arrival of dedicated express mail and other courier services, led by such U.S. companies as Federal Express and United Parcel

Key Dates:

1752: The Netherlands officially establishes a new postal service called the Statenpost.

1799: Dutch postal services are reformed into a single, national system.

1807: The postal service is placed under the administration of the Ministry of Finance.

1850: The Postal Act is passed.

1886: Postal system and telegraph and telephone services are brought together under a single ministry to form the PTT.

1977: Use of postal codes begins.

1989: PTT is privatized; the postal service is renamed PTT Post.

1994: PTT Nederland goes public.

1995: PTT Post acquires TNT.

1998: PTT Nederland splits into two independent companies—Royal KPN and TNT Post Group.

2001: The company changes its name to TPG N.V.

Service and Australia's TNT, presented new challenges to traditional postal services.

The era of government-run monopoly services had reached the beginning of the end. Restructuring was quickly becoming a necessity, not only to enable the PTT to compete in a rapidly transforming marketplace, but also to give the consumer more options—and potentially lower rates. During the 1980s, however, the PTT focused on expansion activities, buying up interests in domestic cable and television networks and moving toward international expansion of its telecommunications services. In 1989, the PTT was finally privatized.

In that year, the PTT was reorganized as a private business, PTT Nederland NV, under direction of CEO Wim Dik. In the new structure, the postal service, renamed PTT Post, joined its larger telecommunications industry sister company, PTT Telecom, as an independently operating subsidiary. Despite being no longer a government agency, the new PTT remained nonetheless wholly owned by the Dutch government. The change, however, allowed the company to pursue its own growth strategy into the 1990s, unhampered by the slower governmental decision-making process. Privatization also enabled the company to seek new international partners, some of which had balked at the prospect of pursuing projects with a government agency.

Changes in the 1990s

One such partnership was established in 1992, when PTT Post joined its time-sensitive mail and freight services with those of Australia's private TNT and the government-owned post offices of Canada, France, Germany, and Sweden in the partnership GD Express Worldwide (GDEW). TNT, which, since its founding in 1946, had expanded to become one of the world's top four express mail and freight delivery businesses, took on a 50 percent ownership of GDEW. Before long, PTT Post bought out GDEW's public post office partners, so that GDEW became a de facto joint venture with TNT.

Faced with the imperatives of the commercial business world, PTT Post, led by Ad Scheepbouwer, underwent a restructuring during the first half of the 1990s, reaching profitability as early as 1993. One important move PTT Post made was to franchise some 1,600 of its smaller post offices, while placing the others under a joint venture operation with the Postbank, a subsidiary of Internationale Nederlanden. The reorganization also led PTT Post to cut some 1,000 jobs. At the same time, the subsidiary began making its first expansion moves, buying up a number of small domestic and international courier and express mail delivery services. PTT Post also was making moves into a new area, that of logistics.

In 1994, PTT Nederland went to the stock market, as the Dutch government sold off some 30 percent of its shares on the Amsterdam Stock Exchange. The public listing of the post-telecommunications business marked the largest offering ever in the Netherlands and was the world's first public listing of a post office. Interest was high in the shares; nonetheless, most investor attention went to PTT Telecom, nearly twice as large as the NLG 5 billion-per-year PTT Post. Two years later, PTT Nederland offered another 25 percent of its shares, effectively ending the Dutch government's control of the country's post and telecommunications services. At that time, PTT Nederland was listed on the New York, London, and Frankfurt stock exchanges.

The following year, PTT Post stepped out of the shadows of its larger sister company when it reached an agreement to acquire the struggling TNT for some NLG 2.7 billion. The purchase, which placed PTT Post roughly on the same revenue footing as PTT Telecom, set the stage for the next evolution of the former state-run monopoly. In 1998, PTT Nederland announced that it was splitting into two entirely independent, publicly listed companies: Royal KPN, which contained the company's telecommunications activities, and TNT Post Group (TPG), which took over the company's postal, logistics, and express mail services wing, including each companies' shares of the GDEW partnership. Both KPN and TPG retained listings on the Amsterdam, New York, London, and Frankfurt stock exchanges.

Among the first activities of the newly independent TPG was to reorganize its operations into two distinct units, PTT Post and TNT Worldwide, while shedding the noncore activities inherited from the TNT acquisition. The company also concentrated on the expansion of its mail handling facilities, including the opening of a state-of-the-art sorting facility in Liege, Belgium, an international road hub and depot in Duiven, Netherlands, and the opening of six new Netherlands-based sorting facilities replacing the 12 facilities that had been in existence since the early 1980s. While expanding its infrastructure, TPG also continued consolidating its international presence, acquiring Jet Services, an express service based in France and operating throughout most of Europe, and in 1999 acquiring Italy's Tecnologistica, with logistics operations in Italy, France, and Germany.

TPG ended its first year as an independent company on the upswing. Not only had its operating revenues swelled to more than NLG 16 billion, with profits of more than NLG 820 million, but the company's PTT Post subsidiary received a new distinction, as it was granted the right to add the moniker Koninglijke (Royal) to its name. To commemorate the occasion, the Royal PTT Post issued a special postage stamp to mark its 200th anniversary. As one of the world's largest postal and express mail services, with a steadily building position in international logistics, TPG had taken center stage in a rapidly changing postal industry.

TPG in the 21st Century

During the early years of the new century, TPG continued look for ways to expand its business. In 2000, the company struck a deal with CSX Corporation to acquire its logistics arm, CTI LOGISTX. The purchase—its largest since gaining independence in 1998—secured TPG's position as the third-largest logistics company in the world.

TPG's appetite for growth was evident in 2001 as the company added CD Marketing Services, Advance Logistics Services, and Lason Inc.'s U.K. division to its arsenal. In 2002, it strengthened its foothold in the Nordic logistics industry when it purchased a 50 percent interest in DFDS Transport Logistics. TPG expanded its German holdings the following year when it bought Werbeagentur Fischer GmbH, an unaddressed mail distribution company.

By now, TPG had its eye on several areas it believed would bolster future growth. The United Kingdom, whose postal market began deregulating in 2003, was one of those areas. In early 2004, TPG partnered with Royal Mail, giving it access to 27 million households in the United Kingdom. With the fastest-growing economy in the world, China also stood as a key growth target for TPG. The firm's joint venture with Shanghai Automotive Industry Corporation, ANJI-TNT, operated as the country's largest logistics provider. In 2003, ANJI-TNT signed China's largest automotive inbound logistics contract with Shanghai Volkswagen. TPG also signed a Memorandum of Understanding with The State Post Bureau of China, which laid the groundwork for future partnerships in mail, express, and logistics services.

The company officially adopted TPG N.V. as its corporate moniker in August 2001. In May 2002, Royal PTT Post changed its name to Royal TPG Post. The company enjoyed continued success as sales and net income rose each year from 2000 to 2002. However, net income fell by 50 percent in 2003, due in part to integration and operational problems at its Logistics division. Despite the drop in income, TPG's management team—lead by CEO Peter Bakker—remained optimistic about the company's overall future, fully confident that TPG would remain a key player in the postal, express, and logistics industries in the years to come.

Principal Operating Units

Royal TPG Post; TNT Express; TNT Logistics.

Principal Competitors

Deutsche Post AG; FedEx Corporation; United Parcel Service Inc.

Further Reading

Bickerton, Ian, "TPG Replaces Logistics Chief," *Financial Times*, August 5, 2003, p. 14.

——, "TPG Unit Back on Track and Hints at Growth," *Financial Times*, December 1, 2003, p. 27.

Dickey, Allan, "Public Services at Private Prices," *Eurobusiness*, March 1994, p. 57.

Dorsey, James M., "Dutch Government Plans to Cut Stake in TNT Post Group," *Wall Street Journal Europe*, March 13, 2001.

Echikson, William, "Privatization: Posts with the Most," *Business Week*, August 17, 1998, p. 18.

——, "This Postal Service Plans to Put Its Stamp on the World," *Business Week*, April 27, 1997, p. 19.

Hastings, Phillip, "Rush to Repackage," *Financial Times*, June 17, 1999.

"Hitting the Mail on the Head," *Economist*, April 30, 1994, p. 69.

"Lex Column—TPG," *Financial Times*, August 6, 2002, p. 18.

Moorhouse, Neil, "TPG Says Growth Will Slow Sharply Due to Economy," *Wall Street Journal Europe*, February 22, 2002, p. A7.

Ratnayaka, Shamal, "Dutch Operator Clinches Delivery Deal with Royal Mail," *Financial Times*, April 8, 2004.

Resener, Madeleine, "How the Dutch Did It," *Institutional Investor*, April 1995, p. 66.

"TNT Sale May Signal Industry Trend," *Logistics Management*, January 1997, p. 26.

Woodford, Julian, "KPN," *Utility Week*, January 23, 1998, p. 24.

—M.L. Cohen
—update: Christina M. Stansell

The Trump Organization

725 Fifth Avenue
New York, New York 10022
U.S.A.
Telephone: (212) 832-2000
Fax: (212) 935-0141
Web site: http://www.trumponline.com

Private Company
Founded: 1974
Employees: 15,000
Sales: $8.5 billion (2003)
NAIC: 531110 Lessors of Residential Buildings and
   Dwellings; 531120 Lessors of Nonresidential
   Buildings (Except Mini-warehouses); 53139 Other
   Activities Related to Real Estate; 23311 Land
   Subdivision and Land Development; 721110 Hotels
   (Except Casino Hotels) and Motels; 721120 Casino
   Hotels; 713210 Casinos (Except Casino Hotels);
   713910 Golf Courses and Country Clubs; 713990 All
   Other Amusement and Recreation Industries

The Trump Organization presides over the assets of the Trump family and serves as the umbrella for the many business interests of the flamboyant realtor Donald Trump. These assets consist of prime residential and commercial properties in New York City, including Trump Tower; the Trump International Hotel and Tower; the office building at 40 Wall Street in Manhattan; Trump World Tower, near the United Nations in New York; and other luxury residential real estate. Other Trump Organization assets include interests in a Florida resort, a skyscraper in Seoul, South Korea, a string of golf courses, and the Miss Universe Organization, which runs the Miss USA, Miss Teen USA, and Miss Universe beauty pageants. The Trump Organization also owns a 56 percent interest in the publicly traded company Trump Hotels & Casino Resorts, Inc. This company owns and manages three casinos in Atlantic City, New Jersey, as well as several other gaming establishments. Donald Trump established a high-profile business empire in the 1980s that almost collapsed under a mountain of debt during the 1990–91 recession. Although forced to divest himself of some properties, he remained an important presence in Manhattan real estate development. The star of a popular television reality show, "The Apprentice," in 2004, and author of hit business books, including *The Art of the Deal* and *How to Get Rich,* Donald Trump's public persona was a key element of his business empire. Even his critics agreed that having his name on a property added significantly to its value. His successful marketing earned him the nickname "the human logo."

Father Fred Trump's Career: 1927–74

Fred Trump represented his life as a climb from poverty to riches, but in his muckraking biography of Donald Trump, Wayne Barrett reported that the elder Trump's father also was engaged in the real estate business, and left a comfortable estate to his widow and children on his death in 1918. Fred Trump built about 300 houses in the New York City borough of Queens from 1927 to 1932, when the market dried up in the depths of the Great Depression. His career revived in 1934, when he was able to acquire a list of serviceable mortgages from a bankrupt Brooklyn realtor. Financing from the newly created Federal Housing Administration enabled Trump to build many more Brooklyn homes, typically selling for $6,000 apiece. During World War II he built FHA-backed housing for naval personnel and shipyard workers near Virginia and Pennsylvania shipyards.

Between 1947 and 1949 Trump completed Shore Haven, a 1,314-unit apartment complex of six-story apartment buildings on a 14-acre site in southern Brooklyn. An even larger development, 2,000-unit Beach Haven, followed. His biggest project was Trump Village in Coney Island. Consisting of 4,600 Brooklyn apartments in seven 23-story buildings—five of them cooperatives, two rental—it was completed in 1965. This one was constructed with state, rather than federal, funding and essentially ended Fred Trump's career as a builder. Previously said to have padded his costs to obtain excessive FHA mortgage money, he was now accused in public testimony of having fraudulently lined his pockets with state funds. Trump ultimately returned $1.2 million and, his reputation under a cloud, was unable to obtain funding for further large residential projects he had planned on the sites of former Coney Island amusement parks.

Donald Trump joined the family business in 1968 upon graduation from the University of Pennsylvania's Wharton School. By 1974 he was president (with his father as chairman of the board) of an assortment of Trump entities, laying claim to the management of 48 privately held corporations and 15 family partnerships. His principal job was managing the apartments, whose number varied between 10,000 and 22,000, according to different estimates. The value of the Trump empire was estimated in the early 1970s at $200 million by Fred Trump and between $40 million and $100 million by other sources.

Acquiring Manhattan Real Estate: 1974–88

Donald Trump was determined to take the enterprise into Manhattan. As head of the Trump Organization—which at the time had no legal existence—he took out, in 1974, an option (with no money down) to purchase railyards along the Hudson River north and south of Midtown, which were owned by the bankrupt Penn Central Transportation Co. Trump planned to build a huge residential complex on the 76-acre northern segment, but opposition by West Side resident groups made the plan unfeasible until the 1990s. He persuaded the city to build a new convention center on the 44-acre southern segment. Although unable to win the construction contract, he collected a $500,000 broker's commission.

Trump also was interested in Penn Central's decaying Commodore Hotel, on East 42nd Street just east of Grand Central Station. Eventually a deal was reached in 1976 whereby a state agency received the property and leased it for 99 years to a Trump entity, which would share in the profits with the city. Trump, who obtained an unprecedented 40-year tax abatement from the city—the first ever granted for a commercial property—then lined up a construction loan guaranteed by his father and the Hyatt Corporation, which became the joint partner. The shell of the hotel was enclosed in a chrome-and-mirrored-glass facade. Completed in 1980, the rehabilitated structure opened as the 1,400-room Grand Hyatt Hotel.

Trump's signature building was the Trump Tower, built on the northeast corner of 56th Street and Fifth Avenue. Assembling lots, purchasing air rights, and securing rezoning enabled him to put up a 58-story office, retail, and residential complex with a six-story atrium shopping mall and a sawtooth exterior shape of 28 different surfaces, cascading in a bronze-and-dark-glass sheath. The Equitable Life Assurance Society of the United States, which owned the land and helped obtain financing from Chase Manhattan Bank, was Trump's joint partner. Completed in 1983 at a cost of $201 million, the building was a hit. By 1986, 251 of the 268 condominium apartments had been sold for a total of $277 million. The partnership retained ownership of the retail and office space and won a ten-year tax abatement in court. Trump installed his family in a penthouse double triplex and bought out Equitable in 1986.

Following on Trump Tower's heels, the 36-story, Y-shaped Trump Plaza residential cooperative at Third Avenue and 61st Street was completed in 1984 at a cost of $125 million. More of a problem was 106 Central Park South, a 15-story apartment building Trump bought in 1981 along with the neighboring, 38-story Barbizon Plaza Hotel (for which he paid only $13 million but received a $65 million mortgage loan). He envisioned a huge condo on the combined sites, but was unable to oust the rent-regulated tenants, who were protected against eviction. When Trump offered to house homeless people in vacated apartments, he was slapped with a tenant harassment suit. In the end the tenants stayed, their building's facade harmonized next to that of the refurbished Barbizon, which became Trump Parc, with 340 condominium units advertised in 1986 at between $180,000 and $4 million. In 1985 Trump paid $72 million for the St. Moritz, the aging hotel across the street from Trump Parc that also faced Central Park.

Trump's last Manhattan hotel purchase was the Plaza, the French Renaissance landmark at the southeastern corner of Central Park, one block east of Trump Parc. He purchased it from the Bass Group in 1988 for a staggering $393 million, or $500,000 per room, making it the most expensive hotel purchase in history. Trump received a $409 million loan from Citibank, and personally guaranteed the $125 million equity portion. Simultaneously, he sold the St. Moritz to Australian magnate Alan Bond, reportedly for $100 million more than he had paid for it.

Trump's option on the northern segment of the Penn Yards had expired in 1979, but after other developers failed to build on the site, he purchased it in 1985 for $115 million. Trump's "Television City" plan for the site included an agglomeration of five buildings extending to a height of 150 stories and a landscaped platform supporting a collection of 8,000 apartments, two office buildings, open space, and parkland above television and film studios, a retail mall, and a massive parking garage. It died in 1987, when NBC decided to renew its quarters in Rockefeller Center. The successor, the 14 million-square-foot "Trump City" development project, did not win the needed city approval.

Atlantic City and Other Ventures: 1980–90

Trump's first investment in Atlantic City came in 1980, when he (with his father) purchased 98-year leases on properties bordering the Boardwalk. After the projected casino was licensed in 1982, Holiday Inns Inc.'s Harrah subsidiary agreed to invest $50 million in a partnership. Trump was responsible for the construction of Harrah's at Trump Plaza (soon shortened to simply Trump Plaza), a 39-story casino-hotel that opened in 1984. Harrah's originally managed it, but in 1986 Trump borrowed $250 million to buy out the company's interest. He had bought the Hilton Corp.'s casino-hotel for $320 million in 1985, which opened as Trump's Castle Casino Resort. An addition to the Castle, a 14-story Crystal Tower of luxury suites, was completed in 1990.

Even these deals paled beside his plan to take over Resorts International, the troubled casino company that was the largest landowner in Atlantic City, and its unfinished Taj Mahal, the world's largest casino. Outbid for voting control of the company in 1988 by television talk show host Merv Griffin, Trump nevertheless obtained his objective—the Taj—for $280 million. He issued $675 million in junk bonds to pay for the acquisition and completion of the casino, which opened in 1990. He spent another $115 million in 1989 to buy two more properties flanking Trump Plaza. One of these was the Atlantis, a 500-room hotel-casino without a gaming license. He renamed it the Trump Regency. The other consisted of the Penthouse, a half-built hotel-casino, and its parking garage site.

Trump indulged his lavish lifestyle by purchasing Mar-A-Lago, a 118-room Palm Beach mansion in 1984, and in 1988 acquiring the world's second largest yacht, a 282-foot-long craft that he renamed the Trump Princess. He docked the craft next to Trump's Castle to entertain high rollers. In partnership with Lee Iacocca, he also paid $41 million for a 32-story residential condominium, which he named Trump Plaza of the Palm Beaches, in West Palm Beach. In 1983 he purchased the New Jersey Generals, of the struggling U.S. Football League, as the opening gambit in a scheme to move the team into an indoor, publicly financed stadium in New York City to be called the "Trumpdome." The league and the stadium proposal folded in 1987. By his own estimates in court papers, Trump lost about $22 million on the venture.

Trump's interest in another glamour business—aircraft—resulted in his purchase of bankrupt Eastern Airlines' Boston-New York-Washington shuttle in 1989 for $365 million. He paid for this with a Citibank loan that accepted as collateral the airline's aging jets and $135 million in equity (backed only by Trump's personal guarantee). Renamed the Trump Shuttle, this venture required $85 million in capital and operating costs in its first year alone. By then he had also paid $23 million for a fleet of helicopters he dubbed Trump Air. Trump also moved ahead with the construction of the Trump Palace, a 55-story residential condominium building on a site at Third Avenue and 69th Street that he had bought in 1985.

Restructuring: 1990–92

When the U.S. economy fell into recession in 1990, Trump's highly leveraged business empire threatened to collapse. Entities of the Trump Organization, or Donald Trump personally, had incurred more than $5 billion in debt—$8.8 billion, according to one source—of which almost $1 billion had been drawn solely on Trump's personal guarantee. Big New York banks had financed $3.75 billion worth of debt. They reduced their risk and collected fees by syndicating the loans to some 70 other banks, including British, French, German, and Japanese institutions. Most of this money was recovered after subsequent restructurings, but some $600 million to $800 million may have been lost. *Forbes* magazine had estimated Trump's worth at $1.7 billion in 1989, making him the nation's 19th richest man. But two years later it assessed his worth at minus $900 million, making him a heavy contender in the world's poorest man category.

An August 1990 bailout pact allowed Trump to defer almost $1 billion in bank debt, but required him to make certain payments on more than $1 billion in additional bank debt. It also gave the banks second and third mortgages on nearly all of Trump's properties. In return for being released from his personal guarantee on about $960 million of debt, Trump gave up ownership of the Trump Shuttle and all but a small stake in the Plaza. Also lost was the West Palm Beach building and the Trump Princess. Trump Air was dissolved and its helicopters sold to pay debts. The Mar-A-Lago was turned into a club. Even Trump's Boeing 727 jet was repossessed (but later repurchased).

Temporarily unaffected was $1.3 billion in casino bonds, but in December 1990 the casinos and property group of the Trump Organization defaulted on a $50 million loan used to fund the Taj Mahal. Trump subsequently agreed to cede half of the casino to bondholders as part of a 1991 restructuring, known as a prepackaged bankruptcy, in which new credit agreements were legally authorized.

During the first part of 1991 the Trump Organization negotiated with creditors of the other casino holdings concerning a revision of the debt. A crucial, mysterious $3.3 million payment on the Trump's Castle debt was traced by a reporter to Fred Trump, who apparently auctioned some of his Brooklyn and Queens apartments to raise the funds. Otherwise, however, Trump could count for help in this quarter only on his own stake in his father's estate, which bankers estimated at a maximum of $150 million. Fred Trump had, according to a biography of Donald Trump by Harry Hurt, turned over the management of his estate to Donald's younger brother, Robert.

Like the Trump Taj Mahal Casino Resort, the Trump Plaza Hotel and Casino and Trump's Castle Casino Resort underwent prepackaged bankruptcies in 1992 to restructure their huge bond debts. Trump Plaza bonds and debt were converted to lower-interest bonds and four million shares of preferred stock for the creditors. In exchange for a reduction in the interest rate on the Trump's Castle bonds, the creditors received half the equity in the property.

Resurgence: 1994–97

Trump also lost the Penthouse and Trump Regency to banks but leased them with options to buy. He reopened the Penthouse—renamed the East Tower—in 1995. He also won a gambling license for the Regency, which was renamed Trump World's Fair. He then exercised his options and bought both properties back for in excess of $200 million. The Trump World's Fair and Plaza East (in the East Tower) casinos opened in 1997.

Trump Plaza Hotel and Casino went public in 1995 as Trump Hotels & Casino Resorts, Inc., selling ten million shares of common stock at $14 a share. A secondary stock offering in April 1996 sold 13.25 million shares at $32.50 a share. This company also included a subsidiary that opened, in 1996, a gambling riverboat, named Trump Indiana, on Lake Michigan at Gary, Indiana.

In April 1996 Trump Hotels & Casino acquired the Taj Mahal for $40.5 million, plus assumption of its debts. The company, through Trump Atlantic City Associates, issued more than $1.1 billion in new mortgage notes to redeem the Taj Mahal's $780 million in mortgage bonds due 1999 and the Trump Plaza's $340 million in mortgage notes due 2001. Five months later, Trump Hotels & Casino acquired the money-losing Trump's Castle (renamed Trump Marina in 1997) for about $490 million in stock, a transaction that included the assumption of about $314 million of the hotel-casino's debt. The acquisition raised Trump's stake in the public company to about 40 percent. Trump Hotels & Casino Resorts grew to six casinos with the integration of the World's Fair and East Tower properties into Trump Plaza in 1997.

Trump Hotels & Casino Resorts was now an awesome agglomeration of Atlantic City properties. Revenues reached $976 million in 1996, but the company lost $65.7 million, mostly because of an extraordinary $59.1 million charge for redemption of notes and the writeoff of deferred financing costs. The company's underlying weakness—a long-term debt that reached $1.7 billion in mid-1997—caused the stock to fall below $10 a share by the end of the year.

Trump's plan for the northern segment of the old Penn Central railyards received approval in 1992 in scaled-down form. The proposed development, renamed Riverside South, now was to consist of 5,700 apartments, 1.8 million square feet of office space, 350,000 square feet of retail space, and parking for 3,500 cars. Trump did not have the financing to develop the property, but in 1994 he signed a joint venture agreement with a consortium of Asian investors, led by two of Hong Kong's biggest developers. He was said to have received a 30 percent stake in the project, with responsibility for constructing and managing the 18 buildings and seeking regulatory approvals, while putting up no cash. According to one source, however, he had no actual equity in the project and would begin to get a share of the profits only after the developer syndicate recovered its investment, plus interest. The first two Riverside South buildings began to rise in 1997, and by 2004 eight of the projected sixteen buildings had been completed.

Again in 1994, Trump's relish for high-profile deals was evident when he formed a joint venture with two foreign investors who had paid $42 million for the Empire State Building. Trump became general partner, but his stake in the venture was unclear. In any case, other realtors had 81 years remaining on a lease of the landmark building that gave them almost complete independence from the owners, who would receive only an annual rental of under $2 million during the life of the lease. In 1995 Trump bought 40 Wall Street, a 72-story office building. He paid less than $8 million for the property, but it was 89 percent vacant, and the remodeling he envisioned would cost at least $100 million.

The Trump International Hotel & Tower, a slender 52-story structure at the north end of Columbus Circle that was formerly the Gulf & Western office building, was converted to luxury residential condominiums, with a Trumpian bronze-and-dark-glass outer skin. Trump Organization units were in charge of construction, sales, and management but provided little or no cash. Aside from fees for these services and the use of his name, Trump received a penthouse in the building and a stake in the hotel's restaurant and garage. Work began in 1995 and was completed in 1997.

In 1996 Trump bought the Miss USA, Miss Universe, and Miss Teen USA pageants from ITT Corp. and then sold half of the property to CBS, which was broadcasting the pageants. He said he wanted to create marketing tie-ins to raise their visibility, possibly including an agreement for a top modeling agency to hire the winners and a new line of Miss Universe cosmetics backed by a major beauty company. Trump sold his half-share in the Grand Hyatt Hotel to the Hyatt Corp. in 1996 for $142 million. This enabled him to extinguish the remainder of his personal indebtedness. *Forbes* estimated his worth at $1.4 billion in October 1997—up from $450 million the previous year.

On to New Heights: The 2000s

Through the late 1990s and early 2000s, Trump projects were rising in New York, sometimes despite protests. The Trump World Tower, on First Avenue in Manhattan between 47th and 48th Streets, was touted as the world's tallest residential structure. The 861-foot tall building dwarfed other residences in the neighborhood, to the dismay of some longtime area denizens. Trump prevailed in a lawsuit brought by the neighborhood association, and the $400 million structure went up. Trump World Tower consisted of 372 luxury apartments priced between $1 million and $11 million, though one sold for $38 million, a record for a New York apartment. Another Trump structure caused neighborhood ire, in a case that went all the way to the New York State Supreme Court. The 31-story sixth tower of Trump's Riverside South project was built only inches away from the historic Chatsworth, a landmarked 13-story apartment house on West 72nd Street. Residents of the Chatsworth tried to stop the sixth tower from going up, and in 2003 appealed the state supreme court's decision against them.

The attacks of September 11, 2001 that brought down the World Trade Center did not stop Trump and others from erecting conspicuous structures in New York. The terrorism issue did, however, force the Trump Organization to reconsider plans for a massive project in Chicago. The Trump Organization had thought of building the world's tallest building in the city, but instead planned Trump Tower Chicago as a more modest skyscraper, which would be the city's fourth tallest. Terrorism insurance also became a big issue after September 2001, complicating financing for high-profile buildings. In 2001, the Trump Organization hoped to swing a $950 million mortgage from Deutsche Banc Mortgage Capital in order to buy the 50 percent portion of the General Motors Building in Manhattan it did not already own. (Trump and Conseco, Inc. jointly bought the building in 1998, with Conseco putting up $211 million and Trump only $11 million.) The deal cooled over the issue of insurance risk in the wake of the attacks. A dispute with Conseco over profits from the General Motors Building led a court in 2003 to order Trump to sell his interest.

In the 2000s, the Trump Organization also moved in altogether new directions. Donald Trump was an avid golfer, and he became a golf mogul as well, building the spectacular Trump National Golf Course in Westchester County, New York, in 2000. Membership in the Trump National club cost $300,000, and the course was studded with lavish features, including a giant waterfall on the 13th hole. Trump also built luxury golf villas adjoining the course. Trump went on to build golf courses in West Palm Beach, Florida and in Bedminster, New Jersey. The Bedminster course, built on farmland formerly owned by automobile magnate John DeLorean, also accommodated 11 cottages and an equestrian center. The golf courses were a new approach to luxury housing, as well as recreation. A fourth course, Trump National Golf Course Los Angeles, was in the works in 2004.

Because the Trump Organization was a private company with no obligation to post financial information, and because many factors made the health of a real estate portfolio hard to evaluate, it was difficult to pin down concretely how well Trump's empire was doing in the early 2000s. Trump had clearly put behind him his missteps of the early 1990s. He had buildings named after him all over Manhattan, and he claimed in 2004 to own at least 50 percent of all the New York buildings with the Trump moniker. His net worth was estimated at between $2 billion and $6 billion, though this was unverified, and some real estate rivals put their own estimates of his worth much lower. Clearly, the Trump name had enormous strength. Sources quoted by *Time* magazine (April 12, 2004) acknowledged that the Trump logo added some $100 per square foot to the value of a building. Trump claimed that his name on his Westchester golf course brought him $300,000, while without the Trump stamp, membership would go for only $25,000. Donald Trump had long been known in the press as simply "The Donald," but by the early 2000s he had acquired another nickname, "the human logo." Akin to Martha Stewart and Oprah Winfrey, Trump was able to extend the cachet of his name into a far-reaching realm. He came out with a Trump Visa card in 2004, as well as his own brand of bottled water, Trump Ice. His biggest publicity coup was his starring role in the 2004 NBC reality show, "The Apprentice." Trump gave a gaggle of contestants business challenges, firing the worst performer every week, until the final contestant won a coveted job with the Trump Organization. This gave Trump huge media exposure, and helped earn him an estimated $5 million advance on his 2004 book, *How to Get Rich*.

Trump's wide exposure seemed like it could only help his branded real estate projects. On the other hand, Trump's publicly held casino and gaming company struggled all through the early 2000s. The company lost money year after year, and its stock sank to $2.50 in mid-2004, compared with a one-time high of more than $35 shortly after the company went public. The casinos were loaded with debt, and hampered by well-heeled competitors. Both Harrah's Entertainment and Park Place Entertainment Corp. owned Atlantic City casinos, and these companies spent lavishly to refurbish their properties, while some slot machines at Trump's casinos did not even have stools. Trump managed to restructure some debt on the casinos in 2001 to get more favorable terms. But by 2004, Trump Hotels & Casino Resorts had a market value of only $41 million, down from more than $500 million in 1996, and it was possible that angry creditors would force the company into bankruptcy. Trump promised to pay more attention to the casino business once his television stint was over. If he managed to save the business, it would not be the first time he had emerged from a seemingly impossible situation. Meanwhile, he churned out real estate development projects. In 2004 these included the Trump Tower at City Center, in White Plains, New York, and a mixed hotel and condominium project in Toronto, the Trump International Hotel & Tower.

Principal Subsidiaries

Trump Sales & Leasing Residential Real Estate; Trump International Hotel & Tower; Trump Hotels & Casino Resorts, Inc. (56%); Trump Golf; Miss Universe Organization (50%).

Principal Competitors

The Lefrak Organization; Harrah's Entertainment, Inc.; Tishman Realty & Construction Co. Inc.; Caesar's Entertainment Inc.

Further Reading

Asbury, Edith Evans, "Housing Windfall Yielded 1.8-Million, Inquiry Here Told," *New York Times,* January 27, 1966, pp. 1, 26.

Barrett, Wayne, *Trump: The Deals and the Downfall,* New York: HarperCollins, 1992.

Bender, Marilyn, "The Empire and Ego of Donald Trump," *New York Times,* August 7, 1983, Sec. 3, pp. 1, 8.

Binkley, Christina, "Stock of Trump Hotels Is Depressed, So Should Donald Buy It Back?," *Wall Street Journal,* August 20, 1997, pp. A1, A8.

"Development in Coney Is Peak of a 40-Year Building Career," *New York Times,* January 5, 1964, Sec. 8, pp. 1–2.

"Donald J. Trump," *Philadelphia Business Journal,* January 3, 1997, p. 18.

"Don Trump's Real Estate Formula," *Business Week,* May 26, 1975, p. 70.

Geist, William E., "The Expanding Empire of Donald Trump," *New York Times Magazine,* April 8, 1984, pp. 28, 30–31, 72–75, 78–79.

Kadlec, Don, and Daren Fonda, "Trump's Reality Woes," *Time,* April 12, 2004, p. 50.

Keith, Natalie, "Trump Tops Off His Legacy," *Real Estate Weekly,* August 9, 2000, p. 1.

Lashinsky, Adam, "For Trump, Fame Is Easier Than Fortune," *Fortune,* February 23, 2004, p. 38.

Linnett, Richard, " 'Human Logo': Reconstructing the Trump Brand," *Advertising Age,* August 18, 2003, p. 1.

"Owners Appeal Court Ruling," *Real Estate Weekly,* April 30, 2003, p. 11.

"The Return of the Manhattan Midas," *Economist,* April 12, 1997, p. 65.

Rowan, Samantha, "Terrorism Insurance, Pricing Unravel Deutsche Banc's $950M Loan for Trump," *Real Estate Finance and Investment,* January 28, 2002, p. 1.

Singer, Marc, "Trump Solo," *New Yorker,* May 19, 1997, pp. 56–62, 64–70.

Sterngold, James, "Trump Shows a Different Profile," *New York Times,* July 26, 1996, pp. D1, D5.

Tell, Lawrence J., "Holding All the Cards," *Barron's,* August 6, 1984, pp. 6–7, 23–25.

"Trump Rolls the Dice with His Creditors," *Business Week,* November 19, 2001, p. 124.

"Trump's Latest Scheme Is Real Beauty, Literally," *Crain's New York Business,* March 17, 1997, p. 4.

Tully, Shawn, "Donald Trump: An Ex-Loser Is Back in the Money," *Fortune,* July 22, 1996, pp. 86–88.

Updike, Edith, "It's a Landmark Trump Deal," *Newsday,* July 8, 1994, p. A47.

Whitman, Alden, "A Builder Looks Back—and Moves Forward," *New York Times,* January 28, 1973, Sec. 8, pp. 1, 9.

—Robert Halasz
—update: A. Woodward

Vance Publishing Corporation

400 Knightsbridge Parkway
Lincolnshire, Illinois 60069
U.S.A.
Telephone: (847) 634-2600
Toll Free: (800) 255-5113
Fax: (847) 634-4350
Web site: http://www.vancepublishing.com

Private Company
Incorporated: 1937
Employees: 350
Sales: $52 million (2000)
NAIC: 511120 Periodical Publishers; 516110 Internet
  Publishing and Broadcasting; 541910 Marketing
  Research and Public Opinion Polling

Vance Publishing Corporation has been producing specialized trade magazines since 1937. Among its most widely circulated titles are *Modern Salon*, offering technical education for hairdressers, *Drovers*, which serves the beef industry, and *Wood & Wood Products*. Other publications target the home decor industry *(Furniture Style)*, fresh produce traders *(The Packer)*, and hog farmers *(Pork)*. The company is not afraid to publish for small markets when it recognizes an unserved readership. For example, recent additions to its collection of 26 magazines include *Process*, for professional hair colorists, *Closets*, for builders of home organizing systems, *Rice Farming*, and *Bovine Veterinarian*. Each magazine has its own editorial and sales team, which ensures that the staff maintains expertise in the targeted industry. Vance Publishing has always been an independent, family-owned business and in 2004 was headed by William Vance, son of founder Herbert Vance. The company has gradually added to its array of publications over the decades either by using profits to acquire existing publications or by starting new titles in-house. Vance Publishing's salon, home decor, and woodworking magazines are produced at the company headquarters near Chicago, while most of its agricultural titles are based in a Lenexa, Kansas, office. In addition to magazines, the company produces some industry-related directories and annual references. Vance Publishing's research division gathers information on the industries the company covers in order to generate relevant editorial content and keep advertisers informed about magazine readership. The company also offers custom publishing for its advertisers and invests in Internet ventures related to the industries it serves.

Early Titles: 1937–57

Herbert A. Vance, founder of Vance Publishing, had a background in banking and the publishing of telephone directories. He started Vance Publishing in New York in 1937 when he bought *Canning Age,* a business magazine serving the food packing field. After a few years he added a second title, *American Lumber,* which became well known decades later under the title *Home Center*. During World War II, Vance joined the Navy and was in charge of the publications branch of the Navy's aeronautics bureau.

After the war, Herbert Vance moved his company's offices to Chicago and founded the firm's first start-up title, *Wood*. The centennial edition of *Wood & Wood Products* reports that Vance wrote to his company attorney in late 1945, "As you know, we have been thinking for a long time about starting a wood-use paper. . . . The paper will cover production and technical developments and the process of wood. . . . We have already discussed this proposition with an outstanding man in the lumber industry, who I think will make an excellent editor because of his background, knowledge and reputation in the field. This is something we have wanted to do for a long time. I think the time is right, and if we can get this individual, our chance of success will be very good." That individual was Robert Turner, who did in fact agree to act as editor for a salary of $600 a month. Turner drew on his industry contacts to gather contributors to the first issue of *Wood,* which appeared in September 1946.

Herbert Vance was never quite satisfied with the magazine's title. He had considered "Wood Age," but, as he wrote to his attorney in February 1946, "Actually talking about a wood age now may not be entirely accurate." "Wood Review" and "Wood Forum" were also possibilities, but Vance finally settled

Company Perspectives:

We believe that we must produce quality business information products that meet the needs of the industries we serve. That means getting involved in those industries, being passionate about their growth and success. It means leading those industries, guiding them to new levels of profitability. And most of all it means caring about and investing in the future of the industries we serve.

on "Wood" even though he worried the title was not distinctive enough for a trademark. That fear proved well-founded when, two weeks after the premiere issue, an English publication also called *Wood* claimed to have copyrighted the name in the United States before the war. The dispute was eventually worked out diplomatically when the two publications agreed to trade articles for reprint in each other's magazines and allow each other to freely sell advertising and subscriptions. Vance's upstart publication had to contend with several well-established competitors, including *Wood Products* and *The Wood-Worker*. In order to increase its credibility and visibility, *Wood* cultivated a relationship with the Forest Products Research Society, which was holding its second annual meeting in 1947. The society's monthly bulletin was published in *Wood*.

In 1951, *Wood* was still a young publication when it found itself in a position to buy one of its major competitors. M.B. Pendleton, owner of the Lumber Buyers Publishing Company, was moving on to other professional opportunities and sold his business to Vance that summer. The sale included the publications *Wood Products, Venetian Blinds,* and *Barrels & Boxes & Packages. Wood Products* was combined with Vance's existing magazine to form *Wood & Wood Products,* giving the magazine the new name Vance had desired. The combined magazine adopted the pedigree of *Wood Products,* which claimed to go back to a publication called *The Stock List* founded in 1896. *Venetian Blinds* was sold within the year; *Barrels & Boxes & Packages* appeared briefly as a department in *Wood & Wood Products* but was soon discontinued.

Adding to the Collection: 1957–70

In 1960, Herbert Vance turned over his duties as publisher of *Wood & Wood Products* to the magazine's editor Jack Koelisch and began devoting more attention to acquiring or starting new publications. In 1957, he had bought *Modern Beauty,* which eventually became known as *Modern Salon.* The magazine featured how-to's for hairdressers as well as reports on industry trends. After this acquisition, growth took off at Vance Publishing. Soon the company took over *The Packer* as well, a weekly newspaper reporting on prices and trends for the fresh produce industry. In 1963, *Wood & Wood Products* launched the Reference Data and Buying Guide, an annual guide for buyers in the woodworking industry. This publication became known as the Red Book Directory, named after its easily visible cover, in 1985.

A venerable addition to Vance Publishing's collection came in 1966 when the company acquired a set of livestock papers known as "The Corn Belt Farm Dailies." The oldest of these

papers had been founded by Harvey Goodall in 1873 as the *Chicago Daily Drovers Journal.* The journal provided a daily report on the cattle trade in Chicago's stockyards. Similar papers were started over the next few years in other river cities that took part in the livestock trade. Eventually, several of these regional papers were bought by the Neff family in Kansas. The papers were a farmer's main source of up-to-date market information for many years, but the rise of radio and television eventually made them obsolete. Vance Publishing bought the papers from a Kansas City bank and revamped them into a weekly publication known as the *Drovers Journal.* Allan McGhee, who had been the paper's editor since the mid-1940s, continued in that position under Vance until 1982.

The company's next acquisition came in 1969 with the purchase of *Industrial Woodworking,* a trade magazine that had been published since 1949. *Industrial Woodworking* merged with *Wood & Wood Products.* At the time, *Wood & Wood Products* had a paid circulation of 11,000, while *Industrial Woodworking* was distributed free of charge. After the publications were combined, they were converted to controlled circulation, which meant that a subscription was free for qualified readers. The magazine's circulation reached 30,000 in 1972 and 50,000 in 1989.

By this time, Vance Publishing was also active as a sponsor of trade shows connected to the industries for which it published. The company's magazine *American Lumber* had evolved into *Home Center,* a publication targeted at retailers of do-it-yourself home products. When the new title was adopted, the industry was just emerging and no trade show yet existed, so Vance started one. It grew into the National Home Center Show, one of the largest such events in the country. Based on that experience, Vance started a special division for trade shows.

Continued Growth in the 1970s–80s

In the mid-1970s, Vance Publishing experimented with pooling the publishing operations of its several independently functioning publications so that salespeople could work in more concentrated areas. However, the company found that advertisers and readers expected sales representatives to have specialized knowledge of a given field, so it returned to a hands-off management style in which each magazine was run as a separate unit. Central management took care of long-range planning and budgets. John O'Neil, who had first joined Vance Publishing in 1957 after his consulting company was called in to work with them, was serving as president. Herbert Vance was chairman.

Vance Publishing's wood division launched *Logging Management* in 1977 under the motto "From Seedling through Sawmill." The magazine was intended to expand the division's coverage to the entire wood products industry. *Logging Management* was particularly strong in its coverage of environmental issues and options for coexisting with the environmental movement. The publication did well for a few years until the country was hit by a housing recession and a subsequent rash of sawmill closings. *Logging Management* stopped publication after October 1981.

A more successful magazine, *Pork,* was founded the same year as a spinoff of *Drovers Journal.* The latter had become focused exclusively on the vertical beef production industry, leaving Vance Publishing with no publication for hog farmers. However, the market was already served with well-established publications such as *Hog Farm Management* and *National Hog Farmer.* Vance would have to develop a new approach to win business from the competitors. The company found an enthusiastic editor in Bill Newham, who had worked with hogs all his life and had a genuine passion for the business. The magazine started out by devoting each issue to in-depth journalism on a single topic; later it responded to the consolidation and financial pressures of the hog industry by developing a more direct focus on profitable management. *Pork* became recognized for exceptionally interesting and well-written articles. In 1987, it became the first agricultural publication to win a Neal award, the Pulitzer Prize of the business press. Snickers broke out among the audience when the award was announced, but the laughs decreased when *Pork* also won awards the next two years.

Vance Publishing had also just started publishing *Modern Jeweler*, which it acquired and redesigned in 1982 despite reports that the industry was depressed. The company joked that its collection went from pigs to pearls. *Modern Jeweler* attained a circulation of about 36,000 by the end of the decade. It reported on everything from store security to sales of famous gems until Vance Publishing sold it in 1996. By 1983, the company had a total of 20 publications and expected annual sales of about $27 million. Vance Publishing's trade show and in-house research divisions were also doing well, and the company had offices in five cities. The diversity of the company's publications helped it weather recessions, since the industries it served were not all suffering at the same time.

In 1986, James Staudt, former executive vice-president, became president of Vance Publishing, and John O'Neil moved on to be vice-chairman. The former vice-chairman was William Vance, Herbert's son. He had been active in the company since

the 1970s and now took over as chairman. The company's latest magazine was *Supermarket Floral*, a narrowly defined publication that nevertheless was published for over a decade. Company-wide sales in 1987 were about $38 million.

More Acquisitions and Start-Ups in the 1990s and Beyond

Vance Publishing carried out a number of acquisitions and start-ups in the early 1990s. *Custom Woodworking Business* was spun off of *Wood & Wood Products* in 1991 to target the formerly overlooked sector that manufactured wood products to customer specifications. The magazine started off as a quarterly and went to monthly production in 1996. Vance also acquired *The Peanut Grower* in 1991 from Agri-Publications Inc. In 1992, the company bought *Hog Farm Management* and *Dairy Herd Management* from Capital Cities/ABC's publishing group. The former was merged with *Pork;* the latter continued as an independent magazine with a controlled circulation of over 70,000.

In 1993, Vance Publishing bought *Salon Today,* which became a sister publication to *Modern Salon. Salon Today* had been founded about a decade earlier by Howard and Vicki Hafetz, salon products sellers who started the magazine to give their clients tips in running a business. The publication was so successful that it became hard to manage for the original founders, who sold it to Vance Publishing. *Salon Today* retained its focus on the aspects of running a business, while *Modern Salon's* strength was technical education. That same year, *Home Improvement Center,* one of Vance Publishing's booming publications during the 1980s, was shut down because of declining revenues and strong competition. The Building, Remodeling and Decor Products Expo, as the company's once highly profitable exposition had come to be known, was sold the following year. A new magazine in the Decor division was *Residential Lighting. Furniture Style* also became part of the Decor division by the end of the decade.

Vance Publishing acquired several agricultural publications in 1995 when it bought Little Publications Inc. of Memphis. The firm's titles included *Cotton Farming, Rice Farming, Soybean South,* and *Custom Applicator,* a magazine for the pesticide industry. Vance had a total of 27 publications in 1996. *Plastics Machining & Fabricating* was founded in 1997 to target the niche for value-added processing of plastic. However, the industry did not thrive as expected and the magazine ceased publication after December 2001. In 1998, Mike Ross was appointed president of Vance Publishing; he had been with the company since 1971. Jim Staudt became chairman of the board.

Vance Publishing became more involved in Internet-related activities by the late 1990s. Vance Internet LLC was founded in 2000 to fund Web-based initiatives in the industries served by Vance publications. For example, the company participated in funding MachineryLink.com, a site where farmers could buy and sell used agricultural equipment. Many of Vance Publishing's magazines made their content available online as well. *Drovers, Pork*, and *Dairy Herd Management* began contributing material to DirectAg.com, a website for the agricultural industry.

Several narrowly targeted magazines were founded around the start of the 21st century. *Process,* started in 2000, was a bimonthly for hair colorists. *Closets* was launched in 2003 to serve the closet and home organization industry, which was booming at the time. *Renew,* a new magazine in the salon division that targeted skin care therapists, started being published in 2004. That January, Vance also acquired a group of agricultural reference books published by C&P Press. The most well-known was the *Crop Protection Reference,* also known as the Greenbook, which offered annually updated information on the usage and specifications of chemicals in agriculture.

Meanwhile, many of Vance's longest-lasting publications were still going strong. *Modern Salon* was the title with the highest circulation (120,000) and the only magazine that required a paid subscription. *The Packer* had been joined by the magazines *Produce Merchandising,* for supermarket retailers, and *Produce Concepts,* for the foodservice industry. *Wood & Wood Products* had celebrated its centennial with a retrospective edition in 1996 and had a circulation of 50,000. *Drovers* continued to be a leader in the beef industry. Vance appeared likely to continue on the steady, specialized and profitable path it had followed for decades.

Principal Divisions

Salon Collection; Industrial Collection; Food Systems Group Collection; Crop Collection; Produce Collection; Decor Collection; Research Services.

Principal Competitors

Penton Media Inc.; Fairchild Publications Inc.; Farm Journal Media; Hanley-Wood LLC; Primedia Inc.

Further Reading

Blankenhorn, Dana, "Vance Mines New Business Model," *Business Marketing*, December 1, 1998, p. 8.
Christianson, Rich, "The Story of *Wood, Wood Products and Wood & Wood Products,*" *Wood & Wood Products* (Centennial Edition), 1996, pp. 23–34.
Conner, Charles, "Illinois Firm to Buy Little Publications," *Commercial Appeal*, July 20, 1995, p. B8.
Cyr, Diane, "High on the Hog," *Folio's Publishing News*, June 15, 1992, p. 21.
Heise, Kenan, "Herbert A. Vance, 89," *Chicago Tribune*, November 10, 1990, p. 20.
Lazarus, George, "Publisher to Buy 2 Farm Magazines," *Chicago Tribune*, June 19, 1992, p. 4.
Mayk, Gary, "Reading Salon Products Distributor Helps Turn Hairdressers into Managers—and Customers," *Eastern Pennsylvania Business Journal*, June 27, 1994, p. 2.
O'Donnell, Maureen, "The Whole Hog," *Adweek's Marketing Week*, May 22, 1989, p. BM34.
Sweet, Neesa, "A Trio Cooks up Profits with the Spice of Life," *Advertising Age*, May 16, 1983, pp. 34–36.
"Vance Adds C&P's Ag Chemical Desk References to Its Six-Title Crop Collection," *MIN's B-to-B*, February 2, 2004, p. 1.
"Vance Internet Formed," *Dairy Herd Management*, October 2000, p. 32.
"Vance Publishing to Launch *Closets,*" *Wood & Wood Products*, July 2003, p. 16.
"Vance Sells Troubled BRDP Expo," *Chilton's Hardware Age*, June 1994, p. 22.
Warren, James, "William Vance Reaches for Narrow Audiences," *Chicago Tribune*, February 3, 1988, p. 3.

—Sarah Ruth Lorenz

Viridian Group plc

120 Malone Road
Belfast
BT9 5HT
United Kingdom
Telephone: (+44) 28 9066 8416
Fax: (+44) 28 9068 9128
Web site: http://www.viridiangroup.co.uk

Public Company
Incorporated: 1931 as the Electricity Board for Northern
    Ireland
Employees: 2,732
Sales: £834.2 million ($1.43 billion)(2003)
Stock Exchanges: London
Ticker Symbol: ISE
NAIC: 221122 Electric Power Distribution

Viridian Group plc is the holding company that controls Northern Ireland Electricity (NIE), which provides electricity procurement, transmission, distribution, and supply services to Northern Ireland. NIE remains Viridian's main operation, accounting for more than £557 million of the group's total turnover of £834 million in 2003–04. NIE represents the regulated side of the Viridian Group. In 1998, the company restructured its operations, splitting off the unregulated parts of NIE. One of these became NIE Powerteam, which became the largest power utility contractor in the Northern Ireland market. NIE Powerteam chiefly provides maintenance and management services for NIE's own transmission network but also provides turnkey services for private power networks. Furthermore, Viridian Group has begun an effort to establish itself as a major power player throughout the Northern Ireland region and has made a push south into the Republic of Ireland itself. As part of that effort, the company's subsidiary Viridian Power & Electricity is building the Huntsdown power generation facility outside of Dublin. The £200 million project uses gas-fired generators and will provide approximately 10 percent of the power generation demand for the entire country upon completion. Viridian P&E is already a major component of the Viridian group, adding more than £206 million to its

revenues in 2003–04. After a brief effort to diversify in the 1990s, Viridian has refocused around its power generation and transmission core. In 2003, the company sold off the last of its non-core holdings, including Fleet Solutions, its share of the Moyle Interconnector, and Lyslyn Ltd. Nonetheless, the company continues to operate two other smaller subsidiaries, Energia, which oversees the group's energy retailing activities, and Sx3, a provider of information technology services. Viridian Group is listed on the London Stock Exchange and is led by CEO Patrick Haren.

Deregulating Energy in Northern Ireland

Northern Ireland turned started using electric power in 1892 when the first commercial power station began operating. Northern Ireland's electrical power market, as in the rest of the United Kingdom, was constructed largely by private and local or regional interests over the next three decades. This led to a patchwork of electrical grids and power generation facilities with little coordination among them. In addition, remote regions of the country were cut off from the electrical power grid—a situation that remained unchanged until the 1950s.

The importance of electrical power to the national infrastructure of the United Kingdom was initially recognized in the 1920s. In 1926, the government formed its first oversight authority, the Central Electricity Board (CEB). The CEB then began building the United Kingdom's national power grid, linking the many power stations then in operation and encouraging the construction of new power stations. By the 1940s, the United Kingdom boasted more than 600 power stations. Yet the country's electricity market remained characterized by widely differing prices and even different voltage standards.

The United Kingdom's control over Northern Ireland meant that it needed to be included in the national power grid. In 1931, legislation created a new regional electricity authority, the Electricity Board for Northern Ireland (EBNI), which worked alongside two other national government bodies, the Corporation Electricity Departments and the Joint Electricity Authority, to develop Northern Ireland's electrical grid.

Private power companies remained in operation through World War II. Following the war, however, the British government moved to nationalize a number of strategic infrastructure and industrial assets, including the country's electrical power and other utilities. This process began in 1947, when the government created an oversight body, as well as new regulations, in order to achieve full national coverage, as well as to standardize not only prices but also voltage rates throughout the United Kingdom. Northern Ireland, along with Scotland, became exceptions when electrical industry was restructured under a single, vertically integrated and nationalized body starting in 1947. Elsewhere in England, power generation and transmission remained separated functions. In 1957, the nationalization of the United Kingdom's electrical market was completed with the creation of a new authority, the Central Electricity Generating Board.

At the same time, the British government launched an ambitious nuclear power generation program, calling for the construction of as many as 19 nuclear power stations to be built by the 1960s. Northern Ireland, too, was slated for its own nuclear plant, with completion expected for 1962. The new atomic energy plants were expected to help reduce Britain's reliance on fossil fuel imports. Nonetheless, these remained an important part of the United Kingdom's power generation grid. In the 1960s, EBNI continued adding new power stations to its network, including a new station at Ballylumford started in 1966. That coal-firing plant was further extended with more than 350 megawatts (MW) of capacity in 1968. Meanwhile, the government's nuclear energy plans had moved ahead, if more slowly than originally planned, and by the end of the 1960s there were nine nuclear power stations in operation.

In 1973, the government created a new authority merging the operations of EBNI and the Northern Ireland activities of the Corporation Electricity Departments and the Joint Electricity Authority into a single body, now called the Northern Ireland Electricity Service (NIES). The government-controlled body then took over the full range of electricity supply, including operation of Northern Ireland's four power stations at Ballylumford, Kilroot, Belfast, and Coolkeeragh. NIES was also responsible for ensuring the transmission, generation, and supply of electricity to Northern Ireland, as well as selling excess capacity to the export market.

The rise of the Conservative Party government under Margaret Thatcher brought impetus to plans to privatize many of the country's nationalized industries. Against opposition, plans were put into place to privatize the United Kingdom's utilities as well.

The first phase of the deregulation process began in 1983, with the passage of a new Electricity Act that allowed the creation of independent power producers in the United Kingdom for the first time since the nationalization of the 1940s. Privatized power generation and transmission appeared to be an especially positive prospect for Northern Ireland, where years of hostilities had led to under-capacity in the province's power generation capacity.

The discovery of a vast lignite deposit in Ulster in the early 1980s promised to reverse some of the province's supply problems. The field, with an estimated 400 million tons of brown coal, including more than 130 million tons immediately available to lower-cost open-cast mining methods, also led to a first test of the government's resolve to privatize the utility market. In 1985, the government began accepting bids from the private sector to build and operate a power-generation plant on the lignite site.

Privatized in the New Century

The 1983 legislation had failed to ignite the private power generation sector, in part because the country's existing government-controlled power generators retained distinct pricing and return rate advantages. At the same time, the legislation did not fully address issues surrounding access to the national power grid by new privately held entrants.

These concerns were finally address in 1989 with the passage of a new Electricity Act. This legislation firmly set in place a process of deregulation and ultimate privatization. An important step toward this end was the restructuring of the electrical industry, separating the power generation component from transmission operations, and at the same time creating a new distribution market composed of twelve new regional electricity companies. The operations of the new companies were further separated into a regulated side—transmission—while marketing activities were slated for full deregulation.

The privatization of the new electrical companies in England and Wales took place in 1990. Northern Ireland's turn came two years later. In 1992, the government restructured NIES, splitting off its four power generation facilities into separate companies, which were then sold to private investors. The remaining operations were regrouped under a new name, Northern Ireland Electricity plc (NIE), created in 1993.

NIE took responsibility for the procurement of electrical power, the development and maintenance of the province's transmission and distribution network, and the delivery of electricity to end users. As in England and Wales, NIE operated along two lines, the regulated transmission component and its non-regulated marketing side, which also included its maintenance and engineering operations.

Faced with constraints on its regulated operations, NIE began an attempt to diversify its business somewhat into the mid- to late 1990s, adding businesses such as Fleet Solutions, which provided fleet management services, and Sx3, an information technology services supplier. NIE also became a partner in the Moyle Interconnector project, laying a sub-sea cable to connect the Northern Ireland and Scottish power grids. The company also entered into the telecommunications sector, acquiring a stake Internet provider nevada. Yet power transmission and marketing remained the group's primary focus.

In 1998, as the United Kingdom moved to full deregulation of the electricity industry, NIE restructured its operations. The

Key Dates:

1892: Commercial electrical power distribution begins in Northern Ireland.
1931: The Electricity Board for Northern Ireland (EBNI) is created.
1947: The British government nationalizes the electricity industry, including EBNI.
1973: EBNI is merged with other components of the Northern Ireland electricity sector to create Northern Ireland Electricity (NIE).
1983: The Electricity Act is passed, deregulating the national electricity industry.
1989: The New Electricity Act sets in motion privatization and deregulation of the UK energy sector.
1992: NIE spins off its four power generation plants as separate companies as part of a restructuring leading to privatization.
1993: NIE is privatized, becoming responsible for procurement, transmission, and distribution of electricity to Northern Ireland.
1998: NIE is broken up into regulated (NIE) and deregulated (Viridian) operations under a new holding company, Viridian Group.
2003: The company completes its divestiture of non-core operations with the sale of Fleet Solutions.

company formally split itself into its regulated and non-regulated components, which were then placed under a new holding company, Viridian Group plc. Where NIE had been barred from the power generation market, Viridian Group faced no such constraints. The company promptly announced its interest in moving south into the Republic of Ireland market. In 1999, Viridian won a bid to construct the new Huntsdown power station outside of Dublin, which came online in 2002.

Into the 2000s, Viridian found itself hard-pressed to maintain profitability in many of its diversified holdings. The company revised its strategy, refocusing itself around its power generation, transmission and marketing core. In 2002, the company began selling off its non-core holdings, which by then included a financial services wing as well as its struggling Internet operation. Viridian's divestment program was completed by the end of 2003 with the sale of Fleet Solutions to AssetCo in November of that year.

The divestment helped refocus Viridian and restore its profitability. The company had also completed more than £650 million in infrastructure improvements between 1992 and 2002, and continued to invest strongly into the middle of the decade. At the same time, Viridian's successful Huntsdown project encouraged the company to eye further growth in the power generation market in the Republic of Ireland. After losing out on a bid to construct two new power stations in Dublin, Viridian announced that it was considering building its own 400 MW facility in North County Dublin.

In May 2004, the British government announced that it would redeem its special shares in a number of the country's energy groups, including Viridian, which effectively shielded these companies from takeover attempts. The removal of the block, in keeping with a ruling from the European Court of Justice, meant the government's consent was no longer a requirement for the purchase of a large stake in Viridian or one of the other companies. The move opened up new possibilities for takeover offers or for mergers among the companies. Meanwhile, Viridian Group continued to power its way into the future as Northern Ireland's dominant electricity company.

Principal Subsidiaries

SONI Ltd.; NIE Powerteam Ltd.; Powerteam Electrical Services Ltd.; Viridian Power and Energy Ltd.; Huntstown Power Company Ltd.; GenSys Power Ltd.; Viridian Power Ltd.; Viridian Energy Supply Ltd.; Viridian Energy Ltd.; Viridian Capital Ltd.; Service and Systems Solutions Ltd.; LearnServe Ltd.; Viridian Enterprises Ltd.; Viridian Properties Ltd.; Viridian Insurance Ltd.

Principal Competitors

National Grid Transco plc; Scottish Power plc; PowerGen plc; Scottish and Southern Energy plc; British Nuclear Fuels plc; EDF Energy plc; British Energy plc; International Power plc; Northern Electric plc.

Further Reading

Bream, Rebecca, "Viridian Eyes Irish Liberalisation," *Financial Times*, September 27, 2003, p. 2.
"Energy Takeover Block Is Removed," *Birmingham Post*, May 6, 2004, p. 23.
Grainge, Zo, "Viridian," *Utility Week*, December 12, 2003, p. 25.
Jones, Matthew, "Viridian to Plug into Irish Electricity Demand," *Financial Times*, May 17, 2001, p. 28.
McCaffrey, Una, "Viridian Set to Meet Expectations," *Irish Times*, September 27, 2003, p. 16.
McGill, Adrienne, "Looking South for New Opportunities," *News Letter*, May 16, 2003, p. 19.
——, "Viridian Surges ahead with New Supply Drive," *News Letter*, January 20, 2004, p.2.
McGrath, Brendan, "Viridian Looks Solid but Has Little Spark," *Sunday Times*, December 22, 2002, p. 13.
Minton, Anna, "Viridian's Non-regulated Growth," *Financial Times*, May 12, 2000, p. 22.
Murray-Brown, John, "Huntsdown Adds Spark to Viridian," *Financial Times*, November 19, 2003, p. 28.
Oliver, Emmet, "Viridian Considers Building Generator," *Irish Times*, March 30, 2004, p. 19.
Power, Edward, "Viridian Chief Warns of Electricity Bottlenecks," *Irish Times*, June 27, 2003, p. 51.
"Viridian Sells of Subsidiary," *Irish Times*, November 28, 2003, p. 51.

—M.L. Cohen

VON MAUR®

Von Maur Inc.

6565 Brady Street
Davenport, Iowa 52806
U.S.A.
Telephone: (563) 388-2200
Fax: (563) 388-2242
Web Site: http://www.vonmaur.com

Private Company
Incorporated: 1872
Employees: 3,000
Sales: $400 million (2003 est.)
NAIC: 452111 Department Stores (Except Discount
   Department Stores)

Based in Davenport, Iowa, family-owned Von Maur Inc. operates a chain of department stores in the Midwest, with stores in Illinois, Indiana, Iowa, Kansas, Kentucky, Michigan, Minnesota, and Nebraska. During the early 2000s, the company operated 22 stores in all. These were tailored to the unique needs and tastes of each market, and ranged in size from 42,000 to 203,000 square feet in size.

1870s Origins

Von Maur's roots can be traced back to 1872, when immigrant J.H.C. Petersen, a native of Germany's Schleswig-Holstein region, established J.H.C. Petersen & Sons. The Petersen family had initially settled in a log cabin in Maysville, Iowa, trying to survive by farming. After enduring a difficult year, however, the family relocated to Davenport, where J.H.C. Petersen unsuccessfully tried to establish a business manufacturing matches. Ultimately, he opened a small store with partner Henry Abel, and the two men sold goods at auction.

By 1872, Petersen had sold his share of the business back to Abel and had opened his own store. With $1,400 in working capital, he based the new venture in a 20-by-50-foot former storeroom on Davenport's West 2nd Street. As partners, Petersen's sons Max, William D., and Henry F. were instrumental in making the new family business a success.

In addition to upholding the motto "Quality Goods at Honest Prices," the three brothers burned the midnight oil. As writer Jim Arpy explained in the April 30, 1972, issue of the *Davenport Times-Democrat:* "In order to lose no more time away from the business than absolutely necessary and to be on hand whenever a customer might appear, the boys at night often made up their beds under the store counters and slept there."

J.H.C. Petersen & Sons did well in its first year, and was soon growing at a healthy clip. The Petersen enterprise was located in the east end of a building that also housed another retailer, T. Richters & Sons. After several years, the Petersens purchased the entire building, followed by an adjacent structure that was home to the Klug store. In 1875 the Petersens ventured into the wholesale trade and added a third story to the former Klug building. In the coming years, other physical expansions occurred at both sites.

In January 1892, J.H.C. Petersen retired from the business, which had evolved considerably during the previous 20 years. Under his sons' management, progress continued as a four-story building was constructed on West 2nd and Main Streets. Behind this new structure, another four-story building was erected several years later. This became the base of operations for the Petersens' wholesale business and allowed them to further expand their retail division.

Ownership Changes in the New Century

In 1905, more than 30 years after establishing his family's retail enterprise, J.H.C. Petersen died at the age of 88. Max and Henry F. Petersen died approximately ten years later, leaving William D. Petersen at the helm of what had become the city's largest retailer. With 400 employees, J.H.C. Petersen's Sons was considered "the finest department store west of Chicago," according to Arpy.

From this solid position, William Petersen and the administrators of his brothers' estates sold the business in 1916. The new owners included three partners: C.J. von Maur, president; R.H. Harned, vice-president; and Cable von Maur, secretary.

Company Perspectives:

Von Maur creates an enjoyable and unique shopping experience through its wide selection of brand-name merchandise, its open and attractive store design, amenities that enhance customer convenience and comfort, and its commitment to customer service.

Prior to acquiring J.H.C. Petersen's Sons, C.J. von Maur got his start in the retail trade at a young age. The son of German immigrant George A. von Maur, a contractor who came to New York from Stuttgart in 1863, C.J. von Maur benefited from educational opportunities that had eluded the Petersens. In addition to attending New York schools, von Maur was educated at a commercial college that helped to prepare him for employment in dry goods retailing. C.J. von Maur's managerial skills were affirmed when he was chosen to manage an entire store in Pittston, Pennsylvania, at the age of 17. Although he established his own store about five years later, von Maur sought employment with another retailer when his partner died from typhoid.

It was around this time that von Maur moved to Peoria, Illinois, where he formed a partnership called Harned, Bergner and Von Maur. After selling that business, von Maur relocated to Davenport, Iowa, where he established The Boston Store in 1887 with partners E.C. Pursel and R.H. Harned on the corner of 2nd and Brady Streets. The new store grew to eight times its original size in only three years. Although Pursel died in 1889, the company continued to prosper under the name of Harned and Von Maur. Expansion included a new facility on West 2nd and Harrison Streets, and ultimately the acquisition of J.H.C. Petersen's Sons in 1916.

Although they shared a common ownership, the two large Davenport retailers, which had both flourished after modest beginnings, continued to operate as separate stores for more than a decade. In 1926, ten years after the acquisition of J.H.C. Petersen's Sons, C.J. von Maur died. In one respect, his death marked the end of one era and the beginning of another.

On May 7, 1928, a major development occurred when J.H.C. Petersen's Sons was combined with Harned and Von Maur to form one retail offering named Petersen Harned Von Maur. The buildings that had housed Harned and Von Maur were leased to a company from New York, and operations moved into the former Petersen store. Presiding over the newly combined enterprise was C.J. von Maur's son, Cable G. von Maur. R.H. Harned was elected chairman, and C.J. von Maur's other sons, James and Richard, both served as officers.

When R.H. Harned died in 1937, his family sold its interest to the von Maurs. Although the store retained the name Petersen Harned Von Maur, members of the von Maur family—including Richard B. von Maur and his sons Charles and Richard B., Jr.—assumed responsibility for guiding it. As the fabric of American society changed from the 1940s through the 1960s, Petersen Harned Von Maur prospered, consistently providing Iowans with quality goods and dependable customer service. Under these principles, the business operated as a downtown department store until its 100th birthday.

Expansion in the 1970s–80s

Petersen Harned Von Maur celebrated a century of operations in 1972. By this time, American shopping malls were beginning to grow in popularity. To capitalize on this trend, the company opened its first mall location in 1972, in Bettendorf, Iowa's Duck Creek Plaza. A second Iowa store opened in West Des Moines' Valley West Mall that same year, followed by one at the SouthPark Mall in nearby Moline, Illinois, in 1974. This steady pattern of growth continued through the 1970s, as locations were added in the Iowa cities of Muscatine (1979) and Cedar Rapids (1980).

By the early 1980s, the migration away from downtown stores and the need for differentiation became increasingly important. As former Von Maur President John R. Arth recalled in the January 1996 issue of *Chain Store Age:* "We asked ourselves how are we going to survive? Several things came to mind. One, we had to do some things [the majors] don't do. And two, we had to leave downtowns for regional malls. But that's not all. It was important that we do more for the customer."

Based on this realization, Petersen Harned Von Maur began making changes. Some, like free year-round gift-wrapping, were small. More dramatic changes included the elimination of entire departments, including bridal, home goods, hair salons, and furniture. By removing these lines, the company was able to focus more strongly on apparel and accessories. In addition, the retailer eventually introduced computer systems that allowed sales associates to locate items for customers at any one of its stores.

In 1981, a new location was established in Davenport's NorthPark Mall, followed by stores in Cedar Rapids' Lindale Mall and Iowa City's Sycamore Mall the same year. As part of its larger strategy, Petersen Harned Von Maur closed its downtown department stores midway through the decade. These closures included a location in Clinton, Iowa, in 1985, followed by the Davenport store in 1986.

One benefit that Petersen Harned Von Maur introduced in the mid-1980s was unprecedented among department store retailers. At that time, the company began offering customers an interest-free store charge card. The well-received customer perk helped the company to secure customers when entering new markets. As proof of the card's popularity, approximately 70 percent of Petersen Harned von Maur's sales were charged on it by the mid-1990s, in contrast to an industry average of about 40 percent.

Not only did Petersen Harned von Maur sacrifice lucrative interest income by offering this benefit to customers, some analysts speculated that the program cost the company a great deal in the way of annual interest charges. Not including delinquent accounts, one August 2000 estimate placed this number between $8.5 and $10 million. While some observers were concerned that the interest-free charge program could lead to financial problems, the company stood by its effectiveness for increasing business.

As the 1980s progressed, Petersen Harned Von Maur continued to expand. Another Iowa store opened its doors in 1987, in Cedar Falls' College Square Mall. In the summer of 1989, the company established a retail foothold in Illinois by purchasing

Key Dates:

1872: J.H.C. Petersen & Sons is established in Davenport, Iowa.

1887: C.J. Von Maur establishes The Boston Store in Davenport, Iowa, with partners E.C. Pursel and R.H. Harned.

1889: After Pursel's death, the renamed Harned and Von Maur continues expanding.

1916: The Petersen business is sold to C.J. von Maur, R.H. Harned, and Cable von Maur.

1928: After operating as separate stores under common ownership, J.H.C. Petersen's Sons is combined with Harned and Von Maur, forming Petersen Harned Von Maur.

1937: After R.H. Harned dies, the von Maurs obtain complete control of the company.

1972: Petersen Harned Von Maur celebrates a century of operation and opens its first mall location in Bettendorf, Iowa.

1986: Von Maur closes its downtown Davenport store.

1989: Petersen Harned Von Maur shortens its name to Von Maur.

1990: Company headquarters relocate from the former Petersen store to a 200,000-square-foot site in north Davenport.

1994: Von Maur enters the Chicago market with a flagship store in Lombard, Illinois' Yorktown Center.

2000: Von Maur enters the Minnesota market, with a new store in Eden Prairie.

2001: James D. von Maur is named company president, representing a fourth generation of family leadership.

2003: Von Maur extends its geographic reach by opening new stores in Kentucky and Michigan.

stores in Decatur's Hickory Point Mall and Normal's College Hills Mall.

As the 1980s came to a close, Petersen Harned Von Maur shortened its name simply to Von Maur. According to the company, this change provided an updated image and better reflected the management of the previous 60 years.

Regional Growth in the 1990s

Von Maur began the 1990s by moving into new headquarters, relocating from the former Petersen store to a 200,000-square-foot site in north Davenport. In addition to corporate offices, the new site also contained Von Maur's distribution center. By the following year, Von Maur employed more than 1,500 people, including 50 buyers who traveled to New York, Los Angeles, Dallas, and Chicago to search for the latest fashions.

As Von Maur emerged as a regional retail competitor, it remained focused on the need to do more for its customers. By the 1990s several differentials had been introduced to set the company apart from such competitors as Younkers and Nordstrom. Instead of advertising specials and weekend sales,

Von Maur relied largely on word-of-mouth promotion. The money it saved from advertising was used to offer unique customer benefits, including interest-free credit, free shopping bags, and complimentary shipping via UPS to any location in the United States. Along with a no-questions-asked return policy that did not require customers to provide receipts, Von Maur also offered to match any competitor's price—without verification or the approval of a store manager.

Von Maur also set itself apart from other retailers by creating a retail environment where customers felt relaxed and at ease. Spacious lounges were provided to women, where they could relax and make complimentary local phone calls, and pianists played melodies on grand pianos for the enjoyment of patrons. In addition to wide aisles, decor included unique antique items and fresh flowers. Singing canaries and shoe departments with fireplaces were other unusual touches that set Von Maur's stores apart from other retailers.

"Our store feels like your home rather than a commercial situation," said Von Maur President Jack Arth in a 1998 issue of the *Indianapolis Star and News*. "We don't have mannequins. We don't have big signs. We don't scream at customers." Instead of discouraging customers from handling items for sale, Von Maur stores included small cards that read: "Please touch the merchandise. You'll love it."

In addition to offering costly customer perks, Von Maur also shouldered higher labor costs than other retailers. The company reportedly paid its sales associates more than other department stores did, hired them in adequate numbers, and rewarded them for efficient and friendly customer service. Sales associates became known for developing relationships with customers, learning about their preferences and keeping the information on file in order to provide personalized service. Although it cost Von Maur more to hire good employees, the strategy increased both productivity and sales.

To compete against the stronger buying power of large national competitors, Von Maur set a goal of being first to market with branded apparel items. In exchange for being the first department store to place an order, the company asked vendors to ship goods to its stores first. With the majority of vendors honoring this request, Von Maur was able to roll out merchandise six or eight weeks ahead of other department store chains. This strategy enabled the retailer to identify bestsellers early and place large reorders before other chains had even introduced the same goods. At the same time, poor sellers were immediately marked down in price.

In July 1994, Von Maur entered the Chicago market for the first time when it opened a 207,000-square-foot flagship store in Lombard, Illinois' Yorktown Center. Rick von Maur, great-grandson of founder C.J. von Maur, was selected to manage the new store, which had a 30,000-square-foot shoe department. Von Maur invested $20 million to renovate the retail space, which had been empty for five years after housing a Wieboldt's Department Store.

Many observers considered Von Maur's Chicagoland debut a litmus test, the results of which would determine if the family-owned company could compete with the likes such Chicago-area heavyweights as Carson Pirie Scott, Marshall Field's, and

Nordstrom. According to the August 16, 1994 issue of *WWD*, the new flagship store achieved a strong start. In its first ten days of operation, mall management revealed that Von Maur generated between four and five times its projected volume. The store continued to do well and soon developed a loyal customer base.

After its foray into the Chicago market, Von Maur opened a store in Omaha, Nebraska in 1995. The following year, the company's 12 stores generated sales of $200 million, or $200 per square foot. Based on National Retail Federation figures, this exceeded the industry average of approximately $169 per square foot. After achieving annual sales of $230 million in 1997, Von Maur added two Indianapolis stores in 1998.

In 1999, Von Maur's sales reached an estimated $248.5 million. By this time, Ric von Maur had been named as the company's president, leading a chain of 15 stores in four states. That year, Von Maur closed what had been its very first mall store, in Bettendorf, Iowa's Duck Creek Plaza. However, it also added a new location in Lincoln, Nebraska.

A Third Century: 2000 and Beyond

By opening new stores in Eden Prairie, Minnesota; Fort Wayne, Indiana; and St. Charles, Illinois; Von Maur began the 21st century by immediately strengthening the midwestern foothold it had established during the previous decade. In particular, the St. Charles store was proof of the company's staying power in the Chicago market.

Despite a weak economic climate in which few department store retailers were expanding, Von Maur continued to extend its geographic reach during the early 2000s. In 2002, the company established a store in Wichita, Kansas. Locations were added in Louisville, Kentucky, and Ann Arbor, Michigan, in September 2003, followed by new stores in Livonia, Michigan, and Glenview, Illinois, in October. Von Maur obtained the two Michigan stores at auction, after Jackson, Michigan-based Jacobson Stores Inc. filed for bankruptcy and opted to liquidate them.

While Von Maur expanded during the early 2000s, an important leadership change occurred at the company. In 2001, James D. von Maur was named company president, representing a fourth generation of family leadership. His father, Richard B. von Maur, as well as Charles R. von Maur, remained involved as co-chairmen.

In the March 11, 2003 issue of *WWD*, James von Maur commented on the road ahead, explaining: "For the short-term, we're expanding in the Midwest, and from there we may take the chain national, depending on economic conditions. Our philosophy is steady, but well-planned growth. We open at least two new stores a year and usually only one or two stores per market. We take a micro-intensive approach to merchandising and buy based on a store's unique local needs. Our plan is always to build trust and loyalty by focusing on customer service, literally from the ground up."

With estimated sales of $400 million and approximately 3,000 employees, Von Maur was poised for continued growth. Although the retail landscape had changed considerably since the company was established, the company remained mindful of the traditions and business practices that had resulted in success for more than a century. Expansion of Von Maur to become a national presence seemed likely.

Principal Competitors

Federated Department Stores Inc.; May Department Stores Company; Nordstrom Inc.

Further Reading

Andrews, Greg, "Lombard, Ill., Department Store Earns Customer Loyalty Through Service," *Indianapolis Star and News*, April 27, 1998.

Arpy, Jim, "Celebrating Their Sagas of Success," *Davenport Times Democrat*, April 30, 1972.

Corfman, Thomas A., "Chicago Tribune Inside Commercial Real Estate Column," *Chicago Tribune*, November 28, 2001.

Fearnley-Whittingstall, Sophy, "Von Maur's Retail Values," *WWD*, August 16, 1994.

Hanson, Holly, "A New Team Enters the Retail Game," *Detroit Free Press*, September 12, 2003.

Hazel, Debra, "The Resurgence of the Regionals," *Chain Store Age*, January 1996.

Howard, Clare, "In Booming Economy, Developers Work Hard to Recruit Retailers," *Peoria Journal Star*, September 8, 1999.

MacDonald, Laurie, "Von Maur Takes On Major Competitors with Opening of Flagship Dept. Store in Chicago," *Footwear News*, August 22, 1994.

McCartney, Jim, "Small, Retro Retail Chain to Open Store in St. Paul, Minn.," *Saint Paul Pioneer Press*, August 6, 2000.

Snavely, Brent, "Von Maur Plans to Fill Shoes at Old Jacobson's Locations," *Crain's Detroit Business*, September 23, 2002.

"Von Maur History," *Scott County Heritage*, Scott County, Iowa: Scott County Heritage Book Committee, 1991.

Williamson, Rusty, "Von Maur Steps Out of the Box; The 18-Unit Midwestern Chain Sets Its Sights on Going National," *WWD*, March 1 2003.

Yue, Loren, "Iowa-Based Retailer Remains Profitable While Department Store Peers Struggle," *Chicago Tribune*, April 25, 2003.

—Paul R. Greenland

WOLSELEY

Wolseley plc

Parkview 1220
Arlington Business Park, Theale
Reading
RG7 4GA
United Kingdom
Telephone: 44 118 929 8700
Fax: 44 118 929 8701
Web site: http://www.wolseley.com

Public Company
Incorporated: 1887 as Wolseley Sheep Shearing Machine
    Company
Employees: 46,000
Sales: £8.2 billion ($13.1 billion) (2003)
Stock Exchanges: New York London
Ticker Symbol: WOS
NAIC: 423710 Hardware Merchant Wholesalers; 326122
    Plastics Pipe and Pipe Fitting Manufacturing; 333414
    Heating Equipment (Except Electric and Warm Air
    Furnaces) Manufacturing; 333996 Fluid Power Pump
    and Motor Manufacturing; 423310 Lumber, Plywood,
    Millwork, and Wood Panel Merchant Wholesalers;
    423410 Photographic Equipment and Supplies
    Merchant Wholesalers; 423720 Plumbing and Heating
    Equipment and Supplies (Hydronics) Merchant
    Wholesalers; 423730 Warm Air Heating and
    Air-Conditioning Equipment and Supplies Merchant
    Wholesalers; 423820 Farm and Garden Machinery
    and Equipment Merchant Wholesalers; 532310
    General Rental Centers; 532412 Construction, Mining
    and Forestry Machinery and Equipment Rental and
    Leasing; 551112 Offices of Other Holding Companies

Wolseley plc has quietly built itself an empire as the world's leading distributor of building materials to professional and governmental building and construction contractors and services. The Reading, England-based company operates 3,500 distribution centers, including nearly 200 showrooms, in 13 countries throughout Europe and in North America. The latter market has become the company's largest, accounting for as much as 65 percent of total sales. In the United States, Wolseley operates through subsidiary Ferguson Enterprises, the leading supplier of plumbing, heating and piping, valves and fittings, and other construction and building materials and supplies in the market, with nearly 750 distribution centers, as well as bathroom and kitchen showrooms, in 49 states. Wolseley Canada is that market's number two building supplies distributor, operating more than 220 branches throughout the country. In the United Kingdom, the company's Lightside Division operates 634 distribution sites under the branch names Plumb Center, Drainage Center, Bathstore.com, and Broughton Crangrove; the Heavyside Division adds 372 Builder Center, Hire Center, and Timber Center sites; the Commercial and Industrial Division operates 207 Pipeline Center, Controls Center, and NRS air-conditioning and refrigeration branches; while the Spares Division supplies HVAC and related parts and supplies through 159 HRPC and Wash-Vac Services centers throughout the United Kingdom. Wolseley also has been steadily expanding into the continental European market. In France, the company owns the 418-branch Brossette plumbing and heating group and the PBM heavyside distribution network; the company also is present in Austria (ÖAG); Ireland (Heatmerchants and Tub and Tile); Switzerland (Tobler); The Netherlands (Wasco); and in Italy, Luxembourg, the Czech Republic, Hungary, and Denmark. Wolseley has long played a motor for the consolidation of the highly fragmented building supplies industry, spending as much as £300 million ($450 million) per year on acquisitions. The company is listed on the New York and London Stock Exchanges. In 2003, the company's sales totaled £8.2 billion ($13.1 billion).

19th Century Innovator

Frederick York Wolseley founded the later Wolseley plc in 1887 at the age of 50 years. Wolseley, a native of Ireland, had emigrated to Australia in his youth, where he began working as a ''jackeroo'' on a sheep ranch near Melbourne. Wolseley later acquired his own sheep ranch, where he formulated the idea for a mechanical sheep shearing machine. By 1886, Wolseley had perfected the design, for which he received a number of patents. In 1887 he set up his own business, the Wolseley Sheep Shearing Machine Company, in Sydney.

Company Perspectives:

The strategic direction of Wolseley is key to its future success. Here are the five main drivers in that overall strategy: Grow through acquisition and organic expansion; develop a European strategy; leverage our international position; enhance business diversity; and develop our people.

Wolseley's invention proved a timely one for the Australian wool industry, meeting with rapid success. Yet Wolseley had lost financial control of the business, having taken on a number of partners and other financial backers. The success of Wolseley's sheep shearer encouraged the company to transfer its operations to England, where Wolseley became managing director of the new Wolseley Engineering Ltd. in Birmingham in 1889. There, Wolseley began developing a variety of other agricultural equipment, such as a stationary engine and tillers. Wolseley was joined by Herbert Austin, who served as the company's foreman and who would lend his name to automotive history.

Wolseley remained in England for just a short while, before returning to Australia and retiring from the company in 1894. Wolseley died just five years later, in Surrey, England. In the meantime, Herbert Austin had been pursuing another of Wolseley's experiments—an automobile. The company's directors and owners, however, refused to provide financing for the development of an invention they believed useless. Instead, Austin worked in secret, and by 1895 had succeeded in producing the company's—and one of the country's—first successful motor cars.

Wolseley now began manufacturing automobiles in addition to its agricultural equipment, and by the dawn of the 20th century had sold more than 100 Wolseley cars. In 1901, however, the company decided to devote itself to its sheep shearing and other agricultural equipment, and sold the automotive business to Vickers Son and Maxim Ltd. The Wolseley name remained highly popular in the British automobile market until production finally ended in 1975. Austin himself left Wolseley in 1905, founding the famed Austin Motor Company and producing the Austin Seven.

Wolseley's sales of its sheep shearing machinery continued to build for some time into the new century—by 1907, the company had sold more than 20,000 in all. Yet over the next several decades, the company's growth remained modest. In the years following World War II, Wolseley clung on as a small-scale manufacturer. In the 1950s, the company began to branch out again, adding a number of new products, such as electric fencing, motorized tillers (such as the Merry Tiller cultivators), clippers, and the like. Over the decade, the company added another operation, HC Webb & Co., adding lawn mowers and hedge trimmers.

Wolseley's product expansion sent it searching for expanded production facilities; the company, with sales of slightly more than £1 million in the late 1950s, also required a larger capital base for expansion. Wolseley's chairman and managing director, Rodney Drake, turned to friend Cyril Hughes, head of Geo H.

Hughes Ltd., with the idea of combining the two companies. Hughes was another modest-sized Birmingham company, specialized in the manufacture of wheels, tires, axles, and casters for baby carriages and strollers, with sales of slightly less than £1 million per year. The companies completed the merger, forming Wolseley-Hughes plc. The company went public in 1960.

That year saw a significant development for the company. Eager for growth, Wolseley-Hughes had begun seeking acquisition targets, and in 1960 the company bought up Nu-way Benson Ltd., a manufacturer of agricultural equipment, with products including air heaters and dries, and mechanical handling equipment. Nu-way also operated a spare parts business, Oil Burner Components (OBC), which provided the company with an entry into the building supplies distribution market.

In the early 1960s, Wolseley-Hughes continued to build up its range of businesses, boosting its engineering side with the purchases of Rapid Magnetic Ltd., a maker of magnetic extracting, separating, detecting, lifting, and conveyancing equipment; and Accles and Shelvoke Ltd., which provided precision engineer services and produced humane slaughtering equipment. Geo H. Hughes Ltd., in the meantime, expanded its own engineering and production businesses to include wheels and tires for the industrial market.

A major moment for the company came in 1965, with the acquisition of two new distribution businesses, Granville Controls and Yorkshire Heating Supplies. Together with OBC, these new businesses were to form the core of one of the company's fastest-growing operations into the early 1970s. By the beginning of the 1970s, the company's revenues had topped £20 million, driven in large part by its distribution business. Yet the company's diversified nature had already led to an under-valuation of the company's stock. This in turn led the company to defend itself against a takeover attempt from Tarmac plc in 1972.

The following year the company made another important step in its evolution, when it merged its distribution businesses into a single company, Wolseley-Hughes Merchants. Originally focused on supplying spare parts for heaters and burners, the Merchants division quickly expanded into other plumbing and heating supplies, such as radiators and boilers. Throughout the 1970s, the company continued to expand its range of products, targeting the larger building contractors community. By the mid-1970s, the company's shift toward distribution was already well under way, as sales topped £76 million in 1976. Distribution by then provided the largest part of the company's sales, reaching 65 percent that year.

U.S. Expansion in the 1980s

The late 1970s marked a new era for the company as it stepped up its focus on distribution, launching an aggressive acquisition campaign that was to mark the company's growth into the next century. In 1979, the company acquired the John James Group of Companies, adding not only manufacturing capacity but especially a distribution network focused on the plumbing market, including sales of industrial pipe, valves, and fittings. That purchase formed the basis for a new distribution brand within Wolseley-Hughes, Pipeline Center. In another area of diversification, Wolseley-Hughes also began producing footwear.

Key Dates:

1887: Frederick York Wolseley invents a mechanical sheep shear and founds Wolseley Sheep Shearing Machine Company.

1889: Wolseley moves to Birmingham, England and reforms the company as Wolseley Engineering with foreman Herbert Austin.

1895: After Wolseley retires to Australia, Austin begins secret development of an automobile, which debuts the following year.

1896: The Wolseley automobile business is sold to Vickers; Wolseley cars remain in production until 1975.

1907: Wolseley sells its 20,000th sheep shearing machine, as it focuses on manufacturing these and other agricultural equipment.

1958: Wolseley merges with Geo H. Hughes, also in Birmingham, and the company becomes Wolseley-Hughes.

1960: The company goes public; it acquires Nu-way Benson, which leads the company into distribution for the first time.

1965: The company acquires Granville Controls and Yorkshire Heating Suppliers.

1973: Distribution operations are combined into a single business, Wolseley-Hughes Merchants.

1979: The company acquires John James, adding manufacturing and pipeline distribution operations.

1982: Ferguson Enterprises in the United States is acquired.

1986: The company changes its name to Wolseley plc; Ferguson acquires Carolina Builders.

1987: Ferguson acquires Familian Corporation and Familian Northwest.

1992: Wolseley expands to France, acquiring the Brossette group; ÖAG in Austria is acquired.

1993: The company acquires Enertech, including HRPC, in Sweden.

1998: The company begins integration of U.S. operations into Ferguson and Stock Builders.

2004: The company enters Switzerland through the acquisition of Tobler.

Wolseley-Hughes's conversion into a distribution giant began in earnest in the 1980s. In 1984, the company sold off its original Wolseley and Hughes engineering businesses. Motivating this decision was the company's acquisition of Ferguson Enterprises in the United States, marking the company's first expansion beyond the United Kingdom.

Ferguson had been founded in 1953 by Charles Ferguson, Ralph Lenz, and Johnny Smither, with the idea of building a network of independent building supply companies. Each member company would retain the name of its owner-manager, yet take advantage of the benefits of being part of a larger group of companies. Ferguson himself acted as more of an investor in the company (he died in 1955) while the group opened it first two companies, Lenz Supply, in Washington, D.C., and Smither Supply Co., in Birmingham, Alabama, in 1953. The following year, Lenz opened a second business, Crossroads Supply, based in Alexandria, Virginia, which acted as the central hub for all three businesses, with Lenz acting as the company's first president.

In 1959, the company signed on a new partner, David Peebles, who opened Peebles Supply in Newport News, Virginia. Over the next decade, the company continued to attract new owner-manager members and made a number of acquisitions as well. In 1969, Peebles took over as president of the company, which had become a prominent East Coast building supply group. Peebles led the group into its next phase, that of becoming a unified building supply. The group changed its name to Ferguson Enterprises, which became the name for its existing distribution centers.

The 1970s marked a period of strong growth for Ferguson, which saw its sales grow from just $10 million to more than $140 million. By the early 1980s, the Ferguson network covered more than 76 locations in 11 states. The company now found itself faced with the need for fresh capital to fund its future expansion. At the same time, Ferguson found itself faced with succession issues. The company began making plans to go public.

Instead, in 1982, Wolseley approached Ferguson with a proposal to buy the company—and a promise to leave Ferguson's direction entirely in the hands of its U.S. managers. Peebles, Lenz, and Smithers quickly agreed, and Ferguson, backed by Wolseley's own strong financial position—by then, Wolseley's sales had risen past £100 million—began a rapid expansion, boosting its own sales to more than $600 million by the end of the decade.

In the mid-1980s, Wolseley continued to shift its emphasis toward distribution. In 1985, the company established a new subsidiary, Wolseley Centers, which became its building supply distribution wing, overseeing its U.K. network of Pipeline Center, Controls Center, and Plumb Center branches. The following year, the company changed its name to Wolseley plc.

Yet the group's fastest growth came from its U.S. wing. In 1986, Ferguson made a significant purchase with the acquisition of Carolina Builders. Based in Raleigh, North Carolina, Carolina Builders formed the basis of Wolseley's largest single operation, Stock Building Supply, which grew to more than 200 branches in 24 states and sales of $2.7 per year by the end of the century.

Ferguson continued its national expansion the following year, buying Familian Corp., based in California, and Familian Northwest, which enabled the company to extend its building supply network to the West Coast as well. In the meantime, David Peebles had been grooming his successor, in the form of Charles Banks, who became Ferguson president in 1989. Under Banks, Ferguson saw even stronger growth, boosting its revenues to more than $3.3 billion, and its branch network to more than 500 sites in 49 states, as well as Puerto Rico and Mexico by the end of the 1990s.

Distribution Specialist for the New Century

Wolseley now targeted expansion onto the European continent, acquiring the Brossette group, the leading supplier of plumbing supplies in France, in 1992. The company then moved to Austria, where it purchased that country's ÖAG Gruppe. In 1993, Wolseley added Sweden, buying Enertech from Trelleborg, which included the HRPC distribution subsidiary.

The success of Wolseley's distribution business convinced the company to transform itself into a specialist in the mid-1990s. The company began selling off its manufacturing businesses, a process completed in 2000. In the meantime, the company began restructuring its U.S. distribution arm, integrating Familian into Ferguson, while transforming Carolina into Stock Building Supply. Wolseley, through Ferguson, also began an aggressive new acquisition program. Over the next several years, the company spent up to $300 million per year making a long series of primarily smaller, bolt-on acquisitions, but also a number of larger-scale purchases, such as 1998's Hall and Co., and the lumber supply specialist Stock Lumber.

In Europe, Wolseley continued to expand its network as well, acquiring CFM in Luxembourg, Heatmerchants in Ireland, and Manzardo in Italy in 1999. Into the 2000s, the company added operations in The Netherlands (Wasco), the Czech Republic (Cesaro), and Denmark (Electro Oil). A major advance in the company's European position came in 2003, when it acquired France's Pinault Bois & Materiaux, part of the Pinault-Printemps-Redoute group. In 2004, the company added another new European market, Switzerland, when it acquired that country's Tobler. Yet European expansion proved more difficult than in the United States, as the company found itself faced with sorting out differing building standards among the many European countries.

By 2004, Wolseley had emerged as the world's leading distributor of building supplies, boasting sales of more than £8.2 billion ($13 billion). The company planned to play a prominent role in driving the consolidation of the heavily fragmented industry, which promised years of growth ahead. At the same time, Wolseley began considering an entry into new markets, including South America and Asia, in the near future.

Principal Subsidiaries

Brossette (France); Cesaro Kft (Czech Republic); Comptoir des Fers et Metaux S.A. (Luxembourg); Electro Oil (Denmark); Ferguson Enterprises (United States); Heatmerchants (Ireland); Manzardo Spa (Italy); Mart Spol SRO (Hungary); ÖAG Gruppe (Austria); PBM (France); Stock Building Supply (United States); Tobler (Switzerland); Tubs and Tiles (Ireland); Wasco (Netherlands); Wolseley Canada.

Principal Competitors

Sears, Roebuck and Company; Lowe's Companies Inc.; Castorama Dubois Investissements S.C.A.; ThyssenKrupp Schulte GmbH; Kesko Oyj; Saud Bahwan Group; BayWa AG; Menard Inc.; Nagase and Company Ltd.; Diethelm Keller Holding Ltd.

Further Reading

"Bumper Growth at Wolseley," *TTJ—The Timber Industry Magazine,* January 24, 2004, p. 4.

Faloon, Kelly, "Ferguson's History: The Ferguson Chronicles; Celebrating 50 Years of Success in the PHCP Wholesale Industry," *Plumbing & Mechanical,* April 2003.

Gow, David, "Building Pounds 1bn Sales But Wolseley Stays Wary," *Guardian,* March 23, 2004, p. 18.

Halstead, Richard, "Wolseley Is Built to Last," *Independent Sunday,* August 18, 1996, p. 6.

Harney, Alexandra, "Wolseley May Spend Pounds 300m to Fuel Growth," *Financial Times,* March 20, 2002, p. 32.

Lenius, Pat, "A Profitable Purchase: Wolseley's Acquisition of Ferguson in 1982 Has Resulted in Growth for Both Sides," *Plumbing & Mechanical,* April 2003.

Morais, Richard C., "I Want It Yesterday," *Forbes,* November 24, 2003, p. 134.

Smith, Peter, "Banks Brings a Sailor's Touch to Wolseley Helm," *Financial Times,* May 10, 2001, p. 26.

"Wolseley Acquires Four Distributors," *Supply House Times,* March 2003, p. 6.

"Wolseley Acquires Swiss HVAC Wholesaler," *Supply House Times,* January 2004, p. 14.

—M.L. Cohen

Zatarain's, Inc.

82 First Street
P.O. Box 347
Gretna, Louisiana 70053-4745
U.S.A.
Telephone: (504) 367-2950
Toll Free: (888) 264-5460
Fax: (504) 362-2004
Web site: http://www.zatarain.com

Wholly Owned Subsidiary of McCormick & Co. Inc.
Incorporated: 1922 as E.A. Zatarain & Sons, Inc.
Employees: 270
Sales: $100 million (2004 est.)
NAIC: 311423 Dried and Dehydrated Food
    Manufacturing; 311822 Flour Mixes and Dough
    Manufacturing from Purchased Flour; 311823 Dry
    Pasta Manufacturing; 311930 Flavoring Syrup and
    Concentrate Manufacturing; 311940 Seasoning and
    Dressing; Mayonnaise, Dressing, and Other Prepared
    Sauce Manufacturing; 311942 Spice and Extract
    Manufacturing; 311999 All Other Miscellaneous
    Food; 422420 Packaged Frozen Food Wholesalers

Zatarain's, Inc., is a leading producer of rice mixes. Based in New Orleans, the company's products tilt toward the spicier side of the flavor spectrum. A Louisiana institution for more than 100 years, Zatarain's first hit the national marketplace in the late 1990s with five rice mixes. These accounted for 65 percent of sales in 2003. Zatarain's produces more than 200 different items, including seafood boil spice mixes, breading mixes for fried food, and sauces, but most are distributed only in New Orleans. A handful of the company's 35 different types of rice mixes—Dirty Rice, Gumbo Mix, Jambalaya Mix, Red Beans and Rice, and Black Beans and Rice—receive national distribution. The company entered the frozen dinner market in 2002 with a dozen varieties, including Red Beans and Rice, Jambalaya, and Blackened Chicken Alfredo Pasta. Minnesota-based Fairmont Foods helped package the frozen dinners, which were based on recipes developed by Zatarain's in New Orleans.

Zatarain's Gretna, Louisiana, facility includes a 30,000-square-foot plant and a 100,000-square-foot warehouse.

New Orleans Origins

The story begins in 1889, when Emile A. Zatarain, Sr. founded a business at 925 Valmont Street, New Orleans. (The name "Zatarain" reportedly means "fishing hole" in the Basque language of Batua.) Root beer extract, seasonings, and bleach were among the first of Zatarain's products. The line-up eventually expanded to include tangy Creole mustard and pickled products.

The business was incorporated on May 29, 1922 as E.A. Zatarain & Sons, Inc. and also did business as Zatarain's Pure Food Products. Ownership of the company passed to Emile A. Zatarain, Jr. and his wife Ida May Bennett Zatarain, who contributed recipes for Remoulade Sauce, Olive Salad, and other products.

By the 1960s, reports *New Orleans CityBusiness,* Zatarain's had fallen low on capital as it relied on outdated, inefficient packaging technology. James Grinstead Viavant, founder of the Avondale Shipyards in New Orleans, acquired Zatarain's Pure Food Products from the Zatarain family in 1963. Viavant merged Zatarain's with his Pa-Poose Products Co., Inc. and another recently acquired business, Pelican State Lab, owner of the Fish-Fri branded mix that would become a Zatarain's best-seller.

Production was modernized as it moved to a five-acre site in Gretna, Louisiana, a suburb of New Orleans. Unprofitable items such as bleach, dye, and pickled goods were dropped from the product line. In 1967, the company name was changed to Zatarain's, Inc. Viavant is credited with building the business into a regional supplier in the 1970s.

Changing Hands in the 1980s

Fort Wayne, Indiana-based Centra Soya Co. bought Zatarain's, Inc. for $24 million in May 1984 as Viviant neared retirement. Annual sales were $10 million at the time and would reach $14 million in 1986. San Francisco holding company Wyndham Foods, Inc. acquired Zatarain's 18 months later. Soon after, Zatarain's entered the institutional food service

Key Dates:

1889: The company is founded in New Orleans.
1963: Zatarain's moves to nearby Gretna and is acquired by James Viavant.
1984: Central Soya Co. buys Zatarain's for $24 million.
1985: Wyndham Foods acquires Zatarain's; boxed rice dinners are introduced.
1987: Martha White Foods buys Zatarain's for $35 million.
1993: Zatarain's is taken private in a leveraged buyout.
2003: McCormick & Co. buys Zatarain's for $180 million.

industry, supplying such markets as hospital cafeterias. Within five years, food service would account for 30 percent of sales.

Zatarain's produced 60 different products at the time. In 1985, the company rolled out the boxed rice dinners that would later be distributed in supermarkets across the country. Dirty Rice and Gumbo Mix were first, followed by Jambalaya Mix.

Zatarain's briefly labeled some of its products with the word "Cajun" in the mid-1980s. However, the word lost much of its meaning due to a number of imitators exploiting this particular food trend. Zatarain's would from then on refer to its products as "Louisiana-style" or "New Orleans-style." (Louisiana is actually home to two distinct styles of cuisine, the Creole of New Orleans being the more refined cousin of Cajun. Both are spicy.)

In December 1987, Zatarain's was acquired by Martha White Foods, Inc. of Brentwood, Tennessee, for about $35 million. Martha White was a unit of E-II Food Specialties Co., which owned several former Beatrice Co. consumer and food businesses.

Zatarain's changed hands a few more times. It was owned for a period by American Brands of Old Greenwich, Connecticut, in the late 1980s. Revenues reached about $16 million in 1989.

Expansion in the 1990s

Zatarain's was identified with the flavor of New Orleans cooking. The company's best-selling mix going into the 1990s was its Crab Boil seasoning blend, while Fish-Fri was number two, reported *New Orleans CityBusiness*. The company, which had 60 employees, was turning out at least four new products a year.

Zatarain's Partnership LP, made up of Citigroup Venture Capital and several Zatarain's employees, took Zatarain's private in a leveraged buyout in 1993. In spite of the numerous changes of ownership, management was relatively stable. Former vice-president of marketing and sales Lawrence Kurzius succeeded Chloe Anderson to become the company's fourth CEO in 1997.

In the early 1990s, Zatarain's products began appearing on grocery shelves throughout the South, where they were well

accepted. Sales reached $26 million in the fiscal year ended July 1995. By 1996, the brand's geographic reach extended into Kansas and Virginia. Revenues were $30.5 million in fiscal 1997, when Zatarain's had 95 employees.

Zatarain's began its push for national distribution in the late 1990s. According to the *Times-Picayune,* of its 200 products, the company chose only five rice mixes to market nationally—jambalaya, gumbo, dirty rice, red beans and rice, and black beans and rice.

The company's first national TV campaign hit the airwaves in January 1999. CEO Lawrence Kurzius told the *Times-Picayune* that increasing acceptance of spicier ethnic foods in the United States seemed to be playing in the company's favor. Nevertheless, some parts of the country, such as New England, proved a harder sell than others.

Sales were $63 million in the fiscal year ended July 1999. With a 7.5 percent market share, Zatarain's was the country's fourth largest purveyor of rice mixes, after Uncle Ben's (10 percent). A $1 million, two-story addition was being constructed next to the company's headquarters in Gretna, Louisiana. In the ramp-up for national distribution, the number of employees had grown from 100 to 150. In 1998, Zatarain's began a five-year run of sales growth in excess of 15 percent a year.

New Horizons in a New Century

Having completed a successful nationwide expansion in the United States, Zatarain's looked to Canada for opportunities. Kurzius pointed out to the *Times-Picayune* the common Acadian heritage that Louisianans shared with French Canadians.

The company extended its product line into pasta dinner mixes, all with New Orleans-type seasonings, in 2000. Zatarain's spent $8 million on advertising in 2001, reported *Adweek*. Sales rose 16 percent to $98.9 million in the fiscal year ended July 2002, and employment was up to 260 people. The company was rolling out a line of frozen rice bowl entrees, beginning in the Southeast.

McCormick & Company Inc. acquired Zatarain's for $180 million in cash in June 2003. Interestingly, McCormick, based in Sparks, Maryland, had also been founded in 1889, operating as a purveyor of root beer. With $2.3 billion in annual sales and

9,000 employees, McCormick was the world's leading spice producer. The buy promised accelerated global expansion for the Zatarain's, which was already found in all 50 states.

While pushing for mainstream acceptance of New Orleans-style food, Zatarain's continued to aim new products towards Louisiana chefs. Offerings included the extra spicy Pro Boil originally developed for professional seafood boilers and a squeeze-bottle version of its Creole mustard.

Principal Competitors

Bruce Foods Corporation; The Golden Grain Company; Lipton; MASTERFOODS USA; Rex Fine Foods Inc.; Tony Chachere's Creole Foods of Opelousas Inc.

Further Reading

Charski, Mindy, and Alicia Griswold, "Packaged-Goods Account in Play," *Adweek*, Midwest Ed., November 25, 2002, p. 6.

Drown, Stuart, "State Food Producers in Stew over Bad Grub Called 'Cajun,'" *Baton Rouge State Times*, June 24, 1988, p. 1B.

"Funeral Notice: Ida May Bennett Zatarain," *Times-Picayune*, March 1, 2004, Metro Sec., p. 5.

Gautreau, Chris, "Zatarain's a Spicy Morsel for Industry Leader McCormick," *Advocate* (Baton Rouge), May 9, 2003, p. 1A.

"James Viviant, One of Avondale Founders," *Times-Picayune* (New Orleans), October 29, 1999, p. 4B.

Karlen, Josh, "McCormick Conjures Cajun Deal," *Daily Deal* (New York), May 9, 2003.

Larroque, Nicole, "Zatarain's Flourishes Despite a Series of Ownership Changes," *New Orleans CityBusiness*, January 15, 1990, p. 10.

Lingle, Rick, "Poucher Funnels Savings into Rice Mixes," *Packaging Digest*, November 1, 1996, p. 108.

Mulvihill, Kathleen, "Zatarain's Adds Spice to Cooking Craze," *New Orleans CityBusiness*, July 7, 1986, p. 18.

Pandolfi, Keith, "N.O.'s Top 100 Private Companies: Zatarain's," *New Orleans CityBusiness*, March 24, 2003.

Pandolfi, Keith, and Elisabeth Butler, "McCormick to Spice up Zatarain's Distribution," *New Orleans CityBusiness*, May 12, 2003, pp. 1f.

Plume, Janet, "'Older Is Better' in the Big Easy," *ADWEEK Southeast*, September 25, 2000, p. 5.

Reichard, Peter, "New Orleans Food Distributors Increasing Revenues and Adding Employees," *New Orleans CityBusiness*, March 18, 2002.

Sentementes, Gus G., "McCormick & Co. to Buy Brand of Louisiana-Style Food Mixes, Spices, Flavorings," *Baltimore Sun*, May 9, 2003.

Sine, Richard, "The Rice Stuff," *Times-Picayune* (New Orleans), November 28, 1999, p. F1.

Sonnier, Cheramie, "Zatarain's: From Rice Mixes to Frozen Foods," *Advocate* (Baton Rouge), April 24, 2003, p. 1F.

——, "Zatarain's Produces Some 200 Products with Louisiana Flair," *Advocate* (Baton Rouge), April 24, 2003, p. 4F.

Treadway, Joan, "N.O. Roots Puzzle Finds Lost Pieces; From Political Heroes and Saints to Old Street Names and Spicy Concoctions, the Basque People's Spanish-French Heritage Runs Deep in Local History," *Times-Picayune*, May 31, 2003, Metro Sec., p. 1.

Yerton, Stewart, and Ronette King, "Zatarain's Sold to McCormick; Food Mix Operation Will Stay in Gretna," *Times-Picayune* (New Orleans), May 9, 2003, Money Sec., p. 1.

Young, Tara, "4th Street Extension May Aid Industries," *Times-Picayune* (New Orleans), Metro Sec., November 27, 2001, p. 1.

—Frederick C. Ingram

INDEX TO COMPANIES ————————————————

Index to Companies

Listings in this index are arranged in alphabetical order under the company name. Company names beginning with a letter or proper name such as Eli Lilly & Co. will be found under the first letter of the company name. Definite articles (The, Le, La) are ignored for alphabetical purposes as are forms of incorporation that precede the company name (AB, NV). Company names printed in bold type have full, historical essays on the page numbers appearing in bold. Updates to entries that appeared in earlier volumes are signified by the notation (**upd.**). Company names in light type are references within an essay to that company, not full historical essays. This index is cumulative with volume numbers printed in bold type.

419

American Steamship Company, **6** 394–95; **25** 168, 170

American Steel & Wire Co., **IV** 572; **7** 549; **13** 97–98; **40** 70, 72

American Steel Foundries, **7** 29–30

American Stock Exchange, **10** 416–17; **54** 242

American Stores Company, **II 604–06**; **12** 63, 333; **13** 395; **17** 559; **18** 89; **22** **37–40 (upd.)**; **25** 297; **27** 290–92; **30** 24, 26–27

American Sugar Refining Company. *See* Domino Sugar Corporation.

American Sumatra Tobacco Corp., **15** 138

American Superconductor Corporation, **41** 141

American Surety Co., **26** 486

American Systems Technologies, Inc., **18** 5

American Teaching Aids Inc., **19** 405

American Technical Services Company. *See* American Building Maintenance Industries, Inc.; ABM Industries Incorporated.

American Telephone and Telegraph Company. *See* AT&T.

American Television and Communications Corp., **IV** 596, 675; **7** 528–30; **18** 65

American Textile Co., **III** 571; **20** 362

American Thermos Bottle Company. *See* Thermos Company.

American Threshold, **50** 123

American Tile Supply Company, **19** 233

American Tin Plate Co., **IV** 572; **7** 549

American Tissue Company, **29** 136

American Tobacco Co., **V** 395–97, 399, 408–09, 417–18, 600; **14** 77, 79; **15** 137–38; **16** 242; **18** 416; **27** 128–29; **33** 82; **43** 126; **50** 116–17, 119, 259–60. *See also* American Brands Inc., B.A.T. Industries PLC.; Fortune Brands, Inc.

American Tool & Machinery, **III** 420

American Tool Companies, Inc., **52** 270

American Tool Company, **13** 563

American Totalisator Corporation, **10** 319–20

American Tourister, Inc., **10** 350; **13** 451, 453; **16 19–21**. *See also* Samsonite Corporation.

American Tower Corporation, 33 34–38

American Tractor Corporation, **10** 379

American Trading and Production Corporation, **7** 101

American Trans Air, **34** 31

American Transport Lines, **6** 384

American Twist Drill Co., **23** 82

American Ultramar Ltd., **IV** 567

American Vanguard Corporation, 47 **20–22**

American VIP Limousine, Inc., **26** 62

American Water Works Company, Inc., **V** 543–44; **6** 443–45; **26** 451; **38 49–52** **(upd.)**

American Wood Reduction Company, **14** 174

American Woodmark Corporation, 31 **13–16**

American Yard Products, **22** 26, 28

American Yearbook Company, **7** 255; **25** 252

American-Strevell Inc., **II** 625

Americana Entertainment Group, Inc., **19** 435

Americana Foods, Inc., **17** 474–75

Americana Healthcare Corp., **15** 522

Americana Ships Ltd., **50** 210

Americom, **61** 272

Ameridrive, 58 67

AmeriFirst Bank, **11** 258

Amerifirst Federal Savings, **10** 340

AmeriGas Partners, L.P., **12** 498, 500; **56** 36

Amerihost Properties, Inc., 30 51–53

AmeriKing Corp., **36** 309

Amerimark Inc., **II** 682

Amerin Corporation. *See* Radian Group Inc.

AmeriServe Food Distribution. *See* Holberg Industries, Inc.

Amerisex, **64** 198

AmeriSource Health Corporation, 37 **9–11 (upd.)**

AmerisourceBergen Corporation, 64 **22–28 (upd.)**

Ameristar Casinos, Inc., 33 39–42

AmeriSteel Corp., **59** 202

AmeriSuites, **52** 281

Amerisystems, **8** 328

Ameritech Corporation, **V 265–68**; **6** 248; **7** 118; **10** 431; **11** 382; **12** 137; **14** 252–53, 257, 259–61, 364; **15** 197; **18** **30–34 (upd.)**; **25** 499; **41** 288–90; **43** 447; **44** 49

Ameritech Illinois. *See* Illinois Bell Telephone Company.

Ameritrade Holding Corporation, 34 **27–30**

Ameritrust Corporation, **9** 476

Ameriwood Industries International **Corp.**, **17 15–17**; **59** 164

Amerock Corporation, **13** 41; **53 37–40**

Amerop Sugar Corporation, **60** 96

Amersham PLC, 50 21–25; **63** 166

Ames Department Stores, Inc., **V** 197–98; **9 20–22**; **10** 497; **15** 88; **19** 449; **30 54–57 (upd.)**

Ametek Inc., **9 23–25**; **12** 88; **38** 169

N.V. Amev, **III 199–202**

AMEX. *See* American Stock Exchange.

Amey Plc, 47 23–25; **49** 320

AMF. *See* American Machinery and Foundry, Inc.

AMF Bowling, Inc., **19** 312; **23** 450; **40** **30–33**

Amfac Inc., **I 417–18**, 566; **IV** 703; **10** 42; **23** 320

Amfac/JMB Hawaii L.L.C., 24 32–35 **(upd.)**

AMFM Inc., **35** 221, 245, 248; **37** 104; **41** 384

Amgen, Inc., **8** 216–17; **10 78–81**; **13** 240; **14** 255; **21** 320; **30 58–61 (upd.)**; **38** 204; **50** 248, 250, 538; **54** 111

Amherst Coal Co., **IV** 410; **7** 309

AMI. *See* Advanced Metallurgy, Inc.

Amiga Corporation, **7** 96

Aminoil, Inc., **IV** 523. *See also* American Independent Oil Co.

AMISA, **IV** 136

Amisys Managed Care Information Systems, **16** 94

Amitron S.A., **10** 113; **50** 43

Amity Leather Products Company. *See* AR Accessories Group, Inc.

AMK Corporation, **7** 85; **21** 111

Amkor, **23** 17

AMLI Realty Company, **33** 418, 420

Amling Co., **25** 89

Ammirati Puris Lintas, **14** 316; **22** 294

L'Ammoniac Sarro-Lorraine S.a.r.l., **IV** 197

Amnesty International, 50 26–29

Amoco Corporation, **IV 368–71**, 412, 424–25, 453, 525; **7** 107, 443; **10** 83–84; **11** 441; **12** 18; **14 21–25 (upd.)**, 494; **18** 365; **19** 297; **26** 369. *See also* BP p.l.c.

AMOR 14 Corporation, **64** 95

Amorim Investimentos e Participaço, **48** 117, 119

Amorim Revestimentos, **48** 118

Amoseas, **IV** 453–54

Amoskeag Company, **6** 356; **8 32–33**; **9** 213–14, 217; **22** 54; **31** 199

Amot Controls Corporation, **15** 404; **50** 394

AMP, Inc., **II 7–8**; **11** 319; **13** 344; **14** **26–28 (upd.)**; **17** 274; **22** 542; **28** 486; **36** 158; **54** 239; **63** 404

Ampad Holding Corporation. *See* American Pad & Paper Company.

AMPAL. *See* American-Palestine Trading Corp.

AMPCO Auto Parks, Inc. *See* American Building Maintenance Industries, Inc.; ABM Industries Incorporated.

Ampeg Company, **48** 353

AMPEP, **III** 625

Ampex Corporation, **III** 549; **6** 272; **17** **18–20**

Amphenol Corporation, 40 34–37

Ampol Petroleum Ltd., **III** 729; **27** 473

Ampro, **25** 504–05

AMR. *See* American Medical Response, Inc.

AMR Combs Inc., **36** 190

AMR Corporation, **6** 76; **8** 315; **22** 252; **26** 427–28; **28 22–26 (upd.)**; **29** 409; **33** 19; **34** 119; **52 21–26 (upd.)**; **54** 4

AMR Information Services, **9** 95

Amram's Distributing Limited, **12** 425

AMRE, **III** 211

AMREP Corporation, **21 35–37**; **24** 78

Amro. *See* Amsterdam-Rotterdam Bank N.V.

Amrop International Australasia, **34** 249

AMS. *See* Advanced Marketing Services, Inc.

Amsbra Limited, **62** 48

Amscan Holdings, Inc., 61 24–26

Amsco International, **29** 450

Amserve Ltd., **48** 23

AmSouth Bancorporation, 12 15–17; **48** **15–18 (upd.)**

Amstar Corp., **14** 18

Amstar Sugar Corporation, **7** 466–67; **26** 122

Amsted Industries Incorporated, 7 29–31

Amsterdam-Rotterdam Bank N.V., **II** **185–86**; **14** 169; **17** 324

Amstrad plc, **III 112–14**; **48 19–23** **(upd.)**

AmSurg Corporation, 48 24–27

AMT. *See* American Machine and Tool Co., Inc.; American Materials & Technologies Corporation.

Amtech. *See* American Building Maintenance Industries, Inc.; ABM Industries Incorporated.

Amtech Systems Corporation, **11** 65; **27** 405

Amtel, Inc., **8** 545; **10** 136

Amtorg, **13** 365

INDEX TO INDUSTRIES

Index to Industries

ENGINEERING & MANAGEMENT SERVICES

FINANCIAL SERVICES: NON-BANKS

HEALTH & PERSONAL CARE PRODUCTS

INSURANCE

MATERIALS

MINING & METALS

PERSONAL SERVICES

PETROLEUM

TEXTILES & APPAREL

UTILITIES

GEOGRAPHIC INDEX

Geographic Index

France

NOTES ON CONTRIBUTORS

Notes on Contributors

BRENNAN, Gerald E. California-based writer.

CAPACE, Nancy K. Detroit-based writer, editor, researcher, specializing in history and biography.

COHEN, M. L. Novelist and business writer living in Paris.

COVELL, Jeffrey L. Seattle-based writer.

DINGER, Ed. Bronx-based writer and editor.

GREENLAND, Paul R. Illinois-based writer and researcher; author of two books and former senior editor of a national business magazine; contributor to *The Encyclopedia of Chicago History* and *Company Profiles for Students.*

HALASZ, Robert. Former editor in chief of *World Progress* and *Funk & Wagnalls New Encyclopedia Yearbook*; author, *The U.S. Marines* (Millbrook Press, 1993).

HAUSER, Evelyn. Researcher, writer and marketing specialist based in Arcata, California; expertise includes historical and trend research in such topics as globalization, emerging industries and lifestyles, future scenarios, biographies, and the history of organizations.

INGRAM, Frederick C. Utah-based business writer who has contributed to *GSA Business, Appalachian Trailway News,* the Encyclopedia of Business, the *Encyclopedia of Global Industries,* the *Encyclopedia of Consumer Brands,* and other regional and trade publications.

LORENZ, Sarah Ruth. Minnesota-based writer.

ROTHBURD, Carrie. Writer and editor specializing in corporate profiles, academic texts, and academic journal articles.

STANSELL, Christina M. Writer and editor based in Farmington Hills, Michigan.

UHLE, Frank. Ann Arbor-based writer; movie projectionist, disc jockey, and staff member of *Psychotronic Video* magazine.

WOODWARD, A. Wiconsin-based business writer.